Business Law

8th Edition

John R. Allison & Robert A. Prentice

THOMSON
™

Australia · Canada · Mexico · Singapore · Spain · United Kingdom · United States

Business Law
John R. Allison & Robert A. Prentice

Executive Editors:
Michele Baird, Maureen Staudt &
Michael Stranz

Project Development Manager:
Linda de Stefano

Marketing Coordinators:
Lindsay Annett and Sara Mercurio

Production/Manufacturing Supervisor:
Donna M. Brown

Pre-Media Services Supervisor:
Dan Plofchan

Project Coordinator:
Jennifer Atwood

Rights and Permissions Specialists:
Kalina Hintz and Bahman Naraghi

Cover Image
Getty Images*

www.thomsonrights.com
The Adaptable Courseware Program
consists of products and additions to
existing Thomson products that are
produced from camera-ready copy.
Peer review, class testing, and
accuracy are primarily the responsibility
of the author(s).

ISBN 0-759-36440-0

International Divisions List

Asia (Including India):
Thomson Learning
(a division of Thomson Asia Pte Ltd)
5 Shenton Way #01-01
UIC Building
Singapore 068808
Tel: (65) 6410-1200
Fax: (65) 6410-1208

Australia/New Zealand:
Thomson Learning Australia
102 Dodds Street
Southbank, Victoria 3006
Australia

Latin America:
Thomson Learning
Seneca 53
Colonia Polano
11560 Mexico, D.F., Mexico
Tel (525) 281-2906
Fax (525) 281-2656

Canada:
Thomson Nelson
1120 Birchmount Road
Toronto, Ontario
Canada M1K 5G4
Tel (416) 752-9100
Fax (416) 752-8102

UK/Europe/Middle East/Africa:
Thomson Learning
High Holborn House
50-51 Bedford Row
London, WC1R 4LS
United Kingdom
Tel 44 (020) 7067-2500
Fax 44 (020) 7067-2600

Spain (Includes Portugal):
Thomson Paraninfo
Calle Magallanes 25
28015 Madrid
España
Tel 34 (0)91 446-3350
Fax 34 (0)91 445-6218

CONTENTS

THE LEGAL ENVIRONMENT OF BUSINESS

CHAPTER 1

NATURE AND SOURCES OF LAW

- Law and Business Strategy
- Law as a Subject of Study
- What Is the Law?
- Rules and Processes
- Requisites of a Legal System
- Some Classifications of Law
- Legal Misconceptions
- Law, Justice, and Morals
- Law, Technology, and Globalization

A.P. Herbert Once wrote: "The general mass, if they consider the law at all, regard it as they regard some monster in the zoo. It is odd, it is extraordinary; but there it is, they have known it all their lives, they suppose that there must be some good reason for it, and accept it as inevitable and natural." (*Uncommon Law*, 1936.)

Law and Business Strategy

In the post-Enron environment, it is clearer than ever before that the subject of business law and its intimately related topic, business ethics, are more important than ever before to business students and businesspeople. The successful manager considers all aspects of the firm's competitive environment. Just as the pricing practices of competitors must be taken into account in formulating long- and short-term strategy, for example, so must the legal environment of business be considered. The successful manager's toolbox includes a facility for factoring legal and regulatory factors into strategic plans.

For example, in considering whether to enter a foreign market, a manager must determine whether contracts entered into in that nation can be enforced, whether intellectual property such as trade secrets, trademarks, and patents can be protected, and whether taxation and threat of expropriation present intolerable risks.

Some managers may view compliance with employment discrimination laws as a low priority, but large companies have lost as much as a billion dollars of market capitalization in a single day following the filing of a class action discrimination lawsuit. Other managers may think compliance with federal securities disclosure requirements should be optional, but Cendant lost $14 billion in market cap in one day upon disclosure of an accounting scandal. It paid more than $2 billion dollars to settle the cases that were later filed. In February, 2005, after Citigroup paid or set aside $10 billion to settle claims stemming from its role in Enron-era scandals, suffered closure of its private bank in Japan due to improper actions, and faced European investigation over its manipulative bond trades, the firm began a major ethics training program to encourage every one of its 300,000 employees to act legally and ethically so that the firm could overcome the competitive disadvantage that it had sustained because of its questionable acts. The strategic manager realizes that money spent to ensure that the company is complying with the law is not only the ethical thing to do, but also a strategic necessity.

Microsoft Corporation, a fabulously successful company in many ways, paid too little attention to the antitrust laws in its early years. Because of that, it suffered several adverse judgments and spent tens of millions of dollars defending lawsuits. That was money that other companies, such as Intel, saved by considering their legal environment more carefully than did Microsoft.

In their book *Edison in the Boardroom*, Julie Davis and Suzanne Harrison point out that many managers are not educated to manage the intellectual property that their companies produce. Yet IBM earns $1.5 billion per year in licensing revenue from its patents, trade secrets and other forms of intellectual property. Increasingly, companies are realizing the huge strategic advantage they can gain from obtaining, maintaining, and exploiting their intellectual capital.

Federal, state, and local governments pay billions of dollars to companies every year. These governmental entities make policy decisions on matters of taxation, regulation, and licensing that make or break entire industry sectors and certainly influence which companies within those sectors succeed or fail. Judicial decisions can have a huge impact on companies. Class action product liability decisions in such industries as tobacco, asbestos, and tires are examples. As Michael Porter noted in his landmark book *Competitive Strategy*, "no structural analysis is complete without a diagnosis of how present and future government policy, at all levels, will affect structural conditions." More than that, intelligent managers don't just analyze governmental policy, they attempt to proactively improve their firms' legal environment by affecting the actors in the political sphere—the executive, legislative, and judicial branches of our various levels of government.

Many other examples could be given, but business law professor George Siedel has pointed out in his book *Using the Law for Competitive Advantage* that "because law is an untapped source of competitive advantage that will continue to be misunderstood by many managers, selected companies should be able to leverage their legal resources into a source of competitive advantage that is sustainable over the long term."

Law As a Subject of Study

Although the law is not nearly as odd or extraordinary as many persons believe, it is undeniably "there"—an integral part of the environment that has been a source of great interest, even fascination, for centuries.

Considering the pervasiveness of the law, this is hardly surprising. Almost all human activity is affected by it in one manner or another, and this alone is adequate explanation for such widespread interest. Certainly, anyone contemplating a business transaction of any magnitude today realizes that he or she must consider not only the physical and financial effort it will entail but—to some extent, at least—the legal ramifications as well. And beyond the practical effect law has on individual conduct in specific situations, it possesses additional characteristics that make its study uniquely rewarding.

First, although the law is by no means an occult language understood only by lawyers, it clearly is a subject that is academically stimulating. For students to get any real benefit from a course in law, they must at the very least learn to recognize precise legal issues, understand the reasoning of the courts as set forth in their decisions, and subject this reasoning to critical analysis. These activities involve varying degrees of mental exercise; and although this is not always pleasurable, it fosters a degree of mental discipline that is not easily acquired elsewhere.

Second, students should have the opportunity to consider the law as a societal institution—to see how it has affected conduct and thought and how it has been influenced by them in return. Whatever the law is, it certainly is not static, and it certainly does not exist in a vacuum.

This approach, which emphasizes the impact of social and economic changes on the law, gives the subject a liberal arts flavor. When viewed in this light, the law and its processes become rewarding to anyone having even a passing interest in economics, sociology, and political science.

What Is the Law?

Ever since the law began to take form, scholars have spent impressive amounts of time and thought analyzing its purposes and defining what it is and what it ought to be—in short, fitting it into a philosophic scheme of one form or another. Although space does not permit inclusion of even the major essays in which these philosophers defend their respective views, their conclusions provide us with useful observations about the nature of law. Consider, for example, the following:

> We have been told by Plato that law is a form of social control, an instrument of the good life, the way to the discovery of reality, the true reality of the social structure; by Aristotle that it is a rule of conduct, a contract, an ideal of reason, a rule of decision, a form of order; by Cicero that it is the agreement of reason and nature, the distinction between the just and the unjust, a command or pro-hibition; by Aquinas that it is an ordinance of reason for the common good, made by him who has care of the community, and promulgated [thereby]; by Bacon that certainty is the prime necessity of law; by Hobbes that law is the command of the sovereign; by Spinoza that it is a plan of life; by Leibniz that its character is determined by the structure of society; by Locke that it is a norm estab-lished by the commonwealth; by Hume that it is a body of precepts; by Kant that it is a harmonizing of wills by means of universal rules in the interests of freedom; by Fichte that it is a relation between human beings; by Hegel that it is an unfolding or realizing of the idea of right. (Huntington Cairns , *Legal Philosophy from Plato to Hegel* (Baltimore: Johns Hopkins University Press, 1949).

Although these early writers substantially agree as to the general purpose of law—the ensuring of orderliness to all human activity—their definitions of the term vary considerably. Today there is still no definition of law that has universal approval, even in legal circles—a fact that is no doubt attributable to its inherent breadth. One can understand how very broad the law is by considering just these few widely varying matters with which the law must deal (1) the standards of care required of a surgeon in the operating room, (2) the determination of whether an "exclusive dealing" provision in a motion picture distributor's contracts constitutes an unfair method of competition under federal law, and (3) the propriety of a witness's testimony when it is challenged as constituting "hearsay" under the rules of evidence.

A brief comment about sources of law is in order at this early point. In our legal system (and in most others throughout the world), there are primary and secondary sources. Primary sources, which contain legally binding rules and procedures, include federal and state constitutions, statutes (legislative enactments), administrative agency regulations, and court decisions; also included are federal treaties and city ordinances. Secondary sources summarize and explain the law, and sometimes criticize and suggest changes in it. Such sources are not legally binding, but are frequently referred to and used by courts, administrative agencies, legislative staff members, and practicing attorneys as aids in determining what the law is or should be. Secondary sources include research articles in academic legal periodicals, restatements (which consist of summaries of and commentary on specific subject areas of law by experts in those areas), legal texts and encyclopedias, and others.

Rules and Processes

At the risk of oversimplification, it can be said that two major approaches to the teaching and study of law exist today. The *rule-oriented approach* views the law as consisting of the rules that are in effect within a state or nation at a given time. This is very likely what practicing attorneys have in mind when they speak about the law, and it is a perfectly respectable view. Witness the following definition adopted by the American Law Institute: "[Law] is the body of principles, standards and rules which the courts . . . apply in the decision of controversies brought before them." (*Restatement, Conflict of Laws* 2d, §4. 1971).

The *process-oriented approach* sees the law in a broader light: The processes by which the rules and principles are formulated (rather than the rules and principles themselves) constitute the major element of law. Because law is necessitated solely by human activity, those who emphasize process contend that the ever-changing problems resulting from this activity and *the ways in which the law attempts to solve them* must receive primary emphasis if one is to gain a proper insight into the subject. The following definition expresses this view: "Law is a dynamic process, a system of regularized, institutionalized procedures for the orderly decision of social questions, including the settlement of disputes." (James I. Houghteling, Jr., *The Dynamics of Law* (New York: Harcourt Brace Jovanovich, 1963).

Obviously, the law is both rule and process. Each approach to the teaching and study of law is legitimate; indeed, each is essential and inevitable. The only difference is in emphasis. In this text, process is emphasized in the first few chapters, and rules in many of the later chapters. Our discussion of rules and principles, however, always includes related legal processes.

Requisites of a Legal System

For a legal system to function properly, particularly within a democratic government such as ours, it must command the respect of the great majority of people governed by it. To do so, the legal rules that compose it must, as a practical matter, possess certain characteristics. They must be (1) relatively certain, (2) relatively flexible, (3) known or knowable, and (4) apparently reasonable.

In the following chapters we consider these requirements more fully and determine the extent to which our legal system satisfies them. For the moment, we give brief descriptions of each of the four.

Certainty

One essential element of a stable society is reasonable certainty about its laws, not only at a given moment but over long periods of time. Many of our activities, particularly business activities, are based on the assumption that legal principles will remain stable into the foreseeable future. If this were not so, chaos would result. For example, no television network would enter into a contract with a professional football league, under which it is to pay millions of dollars for the right to televise league games, if it were not reasonably sure that the law would compel the league to live up to its contractual obligations or to pay damages if it did not. And no lawyer would advise a client on a contemplated course of action without similar assurances.

Because of these considerations, the courts (and to a lesser extent the legislatures) are generally reluctant to overturn principles that have been part of the law for any appreciable length of time. This is not to say, of course, that the law is static. Many areas of American law are dramatically different than they were 50 or even 25 years ago. However, most of these changes resulted from a series of modifications of existing principles rather than from an abrupt reversal of them. The Soldano v. O 'Daniels case later in this chapter illustrates one such modification.

Flexibility

In any nation, particularly a highly industrialized one such as the United States, societal changes occur with accelerating (almost dismaying) rapidity. Each change presents new legal problems that must be resolved without undue delay. This necessity was recognized by Justice Cardozo when he wrote that "the law, like the traveler, must be ready for the morrow." (Benjamin N. Cardozo, The Growth of the Law (Yale University Press-New Haven: 19–201924), pp.19-

Some problems are simply the result of scientific and technological advances. Before Orville and Wilbur Wright's day, for example, it was a well-established principle that landowners had unlimited rights to the airspace above their property, any invasion of which constituted a *trespass*—a wrongful entry. But when the courts became convinced that the flying machine was here to stay, the utter impracticality of this view became apparent and owners' rights were subsequently limited to a "reasonable use" of their airspace.

Other novel problems result from changing methods of doing business or from shifting attitudes and moral views. Recent examples of the former are the proliferating use of the business franchise and of the general credit card. Attitudinal changes involve such questions as the proper ends of government, the propriety of Sunday sales, and the circumstances in which abortions should be permitted.

Some of these problems, of course, require solutions that are more political than legal in nature. This is particularly true where large numbers of the citizenry are faced with a common problem, such as the many difficulties faced by disabled persons in overcoming stereotypical attitudes and physical barriers, and where the alleviation of the problem may well be thought to constitute a legitimate function of either the state or federal government. The passage by Congress of the Americans with Disabilities Act of 1990 is an example of an attempted solution at the federal level of this particular problem.

Regardless of political considerations, however, many problems (particularly those involving disputes between individuals) can be settled only through the judicial process—that is, by one of the parties instituting legal action against the other. The duty to arrive at a final solution in all such cases falls squarely on the courts, no matter how novel or varied the issues. Although we are very fortunate in the U.S. to be able to resort to courts to enforce legal rights, court actions should always be viewed as a last resort. Negotiated settlements, mediation, arbitration, and other non-judicial dispute resolution techniques also play an important role in our society.

Knowability

One of the basic assumptions underlying a democracy—and, in fact, almost every form of government— is that the great majority of its citizens are going to obey its laws voluntarily. It hardly need be said that obedience requires some knowledge of the rules, or at least a reasonable means of acquiring this knowledge, on the part of the governed. No one, not even a lawyer, "knows" all the law or all the rules that make up a single branch of law; that could never be required. But it is necessary for persons who need legal advice to have access to experts on the rules—lawyers. It is equally necessary that the law be in such form that lawyers can determine their clients' positions with reasonable certainty to recommend the most advantageous courses of action.

Reasonableness

Most citizens abide by the law. Many do so even when they are not in sympathy with a particular rule, out of a sense of responsibility, a feeling that it is their civic duty, like it or not; others, no doubt, do so simply through fear of getting caught if they do not. But by and large the rules have to appear reasonable to the great majority of the people if they are going to be obeyed for long. The so-called Prohibition Amendment, which met with such wholesale violation that it was repealed in 1933, is the classic example of a rule lacking widespread acceptance. Closely allied with the idea of reasonableness is the requirement that the rules reflect, and adapt to, changing views of morality and justice. Figure 1.1 summarizes the qualities a legal system must possess to function properly.

Some Classifications of Law

Although the lawmaking and adjudicatory processes are the major concern in Part I, the products that result from the lawmaking process—the rules themselves and the bodies of law that they makeup—must not be overlooked. At the outset, particularly, it is useful to recognize some of the more important *classifications of law*.

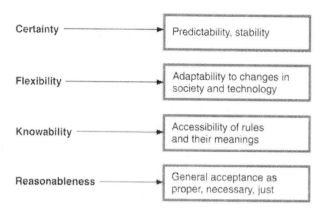

Figure 1.1 Requisites of Properly Functioning Legal System

Subject Matter

One way of classifying all the law in the United States is on the basis of the subject matter to which it relates. Fifteen or 20 branches or subjects are of particular importance, among them

- Administrative law
- Agency
- Commercial paper
- Constitutional law
- Contracts
- Corporation law
- Criminal law
- Domestic relations
- Evidence
- Partnerships
- Intellectual property
- Personal property
- Real property
- Sales
- Taxation
- Torts
- Wills and estates

Two observations can be made about this classification:

1. The subjects of agency, contracts, and torts are essentially *common law* in nature, whereas the subjects of corporation law, criminal law, sales, and taxation are governed by *statute*. Most of the remaining subjects, particularly evidence and property, are mixed in nature.

2. Several of these subjects obviously have a much closer relationship to the world of business than the others; these are the topics that fall within the usual business law or legal environment courses of a business school curriculum. Agency, contracts, corporation law, and sales are typical examples.

Federal and State Law

Another way of categorizing all law in this country is on the basis of the governmental unit from which it arises. On this basis, all law may be said to be either *federal law* or *state law*. Although there are some very important areas of federal law, as we shall see later, the great bulk of our law is state (or "local") law. Virtually all the subjects in the preceding list, for example, are within the jurisdiction of the individual states. Thus it is correct to say that there are 50 bodies of contract law in the United States, 50 bodies of corporation law, and so on. But this is not as bewildering as it appears, because the rules that constitute a given branch of law in each state substantially parallel those that exist in the other states—particularly in regard to common law subjects.

Common Law (Case Law) and Statutory Law

The term *common law* has several different meanings. It sometimes is used to refer only to the judge-made rules in effect in England at an early time—the "ancient unwritten law of England." It sometimes is also used to refer only to those judge-made rules of England that were subsequently adopted by the states in this country. In this text, however, we define the term more broadly to mean *all the rules and principles currently existing in any state, regardless of their historical origin, that result from judicial decisions in those areas of law where legislatures have not enacted comprehensive statutes.* This type of law, examined further in Chapter 4, is frequently referred to as case law, judge-made law, or unwritten law. Also, the term common law is sometimes used to refer to an entire legal system, the English Common Law, a system that prevails in countries having had an early English presence.

The term **statutory law,** by contrast, is generally used to refer to the state and federal *statutes* in effect at a given time—that is, rules that have been formally adopted by legislative bodies rather than by the courts. When *statutory law* is used in contrast to *common law,* it also comprises state and federal constitutions, municipal ordinances, and even treaties. Statutory law is frequently referred to as *written law* in the sense that once a statute or constitutional provision is adopted, its exact wording is set forth in the final text as passed— although the precise meaning, we should recall, is still subject to interpretation by the courts. The subjects of statutory law and judicial interpretation are also covered in Chapter 4.

Civil and Criminal Law

Civil Law

The most common types of controversies are civil actions—that is, actions in which the parties bringing the suits (the **plaintiffs**) are seeking to enforce private obligations or duties against the other parties (the **defendants**). **Civil laws,** then, are all those laws that spell out the rights and duties existing among individuals, business firms, and sometimes even government agencies. Contract law, tort law, and sales law all fall within the civil category.

The usual remedy that the plaintiff is seeking in a civil suit is *damages*—a sum of money roughly equivalent to the loss that he or she has suffered as a result of the defendant's wrong. Another civil remedy is the *injunction*—a court degree ordering the defendant to do or not to do some particular thing. The term civil law is also sometimes used in a broader sense to refer to an entire legal system, the Roman Civil Law, which is based originally on Roman law and more recently on France's Napoleonic Code. This system is used in countries that do not base their law on either the English Common Law or on Islamic law.

Criminal Law

Criminal law, in contrast to civil law, comprises those statutes by which a state or the federal government prohibits specified kinds of conduct and which additionally provide for the imposition of *fines or imprisonment* on persons convicted of violating them. Criminal suits are always brought by the government whose law has allegedly been violated. In enacting criminal statutes, a legislature is saying that certain activities are so inherently inimical to the public good that they constitute wrongs against organized society as a whole.

In addition to the nature of the liability imposed, criminal suits also differ from civil suits in another significant respect. In a criminal action it is necessary that the government's case be proved "beyond a reasonable doubt," whereas in civil actions the plaintif—the person bringing the suit—need prove his or her allegations only by "a preponderance of the evidence."

Crimes are either *felonies* or *misdemeanors*, depending on the severity of the penalty that the statute prescribes. A **felony,** the most serious of the two, is usually defined as a crime for which the legislature has provided a maximum penalty of either imprisonment for more than one year or death, as in the cases of murder, arson, or rape. **Misdemeanors** are all crimes carrying lesser penalties, for example, most traffic offenses.

Finally, it should be noted that some wrongful acts are of a dual nature, subjecting the wrongdoer to both criminal and civil penalties. For example, if X steals Y's car, the state could bring a criminal action against X, and Y could also bring a civil action to recover damages arising from the theft.

Public and Private Law

Some branches of law deal more directly with the relationship between the government and the individual than do others. On the basis of the degree to which this relationship is involved, law is occasionally classified as *public law* or *private law.*

When an area of law is directly concerned with the government-individual (or government- business) relationship, it falls within the *public law* designation. Subjects that are most clearly of this nature are criminal law, constitutional law, and administrative law. Because criminal laws deal with acts that are prohibited by a government itself, the violation of which is a "wrong against the state," such laws more directly affect the government-individual relationship than do any of the other laws. To the extent that our federal Constitution contains provisions substantially guaranteeing that certain rights of the individual or business cannot be invaded by federal and state government activities, the subject of constitutional law falls within the same category. Administrative law— comprising the principles that govern the procedures and activities of government boards and commissions—is of similar nature, in that such agencies are also concerned with the enforcement of certain state and federal statutes (and regulations promulgated thereunder) against individual citizens and businesses.

Many other areas of law, which are primarily concerned with the creation and enforcement of the rights of one individual against another, fall within the private law category. Although a state is indeed concerned that all its laws be properly enforced, even when individuals' or business firms' rights alone are being adjudicated, the concern in these areas is distinctly secondary to the interests of the parties themselves. There also are many areas of law that are of a mixed public-private nature; examples include state or federal statutes that regulate business activities and also create rights and obligations that individuals and businesses themselves may enforce.

Legal Misconceptions

Before proceeding to the more substantive areas of law, we will reflect briefly on two widely held misconceptions about our legal system.

Myth of the One Right Answer

It is widely believed that there is one "correct" legal answer to any legal controversy. This is true in some situations but certainly not as often as many persons believe. The chief reasons for divergent legal opinions are quite explainable:
1. Many rules are expressed in rather general terms to fit varying situations. Consequently, they afford the courts considerable latitude in deciding how they should be applied to specific situations.
2. The ultimate legal processes are in the hands of people, the judges, whose application of rules is always subject, to some extent, to their individual economic and political philosophies and personal moral beliefs. The law, therefore, is not an exact science and never will be.
3. The nature of most legal problems is such that something can be said in behalf of both litigants. The ordinary controversy does not present a clear-cut case of a "good" person suing a "bad" one. In some cases, each party has acted in good faith; in others, each is guilty of some degree of wrong. Additionally, there are some "legal collision" situations, in which one general principle of law may lead to one result while a second will lead to a different result. In such instances each principle will

probably have to undergo some modification when applied to particular cases, with results that are not always harmonious.

Myth of Judicial Eccentricity

The feeling is sometimes expressed that the law is not based on common sense—that its rules are so esoteric and arbitrary, and the judges and lawyers so preoccupied with them, that the results are not in keeping with reality or with what a reasonable person would expect. This indictment, in very large measure, is false. Cases invariably present practical problems for the courts, and the courts keep the practical considerations in mind in choosing the rules that apply.

Take, for example, this situation: C, a contractor, agrees to build a house according to certain specifications for O, the owner, for $60,000. When the house is completed, by which time O has paid $36,000, O discovers that the family room is 10 inches shorter than the plans specified. O refuses to make further payments for this reason, whereupon C brings suit to recover the balance of $24,000.

Now, as far as contract law is concerned, the principle is well established that a person who breaches a contract is not permitted to recover anything from the other party. The question here is, should that rule be applicable to this specific situation, where that would mean that C would not recover any of the balance? The practical person might well say, "I wouldn't think so— where the defect is so slight, it would seem unfair for C to suffer a loss of $24,000." The law reaches the same conclusion: under a view known as the *doctrine of substantial performance,* a person in C's position is usually permitted to recover most of the unpaid balance (even though C did, technically, breach the contract).

The foregoing does not mean, of course, that the law is perfect or that startling or unfair decisions never occur. They do. But by and large the unreasonable result occurs with much less frequency than reports in the news media would indicate; and even in such cases, the possibility usually exists that an appellate court will subsequently repair much of the damage.

Law, Justice, and Morals
Law and Justice

There is a close relationship between law and justice, but the terms are not equivalent. Most results of the application of legal rules are "just"—fair and reasonable. Where this is not so to any degree, the rules are usually changed. Yet it must be recognized that results occasionally "are not fair." Without attempting to defend the law in all such instances, some cautions should nevertheless be voiced.

First, there is never complete agreement as to what is just; there are always some decisions that seem just to some people but not to others. And even if there were unanimity of opinion—a perfect justice, so to speak—the facts in many cases are such that it is simply impossible to attain this end.

In some situations, for example, a legal controversy may arise between two honest persons who dealt with each other in good faith, as sometimes occurs in the area of "mutual mistake." Take this case: P contracts to sell land to G for $40,000, both parties mistakenly believing that a General Motors plant will be built on adjoining land. When G learns that the plant will not be built, he refuses to go through with the deal. If a court rules that the mistake frees G of his contractual obligations, the result might be quite unjust as far as P is concerned. And if it rules otherwise, the decision might seem quite unfair to G. Yet a decision must be made, one way or the other.

Second, in some instances it is fairly clear who is right and who is wrong, but the situation has progressed to the point where it is impossible, either physically or legally, to put the "good" person back into the original position. These "bad check" cases will illustrate: A buys a television from Z, giving Z her personal check in payment. If the check bounces, it is clear that Z should be allowed to recover the set. But what if the television has been destroyed by fire while in A's hands? Here the most the law can do is give Z a *judgment* against A—an order requiring A to pay a sum of money to Z equal to the amount of the check, which A may or may not be financially able to do. Or suppose that A had resold the television to X before Z learned that the check had bounced. Would it not be unfair to permit Z to retake the set from X, an innocent third party?

Because of these considerations, and others to be discussed later, the most the law can seek to accomplish is *substantial* justice in the greatest possible number of cases that come before it.

Law and Morals

Although the terms *law* and *morals* are not synonymous, legal standards and moral standards parallel one another more closely than many people believe. For example, criminal statutes prohibit certain kinds of conduct that are clearly "morally wrong"— murder, theft, arson, and the like. And other rules of law impose civil liability for similar kinds of conduct that, although not crimes, are also generally felt to be wrongful in nature—such as negligence, breach of contract, and fraud. To illustrate: S, in negotiating the sale of a race horse to B, tells B that the horse has run an eighth of a mile in 15 seconds on several occasions within the past month. In fact, the animal has never been clocked under 18 seconds, and S knows this. B, believing the statement to be true, purchases the horse. In such a case, S's intentional misstatement constitutes the tort of *fraud*, and B—assuming he can prove these facts in a legal action brought against S— has the right to set aside the transaction, returning the horse and recovering the price he has paid.

Why, then, are the terms *law* and *morals* not precisely synonymous? First, in some situations moral standards are higher than those imposed by law. For example, a person who has promised to keep an offer open for a stated period of time generally has the legal right to withdraw the offer before the given time has elapsed (for reasons appearing in a later chapter). Yet many persons who make such offers feel morally compelled to keep their offers open as promised, even though the law does not require this. Second, sometimes the law imposes higher standards than do our morals. For example, no religions or philosophies feature the 65-mile-per-hour speed limit as a major tenet, yet it is illegal to drive faster. Third, many rules of law and court decisions are based on statutory or practical requirements that have little or no relationship to moral considerations. For example, in the area of minors' contracts, we will see later that most courts feel, on balance, that it is sound public policy to permit minors to disaffirm (cancel) their contracts until they reach the age of majority, even though the contracts were otherwise perfectly valid and even though the persons with whom the minors dealt did not overreach or take advantage of them in any way. These observations notwithstanding, a society's moral standards will always heavily influence its legal standards. The relationship between legal standards and moral standards, as well as many related questions, is explored thoroughly in Chapter 10.

The interplay between law and morality is illustrated in the following case. Because the study of law involves to a very great extent the ability to reason from cases, students must have some familiarity with court procedures and jurisdiction. For this reason, major emphasis on cases will begin in the following chapter. The case below is our first, and therefore requires a few prefatory comments:

1. This is a *wrongful death* action authorized by statute to allow close relatives of deceased persons to sue those whose wrongful acts have caused a death. Without such statutes, we could be held liable for carelessly or intentionally injuring someone but could escape civil liability if we killed him or her. Under a state wrongful death statute, the *wrongful* act must be a *tort*, such as negligence or assault and battery, for which the deceased could have filed suit if only injury and not death had occurred. In this case, the basis for the wrongful death action is a claim by the *plaintiff* that the *defendant* committed the tort of negligence. The subject of torts is discussed in Chapters 8 and 21. In addition, the plaintiff is seeking to hold both the bartender and his employer legally responsible for damages. Although it is only the bartender's conduct that is in question, under the law of *agency* the bartender's employer also can be held liable if the bartender was acting within the *scope of his employment* at the time of the incident. The bartender clearly was acting within the scope of his employment in this case. If the court finds the bartender liable and the employer pays the judgment to the plaintiff, the employer will have a legal right to reimbursement from the bartender. As a practical matter, however, employers seldom exercise this right. The law of agency is discussed in Chapters 23 and 24.

2. In a civil case, the jury is normally the "judge of the *facts*." The trial judge decides the *law*. However, a judge, for reasons of judicial efficiency, can grant a summary judgment, terminating the case before it is ever tried. Summary judgment is appropriately granted if the evidence in the case so clearly indicates that factually one side or the other is entitled to prevail that a trial would be a waste of time. Only if the judge can conclude that there is "no genuine issue of material fact" should a summary judgment be granted on this ground. The following case involves a situation in which the trial judge had granted a summary judgment for the defendant.

3. If a trial court does grant a summary judgment motion, the losing party can always seek review in an appellate court. If the appellate court finds that the ruling was in error, the case will be returned to the trial court with instructions for a trial on the issue.

SOLDANO V. O'DANIELS
California Court of Appeal, 190 Cal. Rptr. 310 (1983)

On August 9, 1977, Villanueva pulled a gun and threatened the life of Soldano at Happy Jack's Saloon. A patron of Happy Jack's ran across the street to the Circle Inn and informed the bartender of the threat, asking the bartender either to call the police or allow him to use the phone to call the police. The bartender refused both requests. Soon thereafter, Villanueva shot Soldano to death. The plaintiff in this wrongful death action is Soldano's child. The defendants are the bartender and his employer. The trial judge dismissed the claim in response to the defendants' motion for summary judgment. Plaintiff appealed.

Andreen, Associate Justice:
Does a business establishment incur liability for wrongful death if it denies use of its telephone to a Good Samaritan who explains an emergency situation occurring without and wishes to call the police?

... There is a distinction, well rooted in the common law, between action and inaction. It has found its way into the prestigious Restatement Second of Torts, which provides in section 314:

The fact that the actor realizes or should realize that action on his part is necessary for another's aid or protection does not of itself impose upon him a duty to take such action.

The distinction between malfeasance and nonfeasance, between active misconduct working positive injury and failure to act to prevent mischief not brought on by the defendant, is founded on "that attitude of extreme individualism so typical of Anglo-Saxon legal thought." (Bohlen, *The Moral Duty to Aid Others as a Basis of Tort Liability*, part I (1908) 56 U.Pa.L. Rev.217, 219-220.)

Defendant argues that the request that its employee call the police [or permit the requestor to make the call] is a request that it do something. He points to the established rule that one who has not created peril ordinarily does not have a duty to take affirmative action to assist an imperiled person....

The refusal of the law to recognize the moral obligation of one to aid another when he is in peril and when such aid may be given without danger and at little cost in effort has been roundly criticized. Prosser describes the case law sanctioning such inaction as a "refus[al] to recognize the moral obligation of common decency and common humanity" and characterizes some of these decisions as "revolting to any moral sense." (Prosser, *Law of Torts* (4th ed. 1971) §56.)

As noted in Tarasoff v. Regents of University of California, 131 Cal. Rptr. 14(1976), the courts have increased the instances in which affirmative duties are imposed not by direct rejection of the common law rule, but by expanding the list of special relationships which will justify departure from that rule....

In *Tarasoff*, a therapist was told by his patient that he intended to kill Tatiana Tarasoff. The therapist and his supervisors predicted the patient presented a serious danger of violence. In fact he did, for he carried out his threat. The court held the patient therapist relationship was enough to create a duty to exercise reasonable care to protect others from the foreseeable result of the patient's illness.

... Here there was no special relationship between the defendant and the deceased. But this does not end the matter.

It is time to re-examine the common law rule of nonliability for nonfeasance in the special circumstances of the instant case.

Besides well-publicized actions taken to increase the severity of punishments for criminal offenses, the Legislature has expressed a social imperative to diminish criminal action. [The court then referred to laws passed to compensate citizens for injuries sustained in crime suppression efforts, to make it a misdemeanor to refuse to relinquish a party line when informed that it is needed to call the police, and to establish an emergency '911' telephone system.]

The above statutes ... demonstrate that "that attitude of extreme individualism so typical of Anglo-Saxon legal thought" may need limited reexamination in light of current societal conditions and the facts of this case to determine whether the defendant owed a duty to the deceased to permit the use of the telephone. ...

We turn now to the concept of duty in a tort case. The Supreme Court has identified certain factors to be considered in determining whether a duty is owed to third persons. These factors include: "the foreseeability of harm to the plaintiff, the degree of certainty that the plaintiff suffered injury, the closeness of the connection between the defendant's conduct and the injury suffered, the moral blame attached to the defendant's conduct, the policy of preventing future harm, the extent of the burden to the defendant and consequences to the community of imposing a duty to exercise care with resulting liability for breach, and the availability, cost, and prevalence of insurance

for the risk involved." Rowland v. Christian, 443 P.2d 561(Cal. 1968).

We examine those factors in reference to this case. (1) The harm to the decedent was abundantly foreseeable; it was imminent. The employee was expressly told that a man had been threatened. The employee was a bartender. As such he knew it is foreseeable that some people who drink alcohol in the milieu of a bar setting are prone to violence. (2) The certainty of decedent's injury is undisputed. (3) There is arguably a close connection between the employee's conduct and the injury: the patron wanted to use the phone to summon the police to intervene. The employee's refusal to allow the use of the phone prevented this anticipated intervention. If permitted to go to trial, the plaintiff may be able to show that the probable response time of the police would have been shorter than the time between the prohibited telephone call and the fatal shot. (4) The employee's conduct displayed a disregard for human life that can be characterized as morally wrong: he was callously indifferent to the possibility that Darrell Soldano would die as the result of his refusal to allow a person to use the telephone. Under the circumstances before us the bartender's burden was minimal and exposed him to no risk: all he had to do was allow the use of the telephone. It would have cost him or his employer nothing. It could have saved a life. (5) Finding a duty in these circumstances would promote a policy of preventing future harm. A citizen would not be required to summon the police but would be required, in circumstances such as those before us, not to impede another who has chosen to summon aid. (6) We have no information on the question of the availability, cost, and prevalence of insurance for the risk, but note that the liability which is sought to be imposed here is that of employee negligence, which is covered by many insurance policies. (7) The extent of the burden on the defendant was minimal, as noted.

As the [California] Supreme Court has noted, the reluctance of the law to impose liability for nonfeasance, as distinguished from misfeasance, is in part due to the difficulties in setting standards and of making rules workable [citing *Tarasoff*]. Many citizens simply "don't want to get involved." No rule should be adopted which would require a citizen to open up his or her house to a stranger so that the latter may use the telephone to call for emergency assistance. As Mrs. Alexander in Anthony Burgess' *A Clockwork Orange* learned to her horror, such an action may be fraught with danger. It does not follow, however, that use of a telephone in a public portion of a business should be refused for a legitimate emergency call. Imposing liability for such a refusal would not subject innocent citizens to possible attack by the "Good Samaritan," for it would be limited to an establishment open to the public during times when it is open to business, and to places within the establishment ordinarily accessible to the public.

We conclude that the bartender owed a duty to the plaintiff's decedent to permit the patron from Happy Jack's to place a call to the police or to place the call himself.

It bears emphasizing that the duty in this case does not require that one must go to the aid of another. That is not the issue here. The employee was not the Good Samaritan intent on aiding another. The patron was.

It would not be appropriate to await legislative action in this area. The rule was fashioned in the common law tradition, as were the exceptions to the rule.... The courts have a special responsibility to reshape, refine and guide legal doctrine they have created.

The words of the Supreme Court [in Rodriguez v. Bethlehem Steel Corp., 115 Cal. Rptr. 765 (1974)] on the role of the courts in a common law system are well suited to our obligation here:

> The inherent capacity of the common law for growth and change is its most significant feature. Its development has been determined by the social needs of the community which it serves. It is constantly expanding and developing in keeping with advancing civilization and the new conditions and progress of society, and adapting itself to the gradual change of trade, commerce, arts, inventions, and the needs of the country....
>
> In short, as the United States Supreme Court has aptly said, "This flexibility and capacity for growth and adaptation is the peculiar boast and excellence of the common law." [Citation omitted].

The possible imposition of liability on the defendant in this case is not a global change in the law. It is but a slight departure from the "morally questionable" rule of nonliability for inaction absent a special relationship. It is a logical extension of Restatement section 327 which imposes liability for negligent interference with a third person who the defendant knows is attempting to render necessary aid. However small it may be, it is a step which should be taken.

We conclude there are sufficient justiciable issues to permit the case to go to trial and therefore reverse.

Comment

1. As this is our first case, a few comments about the mechanics of case reporting are in order:

   a. The opinion, written by Justice Andreen, is that of an intermediate appellate court in a state system. It hears appeals from California state trial courts, and its decisions can be appealed to the California State Supreme Court. In our state and federal courts, all appeals courts have at least three judges, which decide cases by majority vote. Justice Andreen had the primary responsibility for preparing the appeals court's opinion in this case.

b. The basic facts of the case are summarized by the authors of the text. In the court's opinion, the ellipsis points (...) indicate portions that have been deleted by the authors of this text. Deletions are made to eliminate redundancy or exclude issues irrelevant to points that the case has been selected to illustrate.

c. When a general principle of law is stated in a decision, the court will frequently *cite* (refer to) earlier cases in which that principle has been established. Here, for example, the court has referred to Tarasoff v. Regents of University of California for such a purpose. To facilitate the reading of opinions, the authors have generally omitted such references except where the cited case is heavily relied on to support the decision.

2. A word of caution: It is imperative for readers to acquire the ability to *determine the precise issue* of a case, so they will not leap to unwarranted general conclusions. Could we say, for example, that the instant case establishes the principle that on seeing one person attack another with a knife, a bystander has the legal duty to personally intervene to save the victim? Not at all. This court was very careful in stating the issue narrowly and emphasizing that it was only creating a small exception to the traditional rule.

Law, Technology, and Globalization

The law is always evolving in response to philosophical, practical, social, and other influences. Currently, three forces shaping the law are of overarching importance. One is the interaction of law and morality highlighted in the preceding section (and studied in more detail in Chapter 10). The two other forces dramatically impacting all areas of the law are technology and globalization.

Law and Technology

Creation of the Internet (along with other technological advances) has many implications for how business is done and how it is regulated. In some areas, old principles simply needed to be adapted and reapplied to the new technological reality. In many other areas, the law has been substantially rewritten. As you read through this text, you will see many examples of these changes.

Law and Globalization

As business goes global, so does its regulation. This requires cooperation and coordination on an unprecedented scale. Companies that develop intellectual property in our information age wish to protect that property and exploit it economically, not only in their home country but throughout the world. This necessitates international conventions to establish global rules for patents, copyrights and other forms of intellectual property. It also requires international organizations to enforce those rules. These are explored in Chapter 9.

As another example, consider the Enron scandal which recently rocked confidence in American business. Congress responded by passing the Sarbanes-Oxley Act of 2002, which imposed new rules for corporate disclosure, corporate governance, and audit firm practice (among other changes). These will be discussed in some detail in our chapters on business ethics and securities regulation. Sarbanes-Oxley's provisions were written to govern not only American companies, but also foreign companies that list their shares on American stock exchanges or otherwise access our capital markets and foreign accounting firms that audit those companies. European companies and accounting firms are especially concerned that Sarbanes-Oxley has serious implications for their corporate governance and audit practices. They resent the export of American law. The Securities and Exchange Commission (SEC) that is charged with enforcing American securities laws made some concessions to foreign firms, but generally intends to apply Sarbanes-Oxley's provisions to them. Sarbanes-Oxley subjects executives of German firms, for example, to criminal prosecution in the United States if their financial statements filed with the SEC contain fraudulent statements.

On the other side of things, European Union antitrust laws are stricter than American laws. General Electric was unable to acquire Honeywell because of EU rules, even though both are American companies and U.S. antitrust officials had approved the deal. Japanese rules can make it difficult for American companies to enter certain industries in Japan. Every company hoping to do business abroad, and some that don't, must be concerned with the international legal environment as well as their own domestic rules.

The following case illustrates the complications that can arise when technological and global forces collide.

Yahoo! v. La Ligue Contre Le Racisme Et L'antisemitsme
U.S. District Court, Northern District of California, 169 F.Supp.2d 1181 (2001)

Plaintiff Yahoo! is a leading Internet service provider. Based in the U.S., it has subsidiary corporations operating regional sites and services in 20 other nations, including Yahoo! France. Yahoo!'s auction site allows anyone to post an item for sale and solicit bids from any computer user around the world. Yahoo! is never a party to these transactions, but does monitor them and prohibits certain items from being sold, including stolen goods, body parts, prescription and illegal drugs, weapons, and the like. Yahoo! informs auction sellers that they must comply with Yahoo!'s policies and may not offer items to buyers in jurisdictions where the sale of such item violates applicable laws.

Defendants La Ligue Contre Le Racisme Et l'Antisemitisme (LICRA) and L'Union Des Etudiants Juifs De France are nonprofit French organizations dedicated to eliminating anti-Semitism. In April 2000, LICRA sent a "cease and desist" letter to Yahoo!'s California headquarters informing Yahoo! that the sale of Nazi and Third Reich related goods though its auction services violates French law. LICRA threatened to take legal action unless Yahoo! took steps to prevent such sales within eight days. Defendants subsequently sued Yahoo! in the Trial de Grande Instance de Paris (the "French Court").

The French Court found that 1,000 Nazi and Third Reich related items were being offered for sale on Yahoo.com's auction site. Because any French citizen is able to access these materials on Yahoo.com directly or through a link on Yahoo.fr, the French court concluded that the auction site violates Section R465-1 of the French Criminal Code, which prohibits exhibition of Nazi propaganda and artifacts for sale. In May 2000, the French Court ordered Yahoo! to (1) eliminate French citizens' access to any material on the Yahoo.com auction site that offers for sale any Nazi objects, (2) eliminate French citizens' access to Web pages displaying such items, (3) post a warning to French citizens that searches on Yahoo.fr could lead to cites containing prohibited material, and (4) remove from all browser directories accessible in France various index headings such as "negationists" [people who claim the Holocaust did not occur]. The order subjected Yahoo! to a penalty of 100,000 Euros for each day that it failed to comply with the order.

Yahoo! asked for reconsideration, claiming that while it could (and did) post the required warning to French citizens, it was technologically impossible to comply with the rest of the court's orders. The French Court ordered compliance, prompting Yahoo! to file this suit in California.

Yahoo! asked the federal court to issue a judgment declaring that compliance with the order would impermissibly infringe upon Yahoo!'s rights under the First Amendment to the Constitution because Yahoo! lacked the technology to block French citizens from accessing its auction cite without banning Nazi-related material from Yahoo.com altogether. Yahoo! filed a motion for summary judgment [a court order finding on the merits in its favor].

Fogel, District Judge:

The instant case presents novel and important issues arising from the global reach of the Internet. Indeed, the specific facts of this case implicate issues of policy, politics, and culture that are beyond the purview of one nation's judiciary. Thus it is critical that the Court define at the outset what is and is not at stake in the present proceeding.

This case is not about the moral acceptability of promoting the symbols or propaganda of Nazism. Most would agree that such acts are profoundly offensive. By any reasonable standard of morality, the Nazis were responsible for one of the worst displays of inhumanity in recorded history. This Court is acutely mindful of the emotional pain reminders of the Nazi era cause to Holocaust survivors and deeply respectful of the motivations of the French Republic in enacting the underlying statutes and of the defendant organizations in seeking relief under those statutes. Vigilance is the key to preventing atrocities such as the Holocaust from occurring again.

Nor is this case about the right of France or any other nation to determine its own law and social policies. A basic function of a sovereign state is to determine by law what forms of speech and conduct are acceptable within its borders. In this instance, as a nation whose citizens suffered the effects of Nazism in ways that are incomprehensible to most Americans, France clearly has the right to enact and enforce laws such as those relied upon by the French Court here.

What is at issue here is whether it is consistent with the Constitution and laws of the United States for another nation to regulate speech by a United States resident within the United States on the basis that such speech can be accessed by Internet users in that nation. In a world in which ideas and information transcend borders and the Internet in particular renders the physical distance between speaker and audience virtually meaningless, the implications of this question go far beyond the facts of this case. The modern world is home to widely varied cultures with radically divergent value systems. There is little doubt that Internet users in the United States routinely engage in speech that violates, for example, China's laws against religious expression, the laws of various nations against advocacy of gender equality or homosexuality, or even the United Kingdom's restrictions on freedom of the press. If the government or another party in one of these sovereign nations were to seek enforcement of such laws against Yahoo! or another U.S.-based Internet service provider, what principles should guide the court's analysis?

The Court has stated that it must and will decide this case in accordance with the Constitution and laws of the United States. It recognizes that in so doing, it necessarily adopts certain value judgments embedded in those enactments, including the fundamental judgment expressed in the First Amendment that it is preferable to permit the non-violent expression of offensive viewpoints rather than to impose viewpoint-based governmental regulation upon speech. The government and people of France have made a different judgment based upon their own experience. In undertaking its inquiry as to the proper application of the laws of the United States, the Court intends no disrespect for that judgment or for the experience that has informed it.

The French order prohibits the sale or display of items based on their association with a particular political organization and bans the display of Web sites based on the authors' viewpoint with respect to the Holocaust and anti-Semitism. A United States court constitu-

tionally could not make such an order. The First Amendment does not permit the government to engage in viewpoint-based regulation of speech absent a compelling governmental interest, such as averting a clear and present danger of imminent violence. In addition, the French Court's mandate that Yahoo! "take all necessary measures to dissuade and render impossible any access via Yahoo.com to the Nazi artifact auction service and to any other site or service that may be construed as constituting an apology for Nazism or a contesting of Nazi crimes" is far too general and imprecise to survive the strict scrutiny required by the First Amendment. The phrase, "and any other site or service that may be construed as an apology for Nazism or a contesting of Nazi crimes" fails to provide Yahoo! with a sufficiently definite warning as to what is proscribed. Phrases such as "all necessary measures" and "render impossible" instruct Yahoo! to undertake efforts that will impermissibly chill and perhaps even censor protected speech. The loss of First Amendment freedoms, for even minimal periods of time, unquestionably constitutes "irreparable injury" [that justifies relief].

Rather than argue directly that the French order somehow could be enforced in the United States in a manner consistent with the First Amendment, defendants argue instead that at present there is no real or immediate threat to Yahoo!'s First Amendment rights because the French order cannot be enforced at all until after the cumbersome process of petitioning the French court to fix a penalty has been completed. [However,] there is no dispute that the French order is valid under French law and that the French Court may fix a penalty retroactive to the date of the order.

Defendants also claim that there is no real or immediate threat to Yahoo! because they do not presently intend to seek enforcement of the French order in the United States. [However, the] French order permits retroactive penalties. [Also,] the French order had the immediate effect of inducing Yahoo! to implement new restrictive policies on its auction site. Third, ...the provisions of the French order that require Yahoo! to regulate the content of its Web sites on Yahoo.com never have been waived, suspended or stayed and apparently remain in full force and effect. Under these circumstances, Defendants' assurances that they do not intend to enforce the order at the present time do not remove the threat that they may yet seek sanctions against Yahoo!'s present and ongoing conduct.

Comity. No legal judgment has any effect, of its own force, beyond the limits of the sovereignty from which its authority is derived. However, the United States Constitution and implementing legislation require that full faith and credit be given to judgments of sister states, territories, and possessions of the United States. The extent to which the United States, or any state, honors the judicial decrees of foreign nations is a matter of choice, governed by "the comity of nations." Hilton v. Guyot, 159 U.S. 113(1895). Comity "is neither a matter of absolute obligation, on the one hand, nor of mere courtesy and good will, upon the other." United States courts generally recognize foreign judgments and decrees unless enforcement would be prejudicial or contrary to the country's interests.

As discussed previously, the French order's content and viewpoint-based regulation of the Web pages and auction site on Yahoo.com, while entitled to great deference as an articulation of French law, clearly would be inconsistent with the First Amendment if mandated by a court in the United States. What makes this case uniquely challenging is that the Internet in effect allows one to speak in more than one place at the same time. Although France has the sovereign right to regulate what speech is permissible in France, this Court may not enforce a foreign order that violates the protections of the United States Constitution by chilling protected speech that occurs simultaneously within our borders.

The reason for limiting comity in this area is sound. The protection to free speech and the press embodied in [the First] amendment would be seriously jeopardized by the entry of foreign court judgments granted pursuant to standards deemed appropriate in [another country] but considered antithetical to the protections afforded the press by the U.S. Constitution." Bachchan v. India Abroad Publications, Inc., 585 N.Y.S.2d 661(Sup.Ct. 1992). Absent a body of law that establishes international standards with respect to speech on the Internet and an appropriate treaty or legislation addressing enforcement of such standards to speech originating within the United States, the principle of comity is outweighed by the Court's obligation to uphold the First Amendment.

In light of the Court's conclusion that enforcement of the French order by a United States court would be inconsistent with the First Amendment, the factual question of whether Yahoo! possesses the technology to comply with the order is immaterial. Even assuming for purposes of the present motion that Yahoo! does possess such technology, compliance still would involve an impermissible restriction on speech.

Yahoo! seeks a declaration from this Court that the First Amendment precludes enforcement within the United States of a French order intended to regulate the content of its speech over the Internet. It is so ordered.

This case illustrates the potential complications of doing business internationally in the Internet era perhaps even better than the authors of the text originally thought when including it in earlier editions. In August 2004, a 3-member panel of the Ninth

Circuit Court of Appeals reversed this opinion in Yahoo! Inc. v. La Ligue Contre Le Racisme et L'Antisemitisme, 379 F.3d 1120 (9th Cir. 2004). The appellate court did not address the tricky substantive issues, but held that the trial court did not have personal jurisdiction (a concept we explore in Chapter 2) over the defendants and would not until they attempted to come to the U.S. to enforce the French court's orders. Then, the entire 11-member Ninth Circuit Court of Appeals reviewed the panel decision. In January 2006, by a 6-5 vote, it agreed with the panel decision that the district court decision should be reversed. The reasoning among the 6 judges in the majority differed somewhat, but the ultimate conclusion was that Yahoo!'s lawsuit was premature because the French organizations had not attempted to enforce the French court order in the U.S. If the French organizations do attempt to enforce the French court order in the U.S., the court will almost certainly refuse to do so for the precise reasons set forth in the district court opinion that you just read.

Meanwhile, back in France, Yahoo! has been fined $13,000 per day every day since February 2001, so that it theoretically owes approximately $24 million as of February 2006. Also, a French court has acquitted a Yahoo! executive of criminal charges, while another French court has found that it had jurisdiction over a civil suit arising from the same facts brought against that same executive by the Association of Auschwitz Detainees.

CHAPTER 2

COURT SYSTEMS, JURISDICTION, AND FUNCTIONS

- Court Systems
- Problems of Jurisdiction
- Law, Equity, and Remedies

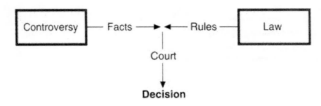

Figure 2.1 Process of Adjudication

LEGAL RULES AND principles take on vitality and meaning only when they are applied to real-life; controversies between real persons, when the rules are *applied tofacts*—when, for example, a particular plaintiff is successful or unsuccessful in his or her attempt to recover a specific piece of land from a particular defendant, or where one company is successful or unsuccessful in recovering damages from another company as a result of an alleged breach of contract on the latter company's part. But the fitting of rules to facts— the settlings of legal controversies—does not occur automatically. This process, which we call **adjudication**, has to be in somebody's hands. Traditionally that "somebody" has been the state and federal courts that hear thousands of cases each year. (Many state and federal administrative agencies also conduct adjudicative types of proceedings.) As Figure 2.1 indicates, rules and facts come together in the adjudication process, leading to a decision.

The primary reason, then, for looking at the courts and the work that they do is to gain an overall awareness of this important legal process. There is, however, another reason for doing so. In the following chapters many actual cases are presented. The reader is given the basic facts of a particular controversy, the judgment entered by the trial court on the basis of those facts, and excerpts of the appellate court's decision in affirming or reversing the trial court's judgment. Obviously, some familiarity with court systems and the judicial process will facilitate one's understanding of the legal significance of each step in these proceedings.

In this chapter, then, we take a brief look at the state and federal court systems and at some problems of jurisdiction arising in those systems. We also examine some additional matters, such as venue, conflict of laws, and the law-equity distinction. In Chapter 3, we will study the litigation process, focusing on the functions of the trial and appellate courts, and then we will discuss some alternative methods of dispute resolution.

Court Systems

As a result of our federal system of government, we live under two distinct, and essentially separate, sovereign types of government—the state governments and the federal government. Each has its own laws and its own court system. For this reason, it is necessary to study both systems to acquire an adequate knowledge of the court structures within which controversies are settled.

The Typical State System

Although court systems vary somewhat from state to state, most state courts fall into three general categories. In ascending order, they are (1) courts of limited jurisdiction, (2) general trial courts, and (3) appellate courts (which frequently exist at two levels).

Courts of Limited Jurisdiction

Every state has trial courts that are limited as to the kinds of cases they can hear and are thus called **courts of limited jurisdiction**. Examples include justice of the peace courts, municipal courts, traffic courts, probate courts (hearing matters of wills and decedents' estates), and domestic relations courts (handling divorce, custody, and child support cases). Numerically speaking, these courts hear most cases that come to trial. However, they need not be discussed in detail here because many of the matters they hear are relatively minor in nature (such as traffic violations) and others involve very specialized subject matter (such as a dispute over a deceased person's estate).

General Trial Courts

The most important cases involving state law, and the ones we will be most concerned with hereafter, commence in the **general trial courts.** These are courts of "general jurisdiction"; they are empowered to hear all cases except those expressly assigned by statute to the courts of limited jurisdiction. Virtually all important cases involving contract law, criminal law, and corporation law, for example, originate in the general trial courts. In some states these courts are called *district courts*, in others *common plea courts,* and in still others *superior courts.* Whatever the specific name, one or more such courts normally exist in every county of every state. Throughout the remainder of the text, we will sometimes refer to these general trial courts simply as state trial courts to distinguish them from federal trial courts. When this is done, we are referring to the state trial courts of general jurisdiction rather than to those of limited jurisdiction.

Appellate Courts

All states have one or more **appellate courts,** which hear appeals from judgments entered by the courts below. In some states there is only one such court, usually called the *supreme court,* but in the more populous states a layer of appellate courts is interposed between the trial courts and the supreme court. Such courts decide legal questions; they do not hear testimony of witnesses or otherwise entertain new evidence.

The Federal Court System

Article III, Section 1 of the U.S. Constitution provides that "the judicial power of the United States shall be vested in one Supreme Court, and in such inferior courts as the

Congress may from time to time ordain and establish." The numerous federal courts that exist today by virtue of this section can, at the risk of oversimplification, be placed into three main categories similar to those of the state courts: (1) specialized trial courts, (2) U.S. district courts, and (3) appellate courts—the courts of appeal and the Supreme Court.

Specialized U.S. Courts

Some federal courts have very specialized subject matter jurisdiction. Examples include the U.S. Tax Court, which hears only federal tax cases, and the U.S. Claims Court, which hears only claims against the U.S. government. These and other specialized federal courts are somewhat analogous to the courts of limited jurisdiction in state court systems.

U.S. District Courts

The basic trial courts within the federal system are the *U.S. district courts*, sometimes called *federal district courts*. Most federal cases originate in these courts.

Congress has created 96 judicial districts, each of which covers all or part of a state or a U.S. territory. The federal districts, with the exceptions noted above, essentially are based on state lines. The less populated states have only one federal district court within their boundaries, whereas most of the remaining states have two, and a few states have three or four. U.S. territories such as Puerto Rico, Guam, and the Virgin Islands each have one federal district court. Every square foot of land in this country and its territories is, geographically speaking, within the jurisdiction of one U.S. district court.

Although the federal district courts are the most important courts in the federal system, they are not really courts of general jurisdiction in the same sense as are the general state courts. State courts of general jurisdiction are essentially a repository of general judicial power; if no other court has jurisdiction over a particular type of case, then a state court of general jurisdiction has power to hear the case. Federal courts, however, are part of the federal government, and the federal government is a government of limited powers under our Constitution. Thus, as we will see shortly, even our most important federal trial courts—the U.S. district courts—have power to hear only those cases that have been specifically placed within their jurisdiction by the Constitution and federal statutory enactments.

Appellate Courts

Above the district courts are two levels of *federal appellate courts*—the U.S. courts of appeal and, above them, the U.S. Supreme Court. There are 13 U.S. courts of appeal. Eleven of these, located in "circuits" across the country, have jurisdiction to hear appeals from the district courts located in the states within their respective boundaries. For example, the U.S. Court of Appeals for the Ninth Circuit in San Francisco hears

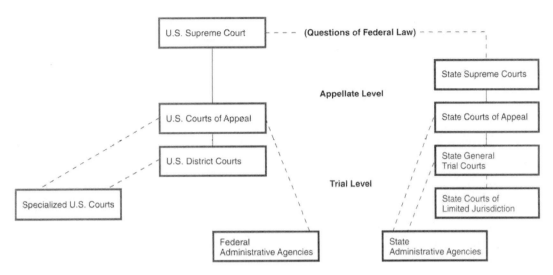

Figure 2.2 Federal and State Court Systems

appeals from decisions of district courts within the states of Alaska, Arizona, California, Hawaii, Idaho, Montana, Nevada, Oregon, and Washington. Each of these 11 appellate courts also hears appeals from the rulings of federal administrative agencies. The jurisdiction of the remaining two appellate courts is somewhat different from that of the others. The U.S. Court of Appeals for the District of Columbia hears appeals from the federal district court located in the District, as well as appeals from rulings of federal agencies that are issued there. The other appellate court is the U.S. Court of Appeals for the Federal Circuit, which hears all appeals from patent applicants whose applications were rejected by the U.S. Patent & Trademark Office, all appeals from patent infringement cases from U.S. District Courts, and appeals from several specialized courts.

Appeals from judgments of the U.S. courts of appeal, like appeals from judgments of the state supreme courts that present federal questions, can be taken to the U.S. Supreme Court. In most cases, however, these appeals are not a matter of right. Rather, the parties who seek review must petition the Supreme Court for a **writ of certiorari,** and the Court has absolute discretion in deciding which of these cases are sufficiently important to warrant the granting of certiorari. (A writ of certiorari is an order of a higher court requiring a lower court to send to it the documentary record of the trial.) In a typical year the Court can hear only about 90 of the several thousand appeals that are made.

Some Observations

The typical state court system and the federal system can be diagrammed as in Figure 2.2. Several general comments can be made about this diagram.

The basic trial courts are the U.S. district courts and the state general trial courts; all courts above this level are appellate courts.

Trial courts must settle questions of both *factand law,* whereas appellate courts rule on questions of law only. Questions of fact are "what happened" questions: for instance, did the defendant corporations expressly or implicitly agree not to sell goods to the plaintiff? Questions of law, by contrast, are "what is the rule applicable to the facts?"

Although most decisions of the trial courts are not appealed, a substantial number are. Hereafter we are concerned primarily with the decisions of the appellate courts. There are several basic reasons for this. First, state trial courts usually enter a judgment without writing a formal opinion as to their reasoning; and, even if there is such an opinion, it is normally not reported (published). (The main exception is that the U.S. District Courts do publish a significant percentage of their opinions.) Appellate courts, however, normally do write opinions that are reported, and access to them is available to anyone wishing to look up the rulings of law involved. Second, appellate courts have more opportunity to delineate the legal issues in their opinions for the benefit of lawyers and others who may read them. Third, if the appellate court disagrees with the result reached by the trial court, the appellate court's decision is, of course, controlling.

Once a case is initiated within a given court system, it will normally stay within that system until a final judgment is reached. Thus, if a case is properly commenced in a state court of general jurisdiction, any appeal from the trial court's judgment must be made to the next higher state court rather than to a federal appellate court. And if a case reaches the highest court in the state, its judgment is usually final. In other words, on matters of state law, state supreme courts are indeed supreme. However, should a state supreme court rule on a case that turns on interpretation of a federal statute or a provision of the U.S. Constitution, an appeal could be taken to the U.S. Supreme Court, which has the final word on matters of *federal law.* Again, however, the U.S. Supreme Court has discretion whether to hear an appeal, whether it is from a U.S. Court of Appeals or from a decision on federal law made by the highest court in a state court system.

The normal terminology is being used here. In a few states, however, the "supreme court" label is given to an intermediate appellate court, with the highest court in the state bearing some other name. The court of last resort in the state of New York, for example, is the Court of Appeals of New York.

With regard to the "title" of an appealed case, the state and federal courts follow somewhat different rules. In most state courts, the original plaintiff's name appears first—just as it did in the trial court. Suppose, for example, that Pink (plaintiff) sues Doe (defendant) in a state trial court, where the case is obviously Pink v. Doe. If the judgment of the trial court is that the title of the case remains Pink v. Doe in the apellate courts, no matter which party is the appellant (the one bringing the appeal). In the federal courts and in a few states, however, the appellant's name appears first. Under this rule, if Doe (defendant) loses in a U.S. district court and appeals to a U.S. court of appeals, the title of the case will be Doe v. Pink in the higher court. For this reason, when one sees a case in a federal appellate court so entitled, one cannot assume that Doe was the party who originated the action in the trial court. That determination must be made by referring to the facts of the case as set forth in the decision of the appellate court. In addition, when there are multiple plaintiffs and/or multiple defendants, the title of the case typically is abbreviated so that only the first listed plaintiff and first listed defendant are named.

Problems of Jurisdiction

In a general sense, the term jurisdiction refers to the legal power of a governmental body or official to take some type of action. With respect to courts, jurisdiction means the power to adjudicate, that is, to hear and decide a case and render a judgment that is legally binding on the parties. A court normally has such power only if it has both **subject matter jurisdiction** and **personal jurisdiction.** Any action taken by a court without complete jurisdiction has no legal effect.

Subject Matter Jurisdiction

Subject matter jurisdiction consists of the power to hear a particular kind of case. In each of our states, provisions in the state constitution specify which types of cases are within the subject matter jurisdiction of which types of courts. Typically, state legislative enactments then provide more detail on the subject matter jurisdiction of particular state courts. As we have already seen, some state courts have very limited jurisdiction, and one set of state courts will have more general jurisdiction. In the federal system, the U.S. Constitution specifies in general terms the kinds of cases that are within the subject matter jurisdiction of the federal courts, and federal statutes provide more detail. The federal courts themselves have also added more detail to the jurisdictional rules through their interpretations of the relevant constitutional and statutory provisions.

Subject Matter Jurisdiction of the Federal Courts

As we have already seen, the federal courts have subject matter jurisdiction over only those kinds of cases that are designated by the U.S. Constitution and then made more specific by federal statutes.

Criminal Cases

Federal courts have jurisdiction over criminal cases in which a violation of a federal criminal statute is alleged. There is a large body of federal criminal law, including statutes making it a crime to smuggle drugs into the United States, hijack an airplane, commit securities fraud, threaten the president, cross state lines after having committed a state law crime, and so on. Some federal statutes, such as the securities and antitrust laws, include both civil liability and criminal penalty provisions. Congress has power to pass criminal laws, like civil ones, only if there is some basis in the Constitution authorizing it to do so. Many federal criminal laws are based on the constitutional provision that empowers Congress to pass laws regulating interstate commerce, but others are enacted under the power granted by different constitutional provisions.

Civil Cases

We are primarily concerned about the jurisdiction and functions of courts in civil cases. Most of the time it will be obvious whether a particular civil case can be heard by a federal court, but sometimes there are difficult questions. These questions may arise when a plaintiff's attorney thinks it would be in the client's best interest to have the case decided by a federal rather than a state court, but where some of the facts relating to the jurisdictional question are not clear. There can be many reasons why a plaintiffs attorney might prefer to file a case in federal court. For example, if the case has to be filed in a state where the attorney normally does not practice, the attorney may be unfamiliar with the procedures of that state's courts and thus may be more comfortable in a federal court in that state, where the procedures are basically the same as in federal courts in other states. Likewise, if a plaintiff has filed in a state court where the defendant's attorney usually does not practice, the latter might attempt to have the case moved to a federal court for the same reason. Sometimes a question about federal versus state court jurisdiction can arise because the plaintiff has filed a case in federal court but the defendant's attorney sees some strategic advantage in having the case decided by a state court. There are two general categories of civil cases that the Constitution and federal statutes have placed within the subject matter jurisdiction of the federal courts.

Federal Question Cases. Federal courts have subject matter jurisdiction over any civil case in which the plaintiff's claim arises from the U.S. Constitution, a federal statute, or a federal treaty. However, a civil lawsuit based on a treaty provision is rare. For example, if a group of environmentally concerned citizens sues a corporation alleging that it was polluting a stream in violation of the federal Clean Water Act, there would be a **federal question.** The plaintiff's claim must directly raise a question of federal law; if the plaintiff's claim does not raise a federal question, the defendant cannot create federal subject matter jurisdiction by raising a federal question in a defense or counterclaim.

It is common for a plaintiff to assert two or more legal claims based on the same set of factual circumstances. If one of these claims raises a federal question and thereby creates federal subject matter jurisdiction, the federal court also has subject matter jurisdiction over any other claim arising out of the same facts, even if the other claim is based on state law rather than federal law. This type of federal subject matter jurisdiction is called "pendent" (or "ancillary") jurisdiction and represents a pragmatic attempt to avoid multiple lawsuits.

Federal jurisdiction based on a federal question may be either *exclusive* or *concurrent*. A claim arising under the U.S. Constitution creates concurrent federal-state jurisdiction, which means that it can be heard by either a federal or state court. A claim arising under a federal statute usually creates concurrent federal-state jurisdiction unless the statute itself says otherwise. A number of federal statutes, such as patent, copyright, antitrust, and securities laws, specifically provide for exclusive federal court jurisdiction; claims thereunder can be filed only in a federal court.

If a federal question case is taken to a federal court, it is normally done at the outset, in one of the federal district courts. However, if (1) a particular federal question case is characterized by concurrent federal-state jurisdiction, (2) the plaintiff chooses to file the case in a state court, and (3) the case proceeds through the state court system until all avenues of appeal in that system are exhausted, either party may ask the U.S. Supreme Court to review the case because of the presence of the federal question. In this situation, as in others, the U.S. Supreme Court has discretion to hear or not hear the case.

Diversity of Citizenship Cases. Diversity of citizenship creates federal subject matter jurisdiction only if the amount in controversy is greater than $75,000. When federal jurisdiction exists because of **diversity of citizenship,** it is always concurrent federal-state jurisdiction, and the plaintiff has a choice of filing in a federal court. If the plaintiff chooses of filing in a federal state court and the case is heard in the state court system, there can be no appeal to the U.S. Supreme Court or any other federal court. (Thus, the situation is different with a diversity case filed in state court than with a federal question case filed in state court.) In the case of an individual, citizenship in a state for federal jurisdiction purposes means U.S. citizenship plus residency in that state. The phrase diversity of citizenship encompasses several different situations. By far the most important situation included within the phrase is one in which the plaintiff and defendant are citizens of different states. Diversity of citizenship also exists when one party is a citizen of a state in the United States and the other is a citizen of another nation.

In several ways, federal courts have interpreted the diversity of citizenship concept rather narrowly to exclude some kinds of cases that logically might have been included. For example, if a case involves multiple plaintiffs and/or multiple defendants, diversity of citizenship exists only if there is *no common statecitizenship on opposite sides of the case.* Thus if P1, a citizen of Nebraska, and P2, a citizen of Kansas, join in a suit against D2, a citizen of New York, and D2, a citizen of Kansas, there is no diversity of citizenship.

If a corporation is a plaintiff or defendant, it is considered to be a citizen of the state where it was *incorporated;* in addition, if it has its *principal place of business* in another state, it is viewed as a citizen of that state as well. Thus, for the purpose of determining whether a federal court has jurisdiction on the basis of diversity of citizenship, it is possible for a corporation to be a citizen of two states. Neither Congress nor the U.S. Supreme Court has defined the term principal place of business. Lower federal courts, however, have held that the state where a company has its headquarters is its principal place of business. Suppose that P, a citizen of New York, sues D Corporation, which was incorporated in Delaware and has its headquarters in New York. Because there is common state citizenship on opposite sides of the case (New York), a federal court would not have subject matter jurisdiction on the basis of diversity of citizenship

The original reason for permitting diversity of citizenship cases to be heard by federal courts was to guard against "hometown verdicts"— decisions by juries or judges that are biased against an out-of-state party. If this ever was a problem, there is little if any evidence that it is still a problem. In any event, if there is such a problem, it is unclear how placing these cases in a federal trial court can solve it. Juries in federal courts are taken from the local population just as they are in state courts, and federal judges are almost always from the state where they serve. For these reasons, and also because diversity of citizenship cases involve questions of state law, bills have been introduced in Congress a number of times over the years to eliminate diversity of citizenship as a basis for federal subject matter jurisdiction. No such bill has passed, however.

What did pass, in early 2005 was the Class Action Fairness Act that, among other things, eliminated the requirement of complete diversity of citizenship for most class action lawsuits where the matter in controversy exceeds $5 million. The purpose of the act was to eliminate perceived forum shopping (choosing to file in states or even counties perceived to be friendly to plaintiffs) by plaintiffs' attorneys in large class action and other mass litigation suits. The law vests subject matter jurisdiction for most such suits in the federal district courts. So, if such a lawsuit is filed in a county in Illinois or Mississippi which has a reputation for handing out huge damage awards, defendants can remove the case to federal court.

Removal From State to Federal Court

When concurrent federal-state jurisdiction exists, the plaintiff has the initial choice of filing in state or federal court. If the plaintiff chooses state court, however, the defendant may have a **right of removal.** This means that, within a short time after the plaintiff files the case in state court, the defendant may have the case moved to a federal district court in the same geographic area. The defendant has a right of removal in any federal question case, so that if the defendant chooses he or she can always have a federal court rule on claims against him or her that are based on federal law. The right also exists in diversity of citizenship cases, except in the situation where the plaintiff filed the suit in the state where the defendant is a citizen.

Personal Jurisdiction

In the great majority of cases, a court must have *personal jurisdiction* in addition to subject matter jurisdiction. Personal jurisdiction is the court's jurisdiction over the parties to the case. In a civil lawsuit, the plaintiff submits to the court's personal jurisdiction by filing the case; thus, any question about personal jurisdiction relates to the defendant. Personal jurisdiction over the defendant is a requirement in so-called *in personam* cases, in which the plaintiff seeks a judgment that will be legally binding against the defendant (whether an individual, corporation, government agency, or other entity). The judgment might be an award of money damages that the defendant has to pay or some other remedy such as an injunction requiring the defendant to take or refrain from taking some particular action. Most cases are of the *in personam* variety. The other type of case is an *in rem* action, which will be discussed after this section on personal jurisdiction is a concept that arises only in civil cases, not in criminal ones, because in a criminal case the defendant must be arrested and bodily brought before the court before he or she can be tried.

Although the rules for a court's acquisition of personal jurisdiction over a defendant vary somewhat from state to state, these rules all have the same objective: compliance with the constitutional requirement of **procedural due process**. What is basically required by procedural due process is (1) adequate notice, (2) a meaningful opportunity to be heard (that is, a hearing), (3) an impartial decision maker (one who does not have a personal stake in the outcome), and (4) in court actions, some substantial contact between the defendant and the *forum state* (the state where the lawsuit has been filed).

Appearance

As we will see, some of the methods for obtaining personal jurisdiction differ depending on whether the defendant is a *resident* of the forum state or a *non-resident*. However, regardless of the residency of the defendant, the defendant automatically submits to the court's personal jurisdiction if he or she makes an **appearance**. In this context, the word *appearance* is a term of art. It does not refer to an actual physical presence in court; instead the term refers to the taking of any formal steps to defend the case. Thus if the defendant, normally acting through an attorney, files a motion to dismiss on the basis that the plaintiff's complaint does not allege facts that establish a legally recognized claim even if proved, an answer to the plaintiff's complaint, or almost any other court papers aimed at defending against the claim, the defendant has made an appearance. Once this has happened the trial court has personal jurisdiction and the defendant cannot thereafter challenge the existence of such jurisdiction.

Therefore, if the defendant wishes to contest the court's personal jurisdiction, this must be completed before taking any other action that would constitute an appearance.

The major exception to this rule is the *specialappearance*—a motion or other formal action taken by the defendant solely for the purpose of challenging the court's personal jurisdiction. If the only action the defendant takes is to challenge the court's personal jurisdiction, this action does not give the court jurisdiction. If the defendant properly makes the special appearance before taking any other formal action in the case but the trial court denies the challenge to its personal jurisdiction, the defendant can then defend the case on its merits without losing the right later to have an appellate court rule on the personal jurisdiction question.

Service of Summons

If the defendant has not made an appearance, the plaintiff must see to it that the court acquires personal jurisdiction. Whether the defendant is a resident or nonresident, the preferred method is *personal service of summons*. The **summons** is the formal notice of the lawsuit. (Although summons is the most commonly used term, courts in a few states call it "process" or "citation." The term "service of process" is also sometimes used in a very general way to refer to delivery of any type of legal papers.) A copy of the plaintiff's complaint is usually attached to the summons. *Personal service* means delivery to the defendant in person while the defendant is physically within the forum state. Traditionally, an officer such as a sheriff, marshal, deputy sheriff or marshal, or constable was always used to deliver the summons. In recent years, however, the rules in many places have been changed to permit other persons, such as the plaintiff's attorney, to deliver a summons. In the federal district courts, for example, the rules were changed in the past few years to place responsibility on the plaintiff's attorney for seeing that the summons is served; the actual delivery of the summons to the defendant can be performed by any person at least 18 years old who is not a party to the lawsuit (such as a clerk in the office of the plaintiff's attorney). Whoever attempts to deliver a summons must make a sworn statement to the court as to whether the attempt was successful or unsuccessful.

In the case of a resident defendant, there are several alternatives to personal service of summons, including (1) permitting the authorized summons server to leave the summons at the defendant's residence with someone older than a specified age (such as 16 or 18 years), (2) permitting the server to leave the summons at the defendant's regular place of business, or (3) permitting the server or the court clerk to mail the summons to the defendant's residence or business. In the latter case, registered or certified mail is required in some places, but only first class mail is required in others. In some states, it is required that personal service first be attempted before one of these alternatives can be used; in other places this is not required. English courts have accepted service of summons via e-mail, but U.S. courts generally have not been receptive to this new practice, although in one case the U.S. Court of Appeals for the Ninth Circuit held that U.S. District Courts may allow service of summons by e-mail when other alternatives have been exhausted, the defendant has evaded being served by other means, and e-mail service is "reasonably calculated to reach to provide notice and an opportunity to respond." (Rio Props. v. Rio Int'l Interlink, 284 F.3d 1007 (9th Cir. 2002)),

Corporate Defendants

Although many of the rules for acquiring personal jurisdiction over a corporation are the same as for an individual, some are a bit different because of the nature of a corporate entity. The rules regarding the making of an appearance are the same for a corporation as for an individual.

If there is no appearance, there are several possible means for serving summons on a corporation. First, if the corporation has a *registered agent* in the forum state, service on that agent is sufficient. This service may be by personal delivery or by some alternative method permitted in that particular court system. A corporation is supposed to have a registered agent for receiving summonses and other legal notices in the state where it is incorporated and in any other state where it does business, but many companies do not actually do this. In this regard, *doing business* usually means having some physical presence in the state, not just advertising or receiving mail or telephone orders. In most places, service of summons also may be accomplished by delivering it to an *officer* of the corporation if one is located within the forum state.

Long-arm Statutes and Due Process

As a general rule, a summons is effective to give a court personal jurisdiction only if it is served on the defendant within the forum state. Thus if P files a suit for breach of contract against D in a state or federal court in Michigan, a summons issued normally must be served on D within Michigan to give the court personal jurisdiction. This requirement presents little problem if D is a resident of Michigan. Not only will it usually be possible personally to deliver the summons to a resident defendant but, as we have already seen, various alternatives are available for accomplishing service of summons to someone who is a resident of the forum state. Also, if a corporate defendant has either its headquarters or a registered agent in the forum state, the requirement is not difficult to meet.

However, if an individual defendant is a resident of some other state or nation or if the out-of-state corporation has no registered agent in the forum state, serving a summons becomes more difficult. The defendant in such a case is not likely to "hang around" in the forum state so that a summons can be served. If personal jurisdiction cannot be obtained, the plaintiff is faced with the prospect of filing suit in a state (or nation) where personal jurisdiction can be obtained; unless the claim is quite large, the substantial extra expense could mean that pursuing the claim is not economically feasible.

There are certain circumstances in which it is possible for a court to gain personal jurisdiction over a defendant even though that defendant has not made an appearance and has not been served with a summons within the forum state. The **procedural due process** guarantee in the Constitution is essentially aimed at ensuring basic procedural fairness when a court or other government entity engages in an adjudicative activity. A number of years ago, the U.S. Supreme Court decided that the due process requirement of basic fairness is satisfied if a nonresident defendant has had substantial prior contact with the forum state. (The Court used the term "minimal" contact, but "substantial" better describes the concept as it has been applied over the years.) In addition to the substantial contact requirement, the Supreme Court said that a particular state had to have a statutory procedure for making sure that a summons was actually forwarded to the nonresident defendant at its out-of-state address.

In response to this Supreme Court decision, every state has adopted a so-called long-arm statute specifying such a procedure. In many states, the **long-arm statute** specifies that personal jurisdiction can be acquired over a nonresident defendant who has "done business" or committed a "tort" (that is, wrongful conduct for which civil liability can be imposed) within the forum state. In other states, the statute simply provides that jurisdiction can be acquired in any circumstances in which the defendant's prior contact with the state is sufficient to comply with the fairness requirement of due process. Regardless of the exact language of the state long-arm statute, however, the ultimate question is whether the nonresident defendant had substantial contact with the forum state because this is the constitutional requirement.

Long-arm statutes provide that, when the evidence shows that the defendant has had sufficient contact with the forum state, the summons is to be sent to a central office in the forum state. In most states, this is the secretary of state's office. The official in charge of that office then has the responsibility to send the summons to the defendant at its out-of-state address. When the nonresident defendant receives the summons, the defendant either has to respond to the merits of the complaint or, if the defendant believes that it has not had substantial contact with the forum state, it will have an attorney make a **special appearance** in the court. A special appearance is simply a motion filed with the court in the forum state asking that the case be dismissed for the sole reason that the defendant has not had substantial contact with the forum state and that there is thus no basis for the court to exercise personal jurisdiction. The defendant must do this before taking any other action to defend itself. If the court in the forum state decides that it does have personal jurisdiction, and the defendant must defend against the plaintiff's complaint, the nonresident defendant has preserved its right to appeal the ruling on personal jurisdiction because it challenged the court's personal jurisdiction before doing anything else in court.

The courts have divided the due process requirement of significant contacts into two categories. The first is usually referred to as **general personal jurisdiction.** This occurs when the nonresident has had "substantial continuing contacts" with the forum state. Or, another way to state it is that the nonresident defendant had a "substantial ongoing presence" in the forum state. In other words, the nonresident has either maintained a physical presence in the forum state or has continually targeted activities at the forum state. In such a case, a state or federal court can acquired personal jurisdiction over the nonresident defendant regardless of the nature of the dispute and regardless of whether the dispute arose from one of the specific contacts the defendant had with the forum state. The second is usually referred to as **specific personal jurisdiction.** Assuming that there is an insufficient basis for general personal jurisdiction, the court may still be able to obtain specific personal jurisdiction over the nonresident defendant. If the nonresident defendant has intentionally engaged in a specific act in the forum state or targeted at the forum state (such as going into the state and committing a tort or making a contract with someone in the forum state, and if the dispute arises out of that specific contact, there is a basis for specific personal jurisdiction. The bottom line is that there are two types of situations in which the nonresident may be said to have had sufficient contact with the forum state to enable a state or federal court there to acquire personal jurisdiction over the nonresident defendant. Again, the reason for the requirement of substantial contacts is to comply with due process under the Constitution. In turn, the objective of the constitutional requirement of procedural due process is to ensure fundamental procedural fairness.

The Internet has given rise to a new set of considerations regarding personal jurisdiction. The courts are still sorting them out. Most courts will not impose personal jurisdiction in, say, California, just because a California computer user can access a passive

New York Web site to gather information. However, if the New York Web site generates substantial revenue from California computer users, perhaps by taking orders and shipping goods to purchasers in California, then courts likely will impose general personal jurisdiction. Or, if a specific transaction is made over the Internet between the New York Web site operator, such as a contract for the sale of merchandise, and the California resident sues the New York resident in California for breach of contract, a California court could acquire specific personal jurisdiction over the New York resident.

The following case illustrates some of the principles we discussed concerning the requirement that a nonresident defendant have had significant contacts with the forum state.

SCHWARZENEGGER V. FRED MARTIN MOTOR CO.
374 F.3d 797 (9th Cir. 2003)

Fred Martin Motor Co., an Ohio car dealership, ran five full-page color ads in the local newspaper Akron, Ohio. Each ad contained a small photograph of Arnold Schwarzenegger (plaintiff), portrayed as the "Terminator," without his permission. The ads feature a cartoon bubble coming from plaintiff's mouth saying: Arnold says 'Terminate early at Fred Martin!'" Plaintiff sued defendant in federal district court in California where plaintiff lives and is, indeed, governor, for $95, 000 for an invasion of privacy tort recognized in California and Ohio (and in other states). Defendant moved to dismiss on grounds of lack of personal jurisdiction. Plaintiff pointed out that defendant has an informational Web site that can be accessed by anyone, including Californians, and that in the past defendant has hired a California direct-mail marketing firm to help it reach customers in Ohio. Fred Martin noted that it has no offices, employees, or bank accounts in California and that as far is it knows it has never sold a car to a California resident. The district judge dismissed the suit and plaintiff appealed.

Fletcher, Circuit Judge:
General Personal Jurisdiction. Schwarzenegger argues, quite implausibly, that California has general personal jurisdiction over Fred Martin. For general jurisdiction to exist over a nonresident, the defendant must engage in "continuous and systematic general business contacts" that approximate physical presence in the forum state. This is an exacting standard, as it should be, because a finding of general jurisdiction permits a defendant to be haled into court in the forum state to answer for any of its activities anywhere in the world.

Schwarzenegger contends that Fred Martin's contacts with California are so extensive that it is subject to general jurisdiction. He points to the following contacts: Fred Martin regularly purchases Asian-made automobiles that are imported by California entities. However, in purchasing these automobiles, Fred Martin dealt directly with representatives in Illinois and New Jersey, but never dealt directly with the California-based importers. Some of Fred Martin's sales contracts with its automobile suppliers include a choice-of-law provision specifying California law. In addition, Fred Martin regularly retains the services of a California-based direct-mail marketing company; has hired a sales training company, incorporated in California, for consulting services; and maintains an Internet Web site accessible by anyone capable of using the Internet, including people living in California.

These contacts fall well short of the "continuous and systematic" contacts; Schwarzenegger has therefore failed to establish a prima facie case of general jurisdiction.

Specific Personal Jurisdiction. Alternatively, Schwarzenegger argues that Fred Martin has sufficient "minimum contacts" with California arising from, or related to, its actions in creating and distributing the Advertisement such that the forum may assert specific personal jurisdiction. We have established a three-prong test for analyzing a claim of specific personal jurisdiction:

> The non-resident defendant must purposefully direct his activities or consummate some transaction with the forum or resident thereof; or perform some act by which he purposefully avails himself of the privilege of conducting activities in the forum, thereby invoking the benefits and protections of its laws; the claim must be one which arises out of or relates to the defendant's forum-related activities; and the exercise of jurisdiction must comport with fair play and substantial justice, i.e. it must be reasonable.

The plaintiff bears the burden of satisfying the first two prongs of the test. If the plaintiff fails to satisfy either of these prongs, personal jurisdiction is not established in the forum state. If the plaintiff succeeds in satisfying both of the first two prongs, the burden then shifts to the defendant to "present a compelling case" that the exercise of jurisdiction would not be reasonable. For the reasons that follow, we hold that Schwarzenegger has failed to satisfy the first prong.

Purposeful Availment or Direction Generally. Under the first prong of our three-part specific jurisdiction test, Schwarzenegger must establish that Fred Martin either purposefully availed itself of the privilege of conducting activities in California, or purposefully directed its activities toward California. We often use the phrase "purposeful availment,"

in shorthand fashion, to include both purposeful availment and purposeful direction, but availment and direction are, in fact, two distinct concepts. A purposeful availment analysis is most often used in suits sounding in contract. A purposeful direction analysis, on the other hand, is most often used in suits sounding in tort.

A showing that a defendant purposefully availed himself of the privilege of doing business in a forum state typically consists of evidence of the defendant's actions in the forum, such as executing or performing a contract there. By taking such actions, a defendant "purposefully avails itself of the privilege of conducting activities within the forum state, thus invoking the benefits and protections of its laws." In return for these "benefits and protections," a defendant must —as a quid pro quo – "submit to the burdens of litigation in that forum." Burger King.

A showing that a defendant purposefully directed his conduct toward a forum state, by contrast, usually consists of evidence of the defendant's actions outside the forum state that are directed at the forum, such as the distribution in the forum state of goods originating elsewhere.

Purposeful Direction. Schwarzenegger does not point to any conduct by Fred Martin in California related to the Advertisement that would be readily susceptible to a purposeful availment analysis. Rather, the conduct of which Schwarzenegger complains—the unauthorized inclusion of the photograph in the Advertisement and its distribution in the *Akron Beacon Journal*–took place in Ohio, not California. Fred Martin received no benefit, privilege, or protection from California in connection with the Advertisement, and the traditional quid pro quo justification for finding purposeful availment thus does not apply. Therefore, to the extent that Fred Martin's conduct might justify the exercise of personal jurisdiction in California, that conduct must have been purposefully directed at California.

We evaluate purposeful direction under the three-part "effects" test traceable to the Supreme Court's decision in Calder v. Jones, 465 U.S.783(1984). Under *Calder*, the "effects" test requires that the defendant allegedly have (1) committed an intentional act, (2) expressly aimed at the forum state, (3) causing harm that the defendant knows is likely to be suffered in the forum state.

Applying the three-part Calder test to this case, Schwarzenegger must first demonstrate that Fred Martin committed an "intention- al act." Fred Martin committed an intentional act when it placed the Advertisement in the *Akron Beacon Journal*.

Second, Schwarzenegger must show that Fred Martin "expressly aimed" its intentional act—the placement of the Advertisement—at California. In *Calder*, the Supreme Court found that the intentional acts of the reporter and editor, though taking place in Florida, were expressly aimed at California: "The allegedly libelous story concerned the Califor- nia activities of a California resident. It impugned the professionalism of an enter- tainer whose television career was centered in California. The article was drawn from Cali- fornia sources. . . . California is the focal point. . . of the story. Petitioner South wrote and petitioner Calder edited an article that they knew would have a potentially devastat- ing impact upon respondent. And they knew that . . . the National Enquirer has its largest circulation [in California]."

The "express aiming" analysis depends, to a significant degree, on the specific type of tort at issue. The reporter and editor in Calder were not accused of "untargeted negligence" that merely happened to cause harm to Jones. Rather, their actions in writing and publishing a false and injurious article about Jones's alleged drinking problem constituted inten- tional behavior directed at Jones in California.

Here, Fred Martin's intentional act–the creation and publication of the Advertise- ment–was expressly aimed at Ohio rather than California. The purpose of the Adver- tisement was to entice Ohioans to buy or lease cars from Fred Martin and, in particular, to "terminate" their current car leases. The Advertisement was never circulated in California, and Fred Martin had no reason to believe that any Californians would see it and pay a visit to the dealership. Fred Martin certainly had no reason to believe that a Californian had a current car lease with Fred Martin that could be "terminated" a s recom- mended in the Advertisement. It may be true that Fred Martin's intentional act eventually caused harm to Schwarzenegger in Califor- nia, and Fred Martin may have known that Schwarzenegger lived in California. But this does not confer jurisdiction, for Fred Martin's express aim was local. We therefore conclude that the Advertisement was not expressly aimed at California.

Because Schwarzenegger has failed to sus- tain his burden with respect to the second part of the *Calder* effects test, we need not, and do not, reach the third part of the test. [Affirmed.]

Foul-ups in Service of Summons

We should note that although it is rather unusual, occasionally something can go wrong in the summons-serving process. This can happen in the case of either a resident or a nonresident defendant. Suppose that the rules for serving a summons have been com- plied with, but for some reason the defendant did not actually receive it. For instance, the summons may have been properly left at the defendant's residence with a friend or family member who lost it and forgot to tell the defendant. Suppose also that the defendant did not know about the lawsuit and thus did not answer the plaintiff's complaint and that the plaintiff then received a default judgment against the defendant because of the latter's failure to respond.

Within a certain period of time thereafter (such as a year or two, depending on the state), the defendant may ask the court to set aside the default judgment and give the defendant a chance to defend against the complaint. The trial judge will do so if convinced that the defendant really did not receive the summons, had no actual knowledge that the lawsuit had been filed, and has some plausible rebuttal or defense to the complaint.

Note: Personal Jurisdiction in Federal Courts

As a general rule, a federal court in a particular state faces the same constraints on its ability to acquire personal jurisdiction as would a state court in that state. Most of the time, a summons issue by a federal district court is effective only if served within the state where the court is located. The federal court can, however, make use of the state's long-arm statute to obtain personal jurisdiction over a nonresident defendant in the same circumstances in which a state court could do so. There are certain exceptional situations in which a federal court summons has a wider reach than one issued by a state court; in a few types of federal question cases, the federal statute that forms the basis of the plaintiff's claim includes a specific provision permitting nationwide service of summons. One example of this is found in the federal laws regulating the issuance and trading of securities in interstate commerce.

In Rem Cases

As mentioned earlier, a court usually must have personal jurisdiction over a defendant because most lawsuits are of the *in personam* variety, in which the plaintiff is seeking a judgment for damages or an equitable remedy against the defendant. However, if the plaintiff's case is characterized as **in rem**, rather than in personam, the court is not required to have personal jurisdiction over a particular party. (It still must have subject matter jurisdiction, however.) State and federal courts inherently have *in rem* jurisdiction over any item of property located in the forum state, whether the property is real estate or an item of tangible or intangible personal property. If a notice of the lawsuit is published in a newspaper of general circulation in the area where the property is located, the court has power to render a judgment affecting the status of title to the property even without having personal jurisdiction over the owner of the property.

Suppose, for example, that D borrowed money from Bank B and executed a document giving B a mortgage on a home or other piece of real estate. The mortgage makes the real estate collateral for the loan and gives B a right to take ownership and possession of the property if D fails to repay the loan on its agreed terms. If D defaults, B will exercise its right by filing a *mortgage foreclosure* action in court. The object of the action is not D, but instead is the acquisition of the title to the property. This is an *in rem* case, and it is not required that the court have personal jurisdiction over D. B can simply have a notice published in a local newspaper, which is not sufficient notice for personal jurisdiction but is sufficient for an *in rem* case to proceed. As a practical matter, if it is possible to get personal jurisdiction over D, B will usually see to it that the court obtains personal jurisdiction, so hat B can also get an *in personam* "deficiency judgment" against D; this is a judgment for any amount of the loan that may remain unpaid if the proceeds from the sale of the property are inadequate.

Other examples of in rem cases include court actions to establish ownership to lost or abandoned property or to give the government title over property that has been forfeited because it was used in connection with certain crimes such as drug dealing.

Related Matters

If we assume that the court has both subject matter and personal jurisdiction, there still may be other preliminary matters to consider. These other matters might include questions regarding venue, *forum non conveniens,* and conflict of laws.

Venue

If a state district court in Texas has subject matter and personal jurisdiction in a case filed by P, *every* district court in Texas has such jurisdiction. The question of where within the state the lawsuit should be heard is a question of **venue.** Every state has statutes that specify which counties are appropriate venues. Typically, venue is appropriate in either the county where the defendant resides or where the accident or transaction took place. Sometimes venue may be proper in other places; if the case involves real estate, an appropriate venue may be the county where the land is located. If there are two or more permissible venues, the plaintiff normally may choose among them when filing the lawsuit. In the federal court system, federal statutes specify which federal districts are appropriate venues.

Although venue is not the same as jurisdiction, the rules governing venue questions have some of the same ultimate objectives as the rules pertaining to personal jurisdiction. The main objective is fairness, and a secondary one is efficiency.

Forum Non Conveniens

A court with both subject matter and personal jurisdiction may decline to exercise them if another court, more conveniently connected to the suit, also has both types of jurisdiction. Under the doctrine of *forum non conveniens,* the court may choose to transfer the suit or even dismiss it, forcing the plaintiff to file in the more convenient court.

For example, in one case arising out of a defendant's agent carelessly causing a fire in the plaintiff's warehouse in Virginia, the plaintiff sued 400 miles away in New York City where the state court had subject matter jurisdiction over the simple tort case and personal jurisdiction because of the defendant corporation's many business contacts in New York. However, the New York court declined to exercise its jurisdiction on grounds that the suit was more conveniently brought in Virginia where the plaintiff and all witnesses were located and where the accident had occurred. The only justification the plaintiff gave for filing in New York—that a New York jury was likely to give a bigger verdict—was inadequate.

In determining the most convenient forum, courts will consider private interest factors such as ease of access to sources of proof, costs of obtaining witnesses' attendance, the possibility of a view of the site of the accident, and the convenience of the parties. Public factors to be considered include the imposition of jury service on residents of the community, the congestion of court dockets, and the interest in having local controversies decided at home.

The *forum non conveniens* doctrine can also be applied internationally. For example, a U.S. court of appeals affirmed a decision of the U.S. district court in New York City that used the doctrine as a basis for transferring a case from that federal court in New York to a court in India. The case involved claims against Union Carbide Corporation arising from the tragic leak of toxic gases from a chemical factory that killed more than 2000 people in Bhopal, India. The federal trial judge took this action only after being convinced that Indian law and procedure were designed to handle such claims and provide substantial justice and that an Indian court would take jurisdiction over the claims. The court also conditioned its dismissal in favor of the Indian courts on Union Carbide's consent to the jurisdiction of the Indian courts and its waiver of any statute of limitations defense. (A statute of limitations specifies a time limit for filing a lawsuit.) *(In re Union Carbide Corp. Gas PlantDisaster at Bhopal, India in Dec. 1984, 809 F.2d 195 (2d. Cir. 1987)).*

It should be noted that although the term venue is not used, the doctrine of *forum nonconveniens* actually involves a very specialized and somewhat ad hoc type of venue question.

Conflict of Laws

Assume D Corporation, formed in Delaware with its principal place of business in Colorado, hires P from California to do subcontracting work on D's condominiums in New Mexico. The contract is negotiated in California, Colorado, and New Mexico before being signed in Colorado. When New Mexico officials ordered P to stop work because he did not have a license to do such work in New Mexico, D fired him. P sued in Colorado to recover for the work he had performed before being stopped. Several states' laws are potentially applicable to this case. If they all lead to the same result, it does not matter which state's rules are applied. However, in this case, New Mexico law bars P from recovery because he had no license. Colorado and California law would allow him to recover despite the lack of a license. Thus, there is a *conflict of laws*. To determine which state's laws to apply, we must resort to **choice of law** rules, which are designed to prevent a plaintiff with multiple jurisdictions from which to choose (because all have subject matter and personal jurisdiction) from "forum shopping" for the jurisdiction with the laws most favorable to him or her. Each state has a set of "choice of law" rules for determining which state's or nation's law should be used to resolve the case.

Conflict of laws questions also can arise in international disputes. Recall for a moment the example of the case against Union Carbide that was transferred from a federal court in New York to a court in India under the doctrine of *forumnon conveniens.* The federal court could have retained jurisdiction and decided the case. If so, it probably would have applied the law of India to decide the case; to do so, the court obviously would have to call on experts in Indian law.

Contract Cases. If the parties stipulate in the contract that, for example, "California law will govern any disputes arising out of this contract," the courts will normally respect that choice if it was fairly bargained and California has at least a passing connection to the parties or the transaction. It is especially desirable for the parties to an international transaction to negotiate and include a clause in their contract specifying which nation's law should be applied to any dispute arising from the deal.

Absent a choice by the parties, the traditional view was to apply the law of the state in which the contract was made to any litigation about the validity of the contract and to apply the law of the state in which the contract was to be performed to any litigation about the performance of the contract.

The strong modern trend, however, is to use an *interest analysis.*

Using an interest analysis to determine which state's law to apply, courts would consider such factors as the relevant policies of the forum and of other interested states, the protection of justified expectations (that is, which state's laws did the parties assume would apply), certainty, predictability, ease of determination of the law to be applied, and uniformity of result.

In contract cases specifically, most modern courts attempt to determine the state with the "most significant relationship" to the parties and the transaction, considering such factors as (1) the place of contracting; (2) the place of negotiation; (3) the place of performance; (4) the location of the subject matter of the contract; and (5) the domicile, residence, nationality, place of incorporation, and place of business of the parties.

In the factual situation outlined previously, the Colorado Supreme Court applied New Mexico's law, reasoning that New Mexico's interest in protecting its citizens from substandard construction by unlicensed subcontractors outweighed Colorado's interest in validating agreements and protecting parties' expectations. (Wood Bros. Homes, Inc. v. Walker Adjustment Bureau, 601 P.2d 1369 (Colo. 1979)).

Tort Cases

Assume that a husband and wife from New Mexico are killed when a plane the husband is piloting crashes in Texas. The parties intended to return to New Mexico and had no other contacts with Texas. The estate of the wife filed suit against the husband's estate in state court in Texas. Texas's doctrine of interspousal immunity would not allow the suit. New Mexico has no such doctrine; its law would allow the suit. Which state's law should apply? The traditional view is to apply the law of the place of the tort—Texas. But why would Texas courts care whether a New Mexico wife's estate can recover from a New Mexico husband's estate? Again, the strong modern trend is to move away from an automatic choice of the law of the place of the tort to

There are always many things to think about when negotiating a substantial contract. Parties should attempt to anticipate and provide in the contract for as many contingencies as possible. As we will see in the next chapter, one of the events that the parties should plan for in advance is a possible future dispute arising out of the transaction. Including a clause in the contract that specifies some type of nonlitigation dispute resolution procedure, such as arbitration, is something the parties should at least consider carefully. Even if they do not agree in advance to resolve future disputes outside the courts, however, there are still some other dispute-related matter they might try to resolve at the outset.

Although such agreements are almost always important, their significance is ever greater when the transaction involves companies from different countries. It is possible and often desirable, for example, to agree where any later lawsuit should be heard. Such a "forum selection" clause will usually be upheld by courts in the United States and other countries so long as the place selected in advance has some connection with the parties or the transaction and the clause is not the product of fraud or an extreme abuse of bargaining power by one party.

A forum selection clause not only constitutes an agreement in advance about where any subsequent lawsuit will be heard, but also serves as consent to the personal jurisdiction of the court in the chosen location. Thus, the parties to a business transaction usually can waive the right to contest a court's personal jurisdiction. Likewise, the parties can agree that a particular state's or nation's law should apply to any future dispute. They also can resolve venue questions in advance. One thing that contracting parties cannot do, however, either in advance or after a dispute has arisen, is create subject matter jurisdiction in a court that does not have it otherwise. Subject matter jurisdiction, whether in a state of federal court in the United States or a court in another country, is a matter of governmental power, and cannot be created by private parties.

an interest analysis. Today, most courts use the following factors in deciding which state has the most significant relationship to the occurrence and the parties: (1) the place where the injury occurred; (2) the place where the conduct causing the injury occurred; (3) the domicile, residence, nationality, place of incorporation, and place of business of the parties; and (4) the place where the relationship, if any, between the parties is centered. In this case, New Mexico law was applied. (Robertson v. McKnight, 609 S.W.2d 534 (Tex. 1980)).

Law, Equity, and Remedies

In the next chapter we will examine the major steps in the process of adjudication, paying particular attention to the roles played by the trial and appellate courts in that process. We will see that in all legal controversies the plaintiff is asking for a **remedy**—an order addressed to the defendant, requiring that person either to pay money or to do (or not to do) a particular act. A remedy, then, is "the means by which a plaintiff's right is enforced or the violation of a right is prevented, redressed, or compensated." (*Black's Law Dictionary*, 5th Edition, © 1979 West Publishing Co.) All remedies are either "legal" or "equitable" in nature, a fact that can be explained only by a brief glimpse at the development of the early court systems in England.

Courts of Law

Over 900 years ago, the first Norman kings of England established a system of courts by designating individuals throughout the country to be their personal representatives in the settling of certain kinds of legal disputes. These representatives could grant only very limited types of relief: (1) money damages, (2) possession of real estate, or (3) possession of personal property.

In settling disputes, the courts made up their own rules as they went along, based largely on the customs and moral standards then prevailing, plus their own ideas of "justice" in particular situations. The formulation of rules in this manner, a process that continues today in some branches of law, gave birth to the *common law* (which we will study in more detail in Chapter 4). The royal courts ultimately became known as **courts of law,** and the remedies that they granted were *remedies at law.*

Courts of Equity

When plaintiffs needed relief other than what the courts of law could grant, they often petitioned the king. Such petitions were frequently decided by the king's chancellor,

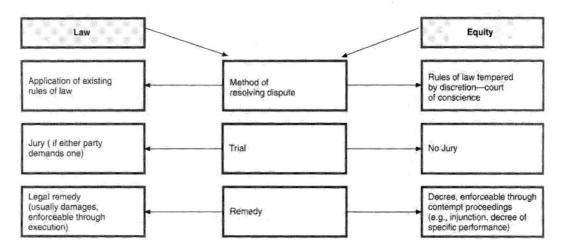

Figure 2.3 Major Differences Between Law and Equity

who granted relief when he thought the claim was a fair one. Out of the rulings of successive chancellors arose a new body of "chancery" rules and remedies for cases outside the jurisdiction of the courts of law. This developed eventually into a system of **courts of equity,** as distinct from the courts of law.

A plaintiff who wanted a legal remedy, such as money damages, would bring an **action at law** in a court of law. A plaintiff wanting some other relief, such as an **injunction** (for example, an order forcing D to stop grazing cattle on land belonging to P) or a **decree of specificperformance** (for example, an order commanding D to live up to a contract to sell land to P), brought an **action in equity** in an equity court. Other common equitable actions, in addition to those asking for injunctions and decrees of specific performance, include (1) divorce actions, (2) mortgage foreclosure suits, and (3) actions for an accounting, brought by one member of a partnership against another.

The Present Scene

Although the distinction between legal and equitable remedies as diagrammed in Figure 2.3 persists today, there has been a fusion of law and equity courts in virtually all states. This means that separate courts of law and equity, as such, have been eliminated. Instead, the basic trial courts in the state and federal systems are empowered to hear both legal and equitable actions.

Today, the basic distinctions between the two kinds of actions are these:
1. Whether an action is one at law or in equity depends solely on the *nature of the remedy* that the plaintiff is seeking.
2. There is *no jury* in an equitable action. Questions of both fact and law are decided by the court, that is, the trial judge. In a case in which a plaintiff is seeking both a legal and an equitable remedy, such as both monetary damages and an injunction, a jury can be impaneled to determine whether the plaintiff has proved its claim and what damages should be awarded, but the decision whether to grant the injunction (or other equitable remedy) is decided solely by the judge.
3. Proceedings in equitable actions are *less formal* than those at law, particularly in regard to the order in which witnesses' testimony can be presented and the determination of admissibility of their evidence.
4. Equitable remedies are considered to be exceptional. Therefore, when determining whether to grant an equitable remedy, a court considers certain factors that it would not consider in a typical money damage suit. For example, even if the plaintiff has proved that the defendant has violated the plaintiff's legal rights, a court may refuse to grant an injunction or other equitable remedy in any of the following situations: (1) The plaintiff does not have "clean hands"—that is, has been guilty of unfair conduct in his or her dealings with the defendant; (2) an award of money damages—a "remedy at law"— would adequately redress the harm done to the plaintiff, so that an equitable remedy is not necessary; or (3) the granting of an equitable remedy might interfere substantially with the rights of some third party who is not involved in the case.

CHAPTER 3

LITIGATION AND ALTERNATIVE METHODS OF DISPUTE RESOLUTION

- The Adversarial System
- Litigation: Pretrial Proceedings
- Litigation: Trial Proceedings
- Litigation: The Appellate Courts
- Note on Performance of Judges
- Alternative Dispute Resolution

Many american novels, movies, and television programs feature courtroom scenes to produce dramatic tension for readers and viewers. This is appropriate, because courtroom battles can produce high drama. Nothing quite matches the tension that litigants and attorneys feel when a jury verdict is about to be announced in open court. This chapter will look at the litigation process, from the initiation of a civil suit through the trial process all the way to final appeal. After this examination, you will be better able to appreciate the context in which these few dramatic moments occur. You will also understand that litigation can be extremely complicated, expensive, and time-consuming. Indeed, litigation is usually something to be avoided. But when you cannot avoid litigation, it pays to understand the process.

Our discussion focuses on procedures in civil lawsuits rather than in criminal prosecutions. Although many of the procedures in the two types of proceedings are the same, there also are a number of important differences. Some of these differences are noted in Chapter 7, Criminal Law and Business. In addition, a few differences between civil and criminal procedures will be mentioned in this chapter.

After we have studied the civil litigation process, we will explore some other ways of resolving disputes, especially those that arise in business. These other methods, which are sometimes grouped together under the name **alternative dispute resolution**, include arbitration, mediation, and other techniques. Such methods are being used with greater frequency today in an effort to resolve disputes more quickly, less expensively, and without destroying valuable relationships.

The Adversarial System

Before studying the process of civil litigation, it is important to note that both civil and criminal proceedings in the United States are based on the so-called **adversarial system**. This approach to litigation is one of the keyfeatures of American law inherited from England.

The term *adversarial* has a very specialized meaning in this context. Even in a nation that does not use the adversarial system, the parties to a lawsuit or a criminal prosecution obviously are adversaries. However, when we use the term*adversarial* to describe the English/American approach to litigation, we are referring primarily to the amount of control that the parties and their attorneys have over the procedure.

Under the adversarial system, the parties themselves (acting through their attorneys) research the law and develop the facts. They decide which issues are going to be presented, which legal arguments are going to be made, what evidence should be gathered and presented, and how the evidence is to be introduced in court. The trial judge does not make these decisions; indeed, the judge normally takes no action unless a party specifically requests it. For example, if one party's attorney attempts to introduce testimony or physical evidence that is not legally admissible, the judge usually will not keep the evidence out unless the other party's attorney makes an objection. If an attorney overlooks a relevant legal argument and fails to make it, the judge normally will not take the initiative to include that argument in the legal analysis of the case.

Although the parties and their attorneys have primary control over the issues and evidence, the trial judge obviously has the duty to exercise ultimate supervisory authority over the entire process. In addition, within the adversarial framework the rules relating to control over issues and evidence can vary somewhat from one court system to another. For example, in some states in the United States, as well as in the federal district courts, trial judges may sometimes ask questions of witnesses if they believe that an attorney's questioning is not eliciting certain important testimony. Similarly, in some states and in the federal courts, trial judges can "comment on the weight of the evidence"—make comments to the jury about the strength of particular testimony or other evidence. In other states, judges cannot do these things. Finally, as case loads and delays increase, more trial judges in the adversarial system probably will take a greater degree of control over the process in the future than they usually have in the past. However, the general idea that the parties and their attorneys should have primary control is so firmly embedded that it will undoubtedly continue as a fundamental elementin our sstem of litigation.

The adversarial system can be contrasted with the so—called **inquisitorial system** of litigation used in European nations and, indeed, in most other parts of the world that did not inherit the English legal system. In general, the trial judge (or, sometimes, a panel of trial judges) in the inquisitorial system has much more control over the process, and the parties have much less than in the adversarial system. The judge often will have the authority to decide which issues will be addressed, although the parties certainly will provide important input. The judges are usually in charge of the investigation and gathering of evidence; they do not do this personally but have investigators who answer directly to them. Judges make rulings and take various other actions on their own initiative rather than merely responding to the parties' requests for action. It should be noted, finally, that there is significant variation in procedural details among the many countries that use the inquisitorial system, just as there is variation within the adversarial system. In some situations, for example, the trial in a country using the inquisitorial system does not consist of a single, highly focused event, but instead consists of a series of several conferences among the judges, parties, and attorneys. The process of investigation and evidence gathering takes place not only before the first conference but also between later conferences. Each meeting brings the case closer to a conclusion. This kind of process can work in these countries because juries of citizens are not used.

There are good and bad points about both of these systems. The adversarial system requires fewer judges and more lawyers than the inquisitorial system. The inquisitorial system requires that more of the time and energy devoted to a case be expended by public officials (judges and investigators) than by the parties and attorneys. Thus, the adversarial system shifts more of the cost to the private sector, whereas the inquisitorial system places more of the cost in the public sector. The adversarial system also puts primary responsibility for developing the facts in the hands of those (parties and their attorneys) who have a natural incentive to do a more thorough job. However, putting this responsibility in the hands of the parties and their attorneys also means that the fact—gathering process may be aimed more at seeking strategic advantage than finding the truth.

Litigation: Pretrial Proceedings

Pretrial proceedings consist of two stages, the *pleading stage* and the *discovery stage*. We will look at each of these steps briefly.

The Pleading Stage

The typical suit is commenced by the plaintiff, through an attorney, filing a **complaint** (or petition) with the court having jurisdiction of the case. At the same time, the plaintiff asks the court to issue a summons to the defendant.

After receiving the summons, the defendant has a prescribed period of time in which to file a response, normally an **answer** to the complaint. After that has been completed, the plaintiff can file a **reply** to the answer if the answer raised new issues. The complaint, answer, and reply make up the pleadings of a case, the main purpose of which is to permit the court and the parties to ascertain the actual points in issue.

The Complaint

The **complaint** sets forth the plaintiff's version of the facts and ends with a "prayer" (request) for a certain remedy based on these facts. The plaintiff alleges those facts that, if ultimately proved by the evidence, will establish a legally recognized claim against the defendant. Suppose, for example, that the plaintiff bought a boat from the defendant, a dealer. The plaintiff claims that the boat leaks badly. After the two parties are unable to resolve their differeces, the plaintiff institutes a lawsuit by filing a complaint. The complaint may allege that the parties made an agreement for the sale of the boat on a particular dat for a particular price, the price was paid and the boat delivered, the plaintiff used the boat and found that it leaked, the defective condition of the boat is in violation of a warranty made by the dealer, and the plaintiff has suffered economic harm because the boat is worth far less in its defective condition than it would have been worth i no defective. If these facts are ultimately proved, the plaintiff has a good claim against the defendant for breach of warrnty. However, the plaintiff might als allege that he defendant intentionally lied about the condition of the boat, thus committing the tort of fraud or perhaps violating a state deceptive trade practice statute.

In most complaints, the remedy requested by the plaintiff is an award of money damages to be paid by the defendant to compensate the plaintiff for his or her loss. If the plaintiff seeks some other remedy, such as an injunction, it will be requested in the complaint. Sometimes the plaintiff's complaint may request multiple remedies, such as damages for past harm and an injunction to prevent future harm. In the boat example, the plaintiff might request money damages for breach of warranty or perhaps fraud. This is not the type of case in which the plaintiff would seek an injunction. The plaintiff might, however, request the equitable remedy of *rescission,* an order of the court canceling the contract, along with *restitution,* a return of the purchase price.

The Answer

The defendant usually responds to the complaint by filing an **answer**. The answer may include several components. One thing it always contains is a *denial* of the plaintiff's allegations. In some places, the defendant is permitted to make a *general denial,* which simply denies all the plaintiff's allegations together. In other court systems, the rules require a defendant to deny each allegation individually; any allegation not denied is deemed to be admitted. The rules in some systems permit a general denial in most cases, but require specific denials of certain types of allegations. Regardless of the form, a denial is essentially a formality that places the plaintiff's allegations in issue and places the burden on the plaintiff to prove the assertions he or she has made.

It must be remembered that the plaintiff in a civil lawsuit (and the prosecution in a criminal case) bears the overall burden of proof. In other words, if the plaintiff does not ultimately produce evidence that convinces the jury (or judge if there is no jury) of the correctness of the allegations in the complaint, the plaintiff loses. Although the defendant must respond with an answer, he or she is not obligated to *prove* anything. Nevertheless, if a defendant believes that the facts create a legally recognized **defense** (sometimes called an *affirmative defense)* against the plaintiff's claim, he or she will assert the defense in the answer after the denial. A defense defeats the plaintiff's claim *even if the plaintiff is able to prove those facts that establish all the elements of his or her claim.* Asserting a defense consists of alleging those facts that, if ultimately proved by the defendant, will establish a legally recognized defense against the plaintiff's claim. For virtually every type of civil claim, the law recognizes one or more defenses. In the boat example, the defendant might allege as a defense to the breach of warranty claim that there was a *disclaimer* in the sale contract stating clearly and conspicuously that the boat was a reconditioned one and was being sold on an "as is" basis. If proved, this allegation would defeat the plaintiff's breach of warranty claim. Such a defense would not defeat a fraud claim, however. (In criminal cases, there are also legally recognized defenses against virtually all types of criminal charges.)

When asserting a defense, the defendant does not make a claim or request a remedy but simply tries to defeat the plaintiff's claim. Sometimes, however, the defendant may wish to assert a claim against the defendant in the form of a **counterclaim.** The defendant will allege facts that, if proved by the defendant, will establish a legally recognized claim against the plaintiff, and the defendant will ask for money damages or some other remedy. Either party alone might prevail on its claim, or both may prevail; in the latter event, the amount of the smaller judgment will be subtracted from the amount of the larger judgment.

Most counterclaims arise from the same set of circumstances that led to the plaintiff's claim (a so-called *compulsory* counterclaim). In such a case, the rules in most court systems require that the defendant assert the claim in this case as a counterclaim if it is to be asserted at all; he or she cannot keep quiet about it now and later sue the plaintiff (with their roles and names obviously reversed) on the claim. However, if the defendant's claim against the plaintiff arises from an unrelated set of circumstances, it is a so-called *permissive* counterclaim, and the defendant has a choice of asserting a counterclaim in the present case or suing separately.

In the boat example, the defendant might assert a counterclaim alleging that the plaintiff had not paid all the boat's purchase price, in violation of the sale contract, and request damages in the amount of the unpaid portion. It is not a rare occurrence for a plaintiff to have the tables turned by a counterclaim and to regret that he or she ever filed a lawsuit. The existence of a potential counterclaim sometimes may persuade a plaintiff not to file a complaint in the first place; at the very least, a realistic possibility that the other party may be able to prove a counterclaim can dramatically affect the bargaining positions of the parties as they attempt to negotiate a settlement.

The Reply

If the defendant raises new matter—additional facts— in the answer, the plaintiff must file a reply. In this pleading, the plaintiff will either deny or admit the new facts alleged in the answer. The most obvious situation in which this occurs is when the defendant asserts a defense and/or counterclaim in the answer.

Motion to Dismiss

Although technically not part of the pleadings, the **motion to dismiss** must be mentioned at this point. (An older term for this motion, which is still used in a few states, is the *demurrer.*) The defendant will file such a motion instead of an answer if he or she believes that the plaintiff has no claim even if all the allegations in the complaint are true. In this motion, the defendant asserts that the plaintiff has not even stated a "cause of action"— that is, that even if the plaintiff's allegations are true (which the defendant is not admitting), the law does not recognize such a claim. The motion does not refer to any evidence but merely takes aim at the allegations made in the plaintiff's complaint. Suppose, for example, that Ralph, the owner of a retail store in Milwaukee, is upset about some of the business practices of a competing retailer in town. In a private conversation between Ralph and George, the president of the other retailer, Ralph says, "You and your people are liars and cutthroats; you screw your customers whenever you think you can get away with it; you have the morals of a gutter rat." The conversation is not overheard by anyone else, and Ralph does not repeat any of it to anyone. If George sues Ralph for the tort of defamation, alleging these facts, Ralph will probably file a motion to dismiss and the court will grant it. Even if what Ralph said about George and his company was false, the tort of defamation (slander or libel) can occur only if false defamatory statements about someone are *communicated* to a third party. Thus, George and his company have no claim against Ralph even if events were exactly as George described in his complaint.

If the court grants the motion to dismiss, the plaintiff will be given an opportunity to amend the complaint. This opportunity is only helpful if the plaintiffs attorney simply forgot to include something. If the problem cannot be corrected by an amendment to the complaint, the court will dismiss the plaintiff's case. However, if the court denies the defendant's motion to dismiss, the defendant will then file an answer.

Like other actions of a trial judge, a ruling on a motion to dismiss can be appealed to a higher court. The plaintiff can begin such an appeal immediately if the trial court grants the motion to dismiss, because this results in a final determination of the case at that level. However, if the trial judge denies the motion to dismiss, the defendant must wait until the case ends at the trial level before appealing; in this situation, the trial judge's ruling on the motion to dismiss probably will be only one of several grounds for the appeal.

The motion to dismiss is the first of several types of motions that give the trial judge an opportunity to end the litigation early when he or she is convinced that there is no doubt about the outcome and thus no reason to continue.

Defendant's Failure to Respond

Assuming that the court has jurisdiction, the defendant must respond within a specified time period by filing either a motion to dismiss or an answer. This time period is 20 days in the federal district courts and about the same amount of time in most state courts. The clock starts ticking when the defendant receives the summons and complaint. If the defendant does not respond during this period, the court may grant a **default judgment** against the defendant. By failing to respond, the defendant has given up the right to contest liability. The only issue to be determined is the amount of money damages to which the plaintiff is entitled, or the appropriateness of some other remedy the plaintiff may be seeking. The court will conduct a hearing at which the plaintiff presents evidence on the question of damages or other requested remedy.

The Discovery Stage

In early years, cases moved directly from the pleading stage to the trial stage. This meant that each party, going into the trial, had little information as to the specific evidence that the other party would rely on in presenting his or her case. Trial proceedings, as a result, often became what was commonly described as a "cat and mouse" game, with the parties often bringing in evidence that surprised their opponents. This situation was a natural outgrowth of the control parties have over evidence gathering and presentation in the adversarial system.

The undesirability of these proceedings was finally perceived by lawyers and judges, with the result that the Federal Rules of Civil Procedure, adopted in 1938, provided means (called *discovery proceedings*) by which much of the evidence that each party was going to rely on in proving his or her version of the facts would be fully disclosed to the other party before the case came to trial. The most common discovery tools recognized by these federal rules, which have now been essentially adopted by the states, are *depositions, interrogatories, and requests for production of documents.*

A deposition is testimony of a witness that is taken outside of court. Such testimony is given under oath, and both parties to the case must be notified so that they can be present when the testimony is given and thus have the opportunity to cross—examine the witness. Depositions are taken for these reasons (1) to learn what the key witnesses know about the case, (2) to gain leads that will help obtain additional information, (3) to preserve the testimony of witnesses who might die or disappear, and (4) to establish a foundation for cross–examination of witnesses who might later change their stories.

Interrogatories are written questions submitted by one party to the other, which must be answered under oath. Use of this device is a primary way by which the questioning party may gain access to evidence that otherwise would be solely in the possession of his or her adversary.

A demand for documents permits a party to gain access to those kinds of evidence—such as business records, letters, and hospital bills—that are in the possession of the other party. Under modern rules of civil procedure, the party seeking the documents has the right to obtain them for purposes of inspection and copying.

A party must make a good faith effort to comply with the other party's legitimate discovery request. The court can impose various sanctions on parties and attorneys who do not make such an effort. These penalties may include the assessment of discovery costs, attorney's fees, or monetary penalties. In cases of flagrant disregard of legitimate discovery requests, the court can even dismiss a claim or defense or grant a default judgment against the offending party. The following case provides an example of such a situation.

FORSYTHE V. HALES
255 F.3d 487 (8th Cir. 2001)

In January 1998, plaintiffs (appellees) filed a securities fraud suit against defendants Comstar Biotechnical and John Hales (appellants). They alleged that defendants had accepted plaintiffs' money to purchase stock, but failed to do so. In February 1999, appellants filed an answer through a California attorney named Lowell who was not licensed to practice law in Minnesota where the lawsuit was filed.

On September 27, 1999, the magistrate judge set a pretrial conference for October 29, 1999. Lowell appeared at the pretrial conference by telephone, but the magistrate judge informed him that because he was not admitted to practice before the court and had not associated with local counsel, he would not be permitted to participate in the conference under Local Rule 83.5. The magistrate judge then afforded Hales and Comstar time to retain counsel in compliance with the rule.

As no attorney had filed a notice of appearance on behalf of Hales and Comstar by November 10, 1999, the magistrate judge issued an order directing all parties to obtain counsel admitted to practice before the court by November 22. Hales personally e–mailed the district court on November 22, requesting an extension until November 29 to retain new counsel. The court granted Hales' request, but Hales nevertheless failed to retain appropriately licensed counsel by the requested date.

By December 1999, Hales and Comstar had committed numerous discovery violations, failing to (1) submit the required pre–discovery disclosures, (2) respond to Appellees' Interrogatories or Document Requests, or (3) appear for a scheduled deposition. Appellees warned Hales and Comstar that their continuing failure to engage in the discovery process could force Appellees to seek a default judgment. When Hales and

Comstar continued to be unresponsive, Appellees moved for various sanctions, including a default judgment.

The magistrate judge scheduled a hearing on Appellees' sanctions motion on January 7, 2000. On January 6, Lowell filed two documents with the court, requesting (1) that his clients be given a two–week continuance to obtain local counsel and respond to Appellees' motion, and (2) that he be permitted to appear by telephone. The court denied permission to appear by telephone. The motion for a continuance was summarily denied, as Lowell had no authority to file such a motion. As a result, the hearing was held as scheduled on January 7, 2000. No appearance was made on behalf of Hales or Comstar. However, the magistrate judge did not grant Appellees' motion for default judgment, but rather entered an order requiring Hales and Comstar to appear before the court on February 2, 2000, and show cause why a default judgment should not be entered against them. The order also required Hales and Comstar to appear at the February 2 hearing with counsel admitted to practice before the court.

During the period between the January 7 and February 2 hearings, Hales and Comstar did not file any discovery responses. On February 2, Hales and Comstar appeared before the court with counsel admitted to practice in the District of Minnesota; however, counsel explained that he had been retained just the day before and had no knowledge of the case. Neither Hales, Comstar, nor their attorney provided the district court with a justification for their failure to respond to discovery, or to engage counsel properly licensed to appear in the case at any time over the preceding twenty–five months. Because he concluded that Hales and Comstar presented no substantive grounds for denying Appellees' motion, the magistrate judge recommended that default judgment be entered against them. The district court reviewed the magistrate's decision

and did enter the default judgment. Appellants appealed.

Magill, Circuit Judge:

Default judgment is appropriate where the party against whom the judgment is sought has engaged in "willful violations of court rules, contumacious conduct, or intentional delays." Akra Direct Mktg. Corp. v. Fingerhut Corp., 86 F.3d 852 (8th Cir. 1996). However, "default judgment is not an appropriate sanction for a 'marginal failure to comply with time requirements.'" Id. Here, defendants' conduct includes a complete failure to engage in discovery and failure to appear at depositions and hearings set by the court. Most significantly, Hales and Comstar failed to engage counsel admitted to practice before the district court for a period of twenty–five months, from the inception of the lawsuit until the very day before the hearing at which they were required to show cause why default should not be entered against them. This conduct provides ample basis for a grant of default judgment. See, e.g., Akra (finding that defendant's failure to obtain substitute counsel, respond to discovery, and comply with orders of the court provided ample basis for district court's grant of default judgment for $ 1.2 million); Comiskey v. JFTJ Corp., 989 F.2d 1007 (8th Cir. 1993) (holding default was the appropriate remedy for failure to comply with numerous court orders and discovery requests).

Hales and Comstar rely primarily on Seventh Circuit authority in support of their argument that the district court abused its authority. See Anilina Fabrique de Colorants v. Aakash Chems. & Dyestuffs, Inc., 856 F.2d 873 (7th Cir. 1988). However, in that case, the district court told the defendant that it faced default if it did not either get counsel and request a continuance or settle the case. The defendant obtained counsel who did appear and request a continuance, but the district court granted default judgment against it nonetheless.

The Seventh Circuit held the district court's action constituted an abuse of discretion. In contrast, in this case, the district court instructed Hales and Comstar that default judgment would be granted if they failed to (1) appear with admitted counsel and (2) show cause why default should not be entered. Though Hales and Comstar appeared with counsel, they failed to show cause why default should not be granted. Thus, unlike the defendants in *Anilina*, Hales and Comstar did not fulfill the requirements of the district court for avoiding a default judgment and therefore *Anilina* is inapposite.

Appellants also argue that their misconduct was far less serious than that of the defendants in *Ackra*, who submitted late and nonresponsive discovery responses for twenty—two months prior to the withdrawal of their counsel, and failed to obtain substitute counsel for over a year thereafter. In fact, the conduct of Hales and Comstar in this case is, if anything, more egregious than that at issue in *Ackra*, as Hales and Comstar failed to retain qualified counsel from the very beginning of the litigation and entirely failed to participate in discovery. Furthermore, rather than immediately granting default judgment when the defendants failed to appear at the default judgment hearing, as did the court in *Ackra*, here, the magistrate judge issued an order affording Hales and Comstar the opportunity to obtain counsel and appear before the court to show cause why Appellees' motion for default should not be granted. Though Hales and Comstar finally obtained counsel and appeared at the hearing, both they and their attorney were unable to show cause why default judgment should not be entered against them. Therefore, under our precedent in *Ackra*, the district court's grant of default judgment was entirely within its discretion.

AFFIRMED.

Electronic Discovery

Formerly document discovery was about exchanging reams of paper, drawers of paperwork, or warehouses full of documents, depending on how complicated the case was. But today, more than 90% of corporate documents are created electronically. Furthermore, employees send approximately three billion e—mails a day. These electronic documents are frequently the keys to proving cases. In an important antitrust case, Microsoft CEO Bill Gates was surprised on cross—examination by an e—mail in which he had asked "How much do we need to pay you to screw Netscape?" Wall Street investment banking firms paid hundreds of millions of dollars of settlements in 2002 and 2003 after disclosure of e—mails indicating that in order to get investment banking business, securities analysts had recommended stocks that they knew were overvalued. Accounting giant Arthur Andersen's demise is largely traceable to an attorney's instructions to follow document retention policies that prosecutors read as an order to destroy Enron—related documents.

E—mails often incriminate corporations. Sometimes they exculpate them. Destruction of them can create liability, especially for securities firms and health—care companies that are required to keep them for a certain time. Attorneys now recommend to their corporate clients that they have document retention, management, and destruction policies, but many companies do not have their IT act sufficiently together to be able to smoothly and efficiently store documents or access them when courts require their production.

Wal–Mart and Dell Computer are among several companies that judges have recently fined or criticized for inadvertently destroying electronic documents.

Because electronic discovery is so expensive, either side could conceivably use it as a tactical weapon. Courts are struggling to adapt to the new issues presented by electronic discovery, as the next case indicates.

Rowe entertainment, inc. v. William morris agency
U.S. District Court, Southern District of New York, 205 F.R.D. 421 (2002)

Plaintiffs, African–American concert promoters, filed suit against 30 booking agencies, claiming that discriminatory booking practices had improperly prevented plaintiffs from promoting events with white bands. Plaintiffs sought access to defendants' e–mails, contending that they would show widespread prejudice. Defendants asked the court for a protective order, contending that production of the electronic documents would be unduly burdensome. A magistrate judge required plaintiffs to pay the costs of production, and plaintiffs appealed.

Patterson, District Judge:

Rules 26(b) and 34 of the Federal Rules of Civil Procedure instruct that computer–stored information is discoverable under the same rules that pertain to tangible, written materials. The 1970 Advisory Committee Notes of Rule 34(a) make clear that electronic data are part of the definition of 'document,' and states that when discovery of e–mail would create an "undue burden or expense" on the respondent the appropriate relief is a motion under Rule 26(c) to shift costs.

Factors considered by Magistrate Judge Francis:

1. *Specificity.* Judge Francis found that plaintiffs' "extremely broad" discovery requests favored shifting the costs of discovery to them. He contrasted plaintiffs' requests to other cases where the plaintiff sought only specific data sets. A review of the record by this Court shows that plaintiffs never made a specific, concrete proposal which narrowed these requests. Judge Francis' finding as to this factor was accurate and certainly not "clearly erroneous."

2. *Likelihood of a Successful Search.* Judge Francis followed the court in McPeek v. Ashcroft, 202 F.R.D.31 (D.D.C. 2001) in using a marginal utility analysis in determining whether to shift costs:

   The more likely it is that the backup tape contains information that is relevant to a claim or defense, the fairer it is that the [responding party] search at its own expense. The less likely it is, the more unjust it would be to make [that party] search at its own expense. The difference is "at the margin."

3. Judge Francis found "there has certainly been no showing that the e–mails are likely to be a gold mine," nonetheless he found there was a high enough possibility that a broad search of the defendants' e–mails would elicit some relevant information so that the search should not be precluded altogether. In particular, Judge Francis pointed out that no witness has testified

about any e—mail communications that allegedly reflect discriminatory or anti-competitive practices. Therefore, he found that the marginal value of searching the e—mails is modest at best, militating in favor of imposing the costs of discovery on the plaintiffs.

4. *Availability from Other Sources.* Judge Francis found that defendants had not shown that their e—mail communications are generally available other than by a search of the defendants' hard drives or back—up tapes and that the moving defendants' representations that "important" e—mails were probably printed out and contained in other files were entirely speculative. He found this factor favored requiring the defendants to produce the e—mail at their own expense. This finding has not been disputed.

5. *Purposes of Retention.* If a party maintains electronic data for business purposes, they will be obligated to produce that same information in discovery. The guiding principle is "information which is stored, used or transmitted in new forms should be available through discovery with the same openness as traditional forms." Daewoo Electronics, Ltd. v. U.S., 650 F.Supp. 1003 (C.I.T. 1986). Conversely, a party that happens to retain data only in case of emergency or simply because it has neglected to discard it, should not be put to the expense of producing it. Judge Francis found that the back-up tapes clearly fell into the latter category as there is no evidence that defendants ever search these tapes for information or even have a means for doing so. Accordingly, he found that cost—shifting is warranted with respect to the back—up tapes. He made the same findings with regard to e—mails that, although deleted from the user's active files, remain on the hard drive. "Just as a party would not be required to sort through its trash to resurrect discarded paper documents, so it should not be obligated to pay the costs of retrieving deleted e—mails."

Purposes of retention was merely one factor in Judge Francis' Order which found that the e—mails are on the backup tapes or remained on the hard drive and were not used by defendants in the course of their business, and therefore that this factor tipped in favor of shifting the costs of discovery to plaintiffs. Plaintiffs did not press this argument at the oral argument on March 19, 2002. Certainly this factor relates to the burden and expense of such discovery. There is no reason to find that Judge Francis' opinion on this point was clearly erroneous.

6. *Benefit to the Parties.* Judge Francis noted that where the responding party itself benefits from the production, there is less rationale for shifting costs to the requesting party. However, he found in this case, since the e—mails are not relevant to any issue on which the defendants bear the burden of proof and cataloguing or searching e—mail would have little business value to them, there is no possible benefit to the defendants making cost—shifting more appropriate.

7. *Total Costs.* Judge Francis found that the costs of the discovery desired by plaintiffs would be substantial by any definition and therefore the magnitude of these expenses favors cost—shifting.

The issue of costs is strongly contested. Plaintiffs project that the costs of WMA would be between $24,000 and $87,000; for Monterey between $10,000 and $15,000; and for SFX and QBQ approximately $64,000. Defendants project that the costs of WMA would be $395,944 if eight selected back—up sessions were produced and as much as $9,750,000 if all of the back—up tapes were produced; for Monterey between $43,110 and $84,060; for CAA a minimum of $395,000; and SFX and QBQ for over

$403,000. Monterey also proffered an estimate of $247,000 to review the e−mails for privilege and CAA approximated $120,000 for their privilege review.

Judge Francis did not base his decision on the substantial costs of the production alone; it was merely one factor in his analysis that favored the shifting of costs. In view of the amount in question, the finding that it was a substantial amount that favored cost−shifting was not "clearly erroneous or contrary to law."

8. *Ability to Control Costs.* Judge Francis found that "where the discovery process is going to be incremental, it is more efficient to place the burden on the party that will decide how expansive the discovery will be." Therefore, he found that plaintiffs are in the best position to decide whether further searches would be justified, militating in favor of costshifting. This factor has not been disputed.

9. *The Parties' Resources.* Judge Francis noted that all of the parties have sufficient resources to conduct this litigation. As to plaintiffs' argument that defendants are some of the most powerful players in the concert promotion business, Judge Francis found that as the plaintiffs purport to be able to compete with them in the market place, the relative financial strength of the parties is at most a neutral factor. Judge Francis' conclusion was not that defendants' and plaintiffs' resources are equal as plaintiffs argue, but that in view of plaintiffs' resources it would not justify an allocation to the defendants.

Judge Francis clearly found the burden or expense of the proposed discovery outweighs its likely benefit, taking into account "the needs of the case, the amount in controversy, the parties' resources, the importance of the issues at stake in the litigation, and the importance of the proposed discovery in resolving the issues." Fed.R.Civ.P. 26(b)(2)(iii). There has been no showing that Judge Francis' finding was "clearly erroneous."

Affirmed.

Summary Judgment

At or near the end of discovery, one party or the other (and sometimes both) may file a motion for **summary judgment** as to one or more of the issues in the lawsuit. In filing such a motion a party is arguing to the judge, in essence, that the evidence produced by discovery makes it so clear that the moving party is legally entitled to prevail that a trial would be a waste of time. A judge should grant such a motion only if a thorough review of the evidence obtained through discovery indicates that there is "no genuine issue as to any material fact"—that is, that there is no real question as to any important factual matter. Although summary judgment can be granted against either party, the fact that the plaintiff has the burden of proof means that summary judgments for the defendant are more common than for the plaintiff. Thus, if a *defendant* files a motion for summary judgment, it will be granted unless the plaintiff has presented at least enough evidence during discovery to create a genuine issue on all the required elements of its claim. If the plaintiff has failed to produce enough evidence to create a genuine fact issue on even one of he elements of its claim, the defendant is entitled to a summary judgment.

However, if a *plaintiff* files the motion, the court will grant it only if (1) the plaintiff has produced evidence so strong that it proves *all* of the elements of its claim so clearly that there is no genuine fact issue on any of these elements, (2) the defendant has failed to present evidence that creates doubt about any of these elements, and (3) the defendant also has failed to present evidence sufficient to create a genuine issue regarding an affirmative defense.

Judges traditionally have been reluctant to grant summary judgment motions, especially when a jury trial has been requested. In recent years, however, the U.S. Supreme Court has urged the federal district courts to make more use of summary judgment when there really does not seem to be much doubt about the ultimate outcome. (Celotex Corp. v. Catrett, 477 U.S. 317 (1986). Not only are federal courts making increasing use of summary judgment, but more state courts also are doing so as heavier case loads put greater pressure on judicial resources.

Litigation: Trial Proceedings
The Trial Stage

Unless a lawsuit is settled out of court or disposed of by the granting of a motion to dismiss or motion for summary judgment, it will eventually come up for trial. In the **trial stage** a jury may be impaneled, evidence presented, a verdict returned, and a judgment entered in favor of one of the parties.

Trial by Jury

In most civil lawsuits in which the plaintiff is seeking a so–called remedy at law, there is a constitutional right to jury trial. Because most lawsuits involve claims for money damages, such a right usually exists. In the federal courts, the right to trial by jury in civil cases is guaranteed by the Seventh Amendment of the U.S. Constitution. (For federal criminal cases, the right to jury trial is found in the Sixth Amendment.) Almost all state constitutions provide similar guarantees for cases tried in state courts; if not guaranteed in a state constitution, the right is guaranteed in state legislation.

When there is a right to jury trial, a jury will be impaneled if either party formally requests one. Failure to demand a jury trial constitutes a waiver of the right to one. The jury is a fact–finding body; its function is to consider all of the evidence and determine to the best of its ability what really happened. The jury determines whether particular testimony or other evidence is believable ("credible") and how much strength it seems to have as proof of the alleged facts. The jury is required to follow the judge's instructions as to the applicable legal principles. If neither party requests a jury, the trial judge performs the fact–finding role in addition to the judicial function. When there is no jury, judge usually is required to prepare formal written "Findings of Fact" and "Conclusions of Law" after hearing the case. Although it is increasingly common today for both parties to waive a jury trial, especially in business disputes, there are still a great many jury trials. Most of the discussion in the remainder of this chapter assumes that there is a jury.

The use of juries drawn randomly from the local population is another unique feature of litigation inherited from the English system. The jury system is sometimes criticized as being inefficient and unpredictable. Critics offer several arguments to support the claim that the jury system is an inferior method for resolving disputes, including the following:

1. Jurors do not have to meet any particular educational requirements.
2. Jurors do not have the experience or training to sift through substantial amounts of evidence, weigh it, and make carefully reasoned decisions.
3. Untrained and inexperienced decision makers are likely to be influenced too easily by irrelevant sympathies or by the rhetoric of a highly skillful attorney.
4. Many of the rules of procedure and evidence that lengthen and complicate lawsuits exist only to accommodate an untrained and inexperienced fact–finding body.
5. There are some types of cases, such as patent infringement suits, that are simply too complex factually and legally for most jurors to understand.

Supporters of the jury system counter with a number of their own arguments, such as the following:

1. General experience in "living" is more important for deciding the average case than is any kind of specialized training or experience.
2. Juries serve as a limited but valuable check on the power of the judicial branch of government.
3. Juries provide a means for direct, continuous input of community values into the legal system.
4. In the case of factually and legally complex cases, the use of juries forces attorneys to simplify the case.

Impaneling a Jury

However one may feel about the jury as an institution, it will no doubt continue to be an integral part of our legal system for a long time to come. When a jury is to be impaneled, names of prospective jurors are drawn from a list of those who have been randomly selected from public records (such as voter registration or driver license) for possible duty during the term. Each prospective juror is questioned in an effort to make sure that the jury will be as impartial as possible. This questioning is conducted by the plaintiffs and defendant's attorneys, by a judge, or by all three, depending on the practice in the particular court system. This preliminary questioning of prospective jurors is called the *voir dire* examination. (*Voir dire,* from the French, means "to speak the truth.")

If questioning indicates that a particular person probably would not be capable of making an impartial decision, the judge will excuse the person by granting a **challenge for cause** made by one of the attorneys. A challenge for cause may be granted, for example, if it is shown that a prospective juror has a close friendship, family relationship, or business association with one of the parties or attorneys, a financial interest in the case, or a clear bias resulting from any other aspect of the action.

The attorney for each party also has a limited number of **peremptory challenges** (or *strikes)*. Such challenges permit the attorney to have a prospective juror removed without giving any reason for doing so. The U.S. Supreme Court has ruled, however, that attorneys in civil or criminal cases, or government prosecutors in criminal cases, violate the **Equal Protection Clause** of the U.S. Constitution if they exclude jurors because of their race. Proving this, of course, can be quite difficult.

Once the number of prospective jurors who have survived both kinds of challenges reaches the number required by law to hear the case, they are sworn in and the case proceeds. Traditionally the number of jurors has been 12, but in recent years courts in quite a few states and in the federal system have reduced the number of jurors in civil cases, with eight being a common number.

Presentation of Evidence

After the attorneys for both sides have made opening statements outlining their cases, the plaintiff begins to present its case. As we have seen, the plaintiff has the *burden of proof*—the duty to prove the facts alleged in the complaint. In a normal civil case, the plaintiff must convince the fact–finder of the truth of the allegations by **a preponderance of the evidence**—in other words, the plaintiff has to convince the fact–finder that it is *more likely than not* that each of its allegations is true. The plaintiff attempts to meet this burden by presenting evidence to support his or her version of the facts. This evidence may consist of the sworn testimony of witnesses, as well as physical evidence such as documents, photographs, and so on. When an item of physical evidence is introduced in court, it is usually required that a witness with personal knowledge about the item give sworn testimony about its authenticity. A witness who gives false testimony while under oath may be convicted of the crime of **perjury.**

The testimony of a witness is normally elicited by questions from an attorney. When a witness is called to testify in court by the plaintiff's attorney, that attorney questions the witness first. This is called the **direct examination.** As a general rule, an attorney cannot ask leading questions during the direct examination. The attorney for the other side must object, however, before the judge will order the attorney to stop asking leading questions. A leading question is one that suggests its own answer, that is, it "puts words into the witness's mouth." "You saw the defendant's car smash into the plaintiff's car while the defendant was going at a high rate of speed, didn't you?" is a leading question. If the attorney calls an **adverse witness,** however, the rule against leading questions does not apply. An adverse witness is either the opposing party to the case or some other witness for the other side. After each of the plaintiff's witnesses testifies, the defendant's attorney has an opportunity to conduct a **cross–examination** of that witness. The attorney is permitted to ask leading questions in cross–examination. The purpose of cross–examination is to discredit or cast doubt on the witness's testimony. For example, a cross–examination might divulge that (1) pertinent facts in the direct examination were omitted, (2) a witness's powers of observation were poor, (3) the witness made a statement in the past (such as in a deposition) that is inconsistent with his or her present testimony, thus creating doubt about his or her credibility, or (4) the witness is not completely disinterested because he or she stands to gain or lose something from the outcome of the case. At the judge's discretion, the plaintifs attorney may then have a chance to conduct a *redirect examination* to deal with any new matters that might have developed during cross–examination. The judge similarly has discretion to permit another cross–examination after the redirect, but this is unusual.

After the plaintiff has completed its presentation of evidence, the defendant then has the same opportunity. The defendant's purpose will be to offer evidence tending to show that the plaintiff's allegations are not correct. If the defendant has asserted a defense or counterclaim, he or she also will offer evidence to meet the burden of proof on those allegations. The procedures and rules are the same when the defendant presents evidence as when the plaintiff was doing so, except that the roles obviously are reversed on direct, cross–, and redirect examination.

Rules of Evidence

Before going on, a brief mention of the **rules of evidence** is necessary. These rules attempt to ensure that the evidence presented in a court of law is relevant to the issues and is as accurate and reliable as possible.

The rules of evidence apply whether there is a jury performing the fact–finding role or whether the trial judge is doing so. The rules are more important, however, and are often applied more strictly in a trial before a jury than in one before a judge. As mentioned earlier, even if evidence is inadmissible under the rules of evidence, it will be excluded only if the attorney for the other side objects. Such an objection is made during the trial when an attempt is made to introduce the evidence. Before trial, however, if an attorney can identify inadmissible evidence that the other side probably will try to present in court and can convince the judge that the other side may be able to "sneak in" some of this evidence before the attorney has a chance to object, the judge may grant a motion ordering the other side not to make the attempt.

Although the rules of evidence are so numerous and complex that a complete treatment is impossible here, we can provide a flavor of them by discussing three kinds of evidence that are commonly excluded by the rules.

Irrelevant Evidence. If witness is asked a question that has no bearing on any of the disputed facts, the opposing attorney may object on the basis that the answer would constitute **irrelevant evidence.** In a negligence suit arising from an auto accident, for example, such matters as the defendant's religious beliefs or the fact that he or she was convicted of a charge of reckless driving several years earlier would have no bearing on the present case. Objections to such evidence would be sustained by the court. Documents or other physical evidence can also be excluded on grounds of irrelevancy.

Hearsay. In our common experience, we all know that second–hand information is usually not as reliable as first–hand information. The law takes this fact into account by holding that, in general, **hearsay evidence** is not admissible in court. Hearsay evidence may take the form of oral testimony by a witness, or it may consist of a statement in a written document that is offered as evidence. Oral or written evidence is

LEGAL FOCUS

International

These days, many suggestions are being put forth for improving out system of civil litigation, some of which consist of ideas borrowed from other nations. One of the changes being proposed is adoption of the so—called "English Rule," or "loser pays" rule. The gist of this proposal is that the United States should borrow from England the rule that whoever loses a civil lawsuit is responsible not only for his or her own attorney fees but also for the other party's attorney fees. Under current U.S. federal and state law, with very few exceptions each party is responsible for its own attorney fees, regardless of who wins the case. Thus, a defendant can run up huge legal bills even if he or she ultimately wins. It is argued by some observers that the current U.S. practice encourages frivolous claims, especially when combined with the fact that many cases are taken by plaintiffs' attorneys on a contingency basis, the plaintiff owing the attorney a fee only if the case is won.

One must always recognize, however, that any such change involves tradeoffs. The current U.S. practice did not develop accidentally; it represents a social policy choice in favor of keeping the courts as available as possible to those who have at least arguable claims. There is no doubt that the loser pays rule discourages the filing of lawsuits. In England, however, those who are relatively poor have much better access to publicly funded legal counsel than in the United States. Large companies and wealthy individuals can afford to take the risks involved in filing a lawsuit under the loser pays system. In addition, trade unions in England usually finance litigation on behalf of their members. Thus, those who are most strongly discouraged from filing lawsuits, even when they have good claims, are the many members of the middle class who do not belong to trade unions.

Some argue that a better solution for the United States is to make trial lawyers more responsible to the court and less responsible to their clients. For example, monetary penalties against plaintiffs' lawyers who file claims that have little factual foundation, and more frequent granting of summary judgments against plaintiffs with weak cases, might serve as solutions that are more narrowly tailored to fit the problem than adopting a loser pays rule. One difficulty with any major change in American litigation that some other nations do not face, however, is that our legal system consists of 51 separate jurisdictions. To accomplish substantial change, rules must be altered in the federal courts and in the courts of 50 different states.

hearsay if (1) it consists of a statement made by some person who is not testifying personally in court and (2) the evidence is offered in court for the purpose of proving the truth of that statement. Thus if an issue in a particular case is whether a trucker delivered a shipment of goods to the X Company on a certain day, witness W (a jogger in the vicinity at the time) could testify that she saw packages being unloaded from a truck on the day in question. But neither W nor any other witness would normally be allowed to testify that she was *told by a third party*, Z, that Z saw goods being unloaded on the day in question. In the latter situation, W's testimony would be inadmissible hearsay because it related a statement of Z, who is not testifying in person, and the evidence is being offered for the purpose of proving that what Z said is true.

There are many situations in which second–hand statements can be placed into evidence because they are not offered for the purpose of proving the truth of the statements. In a breach of contract case, for example, the plaintiff or some other witness may testify in court that the defendant (D) said "I will sell you my car for $10,000." This would not be hearsay, because the witness's testimony is not being offered for the purpose of proving that the internal content of D's statement is true. Indeed, D's statement cannot be characterized as true or false; there may be a question about whether D actually said it, but there can be no issue about the truth or falsity of the statement's content. Sometimes such a statement is called a *verbal act*. Another example would be, in a defamation case brought by P against D, the statement allegedly made by D that "P is a thief, a liar, and a cheat." A witness's testimony in court that D said this would be offered for the purpose of proving that D actually said such a thing and not for the purpose of proving the content of D's statement as a factual matter.

Even if evidence constitutes hearsay, sometimes it is nevertheless admissible under an exception to the hearsay rule. Exceptions exist for situations in which, despite being within the definition of hearsay, particular kinds of evidence are likely to possess a relatively high degree of reliability. For example, a ledger or other business record includes "statements" of the person who made the entry in the record; these statements relate to the factual details of particular actions or business transactions. If the person who made the entry is not testifying personally about his or her recollection of a certain transaction, but instead the business record is offered to prove particular facts about the transaction, the business record is hearsay. There is, however, a well–established exception for business records. Such records are usually made with care because the business firm relies on them for many important purposes. The exception usually applies if a witness in custody of the records can testify under oath that the record was made "in the usual course of business" and was made at or near the time of the act or transaction being recorded. The exception can apply to the regularly kept records of non–business organizations, as well.

Opinion. Sometimes a witness is asked for or volunteers information that he or she believes to be true but that is not based on the witness's personal knowledge. As a general rule, such *opinion evidence*, whether in oral or written form, is not legally admissible. For example, in an auto accident case, a witness properly could testify that he or she had observed the defendant's car weaving back and forth on a highway shortly before the accident. On the basis of this observation, however, the witness could not testify that the defendant was "obviously drunk." Evidence normally is supposed to take the form of information based on direct observation; the drawing of inferences, the forming of opinions, and the reaching of conclusions are tasks for the jury (or the judge if there is no jury).

Opinion evidence is not always excluded. On technical matters that lie outside the knowledge of ordinary jurors, it is frequently necessary that qualified experts be permitted to state their opinions as an aid to the jury's or judge's determination of what facts probably occurred. Thus a physician may give an opinion as to cause of death or as to whether a particular course of medical treatment is generally accepted within the medical community. Similarly, a civil engineer may give an opinion as to the likely cause of a bridge collapsing. An expert must, however, testify as to the factual basis for the opinion. Unless the attorney for one party agrees *(stipulates)* that a particular witness called by the other party is qualified to testify as an expert, the judge must make a ruling on whether the witness is so qualified. In the average situation, a person called as an expert witness is stipulated as such by the other side.

Motion for Directed Verdict

After all the plaintiff's evidence has been presented, the defendant's attorney often makes a motion for directed verdict. In the federal system, this is now called a motion for judgment as a matter of law (JMOL). This motion makes the same assertion as the earlier motion for summary judgment, except that the motion for directed verdict is based on more evidence, including the personal testimony of witnesses in court. The motion asserts that the plaintiff's evidence on one or more of the required elements of its case is either nonexistent or so weak that there is no genuine issue of disputed fact. Thus, "reasonable minds could not differ" on the factual question, and the judge should decide the case "as a matter of law" instead of sending it to the jury. Sometimes it is said that the motion raises the issue of whether there is a "jury question."

If the defendant's motion for directed verdict is denied, the defendant then presents its case as discussed earlier. At the close of the defendant's case, the plaintiff can make a motion for directed verdict. The motion contends that the plaintiff's evidence on the required elements of its claim is so overwhelming and the defendant's rebuttal evidence is so weak that reasonable minds could not differ in the conclusion that the plaintiff has met its burden of proof. Again, the motion asks the judge to decide the case as a matter of law and not send it to the jury. The defendant can also make a motion for directed verdict at this time, regardless of whether he or she had earlier made one after presentation of the plaintiff's case. Motions for directed verdict are denied in most cases, because once a case has progressed this far there usually are genuine issues of fact that must be resolved.

Instructions to the Jury

When a case is submitted to the jury, the judge provides instructions to guide the jury in its deliberations. These instructions are often read aloud to the jury in open court, and in most states, a written copy of these instructions is then given to the jury before they begin their deliberations. The instructions typically contain several parts, including (1) general rules of conduct, such as requirements that the jurors (a) refrain from discussing the case with anyone except other jurors in formal deliberations until the case is over and they are discharged and (b) not speculate about the effect that insurance coverage or attorney fees might have on the ultimate judgment; (2) definitions of certain relevant legal terms; and (3) the court's *charge* to the jury.

The **charge** is the core of the instructions and gives the jury a legal framework for performing its job. A charge may be *general or special* or a combination of the two types, depending on the court system. In the same system, different types of charges may be used in different types of cases; in a particular state, for instance, a special charge might be used in civil cases and a general charge in criminal ones. Although the **general charge** is most common, mixed special general charges are increasing in usage. A general charge outlines and explains the relevant legal principles for the jury; it then asks them to decide the relevant facts and reach a verdict either for the plaintiff or for the defendant. (In a criminal case, the charge would ask for a verdict of guilty or acquittal.) A **special charge** is a series of questions to the jury; each question relates to a disputed fact and asks for a yes or no answer. Regardless of the type of charge used, in a typical case in which the plaintiff is seeking an award of money damages, there will be a question at the end of the charge that asks the jury to determine the amount of damages, assuming that the jury has ruled for the plaintiff (in a general charge) or has answered all questions favorably to the plaintiff (in a special charge).

The following case illustrates the critical importance of the judge's instructions to the jury.

RILEY v. WILLIS
Court of Appeal of Florida, 585 So. 2d 1024 (1991)

Juanita Willis, a minor, and her sister were walking along the side of Highway 50 in Brooksville with their dog between them. The dog was not on a leash. Juanita walked closest to the road. Joseph Riley was driving on Highway 50, which he used every day to travel to and from work. Just as Riley's truck pulled even with the girls, the dog darted toward the road. Juanita leaned into the road and was struck by the front of Riley's truck. Juanita, plaintff filed suit against Riley, defendant, alleging that Riley s negligence was the cause of her injuries. Riley raised the defense of contributory negligence. Under Florida law, as in most states today, if the jury finds that both the plaintiff and the defendant are negligent, the plaintff's damages are reduced by the per-

centage that his her negligence contributed to the occurrence. However, if the plaintiffs negligence contributed more to the occurrence than did the defendant s, the plaintiff cannot receive any money damages.

In the trial, Riley testified that he saw the two girls and slowed from 45 mph to about 35 mph as he approached but did not sound his horn or move to the left of his lane. He also stated that after his truck pulled alongside the girls, he lost sight of them and did not see the dog bolt or Juanita bend into the road.

At the close of the evidence, the trial judge gave the jury instructions about what a plaintiff has to prove to establish a claim of negligence against the defendant and what a defendant has to prove to establish a defense of contributory negligence. In addition, the court included an instruction setting forth a Florida statute detailing the special duty of a motorist to avoid "obstructions" in the roadway by moving to the left of the center of the highway. This instruction had been requested by Juanita's attorney. However, the judge refused to include an instruction, requested by Riley's attorney, concerning a county ordinance that required people to keep their dogs on a leash. The jury found that the plaintiff's negligence contributed 40 percent to the incident and the defendant's 60 percent. The trial judge entered judgment requiring defendant to pay 60 percent of the amount of damages found by the jury to have been suffered by the plaintiff.

Riley appealed on the following grounds: (1) The trial judge should not have included the jury instruction about a motorist's special duty to avoid obstructions. (2) The trial judge should have included the jury instruction about the county ordinance requiring an owner to keep his or her dog on a leash, because Juanita's dog was not on a leash and this contributed substantially to the accident.

Goshorn, Judge:

Riley asserts that an instruction governing a motorist's duty to avoid an obstacle was improperly given. The instruction contained section 316.081(1)(b), Florida Statutes (1987), which provides in relevant part: "(1) Upon all roadways of sufficient width, a vehicle shall be driven upon the right half of the roadway, except as follows: (b) When an obstruction exists making it necessary to drive to the left of the center of the highway; provided any person so doing shall yield the right-of-way to vehicles traveling in the proper direction upon the unobstructed portion of the highway within such distance as to constitute an immediate hazard. . ."

The controversy surrounding the instruction concerns the word "obstruction" and whether evidence of an obstruction hindering Riley was presented at trial. The term "obstruction" is not defined by Chapter 316. Black's Law Dictionary 972 (rev. 5th ed. 1979) defines "obstruction" as "a hindrance, obstacle or barrier." The evidence presented at trial is unrefuted that at the time of the accident Riley's view was unobstructed and the road was clear. It is also unrefuted that Juanita did not bend into the path of Riley's oncoming truck until the truck was practically upon her. Prior to that moment, Juanita and Ebony [her sister] were walking along the side of the road. The obvious inference from the instruction is that Juanita herself was an obstacle that Riley was statutorily obligated to avoid. Yet no testimony or other evidence was presented that Juanita posed an obstacle to the oncoming truck, making it necessary for Riley to drive to the left of the center of the highway.

Jury instructions must be supported by facts in evidence, and an instruction not founded upon evidence adduced at trial constitutes error. Whether that error requires reversal depends on whether the improper instruction in some manner affected the jury's deliberations by misleading or confusing it. . . The instruction at issue in [this case] quite likely confused and misled the jury by creating the erroneous impression that Riley was obligated to somehow avoid Juanita when she reached out into the road and became an "obstacle" simultaneously with Riley's passing. The giving of the improper instruction requires reversal.

Riley also appeals the trial court's refusal to instruct the jury on Hernando County Ordinance 86–2, section 6–5, the local leash law: "The owner, harborer, keeper or person having custody or care of an animal shall ensure that: (1) All dogs, except police dogs on active duty, shall be kept under physical restraint by a responsible person at all times while off the premises of the owner, harborer or keeper." The trial court refused to grant the instruction because no evidence was presented that Juanita owned the dog. However, the ordinance is also applicable to a person who is a "harborer, keeper or person having custody or care of an animal." The record is undisputed that the dog was walking unleashed between Juanita and Ebony until it darted toward the road and Juanita tried to grab it. . .

A party is entitled to have the jury instructed upon its theory of the case when there is evidence to support the theory. In Orange County v. Piper, 523 So. 2d 196 (Fla. 5th DCA) this court set forth three elements that must be met in order to establish that failure to give a requested jury instruction constitutes reversible error: (1) The requested instruction accurately states the applicable law, (2) The facts in the case support giving the instruction, and (3) The instruction was necessary to allow the jury to properly resolve all issues in the case. [The requested instruction met these requirements.] Riley's theory of the case attempted to show that, but for the girls' failure to walk the dog on a leash, the dog would not have darted toward the road and Juanita would not have lunged into Riley's oncoming truck. Riley's requested instruction sought to bolster his claim that Juanita's own negligence resulted in the accident; her failure to comply with the local leash law was a direct and proximate cause of her accident. Indeed, violation of a municipal ordinance is prima facie evidence of negligence. The failure to give the requested instruction was reversible error.

[Reversed and remanded for a new trial.]

After the Verdict

After the jury has reached its verdict, the court usually enters a judgment in conformity with it. Occasionally this does not happen, however, because the losing party still has an opportunity to make two additional types of motions. One is the **motion for judgment notwithstanding the verdict** (or motion for judgment N. O. V, an abbreviation for the Latin equivalent, non obstante veredicto). In the federal system, this motion is now called a renewed motion for judgment as a matter of law (JMOL) and must be filed within 10 days of the verdict. This motion makes the same contention earlier made in the motion for directed verdict (and even earlier in the motion for summary judgment); it essentially asserts that the judge earlier should have granted a directed verdict in favor of the movant and should not have let the case go to the jury because the evidence was so one-sided in the movant's favor. Although a judge rarely grants this motion, it does provide the judge with something of a "safety valve" if a jury goes completely against the evidence. The other post–verdict motion that may be filed by the party who suffered an adverse jury verdict is the **motion for new trial.** This motion alleges that the trial judge committed one or more errors in the trial that probably affected the outcome. The errors alleged in such a motion may include erroneous rulings on objections to evidence, erroneous wording of the instructions that misstated the applicable law, and so on. A motion for new trial is usually a prerequisite for appeal; a party normally must give a trial judge the opportunity to correct his or her own mistakes by granting a new trial before the party can complain about these mistakes to an appellate court.

The following case illustrates the reasoning employed by a court in ruling on a motion for judgment notwithstanding the verdict.

BEEBE-OWEN V. WESTERN OHIO PIZZA, INC.
Court of Appeals of Ohio, 1991 Ohio
App. Lexis 3034 (1991)

Sharon Beebe Owen, the plaintiff, had worked for Western Ohio Pizza for seven years as the director of management information services, managing various computer systems. (Hereafter, the last name Owen will be used, because the appeals court used the shortened version in its decision.) As a result of an incident between Sharon Owen and EricMarcus, another employee of Western Ohio Pizza, she filed a lawsuit against Marcus and Western.

On April 4, 1988, Sharon Owen, Eric Marcus, and six other employees traveled in a van from their place of work in Dayton, Ohio, to Cincinnati to watch a Cincinnati Reds baseball game. In the lawsuit, the evidence established that Eric and Sharon drank beer at the ball game although she denied becoming intoxicated. The evidence also established that Eric at various times during the day kissed and hugged Sharon. Sharon testified that Eric kissed her after the game—"he just reached out and pulled me by the shoulders and embraced me." In cross–examination, she testified: "He hugged me at the ballpark, he kissed me at the ballpark, he hugged me a couple of times in the van, he kissed me a couple of times in the van. He tried to unsnap my bra in the van when I asked him not to. Sure, he had his hands on me more than that." After the game the group returned to Dayton and went to the Olive Garden Restaurant. Sharon testified that while she was walking toward the restaurant she heard footsteps and Eric threw his arms around her shoulders "and hit me really hard and just pushed me to the ground and ended up falling on my leg." However, Eric testified to a different version of the incident, saying that he "put his arms around her to give her a hug and she stumbled and we fell in a heap."

Phyllis Phillips, a secretary at Western Ohio and one of the eight who attended the baseball game, gave the following testimony: She had nothing to drink that day. She sat with three other employees in a different part of the ballpark from Sharon and Eric; when the game ended she went over to where Sharon and Eric were seated and saw Sharon with her arm around Eric and she was kissing his ear. Sharon was staggering when she got up to leave her seat, and she was loud and her speech was slurred. While they were standing by a souvenir stand she observed Sharon go up to Eric and put her arm around him and hug and kiss him. Sharon had her arm around Eric in the van on the return trip and was kissing him. She did not see Sharon and Eric fall in the restaurant parking lot but heard something and saw them lying on the ground laughing.

Janet Heitman, research coordinator for Western Ohio, was the "designated driver" for the trip to the ball game and also did not drink alcohol that day. Her testimony about the conduct of Eric and Sharon during the trip was practically identical to that of Phyllis Phillips. She also stated that both Sharon and Eric appeared to be under the influence of alcohol and that on the way back five people were "smashed into the back seat" and were engaged in horseplay. She stated she did not see Eric and Sharon fall in the parking lot but saw Eric kneeling over her and Sharon was laughing. She said Sharon could not get up. Sharon was taken by ambulance to a hospital, where she underwent surgery for a severe knee injury and remained hospitalized for ten days.

The defendant also introduced into evidence the written notes made by a nurse when Sharon was admitted to the hospital; the notes were made as a regular part of the admission process. One of the nurse's statements in the notes was that Sharon had told her that she had been hurt while "playing with a friend, who had tackled her." The plaintiffs attorney did not challenge the notes as hearsay evidence, so the court made no ruling on this point; however, it is likely that the notes were within the business records exception to the hearsay rule.

Sharon worked three days in June, from mid–July until November 7, 1988, and two weeks in December 1988. She applied for workers' compensation medical benefits and Western Ohio certified her claim on June 16, 1988; she received these benefits. Her full salary was continued by Western until March 12, 1989. Western asked her to obtain information from her physician as to when she could return to full employment. When she failed to provide the requested medical information to her supervisor, her salary was discontinued.

On March 30, 1989, Sharon Owen and her husband filed this lawsuit, asserting various claims against Eric Marcus and Western Ohio Pizza. Shortly thereafter, both she and her husband, who also worked for Western, were terminated. The trial judge granted summary judgment in favor of Western on all claims, and in favor of Eric on most of the claims. The claims of Sharon 's husband also did not survive summary judgment. However, Sharon 's claim against Eric for the tort of assault and battery remained alive and went to trial. A mixed general–special charge was used in the jury instructions. In response to specfc questions, the jury found that Eric had been negligent but that he had not committed the intentional tort of assault and battery, because the jury concluded that Eric was not guilty of an "intentional offensive physical contact without consent" as required by the law for an assault and battery claim.

The jury then awarded Sharon $41, 000 in damages against Eric.

Both sides filed motions for judgment notwithstanding the verdict. Eric's motion asserted that he could not be held liable at all for simple negligence, because he was a coemployee, this social event was within the scope of their employment, and thus workers' compensation benefits were Sharon's only remedy. Sharon's motion argued that the jury's finding that Eric was guilty of only negligence, and not assault and battery, was so contrary to the overwhelming evidence that Eric should have been found guilty of assault and battery by the judge as a matter of law. The trial judge granted Eric's motion and denied Sharon's and entered judgment in favor of Eric.

Sharon appealed.

Brogan, Judge:
[First, the appellate court agreed with the trial court's decision to grant Eric's motion for judgment notwithstanding the verdict. The reason was that, either this outing was within the scope of their employment, or, regardless of whether it was within the scope of their employment, Sharon had actually applied for and received workers' compensation benefits. In either case, an employee has no legal claim against the employer or a fellow employee for mere negligence; the benefits provided under state workers' compensation law are the only remedy. The employee can, however, maintain

a claim for an intentional wrong such as assault and battery, if it can be proved. The jury was properly instructed on these matters but apparently did not adequately understand the instructions and found Eric liable for damages after finding that he was only negligent. Thus, the trial court was correct to grant Eric's motion for judgment N.O.V.]

[Turning to Sharon's claim that the trial court should have granted her motion for judgment N.O.V. because the evidence overwhelmingly proved assault and battery on Eric's part, the court of appeals stated:] The test to be applied by a trial court in ruling on a motion for judgment notwithstanding a verdict is the same as that for a motion for a directed verdict. The evidence must be construed most strongly in favor of the party against whom the motion is made, and where there is substantial evidence to support his side of the case, upon which reasonable minds may reach different conclusions, the motion must be denied. The jury could have reasonably believed Marcus' version of the incident where he fell on Mrs. Owen. The trial court appropriately denied the motion [and submitted this question to the jury]... The judgment will be affirmed.

Litigation: the Appellate Courts
Nature and Role of Appellate Courts

If a party is dissatisfied with the outcome in the trial court, and his or her attorney believes that legally material errors may have been committed in the trial, the party may wish to appeal the trial court's decision to a higher court.

The function of an appellate court is very different from that of a trial court. An appellate court does not hear evidence or make any factual determinations; instead the court seeks to determine whether material errors were committed by the trial court. A material error is one that probably affected the outcome. If a case is appealed to the highest court in a particular system after having been heard by an intermediate level appellate court, the high court essentially "reviews the review" of the intermediate appellate court.

In most appellate courts, the party who is appealing is usually referred to as the *appellant*; the other party is the *appellee*. Sometimes different terms are used, such as *petitioner* and *respondent*. When an appellate court writes its opinion in a case, it normally uses either of these sets of terms to refer to the parties. Occasionally, however, the court's opinion will refer to the parties by their original trial court designations—plaintiff and defendant.

An appellate court always includes at least 3 judges, and often more. When the court has more than 3 members, it sometimes expands its capacity for work by dividing into panels of 3 judges for each case. When this is done, the entire membership of the court has the authority to review the decision of the 3 judge panel, although it usually does not do so. For example, the various U. S. Courts of Appeal, many of which have more than 10 judges, usually divide into 3–member panels to hear cases, and only rarely does the entire membership of one of these courts review a panel decision. The

U.S. Supreme Court, however, does not divide into panels; all nine of its justices participate in deciding each case.

The Process of Appeal

The Record

The appellant's attorney begins the appeal by filing a notice of appeal and by requesting that the clerk of the trial court prepare the *record* of the case and send it to the appellate court. There is a fee for preparation of the record. The most important part of the record is the *transcript* of the trial. During the trial, an official court reporter was recording every word of the proceedings, including all the attorneys' questions, witnesses' answers, attorneys' objections, and the judge's rulings. The transcript is a printed copy of this verbatim account. Copies of the pleadings, motions, jury instructions, and other official papers in the case also are included in the record if they are relevant to some point being raised on appeal. In addition, the record may include items of physical evidence that were introduced and considered in the trial court; such items might include a written contract, business records, or a map or photograph.

Written Briefs

The appellant's attorney prepares an *appellant's brief* and files it with the appellate court. The brief sets forth errors that the appellant claims were made by the trial judge. These alleged errors usually relate to the trial judge's actions in (1) ruling on motions, (2) ruling on objections to evidence, or (3) stating the relevant law in the jury instructions. The remainder of the brief then presents arguments, based on applicable legal principles, that the cited actions of the trial judge amounted to material errors. The appellee's attorney then responds with the *appellee's brief* (or *reply brief*), in which it is argued that under applicable law the trial judge's actions were correct (or even if erroneous, the errors did not affect the outcome and were "harmless").

Oral Arguments

Appellate courts usually schedule several periods of time during the year in which the parties to appeals are permitted to make *oral arguments*. During one two week period, for example, an appellate court might hear oral arguments in 50 or so cases. In each case, the attorney for each side will have a brief period (typically from 30 to 60 minutes) to clarify and emphasize the most important points in the written briefs and to give the appellate court judges an opportunity to ask questions.

Appellate Court's Decision

As was mentioned earlier, an appellate court serves a very different role from that of a trial court. The court studies the record, considers the legal points made in the briefs and oral arguments, does legal research, and decides whether one or more material errors occurred in the trial.

Review of Trial Court's Factual Determinations

Some of the points raised by the appellant may require the appellate court to study the evidence that appears in the record, such as the transcript of witnesses' testimony and physical evidence that has been included in the record. For example, if the appellant claims that the trial judge erred in ruling on a motion for summary judgment, directed verdict, or judgment N.O.V., the appellate court must determine whether the evidence in the record created a genuine fact issue or whether it was overwhelming in the other direction. The court does not, however, decide what the facts are; fact–finding is a trial court function. Indeed, even if the judges on the appellate court believe that they might have reached a different conclusion had they been performing the fact–finding task in the trial court, they normally will not overturn the trial court's (jury's or trial judge's) factual determinations so long as there is any substantial evidence in the record to support those conclusions. Appellate court judges recognize that the jury or judge that performed the fact–finding role was in a better position to assess the evidence, especially when key evidence took the form of testimony from witnesses who testified and were cross–examined in person Moreover, in any multilevel decision–making system, it makes very little sense to redo everything at successive levels.

Review of Trial Court's Legal Determinations

Much of the appellate court's attention is focused on pure legal questions, that is, reviewing the trial judge's rulings on legal questions. For example, when the trial judge rules on a motion to dismiss or frames the instructions to the jury, he or she makes decisions as to what the applicable legal principles are. In some cases, especially when there is no jury, the trial judge makes formal written *conclusions of law.* These legal principles may derive from precedents (prior decisions in other cases), federal or state statutes, administrative agency regulations, or constitutional provisions. In response to the appellant's contentions on appeal, the appellate court decides whether the trial court's interpretations and applications of these legal principles were correct. An appellate court is not so reluctant to overturn the trial court's legal determinations as it is to reverse factual determinations.

Decision Making

The appellate court judges deliberate individually on a case and consult with each other. They decide the case by majority vote. If the majority concludes that no material errors occurred, it *affirms* the lower court's decision, usually sending the case back to the trial court for appropriate action to enforce the judgment. If the court decides that some material error was committed, it *reverses* the lower court's decision. (Sometimes the terms *vacate or set aside* are used instead of reverse.) Occasionally an appellate court may reverse the decision outright and order a contrary judgment. In most cases of reversal, however, the appellate court *remands* the case to the lower court, where some type of further proceeding will be conducted in accordance with the appellate court's opinion. The further proceeding in the lower court may be of a very limited nature, such as merely requiring the trial judge to reconsider some portion of the decision by applying a slightly different legal standard to the already—established facts. Sometimes, however, the additional proceeding necessary to correct the error after remand may be a completely new trial.

Appellate Court's Opinion

One of the judges is assigned the primary responsibility for writing the court's formal opinion; however, the key language of the opinion is the product of agreement among the judges in the majority. If a judge does not agree with some of the reasoning or language of the opinion but still agrees with the overall result, he or she may wish to write a separate concurring opinion setting forth areas of disagreement. If the decision is not unanimous, a judge who disagrees with the majority decision has the opportunity to write a dissenting opinion setting forth his or her views. Although a dissenting opinion has no effect on the outcome of that case, a persuasive dissent on a close and controversial issue may provide "ammunition" for continuing debate on the question in future cases (or in future legislative debates).

As we have already mentioned, an appellate court usually upholds a jury's or a trial judge's factual findings but is not so reluctant to reverse on the basis of errors of law committed by the trial judge.

Sec v. Ginsburg
2004 U.S. App. Lexis 5184 (11th Cir. 2004)

Scott Ginsburg ("Ginsburg") was chairman and CEO of Evergreen Media Corporation. On Friday, July 12, 1996, Ginsburg met with EZ Corporation's CEO about an acquisition of EZ. On Sunday evening, July 14, Ginsburg called his brother Mark and they spoke for 26 minutes. The next day, Mark bought 3800 shares of EZ. Mark spoke with Jordan Ginsburg (his and Scott's father) over the next few days and they admit they talked about buying EZ shares. Over the next week or so, there were more developments in the acquisition, more phone calls from Ginsburg to his brother and father and more purchases of EZ stock by them.

In early 1997, Evergreen was in the process of merging with Chancellor Broadcasting. On March 20, 1997, Ginsburg attended a meeting with senior executives of Katz Media Group and Hicks, Muse, Tate & Furst, an investment firm that owned a majority interest in Chancellor. A potential acquisition of Katz by Chancellor was discussed and a due diligence team headed by Ginsburg was appointed. A confidentiality agreement was signed. On June 16, 1997, a Katz executive met with Ginsburg and urged him to call Katz's chairman to discuss the purchase. He said Ginsburg should act quickly because Katz was having discussions with other companies. That same evening, a call was placed from a cell phone registered to Ginsburg to a phone registered to his brother Mark. The next day, Mark bought 150,000 shares of Katz.

After Mark and Jordan profited substantially by selling EZ and Katz shares once deals were publicly announced, the Securities and Exchange Commission brought civil insider trading charges against Ginsburg, alleging that he had communicated material nonpublic information to his brother and father. A jury found for the SEC, concluding that Ginsburg had violated Section 10b–5's rules against insider trading. However, the district judge entered a judgment as a matter of law [called a judgment notwithstanding the verdict in most state courts] for Ginsburg, concluding that the evidence was insufficient to permit a reasonable jury to find that he had tipped off his brother or father about inside information. The SEC appealed.

Carnes, Circuit Judge:

The nature of a judgment as a matter of law and our review of it is such that we take the evidence at trial in the light most favorable to the party who won before the jury only to have its victory taken away by the court. We draw from the evidence all reasonable inferences in support of the verdict, because the jury could have done so.

We review a decision to grant a motion for judgment as a matter of law de novo, applying the same standards used by the district court. A judgment as a matter of law is warranted only "if during a trial by jury a party has been fully heard on an issue and there is no legally sufficient evidentiary basis for a reasonable jury to find for that party on that issue." Fed. R. Civ. P. 50(a)(1). That means, as we have already said, that we review the evidence, and the inferences arising therefrom, in the light most favorable to the non-moving party. We "may not weigh the evidence or decide the credibility of witnesses." Adler. However, the nonmoving party "must provide more than a mere scintilla of evidence to survive a motion for judgment as a matter of law." Isenbergh v. Knight–Ridder Newspaper Sales, Inc., 97 F.3d 436 (11th Cir. 1996).

The parties disagree about which body of precedent controls the sufficiency of the evidence issue upon which the district court granted judgment as a matter of law. The sufficiency issue in general involves the circumstances in which it will be inferred from A's act following a conversation with B, who knew a given fact, that A had been informed of that fact when he acted. As it arises in insider trading cases, the more specific issue is when it may be inferred from a trade in stock by A, following a conversation with insider B, that B disclosed inside information to A who acted upon it. The SEC argues, logically, that the sufficiency of the evidence and the permissibility of inferences that may be drawn from the evidence in this insider trading case are governed by our insider trading decisions, especially Adler, which is the closest of those cases to the facts we have here. Ginsburg argues, and the district court concluded, that [the decision should be controlled by an employment retaliation decision, Burrell v. Bd. of Trustees of Georgia Military College, 970 F.2d 785 (11th Cir. 1992].

This is what we are talking about. Decision maker A comes into contact with information possessor B and soon thereafter engages in conduct C. When will that factual scenario support an inference that, despite their denials, A was told the information by B and on that basis A did C? More to the point, does an earlier decision of this Court concluding that scenario would not support an inference the information was communicated and acted upon in an employment retaliation case, compel us to conclude that the same scenario would not support an inference of communicated information and action based upon it in insider trading cases?

We think the earlier employment retaliation decision in *Burrell* does not control this case, because insider trading cases are different from employment retaliation cases. The context in which the facts arise and the strength of the competing inferences can differ. As a result, evidence that may appear to be materially identical for purposes of determining whether a decision maker knew a particular fact can actually have different probative force in an insider trading case than in an employment retaliation case.

There are many sound, non-retaliatory business reasons to take some job action that is challenged as retaliatory. That multitude of potential reasons dilutes the strength of any inference that because a decision maker took an action against an employee he must have been told of a fact which could have led him to take the action for a prohibited reason.

By contrast, people do not make large stock trades for as many reasons as businesses take job actions. Although there are exceptions, people generally buy when they believe the price of a stock is going up and sell when they believe it is going down (either absolutely or relative to the expected performance of other stock). The fact finder in an insider trading case need only infer the most likely source of that belief. The temporal proximity of a phone conversation between the trader and one with insider knowledge provides a reasonable basis for inferring that the basis of the trader's belief was the inside information. The larger and more profitable the trades, and the closer in time the trader's exposure to the insider, the stronger the inference that the trader was acting on the basis of inside information. The magnitude of the incentive to trade on insider information is illustrated by the trades that were made in this case. In less than a month Jordan made $412,875 by trading EZ stock in the direction someone with knowledge of the insider information his son possessed would have, and Mark made a total of $1,393,022 by trading EZ and Katz stock as someone privy to the insider information of his brother would have.

It is not at all clear that the same considerations apply with equal force in job discrimination cases. The inference that a job action was based on a retaliatory motive which arose from imparted information may well be weaker than the comparable inferences in insider trading cases for several reasons. For one thing, the incentive to tip and to act on tipped information is usually a great deal stronger than the incentive to impart and act upon information about an employee engaging in legally protected conduct. We expect that most people would rather make $412,875 or $1,393,022 in a short period trading stocks than they would like to see an employee be punished for something the employee had a legal right to do.

Because it is far from clear that employment retaliation cases are interchangeable with insider trading cases, the district court should have looked to the more specifically applicable precedent instead of regarding it as wrongly decided in light of decisions that had nothing to do with insider trading. [The *Adler* insider trading case involved similar trading following similar phone calls and the Court set aside a judgment as a matter of law for the defendant.]

Ginsburg offered evidence of public information about the companies as motivation for Mark's trading, argued that the trades were consistent with prior trading history, and put forward innocent explanations for the calls. The district court commented that "it is plausible that the investments . . . were driven not by tips but rather by public knowledge." It is also plausible that they were driven by insider information. And it was up to the jury to choose between those competing plausible theories of fact.

The jury was free to disbelieve Ginsburg's evidence just as the *Adler* jury was free to disbelieve what we characterized as the "strong" evidence of a preexisting stock trade plan in *Adler*. Evidence of the innocent explanations for the calls between the parties in this case and of Mark's trading habits is not enough to justify overturning the jury's verdict. If it were otherwise, family members who regularly traded in a particular stock or type of stock could trade based on insider information with impunity.

The district court stated that "the phone records are insufficient to compel an inference that Scott Ginsburg conveyed material, non--

public information to Mark," but that is not the issue. The SEC did not have the burden of putting in evidence that compelled the information to Mark. All it was required to do was put in evidence that reasonably permitted that inference. It did that. The call/trade pattern occurrences coupled with the jury's right to disbelieve the innocent explanations of the calls and trades are enough to support the verdict.
Reversed.

Enforcement of Judgments

If a judgment for the plaintiff survives the appellate process (or if no appeal was ever made), the plaintiff may still have to worry about enforcing the judgment. In the relatively unusual case in which the court's judgment grants an injunction or other equitable remedy, the court will enforce the judgment by fining or jailing the defendant for contempt of court if the defendant fails to comply. In the typical case, however, the judgment awards an amount of money damages to the plaintiff. If the defendant is financially well–off, is well–insured for this type of claim, or is a corporation with adequate assets, enforcement of a money judgment will probably present no major obstacles. It can be very difficult, however, to collect a judgment from some people. Indeed, the probable collectability of any judgment is one of the things a party often must take into account in deciding whether to file a lawsuit in the first place.

If the defendant refuses to pay a valid judgment, the plaintiff will ask the court to issue a **writ of execution**. This writ empowers a law enforcement official to seize defendant's nonexempt property and sell it at auction until enough money is raised to satisfy the judgment.

Another procedure is a **writ of garnishment**, which orders a third party holding property belonging to the defendant to deliver the property to the custody of the court. In most cases, the third party is a bank, stock broker, or other entity holding funds or securities belonging to the defendant. A writ of garnishment may also be issued against a third party who owes a debt to the defendant, ordering the third party to pay the debt to the plaintiff instead of the defendant. If the writ of garnishment targets some type of property other than money, a law enforcement officer will sell the property at auction and the proceeds will be applied to pay the judgment. Many (but not all) states even allow garnishment of wages—a court order to the defendant's employer to pay a specified percentage of the defendant's wages or salary to the plaintiff every week or month until the judgment is fully paid. Federal law places a limit on the portion of a person's wages that can be taken by garnishment.

In speaking of *nonexempt* assets, we are referring to the fact that all states have **exemption laws** specifying that certain types of property cannot be seized for the purpose of satisfying a court judgment. The laws vary quite a bit among the states, some states having very liberal statutes exempting much valuable property and others having extremely limited statutes exempting very little. The most common type of property protected by exemption laws is an individual's **homestead,** or residence; however, many states provide for such an exemption only up to a limited dollar amount.

If a defendant has no nonexempt assets in the forum state, the plaintiff can have the judgment enforced by execution or garnishment in any other state where the defendant has such assets. As long as the court that issued the judgment had subject matter and personal jurisdiction, the authorities in other states are required by the U.S. Constitution's **Full Faith and Credit Clause** to enforce the judgment by trying to seize assets located in another nation, it sometimes can be performed if such assets can be identified. The United States is a party to treaties with many countries that obligate each nation to honor the valid court judgments of the other country or countries that have signed the treaty. However, a court in one country will not enforcement would contravene an important public policy of the nation in which enforcement is sought.

Regardless of whether a plaintiff can collect a judgment—in fact, regardless of whether the plaintiff wins or loses the lawsuit once a case is finally concluded, the plaintiff is finished. The doctrine of **res judicata** ("the thing has been adjudicated") specifies that a plaintiff cannot start over by filing another claim against the defendant based on the same general facts. The plaintiff is barred from reasserting not only the same claim, but also any other claim that he or she reasonably could have asserted the first time around. If the later claim arises from the same general events as the earlier claim, the doctrine of *res judicata* applies even if the plaintiff has come up with new evidence. Figure 3.1 pictures the entire process of civil litigation by means of a flow chart.

Alternative Dispute Resolution

We have already noted some of the criticisms directed at the American legal system, as well as some of the responses from the supporters of the system. There can be no question that in the United States, there is an enormous amount of litigation that consumes tremendous resources. Many people, particularly in the business community, argue that Americans are too eager to sue, there are too many lawsuits of questionable merit, and these lawsuits take too much time and cost far too much money. They also commonly assert that there are too many lawyers with too much influence.

Others contend that there is much value in the way we traditionally have resolved many controversies in the United States. One can argue, for instance, that we tend to use formal litigation more than people in most other countries for several legitimate reasons: (1) We are the most heterogeneous, diffuse, and open society the world has ever known. These characteristics tend to produce more use of formal adjudication than in more homogeneous, static societies. (2) We place great value on the "rule of law," rather than the "rule of individuals," another factor that tends to cause people to look to courts for the interpretation and enforcement of rules. (3) We are not, nor would we want to

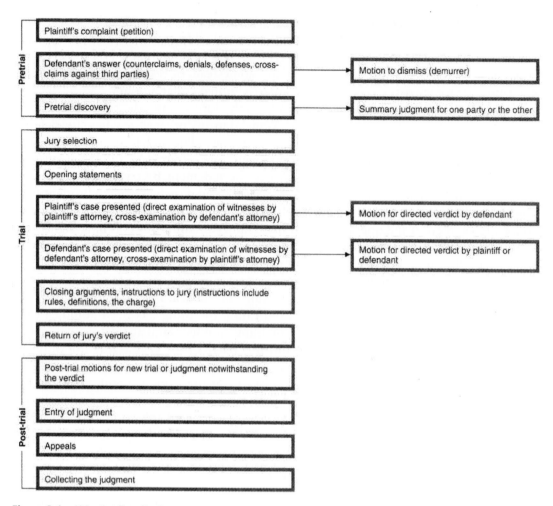

Figure 3.1 Litigation Flow Chart

be, a passive people who accept wrongs with fatalistic resignation as is the custom in some societies. (4) One of the strong legal traditions we inherited from England is the attitude that the courts have authority to formulate legal principles when there is no legislation applicable to a case. Because courts in our system have this limited type of lawmaking power, we naturally use them to set norms of behavior for society to a greater extent than people do in nations with a different system. (5) Our legal profession is much better educated than in most nations, with attorneys being more independent and more readily available to people who feel that their rights have been violated. In some parts of the world, the scarcity of lawyers leads people to obtain help from organized crime syndicates in making and collecting claims.

It also bears mentioning that much of the increase in litigation rates in recent years is not the result of greedy individuals trying to "make a killing" by filing claims against businesses, but instead is attributable to greatly increased filings of cases (1) by corporations against other corporations as a strategic business maneuver and (2) by and against government agencies.

Although there is much disagreement about whether there really are too many lawsuits in the United States, most knowledgeable observers agree that the litigation process is not nearly as efficient as it should be—lawsuits commonly take far too much time and money. In addition, in the case of disputes between business firms, lawsuits tend to decrease the chances that they will be able to maintain a valuable commercial relationship with each other. Although litigation is sometimes necessary and courts will always play a central role in dispute resolution in this country, recent times have witnessed widespread efforts to use other methods.

These other methods are frequently referred to as **alternative dispute resolution (ADR)** techniques. Although these methods do not always work and certainly are not a cure–all for society's problems, they often enable the parties to a dispute to lessen the "sharpness" of the adversarial system, replacing it with an increased emphasis on trust, respect, and win–win solutions.

Negotiated Settlement

Before we address specific methods of ADR, it is important first to point out that most disputes never get to the courtroom. Sometimes a person or business will just "lump it," that is, take a loss rather than pursue a claim. A corporation may do this to keep a valued customer or supplier, perhaps thinking that this particular problem is a one–time occurrence. Also, people sometimes do not pursue claims because they decide that it is not worth it; the perceived likelihood of winning or the size of the claim may lead to a conclusion that pressing a claim will be more trouble and expense than it is worth. Sometimes, instead of lumping it, a party may be able to reach a compromise with the other without ever going to court.

Even when lawsuits are filed, approximately 95 percent of them are resolved without a trial. Some of these are disposed of by some pretrial action of the judge, such as the granting of summary judgment. A large percentage of claims filed in court are resolved by a negotiated out–of–court settlement, with part of the agreement being the dropping of all claims and counterclaims.

The problem with the traditional practice of filing suit and then ultimately settling it out of court is that it usually has been performed very inefficiently. Parties and their attorneys generally have not started thinking seriously about settlement talks until the trial date is very near, thousands of dollars and many months (or years) having already been spent on pretrial discovery and strategic maneuvering. It seems that parties and their attorneys often have felt that they just were not "ready" to talk settlement until just before trial. Thus, enormous time and money traditionally have been spent preparing for an event (the trial) that usually does not happen. In addition, spending so much time, money, and energy battling each other during a lengthy pre-trial process tends to make the parties harden their positions, escalating the intensity of the conflict.

Arbitration

Arbitration is a very old method for resolving disputes that in recent years has become increasingly popular. In arbitration, the parties select an arbitrator (or a panel of three arbitrators), submit very brief pleadings, and present evidence and arguments to the arbitrator. The arbitrator makes a decision, usually called an *award,* which is legally enforceable like a court judgment if the parties had agreed beforehand that it would be binding. Thus, arbitration resembles litigation in that there is actually an adjudication by a third party whose decision is binding.

Despite this superficial resemblance to litigation, arbitration is quite different in many ways. Most of these differences translate into cheaper, faster, and less painful dispute resolution. These differences also increase the chances that the parties can walk away from the process with a commercial relationship still intact. The parties have the ability to control the entire process. They select the decision maker, who may be an expert in the subject matter of the dispute. They also can decide what rules and procedures to use. Unlike litigation, the proceeding can be kept entirely private, which often may be very important to the disputants. There is no required pretrial discovery, although the parties do frequently agree to exchange documents before the arbitration hearing. The parties can decide whether the arbitrator is required to strictly follow particular the rules evidence; most of the time, arbitrators do follow at least the general spirit of the rules of evidence even if they do not follow them strictly. The parties can also agree whether arbitrators are required to follow particular rules of law; most of the time arbitrators do follow the law relatively closely. However, there is essentially no appeal from an arbitrator's award. A court will not review the arbitrator's factual or legal determinations. A court normally will set aside an arbitration award and require a new arbitration hearing only if the evidence shows that the award was affected by fraud or collusion or if there was some serious procedural error such as lack of notice to one of the parties. Although arbitration has a number of advantages over litigation, one can readily see that there are also some important trade−offs that the parties should know about before agreeing to arbitrate.

Arbitration is generally categorized as either *labor arbitration or commercial arbitration.* Labor arbitration involves the resolving of disputes within the labor−management context, usually when the particular group of employees is represented by a union. The relationship between the company and unionized employees is based primarily on a collective bargaining agreement. Almost all collective bargaining agreements include a multistage process for resolving workplace disputes, with legally binding arbitration as the last step. Most of these disputes involve claims by employees that they have been fired or otherwise disciplined without the adequate justification the contract requires. The federal Taft−Hartley Act makes collective bargaining agreements, including arbitration provisions, legally binding.

The term *commercial arbitration* is usually used to describe almost all other forms of arbitration. It includes the use of arbitration to resolve disputes arising from almost any kind of business transaction, including construction contracts, agreements for the sale of goods (such as supplies or equipment), insurance arrangements, joint ventures, and many others. In the United States, the Federal Arbitration Act (FAA) makes commercial arbitration agreements and arbitrator awards legally enforceable if the underlying business transaction affected interstate commerce. If there is no significant effect on interstate commerce, state arbitration statutes in every state usually make the arbitration agreement and award enforceable.

In addition, most of the world's significant trading nations are parties to one or more multilateral treaties under which they agree to enforce arbitration agreements and awards in international commercial transactions involving citizens of other nations that signed the particular treaty. The most important of these treaties is the 1958 United Nations Convention on the Enforcement of Arbitral Awards.

Most commercial arbitration agreements (domestic or international) are of the *predispute* (or *future dispute*) variety; this is a clause in a commercial contract in which the parties agree that if there is any future dispute arising from the transaction, they will submit that dispute to legally binding arbitration. It is also possible for parties to make an agreement to arbitrate after a dispute has already occurred, but this is not usually what happens.

Although the parties to an arbitration agreement can agree as they wish, they usually specify that the arbitration will be coordinated and supervised by an established arbitration organization. In domestic commercial arbitration, the oldest and most frequently used organization is the American Arbitration Association (AAA), which handles about 150,000 commercial arbitration cases per year. In international commercial arbitration, there are several important sponsoring organizations, including the AAA, the International Chamber of Commerce in Paris, and the London Court of Arbitration (which is not a court despite its name).

Although most arbitration is still voluntary, the trial courts in many states and in many federal districts have adopted *court-annexed arbitration*. These programs generally apply to cases involving money damage claims below certain amounts, which range from a few thousand dollars to $150,000 (and a few state programs have no limits). In this form of arbitration, shortly after the lawsuit is filed, the trial judge refers the case to arbitration, with a panel of local attorneys serving as arbitrators. The parties must participate in the arbitration, but the award is not legally binding if either party formally demands a regular trial within a short time after the award (usually 30 days).

In recent years, arbitration has become wildly popular with business as a means of controlling litigation expenses. It is becoming increasingly difficult to buy stock, to open bank accounts, to buy products, to license software, or to get a job without agreeing to arbitrate disputes that might arise. Although courts strongly support the FAA's policy favoring resolution of disputes by arbitration, the following case illustrates that there are some limits that businesses should keep in mind as they draft these agreements.

CIRCUIT CITY STORES, INC. V. ADAMS
Ninth Circuit Court Of Appeals, 279 F.3d 889

Circuit City requires applicants for employment to sign a dispute resolution agreement (DRA) to arbitrate any employment dispute that might arise between the company and one of its employees. Adams signed such an agreement, but later sought to sue Circuit City for employment discrimination under a California fair employment statute [FEHA]. Circuit City sought to stay the lawsuit and asked for a court order to compel arbitration. The trial court found that the arbitration agreement was valid and granted Circuit City's request. Adams appealed.

Nelson, Circuit Judge:

Circuit City has devised an arbitration agreement that functions as a thumb on Circuit City's side of the scale should an employment dispute ever arise between the company and one of its employees. We conclude that such an arrangement is unconscionable under California law.

The Federal Arbitration Act (FAA) was enacted to overcome courts' reluctance to enforce arbitration agreements. The Act not only placed arbitration agreements on equal footing with other contracts, but established a federal policy in favor of arbitration, and a federal common law of arbitrability which preempts state law disfavoring arbitration.

Section 2 of the FAA provides that arbitration agreements "shall be valid, irrevocable, and enforceable, save upon such grounds that exist at law or in equity for the revocation of any contract." In determining the validity of an agreement to arbitrate, federal courts "should apply ordinary state–law principles that govern the formation of contracts." First Optionsof Chicago, Inc. v. Kaplan, 514 U.S. 938 (1995). Thus, although courts may not in-

validate arbitration agreements under state laws applicable only to arbitration provisions, general contract defenses such as fraud, duress, or unconscionability, grounded in state contract law, may operate to invalidate arbitration agreements.

Under California law, a contract is unenforceable if it is both procedurally and substantively unconscionable. When assessing procedural unconscionability, we consider the equilibrium of bargaining power between the parties and the extent to which the contract clearly discloses its terms. A determination of substantive unconscionability, on the other hand, involves whether the terms of the contract are unduly harsh or oppressive.

The DRA is procedurally unconscionable because it is a contract of adhesion: a standard–form contract, drafted by the party with superior bargaining power, which relegates to the other party the option of either adhering to its terms without modification or rejecting the contract entirely. Circuit City, which possesses considerably more bargaining power than nearly all of its employees or applicants, drafted the contract and uses it as its standard arbitration agreement for all of its new employees. The agreement is a prerequisite to employment, and job applicants are not permitted to modify the agreement's terms——they must take the contract or leave it.

[It is] substantively unconscionable as well . . . The DRA unilaterally forces employees to arbitrate claims against the employer. The claims subject to arbitration under the DRA include "any and all employment–related legal disputes, controversies or claims of an Associate arising out of, or relating to, an Associate's application or candidacy for employment, employment or cessation of employment with Circuit City." The provision does not require Circuit City to arbitrate its claims against employees. Circuit City has offered no justification for this asymmetry, nor is there any indication that "business realities" warrant the onesided obligation. This unjustified one–sidedness deprives the DRA of the "modicum of bilaterality" that the California Supreme Court requires for contracts to be enforceable under California law.

The asymmetry is compounded by the fact that the agreement limits the relief available to employees. Under the DRA, the remedies are limited to injunctive relief, up to one year of back pay and up to two years of front pay, compensatory damages, and punitive damages in an amount up to the greater of the amount of back pay and front pay awarded or $ 5,000. By contrast, a plaintiff in a civil suit for sexual harassment under the FEHA is eligible for all forms of relief that are generally available to civil litigants——including appropriate punitive damages and damages for emotional distress. The DRA also requires the employee to split the arbitrator's fees with Circuit City. This fee allocation scheme alone would render an arbitration agreement unenforceable. [Author's note: most courts probably would not hold that the fee–splitting provision by itself would be enough to support a finding of substantive unconscionability.] But the DRA goes even further: it also imposes a strict one year statute of limitations on arbitrating claims that would deprive Adams of the benefit of the continuing violation doctrine available in FEHA suits. In short, the DRA forces Adams to arbitrate his statutory claims without affording him the benefit of the full range of statutory remedies.

In addition, our decision is entirely consistent with federal law concerning the enforceability of arbitration agreements. The Supreme Court, in Gilmer v. Interstate/Johnson Lane Corp., 500 U.S. 20(1991), held that "by agreeing to arbitrate a statutory claim, [an employee] does not forgo the substantive rights afforded by the statute; [he] only submits to their resolution in an arbitral, rather than a judicial forum." While the Court in *Gilmer* affirmed that statutory rights can be resolved through arbitration, the decision also recognized that the arbitral forum must allow the employee to adequately pursue statutory rights.

Courts have since interpreted *Gilmer* to require basic procedural and remedial protections so that claimants can effectively pursue their statutory rights. Cole v. Burns Inter'l Security Services, 105 F.3d 1465(D.C.Cir. 1997) [holding that an employment arbitration agreement must: (1) provide the same rights and remedies available to the individual under applicable federal, state, and local law; (2) permit the employee to participate in the selection of a neutral arbitrator; (3) allow the employee the right to be represented by counsel; (4) allow reasonable discovery prior to the arbitration hearing; and (5) ensure that the employee has the right to present his or her proof through testimony, documentary evidence, and cross-examination.] We note that here, Circuit City's arbitration agreement fails to meet two of Cole's minimum requirements: it fails to provide for all of the types of relief that would otherwise be available in court, or to ensure that employees do not have to pay either unreasonable costs or any arbitrators' fees or expenses as a condition of access to the arbitration forum.

Nor does our decision run afoul of the FAA by imposing a heightened burden on arbitration agreements. Because unconscionability is a defense to contracts generally and does not single out arbitration agreements for special scrutiny, it is also a valid reason not to enforce an arbitration agreement under the FAA.

Because we find that the DRA is an unconscionable contract of adhesion under California law, the order compelling arbitration is REVERSED.

Mediation

Other forms of ADR are quite different from arbitration. The various other types do not produce a decision that is legally binding on the parties. Instead, these methods are aimed at facilitating agreed settlements by (1) creating a structure that encourages the parties to get together and seriously negotiate much earlier, before they have hardened their positions and spent so much time and money, (2) trying to build trust and respect between the parties, (3) making the parties more realistic about the weaknesses of their positions and the strengths of the other side's positions before the dispute has escalated very far, and (4) creating an environment in which the parties are more likely to think of creative solutions to their problems that can benefit both sides rather than thinking about the dispute only in legalistic and dollar terms.

The most important version of this type of ADR is **mediation,** another old method being used much more in recent years. Like ADR generally, most mediation is entirely voluntary; it is created and controlled by the parties. The third party chosen by the disputants to help them find a solution to their differences is called a *mediator.* A mediator does not impose a solution but tries to help the parties themselves achieve one. Various approaches are used in mediation, depending on the wishes of the parties, the nature of the dispute, and the skill and personality of the mediator. The mediator may do as little as persuade the parties to talk to each other. Going further, he or she might help the parties agree on an agenda for a meeting and provide a suitable environment for negotiation. The mediator might point out that particular proposals are unrealistic, help the parties formulate their own proposals, and even make proposals for them to consider. In some situations, the mediator may try very hard to persuade them to accept a settlement he or she believes is reasonable.

Mediation has facilitated resolution of a wide range of disputes, such as many kinds of business disputes, international political conflicts, labor disputes, landlord–tenant disagreements, disputes between divorcing spouses, and multiparty controversies over environmental protections. It also can be very useful in combination with some other form of ADR, such as arbitration. For example, when IBM claimed that Fujitsu had illegally copied the former's mainframe operating system software, they spent several years and a great deal of time, money, and energy unsuccessfully trying to negotiate a settlement. They reached certain settlement agreements, but disagreements continued to break out, largely because of the technical complexity of the problem. The parties agreed to arbitration by a law professor experienced in dispute resolution and a retired computer industry executive. (The use of a two member panel was unusual.) The arbitrators recognized that the controversy presented factual disputes about past copying that would be almost impossible to resolve. They focused primarily on the future, ordering Fujitsu to provide a complete accounting of its use of programs under the earlier settlement agreement and requiring the parties to participate in mediation regarding programs falling outside the earlier agreement. The arbitrators became mediators; through mediation, new agreements were reached, after which the professor and executive resumed their roles as arbitrators and incorporated the new agreements into a binding arbitration order.

Although most mediation is voluntary, a number of states and a few federal districts are using courtannexed mediation, in which a trial judge refers the parties to mediation shortly after the case is filed. Although participation in this type of mediation is required, the mediator still does not impose an outcome on the parties.

Summary Jury Trial

Unlike most ADR techniques, the **summary jurytrial (SJT)** can be used only after a lawsuit has been filed. The trial judge usually selects cases for SJT that he or she thinks (1) are unlikely to be settled by the parties through normal negotiation and (2) will probably require substantial trial time. Either the parties have performed some amount of pretrial discovery already, or if not, they are given an opportunity to conduct limited discovery before the SJT. A small (such as six—member) jury is selected in the same way that regular juries are chosen. To ensure that the jurors take their responsibility seriously, they are not informed that their decision is nonbinding.

The parties are then given a few hours to summarize their positions and their evidence (sometimes including key portions of videotaped deposition testimony) and to give closing arguments. After the jury renders a verdict, the parties are urged to negotiate a settlement based on the additional guidance that the jury's reaction to the case provides. Despite the fact that difficult cases are usually chosen for SJT, it has generally enjoyed a very high success rate, with most of the cases settling shortly after the SJT. The procedure tends to puncture inflated expectations and make parties choose more realistic settlement positions.

Minitrial

The **minitrial,** which has been used almost exclusively in disputes between corporations, involves summary presentations of evidence and arguments (similar to the presentations in an SJT) by opposing attorneys to a panel consisting of a neutral advisor and high-ranking executives from each company. The company representatives, who should have settlement authority, retire for direct settlement negotiations shortly after the presentations. They may seek the opinion of the neutral advisor before beginning settlement talks or only after negotiations have stalled. The exact design of the procedure, like the decision to use it in the first place, depends on the agreement of the parties. The minitrial has had a number of notable successes in complex, difficult disputes involving some of America's largest and best known companies. For example, almost immediately after a minitrial, Allied Corporation and Shell Oil settled a contract dispute that had been dragging on for almost ten years, including four years of expensive litigation.

Regulatory Negotiation

Regulatory negotiation, sometimes called *reg-neg* or *negotiated rule making*, has been a reasonably successful alternative to traditional administrative agency rule making. Agency regulations are often challenged in court, commonly taking years finally to receive court approval or disapproval. A number of federal and state agencies have avoided such litigation through a process in which the agency meets with representatives from interested groups to negotiate the content of regulations before they are formally proposed. The negotiations frequently involve a neutral third party acting as a mediator. The scope and validity of a rule produced through this process is much less likely to be challenged; in fact, the procedure sometimes produces both an agreed—on regulation and an agreement not to file a lawsuit challenging the regulation. The Environmental Protection Agency has been one of the leaders among federal agencies in using regulatory negotiation for new water and air quality regulations.

Future of ADR

Other forms of ADR have been used, often consisting of variations or hybrids of the methods we have discussed. Given the time and expense associated with traditional litigation and non—ADR negotiation, the use of ADR is likely to increase. In Texas, for example, the legislature stated that "it is the policy of the State to encourage the peaceable resolution of disputes . . . and the early settlement of pending litigation through voluntary settlement procedures." The legislation charges the courts of the state with the responsibility to carry out that policy by encouraging use of arbitration, mediation, SJTs, minitrials, and the like.

CHAPTER 4

COMMON AND STATUTORY LAW

There are several basic processes by which law is made: (1) the formulation of rules by the courts—the judges—in deciding cases coming before them in those areas of law in which no statutes apply; (2) the enactment and interpretation of statutes; (3) the interpretation and application of constitutional provisions; and (4) the promulgation of rules and regulations by administrative agencies. In this chapter we look at the first and second of these lawmaking processes. First we show how common law (or case law) is formed by the courts. Then we turn our attention to the enactment and interpretation of statutory law.

Origin of Common Law

As we described in Chapter 2, the early king's courts in England largely made up the law on a case-by-case basis. If, for example, a plaintiff asked for damages for breach of contract in a situation in which the defendant denied that a contract ever existed, the court had to spell out the nature of a contract—that is, specify the minimum elements that the court felt must exist for it to impose contractual liability on the defendant. Similarly, if a defendant admitted making the contract in question but sought to escape liability for reasons of illness or military service, the court had to decide what kinds of defenses ought to be legally recognizable—defenses that should free the defendant from his or her contractual obligations.

Over a period of time, as more and more cases were settled, a rudimentary body of contract law came into being. Thereafter, when other cases arose involving contractual matters, the courts quite naturally looked to the earlier cases to see what principles of law had been established. The same procedure was followed in many other branches of law, and the legal rules that arose in this manner constituted the common law, or **case law,** of England.

The common-law rules that had developed in England became the law of our early colonies. When those colonies achieved statehood, they adopted those rules as a major part of their respective bodies of law. As the territories became states, they followed suit so that at one time the major portion of the law of all states. There is one exception—Louisiana continues to be governed by the civil law (rather than common law) system adopted in most European countries. In a civil law system, virtually all law is codified.

The Current Scene

Gradually, the state legislatures began to pass increasing numbers of statutes, with the result that today most branches of the law are statutory in nature. For example, all states now have comprehensive statutes governing the areas of corporation law, criminal law, tax law, municipal corporations, and commercial law. Some of these statutes have been based largely on the common-law principles that were in effect earlier. Others, however, have been passed to create bodies of rules that did not exist previously or that expressly overrule common-law principles.

Despite the ever-increasing amount of statutory law in this country (which we examine in some detail later in this chapter), several branches of law today are still essentially common law in nature in 49 states—particularly the subjects of *contracts, torts,* and *agency.* In these areas, in which the legislatures have not seen fit to enact comprehensive statutes, the courts still settle controversies on the basis of judge-made or *case law*—the rules formulated by the courts in deciding earlier cases over the years, as illustrated in Figure 4.1. (Although many of these rules had their origin in England, as has been indicated, our definition of common law also includes those additional rules that have originated in the state courts in this country.)

In deciding each case, judges bear the twin burden of attempting to provide "justice" for the case at hand while at the same time setting a precedent that will serve the greater interests of society when applied in future cases. The common-law rules, like legislative statutes, must serve public policy interests—the "community common sense and common conscience." Therefore, courts have laid great stress on the customs, morals, and forms of conduct that are generally prevailing in the community at the time of decision. There is no doubt that occasionally the judge's personal feelings as to what kinds of conduct are just and fair, what rule would best serve societal interests, and simply what is "right" or "wrong" enter the picture.

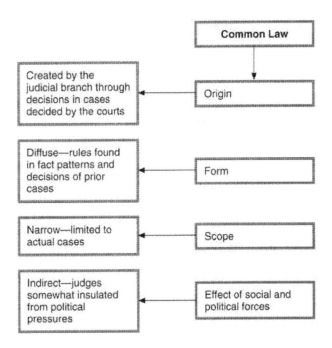

Figure 4.1 Common Law

Role of the Judge

Famous jurist Benjamin Cardozo in his book The Nature of the Judicial Process, contended that four "directive forces" shaped the law, and especially the common law, as follows: (1) philosophy (logic), (2) history, (3) custom, and (4) social welfare (or sociology).

In a lecture on the role of philosophy in the law, Cardozo briefly commented on the special tasks of the judge in interpreting statutes and constitutions, and then continued:

> We reach the land of mystery when constitution and statute are silent, and the judge must look to the common law for the rule that fits the case. . . The first thing he does is to compare the case before him with the precedents, whether stored in his mind or hidden in the books. . . Back of precedents are the basic juridical conceptions which are the postulates of judicial reasoning, and farther back are the habits of life, the institutions of society, in which those conceptions had their origin, and which, by a process of interaction, they have modified in turn. . . If [precedents] are plain and to the point, there may be need of nothing more. Stare decisis ("to stand by decisions") is at least the everyday working rule of the law.

Early in that same lecture, however, Cardozo cautioned that the finding of **precedent** was only part of the judge's job and indicated how the law must grow beyond the early precedents:

> The rules and principles of case law have never been treated as final truths, but as working hypotheses, continually retested in those great laboratories of the law, the courts of justice. . . In [the] perpetual flux [of the law,] the problem which confronts the judge is in reality a twofold one: he first must extract from the precedents the underlying principle, the ratio decidendi [the ground of decision]; he must then determine the path or direction along which the principle is to move and develop, if it is not to wither and die. . .
>
> The directive force of a principle may be exerted along the line of logical progression; this I will call the rule of analogy or the method of philosophy, along the line of historical development; this I will call the method of evolution; along the line of the customs of the community; this I will call the method of tradition; along the lines of justice, morals and social welfare, the mores of the day; and this I will call the method of sociology. . .

Common Law—the Doctrine of Stare Decisis

The heart of the common-law process lies in the inclination of the courts generally to follow precedent—to stand by existing decisions. This policy, as we were told by Cardozo, is referred to as the doctrine of *stare decisis.* Under this approach, when the fact pattern of a particular controversy is established, the attorneys for both parties search for earlier cases involving similar fact patterns in an effort to determine whether applicable principles of law have been established. If this research produces a number of similar cases (or even one) within the state where a rule has been applied by the appellate courts, the trial court will ordinarily feel constrained to follow the same rule in settling the current controversy. (But, as we will see later, this does not mean that the courts are reluctant to abandon a precedent if it produces clear injustice under "contemporary conditions.")

Types of Precedent

Authority originating in courts above the trial court in the appellate chain is called **mandatory authority.** The judge must follow it. Thus, a state trial judge in Ohio will follow the rulings of the Ohio Supreme Court if there are any precedents from this court; if not, the judge will follow the prior decisions of Ohio's intermediate appellate courts. The intermediate appellate courts will do the same thing, and the Ohio Supreme Court will follow its own precedents. In matters of federal law, the Ohio Supreme Court will follow the holdings of the U.S. Supreme Court. A judge who does not follow mandatory authority is not impeached or shot at dawn but certainly runs a strong risk of reversal.

So strong is the hold of mandatory authority that judges will usually follow it even though they violently disagree with its reasoning and result. The following case illustrates this fact. The case involves a claim of *negligence*, which we shall study in detail in Chapter 8. It means simply that the defendant was more careless than a reasonable person would have been under the circumstances and should be liable for injuries that result. The case also involves a defense of governmental immunity, which stems from the ancient English doctrine that the King (or in this case the government) "can do no wrong" and therefore cannot be sued absent his consent. The decision is by a Michigan intermediate appellate court, sitting between the trial court and the Michigan Supreme Court in the appellate chain.

EDWARDS V. CLINTON VALLEY CENTER
Court of Appeals of Michigan, 360 N.W. 2d 606 (1984)

The plaintiff is the estate of JeanEdwards, who was fatally stabbed by a former mental patient. The defendant is a government mental hospital that refused to admit the killer after she was brought to the facility by police when she threatened to "kill someone." The plaintiff alleges that the defendant's refusal to admit the killer was negligent. The trial judge dismissed the suit on a purely legal ground...governmental immunity. The plaintiff appealed.

Bronson, Presiding Judge:
Under the rule of *stare decisis*, this Court is bound to follow decisions of the Michigan Supreme Court, even if we disagree with them. The rule of *stare decisis*, founded on considerations of expediency and sound principles of public policy, operates to preserve harmony, certainty, and stability in the law. However, the rule "was never intended to perpetuate error or to prevent the consideration of rules of law to be applied to the ever-changing

business, economic, and political life of a community." Parker v. Port Huron Hospital, 105 N.W.2d 1(1960).

In Perry v. Kalamazoo State Hospital,273 N.W.2d 421(1978), the majority of the Supreme Court held that governmental immunity for tort liability extends to the day-to-day care public mental hospitals provide. An attempt to distinguish the instant case from Perry could not possibly withstand logical or honest analysis. As a member of the Court of Appeals, I am obligated to follow the decisions of our higher court. For that reason, and that reason alone, the order of summary judgment is affirmed.

I feel compelled, however, to register my fundamental disagreement with the result adopted by the Perry majority I am much more inclined to follow the narrow interpretation of governmental immunity advanced by the dissenters, because the operation of a mental hospital is not an activity which can be done only by the government, it is not a governmental function within the meaning of [the Michigan statutes establishing governmental immunity], and, therefore, a mental hospital should not be immune from liability for its torts.

If ever a factual situation invited reconsideration of the wisdom of a broad interpretation of what is, in the first place, an archaic doctrine, it is presented in the instant case. The Pontiac police bring Wilma Gilmore to the state-operated Clinton Valley Center. Gilmore threatens to kill someone. Gilmore had been previously institutionalized at the center. The center refuses to admit Gilmore.

Four days later, Gilmore once again goes to the police and repeats her homicidal threats. She is told to leave. Two days later, Gilmore enters the apartment of Jean Edwards and fatally stabs her in the arms, throat, and abdomen. Of note is that nowhere in the record does the center offer a reason for its refusal to admit Gilmore.

I fail to see how summarily relieving the hospital of responsibility for such obvious gross negligence, without requiring of it even the slightest explanation, serves any viable public interest or protects the people of our state. Instead, it harshly imposes the entire risk of the center's negligence on JeanEdwards and her family. The time has come for either the Legislature or our Supreme Court to preserve and promote justice by modifying the doctrine of governmental immunity.

Affirmed.

What if a trial judge searches the law books and discovers that there is no precedent in the state on the legal question presented? In such a case, the judge may examine the decisions of courts of other states. For example, assume a state trial judge in Oregon is faced with the question of whether a landlord who did not attempt to lease an apartment after a tenant moved out in the middle of a lease should be barred from suing the tenant for damages. No Oregon cases address the issue, and the only case "on point" was rendered by the Alabama Supreme Court. Must the Oregon judge follow the Alabama precedent? No. Because the Oregon judge's decision cannot be appealed to the Alabama Supreme Court, the latter's rulings are not mandatory authority.

The Alabama decision would constitute **persuasive authority**. That is, the Oregon judge can study the Alabama decision and, on finding it persuasive, may choose to follow it. However, if the judge finds the decision not to be persuasive, the judge need not apply its rationale in Oregon.

What if there are two existing precedents, that of the Alabama Supreme Court and one from the North Dakota Supreme Court, that reach diametrically opposed results on the same issue? Again, they are both only persuasive authority for the Oregon judge who can study them and follow the one that seems more reasonable. Of course, the judge can also reject both persuasive precedents and create yet a third approach to the issue. Despite the importance of stability to the law, the majesty of the common law lies in its flexibility and adaptability. Although judges revere stability, they will change a rule when they become convinced that it was wrongly established and never served society's interests or that, although it was a good rule when established, changing social, moral, economic, or technological factors have rendered it outmoded. If no valid reason supports a common-law rule, no matter how long it has been established, the judges should and usually will change it.

Sometimes common-law rules change slowly. Exceptions or qualifications to a rule will slowly appear in the case law. Most of the history of the common law is of a slow evolution as the law keeps pace with a changing society. Refer back to Soldano v. O'Daniels in Chapter 1. That case not only illustrates a minor change in the slow evolution of the law regarding our duties to our fellow citizens, but it also contains some eloquent language extolling the virtues of our flexible common law.

Sometimes the law will change dramatically, as when modern judges decide an established rule no longer serves society and must be scrapped, as the following case illustrates.

FLAGIELLO V. PENNSYLVANIA HOSPITAL
Supreme Court of Pennsylvania, 208 A.2d 193 (1965)

Mrs. Flagiello fell and broke an ankle while being moved by two of employees of the Pennsylvania Hospital. She brought this action against the hospital to recover damages, alleging that the employees were guilty of negligence. The defendant hospital moved for a judgment on the pleadings, contending that under the case law of Pennsylvania, it was well established that a charitable institution was not responsible for the wrongs of its employees. The trial court sustained this motion and entered judgment for the defendant. The plaintiff appealed to the Supreme Court of Pennsylvania.

Musmanno, Justice:

... The hospital has not denied that its negligence caused Mrs. Flagiello's injuries. It merely announces that it is an eleemosynary institution, and, therefore, owed no duty of care to its patient. It declares in effect that it can do wrong and still not be liable in damages to the person it has wronged. It thus urges a momentous exception to the generic proposition that in law there is no wrong without a remedy. From the earliest days of organized society it became apparent to man that society could never become a success unless the collectivity of mankind guaranteed to every member of society a remedy for a palpable wrong inflicted on him by another member of that society. In 1844 Justice Storrs of the Supreme Court of Connecticut crystallized into epigrammatic language that wise concept, as follows: "An injury is a wrong; and for the redress of every wrong there is a remedy; a wrong is a violation of one's right; and for the vindication of every right there is a remedy." Parker v. Griswold, 17 Conn. 288.

[The court addressed itself to several specific arguments advanced by the defendant to support its contention that charitable institutions were not and should not be, subject to the general rule stated above. One of these arguments was that, on economic grounds alone, the imposition of liability on charitable institutions would be financially ruinous to them. The court rejected this argument, noting first that, as a general rule, a defendant is never permitted to escape liability as to valid claims solely on the ground that an entry of a judgment against the defendant would be financially burdensome, or might even force the defendant into bankruptcy. The court also noted that the rule of immunity as to charitable institutions originated in this country at a time when most of their patients paid nothing for the services they received and that the rule was an effort by the courts to preserve the meager assets of such institutions. Judge Musmanno further observed that conditions have now changed; that so-called charitable hospitals operate on the same basis as ordinary business establishments; that in 1963 "the fees received from patients in the still designated charitable hospitals in Pennsylvania constituted 90.92 percent of the total income of such hospitals," and the plaintiff did, in fact, pay the defendant $24.50 a day for services rendered her.

On these facts, the court rejected defendant's claim of immunity based on financial considerations. The court then turned to the remaining major contention of the defendant, specifically, that the rule of immunity as to charitable hospitals was so firmly established in the case law of Pennsylvania, including cases decided by the Pennsylvania Supreme Court, that, under the doctrine of stare decisis, the rule could not now be abandoned by the courts. In that regard Judge Musmanno, in a lengthy examination of cases, concluded that

the immunity doctrine originated in an early English case that was soon overruled there, that the American courts seemed to adopt the rule of that case blindly, without examining the validity of the reasons ostensibly underlying it, and further noted that approximately half the states in this country have now rejected the doctrine of immunity. The court then continued:]

Failing to hold back both the overwhelming reasons of rudimentary justice for abolishing the doctrine, and the rising tide of out-of-state repudiation of the doctrine, the defendant hospital and the Hospital Association of Pennsylvania fall back for defense to the bastion of *stare decisis*. It is inevitable and proper that they should do so. Without *stare decisis*, there would be no stability in our system of jurisprudence.

Stare decisis channels the law. It erects lighthouses and flies the signals of safety. The ships of jurisprudence must follow that well-defined channel which, over the years, has been proved to be secure and trustworthy. But it would not comport with wisdom to insist that, should shoals rise in a heretofore safe course and rocks emerge to encumber the passage, the ship should nonetheless pursue the original course, merely because it presented no hazard in the past. The principle of stare decisis does not demand that we follow precedents which shipwreck justice...

There is nothing in the records of the courts, the biographies of great jurists, or the writings of eminent legal authorities which offers the slightest encouragement to the notion that time petrifies into unchanging jurisprudence a palpable fallacy. [Emphasis added.] As years can give no sturdiness to a decayed tree, so the passing decades can add no convincing flavor to the withered apple of sophistry clinging to the limb of demonstrated wrong. There are, of course, principles and precepts sanctified by age, and no one would think of changing them, but their inviolability derives not from longevity but from their universal appeal to the reason, the conscience and the experience of mankind. No one, for instance, would think of challenging what was written in Magna Charta, the Habeas Corpus Act or the Bill of Rights of the Constitution of the United States...

While age adds venerableness to moral principles and some physical objects, it occasionally becomes necessary, and it is not sacrilegious to do so, to scrape away the moss of the years to study closely the thing which is being accepted as authoritative, inviolable, and untouchable. The Supreme Court of Michigan said sagaciously in the case of Williams v. City of Detroit, 364 Mich. 231, that "it is the peculiar genius of the common law that no legal rule is mandated by the doctrine of stare decisis when that rule was conceived in error or when the times and circumstances have so changed as to render it an instrument of injustice."

The charitable immunity rule proves itself an instrument of injustice and nothing presented by the defendant shows it to be otherwise. In fact, the longer the argument for its

preservation the more convincing its purpose if, indeed, it ever had a purpose consonant with sound law. "Ordinarily, when a court-made rule of long standing, it starts out by saying that the reason for the rule no longer exists. In this case, it is correct to say that the 'reason' originally given for the rule of immunity never did exist." Pierce v. Yakima Valley Hospital Ass'n, 260 P.2d 765.

A rule that has become insolvent has no place in the active market of current enterprise. When a rule offends against reason, when it is at odds with every precept of natural justice, and when it cannot be defended on its own merits, but has to depend alone on a discredited genealogy, courts not only possess the inherent power to repudiate, but, indeed, it is required, by the very nature of judicial function, to abolish such a rule.

We, therefore, overrule Michael v. Habnemann, 404 Pa. 424, and all other decisions of identical effect, and hold that the hospital's liability must be governed by the same principles of law as apply to other employers...

Reversed and remanded.

Profile of Our Federal and State Statutory Law

Although a significant portion of our law is still common law in nature, most of our federal and state law today results from the enactment of **statutes** by legislative bodies. These are the formally adopted rules that constitute our *statutory law,* the second of the major sources of law. All states, for example, have comprehensive statutes governing such subjects as banking law, criminal law, education, consumer sales, and motor vehicle law.

Similarly, at the federal level, sweeping statutes in the areas of antitrust law, labor law, food and drug regulation, and securities law have long been in effect. Newer (and usually narrower) statutes are added every year, including, for example, the Federal Trademark Dilution Act of 1995, the Digital Millennium Copyright Act of 1998, and the Sarbanes-Oxley Act of 2002.

In this section our first objectives are to look at the reasons for the existence of statutory law, to become acquainted with the basic rules that delineate the jurisdictions of the federal and state governments, and to note the contrasts between statutory and common law. We then turn our attention to the closely related area of statutory interpretation...the process by which the courts spell out the precise meaning of statutes that are applicable to the particular cases coming before them...and conclude

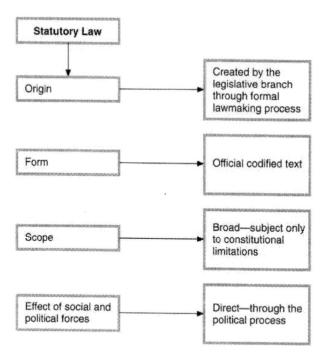

Figure 4.2 Statutory Law

with a summary of selected state statutes that are of special significance to the business community. As a backdrop for a better understanding of the issues that are addressed in this chapter, however, a brief description of the vast scope of our statutory law is first in order.

Statutory Law...the Rationale

There are many reasons for the existence of statutory law, three of which deserve special mention.

1. One of the primary functions of any legislative body is to adopt measures having to do with the *structure and day-to-day operation* of the government of which it is a part. Thus many federal statutes are of the "nuts and bolts" variety, relating to such matters as the operation of the federal court system, the Internal Revenue Service, and the administration and employment rules of the U.S. Civil Service Commission. In a similar vein, many state statutes relate to such matters as the property tax laws, the operation of school systems, and the setting forth of powers of municipalities within their borders.

2. Many activities are of such a nature that *they can hardly be regulated by common-law principles* and the judicial processes. In the area of criminal law, for example, it

is absolutely essential for the general populace to know what acts are punishable by fine and imprisonment; the only sure way to set forth the elements of specific crimes is through the enactment of federal and state criminal statutes. Similarly, the activities of corporations are so complex and so varied that they do not lend themselves to judicial regulation. Few judges, for example, have either the expertise to deal with such questions as the conditions under which the payment of corporate dividends should be permitted or the time to deal with the spelling out of such conditions on a case-by-case basis. Thus the only practical way to deal with these and other problems is by the drafting of detailed statutes, which, in total, make up the comprehensive corporation laws of the states.

3. A third function of a legislature is to change expressly (or even overrule) common-law rules when it believes such modifications are necessary, and...even more commonly...to enact statutes to *remedy new problems* to which common-law rules do not apply. Thus a state legislature might pass a statute making nonprofit corporations (such as hospitals) liable for the wrongs of their employees to the same extent as are profit-making corporations, thereby reversing the early common-law rule of nonliability for such employers. Or a legislature, aware of increasing purchases of its farmlands by foreign citizens...a situation not covered by common-law rules... might react to this perceived evil by passing a statute placing limits on the number of acres aliens may own or inherit.

Limitations on Legislative Bodies
Procedural Requirements

All state constitutions (and, to a lesser extent, the federal Constitution) contain provisions about the manner in which statutes shall be enacted. As a general rule, acts that do not conform to these requirements are void. For example, virtually all state constitutions provide that revenue bills "shall originate in the House of Representatives," a requirement that also appears in the federal Constitution. Typical state constitutions also contain provisions (1) restricting the enactment of "special" or "local" laws that affect only a portion of the citizenry, (2) requiring that the subject of every act be set forth in its title, and (3) prohibiting a statute from embracing more than one subject. Additionally, all constitutions prescribe certain formalities in regard to the enactment processes themselves, such as specific limitations on the time and place of the introduction of bills, limitations on the amendment of bills, and the requirement that bills have three separate readings before final passage.

These kinds of provisions, although appearing to be unduly technical, actually serve meritorious purposes. For example, although legislatures normally strive to pass statutes of general application, it is necessary that some laws operate only on certain classes of persons or in certain localities of a state. Such special or local laws are valid only if the basis of their classification is reasonable; two of the purposes of the constitutional provisions just mentioned are to ensure such reasonableness and to guarantee that the classes of persons covered be given notice of the consideration of the bill before its passage. Similarly, the purpose of requiring that the subject of an act be expressed in its title is to ensure that legislators voting on a bill are fully apprised as to its subject, thereby guarding against the enactment of "surprise" legislation. And the purpose of the requirement that a bill contain one subject is to prevent the passage of omnibus bills (those that bring together entirely unrelated, or incongruous, matters).

Requirement of Certainty

All statutes are subject to the general principle of constitutional law that they be "reasonably definite and certain." Although the Constitution itself does not expressly contain such a provision, the courts have long taken the view that if the wording of a statute is such that persons of ordinary intelligence cannot understand its meaning, the statute violates the due process clause of the Constitution and is thus invalid. In such instances, it is said that the statute is "unconstitutionally vague."

As a practical matter, most statutes that are challenged on the ground of vagueness or uncertainty are upheld by the courts. This is because most statutes are, in fact, drafted carefully and because the courts are extremely reluctant to declare a statute unconstitutional if they can avoid doing so. Thus, if the wording of a statute is subject to two possible but conflicting interpretations, one of which satisfies constitutional requirements and the other of which does not, the former interpretation will be accepted by the courts if they can reasonably do so.

An application of the vagueness analysis in a criminal case occurred in Kolender v. Lawson, 461 U.S. 352 (1983), in which the U.S. Supreme Court struck down, on the ground of vagueness, a California statute that required persons who loitered or wandered on the streets to provide "credible and reliable" identification and to account for their presence when requested to do so by a peace officer. The court said, "It is clear that the full discretion accorded to the police to determine whether the suspect has provided a 'credible and reliable' identification necessarily entrusts lawmaking to the moment-to-moment judgment of the policeman on his beat," and "furnishes a convenient tool for harsh and discriminatory enforcement by local prosecuting officials against particular groups deemed to merit their displeasure."

In a case involving regulation of business, rather than criminal charges, the courts will not be as demanding in applying the vagueness test, as the next case illustrates.

FORD MOTOR CO. v. TEXAS DEPARTMENT OF TRANSPORTATION
Fifth Circuit Court of Appeals, 264 F.3d 493 (2001)

Plaintiff Ford Motor Co. attempted to market preowned cars in Texas via its Internet cite,

The Showroom. The State filed an administrative complaint alleging that Ford violated the Texas Motor Vehicle Commission Code by controlling an automobile "dealer" while acting as a manufacturer of automobiles. Ford responded by filing suit in federal court, claiming that the law was unconstitutional on several grounds, including vagueness. The district court granted summary judgment for the State, and Ford appealed.

Benavides, Justice:

Section 5.02C(c) provides that a manufacturer may not directly or indirectly, operate or control a dealer or act in the capacity of a dealer. In its administrative complaint, the State alleged that Ford, through the operation of the Showroom, acted in the capacity of a dealer. Ford counters that § 5.02C(c) is unconstitutionally vague and does not provide it fair notice of what conduct constitutes "operating or controlling a dealer" or "acting in the capacity of a dealer." In this regard, Ford correctly notes that neither of these phrases [is] defined in the Code. The term "dealer" is, however. Additionally, during her deposition, Carol Kent, the Director of the Texas Department of Transportation, Enforcement Section, indicated that if a company had any questions regarding whether their conduct violated the Code, they could contact the Motor Vehicle Division. Ford attacks this position as unreasonable.

Under this Court's precedent, the appropriate test for a vagueness challenge depends on whether the statute at issue is civil or criminal. For criminal statutes we employ the two-part void-for-vagueness test:

Vagueness may invalidate a criminal law for either of two independent reasons. First, it may fail to provide the kind of notice that will enable ordinary people to understand what conduct it prohibits; second, it may authorize and even encourage arbitrary and discriminatory enforcement. U.S. v. Escalante, 239 F.3d 678 (5th Cir. 2001).

A less stringent standard is applied to civil statutes that regulate economic activity. An economic regulation is invalidated "only if it commands compliance in terms 'so vague and indefinite as really to be no rule or standard at all' . . .or if it is 'substantially incomprehensible.'" U.S. v. Clinical Leasing Service, Inc., 925 F.2d 120 (5th Cir. 1991). There is, however, a caveat to this general rule. Civil statutes or regulations that contain quasi-criminal penalties may be subject to the more stringent review afforded criminal statutes.

The Supreme Court applied the more stringent standard in reviewing an ordinance that required stores to obtain a license to sell "any items, effect, paraphernalia, accessory or thing which is designed or marketed for use with illegal cannabis or drugs . . . ." Hoffman Estates v. Flipside, 455 U.S. 489 (1982). Customers that purchased such goods were forced to sign their names and addresses to a register that would be available to police. The Court concluded that, while the statute nominally imposed civil penalties, its prohibitory and stigmatizing effect warranted quasi-criminal treatment.

In the present case, the Code only provides for civil monetary damages in the event of a violation. And while the potential fines are substantial, no prohibitory effect or quasi-criminal penalties are associated with a violation of the Code. Thus, Ford must show that §5.02C(c) is vague, "not in the sense that it requires a person to conform to an imprecise, but comprehensible normative standard, but rather in the sense that no standard of conduct is specified at all." Coates v. Cincinnati, 402 U.S. 611 (1971).

The Motor Vehicle Code provides that for purposes of § 5.02 "dealer" means "franchised dealer." A franchised dealer is [defined in the Code as] "any person . . . who is engaged in the business of buying, selling, or exchanging new motor vehicles and servicing or repairing motor vehicles . . ." A new motor vehicle means "a motor vehicle which has not been the subject of a 'retail sale' without regard to the mileage of the vehicle." A retail sale means "the sale of a motor vehicle except a sale in which the purchaser acquires a vehicle for the purpose of resale." Ford argues that, based on these definitions, it did not technically engage in a retail sale because it sold the automobile to the dealer who then sold it to the customer. Because the purchaser, the dealer, purchased the vehicle for the purpose of resale, the transaction is excepted from the definition of a retail sale. Or, in any event, [Ford claims it] could not know if such an arrangement was prohibited by § 5.02C(c).

Ford essentially argues that § 5.02C(c) is vague because Ford was unsure whether its operation of the Showroom constituted acting the capacity of a dealer. Ford's argument misapprehends the basic purpose behind prohibiting vague statutes. Vague statutes violate due process, because laws must "give the person of ordinary intelligence a reasonable opportunity to know what is prohibited, so that he may act accordingly." Grayned v. City of Rockford, 408 U.S. 104 (1972). Ford knew, that as a manufacturer, it was prohibited from selling automobiles and it had fair notice that its conduct may violate § 5.02C(c). In drafting § 5.02C(c), the legislature probably intended, permissibly so, to capture whatever creative conduct could be imagined by manufacturers to circumvent the statute's intended prohibition. A statute is not unconstitutionally vague merely because a company or an individual can raise uncertainty about its application to the facts of their case. A statute is unconstitutionally vague only where no standard of conduct is outlined at all; when no core of prohibited activity is defined.

The level of precision a statute must contain depends, in part, upon the nature of the enactment. Broader proscriptions are permitted in economic regulations because businesses, which face economic demands to plan behavior carefully, can be expected to consult relevant legislation in advance of action. Indeed, the regulated enterprise may have the ability to clarify the meaning of the regulation by its own inquiry, or by resort to an administrative process. By making an inquiry in this case, Ford could have obtained a preenforcement ruling on whether the Showroom complied with Texas law. In fact, negotiations between the State and General Motors allowed GM to become involved in running a Web site in compliance with Texas law. Even absent an administrative procedure, § 5.02C(c) is not unconstitutionally vague. Section 5.02C(c) provides a comprehensible standard of the proscribed conduct — acting in the capacity of a dealer. The phrase "in the capacity of a dealer" is naturally read to include those activities performed by a licensed dealer. The Code defines exactly what activities are performed by a dealer – buying, selling, or exchanging motor vehicles. Thus, it is clear under § 5.02C(c) what conduct is proscribed. Accordingly, Ford's argument that § 5.02C(c) is unconstitutionally vague fails. AFFIRMED.

Statutory Law and Common Law. . .a Contrast

Statutory law and common law differ in several significant respects. The most obvious of these are the *processes* by which each comes into being and the form of each after it becomes operative.

Processes and Form

Legislative acts become law only after passing through certain formal steps in both houses of the state legislatures (or of Congress) and, normally, by subsequent approval of the governor (or the president). The usual steps are (1) introduction of a bill in the house or senate by one or more members of that body; (2) referral of the bill to the appropriate legislative committee, where hearings are held; (3) approval of the bill by that committee and perhaps others; (4) approval of the bill by the house and senate after full debate; and (5) signing of the bill by the executive (or legislative vote overriding an executive veto). At each of these stages the opponents of the bill are given considerable opportunity to raise objections, with the result that the bill may be voted down or may pass only after being substantially amended. *Common-law rules,* by contrast, are creatures of the judicial branch of government; they are adopted by the courts for settling controversies involving points of law on which the legislature has not spoken.

In addition to these obvious contrasts between the two types of law, others are equally significant. We note these briefly.

Social and Political Forces

The social and political forces within a state have a greater and more evident impact on statutory law than on common law. Judges are somewhat more insulated from such pressures than are legislatures. Additionally, the steps required in the enactment of statutes enable representatives of vocal special interest groups (who are frequently at odds with one another) to attract considerable publicity to their causes. And, of course, the raw political power that each is able to exert on the legislators plays a significant, although not always controlling, part in the final disposition of a bill.

In addition to the political and financial pressures that have always been wielded by lobbyists, the past 20 years have seen an enormous increase in the activities of political action committees (PACs). Whereas lobbyists' activities are intended to sway the votes of lawmakers, PACs direct their efforts to raising funds for the election of candidates who will support their particular causes. Recent scandals involving Jack Abramoff, Tom DeLay, and many others indicate to many that campaign and reform is seriously needed. As governments grow more powerful, more and more is at stake, meaning that huge amounts of money enter the processes. Money creates opportunity for abuse, yet the First Amendment means that there are Constitutional limitations on the reform that can be undertaken. Over the years the Supreme Court has frequently addressed the difficult issues that arise in the collision between values in this area. In McConnell v. Federal Election Commission, 540 U.S. 93 (2003), for example, the Court upheld sweeping limitations on campaign donations, but in other decisions the Court has ruled in favor of the right to make donations as an expression of free speech.

Legislative Options

Although judges are required to settle controversies that come before them, legislatures generally have no duty to enact legislation. Thus legislatures have the option of refraining from the passage of laws when there is little public sentiment for them or when competing groups are so powerful that inaction is, politically, the better part of valor.

Legislative Scope

Subject only to the relatively few constitutional limitations placed on it, the legislative power to act is very broad. Thus legislatures are not only free to enact statutes when case law is nonexistent, but they also can pass statutes that expressly overrule common-law principles. Examples of the latter are those statutes involving the legality of married women's contracts. Under English and early American common law, it was firmly established that married women lacked the capacity...the legal ability...to contract, and thus any agreements they entered into while married had no effect. Today, all states have enacted statutes that give married women the same rights to contract as those enjoyed by other citizens.

As for jurisdictional scope, legislatures have the power to pass broad statutes encompassing all aspects of a given subject, whereas the courts can "make law" only in deciding the cases that come before them. Every state, for example, has comprehensive corporation acts, in which virtually all aspects of corporate activities, from incorporation procedures to dissolution procedures, are specified in detail. Similarly, every state has an all-encompassing criminal code, within which the criminal offenses in the state are defined.

Statutory Interpretation

We have seen that legislative bodies make law whenever they enact statutes. By doing so, they formally state what kinds of conduct they are requiring or prohibiting in specified situations and what results they expect from the passage of these laws on the rights and duties of affected parties.

But the true scope and meaning of a particular statute is never known with precision until it is formally construed by the courts in settling actual disputes arising under it. This search for legislative intent, which usually necessitates a *statutory interpretation*, is thus another major source of our law. **Interpretation** is the process by which a court determines the precise legal meaning of a statute as it applies to a particular controversy.

Interpretation: a Necessary Evil?

Whenever a dispute arises in which either of the parties is basing his or her case on the wording of a particular statute, one might think that the court's job would be mechanical in nature. That is, once the facts were established, a careful reading of the statute would make it clear what result the legislature intended in such a situation. Although this is often true, there are many instances in which it is not.

To bring the nature of the problem into sharper focus, consider the following situation. X flies a stolen airplane from one state to another and is convicted under a U.S. statute that makes the interstate movement of stolen motor vehicles a federal crime. In this statute, a motor vehicle is defined as "an automobile, automobile truck, automobile wagon, motorcycle, or any other self-propelled vehicle not designed for running on rails." Is an airplane a "motor vehicle" under this law? The problem is that the words of the statute are broad enough to embrace aircraft if they are given a literal interpretation; yet it is at least arguable that Congress did not really intend such a result. The U.S. Supreme Court answered no to the question in McBoyle v. U.S., 283 U.S. 25 (1931), holding that the term vehicle is "commonly understood as something that moves or runs on land, not something which flies in the air"... although it admitted that "etymologically the term might be considered broad enough to cover a conveyance propelled in the air."

Plain Meaning Rule

The primary source of legislative intent is, of course, the language that makes up the statute itself. In the relatively rare case when a court feels that the wording of an act is so clear as to dictate but one result and that the result is not "patently absurd," the consideration of other factors is unnecessary. If, for example, a state statute provides that "every applicant for examination and registration as a pharmacist shall be a citizen of the United States," a state pharmacy board would have to refuse to process the application of an alien even though he or she may have *applied for* U.S. citizenship as of the date of the pharmaceutical examination (State v. Dame, 249 P.2d 156 (Wyo. 1952). In cases of this sort (and occasionally in others in which the language is somewhat less precise), the courts say that the statute possesses a **plain meaning** and that interpretation is thus unnecessary.

Aids to Interpretation

Many statutes, however, do not easily lend them themselves to the plain meaning rule. There are several reasons why courts frequently must interpret statutes before applying them, including the following: (1) Legislatures sometimes draft statutes with an element of "deliberate imprecision," intentionally giving courts a degree of latitude in applying the statute. They may do this because they legitimately recognize the difficulty of defining certain concepts in the abstract or because they want to avoid making a specific decision on a controversial political issue. (2) Even if a legislature tries to define all the key elements of a statute with great precision, the effort sometimes fails because some concepts are extremely difficult to define without reference to a specific set of facts. (3) The complex process of amendment and deletion as a bill goes through the legislature sometimes leads to a product that is less clear than the originally introduced bill. (4) The choice of particular language may have been the result of compromise among factions in the legislature, which sometimes leads to a lack of clarity. (5) At its best, language is imperfect, and few words are susceptible to but one meaning.

Therefore, in many cases a court must interpret a statute before using it as a basis for deciding a case. Even when a court asserts that a statute has a plain meaning, it often bolsters its conclusion by resorting to various interpretive aids. The aids or devices used by a court to ascertain the legislative intent may be grouped into several categories.

First, a court sometimes refers to a dictionary or other standard reference source. It is presumed that legislative bodies use words in their common, ordinary sense, and a standard dictionary may be the best starting point to determine common English usage. If anyone claims that the legislature used a word in an unusual or technical sense, that party has the burden of proving it. General rules of grammar and punctuation are also usually followed unless there is a clear indication that the legislature intended otherwise.

Second, the court will examine the law's **textual context,** which involves reading the statute as a whole rather than concentrating solely on the language in question. Sometimes other language in that section of the statute, or perhaps similar language in another section of the same statute, may provide a clue as to what the legislature intended. This is simply an application of one of the cardinal principles of communication... do not take words out of their context.

Third, a court might examine the statute's **legislative history.** Comprehensive legislative histories are available for federal statutes, and less comprehensive histories are available for the statutory enactments of several states. A statute's legislative history may consist of several components. All bills are considered by one or more committees of the legislature, which hold hearings on the bill at which testimony and other evidence is presented by proponents and opponents of particular positions. Sometimes a verbatim *transcript* of all the oral testimony, written statements, and other evidence is published. After the committee has held hearings and deliberated, it will vote on whether to send the bill to the full body (house or senate) with a favorable or unfavorable recommendation. The committee often prepares a written report to accompany its recommendation. Dissenting committee members may also write a minority report. These *committee reports* are also part of the legislative history. Finally, the transcript of the *floor debates* when the entire body considers the bill forms part of the legislative history, as well. In the case of federal legislation, these transcripts are published in the *Congressional Record.* The legislative history, especially the hearing transcripts and committee reports, can provide a wealth of information about the background and purpose of the law, the reasons for using particular language, how and why amendments and deletions were made, and other relevant matters. Presidents have begun issuing "presidential signing statements" giving their interpretation of the meaning of the statutes they sign into law. Whether these should be given any legitimate weight by the courts is currently unsettled.

Fourth, the statute's **circumstantial context** may be taken into account by a court seeking to discern the meaning of legislative language. This term simply describes the conditions or social problem that led the legislature to act. If, for example, the law was passed to fight organized crime, the courts will construe ambiguous language to help achieve that purpose. Evidence of the circumstantial context may be derived from several sources, including the legislative history.

Fifth, a court will consider *precedent* when interpreting a statute. Thus, prior judicial interpretations of the same statute, or of similar language in another statute, may be taken into account.

Regardless of the reason why a particular statute needs to be interpreted, and regardless of the particular interpretive aids employed, the court's sole task is to do the best it can to determine the legislative intent. The court's job is not to improve on what the legislature said or to make the statute mean what the court thinks it *should* mean. Even though determining what the legislature meant can be an elusive goal, the courts must do the best they can.

A final comment on statutory interpretation relates to the concept of *implied repeal.* Sometimes a party to a case will contend that some provision of a statute was implicitly repealed by later action of the same legislative body. The courts operate from a strong presumption against implied repeal; a court will find that a legislature intended to amend, repeal, or make an exception to an earlier statute only if the evidence of such intent is very clear.

SOLDANO V. O'DANIELS
California Court of Appeal, 190 Cal. Rptr. 310 (1983)

Beginning with the Homestead Act of 1862, Congress enacted a series of land-grant statutes aimed at settling the American frontier. One of these was the Pittman Act, which sought to promote development and population growth in the State of Nevada by encouraging private citizens to prospect for water in Nevada. The Act authorized the Secretary of the Interior to designate certain "nonmineral" lands in Nevada, on which settlers could obtain permits to drill for water. Any settler who could demonstrate successful irrigation of at least 20 acres of crops was eligible for a land grant, or "patent" [not the same as a patent on an invention], of up to 640 acres. Importantly, each patent issued under the Act was required to contain "a reservation to the United States of all the coal and other valuable minerals in the lands . . ., together with the right to prospect for, mine and remove the same." By virtue of this reservation, the United States was free to dispose of the "coal and other valuable mineral deposits in such lands" in accordance with "the provisions of the coal and mineral land laws in force at the time of such disposal."

The Pittman Act failed to significantly advance agricultural development in Nevada, but when Congress repealed it in 1964, it expressly reserved the rights of existing pat-

entees. In 1940 petitioner BedRoc's predecessors in interest obtained a patent for 560 acres of land some 65 miles north of Las Vegas. As required by the Act, the patent reserved the "coal and other valuable minerals" to the United States. Common sand and gravel were plentiful and visible on the surface of the land, but there was no commercial market for them due to Nevada's sparse population and the land's remote location. However, by 1993 the expansion of Las Vegas had created a commercial market for the sand and gravel on the land. Shortly after BedRoc's predecessor in interest (Williams) began extracting the sand and gravel, however, the Bureau of Land Management (BLM) served him with trespass notices pursuant to a federal rule providing that any unauthorized removal of "mineral materials" from public lands is "an act of trespass." The BLM ruled that by removing sand and gravel Williams had trespassed against the Government's reserved interest in the "valuable minerals" on the property. The Interior Board of Land Appeals affirmed that decision. Meanwhile, petitioner BedRoc Limited, LLC (BedRoc), acquired the property from Williams in 1995.

BedRoc filed an action in the United States District Court seeking to quiet title to the sand and gravel on the property. The District Court granted summary judgment to the Government, holding that the contested sand and gravel are "valuable minerals" reserved to the United States by the Pittman Act. The Ninth Circuit affirmed and the Supreme Court granted certiorari.

Rehnquist, Chief Justice:

The question here is whether sand and gravel are "valuable minerals" reserved to the United States in land grants issued under the Pittman Underground Water Act of 1919. We hold they are not.

In Watt v. Western Nuclear, Inc., 462 U.S. 36 (1983), we construed the mineral reservation in the Stock-Raising Homestead Act of 1916 (SRHA)–"the most important land-grant statute enacted in the early 1900's." Unlike the Pittman Act, the SRHA was not limited to Nevada; it applied to any "public lands" the Secretary of the Interior designated as "stock-raising lands." A person could obtain a patent under the SRHA if he resided on stock-raising lands for three years, and "made permanent improvements upon the land . . . tending to increase the value of the [land] for stock-raising purposes." The SRHA's mineral reservation was identical to the Pittman Act's in every respect, save one: Whereas the SRHA reserved to the United States "all the coal and other minerals," the Pittman Act reserved "all the coal and other valuable minerals."

The question before us in Western Nuclear was "whether gravel found on lands patented under the [SRHA] is a mineral reserved to the United States." A closely divided Court held that it is. After determining that "neither the dictionary nor the legal understanding of the term 'minerals' that prevailed in 1916 sheds much light on the question before us," we turned to the purpose and history of the SRHA. We observed that the SRHA, like other land-grant Acts containing mineral reservations, sought to "facilitate development of both surface and subsurface resources." We

therefore reasoned that "the determination of whether a particular substance is included in the surface estate or the mineral estate should be made in light of the use of the surface estate that Congress contemplated." Accordingly, we interpreted the SRHA's mineral reservation to include "substances that are mineral in character (i.e., that are inorganic), that can be removed from the soil, that can be used for commercial purposes, and that there is no reason to suppose were intended to be included in the surface estate." Because we thought it unlikely that Congress would have made the exploitation of gravel deposits dependent on farmers and ranchers "whose interests were known to lie elsewhere," and because gravel met our other criteria, we concluded that it is indeed a "mineral" reserved to the United States.

The Government argues that our rationale in Western Nuclear compels the outcome in this case, notwithstanding the Pittman Act's seemingly narrower reservation of "valuable" minerals. Whatever the correctness of Western Nuclear's broad construction of the term "minerals," we are not free to so expansively interpret the Pittman Act's reservation. In *Western Nuclear*, we had no choice but to speculate about congressional intent with respect to the scope of the amorphous term "minerals." Here, by contrast, Congress has textually narrowed the scope of the term by using the modifier "valuable."

The preeminent canon of statutory interpretation requires us to "presume that [the] legislature says in a statute what it means and means in a statute what it says there." Connecticut Nat. Bank v. Germain, 503 U.S. 249 (1992). Thus, our inquiry begins with the statutory text, and ends there as well if the text is unambiguous. We think the term "valuable" makes clear that Congress did not intend to include sand and gravel in the Pittman Act's mineral reservation. In interpreting statutory mineral reservations like the one at issue here, we have emphasized that Congress 'was dealing with a practical subject in a practical way' and that it intended the terms of the reservation to be understood in 'their ordinary and popular sense.'" Amoco Production Co. v. Southern Ute Tribe, 526 U.S. 865(1999), quoting Burke v. Southern Pacific R. Co., 234 U.S. 669(1914). Importantly, the proper inquiry focuses on the ordinary meaning of the reservation at the time Congress enacted it. Amoco. Because the Pittman Act applied only to Nevada, the ultimate question is whether the sand and gravel found in Nevada were commonly regarded as "valuable minerals" in 1919.

Common sense tells us, and the Government does not contest, that the answer to that question is an emphatic "No." Sand and gravel were, and are, abundant throughout Nevada; they have no intrinsic value; and they were commercially worthless in 1919 due to Nevada's sparse population and lack of development. Thus, even if Nevada's sand and gravel were regarded as minerals, no one would have mistaken them for valuable minerals. The Government argues only that sand and gravel were commercially marketable in other parts of the United States during World War I and that there is now a market for sand and gravel in some parts of Nevada. As we have explained, this evidence is simply irrelevant to the proper inquiry into the meaning of the statutory mineral reservation.

The statutory context of the Pittman Act's mineral reservation further confirms its ordinary meaning. The sentence directly following the reservation provides that the reserved "valuable mineral deposits . . . shall be subject to disposal by the United States in accordance with the provisions of the . . . mineral land laws in force at the time of such disposal." Here, Congress was explicitly cross-referencing the General Mining Act of 1872. Then, as now, the General Mining Act provided that "all valuable mineral deposits in lands belonging to the United States. . . shall be free and open to exploration and purchase . . . under regulations prescribed by law." We can therefore infer that the reserved "valuable minerals" in Pittman Act lands were the same class of minerals that could be located and disposed of under the General Mining Act.

It is beyond dispute that when the Pittman Act became law in 1919, common sand and gravel could not constitute a locatable "valuable mineral deposit" under the General Mining Act.

Notwithstanding the contemporaneous plain meaning of the Pittman Act's mineral reservation, the Government argues that the Act's legislative history counsels us to give "valuable minerals" precisely the same meaning we ascribed to "minerals" in Western Nuclear. Because we have held that the text of the statutory reservation clearly excludes sand and gravel, we have no occasion to resort to legislative history. Having declined to extend Western Nuclear's rationale to a statute where the plain meaning will not support it, we will not allow it in through the back door by presuming that "the legisature was ignorant of the meaning of the language it employed." Montclair v. Ramsdell, 107 U.S. 147(1883). While Justice Stevens [in his dissent] does not contest the plain meaning of the ittman Act's mineral reservation, he nonetheless takes us to task for "refusing to examine" the legislative history proffered by the Government and thereby engaging in a "deliberately uninformed" and "unconstraned" method of statutory interpretation. Of course, accepting this approach would require a radical abandonment of our longstanding precedents that permit resort to legislative history only when necessary to interpret ambiguous statutory text. Chief Justice Marshall in 1805 stated the principle that definitively resolves this case nearly 200 year later: "Where a law is plain and unambiguous, whether it be expressed in general or limited terms, the legislature should be intended to mean what they have plainly expressed, and consequently no room is left for construction." U.S. v. Fisher, 6 U.S. 358. We thus cannot accept ustice Stevens' invitation to presume that Congress expressed itself in a single House Committee Report rather than in the unambiguous statutory text approved by both Houses and signed by the resident. We fail to see, moreover, how a court exercises unconstrained discretion when it carries out its "sole function" with respect to an unambiguous statute, namely to "enforce it according to its terms." Caminetti v. U.S., 242 U.S. 470 (1917).

Reversed.

Dissent by Justice Stevens:

The Stock-Raising Homestead Act of 1916 (SRHA or Act) authorized the settlement of homesteads on "lands the surface of which" was "chiefly valuable for grazing and raising forage crops" and "not susceptible of irrigation from any known source of water supply." Congress included in the statute "a reservation to the United States of all the coal and other minerals in the lands . . . entered and patented" under the Act. Two decades ago, in a closely divided decision in *Western Nuclear*, we held that gravel found on lands patented under the Act is a mineral reserved to the United States.

The Pittman Act, enacted just three years after the SRHA, was designed to encourage the reclamation of lands in the State of Nevada that were "not known to be susceptible of successful irrigation at a reasonable cost from any known source of water supply." Today the Court decides that the reservation of minerals in § 8 of the Pittman Act does not include gravel. I think it highly unlikely that Congress would reserve its ownership of sand and gravel in the millions of acres of land in the West that were covered by the SRHA and not do so for the land in Nevada covered by the Pittman Act. Indeed, the House Committee Report describing the scope of the mineral reservation in § 8 of the Pittman Act plainly states: "Section 8 of the bill contains the same reservations of minerals, with the facility for

prospecting for and developing and mining such minerals as was provided in the [SRHA]." A clearer expression of Congress' intent would be hard to find.

The plurality opinion rests entirely on the textual difference between the SRHA's reservation of "all the coal and other minerals" and the Pittman Act's reservation of "all the coal and other valuable minerals." But that holding ignores the fact that in Western Nuclear the Court's interpretation of the term "mineral" in the SRHA included the requirement that the material be valuable. Moreover, the term "mineral" or "minerals" appears eight times in § 8 of the Pittman Act, and only twice is it modified by the adjective "valuable," strongly suggesting that the terms "valuable minerals" and "minerals" were intended to be synonymous. Thus, the text of § 8 and its legislative history, as well as both the reasoning and the result in *Western Nuclear,* all support the conclusion that Congress intended the mineral reservation in these two statutes to be the same. The single word "valuable," in short, cannot support the weight the Chief Justice places on it.

In refusing to examine the legislative history that provides a clear answer to the question whether Congress intended the scope of the mineral reservations in these two statutes to be identical, the plurality abandons one of the most valuable tools of judicial decision-making. As Justice Aharon Barak of the Israel Supreme Court perceptively has explained, the "minimalist" judge "who holds that the purpose of the statute may be learned only from its language" retains greater discretion than the judge who "will seek guidance from every reliable source." Judicial Discretion 62 (Y. Kaufmann transl. 1989). A method of statutory interpretation that is deliberately uninformed, and hence unconstrained, increases the risk that the judge's own policy preferences will affect the decisional process. Accordingly, I respectfully dissent.

Uniform State Statutes

Before leaving the subject of statutory law, several widely adopted state statutes deserve brief mention. Our federal system of governments permits great variation in law from state to state. This variation has advantages; the states have been termed the "laboratories of democracy" because a few can try a particular approach to a legal or regulatory problem. If the approach doesn't work well, it can be abandoned. If it does work well, other states will likely copy the success.

However, the variation obviously causes problems, especially for companies that do business in many states. Therefore, many in the legal and business community press for increased state-to-state uniformity of approach to important legal problems. The National Conference of Commissioners on Uniform State Laws (NCCUSL) is an organization that drafts uniform or model laws with the hope that many states will adopt them, thereby decreasing the variability of regulation.

The most successful and probably most important of these uniform acts is the Uniform Commercial Code, adopted in whole (with little variation) in all states except Louisiana (which has adopted parts). The UCC features Article 2, which governs contracts for the sale of goods in this country. That article receives substantial attention later in this book. Article 2A governs leases of goods. Article 3 provides the law of commercial paper, governing the rights and obligations of the makers of notes, drawers of checks, and endorsers of negotiable instruments. Articles 4 through 8 deal with more specialized situations, such as the duties that exist between depositary and collecting banks and the transfers of bills of lading and other documents of title. Article 9 covers all kinds of secured transactions, which arise when creditors seek to retain a security interest in goods physically in the possession of a debtor.

The law of business organizations is largely contained in the Revised Uniform Partnership Act, the Revised Uniform Limited Partnership Act, and the Revised Model Business Corporation Act. However, there is less uniformity in these areas than under the UCC, especially because many states pattern their corporation law after Delaware's Corporation Code rather than the RMBCA.

The NCCUSL has promulgated uniform laws and model codes that address trusts, probate, securities, electronic transactions, arbitration, and many other areas. Some of the uniform acts have been adopted by all states; some by just a few. The organization's Web site contains texts of all the acts and lists of the states that have adopted them. http://www.law.upenn.edu/bll/ulc/ulc_frame.htm

Federal Statutes

Federal statutes naturally play an important role governing business as well. Federal tax laws, securities laws, environmental laws, antitrust laws, bankruptcy laws, employment laws, labor laws, and others play influential roles in the competitive environment of businesses. Technological developments related to the Internet have prompted passage of several federal laws, including the Federal Electronic Signatures Act (aimed at facilitating electronic commerce by enforcing agreements made electronically), the Electronic Communications Privacy Act (intended to encourage people to use the Internet by protecting their privacy), the Digital Millennium Copyright Act (aimed, in part, at preventing the Internet from being used to destroy the values of copyrights), and the Anticybersquatting Act (intended to prevent cyber damage to trademarks). These statutes are featured in later chapters of this book.

Businesses are keenly aware of the critical role that federal statutes play in their business environment. Therefore, they make campaign contributions, hire lobbyists, and otherwise attempt to influence this environment. For examples, because of intense lobbying by major accounting firms and Silicon Valley firms that were targets of large numbers of federal securities lawsuits, Congress passed the Private Securities Litigation Reform Act of 1995. The PSLRA made it much more difficult for investors who thought they had been defrauded to recover against the alleged wrongdoing companies, officers, directors, and auditors. Of course, that relief was shortlived, because the Enron scandal prompted Congress to pass the Sarbanes-Oxley Act of 2002. SOX increased penalties for securities fraud, required more and prompter disclosures of financial information by companies, banned auditors from providing many forms of nonaudit services to their audit clients, and made many other significant changes. Already companies are attempting to influence Congress and the SEC to water down SOX's more stringent provisions.

CHAPTER 5

CONSTITUTIONAL LAW

- Organization of The Federal Government
- Authority of Federal and State Governments
- Protecting Basic Rights

THE MOST IMPORTANT SINGLE document in the United States and, arguably, the world, is the U.S. Constitution. This document is the foundation of our democratic system of government and the basis of our many freedoms. Although drafted in a simpler time, the Constitution has evolved over the past 200 years to keep pace with changes in American society. Partly through amendment, but more importantly through flexible Supreme Court interpretations, the Constitution has remained as vital and timely as it was when originally written.

Few areas of the law can be studied without reference to the Constitution. For example, Chapter 2 discussed the structure of the federal court system, which is established in the Constitution, as well as the exercise of personal jurisdiction by state and federal courts, which is constrained by the Constitution's due process provisions. The Constitution governs the ability of the government to intervene in business activities; for example, Chapter 6 points out that the government's power to conduct inspections and searches of business firms is limited by the Fourth Amendment of the Constitution. The Constitution contains several protections for defendants charged with crimes, as discussed in Chapter 7. The Constitutional right to freedom of speech affects the principles of defamation law discussed in Chapter 8 and the rules of trademark and copyright law discussed in Chapter 9. Although not everyone realizes this fact, the Constitution has at least as much relevance to the operation of business enterprises as it does to the personal affairs of individuals. Our discussion of constitutional law in this chapter is fairly broad, but it will emphasize the role the Constitution plays in both empowering the government to regulate business and placing limits on the exercise of these regulatory powers.

Before turning to a discussion of the U.S. Constitution, it bears mentioning that every state in this country also has a constitution. These documents include many provisions similar to those found in the federal Constitution, such as those separating state governments into three branches and protecting fundamental liberties. Most state constitutions are much more detailed than the U.S. Constitution. A state constitutional provision is the supreme law within that state, unless it conflicts with the U.S. Constitution or some other federal law.

The U.S. Constitution contains three general categories of provision:

- It prescribes the basic organization of the federal government into legislative, executive, and judicial branches.
- It delineates the authority of the federal government, in contrast with the states, by granting specific powers to the three branches of the federal government.
- It protects certain basic rights of individuals and businesses by placing limitations on federal and state governmental power.

Organization of the Federal Government

One major function of the Constitution is to establish the basic organization of the federal government into legislative, executive, and judicial branches. The essential function of the legislative branch, Congress, is to make laws, as well as to collect revenue and appropriate funds for carrying out those laws.

The main function of the executive branch is to enforce these laws; however, the executive branch also plays the primary role in conducting foreign relations and directing our military forces. The basic task of the judicial branch is to decide how particular laws should be applied to actual disputed cases.

Separation of Powers

As a general proposition, each branch of the federal government is supposed to exercise only those types of powers expressly given to it by the Constitution. Stated somewhat differently, one branch generally is not supposed to encroach on the powers of another branch. The doctrine of **separation of powers** is, however, a flexible one that is subject to various exceptions based on practicality.

Checks and Balances

To begin with, the Constitution expressly provides for a number of "checks and balances" to insure against any single branch of government developing an excessive degree of power. Examples include the requirement that the president sign legislation passed by Congress (the executive veto power) and the ability of Congress to override a presidential veto by a two–thirds vote in both houses.

Judicial Review

Another type of permissible interplay among the three branches of government is *judicial review*. Although this could be characterized as another form of "check and balance," the concept of judicial review is not expressed in the Constitution. During the early days of the Republic, the question of which branch had ultimate authority to determine constitutional is sues was unsettled. In Marbury v. Madison, 5 U.S. 137 (1803), the U.S. Supreme Court assumed this power for the judicial branch of government. Because of the practicality and logic of placing this task in the hands of the federal courts and because of the stature of Chief Justice John Marshall, the author of the opinion in *Marbury*, the doctrine of judicial review is generally accepted without question today. Under the principle of judicial review, the federal courts have the final say in deciding whether the Constitution has been violated by a congressional law or executive action. It is no exaggeration to say that "the Constitution means what the Supreme Court says it means."

Although not involving a federal separation of powers question, it also should be noted that the doctrine of judicial review later expanded to include the power of the federal courts to determine whether actions of *state* courts, legislatures, and executive officials violate the U.S. Constitution. In a similar vein, it also has come to be an accepted principle in our law that state courts have the power to determine whether state legislative or executive actions are valid under that particular state's constitution. Moreover, state courts have power to review state legislative and executive actions for conformity to the U.S. Constitution, subject only to possible ultimate review by the U.S. Supreme Court.

Reasonable Overlap of Functions

It is sometimes necessary for one branch of government to engage in an activity that closely resembles the type of function that the Constitution has assigned to another branch of government. For example, in providing for the implementation of many of its regulatory laws, Congress has found it necessary to give judicial–like powers to government agencies that are not part of the federal judiciary.

These agencies may be part of the executive branch, such as the Social Security Administration (part of the Department of Health and Human Services), or they may be relatively independent of the executive branch, such as the Securities and Exchange Commission. In any event, such an agency frequently performs an adjudicative type of function, that is, deciding whether an individual meets the requirements for Social Security disability benefits or whether a corporation has made misleading statements in connection with the issuance of stocks or bonds. Similarly, Congress sometimes has to exercise investigative powers that traditionally have been considered executive in nature. Also, the federal courts engage in a form of "lawmaking" when they interpret provisions of the Constitution and federal statutes.

There are many other examples of situations in which one branch, to effectively carry out its primary role, may find it necessary to perform tasks similar to those of another branch. Performing such a "borrowed" function is permissible under the separation of powers doctrine so long as (1) it is reasonably necessary and incidental to the primary functions of that branch of government, and (2) the power of one branch is not substantially enlarged at the expense of another branch.

The Supreme Court is often called upon to settle clashes over the roles of the three branches of government. It has held that although separation of powers does not mean that the three branches ought have no partial control over the acts of others, they still should not intrude upon each other's central prerogatives. Thus, the Court has held, for example, that Congress may not revise judicial determinations by retroactive legislation reopening judgments, may not enact laws without bicameral passage and presentment of the bill to the President, may not remove executive officers except by impeachment, and may not deprive a court of jurisdiction based on the outcome of a case or undo a Presidential pardon.

Delegation of Powers

The final category of exception to the separation of powers doctrine is found in the principle that Congress may expressly delegate legislative powers to the other two branches. Congress often delegates rulemaking powers, for example, to federal administrative agencies that are outside the legislative branch. For example, in the Securities Exchange Act of 1934, Congress prohibited fraudulent and deceptive practices in connection with the sale of securities and delegated to the Securities and Exchange Commission the power to make rules specifying in more detail the types of conduct that would violate this prohibition. Congress also has delegated certain rule–making powers to the federal courts, namely, the limited power to prescribe rules of procedure and evidence. Express delegations of legislative power are normally valid so long as Congress (1) indicates the basic policy objectives it is seeking to achieve and (2) provides some degree of guidance as to how the power is to be exercised. (At the state government level, the same general principles typically are applied to the separation of powers doctrine and its exceptions.)

Authority of Federal and State Governments

A second major function of the U.S. Constitution is to delineate the authority of the federal government, in contrast with that of the states. In our dual system of sovereignty, there are 51 primary governments— the federal government and the 50 state governments. When the original 13 colonies ratified the Constitution, they agreed to cede certain important sovereign powers to the federal government; as other states were added they similarly agreed. Under our system of federalism, the federal government has those powers that are specifically given to it in the Constitution—the so–called **delegated powers** (or *enumerated powers)*. Those powers not granted to the federal government continue to reside with the states—the so –called **reserved powers.**

Our discussion of federal authority will focus on the power of Congress and primarily on the power of 3 that federal legislative body to regulate business activities. Article I, section 8 of the Constitution spells out the powers of the U.S. Congress, the most important of which include the power:

> To lay and collect Taxes, Dues, Imposts and Excises, to pay the Debts and provide for the common Defense and general Welfare of the United States; . . .
>
> To borrow Money on the Credit of the United States;
>
> To regulate Commerce with foreign Nations, and among the several States, and with the Indian Tribes;
>
> To establish an uniform rule of Naturalization, and uniform Laws on the subject of Bankruptcies throughout the United States;
>
> To coin Money, regulate the Value thereof, and of foreign Coin, and fix the Standard of Weights and Measures, . . .
>
> To establish Post Offices and post Roads;
>
> To promote the Progress of Science and useful Arts, by securing for limited Times to Authors and Inventors the exclusive right to their respective Writings and Discoveries;
>
> To constitute Tribunals inferior to the Supreme Court;. . .
>
> To declare War, grant Letters of Marque and Reprisal, and make Rules concerning Captures on Land and Water;
>
> To raise and support Armies, but no Appropriation of Money to that Use shall be for a longer Term than two Years;
>
> To provide and maintain a Navy;

To make Rules for the Government and Regulation of the land and naval forces;

To provide for calling forth the Militia to execute the Laws of the Union, suppress Insurrections and repel Invasions;

To provide for organizing, arming, and disciplining the Militia, and . . .

To make all Laws which shall be necessary and proper for carrying into Execution the foregoing Powers, and all other Powers vested by this Constitution in the Government of the United States, or in any Department or Officer thereof.

State Police Power

In most circumstances, the lines of demarcation between the authority of the federal and state governments are quite clear. Most of the legislative powers delegated to the federal government under article I, section 8—such as the power to operate post offices and to maintain the various armed forces—involve such obviously federal powers that no state reasonably could claim to possess any regulatory authority over them.

By the same token, the powers reserved to the states are also relatively clear and well established.

Virtually all the powers of a particular state derive from the **state police power**—a term referring to the inherent governmental power to regulate the health, safety, morality, and general welfare of its people. Statutes relating to the operation of motor vehicles, the manufacture and sale of alcoholic beverages, and the regulation of crime obviously fall within the police power, because they are directly involved with matters of health, safety, and morals. Typical state laws based on the "general welfare" component of the police power are those that regulate such matters as marriage and divorce, the inheritance of property, and landlord–tenant relationships.

The power to enact zoning laws specifying restrictions on the use of real estate also falls within the state police power, but state legislatures normally delegate this power to their cities; thus, most zoning regulations are actually found in city ordinances or the regulations of city zoning commissions. In fact, state legislatures may delegate any part of the police power to local political subdivisions such as cities or counties. They also sometimes delegate very limited police powers to specialized political subdivisions of the state, such as port authorities, flood control districts, school districts, water supply and conservation districts, hospital districts, and so forth. Later, when we discuss limits that the U.S. Constitution places on state governmental powers, it should be understood that these limits are the same whether the state power is exercised directly by the state or is delegated to a local government entity.

Federal Power—the Commerce Clause

In examining the authority of the federal government, we are primarily concerned here with the power to regulate business. Although in many areas there is a clear delineation between the powers of the federal government on one hand and the state governments on the other, one area presents difficult problems—regulation of commercial activities. Despite the fact that the federal power to regulate commerce is very broad, the states also have a substantial amount of regulatory power over commerce. The dual nature of the power to regulate commerce has created many instances of state–federal friction. Seldom does a year go by in which the U.S. Supreme Court does not decide an important case bearing on the respective spheres of authority to regulate commerce.

Federal Regulation of Interstate Commerce

Article I, section 8 of the U.S. Constitution grants to Congress the power "to regulate Commerce with foreign Nations, and among the several States." Many provisions of the Constitution were aimed at preventing various kinds of provincialism and thus at making the United States truly "united." By giving Congress the primary authority to regulate interstate commerce, the **Commerce Clause** was intended to make the United States a common market, with the many economic advantages of trade that is unhindered by state boundaries. Before the adoption of the Constitution, economic "Balkanization" had plagued trade relations among the Colonies under the Articles of Confederation, the Colonies having erected various barriers to free trade among themselves.

By giving Congress the power to regulate trade with foreign nations, the framers of the Constitution recognized that the nation could not join the international trading community unless it could speak with one voice in maintaining international trade relations.

Until the late 1930s, the Supreme Court interpreted the commerce clause very narrowly with respect to the power of Congress over interstate and foreign commerce. The Court took the view that Congress could regulate a commercial activity only to the extent that it actually occurred *in the course* of interstate or foreign commerce. To the extent that an activity took place within the borders of a particular state, Congress could not normally regulate it, no matter how great the activity's ultimate effect on interstate or foreign commerce might be. Thus, under this older interpretation, Congress had no constitutional power to regulate manufacturing or other productive activities within a state; for example, it could not regulate wages, hours, or working conditions of manufacturing employees.

Beginning in the late 1930s, the Supreme Court took an almost 180-degree turn in its interpretation of the Commerce Clause. Since that time, the power of Congress in this area has been interpreted very broadly. It is still true that any commercial activity that actually crosses state or national boundaries is within the scope of the commerce clause. In addition, the regulatory power of Congress today extends to any activity that has "any appreciable effect" on interstate or foreign commerce, even though the activity took place solely within a particular state.

In the increasingly interdependent national and international economy in which we find ourselves, most significant commercial activities have an "appreciable" (that is, meaningful or significant) effect on either interstate or foreign commerce. Today, most of our federal regulatory laws have been passed by Congress under this expanded

Commerce Clause power. Examples include the federal laws regulating securities markets, workplace safety, wages and hours, and competition (antitrust laws). Indeed, Congress often uses the Commerce Clause as a constitutional foundation for enacting legislation even when its primary goal is not an economic one. Examples of this include laws aimed at protecting the environment and prohibiting employment discrimination.

"Commerce" includes almost anything remotely related to an economic activity, including manufacturing, advertising, contracting, sales and sales financing, transportation, capital–raising, and so on. Because the federal regulatory power encompasses intrastate commercial activity that affects *interstate* or foreign commerce, few local businesses can escape the reach of the federal government.

For example, in McLain v. Real Estate Board of New Orleans, 444 U.S. 232 (1980), a question arose whether a number of New Orleans real estate firms and trade associations had violated the federal antitrust laws by entering into several price–fixing contracts. The lower courts dismissed the action, ruling that the defendants' actions, which involved sales of land in New Orleans, were "purely local" in nature and thus not subject to federal law. The Supreme Court reversed, finding that the indirect effects of the defendants' activities were sufficiently related to interstate commerce to justify application of federal law. This finding of sufficient effect—a "not insubstantial effect"—was based primarily on the fact that (1) significant amounts of money lent by local banks to finance real estate purchases came from out–of–state banks, and (2) most of the mortgages taken by the local banks were "physically traded" by them to financial institutions in other states.

Although there are very few businesses today whose activities are so completely local (intrastate) in nature as to be outside the power of Congress to regulate, it is important to note that Congress has not exercised all its regulatory power. The fact that an activity affects, or even directly involves, interstate or foreign commerce does not necessarily mean that Congress has chosen to regulate the activity. The power granted by the commerce clause, as interpreted by the Supreme Court, can be viewed as a reservoir of law–making power. In any given situation, Congress may or may not have drawn from that reservoir to enact legislation. The same is true of other powers granted by the Constitution.

In addition, when Congress decides to regulate a particular commercial activity, it sometimes chooses to exercise less than its full constitutional authority. For example, Congress might choose to include within a particular law only certain activities that actually cross state or national boundaries, even though it could regulate activities not crossing these boundaries because of their effect on interstate or foreign commerce. For instance, Congress has expressly exempted "intrastate offerings" of stocks and bonds from many of the document–filing requirements of the Securities Act of 1933, leaving the regulation of intrastate sales of new securities to the discretion of the particular state. Congress may choose to exempt certain activities in other ways, as well. Thus, the employment discrimination prohibitions found in Title VII of the 1964 Civil Rights Act apply only to employers whose businesses affect interstate commerce *and* who have 15 or more employees, thus exempting employers with a smaller number of workers.

Similarly, other laws might expressly exclude from coverage businesses with assets below a certain value or transactions below a stated amount.

The following case is a recent application of the law in this area.

GONZALES V. RAICH
U.S. Supreme Court, 125 S. Ct. 2195 (2005)

California authorizes the use of marijuana for medicinal purposes. The question presented in this case is whether the power vested in Congress by [the Commerce Clause] includes the power to prohibit the local cultivation and use of marijuana in compliance with California law. Respondents Raich and Monson are California residents who suffer from a variety of serious medical conditions and have sought to avail themselves of medical marijuana pursuant to the terms of California's Compassionate Use Act. They are being treated by licensed, board–certified family practitioners, who have concluded, after prescribing a host of conventional medicines to treat respondents' conditions and to alleviate their associated symptoms, that marijuana is the only drug available that provides effective treatment. Both women have been using marijuana as a medication for several years pursuant to their doctors' recommendation, and both rely heavily on cannabis to function on a daily basis. Indeed, Raich's physician believes that forgoing cannabis treatments would certainly cause her excruciating pain and could very well prove fatal. Respondent Monson cultivates her own marijuana, but Raich is unable to cultivate her own, and thus relies on two caregivers to provide her with locally grown marijuana at no charge. After federal agents raided Monson's house and destroyed her plants, respondents sued the U.S. Attorney General Gonzales and the head of the DEA seeking injunctive and declaratory relief prohibiting the enforcement of the federal Controlled Substances Act (CSA), to the extent it prevents them from possessing, obtaining, or manufacturing cannabis for their personal medical use. The district court ruled against respondents and the Ninth Circuit reversed. Attorney General Gonzales appealed.

Stevens, Justice:

The case is made difficult by respondents' strong arguments that they will suffer irreparable harm because, despite a congressional finding to the contrary, marijuana does have valid therapeutic purposes. The question before us, however, is not whether it is wise to enforce the statute in these circumstances; rather, it is whether Congress' power to regulate interstate markets for medicinal substances encompasses the portions of those markets that are supplied with drugs produced and consumed locally.

[The Court first reviewed the lengthy history of Congressional efforts to regulate the selling of illicit drugs, including marijuana.] To effectuate these goals, Congress devised a closed regulatory system making it unlawful to manufacture, distribute, dispense, or possess any controlled substance except in a manner authorized by the CSA. Respondents in this case do not dispute that passage of the CSA was well within Congress' commerce power. Rather, they argue that the CSA's categorical prohibition of the manufacture and possession of marijuana as applied to the intrastate manufacture and possession of marijuana for medical purposes pursuant to California law exceeds Congress' authority under the Commerce Clause.

In assessing the validity of congressional regulation, none of our Commerce Clause can be viewed in isolation. Our understanding of the reach of the Commerce Clause, as well as Congress' assertion of authority thereunder, has evolved over time. The Commerce Clause emerged as the Framers' response to the central problem giving rise to the Constitution itself: the absence of any federal commerce power under the Articles of Confederation. For the first century of our history, the primary use of the Clause was to preclude the kind of discriminatory state legislation that had once been permissible. Then, in response to rapid industrial development and an increasingly interdependent national economy, Congress ushered in a new era of federal regulation under the commerce power, beginning with the enactment of the Interstate Commerce Act in 1887, and the Sherman Antitrust Act in 1890.

Cases decided during that "new era," which now spans more than a century, have identified three general categories of regulation in which Congress is authorized to engage under its commerce power. First, Congress can regulate the channels of interstate commerce. Second, Congress has authority to regulate and protect the instrumentalities of interstate commerce, and persons or things in interstate commerce. Third, Congress has the power to regulate activities that substantially affect interstate commerce. Only the third category is implicated in the case at hand.

Our case law firmly establishes Congress' power to regulate purely local activities that are part of an economic "class of activities" that have a substantial effect on interstate commerce. See, *e.g.*, Wickard v. Filburn, 317 U.S. 111(1942). As we stated in *Wickard*, "even if appellee's activity be local and though it may not be regarded as commerce, it may still, whatever its nature, be reached by Congress if it exerts a substantial economic effect on interstate commerce." We have never required Congress to legislate with scientific exactitude. When Congress decides that the

"total incidence'" of a practice poses a threat to a national market, it may regulate the entire class. In this vein, we have reiterated that when "'a general regulatory statute bears a substantial relation to commerce, the de *minimis* character of individual instances arising under that statute is of no consequence.'"

In *Wickard*, we upheld the application of regulations promulgated under the Agricultural Adjustment Act of 1938, which were designed to control the volume of wheat moving in interstate and foreign commerce in order to avoid surpluses and consequent abnormally low prices. The regulations established an allotment of 11.1 acres for Filburn's 1941 wheat crop, but he sowed 23 acres, intending to use the excess by consuming it on his own farm. Filburn argued that even though we had sustained Congress' power to regulate the production of goods for commerce, that power did not authorize "federal regulation [of] production not intended in any part for commerce but wholly for consumption on the farm." [The Court rejected this argument, noting]: "The effect of the statute before us is to restrict the amount which may be produced for market and the extent as well to which one may forestall resort to the market by producing to meet his own needs. That appellee's own contribution to the demand for wheat may be trivial by itself is not enough to remove him from the scope of federal regulation where, as here, his contribution, taken together with that of many others similarly situated, is far from trivial."

Wickard thus establishes that Congress can regulate purely intrastate activity that is not itself "commercial," in that it is not produced for sale, if it concludes that failure to regulate that class of activity would undercut the regulation of the interstate market in that commodity. The similarities between this case and *Wickard* are striking. Like the farmer in *Wickard*, respondents are cultivating, for home consumption, a fungible commodity for which there is an established, albeit illegal, interstate market. Just as the Agricultural Adjustment Act was designed "to control the volume [of wheat] moving in interstate and foreign commerce in order to avoid surpluses . . ." and consequently control the market price, a primary purpose of the CSA is to control the supply and demand of controlled substances in both lawful and unlawful drug markets. In *Wickard*, we had no difficulty concluding that Congress had a rational basis for believing that, when viewed in the aggregate, leaving home–consumed wheat outside the regulatory scheme would have a substantial influence on price and market conditions. Here too, Congress had a rational basis for concluding that leaving home–consumed marijuana outside federal control would similarly affect price and market conditions. Even respondents acknowledge the existence of an illicit market in marijuana; indeed, Raich has personally participated in that market, and Monson expresses a willingness to do so in the future.

More concretely, one concern prompting inclusion of wheat grown for home consumption in the 1938 Act was that rising market prices could draw such wheat into the interstate market, resulting in lower market prices. The parallel concern making it appropriate to include marijuana grown for home consumption in the CSA is the likelihood that the high demand in the interstate market will draw such marijuana into that market. While the diversion of homegrown wheat tended to frustrate the federal interest in stabilizing prices by regulating the volume of commercial transactions in the interstate market, the diversion of homegrown marijuana tends to frustrate the federal interest in eliminating commercial transactions in the interstate market in their entirety. In both cases, the regulation is squarely within Congress' commerce power because production of the commodity meant for home consumption, be it wheat or marijuana, has a substantial effect on supply and demand in the national market for that commodity.

In assessing the scope of Congress' authority under the Commerce Clause, we stress that the task before us is a modest one. We need not determine whether respondents' activities, taken in the aggregate, substantially affect interstate commerce in fact, but only whether a "rational basis" exists for so concluding. Given the enforcement difficulties that attend distinguishing between marijuana cultivated locally and marijuana grown elsewhere, and concerns about diversion into illicit channels, we have no difficulty concluding that Congress had a rational basis for believing that failure to regulate the intrastate manufacture and possession of marijuana would leave a gaping hole in the CSA. Thus, as in *Wickard*, when it enacted comprehensive legislation to regulate the interstate market in a fungible commodity, Congress was acting well within its authority to "make all Laws which shall be necessary and proper" to "regulate Commerce . . . among the several States." That the regulation ensnares some purely intrastate activity is of no moment. As we have done many times before, we refuse to excise individual components of that larger scheme.

To support their contrary submission, respondents rely heavily on two of our more recent Commerce Clause cases. In their myopic focus, they overlook the larger context of modern–era Commerce Clause jurisprudence preserved by those cases. Moreover, even in the narrow prism of respondents' creation, they read those cases far too broadly.

Those two cases, of course, are U.S. v. Lopez, 514 U.S. 549 (1995) and U.S. v. Morrison, 514 U.S. 549 (2000). As an initial matter, the statutory challenges at issue in those cases were markedly different from the challenge respondents pursue in the case at hand. Here, respondents ask us to excise individual applications of a concededly valid statutory scheme. In contrast, in both *Lopez* and *Morrison*, the parties asserted that a particular statute or provision fell outside Congress' commerce power in its entirety. This distinction is pivotal for we have often reiterated that "[w]here the class of activities is regulated and that class is within the reach of federal power, the courts have no power 'to excise, as trivial, individual instances' of the class." Perez v. U.S., 400 U.S. 146 (1971).

At issue in *Lopez* was the validity of the Gun—Free School Zones Act of 1990, which was a brief, single—subject statute making it a crime for an individual to possess a gun in a school zone. The Act did not regulate any economic activity and did not contain any requirement that the possession of a gun have any connection to past interstate activity or a predictable impact on future commercial activity. Distinguishing our earlier cases holding that comprehensive regulatory statutes may be validly applied to local conduct that does not, when viewed in isolation, have a significant impact on interstate commerce, we held the statute invalid. We explained [that the statute] "is a criminal statute that by its terms has nothing to do with 'commerce' or any sort of economic enterprise, however broadly one might define those terms."

The statutory scheme that the Government is defending in this litigation is at the opposite end of the regulatory spectrum. As explained above, the CSA, enacted in 1970 as part of the Comprehensive Drug Abuse Prevention and Control Act, was a lengthy and detailed statute creating a comprehensive framework for regulating the production, distribution, and possession of "controlled substances. The regulatory scheme is designed to foster the beneficial use of those medications, to prevent their misuse, and to prohibit entirely the possession or use of substances listed in Schedule I of the CSA. Our opinion in *Lopez* casts no doubt on the validity of such a program.

Nor does this Court's holding in *Morrison*. The Violence Against Women Act of 1994, created a federal civil remedy for the victims of gender—motivated crimes of violence. Despite congressional findings that such crimes had an adverse impact on interstate commerce, we held the statute unconstitutional because, like the statute in *Lopez*, it did not regulate economic activity. We concluded that "the noneconomic, criminal nature of the conduct at issue was central to our decision" in *Lopez*, and that our prior cases had identified a clear pattern of analysis: "'Where economic activity substantially affects interstate commerce, legislation regulating that activity will be sustained.'"

Unlike those at issue in *Lopez* and *Morrison*, the activities regulated by the CSA are quintessentially economic. The CSA is a statute that regulates the production, distribution, and consumption of commodities for which there is an established, and lucrative, interstate market. Prohibiting the intrastate possession or manufacture of an article of commerce is a rational (and commonly utilized) means of regulating commerce in that product. Because the CSA is a statute that directly regulates economic, commercial activity, our opinion in *Morrison* casts no doubt on its constitutionality.

We acknowledge that evidence proffered by respondents in this case regarding the effective medical uses for marijuana, if found credible after trial, would cast serious doubt on the accuracy of the findings that require marijuana to be listed [as a prohibited substance]. But the possibility that the drug may be reclassified in the future has no relevance to the question whether Congress now has the power to regulate its production and distribution. Respondents' submission, if accepted, would place all homegrown medical substances beyond the reach of Congress' regulatory jurisdiction.

The Ninth Circuit's decision is vacated and remanded.

State Regulation of Commerce

Despite the dominant federal role, the states retain substantial authority to regulate commercial activities. A state's police power permits it to protect the health, safety, and general welfare of its citizens. This power includes the authority to regulate commercial activities within the state, even if those activities have a substantial effect on interstate or foreign commerce and even if they originated outside the state. To give effect to the primary power of the federal government in these areas, however, the courts have developed several principles that limit the power of the states These include preemption, discrimination against interstate commerce, and unduly burdening interstate commerce. Although different, all these concepts are closely related, and more than one of them may sometimes be at issue in the same case. (These principles also apply to state laws that affect foreign commerce—that is, international trade. Unless indicated otherwise in this discussion, international commerce will be included within the term *interstate commerce*.)

Federal Preemption. The concept of **federal preemption** is a general principle of constitutional law that applies to any state–federal conflict. The doctrine of preemption is relevant regardless of whether a particular federal power comes from the Commerce Clause or from some other provision of the Constitution. However, we discuss the preemption doctrine in the context of the federal Commerce Clause power because it is in this context that most of the issues arise.

If a particular governmental power is exclusively federal, we say that there is federal preemption of this field of government activity. Federal preemption may be either express or implied, or it may result from a direct conflict between state and federal law. As we mentioned in the previous section, some federal powers in the Constitution are obviously of an exclusively federal nature, such as conducting foreign affairs, maintaining an army, and establishing a monetary system. The state governments have no power to act in such matters. In the case of other powers granted to the federal government, however, it may not be so obvious that the power is exclusively federal. When the Constitution gives the federal government a certain type of authority and a state attempts to exercise a similar or related power, the courts may have to determine whether there actually is federal preemption.

Express Preemption. When a preemption question arises, we begin with one basic proposition: the **Supremacy Clause** found in article VI, section 1 of the Constitution makes federal law the "supreme law of the land." The Supremacy Clause applies regardless of the specific source of the state or local law and regardless of the specific source of the federal law. The Supremacy Clause means, among other things, that if the Constitution gives a power to the federal government, the federal government also has the authority to prohibit the states from exercising a similar power. For example, the Constitution specifically gives Congress the power to enact patent laws that protect the creative work of inventors. When using this power to pass patent legislation, Congress can engage in *express preemption* by specifying in the legislation that the states have no power to adopt similar laws. If Congress exercises its authority expressly to preempt the states, no state can adopt a law that provides to inventors any legal protection for their inventions that is basically the same as the protection provided by the federal patent laws.

Although Congress has this power of express preemption, it usually does not use it. In fact, when passing a law, Congress often provides expressly that states retain the power to adopt similar or related laws so long as those laws do not conflict with or hinder the objectives of the federal law.

Implied Preemption. When Congress has chosen to regulate some activity but has said nothing about whether the states do or do not have power to pass related laws, a question of *implied preemption* may arise. For example, Congress has extensively regulated labor –management relations, as discussed in Chapter 29. Federal law establishes a framework within which groups of employees may fairly and democratically decide whether they want to form a union and, if so, which labor organization they wish to represent them in negotiating with the employer about wages, hours, and working conditions. The conduct of both employers and unions is closely regulated during this process. Once a group of employees decides to be represented by a particular union and the union is officially certified, the employer is under a legal obligation to bargain with the union in good faith. The objective of the regulated negotiation process is to achieve a collective bargaining agreement governing the rights and responsibilities of the employer and employees during the term of the contract. Suppose that, in State X, there has been a history of labor strife in a particular industry that is important to the state's economy. Strikes by employees and lockouts by employers have sometimes resulted, causing economic harm to the state. In response, State X's legislature passes a statute authorizing the state governor to issue an executive order ending a strike or lockout in that industry after a stated time period if the governor finds that serious harm is being done to the state's economy. Assume that, when the governor later exercises this power, a union or employer challenges the validity of the state law under which the governor acted. Because the federal labormanagement relations laws say nothing about state authority to engage in similar a challenge to the state law is likely to be based of implied preemption. (The employer or union claim that the law places an undue burden on commercethis concept will be discussed shortly.)

When a claim of implied preemption is made, the one challenging the state law is asking the court to draw an inference about the intent of Congress—in other words, that party tries to prove that Congress implicitly intended to preempt the regulation of this general area. The challenger usually must prove two conditions before a court will conclude that implied preemption exists. First, it must be shown that the federal regulation is relatively *comprehensive*. In other words, the court must be convinced that Congress attempted to impose a fairly complete regulatory structure on this type of activity. Otherwise, it makes no sense to infer a preemptive intent on the part of Congress. This first condition is clearly met in the case of federal labor –management relations laws.

Second, it also must be shown that there is a very strong need for a uniform national regulatory policy in this area, so that individual state laws of this type are likely to interfere with the objectives of the federal regulatory effort. Most unions represent employees in several states, and many of the employers that negotiate with unions also operate in more than one state. Moreover, a group of employers may negotiate with one large union, and sometimes one large employer must negotiate with several unions. In other words, relationships between companies and unions generally transcend state boundaries, but the objective of a particular negotiation is a single contract. If these often—sensitive negotiations had to be conducted within a framework of several different sets of state regulations, it would be extremely difficult for the parties ever to achieve a collective bargaining agreement, and the collective bargaining agreement is the cornerstone of federal regulation in this area. Thus, the second condition for implied preemption also exists. Because both conditions are met, the Supreme Court has concluded that the states are preempted from adopting laws dealing with the company—union relationship.

It should be noted that, even in a situation in which there is implied federal preemption, states still may protect important state interests by passing laws that are only peripherally related to the federally regulated area and that are not likely to interfere with the federal regulatory objectives. For example, despite implied preemption, an employee may be punished under state criminal or tort law for assault and battery or property destruction even though the wrongful conduct occurred during the course of a union—sponsored strike.

Direct Conflict. A much narrower form of preemption occurs when a specific state law is in *direct conflict* with a specific provision of federal law. In the labor—management relations setting, recall that there is no express federal preemption. For the sake of illustration, now let us also assume that either (or both) of the requirements for implied preemption were not met. What this would mean is that there is no federal preemption of this general field of regulatory activity, and the states could enact laws regulating company—union relations. However, if a particular state provision comes into direct conflict with a federal law, the state law is void to the extent of the conflict. Suppose that, even if there is no express or implied federal preemption, there is a specific federal statute that empowers the U.S. president to seek a federal court injunction ending a strike or lockout under certain carefully prescribed conditions. In such a case, the law in State X authorizing its governor to halt strikes or lockouts might very well be void because of a direct conflict with the federal law.

A state law is not void because of direct conflict just because the state provision deals with the same type of activity. Moreover, the mere fact that a state law is more stringent than a similar federal law does not make the state law void. For example, the fact that California law places stricter pollution control standards on automobiles does not mean that this state law is in conflict with federal auto emission control regulations. A state law is void because of direct conflict in only two situations. First, there is a direct conflict if it is impossible to comply with both the state and federal laws. An example of this would be a state law *requiring* wholesalers to grant quantity discounts to retailers in the state even in circumstances in which the discounts are not justified by any lower costs of selling in larger quantities. This state law would require conduct that violates the federal RobinsonPatman Act's prohibition of price discrimination.

Second, even if it is literally possible to comply with both laws, there nevertheless is a direct conflict if the state law substantially interferes with the purpose of the federal law. For example, suppose that when Congress passed the law giving the president authority to stop strikes or lockouts in certain carefully defined situations, it clearly indicated an intent to permit government interference in company–union confrontations only when national defense is threatened or when a national economic emergency exists. In such a case, the hypothetical law giving the governor of State X the power to stop strikes when economic injury to the state is threatened might be void for direct conflict because it interferes with objectives of the federal law.

It should be reemphasized that either type of direct conflict is really just a narrower form of implied preemption applying only to a specific state law and a specific federal law rather than to an entire field of regulated activity.

One final note on the concept of preemption is worth mentioning. In this country, there is a presumption *against* preemption. Thus, a court will normally find federal preemption only if Congress or a federal agency clearly expressed that intent or if the evidence of implied preemption or direct conflict is very strong. In the European Union (EU), however, the presumption is reversed. When the EU adopts a regulation of some kind, there is a presumption that this law was intended to preempt related laws of member nations.

The following case illustrates the concept of implied preemption in the case of a federal regulatory system aimed at encouraging the use of American ports in international trade.

XEROX CORP. V. HARRIS COUNTY
U.S. Supreme Court, 459 U.S. 145 (1982)

Pursuant to its powers under the commerce clause, Congress established a comprehensive customs system aimed at placing certain controls on the flow of goods into and out of the country, while at the same time encouraging international trade between the United States and other countries. For many years, federal customs law has provided for a system of "customs bonded warehouses" at various U.S. ports of entry. These warehouses are owned and run by private operators but are under the continuous control and supervision of the federal customs officials at that port. Ordinarily, imported goods are subject to a federal tax known as a "duty." However under certain conditions federal customs law permits goods to be imported duty–free if they are stored in a customs bonded warehouse. The owner of imported goods is permitted to store them in such a warehouse when they are intended for ultimate sale somewhere outside the United States—in other words, when the United States is just a stop over for goods that are destined for sale in some other country. Such goods can remain duty–free in the customs bonded warehouse for up to five years. If they are stored for more than five years or if the owner changes its plans and markets the goods within the United States, an import duty must be paid. Congress established this system for the purpose of encouraging the use of American ports as a stop over for goods in international trade when the owner finds it efficient to do so.

Increased use of American ports produces more economic activity in the vicinity of those ports.

Xerox Corporation manufactured parts for copying machines in Colorado and New York. These parts were then shipped to Mexico for assembly. After assembly, the copiers were imported into the United States and stored in a customs bonded warehouse in Houston, Texas, while awaiting shipment to various destinations in Latin America. The copiers were designed especially for sale in the Latin American market; the machines operated on an electric current of 50 cycles per second as is common in Central and South America, rather than the 60 cycles per second that is standard in the United States. In addition, all printing on the machines and instructions was in either Spanish or Portuguese; thus there was no question about Xerox's claim that the goods were not intended for sale in the United States. (Until 1974, Xerox had shipped its Mexican–assembled copiers to the Free Trade Zone of Panama, where they were stored tax–free. In 1974, rising anti-American sentiment in Panama caused Xerox to look for another storage facility. It decided on the Houston customs bonded warehouse because of the excellent port facilities at Houston and its proximity to Latin America.)

Beginning in 1977, Harris County (where Houston is located) assessed local property taxes on Xerox's copiers in the customs bonded warehouse. (The city and school district also levied these taxes.) The taxes were nondiscriminatory—they applied to all goods in described categories for the period of time they were physically located within the county,

regardless of where the goods originated or where they came from. The county did not place a tax directly on imports or exports as the goods entered or exited but instead based the tax on the physical location of the goods within the county for the duration of their stay. Thus, the local property tax was not automatically void under the constitutional prohibition against state or local taxes on imports or exports. Xerox filed suit in a state trial court in Houston, alleging that the tax measure was unconstitutional because it was impliedly preempted by the federal regulations setting up the system of customs bonded warehouses. The trial court ruled for Xerox, but the intermediate level state appellate court reversed and upheld the tax. The Texas Supreme Court refused to review the decision, and the U.S. Supreme Court agreed to hear Xerox's appeal of the federal constitutional question.

Burger, Chief Justice:

Government regulated, bonded warehouses have been a link in the chain of foreign commerce since "a very early period in our history." Fabbri v. Murphy, 95 U.S. 191, 197 (1877). A forerunner of the present statute was the Warehousing Act of 1846, ch. 84, 9 Stat. 53 (1846). A major objective of the warehousing system was to allow importers to defer payment of duty until the goods entered the domestic market or were exported. The legislative history explains that Congress sought to reinstate:

> "the sound though long neglected maxim of Adam Smith , 'that every tax ought to be levied at the time and in the manner most convenient for the contributor to pay it;' [by providing] that the tax shall only be paid when the imports are entered for consumption . . ." H.R. Rep. No. 411, 26th Cong., 1st Sess. 3 (1846).

The Act stimulated foreign commerce by allowing goods in transit in foreign commerce to remain in secure storage, duty free, until they resumed their journey in export. The geographic location of the country made it a convenient place for transshipment of goods within the Western Hemisphere and across both the Atlantic and the Pacific. A consequence of making the United States a center of world commerce was that:

"...our carrying trade would be vastly increased; that shipbuilding would be stimulated; that many foreign markets would be supplied, wholly or in part, by us with merchandise now furnished from the warehouses of Europe; that the industry of our seaports would be put in greater activity; [and] that the commercial transactions of the country would be facilitated..." App. to Cong. Globe, 29th Cong., 1st Sess. 792 (1846)(remarks of Sen. Dix).

To these ends, Congress was willing to waive all duty on goods that were reexported from the warehouse, and to defer, for a prescribed period, the duty on goods destined for American consumption. This was no small sacrifice at a time when customs duties made up the greater part of federal revenues, but its objective was to stimulate business for American industry and work for Americans.

In short, Congress created secure and duty free enclaves under federal control in order to encourage merchants here and abroad to make use of American ports. The question is whether it would be compatible with the comprehensive scheme Congress enacted to effect these goals if the states were free to tax such goods while they were lodged temporarily in government regulated bonded storage in this country.

In McGoldrick v. Gulf Oil Co., 309 U.S. 414 (1939), the City of New York sought to impose a sales tax on imported petroleum that was refined into fuel oil in New York and sold as ships' stores to vessels bound abroad. The crude oil was imported under bond, and refined in a customs bonded manufacturing warehouse and was free from all duties. We struck down the state tax, finding it preempted by the Congressional scheme.

The Court determined that the purpose of the exemption from the tax normally laid upon importation of crude petroleum was "to encourage importation of the crude oil for [refinement into ships' stores] and thus to enable American refiners to meet foreign competition and to recover trade which has been lost by the imposition of the tax." The Court went on to note that, in furtherance of this purpose,

"Congress provided for the segregation of the imported merchandise from the mass of goods within the state, prescribed the procedure to insure its use for the intended purpose, and by reference confirmed and adopted customs regulations prescribing that the merchandise, while in customs bonded warehouse, should be free from state taxation.'

The Court concluded that

"the purpose of the Congressional regulation of commerce would fail if the state were free to impose a tax which would lessen the competitive advantage conferred on the importer by Congress, and which might equal or exceed the remitted import duty."...

The analysis in *McGoldrick* applies with full force here. First, Congress sought, in the statutory scheme reviewed in *McGoldrick*, to benefit American industry by remitting duties otherwise due. The import tax on crude oil was remitted to benefit oil refiners employing labor at refineries within the United States, whose products would not be sold in domestic commerce. Here, the remission of duties benefited those shippers using American ports as transshipment centers. Second, the system of customs regulation is as pervasive for the stored goods in the present case as it was in *McGoldrick* for the refined petroleum. In both cases, the imported goods were segregated in warehouses under continual federal custody and supervision. Finally, the state tax was large enough in each case to offset substantially the very benefits Congress intended to confer by remitting the duty. In short, freedom from state taxation is as necessary to the Congressional scheme here as it was in *McGoldrick*.

Although there are factual distinctions between this case and McGoldrick, they are distinctions without a legal difference. We can discern no relevance to the issue of Congressional intent in the fact that the fuel oil in *McGoldrick* could be sold only as ships' stores whereas Xerox had the option to pay the duty and withdraw the copiers for domestic sale, or that in *McGoldrick* the City sought to impose a sales tax and here appellees assessed a property tax...

[The state appeals court decision is reversed; the tax is unconstitutional and thus void. Because of this holding, there is no need to address the additional argument of Xerox that the tax is, in practical effect, a constitutionally prohibited tax on imports.]

Discrimination Against Interstate Commerce. Even when there is no preemption of any kind, a state cannot pass a law that discriminates against interstate commerce (or international commerce). Such discrimination interferes with the primary authority of Congress over interstate and foreign commerce, and thus violates the Supremacy Clause. States may not, for example, shelter their own industries from competition emanating from other states or nations. (Although it may not be wise to do so, Congress does have the power to shelter American companies from foreign competition.)

Although states may act to preserve their own natural resources, they cannot do so by discriminating against out–of–state buyers. They also cannot require that business operations that could be conducted more efficiently elsewhere take place within the state. For example, a state could not require that shellfish caught off its shores be processed in–state before being shipped elsewhere for sale.

A state's intent to discriminate might be explicit or it might be inferred from surrounding circumstances. For example, in Philadelphia v. New Jersey, 437 U.S. 617 (1978), the state legislature of New Jersey explicitly prohibited garbage from being imported into the state. Operators of several landfills in New Jersey, as well as several cities from other states that had agreements with these landfill operators for waste disposal, challenged the law. The Supreme Court held that the law unconstitutionally discriminated against interstate commerce; even a desire on the part of New Jersey to conserve landfill space was not a strong enough state interest to justify an explicit discrimination against the interstate transportation of solid waste. In its opinion the Court also distinguished the so –called quarantine cases, in which state quarantine laws had been upheld. The Court said that these laws, which forbade the transportation of diseased livestock or plants, had been held to be constitutional because they were aimed primarily at the act of moving the livestock or plants from one place to another, whether the movement was totally within the state or into it from another state.

Sometimes the circumstances may lead a court to conclude that a state intended to discriminate against interstate commerce even though the intent was not made explicit. As with any question of intent in the law, the court attempts to draw the most logical inference from surrounding circumstances. An example is Hunt v. Washington State

Apple Advertising Commission, 432 U.S. 333 (1977), which involved a North Carolina law, unique in the 50 states, that required all apples sold in the state to have only the applicable grade under U.S. Department of Agriculture grading standards stamped on the crates; state grades were expressly prohibited. For many years all apples shipped from the state of Washington had been stamped with grades under that state's grading system. In all cases, Washington state grades were superior to the comparable federal ones. The state of Washington and its apple industry had spent decades developing the quality and national reputation of its apples. If they still wanted to sell apples in North Carolina, Washington apple growers would have to segregate apples intended for shipment there and package them differently, in addition to losing the competitive advantage of being able to use their well known grading standards. North Carolina asserted that the law was adopted to protect consumers in the state from deception and confusion caused by multiple grading systems. The evidence was very convincing, however, that North Carolina was really engaging in economic protectionism by placing Washington apples at a disadvantage in the North Carolina market. The factors indicating an intent to discriminate against interstate commerce included (1) the complete lack of evidence that any consumers in North Carolina had ever been confused or deceived by multiple apple grading standards, (2) the fact that customers do not normally buy apples in the crates on which grades are stamped, and (3) the fact that the local North Carolina apple industry would clearly benefit from the Washington apple industry's increased costs of selling in North Carolina and its inability to use its highly reputed grading system. The law was found unconstitutional.

When a court concludes that a state has intentionally discriminated against interstate commerce, the state action is almost always void. It would be a rare case indeed in which a state could prove a sufficiently important state interest to justify such discrimination, because the interest could almost always be promoted by less restrictive means that do not discriminate in this way.

Most questions about state power over commerce involve attempts by a state to regulate the activities of business firms. However, if the state government itself actually becomes a *participant* in the market, the state has much more latitude. In fact, the Supreme Court has held that the general rule prohibiting discrimination against interstate commerce does not apply when a state or local government is a seller or buyer. For example, when a state or a city makes contracts for the purchase of goods or services, it may grant preferences to in-state companies or individuals. The same exception applies when the state is a seller. For example, in Reeves, Inc. v. Stake, 447 U.S. 429 (1980), the state of South Dakota owned a large cement factory, and during times of short supply state law required that a preference be given to in-state buyers over those from outside the state. The Supreme Court upheld the state's discriminatory policy.

Unduly Burdening Interstate Commerce. Another restriction on the power of the states to regulate commercial activities is that they may not unduly burden the free flow of interstate or international commerce. The concept we just discussed, discrimination against interstate commerce, involves a question of intent, whereas the concept of unduly burdening involves a question of impact. The two concepts are closely related, often both being raised by a challenger in the same case. Some of the same information will often be relevant to both types of claims. Despite their close relationship, however, the two concepts provide separate grounds for invalidating a state regulatory measure.

If a state law challenged on this basis is shown to hinder the free flow of interstate commerce in some way, the court uses a balancing analysis to determine whether the law is constitutional. The analysis is very similar to the balancing of competing interests that takes place throughout constitutional law and, indeed, throughout the law generally. To determine whether there is an undue burdening of interstate commerce, the court balances the local interest being furthered by the state law against the degree of burden it places on interstate commerce. In general, the stronger the state interest, the greater will be the burden that can be tolerated under the Constitution. Purely economic interests of a state are certainly legitimate, but such interests typically do not weigh as heavily as a state's interest in protecting the safety and health of its citizens or protecting them against fraudulent or other wrongful practices. In addition, some economic interests are stronger than others; thus, a state law aimed at preventing the spread of a citrus fruit disease that could wipe out a major industry in the state could permissibly burden interstate commerce to a greater extent than one aimed at protecting an economic interest of less magnitude.

The *Hunt* case discussed in the previous section also illustrates the undue burdening concept. There, the local interest did not weigh very heavily in the balancing process because there was no evidence to indicate that consumers actually had been deceived or confused by multiple apple grading standards, and the regulation would not have solved such a problem if there had been one. On the other side, the evidence demonstrated that the North Carolina law would impose substantial economic inefficiency on the selling of Washington apples in North Carolina. The Washington apple industry had developed substantial economies of scale in packaging, storing, and shipping its apples, and compliance with the North Carolina law would destroy much of these scale economies. In the *Hunt* case, the Supreme Court ultimately struck down the statute because it unduly burdened interstate commerce. Even though there was ample evidence to infer intentional discrimination against interstate commerce, the Court said that it was not necessary to make a ruling on that separate contention.

Another example is Kassell v. Consolidated Freightways Corp., 450 U.S. 662 (1981), which involved an Iowa law that prohibited the use of 65–foot double–trailer trucks on its highways, while allowing 55–foot single trailers and 60–foot double trailers. States around Iowa all allowed 65–foot double trailers, but Iowa claimed that the law was a safety measure. However, statistics showed no relationship between truck length and accident rates. Instead, studies showed a strong positive correlation between mileage driven and truck accident rates. Thus, the evidence of a legitimate state interest was quite weak; in fact, the law actually worked against safety interests by requiring use of smaller trucks that would have to travel more total miles to deliver the same amount of cargo. However, interstate commerce was substantially burdened because trucks with the more efficient 65–foot double trailers either had to go around the state or unload onto smaller trucks when reaching the Iowa border. The law was found unconstitutional.

(After the *Kassell* case, Congress stepped in to provide a degree of national uniformity to the regulation of truck–trailer lengths on interstate highways and on other "primary" highways built or maintained with any federal funds. The congressional enactment, which applies to about 42,000 miles of interstate highways and 140,000 miles of other highways, requires states to permit double–trailor rigs with each trailer having a length up to 28 feet, an approximate total rig length of 65 feet. The law also requires states to permit such rigs to have a width up to 102 inches, with exceptions for particular highways specifically found to be too narrow for rigs of such width to operate safely.)

Finally, many of the cases involving the undue burdening concept have challenged various state and local taxes on property items used in interstate commerce. Examples include state road use taxes on trucks used in interstate transportation, and state or local property taxes on items such as railroad cars, airplanes, barges on inland waterways, and shipping containers. As we saw in the *Xerox* case, a local property tax was found unconstitutional because it was preempted by the federal law setting up a system of customs bonded warehouses. Usually, however, there is no federal regulatory scheme that preempts state or local taxes on the instrumentalities of interstate commerce. In most cases, state and local government entities do have the right to tax such items located or used within their jurisdiction. It usually is only fair that the owners should pay some type of tax to contribute to the cost of police and fire protection and other services they receive within the taxing jurisdiction.

Such a tax must be carefully designed, however, to avoid being invalidated by the courts. First, it is obvious that the tax must not discriminate against interstate commerce by being higher for items used in interstate commerce than for items used only within the state. Assuming that the tax is nondiscriminatory, the Supreme Court has held that such a tax must meet three additional requirements to avoid being invalid under the undue burdening theory. The tax (1) can only be applied to property or activities that have a substantial "nexus" (that is, connection) with the taxing jurisdiction, (2) must be reasonably related to the services provided by the taxing jurisdiction, and (3) must be "apportioned" so that the item is not subjected to multiple taxation in the various places in which it is used or located. This last condition, the requirement of apportionment, has been an issue in a great many cases. It basically requires a formula that bases the tax only on the degree of connection the item has with the particular taxing jurisdiction. For example, a state might apportion a property tax on railroad cars by taxing only a fraction of the value of the cars that corresponds to the average fraction of a tax year the cars are located in the state.

Regarding taxation, in Japan Line, Ltd. v. County of Los Angeles, 441 U.S. 434 (1979), the Supreme Court held that a local property tax could not be levied on an item owned by a *foreign* company or individual and used exclusively in foreign commerce. The items in question were modular shipping containers owned by a Japanese corporation. The nondiscriminatory property tax imposed by Los Angeles County was based on only the time the containers spent in that county and would have been valid if the containers were used in interstate rather than international commerce. For two reasons, however, the Supreme Court concluded that the tax unduly burdened international commerce and was thus unconstitutional. First, in the case of property owned by a foreign citizen, U.S. courts have no power to require the foreign jurisdiction to apportion its own taxation of the item; consequently, permitting a state or local property tax in this country would create a risk of subjecting the property to taxation on more than its total value. Second, such a tax might interfere with the ability of the United States to "speak with one voice" in matters of international trade.

The following case addresses the matter of discrimination against interstate commerce in a setting that is becoming increasingly prevalent in our Internet economy.

GRANHOLM V. HEALD
U.S. Supreme Court, 125 S.Ct. 1885 (2005)

Like many other States, Michigan and New York regulate the sale and importation of alcoholic beverages, including wine, through a three-tier distribution system. Separate licenses are required for producers, wholesalers, and retailers. The three-tier scheme is preserved by a complex set of overlapping state and federal regulations. For example, both state and federal laws limit vertical integration between tiers. States have been permitted to mandate a three-tier distribution scheme in the exercise of their authority under the 21st Amendment. However, the three-tier system is mandated by Michigan and New York only for sales from out-of-state wineries. In-state wineries, by contrast, can obtain a license for direct sales to consumers.

Separate plaintiffs, out of state wineries that wished to be able to ship their wine directly to customers in Michigan and New York, filed lawsuits challenging those states' laws. Both district courts ruled for plaintiffs. The Sixth Circuit Court of Appeals also ruled for the plaintiffs in the Michigan case, but the Second Circuit Court of Appeals ruled for defendants in the New York case. The losing parties appealed, and the Supreme Court consolidated the appeals.

Kennedy, Justice:

We consolidated these cases and granted certiorari on the following question: "'Does a State's regulatory scheme that permits in-state wineries directly to ship alcohol to consumers but restricts the ability of out-of-state wineries to do so violate the dormant Commerce Clause in light of Section 2 of the 21st Amendment?

Time and again this Court has held that, in all but the narrowest circumstances, state laws violate the Commerce Clause if they mandate "differential treatment of in-state and out-of-state economic interests that benefits the former and burdens the latter." Oregon Waste Systems, Inc. v. Dept. of Environmental Quality of Ore., 511 U.S. 93 (1994). This rule is essential to the foundations of the Union. The mere fact of nonresidence should not foreclose a producer in one State from access to markets in other States. States may not enact laws that burden out-of-state producers or shippers simply to give a competitive advantage to in-state businesses. This mandate "reflect[s] a central concern of the Framers that was an immediate reason for calling the Constitutional Convention: the conviction that in order to succeed, the new Union would have to avoid the tendencies toward economic Balkanization that had plagued relations among the Colonies and later among the States under the Articles of Confederation." Hughes v. Oklahoma, 441 U.S. 322(1979).

Laws of the type at issue in the instant cases deprive citizens of their right to have access to the markets of other States on equal terms. The perceived necessity for reciprocal sale privileges risks generating the trade rivalries and animosities, the alliances and exclusivity, that the Constitution and, in particular, the Commerce Clause were designed to avoid. State laws that protect local wineries have led to the enactment of statutes under which some States condition the right of out—of—state wineries to make direct wine sales to in—state consumers on a reciprocal right in the shipping State. California, for example, passed a reciprocity law in 1986, retreating from the State's previous regime that allowed unfettered direct shipments from out—of—state wineries. Prior to 1986, all but three States prohibited direct—shipments of wine. The obvious aim of the California statute was to open the interstate direct—shipping market for the State's many wineries. The current patchwork of laws——withsome States banning direct shipments altogether, others doing so only for out-of—state wines, and still others requiring reciprocity——is essentially the product of an ongoing, low—level trade war. Allowing States to discriminate against out—of—state wine "invite[s] a multiplication of preferential trade areas destructive of the very purpose of the Commerce Clause." Dean Milk Co. v. Madison,340 U.S. 349(1951).

The discriminatory character of the Michigan system is obvious. Michigan allows in—state wineries to ship directly to consumers, subject only to a licensing requirement. Out—of—state wineries, whether licensed or not, face a complete ban on direct shipment. The differential treatment requires all out—of—state wine, but not all in—state wine, to pass through an in—state wholesaler and retailer before reaching consumers. These two extra layers of overhead increase the cost of out—of—state wines to Michigan consumers. The cost differential, and in some cases the inability to secure a wholesaler for small shipments, can effectively bar small wineries from the Michigan market.

The New York regulatory scheme differs from Michigan's in that it does not ban direct shipments altogether. Out—of—state wineries are instead required to establish a distribution operation in New York in order to gain the privilege of direct shipment. This, though, is just an indirect way of subjecting out-of—state wineries, but not local ones, to the three—tier system. New York defends the scheme by arguing that an out—of— state winery has the same access to the State's consumers as in—state wineries: All wine must be sold through a licensee fully accountable to New York; it just so happens that in order to become a licensee, a winery must have a physical presence in the State. There is some confusion over the precise steps out—of—state wineries must take to gain access to the New York market, in part because no winery has run the State's regulatory gauntlet. New York's argument, in any event, is unconvincing.

The New York scheme grants in—state wineries access to the State's consumers on preferential terms. The suggestion of a limited exception for direct shipment from out-of—state wineries does nothing to eliminate the discriminatory nature of New York's regulations. In—state producers, with the applicable licenses, can ship directly to consumers from their wineries. Out—of—state wineries must open a branch office and warehouse in New York, additional steps that drive up the cost of their wine. For most wineries, the expense of establishing a bricks—and—mortar distribution operation in 1 State, let alone all 50, is prohibitive. It comes as no surprise that not a single out–of–state winery has availed itself of New York's direct–shipping privilege. We have "viewed with particular suspicion state statutes requiring business operations to be performed in the home State that could more efficiently be performed elsewhere." Pike v. Bruce Church, Inc., 397 U.S. 137(1970). New York's in–state presence requirement runs contrary to our admonition that States cannot require an out–of–state firm "to become a resident in order to compete on equal terms." Halliburton Oil Well Cementing Co. v.Reily, 373 U.S. 64(1963).

We have no difficulty concluding that New York, like Michigan, discriminates against interstate commerce through its direct–shipping laws. State laws that discriminate against interstate commerce face a virtually *per se* rule of invalidity." Philadelphia v. New Jersey, 437 U.S. 617(1978). The Michigan and New York laws by their own terms violate this proscription. The two States, however, contend their statutes are saved by Sec. 2 of the 21st Amendment, which provides: "The transportation or importation into any State, Territory, or possession of the United States for delivery or use therein of intoxicating liquors, in violation of the laws thereof, is hereby prohibited." The aim of the 21st Amendment was to allow States to maintain an effective and uniform system for controlling liquor by regulating its transportation, importation, and use. The Amendment did not give States the authority to pass nonuniform laws in order to discriminate against outofstate goods, a privilege they had not enjoyed at any earlier time. Our recent cases confirm that the 21st Amendment does not supersede other provisions of the Constitution and, in particular, does not displace the rule that States may not give a discriminatory preference to their own producers.

Our determination that the Michigan and New York direct–shipment laws are not authorized by the 21st Amendment does not end the inquiry. We still must consider whether either State regime "advances a legitimate local purpose that cannot be adequately served by reasonable nondiscriminatory alternatives." New Energy Co. of Ind., 486 U.S. 269(1988). The States offer two primary justifications for restricting direct shipments from out–of–state wineries: keeping alcohol out of the hands of minors and facilitating tax collection.

The States claim that allowing direct shipment from out–of–state wineries undermines their ability to police underage drinking. Minors, the States argue, have easy access to credit cards and the Internet and are likely to take advantage of direct wine shipments as a means of obtaining alcohol illegally.

The States provide little evidence that the purchase of wine over the Internet by minors is a problem. Indeed, there is some evidence to the contrary. A recent study by the staff of the FTC found that the 26 States currently allowing direct shipments report no problems with minors' increased access to wine. This is not surprising for several reasons. First, minors are less likely to consume wine, as opposed to beer, wine coolers, and hard liquor. Second, minors who decide to disobey the law have more direct means of doing so. Third, direct shipping is an imperfect avenue of obtaining alcohol for minors who, in the words of the past president of the National Conference of State Liquor Administrators, "'want instant gratification.' Without concrete evidence that direct shipping of wine is likely to increase alcohol consumption by minors, we are left with the States' unsupported assertions. Under our precedents, which require the "clearest showing" to justify discriminatory state regulation, C&A Carbone, Inc. v. Town of Clarkstown, 511 U.S. 383(1994) this is not enough.

Even were we to credit the States' largely unsupported claim that direct shipping of wine increases the risk of underage drinking, this would not justify regulations limiting only out-of-state direct shipments. As the wineries point out, minors are just as likely to order wine from in-state producers as from out-of-state ones. Michigan, for example, already allows its licensed retailers (over 7,000 of them) to deliver alcohol directly to consumers.

The States' tax-collection justification is also insufficient. Increased direct shipping, whether originating in state or out of state, brings with it the potential for tax evasion. With regard to Michigan, however, the tax-collection argument is a diversion. That is because Michigan, unlike many other States, does not rely on wholesalers to collect taxes on wines imported from out-of-state. Instead, Michigan collects taxes directly from out-of-state wineries on all wine shipped to in-state wholesalers. If licensing and self-reporting provide adequate safeguards for wine distributed through the three-tier system, there is no reason to believe they will not suffice for direct shipments.

New York and its supporting parties also advance a tax-collection justification for the State's direct-shipment laws. While their concerns are not wholly illusory, their regulatory objectives can be achieved without discriminating against interstate commerce. In particular, New York could protect itself against lost tax revenue by requiring a permit as a condition of direct shipping. This is the approach taken by New York for in-state wineries. The State offers no reason to believe the system would prove ineffective for out-of-state wineries. Licensees could be required to submit regular sales reports and to remit taxes. Indeed, various States use this approach for taxing direct interstate wine shipments and report no problems with tax collection.

Michigan and New York benefit, furthermore, from provisions of federal law that supply incentives for wineries to comply with state regulations. The Tax and Trade Bureau has authority to revoke a winery's federal license if it violates state law. Without a federal license, a winery cannot operate in any State. In addition the 21st Amendment Enforcement Act gives state attorneys general the power to sue wineries in federal court to enjoin violations of state law. These federal remedies, when combined with state licensing regimes, adequately protect States from lost tax revenue. The States have not shown that tax evasion from out-of-state wineries poses such a unique threat that it justifies their discriminatory regimes.

[Both laws are invalidated. The opinion of the Sixth Circuit is affirmed and that of the Second Circuit reversed.]

Other State Limitations

At this point, two other constitutional limitations on the discretion of states are appropriately mentioned— the full faith and credit clause, and the contract clause.

Article IV, section 1 of the Constitution provides in part that "full faith and credit shall be given in each State to the public acts, records, and judicial proceedings of every other State," The import of the **full faith and credit clause** is quite clear: The courts of one state must recognize court judgments and other public actions of its sister states. Thus a business firm that obtains a valid judgment against a debtor in one state may enforce that judgment in the courts of any other state in which that debtor's property may be located. The requirement is, however, subject to two important limitations. First, if the court that entered the judgment originally did not have jurisdiction, the courts of other states are not obligated to (and will not) recognize the judgment. Second, if the judgment violates the public policy of the state where enforcement is sought, the courts of that state will not enforce it. For example, if a court in State A awards damages for breach of a loan contract that included a rate of interest that was valid in State A and the creditor then tries to enforce the judgment against the debtor's property in State B, where that interest rate is higher than allowed by State B's law, the courts of State B may well refuse to enforce the judgment on public policy grounds.

Our Constitution's full faith and credit clause obviously has no applicability to the enforcement of American state or federal court judgments in other nations or to the enforcement in this country of court judgments from other nations. Similar principles are generally applied, however. Under customary international law, the doctrine of *comity* generally calls for the enforcement of another nation's court judgments subject to the two exceptions for lack of jurisdiction and public policy. This doctrine and its exceptions have also been embodied in a number of bilateral and multilateral treaties to which the United States is a party.

Article I, section 10 of the Constitution provides that "no State shall ...pass any ... Law impairing the Obligation of Contracts. . ." The **Contract Clause,** which applies only to the states and not to the federal government, is intended to prevent states from changing the terms of existing contracts by passage of subsequent legislation. When a state passes a statute that might affect contractual obligations, it normally includes a "grandfather clause" specifying that the new law applies only to transactions entered into after the effective date of the law. This not only ensures compliance with the Contract Clause, but also makes the law fairer. However, even if a state law does have an effect on preexisting contractual rights and obligations, it does not violate the contract clause if the law promotes an important state government interest and interferes with contracts only to an extent that is reasonably necessary to further the state interest.

Protecting Basic Rights

The Constitution contains numerous provisions aimed at protecting individuals and businesses by limiting the powers of the federal and state governments to regulate our affairs. Many of our basic rights are guaranteed in the Bill of Rights—the first 10 amendments to the Constitution. Other protective provisions are found in the body of the original Constitution itself and in subsequent amendments.

Before we look at several of the most important rights–protecting provisions of the Constitution, two preliminary observations are necessary. First, by its express terms, the Bill of Rights applies only to the *federal* government and not to state or local governments. Nothing in the Constitution specifically prohibits the states from infringing freedom of speech, for example. However, the U.S. Supreme Court has used the Fourteenth Amendment's due process clause as a vehicle for applying almost everything in the Bill of Rights to state and local governments. The Fourteenth Amendment, which was passed in 1868 shortly after the Civil War, includes several provisions that expressly limit the powers of the states. As we will see later, one of these provisions—the due process clause—directly guarantees certain important rights. In addition, under the **doctrine of incorporation,** the Supreme Court has concluded that the concept of due process includes many other basic rights. Thus, the Fourteenth Amendment's due process clause implicitly incorporates almost all the protections in the Bill of Rights and applies them to state and local governments. Among the many guarantees applied to the states in this way are freedom of speech, freedom of the press, freedom of religion, right to an attorney, privilege against self–incrimination in criminal cases, and freedom from unreasonable searches and seizures. (The only two important guarantees in the Bill of Rights that the Supreme Court has held inapplicable to the states are (1) the right to jury trial in civil cases and (2) the requirement that a person be indicted by a grand jury before being tried for a criminal offense. The states are free to devise their own rules regarding these two matters; in fact, state constitutional and statutory provisions guarantee these rights in most circumstances.) Although the doctrine of incorporation has always been very controversial among constitutional scholars, it is now so firmly embedded in our law as to be beyond question.

Second, it must be emphasized that the protective provisions of the Constitution are limitations on government; thus, these provisions apply only to governmental actions and not to actions by individuals or business firms. Thus, the Constitution's free speech and assembly provisions do not prevent a private employer from restricting the speech of its employees or a private university from banning a political rally on its campus. However, Constitutional protections apply when a governmental body either compels the private action or substantially participates in it or when governmental power is used to enforce the private action against others. For example, there is a violation of the equal protection clause of the Fourteenth Amendment when a private attorney in a criminal or civil case intentionally excludes potential jurors on the basis of race. The reason for the Constitution's applicability is that jury selection is such an integral part of a governmental process that the government is essentially a co–participant with the private attorney. Another example is found in the rule that a court—an arm of the government—will not enforce a private deed restriction that excludes those of a particular race from purchasing property in a subdivision on the basis of their race; to do so would violate the equal protection clause. However, the mere fact that a particular business or industry is subject to substantial government regulation does not turn the actions of the regulated business firms into governmental actions. For example, public utilities such as telephone and electric companies are very closely regulated by the states, but their actions are not subject to the Constitution unless the government in a particular situation has actually compelled, substantially participated in, or enforced those actions.

Even though the Constitution does not prohibit private actions, a federal or state statute might. For example, racial discrimination by a private employer or restaurant does not violate the equal protection clause, but it does violate a federal statute—the

Civil Rights Act of 1964. We will now turn to a discussion of several important Constitutional guarantees.

Privileges and Immunities

Article IV, section 2 of the Constitution states, in part, that "the citizens of each State shall be entitled to all privileges and immunities of the several states."

The basic aim of the **Privileges and Immunities Clause** is to prohibit states from discriminating against residents of other states merely because of their residency. Thus a state cannot prohibit travel by nonresidents within its borders, nor can it deny nonresident plaintiffs access to its court system. The Privileges and Immunities Clause is yet another provision of the Constitution intended to prevent states from erecting barriers around their borders. The fundamental individual right (and also the national interest) that the clause protects from state infringement is that of moving freely among the states without being unreasonably disadvantaged because of the state of residency.

Like other constitutional guarantees, the Privileges and Immunities Clause is not an absolute limitation on governmental power. A state law may treat residents of other states differently if the law protects a legitimate "local" (state) interest and does not discriminate more than is necessary. For example, because state universities are substantially assisted by the taxes that state residents pay, the charging of higher tuition for nonresident students does not violate the Privileges and Immunities Clause. The balancing of a state's local interest against the national interest in individual freedom of travel is a familiar process; the form of the analysis closely resembles the process of resolving claims that state laws unduly burden interstate commerce.

The Privileges and Immunities Clause is one of the few constitutional protections that applies only to individuals and not to corporations. Even though the Privileges and Immunities Clause does not apply, however, a state's discriminatory treatment of companies incorporated in other states will often have a negative impact on interstate commerce and thus is likely to violate the Commerce Clause unless it furthers a legitimate state interest and is reasonably limited so as to discriminate no more than necessary.

The following case involves a Privileges and Immunities Clause challenge to a state law in Alaska, in which the Supreme Court balanced the local interest against the individual and national interest, paying careful attention to whether the law was narrowly tailored to fit the state's problem.

The Alaska legislature passed a statute in 1972 (known as "Alaska Hire") for the stated purpose of reducing unemployment within the state. The key provision of the statute required all employers engaged in specified lines of work to hire qualified Alaska residents in preference to nonresidents. The types of work related to construction of the TransAlaska pipeline after discovery of the huge North Slope oilfield. To implement the law, persons who had resided in the state for a minimum of one year were furnished "resident cards" as proof of their preferred status.

Hicklin and others, the plaintiffs, were nonresidents who had worked on the Trans–Alaska pipeline for short periods until late 1975, when the law was first enforced. In 1976, when the plaintiffs were refused employment on the pipeline, they brought this action against Orbeck, the state official charged with enforcing Alaska Hire, contending that the law violated the privileges and immunities clause. The Alaska Supreme Court, by a 3–2 vote, upheld the law, and the U.S. Supreme Court granted the plaintiffs request for review.

HICKLIN V. ORBECK
U.S. Supreme Court, 437 U.S. 518 (1978)

The Alaska legislature passed a statute in 1972 (known as "Alaska Hire ") for the stated purpose of reducing unemployment within the state. The key provision of the statute required ll mployers engaged in specified lines of work to hire qualified Alaska residents in preference to nonresidents. The types of work related to construction of the TransAlaska pipeline after discovery of the huge North Slope oilfield. To implement the law, persons who had resided in the state for a minimum of one year were furnished "resident cards" as proof of their preferredstatus.

Hicklin and others, the plaintiffs,were nonresidents who had worked on the Trans-Alaska ipeline or short periods until late 1975, when the law was first enforced. In 1976, when the plaintiffs were refused employment on the pipeline, they brought this action against Orbeck, the state official charged with enforcing Alaska Hire,contending that the law violated the privileges and mmunities clause. The Alaska Supreme Court, by a 3-2 vote,u-pheld the law, and the U.S. Supreme Court granted the plaintiffs request for review.

Brennan, Justice:

...The Privileges and Immunities Clause ...establishes a norm of comity that is to prevail among the States with respect to their treatment of each other's residents...Appellants' appeal to the protection of this Clause is strongly supported y this Court's decisions holing violative of the Clause state discrimination against nonresidents seeking to ply their trade, practice their occupation, or pursue a common calling within the State. For example, [an early case in this Court] ...recognized that a resident of one State is constitutionally entitled to travel to another State for purposes of employment free from discriminatory restrictions in favor of state residents imposed by the other State.

Again, [in] Toomer v. Witsell, 334 U.S. 385 (1948), the leading exposition of the limitations the Clause places on a State's power to bias employment opportunities in favor of its own residents, [this Court] invalidated a South Carolina statute that required nonresidents to pay a fee 100 times greater than that paid by residents for a license to shrimp commercially in the three–mile maritime belt off the coast of that state. The Court reasoned that although the Privileges and Immunities Clause "does not preclude disparity of treatment in the many situations where there are perfectly valid independent reasons for it, it does bar discrimination against citizens of other States where there is no substantial reason for the discrimination beyond the mere fact that they are citizens of other States." A "substantial reason for the discrimination" would not exist, the Court explained, "unless there is something to indicate that noncitizens constitute a peculiar source of the evil at which the statute is aimed.". . .

Even assuming that a State may validly attempt to alleviate its unemployment problem by requiring private employers within the State to discriminate against nonresidents—an assumption made at least dubious [by prior cases]—it is clear under the *Toomer* analysis that Alaska Hire's discrimination against nonresidents cannot withstand scrutiny under the Privileges and Immunities Clause. For although the Statute may not violate the Clause if the State shows [in the words of *Toomer*] "something to indicate that noncitizens constitute a peculiar source of evil," *certainly no showing was made on this record that nonresidents were a peculiar source of the evil [that] Alaska Hire was enacted to remedy, namely, Alaska's uniquely high unemployment.* [Emphasis added.] What evidence the record does contain indicates that the major cause of Alaska's high unemployment was not the influx of nonresidents seeking employment, but rather the fact that a substantial number of Alaska's jobless residents—especially the unemployed Eskimo and Indian residents— were unable to secure employment either because of their lack of education and job training or because of their geographical remoteness from job opportunities. The employment of nonresidents threatened to deny jobs to Alaska residents only to the extent that jobs for which untrained residents were being prepared might be filled by nonresidents before the residents' training was completed.

Moreover, even if the State's showing is accepted as sufficient to indicate that nonresidents were "a peculiar source of evil," *Toomer* compels the conclusion that Alaska Hire nevertheless fails to pass constitutional muster, [because] the discrimination the Act works against nonresidents does not bear a substantial relationship to the particular "evil" they are said to present. Alaska Hire simply grants all Alaskans, regardless of their employment status, education, or training, a flat employment preference for all jobs covered by the Act. A highly skilled and educated resident who has never been unemployed is entitled to precisely the same preferential treatment as the unskilled, habitually unemployed Arctic Eskimo enrolled in a job–training program. If Alaska is to attempt to ease its unemployment problem by forcing employers within the State to discriminate against nonresidents—again, a policy which [itself] may present serious constitutional questions—the means by which it does so must be more closely tailored to aid the unemployed the Act is intended to benefit. Even if a statute granting an employment preference to unemployed residents or to residents enrolled in job–training programs might be permissible, Alaska Hire's across the–board grant of a job preference to all Alaskan residents clearly is not. . . [For these reasons,] Alaska Hire cannot withstand constitutional scrutiny.

[Judgment reversed.]

Freedom of Religion

The First Amendment contains two clauses protecting freedom of religion. It provides that "Congress shall make no law (1) respecting an establishment of religion, or (2) prohibiting the free exercise thereof." Although the Establishment and Free Exercise clauses overlap (and sometimes even conflict), they clearly create two separate guarantees. Both guarantees provide that the government's role is to be one of "benevolent neutrality," neither advancing nor inhibiting religion.

Establishment Clause

A large part of the metaphoric "wall" between church and state arises from the **Establishment Clause,** which prohibits the government from establishing a state religion and, according to the Supreme Court, from financially supporting religion, becoming actively involved in religion, or favoring one religion over another.

The most controversial manifestation of the Supreme Court's view of the Establishment Clause is probably the "school prayer" case, Engel v. Vitale, 370 U.S. 421 (1962). The New York State Board of Regents had written a nondenominational prayer to be recited by students in school on a voluntary basis. The Supreme Court found an Establishment Clause violation, saying, in part, that "the constitutional prohibition against laws respecting an establishment of a religion must at least mean that in this country it is no part of the business of government to compose official prayers for any group of the American people to recite as a part of a religious program carried on by any government."

An attempt to circumvent Engel v. Vitale by institution of a "moment of silence" in the public schools "for meditation or voluntary prayer" was declared unconstitutional in Wallace v. Jaffree, 472 U.S. 38 (1985). The legislative history of the law in question made it clear that its primary purpose was to promote religion.

When a state or federal law is challenged as violative of the Establishment Clause, it will be evaluated by a three–pronged test, known as the *Lemon* test. First, the court will ask whether the law has a secular (nonreligious) purpose. If there is no such purpose, the law is invalid. Even if the law has a secular purpose, the court will ask, second, whether its *primary* purpose is to advance or inhibit religion. If the answer is in the affirmative, the law is unconstitutional. If the answer is in the negative, the court will ask, third, whether the law fosters excessive government entanglement with religion. Such entanglement might include government evaluation of religious practices, extensive government involvement in church finances and operations, or government attempts to classify what is religious and what is not. Presence of such entanglement obviously indicates an Establishment Clause violation.

In Van Orden v. Perry, 125 S.Ct. 2854 (2005), the Supreme Court held that the *Lemon* test was not helpful in deciding a claim that a Ten Commandment monument's placement on the Texas State Capitol grounds violated the Establishment Clause. The Court rejected the claim because the monument's placement was a far more passive use of those the Commandments than their mandatory placement in elementary schools and was quite different from requiring prayers in school. The Capitol grounds had many monuments representing several strands of the State's political and legal history, and in this context the inclusion of the Ten Commandments monument had a dual significance, partaking of both religion and government. Had the monument been placed for the purpose of celebrating America's devotion to religion, a different result would have followed.

An Establishment Clause case affecting business is Estate of Thornton v. Caldor, Inc., 472 U.S. 703 (1985), which involved a Connecticut statute guaranteeing every employee who "states that a particular day of the week is observed as his Sabbath," the right not to work on his or her chosen day. Because the law gave an absolute preference to the worker's religious practice, no matter how severe the hardship to the employer, the Court held that its primary purpose was to advance religion. Federal law validly requires that employers subject to Title VII, discussed in our later chapter on employment law, make "reasonable accommodations" for the religious practices of employees. But an absolute preference is invalid.

Free Exercise Clause

The general thrust of the **Free Exercise Clause** is to guarantee to all persons the right of religious belief and the freedom to practice their beliefs without governmental interference. The government may not single out any particular religion for discrimination. To claim the protection of the Free Exercise Clause, a plaintiff must normally prove that he or she is a sincere adherent of an established religion and that a fundamental tenet of that religion is at stake in the case. These requirements weed out spurious, insincere, and trivial claims.

Under the Free Exercise Clause, plaintiffs, frequently belonging to religious minorities, have paved the way for the religious freedoms we all enjoy. For example, in West Virginia State Board of Education v. Barnette, 319 U.S. 624 (1943), the Supreme Court held that a board of education requirement that students salute the flag and say the pledge of allegiance was unconstitutional as applied to the plaintiff, a member of the Jehovah's Witnesses. The court said: "If there is any fixed star in our constitutional constellation, it is that no official, high or petty, can prescribe what shall be orthodox in politics, nationalism, religion, or other matters of opinion, or force citizens to confess by word or act their faith therein. If there are any circumstances which permit an exception, they do not now occur to us.

To overcome the very important interest in free exercise of religious beliefs, the government must demonstrate that an unusually important interest is at stake (denominated in various cases "compelling," "of the highest order," or "overriding") and that granting an exemption to the plaintiff will do substantial harm to that interest. The government has succeeded in cases requiring vaccinations for children against their parents' religious objections in furtherance of public health, in cases requiring medical treatment for children over their parents' objections when such treatment was necessary to save the child's life, and in cases banning the handling of poisonous snakes in religious services.

The Supreme Court reduced the government's burden where incidental effects of government programs interfere with religious practices but do not coerce individuals to act contrary to their religious beliefs. In such cases, the government need not show a "compelling justification" to prevail. Thus, in Oregon v. Smith, 494 U.S. 872 (1990), the Supreme Court held that a state's interest in fighting drugs validated its decision to deny unemployment compensation on grounds of "misconduct" to two men who had been fired by a private employer because they ingested peyote, a hallucinogenic drug, for sacramental purposes at a ceremony of their Native American church. The balancing test approach was held inapplicable to an across–the–board criminal prohibition on a particular form of conduct.

Freedom of Speech

No right of Americans receives greater protection than freedom of speech. As with most other constitutional guarantees, the First Amendment's **Free Speech Clause** has been expanded to limit not only the actions of the federal government but also the actions of state and local governments. Unlike citizens in so many other countries, we may freely criticize public officials and the laws of our government.

All methods of expression are within the scope of the Free Speech Clause, including oral and written communications, and those recorded on tape, film, and so on. Moreover, *symbolic expression* is also protected. In other words, expression by nonverbal means such as wearing black arm bands or picketing is protected from government suppression. The giving of money to political candidates, charitable organizations, or various other entities is even treated as a form of protected expression.

However, a government limitation of symbolic expression is somewhat more likely to be upheld than a limitation on verbal expression, simply because the conduct that constitutes symbolic expression is somewhat more likely to interfere substantially with some important public interest. If symbolic expression does not substantially interfere with an important public interest, however, it is fully protected.

The right of association is also viewed as a component of free speech. The groups and organizations we join often provide us with one of our most effective means of expressing our beliefs and opinions. Thus, a government limitation on our ability to associate with groups of our choice is a limitation on free speech.

Not only does free speech include the right to express oneself, but it also includes the right to avoid expressing opinions that we do not agree with. For example, in Pacific Gas & Electric Co. v. Public Utilities Commission of California, 475 U.S. 1 (1986), the Supreme Court overturned on free speech grounds an order of the California utility regulatory agency that had required an investor–owned utility to include in its billing envelopes a leaflet expressing the views of a consumer group with which the utility disagreed. The Court held that the agency's order unconstitutionally burdened the utility's freedom not to speak, a right that is protected because all speech inherently involves choices of what to say and what to leave unsaid.

Corporate Speech

In addition to protecting the speech of individuals, the First Amendment has also been interpreted to protect the expressions of corporations. This proposition was evident in the above reference to the *Pacific Gas & Electric* case. Corporate speech, like individual speech, has informational value—it contributes to the public debate on important issues. Thus, in First National Bank of Boston v. Bellotti, 435 U.S. 765 (1978), the Supreme Court struck down a state statute that prohibited expenditures by business corporations for the purpose of influencing the vote on state referendum proposals, unless a particular proposal "materially affected" the business or property of the corporation. The law was passed to silence the voice of corporations in the public debate over an upcoming referendum concerning a personal income tax. Because the referendum did not deal with a corporate income tax, it did not materially affect the business or property of corporations; thus the statute prohibited corporations from issuing press releases, publishing advocacy advertisements, or otherwise speaking out on the personal income tax issue. The First National Bank of Boston wished to speak out because it felt that a personal income tax would harm the overall economic climate of the state. In overturning the law, the Supreme Court noted that "the inherent worth of the speech in terms of its capacity for informing the public does not depend upon the identity of its source, whether corporation, association, union, or individual."

Unprotected Speech

Although almost all expression is constitutionally protected, a few categories are not. If a particular type of expression is unprotected, this simply means that the government may limit or prohibit it without violating the First Amendment.

The first category of unprotected speech is obscenity. A local, state, or federal law that punishes the dissemination of obscene material is constitutional if the particular material to which the law is applied in a given case meets the Supreme Court's definition of obscenity. In Miller v. California, 413 U.S. 15 (1973), the Supreme Court held that, for a book, movie, or other material to be considered obscene, a court must determine that (1) "the average person, applying contemporary community standards" would find that the work, taken as a whole, appeals to the prurient interest; (2) the work depicts or describes, in a patently offensive way, sexual conduct specifically defined by the applicable law; and (3) the work, taken as a whole, lacks serious literary, artistic, political, or scientific value. Under today's community standards in most places, it is very difficult if not impossible to prove that most pornographic material is obscene. When pornography involves children or when children are exposed to such material, however, there is a much higher probability that it will be within the definition of obscenity.

A second category of unprotected speech is *defamation*. Thus it is constitutionally permissible for state tort or criminal laws to be applied to libel or slander—false statements that defame a person's character.

The third category of unprotected speech is a rather amorphous one commonly referred to as *fighting words:* threats, epithets, profanity, false alarms, and the like, which by their nature are likely to lead to violence. Their minimal social value is viewed as being outweighed by the danger to civilized society. This unprotected category of speech is narrowly construed, however; to be outside the scope of constitutional protection, fighting words must contain no significant informational content, must be apparently calculated to lead to violence, and must be made under circumstances in which actual violence is a very real danger.

Unpopular Views

The fact that particular speech is unpopular, or even highly offensive to many people, does not take it out of the zone of constitutional protection. As the Supreme Court said in Cox v. Louisiana, 379 U.S. 536 (1965), "Mere expression of unpopular views cannot be held to be a breach of peace." In fact, sometimes the government has an obligation to provide protection for those who express unpopular positions.

Many examples of government attempts to suppress unpopular views have been found unconstitutional. For instance, speech that is critical of the government, even to the point of being very disrespectful or "unpatriotic," is normally protected. In Texas v. Johnson, 491 U.S. 397 (1989), the Supreme Court struck down a state law making it a criminal act to "desecrate" the American flag. The Court invalidated the conviction of a communist protester who had burned the flag at a Republican National Convention, saying: "If there is a bedrock principle underlying the First Amendment, it is that the Government may not prohibit the expression of an idea simply because society finds the idea itself offensive or disagreeable." Indeed, in Brandenburg v. Ohio, 395 U.S. 444 (1969), the Supreme Court held that even speech calling for the overthrow of the government is protected by the First Amendment unless it is "directed to inciting or producing imminent lawless action and is *likely* to incite or produce such action." This is really just another example of the narrowness of the "fighting words" exception. Among other reasons, providing constitutional protection for the expression of views that are unpopular, distasteful, or offensive to the majority helps to guarantee that the public debate on important issues will be as fully informed and undistorted as possible. The greater number of varied ideas (even bad ones) people are exposed to, the better equipped they will be to recognize worthy ideas.

Scope of Protection

Assuming that speech is protected, a court faced with a First Amendment issue must engage in further analysis to determine the scope of protection to which the expression is entitled under the circumstances. Although powerful, the right of free expression is not absolute and occasionally must yield in limited ways to other public interests.

Commercial Speech. A court must determine whether speech is commercial or noncommercial. **Commercial speech** is intended primarily to propose a commercial transaction. Advertising is the most obvious form of commercial speech. Until the mid–1970s, the general assumption was that commercial expression was not protected. However, the Supreme Court held that it is indeed protected in Virginia Board of Pharmacy v. Virginia Citizens Consumers Council, 425 U.S. 748 (1976); in that case, the Court struck down a state law that banned the advertising of prices for prescription drugs. A state law prohibiting advertising by lawyers was invalidated in Bates v. Arizona State Bar, 433 U.S. 350 (1977). A city ordinance forbidding the posting of "for sale" signs on real estate was found to violate free speech in Linmark Associates v. Township of Willingboro, 431 U.S. 85 (1977), despite the fact that the city had the laudable goal of preventing "white flight" from racially integrated neighborhoods.

According to the Supreme Court, commercial speech is protectable primarily because of its informational value. Prescription drug consumers in the *Virginia Pharmacy* case could not learn, before the advertising ban was struck down, that price variations of up to 600 percent existed among competing pharmacies.

Commercial speech is only protected if it relates to a lawful activity and if it is not misleading. Thus, commercial speech that either relates to an unlawful activity or is misleading could be listed as another category of unprotected speech. Although most commercial speech is protected by the First Amendment, it receives a lower level of protection than noncommercial speech. A restriction on commercial speech will be valid if the government can show that it is necessary to further a significant governmental interest and that the restriction is reasonably related to that interest. The following case applies this legal standard for restrictions on commercial speech.

PITT NEWS V. PAPPERT
379 F.3d 96 (3d Cir. 2004)

Pitt News is the University Pittsburgh's student newspaper. When the Commonwealth of Pennsylvania enacted a statute, Sec. 4–498 that banned media affiliated with universities and other educational institutions from accepting advertisements for alcoholic beverages, Pitt News lost around $17,000 in advertising revenue. It brought suit to have the law declared unconstitutional as a violation of the newspaper's First Amendment right to freedom of expression. The trial judge upheld the law on grounds that the paper remained free to say whatever it wished about alcoholic beverages as long as it was not paid. The paper appealed.

Alito, Circuit Judge:
Although the Commonwealth makes much of the fact that Section 4–498 does not prohibit The Pitt News from printing alcoholic beverage ads but simply prevents the paper from receiving payments for running such ads, Section 4–498 clearly restricts speech. Its very purpose is to discourage a form of speech (alcoholic beverage ads) that the Commonwealth regards as harmful. If government were

free to suppress disfavored speech by preventing potential speakers from being paid, there would not be much left of the First Amendment.

Consequently Section 4–498 must be analyzed as a content–based restriction of speech, and at a minimum must satisfy the test for restrictions on commercial speech set out in Central Hudson Gas & Elec. Corp. v. Pub. Serv. Comm'n of New York,447 U.S. 557 (1980). Under Central Hudson, we must engage in "a four–part analysis." First, "we must determine whether the expression is protected by the First Amendment," and this means that "it at least must concern lawful activity and not be misleading." Second, "we ask whether the asserted governmental interest is substantial." If the first and second "inquiries yield positive answers, we must determine [third] whether the regulation directly advances the governmental interest asserted, and [fourth] whether it is not more extensive than is necessary to serve that interest."

Here, the first and second prongs are satisfied. As noted, Section 4–498 burdens speech. In addition, the law applies to ads that concern lawful activity (the lawful sale of alcoholic beverages) and that are not misleading, and we see no other ground on which it could be argued that the covered ads are outside the protection of the First Amendment. There can also be no dispute that the asserted government interests—preventing underage drinking and alcohol abuse—are, at minimum, "substantial."

Section 4–498 founders, however, on the third and fourth prongs of the *Central Hudson* test. To satisfy the third prong, the government must demonstrate that the challenged law "alleviates" the cited harms "to a material degree." Although the government has considerable latitude in the sources on which it may draw to make this showing, "this burden is not satisfied by mere speculation or conjecture." Furthermore, it is not enough if a law "provides only ineffective or remote support for the government's purposes, or if there is "little chance" that the law will advance the state's goal. The Supreme Court has noted that the third prong of the *Central Hudson* test "is critical; otherwise, 'a State could with ease restrict commercial speech in the service of other objectives that could not themselves justify a burden on commercial expression.'" Rubin v. Coors Brewing Co., 514 U.S. 476(1995).

In this case, the Commonwealth has not shown that Section 4–498 combats underage or abusive drinking "to a material degree," or that the law provides anything more than "ineffective or remote support for the government's purposes." We do not dispute the proposition that alcoholic beverage advertising in general tends to encourage consumption, and if Section 4–498 had the effect of greatly reducing the quantity of alcoholic beverage ads viewed by underage and abusive drinkers on the Pitt campus, we would hold that the third prong was met. But Section 4–498 applies only to advertising in a very narrow sector of the media (i.e., media associated with educational

institutions), and the Commonwealth has not pointed to any evidence that eliminating ads in this narrow sector will do any good. Even if Pitt students do not see alcoholic beverage ads in The Pitt News, they will still be exposed to a torrent of beer ads on television and the radio, and they will still see alcoholic beverage ads in other publications, including the other free weekly Pittsburgh papers that are displayed on campus together with The Pitt News. The suggestion that the elimination of alcoholic beverage ads from The Pitt News and other publications connected with the University will slacken the demand for alcohol by Pitt students is counter intuitive and unsupported by any evidence that the Common–wealth has called to our attention. Nor has the Commonwealth pointed to any evidence that the elimination of alcoholic beverage ads from The Pitt News will make it harder for would–be purchasers to locate places near campus where alcoholic beverages may be purchased. Common sense suggests that would–be drinkers will have no difficulty finding those establishments despite Section 4–498, and the Commonwealth has not pointed to any contrary evidence. In contending that underage and abusive drinking will fall if alcoholic beverage ads are eliminated from just those media affiliated with educational institutions, the Commonwealth relies on nothing more than "speculation" and "conjecture.

Section 4–498 is also not adequately tailored to achieve the Commonwealth's asserted objectives. The fourth step of the *Central Hudson* test does not require government to use the least restrictive means to achieve its goals, but it does demand a "reasonable ft between the legislature's ends and the means chosen to accomplish those ends a means narrowly tailored to achieve the desired objective." Here, Section 4–498 is both severely over–and under–inclusive. As noted, more than 67% of Pitt students and more than 75% of the total University population is over the legal drinking age, and, in Lorillard Tobacco Co. v. Riley, 533 U.S. 525 (2001), the Supreme Court held that a restriction on tobacco advertising was not narrowly tailored in part because it prevented the communication to adults of truthful information about products that adults could lawfully purchase and use. Not only does Section 4–498 suffer from this same defect, but the Commonwealth can seek to combat underage and abusive drinking by other means that are far more direct and that do not affect the First Amendment. The most direct way to combat underage and abusive drinking by college students is the enforcement of the alcoholic beverage control laws on college campuses.

However, studies have shown that enforcement of these laws on college campuses is often halfhearted, and the Commonwealth has not demonstrated that its law enforcement officers, at either the state or local level, or the administrators of its colleges and universities engage in aggressive enforcement of these laws on college and university campuses.

We hold that Section 4–498 fails the *Central Hudson* test. Section 4–498 violates the First Amendment for an additional, independent reason: it unjustifiably imposes a financial burden on a particular segment of the media, i.e., media associated with universities and colleges. The Supreme Court recognized long ago that laws that impose special financial burdens on the media or a narrow sector of the media present a threat to the First Amendment.

Laws that impose financial burdens on a broad class of entities, including the media, do not violate the First Amendment. At the same time, however, courts must be wary that taxes, regulatory laws, and other laws that impose financial burdens are not used to undermine freedom of the press and freedom of speech. Government can attempt to cow the media in general by singling it out for special financial burdens. Government can also seek to control, weaken, or destroy a disfavored segment of the media by targeting that segment. [Reversed.]

Noncommercial Speech. If a court determines that particular expression is noncommercial in nature, the degree of constitutional protection is considerably greater than it is for commercial speech. Often the courts use the term *political speech* to refer to noncommercial expression. It should be understood that when the term *political speech* is used, it includes virtually all noncommercial speech—the term is not limited to discussion of political issues.

When noncommercial speech is at issue, a court first must determine whether the restriction merely limits the *time, place, or manner* of expression. (Here, *manner* essentially means method.) A governmental body is entitled to place reasonable limits on the time, place, or manner of speech. A time, place, or manner restriction is not based on the content of the expression. For such a restriction to be valid, the government must show that it is necessary to further a significant governmental interest and necessary to protect a "compelling" government interest— one that is of extreme importance to society—and the restriction must be "narrowly tailored" to limit expression only to the extent needed to further the government interest. Several examples of compelling government interest are the needs to preserve security and order in prisons, prevent disruptions in public schools, maintain a quiet and reflective environment at the place where election votes are cast, maintain discipline in the armed forces, efficiently and effectively

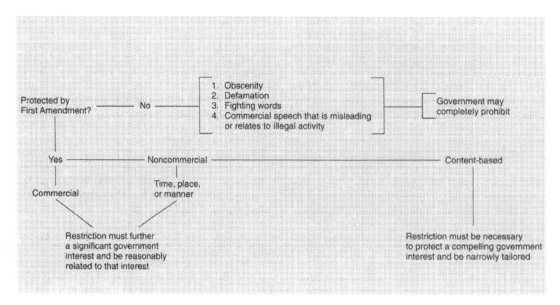

Figure 5.1 Analysis of a Free Speech Question

manage the work force at a government agency, protect the national security, and protect the security of a foreign embassy in the United States.

Even if a compelling interest is involved, however, the narrow tailoring requirement can be very difficult for the government to satisfy. For example, in Boos v. Barry, 485 U.S. 312 (1988), the asserted government interest was protecting the security of foreign embassies in

Equal Protection

The Fourteenth Amendment was passed in 1868, shortly after the Civil War. It states, in part, that "no State shall ...deny to any person within its jurisdiction the equal protection of the laws." Although no provision of the Constitution explicitly mentions equal protection in connection with the federal government, the concept has been found to be implicit in the Fifth Amendment's due process clause, which does apply to the *federal* government. Thus, the guarantee of equal protection acts as a limitation on all levels of government—federal, state, and local.

The fundamental thrust of the **Equal Protection Clause** is to prohibit the government from making arbitrary and unreasonable distinctions among persons. Because virtually every law and regulation involves distinctions and classifications—for example, applying to some industries but not to others, applying to larger companies but not to smaller ones, giving benefits to older people but not to younger ones—legal questions involving the Equal Protection Clause arise frequently. Unfortunately, the Supreme Court's interpretations of the clause have not been as clear or consistent as we would

LEGAL FOCUS

International

As newly independent nations have sought to develop democratic forms of government, it has been relatively common for them to look to the U.S. constitution as a model. Likewise, emerging democracies often have sought the advice of American constitutional experts when drafting their own new constitutions. For example, former U.S. Supreme Court Justice Thurgood Marshall played a substantial role in drafting a constitution for Kenya in 1960, not long after it became an independent nation.

This is not to say, however, that other nations have simply adopted out Constitution's structure and language. Many countries in such a situation correctly point out, for example, that the real meaning of our Constitution includes 200 years of Supreme Court interpretations. As a consequence, Eastern European nations such as Poland, Hungary, Czechoslovakia, and the Baltic states have embraced many of the fundamental tenets of the U.S. Constitution, such as freedom of speech and the press, freedom of religion, and due process, but they are not satisfied with the broad generalities of the American Constitution. They may agree that the generality and breadth of the U.S. Constitution were appropriate for the late eighteenth century when many of the ideas in that document were novel, but assert that a democratic constitution for the late twentieth and early twenty—first centuries must include more detail than was included in the U.S. Constitution. Many of these nations, while relying heavily on the advice of American constitutional experts, insist on more detail in their modern constitutions than is found in the American Constitution. In setting out basic principles such as free speech, these nations are insisting on the inclusion of exceptions that U.S. courts have created during the 200 years of the U.S. Constitution's existence, such as those permitting government restrictions on the time, place, and method of expressing one's opinions.

The real difficulty, of course, is in the clash of cultures. In Bulgaria, for example, there were proposals that the new constitution include an exception to the free speech guarantee that prohibits anyone from injuring the reputation of another. This exception goes far beyond the exception in U. S. constitutional protection for defamatory statements; such statements in our system are outside the realm of constitutional protection only if they defame a person or business (injure its reputation) and if they are proved to be false, to have been communicated to a third party, and to have caused actual damage. This process of blending and compromising firmly held ideals is, in itself, as integral part of the democratic process that is both inevitable and healthy.

like. The Court has definitely identified two different levels of protection under the clause and has probably identified a third. For our purposes, we will characterize the Equal Protection Clause as providing three different levels of protection against unreasonable distinctions. We will first examine those aspects of the law under the Equal Protection Clause that are relatively certain and then look briefly at those that are less clear.

Economic and Social Regulation

One area that is quite clear is the application of the Equal Protection Clause to economic and social regulation. The Supreme Court realizes that legislatures must make distinctions in passing such legislation. Only the poor need welfare; the rich do not. Some industries cause pollution; others do not. Some jobs imperil the safety of workers; others do not. Therefore, the Supreme Court uses a lax standard for economic and social legislation when equal protection challenges are raised. This standard is often referred to as the *rational basis test*. The distinction or classification merely has to have a rational basis; in other words, there merely has to be a legitimate government interest (not even a strong one), and the distinction must have some rational relationship with that interest. If a state legislature, for example, has identified a problem and has made a good faith effort to solve it, the test is normally met. Only if the court can conceive of no reasonable set of facts that would justify the distinction and it is clearly a display of arbitrary power and not a matter of judgment will the distinction be invalidated on equal protection grounds.

To decide that the rational basis test applies to economic or social regulation is almost to decide the case. There is such a strong presumption of reasonableness that discrimination in such regulations is almost always upheld. Distinctions need not be drawn with "mathematical nicety," nor must a legislature attack all aspects of a problem at once. Thus, a law requiring operators of "flea markets" who leased space to persons wishing to sell automobiles to have a type of license not required of persons who leased land to regular car dealers constituted permissible discrimination. The state has a legitimate interest in preventing fraud, and it is rational to presume that fraud will be a bigger problem in a flea market than in a stationary car dealership that will probably still be there when a defrauded customer goes back to complain. (North Dixie Theatre, Inc. v. McCullion, 613 F. Supp. 1339 (S.D. Ohio 1985)). Similarly, in Minnesota v. Clover Leaf Creamery Co., 449 U.S. 456 (1981), the Supreme Court upheld a state statute that banned the retail sale of milk in nonreturnable, nonrefillable plastic containers but permitted such sale in paperboard containers. The law also did not prohibit the sale of other kinds of products in plastic containers. The state legislature had identified an environmental problem—solid waste disposal—and had made a good faith effort to solve part of the problem. The legislature wanted to encourage the development of environmentally superior containers and had chosen one major industry as a basis for its experiment. Whether the law would work as intended was not the Supreme Court's business; the distinctions in the law did have a rational basis.

Strict Scrutiny

Another relatively clear area of law under the equal protection clause today involves governmental distinctions based on race or national origin or that affect fundamental rights. The highest level of protection applies in such cases. If a law or other government action discriminates against someone because of the person's ethnic group or ancestral origin, the courts apply what they refer to as *strict scrutiny*. The test is essentially the same one that courts apply to content–based restrictions on noncommercial speech. The government must demonstrate that the distinction is necessary to protect a compelling interest and that the distinction is narrowly tailored to discriminate no more than is absolutely needed. A governmental body can almost never meet this test, and a distinction based on race or national origin will almost always be void.

The courts have also applied the strict scrutiny standard to government distinctions and classifications that interfere with fundamental rights such as free speech, right to privacy, and right to travel interstate. The Equal Protection Clause has no independent significance when applied to such matters, however, because these fundamental rights are protected by other constitutional provisions.

Perhaps the most well–known application of the Equal Protection Clause to a racial classification by the government was the Supreme Court's decision in Brown v. Board of Education, 347 U.S. 483 (1954), in which racially segregated public school systems were found to be unconstitutional. And in Palmore v. Sidoti, 466 U.S. 429 (1984), the Supreme Court invalidated the action of a state trial judge who took a child away from its mother in a custody fight, because the white mother had married a black man. The legal standard normally applied in child custody cases involves a determination of what is in the best interests of the child; the trial judge had concluded that, in many locales, prevailing societal attitudes against interracial families would make life difficult for the child. However, the Supreme Court said that attempting to shield the child from "the reality of private biases" was not a sufficient justification for a racial distinction.

The courts apply the strict scrutiny test primarily to intentional racial or national origin distinctions by the government. If a distinction or classification is neutral on its face but happens to have a disproportionate impact on a particular ethnic group, strict scrutiny does not apply. In such a case of *de facto* discrimination, the courts apply the rational basis test. Examples include public school districts that follow a "neighborhood school" concept, which may result in particular schools having predominantly white or predominantly black enrollments solely because of housing patterns and not because of any discriminatory act by the school district. There is no violation of the equal protection clause. (A word of caution is in order, however: If government *employment* practices are challenged for being discriminatory, de facto discrimination might be illegal under Title VII of the 1964 Civil Rights Act. Although the equal protection clause of the Constitution would not apply, de facto employment discrimination can be illegal under this federal statute whether a government or private employer is involved. Employment discrimination is discussed in Chapter 29.)

Thus far, the only form of racially based distinction that has been upheld is *affirmative action*. Sometimes referred to as "benign" discrimination, affirmative action programs grant limited preferences to ethnic minorities. Affirmative action in the employment setting, by either government or private employers, is governed by Title VII of the 1964 Civil Rights Act, our most important employment discrimination law. Affirmative action occurs in several other contexts, as well; in any nonemployment situation in which an affirmative action program is instituted by a governmental body, the equal protection clause applies. Examples include programs that give limited preferences to minorities in admission to state universities or in the awarding of government contracts for the purchase of goods or services. The purposes of such programs include increasing diversity in state–supported higher education, helping minority–owned businesses become established by enabling them to break into government contract work, and assisting minorities in overcoming the effects of past discrimination in various endeavors.

Although affirmative action has proved to be the only situation in which racial or national origin distinctions have been permitted under the equal protection clause, the government must meet stringent requirements to justify them. For example, in Richmond v. J. A. Croson Co., 488 U.S. 469 (1989), the Supreme Court struck down the minority business enterprise (MBE) set–aside program for awarding city government contracts in Richmond, Virginia. Under this program the City of Richmond required that 30 percent of the dollar volume of all city construction contracts be awarded to businesses that were owned and controlled by blacks, Hispanics, Asians, or Native Alaskans. The percentage could be met by a white–owned general contractor subcontracting work to MBEs. The MBE program was challenged by a white-owned construction company that lost a small contract to install guard rails on a highway, even though its bid was slightly lower than the successful bid of the MBE. The Supreme Court held that the city did have compelling interests in both remedying the effects of past discrimination and making sure that city tax money was not spent to support an industry that engaged in discriminatory practices (that is, discriminatory subcontracting). However, the Court held that for an MBE program to be valid, the city had to produce evidence demonstrating (1) that discrimination against MBEs in the awarding of city contracts and subcontracts had occurred in the past, (2) a reasonable estimate of the extent of that discrimination, and (3) that it had narrowly tailored the program to take race into account to the least extent possible to serve the city's compelling interest. The city had not fulfilled these requirements. In light of this decision, Richmond let its MBE program expire; thereafter, the amount of MBE participation in city construction contracts dropped to almost zero in Richmond. This result has been repeated in a number of other places. However, many other state and local government agencies are attempting to satisfy the requirements of the *Croson* case.

The following case, although it does not involve employment law, will be of interest to students and shed light on courts' current thinking on affirmative action.

GRUTTER V. BOLLINGER
Grutter v. Bollinger

Plaintiff Grutter, a Caucasian, applied for admission to the University of Michigan Law School, a state educational institution receiving federal funds. She filed this lawsuit alleging that her application was rejected because defendants (the law school, its dean and director of admissions, and the university president and regents) illegally used race as a predominant factor in determining law school admissions.

After a bench trial, the trial judge found that defendants explicitly considered the race of applicants in order to enroll a critical mass of underrepresented minority students. Specifically, defendants desire that each entering class contain 10% to 17% African American, Native American, and Hispanic students. Thus, in 1995, for example, all African American applications with an LSAT score of 159–160 and a GPA of 3.00 and above were admitted, whereas only one of 54 Asian applicants and four of 190 Caucasian applicants with these qualifications were admitted.

The United States District Court held that the law school's consideration of race and ethnicity in its admissions decisions was unlawful and enjoined law school from using race as a factor in its admissions decisions. The United States Court of Appeals for the Sixth Circuit reversed the District Court's judgment and vacated the injunction. The Supreme Court granted certiorari.

Supreme Court, Justice O'Connor:

The [University of Michigan] Law School ranks among the Nation's top law schools. It receives more than 3,500 applications each year for a class of around 350 students. The Law School seeks "a mix of students with varying backgrounds and experiences who will respect and learn from each other." In 1992,

the dean of the Law School charged a faculty committee with crafting a written admissions policy to implement these goals. In particular, the Law School sought to ensure that its efforts to achieve student body diversity complied with this Court's most recent ruling on the use of race in university admissions. *See* Regents of Univ. of Cal. v. Bakke, 438 U.S. 265 (1978).

The hallmark of that policy is its focus on academic ability coupled with a flexible assessment of applicants' talents, experiences, and potential "to contribute to the learning of those around them." The policy requires admissions officials to evaluate each applicant based on all the information available in the file, including a personal statement, letters of recommendation, and an essay describing the ways in which the applicant will contribute to the life and diversity of the Law School. In reviewing an applicant's file, admissions officials must consider the applicant's undergraduate grade point average (GPA) and Law School Admissions Test (LSAT) score because they are important (if imperfect) predictors of academic success in law school. The policy stresses that "no applicant should be admitted unless we expect that applicant to do well enough to graduate with no serious academic problems."

The policy aspires to "achieve that diversity which has the potential to enrich everyone's education and thus make a law school class stronger than the sum of its parts." The policy does not restrict the types of diversity contributions eligible for "substantial weight" in the admissions process, but instead recognizes "many possible bases for diversity admissions." The policy does, however, reaffirm the Law School's longstanding commitment to "one particular type of diversity," that is, "racial and ethnic diversity with special reference to the inclusion of students from groups which have been historically discriminated against, like African Americans, Hispanics and Native Americans, who without this commitment might not be represented in our student body in meaningful numbers." By enrolling a " 'critical mass' of [underrepresented] minority students," the Law School seeks to "ensur[e] their ability to make unique contributions to the character of the Law School."

We last addressed the use of race in public higher education over 25 years ago. In the landmark *Bakke* case, we reviewed a racial set—aside program that reserved 16 out of 100 seats in a medical school class for members of certain minority groups. The decision produced six separate opinions, none of which commanded a majority of the Court. The only holding for the Court in *Bakke* was that a "State has a substantial interest that legitimately may be served by a properly devised admissions program involving the competitive consideration of race and ethnic origin."

The Equal Protection Clause provides that no State shall "deny to any person within its jurisdiction the equal protection of the laws." Because the Fourteenth Amendment "protect[s] persons, not groups," all "governmental action based on race——a group classification long recognized as in most circumstances irrelevant and therefore prohibited——should be subjected to detailed judicial inquiry to ensure that the personal right to equal protection of the laws has not been infringed." Adarand Constructors, Inc. v. Peña, 515 U.S. 200 (1995).

We have held that all racial classifications imposed by government "must be analyzed by a reviewing court under strict scrutiny." *Ibid*. This means that such classifications are constitutional only if they are narrowly tailored to further compelling governmental interests. "Absent searching judicial inquiry into the justification for such race—based measures," we have no way to determine what "classifications are 'benign' or 'remedial' and what classifications are in fact motivated by illegitimate notions of racial inferiority or simple racial politics." Richmond v. J.A. Croson Co., 488 U.S. 469 (1989).

Today, we hold that the Law School has a compelling interest in attaining a diverse student body. These benefits [of racial balancing] are substantial. As the District Court emphasized, the Law School's admissions policy promotes "cross —racial understanding," helps to break down racial stereotypes, and "enables [students] to better understand persons of different races." These benefits are "important and laudable," because "classroom discussion is livelier, more spirited, and simply more enlightening and interesting" when the students have "the greatest possible variety of backgrounds."

The Law School's claim of a compelling interest is further bolstered by [parties who filed amicus curiae briefs], who point to the educational benefits that flow from student body diversity. In addition to the expert studies and reports entered into evidence at trial, numerous studies show that student body diversity promotes learning outcomes, and "better prepares students for an increasingly diverse workforce and society, and better prepares them as professionals."

We have repeatedly acknowledged the overriding importance of preparing students for work and citizenship, describing education as pivotal to "sustaining our political and cultural heritage" with a fundamental role in maintaining the fabric of society. Plyler v. Doe, 457 U.S. 202 (1982). For this reason, the diffusion of knowledge and opportunity through public institutions of higher education must be accessible to all individuals regardless of race or ethnicity. Moreover, universities, and in particular, law schools, represent the training ground for a large number of our Nation's leaders. Sweatt v. Painter, 339 U.S. 629(1950) (describing law school as a "proving ground for legal learning and practice"). Individuals with law degrees occupy roughly half the state governorships, more than half the seats in the United States Senate, and more than a third of the seats in the United States House of Representatives.

In order to cultivate a set of leaders with legitimacy in the eyes of the citizenry, it is necessary that the path to leadership be visibly open to talented and qualified individuals of every race and ethnicity. All members of our heterogeneous society must have confidence in the openness and integrity of the educational institutions that provide this training. As we have recognized, law schools "cannot be effective in isolation from the individuals and institutions with which the law interacts." See Sweatt v. Painter. Access to legal education (and thus the legal profession) must be inclusive of talented and qualified individuals of every race and ethnicity, so that all members of our heterogeneous society may participate in the educational institutions that provide the training and education necessary to succeed in America.

Even in the limited circumstance when drawing racial distinctions is permissible to further a compelling state interest, government is still "constrained in how it may pursue that end: [T]he means chosen to accomplish the [government's] asserted purpose must be specifically and narrowly framed to accomplish that purpose." Shaw v. Hunt,517 U.S. 899 (1996). The purpose of the narrow tailoring requirement is to ensure that "the means chosen 'fit' . . . th[e] compelling goal so closely that there is little or no possibility that the motive for the classification was illegitimate racial prejudice or stereotype." Croson. Since Bakke, we have had no occasion to define the contours of the narrow— tailoring inquiry with respect to race—conscious university admissions programs. That inquiry must be calibrated to fit the distinct issues raised by the use of race to achieve student body diversity in public higher education.

To be narrowly tailored, a race—conscious admissions program cannot use a quota system——it cannot "insulat[e] each category of applicants with certain desired qualifications from competition with all other applicants." Bakke.

Instead, a university may consider race or ethnicity only as a " 'plus' in a particular applicant's file," without "insulat[ing] the individual from comparison with all other candidates for the available seats." In other words, an admissions program must be "flexible enough to consider all pertinent elements of diversity in light of the particular qualifications of each applicant, and to place them on the same footing for consideration, although not necessarily according them the same weight."

We find that the Law School's admissions program bears the hallmarks of a narrowly tailored plan. As Justice Powell made clear in Bakke, truly individualized consideration demands that race be used in a flexible, non-mechanical way. It follows from this mandate that universities cannot establish quotas for members of certain racial groups or put members of those groups on separate admissions tracks. Nor can universities insulate applicants who belong to certain racial or ethnic groups from the competition for admission. Universities can, however, consider race or ethnicity more flexibly as a "plus" factor in the context of individualized consideration of each and every applicant.

The Law School's goal of attaining a critical mass of underrepresented minority students does not transform its program into a quota. "[S]ome attention to numbers," without more, does not transform a flexible admissions system into a rigid quota. Bakke. Nor, as Justice Kennedy posits [in his dissenting opinion], does the Law School's consultation of the "daily reports," which keep track of the racial and ethnic composition of the class (as well as of residency and gender), "suggest[ ] there was no further attempt at individual review save for race itself" during the final stages of the admissions process. To the contrary, the Law School's admissions officers testified without contradiction that they never gave race any more or less weight based on the information contained in these reports.

That a race–conscious admissions program does not operate as a quota does not, by itself, satisfy the requirement of individualized consideration. When using race as a "plus" factor in university admissions, a university's admissions program must remain flexible enough to ensure that each applicant is evaluated as an individual and not in a way that makes an applicant's race or ethnicity the defining feature of his or her application. The importance of this individualized consideration in the context of a race–conscious admissions program is paramount. *See Bakke* (identifying the "denial . . . of th[e] right to individualized consideration" as the "principal evil" of the medical school's admissions program).

What is more, the Law School actually gives substantial weight to diversity factors besides race. The Law School frequently accepts nonminority applicants with grades and test scores lower than underrepresented minority applicants (and other nonminority applicants) who are rejected. This shows that the Law School seriously weighs many other diversity factors besides race that can make a real and dispositive difference for nonminority applicants as well. By this flexible approach, the Law School sufficiently takes into account, in practice as well as in theory, a wide variety of characteristics besides race and ethnicity that contribute to a diverse student body.

Petitioner and the United States argue that the Law School's plan is not narrowly tailored because race–neutral means exist to obtain the educational benefits of student body diversity that the Law School seeks. We disagree. Narrow tailoring does not require exhaustion of every conceivable race–neutral alternative. Nor does it require a university to choose between maintaining a reputation for excellence or fulfilling a commitment to provide educational opportunities to members of all racial groups. Wygant v. Jackson Bd. of Ed., 476 U.S. 267 (1986). Narrow tailoring does, however, require serious, good faith consideration of workable race–neutral alternatives that will achieve the diversity the university seeks. Id.

The Law School's current admissions program considers race as one factor among many, in an effort to assemble a student body that is diverse in ways broader than race. Because a lottery would make that kind of nuanced judgment impossible, it would effectively sacrifice all other educational values, not to mention every other kind of diversity. So too with the suggestion that the Law School simply lower admissions standards for all students, a drastic remedy that would require the Law School to become a much different institution and sacrifice a vital component of its educational mission. We are satisfied that the Law School adequately considered race–neutral alternatives currently capable of producing a critical mass without forcing the Law School to abandon the academic selectivity that is the cornerstone of its educational mission.

In summary, the Equal Protection Clause does not prohibit the Law School's narrowly tailored use of race in admissions decisions to further a compelling interest in obtaining the educational benefits that flow from a diverse student body. AFFIRMED.

In a related case, Gratz brought a discrimination suit against the University of Michigan after she had been denied admission as an undergraduate. Although the Supreme Court upheld the University of Michigan Law School's affirmative action plan in *Grutter*, it found the undergraduate admission system to be unconstitutional. Gratz v Bollinger, 539 U.S. 244 (2003).

The undergraduate program awarded points to applicants based on ethnicity and race. While the Court felt there was a compelling interest in achieving a diverse student body, the undergraduate scheme was not narrowly tailored to achieve this compelling interest. The point system, which automatically awarded 20 points to minorities regardless of other factors and made race the decisive factor for virtually every minimally qualified underrepresented minority applicant, was held not to flow from the sort of individualized review that was required in Grutter.

When read together, these decisions reinforce a longstanding standard that a compelling justification to consider race in admissions decisions can be established, but that such consideration must be done in a restrictive manner. The Court has provided at least general guidelines for colleges and universities to use race in determining admissions, financial aid, and in other areas.

Intermediate Scrutiny

We know that the rational basis test applies to classifications in economic regulations and most social legislation, and we also know that the strict scrutiny test applies to government distinctions based on race or national origin. There are a number of other types of distinctions, however, about which the law is not very clear. There appears to be a "middle tier" of protection that applies to distinctions based on important personal characteristics other than race or national origin. Sometimes courts refer to an "intermediate" level of scrutiny. It is fairly clear that this middle tier of protection applies to gender-based distinctions; in such a case, the government must prove that the classification *substantially* advances an *important* government interest." This test is stricter than the rational basis test but not as stringent as the strict scrutiny test.

When such a test is applied, however, most gender-based distinctions will violate the equal protection clause. For example, in Arizona v. Norris, 463 U.S. 1073 (1983), the Supreme Court struck down an Arizona state employees' retirement plan that paid women smaller monthly benefits than men because actuarial tables predicted that the average woman would live longer then the average man. The plan was deemed unfair to the plaintiff, who could not count on living as long as the "average" woman. (If this same type of sex-discriminatory employee benefit plan is used by a private employer, the equal protection clause obviously does not apply. However, such a benefit plan in private employment will violate the prohibition against sex discrimination in Title VII of the 1964 Civil Rights Act.)

Several other kinds of distinctions also apparently fall within this middle tier of protection, including those based on "alienage" (whether a person is a U. S. citizen or merely a legal resident), age, a child' s legitimacy or illegitimacy, and a few others involving important personal characteristics. The Supreme Court has not given clear guidance, however. Sometimes it seems to recognize that an intermediate level of scrutiny is being applied; in other cases it claims to be applying only the rational basis test but reaches conclusions indicating that it actually is applying an intermediate level of scrutiny. For example, in City of Cleburne v. Cleburne Living Center, 473 U.S. 432 (1985), the plaintiffs wished to establish a closely supervised and highly regulated home for the mentally retarded in Cleburne, Texas. The city required a special use permit for "homes for the lunatic" and denied the plaintiff's request. The Supreme Court specifically stated that it was applying the rational basis test and concluded that there was no rational basis for prohibiting a residential–type home for the mentally retarded within the city. The Court was obviously scrutinizing the city ordinance more closely than it would if it had been an economic regulation. An economic regulation can be practically nonsensical and still pass the rational basis test. Thus, despite the Court's claim that it was merely applying the rational basis test, it was providing some type of middle–tier protection against government distinctions based on mental retardation.

Due Process of Law

Among other clauses in the Fifth Amendment, the Due Process Clause states that "no person shall . . .be deprived of life, liberty, or property without due process of law." The provision applies to actions of the federal government. Among the several provisions of the Fourteenth Amendment, there is also a due process clause that applies to actions of state and local governments. The two clauses are identical, both in their language and in the way they have been interpreted by the courts; thus, there is no reason for distinguishing between the two and people usually refer to the Due Process Clause as a single provision that applies to all levels of government. The courts have interpreted the due process clause as limiting government action in two different ways: the first kind of limitation is referred to as **substantive due process; the second is called procedural due process. Today, procedural due process** is much more important than substantive due process.

Substantive Due Process

The substantive component of due process prohibits statutes, regulations, and other kinds of government action that are arbitrary and irrational. Until the late 1930s, the Supreme Court used substantive due process as a basis for invalidating many economic regulations; basically, if the Court disagreed with the law's underlying rationale, it found the law to be arbitrary and irrational. For example, in one leading case, a law limiting the number of hours that bakers could work was found violative of substantive due process because it unreasonably interfered with "the freedom of master and employee to contract in relation to their employment." Since the late 1930s, the Supreme Court has taken a dramatically different view of substantive due process. Under the modern interpretation, the Court refuses to "sit as a superlegislature second–guessing the wisdom of legislation." The standard the Court applies today is essentially the same "rational basis" test that is applied to economic classifications under the equal protection clause. Thus, substantive due process is used only rarely to invalidate economic regulation.

Today, substantive due process still plays a role in several situations, although that role is rather limited:

Substantive due process incorporates the standards of the equal protection clause and applies them to the federal government. Thus, the different levels of protection that apply under the equal protection clause to classifications by state and local governments are applied to federal government distinctions by means of substantive due process.

As mentioned earlier, under the doctrine of incorporation, the protections in the Bill of Rights have been extended to the states by means of the Fourteenth Amendment's Due Process Clause. Substantive due process is the means by which this has been accomplished.

Substantive due process protects against extreme instances of statutory vagueness. If a statute is so vague or incomplete that a reasonable person, even after consulting an attorney, would have to engage in sheer guesswork to determine what conduct is permitted or prohibited, the statute violates substantive due process. Sometimes the courts say that a statute must "establish a reasonably ascertainable standard for conduct" to comply with substantive due process. Claims of statutory vagueness are frequently made but are successful only in unusual cases of extreme vagueness.

Substantive due process protects against "irrational presumptions." As a matter of practical necessity, the law must make presumptions—presuming the existence of Fact B from proof of Fact A. Presuming one fact because another has been proved is legitimate so long as there is a logical connection between the two. Suppose, for example, that a state law makes it a crime either to steal property or knowingly to take possession of stolen property. Suppose also that, if someone is found in possession of stolen property, the law presumes that the person either stole it or else took possession of it with knowledge that it was stolen. This has been held to be a valid presumption, because the possessor of the property is in a better position than anyone else to explain how he or she acquired it, and he or she is given ample opportunity to explain the circumstances. Thus, he or she is in the best position to explain why the presumption should not be applied in this case. Another example, with an opposite result, involved a federal statute providing that if a kidnapping occurred and nothing was heard from either the kidnapper or the victim for 24 hours after the crime, it was presumed that the kidnapper had crossed state lines. This presumption caused a federal criminal statute to become applicable, thus giving investigative jurisdiction to the Federal Bureau of Investigation. This presumption was found to violate substantive due process, because of the Supreme Court's view that there was no rational connection between a 24 hour period of silence and the act of crossing state lines.

Procedural Due Process

Of much greater importance today is the procedural component of due process. When procedural due process applies, it essentially guarantees that the government will follow fair procedures before taking certain actions against individuals or companies.

Deprivation of Life, Liberty, or Property. The Due Process Clause applies only if particular government action "deprives" a person of "life, liberty, or property." This prerequisite exists whether substantive or procedural due process is at issue; however, most of the problems in determining whether this requirement has been met arise in the procedural due process context. Due process questions almost never involve governmental deprivation of "life," the obvious exception being a criminal prosecution in which the death penalty is a possibility. Thus, the question normally is whether particular government action constitutes a deprivation of "liberty" or "property." These terms are interpreted rather broadly. The term *deprivation of liberty* includes virtually any substantial restriction on the freedom of an individual or company, and the term *deprivation of property* includes virtually any substantial negative effect on any type of property interest. It can be seen from this statement that the term deprivation really just means a substantial adverse impact; there does not have to be total destruction of a liberty or property interest to constitute a deprivation. One example of the breadth of the term *property* is that a person can even be viewed as having a property interest in a job with a local, state, or federal government agency. If there is a statutory provision or an agency regulation that gives the employee some type of legally enforceable job security, the person has a property interest in the job and must be given procedural due process before the job can be terminated. The statute or regulation might, for example, provide that the employee can be terminated only for "good cause" or only in other described conditions. Such a guarantee creates a property interest. There are many other examples of situations in which individuals or corporations have legal rights that rise to the level of property interests.

Basic Procedural Requirements. When procedural due process applies to government action, the government must provide the affected party with (1) advance notice of the proposed action, (2) an "opportunity to be heard," that is, a hearing of some type, and (3) an impartial decision maker. If this same type of sex–discriminatory employee benefit plan is used by a private employer, the equal protection clause obviously does not apply. However, such a benefit plan in private employment will violate the prohibition against sex discrimination in Title VII of the 1964 Civil Rights Act.

These requirements are very flexible. The type of notice that will be sufficient may vary with the circumstances. The general rule is simply that the timing and content of the notice must be such that the affected party is reasonably apprised of the nature of the proposed action and has an adequate opportunity to prepare a response.

The requirement of a hearing is also very flexible; the fact that procedural due process applies does not mean that there has to be a full–blown court–like hearing. The hearing must be "meaningful under the circumstances" and might range from a very informal face–to–face meeting between the affected party and the decision maker all the way to a very formal trial–type hearing. The kind of hearing required in a particular case depends on how important the affected party's interest is, how important the government's interest is, and what seems to be the best way to optimize those conflicting interests under the circumstances.

The requirement of an impartial decision maker usually just means that a person having the responsibility for making the decision (either alone or as a member of a decision—making group) should not have prejudged the case and should not have a substantial monetary or emotional stake in the outcome of the decision. The mere fact that a decision maker has a particular ideology or has very strong views about the general subject of the decision does not disqualify him or her.

There are several reasons for requiring fair procedures in any decision—making process, including those in government. The most important reason is that fair procedures generally tend to produce better decisions because these procedures improve the chances that all relevant issues will be identified, all important positions will be presented and considered, and relevant information will be adequately screened and tested.

Another important reason for fair procedures is making people feel as if their views count for something, thus increasing their acceptance of decisions even when those decisions go against them. It is much easier to get the compliance and cooperation necessary to carry out decisions when people accept those decisions as being legitimate.

Adjudicative—Legislative Distinction. It is also important to note that the courts have made an important distinction between adjudicative and legislative types of governmental actions. In general, procedural due process applies only to adjudicative types of governmental actions and not legislative ones. The most obvious example of such an action is a court proceeding. Many other kinds of action at all levels of government, however, fall within the definition of adjudicative. Most of the decisions made by government officials, even informal decisions, are of an adjudicative nature. The essential characteristics of an adjudicative process are that (1) it usually seeks to determine a very specific set of facts relating to the prior conduct of an individual or business (or a relatively small number of individuals or businesses); (2) it applies some already established rule or guideline to these facts; and (3) based on the application of the rule to these facts, it produces a decision and imposes legal consequences on an individual or business (or a relatively small group of them).

The most obvious example of a legislative type of action is the enactment of a statute by Congress or a state legislature. Again, however, many other kinds of action at all levels of government are legislative in character. For instance, when a federal agency adopts regulations that will apply in the future to an industry or when a city zoning board adopts a zoning plan to guide future land uses in the city, the action is basically legislative. The essential characteristics of a legislative process are that (1) if it involves fact—finding, those facts are usually of a very general nature; (2) it seeks to develop policies or rules that will apply either to the general population or to a relatively large group of individuals or businesses; and (3) it usually imposes legal consequences only for future conduct and not for prior conduct

Like most other distinctions, the adjudicative legislative distinction is sometimes obvious and sometimes not. Some government actions are hybrids. Actually, government decision—making processes run along a continuum from purely adjudicative to purely legislative. The more a particular action looks like an adjudicative one, the more likely it is that a court will find that procedural due process applies. Even when a governmental body takes action that is essentially legislative in nature, it may provide notice, hearing, and other procedural safeguards if it so chooses. Thus,

Congress has passed legislation requiring federal agencies to provide notice and hearing before certain kinds of agency rule–making activities—this was simply a choice made by Congress despite the fact that the Due Process Clause of the Constitution would not require these procedures. Fair procedures can have great value even if not required by the Constitution.

The basic reasons why the courts have generally applied procedural due process guarantees to adjudicative actions but not to legislative ones are that (1) fundamental fairness usually demands more procedural safeguards when legal consequences are imposed for past conduct than when rules are developed to guide future conduct; (2) providing advance notice and an opportunity for a hearing becomes extremely difficult and expensive when very large numbers of parties are affected, as is usually the case with legislative actions; and (3) the fact that legislative actions affect a large number of parties usually means b that there will be more publicity and more collective economic and political power to guard against arbitrary actions by the government.

As noted, distinguishing between legislative actions which do not require procedural due process and judicial actions which do can be difficult, as the following case illustrates.

L C & S, INC. V. WARREN COUNTY AREA PLAN COMMISSION
Seventh U.S. Circuit Court of Appeals, 244 F.3d 601 (2001)

In this case, plaintiffs sought to open a bar in a rural Indiana town. The town amended its zoning law even before plaintiffs could open the bar. Plaintiffs sued on several grounds, including procedural due process. The trial court granted summary judgment to defendant government officials and agencies. Plaintiffs appealed. The facts are spelled out in more detail in the court opinion.

Posner, Circuit Judge:

"Legislative due process" seems almost an oxymoron. Legislation is prospective in effect and, more important, general in its application. Its prospective character enables the persons affected by it to adjust to it in advance. Its generality offers further, and considerable, protection to any individual or organization that might be the legislature's target by imposing costs on all others who are within the statute's scope. The prospect of such costs incites resistance which operates to protect what might otherwise be an isolated, vulnerable, politically impotent target of the legislature's wrath or greed. The right to notice and a hearing, the essence of the concept of procedural due process, are substitutes for the prospectivity and generality that protect citizens from oppression by legislators and thus from the potential tyranny of electoral majorities. The generality of legislation makes notice by service or otherwise impracticable; many of the persons affected by the legislation will be unknown and unknowable. Unfortunately the line between legislation and adjudication is not always easy to draw, especially when the extent of the legislative domain is extremely limited, as is often the case with zoning.

In 1996 the plaintiffs obtained from the state a liquor license for use in Williamsport, and they leased a building in anticipation of opening a restaurant in it where liquor would be served. The building was in a part of the town zoned for commercial use, and the operation of a "tavern" was a permitted use in that zoning district, meaning that the permission of the zoning board was not required. In 1998, before the plaintiffs' restaurant had opened, rumors swept Williamsport that a topless bar, or perhaps even a gay bar, was coming to the town—and that in fact it would be opening in the building the plaintiffs had leased, so presumably would be operated by them. So far as appears, there was no basis for the rumors. They were not even plausible, since topless (or at least fully topless) bars are illegal in Indiana and small country towns are unlikely venues for openly homosexual conclaves. Nevertheless, in response to the rumors the county's planning commission (one of the defendants) recommended that the town council amend its zoning ordinance to make "taverns" "special exceptions" to the uses permitted in the commercial zoning district. This would require the plaintiffs, if they wanted to open a "tavern" in the building they had leased, to apply to the planning commission's board of zoning appeals for permission. The town council amended the ordinance accordingly, but grandfathered the only existing bar in Williamsport.

Neither the planning commission nor the town council notified the plaintiffs of the change in the ordinance. When the plaintiffs discovered what had happened they applied for a special exception for their proposed "tavern." At the hearing before the board of zoning appeals they denied intending to open either a topless or a gay bar. Nevertheless their application for a special exception was turned down, so far as appears without any statement of reasons.

The plaintiffs argue that the amending of the ordinance, though nominally a legislative act, should be treated as adjudicative because it was aimed solely at them and constituted in effect an adverse "judgment" based on a "finding" that they intended to open a topless or gay bar. They were, therefore, the argument continues, entitled to notice of the proposed amendment and an opportunity for a hearing on the proposal. To complete their due process argument they claim that the effect of the ordinance was to take away a property right, the right granted by the state to sell liquor in Williamsport. This is doubtful, but it will be convenient to postpone consideration of the property question for a bit.

That the plaintiffs were the target, and so far as appears the only target, of the amendment is plain. The ordinance was amended solely because of rumors that they were intending to use their liquor license and building lease to open either a topless bar or a gay bar, either use being anathema to the burghers of Williamsport. But this does not establish that the amendment was not a bona fide legislative measure. It is utterly commonplace for legislation to be incited by concern over one person or organization. The Sherman Act, for example, was intended in large measure to curb John D. Rockefeller's Standard Oil Trust, and, sure enough, some years after it was passed a successful suit was brought under it to dismember the trust. Standard Oil Co. of New Jersey v. U.S.,221 U.S. 1(1911).

Williamsport cannot be criticized for having taken a long time to wake up to the need to treat taverns differently from other commercial establishments. The rumors, unfounded though they were, operated as a wake-up call. Because of the association between striptease and prostitution, a topless bar can strain the resources of a small town's police force. Gay bars can require increased law enforcement as well; they may become sites of male prostitution and arouse the hostility of "straights." The consumption of alcohol, particularly in public places, is a rich source of social problems, of which toplessness and the flaunting of homosexual preference may be far from the most serious, yet these exotic venues for the sale of alcoholic beverages may have stimulated a sharp if belated awareness of the problematic character of adding to the number of local taverns. There is as yet no constitutional right to operate or patronize either type of bar; and the plaintiffs do not challenge the amendment as a denial of equal protection on the theory that the defendants singled out the plaintiffs for adverse treatment out of unreasoned hostility.

Not the motive or stimulus, but the generality and consequences, of an enactment determine whether it is really legislation or really something else. If the Williamsport town council had imposed a fine on the plaintiffs, or provided that only the plaintiffs had to apply for permission to operate a tavern in the town's commercial district, the amendment would have lacked either prospectivity (in the first example) or generality (in the second); it might even have been a bill of attainder. But the amendment operated prospectively, regulating a future use but not imposing a sanction for past conduct. Far from being punitive, the amendment is not even prohibitory. It subjects taverns to regulation; it does not ban them. And it applies to anyone who might want to open a new tavern in Williamsport, not just the plaintiffs. There must be a market demand for a second tavern in the town; otherwise the plaintiffs would not have sought a liquor license for use in Williamsport or leased the building. No doubt, therefore, someone else will want to open a tavern in Williamsport, and that someone else will have to apply to the board of zoning appeals for a special exception, just as the plaintiffs had to do. Obviously the domain of this legislation is limited, but it is limited basically by the size of Williamsport. It cannot be the law that small towns cannot legislate because they are likely to know just who is likely to be hurt by the legislation, and the who may indeed be singular. We conclude that the amendment to the ordinance was bona fide legislation; therefore no notice or opportunity to be heard was constitutionally required.

The foregoing discussion implies, moreover, that the amendment to the ordinance did not deprive the plaintiffs of property within the meaning of the due process clause of the Fourteenth Amendment. The liquor license was, we may assume, their property within the amendment's meaning, but it was not taken away from them. The grant of the license did not preempt local zoning laws. A liquor licensee is always at risk that he will not be able to use the license because he can't find suitable premises zoned for the sale of liquor. He has no right, vested or otherwise, to freeze zoning law as of the date on which he obtains the license. He assumes the risk that the zoning laws will be tightened up and make it more difficult for him to use his license. That is all that happened here. The amendment to the ordinance did not revoke the license that is the claimed property right; it curtailed an expectation of unchanged zoning law, and such an expectation is not a property right, or even reasonable.

Our conclusion that the amendment did not deprive the plaintiffs of a property right or deny them due process of law does not leave people in their position remediless against rural prejudice, if that is how the defendants' response to the baseless rumors of an impending challenge to local moral sentiment should be interpreted. The plaintiffs could have appealed the zoning decision to an Indiana court. Perhaps they still can, by reapplying for the special exception and, if it is again denied, appealing that denial. Affirmed.

Takings Clause

The final constitutional provision we will examine is the **Takings Clause** of the Fifth Amendment. It applies explicitly to the federal government and, through the doctrine of incorporation, also applies to state and local governments. The Takings Clause states that private property shall not "be taken for public use without just compensation." The clause recognizes the ancient principle that a sovereign may take private property for public purposes. This long recognized governmental power is referred to as the power of **eminent domain.** The Takings Clause, however, also places limitations on this power. Private property can be taken only for a public purpose, but this requirement is interpreted so broadly that almost any governmental objective will suffice. The most important limitation is that the government must pay "just compensation"—the fair market value—of the property it takes.

The concept of property is very broad under the Takings Clause. It obviously includes land, as well as the many different types of interests in land such as subsurface mineral rights, easements, and "air rights" (the right to use the air space above land). It also includes any other tangible property, such as a boat or piece of equipment, and intangible property rights such as those that exist in a company's trade secret information.

The government is required to pay the owner when there has been a "taking." It will be remembered that procedural due process applies to any government action that has a significant negative effect on a property interest. To be a taking for which compensation must be paid, however, there must be much more than just a significant negative effect on the property interest. All or most of the property's value and utility must have been appropriated by the government's action. When the government physically appropriates the ownership of property, as when it builds a highway on your land, there obviously is a taking. If you do not agree to sell the land, the government must take legal action to condemn the property and have a court determine its fair value.

Difficult questions can arise, however, when the government does something that has a substantial negative effect on the utility and value of a property interest, without actually appropriating the property. When the government engages in some physical act that greatly diminishes the utility and value of someone's property, courts sometimes view the action as a taking. For example, the government might extend an airport runway so that takeoffs and landings are now very low over an adjoining tract of land. If the government has not bought the adjoining land, either through negotiated purchase or condemnation, the property owner is likely to file suit claiming a de facto, taking of his or her property. If the court concludes that the government's actions substantially destroyed the owner's ability to make productive use of his or her property, the court usually decides that there has been a taking for which compensation is due. Although the government's action can constitute a taking without totally destroying all possible uses of the property, one of the factors a court will consider in determining whether there has been a sufficiently large destruction of value is whether there are other comparably productive uses for the property.

The issue of whether there has been a taking can also arise when some law or regulation affects the value of property. Most of the time, a regulation that limits the uses an owner can make of his or her property or that otherwise affects its value will not constitute a taking. Courts usually view these regulations as one of the burdens a person or company must bear in return for the many benefits of living in an organized society. The most obvious example is a city zoning law that permits only single–family homes in certain areas, multifamily dwellings in other areas, retail stores elsewhere, and various categories of industry in yet other sections. Despite occasional claims by property owners that they are deprived of the greater financial return they could receive by putting their property to some other use, zoning laws almost never constitute takings. Among other reasons for this conclusion, zoning usually benefits property values on the whole because of the predictability it creates.

The Supreme Court's many cases involving application of the Takings Clause to regulations have not provided very clear guidance. Unfortunately, the cases in this area are of a rather ad hoc nature. Generally speaking, a regulation that limits use will only constitute a taking in circumstances in which a particular property owner is forced to bear an unusual financial burden that is totally out of proportion with the benefits to be received by either the property owner or the community. For example, in Nollan v. California Coastal Commission, 483 U.S. 825 (1987), the Supreme Court held that a state agency had committed a taking when it required a landowner to grant public access across a section of the owner's private beach; the requirement was imposed as a condition before the agency would permit the landowner to demolish an old structure and replace it with a house on the property. The Court found a taking because of a combination of factors: (1) the landowner was singled out for a special burden not imposed on a general community of landowners; (2) the restriction on the owner's ability to demolish and build was not really related to the condition of granting public access; and (3) the granting of access to the public resembled the actual appropriation of an easement by the government (an easement—the right to do something on someone else's land—is a property interest).

The following case is a controversial example of how difficult takings cases can be to decide fairly.

LAWMAKING BY ADMINISTRATIVE AGENCIES

In The Preceding Chapters we have studied the major processes by which law is made—the formulation of common-law rules by the courts, the enactment of statutes by the legislative bodies, and the interpretation of statutes by the courts. But this examination does not present the total lawmaking picture.

Administrative agencies—the hundreds of boards and commissions existing at all levels of government—also "make law" by their continual promulgation of rules and regulations. The number of administrative agencies has grown so rapidly in the past 60 years that the practical impact of local, state, and federal agencies on the day-to-day activities of individuals and businesses is today probably at least as great as that of legislatures and courts. Every day, boards and commissions across the country engage in such traditional functions as assessing properties for tax purposes, granting licenses and business permits, and regulating rates charged in the transportation and public utility industries—actions that affect millions of Americans. And, more recently, newer agencies such as the Environmental Protection Agency (EPA), Occupational Safety and Health Administration (OSHA), and the National Highway Traffic and Safety Administration (NHTSA) have spawned regulations having a broad impact on the nation's businesses. Justice Jackson was right when he wrote in FTC v. Ruberoid Co., 343 U.S. 470 (1952):

The rise of administrative bodies probably has been the most significant legal trend of the last century and perhaps more values today are affected by their decisions than by those of all the courts. . . . They also have begun to have important consequences on personal rights. . . . They have become a veritable fourth branch of the Government, which has deranged our three-branch legal theories as much as the concept of a fourth dimension unsettles our three-dimensional thinking.

Rise of the Administrative Agency

At the risk of oversimplification, we can say that two major factors are responsible for the dramatic growth of the administrative agency in recent years. First was a change in attitude toward government regulation of business. Until about 1880 the basic attitude of the state and federal governments toward business firms was that of "hands-of"—a philosophy frequently characterized by the *laissez faire* label. The theory was that trade and commerce could best thrive in an environment free of government controls. By the end of the nineteenth century, however, various monopolistic practices had begun to surface. The passage of the Sherman Act in 1890 reflected the growing idea that a certain amount of government regulation of, business was necessary to preserve minimum levels of competition.

A second, and perhaps even more powerful, reason for the emergence of the modern administrative agency is that as our nation grew and became more industrialized, many complex problems sprang up t. that did not easily lend themselves to traditional types of regulation. Some were posed by technological advances such as the greatly increased generation, and distribution of electrical power and the rapid growth of the airline industry. Others resulted from changes in social and economic conditions, particularly the rise of the giant manufacturers and the new methods by which they marketed their products on a national basis. The solution of these problems required expertise and enormous amounts of time for continuous regulation, which the courts and the legislatures simply did not possess. Faced with this situation, the legislative bodies sought new ways to regulate business (and to implement nonbusiness government programs, such as Social Security) that would be more workable.

The Agency—an Overview

To understand the basic workings of administrative agencies and the nature of the legal problems we will discuss later, it will be helpful to see how the typical agency is created and how it receives its powers. For this purpose, the Federal Trade Commission provides a good example.

By the turn of the century, it was apparent that some firms in interstate commerce were engaging in practices that, although not violating the Sherman Act, were nonetheless felt to be undesirable.

Although persons who were injured by these practices were sometimes able to obtain relief in the courts, the relief was sporadic, and there was no single body that could maintain surveillance of these practices on a continuing basis.

Accordingly, in 1914 Congress passed the Federal Trade Commission Act, which created the *Federal Trade Commission (FTC)* and authorized it (among other things) to determine what constituted "unfair methods of competition" in interstate commerce. Not only could the commission issue regulations defining and prohibiting such practices, but additionally, it could take action against companies that it believed to be violating such regulations.

Several federal agencies are considered to be part of the executive branch, such as the Small Business Administration (SBA), OSHA, and the Federal Aviation Administration (FAA). Others are structurally independent of the executive branch; once the president's appointment of agency heads and members is confirmed by the Senate, the president has no direct control over the appointee and cannot remove him or her from office. Examples of independent regulatory agencies include the FTC, the Securities and Exchange Commission (SEC), the National Labor Relations Board (NLRB), and the Federal Reserve Board (FRB).

Legislative Delegation of Lawmaking Power

The administrative agency sits somewhat uncomfortably in our tripartite (legislative-executive-judicial) system of government. An agency that is technically part of the executive branch or perhaps an "independent regulatory agency" may exert powers that entail adjudication and rule making as well as traditional executive functions such as investigation and enforcement. A constitutional problem arises because the Constitution in article I, section 1, clearly vests all legislative powers in the Congress and does not provide for delegation of those powers. Therefore, rules and regulations that have been promulgated by agencies and that have the force and effect of law have been challenged as resulting from an unconstitutional delegation of legislative power.

Only in a couple of cases decided during the 1930s, in which the Supreme Court found "delegation running riot," have such challenges succeeded.

The courts are well aware of the very practical need for administrative agencies that was described earlier in this chapter. Therefore, they will uphold any agency ruling, regulation, or act that is within standards set forth in an enabling act if that act contains "reasonable standards" to guide the agency. What are reasonable standards? Courts have upheld as constitutional delegations of power "to promulgate regulations fixing prices of commodities," to institute rent controls on real property anywhere in the nation under specified circumstances, and even "to issue such orders and regulations as he [the President] deems appropriate to stabilize prices, rents, wages and salaries." Indeed, the doctrine of unconstitutional delegation of legislative power appears moribund at the federal level, although it still has some vitality in litigation involving state agencies.

Functions and Powers
Ministerial and Discretionary Powers

Before addressing the legal problems that are presented when agencies' rules or orders are appealed to the courts, we will briefly look at the nature of agency activities. The activities of these government boards and commissions vary widely. The functions and powers of some agencies are only **ministerial**— concerned with routinely carrying out duties imposed by law. Boards that issue and renew drivers' licenses fall within this category, as do the many Social Security offices that give information or advice to persons filing for Social Security benefits.

But most agencies also possess broad **discretionary powers**—powers that require the exercise of judgment and discretion in carrying out their duties. Again there is variety in the specific powers of these agencies. Some agencies' discretionary power is largely **investigative** in nature. Two examples are the authority granted to the Internal Revenue Service to inquire into the legality of deductions on taxpayers' returns and the authority of some commissions to make investigations for the purpose of recommending needed statutes to legislatures. Other agencies have largely **rule making powers,** with perhaps some investigative but little **adjudicative power** (enforcement power).

"Full-fledged" federal agencies, such as the FTC and the NLRB, possess all three types of discretionary power—investigative, rule-making, and adjudicative. Thus, typically a board will conduct investigations to determine if conditions warrant the issuance of rules to require (or prohibit) certain kinds of conduct; then it will draw up the regulations and thereafter take action against individuals or firms showing evidence of violating them. In drawing up the rules the board acts quasi-legislatively, and in enforcing them it acts quasi-judicially.

Investigative Power

Agencies frequently hold hearings before drafting regulations, and the investigative powers they possess in connection with such hearings are largely determined by the statutes by which they are created. Normally, agencies can order the production of accounts and records relative to the problem being studied and can **subpoena** witnesses and examine them under oath. More disruptive to businesses are the powers most major agencies have to investigate whether statutes they are charged with enforcing and rules they have promulgated are being violated. The two most intrusive forms of investigative power are the subpoena and the physical search and seizure.

Subpoena Power

In the exercise of its adjudicative powers, which are soon to be discussed, agencies may issue subpoenas compelling witnesses to appear and give testimony at an agency hearing.

In any sort of investigation, agencies also may issue **subpoenas duces tecum**, which order the production of books, papers, records, and documents. Agency authority is construed very broadly in this area. According to United States v. Powell, 379 U.S. 48 (1964), an agency must demonstrate that (1) the investigation will be conducted for a legitimate purpose, (2) the inquiry is relevant to the purpose, (3) the information sought is not already possessed by the agency, and (4) the administrative steps required by law have been followed. The agency does not, however, have to prove that there is "probable cause" to believe that a violation of the law has occurred, as is usually required in criminal investigations by the police.

Once the agency has established an apparently valid purpose for the investigation, the burden shifts to the company or individual being investigated to show that the purpose is illegitimate (for example, undertaken for harassment). The following case illustrates the difficulty that the target of a federal agency's investigation may have in attempting to block enforcement of such a subpoena.

EEOC v. PEAT, MARWICK, MITCHELL AND CO.
U.S. Eighth Circuit Court of Appeals
775 F.2d 928 (1985)

In May 1982, the Equal Employment Opportunity Commission (EEOC) began investigating the retirement practices and policies of Peat, Marwick, Mitchell and Co. (PM) in an effort to determine whether those policies violated the Age Discrimination in Employment Act (ADEA). In accord with its statutory investigative powers, the EEOC subpoenaed from PM documents bearing on the relationship of members to the firm and documents relating to PM's retirement practices and policies.

PM refused to comply with the subpoena, so the EEOC initiated an enforcement proceeding in the district court. The district court ordered enforcement of the subpoena, and PM appealed.

Fagg, Circuit Judge:

PM's primary argument on appeal is that the subpoena should not be en- forced because the EEOC s investigation is not for a legitimate purpose authorized by Congress. The ADEA prohibits discrimination by an employer against an employee or prospective employee on the basis of age. PM contends that its partners are not employees under the ADEA but rather they fall within the definition provided for employers in the Act. Thus, according to PM, the EEOC's investigation of the relationship of PM partners as employers, to the firm and to each other and its investigation of the retirement practices and policies of the partnership is not for a legitimate purpose authorized by Congress.

EEOC maintains that it has subpoenaed the records of PM in an effort to determine whether individuals that PM classifies as "partners" fall within the definition of "employees" for purposes of the ADEA.

Congress has established the EEOC as the administrative body empowered to investigate violations of the ADEA and has given the EEOC subpoena power in order to carry out its investigations. The authority to investigate violations includes the authority to investigate coverage under the statute. Donovan v. Shaw, 668 F.2d 985 (8th Cir. 1982). It can no longer be disputed that "a subpoena enforcement proceeding is not the proper forum in which to litigate the question of coverage under a particular federal statute." *Id.* The initial determination of the coverage question is left to the administrative agency seeking enforcement of the subpoena. Often a coverage question cannot be resolved until the administrative agency has

had an opportunity to examine the subpoenaed records.

"The showing of reasonable cause required to support an application for enforcement of a subpoena duces tecum 'is satisfied . . . by the court's determination that the investigation is authorized by Congress, is for a purpose Congress can order, and the documents sought are relevant to the inquiry.'" *Donovan,* 668 F.2d at 989. *See also* United States v. Powell, 379 U.S. 48(1964). The EEOC's investigation of PM is in an effort to determine whether PM's retirement practices and policies discriminate against individuals classified as employees for purposes of the ADEA. Thus, EEOC's investigation is for a legitimate purpose authorized by Congress. PM has not questioned the relevancy of the documents subpoenaed by the EEOC to a determination of this question.

PM also argues that the district court committed error in enforcing the subpoena because it is abusive, unreasonable, not in good faith, and violative of the constitutional rights of PM and its members. In this regard, PM argues that the EEOC has never made or attempted to make a showing that PM's partners may in fact be employees for purposes of the ADEA, or that it has reason to believe that PM's retirement practices and policies may be violative of the ADEA.

The EEOC is not required to make such a showing. As previously indicated, the EEOC must show that its investigation is for a legitimate purpose authorized by Congress and that the documents subpoenaed are relevant to its inquiry. If this demonstration is made, the EEOC is entitled to the documents subpoenaed unless PM demonstrates that judicial enforcement of the subpoena would amount to an abuse of the court's process. PM has presented no evidence of bad faith or an abuse of the court's process by the EEOC.

[We affirm.]

Search and Seizure

Many agencies carry out on-site inspections or searches when investigating matters under their jurisdiction. From city health inspectors checking a restaurant's kitchen to OSHA personnel investigating trenches at a construction site to federal mine safety inspectors probing underground coal mines, such investigations are a frequent and, for the investigated company, troublesome occurrence.

These searches have constitutional implications, because the warrant clause of the Fourth Amendment protects commercial buildings as well as private homes. As the Supreme Court pointed out in Marshall v. Barlow's, Inc., 436 U.S. 307 (1978), the searching of businesses by the British immediately preceding the American Revolution was particularly offensive to the colonists and provided part of the rationale for the warrant requirement.

However, we are not accorded as great an expectation of privacy for our businesses as for our homes. For example, several types of businesses, including gun dealers, stone quarries, day care centers, and fishing vessels, have been held to be so "pervasively regulated" that they can have little or no reasonable expectation of privacy. This doctrine appears to be shrinking the protection that businesses have from warrantless searches and seizures, as the following case illustrates.

NEW YORK V. BURGER
U.S. Supreme Court, 482 U.S. 691 (1987)

Burger owned a junkyard that dismantled cars and sold their parts. Pursuant to a New York statute [Sec. 415-a] authorizing warrantless inspections of such junkyards, police officers entered Burger's junkyard and asked to see his license and records. He replied that he did not have such documents though they are required by the statute. The officers then announced their intent to search the premises Burger did not object. The officers found stolen vehicles and parts. Burger was charged in state court with possession of stolen property and unregistered operation of a vehicle dismantler. He moved to suppress the evidence, claiming that the administrative inspection statute was unconstitutional. The trial court denied the motion, but the New York Court of Appeals reversed. The Supreme Court granted the State's application for certiorari.

Blackmun, Justice:
The Court long has recognized that the Fourth Amendment's prohibition on unreasonable searches and seizures is applicable to commercial premises, as well as to private homes. An owner or operator of a business thus has an expectation of privacy in commercial property, which society is prepared to consider to be reasonable. An expectation of privacy in commercial premises, however, is different from and indeed less than a similar expectation in an individual's home. This expectation is particularly attenuated in commercial property employed in "closely regulated" industries.

[A] warrantless inspection, however, even in the context of a pervasively regulated business, will be deemed to be reasonable only so long as three criteria are met. First, there must be a "substantial government interest" that informs the regulatory scheme. Second, the warrantless inspections must be "necessary to further [the] regulatory scheme." Donovan v. Dewey, 452 U.S. 594, 600 (1981). Finally, "the statute's inspection program, in terms of the certainty and regularity of its application, [must] provid[e] a constitutionally adequate substitute for a warrant." In other words, the regulatory statute must perform the two basic functions of a warrant: it must advise the owner of the commercial premises that the search is being made pursuant to the law and has a properly defined scope, and it must limit the discretion of the inspecting officers. To perform this first function, the state must be "sufficiently comprehensive and defined that the owner of commercial property cannot help but be aware that his property will be subject to periodic inspections undertaken for specific purposes." *Ibid*. In addition, in defining how a statute limits the discretion of the inspectors we have observed that it must be "carefully limited in time, place and scope." United States v. Biswell 406 U.S. 311, 315 (1972).

Searches made pursuant to Sec. 415-a, in our view, clearly fall within this established exception to the warrant requirement for administrative inspections in "closely regulated" businesses. First, the nature of the regulatory statute reveals that the operation of a junkyard, part of which is devoted to vehicle dismantling, is a "closely regulated" business in the State of New York. The provisions regulating the activity of vehicle dismantling are extensive. [The Court then described these regulations in detail.]

The New York regulatory scheme satisfies the three criteria necessary to make reasonable warrantless inspections pursuant to Sec. 415-a5. First, the State has a substantial interest in regulating the vehicle-dismantling and automobile junkyard industry because motor vehicle theft has increased in the State and because the problem of theft is associated with this industry. In this day, automobile theft has become a significant social problem, placing enormous economic and personal burdens upon the citizens of the United States.

Second, regulation of the vehicle dismantling industry reasonably serves the State's substantial interest in eradicating automobile theft. It is well established that the theft problem can be addressed effectively by controlling the receiver of, or market in, stolen property.

Moreover, the warrantless administrative inspections pursuant to Sec. 415-a5 "are necessary to further [the] regulatory scheme." Donovan v. Dewey, 452 U.S., at 600. We explained in *Biswell*:

"If inspection is to be effective and serve as a credible deterrent, unannounced, even frequent inspections are essential. In this context, the prerequisite of a warrant could easily frustrate inspection; and if the necessary flexibility as to time, scope, and frequency is to be preserved, the protections afforded by a warrant would be negligible."

Third, Sec. 415-a5 provides a "constitutionally adequate substitute for a warrant." The statute informs the owner of a vehicle-dismantling business that inspections will be made on a regular basis. Thus, the vehicle dismantler knows that the inspections to which he is subject do not constitute discretionary acts by a government official but are conducted pursuant to statute. Section 415-a5 also sets forth the scope of the inspection and, accordingly, places the operator on notice as to how to comply with the statute. In addition, it notifies the operator as to who is authorized to conduct an inspection.

Finally, the "time, place, and scope" of the inspection is limited to place appropriate restraints upon the discretion of the inspecting officers. The officers are allowed to conduct an inspection only "during [the] regular and usual business hours." The inspections can be made only of vehicle-dismantling and related industries. And the permissible scope of these searches is narrowly defined: the inspectors may examine the records, as well as "any vehicle or parts of vehicles which are subject to the record-keeping requirements of this section and which are on the premises."

The Court of Appeals, nevertheless, struck down the statute as violative of the Fourth Amendment because, in its view, the statute had no truly administrative purpose but was "designed simply to give the police an expedient means of enforcing penal sanctions for possession of stolen property." In arriving at this conclusion, the Court of Appeals failed to recognize that a State can address a major social problem both by way of an administrative scheme and through penal sanctions. Administrative statutes and penal laws may have the same *ultimate* purpose of remedying the social problem, but they have different subsidiary purposes and prescribe different methods of addressing the problem.

Nor do we think that this administrative scheme is unconstitutional simply because, in the course of enforcing it, an inspecting officer may discover evidence of crimes, besides violations of the scheme itself. The discovery of evidence of crimes in the course of an otherwise proper administrative inspection does not render that search illegal or the administrative scheme suspect.

Finally, we fail to see any constitutional significance in the fact that police officers, rather than "administrative" agents, are permitted to conduct the Sec. 415-a5 inspection. [W]e decline to impose upon the States the burden of requiring the enforcement of their regulatory statutes to be carried out by special agents.

[Reversed.]

Obviously, warrantless searches may occur in motel lobbies, bars, and other business premises open to the public. The business has no expectation of privacy there. Additionally, the "open field" doctrine allows warrantless searches of areas that are so open to plain view that no reasonable expectation of privacy can exist. For example, the Supreme Court approved a warrantless EPA search carried out by a commercial aerial photographer flying over a 2000-acre chemical plant consisting of numerous covered buildings with outdoor manufacturing equipment and piping conduits.

Although the company had substantial ground level security, the Court concluded that the plant was more like an open field than it was like "curtilage" — open space in the immediate vicinity of a dwelling, such as a yard. In Dow v. Chemical Co. v. U.S., 426 U.S. 227 (1986), the Court noted that a commercial property owner has to expect less privacy than a homeowner so that, correspondingly, the government's latitude to conduct warrantless searches is greater.

Rule Making

Much of the legislative-type activity of federal agencies is carried out through their rule-making function. Sometimes Congress spells out the procedures for rule-making by a particular agency in that agency's enabling statute. Sometimes the agency is left to follow the Administrative Procedure Act (APA), which the more specific statutes normally follow anyway. The APA provides a comprehensive set of procedural guidelines for a variety of agency activities. In the rule-making area, the APA provides for two basic types—*informal* and *formal*. A third type, called hybrid rule-making, has also developed.

Informal Rule Making

Sometimes Congress will authorize informal rule making. To properly promulgate a rule under these procedures, the agency usually publishes a notice of the proposed rule in the *Federal Register*. There follows a comment period, typically of 30 days, in which any interested citizen or company may send written comments to the agency regarding the rule. Such comments might argue that the rule is unnecessary, is unduly burdensome to business, does not go far enough to remedy the problem, goes too far, and the like. The agency is then supposed to digest and react to the comments, perhaps by altering or even scrapping the proposed rule. Normally the rule is modestly altered, and then published in final form in the *Federal Register* At that point, it becomes effective. Ultimately it will be codified in the *Code of Federal Regulations* along with the rules of all other federal administrative agencies.

Formal Rule Making

Formal rule making also involves "notice and comment," but it supplements these with formal hearings at which witnesses testify and are cross-examined by interested parties. Transcripts of the testimony are preserved and become part of the public record. Formal rule making can be very expensive and time-consuming but theoretically leads to especially well-considered results.

Hybrid Rule Making

Hybrid rule making closely resembles formal rule making, except that there is no right to cross-examine the agency's expert witnesses, and, as we shall soon see, a different standard of review is applied by the courts if the rule-making procedure is challenged.

Judicial Review of Rule Making

Naturally some parties are likely to be aggrieved by promulgation of rules that affect them adversely. Few important rules are issued without a subsequent court challenge. Courts will invalidate rules issued pursuant to an unconstitutional delegation of legislative power (as noted above, an extremely rare occurrence) and rules that are unconstitutional (perhaps because they discriminate on the basis of race in violation of equal protection principles).

Courts will also invalidate rules not issued in accordance with applicable procedural standards. For example, if an agency engaged in informal rule making fails to publish a proposed version of the rule in the Federal Register so that comments may be received, the rule will likely be invalidated if challenged. The courts will permit minor deviations from APA procedures, but major ones are risky.

Standards of Review. In issuing rules, an agency will have to make several types of decisions. One type of decision will likely turn on a pure **question of law** regarding its powers and the scope of its charge under a law passed by Congress. Courts are experts on the law. Therefore, they have the authority to substitute their interpretations for the meaning of laws passed by Congress for the interpretations made by the agency.

Nonetheless, in Chevron U.S.A., Inc. v. Natural Resources Defense Council, 467 U.S. 837 (1984), the Supreme Court has concluded that it makes sense to give deference to the expertise developed by the agency, noting:

When a court reviews an agency's construction of the statute which it administers, it is confronted with two questions. First, always, is the question whether Congress has spoken to the precise question at issue. If the intent of Congress is clear, that is the end of the matter; for the court, as well as the agency, must give effect to the unambiguously expressed intent of Congress. If, however, the court determines Congress has not directly addressed the precise question at issue, the court does not simply impose its own construction on the statute, as would be necessary in the absence of an administrative interpretation. Rather, if the statute is silent or ambiguous with respect to the specific issue, the question for the court is whether the agency's answer is based on a permissible construction of the statute . . . .

We have long recognized that considerable weight should be accorded to an executive department's construction of a statutory scheme it is entrusted to administer, and the principles of deference to administrative interpretations.

An agency issuing rules must also make decisions as to facts and policy. Two tests predominate review of these types of decisions. The *arbitrary and capricious test* assumes the correctness of an agency's decision, placing the burden on any challenger to prove that the decision was not simply erroneous but so far off the mark as to be arbitrary and capricious. The *substantial evidence test* requires that an agency's decision be based not just on a scintilla of evidence, but on such relevant evidence as a reasonable mind might accept as adequate to support a conclusion.

The arbitrary and capricious test is usually used to judge any policy decision by an agency. Findings of fact made pursuant to formal rule making are judged by the substantial evidence test. Factual determinations made in informal rule making are gauged by the arbitrary and capricious test unless an agency's authorizing act calls for use of the substantial evidence test. Many courts have noted that there is little practical difference in how the two tests are usually applied. Both require court deference to agency decision making, but the following case shows that such deference is not unlimited.

MOTOR VEHICLE MANUFACTURERS ASSN. V. STATE FARM MUTUAL AUTO. INS. CO.
U.S. Supreme Court, 463 U.S. 29 (1983)

To improve highway safety, Congress passed the National Traffic and Motor Vehicle Safety Act of 1966, which directs the Secretary of Transportation or a designated representative to issue motor vehicle safety standards. In *1967, the Secretary's representative, the National Highway Traffic Safety Administration (NHTSA) issued Standard 208, which required installation of seatbelts in all new automobiles. Because usage by consumers was quite low, NHTSA studied passive restraints in the form of automatic seatbelts and airbags, which it estimated could prevent approximately 12,000 deaths and more than 100,000 serious injuries annually. Deadlines for implementation of the passive restraint systems were repeatedly extended until, in 1977, the Secretary promulgated Modified Standard 208, which ordered a phase-in on all new cars to take place between 1982 and 1984. The Secretary assumed that 60 percent of new cars would have airbags and 40 percent would have automobile seat-belts.*

However, it soon became apparent that 99 percent of American cars would have detachable seatbelts. In light of this fact and of economic difficulties in the auto industry, the Secretary began in 1981 to reconsider the passive restraint requirement of Modified Standard 208 and ultimately rescinded it.

State Farm Mutual and other insurance companies sued for review of the rescission order. The federal district court and court of appeals held the rescission to be arbitrary and capricious in violation of law. The petitioner Motor Vehicle Manufacturers Association brought the case to the Supreme Court.

White, Justice:

Both the Motor Vehicle Safety Act and the 1974 Amendments concerning occupant crash protection standards indicate that motor vehicle safety standards are to be promulgated under the informal rule-making procedures of Sec. 553 of the Administrative Procedure Act. The agency's action in promulgating such standards therefore may be set aside only if found to be "arbitrary, capricious, an abuse of discretion, or otherwise not in accordance with law." We believe that the rescission or modification of an occupant protection standard is subject to the same test.

The Department of Transportation argues that under this standard, a reviewing court may not set aside an agency rule that is rational, based on consideration of the relevant factors and within the scope of the authority delegated to the agency by the statute. We do not disagree with this formulation. The scope of review under the "arbitrary and capricious" standard is narrow and a court is not to substitute its judgment for that of the agency. Nevertheless, the agency must examine the relevant data and articulate a satisfactory explanation for its action including a "rational connection between the facts found and the choice made." Burlington Truck Lines v. U. S., 371 U.S. 156 (1962). In reviewing that explanation, we must "consider whether the decision was based on a consideration of relevant factors and whether there has been a clear error of judgment." Bowman Transp. Inc. v. Arkansas-Best Freight System, Inc., 419 U.S. 281 (1974). Normally, an agency rule would be arbitrary and capricious if the agency has relied on factors which Congress has not intended it to consider, entirely failed to consider an important aspect of the problem, offered an explanation for its decision that runs counter to the evidence before the agency, or is so implausible that it could not be ascribed to a difference in view or the product of agency expertise. The reviewing court should not attempt itself to make up for such deficiencies: 'We may not supply a reasoned basis for the agency's action that the agency itself has not given." SEC v. Chenery Corp., 332 U.S. 194 (1947). 'We will, however, uphold a decision of less than ideal clarity if the agency's path may reasonably be discerned." *Bowman Transp.*

The ultimate question before us is whether NHTSA's rescission of the passive restraint requirement of Standard 208 was arbitrary and capricious. We conclude, as did the Court of Appeals, that it was. We also conclude but for somewhat different reasons that further consideration of the issue by the agency is therefore required. We deal separately with... airbags and seat-belts.

The first and most obvious reason for finding rescission arbitrary and capricious is that NHTSA apparently gave no consideration whatever to modifying the Standard to require that airbag technology be utilized. Not one sentence of its rulemaking statement discusses the airbags-only option. [W]hat we said in Burlington Truck Lines v. United States,371 U.S., at 167, is apropos here:

There are no findings and here to justify the choice indication of the basis on [agency] exercised its expert We are not prepared to and the Administrative Procedures Act will not permit us to accept such ... practice.... Expert discretion is the lifeblood of the administrative process, but "unless we make the requirements for administrative action strict and demanding, expertise, the strength of monster which rules with no practical limits on its discretion." New York v. United States, 342 U.S. 882.

We have frequently reiterated that an agency must cogently explain why it has exercised its discretion in a given manner. [T]he airbag is more than a policy alternative to the passive restraint standard; it is a technological alternative within the ambit of the existing standard. We hold only that given the judgment made in 1977 that airbags are an effective and cost beneficial life-saving technology, the mandatory passive-restraint rule may not be abandoned without any consideration whatsoever of an airbags-only requirement.

Although the issue is closer, we also find that the agency was too quick to dismiss the safety benefits of automatic seatbelts. NHTSA's critical finding was that, in light of the industry's plans to install readily detachable passive belts, it could not reliably predict "even a 5 percentage point increase as the minimum level of expected usage increase." The Court of Appeals rejected this finding because there is "not one iota" of evidence that

Modified Standard 208 will fail to increase nationwide seatbelt use by at least 13 percentage points, the level of increased usage necessary for the standard to justify its cost.

Recognizing that policymaking in a complex society must account for uncertainty ... does not imply that it is sufficient for an agency to merely recite the terms "substantial uncertainty" as a justification for its actions. The agency must explain the evidence which is available and must offer a rational connection between the facts and found and the choice made." *Burlington Truck Lines*. Generally, one aspect of that explanation would be a justification for rescinding the regulation before engaging in a search for further evidence.

The agency is correct to look at the costs as well as the benefits of Standard 208 [but i]n reaching its judgment, NHTSA should bear in mind that Congress intended safety to be the preeminent factor under the Act.

The agency also failed to articulate a basis for not requiring nondetachable belts under Standard 208. By failing to analyze the continuous seatbelt in its own right, the agency has failed to offer the rational connection between facts and judgment required to pass muster under the arbitrary and capricious standard. We agree with the Court of Appeals that NHTSA did not suggest that the emergency release mechanisms used in nondetachable belts are any less effective for emergency egress than the buckle release system used in detachable belts.

"An agency's view of what is in the public interest may change, either with or without a change in circumstances. But an agency changing its course must supply a reasoned analysis. ...." Greater Boston Television Corp. v. FCC, 444 F.2d 841(CADC).

[Remand to Court of Appeals with directions to remand to NHTSA for further consideration consistent with this opinion.]

LEGAL FOCUS

As we saw in Chapter 3, various methods of alternative dispute resolution (ADR) are becoming increasingly popular for resolving many kinds of conflicts. In the area of administrative law, on important use of ADR is negotiated *rule making*, sometimes referred to as *regulatory negotiation* or *reg-neg*. Under such a process, the agency proposing to adopt a particular regulation attempts to identify and bring together representatives of various interest groups that might be affected by the regulation. Negotiated rule making is essentially a form of multiparty mediation, with either agency representatives or professional mediators performing the mediation function. The objective is to reach agreement on as many aspects of the regulation as possible, producing rules that accommodate the concerns of affected parties to the greatest extent feasible and reducing the probability of legal challenges to the validity of the rules.

One example of an apparently successful use of negotiated rule making involved the U.S. Coast Guard. The 1990 Oil Pollution Act provided that the Coast Guard must adopt regulations requiring operators of oil tankers and barges to develop individual oil spill response plans. Although the Coast Guard could have gone through a typical formal or informal rule-making process, it chose to use a negotiated rule-making process that brought together oil tanker and barge operators, representatives of several environmental groups, and officials from the Coast Guard and other government agencies. Ultimately, the group was able to reach a consensus on a detailed regulation concerning the necessary equipment and personnel to be abroad tankers and barges, the required training for crew members assigned emergency spill response duties, procedures for "lightering" (off-loading oil from a tanker to barges or other vessels in the event of a spill or leakage), procedures for coordinating responses with federal officials, and other matters. The agreement reached by the group was then used as the basis for a regulation proposed and issued by the Coast Guard.

Adjudication

Most major federal agencies also exercise substantial, powers of adjudication. That is, they not only issue rules and investigate to uncover violations, they may also charge alleged violators and try them to determine whether a violation has actually occurred.

Because the agency is acting as legislator, police officer, prosecutor, *and* judge and jury, care must be taken to avoid abuse. For that reason, the APA and the courts demand that formal procedural requirements be followed,

Over the years, procedures have evolved such that a person or company brought before an administrative agency for adjudication of a charged violation will usually have the right to notice, the right to counsel, the right to present evidence, and the right to confront and cross-examine adverse witnesses.

A jury trial is not allowed, but the case is heard by an administrative law judge (ALJ), who is the finder of fact in the first instance. Although the 1000-plus ALJs in the federal system are employees of the agencies whose cases they hear, they cannot be disciplined except for good cause as determined by the federal Merit System Protection

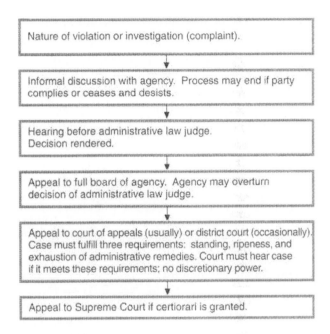

Figure 6.1 Administrative Law Process

Board. Thus, the ALJs exercise substantial autonomy and are seldom puppets of the agency employing them.

Under the APA, all ALJ decisions are reviewable by the employing agency. The agency reviews the record developed in the hearing that was conducted by the ALJ, and reviews the ALJ's fact-findings and legal conclusions. Although the agency usually conducts a limited appellate-type review of the ALJ's findings and conclusions, it does have the power to substitute its own findings and conclusions for those of the ALJ. If the agency does so, however, it still must base its decision on the evidence that appears in the ALJ-hearing record—it cannot disregard this record.

Adjudication is a very influential process. Not only are findings of fact required (for example, did the employer consult the union before deciding to move the plant?), but the ALJ and the agency must also interpret the applicable law (for example, is the employer required to consult the union before deciding to move the plant?). During the Reagan administration, the NLRB largely rewrote American labor policy through the process of adjudication. Although this was done piecemeal through several decisions involving unfair labor practice charges, the change in the law was as complete as if major rule making had been undertaken.

The quasi-judicial powers of major federal agencies are so significant that such decisions are normally reviewed directly by the circuit courts of appeal. Other types of decisions—such as the decision to issue a subpoena or to promulgate a new rule—are normally reviewed in the first instance by federal district courts. (Figure 6.1 helps illustrate the adjudicatory process of a federal agency.)

Many different kinds of agency action obviously can have an effect on the liberty or property of individuals and companies. As we saw in the previous chapter, procedural due process requires that many of these actions be preceded by notice and a hearing of some type. These principles were discussed and illustrated at length. The following case involves a procedural due process challenge to an agency action. Because the agency's action was of an adjudicative type—aimed at a particular company based on specific facts—procedural due process applied. The question that remained, however, was whether the agency had provided sufficient procedural protections under the circumstances.

Gun south inc. v. Brady
U.S. Eleventh Circuit Court of Appeals, 877 F.2d 858 (1989)

Gun South, Inc. (GSI), is a wholesale gun dealer licensed by the Treasury Department's Bureau of Alcohol, Tobacco, and Firearms. In late 1988 and again in early 1989, GSI applied for and was granted permits to import semiautomatic rifles for sporting purposes. On January 23, 1989, GSI ordered 800 AUG-SA semiautomatic rifles and obligated itself to pay $700,000 toward a larger total purchase price. On March 21, 1989, William Bennett, the "Drug Czar," speaking for the secretary of the treasury, announced a temporary 90-day suspension on the importation of five "assault-type" weapons, including those ordered by GSI, so that the bureau could review its conclusion that such rifles are "generally suitable for sporting purposes." Although the bureau assured GSI that the suspension did not apply to weapons purchased under preexisting permits, the Customs Service intercepted GSI's shipment of the aforementioned rifles at the Birmingham Airport.

GSI brought this action to enjoin the government from interfering with the delivery of firearms imported under permits issued before the suspension. The district court issued such an injunction, Brady, Secretary of the Treasury, appealed. The appellate court's discussion of the due process issue follows.

Hatchett, Circuit Judge:

According to GSI, the Government's failure to give it notice of the suspension and an opportunity to respond prior to imposing the suspension deprived GSI of its due process rights. GSI reaches this conclusion by arguing that the Government may not deprive an individual of property without giving such individual an opportunity to be heard. Although GSI correctly argues the general rule, GSI fails to recognize that the Constitution does not always require such predeprivation procedural protection. Hodel v. Virginia Surface Mining and Reclamation Assoc., 452 U.S. 264, 300 (1981) ("summary administrative action may be justified in emergency situations"). See Barry v. Barchi, 443 U.S. 55 (1979) (pending prompt judicial or administrative hearing to determine issue, state's board could properly temporarily suspend horse trainer's license prior to hearing); Ewing v. Mytinger and Casselberry, Inc., 339 U.S. 594 (1950) (allowing seizure of misbranded articles by enforcement agency prior to hearing).

Rather than setting categories of mandatory procedural protections in all cases, the Supreme Court decides the nature and timing of the requisite process in an individual case by accommodating the relevant competing interests.

The Supreme Court's balancing test essentially requires us to weigh three factors: (1) the nature of the private interest; (2) the risk of an erroneous depriviation of such interest; and (3) the government's interest in taking its action, including the burdens that any additional procedural requirement would entail. Mathews v. Eldridge, 424 U.S. 319, 335 (1976). Balancing these considerations, we conclude that the Bureau's summary action did not violate GSI's due process rights.

The Bureau imposed the temporary suspension to protect the public by ensuring that nearly three-quarters of a million rifles do not improperly enter the country. The protection of the public's health and safety is a paramount government interest which justifies summary administrative action:

Protection of the health and safety of the public is a paramount governmental interest which justifies summary administrative action. Indeed, deprivation of property to protect the public health and safety is '[o]ne of the oldest examples' of permissible summary action.

Hodel, 452 U.S. at 300 (safety concerns justified summary seizure of vitamin product). The public interest in avoiding the import of possible illegal assault rifles which could contribute significantly to this country's violent crime epidemic is clearly substantial, especially given the large number of rifles approved for importation under the current outstanding permits. The Government could not protect the public interest without imposing the temporary suspension.

On the other side of the balancing equation, we consider the nature of the private interest, including the deprivation's length and finality. GSI has not suffered a permanent loss because the government has not revoked GSI's license or its permits. The Government has merely deprived GSI of the ability to import the AUG-SA rifle for ninety days. The Government has further reassured the court that it will not revoke GSI's permits without giving GSI the right to participate in a hearing.

In addition to being a non-final, temporary deprivation, the ninety-day suspension does not affect a significant portion of GSI's imports. The rifles which GSI seeks to import during this ninety-day period are only a small percent of the number of fire-arms it plans to import under its permits this year.

Considering the final factor, we do not find that the Government's summary action presents a significant risk of an erroneous deprivation of GSI's right to import the rifles. First, GSI only loses its right to import the rifles for ninety days. Second, as discussed above, the Bureau considered ample evidence before imposing the temporary suspension, and therefore, it minimized the risk that its action would erroneously deprive GSI of its right to import the AUG-SA rifles.

Balancing GSI's temporary nonfinal loss of its right to import one type of rifle against the Government's interest in preventing the unlawful importation of firearms, we conclude that the Government did not err by suspending the importation of the AUG-SA rifle prior to giving GSI an opportunity to respond. The strong public interest in the immediate action outweighs the temporary and limited impact on GSI's alleged property interest. We find support for this decision in other cases which have subordinated more substantial property interests to the Government interest in protecting the public. *See* Mackey v. Montrym, 443 U.S. 1 (1979) (although license to operate motor vehicle is substantial property interest, the substantial nature of such interest is diminished measurably by maximum duration of suspension being ninety days and availability of immediate post-suspension hearing). Furthermore, the availability of a hearing at the end of this temporary suspension provides adequate procedural protection. Thus, the summary imposition of the import suspension does not violate GSI's due process rights.

[Reserved]

Estoppel

Often businesses that deal with the government seek advice from government officials, asking such questions as the right way to fill out tax returns, the correct interpretation of a zoning ordinance, or the legality of a securities sale. What all businesspersons must keep in mind is that government officials may from time to time give erroneous advice, but that does not relieve the businesses from culpability.

\The legal doctrine of **estoppel** provides in many areas that an entity that takes a particular position that others rely on cannot later change that original position when to do so would injure the party that relied on it. Unfortunately, the general rule is that the doctrine of estoppel does not operate against the government. That is to say, if the government gives erroneous advice, it is not later "estopped to deny" its original position. The leading case on this subject is Federal Crop Insurance Corp. v. Merrill, 322 U.S. 380 (1947), in which a government official told farmer Merrill that reseeded spring wheat would be covered by federal crop insurance. Unfortunately, the agency's regulations, printed in the Federal Register, stated that insurance would not be provided for reseeded crops. Merrill, not knowing of the regulation, relied on the advice. When the crop was destroyed, however, Merrill was unable to recover insurance. The government was not estopped to deny its original position. It was allowed to change its position in a way that the doctrine of estoppel would probably prevent a private insurance company from doing.

The reasoning behind the government exclusion lies, in part, in the notion that federal statutes are contained in the *United States Code* and federal regulations are printed in the *Federal Register* and codified in the *Code of Federal Regulations*, and therefore all citizens are "on notice" of these rules. Still, the exclusion seems unjust to many people, so some exceptions have developed. For example, some courts will invoke estoppel against the government when an official has intentionally misled someone. Others create an exception when the government is acting in a proprietary (business-like) capacity. Today, for example, many courts might decide the 1947 Merrill case differently, because in that case the agency was acting more in the role of a private insurance company than as a government agency.

The doctrine's impact when lower levels of government are involved is less clear but cannot be ignored. This lesson was brought home recently when builders given the "go-ahead" by local government officials to build a 31-story building were, after substantial construction, forced to remove everything above the nineteenth floor because the officials had misread a zoning ordinance. The court said in Parkview Assoc. v. City of New York, 513 N.Y.S.2d 342 (1988), that estoppel is not available "for the purpose of ratifying an administrative error."

Other Developments

The federal administrative process has been closely scrutinized from several angles in recent years. To make federal agencies more open to public view and more responsive to the needs of constituents and to fiscal and economic concerns, many changes have been made.

Freedom of Information Act

The Freedom of Information Act of 1967 (FOIA), with significant amendments in 1974, is codified as section 552 of the Administrative Procedure Act. Before its enactment it was extremely difficult for a private citizen to obtain and examine government-held documents. The agency from which the information was requested could deny the applicant on the grounds that he or she was not properly and directly concerned or that the requested information should not be disclosed because to do so would not be in the public interest. Under the FOIA, any person may reasonably describe what information is sought, and the burden of proof for withholding information is on the agency. A response is required of the agency within 10 working days after receipt of a request, and denial by the agency may be appealed by means of an expeditable federal district court action. There are, of course, exemptions—nine specific areas to which the disclosure requirements do not apply. That is, if the information concerns certain matters, the agency is not required to comply with the request. The nine exemptions apply to matters that are:

1. Secret in the interest of national defense or foreign policy;
2. Related solely to internal personnel rules and practices of an agency;
3. Exempted from disclosure by statute;
4. Trade secrets and commercial or financial information obtained from a person and privileged or confidential;
5. Interagency or intraagency memoranda or letters;
6. Personnel and medical files, the disclosure of which would constitute an invasion of personal privacy;
7. Certain investigatory records compiled for law enforcement purposes;
8. Related to the regulation or supervision of financial institutions;
9. Geologic and geophysical information and data, including maps concerning wells.

With regard to the exemptions, Chief Judge Bazelon had this to say in Soucie v. David, 448 F.2d 1067 (D.C.Cir. 1971):

> The touchstone of any proceedings under the Act must be the clear legislative intent to assure public access to all governmental records whose disclosure would not significantly harm specific governmental interests. The policy of the Act requires that the disclosure requirements be construed broadly, the exemptions narrowly.

Businesses have often complained that confidential information they were required to disclose to the government pursuant to regulatory programs might be vulnerable to disclosure to competitors through the FOIA. In 1987, regulations were issued that require federal agencies to provide early notification to businesses whenever "arguably" confidential business data in government hands are about to be released under the FOIA. Those businesses are given an opportunity to object to the disclosure. Agencies are required to explain in writing if they choose to override such an objection.

Privacy Act

The Federal Privacy Act of 1974 seeks to protect individuals from unnecessary disclosures of facts about them from files held by federal agencies. Although the need of federal agencies for information is recognized through a large series of exceptions and qualifications, the general thrust of the Privacy Act is to prohibit federal agencies from disclosing information from their files about an individual without that individual's written consent. Federal agencies are specifically forbidden from selling or renting an individual's name and address, unless authorized by another law.

Government in the Sunshine Act

A further effort to open up the government is provided by the 1976 Government in the Sunshine Act, codified as section 552b of the Administrative Procedure Act. The purpose of the Act is to assure that "every portion of every meeting of an agency shall be open to public observation." There are, however, exceptions to the open meeting requirement. If the meeting qualifies for one of ten specified exemptions and the agency by majority vote decides to do so, the meeting may be closed to the public. The exemptions of the Act are similar to the nine provided for in the FOIA but are not identical.

Most states have passed some form of open meetings laws. There is considerable diversity, but the common purpose is to permit the public to view the decision-making process at all stages.

Regulatory Flexibility Act

We are all presumed to know the law and when final versions of rules are published in the *Federal Register,* legally speaking, we are all put on notice of their existence. Congress realized, however, that as a practical matter many persons, especially small businesses, do not closely follow proposed and final rules printed in the *Federal Register.* Therefore, Congress passed the Regulatory Flexibility Act (RFA) in 1980. Among other provisions, the RFA requires most federal agencies to transmit to the Small Business Administration on a semiannual basis agendas briefly describing areas in which they may propose rules having a substantial impact on small entities (including small businesses, small governmental units, and nonprofit organizations). In this way the small businesses may be on the lookout for potential changes. Also, when any rule is promulgated that will have a significant economic impact on a substantial number of small entities, the agency proposing the rule must give notice not only through the *Federal Register* but also through publications of general notice likely to be obtained by small entities, such as trade journals.

The RFA initially provided little help to small business because it allowed agencies to avoid a cost-benefit analysis by certifying (with very little supporting data) that their regulation would not have a disparate impact on small entities. Congress then added the Small Business Regulatory Enforcement Fairness Act of 1996 (SBREFA), which contained a judicial review provision giving individuals or entities the power to sue federal agencies if they do not adequately take into account the disparate impact their proposed regulations will have on small businesses. In subsequent litigation, small businesses have often prevailed where there was a gross violation of federal rulemaking procedures by an agency, but have usually lost in cases where the agency made some effort to comply with the procedural requirements. Although agency actions are usually upheld, most major EPA initiatives in recent years have been challenged as violating the RFA as amended.

Deregulation

The economic efficiency of many programs of federal regulation is easily questioned. Furthermore, the paperwork burden on many companies attempting to comply with complex federal regulatory schemes can be overwhelming. For these and other reasons, recent administrations have attempted to "deregulate" the economy.

Congress has, at times, assisted the deregulation movement, as evidenced by the Airline Deregulation Act of 1978, the CAB Sunshine Act of 1984, and the Motor Carrier Act of 1980. Various executive orders and agency interpretations have supplemented the effort. During the Reagan administration, for example, there was a noticeably less aggressive enforcement attitude in such agencies as OSHA, the Consumer Products Safety Commission (CPSC), and the EPA.

The advantages and disadvantages of deregulation will be debated for years. Proponents point to the cost savings and the general fare reductions that have occurred in the airline industry through introduction of free competition and elimination of government rate setting. Opponents point to a recent rise in injuries from products and in the work place, the provinces of OSHA and the CPSC, and to alleged increases in various types of pollution caused by EPA inactivity. Neither increases in regulation nor decreases in regulation (as the Motor Vehicle Manufacturers Ass'n v. State Farm Mutual Auto. Ins. Co. case shows) come without cost. To a large extent, the positions taken on the deregulation debate are determined by political philosophies and "whose ox is being gored."

CHAPTER **7**

CRIMINAL LAW AND BUSINESS

- Nature of Criminal Law
- Constitutional Protections
- General Elements of Criminal Responsibility
- General Criminal Defenses
- State Crimes Affecting Business
- Federal Crimes Affecting Business
- Computer Crime
- White Collar Crime

Businesses Are The victims of crime. Businesses commit crimes. This sad reality necessitates a general overview of the role of criminal law in the legal environment of business. Armed robberies, bad checks, employee pilfering, and other criminal acts cost businesses billions of dollars annually. Consumers suffer as well, because these losses are manifested either in the form of higher prices or, worse, failed businesses.

Criminal acts committed by businesses also cause enormous losses to our society. Though crimes committed by businesses received little attention in the criminal law until recently, that situation has changed dramatically as we have become aware of such wrongful acts as stifling competition by fixing prices, selling stock based on contrived financial statements, using false advertising to lure customers into buying inferior products, and the like.

The strong interrelationship between criminal law and the vital interests of business is highlighted by frequent references to criminal acts in other chapters of this text. For example, there is discussion of contracts calling for criminal acts in Chapter 14, of criminal securities law violations in our discussion of securities laws, of illegal competitive acts in the antitrust chapter, and of criminal violation of environmental laws.

Nature of Criminal Law

A **crime** is a wrong committed against society. Indeed, that wrong is also defined by society, because the criminal law is one of a civilized society's primary tools for conforming the behavior of its citizens to societal norms. Even in a society with as many freedoms as America's, limits must be placed on individual and corporate actions. Today's drug epidemic is a vivid reminder of the damage that certain types of individual activity can inflict on society as a whole. Criminalizing activity is often far from the best way to address the causes of that activity or to solve the problems that arise from it. Nonetheless, criminal law is one of society's most important mechanisms for controlling individual behavior, and that will not change anytime soon.

Civil and Criminal Law Contrasted

Most of this text discusses civil law matters. While there are many similarities between criminal law and civil law, there are also important distinctions. The civil law adjusts rights between or among individuals. The basis of the controversy may be a broken commercial promise, an injury caused by someone's careless driving, or a loss caused by a defective product. The focus is on adjusting the rights of the parties to the transaction. The criminal law, on the other hand, focuses on the individual's relationship to society. In enacting criminal statues, a government is saying that there are certain activities so inherently contrary to the public good that they must be flatly prohibited in the *best interests of society.*

A civil lawsuit is brought by one individual or company (the plaintiff) against another (the defendant). A criminal action, on the other hand, is always brought by an

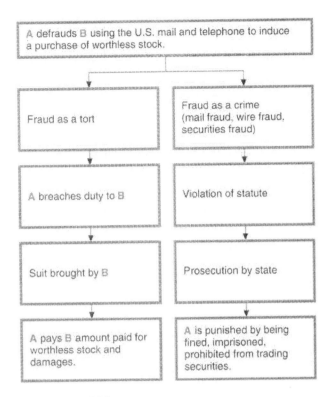

Figure 7.1 A Single Act as Both Tort and Crime

agent of the government (the prosecutor or district attorney) against the alleged wrong-doer. The essence of the civil suit is an injury that the defendant's wrongful act caused to the individual plaintiff. The essence of a criminal prosecution is the injury that the defendant's wrongful act caused society. Of course, there are usually individual victims of criminal acts. The suffering of those victims is not ignored by the criminal law, but greater emphasis is placed on the implications that such conduct has for society at large.

A plaintiff in a civil suit usually requests money damages as compensation for injuries sustained by the defendant's wrongful conduct. In a criminal action, however, even a successful prosecution will not usually produce a dime for the plaintiff. Rather, the remedy sought by the prosecutor typically is punishment for the defendant, such as a fine (which usually goes to the state), imprisonment, or both.

Of course, many types of acts (such as battery) constitute both criminal wrongs and actionable torts. As illustrated in Figure 7.1, the same activity might be the subject of both a civil suit by the victim and a criminal action by the state. A critical difference in such actions lies in the burden of proof. A plaintiff in a civil action must prove the elements of recovery by only "a preponderance of the evidence." Because the consequences of a criminal conviction are generally considered much more severe, a higher standard of proof must be met by prosecutors. Jurors must be convinced of the defendant's guilt

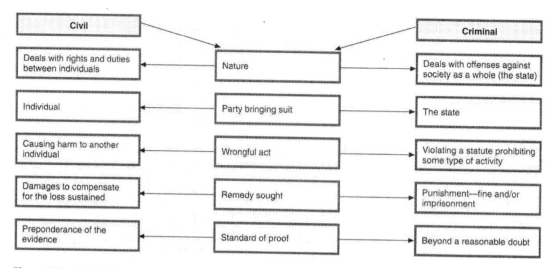

Figure 7.2   Major Differences Between Civil and Criminal Law

"beyond a reasonable doubt" before the guilty verdict is appropriate. Figure 7.2 outlines major differences between civil and criminal law.

Classification of Crimes

Degree of Seriousness

Except for the most serious crime of treason, crimes are either *felonies* or *misdemeanors,* depending on the severity of the penalty that the statute provides. The definition of **felony** varies from state to state, but it is usually defined as any crime in which the punishment is either death or imprisonment for more than one year in a state penitentiary, as in the cases of murder, robbery, or rape. **Misdemeanors** are all crimes carrying lesser penalties (such as fines or confinement in county jails)— for example, petit larceny and disorderly conduct. In the federal system, felonies are crimes for which the designated penalty is more than one year in prison; misdemeanors are crimes with lesser designated penalties. Yet another category used in some states is *petty offenses,* covering such infractions as traffic and building code violations.

The distinction between felonies and misdemeanors can be important because of various penalties often imposed on persons convicted of the former, such as loss of the right to vote, to hold public office, or to pursue various careers.

Degree of Moral Turpitude

Crimes such as murder, rape, arson, or robbery are evil in and of themselves. Such acts are called *malum in se,* meaning that they are criminal because they are inherently wicked. Other acts, such as jaywalking or speeding, are *malum prohibitum,* meaning that they are crimes merely because the legislature has said that they are wrong. Typically, greater punishments attach to crimes that involve moral turpitude.

Jurisdiction

As has already been noted, in America a federal criminal justice system is superimposed over state and local systems. These systems generally address different concerns. Murder is usually a concern only of the state in which it occurred unless, for example, it occurred on federal property, the victim was a federal official, or it occurred as part of an interstate kidnapping. Still, there are several areas of overlap and actions that might well violate both federal and state laws. For example, during the wave of bank robberies during the 1930s Depression, a federal law against bank robberies was passed so that the Federal Bureau of Investigation and federal prosecutors could supplement the efforts of state police and judicial systems.

Purpose of Punishment

Perhaps the most salient feature of the criminal justice system is the punishment that it imposes on wrongdoers. As noted earlier, the punishment is not imposed to compensate the victim. That is the province of the civil tort system. Rather, there are four primary purposes of criminal punishment. First, there is *rehabilitation* or reformation. Although published rates of recidivism (relapse into crime) indicate that this is the most difficult of the punishment goals to attain, it is important that our system at least attempt to reform wrongdoers.

A second, less ambitious, purpose of punishment is simply *restraint* or incapacitation, on the theory that a robber cannot rob and a rapist cannot rape while they are locked up. A third purpose of punishment, and a somewhat controversial one, is that of *retribution*. The concept of retribution predates the Bible's admonition of "an eye for an eye," and society's infliction of retribution on criminals still has strong popular support.

A final purpose of punishment is *deterrence*. The law seeks to persuade the wrong-doer being punished not to err again and, at the same time, to provide an example that might generally deter other potential lawbreakers. The effectiveness of various types of criminal sanctions in deterring crime is not clear. One very controversial subject is the death penalty. Although the evidence regarding whether a state will reduce its murder rate by adopting the death penalty is mixed, advocates justify the ultimate punishment on restraint and retribution grounds.

Constitutional Protections

Once arrested, a criminal defendant has the considerable power and resources of the government lined up against him or her. The potential for abuse of that power is considerable, and one need not be a student of history to discover blatant examples of such abuses. Because our system operates on the theory that it is better that a guilty man or woman go free than that an innocent man or woman should suffer unjust punishment, we provide manifold protections for criminal defendants. Many of these protections are set forth in the Bill of Rights. Through the controversial process of "incorporation," most of these rights have been applied to the states as well. Additionally, many state constitutions contain parallel protections. The following discussion will help complete the examination of constitutional law begun in Chapter 5.

Fourth Amendment

The Fourth Amendment protects people (and, as we saw in Chapter 6, businesses) against "unreasonable searches and seizures," requiring that search warrants not be issued absent "probable cause." A search warrant will be issued by a judge if the police have produced evidence that would lead a reasonably prudent person to believe there is a substantial likelihood that the defendant is guilty of the offense the police charge. The Fourth Amendment requires that the warrant "particularly describe" the place to be searched and the persons or things to be seized.

A controversial question regards enforcement of this prohibition. What happens to evidence that the police seize without a valid warrant? In Mapp v. Ohio, 367 U.S. 643 (1961), the Supreme Court held that "all evidence obtained by searches and seizures in violation of the Constitution is... inadmissible in a state court." This holding was very controversial, opponents arguing that "the crook should not go free just because the constable has erred." In recent year the increasingly conservative Supreme Court has fashioned a number of exceptions to this "exclusionary rule," weakening its impact substantially. For example, in United States v. Leon, 468 U.S. 189 (1984), the Court created a "good faith" exception for situations in which the police searched pursuant to an apparently valid search warrant that was later determined to have been improperly issued. The Court reasoned, in part, that the exclusionary rule was meant to deter police abuses rather than to correct errors by judges.

Fifth Amendment

The Fifth Amendment contains a number of provisions that protect criminal defendants from government abuse. For example, individuals cannot be held to answer for major federal criminal charges unless they have been indicted by a **grand jury.** A grand jury typically consists of 23 members of the community who hear evidence presented by the prosecution. If a majority concludes that there is probable cause to believe that the defendant has committed a crime alleged, the grand jury issues a true bill. The right to indictment by grand jury is one of the few protections in the Bill of Rights that the Supreme Court has not applied to the states. However, many state constitutions have similar provisions.

The Fifth Amendment also protects defendants from **double jeopardy,** which is being tried twice for the same offense. This means that when a jury finds a defendant "not guilty," the government cannot simply reindict the defendant for the same crime and try again to convict him or her. However, it does not mean that a defendant acquitted of criminal assault and battery could not be sued civilly by his or her alleged victim. Because of the different burden of proof, the same body of evidence that did not convince a criminal jury beyond a reasonable doubt might convince a civil jury applying a preponderance of evidence standard. The fact that a state prosecution will not bar a subsequent federal prosecution and vice versa constitutes another major exception to the double jeopardy prohibition. Thus, theoretically, a defendant who was acquitted of a federal bank robbery charge might be prosecuted by a state claiming that the same alleged robbery violated a state statute.

The Fifth Amendment mandates that no person be deprived of life, liberty, or property without **due process** of law. We know quite a bit about due process from previous chapters. One aspect of due process, for example, is that no one should be convicted of violating a statute that is unduly vague, so that a well-intentional person could not conform his or her conduct to comply with the law. Kolender v. Lawson, 461 U.S. 352 (1981), is a good example. In that case, a California criminal statute requiring persons on the street to provide "credible and reliable" identification and to account for their presence when requested to do so by a police officer was held to be unduly vague.

As another example, it would be a due process violation for a prosecutor intentionally to suppress material evidence favorable to the accused. Brady v. Maryland, 373 U.S. 83 (1963). But the Supreme Court recently held that the government's accidental destruction of evidence that might have supported the defendant's innocence did not violate due process. Nor was due process violated by the government's innocent failure to use the most modern, sophisticated scientific methods of examining evidence. Arizona v. Youngblood, 488 U.S. 51(1988).

The most controversial part of the Fifth Amendment, as interpreted by the Supreme Court, is its protection against self–incrimination. No person "shall be compelled in any criminal case to be a witness against himself." This includes matters of document production as well as of oral testimony. The right is not available to corporations and is individual to the person charged. In a case of interest to all businesspersons, United States v. Doe, 465 U.S. 605 (1984), the court held that the sole owner of a corporation could not claim the privilege against self-incrimination to avoid producing records that belong *to the corporation.* Had the business been a sole proprietorship, the owner could have claimed the privilege because the records would have been the owner's, not a separate entity's.

The most famous self–incrimination case is Miranda v. Arizona, 384 U.S. 436 (1966), which excluded from evidence any incriminating statements made by a defendant (and evidence to which those statements led police, called "fruit of the poisonous tree") who had not been fully warned of his constitutional right against self-incrimination (and his right to counsel). Thus, the famous "Miranda warning" was born.

Although the Supreme Court has riddled Miranda with exceptions over the years, in 2000 it reversed a lower court opinion holding that *Miranda* had been abolished by a Congressional enactment. The Court held that Miranda is constitutionally based and therefore cannot be abolished by legislative enactment. Dickerson v. U.S., 530 U.S. 428 (2000). The Court noted that "Miranda has become embedded in routine police practice to the point where the warnings have become part of our national culture."

Sixth Amendment

The Sixth Amendment contains a litany of constitutional protections for criminal defendants, including the important right to counsel that was mentioned in the previous discussion of the *Miranda* case. Generally speaking, any individual facing potential incarceration has the right to consult an attorney and to have one provided if he or she cannot afford one. The right to counsel is made more meaningful by the defendant's Sixth Amendment rights to be informed of the nature of the accusation, to confront witnesses against him or her, and to call witnesses on his or her own behalf.

There is also the right to a "speedy and public trial." Court backlogs have threatened to make a mockery of the right to a "speedy" trial, but the federal government and most states have now passed "speedy trial" acts that place time limits on the government and give criminal cases priority over civil cases on crowded court dockets.

Importantly, there is also a right to trial by an impartial jury that applies in cases involving "serious" criminal charges. Juries, serving as the "conscience of the community," are a critical safeguard against the heavy hand of the government.

Eighth Amendment

The Eighth Amendment contains important protections for criminal defendants. It states that "excessive bail" shall not be required. Thus, when a judge sets bail before trial, the aim should be not to punish the defendant who is presumed innocent, but simply to guarantee the defendant's appearance at trial. In recent years, Congress has increased the courts' authority to deny bail in situations in which defendants pose special harm to the public.

The Eighth Amendment also bans "excessive fines" and "cruel and unusual punishment." The Supreme Court has held that the Eight Amendment bars the death penalty for minors and the mentally retarded, but not for the mentally ill.

Miscellaneous Protections

Other protections for criminal defendants are scattered throughout the Constitution. For example, there is a ban on *ex post facto* laws—laws that are passed to criminalize conduct after the conduct has occurred. Obviously, criminal laws must also be scrutinized to ensure that they do not violate basic freedoms, such as religion and speech. The government could not, for example, make it a crime to be a Baptist. Nor, the court has held, can a state criminalize the burning of the American flag when performed as a form of political expression. Texas v. Johnson, 491 U.S. 397(1989).

General Elements of Criminal Responsibility

As a general rule, the prosecutor in a criminal case must do three things to obtain a valid conviction: (1) show that the defendant's actions violated an existing criminal statue, (2) prove beyond a reasonable doubt that the defendant did do the acts alleged, and (3) prove that the defendant had the requisite intent to violate the law. The first element is important because although many of our crimes have strong common-law roots, today almost all crimes are statutory in nature. The other two elements of act and intent deserve separate consideration.

Guilty Act

A basic element of a criminal conviction is the ***actus reus,*** a Latin term meaning "guilty act." This is a critical part of a criminal conviction because our legal system generally does not punish persons for their thoughts. Evil thoughts alone normally do not injure society and therefore do not justify bringing to bear the full power of the government's criminal justice system. This does not mean that a defendant must always successfully complete a criminal act to be guilty. Generally any act that clearly is a step in the commission of a crime will be sufficient for a conviction for *attempted* larceny, murder, and so on, if the intent requirement is also present.

The guilty act must be voluntary and generally must be an act of commission rather than mere omission. However, there are exceptions. Failure to perform a legally imposed duty will constitute a sufficient *actus reus.* An example is failure to fulfill the legally required duty to file an income tax return.

Guilty Mind

Generally, a defendant is not guilty unless his or her guilty act is coupled with a guilty mind, that is, unless the defendant had ***mens rea,*** an intent to do wrong. A murder conviction, for example, requires the act of killing the victim plus the evil intent to take a life.

Because a person's actual intent can rarely be known with absolute certainty, juries may often presume a criminal intent on the part of the defendant based on the established facts. Thus a jury may presume that an armed prowler apprehended at night entered the house "with the intention of committing a felony," one of the usual statutory elements of the crime of burglary. Intent is often a difficult element to prove beyond a reasonable doubt, but as Justice Oliver Wendell Holmes once stated, "even a dog distinguishes between being stumbled over and being kicked."

Many crimes are called *specific intent* crimes, in that conviction is appropriate only if the defendant had the intent to commit the exact forbidden act charged. For other crimes, *general intent* will suffice, meaning that the defendant had the general intent to commit a wrongful act even though he or she did not intend to bring about the specific result. First degree murder is typically a specific intent crime; to be guilty the defendant must have intended to take a human life. However, if a defendant became very drunk and went on a rampage, killing a man with a gun, he may be found guilty of second degree murder even though he was so drunk he did not know he had a gun. This is an example of general intent.

There are a few crimes for which negligence will suffice and no intent need be proven. Negligent vehicular homicide is an example. There are even some *strict liability* crimes, in which defendants can be found guilty absent intent or even careless behavior. These are typically misdemeanors. Examples include selling liquor to minors, violating traffic rules, and violating pure food and drug laws.

In the following case, the Supreme Court addressed the question of whether a good faith, but objectively unreasonable, belief could negate the intent element in a case involving an intent–based crime.

Cheek v. United States
U.S. Supreme Court, 498 U.S. 192 (1991)

Petitioner Cheek was charged with multiple counts of willfully failing to file a federal income tax return in violation of section 7203 of the Internal Revenue Code and of willfully attempting to evade his income taxes in violation of section 7201. Cheek admitted that he had not filed the returns but testified that he had not acted willfully because he sincerely believed, based on his indoctrination by a tax protest organization and his own study, that the tax laws were being unconstitutionally enforced and that his actions were lawful. The court of appeals affirmed Cheek's conviction, rejecting his challenge to the trial judge's instructing the jury that an honest but unreasonable belief is not a defense and that Cheek's beliefs that wages are not income and that he was not a taxpayer within the meaning of the code were not objectively reasonable. Cheek appealed.

White, Justice:

The general rule that ignorance of the law or a mistake of law is no defense to criminal prosecution is deeply rooted in the American legal system. Based on the notion that the law is definite and knowable, the common law presumed that every person knew the law.

The proliferation of statutes and regulations has sometimes made it difficult for the average citizen to know and comprehend the extent of the duties and obligations imposed by the tax laws. Congress has accordingly softened the impact of the common—law presumption by making specific intent to violate the law an element of certain federal tax offenses. Thus, the Court almost 60 years ago interpreted the statutory term "willfully" as used in the federal criminal tax statutes as carving out an exception to the traditional rule.

This special treatment of criminal tax offenses is largely due to the complexity of the tax laws.

Willfulness, as construed by our prior decisions in criminal tax cases, requires the Government to prove that the law imposed a duty on the defendant, that the defendant knew of his duty, and that he voluntarily and intentionally violated that duty. We deal first with the case where the issue is whether the defendant knew of the duty purportedly imposed by the provision of the statute or regulation he is accused of violating, a case in which there is no claim that the provision at issue is invalid. In such a case, if the Government proves actual knowledge of the pertinent legal duty, the prosecution, without more, has satisfied the knowledge component of the willfulness requirement. But carrying this burden requires negating a defendant's claim of ignorance of the law or a claim that because of a misunderstanding of the law, he had a good faith belief that he was not violating any of the provisions of the tax laws. This is so because one cannot be aware that the law imposes a duty on him and yet be ignorant of it, misunderstand the law, or believe that the duty does not exist. In the end, the issue is whether, based on all the evidence, the Government has proved that the defendant was aware of the duty at issue, which cannot be true if the jury credits a good-faith misunderstanding and belief submission, whether or not the claimed belief or misunderstanding is objectively reasonable.

It was therefore error to instruct the jury to disregard evidence of Cheek's understanding that, within the meaning of the tax laws, he was not a person required to file a return or to pay income taxes and that wages are not taxable income, as incredible as such misunderstandings of and beliefs about the law might be. Of course, the more unreasonable the asserted beliefs or misunderstandings are, the more likely the jury will consider them to be nothing more than simple disagreement with known legal duties imposed by the tax laws and will find that the Government has carried its burden of proving knowledge.

[Cheek's] claims that some of the provisions of the tax code are unconstitutional are submissions of a different order. They do not arise from innocent mistakes caused by the complexity of the Internal Revenue Code. Rather, they reveal full knowledge of the provisions at issue and a studied conclusion, however wrong, that those provisions are invalid and unenforceable. Thus in this case, Cheek paid his taxes for years, but after attending various seminars and based on his own study, he concluded that the income tax laws could not constitutionally require him to pay a tax.

We do not believe that Congress contemplated that such a taxpayer, without risking criminal prosecution, could ignore the duties imposed upon him by the Internal Revenue Code and refuse to utilize the mechanisms provided by Congress to present his claims of invalidity to the courts and to abide by their decisions. There is no doubt that Cheek, from year to year, was free to pay the tax that the law purported to require, file for a refund and, if denied, present his claims of invalidity, constitutional or otherwise, to the courts. Also, without paying the tax, he could have challenged the claims of tax deficiencies in the Tax Court, with the right to appeal to a higher court if unsuccessful. Cheek took neither course in some years, and when he did was unwilling to accept the outcome. As we see it, he is in no position to claim that his good-faith belief about the validity of the Internal Revenue Code negates willfulness or provides a defense to criminal prosecution.

[T]he judgment of the Court of Appeals is vacated, and the case is remanded for further proceedings consistent with this opinion.

General Criminal Defenses
Defenses Negating Intent

Many defenses raised in a criminal case are aimed at negating the *mens rea* element by showing that the defendant did not intend to commit a crime. Several such defenses exist. We will learn in Chapter 15 that many of these concepts also provide grounds for escaping contractual obligations.

Infancy

The common-law rule was that children younger than seven years were *conclusively* presumed to be incapable of forming criminal intent. Children between seven and fourteen years were accorded the same presumption but in a *rebuttable* form. The presumption could be overcome by proof that the child understood the wrongful nature of his or her act. Many states still follow these basic notions in their criminal statutes. However, virtually all states have created juvenile courts, which treat juveniles as delinquents rather than criminals with the purpose of reforming rather than punishing them. Therefore, infancy as a criminal defense is not as important as it once was, although prosecutors usually have the option of attempting to convince a court to try a juvenile as an adult when a particularly heinous crime has been committed.

Insanity

There are several approaches, none satisfactory, to handling defendants who "plead insanity." Some states use the *M'Naghten* test, which excuses a defendant whose mental defect renders him or her incapable of appreciating the difference between right and wrong. Others excuse defendants who may appreciate the difference between right and wrong but who suffer a mental defect causing an "irresistible impulse" to commit the crime. The District of Columbia courts developed the *Durham* rule, which simply asks whether the defendant was insane at the time of the crime and, if so, whether the crime was a product of that insanity. Finally, the Model Penal Code provides that a defendant "is not responsible for criminal conduct if at the time of such conduct as a result of a mental disease or defect he lacks substantial capacity either to appreciate the wrongfulness of his conduct or to conform his conduct to the requirements of the law." In whatever form, the insanity defense seldom succeeds.

Intoxication

If a person *voluntarily* becomes intoxicated (or "high" on drugs), the general rule is that this may negate specific intent but will not negate general intent, as discussed above. Voluntary intoxication is generally no defense to crimes requiring mere negligence or recklessness.

In voluntary intoxication, however, is generally treated as equivalent to insanity. Thus, if a defendant unforeseeably became intoxicated because of an unusual reaction to prescribed medication, courts would be reluctant to hold him or her responsible for crimes he or she might commit under the influence of that medication.

Duress

Occasionally, persons will be forced to commit crimes against their will. When the wrongful threat of others causes a person to commit a crime, mens rea is negated. Duress is generally shown when an immediate and inescapable threat of serious bodily injury or death (that is greater than the harm to be caused by the crime) forces a person to commit a crime that he or she does not wish to commit. The threat must come through no fault of the defendant's. If, for example, a defendant voluntarily joins a criminal gang, he or she has no duress defense if the gang leader forces him or her to help in one of the gang's planned crimes.

Mistake

Because ignorance of the law is no excuse, a *mistake of law* is generally no defense to a criminal charge. Thus, a defendant who has intentionally performed a specific act cannot usually defend by saying: "I didn't know that it was illegal," or even "My attorney told me that it was okay." The courts' refusal to hold an attorney's advice to be a valid defense discourages "attorney shopping." However, many courts will find that a mistake of law negates the intent element if (1) the law was not reasonably made known to the public, or (2) the defendant reasonably relied on an erroneous but official statement of the law (such as in a judicial opinion or administrative order).

A defense based on *mistake of fact* is more likely to succeed. Thus, a defendant charged with stealing a blue 12-speed bicycle might successfully defend by showing that he or she owned an identical blue 12- speed bicycle parked at the next rack and mistakenly rode off on the wrong one.

Other Defenses

Entrapment

Police undercover work is often aimed at catching criminals "in the act." If the police not only create an opportunity for a criminal act but also persuade the defendant to commit a crime that he or she would not otherwise have committed, the defendant may have a good **entrapment** defense. The entrapment defense presents difficult factual questions, for the court must draw the line between an unwary innocent and an unwary criminal. The key issue is whether the defendant was *predisposed* to commit the crime. That is, the criminal idea must originate with the defendant, not with the police officer. The Supreme Court has held that entrapment results "[w] hen the criminal design originates with the [police who] implant in the mind of an innocent person the disposition to commit the alleged offense and induce its commission in order that they may prosecute." Sorrells v. United States, 287 U.S. 435 (1932). This standard is applied to the following recent case.

JACOBSON v. UNITED STATES
U.S. Supreme Court, 503 U.S. 540 (1992)

Petitioner Jacobson ordered two "Bare Boys" magazines containing photos of nude preteen and teenage boys at a time when it was legal to do so. Later, the Child Protection Act of 1984 made it illegal to receive through the mails sexually explicit depictions of children. Noticing Jacobson's name on the bookstore mailing list, two government agencies sent mail to him through five fictitious organizations and a bogus pen pal in order to explore his willingness to break the new law. The organizations purported to promote sexual freedom, freedom of choice, and free speech. Jacobson responded to some of the letters. After two and a half years on the government mailing list, Jacobson was solicited to order child pornography. He answered a letter that described concern about child pornography as hysterical nonsense and condemned international censorship, and then received a catalog and ordered a magazine depicting young boys, engaged in sexual activities. Jacobson was arrested; a search of his house found no materials other than those sent by the government.

Jacobson was convicted and his conviction was affirmed, despite his entrapment defense. He then petitioned the Supreme Court for review.

White, Justice:

In their zeal to enforce the law, . . . Government agents may not originate a criminal design, implant in an innocent person's mind the disposition to commit a criminal act, and then induce commission of the crime so that the Government may prosecute. Sorrells v. United States, 287 U.S. 435, 442 (1932). Where the Government has induced an individual to break the law and the defense of entrapment is at issue, as it was in this case, the prosecution must prove beyond reasonable doubt that the defendant was disposed to commit the criminal act prior to first being approached by Government agents.

Thus, an agent deployed to stop the traffic in illegal drugs may offer the opportunity to buy or sell drugs, and, if the offer is accepted, make an arrest on the spot or later. In such a typical case, or in a more elaborate "sting" operation involving Government-sponsored fencing where the defendant is simply provided with the opportunity to commit a crime, the entrapment defense is of little use because the ready commission of the criminal act amply demonstrates the defendant's predisposition. Had the agents in this case simply offered petitioner the opportunity to order child pornography through the mails, and petitioner— who must be presumed to know the law—had promptly availed himself of this criminal opportunity, it is unlikely that his entrapment defense would have warranted a jury instruction.

But that is not what happened here. By the time petitioner finally placed his order, he had already been the target of 26 months of repeated mailings and communications from Government agents and fictitious organizations

Therefore, although he had become predisposed to break the law by May 1987, it is our view that the Government did not prove that this predisposition was independent and not the product of the attention that the Government had directed at petitioner since January 1955.

[The fact that petitioner had previously ordered such magazines does not indicate a predisposition to act illegally because] petitioner was acting within the law at the time he received [those] magazines . . . When the Government's quest for convictions leads to the apprehension of an otherwise law-abiding citizen who, if left to his own devices, likely would have never run afoul of the law, the courts should intervene [Reversed.]

Self-Defense

Self-defense and defense of others may justify acts of violence that otherwise would be criminal. Although the courts do not require "detached reflection in the presence of an uplifted knife," Brown v. United States, 256 U.S. 335 (1921), the general rule permits only that degree of force reasonable under the circumstances. Deadly force can be used if the defendant has a reasonable belief that imminent death or grievous bodily injury will otherwise result. The law does not allow one to shoot an assailant in the back once that assailant is clearly fleeing and poses no further threat. In some cases, retreat might even be required as preferable to deadly force. Non-deadly force can be used in the degree reasonably believed necessary to protect persons or property from criminal acts, although obviously, a lesser degree of force will be viewed as "reasonable" in defense of property.

Immunity

Through the process of *plea bargaining,* defendants often agree to testify against other criminals in return for consideration at time of sentencing and perhaps **immunity** from prosecution of certain potential charges. It is often said that such persons are "turning state's evidence" to help the prosecutor's case.

State Crimes Affecting Business

So many crimes against persons and property are contained in state criminal codes that it would be impossible to list them all. Furthermore, there is such variation from state to state that it is difficult to generalize about criminal law. Nonetheless, this section briefly describes a few of the more common crimes against businesses.

Theft

Many state statutes criminalize the unlawful taking of another's property under a general statute that often terms the crime "theft." Such statutes consolidate a variety of related crimes that developed separately at the common law, such as larceny, burglary, false pretenses, and embezzlement.

Larceny

At common law, **larceny** was the trespassory taking away of the personal property of another with wrongful intent permanently to deprive that person of the use of the property. Larceny is viewed as an injury to the owner's interest in possessing the goods. Shoplifting is a good example. Promising to sell someone your car, taking the money, and then refusing to turn over the car is not larceny, because there is no wrongful taking. The concept of personal property generally does not include trees or personal services but would include computer programs and trade secrets.

There are degrees of larceny. Petit larceny covers theft of smaller amounts (for example, less than $500). Thefts of property worth more would be grand larceny. These statutory distinctions vary in amount from state to state.

Burglary

At common law, **burglary** was the trespassory breaking and entering of the dwelling house of another during the nighttime with intent to commit a felony. Over time, many of the technical requirements have been dropped. Now, most statutes would find burglary even though the building broken into was not a dwelling house and even though it occurred during the day. Burglary with use of a weapon is called aggravated burglary.

False Pretenses

Obtaining goods by **false pretenses** was defined by the common law as obtaining title to someone else's property by knowingly or recklessly making a false representation of existing material fact that is intended to and does defraud the victim into parting with his or her property. Technically, false pretenses is an injury to title, not mere possession. Title passes to the thief, quite unlike larceny. Examples of such conduct are the filing of false claims with insurance companies, the buying of a VCR with a check the purchaser knows will "bounce," and the taking of buyers' money for goods or services with no intent of delivering such goods or services.

Embezzlement

A wholly statutory offense, **embezzlement** is the fraudulent conversion of the property of another by one who has lawful possession of it. This crime somewhat overlaps with larceny, but the original possession by the wrongdoer is lawful. An example is an attorney who receives funds from a client for payment of a settlement but later decides to spend the money on her- or himself instead.

Some of the key elements of an embezzlement charge are discussed in the following case.

STATE v. JOY
Supreme Court of Vermont, 549 A.2d 1033 (1988)

Defendant Joy was president and sole shareholder of Credit Management Services (CMS), a debt collection agency that collected delinquent accounts for businesses in exchange for 40 percent of the amount collected. CMS was entitled to this percentage regardless of whether the debtor paid CMS or settled with the client directly. When CMS received a payment from a debtor, it would deposit the money with the Barre bank, and within a month an invoice detailing the transaction would be sent to the client. If monies were due the client, a check would accompany the invoice. In addition, CMS maintained an account with a Montpelier bank from which it drew operating expenses.

In early 1981, CMS, suffering financial difficulties, began transferring funds from the

Barre account to the Montpelier account to cover its operating expenses. In June 1981, CMS was hired by Stacey Fuel to collect several delinquent accounts. On August 14, CMS received a check from one of Stacey's debtors in the amount of $1,920.25. CMS never forwarded any of this money to Stacey, nor did it inform Stacey that the money had been received. Stacey ended its relationship with CMS in August 1982 and only later learned that CMS had filed for bankruptcy and had listed Stacey as one of its creditors.

Joy was convicted of embezzlement and appealed.

Dooley, Justice:
In his first claim on appeal, defendant suggests that the trial court improperly refused to

charge the jury that "[t]he mere fact that C.M.S. Corporation failed or was unable to pay its creditors is not a sufficient showing of intent to justify conviction [of embezzlement]."

Defendant's main objection to the charge is that it failed to state that the jury could consider intent to repay as evidence that the defendant had no fraudulent intent. The elements of embezzlement are detailed in 13 V.S.A. § 2531, which states in pertinent part that:

An officer, agent, bailee for hire, clerk or servant of a banking association or an incorporated company... who embezzles or fraudulently converts to his own use, or takes or secretes with intent to embezzle or fraudulently convert to his own use, money or other property which comes into his possession or is under his own care by virtue of such employment, notwithstanding he may have an interest in such property, shall be guilty of embezzlement....

The law is clear that intent to repay is not a defense to embezzlement under a statute like ours. *See, e.g.,* 3 Wharton's Criminal Law § 397, at 405-07(14th ed. 1980). Further, the proposition that defendant's intent to repay should have been considered by the jury in its determination of whether or not he possessed the necessary mens rea is inconsistent with the state of the law. A leading authority on criminal law has observed that "[g]iven a fraudulent appropriation or conversion, an embezzlement is committed even if the defendant intends at some subsequent time to return the property or to make restitution to the owner." 3 Wharton's Criminal Law § 397, at 405-06.

The rationale for this rule was stated by the Pennsylvania Supreme Court in Commonwealth v. Bovaird:

Where one is charged with embezzlement or fraudulent conversion, the intention to abstract the money and appropriate it to his own use has been fully executed upon its wrongful taking; the ability and intention to indemnify the party from whom it has been withdrawn remains unexecuted, and such intention, even if conscientiously entertained, may become impossible of fulfillment. The crime is consummated when the money is intentionally and wrongfully converted, temporarily or permanently, to the defendant's own use.

The trial judge properly charged the elements of the offense of embezzlement. Regarding intent, the judge stressed that "there must be a fraudulent intent and the State must prove fraudulent intent beyond a reasonable doubt." And the court properly noted that "the intent to embezzle is a state of mind which can be shown by words or conduct."

Defendant also argues that the trial court erred by not instructing the jury that a mere inability or failure to pay creditors is not sufficient to demonstrate the fraudulent intent necessary for the crime of embezzlement. For the same reasons that intent to repay is not relevant to the existence of fraudulent intent, neither is the ability or inability to repay. Moreover, the charge urged by the defendant misstates the facts of this case and mischaracterizes his relationship with Stacey.

There is no question that "[in] a debtor-creditor relation, the debtor's failure to pay the creditor does not constitute embezzlement." 3 Wharton's Criminal Law § 402, at 417. However, defendant's relationship with Stacey was not that of debtor-creditor, but rather it was one of agent and principal. We are satisfied that the facts and circumstances of this case support defendant's status as an agent of Stacey. The trial court instructed the jury that an agency relationship was critical to the offense charged and that the State was burdened with proving beyond a reasonable doubt that such relationship existed. The court also instructed that "[a] debtor-creditor relationship alone is insufficient to create an agency relationship." The evidence supports a finding of an agency relationship, and the jury so found. Moreover, on appeal, defendant does not argue that he was anything other than an agent of Stacey.

As an agent, rather than a debtor, of Stacey, defendant was obligated to hold and remit to Stacey its percentage of any amounts collected. Given the existence of an agency relationship— as found by the jury—defendant's conversion of the money credited to Stacey's account was precisely the activity prohibited by the embezzlement statute.

[Affirmed.]

Specialized Statutes

The common-law classifications and general theft statutes have been supplemented by a variety of more specific laws aimed at the same types of conduct. For example, although obtaining money or property by the giving of a bad check would constitute false pretenses or general theft, all states have specific statutes relating to the issuance of bad checks, which impose criminal liability on persons who, with intent to defraud, issue or transfer checks or other negotiable instruments knowing that they will be dishonored. Such knowledge is presumed to exist, under the typical statute, if the drawer had no account with the drawee bank when the check was issued, or if the check was refused payment because of insufficient funds in the drawer's account when it was presented to the bank for payment. Similarly, most states have separate statutes relating to a number of special offenses, such as the setting back of automobile odometers with the intent to defraud and the knowing delivery of "short weights"—the charging of buyers for quantities of goods that are greater than the quantities that were actually delivered.

Robbery

Robbery is stealing from a person or in his or her presence by use of force or threat of force. It is, essentially, a form of larceny but the extra element of force makes it a more serious offense. Removing someone's earring by stealth would be larceny; ripping it from the victim's earlobe would be robbery. Use of a weapon escalates the crime to aggravated robbery.

Forgery

Forgery is the false making or altering of a legally significant instrument (such as a check, credit card, deed, passport, mortgage, or security) with the intent to defraud. Writing an insufficient funds check is not forgery, although it may constitute false pretenses or violate a state bad check law. But changing the true payee's name as written on a check to your own and cashing the check is certainly forgery.

Forgery is a crime with roots deep in the common law, but changing technologies can challenge traditional rules, as the following case illustrates.

PEOPLE V. AVILA
Colorado Court of Appeals, 770 P.2d 1330 (1988)

For fees of between $1500 and $3000, Avila, a lawyer, altered the driver records of his clients whose driver's licenses were under revocation for alcohol-related offenses. Avila would instruct his contact in the Motor Vehicle Division (MVD) Office, who had access to the data base where the driving records were maintained on computer disk, to delete the clients' records. The client would later apply for a driver's license, stating that he had no previous driver's license, which the altered computer records would verify. Avila was convicted of two counts of second degree forgery. He appealed.

Van Cise, Judge:

Initially, we note that much of Avila's argument relies on the assertion that forgery cannot be committed on a computer. We reject that contention.

A forgery can be made by any number of artificial means. Indeed, "whether [the forgery] is made with the pen, with a brush[,] . . . with any other instrument, or by any other device whatever; whether it is in characters which stand for words or in characters which stand for ideas. . . is quite immaterial. . ." Benson v. McMahon, 127 U.S. 457 (1888).

Avila also contends, in essence, that there was insufficient evidence to sustain his convictions. We disagree.

The elements of second degree forgery pertinent to this case are that (1) the defendant, (2) with intent to defraud, (3) falsely alters, (4) a written instrument, (5) which is or purported to be, or which is calculated to become or to represent if completed, a "written instrument officially issued or created by a public office, public servant, or government agency." Section 18-5-103(1)(c).

Avila contends that there was no written instrument in this case so the forgery conviction cannot stand. We disagree.

Section 18-5-101(9) defines "written instrument" as follows:

> Written instrument" means any paper, document, or other instrument containing written or printed matter or the equivalent thereof, used for purposes of reciting, embodying, conveying, or recording information . . . which is capable of being used to the advantage or disadvantage of some person. (Emphasis supplied.)

A fair reading of the statute indicates that a computer disc is included in the definition of a "written instrument."

Next, Avila contends that, since the driving records were deleted, the evidence at trial does not support the finding that he falsely altered a written instrument. He argues that "alter" means to change, while "delete" means to cause to vanish completely. Therefore, he claims he committed no forgery. We are not persuaded.

Section 18-5-101(2) states:

To "falsely alter" a written instrument means to change a written instrument without the authority of anyone entitled to grant such authority, whether it be in complete or incomplete form, by means of erasure, obliteration, deletion, insertion of new matter, transposition of matter, or any other means, so that such instrument in its thus altered form falsely appears or purports to be in all respects an authentic creation of or fully authorized by its ostensible maker.

The record shows that the driving records of two of Avila's clients were deleted so that instead of containing their history of driving violations, the computer found no driving records and thus would display the message "no record found."

Under the plain language of the statute, Avila's actions constituted a false alteration within the meaning of 18-5-101(2).

Next, Avila asserts that there is a distinction between a document falsely made and a genuine document that contains false information. Based on this distinction, he contends that the written instruments were not false but rather were genuine MVD documents which contained false information and, as such, they cannot form the basis for a forgery conviction. We disagree.

In DeRose v. People, 64 Colo. 332, 171 P. 359(1918), the court held that a false statement of fact in an instrument which is genuine is not forgery. It stated:

This writing is what it purports to be—a true and genuine instrument, although it contains false statements. It is not a false paper, and the execution of such a document does not constitute forgery.

In *DeRose*, defendant was a railroad foreman whose job was to draft and submit the time rolls for his men. He was charged with forgery because he credited one of his men with more days than the man had worked. Because the defendant was authorized to draft and submit the time roll, the court found that the document was not "falsely made." It was a genuine railroad time roll prepared by one authorized to do so, but which contained false information.

In *DeRose* the defendant had the authority to perform the general act that led to the production of the document containing the false information. In contrast, in the instant case, testimony showed that Avila's confederate at the MVD had no authority to delete driver histories. Therefore, under *DeRose*, the documents were forged.

[Affirmed.]

Arson

At common law, **arson** was the malicious burning of the dwelling house of another. Today, the building burned need not be a dwelling house. And, as all too commonly occurs, people who burn their own house (or other building or personal property) for purposes of defrauding an insurance company are almost certainly violating a state criminal statute prohibiting such fraud.

Federal Crimes Affecting Business

As with state crimes, there are so many federal criminal statutes that it would be impossible to list them all. Many have been passed in response to perceived crises. In the era of the giant trusts in the late 1800s, Congress passed many antitrust laws, including some carrying criminal penalties (discussed in Chapter 28). In the wake of the Watergate scandal in the early 1970s, investigation disclosed widespread bribery of foreign officials by U.S. companies, leading to enactment of the Foreign Corrupt Practices Act (discussed in Chapter 26). After the Ivan Boesky case and other insider trading scandals in the late 1980s, Congress increased the criminal penalties for that fraudulent activity (also discussed in Chapter 26). Congress responded to the savings and loan scandal of the 1980s by enacting criminal penalties to punish several types of fraudulent activity that had necessitated a multi-billion dollar taxpayer bailout of savings & loans (see the Financial

Institutions Reform, Recovery, and Enforcement Act of 1989). Instead of trying to list all such federal criminal statutes, we will briefly address a few of the more general ones.

Mail and Wire Fraud

Two very general federal statutes punish **mail fraud** (use of the mails to defraud or swindle) and **wire fraud** (similar use of telephone, telegraph, radio, or television). The typical mail or wire fraud case would involve use of the mails or telephones to make false representations to sell products or securities. For example, the mail fraud law has been used to punish fraudulent representations in the use of the mails to advertise such articles as hair-growing products that proved to be worthless, retrofit carburetors that totally failed to improve automobile fuel economy, and false identification cards that the sellers knew were ordered by purchasers for the purpose of deceiving third parties. Similarly, schemes for the operation of "mail-order" schools, where degrees or diplomas are awarded "without requiring evidence of education or experience entitled thereto," and where the operators know such documents are likely to be used by purchasers to misrepresent their qualifications to prospective employers, violate these sections of the law. However, the statutes have been construed to cover a wide variety of factual situations.

For example, in Carpenter v. United States, 484 U.S. 19 (1987), a Wall Street Journal reporter tipped material nonpublic information (the contents of his columns that were about to be published) to confederates who profitably traded on it. Although the Supreme Court split 4-4 regarding the specific insider trading theory offered by the prosecution, it unanimously affirmed the defendant's conviction for mail and wire fraud. The fraudulent scheme's connection to the mails and wire services used to distribute the newspaper was deemed sufficient to support the conviction.

In the following case the Supreme Court dealt with a difficult mail fraud issue.

SCHMUCK V. UNITED STATES
U.S. Supreme Court, 489 U.S. 705 (1989)

Petitioner Schmuck, a used-car distributor, purchased used cars, rolled back their odometers, and then sold the automobiles to Wisconsin retail dealers for prices artificially inflated because of the low mileage readings. These unwitting car dealers, relying on the altered odometer figures, then resold the cars to customers, who in turn paid prices reflecting Schmuck's fraud. To complete the resale of each car, the dealer who bought it from Schmuck would submit a title-application form to the Wisconsin Department of

Transportation on behalf of the retail customer. The receipt of a Wisconsin title was a legal prerequisite for transferring title and obtaining car tags.

Schmuck was convicted on 12 counts of mail fraud. He appealed, alleging that the mailings that were the crux of the indictment—the submissions of the title-application forms by the auto dealers—were not in furtherance of the fraudulent scheme and, thus, did not satisfy the mailing element of the crime of mail fraud. The circuit court rejected Schmuck's claim but reversed on other grounds. The Supreme Court granted certiorari to resolve both issues. (The following excerpt addresses only the mail fraud issue.)

Blackmun, Justice:

"The federal mail fraud statute does not purport to reach all frauds, but only those limited instances in which the use of the mails is a part of the execution of the fraud, leaving all other cases to be dealt with by appropriate state law." Kann v. United States, 323 U.S. 88, 95 (1944). To be part of the execution of the fraud, however, the use of the mails need not be an essential element of the scheme. Pereira v. United States, 347 U.S. 1, 8 (1954). It is sufficient for the mailing to be "incident to an essential part of the scheme," or "a step in [the] plot." Badders v. United States, 240 U.S. 391, 394 (1916).

Schmuck argues that mail fraud can be predicated only on a mailing that affirmatively assists the perpetrator in carrying out his fraudulent scheme. The mailing element of the offense, he contends, cannot be satisfied by a mailing, such as those at issue here, that is routine and innocent in and of itself, and that, far from furthering the execution of the fraud, occurs after the fraud has come to fruition, is merely tangentially related to the fraud, and is counterproductive in that it creates a "paper trail" from which the fraud may be discovered. We disagree both with this characterization of the mailings in the present case and with this description of the applicable law.

We begin by considering the scope of Schmuck's fraudulent scheme. Schmuck was charged with devising and executing a scheme to defraud Wisconsin retail automobile customers who based their decisions to purchase certain automobiles at least in part on the low-mileage readings provided by the tampered odometers. This was a fairly large-scale operation. Evidence at trial indicated that Schmuck had employed a man known only as "Fred" to turn back the odometers on about 150 different cars. Schmuck then marketed these cars to a number of dealers, several of whom he dealt with on a consistent basis over a period of about 15 years. Thus, Schmuck's was not a "one-shot" operation in which he sold a single car to an isolated dealer. His was an ongoing fraudulent venture. A rational jury could have concluded that the success of Schmuck's venture depended upon his continued harmonious relations with and good reputation among retail dealers, which in turn required the smooth flow of cars from the dealers to their Wisconsin customers.

Under these circumstances, we believe that a rational jury could have found that the title-registration mailings were part of the execution of the fraudulent scheme, a scheme which did not reach fruition until the retail dealers resold the cars and effected transfers of title. Schmuck's scheme would have come to an abrupt halt if the dealers either had lost faith in Schmuck or had not been able to resell the cars obtained from him. These resales and Schmuck's relationships with the retail dealers naturally depended on the successful passage of title among the various parties. Thus, although the registration-form mailings may not have contributed directly to the duping of either the retail dealers or the customers, they were necessary to the passage of title, which in turn was essential to the perpetuation of Schmuck's scheme. As noted earlier, a mailing that is "incident to an essential part of the scheme," Pereira, 347 U.S., at 8, satisfies the mailing element of the mail fraud offense. The mailings here fit this description. See, e.g., United States v. Locklear, 829 F.2d 1314, 1318-1319 (CA4 1987) (retail customers obtaining title documents through the mail furthers execution of wholesaler's odometer tampering scheme).

Once the full flavor of Schmuck's scheme is appreciated the critical distinctions between this case and the three cases in which this Court has delimited the reach of the mail fraud statute— Kann, Parr, and Maze—are readily apparent. In other cases, the Court has found the elements of mail fraud to be satisfied where the mailings have been routine.

We also reject Schmuck's contention that mailings that someday may contribute to the uncovering of a fraudulent scheme cannot supply the mailing element of the mail fraud offense. The relevant question at all times is whether the mailing is part of the execution of the scheme as conceived by the perpetrator at the time, regardless of whether the mailing later, through hindsight, may prove to have been counterproductive and return to haunt the perpetrator of the fraud. The mail fraud statute includes no guarantee that the use of the mails for the purpose of executing a fraudulent scheme will be risk free. Those who use the mails to defraud proceed at their peril.

For these reasons, we agree with the Court of Appeals that the mailings in this case satisfy the mailing element of the mail fraud offenses.

Travel Act

Section 1952 of Title 18 of the *United States Code* is called the Travel Act. It punishes anyone who travels in interstate or foreign commerce or uses any facility in such commerce to (1) distribute the proceeds of illegal activity, (2) commit any crime of violence or further any unlawful activity, or (3) promote, manage, establish, carry on, or facilitate any unlawful activity. Obviously, this is a very broad act that federalizes all sorts of traditionally state crimes. The "interstate commerce" element can be met by simply mailing a letter or using a telephone, for these are instrumentalities of interstate commerce. The Act has been used, for example, to convict a city electrical inspector who took bribes from private electrical contractors to overlook code violations and to facilitate departmental paperwork even though all the letters mailed by the defendant stayed in one state. The mail is a facility of interstate commerce because it can be used to send letters from state to state.

Hobbs Act

The Hobbs Act, 18 U.S.C. Sec. 951, punishes anyone who "in any way or degree obstructs, delays, or affects commerce or the movement of any article or commodity in commerce, by robbery or extortion...." This law punishes extortion (obtaining money or something else of value by use of violence or threat of violence) but not merely accepting bribes. The distinction between the two can be difficult to draw but has been characterized as the difference between "pay me and be assisted" (commercial bribery) and "pay me or be precluded" (extortion).

Because the law punishes those who "in any way" affect commerce, the reach of the federal statute is very broad. In one case, a county sheriff who extorted bribes to protect gamblers and prostitutes was convicted under the Hobbs Act after he solicited payments from an FBI undercover bookie operation. The court held that because the FBI operation bought furniture, paper, food, and natural gas and could have bought more had it not given money to the defendant, interstate commerce was affected. United States v. Frasch, 818 F.2d 631(7th Cir. 1987).

Racketeer Influenced and Corrupt Organizations Act

In 1970 Congress passed the Racketeer Influenced and Corrupt Organizations Act (RICO) to attack organized crime, especially its infiltration into legitimate business. RICO is an unusual criminal statute in that it expressly contains parallel civil provisions. In other words, it provides for both criminal penalties and private civil suits for damages. However, RICO neither included a definition of "organized crime" nor expressly required a link between a defendant's activities and organized crime. Therefore, about nine-tenths of the civil suits and many of the criminal prosecutions brought under RICO have had no connection with professional criminals (as thought of in the common sense) but have, instead, named as defendants accounting firms, banks, law firms, manufacturing corporations, anti-abortion protestors, and a wide variety of others.

Fortunately, most of the criminal prosecutions brought under RICO have attacked the more traditional manifestations of organized crime. Prosecutors have secured RICO criminal convictions in cases involving marijuana smuggling, kickbacks to judges, extortion of "protection money" by police officers loan sharking, gambling, and the like. However, even in criminal prosecutions the government has occasionally pushed RICO to its limits by prosecuting actions in circumstances it is difficult to believe Congress had in mind when passing RICO.

Computer Crime

The explosive growth of the use of computers in the business world in the past few years has brought with it a corresponding increase in computer misuse. The *Avila* forgery case mentioned earlier in this chapter is a good example. Burgeoning computer crime and corresponding government responses justify separate discussion of the area of computer crime. Traditional (precomputer) state and federal laws applicable to such crimes as larceny are not necessarily appropriate for prosecution of cases of computer fraud and computer theft. For example, some cases held that an employee's unauthorized use of his or her employer's computer facilities in private ventures could not support a theft conviction because the employer had not been deprived of any part of value or use of the computer. Other cases have held that use of a computer is not "property" within traditional theft statutes.

Computer crimes fall mainly into three broad categories: unauthorized access, theft of information, and theft of funds. Among schemes that have been subject to prosecution are (1) stealing a competitor's computer program, (2) paying an accomplice to delete adverse information and insert favorable false information into the defendant's credit file, (3) a bank president's having his or her ccount computer coded so that his or her checks would be remoed and held rather than posted so he or she could later remove the actual checks without their bein debited, (4) a disgruntled exemployee's inserting a "virus" into his former employers computer to destroy its records, and (5) three computer "hackers" foray into the forbidden recesses of computers that run BellSouth Corporation's phone network.

Computer crime costs business an estimated $70 billion or so per year. (including thefts of funds, losses of computer programs and data, losses of trade secrets, and damage to computer hardware). Furthermore, a substantial amount of computer crime is never discovered, and a high percentage of that which is discovered is never reported because (1) companies do not want publicity about the inadequacy of their computer controls and (2) financial institutions such as banks and savings and loans fear that reports of large losses of funds, even when insured, are likely to cause customers to withdraw their deposits.

Whatever the actual loss caused by computer misuse, both Congress and the state legislators have passed statutes to deal specifically with computer crime.

Federal Laws

Although there have been convictions for computer crimes under general federal statutes—such as those dealing with wire fraud, theft, and misappropriation, Congress has enacted laws aiming specifically at criminal activity involving computers. For example, the Comprehensive Crime Control Act of 1984 contained a section on the use of computers in credit card fraud and established penalties for violation. The Electronic Communications Privacy Act of 1986 updated federal rules against intercepting wire and electronic communications (formerly known as "wiretapping") to cover e-mails, encrypted satellite-transmitted television broadcasts, cable television signals, and other electronic communications. The Child Pornography Prevention Act of 1996 criminalized the production and distribution of computer-generated, sexual images of children.

The most important federal statute in this area may be the Access Device and Computer Fraud and Abuse Act of 1984, which has been amended several times (most importantly by the National Information Infrastructure Protection Act of 1996). This act protects any computer attached to the Internet (even if all the computers involved are located in the same state). The current version of the law makes it a crime to (a) access computer files without authority and subsequently to transmit classified government information; (b) access without authority information from financial institutions, the U.S. government, or (importantly) private sector computers used in interstate commerce; (c) intentionally access a U.S. department or agency nonpublic computer without authorization in such a way as to affect the government's use of the computer; (d) access a protected computer, without or beyond authorization, with the intent to defraud and obtain something of value; (e) cause damage in one of several forms (e.g., sending damaging viruses) by computer hacking; (f) knowingly and with intent to defraud traffic in passwords which would permit unauthorized access to a government computer or affect interstate or foreign commerce; and (g) transmit in interstate or foreign commerce any threat to cause damage to a protected computer with intent to extort something of value.

The Computer Fraud and Abuse Act has been used to punish hackers who sent out worm viruses to crash computers and who broke into company data bases and deleted information. A spammer who inundated a company with thousands of e-mail messages, forcing it to shut down its computers, was also convicted under the CFAA. The following case represents another application.

EF Cultural Travel BV v. Explorica
U.S. Court of Appeals, First Circuit, 274 F.3d 577 (2001)

Plaintiff EF and Defendant Explorica are competitors in the student travel business. Explorica was founded by former EF employees (including Gormley) who aimed to compete in part by copying EF's prices from EF's Web site and setting Explorica's own prices slightly lower. EFs Web site permits a visitor to the site to search its tour databases and view the prices for tours meeting specified criteria such as gateway (e.g., departure) cities, destination cities, and tour destination. In June 2000, Explorica hired Zefer to build a scraper tool that could scrape" the prices from EFs Web site and download them into an Excel spreadsheet. A scraper, also called a "robot" or "ot,"is nothing more than a computer program that accesses information contained in a succession of Web pages stored on the accessed computer. Strictly speaking, the accessed information is not the graphical interface seen by the user but rather the HTML source code– available to anyone who views the site– that generates the graphical interface. This information is then downloaded to the user's computer. The scraper program used in this case was not designed to copy all of the information on the accessed pages (e.g., the descriptions of the tours), but rather only the price for each tour through each possible gateway city.

Zefer built a scraper tool that scraped two years of pricing data from EF's Web site. After receiving the pricing data from Zefer, Explorica set its own prices for the public, undercutting EF's prices an average of five percent. EF discovered Explorica's use of the scraper tool and filed suit against Explorica, some of its employees, and Zefer, alleging, among other things, violations of various provisions of the CFAA. The trial court granted EF a prelimi-nary injunction based on one provision of the CFAA, ruling that the use of the scraper tool went beyond the "reasonable expectations" of ordinary users. The defendants appealed.

Coffin, Circuit Judge:

Although appellees alleged violations of three provisions of the CFAA, the district court found that they were likely to succeed only under section 1030(a)(4). That section provides that "[Whoever] knowingly and with intent to defraud, accesses a protected computer without authorization, or exceeds authorized access, and by means of such conduct furthers the intended fraud and obtains anything of value... shall be punished...."

Appellees allege that the appellants knowingly and with intent to defraud accessed the server hosting EF's Web site more than 30,000 times to obtain proprietary pricing and tour information, and confidential information about appellees' technical abilities. [Because defendants did not argue in the trial court that they lacked intent to defraud, the key issue is] whether appellants' actions either were "without authorization" or "exceeded authorized access" as defined by the CFAA. We conclude that because of the broad confidentiality agreement appellants' actions "exceeded authorized access," and so we do not reach the more general arguments made about statutory meaning, including whether use of a scraper alone renders access unauthorized.

Congress defined "exceeds authorized access," as accessing "a computer with authorization and [using] such access to obtain or alter information in the computer that the accesser is not entitled so to obtain or alter." EF is likely to prove such excessive access based on the confidentiality agreement between defendant Gormley and EF. [In that standard nondisclosure agreement, Gormley agreed never to disclose to third parties or use for his own benefit EF's confidential or proprietary information.]

The record contains at least two communications from Gormley to Zefer seeming to rely on information about EF to which he was privy only because of his employment there. First, in an email to Zefer employee Joseph Alt exploring the use of a scraper, Gormley wrote: "might one of the team be able to write a program to automatically extract prices. . . ? I could work with him/her on the specification." Gormley also sent the following email to Zefer employee JohnHawley:

Here is a link to the page where you can grab EF's prices. There are two important drop down menus on the right.... With the lowest one you select one of about 150 tours. * * * You then select your origin gateway from a list of about 100 domestic gateways (middle drop down menu). When you select your origin gateway a page with a couple of tables comes up. One table has 1999-2000 prices and the other has 2000-2001 prices. * * * On a high speed connection it is possible to move quickly from one price table to the next by hitting backspace and then the down arrow.

This documentary evidence points to Gormley's heavy involvement in the conception of the scraper program. Furthermore, the voluminous spreadsheet containing all of the scraped information includes the tour codes, which EF claims are proprietary information. Each page of the spreadsheet produced by Zefer includes the tour and gateway codes, the date of travel, and the price for the tour. An uninformed reader would regard the tour codes as nothing but gibberish. Although the codes can be correlated to the actual tours and destination points, the codes standing alone need to be "translated" to be meaningful.

Explorica's wholesale use of EF's travel codes to facilitate gathering EF's prices from its Web site reeks of use—and, indeed, abuse—of proprietary information that goes beyond any authorized use of EF's Web site.

Gormley voluntarily entered a broad confidentiality agreement prohibiting his disclosure of any information "which might reasonably be construed to be contrary to the interests of EF." Appellants would face an uphill battle trying to argue that it was not against EF's interests for appellants to use the tour codes to mine EF's pricing data. If EF's allegations are proven, it will likely prove that whatever authorization Explorica had to navigate around EF's site (even in a competitive vein), it exceeded that authorization by providing proprietary information and know-how to Zefer to create the scraper.

[Affirmed.]

State Laws

Almost all states have passed laws dealing with computer crime. Most of the statutes comprehensively address the problem, outlawing (1) computer trespass (unauthorized access), (2) damage to computers or software (for example, use of "viruses"), (3) theft or misappropriation of computer services, and (4) obtaining or disseminating information by computer in an unauthorized manner.

White Collar Crime

The term **white collar crime** generally encompasses nonviolent acts by individuals or corporations to obtain a personal or business advantage in a commercial context. Many of the crimes discussed earlier in this chapter are examples of white collar crime. White collar crime has become an extremely controversial subject in recent years for at least two reasons. First, there is evidence that the economic losses caused by white collar crime are at a staggering level (often estimated at more than $100 billion annually) and growing rapidly. Second, there is a perception, based on substantial fact, that criminal penalties for white collar crimes costing the public millions of dollars are often much less severe than criminal penalties imposed on the average street hood who steals a $75 pair of shoes.

Traditional criminal law did not punish corporations for crimes, reasoning that because a corporation is an artificial entity, it could not form the intent required to supply *mens rea*, and it could not be punished by incarceration. Also American law was slow to punish corporate officials who committed crimes. One reason is illustrated by the oft-quoted sentiment of a federal judge who said that he would not "penalize a businessman trying to make a living when there are felons out on the street."

In recent years, however, the traditional views have changed rather dramatically. Potential criminal liability must now be a significant concern for both corporations and their officials.

Criminal Liability of Corporations

Today, most criminal statutes include corporations in their definition of "persons" who may violate the statute. The traditional reluctance to impose criminal sanctions on corporations has been overcome by modern reasoning that suggests (1) that the mens rea necessary to convict a corporation can be supplied by imputing the intent of the corporation's agents who physically commit the crimes to the corporation (as has long been done in the area of tort law), and (2) that corporations can be punished by fines and by innovative punishments that might, for example, require a corporation that has been caught polluting to fund an environmental education course at a local high school.

The general rule today is that corporations can be held criminally liable for any acts performed by an employee if that employee is acting within the scope of his or her authority for the purpose of benefitting the corporation. The basic idea is that the corporation receives the benefit when the agent acts properly and must bear the responsibility when the agent errs. This is simply an application of the respondeat superior doctrine (let the master answer for the wrongs of the agent) that is discussed in more detail in Chapter 24. The corporation can even be held liable when the agent is violating company policy or disobeying a specific order from a superior. Some jurisdictions refuse to hold the corporation criminally liable for crimes committed by lower-level employees, but many states find the corporation responsible no matter how far down the ladder the actual wrongdoer is.

Corporations have been indicted for homicide and a wide variety of lesser offenses, including health and safety violations arising out of toxic waste disposal, failure to remove asbestos from buildings, and construction-site accidents.

Federal sentencing guidelines contain provisions that apply specifically to corporate defendants. A sentencing judge now has the prerogative to place a corporation on probation in order to supervise it for a time to ensure that criminal activity is eradicated.

Fortunately for corporations, the suggested punishment structure is mitigated substantially if the defendant company has in place an "effective program to prevent and detect violations of law." The purpose of this mitigation factor is to induce corporations to "police their own" by establishing standards of conduct for employees and using various means to enforce those standards.

Criminal Liability of Corporate Officials

The increase in prosecutions of corporations has been matched by an increase in prosecutions of corporate officers as well. Corporate officers will definitely be held liable for criminal acts that they participate in or authorize. In addition, they will be held liable for acts that they aid and abet through any significant assistance or encouragement. Some courts find sufficient encouragement in mere acquiescence of a superior (which a subordinate may read as tacit approval) and even in failure to stop criminal activity that the official knows is occurring. In rare instances involving *strict liability* statutes, corporate officers have been held criminally liable because they failed to control the criminal acts of subordinates (even where they had no knowledge of the acts or had been assured that the acts had stopped). United States v. Park, 421 U.S. 658(1975).

Indicative of the trend toward increased criminal liability are some recent cases in which corporate officials have been tried for *murder* in the deaths of employees exposed to hazardous conditions in the work place. Additionally, federal laws have recently been enacted or beefed up to encourage criminal actions against individuals who engage in insider trading, environmental pollution, savings and loan fraud, defrauding of the Defense Department, and a host of other activities that have been in the news recently.

Sarbanes-Oxley Act of 2002

As an illustration of federal actions to stop white collar crime, consider that after the wave of corporate scandals involving Enron, Global Crossing, WorldCom, Adelphia, Tyco, HealthSouth, and other companies occurred in late 2001 and early 2002, Congress responded by passing the Sarbanes-Oxley Act (SOX). SOX had many non-criminal components: creation of the Public Company Accounting Oversight Board (PCAOB) to regulate public auditing firms, creation of new rules for auditor independence and corporate governance, institution of new rules to minimize conflicts of interest in Wall Street investment banking firms, SOX also included several provisions that either created new white collar crimes or stiffened penalties for old ones, including:

- Requiring CEOs and CFOs to certify their belief in the accuracy of their companies' quarterly and annual financial statements as well as the effectiveness of their companies' internal controls and punishing them criminally if they lie. The punishment is as much as a five million dollar fine and 20 years imprisonment.
- Addressing alteration of documents by adding two criminal provisions. The first punishes with a penalty of up to 20 years in prison the destruction, alteration, and falsification of records in federal investigations and bankruptcy. The second requires auditors who audit a reporting company to maintain all audit or review workpapers for 7 years and punishes willful noncompliance with a penalty of up to 10 years imprisonment.
- Mandating the United States Sentencing Commission to alter sentencing guidelines to enhance punishment in cases involving obstruction of justice or abuse of a position of trust.
- Adding a criminal securities fraud provision to Title 18 of the United States Code, the title that contains most federal criminal provisions. A similar provision was already contained in the portion of the U.S. Code that contains most securities laws. The punishment for that provision was increased to as much as 20 years in jail and/or a $2.5 million fine for individuals.
- Increasing the penalties for several existing criminal acts that are often related to securities fraud, including mail fraud, wire fraud, and ERISA violations
- Adding a new criminal provision punishing attempts and conspiracies to commit federal criminal fraud.
- Making it a crime to retaliate against an informant who provided truthful information relating to the commission of any Federal offense to law enforcement officers.

CHAPTER 8

THE LAW OF TORTS

A Preface

Two areas of law, criminal law and contract law, developed at an early time in England. Although both were intended to eliminate, insofar as possible, various kinds of wrongful conduct, each was concerned with markedly different wrongs. The major purposes of criminal law were to define wrongs against the state—types of conduct so inherently undesirable that they were flatly prohibited—and to permit the state to punish those who committed such acts by the imposition of fines or imprisonment. The major purposes of contract law, however, were (1) to spell out the nature of the rights and duties springing from *private agreements between individuals* and (2) in the event that one party failed to live up to these duties, to compensate the innocent party for the loss resulting from the other's breach of contract.

When criminal law and contract law were still in their initial stages of development, it became apparent that neither one afforded protection to the large numbers of persons who suffered losses resulting from other kinds of conduct equally unjustifiable from a social standpoint— acts of carelessness, deception, and the like. Faced with this situation, the courts at an early time began to recognize and define other "legal wrongs" besides crimes and breaches of contract—and began to permit persons who were injured thereby to bring civil actions to recover damages against those who committed them. Acts that came to be recognized as wrongs under these rules, which were formulated by judges over the years on a case–by–case basis, acquired the name of **torts** (the French word for *wrongs)*.

Because tort law applies to such a wide range of activities, any introductory definition of tort must necessarily be framed in general terms—as, for example, "any wrong excluding breaches of contract and crimes," or "any noncontractual civil wrong committed upon the person or property of another." Although such definitions are of little aid in illustrating the specific kinds of torts that are recognized, they do, at least, reflect the historic lines of demarcation between breaches of contract, crimes, and torts.

Scope and Complexity of Tort Law

As our society has become increasingly industrialized and complex, with many relationships existing among individuals that were perhaps unthought of 50 years ago, the legal duties owed by one member of society to others have become considerably more numerous and varied. As a result, tort law encompasses such a wide range of human conduct that the breaches of some duties have little in common with others. For example, some actions are considered tortious (wrongful) only when the actor intended to cause an injury, whereas in other actions— especially those involving negligence—the actor's intentions are immaterial. Similarly, in some tort actions the plaintiff is required to show physical injury to his or her property as a result of the defendant's misconduct, whereas in other actions such a showing is not required. In the latter situations other kinds of legal injury are recognized, such as damage to reputation or mental suffering.

A somewhat clearer picture of the broad sweep of tort law can be gained from the realization that the rules making up this area of law must deal with such diverse matters as the care required of a surgeon in the operating room, the circumstances in which a contracting party has a legal obligation to inform the other party of facts that he or she knows that the other party does not possess, and the determination of the kinds of business information (trade secrets) that are entitled to protection against theft by competitors.

The courts clearly engage in some degree of social engineering as they shape the common law of torts. Common to all successful tort actions are the twin concepts of *interest* and *duty*. Each time a court allows a plaintiff to receive damages for a tort committed by a defendant, it is saying that the plaintiff has an interest (for example, in bodily integrity, in enjoying the benefits of private property, in a good reputation, etc.) sufficiently important for the law to furnish protection and that, correspondingly, in a civilized society the defendant has a duty (for example, not to strike the plaintiff, not to steal the plaintiff's property, not to falsely injure the plaintiffs reputation, etc.) that was breached. As society evolves technologically, morally, philosophically, and otherwise, tort law evolves also. For example, 100 years ago, Americans had very little privacy. However, as increased wealth has allowed us to purchase and enjoy privacy, most of us have come to value privacy very much. In recent years most courts have come to recognize privacy as an interest worth protecting and, as we shall see, have imposed a duty on others not to invade our privacy.

The present chapter focuses primarily on the law of negligence and on selected intentional torts. At the end of the chapter, however, we also discuss two examples of so–called "business torts"—torts that arise directly from competitive rivalry. The law of torts is so broad and pervasive that it cannot be covered in a single chapter. For example, lawsuits arising out of the sale of defective products are also primarily tort–related; they are discussed in Chapter 21. In addition, Chapter 9 discusses intellectual property—trademarks, trade secrets, patents, and copyrights. Infringement of another's intellectual property is also a tort, and Chapter 9 is devoted to this area of the law.

Negligence

Negligence, to oversimplify, is carelessness. The courts long ago decided that our interests in economic well–being and personal safety are sufficiently important to be protected from the careless acts of others. Correspondingly, each of us has a duty as we live our lives and carry on our professions to exercise care not to injure others. Even though we may not intend to injure, the harm is just as real to the victim who is struck by the careless driver, burned by the carelessly designed product, crippled by the careless surgeon, or ruined financially by embezzlement that an accountant carelessly failed to detect.

The negligence cause of action is the most important method of redress existing today for persons injured accidentally. The newspapers are filled with accounts of negligence actions involving asbestos exposure, tobacco warnings, marketing of handguns, Firestone tires, and the like. Whether a plaintiff was injured by a careless driver, a careless product designer, a careless surgeon, or a careless accountant, the same basic elements must be proved to establish a right of recovery: (1) that the defendant owed the plaintiff a *duty* of due care, (2) that the defendant *breached* that duty of due care, (3) that the defendant's breach *proximately caused* the injury, and (4) that the plaintiff suffered injury.

Duty

Few concepts are more fraught with difficulty than that of "duty" in the negligence cause of action. As a general rule, it may be said that we each owe a duty to every person who we can *reasonably foresee* might be injured by our carelessness. If we drive down the street carelessly, pedestrians and other drivers are within the class of foreseeable plaintiffs we might injure. That we do not know the exact names of our prospective victims is unimportant.

To illustrate quickly, in Burke v. Pan American World Airways, Inc., 484 F.Supp. 850 (S.D.N.Y. 1980), the plaintiff sued the defendants allegedly responsible for a terrible plane collision in the Canary Islands, claiming that she, although in California at the time, felt as though she were being "split in two" and felt an emptiness "like a black hole" at the exact instant of the crash. The plaintiff claimed that in that instant she knew that something terrible had happened to her identical twin sister, who was, in fact, killed in the collision. The plaintiff was prepared to document the phenomenon of "extrasensory empathy" between some pairs of identical twins. Even assuming the plaintiff could establish the point, the court dismissed the suit. When a plane crashes because of an airline's negligence, its passengers are certainly foreseeable plaintiffs, as are any persons on the ground hit by falling wreckage. However, Burke's injuries were too bizarre to be reasonably foreseeable, even if she did sustain them. The defendants owed no legal duty to the plaintiff.

Although foreseeability is a very important consideration in establishing the parameters of a careless actor's duty, it is not the only one. The California courts, which have extended the notion of duty about as far as any jurisdiction, have taken into account such factors as (a) the foreseeability of harm to the plaintiff, (b) the degree of certainty that the plaintiff suffered injury, (c) the closeness of the connection between the defendant's conduct, (e) the policy of preventing future harm, (f) the extent of the burden to the defendant and consequences to the community of imposing a duty to exercise care with resulting liability, and (g) the availability, cost, and prevalence of insurance for the risk involved. Indeed, these are factors the court used in Soldano v. O'Daniels, a case discussed in Chapter 1, to impose a duty not to interfere with a Good Samaritan's attempt to aid a victim in distress.

The following case is just one illustration of a court's struggle to meld foreseeability and public policy factors to produce a proper scope of duty.

Otis Engineering Corp. v. Clark
Texas Supreme Court, 668 S.W. 2d 307 (1983)

Matheson, an employee of defendant Otis Engineering Corporation, had a history of being intoxicated on the job. One night he was particularly intoxicated, and his fellow employees believed he should be removed from the machines. Roy, Matheson's supervisor, suggested that Matheson go home, escorted him to the company parking lot, and asked him if he could make it home. Matheson answered that he could, but 30 minutes later and some three miles away he caused an accident killing the wives of plaintiffs Larry and Clifford Clark.

The Clarks sued Otis in a wrongful death action, but the trial court dismissed the suit, holding that Otis could not be liable because Matheson was not acting within the scope of his employment at the time of the accident. The intermediate court of appeals reversed, and Otis appealed to the Texas Supreme Court.

Kilgarlin, Justice:

The Clarks contend that under the facts in this case Otis sent home, in the middle of his shift, an employee whom it knew to be intoxicated. They aver this was an affirmative act which imposed a duty on Otis to act in a non−negligent manner.

In order to establish tort liability, a plaintiff must initially prove the existence and breach of a duty owed to him by the defendant. As a general rule, one person is under no duty to control the conduct of another, *Restatement (Second) of Torts* §315 (1965), even if he has the practical ability to exercise such control. Yet, certain relationships do impose, as a matter of law, certain duties upon parties. For instance, the master−servant relationship may give rise to a duty on the part of the master to control the conduct of his servants outside the scope of employment. This duty, however, is a narrow one.

Though the decisional law of this State has yet to address the precise issues presented by this case, factors which should be considered in determining whether the law should impose a duty are the risk, foreseeability, and likelihood of injury weighed against the social utility of the actor's conduct, the magnitude of the burden of guarding against the injury and consequences of placing that burden on the employer.

While a person is generally under no legal duty to come to the aid of another in distress, he is under a duty to avoid any affirmative action which might worsen the situation. One who voluntarily enters an affirmative course of action affecting the interests of another is regarded as assuming a duty to act and must do so with reasonable care.

Otis contends that, at worst, its conduct amounted to nonfeasance and under established law it owed no duty to the Clarks' respective wives. Traditional tort analysis has long drawn a distinction between action and inaction in defining the scope of duty. However, although courts have been slow to recognize liability for nonfeasance, "[d]uring the last century, liability for 'nonfeasance' has been extended still further to a limited group of relations, in which custom, public sentiment and views of social policy have led the courts to find a duty of affirmative action" W. Prosser, *The Law of Torts* at 339. Be that as it may, we do not view this as a case of employer nonfeasance.

What we must decide is if changing social standards and increasing complexities of human relationships in today's society justify imposing a duty upon an employer to act reasonably when he exercises control over his servants. Even though courts have been reluctant to hold an employer liable for the off-duty torts of an employee, "[a]s between an entirely innocent plaintiff and a defendant who admittedly has departed from the social standard of conduct, if only toward one individual, who should bear the loss?" W. Prosser, *supra*, at 257. Dean Prosser additionally observed that "[t]here is nothing sacred about 'duty,' which is nothing more than a word, and a very indefinite one with which we state our conclusion."

During this year, we have taken a step toward changing our concept of duty in premises cases. In Corbin v. Safeway Stores Inc., 648 S.W.2d 292 (Tex. 1983), we held that a store owner has a duty to guard against slips and falls if he has actual or constructive knowledge of a dangerous condition and it is foreseeable a fall would occur. Following Corbin, why should we be reluctant to impose a duty on Otis? As Dean Prosser has observed, "[c]hanging social conditions lead constantly to the recognition of new duties. No better general statement can be made than the courts will find a duty where in general, reasonable men would recognize and agree that it exists."

Therefore, the standard of duty that we now adopt for this and all other cases currently in the judicial process, is: when, because of an employee s incapacity, an employer exercises control over the employee, the employer has a duty to take such action as a reasonably prudent employer under the same or similar circumstances would take to prevent the employee from causing an unreasonable risk of harm to others. The duty of the employer is not an absolute duty to insure safety, but requires only reasonable care.

Therefore, the trier of fact in this case should be left free to decide whether Otis acted as a reasonable and prudent employer considering the following factors: the availability of the nurses' aid station [on the plant premises], a possible phone call to Mrs. Matheson, having another employee drive Matheson home, and the foreseeable consequences of Matheson's driving upon a public street in his stuporous condition.

[Affirm judgment of court of appeals and remand to trial court.]

Duty of Landowners

A recurring problem in establishing the nature of a duty exists regarding the responsibility of owners or occupiers (such as tenants) of land. How much of a duty they owe to visitors to their property has traditionally turned on whether the visitor was a trespasser (one who enters the land with no right to do so), a licensee (one who has a right to come onto the property for self–benefit, such as a door–to–door salesman or a neighbor dropping in uninvited), or an invitee (one invited by the owner or occupier or who enters for the benefit of the owner or occupier, such as a customer at a store). Under this traditional approach (which is still the majority view), trespassers may sue only for intentional torts, licensees may sue also for hidden dangers they should have been warned about, and invitees may sue under the ordinary rules of negligence. An increasing number of more recent cases have rejected this tripartite approach, not differentiating between plaintiffs and treating all defendants in this context under the general rules of negligence "governed by the test of reasonable care under all the circumstances in the maintenance and operation of their property." Oulette v. Blanchard, 364 A.2d 631 (N.H. 1976). Using this alternative approach, which is not yet the majority rule, the status of the plaintiff (such as being a trespasser) may still have an effect on the court's analysis of what a reasonable landowner should foresee, but the rigid categories are dispensed with.

Breach

To be liable for negligence, a defendant must *breach* an existing duty. A breach occurs when the defendant fails to exercise the same care as a "reasonable person under similar circumstances" would have exercised. This hypothetical "reasonable person" or "reasonable man" standard can be fairly strict because of a jury's tendency, confronted with a seriously injured plaintiff, to use 20–20 hindsight:

> [The reasonable man] is one who invariably looks where he is going and is careful to examine the immediate foreground before he executes a leap or bound; who neither stargazes nor is lost in meditation when approaching trap doors or the margin of a dock; . . . who never mounts a moving omnibus, and does not alight from any car while the train is still in motion . . . and who informs himself of the history and habits of a dog before administering a caress. [A.P. Herbert , UNCOMMON LAW (1991)]

All the Circumstances

Whether or not a defendant's conduct met the "reasonable person" standard of care should be examined in light of all the circumstances of the case. Emergency conditions, for example, may be considered. Normally it would be a clear breach of due care to abandon a moving vehicle, but if a cab driver does so because a robber in the back seat has pulled a gun, a jury might determine that, under all the circumstances, there was no breach of due care to render the cab company liable to a pedestrian who was struck by the driverless cab. An unexpected bee sting might cause a bus driver unavoidably to lose control of a bus, though she was a most careful driver.

The custom of others in the community or of other companies in the industry may also shed light on the proper standard of due care. If the defendant has acted in the same manner as most others in the same situation, it is difficult to conclude that a reasonable person standard was breached. However, custom is not always binding. In one famous case, barges were lost at sea because the tugs towing them had no radio sets to listen to weather reports that would have warned them to take shelter from an approaching storm. That few tug companies used the radio set was not proof that the "reasonable person" standard was met, because "a whole calling may have unduly lagged in the adoption of new and available devices." (The T.J.Hooper, 60 F.2d 737 (2d Cir. 1932).

Conduct of Others

Traditionally the courts allowed people to assume that other members of society would act carefully and lawfully. In other words, citizens had no duty to anticipate the negligent or criminal acts of others. However, increasingly courts and juries are concluding that such acts can and must be anticipated in certain circumstances. Thus, operators of a motel located in a high crime area that has itself been the scene of criminal acts in the past may be held to have breached a duty of due care by not providing adequate security for guests who are victimized by crime. Though some courts refuse to impose a duty in such circumstances, providing adequate security is increasingly a concern for motel owners, common carriers, store owners, concert promoters, and even universities.

Negligence Per Se

Although the standard of care to which a defendant will be held in a negligence case is usually formulated by the jury's assessment of what a reasonable person would have done, in some cases the conduct is measured in accordance with legislative imposed standards.

One example is a "dram shop" act, which many states have passed making it illegal to sell liquor to an intoxicated person. Another is the posted speed limit on a roadway.

A majority of courts have held that if a defendant violates such a statute, it is **negligence per se.** That is, if the plaintiff can show that he or she is within the class of persons that the statute was meant to protect and the harm sustained was the type the statute was meant to prevent, the issue of breach of due care is conclusively resolved against the defendant. The jury can be instructed that the defendant had breached the duty of due care. Lack of damages or proximate causation still might prevent recovery. A few courts do not go quite so far, holding only that violation of a statute is one factor the jury may consider among all others in deciding whether the defendant breached the duty of due care.

Proximate Cause

After proving existence and breach of a duty of due care, the plaintiff in a negligence action must demonstrate that the breach proximately caused the plaintiff's alleged injuries. There are many different labels and many different approaches to the proximate cause concept. Fundamentally, **proximate cause** means direct cause—that there is a direct causal connection between the defendant's act of carelessness and the plaintiff's injury—but it is more complicated than that.

"Legal cause," according to many courts, has two requirements. First, *causation in fact* must be shown. Some courts stress that the defendant's carelessness must be an act without which no harm would have occurred. In other words, can we say that "but for" the defendant's act the injuries would not have happened? For example, assume that Jill is driving her car at 40 miles per hour on a street where the speed limit is 30 miles per hour when a small child darts into the street from between two cars and is hit by Jill's car. Assume further that the child was so close to Jill's car when he darted into the street that even had Jill been driving 30 miles per hour, or even 20, she could not have avoided striking the child. In such a case we cannot say that "but for" Jills speeding the accident would not have happened. Jill's careless speeding was not a proximate cause of the accident, and Jill would not be liable.

Other courts addressing the *causation in fact* element stress that the defendant's carelessness must be a *substantial factor* in bringing about the injury, but not necessarily a "but for" cause, although the two will often overlap.

Factual causation ("but for" or "substantial factor") is insufficient in and of itself, however. Almost every act has consequences that ripple throughout society, and many incidents have several causes. Perhaps "but for" your carelessly running a stop sign, ambulance driver A would never have met nurse B and had child C who at the age of 14 years murdered D. May D's family sue you? Obviously not. For policy reasons, we must limit the liability stemming from our actions in some fashion.

Most courts return to the notion of *foreseeability* in establishing the second element of legal causation. Factual causation ("but for") plus foreseeability will establish *legal causation*. (Because foreseeability is an important factor in the establishment of both duty and proximate cause, court discussions of the two concepts tend to overlap.) Factual causation plus legal causation equals **proximate causation.**

The most famous tort case of all time is perhaps Palsgraf v. Long Island R.R., 163 N.E. 99 (1928), in which railway employees carelessly pushed a passenger who was trying to board a train. This caused him to drop a package he was carrying which, it turned out, contained fireworks that exploded beneath the wheels of the train. The force of the concussion knocked over a scale at the far end of the train station, injuring Mrs. Palsgraf. Injury to the boarding passenger and his property was a foreseeable result of the negligence of the railroad employees. They owed a duty of care to him, and any injuries to him would have been proximately caused by their actions. However, the court found the injury to Mrs. Palsgraf unforeseeable. The duty owed to the boarding passenger did not protect her. Sometimes the concept of reasonable foreseeability is interpreted rather broadly. For example, if we carelessly injure a person who turns out to be a hemophiliac and who then bleeds to death when most people would not have, we are still liable for the death. Courts say that we must "take our victims as we find them." Although it may not be reasonably foreseeable to us that our victim would be a hemophiliac, it is reasonably foreseeable that if we negligently cause harm, any particular victim might have any number of conditions making him or her more vulnerable. In a similar vein, we often are liable for harm to the victim of our negligence if our negligence resulted in greater harm because we placed that victim into a hazardous situation (such as our negligent driving not only causing direct damage but also placing the victim in a situation in which he or she is more vulnerable to other common road hazards, such as being hit by someone else). Likewise, we often will be liable to our victim for harm that is made worse by relatively common kinds of negligent medical care (although the negligent medical care provider also is liable, of course.)

Independent Intervening Cause

Especially in terms of foreseeability, the concept of independent intervening cause is important. Such a cause is one that emanates from a third party or source to disrupt the causal connection between the defendant's careless act and the plaintiff's injury. Assume that Sue is driving down the street when she comes to an intersection that is blocked by an accident caused by Joe's having run a stop sign. Sue turns her car around and while driving away is hit by a tree that is blown down by a strong wind. Sue can argue that "but for" Joe's carelessness the intersection would not have been blocked and she would have been several miles away from the tree at the time it fell over. But should we hold Joe liable for Sue's injury? No, because the tree's falling is an independent, intervening cause that breaks up the causal chain between Joe's careless driving and Sue's injury. The key, again, is foreseeability. An intervening cause that can reasonably be foreseen by the defendant is usually insufficient to break the causal chain.

BROWN V. PHILADELPHIA COLLEGE OF OSTEOPATHIC MEDICINE
Superior Court of Pennsylvania, 760 A.2d 863 (2000)

Yvette Brown delivered a child at Philadelphia College of OsteopathicMedicine (PCOM) on August 29, 1991. Soon after her delivery, the child was given a blood test to detect congenital syphilis. A PCOM physician told Mrs. Brown that the test results revealed her daughter had been born with syphilis, and that the baby only could have contracted the disease from her. When her husband arrived at the hospital, Mrs. Brown confronted him with the diagnosis and questioned whether he had been faithful to her. Although Mr. Brown initially denied infidelity, he subsequently admitted to having begun an affair with a co–worker during the last trimester of his wife's pregnancy, an affair that did not terminate until after the birth of the child.

Sometime after the baby was released from the hospital, the Browns requested that she be tested again for syphilis. They learned in October 1991 that the child, in fact, did not have syphilis. In addition, results of a test performed on Mr. Brown, which were received by the Browns in December 1991, revealed that Mr. Brown did not have syphilis.

The Browns filed a negligence suit against PCOM. Mrs. Brown testified that after the diagnosis the couple experienced "a lot of arguing, a lot of accusations, distrust" which they had not previously experienced in their marriage. Eventually, Mr. Brown became

physically abusive to his wife. Central to the Browns' damage claims in this litigation was an episode of abuse in November 1991 that began when Mrs. Brown received a telephone call at her home from her male partner on the police force. According to Mrs. Brown, upon hearing a man's voice on the line, Mr. Brown became suspicious and "snatched the phone out of the wall and hit me, and he hit me several times." Mrs. Brown then retrieved her service revolver and while bleeding and wearing only her underwear pursued Mr. Brown out of the house. She fired several shots at him, hitting his car. As a result of this incident, both of the Browns were arrested and Mrs. Brown obtained a restraining order against her husband. Subsequently, Mrs. Brown was discharged from the Philadelphia police force for conduct unbecoming an officer. The Browns lived separately thereafter.

A jury returned a verdict in favor of $510,000 in favor of the Browns. PCOM appealed.

Todd, Justice:

In this negligence action, we are called upon to determine whether an erroneous syphilis diagnosis was the proximate cause of the breakdown of a marriage, physical violence and loss of employment. The element of causation lies at the heart of this matter. For purposes of this appeal, we assume that PCOM owed a duty to the Browns and that in delivering the erroneous test results it breached that duty. In addition, we accept, as found by the jury, that PCOM's conduct was an actual cause of the eventual harm suffered by the Browns.

It is not sufficient, however, that a negligent act may be viewed, in retrospect, to have been one of the happenings in the series of events leading up to an injury. Even if the requirement of actual causation has been satisfied, there remains the issue of proximate or legal cause. ...While actual and proximate causation are "often hopelessly confused", a finding of proximate cause turns upon: "whether the policy of the law will extend the responsibility for the [negligent] conduct to the consequences which have in fact occurred. ...The term 'proximate cause' is applied by the courts to those more or less undefined considerations which limit liability even where the fact of causation is clearly established." Bell v.Irace, 619 A.2d 365 (Pa. Super. 1993)(*quoting* W.P. Keeton, Prosser & Keeton, The Law of Torts (5th ed.1984)).

Proximate cause "is primarily a problem of law." As a threshold issue, therefore, the trial judge must determine whether the alleged tortfeasor's conduct could have been the proximate, or legal, cause of the complainant's injury before sending the case to the jury. In the present case, the learned trial judge made no such threshold determination at any of the appropriate junctures for him to have done so. Instead, the trial court denied PCOM's motions for a nonsuit, a directed verdict and judgment notwithstanding the verdict. This was an error of law that controlled the outcome of the present case and on this basis we are constrained to reverse.

The law of this Commonwealth will not support a finding of proximate cause if, as in the present case, "the negligence, if any, was so remote that as a matter of law, [the actor] cannot be held legally responsible for [the] harm which subsequently occurred." Reilly v.

Tiergarten, 633 A.2d 208 (Pa.Super. 1993). Accord *Bell*, 619 A.2d at 367 ("At the point in the causal chain when the consequence of the negligent act is no longer reasonably foreseeable, 'the passage of time and the span of distance mandate a cut-off point for liability.'")

To determine proximate cause, the Supreme Court of Pennsylvania has stated that "the question is whether the defendant's conduct was a 'substantial factor' in producing the injury." Vattimo v. Lower Bucks Hosp., Inc., 502 Pa. 241, 246, 465 A.2d 1231, 1233 (1983). To determine whether an actor's conduct constitutes the proximate cause of an injury, the courts of the Commonwealth have adopted and relied upon the factors set forth in Section 433 of the Restatement (Second) of Torts. This section provides:

The following considerations are in themselves or in combination with one another important in determining whether the actor's conduct is a substantial factor in bringing harm to another: the number of other factors which contribute in producing the harm and the extent of the effect which they have in producing it; whether the actor's conduct has created a force or series of forces which are in continuous and active operation up to the time of the harm, or has created a situation harmless unless acted upon by other forces for which the actor is not responsible; lapse of time.

Applying these factors to the present case, it is abundantly clear that factors other than the negligence of PCOM had a far greater effect in producing the harm complained of by the Browns. Mr. Brown conducted an extramarital affair and confessed this to his wife at a time when the affair was still ongoing. It is this affair and his confession to it, together with Mr. Brown's suspicions that his wife was having an affair herself, not the false diagnosis of syphilis, that had the greatest effect in bringing about the marital discord and eventual breakdown for which the couple seeks compensation. Under the first of the Restatement factors, therefore, the actions of PCOM are not a substantial factor in bringing about these alleged damages.

Even the allegations of the Brown's Complaint show that forces other than the negligence of PCOM were the proximate cause of their damages. The Complaint alleges that:

"As a direct and proximate result of the negligence of PCOM, wife Plaintiff suffered serious and severe physical and psychological damages as a consequence. Because of the nature of the disease and its communicability, wife Plaintiff accused husband Plaintiff of infecting her with a venereal disease, which husband Plaintiff denied. These accusations took place over several days in the course of which, husband Plaintiff admitted to an extramarital affair. As a consequence of this admission, that marital relationship became extremely strained and at one point, resulted in physical violence. In self—defense, wife Plaintiff was caused to discharge a firearm in the direction of husband Plaintiff on the public streets of Philadelphia. As a consequence of this action, wife Plaintiff was terminated from her employment as a Philadelphia Police officer."

Under the second factor, it is clear that PCOM's conduct did not create "a force or series of forces which [were] in continuous and active operation up to the time of the harm." Instead, Mr. Brown confessed his adultery shortly after Mrs. Brown received the erroneous test results, before any retesting or verification of the results could be accomplished.

The third factor is lapse of time. In the present case, the child was born August 29, 1991 and was tested for syphilis shortly thereafter. The erroneous test results were delivered to the Browns, and Mr. Brown confessed his adultery while Mrs. Brown was still hospitalized recovering from the birth. By some time in October, they had learned that the diagnosis had been made in error. The primary physical altercation between the couple that resulted in Mrs. Brown's physical injury, the arrest of

both parties, the filing of a protection from abuse order against Mr. Brown and the couples separation, occurred more than two months after the receipt of the erroneous diagnosis and in the month after they learned that the diagnosis had been in error. Thus, the lapse of more than two months, between the erroneous diagnosis and the initial break up of their marriage, point to a finding that PCOM's negligence was not a substantial factor in bringing about this harm. Accordingly, under all three factors set forth in the Restatement analysis, PCOM's negligence was not a substantial factor in bringing about the breakdown of the Browns' marriage and, thus, was not a proximate cause of this harm.

Even more clearly, the erroneous test results were not the proximate cause of Mrs. Brown's alleged loss of income and earning capacity during the more than six years between the erroneous test and the trial. Instead, her independent act of discharging her service revolver in the direction of her husband on a public street (the month after she learned that the syphilis test results were erroneous) and the subsequent determination of the Philadelphia Police Department that such an action constituted conduct unbecoming an officer were the proximate causes of the termination of her employment as a police officer. This, combined with her difficulties in finding adequate child care that would permit her to pursue full—time employment, are the proximate causes of her alleged reduction in income and earning capacity.

Our decision that the damages alleged to have been suffered by the Browns are so remote from the actions of PCOM that PCOM cannot be held legally responsible for the harm is dictated by our prior jurisprudence on this issue wherein this Court has rejected similar attempts by plaintiffs to link damages to acts well beyond the point of reasonable foreseeability.

Reversed, judgment vacated, and remanded for entry of judgment notwithstanding the verdict in favor of Appellant.

Injury

As the final element of a negligence cause of action, the plaintiff must prove injury. Negligence recovery is allowed primarily for injury to person or property. Recovery for economic loss not related to personal injury or property damage is generally not allowed, although there are several exceptions for special situations.

Courts traditionally have also been reluctant to allow recovery for emotional distress on grounds that such injuries are too intangible and too easily faked. Over the years, most courts have changed their views as psychiatric testimony regarding the actual existence of emotional distress has become more dependable.

At first, courts allowed recovery for negligently caused emotional distress when the plaintiff also sustained a physical injury in the accident. It was easier to believe that the plaintiff suffered emotional distress if there were accompanying physical injuries. Later courts also awarded recovery to plaintiffs who were not physically injured but were in the "zone of danger." Thus, a pedestrian who was narrowly missed by an automobile that ran down a fellow pedestrian could sue the careless driver for emotional damages.

Because application of the "zone of danger" test sometimes leads to rather arbitrary distinctions, many courts have taken an additional step by allowing "bystander recovery." Thus, a parent who sees or hears an accident killing the parent's child may be allowed to recover for emotional distress although not within the zone of danger. Three factors to be weighed in deciding whether to allow recovery are: (1) whether the plaintiff was located near the scene of the accident; (2) whether the emotional shock resulted from a contemporaneous perception of the accident, as opposed to hearing about it later; and (3) whether the plaintiff and the victim were closely related. Many courts have rejected bystander recovery, which obviously entails an extension of the concept of duty. But the modern trend is to recognize that if an actor's carelessness causes an injury that kills or seriously injures someone, the victim's loved ones are almost certain to suffer emotional trauma.

Punitive damages, also known as exemplary damages, are not recoverable in mere negligence cases. These are monetary damages, over and above the sums necessary to compensate for the plaintiff's injuries, that are assessed against the defendant to punish for wrongdoing and to deter the defendant and others from engaging in such wrongful conduct.

A defendant in a negligence action is guilty of mere carelessness, so punitive damages are viewed as inappropriate. However, punitive damages are generally available to plaintiffs injured by the intentional torts that we will discuss later in the chapter.

Defenses

Even if the plaintiff establishes all four elements of a negligence cause of action, the defendant may avert or reduce recovery by establishing certain defenses.

Comparative Fault

If the plaintiff is guilty of fault that contributed to the accident, a defense may exist. Under the old system of **contributory negligence,** a plaintiff who was guilty of carelessness that contributed in any material way to the accident was barred from recovery altogether. Even if the jury concluded that the plaintiff was 1 percent at fault and the defendant 99 percent, the plaintiff could recover nothing, no matter how serious the injuries were.

Because of the harshness of the contributory negligence system, most jurisdictions have replaced it with a system of **comparative negligence.** Comparative negligence or comparative fault systems vary widely from jurisdiction to jurisdiction, so it is difficult to generalize. Some states have "pure" comparative negligence systems under which, no matter how great a share of the fault is attributable to the plaintiff, the plaintiff still is entitled to recover the portion of damages caused by the defendant's carelessness. For example, let's assume that in a case arising out of an auto colision between P and D, a jury assesses P's damages at $100,000 and finds P 40 percent at fault and D 60 percent at fault. Rather than being barred from recovery as in a contributory negligence system P would recover $60,000—that portion of the damages caused by D's fault. Indeed, in a pure system, even if P is found 99 percent at fault and D 1 percent, P would still recover $1,000. That P is many times more at fault than D does not bar recovery for that portion of the loss caused by D's carelessness.

Most jurisdictions have not adopted a pure comparative negligence system. Many allow a plaintiff to recover whatever percentage of damages were caused by the defendant, unless the plaintiff's share of the fault is assessed at 51 percent or higher. If the plaintiff's fault exceeds 50 percent, recovery is barred altogether on the theory that the plaintiff should recover nothing if he or she is more at fault than the defendant. Other states set 49 percent as the cap, not allowing proportionate recovery to a plaintiff found 50 percent or more at fault.

Statute of Limitations

In negligence, as in other causes of action, every state has a **statute of limitations** within which the suit must be filed or forever barred. A typical tort statute of limitations is two years. Thus, a plaintiff injured by a defendant's negligence must file suit within two years of the occurrence. Occasionally a plaintiff may not even know of the injury until more than two years after the occurrence, for example, when carelessly designed drugs with side effects that will not show up for years are sold. Most states have applied tolling devices that provide that in such a case the statute of limitations is tolled; that is, will not begin to run, until the plaintiff knows or should know of the injury. In response to the medical malpractice and products liability "crises," several states have passed statutes of "repose" that bar certain actions after, say, 15 years, whether the injuries sustained were discoverable or not during that period.

No Fault Systems

Negligence has been eliminated as a basis for lawsuits in at least two contexts that should be mentioned here. Every state has a *workers' compensation* system that allows injured employees to recover benefits from their employers when injured on the job. The employee can recover regardless of the presence of employer fault but forfeits the right to sue the employer even if the employer has been careless. Most jurisdictions, however, allow an employee covered by workers' compensation to sue his or her employer in tort if injured by the employer's gross negligence (for example, if the employer has allowed several employees to be injured by the same defective machine without replacing it) or intentional tort. Workers' compensation plays a role in the Caudle v. Betts case in the next section and is discussed in more detail in Chapter 29.

Several states have enacted "no fault" automobile statutes. The thrust of these statutes is to reduce litigation by allowing persons who suffer only minor injuries in car accidents to recover only from their own insurance company. Although these laws vary widely from jurisdiction to jurisdiction, in most the plaintiffs' losses must exceed a certain statutory threshold before resort to litigation is allowed.

Major Intentional Torts
Assault and Battery

Assault and battery are similar torts that may be treated together. Although modern courts and statutes frequently use the two terms interchangeably, technically a **battery** is a rude, inordinate contact with the person of another. An **assault,** basically, is any act that creates an apprehension of an imminent battery. That we can sue for assault and battery protects our personal dignity from intrusions of the mind (assault) and body (battery). The courts long ago concluded that we have a legitimate interest in being protected from offensive bodily contacts and from fear of them. Indeed, assault and battery also constitute crimes.

Elements

One way to formulate the basic elements of the torts of assault and battery is to require the plaintiff to prove (1) the defendant's affirmative conduct, (2) intent, and (3) the plaintiff's injury.

Affirmative Conduct and Intent. If Sue is carefully driving down the street and is hit by a car that runs a red light, and as a result Sue's car is pushed into a pedestrian, Sue has not committed assault or battery. Although the pedestrian has sustained both apprehension (assuming she saw the accident as it happened) and rude contact, Sue committed no affirmative act that caused the injuries. The driver of the car that ran the red light did commit an affirmative act that was tortious, but that act was negligence, not assault or battery. However, if, while driving down the street, Sue spotted an enemy and deliberately ran down that person in a crosswalk, an assault and battery would have occurred.

The intent required for both assault and battery is the intent either to create an offensive contact to the plaintiff's body or the apprehension of it in the plaintiff. Furthermore, a person is presumed to intend the natural consequences of his or her actions. Thus, if A points an unloaded gun at B and utters threats to use it, an assault occurs if B does not know the gun is unloaded even if A's intent is simply to play a harmless prank. The natural consequences of A's act of pointing the gun is to create an apprehension in B.

Under the doctrine of transferred intent, if Sam shoots at Bill, but Bill ducks and the bullet hits Carlos, Carlos has an assault (assuming he saw the incident happening) and battery claim against Sam even if he is Sam's best friend and Sam would not intentionally hurt him for the world. The law transfers the intent Sam had to injure Bill to Carlos.

Injury. If a plaintiff seeks to establish an assault, the injury sustained must be in the nature of an apprehension of imminent bodily contact of an offensive nature. A threat of future contact or a threat by a defendant far away is insufficient. Threats or even attempts at violence that the intended victim does not know about until much later do not create the requisite apprehension, as where D shoots and misses P from so far away that P never realizes the shot was fired. Usually the plaintiff's reactions are judged by what would have caused apprehension in a reasonable person, but if the defendant knows that the plaintiff is an unusually sensitive person and threatens contact that the plaintiff finds offensive although most persons would not, an assault occurs.

If the plaintiff sues for battery, the injury that must be demonstrated is an offensive contact. Being struck with a fist, a knife, or a bullet obviously satisfies the requirement. So does being spat on, poisoned, and having one's clothes ripped or cane knocked away.

The following case illustrates the tort of battery in an employment context, thereby raising also some important workers' compensation issues.

CAUDLE V. BETTS
Supreme Court of Louisiana, 512 So.2d 389 (1987)

Plaintiff Ruben Caudle was a salesman at Betts Lincoln–Mercury, Inc. Shortly before an office Christmas party on December 23, 1983, other employees engaged in horseplay with an electric automobile condenser after discovering that it could be charged by touching one end to a car's spark plug wire and turning the engine over. Once charged, the condenser would deliver a slight electric shock when touched at both ends. Several employees played catch with the charged condenser. Peter Betts, president of the corporation, shocked the back of Caudle's neck with the charged condenser and chased Caudle with it until Caudle escaped by locking himself in an office. After the incident, Caudle suffered headaches and passed out 30 to 40 times in the following months. The condition finally required occipital nerve surgery leaving a slight numbness on the right side of the plaintiff's head.

Caudle sued Betts individually and Betts Lincoln–Mercury, Inc., for battery, seeking damages for, among other things, pain and suffering, past medical expenses, and loss of earnings. The trial court held that the injury to the plaintiff was not an intentional injury and, therefore, that workers' compensation benefits were the plaintiff's sole remedy. The appellate court affirmed the dismissal of the plaintiff's tort suit, and the plaintiff's appealed to the Louisiana Supreme Court.

Dennis, Justice:

The Louisiana Worker's Compensation Act provides for compensation if an employee receives personal injury by accident arising out of and in the course of his employment. As a general rule, the rights and remedies granted to an employee therein are exclusive of all rights and remedies against his employer, any officer or principal of the employer, or any co–employee. However, an exception to this rule provides that nothing therein shall affect the liability of an employer, principal, officer, or co–employee resulting from an "intentional act." ... [I]n drawing a line between intentional and unintentional acts the legislative aim was to make use of the well established division between intentional torts and negligence.

A harmful or offensive contact with a person, resulting from an act intended to cause the plaintiff to suffer such a contact, is a battery. ... The intention need not be malicious nor need it be an intention to inflict actual damage. It is sufficient if the actor intends to inflict either a harmful or offensive contact without the other's consent.

The original purpose of the courts in providing the action for battery undoubtedly was to keep the peace by affording a substitute for private retribution. F. Stone, Louisiana Civil Law Treatise, Tort Doctrine, Sec. 125 (1977). The element of personal indignity always has been given considerable weight. Consequently, the defendant is liable not only for contacts that do actual physical harm, but also for those relatively trivial ones which are merely offensive and insulting. W. Prosser and W. Keeton, The Law of Torts, Sec. 9 (5th ed. 1984).

The intent with which tort liability is concerned is not necessarily a hostile intent, or a desire to do any harm. ... Rather it is an intent to bring about a result that will invade the interests of another in a way that the law forbids.

The defendant may be liable although intending nothing more than a good–natured practical joke, or honestly believing that the act would not injure the plaintiff, or even though seeking the plaintiff s own good. [Id.]

Bodily harm is generally considered to be any physical impairment of the condition of a person's body, or physical pain or illness. Restatement (Second) of Torts, American Law Institute, Sec. 15 (1965). The defendant's liability for the resulting harm extends, as in most other cases of intentional torts, to consequences which the defendant did not intend, and could not reasonably have foreseen, upon the obvious basis that it is better for unexpected losses to fall upon the intentional wrongdoer than upon the innocent victim. ...

Applying these precepts to the facts found and affirmed by the lower courts, we conclude that the plaintiff employee proved that a battery had been committed on him by another employee and that he is entitled to recovery for all injuries resulting therefrom including his occipital nerve impairment. It is undisputed that when Mr. Betts shocked the employee, Mr. Caudle, with the condenser, he intended the contact to be offensive and at least slightly painful or harmful. The fact that he did so as a practical joke and did not intend to inflict actual damage does not render him immune from liability. Further, as between the innocent employee victim and the wrongdoer, it is better for unexpected losses to fall upon the intentional wrongdoer. Mr. Caudle is entitled to recover for all consequences of the battery, even those that Mr. Betts did not intend and could not reasonably have foreseen. [Reversed and remanded.]

Defenses

In addition to the statute of limitations, which typically is two years in such cases, the two primary defenses to assault and battery are **consent** and **self-defense.** A plaintiff who has consented to offensive contacts and the threat of them cannot sue for assault and battery. Thus, a boxer who steps into the boxing or the quarterback who steps onto the football field consents to the normal contacts that go with the rules of the game. However, a football player who is forearmed from behind by an opposing player after the play was over, he might have a good battery claim because his consent does not extend to this contact outside the rules of the game any more than it would extend to being shot by an opponent.

Consent cannot be procured by fraud, nor can it be ill– informed. Thus, if M procures F's consent to sexual intercourse by hiding the fact that he has herpes, her consent to intercourse does not constitute consent to the harmful contact with the disease. She may sue for battery. Doctors performing surgery must be very careful to fully inform their patients regarding the contacts that will take place during the surgery to avoid liability for battery. Consent to an appendectomy does not extend to the removal of some of the reproductive organs even though it may be the doctor's best medical judgment that they should be removed.

Self–defense creates a well–recognized privilege to assault and battery. Generally, the courts restrict one to that degree of force considered reasonable under all the circumstances.

Defamation

Long ago the courts decided that we have a legitimate interest in preserving our good reputation in the community. Those who damage our reputation by spreading falsehoods commit the tort of **defamation** and may be liable in damages. Although defamation has historic common-law roots, its development in recent years has been strongly influenced by a series of Supreme Court decisions that have molded the tort in accordance with First Amendment principles.

Libel Versus Slander

Defamation takes two basic forms. **Libel** is written defamation; **slander** is oral. Television and radio broadcasts have generally been categorized as libel. The distinction is important because, traditionally, libel, perhaps because of its more permanent form, was considered more damaging than slander. At common law, a person who proved libel was able to recover damages without any proof of special damages; that is, the very proof that something potentially damaging to the reputation was circulated in public led the court to presume injury. The jury could assess damages without evidence of any specific loss.

Slander, however, required proof of special damages. Generally, a plaintiff had to prove some sort of economic loss stemming from the damage to reputation. Once that was proved, the plaintiff could recover for all sorts of injuries, including humiliation, loss of friendship, and the like. However, in four special categories known as *slander per se*, no special damages needed to be proved. These categories were imputation of serious crime, of loathsome disease, of incompetence in the plaintiff's profession, and of sexual misconduct.

However, as we shall see, the Supreme Court's First Amendment decisions have had an impact on this traditional distinction.

Elements

In a defamation case, the plaintiff must generally establish four elements to prevail: (1) defendant made a statement about the plaintiff as though it were a fact (rather than an opinion), (2) the statement about plaintiff was defamatory, (3) the statement was false, (4) the statement was communicated (sometimes the courts say "published") by the defendant to at least one other person, and (5) the plaintiff's reputation was harmed. Questions of the defendant's fault, as we shall see, also arise.

Fact vs. Opinion. Under the First Amendment, there is no such thing as a false idea. We are all entitled to our opinions. Thus, "I think Joe is a jerk" is not actionable. Neither is " just don't trust Joe; he looks sneaky to me." However, when an editorial writer stated that a plaintiff had lied under oath, the Supreme Court rejected a defense of opinion because the statement was "sufficiently factual to be susceptible of being proved true or false." Milkovich v. Lorain Journal Co., 497 U.S. 1(1990).

Defamatory. To be defamatory, a statement must be of such a nature as to tend to lower the plaintiff's esteem in the eyes of others, that is, to damage plaintiff's reputation. An infinite variety of statements have been held defamatory, but if the defendant falsely tells others that the plaintiff is a thief, a bankrupt, a Nazi, a communist, or a homosexual, it is likely that the plaintiff's esteem in the eyes of others will be lowered. Although most defamation actions are brought by individuals, they can also be brought by corporations and other organizations.

The defamatory statement must be one that the readers or hearers will associate with the plaintiff. Although not mentioned by name, a person who is obviously referred to in a disparaging way in a "novel" that is closely based on reality may have a claim against the author. So may a member of a small group when the defendant defames the entire group (for example, "All the male clerks at this store have AIDS") although the plaintiff is not mentioned by name. When larger groups are referred to (such as "All Republicans are fascists"), the courts will not hold the defendant liable.

The defamatory statement not only must tend to lower the plaintiff's esteem in the eyes of others, but also must be false. The most defamatory statement in the world does not constitute the tort of defamation if it is true. The question may be: Who has the burden of proving truthfulness or falsity? The common law presumed that everyone was a good person; therefore, if the plaintiff proved that a statement tending to defame him or her had been published by the defendant, the burden of proof was on the defendant to prove the truthfulness of the statement. Truth, in other words, was an absolute defense to a defamation claim.

A recent Supreme Court case redistributed this burden of proof, at least in some cases, on First Amendment grounds. In Philadelphia Newspaper, Inc. v. Hepps, 475 U.S. 767(1986), the Court held that if the plaintiff is a public figure (such as a famous actress or athlete), a public official (such as a governor), or a "limited" public figure (a private citizen caught up in a public controversy, such as a businessman whose name appears in a newspaper article about the Mafia), free speech concerns require that the plaintiff be given the burden of proof to demonstrate falsity. The common–law presumption that defamatory speech is false was rejected, at least when the defendant is a member of the media. The implications for a nonmedia defendant or a case involving a private plaintiff not involved in any public controversy are unclear.

Communication. To be defamatory, a statement must be "published" or communicated by the defendant—that is, overheard or read by a third party. If Joe and Kim are standing alone in a field miles from anyone else, Joe can say all the nasty things he wants to Kim without committing defamation. Kim's reputation in the community cannot be hurt if no one else hears the statements. If Kim goes back into town and repeats the statements for others, it is Kim doing the communicating, not Joe.

Injury. As noted earlier, the traditional common–law rule presumed damages in libel and the four special types of slander. If a false statement tending to lower the plaintiff's esteem in the eyes of others appeared in a local newspaper, it was sensible to presume that persons read it and that their impressions of the plaintiff were adversely affected. Injury was presumed, and it made no difference that the defendant did not intend to injure the plaintiff. Because injury is typically presumed in a case of libel or slander per se, the court (jury, if there is one) may award substantial damages to the plaintiff even if the plaintiff has not produced evidence of actual harm to his reputation. Even if not required, however, it will always be in the plaintiff's best interest to produce evidence of actual reputational harm (and evidence of any economic loss resulting from the damage to his reputation) if such evidence exists.

The Supreme Court has indicated that this presumption of injury is inconsistent with the First Amendment, at least when the media are reporting about public officials, public figures, or private figures involved in public controversies. In these cases, at least, plaintiffs must introduce some evidence to show that the defamatory publication injured their reputations.

Defenses

Several noteworthy defenses are available in defamation cases.

Statute of Limitations. In most jurisdictions, the statute of limitations for defamation cases is one year, only half the two–year statute of limitations typically found for other types of tort claims.

Absolute Privilege. To encourage certain types of activity, the courts have created an absolute privilege for the potential defendant in several contexts. That is, even if the plaintiff could prove all the elements of defamation just discussed, no liability would attach. The two most important of these are the privileges for judicial and legislative proceedings. To encourage judges to judge, witnesses to testify, lawyers to advocate, and legislators to debate the issues aggressively, all are protected absolutely when involved in their respective activities. Note, however, that the absolute privilege is narrow in scope. An attorney who wrote a book about a case after the trial was over or a legislator making statements not while debating a bill but while campaigning would not be protected.

Qualified Privileges. There are also several qualified privileges when the defendant will be protected if he or she acted *in good faith;* that is, malice must be proved as a prerequisite for recovery. The primary example of this is when the plaintiff is a public figure or public official. Others include, according to some jurisdictions, communications to those who can act in the public interest (for example, complaints to a school board about a teacher) and fair comment on matters of public interest by news commentators.

Many states have provided a business-related good faith privilege for those who traffic in commercially useful information such as credit reports and employee references. Thus, in many jurisdictions, a job applicant's former employer is protected if he tells the applicant's prospective employer that "We think she stole from us." The plaintiff would have to prove malice to prevail. Note, however, that Dun & Bradstreet, Inc. v. Greenmoss Builders, 472 U.S. 749 (1985), makes it clear that this privilege is not constitutionally mandated.

Injurious Falsehood

Closely related to defamation (and perhaps equally as closely connected to the business torts discussed at the end of this chapter) is the tort of **injurious falsehood,** also known as disparagement of goods, slander of goods, and trade libel. The elements are generally the same as for traditional defamation, but the subject matter relates not to an individual's reputation, but to the plaintiff's title to property or to the quality or conduct of the plaintiff's business. The tort is aimed at protecting economic interests and would allow suit against a defendant who, for example, falsely stated that the plaintiff's business was no longer in existence. One major difference between this tort and defamation is that a plaintiff in an injurious falsehood case cannot receive any damages unless the plaintiff proves actual economic loss.

False Imprisonment

The privilege to come and go as we please is important in our society. The courts protect that interest by recognizing the right to sue for the tort of **false imprisonment** when persons are unlawfully confined or restrained without their consent. If the defendant purports to arrest the plaintiff as well, the nearly identical claim of **false arrest** is applicable.

Elements

To prove a false imprisonment claim, the plaintiff must usually prove that the defendant (1) confined or restrained the plaintiff, (2) with intent, (3) without the plaintiff's consent, (4) thereby injuring the plaintiff.

Confinement. False imprisonment can occur when the plaintiff is confined in a room, a building, a car, or even a boat. It can even occur in the wide open spaces if the plaintiff is held in one spot against his or her will by force or threat. If the defendant blocks one exit to a room but another is available to the plaintiff, the confinement requirement is not met.

Intent. If someone accidentally locks another in a room, perhaps negligence is involved, but not false imprisonment. False imprisonment requires a wrongful intent on the defendant's part. As with assault and battery, an intent to injure will suffice, as well as an intent to confine. If the defendant stands outside the plaintiff's house with a gun, issuing threats of bodily injury should the plaintiff emerge, the intent requirement is met. Although the defendant would like nothing better than for the plaintiff to come out of the house, the natural consequence of the defendant's actions is to force the plaintiff to remain in the house.

Without Consent. The same force and threats of force that create an assault may force a person to remain in one place against his or her will. A large man could easily intimidate a small person into staying involuntarily in one place. However, if the plaintiff stays in one place as an accommodation or to clear up an accusation with police, there is no involuntary confinement. If, for example, a store clerk told a customer only "We believe you have stolen from the cash register and we have called the police," and the customer voluntarily stayed in the store to give his or her side of the story, there would be no false imprisonment.

Injury. The injury necessary for a valid false imprisonment claim arises automatically from the confinement, even if it is brief. A restraint of hours or days is not required for the necessary injury to occur. However, because the injury is somewhat mental in nature, it will not occur if the plaintiff is unaware of the confinement. Thus, if the plaintiff sleeps through a confinement, there would be no cognizable injury. But if the plaintiff knows of the confinement, actual and punitive damages are available.

Defenses

In addition to the statute of limitations (typically two years), the defendant's best chance in a false imprisonment case is to prove legal right. Obviously, police officers in possession of probable cause have the right to detain or confine suspects.

Many false imprisonment claims involve shopkeepers. Shoplifting, unfortunately, is a problem of epidemic proportions in the United States. When a shopkeeper detains a suspected shoplifter and presses charges, any number of things can prevent a conviction from being obtained, including prosecutorial or police error, or the failure of a witness to appear. At common law, even a well–founded belief by a shopkeeper that a theft had occurred frequently would not prevent the success of a later false imprisonment claim if, for whatever reason, no criminal conviction was obtained. However, many state legislatures have acted to protect shopkeepers with legislation such as that discussed in the following case. Additionally, some states have updated their protective statutes to reflect usage of moder technology, as the following case illustrates.

ESTES V. JACK ECKERD CORPORATION
Court of Appeals of Georgia, 360 S.E.2d 649 (1987)

As she left Eckerd's store after purchasing some items, the plaintiff Estes activated an anti—shoplifting device's buzzer. Posters warned customers that such devices were in use. Estes was approached by the store manager who told her that he had to look in her shopping bag because the alarm had gone off. His inspection of the bag and the plaintiff's receipt indicated that Estes had paid for all the items, but the sales clerk had not deactivated a special tag on a bottle of shampoo. Estes was soon released. The parties' version of events differed on whether the store manager had treated Estes in a rude and derogatory fashion. The jury apparently believed that he had not, returning a verdict for the defendant on Estes' false imprisonment claim. Estes appealed.

Beasley, Judge:

False imprisonment is "the unlawful detention of the person of another, for any length of time, whereby such person is deprived of his personal liberty." By OCGA 51–7–60, the [legislature] provided a qualified immunity to merchants from tort liability for false arrest or false imprisonment. No recovery is permitted where plaintiffs conduct is such "as to cause a man of reasonable prudence to believe" that the plaintiff was shoplifting or where the manner of detention or arrest and the length of the detention was reasonable under all the circumstances.

Later, OCGA 51–7–61 was added to provide that where a store used an anti—shoplifting or inventory control device "the automatic activation of the device as a result of a person exiting the establishment or a protected area within the establishment shall constitute reasonable cause for the detention of the person so exiting by the owner or operator . . . or employee. . . . Each detention shall be made only in a reasonable manner and only for a reasonable period of time sufficient for any inquiry into the circumstances surrounding the activation of the device." [Emphasis added.]

This applies only when a warning notice is conspicuously posted.

In response to Eckerd's position that the statute acts as an absolute bar to Mrs. Estes' recovery, she asserts that immunity is granted only if Eckerd used all reasonable care and due diligence in the use of the device and did not cause harm to her through its negligence.

"False imprisonment is an intentional tort, not a tort of negligence." Williams v. Smith, 348 S.E.2d 50 (Ga.App. 1986). . . . The present case is governed by OCGA 51–7–61, not by 517– 60. . . . A Louisiana court considered a similar Louisiana antishoplifting device statute . . . [and] reasoned that . . . the legislature's clear intention was "to afford to the merchant a right, within statutory limitations, to detain a person when the electronic device has been triggered." The conclusion was that the essential question under such a statute was "not whether 'reasonable cause' exists, but whether the method and extent of plaintiff's detention was reasonable under the circumstances. . . ."

The reasoning of the Louisiana court is persuasive and substantiates our construction of the language of the Georgia statute, which is mandatory, inasmuch as it states that "automatic activation of the device . . . shall constitute reasonable cause. . . ." That is, it makes no difference to "reasonable cause" whether or not negligence on the part of Eckerd's employee in failing to deactivate the special tag on the bottle of shampoo set the device off. What matters is whether the method and time of detention were reasonable within the statutory limitations. Defendant's right to detain is lawful once the device is activated.

Having determined that the defendant's alleged precursor negligence is immaterial when an anti—shoplifting device has been automatically activated, the only issue under OCGA 51—7—61 is whether the detention was made in a reasonable manner, as she does not contend that it was not for a reasonable period of time, and if proper notice was posted as required. The latter is undisputed as there were at least two warning signs prominently displayed in the store near the entrance and exit.

While the testimony of Estes and Eckerd's manager was conflicting as to what he said when he approached her, there is no dispute that he searched her bag without any objection on her part, and that the episode lasted only five to ten minutes. Clearly there was no restraint by force or fear here. . . .

We find the evidence sufficient to support the jury's apparent conclusion that Mrs. Estes was not detained unreasonably.

[Affirmed].

Box 8.1 illustrates another remedy given to merchants victimized by shoplifters.

Trespass

We work hard for our money, and when we spend it on property we should have the right to use that property without interference from others. When others infringe on our right to use real property— land and those things attached to it, such as houses—the tort of **trespass** to real property is committed. The tort has a convoluted common—law history that protects property owners from innocent as well as mean—spirited invasions of the right to use real property.

Elements

Generally speaking, to prevail in a trespass case the plaintiff must establish the following elements: (1) affirmative conduct by the defendant, (2) with intent to enter onto realty in the possession of another, and (3) resulting in actual entry.

Affirmative Conduct. If Joe is driving down the street when Alan runs a stop sign with his car, smashes into Joe, and pushes Joe up onto Ed's lawn, no trespass has been committed by Joe. He invaded Ed's real property but not through any affirmative act of his own.

Intent. Unlike most other intentional torts, the intent element of a trespass cause of action requires the plaintiff to demonstrate only that the defendant intended to enter the place and that the place belonged to the plaintiff. No intent to do harm is required. Thus, if Cindy walks across Ann's land believing that she is walking across her own or across land belonging to her friend Sally who has given her permission to cross it, Cindy commits

The Law at Work

Shoplifting is a problem of immense proportions, costing American retailers (and, by extension, American consumers) as much as $20 billion each year. The text describes antishoplifting statutes that protect merchants from false imprisonment lawsuits when they act reasonably in lodging criminal complaints against suspected shoplifters.

Another tool for merchants, which many believe is less complicated and more effective than the criminal complaint, is the civil fine. More than 40 states have enacted statutes allowing merchants to file civil actions against suspected shoplifters. If the action succeeds, the court may assess "fines" (which are paid to the merchant) against the shoplifters ranging from relatively small amounts (such as $40) to three times "actual damages" (including, generally, the price of the item and the wages of the employees whose time is consumed processing the case). Fines are typically higher if goods are not returned or are damaged, and often the shoplifter must pay the merchant's court costs and attorney's fees.

Many merchants prefer the civil approach rather than pressing criminal charges because the criminal lawsuits are often delayed for long periods as courts struggle to handle more serious cases. Also, merchants seldom recover any money through criminal proceedings. One national retailer recovered more than $50,000 in one year through such fines, although this was just a drop in the bucket compared to real losses caused by shoplifting.

a trespass actionable by Ann. Cindy's good faith is no defense. However, if Mark has a heart attack and dies instantly while driving down the street, and his car runs onto Ed's lawn, the affirmative conduct element is arguably not met and certainly the intent element is missing. The same may be said of a person who, driving too fast on slick streets, loses control of the car and winds up on someone's lawn. The intent element is missing.

Actual Entry. Entry is required for completion of the tort, but *usually* no real injury. Damage is presumed from the fact of entry, even if the only injury is trampled blades of grass. A judgment in the form of nominal damages of a dollar or so would still be warranted. According to most courts, the invasion need only be slight, including throwing a rock onto the plaintiffs property, shooting a bullet over it, or tunneling under it. Some courts refuse to recognize injury where the invasion is truly minor, such as where A's tree limb grows so far that it extends over B's property line.

The court must sometimes balance competing interests. For example, in Bradley v. American Smelting and Refining Co., 709 P.2d 782 (Wash. 1985), the defendant operated a copper smelter that emitted particulate matter, including arsenic, cadmium, and other metals. Although undetectable by human senses and not harmful to health, this matter did sometimes settle on the plaintiff's property. The court felt constrained to create an exception to the general rule that any entry constitutes an injury, stating:

When [airborne] particles or substance accumulates on the land and does not pass away, then a trespass has occurred. While at common law any trespass entitled a landowner to recover nominal and punitive damages for the invasion of his property, such a rule is not appropriate under the circumstances before us. No useful purpose would be served by sanctioning actions in trespass by every landowner within a hundred miles of a manufacturing plant. Manufacturers would be harassed and the litigious few would cause the escalation of costs to the detriment of the many. . ... The plaintiff who cannot show actual and substantial damages should be subject to dismissal.

A claim of trespass is normally recognized as belonging to the lawful possessor of the land even if he is not the owner. Thus, if T were renting a farm from L, and X trespassed on the farm, T would normally have the right to sue for trespass rather than L.

Defenses

In addition to the typical two-year statute of limitations (which is extended if the trespass is a continuing one, as when the trespasser has erected a small building on the plaintiff's property), the main defenses to a trespass cause of action are consent and legal right. Thus, a tenant has the landlord's consent, pursuant to a lease, to remain on the landlord's property. However, if the tenant stays beyond the term of the lease and refuses to leave, a trespass is committed because consent has expired.

A legal right might arise from, for example, an easement, which is a right to use someone's property for a limited purpose. Thus, if M's land is between N's land and a major highway, N might negotiate an easement from M, paying M a sum of money in exchange for the limited right to travel over M's land going to and from the highway.

Other Intentional Torts
Invasion of Privacy

Slowly over the past 75 years or so, the courts have begun to recognize privacy as an interest worthy of legal protection. Today, many jurisdictions have recognized one or more of the following varieties of tort that come under the umbrella of **invasion of privacy.**

Intrusion

Intrusion occurs whenever a defendant intrudes into an area where a plaintiff has a reasonable expectation of privacy. The invasion must be highly offensive to a reasonable person to be actionable. Secretly placing a microphone under the plaintiffs bed to overhear the goings-on would be actionable. So might an employer's secretly searching an employee's locker (where the employee provided his or her own lock and therefore had a justifiable expectation of privacy) without reasonable grounds for doing so.

Disclosure of Embarrassing Private Facts

Where no justification exists, it may be actionable to disclose to the public facts that the plaintiff finds embarrassing or offensive. Because they are "true," the disclosures do not constitute defamation; they may be more akin to blackmail However, a newsworthiness defense exists, at least for the media. In one case, a woman sued for the embarrassment she was caused by a newspaper's disclosing that her husband was killed in a fire in a motel while accompanied by another woman. The court held that fires are newsworthy events, and the newspaper could not be liable for accurately reporting the names of the victims. (Fry v. Ionia Sentinel Standard, 300 N.W.2d 867 (Mich.App. 1980)).

False Light

Very similar to the tort of defamation, the action for "false–light" privacy renders liable a defendant who makes statements or does acts that place the plaintiff in a false light in the public eye. Although usually these statements or actions would injure the plaintiffs reputation and also be actionable as defamation, occasionally they might involve false statements that the plaintiff had performed many wonderful deds. Rather than suing for injury to reputation as in defamation suits, a false–light plaintiff seeks compensation for shame, embarrassment, mental anguish, or humiliation. An attraction of this tort is that it frequently has a two–year statute of limitations, longer than the one–year statutes typical for defamation. The tort of placing someone else in a false light is very uncommon.

Appropriation of Name or Likeness

A final type of privacy tort protects the economic interests that persons have in the potential exploitation of their names and faces. Thus, if a company uses the name or picture of a famous actress in its advertising campaign without her permission, it has appropriated her name or likeness to her economic detriment. The company should have acquired her consent and paid her for such use. After singer Bette Midler refused to sing for a company's television commercial, it hired one of her back–up singers and asked her to sound as much like Midler as possible. Many listeners thought they were hearing the real Bette Midler, which formed the basis for a successful appropriation suit by Midler. (Midler v. Ford Motor Co., 849 F.2d 460 (9th Cir. 1988))

Several employer–employee disputes have involved claims of invasion of privacy, as the following case illustrates.

YOUNG V. JACKSON
Supreme Court of Mississippi, 572 So.2d 378 (1990)

Plaintiff Young worked at a nuclear power station operated by the defendant, Mississippi Power & LightCo. One day while Young, wearing protective gear, was working in an area highly contaminated by radioactivity, *she lost consciousness and was transported to the hospital. Co–worker and defendant Jackson called and visited her at the hospital to inquire about her status. The substance of what happened is disputed. Young claimed that Jackson told her that government safety officials were inquiring about the incident and she needed to tell what happened. Young further claimed that she told Jackson that it was not a safety matter but stemmed from a partial hysterectomy she recently had. The operation was very upsetting to Young, who felt like "half a woman now. Young testified that she made Jackson promise to keep the information secret because she had not even told her husband. Jackson, however, testified that Young volunteered the information about her hysterectomy, telling him not to worry about any radiation.*

Word spread quickly throughout the plant that Young had collapsed and been taken to the hospital. Rumors spread that Young was a victim of radiation and other employees might be also. In this setting, Jackson told his boss about the hysterectomy and Jackson's boss called employees together and told them there was no reason to worry about radiation because Young had passed out because of the aftereffects of her recent partial hysterectomy.

Later, Young filed this action against the defendants claiming invasion of privacy. The trial court granted the defendants' motion for summary judgment and Young appealed.

Robertson, Justice:

The positive law of this state affords each person a substantial zone of freedom which, at his election, he may keep private. The zone surrounds person and place and without his consent may not be invaded by other persons. We have made no effort to identify the outer limits of a person's right of privacy and certainly make none here. Suffice it to say that where, as here, the invasion is by private parties, we have recognized a right of action in at least three contexts: (1) the portrayal of Plaintiff in a false light; (2) appropriation of Plaintiff's likeness and unpermitted use; (3) public disclosure of private facts, and (4) intrusion into seclusion. It is theory (3) that Betty Young invokes and

we accept its more precise statement in Restatement (Second) of Torts Sec. 652D (1977): "One who gives publicity to a matter concerning the private life of another is subject to liability to the other for invasions of his privacy, if the matter publicized is of a kind that (a) would be highly offensive to a reasonable person, and (b) is not of legitimate concern to the public."

No doubt an objective test obtains. A person may not be held liable for public disclosure of facts about another unless he should reasonably have foreseen that the person would be likely offended. It requires little awareness of personal prejudice and human nature to know that, generally speaking, no aspects of life [are] more personal and private than those having to do with one's sexual organs and reproductive system. It may be the fact that many women who have undergone a hysterectomy do not keep that fact secret, but this is not the test. We do not regard it unreasonable that a woman would consider the fact a private matter, nor unforeseeable that she would so consider it.

Without further ado, we hold that the fact that she has undergone a hysterectomy is a fact that a woman ordinarily has the right to keep private if she wishes and that public disclosure of that fact by unauthorized persons and without her consent may be actionable.

The [trial court] did not hold Young stated no claim but rather that, in the present state of the record, Defendants' qualified privilege defense prevailed as a matter of law. The defense of qualified privilege has long been accepted in our law of defamation, but we have had no occasion to consider it in an invasion of privacy context. The settings are certainly analogous. We hold that actions for invasion of privacy are subject to the defense of privilege the same as defamation actions. Turning to the contours of the qualified privilege defense as it has evolved in the law of defamation, we can improve little on this Court's early statement:

A communication made in good faith and on a subject—matter in which the person making it has an interest or in reference to which he has a duty, is privileged if made to a person or persons having a corresponding interest or duty, even though it contains matter which without this privilege would be slanderous. There are certain occasions on which a man is entitled to state what he believes to be the truth about another, and in doing so public policy requires that he shall be protected, provided he makes the statement honestly and not for any indirect or wrong motive. Such occasions are called occasions of qualified privilege, for the reason that the protection is not absolute, but depends entirely upon the honesty of purpose with which the statement is made. Among such statements is one made on a subject—matter in which the person making it, and the person to whom it is made, have a legitimate common interest. The underlying principle is public policy.

Specifically, this Court has recognized that a public policy reason of the sort contemplate[d] exists in the context of the employer/employee relationship.

Today's case arises in such an employer/employee context, and the statements concerning Young's hysterectomy were made against the backdrop of that relationship. The work at [the nuclear power station] was disrupted by rumors concerning Young's accident. Young's co—workers were concerned for her welfare, but for their own as well. Disclosing the true facts of Young's operation could reasonably have been seen likely to allay the fears of her co—workers of excessive levels of radiation in the areas in which they worked.

[Affirmed.]

Intentional Infliction of Mental Distress

As noted earlier, because emotional injuries are difficult to prove and to value, courts have traditionally been reluctant to allow recovery for them. But just as they are now allowed in suitable cases of negligence they are also allowed when intentionally caused. The turning point may have been cases such as Wilkinson v. Downtin, 2 Q.B.D. 57 (1897), in which, as a practical joke, the defendant called the plaintiff, a woman whose mental state was somewhat suspect anyway, and told her that her husband had been in a serious accident. This so upset the plaintiff that she had to be hospitalized. Recovery for her emotional distress was allowed.

The requisite elements for proof for the tort of **intentional infliction of mental distress** are generally formulated as follows. First, the defendant must be guilty of extreme and outrageous conduct. Mere insults are usually insufficient, as are profanity and other abuses of a relatively minor nature. Second, the defendant must have intended to cause the plaintiff severe emotional distress. Again, the defendant will be presumed to intend the natural consequences of his or her actions. And a defendant who is aware of a particular plaintiff's susceptibilities to mental distress will be judged accordingly. Finally, the plaintiff must actually suffer such severe distress. Physical consequences are not required, but their presence does assist in establishing proof of severe emotional anguish.

Today, such suits frequently involve attempts by collection agencies to force debtors to pay bills. Thus, in Turman v. Central Billing, Inc. , 568 P.2d 1382 (1977), the collection agency was held liable to Turman, who was blind, when it badgered her in trying to collect a small debt assigned to it for collection, even after it knew that she and the creditor had come to a satisfactory settlement. This harassment, which resulted in the plaintiff's hospitalization for anxiety and severe stress, was carried out by repeated phone calls—sometimes twice a day—in which the defendant's agent "shouted" at her, used profanity, told her several times that her husband would lose his job and the house if she did not pay, and called her "scum" and a "deadbeat." (Such egregious acts also violate the Federal Debt Collection Practices Act.)

This tort cannot be used to evade First Amendment restrictions on recovery for defamation. When the Reverend Jerry Falwell sued *Hustler* magazine over an extremely rude parody, showing that it had caused him emotional distress, the Supreme Court held that freedom of expression considerations barred recovery. Hustler Magazine v. Falwell, 485 U.S. 46(1988).

While some courts have indicated that they recognize that feelings can be severely hurt when someone is fired or laid off, they do not want every employment dispute to be turned into a lawsuit for intentional infliction of emotional distress. Still, some employers' activities can be found to be beyond the pale.

GTE SOUTHWEST V. BRUCE
998 S.W.2d 605 (Tex. 1999)

Three GTE employees, Rhonda Bruce, Linda Davis, and Joyce Poelstra, sued GTE for intentional infliction of emotional distress premised on the constant humiliating and abusive behavior of their supervisor, Morris-Shields. Shields is a former U.S. Army supply sergeant who began working for GTE in 1971. Between 1981 and May 1991, Shields worked as a supervisor in GTE's supply department Jacksonville, Arkansas. During his tenure there, four of Shields's subordinate employees (none of the employees involved in this case) filed formal grievances against Shields with GTE, alleging that Shields constantly harassed them. As a result of these complaints, GTE investigated Shields's conduct in 1988 and 1989, but took no formal disciplinary action against him.

In May 1991, GTE transferred Shields from Jacksonville to Nash, Texas, where he became the supply operations supervisor. The supply department at Nash was small, consisting of two offices and a store room. There were approximately eight employees other than Shields. Bruce, Davis, and Poelstra ("the employees") worked under Shields at the Nash facility. Like the GTE employees in Jacksonville, Bruce, Davis, and Poelstra complained to GTE of Shields's conduct, alleging that Shields constantly harassed and intimidated them. The employees complained about Shields daily use of profanity, short temper, and his abusive and vulgar dictatorial manner. The employees complained that, among other offensive acts, Shields repeatedly yelled, screamed, cursed, and even "charged" at them. In addition, he intentionally humiliated and embarrassed the employees.

GTE investigated these complaints in April 1992, after which GTE issued Shields a "letter of reprimand. "After the reprimand, Shields discontinued some of his egregious conduct, but did not end it completely.

Eventually, Bruce, Davis, and Poelstra sought medical treatment for emotional distress caused by Shields's conduct. In March 1994, the employees filed suit, alleging that GTE intentionally inflicted emotional distress on them through Shields. A jury ruled for plaintiffs and the Texas Court of Appeals affirmed. GTE appealed to the Texas Supreme Court.

Abbott, Justice:

To recover damages for intentional infliction of emotional distress, a plaintiff must prove that: (1) the defendant acted intentionally or recklessly; (2) the conduct was extreme and outrageous; (3) the actions of the defendant caused the plaintiff emotional distress; and (4) the resulting emotional distress was severe. Standard Fruit & Vegetable Co. v. Johnson, 985 S.W.2d 62 (Tex. 1998). In addition, "[a] claim for intentional infliction of emotional distress cannot be maintained when the risk that emotional distress will result is merely incidental to the commission of some other tort." Id. Accordingly, a claim for intentional infliction of emotional distress will not lie if emotional distress is not the intended or primary consequence of the defendant's conduct.

GTE first argues that Shields's conduct is not extreme and outrageous. To be extreme and outrageous, conduct must be "so outrageous in character, and so extreme in degree, as to go beyond all possible bounds of decency, and to be regarded as atrocious, and utterly intolerable in a civilized community." Natividad v. Alexsis, Inc., 875 S.W.2d 695 (Tex. 1994). Generally, insensitive or even rude behavior does not constitute extreme and outrageous conduct. Similarly, mere insults, indignities, threats, annoyances, petty oppressions, or other trivialities do not rise to the level of extreme and outrageous conduct.

In determining whether certain conduct is extreme and outrageous, courts consider the context and the relationship between the parties. In the employment context, some courts have held that a plaintiffs status as an employee should entitle him to a greater degree of protection from insult and outrage by a supervisor with authority over him than if he were a stranger. This approach is based partly on the rationale that, as opposed to most casual and temporary relationships, the workplace environment provides a captive victim and the opportunity for prolonged abuse.

In contrast, several courts, including Texas courts, have adopted a strict approach to intentional infliction of emotional distress claims arising in the workplace. Texas courts have held that a claim for intentional infliction of emotional distress does not lie for ordinary employment disputes. The range of behavior encompassed in "employment disputes" is broad, and includes at a minimum such things as criticism, lack of recognition, and low evaluations, which, although unpleasant and sometimes unfair, are ordinarily expected in the work environment. Thus, to establish a cause of action for intentional infliction of emotional distress in the workplace, an employee must prove the existence of some conduct that brings the dispute outside the scope of an ordinary employment dispute and into the realm of extreme and outrageous conduct. *See* Ramirez v. Allright Parking El Paso, Inc., 970 F.2d 1372 (5th Cir. 1992) (requiring employee to show conduct "elevating [the employer's] actions above those involved in an 'ordinary employment dispute'"). Such extreme conduct exists only in the most unusual of circumstances. For example, in Dean v. Ford Motor Credit Co., 885 F.2d 300 (5th Cir. 1989), the court recognized that the supervisor's act of placing checks in the employee's purse to make it appear that she was a thief and to put her in fear of criminal prosecution was extreme and outrageous. In addition, in

Wilson v. Monarch Paper Co., 939 F.2d 1138 (5th Cir. 1991), the court held that the employer's intentional and systematic actions to humiliate the plaintiff, a long-time executive with a college education and 30 years experience, and to force him to quit by requiring him to do menial, janitorial duties was extreme and outrageous.

GTE contends that the evidence establishes nothing more than an ordinary employment dispute. To the contrary, the employees produced evidence that, over a period of more than two years, Shields engaged in a pattern of grossly abusive, threatening, and degrading conduct. Shields began regularly using the harshest vulgarity shortly after his arrival at the Nash facility. In response, Bruce and Davis informed Shields that they were uncomfortable with obscene jokes, vulgar cursing, and sexual innuendo in the office. Despite these objections, Shields continued to use exceedingly vulgar language on a daily basis. Several witnesses testified that Shields regularly heaped abusive profanity on the employees. Linda Davis testified that Shields used this language to get a reaction. Gene Martin, another GTE employee, testified that Shields used the words "f———" and "mother f———er" frequently when speaking with the employees. On one occasion when Bruce asked Shields to curb his language because it was offensive, Shields positioned himself in front of her face, and screamed, "I will do and say any damn thing I want. And I don't give a s———who likes it." There was further evidence that Shields' harsh and vulgar language was not merely accidental, but seemed intended to abuse the employees.

More importantly, the employees testified that Shields repeatedly physically and verbally threatened and terrorized them. There was evidence that Shields was continuously in a rage, and that Shields would frequently assault each of the employees by physically charging at them. When doing so, Shields would bend his head down, put his arms straight down by his sides, ball his hands into fists, and walk quickly toward or "lunge" at the employees, stopping uncomfortably close to their faces while screaming and yelling. The employees were exceedingly frightened by this behavior, afraid that Shields might hit them. Linda Davis testified that Shields charged the employees with the intent to frighten them. At least once, another employee came between Shields and Poelstra to protect her from Shields's charge. A number of witnesses testified that Shields frequently yelled and screamed at the top of his voice, and pounded his fists when requesting the employees to do things. Bruce testified that Shields would "come up fast" and "get up over her" —— causing her to lean back —— and yell and scream in her face for her to get things for him. Shields included vulgar language in his yelling and screaming. Bruce stated that such conduct was not a part of any disciplinary action against her. Further, the incidents usually occurred in the open rather than in private. Bruce testified that, on one occasion, Shields began beating a banana on his desk, and when he jumped up and slammed the banana into the trash, Bruce thought he would hit her. Afterwards, Shields was shaking and said "I'm sick."

Bruce also told of an occasion when Shields entered Bruce's office and went into a rage because Davis had left her purse on a chair and Bruce had placed her umbrella on a filing cabinet in the office. Shields yelled and screamed for Bruce to clean up her office. Shields yelled, "If you don't get things picked up in this office, you will not be working for me." He later said that Bruce and Davis would be sent to the unemployment line and "could be replaced by two Kelly girls" that were twenty years old. On another occasion, Shields came up behind Bruce and said, "You're going to be in the unemployment line." Once he told Bruce that he had been sent to Nash to fire her. Another time, he typed "quit" on his computer and said, "That's what you can do." Davis testified that Shields threatened to "get them" for complaining about his behavior. And both Bruce and Martin testified that Shields had stated that "he was in a position to get even for what [the employees] had done."

Bruce also testified that Shields called her into his office every day and would have her stand in front of him, sometimes for as long as thirty minutes, while Shields simply stared at her. Bruce was not allowed to leave Shields' office until she was dismissed, even though Shields would periodically talk on the phone or read papers. This often occurred several times a day. Bruce testified that it made her nauseated and intimidated her. On one occasion, Shields backed Bruce into a corner, leaned over her, and said, "Rumor has it that you know how to get anything you want out here." During an annual review, Shields said to Bruce, "You're mean and you're deadly, very deadly." Davis also testified that Shields would stand over her desk and stare at her.

Shields required Bruce and Davis, both general clerks at GTE, to purchase vacuum cleaners with company funds and to vacuum their offices daily, despite the fact that the company had a cleaning service that performed janitorial services such as vacuuming. The purpose of this seemed not to clean, but to humiliate. Bruce testified that she was ridiculed by other employees. Shields also yelled and screamed when he discovered a spot on the carpet; he made Bruce get on her hands and knees and clean the spots while he stood over her yelling. Poelstra testified that Shields required her to clean tobacco stains from a wall in the warehouse. Poelstra testified that, after she forgot her paperwork for a driving test, Shields ordered her to wear a post—it note on her shirt that said, "Don't forget your paperwork." Other witnesses corroborated the employees' testimony about Shields' conduct.

In considering whether the evidence establishes more than an ordinary employment dispute, we will also address GTE's argument that because none of Shields's acts standing alone rises to the level of outrageous conduct, the court of appeals erred in holding that, considered cumulatively, the conduct was extreme and outrageous.

As already noted, the employees demonstrated at trial that Shields engaged in a course of harassing conduct directed at each of them, the totality of which caused severe emotional distress. It is well recognized outside of the employment context that a course of harassing conduct may support liability for intentional infliction of emotional distress. In such cases, courts consider the totality of the conduct in determining whether it is extreme and outrageous. Similarly, in the employment context, courts and commentators have almost unanimously recognized that liability may arise when one in a position of authority engages in repeated or ongoing harassment of an employee, if the cumulative quality and quantity of the harassment is extreme and outrageous. When such repeated or ongoing harassment is alleged, the offensive conduct is evaluated as a whole. We agree with the overwhelming weight of authority in this state and around the country that when repeated or ongoing severe harassment is shown, the conduct should be evaluated as a whole in determining whether it is extreme and outrageous.

We now consider whether Shields' conduct, taken as a whole, amounts to extreme and outrageous conduct. When reasonable minds may differ, however, it is for the jury, subject to the court's control, to determine whether, in the particular case, the conduct has been sufficiently extreme and outrageous to result in liability. To support liability for intentional infliction of emotional distress, it is not enough that the defendant has acted with an intent that is tortious, malicious, or even criminal, or that he has intended to inflict emotional distress.

GTE argues that the conduct complained of is an ordinary employment dispute because the employees' complaints are really that Shields was a poor supervisor with an objectionable management style. GTE also contends that the actions are employment disputes because Shields committed the acts in the course of disciplining his employees. But Shields' ongoing acts of harassment, intimidation, and humiliation and his daily obscene and vulgar behavior, which GTE defends as his "management style," went beyond the bounds of tolerable workplace conduct. The picture painted by the evidence at trial was unmistakable: Shields greatly exceeded the necessary leeway to supervise, criticize, demote, transfer, and discipline, and created a workplace that was a den of terror for the employees. And the evidence showed that all of Shields' abusive conduct was common, not rare. Being purposefully humiliated and intimidated, and being repeatedly put in fear of one's physical well–being at the hands of a supervisor is more than a mere triviality or annoyance.

Occasional malicious and abusive incidents should not be condoned, but must often be tolerated in our society. But once conduct such as that shown here becomes a regular pattern of behavior and continues despite the victim's objection and attempts to remedy the situation, it can no longer be tolerated. It is the severity and regularity of Shields's abusive and threatening conduct that brings his behavior into the realm of extreme and outrageous conduct. Conduct such as being regularly assaulted, intimidated, and threatened is not typically encountered nor expected in the course of one's employment, nor should it be accepted in a civilized society. An employer certainly has much leeway in its chosen methods of supervising and disciplining employees, but terrorizing them is simply not acceptable. If GTE or Shields was dissatisfied with the employees' performance, GTE could have terminated them, disciplined them, or taken some other more appropriate approach to the problem instead of fostering the abuse, humiliation, and intimidation that was heaped on the employees. Accordingly, the trial court properly submitted the issue to the jury, and there was some evidence to support the jury's conclusion that Shields' conduct was extreme and outrageous.

[The court then concluded that there was ample evidence to support the jury's conclusion that the other elements of the cause of action were present, including that plaintiffs had indeed sustained severe emotional distress.] Affirmed.

Fraud

The essence of the tort of *fraud* is the intentional misleading of one person by another, which results in a loss to the deceived party. Because many kinds of fraudulent conduct occur when the sole purpose of the wrongdoer is to cause the innocent party to enter a contract that the person otherwise would not make, additional consideration of this subject will be undertaken in Chapter 15.

Conversion and Trespass to Personal Property

The tort of **conversion** renders actionable certain invasions of personal property interests, just as trespass protects real property interests. Conversion remedies invasions so serious that they justify forcing the defendant to compensate the plaintiff for the reasonable value of the item involved. An example would be the defendant's theft of the plaintiff's automobile.

A tort that generally covers more minor invasions of personal property rights is frequently called **trespass to personal property** (or, "trespass to chattels"). This tort would remedy, for example, the defendant's minor vandalism of the plaintiff's car. Recently, the tort of trespass to personal property has arisen in situations in which the defendant has "hacked" into plaintiff's computer system (which is also a crime). In addition, someone who intentionally transmits a software virus, or who floods plaintiff's e–mail system with unsolicited e–mail to such an extent that it either causes problems with the plaintiff's e–mail server or interferes with the ability of plaintiff's employees to do their jobs, has committed the tort of trespass to personal property.

Nuisance

Like trespass to real property, the tort of **nuisance** protects the enjoyment of such property. Frequently nuisance is used to compensate an intangible disruption of the enjoyment of property, as when the plaintiff is injured by the defendant's invasion through light (erection of tall light poles), noise (rock concerts), vibrations (blasting with dynamite), or smells (pig farming). The courts will consider such factors as the type of neighborhood, the nature of the wrong, its proximity to the plaintiff, its frequency or continuity, and the nature and extent of the injury in deciding whether an actionable nuisance exists.

Special Problems
Employer Liability

Ordinarily, the application of the principles of tort law results in the imposition of liability on the wrongdoer alone. There is one major exception, however, which springs from the principles comprising our master-servant law and our law of agency.

Under these principles, an employer is uniformly held liable for the torts of employees if the employees are acting "within the scope of their employment" at the time of the injury. Thus, if T, a truck driver employed by the D Furniture Company, negligently injures P while delivering a piece of furniture to a customer's home, P has a cause of action against both T and the D Company, as illustrated in Figure 8.1.

Ordinarily, in such a case, P brings just one action against both defendants; if he is successful in proving the facts as alleged, he obtains a "joint and several" judgment against T and the D Company. This means that if he is awarded a judgment of $4000, he can enforce the judgment against the assets of either party, or of both, until that sum is recovered. (The "scope of employment" problem is covered further in Chapter 24.)

Joint and Several Liability

When two defendants' actions together contribute to a plaintiffs injury, they are frequently held jointly and severally liable. The "joint" portion of this liability means that each defendant may be held responsible for the entire loss caused to the plaintiff. Thus, theoretically one defendant who is only 10 percent at fault might have to pay also for

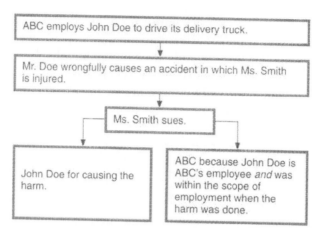

Figure 8.1 Employer's Liability for Employee's Tort

the 90 percent fault of another defendant, especially if the latter defendant is judg-ment–proof (lacking assets or insurance to pay). The relatively harsh result that this can have for "deep pocket" defendants is a major cause of criticism of our present tort system. Most states have abolished or enacted limits on joint and several liability in many types of cases.

Business Torts

As we have seen in our discussion of negligence and intentional torts, all of tort law has applicability to businesses. Certain kinds of torts, however, are often referred to as "business torts" because they arise directly from the competitive rivalry between businesses. We discuss two of the main areas of tort law involving business torts. The first is Intentional Interference with Business Relationships. This tort is sometimes referred to as "tortious interference." Like almost all other tort law, it has been developed by courts as part of the law of intentional torts. The second is Unfair Competition, which is quite a bit broader and actually encompasses several closely related torts. The law of unfair competition has many sources, including state court decisions (common law) and both state and federal statutes. Finally, the subject of the next chapter, Chapter 9—Intellectual Property Law—is very closely related. This area of law— misappropriation of trade secrets and infringement of patents, copyrights, and trademarks— also encompasses allegedly wrongful conduct arising from competitive rivalry. As with all areas of law, categorization can be difficult and imprecise.

Intentional Interference with Business Relationships

Beginning with an old English case, Lumley v. Gye, 118 Eng.Rep. 749 (Q.B. 1853), in which an opera singer was induced by the defendant theater owner to breach her contract to sing at the plaintif's theater and appear at the defendant's instead, courts have recognized the general principle that a third party who wrongfully interferes with an existing contract has committed a tort. Most courts have even stretched the concept to hold defendants liable for intentionally interfering with contracts that do not yet exist but are reasonably certain to be entered into, and with certain other kinds of business relationships that have not yet attained the status of binding contracts.

Elements of the Tort

The law in this area varies quite a bit among courts in different states. Even the name of the tort—variously tortious interference with contract, tortious interference with business relationships, tortious interference with prospective economic advantage—varies among jurisdictions.

The basic elements of the tort, however, are similar in most states. The factual scenario in such cases typically involves a plaintiff and defendant who are competitors, the plaintiff has a contractual relationship with a third party, and plaintiff contends that the defendant intentionally took actions that led the third party to breach its contract with the plaintiff. In the case of an existing contract, a common formulation of the elements of the tort would be that plaintiff must prove: (a) the existence of a binding contract subject to interference; (b) an intentional act of interference; (c) proximate cause; and (d) actual damage or loss occurred. The intent involved need not be malicious. The simple fact that defendant knew such a contract existed and proceeded to interfere suffices.

Texaco, Inc. v. Pennzoil Co., 729 S.W.2d 768 (Tex.App. 1987), one of the most controversial cases in recent legal history, involved a situation in which the court found that the defendant had knowingly interfered with an existing contract. Pennzoil sued Texaco for intentional interference with contract rights when Texaco bought a controlling interest in the stock of Getty Oil Co. after, according to Pennzoil, it had already made a contract to acquire Getty. Agreeing with Pennzoil, a jury awarded the largest judgment in American legal history—$11.1 billion in compensatory and punitive damages. (That verdict and trial court judgment were affirmed on appeal and later settled out of court when Texaco paid $3 billion to Pennzoil.)

But what if there is no binding contract, but simply the prospect that plaintiff might have entered into a binding contract or a beneficial economic relationship with the third party? In this setting, a common formulation of the elements of a cause of action requires: (a) a reasonable probability that the parties would have entered into a contractual relationship; (b) an intentional *and malicious* act by defendant that prevented the relationship from occurring, with the purpose of harming plaintiff; (c) defendant lacked privilege or justification to do the act; and (d) actual damage or loss occurred. Because no binding contract exists, it is fair for defendant to compete with plaintiff for the third party's business and therefore, defendant will not be liable in this setting unless it acted with "malice." Indeed, as we shall soon see many courts require a vague showing of "malice." They require that defendant committed an independent tort or violation of law.

One case illustrating the tort of intentional interference with a business relationship that had not yet ripened into a legally enforceable contract involved the following situation. A real estate salesman followed customers away from his former employer's business premises and convinced them to rescind their contracts with that business and to purchase less expensive real estate from him. Although the customers had the right under the federal Truth–in–Lending Act (these were credit sales) to rescind their contracts with the former employer within three days, the salesman was found liable to his former employer for committing this tort. Although there was arguably no interference with a binding contract, there was interference with prospective advantage flowing from an advantageous business relationship. One can see that the relationship came very close to being a legally enforceable contract, however. Other examples of circumstances in which most courts would hold the defendant liable for interference with a business relationship that was not valid contract include situations in which there was a contract between the plaintiff and a third party, but the contract was not legally enforceable because it was required to be in writing under the Statute of Frauds (discussed in Chapter 16 or was not a valid contract because the plaintiff or the third party had committed fraud in the creation of the contract (or was not valid for similar reasons discussed in Chapter 15).

Because this is an intentional tort, plaintiffs often recover punitive damages as well as compensatory damages.

Privilege of Competition

As noted earlier, the courts in a majority of states do not require the plaintiff to prove that the defendant acted with malice when the defendant knowingly induced someone to breach an existing contract with the plaintiff. A larger number of courts do require proof of (at least) malice, however, when the relationship that the defendant interfered with was not yet a legally enforceable contract or when the contract is terminable at will and therefore either party may withdraw without breach.

In such cases, the defendant is protected by the **privilege of competition**—the right to compete—as long as the defendant did not use clearly improper means to achieve his purpose. Assume that P Co. has an at–will contract to supply ABC Co. with widgets. D Co. is entitled to go to ABC to offer a better price or better quality in order to win ABC's business away from P Co. However, D Co. may not lie about the quality of P's products or its own or defame P's owners in an attempt to win away ABC's business.

Note, however, that if P Co. has a two–year term contract to supply ABC with widgets, D Co. cannot invoke the competition privilege in order to induce ABC to breach its contract with P Co. P Co.'s right to see its contract with ABC enforced outweighs D's right to compete. But D Co. is entitled to induce ABC to switch away from P's products to its own as soon as the two–year contract expires.

Justification Defense

Malice also would not be found if the defendant's actions are legally justifiable. **Justification** for a defendant's interference may be found if it is aimed at protecting a third person's legitimate interests, such as when an independent construction inspector hired by a city recommended that the city terminate the plaintiff's construction contract for substandard work, or at protecting the public interest in general.

Furthermore, the defendant can claim justification for interference to protect its own existing legitimate contractual or property interests. For example, assume that X gets a new car franchise from D, an auto manufacturer. Later X makes a contract with P, a motorcycle wholesaler, under the terms of which P is permitted to sell motorcycles in a limited area in X's showroom. D subsequently causes X to break the contract with P because of complaints from new car buyers about dirt and noise associated with P's operation. D's interest in the proper conduct of the new car dealership would likely justify its actions, providing a defense to any tortious interference claim P might bring. Thus, P's only recourse would be a breach of contract action against X.

The following case shows one court's analysis of a case in which the defendant induced several third parties to make contracts with him, when doing so necessarily meant that they would breach their contracts with the plaintiff, a competitor of defendant.

SPEAKERS OF SPORT, INC. V. PROSERV, INC.
Seventh Circuit Court of Appeals, 178 F.3d 862 (1999)

Ivan Rodriguez, a highly successful major league catcher, in 1991 signed the first of several one-year contracts making plaintiff Speakers of Sport his agent. Defendant Pro-Serv wanted to expand its representation of baseball players and to this end invited Rodriguez to its office in Washington and there promised that it would get him between $2 and $4 million in endorsements if he signed with ProServ—which he did, terminating his contract (which was terminable at will) with Speakers. This was in 1995. ProServ failed to obtain significant endorsement for Rodriguez and after just one year he switched to another agent who the following year landed him a five-year $42 million contract with the Texas Rangers. Speakers brought this suit a few months later, charging that the promise of endorsements that ProServ had made to Rodriguez tortiously induced him to terminate his contract with Speakers.

The district court ruled against plaintiff Speakers, and Speakers appealed.

Posner, Chief Judge:

Speakers could not sue Rodriguez for breach of contract, because he had not broken their contract, which was, as we said, terminable at will. Nor, therefore, could it accuse ProServ of inducing a *breach* of contract. But Speakers did have a contract with Rodriguez, and inducing the *termination* of a contract, even when the termination is not a breach because the contract is terminable at will, can still be actionable under the tort law of Illinois as an interference with prospective economic advantage.

There is in general nothing wrong with one sports agent trying to take a client from another if this can be done without precipitating a breach of contract. That is the process known as competition, which though painful, fierce, frequently ruthless, sometimes Darwinian in its pitilessness, is the cornerstone of our highly successful economic system. Competition is not a tort, but on the contrary provides a defense (the "competitor's privilege") to the tort of improper interference. It does not privilege inducing a breach of [a term] contract, but it does privilege inducing the lawful termination of a contract that is terminable at will. Sellers do not "own" their customers, at least not without a contract with them that is not terminable at will.

There would be few more effective inhibitors of the competitive process than making it a tort for an agent to promise the client of another agent to do better by him——which is pretty much what this case comes down to. It is true that Speakers argues only that the competitor may not make a promise that he knows he cannot fulfill, may not, that is, compete by fraud. Because the competitor's privilege does not include a right to get business from a competitor by means of fraud, it is hard to quarrel with this position in the abstract, but the practicalities are different. If the argument were accepted and the new agent made a promise that was not fulfilled, the old agent would have a shot at convincing a jury that the new agent had known from the start that he couldn't deliver on the promise. Once a case gets to the jury, all bets are off. The practical consequence of Speakers' approach, therefore, would be that a sports agent who lured away the client of another agent with a promise to do better by him would be running a grave legal risk.

The promise of endorsements was puffing not in the most common sense of a cascade of extravagant adjectives but in the equally valid sense of a sales pitch that is intended, and that a reasonable person in the position of the "promisee" would understand, to be aspirational rather than enforceable——an expression of hope rather than a commitment. So understood, the "promise" was not a promise at all. But even if it was a promise (or a warranty), it cannot be the basis for a finding of fraud because it was not part of a scheme to defraud evidenced by more than the allegedly fraudulent promise itself [which must be shown to establish promissory fraud under Illinois law].

It can be argued, however, that competition can be tortious even if it does not involve an actionable fraud or other independently tortious act, such as defamation, or trademark or patent infringement, or a theft of a trade secret; that competitors should not be allowed to use "unfair" tactics; and that a promise known by the promisor when made to be unfulfillable is such a tactic, especially when used on a relatively unsophisticated, albeit very well to do, baseball player. Considerable support for this view can be found in the case law. But the Illinois courts have not as yet embraced the doctrine, and we are not alone in thinking it pernicious. The doctrine's conception of wrongful competition is vague—— "wrongful by reason of . . . an established standard of a trade or profession" or "a violation of recognized ethical rules or established customs or practices in the business community." Worse, the established standards of a trade or profession in regard to competition, and its ideas of unethical competitive conduct, are likely to reflect a desire to limit competition for reasons related to the self-interest of the trade or profession rather than to the welfare of its customers or clients. We agree with Professor Perlman that the tort of interference with business relationships should be confined to cases in which the defendant employed unlawful means to stiff a competitor, Harvey S. Perlman, "Interference With Contract and Other Economic Expectancies: A Clash of Tort and Contract Doctrine," 49 U. Chi. L. Rev. 61 (1982), and we are reassured by the conclusion of his careful analysis that the case law is generally consistent with this position as a matter of outcomes as distinct from articulation.

Invoking the concept of "wrongful by reason of . . . an established standard of a trade or profession," Speakers points to a rule of major league baseball forbidding players' agents to compete by means of misrepresentations. The rule is designed to protect the players, rather than their agents, so that even if it established a norm enforceable by law Speakers would not be entitled to invoke it; it is not a rule designed for Speakers' protection. In any event its violation would not be the kind of "wrongful" conduct that should trigger the tort of intentional interference; it would not be a violation of law. Affirmed.

Manager's Privilege

When a corporation breaches a contract, the other party will frequently sue not only the corporation for breach of contract but also will assert a tortious interference claim against any corporate manager who participated in the decision to breach the contract. Corporate officers or other managers are usually protected from liability by a doctrine called the "manager's privilege" if their decision to have the corporation breach the contract was based solely or essentially on the best interests of the corporation. Such would be the case when it would be far more advisable for a corporation to pay damages resulting from a breach of contract than to live up to a contract that might be financially disastrous. However, if the officer is acting primarily to further his or her own personal interests, tort liability will be imposed. If a consultant recommends in good faith that a client breach its contract with ABC Computer and begin buying XYZ's computers, an analogous "consultant's privilege" will protect the consultant from liability if ABC sued it for tortious interference with contract.

The following case addresses the question of what plaintiffs must prove in a case where there is no binding term contract.

Unfair Competition

The term unfair competition is an imprecise one. In its broadest sense, it covers all torts arising from competitive rivalry. In its most common usage, however, the term refers only to those business practices that are based on deception. It includes a number of common–law torts, such as (1) falsely causing consumers to believe a product is endorsed by another, and (2) "palming off'—palming off refers to any word or deed causing purchasers to be misled into thinking that defendant's product was produced by someone else for the purpose of taking a free ride on the plaintiff's brand name and reputation. Both (1) and (2) are a form of intentional trademark infringement that constituted a tort long before the development of modern federal trademark law.

State Deceptive Trade Practices Acts

A consumer who is misled by false advertising or other deceptive practices may have the right to sue under a common–law fraud theory or perhaps a breach of express warranty theory if the advertising involved a product. These theories are discussed in other chapters. However, additional consumer protection legislation, passed at both the state and federal levels, also addresses such activity.

Misleading advertising is often prohibited by **state deceptive trade practices** acts. In states having such statutes, the wrongs are thus statutory rather than common law torts. Other types of unfair competition that are usually prohibited by such statutes are the advertising of goods or services with the intent not to sell them on the advertised terms, representing goods as new when they are used or second–hand, and disparagement— making false statements of fact about competitors' goods or services.

Lanham Act

The federal government has also passed various acts that prohibit unfair competition, such as misleading advertising. In this chapter, our focus is on section 43(a) of the Lanham Act, which outlaws "any false description or representation." Although this section is frequently used to allow trademark owners to sue competitors for trademark infringement, it has also created a general federal law of unfair competition, which is frequently applied to deceptive advertising. Designed in large part to protect consumers from being misled, the cause of action is given primarily to the competitors of the deceptive advertiser.

Illegal Acts Under Section 43(a)

Section 43(a) of the Lanham Act has supported suits against companies that (1) used pictures of the plaintiff's product to advertise their own inferior brand; (2) used a confusingly similar color and shape of drug capsule that could mislead consumers into thinking that they were buying the plaintiff's nontrademarked brand; (3) printed "$2.99 as advertised on TV" when only the plaintiff had run such ads; (4) claimed that their pain reliever worked faster than the plaintiff's when it did not; and (5) displayed a rock star's picture on an album creating the impression that the star was a featured performer when, in fact, he or she was not.

As in all advertising, some "puffing" is permitted by the Lanham Act. For example, when a computerized chess game was advertised as "like having Karpov [a famous Russian chess master] as your opponent," mere puffing was found . Data Cash Systems v. JS&A Group, Inc. 223U.S.P.Q. 865(N.D.Il1. 1984)

Enforcement

Most courts have not allowed deceived consumers to bring section 43(a) claims. Instead, suit is usually brought by competitors who, while redressing their own injuries, seek to end false advertising that also injures consumers. These competitors have been termed vicarious avengers of the consumer interest. The following case contains a common fact pattern in Lanham Act litigation.

Commercial Defamation

Through passage of the Trademark Revision Act of 1988, Congress established a cause of action for commercial defamation, thereby increasing the volume of this type of litigation. The Lanham Act now bans false descriptions or representations about the

AMERICAN ITALIAN PASTA CO. v. NEW WORLD PASTA CO.

Eighth Circuit Court of Appeals, 371 F.3d 387 (2004)

From 1997 to 2000, American Italian Pasta Co. (American) manufactured Mueller's brand (Mueller's) dried pasta for Best Foods. In the fall of 2000, American purchased Mueller's and began placing the phrase "America's Favorite Pasta" on Mueller's packaging. On various packages, the phrases "Quality Since 1867," "Made from 100% Semolina," or "Made with Semolina" accompany the phrase "America's Favorite Pasta." The packaging also contains a paragraph in which the phrase "America's Favorite Pasta" appears. The paragraph states (1) pasta lovers have enjoyed Mueller's pasta for 130 years (2) claims Mueller's pasta cooks to perfect tenderness every time," because Mueller's uses "100% pure semolina milled from the highest quality durum wheat;" and (3) encourages consumers to "taste why Mueller's is America's favorite pasta."

In this litigation, New World claims that American's use of the phrase "America's Favorite Pasta" violates Section 43(a) of the Lanham Act. The district court ruled for American, and New World appealed.

Riley, Circuit Judge:

The district court concluded the phrase "America's Favorite Pasta" constitutes nonactionable puffery as a matter of law, and the phrase is not actionable under the Lanham Act. New World contends that the phrase "America's Favorite Pasta" is not puffery, but is a deceptive factual claim.

A purpose of the Lanham Act is "to protect persons engaged in commerce against false advertising and unfair competition." United Indus. Corp. v. Clorox Co., 140 F.3d 1175 (8th Cir. 1998). To establish a false or deceptively misleading advertising claim under section 43(a) of the Lanham Act, New World must establish:

(1) a false statement of *fact* by [American on its packaging] about its own or another's product; (2) the statement actually deceived or has the tendency to deceive a substantial segment of its audience; (3) the deception is material, in that it is likely to influence the purchasing decision; (4) the defendant caused its false statement to enter interstate commerce; and (5) the plaintiff has been or is likely to be injured as a result of the false statement. The failure to establish any element of the prima facie case is fatal.

Under section 43(a), two categories of actionable statements exist: (1) literally false factual commercial claims; and (2) literally true or ambiguous factual claims "which implicitly convey a false impression, are misleading in context, or [are] likely to deceive consumers." *United Indus.* Besides actionable statements, a category of non-actionable statements exists. Many statements fall into this category, popularly known as puffery. Puffery exists in two general forms: (1) exaggerated statements of bluster or boast upon which no reasonable consumer would rely; and (2) vague or highly subjective claims of product superiority, including bald assertions of superiority.

Juxtaposed to puffery is a factual claim. A factual claim is a statement that "(1) admits of being adjudged true or false in a way that (2) admits of empirical verification." Pizza Hut v. Papa John's, 227 F.3d 489 (5th Cir. 2000). To be actionable, the statement must be a "specific and measurable claim, capable of being proved false or of being reasonably interpreted as a statement of objective fact." Coastal Abstract Serv., Inc. v. First Am. Title Ins. Co., 173 F.3d 725 (9th Cir. 1999) Generally, opinions are not actionable.

Puffery and statements of fact are mutually exclusive. If a statement is a specific, measurable claim or can be reasonably interpreted as being a factual claim, i.e., one capable of verification, the statement is one of fact. Conversely, if the statement is not specific and measurable, and cannot be reasonably interpreted as providing a benchmark by which the veracity of the statement can be ascertained, the statement constitutes puffery. Defining puffery broadly provides advertisers and manufacturers considerable leeway to craft their statements, allowing the free market to hold advertisers and manufacturers accountable for their statements, ensuring vigorous competition, and protecting legitimate commercial speech.

The phrase "America's Favorite Pasta," standing alone, is not a statement of fact as a matter of law. The key term in the phrase "America's Favorite Pasta" is favorite." Used in this context, "favorite" is defined as "markedly popular especially over an extended period of time." Webster's Third New International Dictionary, p. 830. Webster's definition of "favorite" begs the question of how "popular" is defined. In this context, "popular" is defined as "well liked or admired by a particular group or circle." By combining the term "favorite" with "America's," American claims Mueller's pasta has been well liked or admired over time by America, a non-definitive person.

"America's Favorite Pasta" is not a specific, measurable claim and cannot be reasonably interpreted as an objective fact. "Well liked" and "admired" are entirely subjective and vague. Neither the words "well liked" nor "admired" provide an empirical benchmark by which the claim can be measured. "Well liked" and "admired" do not convey a quantifiable threshold in sheer number, percentage, or place in a series. A product may be well liked or admired, but the product may not dominate in sales or market share.

America's Favorite Pasta" also does not imply Mueller's is a national brand. First, "America's" is vague, and "America's," as well as "America" and "American" used in a similar context, is a broad, general reference. Second, a brand, chain, or product could be America's favorite without being national. Because "America's Favorite" depends on numerous characteristics, many of which may be intrinsic, a product need not be sold nationally to be America's favorite.

Having decided the phrase "America's Favorite Pasta," standing alone, is not a statement of fact, we consider whether the context in which the phrase is used by American transforms it into a statement of fact. "America's Favorite Pasta" appears on Mueller's packaging in two places. First, Mueller's packaging contains the phrase "America's Favorite Pasta" in the following paragraph (Paragraph): "For over 130 years, pasta lovers have enjoyed the great taste of Mueller's. Our pasta cooks to perfect tenderness every time because it's made from 100% pure semolina milled from the highest quality durum wheat. Taste why Mueller's is America's favorite pasta." Second, "America's Favorite Pasta" appears directly above "Quality Since 1867" on some packaging, and directly above "Made from 100% Semolina" or "Made with Semolina" on other packaging (Phrases).

The Paragraph and the Phrases fail to transform "America's Favorite Pasta" into a statement of fact. The Paragraph does not suggest a benchmark by which the veracity of American's statement can be verified. The Paragraph generally declares the brand has existed for

130 years, Mueller's tastes great, cooks to perfect tenderness, and is manufactured from high quality grain. Two attributes listed in the Paragraph are subject to verification: Mueller's is made from 100% pure semolina, and the brand is more than 130 years old. New World does not contend these claims are false. The remaining attributes listed in the Paragraph are unquantifiable and subject to an individual's fancy.

Similarly, the Phrases do not convey a benchmark for "America's Favorite Pasta." The term "quality" is vague, entirely subjective, and a bare assertion of product superiority. In the context used, "quality" means "inherent or intrinsic excellence of character or type" or "superiority in kind." Webster's Third New International Dictionary, p. 1858. The only portion of "Quality Since 1867" that can be verified is "Since 1867," but "Since 1867" does not provide a methodology or a reason why Mueller's is America's favorite. The words simply state, accurately, when the brand was founded. Likewise, while presenting factual claims, the phrases "Made from 100% Semolina" and "Made with Semolina" do not define a methodology by which to ascertain the veracity of American's claim that Mueller's is "America's Favorite Pasta." The two phrases simply, and correctly, list characteristics of the pasta.

In its survey, New World asked consumers if the phrase "America's Favorite Pasta" conveyed a meaning. According to New World, thirty-three percent of those surveyed allegedly perceived the phrase "America's Favorite Pasta" to mean Mueller's is the number one brand. Fifty percent of those surveyed allegedly perceived the phrase "America's Favorite Pasta" to mean Mueller's is a national brand. The Seventh Circuit confronted a similar question in Mead Johnson & Co. v. Abbott Laboratories, 201 F.3d 883 (7th Cir. 2000). Having concluded the phrase "1st Choice of Doctors" conveyed more

doctors prefer this product over its rivals, the Seventh Circuit considered whether a consumer survey can assign a different meaning to a phrase. Mead Johnson's survey indicated consumers perceived the phrase "1st Choice of Doctors" to mean a majority of doctors. Concluding the district court erred in using the survey to assign such a meaning, the Seventh Circuit noted, "never before has survey research been used to determine the meaning of words, or to set the standard to which objectively verifiable claims must be held." While acknowledging dictionaries are surveys by people who devote their entire lives to discovering the usage of words, the Seventh Circuit cogitated "it would be a bad idea to replace the work of these professionals with the first impressions of people on the street." The Seventh Circuit reasoned that using consumer surveys to determine the benchmark by which a claim is measured would remove otherwise useful words from products and would reduce ads and packaging to puffery.

To allow a consumer survey to determine a claim's benchmark would subject any advertisement or promotional statement to numerous variables, often unpredictable, and would introduce even more uncertainty into the market place. A manufacturer or advertiser who expended significant resources to substantiate a statement or forge a puffing statement could be blind-sided by a consumer survey that defines the advertising statement differently, subjecting the advertiser or manufacturer to unintended liability for a wholly unanticipated claim the advertisement's plain language would not support. The resulting unpredictability could chill commercial speech, eliminating useful claims from packaging and advertisements. As the Seventh Circuit noted, the Lanham Act protects against misleading and false statements of fact, not misunderstood statements. Affirmed.

"nature, characteristics [or] qualities of any person's goods, services or commercial activities." Therefore, if Company A runs an ad comparing its products to those of Company B, and in so doing misleadingly describes the characteristics of Company B's products, Company B will be able to recover damages, perhaps including treble damages. For First Amendment reasons, the Act contains express protection for two broad types of activities: (1) political speech, consumer or editorial comment, and satire, and (2) "innocent infringement" (thereby insulating news media that innocently disseminate false advertising).

CHAPTER **9**

INTELLECTUAL PROPERTY

- Trademarks
- Trade Secrets
- Patents
- Copyrights

The law of intellectual property—trademarks, trade secrets, patents, and copyrights—has always been important, but has become far more important in modern times because the value of these types of intangible assets has increased tremendously in comparison with the value of tradition capital assets. Individuals and companies today spend far more money and time than just a few years ago in creating and protecting intellectual property. The modern economy is based much more on knowledge, in contrast with capital and labor, than it once was. The natural result of the evolutionary economic process is that knowledge–based assets are simply worth more than they used to be.

Intellectual property law is based on several fundamental concepts. First, intellectual property law protects certain types of knowledge, ideas, and expressions by granting exclusive rights to creators. These exclusive rights are a type of intangible property right.

Second, when someone else violates these rights, the violator is actually engaging in a form of competition. It is a type of competition that has been declared unlawful, but it is competition nonetheless. In general, of course, competition is necessary for markets to function properly, and is viewed as being very desirable for consumers. Experience has taught us, however, that some conduct that is competitive in the short run may actually harm competition in the long run. Suppose, for example, that X (or the company he works for) invests time, energy, and money in coming up with a new invention that provides a benefit to society. Using the knowledge that X developed, Y then begins making and selling a new a product that is the same as X's invention. If X has no way to protect his investment in inventing, he is less likely to make these kinds of investments in the future. If we have patent laws, if his invention meets the requirements for obtaining a patent, and if he is able to successfully sue Y for patent infringement, X is more likely to continue investing in the inventive process in the future. In many sectors of the economy, the most important type of competition is the competitive rivalry to innovate and create. The same can be said for investing time and money in creative efforts such as writing books, music, and software. Here, copyright law creates certain exclusive rights that are intended to encourage people to continue engaging in these socially desirable creative activities. Thus, intellectual property laws essentially prohibit certain kinds of conduct (such as infringing on someone else's patent, copyright, trade secret, or trademark) that are competitive in the short run, with the objective of creating greater incentives for people and companies to engage in innovative and creative activities that tend to promote competition and also benefit society in other ways (such as the cultural value of creativity) in the long run.

Third, even though there is a general consensus that intellectual property laws benefit society in the long run, such laws can go too far. If, for example, very many patents are granted to inventions that really don't deserve such protection, society pays the short–term price of less competition but does not receive the long–term benefits from genuine innovation. Likewise, if copyright law protects too much or protects it for too long (which many knowledgeable observers believe to be the case today), society gives up a lot in the short run without receiving properly corresponding benefits in the long run.

An ideal system provides protection to intellectual property that is no greater than is necessary to create and maintain the desired incentives to innovate and create over time. No system is ideal. No nation's intellectual property laws, including those of the U.S., are ideal. Most experts continue to believe, however, that societies are better off with these laws than without them, and most of the debate is not concerned with whether there should be protection for intellectual property, but rather with how much protection these laws should provide.

Moreover, a country cannot fully participate in today's global economy without a full slate of intellectual property laws and effective means for enforcing them. This is one of the fundamental obligations of all nations that are members of the World Trade Organization (WTO). Currently, 144 countries are members, China and Taiwan being the most recent. The WTO was created by the Uruguay Round of Negotiations on GATT (General Agreement on Trade & Tariffs), which concluded in 1994. One of the main agreements resulting from the Uruguay Round was TRIPS (Trade–Related Intellectual Property Rights), which set a number of minimum requirements for intellectual property protection in all member nations.

Trademarks

A trademark is any distinctive word, phrase, symbol, or design adopted for the purpose of identifying the origin of goods being offered for sale. A trademark benefits consumers by acting as a symbol enabling them to identify goods or services that have been satisfactory in the past and to reject those that have been unsatisfactory. A trademark also motivates businesses to maintain or improve the quality of their goods or services over time to reap the benefits of a well–earned public trust in a mark. Trademark infringement occurs, therefore, when a competitor of the trademark owner uses a mark so similar to the owned trademark that purchasers of the competitor's goods are likely to be misled as to the origin of the goods that they are purchasing. In other words, a deception is accomplished that permits the competitor (typically a manufacturer or other seller) to take a "free ride" on the reputation and goodwill of the trademark owner (who is, typically, another manufacturer or seller). Although a deception is accomplished, trademark infringement can occur even if the defendant did not intend it (or even if the defendant didn't know about the plaintiff's mark).

Trademark law also governs service marks, used to identify the origin of services such as car rental, video rental, computer repair, insurance, and so on. The legal principles are the same for both trademarks and service marks and, thus, most people simply use the word trademark to refer to either.

A company's name—its business name (or "trade name")—may or may not be protected as a trademark. If the company uses its name, such as Microsoft or IBM, to serve trademark (branding) purposes, the name is protectable as a trademark or service mark.

Finally, trademark law also protects "trade dress"—the total image and overall appearance of a product or business created by its design or packaging if it serves the same purpose as a trademark. For example, the U.S. Supreme Court held in Two Pesos, Inc. v. Taco Cabana, Inc., 112 S.Ct. 2753 (1992), that the distinctive design of a restaurant's exterior and interior decor were protected as trade dress.

Early trademark law was developed by courts as part of the common law of torts. Later, federal statutes were passed that embodied these early principles and modified them in a number of ways. The most recent federal trademark statute is the Lanham Act, passed by Congress in 1946 and amended several times since then. This is, of course, the same pattern we have seen in many other areas of law. The Lanham Act governs marks that are used in connection with the sale of goods and services in interstate commerce. Each state also has a trademark statute that deals with marks that are used only in connection with intrastate commerce within that state. State trademark statutes are essentially identical to the Lanham Act.

Protectability of Marks

For a mark (trademark or service mark) to be legally protectable, it must serve as a "source identifier." This means that, when a substantial number of buyers see or hear the mark, they associate it with a particular source—a particular seller, even if most buyers cannot recall the name of the seller. In trademark law, several different phrases are often used to describe the same concept. Courts often say that a mark must have "secondary meaning." This means that, although a term may have some original meaning of its own, when a lot of customers see or hear it they mentally associate it with a particular seller; thus, the term "secondary meaning" describes the same idea as "source identifier." If we get rid of the legalese, what both phrases mean in common English is that, for a mark to be protectable, it must serve a branding function. When suing for trademark infringement or when applying for federal registration of a mark with the U.S. Patent & Trademark Office (PTO), the owner must first establish that it has a protectable mark.

Courts have developed four categories of trademarks to assist them in determining whether marks are protectable. A potential trademark may be classified as (1) generic, (2) descriptive, (3) suggestive, or (4) arbitrary or fanciful. These categories, like the tones in a spectrum, tend to blur at the edges.

A generic term is a word or phrase used to describe an entire class of goods or services rather than a particular seller's version of a good or service. Generic terms like car, wood, paper, and other nouns can never become protectable marks when used in their generic sense. (As noted below, however, when a generic term is used in connection with a product or service totally unrelated to its original meaning and does serve a branding purpose, it can be a protectable mark.)

A descriptive term merely identifies a characteristic or quality of a product or service, such as its color, odor, function, dimensions, or ingredients. A seller of goods or services cannot protect a descriptive term as a trademarks unless that seller can produce evidence (such as consumer surveys) proving that the term has acquired secondary meaning (that is, has come to serve a branding purpose) because a substantial portion of the relevant population of consumers have come to treat the term as the seller's particular brand. An example of a descriptive mark is "Vision Center" in reference to a business offering optical goods and services.

In Zatarains, Inc., v. Oak Grove Smokehouse, Inc., 698 F.2d 786 (1983), the main question was whether Zatarains' use of the term "FISH FRI" for its packaged batter for frying fish was so descriptive of batters generally that it could not be protected against the use of the term "FISH FRY" for frying batters by the defendant Oak Grove. The court held that the term "FISH FRI" was indeed a descriptive mark, but that Zatarains' consumer surveys and evidence of substantial advertising and sales over many years proved that the term had acquired secondary meaning as its own brand of batter mix in the New Orleans area. However, the court also concluded that Oak Grove had not committed trademark infringement because Oak Grove had not used the term "FISH FRY" in a trademark sense but instead had merely used it to help describe its own product. Oak Grove had, consequently, made a "fair use" of a term that was almost identical to Zatarain's trademark. It should be emphasized that the "fair use" in trademark law does not mean what it means in copyright law. In trademark law it refers only to the use by a defendant of a term that is identical or very similar to the plaintiff's descriptive (but protectable because of acquired secondary meaning) mark to help it describe its own product or service. Another example of a descriptive mark with proof of secondary meaning is given in Box 9.1.

If a mark consists primarily of a geographic designation ("West Coast Video" for a chain of video rental/sale stores), or if it consists primarily of someone's last name (Dell Computers), the law treats it in the same way as a descriptive mark, and secondary meaning must be proved.

A suggestive term suggests, rather than describes, some particular characteristic of the goods or services to which it applies and requires the consumer to exercise the imagination in order to draw a conclusion as to the nature of the goods and services. "Coppertone" has been held suggestive in regard to sun tanning products, as has "Roach Motel" for a roach bait device. A suggestive term can be a protectable mark even without actual proof of acquired secondary meaning because courts view suggestive terms as being "inherently distinctive."

Arbitrary or fanciful terms bear no relationship to the products or services to which they are applied. Like suggestive terms, these marks are protectable without proof of secondary meaning. "Coined" words that were created to serve as trademarks, such as Kodak, Xerox, and Exxon are fanciful marks. Terms that were generic or descriptive in their original meaning, but that are used as marks in connection with the sale of products or services totally unrelated to that original meaning, are arbitrary marks. Examples include Ivory for soap or Apple for computers. Trademark law treats arbitrary or fanciful marks in the same way—they are so inherently distinctive that they are necessarily protectable, and indeed are the strongest type of marks.

Geography, Priority, and Registration

Trademark law in the U.S. is a hybrid system that provides protection based on the geographic area in which a mark has been used in connection with the sale of goods or

Chewing gum carrying American major league baseball team logos sells well in Japan. However, the Japanese patent office barred registration of the Los Angeles baseball team's name in this connection because the name "Dodgers" to Japanese ears sounded too much like "Rogers," a name already in use by a Japanese food company. However, the Japanese High Court ruled in 1992 that the Dodgers mark can indeed be registered, much to the delight of Japanese baseball fans. A suit for Nullification of the Patent office's Dismissal of the Demand for Retrial of Trademark Application, 71256/1978.

services, and then provides expanded protection when the mark is registered with the trademark branch of the PTO. In almost all other countries, protection for a trademark is established by registration. In some of these countries, this is all that is required, but in others there is a requirement that the mark actually be used in connection with the sale of goods or services within a designated time.

Suppose that X Co. begins to use the mark "Morpheus" for its computer services business in northern California. If no one else already uses the same or very similar mark in connection with the sale of the same or closely related services (even closely related products) in the area where X is using it, X's mark is protected in that area plus a surrounding zone to account for reasonably expected future expansion. In such a case, Y Co. could use the same or similar mark in a different geographic area.

In the same scenario, suppose that X Corp. expands its business and the use of its mark to other states such as Oregon and Washington. Assuming that its expansion does not take it into an area in which there is an earlier user of the same or a similar mark on the same or related services or goods, X's mark is now protected in this wider geographic area (plus a future expansion zone). In addition, once X has made a substantial use of the mark in interstate commerce (in more than one state), X can seek federal registration for its mark. X's mark obviously cannot be registered if it is generic. Also, if the mark is descriptive (or primarily geographic or primarily someone's last name), X must prove secondary meaning to obtain registration. Assuming that these principles provide no obstacle, X can obtain federal registration for its "Morpheus" mark IF there is not another mark regesitered either with the PTO or with a state trademark registration authority that is the same or confusingly similar for the same or related goods or services.

If X Co. was both the first to use the mark and the first to register it, X has nationwide exclusive rights. Suppose, however, that Y Co. had used the same or a

LEGAL FOCUS

The Hard Rock Café, founded in 1982, has sold barbecued pork sandwiches under the name "pig sandwich" from Tennessee to New York to Stockholm. However, in 1986, when founder Isaac Tigrett opened up a Hard Rock Café in Dallas, he was notified in writing that the Texas Pig Stands (TPS) claimed the trademark for the term "pig sandwich." Litigation ensued.

It seems that TPS had sold barbecued pork sandwiches as "pig sandwiches" since the 1920's. At one time, more than 100 TPS restaurants spanned the continent, but by 1986 only 10 were left operating in Texas (and none in Dallas). Still, the jury found for TPS.

On appeal, the Fifth Circuit Court of Appeals, a court that apparently has too much time on its hands, issued a pun–filled ruling that upheld TPS's recovery on the merits. In a section entitled "This Little Piggy Went to See His Lawyer," the court framed the issue as "[w]hether Hard Rock's legal edifice is made of brick, twigs, or straw. . .."

The court concluded that the terms "pig" and "sandwich" may be generic, but when combined they form a descriptive mark that is protectible with a showing of secondary meaning. The court affirmed the jury's finding the TPS had demonstrated secondary meaning, noting that "[s]everal Texas citizens testified to having fond memories of TPS' porcine specialty, supporting TPS' contention that over sixty years of 'pig sandwiches' and 'The Sign of the Pig' had linked the swinging and dining. For these reasons, we cannot say that the jury's decision was unfounded."

In its conclusion, entitled "D–D–Dt D–D–Dt That's All, Folks!" the court found that TPS's evidence merited an injunction ordering Hard Rock to cease using the term "pig sandwich," but did not support any award of damages because there was insufficient evidence that TPS had lost any sales or Hard Rock had gained any sales because of the infringement. Texas Pig Stands v. Hard Rock Cafe International, 951 F.2d 684 (5th Cir. 1992).

similar mark in connection with the same or related goods or services in New York before X had begun using the Morpheus mark in California. Thus, X was not the first user, but it is the first to register. In this case, X could obtain federal registration that would give it exclusive rights throughout the nation except for the geographic area in New York in which Y was the first user. Y retains the right to use its mark in that area in New York plus a reasonable expansion zone. Y's area of use is frozen as of the time that Y applied for federal registration. This assumes that there is no evidence showing that Y had actual knowledge of X's first use and that X had not obtained a state registration.

Finally, Congress amended the Lanham Act in 1988 to permit "Intent–to–Use" (ITU) registration applications for those who have not yet made a substantial interstate use of a mark but intend to do so in the reasonably near future. In an ITU application, the owner of the mark must declare that it has "good faith intent" ("bona fide intent") to use the mark at a future date. Assuming that there is no other obstacle to registration, the owner may then obtain a regular registration if there is a substantial interstate use of the mark within 3 years after filing the ITU application. The important thing about an ITU application is that, if there is a contest over who was first to register (and obtain nationwide rights), the "priority" date is the date on which the ITU was filed. If there was no previous ITU, but only a regular application, the priority date is the date on which the regular application was filed. However registration is achieved, the term of registration is ten years from the time the mark was actually registered and may be renewed in ten–year increments by registrants who show that they are still genuinely using the mark.

Likelihood of Confusion

In most infringement actions, the plaintiff mark owner has the burden of proving that the defendant's mark is so similar to the plaintiff's that the defendant's use will produce a "likelihood of confusion" in buyers' minds as to the true origin of the goods or services. Even if the evidence does not prove that the defendant's use of the same or a confusingly similar mark is likely to cause customer confusion as to actual source, there may still be trademark infringement if the evidence shows that consumers are likely to confused about affiliation, sponsorship, or endorsement—that is, they are likely to be misled into believing that the plaintiff is associated with defendant or sponsors what the defendant is doing.

Whether such likelihood exists is a question of fact in any particular case and is determined by such factors as similarity of design of the marks, similarity of product, proof of confusion among actual buyers, and marketing surveys of prospective purchasers showing an appreciable misassociation of the defendant's mark with the plaintiff's product. On the basis of these factors, for example, Rotary DeRooting was held to be a mark so similar to Roto–Rooter that the owner of Roto–Rooter was successful in recovering damages from the owner of Rotary DeRooting. Roto–Rooter Corp. v. O'Neal, 513 F.2d 44 (5th Cir. 1975).

If the products are dissimilar and unrelated, however, even identical marks may not cause confusion. Thus, where a clothing manufacturer had purchased the right to use the mark "Here's Johnny," a court held that the use of that mark by a manufacturer of portable toilets was not likely to cause purchasers of the toilets to associate them with the producer of "Here's Johnny men's suits. (Carson v. Here's Johnny Portable Toilets, Inc., 698 F.2d 831 (6th Cir. 1983) (involving the trademarked introduction for Johnny Carson, Jay Leno's predecessor on "The Tonight Show," a phrase that Carson then used as mark for a line of men's clothing)).

SULLIVAN V. CBS CORPORATION
385F3d 772 (7th Cir. 2004)

Sullivan and others formed a band they named "Survivor" in 1977. Throughout the 80s, the Band had a number of hit songs, including "Eye of the Tiger," the theme song for the well–known movie Rocky III. After the Band broke up, Sullivan applied for a trademark registration for the name "Survivor" in March 1994, seeking to use the name in connection with "Entertainment services: namely providing band and/or musical services." The registration did not encompass merchandising.

Sullivan continues to perform as Survivor, though the Band has not released any new music in the United States since 1993. At concerts, Survivor sells its CDs and other products like t–shirts. Survivor also licenses music to television shows and commercials. Record stores sell the Band's CDs and radio stations continue to play the Band's music.

In May 2000, CBS debuted a weekly reality television series called "Survivor," featuring castaways facing various trials and contests, all while trying to survive the harsh realities of life in a deserted location. The Series has been a great success. Before the Series first aired, CBS developed a logo for use in promotions and advertising. The logo features an oval with the word "SURVIVOR" across the center, surrounded by a scene reflecting the current season's location. The words "OUTWIT," "OUTPLAY," and "OUTLAST" surround the perimeter of the oval. In the second season, for example, the inside scene showed a kangaroo and sunset on an Australian outback scene. The inside phrase was changed from "SURVIVOR," to "SURVIVOR—AUSTRALIAN OUTBACK."

In August 2000, CBS released a soundtrack featuring a compilation of original music from the Series. The word "SURVIVOR" is printed in large block letters across the front of the album, while the words "THE OFFICIAL SOUND–TRACK TO THE HIT CBS TV SERIES" are printed underneath. The lower right of the CD shows the Series' oval logo. CBS released a second CD in November 2000, this one proclaiming that it featured music "inspired" by the Series. The front of the second CD shows the oval Series logo, with frames coming through the top of the oval, and the words "OFFICIAL PARTY SURVIVAL KIT" printed below the logo. This CD contains previously recorded songs with survival and island themes. Both CDs are marketed primarily to Series viewers and are classfied as soundtracks. In June 2000, CBS launched a line of merchandise, including t–shirts, mugs, bags, calendars, and books, all bearing the oval Series logo.

Sullivan filed this trademark infringement suit against CBS, but the trial court granted summary judgment to CBS on grounds that Sullivan could not show a likelihood of confusion. Sullivan appealed.

Wood, Circuit Judge:

To prevail, Sullivan must show that his mark is entitled to protection and that there is a likelihood of confusion between his mark and CBS's mark. Although CBS does not contest the district court's classification of Sullivan's mark as descriptive, in our view that classification is incorrect. Ultimately, this does not change the outcome for Sullivan, but the mark, "Survivor," for a band, is properly classified as arbitrary, not descriptive. Trademarks are classified in one of four categories—fanciful/arbitrary, suggestive, descriptive, and generic. The amount of protection inherently available tends to increase from generic to fanciful. The word "survivor" when used as a band name is arbitrary; there is nothing about the word which is necessary to the description of a band, or of Sullivan's band. Because the word "survivor" is a common word that is being applied to a service unrelated to its meaning, the Band name, properly considered, is an arbitrary mark.

Classifying "Survivor" as an arbitrary mark does not, however, automatically mean that the mark is entitled to strong protection. The strength of a mark is determined partly by its classification, but the courts are still free to examine the strength of a mark outside its area of use. In other words, just because a trademark is arbitrary, if it is used only in a narrow area, others may use a similar mark for different goods without any trademark infringement. We can assume that Sullivan's mark is entitled to strong protection as against other band names, but there is no presumption that his mark is equally strong outside that realm.

This case turns, in our view, on Sullivan's failure to submit enough evidence on the likelihood of confusion point to survive summary judgment.

Sullivan had to submit evidence that, if believed by a trier of fact, would show that consumers are likely to be confused as to the source of the CDs and merchandise at issue. In assessing the likelihood of confusion, courts have identified seven relevant factors that help in deciding the ultimate question: (1) the similarity of the marks; (2) the similarity of the products; (3) the area and manner of concurrent use; (4) the degree of care likely to be used by consumers; (5) the strength of the plaintiff's mark; (6) whether any actual confusion exists; and (7) the defendant's intent to palm off its goods as those of the plaintiff.

We begin by considering the strength of Sullivan's mark. Sullivan contends that because "Survivor" is arbitrary as a band name, it is entitled automatically to wide protection in any field as against any competitor. The law draws finer lines than this. A mark can be arbitrary for one purpose but it may still be used extensively in other areas. As applied to

Sullivan, this means that he might enjoy strong protection for his mark as against other aspiring rock bands or musical groups, but that he would have only weak or nonexistent protection outside that particular niche.

The ultimate concern in a trademark case like this one is the tendency of the mark to indicate the origin of the product in the eyes of the purchasing public. The crucial question is whether the mark is strong enough that the public will form an association between the mark and the source of that particular good. Sullivan claims that his mark is famous enough to make consumers think the Series' merchandise is likely to come from his band. But he offered no evidence to back up this guess. He might have offered specifics on how well–known the name "Survivor" still is today as the identifier of a rock band, but he did not. Survivor has not released a new album in the United States since 1993. Sullivan offered nothing about how much money he spends promoting the Band, or on advertising for the Band, nor did he provide any evidence of how much money the Band has earned. There is simply no evidence that "Survivor" the Band enjoys fame and recognition as the originator of any products other than rock albums and concert t–shirts.

Looking next at the similarity of the two marks, we make the comparison "in light of what happens in the marketplace and not merely by looking at the two marks side–by–side." Ty, Inc. v. The Jones Group, Inc., 237 F.3d 891(7th Cir. 2001) . "If one word or feature of a composite trademark is the salient portion of the mark, it may be given greater weight than the surrounding elements." Henri's Good Prods. Co. v. Kraft, Inc., 717 F.2d 352(7th Cir. 1983) . Sullivan encourages us to focus our analysis only on the word "Survivor," which obviously appears in both marks. Sullivan argues that CBS's version of the mark, which includes an oval background containing a drawing relevant to the season's location, and the words, "outplay, outlast, outwit," adds only minor, stylistic differences. Sullivan is correct that the dominant portion of CBS's mark is the word, "Survivor" never appears alone on any of CBS's merchandise at issue. The term always appears over a relevant scene of some kind and surrounded by the words, "outplay, outlast, outwit." Consumers in the marketplace never see CBS's mark as the word "Survivor" alone.

CBS responds that when we focus on the ultimate question, it is plain that despite the similarity of the dominant portion of the marks, there can be no confusion. We agree. In a case comparing the marks "Yogowhip" and "Miracle Whip," the court acknowledged that the word "whip," was prominent and identical, but it held that when consumers viewed the labels as a whole, as they always would at the grocery store, there could be no confusion. *Henri's Good Prods.*, 717 F.2d at 355. The court explained, "based on our examination of the marks, we think that a purchaser, even a supermarket shopper who will make a selection quickly and without careful examination, is likely to differentiate between the products." We find the same to be true here. The marks, when viewed in their entirety, are quite different. Additionally, on the two products that give rise to the greatest concern—the music CDs—CBS has taken additional steps to associate the CDs with the television show.

On both of the CDs issued by CBS, not only is the "Survivor" mark on display in its entirety, but each CD announces its affiliation with the CBS television show. The first CD, which contains music composed for the show, states that it is "The official Soundtrack to the Hit CBS TV Series." The second CD announces that it is "Music Inspired by the Hit CBS TV Series." CBS has, in short, taken substantial steps to make the association between its CDs and its television show readily apparent from the face of the CD. Although the marks are similar, the prominent display of different names on the marks reduces any likelihood of confusion.

The district court thought that the "similarity of products" factor also favored CBS, but we are not so sure. We have held that "a closely related product is one which would reasonably be thought by the buying public to come from the same source, or thought to be affiliated with, connected with, or sponsored by, the trademark owner." *Ty, Inc.*, 237 F.3d at 900. The similarity between products focuses on whether the buying public thinks or expects the products to come from the same source. Sullivan asserts that because both he and CBS sell CDs and merchandise like t–shirts and hats, that their products are necessarily similar. He comes closer to creating a genuine issue of fact on the similarity factor, with respect to the CDs only. But even giving him the benefit of the doubt with respect to this factor is not enough to carry the day for him here. First, there is nothing magical about these "factors"; they operate only as a heuristic device to assist in determining whether confusion exists. Moreover, it is not as if the Band's CDs are identical to the Series' CDs; they are not. The Band CDs are placed in the "rock music" section of stores (both physical and virtual), while CBS's CDs are grouped with soundtracks. There is no indication that CBS has tried to suggest that all the music on its CDs comes from an eponymous band.

Both Sullivan and CBS market similar merchandise, but Survivor the Band sells t–shirts only at their concerts, whereas CBS sells Survivor the Series t–shirts, hats, and other merchandise through various outlets. As with the CDs, Survivor the Series' merchandise prominently displays the entire "Survivor" mark. Taking these facts as a whole, we conclude that no rational fact finder could conclude that any consumer would be confused as to the source of the merchandise. Series' merchandise is not sold through the same outlets as the Band's merchandise, nor is it advertised in the same manner or in similar outlets.

Sullivan finally takes issue with the district court's finding that no evidence of actual confusion exists. Sullivan asks us to disregard the results of a CBS survey demonstrating no actual confusion. That survey, he claims, improperly focused on confusion about music, not trade identities; it was limited to only one CD; and it failed to include any questions about other merchandise. This court has upheld similar surveys, however. Sullivan had ample opportunity to conduct his own survey, but he chose not to.

Because there is no triable issue of fact on likelihood of confusion, we conclude that CBS's "Survivor" mark does not infringe Sullivan's "Survivor" mark. Sullivan, through his band Survivor, has been fortunate enough to have a successful rock band, succeeding in a business where many fail. CBS, through its show Survivor, has (for better or for worse) revolutionized the world of reality television. Both Sullivan and CBS are using the same mark, but we hold that there is no likelihood of confusion in the minds of consumers. We therefore AFFIRM the judgment of the district court.

Genericide

In addition to the fact that a generic term cannot be protected in the first place, a formerly protectable mark can become generic through usage over time. This concept is discussed later. Terms such as aspirin, cellophane, and escalator, which were at one time protected trademarks, have been held to have become generic through usage and therefore unprotectable. Many people use the term "genericide" to refer a mark's loss of protection by becoming generic. In most cases in which this has happened, the owner of the mark was simply complacent and took few if any steps to make sure that consumers understood that the mark was the owner's brand rather than identifying an entire class of goods or services. In most cases, this complacency occurred because the owner of the mark had a leading position in the market, either because of patent protection or simply because the owner was the first to be extremely successful in the particular market and was able to hold on to its head-start for a long period of time.

Although a number of trademarks have lost their protection through genericide, such an occurrence has now become uncommon because companies in recent years have better recognized the danger and have been proactive in preventing genericide. Companies with valuable brand names have taken a variety of preventive measures such as emphasizing in advertising and packaging that the mark is a brand name, that there is another term that is generic, and that the two should not be confused. For example, in Kimberly-Clark Corp.'s advertising and packaging of its market-leading "Kleenex" tissues, it no longer just uses the term Kleenex by itself, but instead identifies the product as "Kleenex Brand Tissues." Xerox Corp. devotes substantial advertising to the purpose of reminding consumers that "Xerox" is a brand name and should not be used as a noun (for a photocopy or photocopy machine) or as a verb (for making a photocopy). Coca-Cola Corp. spends large amounts of money paying employees to watch TV, listen to radio, go through magazines, etc. to find improper generic uses of its "Coca-Cola," "Coke," "Diet Coke," and other trademarks. Improper uses typically result in letters from Coke's trademark lawyers. Sometimes it also been known to send employees to places that sell or serve soft drinks and ask for a "Coke." If the Coca–Cola representative is served another brand, Coca–Cola's trademark lawyers are again likely to be heard from.

Remedies

Where likelihood of confusion is established, the plaintiff's usual remedies under the Lanham Act or common-law principles are an injunction and damages. The injunction is an order prohibiting or placing limitations on the defendant's further use of the mark, and damages is a recovery of money to compensate the plaintiff for the economic loss (if any) sustained as a result of the infringement.

Because of a tremendous increase in the trafficking of counterfeit designer goods, Congress passed the Trademark Counterfeiting Act of 1984, which provides escalating criminal penalties for multiple offenders. For example, a second offender, if an individual, can be fined up to $1 million, imprisoned for up to 15 years, or both.

Anti-Dilution Statutes

Approximately half the states have extended trademark protection beyond situations where a "likelihood of confusion" exists by enacting anti-dilution statutes. Anti dilution laws prohibit uses of some marks even where the goods or services are not similar and thus where there is no likelihood of confusion. In 1995, Congress passed the Federal Trademark Dilution Act (FTDA). Like the state statutes, the FTDA protects trademarks from unauthorized use in connection with goods or services that are neither the same nor similar.

Like earlier state laws, the FTDA does not protect all marks, but protects only those that a court determines to be "famous." A famous mark is one that is more than just distinctive. In the FTDA, Congress itemized eight factors that tend to show that a mark is famous: (1) The degree of inherent or acquired distinctiveness of the mark; (2) The duration and extent of use of the mark in connection with the goods or services with which the mark is used; (3) The duration and extent of advertising and publicity of the mark; (4) The geographical extent of the trading area in which the mark is used; (5) The channels of trade for the goods or services with which the mark is used; (6) The degree of recognition of the mark in the trading areas and channels of trade used by the marks' owner and the person against whom the injunction is sought; (7) The nature and extent of use of the same or similar marks by third parties; and (8) Whether the mark was registered.

One example of the application of an anti–dilution case law is Tiffany v. Boston Club, 231 F. Supp. 836 (D.Mass. 1964) . This case, which was decided according to a state anti-dilution law but which would be decided the same way under the FTDA, involved the old and very well– known "Tiffany" trademark for jewelry, fine glassware, and related products. Over time, the mark has come to be associated with luxury and excellence. The defendant used the "Tiffany" name for a bar. The public is certainly not likely to believe that the owners of the "Tiffany" trademark were also responsible for the bar, and thus there would be no likelihood of confusion. However, use of the name "Tiffany" on the bar may injure the holder of the "Tiffany" trademark in two ways: (1) Such use weakens the mark by diminishing (diluting) its distinctiveness. Moreover, if the bar is allowed to use the mark, others also would be able to use it for unrelated goods or services, thus having a cumulative effect of further dilution over time. This type of harm is sometimes called "blurring." (2) This type of use also undermines the positive image of the mark if it is no longer restricted to luxury–type products. This type of harm is often called "tarnishment." Tarnishment could also be proved by evidence showing that defendant's use of a mark identical or confusingly similar to the plaintiffs famous mark casts the mark in an unsavory light, such as using the famous "Barbie" trademark for dolls in connection with a pornographic Web site. Anti–dilution laws protect against either type of harm.

In addition to protecting traditional marks from dilution or tarnishment, federal courts applying the FTDA have also given protection to famous trade dress such as the color and shape of the Goldfish cracker, as well as to famous slogans such as American Express's "Don't Leave Home Without It."

The FTDA has been very important since its enactment, having been used by plaintiffs in a large number of cases. Most lower federal courts had concluded that the law could be used to enjoin a defendant from continuing its use of plaintiff's famous mark even without proving economic harm resulting from the actual blurring of the mark's high level of distinctiveness. Indeed, the objective behind the anti–dilution law was preventive—to prevent the gradual erosion of a famous mark's distinctiveness by cumulative uses over time (even though the uses do not cause a likelihood of confusion). In Moseley v. V Secret Catalogue, Inc., 123 S. Ct. 1115 (2003), the US Supreme Court held that a plaintiff could prevail in an anti–dilution case only if it proved that the defendant's use of the mark actually blurred the distinctiveness of the mark.or actually tarnished the mark. Trademark lawyers told the authors that they knew of no way to prove actual blurring and had not been able to do so. Then, in the fall of 2005, Congress passed legislation to overturn the Supreme Court's decision by requiring only that a likelihood of blurring be proved. In addition, the legislation cleared up some lower court conflicts by stating that a mark is protected by the anti–dilution law only if it is "famous" in all or most of the U.S., and not just in a small niche market. Furthermore, the legislation stated that a mark can be "famous" based on "acquired distinctiveness" over time, even if it was not inherently distinctive originally. Both of these propositions make very good sense, but a few lower courts had held otherwise prior to this legislation.

Anti–Cybersquatting Consumer Protection Act

A "cybersquatter" is someone who registers an Internet domain name (1) that is the same as or confusingly similar to someone else's protected trademark, (2) where there is a bad faith intent to commercially exploit the trademark, and (3) the likely effect is to either cause confusion, or, if the mark is famous, to cause dilution. Because of the widespread prevalence of cybersquatting in recent years, Congress passed the Anti–cybersquatting Consumer Protection Act (ACPA) in 1999.

The ACPA lists nine factors for courts to considere in determining whether the defendant has registered a domain name with a bad–faith intent to exploit the planitff's trademark, although only eight of these factors seem relevant. The first four of these factors tend to show good faith, and the next four factors tend to show bad faith. The factors tending to show that defendant acted in good faith and is not a cybersquatter are: (1) The defendant itself had preexisting trademark or other intellectual property rights in the words used in the domain name; (2) The domain name consists of the defendant's name; (3) The defendant had made previous use of the word or words in the domain name in connection with the legitimate sale of goods or services; or (4) The defendant is making a genuine noncommercial or fair use of the mark at a Web site reached by the domain name.

The factors tending to show that defendant was acting in bad faith and thus was an illegal cybersquatter are: (1) The defendant apparently intended to divert consumers from the trademark owner's online location to the defendant's Web site in a way that could harm the plaintiff either causing a likelihood of confusion or, if the plaintiff's mark is famous, by causing dilution; (2) The defendant has offered to sell the domain name it registered to someone else without having made a legitimate business use of it (offering goods or services), and without any apparent intent to make a legitimate business use of it; (3) The defendant has given misleading contact information when applying for the registration of the domain name, or has intentionally failed to maintain accurate information for contacting him; or (4) The defendant's prior conduct shows a pattern of registering or acquiring domain names the same as or confusingly similar to the preexisting trademarks of others.

Trademark owners may recover statutory damages of up to $100,000 and an injunction where personal jurisdiction over the defendant is acquired over the defendant. When the court has only *in rem* jurisdiction (discussed in Chapter 2), the court can cancel the domain name registration or transfer it to the plaintiff. Dell Computer, for example, succeeded in an ACPA claim against a seller using the site "www.DellKorea.com" to sell non–Dell computer parts online to Korean purchasers. Dell filed an *in rem* case against the domain name in federal court in Virginia, where the name was registered. A state or federal court has *in rem* jurisdiction over any kind of property located within the state where the court is located, and can grant judgments that affect the title to that property even when the court has no personal jurisdiction over a particular individual or company and could not issue a judgment against them for damages or an injunction. A domain name is an item of intangible personal property, and in this case it resided on a server in Arlington, Virginia. Even though the court had not acquired personal jurisdiction over the owner of the domain name, who lived in Seoul, Korea, the court had jurisdiction over the domain name itself. After publication of a notice in a newspaper of general circulation in the Arlington, Virginia area, the court found that a violation of the ACPA had occurred and, in just a few days, transferred ownership of the domain name to Dell.

International Trademark Concerns

Several years ago, the United States became a signatory to the Madrid Agreement Concerning the International Registration of Marks ("Madrid Agreement"), a multi–lateral treaty sponsored by the the World Intellectual Property Association (an agency of the U.N.). In 2003, the U.S. also ratified the "Madrid Protocol," which supplements the Madrid Agreement. In combination, these two treaties allow for one centralized filing of a trademark application in a member country (in the U.S., this is done in the U.S. Patent & Trademark Office (PTO)), and the payment of a single filing fee. The application is then forwarded to the other member countries designated by the applicant, and no language translation is required. Over 65 countries are now members of both treaties.

NORTHERN LIGHT TECHNOLOGY INC. v. NORTHERN LIGHTS CLUB
U.S. Court of Appeals, First Circuit, 236 f.3d 57 (2001)

On September 16, 1996, plaintiff Northern Light Technology, Inc. registered the Internet domain names on the World Wide Web. That same month plaintiff registered "Northern Light" as a service mark with the U.S. Patent and Trademark Office. Nearly a year later in August 1997, plaintiff began operation of the "northernlight.com" Web site as an Internet search engine.

Defendant Burgar who lives in Alberta, Canada, is president and shareholder of defendant 641271 Alberta, Ltd. Burgar, a self–described Internet entrepreneur, registered thousands of "catchy" domain names, appropriating in identical or slightly modified forms the names of popular people and organizations. Burgar was also president of Northern Lights Club, an unincorporated association with a listed address in Las Vegas. Although the stated mission of the Northern Lights Club was to bring together devotees of the Northern Lights, or aurora borealis, including businesses that take their names from the famous celestial phenomenon, Burgar's later testimony in court indicated that the club actually had no members. A month

after plaintiff registered "northernlight. com" as a domain name, Burgar and his company (defendants) registered "northernlights.com" as a domain name. Not long after defendant's registration of the domain name, defendants transferred ownership of it to "FlairMail," a vanity e–mail service that Burgar managed and that was owned by a local Alberta newspaper. He later testified that he "believed" that the newspaper was owned by his wife.

The two domain names peacefully co–existed until March 1999, when a USA Today story on Internet search engines erroneously identified plaintiff's Web site as northern-lights.com. Plaintiff contacted defendants and sought to buy the latter's domain name, but no agreement resulted. In April 1999, defendants posted an active page on the site with a site–search function. In July 1999, plaintiff sent Burgar a cease–and–desist letter. He did not respond. Plaintiff then asked NSI (the registrar for the .com domain) to strip defendants of the northernlights.com address in light of plaintiff's trademark, but NSI declined. Plaintiff then filed suit alleging trademark infringement and other claims. In

December 1999, plaintiff amended its com-
plaint to add a claim under the Anti–cybers-
quatting Consumer Protection Act (ACPA).
After concluding that plaintiff would prob-
ably win the case, the trial judge quickly
granted a temporary restraining order (TRO)
requiring the defendants to largely deactivate
their site pending a fuller hearing. Defendants
appealed.

Stahl, Circuit Judge:

Defendants vehemently contest the district court's finding that the registration and maintenance of the northernlights. com domain name represented a bad–faith effort to profit from plaintiff's Northern Light trademark. The issue of bad faith is . . . relevant to the merits of plaintiff's suit in so far as "bad faith intent to profit from [another's] mark" constitutes an essential element of the cause of action under ACPA. . . . We review the district court's finding of bad faith for clear error.

Along with its inclusion bad faith among the essential elements of the ACPA cause of action, Congress provided nine nonexhaustive guideposts that the courts may use to divine whether or not bad faith exists. . . . In this case, the district court determined that defendants' myriad explanations for their use of the northernlights.com site – e.g., as an experimental new business model, as a site for aurora borealis admirers, and as a compilation of businesses that contain the phrase "Northern Lights" – undermined Northern Lights' claim of [good faith]. Additionally, the court concluded that the defendants' numerous registrations of domain names containing the trademarks of others, which defendants accomplished in some

cases by creating financial "fan clubs" so that they could present a mantle of legitimacy in their registration requests to NSI, represented powerful evidence of defendants' bad faith in operating the northernlights.com site. This conclusion of bad faith was reinforced, according to the district court, by defendants' history of disregarding cease–and–desist letters from legitimate trademark owners, and their apparent openness to sell the northernlight.com registration to the plaintiff.

Although defendants are correct in asserting that their multiple registrations alone are not dispositive of the bad–faith issue, their well–established pattern of registering multiple domain names containing famous trademarks, such as rollingstones.com, evinrude.com, and givenchy.com, has been made highly relevant to the determination of bad faith by the list of factors in ACPA. One relevant factor pointing to bad faith is "the person's registration or acquisition of multiple domain names which the person knows are identical or confusingly similar to marks of others that are distinctive at the time of registration of such domain names." Those facts are not clearly trumped by facts favoring defendants' side of the story, such as their use of northernlights.com as a domain name used solely as an e–mail address for several years prior to the dispute with the plaintiff and Burgar's initial resistance to the plaintiff's efforts to acquire defendants' domain name registration. . . ..

Accordingly, we determine that the district court did not err in finding that defendants will likely be found to have acted in bad faith in operating their northernlights.com Web site. AFFIRMED.

Trade Secrets

It is an information age, and nothing is more important to most businesses than information. By means of economic espionage and the hiring of competitors' employees, companies annually acquire from competitors billions of dollars worth of confidential information. A trade secret is "any formula, pattern, device or compilation of information which is used in one's business, and which gives him an opportunity to obtain an advantage over competitors who do not know or use it." Examples of protectable trade secrets include detailed customer information that is not easily available to others, manufacturing processes, chemical formulas, operating and pricing policies, marketing strategies, raw materials sources, and the functional ideas in computer software. Trade secrets traditionally were protected by common law principles (as embodied in the Restatement of Torts), but in recent years 45 states and the District of Columbia have adopted the Uniform Trade Secrets Act (UTSA). Whether a given state has enacted the UTSA or still relies on common–law principles will almost never affect the outcome of a particular case because the principles are essentially the same.

Although both trade secret and patent law can be used to protect knowledge, the definition of what kind of knowledge can be protected is much broader in trade secret law. In situations where a company has knowledge (in the form of an "invention" such as a new process or product) that can potentially be protected either by trade secret or patent law, the company cannot protect the same thing as both a trade secret and as a patented invention. The public disclosure required for a patent destroys secrecy, and the company must choose which form of protection it wants.

To successfully bring a trade secret misappropriation case, a plaintiff must prove (1) The information actually was a trade secret; (2) The plaintiff had maintained reasonable measures to protect secrecy; and (3) The defendant improperly disclosed or acquired the trade secret information.

Existence of a Trade Secret

Courts take into account a variety of factors in deciding whether information qualifies as a trade secret. These factors may include (1) the extent to which the information is or is not known outside the company; (2) how easy or difficult it would be for someone else to independently develop the information or to acquire it properly; (3) the value of the information to the company; (4) the amount of time and money it took the company to create the information; and (5) how well the company has protected the information. Factor (5) is treated by most courts as a separate requirement for trade secret protection, as seen below, but the extent to which the company has maintained secrecy is also closely related to the initial question of whether there is a trade secret at all. The reason is simple. If a court is faced with a close factual question whether a trade secret exists, the fact that the owner took substantial measures to protect the knowledge strongly tends to show that there was a trade secret, and vice–versa. Secrecy measures are expensive to establish, monitor, review, and enforce. Rational company managers are not likely to devote substantial time and money to protecting something that is not valuable and confidential.

Courts have concluded that a combination of things can be a trade secret, even if none of the individual elements qualifies as a trade secret. For example, in Metallurgical Industries, Inc. v. Fourtek, Inc., 790 F.2d 1195 (5th Cir. 1986) , the court concluded that a company's combination of improvements to a furnace using a "zinc recovery" method for separating and recycling expensive carbide from scrap metal was a trade secret even though each individual improvement was not. In a furnace using this process, molten zinc interacts with carbide in the scrap metal, causing the carbide to separate and become brittle so that it can then be ground into a powder and used as a substitute for virgin carbide. Metallurgical had ordered a furnace from a manufacturer, but the furnace that was delivered did not work properly because of several design problems. After experimentation and trial–and–error, Metallurgical modified the furnace by (1) inserting chill plates in one part of the furnace to create a better temperature differential for distilling the zinc, (2) replacing the one large crucible with several smaller ones to prevent the zinc from dispersing in the furnace, (3) replacing segmented heating elements that had caused undesired electric arching with unitary graphite heating elements, and (4) installing a filter in the furnace's vacuum–pumps where clogging of zinc particles had been a serious problem. There was nothing new about any single modification, but the combination was new and not readily known or available. This concept is just common sense, because almost everything is a combination of elements. As we will see in patent law, a patentable invention may also consist of a new combination of previously known elements.

A final observation regarding the existence of a trade secret is worth noting. When a trade secret consists of the solution to some problem, it is not just the final results of a knowledge–development effort that are protectable. In many such cases, most of the time, money, and effort are expended in running into blind–alleys; in other words, a lot of the knowledge gained is in the form of figuring out what does not work. Often referred to as "negative know–how," such knowledge is also protectable as a trade secret if other requirements for protection are satisfied.

Reasonable Security Measures

A prototypical trade secret is the formula for Coca–Cola. With regard to how the company protects the secrecy of the formula, a Coca–Cola company executive testified by affidavit in Coca-Cola Bottling Co. v. Coca–Cola Co., 227 U.S.P.Q. 18 (D.Del. 1985) that "[t]he written version of the secret formula is kept in a security vault at the Trust Company Bank in Atlanta, and that vault can only be opened by a resolution from the company's Board of Directors. It is the company's policy that only two persons in the company shall know the formula at any one time, and that only those persons may oversee the actual preparation of [the product]. The Company refuses to allow the identity of those persons to be disclosed or to allow those persons to fly on the same airplane at the same time."

Although a company often will not be required to use the extreme measures adopted by Coca–Cola, you get the idea. A trade secret owner is not required to keep the information absolutely secret (which in most cases would be impossible, anyway), but does have to employ protective measures that are reasonable under the circumstances. The requirement of reasonable security measures closely resembles a requirement that the owner not be negligent in protecting this intangible property. The extent to which the law expects a trade secret owner to go in protecting the secret depends on a variety of factors: (1) How valuable is the information? (2) How much would additional protective measures cost? (3) How much would additional security efforts interfere with employees' ability to do their jobs? (4) How much additional protection would extra security measures actually provide? One can see from these factors that courts often use a rough "cost–benefit" analysis to determine whether the trade secret owner used adequate protective measures. That is, the court weighs the relative costs and benefits of additional protection.

Although the exact type of security required depends on the type of information being protected, typical measures might include providing access to the trade secret information only in restricted areas, keeping doors and gates locked, requiring ID's and passwords, using surveillance cameras or other appropriate devices such as motion detectors, having fences that outsiders can't see through, only allowing access to the information to employees who must know it to do their jobs (access on a "need–to–know" basis), disclosing information to outsiders (such as another company that must be relied on to do the manufacturing) only when it is necessary for the owner to do so in order to use it for commercial benefit and only when confidentiality obligations are imposed on the outsider. Also, even though the courts in most states impose an implied obligation of confidentiality on employees, requiring employees to sign written confidentiality, nondisclosure agreements (CNDA's) is a very good idea for several reasons, including the fact that this may be viewed as a reasonably necessary security measure.

A good example of the way in which courts balance the relative costs and benefits of additional security measures when deciding whether the owner should have made more protective efforts is E.I. duPont de Nemours & Co. v. Christopher, 431 F.2d 1012 (5th Circ. 1970) . There, duPont was constructing a large petrochemical refining plant that included facilities designed to enable duPont to use its new, secret process for producing methanol. Apparently, someone who knows a great deal about such refining processes could figure out how duPont's new process worked by seeing and studying the facility under construction. The type of security that one would reasonably expect in a case like this would include things like a tall privacy fence around the construction site, restricted access by having locked gates and requiring I.D.'s, using guards who patrolled the perimeter, and so on. In a small airplane, the defendants flew over the construction site and took aerial photographs. The court held that the requirement of reasonable protective efforts did not mean that duPont was required to build a dome over the construction site. This would have been an extraordinary step, and an exceptionally expensive one, and would be necessary only to protect against an intentional effort to spy. The defendants were found to have misappropriated duPont's trade secret.

Improper Disclosure, Acquisition, or Use

After Manville Corporation spent $9 million over seven years to develop a new method of insulation, one of its competitors hired six key Manville employees and was able to enter the market in less than two years. Manville later prevailed in a lawsuit against the competitor. This is just one of countless examples of improper disclosure (by former employees), acquisition, or use of trade secret information.

Conduct obviously will amount to misappropriation if it is independently illegal, such as bribery, burglary, trespassing, tapping telephones or other electronic message interception, or fraudulent misrepresentations (e.g., as a spy probably would have to make). However, conduct may be "improper," and thus constitute misappropriation, even though it is not illegal by itself. The best known example is found in the *duPont* case, discussed above, in which the court held that the aerial photography was not illegal and was not a tort, but was nevertheless an act of misappropriation because its only purpose was to intentionally overcome the reasonable security measures that duPont had put into place. One of the most common forms of misappropriation is the breach of a duty of confidentiality. Although confidentiality obligations may exist in a number of circumstances, the most common example of such an obligation exists in the employment context. As noted earlier, courts treat employees as having an implied obligation of confidentiality to their employers in almost all cases. Whether the duty is implied or express in a given case, an employee who acquires trade secret knowledge as a result of the employment relationship commits an act of misappropriation if she intentionally discloses the information for her own benefit either while still an employee or afterwards. If the employee goes to work for another company and discloses or uses the information in her subsequent job, the new employer also will be liable for misappropriation if a manager or supervisor knows about it or as a reasonable person should know about it.

There are two methods of trade secret acquisition that are not misappropriation. First, if someone else independently develops the same knowledge there is no misappropriation. Second, there likewise is no misappropriation if (1) the information is embodied in a product, and (2) someone else lawfully acquires the product and "reverse engineers" (dissembles and works backwards) to discover the trade secret. This is in contrast with patent law, under which there can be patent infringement regardless of how the knowledge is acquired.

The first of the two cases that follow illustrates the care that one must take when disclosing a new idea. The second illustrates the all–too–common situation of former employees who took confidential information with them when they left a company.

SMITH V. SNAP–ON TOOLS CORP
United States Court of Appeals, Fifth Circuit, 833 F.2d 578 (1987)

Smith made a ratchet by combining parts of two existing tools. Hoping to see his ratchet made available for sale, he brought it to the attention of Snap-on Tools, Inc., by showing the ratchet to an independent Snap-on dealer and then submitting a tool suggestion form to Snap-on's Wisconsin headquarters.

Snap-on began making and selling the ratchet without paying anything to Smith.

Smith sued, claiming that Snap–on had misappropriated a trade secret. The trial court, applying Wisconsin law, ruled for Smith but did not give him as large a judgment as he desired. Both sides appealed.

Wisconsin law prescribes two essential elements in a cause of action for misappropriation of trade secrets: an actual trade secret and a breach of confidence. The essence of the tort of trade secret misappropriation is the inequitable use of the secret. Even when a trade secret exists, a person who learns the secret legitimately, without any duty of confidentiality, is free to use it.

Rubin, Circuit Judge:

Wisconsin therefore follows trade secret law as set out in Sec. 757 of the Restatement of Torts. Under the Restatement, "[o]ne who discloses or uses another's trade secret, without a privilege to do so, is liable to the other if . . . his disclosure or use constitutes a breach of confidence reposed in him by the other in disclosing the secret to him." As the comment to this provision states, the proprietor of a trade secret may not unilaterally create a confidential relationship without the knowledge or consent of the party to whom he discloses the secret. No particular form of notice is necessary, however; the question is whether the recipient of the information knew or should have known that the disclosure was made in confidence.

Smith concedes that he never explicitly requested that his disclosure to Snap–on be held in confidence. Nonetheless, he argues, Snap–on knew or should have known that the disclosure was confidential. According to Smith, a "special relationship existed between himself and Snap–on, based on the fact that he, as a relatively unsophisticated individual, submitted his invention to Snap–on, a large corporation. Under the circumstances, Smith contends, the manufacturer should have known that he, as the inventor, expected compensation even if he did not request it.

The district court accepted this argument . . ., [but t]his does not reflect Wisconsin law. The Supreme Court of Wisconsin has held [in RTE Corp. v. Coatings, Inc., 267 N.W.2d 226 (1978)] that, when parties are dealing at arm's length, one party's disclosure of an alleged trade secret to another does not automatically create a confidential relationship. Although [RTE] involved two corporations, we see no reason to believe that it would have applied a different rule if the inventor had been an individual rather than a corporation.

Under certain circumstances, courts have found liability for misappropriation of trade secrets in cases involving implied confidentiality between an inventor and a manufacturer. When a manufacturer has actively solicited disclosure from an inventor, then made use of the disclosed material, the manufacturer may be liable for use or disclosure of the secret in the absence of any expressed understanding as to confidentiality. In this case, however, Smith disclosed the invention on his initiative, without any prompting from Snap–on. Alternatively, courts have imposed liability when the disclosing inventor did not specifically request confidentiality from the manufacturer, but did make clear that the disclosure was intended as part of a course of negotiations aimed at creating a licensing agreement or entering into a similar business transaction. These cases are also distinguishable because Smith did not indicate that he wanted any pecuniary recompense for his suggestion. . . . When Smith sent Snap–on a tool suggestion report describing the ratchet, he did not in any way indicate that he wanted compensation, and indeed wrote on the suggestion form, "I would like to be able to buy a nice new shiney [sic] one from the Snap–on truck." In none of his dealings with Snap–on over the next two years did Smith ever request confidentiality or indicate that he expected or desired any commercial arrangement based on his submission of the ratchet suggestion to Snap–on.

In February 1978, more than two years after Smith showed the ratchet to Clark, Smith's lawyer sent a letter to the supervisor of Snap–on's Product Management Division in which he asked that Smith receive compensation.

Reliance on confidentiality, however, must exist at the time the disclosure is made. An attempt to establish a special relationship long after an initial disclosure comes too late.

Because there was no confidential relationship between Smith and Snap–on, Snap–on violated no obligation to Smith by manufacturing the ratchet. We therefore reverse.

Economic Espionage Act

Although trade secret law still is primarily state law, in 1996 Congress passed the Economic Espionage Act (EEA) that makes it a federal crime to steal trade secrets. The primary concern of Congress was trade secret theft by agents of foreign companies or governments, but the law applies to everyone, including U.S. nationals. The EEA contains a broad definition of trade secrets and an even broader definition of misappropriation in an attempt to punish every form of unauthorized misappropriation. Just as importantly, the EEA adopts the traditional view that a trade secret loses its protected status if its owner does not take reasonable measures to protect it from disclosure. Prosecutors must prove not only that the purloined information was a trade secret, but also (a) that the defendant knew the information was a trade secret, (b) that the defendant intended to provide an economic benefit to a person other than the rightful owner, and (c) that the defendant intended to injure the owner of the trade secret. Domestic corporate espionage can be punished by fines of up to $500,000 for individuals and up to $5 million for organizations. Individuals defendants also face prison terms of up to ten years. If the trade secret theft is meant to benefit foreign entities, the penalties are even stiffer. Furthermore, any proceeds derived from the violation may be ordered forfeited.

In one of the earliest EEA cases, a maintenance supervisor at PPG–Industries offered to sell trade secrets to a competitor, Owens–Corning. Owens–Corning notified the FBI, which set up a sting operation. After being arrested attempting to sell trade secrets to an undercover agent, the PPG employee pled guilty and received a 15–month prison sentence.

INTEGRATED CASH MANAGEMENT SERVICES V. DIGITAL TRANSACTIONS, INC.
United States Court of Appeals, Second Circuit, 920 F.2d 171 (1990)

Plaintiffs–appellees Integrated Cash Management Services, Inc. and Cash Management Corporation (collectively, "ICM") design and develop computer software. ICM's programs are marketed to banks that, in turn, market the programs to the financial and treasury depatments of various corporations. CM develops generic programs that are readily customized to suit a particular client s specifications. It invests millions of dollars in the research and development these generic programs and in structuring these programs to create its software product.

The ICM programs at issue in the present case are: SEUNIMNT, a generic universal database management system; Telefon, a generic communications program; Menu System/Driver, a treasury work station program; and Report Writer, a financial report customizing program. ICM claims to employ a "winning combination" of these generic programs that, it argues, deserves protection as a trade secret.

Individual defendants Newlin and Vafa each worked for ICM. Alfred Newlin was employed by ICM as a computer programmer between September 1984 and March 1987.

While an ICM employee, Newlin wrote the Communications and Menu modules of the ICM system. He also assisted in writing the SEUNIMNT program in the computer language called "C" and in writing an initial version of the Report Writer module for ICM. Behrouz Vafa was employed by ICM as a computer programmer between June 1986 and March 1987. Vfa's projects as an ICM employee included writing, with Newlin's assistance, the "C" language version of SEUNIMNT. Vafa also collaborated with Newlin and others in the early stages of creating Report Writer. For both Newlin and Vafa, working at ICM was their first full–time position after completing graduate degrees. Both Newlin and Vafa signed nondisclosure agreements with ICM in which they agreed not to disclose or use any confidential or proprietary information of ICM upon leaving the company's employ.

Newlin and Vafa left ICM on March 13, 1987 and began working at DTI three days later. Before leaving ICM Newlin copied certain ICM files onto a personal diskette. He took that diskette with him without informing ICM. Vafa also left ICM with a copy of source code he had written for ICM. He later destroyed that file, however, because of personal doubts about the propriety of using the code at DTI.

Within two weeks of the individual defendants' commencement of work at DTI, it had created a prototype database manager program. This program, and other generic programs subsequently produced for DTI by Newlin and Vafa, were found by the district court to "operate in substantially the same manner as comparable ICM generic programs." The products developed by DTI were similar to those produced by ICM in both the design of component utilities and in overall structure or "architecture." Newlin and Vafa did not copy any of ICM's source code in creating their new programs. Instead, they used the same functional ideas and wrote new computer code that was neither identical nor substantially similar in its expressive elements. Thus, there was no copyright infringement.

ICM sued DTI, Newlin, and Vafa in federal district court, alleging trade secret misappropriation and copyright infringement. ICM originally sought both damages and an injunction. At the end of trial, ICM dropped its copyright claim and, for unexplained reasons, dropped its claim for damages. The district court found that defendants had misappropriated trade secrets from ICM and had used the secrets in developing DTI's computer programs. Accordingly, it enjoined, for a period of six months, the defendants from utilizing as part of DTI's systems any version of the four utility programs found to include misappropriated trade secret, or from contributing to the creation of any new programs embodying any of these four utility programs. Also, the court permanently enjoined defendants from distributing the four utility *programs as they existed on the date of court's decision. Defendants appealed.*

Altimari, Circuit Judge:

The central question presented by this appeal is whether trade secret protection extends to the manner in which several non–secret utility programs are arranged to create a computer software product.

A plaintiff claiming misappropriation of a trade secret must prove: (1) It possessed a trade secret, (2) It maintained reasonable security measures to protect secrecy (which is not an issue in this case), and (3) Defendant has disclosed, acquired, or used the trade secret by improper means, which includes breach of a duty of confidentiality. Defendants do not dispute the claim that, if the functional ideas causing the four computer programs were indeed trade secrets, they breached a duty of confidentiality. [Not only did they sign confidentiality agreements, but almost all circumstances the courts view employees as owing an implied duty of confidentiality even if there is no explicit agreement.] Instead, DTI and the individual defendants contend that the district court erred in finding that the "architecture" of ICM's system was a protectable trade secret. We disagree.

The most comprehensive and influential definition of a trade secret is that set out in § 757, comment b of the Restatement of Torts.... That definition, in pertinent part, provides: "A trade secret may consist of any formula, pattern, device or compilation of information which is used in one's business, and which gives him an opportunity to obtain an advantage over competitors who do not know or use it."

In determining whether a trade secret exists, the New York courts have considered the following factors to be relevant: (1) the extent to which the information is known outside of his business; (2) the extent to which it is known by employees and others involved in his business;

(3) the extent of measures taken by him to guard the secrecy of the information; (4) the value of the information to him and to his competitors; (5) the amount of effort or money expended by him in developing the information; (6) the ease or difficulty with which the information could be properly acquired or duplicated by others.

Applying these factors to the software program at issue in this case, it is evident that ICM retains a protectable trade secret in its product. The manner in which ICM's generic utility programs interact, which is the key to the product's success, is not generally known outside of ICM. Contrary to defendants' suggestion, the non–secret nature of the individual utility programs that comprise ICM's product does not alter this conclusion. A trade secret can exist in a combination of characteristics and components, each of which, by itself, is in the public domain, but the unified process, design and operation of which, in unique combination, affords a competitive advantage and is a protectable secret. As the district court found, the architecture of ICM's product, or the "way in which [ICM's] various components fit together as building blocks in order to form the unique whole."

Moreover, ICM's combination of programs was not disclosed in ICM's promotional literature, which contains merely a user–oriented description of the advantages of ICM's product. The defendants have not shown that the limited information available in the promotional literature contains sufficient technical detail to constitute disclosure of the product's architecture. The district court's finding that "the package as a whole, and the specifications used by ICM to make the parts of that package work together, are not in the public domain," was based on extensive expert testimony.

The remaining factors to be considered in ascertaining the existence of a trade secret are also satisfied in this case. ICM has taken measures to protect the secrecy of its product architecture. The doors to the premises were kept locked.

Employees, including Newlin and Vafa, were required to sign nondisclosure agreements which provided that "when employment is terminated, the [former employee] agrees not to use, copy or disclose any of ICM's secrets, software products, software tools or any type of information and software which belongs to ICM." The large investment in research and development of ICM's product has not been challenged by the defendants. Finally, the expert testimony reveals that the ICM product's architecture could not be readily duplicated without the secret information acquired by CM through years of research. The architecture of the ICM system was not "readily ascertainable," other than by the improper disclosure and use by Newlin and Vafa. Accordingly, the district court found ICM's "winning combination" of generic utility programs to be a trade secret, on the record before us, these findings are not clearly erroneous and, therefore, will not be disturbed . . . .

The district court further found that the defendants made use of this information in designing similar software. Newlin and Vafa "made use of information learned while at ICM concerning which functions and relationships among the modules would and would not work in the generic program." Contrary to defendants–appellants' suggestion, the court's statement that Vafa "was certainly capable of writing the source code in his own right," does not contradict the finding that Vafa and Newlin, in fact, used ICM's trade secrets.

Defendants–appellants contend that two aspects of the district court's injunction against them are improper. First, they challenge the court's six–month injunction prohibiting Newlin and Vafa from becoming involved in the development of programs similar to ICM's product. They argue that this injunction unfairly precluded Newlin and Vafa from utilizing their training and general experience in the field of computer programming. We believe that the court crafted this aspect of its injunction with a careful eye toward the balance between the right of a former employer to protect trade secrets and the right of a former employee to utilize his skills and experience. However, we do not reach the propriety of this aspect of the district court's injunction at this time. By its terms, the injunction against the involvement of Newlin and Vafa in DTI's programming efforts expired on April 26, 1990.

Second, the defendants–appellants challenge the district court's perpetual injunction against their distribution of any version of ICM's four generic utility programs in existence as of October 26, 1989, the date decision was rendered.

They contend that this perpetual injunction gives ICM an undeserved windfall by extending the restriction beyond the six–month period which the court considered necessary "to neutralize the 'head start" gained by DTI from the improper use of ICM's trade secrets." We disagree.

In contrast to the district court's six month injunction against the defendants' use of ICM's programs, the court's perpetual injunction is aimed at preventing defendants' distribution of those programs as they existed on October 26, 1989. Defendants are thereby prevented from simply shelving the misappropriated information for six months, and then distributing the ICM product as their own. Following the six month period, defendants may internally use ICM's four generic programs and may alter or modify them as they choose. However, defendants may not distribute any unmodified ICM programs either during or after the six–month period. The district court's injunction, when considered in toto, is a reasonable and wise exercise of discretion. Affirmed.

Patents

To encourage creation and disclosure of inventions, the Constitution authorizes the federal government to grant patents to inventors. The first U.S. patent law was adopted by Congress in 1790, and the current statute is the Patent Act of 1952 (including many amendments since its passage). In exchange for disclosing the invention, the inventor patentee receives a 20–year exclusive right to make, use, or sell the patented invention. The 20–year patent is nonrenewable; after expiration of the period the item goes into the public domain and may be made, used, or sold by anyone. Until 1995 the term of patent protection was 17 years from the date the patent was issued, but Congress changed it to 20 years from the date the patent application was first filed. Congress made this and several other changes in order to implement the provisions of the international agreements that created the WTO.

Applying for a Patent

An application for a U.S. patent must be filed with the U.S. Patent & Trademark Office (PTO). The application specifies the names of the inventors and indicates who owns the patent if the owner is someone other than the inventors. Much more often than not, there will be an "assignee–at–issue," which is usually a corporation that employed the inventors. The application must contain a thorough and concise description of the invention and drawings. The description and drawings together must meet the **enablement** requirement, which means that they must describe the invention with sufficient thoroughness and conciseness to enable a hypothetical "ordinarily skilled practitioner of the art" (art refers to the relevant field of technology) to make the invention and put it into practice without undue experimentation. The applicant is not required to have actually made the invention physically, and many patents are granted even thought the applicant has not created a physical embodiment of the invention. However, physically making the invention is a practical necessity in some situations in order for the inventor to know that the invention works and to be able to write an "enabling" description of the invention.

In the patent law of the U.S. and a few other countries, the application also must disclose the **best mode** for putting the invention into practice. Obviously, the application must disclose at least one mode (method for making and putting into practice) or it will not be enabling. In addition, if the inventor(s) believe at the time the application is filed that a particular mode is the best one for making the invention and putting it into practice this method must be disclosed in the application. Thus, even if the inventors are not claiming a particular technique for making or using the invention as part of the invention itself (often the case), they must disclose it if they believe it to be the best method at the time they file. Because this is a subjective requirement (unlike enablement), it usually is not an issue in the PTO, but sometimes is a basis for a court judgment that later declares the patent invalid. When the best mode must be disclosed, its disclosure must be thorough and concise. Sometimes the "best mode" is referred to as the *"preferred embodiment."*

After the written description and drawings, the patent includes "claims," which precisely delineate the intangible property right the applicant is asking the PTO to grant. To determine exactly what the invention is, one must look at the precisely drafted claims. When a patent owner sues for patent infringement, the owner is actually suing for infringement of one or more claims within the patent.

In addition to a regular application, since 1995 U.S. law has permitted a "provisional application," which can be especially advantageous for individuals, small businesses, and nonprofits like universities because it allows for the deferral of many patenting costs for up to a year—this gives the applicant an all-important filing date but provides extra time to do things like seek additional funding and further explore market potential. A provisional application can be filed without including any claims, and the PTO takes no action on it. If the applicant files a regular application within one year (including claims) and does not make any material change in the description, any resulting patent traces its filing date back to the filing of the provisional. Having as early a filing date as possible is important for many reasons, one of which will be seen below in our discussion of the requirements of patentability.

Requirements for Patentability

For an invention to be patentable, it must be (1) patentable subject matter, (2) useful, (3) novel, (4) the result of a patent application that was originally filed less than one year after certain actions that revealed the invention, and (5) "nonobvious" (not obvious to an ordinarily skilled practitioner in this area of technology).

Patentable Subject Matter

Inventions that may be patented include (1) processes, (2) machines, (3) manufactures (that is, products), (4) compositions of matter (for example, new compositions of elements in a metal alloy), and (5) any improvement on the first four categories that itself meets all of these requirements. Patents also may be granted on certain new plant varieties. Regular patents are sometimes referred to as "utility" patents. Patent law also recognizes so-called "design patents" for non-functional ornamental design elements in a functional product. We will not discuss design patents. One cannot patent naturally occurring substances or abstract ideas such as formulas or scientific principles. Particular applications of formulas or principles, however, can be patented.

For a number of years, there was legal debate about whether patent law can protect biotechnology processes and products. This debate was resolved in the affirmative by the Supreme Court in Diamond v. Chakrabarty, 447 U.S. 303 (1980), in which the Court upheld the validity of a patent on new bacteria created by genetic engineering that would "eat" crude oil in an oil spill. The court observed that Congress had intended to provide protection to "anything under the sun made by man" if it meets other patentability requirements. Since then, many patents have been granted by the PTO on things like genetically altered mice and rabbits (for applications in medical research). The dividing line is between discovery and invention. If something originally found in nature has been so altered by human intervention that it now is really something quite different, it is patentable subject matter.

Whether computer software is patentable subject matter also was debated hotly for some time. Copyright law protects the expressive elements in software, mainly the source code and object code. But what about the functional ideas in software that can cause the software to be viewed as an "invention"? The question arose because software consists of a large number of algorithms (formulas for solving problems). After many confusing decisions by both the Supreme Court and the Court of Appeals for the Federal Circuit (the intermediate appeals court that hears all patent cases), it now is firmly settled that software can be a patentable invention as long as it has a practical application and meets the other requirements of patentability. Algorithms in the abstract cannot be patented, but their specific applications to accomplish certain results can be.

About the same time that the courts finally resolved the question about the patentability of software generally, the Federal Circuit Court of Appeals also settled a subsidiary debate by concluding that software–implemented methods of doing business also can be patented. The most notable case reaching this conclusion was State Street Bank & Trust v. Signature Financial Services, 149 F.3d 1368 (Fed. Cir. 1998), in which a patent was upheld on a software program that enabled several mutual funds to achieve substantial efficiencies in financial calculation and financial reporting by forming a computerized partnership for these limited purposes.

Utility

The requirement that an invention be useful is typically referred to as the "utility" requirement. This requirement merely means that the invention must be operable and achieve a useful result. "Operable" and "useful result" essentially mean that it actually does something, and does not defy the laws of physics (like a perpetual motion machine). It does not have to be commercially successful; as earlier mentioned, it is not even required that the inventor has actually made a working version as long as thorough details are disclosed in the patent application. In recent years, the PTO finally rejected a patent application on a process for supposedly achieving "cold fusion" because the experimental results (which were highly questionable and rejected by others in the scientific community) could never be replicated by anyone. Other scientists concluded that the patent applicant had achieved only a chemical reaction rather than an atomic reaction.

One can see that the utility requirement has a very low threshold and will almost always be fulfilled. In a few areas of technology, however, such as biotechnology and some areas of organic chemistry, the inventor must go significantly farther in order to demonstrate operability and a useful result because experimentation in these areas is prone to highly unpredictable results.

A Note on "Prior Art"

Before further discussion of the requirements of patentability, it is necessary to explain the concept of "prior art" in patent law. With some simplification, prior art consists of either of the following: (1) A patent anywhere in the world; (2) A printed publication anywhere in the world; (3) Evidence of a "public use" of the invention that took place in the U.S.; or (4) Evidence that the invention was placed "on sale" (sold or offered for sale) in the U.S.

By definition, a patent issued in any country is publicly available. A document (either in traditional hard copy or in any other tangible form) is treated as a printed publication when it is accessible to anyone who is interested and willing to take the time to find it. "Public use" is an elusive concept, but essentially means either that the invention was used by someone else who was not under a duty of confidentiality to the inventor or to the inventor's employer, that its used was viewed by such a person, or that it was demonstrated to such a person. An invention is placed on sale if it is either sold, subject to a contract of sale, or offered for sale, regardless of confidentiality. A patent or a printed publication is treated as prior art if was "enabling"— that is, only if it revealed all of the elements of the later invention that is now in question, with sufficient detail so that a hypothetical ordinarily skilled practitioner in this technology area could have made the invention by studying these revealed details. A prior public use of an invention that is the same as the current one can be prior art even if the use did not reveal enough detail to have been enabling. With respect to the fourth type of prior art, an invention the same as this one having been placed on sale, the actions involved in making the sale or offer are also not required to have been enabling (although, as a practical matter, such actions usually do reveal enough to be enabling). Also, a public use is the only one of the four types of prior art that can come into existence only if a physical embodiment of the invention has been created— there must be a physical embodiment for it to be "used." The practical importance of these concepts of prior art is discussed further in the following section on the requirements of novelty and timely application filing.

Novelty and Delayed Filing

In the Patent Act there are two related provisions dealing with the requirement of novelty, and with the requirement that an inventor file a patent application within one year after a piece of prior art came into existence. The first section states that an inventor should not receive a patent if someone else (other than this inventor) had a patent issued, created a printed publication, made a public use, or put an invention on sale before this inventor *invented*, where the prevous invention contained all of the same functional elements as the current one.

Suppose, for example, that Inventor X has invented a new device for improving automobile fuel efficiency. When X applies for a patent, the patent examiner in the PTO will search for and study relevant prior art. Obviously, X should have done a prior art search before filing, to determine whether his invention probably is patentable (but this can be a very difficult determination). Although X should have done this, in reality the quality of applicant prior art searches varies greatly. If it is found that, before X invented, Y had received a patent on an invention that included all of the elements of X's invention, then X's invention does not meet the requirement of **novelty**. The same would be true if it is found that Y had created one of the other types of prior art before X invented. Although novel means "new," it is possible for X to receive a valid patent on an invention even if someone else had created the same invention first. If, for instance, Y had invented before X did, but Y kept its invention secret (did not get a patent, did not disclose the invention in a prior printed publication, and did not create one of the other types of prior art before X invented), then X's invention is still treated as being novel.

The second section in the Patent Act specifies that, if either Inventor X or someone else created one of these pieces of prior art more than one year before X filed her patent application, X is not entitled to a patent. In the example above, suppose that Y had received a patent or created one of the other pieces of prior art more than one year before X filed his patent application. This provides another reason for denying X a patent. Suppose that the evidence did not establish when X actually invented—inventors should keep excellent records of their activities leading to an invention, but often they do not. In such a case, even if we don't know whether Y's prior art came into existence before X invented, this prior art destroys X's ability to get a patent if it came into existence more than one year before X filed his patent application. If we know when X invented, and Y's prior art is both before X invented and more than one year before X filed his patent application, there are two alternative reasons for denying X's patent.

Although the rule requiring X to file a patent application within one year after certain events can be applied to something someone else has done, as we have just seen, the most important application of this filing–within–one–year rule is to things that Inventor X has done himself. Assume again, for example, that Inventor X invents the new fuel efficiency device, and has not yet filed an application for a patent. X makes a public use of the invention, places it on sale, or makes a written disclosure of the invention's details to someone who does not owe him a confidentiality obligation. X must file an application within one year after doing one of these things or he loses the right to obtain a patent. This is often referred to as the one–year "grace period," and allows X to engage in some preliminary efforts to seek financing or gauge the market even before. At the present time, other countries do not have this grace period and in those countries a patent cannot be obtained if any of these activities occurred anytime before the application is filed in such a country. Thus, X might be able to get a U.S. patent if he files a patent application within a year after a public use, etc., but he cannot get a patent in another country.

It is relatively common for the PTO to miss a relevant piece of prior art. One can easily see that the PTO is much more likely to discover a relevant prior patent or printed publication than it is to discover evidence of a prior public use or a sale or offer to sell. Thus, even if the PTO issued a patent to X, when X later sues someone else for patent infringement, the defendant usually challenges the validity of X's patent; if the defendant presents to the court evidence of prior art not considered by the PTO showing that X's invention lacked novelty or that X failed to file within a year after a triggering event, the court will declare X's patent to be void.

An example helps illustrate all of the above principles. In the East Texas oil fields during the mid–1930s, a group of Gulf oil employees developed and used a new technique for oil and gas exploration. The employees owed a confidentiality obligation to Gulf, and use of the newly developed process solely by them was not a public use. However, they used the new process out in the open, without any fences or other barriers to prevent someone else from coming to see what they were doing. Although there was no evidence that someone who was not a Gulf employee had actually observed what they were doing, such a person could have done so. Because the use could have been viewed by someone who did not owe a confidentiality obligation to Gulf, this was treated as a public use. A man named Rosaire was also developing new exploration techniques somewhere else. About a year after the public use by Gulf, Rosaire independently invented the same new process. Rosaire obtained a patent on the process and later sued two companies for infringing it. The defendants produced evidence of the Gulf public use and the court held Rosaire's patent to be invalid because his invention lacked novelty. Although the validity of Gulfs own patent was not an issue in the case, the evidence revealed that Gulf itself had not applied for a patent until about four years after it made the public use; thus Gulf exceeded the grace–period and was not entitled to a patent on its invention. This means that no one had a patent on the new exploration process and it could be used freely by anyone. If Gulf had kept its use secret, as by using the process only within a fenced area with locked gates, restricted access, guards, and so forth, Gulfs use would not have been prior art that destroyed the patentability of Rosaire's later identical invention, and would not have triggered the one–year clock for Gulf itself.

The foregoing example naturally raises the question of how we sort out patent rights when two inventors invent the same thing and try to patent it within a closely contemporaneous time period. In most countries, when there is a contest between two inventors as to who is entitled to patent protection on their identical but independently developed inventions, the right goes to the first one to file a patent application. In the U.S., however, the rule is that the patent rights go to the first one who invented. Thus, when there is such a contest, either in the PTO or in court, the two inventors seek to prove who was actually the first to invent. Although the U.S. first–to–invent system is unusual in theory, it is not as different in actual practice, because when there is such a contest, the inventor who first filed a patent application wins a large majority of the time. Often, the reason is that the one claiming to have been the first to invent is unable to produce records that are sufficient to prove his contention.

The following case illustrates a situation in which an inventor makes a public use and then waits too long to file a patent application. The court not only discusses what constitutes a public use, but also discusses the so–called "experimental use" exception to the one–year rule. If the inventor's use was public, but was being done for genuine experimental purposes to ascertain whether the invention works as intended, the one–year clock is postponed for a reasonable time to allow for this experimentation.

LOUGH V. BRUNSWICK CORP.

U.S. Court of Appeals, Federal Circuit, 86 F.3d 1113 (1996)

Stern drives are marine propulsion devices for boats in which the engine is located inside the boat and is coupled to an outdrive, which includes a propeller located outside the boat ("inboard/outboard boat"). In 1986, Steven Lough worked as a repairman for a boat dealership and marina in Sarasota, Florida.

While repairing Brunswick inboard/outboard boats, he noticed that the upper seal assembly in the stern drives often failed due to corrosion.

Lough determined that the corrosion in the upper seal assembly occurred due to contact between the annular seal and the bell housing aperture. He designed a new upper seal assembly that isolated the annular seal from the aluminum bell housing in order to prevent such corrosion. After some trial and error with his grandfather's metal lathe, he made six usable prototypes in the spring of 1986. He installed one prototype in his own boat at home.

Three months later, he gave a second prototype to a friend who installed it in his boat. He also installed prototypes in the boat of the owner of the marina where he worked and in the boat of a marina customer. He gave the remaining prototypes to longtime friends who were employees at another marina in Sarasota. Lough did not charge anyone for the prototypes. For over a year following the installation of these prototypes, Lough neither asked for nor received any comments about the operability of the prototypes. During this time, Lough did not attempt to sell any seal assemblies.

On June 6, 1988, Lough filed a patent application entitled "Liquid Seal for Marine Stern Drive Gear Shift Shafts," which issued as U.S. Patent 4,848,775 (the '775 patent) on July 18, 1989. After learning of Lough's invention, Brunswick designed its own improved upper seal assembly. Lough sued Brunswick on June 12, 1993, alleging infringement of the '775 patent. Brunswick counterclaimed for a declaratory judgment of non–infringement and invalidity. A jury found that Brunswick failed to prove that Lough's invention was in public use before the critical date on June 6, 1987, one year prior to the filing date of the '775 patent. The jury also found that Brunswick infringed claims 1–4 of '775 patent. Based on its infringemen finding, the juy awarded Lough $1,500,000 in lost profits. After trial, Brunswick filed a Motion for Judgent as a Matter of Law JMOL the same thing as a judgment N.. V.] in which it argued that the claimed invention was invalid because it had been in public use before the critical date. The district court denied Brunswick s motion, and Brunswick appealed.

Lourie, Circuit Judge:

Brunswick challenges, inter alia, the court's denial of its motion for JMOL on the issue of public use. Brunswick argues that the district court erred in denying its motion for JMOL because the uses of Lough's prototypes prior to the critical date were not experimental. Brunswick asserts that Lough did not control the uses of his prototypes by third parties before the critical date, failed to keep records of the alleged experiments, and did not place the parties to whom the seals were given under any obligation of secrecy. Based on this objective evidence, Brunswick argues that the uses of Lough's prototypes before the critical date were not "experimental." Therefore, Brunswick contends that the jury's verdict was incorrect as a matter of law and that the court erred in denying its JMoL motion.

Lough counters that the tests performed with the six prototypes were necessary experiments conducted in the course of completing his invention. He argues that when the totality of circumstances is properly viewed, the evidence supports the jury's conclusion that those uses were experimental. Lough maintains that a number of factors support the jury's experimental use conclusion, including evidence that he received no compensation for the prototypes, he did not place the seal assemblies on sale until after he filed his patent application, and he gave the prototypes only to his friends and personal acquaintances who used them in such a manner that they were unlikely to be seen by the public. He further argues that, to verify operability of the seal assemblies, prototypes had to be installed by mechanics of various levels of skill in boats that were exposed to different conditions. Thus, he asserts that the court did not err in denying Brunswick's JMoL motion. We disagree with Lough.

One is entitled to a patent unless, [among other things], the invention was . . . in public use . . . in this country, more than one year prior to the date of the application for patent in the United States. We have defined public use as including "any use of [the claimed] invention by a person other than the inventor who is under no limitation, restriction or obligation of secrecy to the inventor." An evaluation of a question of public use depends on "how the totality of the circumstances of the case comports with the policies underlying the public use bar."

These policies include: (1) discouraging the removal, from the public domain, of inventions that the public reasonably has come to believe are freely available; (2) favoring the prompt and widespread disclosure of inventions; (3) allowing the inventor a reasonable amount of time following sales activity to determine the potential economic value of a patent; and (4) prohibiting the inventor from commercially exploiting the invention for a period greater than the statutorily prescribed time.

A patentee may negate a showing of public use by coming forward with evidence that its use of the invention was experimental. Neither party disputes that Lough's prototypes were in use before the critical date. Thus, both parties agree that the issue presented on appeal is whether the jury properly decided that the use of Lough's six prototypes in 1986, prior to the critical date, constituted experimental use so as to negate the conclusion of public use.

The law requires that an inventor must file a patent application within one year after his invention is publicly used. Public use means any use of Mr. Lough's invention by any person other than Mr. Lough who was not limited or restricted in their activities regarding the invention, or not obligated to secrecy by Mr. Lough. Such use, however does not invalidate Mr. Lough's patent if the use was primarily for bona fide experimental purposes. . . .

The parties do not dispute that the five seal assemblies were used by others before June 6, 1987. The only dispute is whether these uses qualify as experimental uses. Whether an invention was in public use prior to the critical date within the meaning of § 102(b) is a question of law. "The use of an invention by the inventor himself, or of any other person under his direction, by way of experiment, and in order to bring the invention to perfection, has never been regarded as [a public] use." City of Elizabeth v. American Nicholson Pavement Co., 97 U.S. 126, 134(1877) . This doctrine is based on the underlying policy of providing an inventor time to determine if the invention is suitable for its intended purpose, in effect, to reduce the invention to practice.

To determine whether a use is "experimental," a question of law, the totality of the circumstances must be considered, including various objective indicia of experimentation surrounding the use, such as the number of prototypes and duration of testing, whether records or progress reports were made concerning the testing, whether the patentee received compensation for the use of the invention, and the extent of control the inventor maintained over the testing. The last factor of control is critically important, because, if the inventor has no control over the alleged experiments, he is not experimenting. If he does not inquire about the testing or receive reports concerning the results, similarly, he is not experimenting. In order to justify a determination that legally sufficient experimentation has occurred, there must be present certain minimal indicia. The framework might be quite formal, as may be expected when large corporations conduct experiments, governed by contracts and explicit written obligations. When individual inventors or small business units are involved, however, less formal and seemingly casual experiments can be expected. Such less formal experiments may be deemed legally sufficient to avoid the public use bar, but only if they demonstrate the presence of the same basic elements that are required to validate any experimental program. Our case law sets out these elements. The question framed on this appeal is whether Lough's alleged experiments lacked enough of these required indicia so that his efforts cannot, as a matter of law, be recognized as experimental.

Here, Lough either admits or does not dispute the following facts. In the spring of 1986, he noted that the upper seal assembly in Brunswick inboard/outboard boats was failing due to galvanic corrosion between the annular seal and the aperture provided for the upper seal assembly in the aluminum bell housing. He solved this problem by isolating the annular seal from the aluminum bell housing in order to prevent corrosion. After some trial and error, Lough made six prototypes. He installed the first prototype in his own boat. Lough testified at trial that after the first prototype had been in his boat for three months and he determined that it worked, he provided the other prototypes to friends and acquaintances in order to find out if the upper seal assemblies would work as well in their boats as it had worked in his boat. Lough installed one prototype in the boat of his friend, Tom Nikla. A prototype was also installed in the boat of Jim Yow, co-owner of the dealership where Lough worked. Lough installed a fourth prototype in one of the dealership's customers who had considerable problems with corrosion in his stern drive unit. The final two prototypes were given to friends who were employed at a different marina in Florida. These friends installed one prototype in the boat of Mark Liberman, a local charter guide. They installed the other prototype in a demonstration boat at their marina. Subsequently, this boat was sold. Neither Lough nor his friends knew what happened with either the prototype or the demonstration boat after the boat was sold. After providing the five prototypes to these third parties, Lough neither asked for nor received any comments concerning the operability of these prototypes.

It is true that Lough did not receive any compensation for the use of the prototypes. He did not place the seal assembly on sale before applying for a patent. Lough's lack of commercialization, however, is not dispositive of the public use question in view of his failure to present objective evidence of experimentation. Lough kept no records of the alleged testing. Nor did he inspect the seal assemblies after they had been installed by other mechanics. He provided the seal assemblies to friends and acquaintances, but without any provision for follow–up involvement by him in assessment of the events occurring during the alleged experiments, and at least one seal was installed in a boat that was later sold to strangers. Thus, Lough did not maintain any supervision and control over the seals during the alleged testing.

Lough argues that other evidence supports a finding that his uses were experimental, including his own testimony that the prototypes were installed for experimental purposes and the fact that the prototypes were used in such a manner that they were unlikely to be seen by the public. However, the expression by an inventor of his subjective intent to experiment, particularly after institution of litigation, is generally of minimal value. In addition, the fact that the prototypes were unlikely to be seen by the public does not support Lough's position. As the Supreme Court stated in Egbert v. Lippman: "[S]ome inventions are by their very character only capable of being used where they cannot be seen or observed by the public eye. An invention may consist of a lever or spring, hidden in the running gear of a watch, or of a ratchet, shaft, or cog-wheel covered from view in the recesses of a machine for spinning or weaving. Nevertheless, if its inventor [publicly uses] a machine of which his invention forms a part, and allows it to be used without restriction of any kind, the use is a public one."

We do not dispute that it may have been desirable in this case for Lough to have had his prototypes installed by mechanics of various levels of skill in boats that were exposed to different conditions. Moreover, Lough was free to test his invention in boats of friends and acquaintances to further verify that his invention worked for its intended purpose; however,

Lough was required to maintain some degree of control and feedback over those uses of the prototypes if those tests were to negate public use. Lough's failure to monitor the use of his prototypes by his acquaintances, in addition to the lack of records or reports from those acquaintances concerning the operability of the devices, compel the conclusion that, as a matter of law, he did not engage in experimental use. Lough in effect provided the prototype seal assemblies to members of the public for their free and unrestricted use. The law does not waive statutory requirements for inventors of lesser sophistication. When one distributes his invention to members of the public under circumstances that evidence a near total disregard for supervision and control concerning its use, the absence of these minimal indicia of experimentation require a conclusion that the invention was in public use.

We conclude that the jury's determination that Lough's use of the invention was experimental so as to defeat the assertion of public use was incorrect as a matter of law. The court thus erred in denying Brunswick's JMoL motion on the validity of claims 1–4 of the "775 patent under § 102(b). REVERSED.

Nonobviousness

Even if there is not a single item of prior art that, by itself, invalidates Inventor X's patent, there is still the chance that X's invention may not meet the requirement of "nonobviousness." This requirement provides that an inventor is not entitled to a patent on an invention if, at the time of invention, a hypothetical ordinarily skilled practitioner in this art (technology) would have viewed the invention as representing only a trivial, or obvious, advance over the cumulative prior art.

When a question of nonobviousness arises, either in the PTO or later in court, the first step is to analyze the relevant prior art. Although a single piece of prior art may cause X's invention to be obvious (X's invention is too minor a step beyond what was in the prior art), it is common for the PTO and the courts to combine two or more pieces of prior art in the same field of technology and say something like "the teachings of this prior patent, when read in the light of the teachings of this other prior printed publication, cause X's invention to be obvious."

The following example may help. Lockwood produced an invention that allowed people to make multiple reservations with airlines, rental car companies, hotels, and so on. His invention was referred to as a "terminal," but it was actually a software invention. He sued American Airlines, claiming that AA's Sabre reservation system infringed on his patent. The court first concluded that AA had not infringed because its Sabre system did not have an audio–visual feature that was an integral part of Lockwood's patented invention. The court then concluded that Lockwood's patent was invalid because his invention was obvious in light of the teachings of two pieces of prior art that were closely enough related that they should be viewed together for this purpose. The first was AA's original reservation system that had been introduced in the early 1960s and used by many thousands of customers, travel agents, and others. The court found that this was prior art because there had been a public use of the system even though the users could not have figured out the details of the software that made the system work (a public use does not have to be enabling). The second was one of Lockwood's own earlier patents. The original AA system included many of the functional ideas in Lockwood's patented invention and the older Lockwood patent disclosed the audio–visual feature. The invention in Lockwood's patent was merely an obvious step beyond the combination of the AA system and the older Lockwood patent.

After studying the relevant prior art, a court sometimes will still be on the fence regarding the nonobviousness question. If there is evidence of so–called "objective factors"—evidence of what actually happened after a patented product or process was marketed—such evidence may help the court resolve the question. This type of evidence could not have been available to the PTO when considering whether to grant the patent. Such evidence can take several forms, but it all focuses on the following question: If X's invention was so obvious, then why did this happen? For example, if X's invention was so obvious, then: a. Why was the product so commercially successful? b. Why had there been such a long–felt need for solving the problem that Inventor X solved? Why had others tried and failed after substantial efforts to find the solution that Inventor X found? or Why did one or more competitors start copying X's invention rather than relying on their own solutions?

In addition, if there is evidence to show that X's invention produced a result that was surprising or that was contrary to conventional teachings in this area of technology, this very strongly points toward nonobviousness. Inventor X is certainly not required to show that his invention produces an unexpected result, because most patentable inventions actually produce the results that were theorized, but an unexpected technical result almost compels a conclusion of nonobviousness. For example, Dr. Robert Gore was searching for a better method of stretching Teflon™ into tubing, tape, and other products through a combination of temperature and stretching speed variations. Conventional wisdom taught that, as the temperature was increased, more stretching without breaking could be accomplished by slowing down the stretching speed. Dr. Gore's experiments showed, to the contrary, that increasing the stretching speed increased the amount of stretching without breaking. This evidence helped show that the new process he invented was not obvious.

Ownership of Patent Rights

Although patent law is federal law, questions regarding ownership of patented inventions or rights to use them are determined by state law. An owner can sell or otherwise transfer patent ownership to someone else by executing a written assignment. A patent assignment must be recorded with the PTO.

An owner can keep the patent and grant exclusive or nonexclusive licenses that give others the right to make specified uses of the patented technology in return for royalty payments. Licensing of all kinds of intellectual property rights is very common.

If an employee is hired for creative or inventive work ("hired to invent") and invents something on company time while using company resources, the invention and any resulting patent belong to the company. The company will file the application in the employee's name, but the company will own it (as the "assignee–at–issue"). Even if the employee was not hired for creative or inventive work, if she invents something on company time or using company resources, the company will be granted a nonexclusive license to use the patented invention within its business without payment of a royalty. In this latter case, the employer's implied nonexclusive license is called a "shop right." Of course, many employers have their employees sign "pre–invention assignment agreements" that obligate them to assign title to the employer of all patents generated on company time or using company resources. Under such an obligation, if the inventor–employee later refuses to actually execute the assignment, it will be done for him.

Infringement

As observed earlier, when a patent owner sues for infringement, he is alleging that the defendant infringed one or more of the claims in the patent. The invention is actually defined most precisely in the claims. For example, Inventor X may have a patent on his new device for improving auto fuel efficiency that includes as its first, broadest claim:

"A device for enhancing the fuel efficiency of an internal combustion engine, comprising
a.   A widget, disposed laterally across two gadgets; and
b.   A froozmit coupled with each gadget at an angle no greater than 17 degrees; and
c.   A plurality of diazapod schlingers extending radially from the froozmit; and
d.   A cornplow dinger adjoined to the proximal end of each diazapod schlinger.

If the defendant's product contains all of these elements, a–d, it infringes (even if it includes other things). If it doesn't include one element, such as c., it does not infringe. If defendant's product contains elements that are identical to a., b., and c., but substitutes something else for element d., the defendant's product may or may not infringe on plaintiff's patent. In such a case, the court will apply the "doctrine of equivalents," which finds infringement if what the defendant is doing, on an element–by–element basis, "performs substantially the same function in substantially the same way to achieve substantially the same result." In this example, defendant's first 3 elements are the same, so the question is whether its substitute for element d. performs substantially the same function as d. in substantially the same way to achieve substantially the same result. If so, it infringes. The same infringement analysis is used for other types of inventions such as processes, machines, and compositions of matter.

LARAMI CORP. V. ALAN AMRON & TALK TO ME PPRODUCTS, INC.
United States District Court, Eastern District of Pennsylvania, 1993 U.S. Dist. LEXIS 3097 (1993)

Plaintiff Larami Corp. manufactures a line of toy water guns called "SUPER SOAKERS," that includes five models: SUPER SOAKER 20, SUPER SOAKER 30, SUPER SOAKER 50, SUPER SOAKER 100, and SUPER SOAKER 200. All use a hand-operated air pump to pressurize water and a "pinch trigger" valve mechanism for controlling the ejection of the pressurized water. All feature detachable water reservoirs prominently situated outside and above the barrel of the gun. Alan Amron and Talk To Me Products, Inc. (hereinafter referred to collectively as "TTMP") claim that the SUPER SOAKER guns infringe on U.S. patent 4,239,129 (the '129 patent), which TTMP obtained by assignment from Gary Esposito ("Esposito"), the inventor. [Esposito was almost certainly an employee of TTMP when he invented.] The '129 patent covers a water gun which, like the SUPER SOAKERS, operates by pressurizing water housed in a tank with an air pump. In the '129 patent, the pressure enables the water to travel out of the tank through a trigger–operated valve into an outlet tube and to squirt through a nozzle. Unlike the SUPER SOAKERS, the '129 patent also contains various electrical features to illuminate the water stream and create noises. Also, the water tank in the '129 patent is not detachable, but is contained within a housing in the body of the water gun.

After being threatened by TTMP with an infringement suit, Larami brought this action seeking a declaratory judgment that the "SUPER SOAKER" does not infringe the '129 patent, and that the '129 patent is invalid. TTMP counter–claimed for infringement of the '129 patent. Larami moved for partial summary judgment of noninfringement of the '129 patent and for partial summary judgment on TTMP's counterclaim for infringement of the '129 patent.

Reed, Jr., U.S. District Judge:

A patent owner's right to exclude others from making, using or selling the patented invention is defined and limited by the language in that patent's claims. Thus, establishing infringement requires the interpretation of the "elements" or "limitations" of the claim and a comparison of the accused product with those elements as so interpreted. The words in a claim should be given their "ordinary or accustomed" meaning. An inventor's interpretations of words in a claim that are proffered after the patent has issued for purposes of litigation are given no weight. A patent holder can seek to establish patent infringement in either of two ways: by demonstrating that every element of a claim (1) is literally infringed or (2) is infringed under the doctrine of equivalents. To put it a different way, because every element of a claim is essential and material to that claim, a patent owner must, to meet the burden of establishing infringement, show the presence of every element or its substantial equivalent in the accused device. If even one element of a patent's claim is missing from the accused product, then there can be no infringement as a matter of law. Larami contends, and TTMP does not dispute, that 28 of the 35 claims in the '129 patent are directed to the electrical components that create the light and noise. Larami's SUPER SOAKER water guns have no light or noise components. Larami also contends, again with no rebuttal from TTMP, that claim 28 relates to a "poppet valve" mechanism for controlling the flow of water that is entirely different from Larami's "pinch trigger" mechanism. Thus, according to Larami, the six remaining claims (claims 1, 5, 10, 11, 12 and 16) are the only ones in dispute. Larami admits that these six claims address the one thing that the SUPER SOAKERS and the '129 patent have in common — the use of air pressure created by a hand pump to dispense liquid. Larami argues, however, that the SUPER SOAKERS and the '129 patent go about this task in such fundamentally different ways that no claim of patent infringement is sustainable as a matter of law. TTMP points to evidence to support its assertion that only SUPER SOAKER 20 literally infringes claim 1 and that SUPER SOAKERS 20, 30, 50, 100 and 200 infringe claim 10 under the doctrine of equivalents. TTMP has neither produced nor referred to evidence contradicting facts averred by Larami on all other claims of the '129 patent. I conclude, therefore, that TTMP has not met its burden of coming forward with specific evidence showing that there is a genuine issue of material fact as to these claims. Accordingly, this memorandum will address only claims 1 and 10.

1. Literal Infringement of Claim 1

TTMP claims that SUPER SOAKER 20 literally infringes claim 1 of the '129 patent. Claim 1 of U.S. Patent No. 4,239,129 describes the water gun as:

A toy comprising an elongated housing having a chamber therein for a liquid, a pump including a piston having an exposed rod and extending rearwardly of said toy facilitating manual operation for building up an appreciable amount of pressure in said chamber for ejecting a stream of liquid therefrom an appreciable distance substantially forwardly of said toy, and means for controlling the ejection.

[Authors' note: The term "appreciable" would be too indefinite except that (a) the claim reveals that an appreciable amount of pressure is the amount of pressure necessary to eject a stream of water "an appreciable distance," and (b) the patent's written description states that "an appreciable distance" is approximately 30 feet.] [The court concluded that Larami's water guns do not literally infringe claim 1 of TTMP's '129 patent because one of the elements in claim 1 is "a chamber therein for a liquid," i.e., a water tank inside the housing of the gun, but Larami's water guns do not have a chamber or tank inside the gun. Instead, Larami's water guns have water tanks attached to the outside of the water gun. The court granted Larami's motion for summary judgment that Larami's water guns did not literally infringe claim 1 of TTMP's '129 patent.]

2. Infringement by Equivalents of Claim 10

TTMP claims that all five of the SUPER SOAKER water guns infringe claim 10 of U.S. Patent No. 4,239,129. Claim 10 describes the arrangement of several components of the water gun as follows:

A toy simulating a pistol comprising wall structure forming an elongated barrel of appreciable cross section dimensions, a tank in the barrel for a liquid and a hollow handle, a cylinder disposed axially in said tank and provided with a check valve, a piston mounted in said cylinder for manual reciprocation for pumping air into said tank, conduit means connected to said tank and having an outlet located at the front of said barrel, valve means interposed in said conduct means, and a trigger operable independently of said piston carried by said handle for operating said valve means for controlling the forced flow of liquid through said outlet.

To show infringement under the doctrine of equivalents, the patent owner bears the burden of proving that the accused product has the "substantial equivalent" of every limitation or element of a patent claim. Put another way, the patent owner must show that the accused product "performs substantially the same overall function or work, in substantially the same way, to obtain substantially the same overall result as the claimed invention." The doctrine of equivalents is used to hinder the unscrupulous copyist who could otherwise imitate a patented invention as long as s/he was careful not to copy every inconsequential detail of the claimed inventions, or to make some unimportant and insubstantial change to the claimed invention. The doctrine [must be used with care, however, or members of the public will not be able to depend on the claims in a patent to inform them of what is prohibited.] As the U.S. Court of Appeals for the Federal Circuit, recently stated: "If the public comes to believe (or fear) that the language of patent claims can never be relied on, and that the doctrine of equivalents is simply the second prong of every infringement charge, regularly available to extend protection beyond the scope of the claims, then claims will cease to serve their intended purpose. Competitors will never know whether their actions infringe a granted patent."

TTMP argues that claim 10 "defines" a novel relationship among three components to any air pressurized water gun: the tank, air pump and outlet nozzle. TTMP asserts that Claim 10 provides that the tank, air pump and outlet nozzle be situated along the same axis. TTMP alleges that axial arrangement of these three components is novel because the prior art describes water guns with outlet nozzles located higher than their tanks.

TTMP claims that. . . the most significant feature [the most significant feature shown in Claim 10] is this axial arrangement of the components which obviates the need to overcome the force of gravity upon the water. According to TTMP, Larami's SUPER SOAKER series has simply taken the construction of the '129 patent and relocated the water tank from inside the housing to the top of the housing which changes the look of the gun but does not affect its unique operating characteristics. [However], even if claim 10 were to require that the outlet nozzle be placed on the same axis as the water tank and air pump, at least one other element of the '129 patent is absent from the SUPER SOAKER water guns. Claim 10 requires, among other things, "a tank in the barrel for a liquid." As discussed above with regard to claim 1, the SUPER SOAKER water guns have external water reservoirs that are detachable from the gun housing, and not contained within the housing or barrel. No SUPER SOAKER water gun has a "tank in the barrel for a liquid" as described in claim 10 of the '129 patent. To establish that a water tank outside of the housing or barrel is the substantial equivalent of a water tank inside the housing or barrel, TTMP must muster evidence which would create a genuine issue of material fact as to whether the outside tank would have a substantially similar function and use substantially similar means to yield a substantially similar result as the inside tank. TTMP claims that the "movement of the water reservoir upwardly simply serves as a cosmetic alteration for the aesthetic looks of the water gun, and does not alter the novel operational characteristics of the water gun covered by the '129 patent." The evidence, however, is to the contrary. The SUPER SOAKER design improved on the '129 patent and other prior art by locating the tank outside the housing. First, the external and detachable tank makes manufacturing the device simpler because it is not necessary to make the entire housing pressure tight. Second, this design makes it easier for the consumer to fill the tank because it is detachable. Third, the size and volume of the external water reservoirs are not limited by the size of the housing. Fourth, the external tanks are replaceable if they should become damaged without replacing the entire toy. Finally, users of the SUPER SOAKERS can carry additional, filled tanks on a belt or backpack and replace an empty tank without going back to a source of water. Thus, the external tanks at least function in a very different manner from the '129 patent. Larami's motion for partial summary judgment of noninfringement of the '129 patent will be granted.

Remedies

A patent owner who successfully sues for infringement can obtain an injunction and damages. Damage awards in patent cases, which can be in the many millions of dollars, can include lost profits on sales of a patented item that the owner would have made if it hadn't been for the infringement, lost profits on sales of unpatented items that customers would have bought along with the patented items, a reasonable royalty on the defendant's sales that the patent owner probably would not have made for various reasons, plaintiff's losses because it had to drop prices as a result of the illegal competition, and interest on these amounts. If the court concludes that the defendant willfully infringed (knew or should have known it was infringing), the court may multiply the plaintiff's damages by a factor of up to three, and may award attorneys' fees. As in other types of lawsuits, the losing party typically pays court costs.

International Patent Law

As with other types of intellectual property, patent rights are granted under the law of a particular nation. Although there have been many efforts to "harmonize" the patent laws of various nations, there still is no "international" patent. Even in the European Union (EU), where there is the greatest degree of commonality, and where there is a unified system for filing patent applications, patent rights are still governed by the law of each member nation. The EU probably will be the first place to adopt a common patent law for multiple nations, but that is still several years away.

The Paris Convention is the most important international treaty dealing with patent application filing. It provides that, if someone files an application in one member nation, the applicant can file for a patent in another member nation within one year and keep the original filing date. The Paris Convention recently became even more important because all members of the WTO must also be members of the Paris Convention.

The Patent Cooperation Treaty (PCT) is also very important to those who wish to file for patents on an invention in multiple countries. If an inventor files in one member country, then indicates within one year that this is an international application, he may have up to 30 months total (18 months added to the first 12) to file applications in other member countries.

Copyrights
Term of Copyright Protection

The first U. S. copyright law was passed by Congress in 1790, and the most recent enactment is the Copyright Act of 1976, which has been amended numerous times since. Copyright law protects original expression. The term of copyright protection has been extended numerous times, beginning with a term of 14 years (renewable once, for a total of 28 years), then 28 years (renewable once, for a total of 56 years), then life of the author plus 50 years. In 1998, Congress extended the term once more, adding 20 years of protection to not only those expressive works produced in the future but also to any work then still protected. Thus, the term of protection is now life of the author plus 70 years. Many recent changes to copyright law are controversial, and adding 20 years of protection retroactively is one of these.

The term of copyright protection is different for a **work–for–hire**. The current term (after the 1998 addition of 20 years) for a work for hire is 95 years from the date of publication or 120 years from the date of creation, whichever is shorter. A work created by an employee while acting in the scope of his employment is a work–for–hire, with ownership of the copyright automatically and immediately vesting in the employer. In addition, a work created for the employer by an independent contractor can be a work–for–hire if: (1) the employer and independent contractor made a written agreement before the independent contractor started work, (2) the agreement "specially commissioned the work as a work–for–hire" (expressly using the term work–for–hire), and (3) the work was within one of nine categories— (a) a contribution to a collective work, (b) a part of a motion picture or other audiovisual work, (c) a translation, (d) a supplementary work, (e) a compilation, (f) an instructional text, (g) a test, (h) answer material for a test, or (i) an atlas. If there was no such agreement before work started, or if the work is not one of the specified types, the independent contractor owns the copyright, although in such a case there will be an implied license allowing the employer to make use of the work without paying a royalty. In such a case, the employer also may acquire ownership by means of an assignment, although the rights of a copyright assignee are often less than those of original owners because the creator or his heirs can terminate the assignment at any point between 35 and 40 years after the assignment was executed. This is true of any copyright assignment, not just one that transfers ownership to an employer.

Copyright assignments transferring ownership must be in writing. It is possible for the parties' conduct to create an implied license granting certain rights to a copyrighted work, but it is impossible to create an implied assignment because of the writing requirement.

Subject Matter

The Copyright Act enumerates several types of protected works:
1. Literary works. The term "literary" is used very broadly, and includes things like books, poems, stories, newspapers, magazines, Web pages, computer software, etc.

2. Musical works, including any accompanying words.
3. Dramatic works, including any accompanying music.
4. Pantomimes and choreographic works.
5. Pictorial, graphic, and sculptural works.
6. Motion pictures and other audiovisual works.
7. Sound recordings (protected by a separate copyright since 1972).
8. Architectural works (since 1990, architects have been able to protect not only the blueprints but also the original expression in building designs themselves, although they cannot prevent someone from photographing, painting, or drawing a building from a place commonly accessible to the public).

This list was not intended to be exclusive, however, because the law is meant to protect all "original works of authorship" ("authorship" obviously referring to any creation of original expression).

In copyright law, "original" does not mean the same thing as novel, but it simply means that the expression was original to this particular person. Stated somewhat differently, original expression is expression that was not copied from some other source. It is easier to discuss what is not protected by copyright than it is to discuss what is protected. Following are some examples of things not protected by copyright law; note that some of these are closely related and overlapping.

Facts. Facts are not protected by copyright. Thus, if I write a book that includes statements of facts, someone else can copy the facts from my book without being guilty of copyright infringement. I may be able to find original ways to express statements about facts and, if so, my original expressions are protected, but the facts themselves are not.

The lack of protection for facts has implications for those who compile databases and market them. Data are facts. No matter how much time and money the compiler has devoted to developing a database, the data are not protected by copyright law. As the Supreme Court discusses below in the Feist case, a database compiler has a "compilation copyright" in any original expression manifested in its selection and arrangement of the data, but that still does not protect the data themselves.

Ideas. Copyright protects original expressions of ideas, but not the ideas themselves. Someone else may freely take the ideas from my book, article, or other work, but not my expression of those ideas. Although not infringement, it is, of course, intellectually dishonest "plagiarism" to knowingly use another's ideas without giving them credit.

"Merger Doctrine." An expression of an idea may not be protected by copyright if there is only one way, or only a very small number of ways, to express the idea. Under the "merger doctrine," courts say that in such circumstances the expression "merges" with the idea. Protecting the expression would have the practical effect of protecting the idea itself. Protecting ideas is within the purview of trade secret and patent law, not copyright law. For example, the expression contained in a set of rules on the packaging of a consumer product for entering a contest will typically be very simple, and there probably are not very many ways to effectively express the functional ideas on which the contest is based. Here, the expression probably has merged with the ideas and is not protectable by copyright law. Although the merger doctrine can apply to portions of any type of expressive work, it is more commonly encountered in works that are motivated mainly by a desire to achieve effective and efficient functionality. For example, works such as maps, directories, software, and others whose main value is in the functions it performs rather than in its creative expressions, the need to achieve certain functions in a relatively effective and efficient way greatly limits the way that certain ideas can be expressed. These types of works will include original expressions that are protected by copyright, but they usually will include a large number of uncopyrightable elements, including expressions that are treated as unprotectable ideas because of the merger doctrine.

Scenes a faire. Very closely related to the lack of protection for ideas is the lack of protection for scenes a faire. Scenes a faire are standard techniques necessary to convey particular ideas, such as descriptions of the stereotypical Jewish mother or the stereotypical Irish father. If one writes a story in a particular genre, such stock characters are standard and they, along with stereotypical descriptions, mannerisms, and speech are not protected because they are treated as having fallen into the public domain.

The following case explains the originality requirement, why facts cannot meet the originality requirement, and how databases (factual compilations) can receive some degree of copyright protection.

FEIST PUBLICATIONS, INC. V. RURAL TELEPHONE SERVICE CO.
U. S. Supreme Court, 499 U. S. 340 (1991)

Rural Telephone Service Company, Inc., is a certified public utility that provides telephone service to several communities in northwest Kansas. It is subject to a state regulation that requires all telephone companies operating in Kansas to issue annually an updated telephone directory. Accordingly, as a condition of its monopoly franchise, Rural publishes a typical telephone directory, consisting of white pages and yellow pages. The white pages list in alphabetical order the names of Rural's subscribers, together with their towns and telephone numbers. The yellow pages list Rurals business subscribers alphabetically by category and feature classified advertisements of various sizes. Rural distributes its directory free of charge to its subscribers, but earns revenue by selling yellow pages advertisements.

Feist Publications, Inc., is a publishing company that specializes in wide–area telephone directories. Unlike a typical directory, which covers only a particular calling area, Feist's wide area directories cover a much larger geographical area, reducing the need to call directory assistance or consult multiple directories. The Feist directory that is the subject of this litigation covers 11 different telephone service areas in 15 counties and contains 46,878 white pages listings — compared to Rural's approximately 7,700 listings. Like Rural's directory, Feist's is distributed free of charge and includes both white pages and yellow pages. Feist and Rural compete vigorously for yellow pages advertising.

As the sole provider of telephone service in its service area, Rural obtains subscriber information quite easily. Persons desiring telephone service must apply to Rural and provide their names and addresses; Rural then assigns them a telephone number. Feist is not a telephone company, let alone one with monopoly status, and therefore lacks independent access to any subscriber information. To obtain white pages listings for its area–wide directory, Feist approached each of the 11 telephone companies operating in northwest Kansas and offered to pay for the right to use its white pages listings.

Of the 11 telephone companies, only Rural refused to license its listings to Feist. Rural's refusal created a problem for Feist, as omitting these listings would have left a gaping hole in its area–wide directory, rendering it less attractive to potential yellow pages advertisers.

Unable to license Rural's white pages listings, Feist used them without Rural's consent. Feist began by removing several thousand listings that fell outside the geographic range of its wide–area directory, then hired personnel to investigate the 4,935 that remained. These employees verified the data reported by Rural and sought to obtain additional information. As a result, a typical Feist listing includes the individual's street address; most of Rural's listings do not. Notwithstanding these additions, however, 1,309 of the 46,878 listings in Feist's 1983 directory were identical to listings in Rural's white pages. Four of these were fictitious listings that Rural had inserted into its directory to detect copying. Rural sued for copyright infringement in federal district court. The district court and the court of appeals held that Rural's white pages were protected by copyright and that Feist had infringed. Feist appealed to the Supreme Court.

O'Connor, Associate Justice:

This case concerns the interaction of two well–established propositions. The first is that facts are not copyrightable; the other, that compilations of facts generally are. That there can be no valid copyright in facts is universally understood. The most fundamental axiom of copyright law is that no author may copyright his ideas or the facts he narrates. At the same time, however, it is beyond dispute that compilations of facts are within the subject matter of copyright.

There is an undeniable tension between these two propositions. Many compilations consist of nothing but raw data—wholly factual information not accompanied by any original written expression. On what basis may one claim a copyright in such a work? Common sense tells us that 100 uncopyrightable facts do not magically change their status when gathered together in one place. Yet copyright law seems to contemplate that compilations that consist exclusively of facts are potentially within its scope.

The key to resolving the tension lies in understanding why facts are not copyrightable. The sine qua non of copyright is originality. To qualify for copyright protection, a work must be original to the author. Original, as the term is used in copyright, means only that the work was independently created by the author (as opposed to copied from other works), and that it possesses at least some minimal degree of creativity. To be sure, the requisite level of creativity is extremely low; even a slight amount will suffice. The vast majority of works make the grade quite easily, as they possess some creative spark, "no matter how crude, humble or obvious" it might be. originality does not signify novelty; a work may be original even though it closely resembles other works so long as the similarity is fortuitous, not the result of copying.

Originality is a constitutional requirement. The source of Congress' power to enact copyright laws is Article I, § 8, cl. 8, of the Constitution, which authorizes Congress to "secure for limited Times to Authors . . . the exclusive Right to their respective Writings." In two decisions from the late 19th century—The TradeMark Cases, 100 U.S. 82(1879); and Burrow-Giles Lithographic Co. v. Sarony, 111 U.S. 53(1884)—this Court defined the crucial terms "authors" and "writings." In so doing, the Court made it unmistakably clear that these terms presuppose a degree of originality. It is this bedrock principle of copyright that mandates the law's seemingly disparate treatment of facts and factual compilations. No one may claim originality as to facts. This is because facts do not owe their origin to an act of authorship. The distinction is one between creation and discovery: The first person to find and report a particular fact has not created the fact; he or she has merely discovered its existence.

Factual compilations, on the other hand, may possess the requisite originality. The compilation author typically chooses which facts to include, in what order to place them, and how to arrange the collected data so that they may be used effectively by readers. These choices as to selection and arrangement, so long as they are made independently by the compiler and entail a minimal degree of creativity, are sufficiently original that Congress may protect such compilations through the copyright laws. Thus, even a directory that contains absolutely no protectible written expression, only facts, meets the constitutional minimum for copyright protection if it features an original selection or arrangement.

This protection is subject to an important limitation. The mere fact that a work is copyrighted does not mean that every element of the work may be protected. Others may copy the underlying facts from the publication, but not the precise words used to present them. In *Harper & Row*, for example, we explained that President Gerald Ford could not prevent others from copying bare historical facts from his autobiography, but that he could prevent others from copying his "subjective descriptions and portraits of public figures." Where the compilation author adds no written expression but rather lets the facts speak for themselves, the expressive element is more elusive. The only conceivable expression is the manner in which the compiler has selected and arranged the facts. Thus, if the selection and arrangement are original, these elements of the work are eligible for copyright protection. No matter how original the format, however, the facts themselves do not become original through association.

This inevitably means that the copyright in a factual compilation is thin. Notwithstanding a valid copyright, a subsequent compiler remains free to use the facts contained in another's publication to aid in preparing a competing work, so long as the competing work does not feature the same selection and arrangement. As one commentator explains it: "No matter how much original authorship the work displays, the facts and ideas it exposes are free for the taking. . . . The very same facts and ideas may be divorced from the context imposed by the author, and restated or reshuffled by second comers, even if the author was the first to discover the facts or to propose the ideas."

It may seem unfair that much of the fruit of the compiler's labor may be used by others without compensation. As Justice Brennan has correctly observed, however, this is not "some unforeseen byproduct of a statutory scheme." Harper & Row 471 U.S., at 589. It is, rather, "the essence of copyright," and a constitutional requirement. The primary objective of copyright is not to reward the labor of authors, but "to promote the Progress of Science and useful Arts." To this end, copyright assures authors the right to their original expression, but encourages others to build freely upon the ideas and information conveyed by a work. This principle, known as the idea/expression or fact/expression dichotomy, applies to all works of authorship.

[Some lower federal courts] developed a theory to justify the protection of factual compilations, known as "sweat of the brow" or "industrious collection," the underlying notion was that copyright was a reward for the hard work that went into compiling facts. The "sweat of the brow" doctrine had numerous flaws, the most glaring being that it extended copyright protection in a compilation beyond selection and arrangement — the compiler's original contributions — to the facts themselves. Under the doctrine, the only defense to infringement was independent creation. Without a doubt, the "sweat of the brow" doctrine flouted basic copyright principles.

There is no doubt that Feist took from the white pages of Rural's directory a substantial amount of factual information. At a minimum, Feist copied the names, towns, and telephone numbers of 1,309 of Rural's subscribers. Not all copying, however, is copyright infringement. To establish infringement, two elements must be proven: (1) ownership of a valid copyright, and (2) copying of constituent elements of the work that are original. The first element is not at issue here; Feist appears to concede that Rural's directory, considered as a whole, is subject to a valid copyright because it contains some foreword text, as well as original material in its yellow pages advertisements.

The question is whether Rural has proved the second element. In other words, did Feist, by taking 1,309 names, towns, and telephone numbers from Rural's white pages, copy anything that was "original" to Rural? Certainly, the raw data do not satisfy the originality requirement. The question that remains is whether Rural selected, coordinated, or arranged these uncopyrightable facts in an original way. As mentioned, originality is not a stringent standard; it does not require that facts be presented in an innovative or surprising way. It is equally true, however, that the selection and arrangement of facts cannot be so mechanical or routine as to require no creativity whatsoever. The standard of originality is low, but it does exist. As this Court has explained, the Constitution mandates some minimal degree of creativity, and an author who claims infringement must prove the existence of intellectual production, of thought, and conception.

The selection, coordination, and arrangement of Rural's white pages do not satisfy the minimum constitutional standards for copyright protection. As mentioned at the outset, Rural's white pages are entirely typical. Persons desiring telephone service in Rural's service area fill out an application and Rural issues them a telephone number. In preparing its white pages, Rural simply takes the data provided by its subscribers and lists it alphabetically by surname. The end product is a garden–variety white pages directory, devoid of even the slightest trace of creativity.

Rural's selection of listings could not be more obvious: It publishes the most basic information—name, town, and telephone number—about each person who applies to it for telephone service. This is "selection" of a sort, but it lacks the modicum of creativity necessary to transform mere selection into copyrightable expression. Rural expended sufficient effort to make the white pages directory useful, but insufficient creativity to make it original. [Selection of the company's subscribers and alphabetical arrangement] is not only unoriginal, it is practically inevitable.

Because Rural's white pages lack the requisite originality, Feist's use of the listings cannot constitute infringement. This decision should not be construed as demeaning Rural's efforts in compiling its directory, but rather as making clear that copyright rewards originality, not effort.

The judgment of the Court of Appeals is Reversed.

Fixation in a Tangible Medium

To be protected by copyright, original expression must be "fixed in a tangible medium." The Copyright Act provides that the fixation is sufficient if the work "can be perceived, reproduced, or otherwise communicated, either directly or with the aid of a machine or device." This simply means that the expression must be recorded on paper, audio tape, video tape, film, a magnetic storage medium such as any of the types of computer disks, carved in stone or other material, or any other medium.

The requirement of fixation can be illustrated by live speeches or lectures, live news or sports broadcasts, and live musical or dance or dramatic performances. If the live expressions have not been previously fixed in a tangible medium (such as choreographic or music notation), the requirement can nevertheless be fulfilled if the author of the expressions simultaneously records them or authorizes someone else to do so. An unauthorized recording is not a fixation and, if the author has not previously fixed the expressions, neither the author nor the unauthorized recorder has a copyright. Although unfixed works are not protected by the 1976 Copyright Act, state law can provide protection; this is the only instance in which state law can play any role in providing copyright protection. (For works created prior to the 1978 effective date of the 1976 Act, state law played a somewhat greater role because the federal law did not protect unpublished works and state law could do so.)

With regard to live musical performances, regardless of whether they have been fixed in a tangible medium, it is illegal under a separate provision of the Copyright Act to record them without authorization. Although this provision was added to the Copyright Act, it actually has nothing to do with copyright law itself.

The Copyright Owner's Exclusive Rights

When most people think about copyright protection, they think only of actual copying. The exclusive right to make reproductions is certainly one of the most important rights of a copyright owner, but it is by no means the only one. Section 106 of the Copyright Act states that "the owner of a copyright under this title has the exclusive rights to do and to authorize any of the following:"

1. to reproduce the copyrighted work in copies or phonorecords;
2. to prepare derivative works based upon the copyrighted work;
3. to distribute copies or phonorecords of the copyrighted work to the public by sale or other transfer of ownership, or by rental, lease, or lending;
4. in the case of literary, musical, dramatic, and choreographic works, pantomimes, and motion pictures and other audiovisual works, to perform the copyrighted work publicly;
5. in the case of literary, musical, dramatic, and choreographic works, pantomimes, and pictorial, graphic, or sculptural works, including the individual images of a motion picture or other audiovisual work, to display the copyrighted work publicly; and
6. in the case of sound recordings, to perform the copyrighted work publicly by means of a digital audio transmission.

Formalities

Registration with the U.S. Copyright Office is not required for copyright protection. Moreover, since 1989 there is no longer any requirement that a copyright notice be placed on a work. For works first published before 1989, each published copy had to contain the word "copyright," the abbreviation "Copr.," or the symbol ©, along with the date of first publication and the name of the copyright owner. Thus, prior to 1989 a person who observed a published work that did not contain a copyright notice could feel assured that the work was in the public domain. For works published after that date, however, this is not the case. Congress abandoned the notice requirement in 1989 because the U.S. became a member of the 100–year–old Berne Convention, an international treaty that provides that copyright protection should be granted in all member nations without the necessity of any formalities.

Although registration and notice are no longer necessary for copyright protection, they are a very good idea. A copyright notice, for example, can serve the practical purpose of emphasizing to others that the work is protected. Registration, which can be accomplished by filling out a form and sending it to the Copyright Office, along with two copies of a published work or one copy of an unpublished work, and a modest fee, has an even more important practical effect. A copyright owner who is a U.S. national cannot file suit in federal court for copyright infringement unless the copyright has been registered.

Infringement

To prove copyright infringement, the owner must first prove that the defendant had access to the plaintiff's copyrighted work. Courts presume access, however, in the case of works that have been distributed in a relatively wide fashion. After proving access, in most cases the plaintiff can prove infringement by showing that the defendant's work is "substantially similar" to the plaintiff's work. In some cases, however, the test for infringement is "virtual identity" rather than substantial similarity. The defendant's work must be virtually identical to the plaintiff's in cases where the plaintiff's copyrighted work has only a so–called "thin copyright," such as the copyright in a map or directory or the compiler's copyright in the original selection and arrangement of a database. Thin copyright protection exists in works in which there are relatively few copyrightable elements relative to uncopyrightable elements.

The plaintiff does not have to prove intent and thus, an innocent infringer can be held liable. For example, in Bright Tunes Music Corp. v. Harrisongs Music, Ltd, 420 F. Supp. 177 (S.D.N.Y. 1976), the judge did not believe that former Beatle George Harrison intentionally copied the music from an earlier song, "He's So Fine," when he composed "My Sweet Lord" in 1970. Nonetheless, Harrison had access to the earlier song (which was widely played on popular radio during the 1960s), and the music in his song was substantially similar. The court held that Harrison infringed the owner's copyright.

Defenses

The Copyright Act provides for several defenses to copyright infringement. For example, a nonprofit library may make a copy of a work for archival purposes. Also, an owner of a lawful copy of computer software may make a copy that is necessary for the software to be used (such as copying from a CD to the computer's hard drive), as well as one backup copy. This does not mean, however, that it is legal to give copies of a software program to friends and family.

One very important defense is embodied in the "first sale doctrine." According to this rule, someone who buys or otherwise lawfully acquires a copy of a book or other copyrighted work may resell or give away his copy. The person bought ownership of that physical copy, although he did not acquire any rights in the underlying copyright.

The most widely debated and litigated defense is "fair use," which was developed by the courts and then codified in section 107 of the 1976 Copyright Act. The fair use defense is discussed and illustrated below.

Fair Use Defense

Section 107 of the Copyright Act of 1976 states:

[T]he fair use of a copyrighted work, including such use by reproduction in copies or phono–records or by any other means specified by [§ 106], for purposes such as criticism, comment, news reporting, teaching (including multiple copies for classroom use), scholarship, or research, is not an infringement of copyright. In determining whether the use made of a work in any particular case is a fair use the factors to be considered shall include—

1. the purpose and character of the use, including whether such use is of a commercial nature or is for nonprofit educational purposes;
2. the nature of the copyrighted work;
3. the amount and substantiality of the portion used in relation to the copyrighted work as a whole; and
4. the effect of the use upon the potential market for or value of the copyrighted work.

Although the applications of this doctrine are controversial, the Copyright Office has issued supplemental guidelines dealing with photocopies: obviously copies of all or part of a work for the purpose of literary criticism, classroom teaching, academic research, or parody are more likely to fare better than those used for commercial purposes.

If a court concludes that the defendant's use of the plaintiff's work is a true parody, the defendant usually will be able to use the fair use defense because parodies enjoy a high level of First Amendment free speech protection. A parody is a type of satire that holds up the original to contempt, ridicule, or scorn. For example, in Campbell v. Acuff-Rose Music, Inc., 510 U.S. 569(1994), the Supreme Court concluded that the rap group 2 Live Crew had engaged in a legally justified fair use when it composed and recorded its rap version of the 1960s song "oh, Pretty Woman" in the 1980s. The mere fact that they made a rap version did not prove fair use. The Court found fair use in the fact that the rap version made fun of the original.

The following case illustrates how courts apply these factors in analyzing a defendant's claim that its infringement is justified by the fair use defense.

CASTLE ROCK ENTERTAINMENT, INC. v. CAROL PUB. GROUP, INC.
U.S. Court of Appeals, Second Circuit, 150 F.3d 132 (1998)

Plaintiff Castle Rock is the producer and copyright owner of each episode of the Seinfeld television series. The series revolves around the petty tribulations in the lives of four single, adult friends in New York: Jerry Seinfeld, George Costanza, Elaine Benes, and Cosmo Kramer.

Defendants are Beth Golub, the author, and Carol Publishing Group, Inc., the publisher, of The SAT, a 132– page book containing 643 trivia questions and answers about the events and characters depicted in Seinfeld. These include 211 multiple choice questions, in which only one out of three to five answers is correct; 93 matching questions; and a number of short–answer questions. The questions are divided into five levels of difficulty, labeled (in increasing order of difficulty) "Wuss Questions," "This, That, and the other Questions,"

"Tough Monkey Questions,"

"Atomic Wedgie Questions," and "Master of Your Domain Questions." Selected examples from level 1 are indicative of the questions throughout The SAT:

1. To impress a woman, George passes himself off as
a gynecologist
a geologist
a marine biologist
a meteorologist

11. What candy does Kramer snack on while observing a surgical procedure from an operating-room balcony?
12. Who said, "I don't go for those nonrefundable deals ... I can't commit to a woman ... I'm not committing to an airline."?

Jerry
George
Kramer

An example of the trivia quiz book's matching questions (entitled "Family Trees") is as follows:

1. Cousin Jeffrey 2. Uncle Leo 3. Manya 4. Isaac 5. Mr. Seinfeld 6. Mrs. Seinfeld 7. Mr. Benes 8. Mr. Costanza 9. Mrs. Costanza 10. Mrs. Kramer.

a. Former condo association president
b. Drinks Colt 45 in the nude
c. Arm–grabbing, loquacious garbage can picker
d. Leaves a rent–controlled New York City apartment for the Phoenix sunshine
e. Gruff–talking, well–known novelist
f. New York City employee who watches the Nature Channel
g. Wears sneakers in the swimming pool and has to "get the good spot in front of the good building in the good neighborhood"
h. Enjoys the heat and never uses air conditioning

i. Elderly immigrant whose beloved pony was "the pride of Krakow"

j. Nagging, shrill–voiced Glamour magazine reader who was hospitalized for a back injury

The book draws from 84 of the 86 Seinfeld episodes that had been broadcast as of the time The SAT was published. Although Golub created the incorrect answers to the multiple choice questions, every question and correct answer has as its source a fictional moment in a Seinfeld episode. Forty–one questions and/or answers contain dialogue from Seinfeld. The single episode most drawn upon by The SAT, "The Cigar Store Indian," is the source of 20 questions that directly quote between 3.6% and 5.6% of that episode (defendants' and plaintiff's calculations, respectively).

Golub described The SAT as a "natural outgrowth" of Seinfeld which, "like the Seinfeld show, is devoted to the trifling, picayune and petty annoyances encountered by the show's characters on a daily basis." According to Golub, she created The SAT by taking notes from Seinfeld programs at the time they were aired on television and subsequently reviewing videotapes of several of the episodes, as recorded by her or various friends.

Castle Rock had been highly selective in marketing products associated with Seinfeld, rejecting numerous proposals from publishers seeking approval for a variety of projects related to the show. Castle Rock licensed one Seinfeld book, The Entertainment Weekly Seinfeld Companion, and has licensed the production of a CD–ROM product that includes discussions of Seinfeld episodes; the CD–ROM allegedly might ultimately include a trivia bank. Castle Rock claims in this litigation that it plans to pursue a more aggressive marketing strategy for Seinfeld–related products, including "publication of books relating to Seinfeld."

Castle Rock sued Carol Publishing and Golub, claiming that the defendants had infringed on Castle Rock's exclusive right to create derivative works from the original episodes of Seinfeld. The defendants claimed that they were protected by the fair use defense. The district court granted summary judgment to Castle Rock, awarded Castle Rock $ 403,000 with interest, permanently enjoined defendants from publishing or distributing The SAT, and ordered defendants to destroy all copies of The SAT in their custody or control. Defendants appealed.

Walker, J.:

The Copyright Act of 1976 grants copyright owners a bundle of exclusive rights, including the rights to "reproduce the copyrighted work in copies" and "to prepare derivative works based upon the copyrighted work." Copyright infringement is established when the owner of a valid copyright demonstrates unauthorized copying. There are two main components of this prima facie case of infringement: a plaintiff must first show that his work was actually copied and then must show that the copying amounts to an improper or unlawful appropriation. Actual copying may be established either by direct evidence of copying or by indirect evidence, including access to the copyrighted work, similarities that are probative of copying between the works, and expert testimony. It is only after actual copying is established that one claiming infringement then proceeds to demonstrate that the copying was improper or unlawful by showing that the second work bears "substantial similarity" to protected expression in the earlier work.

[There is no question that copying occurred.] Golub freely admitted that she created The SAT by taking notes from Seinfeld programs at the time they were aired on television and subsequently reviewing videotapes of several of the episodes that she or her friends recorded. [The court then concluded that the SAT was substantially similar to the Seinfeld TV series and, thus, that there was copyright infringement unless the defendants could prove the fair use defense.]

From the infancy of copyright protection, the fair use doctrine has been thought necessary to fulfill copyright's very purpose, "promote the Progress of Science and useful Arts." As noted in Campbell v. Acuff–Rose, "in truth, in literature, in science and in art, there are, and can be, few, if any, things which in an abstract sense, are strictly new and original throughout. Every book in literature, science and art, borrows, and must necessarily borrow, and use much which was well known and used before." Until the 1976 Copyright Act, the doctrine of fair use grew exclusively out of the common law.

In the Copyright Act, Congress restated the common law tradition of fair use:

"The fair use of a copyrighted work . . . for purposes such as criticism, comment, news reporting, teaching (including multiple copies for classroom use), scholarship, or research, is not an infringement of copyright. Fair use analysis always calls for case–by–case analysis. The factors contained in Section 107 are merely by way of example, and are not an exhaustive enumeration. The ultimate test of fair use is whether the copyright law's goal of "promoting the Progress of Science and useful Arts," U.S. Const., art. I, § 8, cl. 8, would be better served by allowing the use than by preventing it. [The court then turned to an analysis of the four fair–use factors.]

a.   **A. Purpose/Character of Use**

The first fair use factor to consider is "the purpose and character of the [allegedly infringing] use, including whether such use is of a commercial nature or is for nonprofit educational purposes." The fact that the SAT's use is commercial tends to weigh against a finding of fair use. But we do not make too much of this point. As noted in the *Campbell* case, "nearly all of the illustrative uses listed in the preamble paragraph of § 107, including news reporting, comment, criticism, teaching, scholarship, and research . . . are generally conducted for profit in this country." We therefore do not give much weight to the fact that the secondary use was for commercial gain.

The more critical inquiry under the first factor and in fair use analysis generally is whether the allegedly infringing work merely supersedes the original work or instead adds something new, with a further purpose or different character, altering the first with new meaning or message, in other words whether and to what extent the new work is transformative. If the secondary use adds value to the original— if copyrightable expression in the original work is used as raw material, transformed in the creation of new information, new aesthetics, new insights and understandings—this is the very type of activity that the fair use doctrine intends to protect for the enrichment of society. In short, the goal of copyright, to promote science and the arts, is generally furthered by the creation of transformative works.

Any transformative purpose possessed by The SAT is slight to nonexistent. We reject the argument that The SAT was created to educate Seinfeld viewers or to criticize, "expose," or otherwise comment upon Seinfeld. The SAT's purpose, as evidenced definitively by the statements of the book's creators and by the book itself, is to repackage Seinfeld to entertain Seinfeld viewers. The SAT's back cover makes no mention of exposing Seinfeld to its readers, for example, as a pitiably vacuous reflection of a puerile and pervasive television culture, but rather urges SAT readers to "open this book to satisfy their between–episode Seinfeld cravings." The SAT's author described the trivia quiz book not as a commentary or a Seinfeld research tool, but as an effort to "capture Seinfeld's favor in quiz book fashion." Finally, even viewing The SAT in the light most favorable to defendants, we find scant reason to conclude that this trivia quiz book seeks to educate, criticize, parody, comment, report upon, or research Seinfeld, or otherwise serve a transformative purpose. The book does not contain commentary or analysis about Seinfeld, nor does it suggest how The SAT can be used to research Seinfeld; rather, the book simply poses trivia questions. The SAT's plain purpose, therefore, is not to expose Seinfeld's "nothingness," but to satiate Seinfeld fans' passion for the "nothingness" that Seinfeld has elevated into the realm of protectable creative expression.

b.   **B. Nature of the Copyrighted Work**

The second statutory factor, "the nature of the copyrighted work," calls for recognition that some works are closer to the core of intended copyright protection than others, with the consequence that fair use is more difficult to establish when the former works are copied. Defendants concede that the scope of fair use is somewhat narrower with respect to fictional works, such as Seinfeld, than to factual works. Thus, the second statutory factor favors the plaintiff.

c.   **C. Amount and Substantiality of the Portion Used in Relation to the Copyrighted Work as a Whole**

In Campbell v. Acuff–Rose, the Supreme Court clarified that the third factor—the amount and substantiality of the portion of the copyrighted work used—must be examined in context. The inquiry must focus upon whether "the extent of copying" is consistent with or more than necessary to further "the purpose and character of the use." By focusing on the amount and substantiality of the original work used by the secondary user, we gain insight into the purpose and character of the use as we consider whether the quantity of the material used was reasonable in relation to the purpose of the copying. In *Campbell,* for example, the Supreme Court determined that a "parody must be able to 'conjure up' at least enough of the original work to make the object of its critical wit recognizable" and then determined whether the amount used of the original work was "no more than necessary" to satisfy the purpose of parody.

In the instant case, it could be argued that The SAT could not expose Seinfeld's "nothingness" without repeated, indeed exhaustive examples deconstructing Seinfeld's humor, thereby emphasizing Seinfeld's meaninglessness to The SAT's readers. That The SAT posed as many as 643 trivia questions to make this rather straightforward point, however, suggests that The SAT's purpose was entertainment, not commentary. Accordingly, the third factor weighs against fair use.

d.   **D. Effect of Use Upon Potential Market for or Value of Copyrighted Work**

Defendants claim that the fourth factor favors their case for fair use because Castle Rock has offered no proof of actual market harm to Seinfeld caused by The SAT. To the contrary, Seinfeld's audience grew after publication of The SAT, and Castle Rock has evidenced no interest in publishing Seinfeld trivia quiz books and only minimal interest in publishing Seinfeld–related books.

Under this factor, we consider not only the extent of market harm caused by the particular actions of the alleged infringer, but also whether unrestricted and widespread conduct of the sort engaged in by the defendant would result in a substantially adverse impact on the potential market for the original. The fourth factor must also take account of harm to the market for derivative works, defined as those marketsthat creators of original works would in general develop or license others to develop.

In considering the fourth factor, our concern is not whether the secondary use suppresses or even destroys the market for the original work or its potential derivatives, but whether the secondary use usurps or substitutes for the market of the original work. The more transformative the secondary use, the less likelihood that the secondary use substitutes for the original. As noted by the district court, "by the very nature of transformative endeavors, persons other than the copyright holder are undoubtedly better equipped, and more likely, to fill these particular market and intellectual niches." And yet the fair use, being transformative, might well harm, or even destroy, the market for the original. A lethal parody, like a scathing theater review, may kill demand for the original, but does not produce a harm cognizable under the Copyright Act, and the evidence of harm would not cause such a parody to lose its fair use defense.

Unlike parody, criticism, scholarship, news reporting, or other transformative uses, The SAT substitutes for a derivative market that a television program copyright owner such as Castle Rock would in general develop or license others to develop. Because The SAT borrows exclusively from Seinfeld and not from any other television or entertainment programs, The SAT is likely to fill a market niche that Castle Rock would in general develop. Moreover, as noted by the district court, this "Seinfeld trivia game is not critical of the program, nor does it parody the program; if anything, SAT pays homage to Seinfeld."

Although Castle Rock has evidenced little if any interest in exploiting this market for derivative works based on Seinfeld, such as by creating and publishing Seinfeld trivia books or at least trivia books that endeavor to "satisfy" the between–episode cravings of Seinfeld lovers, the copyright law must respect that creative and economic choice. It would not serve the ends of the Copyright Act—i.e., to advance the arts—if artists were denied their monopoly over derivative versions of their creative works merely because they made the artistic decision not to saturate those markets with variations of their original.

We therefore reject defendants' fair use defense. Undoubtedly, innumerable books could "expose" the "nothingness" or otherwise comment upon, criticize, educate the public about, or research Seinfeld and contemporary television culture. The SAT, however, is not such a book. For the reasons set forth above, the judgment of the district court is affirmed.

Remedies

A successful plaintiff in a copyright infringement action usually receives actual damages plus the defendant's profits to the extent they were not calculated into the damage award. If the plaintiffs have registered their copyright, they may elect between proving actual damages or receiving "statutory damages" in an amount between $750 and $30,000 per act of infringement "as the court considers just." The amount can be up to $150,000 per infringing act for willful infringement. Copyright infringement can also constitute a federal crime which, depending on various circumstances, can be punishable by fines or imprisonment of up to 5 years for a first offense and up to 10 years for second or subsequent offenses.

Digital Millennium Copyright Act

In 1998 Congress passed the Digital Millennium Copyright Act (DMCA). The most far–reaching and controversial aspect of the DMCA are its so–called "anti–circumvention" provisions, which were enacted mainly in response to heavy lobbying from the movie industry. They apply when an owner of copyrighted material in digital form uses a technological measure (such as encryption, initialization codes, etc.) to effectively limit access to its work or protect the work from being copied. If someone else circumvents this protective measure, such as decrypting the encryption or copying the initialization (start–up) code, there is a violation of the DMCA. This is analogous to picking the lock on the door to a room that contains copyrighted material.

Most people outside the movie, music, and software industries have criticized this provision of the DMCA because it sweeps so broadly. There can be a DMCA violation, for example, even if the one who circumvented the access control intends to use the protected material in a completely legitimate way once gaining access to it. There is no fair use defense to the DMCA and, thus, there can be a violation even if the one gaining access through circumvention makes a fair use of the copyrighted material.

Not only is it illegal to engage in circumvention, but it also is illegal to "traffic in" anti–circumvention measures by making such measures available to others. For example, a teenager in Norway developed a program he called DeCSS that decrypted the encrypted code that prevented copying of DVDs. The encryption protecting the DVDs was called CSS for "content scrambling system." Although he was outside the reach of the DMCA in Norway, a magazine in the US ("2600 Magazine") was found by US courts to have violated the DMCA by posting the DeCSS source code on its Web site and also providing a hypertext link in to a place where readers could download the DeCSS program. This program was a circumvention measure and the magazine made it available to others. Thus, there was a DMCA violation.

CHAPTER 10

BUSINESS ETHICS, CORPORATE SOCIAL RESPONSIVENESS, AND THE LAW

Jill Is A Regional sales manager for a nationwide chain of retail consumer electronics stores. She and her assistants at company headquarters design promotional programs for stores in the region, supervise store managers' implementation of company marketing strategies, and conduct sales seminars for salespeople at these stores. Questions continually arise about how far promotional materials and the statements of individual salespeople can go in pushing their products. These questions relate not only to what is legal, but also to what is "appropriate" or "ethical." If particular statements are legal, is there any reason at all to be concerned about them? Are there any other standards? Jill and her associates know that it usually will be illegal to brazenly lie about the quality of a product. But they also know that it is often very difficult for a buyer to prove that a seller made intentionally deceptive statements, so the legal risk is small even in such a case. Jill understands that a company's reputation, and ultimately its sales, may suffer if it becomes known for dealing dishonestly. She also knows, however, that if some forms of subtle deception are practiced with skill, most customers will never know. Although a few customers may discover the deception, the company does not depend on repeat business in most of its product lines.

Even if the legal or financial risks are not great, Jill feels that it is "wrong" to lie to a customer. When she receives a lot of pressure from her superiors to increase sales, however, she begins to ask herself various questions: "Why is it wrong, really?" "Who, after all, defines what is wrong if it isn't illegal?" "We're selling to adults; aren't they supposed to look after themselves?" "Isn't this just the free market at work, and doesn't the market operate impersonally on the assumption that all sellers and buyers pursue their own economic self-interests?" "Isn't it okay to do it if I feel okay about it?" "But what if I feel good about it only after some strained rationalizing?" "And ... let's face it—I don't always feel good about what happens."

When Jill tries to define what is "wrong," she finds it difficult to come up with any standards or any systematic way to develop such standards. Not only that but she cannot even decide whether there is a rational way to analyze problems of this nature.

Assuming, again, that there are no significant legal risks, Jill wonders how much latitude a salesperson should have in extolling the virtues of a product. Must every shortcoming of the item be revealed? Surely not. But why not? May the sales pitch be couched in vague, laudatory terms or must all responses be absolutely factual, precise, and to-the-point? Should the salesperson be concerned about the customer's real need for the product, or is the customer's apparent willingness to purchase the only thing that matters? Should there be any regard for the customer's particular susceptibilities to advertising? What if the advertising campaign that brought the customer into the store was full of "subliminal" messages that subconsciously persuaded him that this product would improve his love life? Jill finally decides that she does not have the time or energy to worry about such things, and that she will just be guided by the opinion of the company's attorneys about the legal risks of particular strategies and statements. Over a period of time, however, she is increasingly bothered by some of the promotional strategies that she initiates or approves. After doing some reading, she realizes that she has been grappling with age-old questions and that there is an entire field of study concerned with questions of this nature. Jill has discovered "business ethics."

In the wake of the Enron/Arthur Andersen debacle, many people have discovered business ethics. Indeed, there has never been more pressure for business schools to teach business ethics to their students (59% of college students recently admitted to cheating on exams) or for corporations to get their ethical houses in order (47% of 400 executives recently surveyed were willing to commit fraud by understating write-offs that reduced their firms' profits). The Sarbanes-Oxley Act that Congress passed in 2002 to respond to the Enron scandal directly addressed practices that are arguably unethical, including earnings management and off-balance sheet accounting by public companies and the conflicts of interest that prevented audit firms, stock analysts, and attorneys from serving as the investing public's protectors. Sarbanes-Oxley increased penalties for wrongdoing and required companies to adopt codes of ethics for their top financial officers.

What is Ethics?

In a formal sense, the term **ethics** refers to the study of **morality** by systematically exploring moral values, moral standards and obligations, moral reasoning, and moral judgments. The terms morality and morals refer to the appropriate treatment of our fellow human beings. Although some people observe a technical distinction between "ethics" and "morals," these terms are often used interchangeably. When someone says, for example, that "Joe did not act ethically in that situation," the word "ethically" means the same thing as "morally." In this chapter, we are not very fussy about the use of these terms. Sometimes we will use them in their technical sense, and sometimes we will not. The context will make the meaning clear.

Is Business Ethics Different?

Should a study of "business ethics" differ from a more general study of the subject? Questions about how we ought to interact with and treat others arise in all aspects of life. Moral issues arise in the realm of the family, social groups, neighborhoods, politics and government, interactions between nations, professional associations, and other relationships, as well as in business. The basic questions, arguments, and problem-solving methods remain the same for all these domains. The factual contexts will vary, of course, depending on the nature of the relationship. In studying "business" ethics, we focus on business relationships and use examples of business problems that raise ethical questions. In other words, business ethics consists of the application of moral principles to people in a business setting.

The Relationship Between Law and Ethics

One might legitimately ask why a study of business ethics should be included as a unit in a business course about law and the legal system. The material is admittedly somewhat different from the rest of the material in this book, and one could argue that the subject represents a digression from the main focus of the course. There are, however, a number of ways in which ethics and law fit together very naturally. As a result, there are several excellent reasons for dealing with the subject in the context of law. We will first recognize and discuss some of the differences between law and ethics, and then examine the close relationship between the two.

Differences Between Legal and Moral Standards

As we will see shortly, legal standards often have their counterparts in the ethical domain, and vice-versa. For example, lying not only may violate a fundamental moral standard but also may constitute fraud under the law of torts and under various criminal statutes. Similarly, breaking a promise not only may be unethical but also may constitute a legally impermissible breach of contract in some circumstances. There are, however, several basic differences between legal and moral standards.

First, legal standards have a different source than moral ones. Whether found in a constitution, statute, judicial decision, or administrative agency regulation, legal standards are defined and applied by governmental processes. It takes governmental power to adopt and enforce laws.

Moral standards, on the other hand, are internal; they are developed within each person. It is true that people develop their moral standards from input they receive from external sources, such as the tenets of their religion and instructions from parents, teachers, friends, and others under whose influence they fall during their formative years. People even pick up information about appropriate and inappropriate moral behavior by observing the conduct and speech of strangers. These moral perceptions are formed, modified, and reinforced over time as we go through the process of having to give rational support and justification for our conduct when it affects others. Despite external influences, people ultimately develop, apply, and modify their own moral standards. Legal authority may be complex, even murky, but it is always there. In the personal realm of morality, however, we simply cannot get off the hook by referring to outside authority. Our only human source of authority is our rational thought processes: clear and objective thinking about the dignity, worth, and integrity of people around us and our impact on their lives. Even when one derives his or her basic moral standards from religion, thus referring to a higher authority, conformity with those standards involves an individual choice—an exercise of the will.

Second, the consequences of violating legal and moral standards are different. Violations of the law, if detected, result in concrete sanctions. When lying violates the law against fraud, for example, the guilty person may have to pay damages to the victim in a civil action, and may even be prosecuted in a criminal action and forced to pay a fine to the state or serve a jail term. There are no externally imposed sanctions for violating moral standards, however. Although lying usually is clearly unethical even if it does not meet the legal definition of fraud, the violation of ethical norms by itself is not subject to any definite penalties. It is true that unethical conduct sometimes can result in tangible consequences such as lost business because of a damaged reputation. Mostly, however, the consequences are like the standards themselves, internal and difficult to define.

Third, even though legal standards sometimes need to be a bit vague in order to be flexible, they must be more clearly defined than moral standards. The obvious reason is that legal standards are imposed on us by society and we can be punished for violating them; because of this, legal standards must be expressed with enough clarity to give us reasonable notice of society's expectations.

Fourth, moral standards usually require more of us than legal standards. The law tends to seek out the average in human behavior, for at least three reasons: (1) Although people's ideas about what is appropriate behavior vary, the law attempts to prescribe and enforce norms for an entire society. (2) The enforcement of laws requires the use of scarce public resources to support courts, police, and so on. As a result, in order for legal standards to be effective, they must survive a rough cost/benefit analysis. In other words, we should generally allocate society's scarce resources to the enforcement of legal standards only if we feel that the costs of that enforcement are outweighed by the benefits to society of upholding those standards. This is one of the reasons why our legal system often does not do a very good job of providing remedies for small claims. (3) The law must be practical. It may be unethical to break a vaguely expressed promise, for example, but a court can require someone to pay monetary damages for breaking a promise only where the promise describes obligations with reasonable certainty.

Fifth, some laws have little or nothing to do with moral behavior because they exist for other purposes. Some laws, for instance, are adopted solely for the purpose of bringing order to our affairs. There is nothing inherently moral or immoral about driving on one side of the road rather than the other. To prevet chaos, however, a society must decide one way or the other.

The Legal/Ethical Overlap

Despite their differences, law and ethics have much in common. They both represent society's expression of its most basic values. Naturally, then, they largely overlap. In constructing a decision tree for the ethical manager, Harvard Business School's Constance Bagley recently noted that the first question the ethical decision maker must always ask is: "Is it legal?" Not only is this the first question that the ethical decision maker must ask, more than ninety percent of the time it will also be the last question that need be asked. Our society's ethical and legal standards are sufficiently conflated that it is rare that an illegal action will be ethical. That is one reason that a course in business law is so important for students.

Importantly, law not only expresses our society's ethical values, it can shape them as well. After laws were passed outlawing racial discrimination in employment and insider trading, studies showed that a much higher percentage of people viewed those activities as improper than had held that view before the laws were passed.

Also, as we shall soon see, sound moral reasoning is quite similar in methodology to sound legal reasoning. The methods that businesspeople can use to identify and analyze ethical issues are very much the same as methods for dealing with legal issues.

Are There Any Moral Standards?

There are those who believe that it is impossible to identify any concrete rules or standards to serve as a general foundation for evaluating the morality of behavior. The existence and content of particular ethical standards is too personal and individualized to formulate generally applicable rules. Moreover, they argue that what is "ethical" depends a great deal on what is viewed as acceptable behavior in a particular culture and that norms vary greatly from one culture to another. They assert that the formal study and practical application of ethics can consist only of defining and improving the processes by which moral issues are identified and analyzed.

Others argue that, although there are no overarching moral "rules" that can be applied to all human behavior, the general standard of utilitarianism can serve as a guide for moral behavior. Advanced by noted philosophers such as Jeremy Bentham and John Stuart Mill, utilitarianism is an ethical theory that is committed solely to the purpose of promoting "the greatest good for the greatest number." Utilitarianism essentially permits all conduct that will serve the objective of maximizing the social utility (i.e., the social "benefit" or "good"). As an abstract theory, utilitarianism makes a lot of sense. In actual practice, however, it can be all but impossible to predict, even roughly, which specific actions are likely to provide the greatest benefit to society. Moreover, even deciding how to define "benefit" to society can be an exercise in futility because of the many possible value judgments that may be involved. What one person views as a benefit to society may be quite different from the view of another person. In large part because of these difficulties, other ethicists view utilitarianism as being just one useful component in a rational process of ethical reasoning.

Some well-known philosophers do feel that certain threshold standards of moral behavior can be identified and applied to real problems across various circumstances and cultures. The German philosopher Immanuel Kant wrote that every person's actions should be judged morally by asking the question: "Can this action be justified by reasons that are uniformly applicable to all other persons?" In other words, he suggested as an overarching standard of moral behavior the rule that people cannot make exceptions of themselves; one's behavior is morally defensible only if everyone else could do the same thing without interfering with the optimal functioning of an organized society. This means, among other things, that we should all treat others as we would wish to be treated, a wisdom embodied in the so-called Golden Rule. Each person should be treated as an end in himself, not as a means to an end.

We think there is merit in all of these positions, and that the best approach to questions about ethical behavior includes elements of each. Process is extremely important. It is essential to employ a rational process for analyzing these kinds of questions. (We will present such a process later in this chapter.) We also think, as did Kant, that there are certain fundamental moral standards that are virtually universal. As we discuss these principles, it will become apparent that some elements of utilitarianism are included; we recognize that costs and benefits of alternative courses of action may have to be taken into account when there are extenuating circumstances or conflicting moral obligations.

The "Moral Minimum"

As we observe human interactions and learn more about human nature, examine and think deeply about the effects that our own actions have on others, and perhaps study the writings of those philosophers who have pondered moral questions over the years, we may begin to discover that certain basic values and standards of conduct are truly necessary for the existence of an advanced civilization. What form do these principles take? LawrenceKohlberg writes that the morally mature individual bases his actions on "principles chosen because of their logical comprehensiveness, their universality, and their consistency." He then adds: "These ethical principles are not concrete like the Ten Commandments but abstract universal principles dealing with justice, society's welfare, the equality of human rights, respect for the dignity of individual human beings, and with the idea that persons are ends in themselves and must be treated as such." (Lawrence Kohlberg in Business Ehics: Concepts And Cases 20(1982).

In our search for generally applicable moral standards, let us assume that we are looking only for those guideposts that are relatively comprehensive, universal, and consistent. We can also assume that the foundation for this search is a view of each human being as unique and as deserving to be treated as we ourselves would wish to be treated. Important questions remain, however: Exactly where do we find these standards? If they can be found, can they ever be expressed with enough certainty to provide meaningful guidance for our conduct?

The answer to the first question is that, in order to satisfy the requirements of comprehensiveness, universality, and consistency, we must rely on the rational human thought process as our source. Any other source is likely to produce results that are too variable across cultures, beliefs, circumstances, and even across time.

One approach to the second question is to determine whether there are any standards of behavior that do not need to be defended by a rational person. In other words, from the perspective of a rational mind, are there any general categories of behavior that stand on their own moral foundation, without any need for justification? If so, they could be identified as the **moral minimum**—a set of general standards that constitute the ethical minimum necessary for the functioning of civilization. Stated somewhat differently, violation of these standards is *prima facie* (on its face) wrong. Compliance with such standards requires no defense or justification. To the contrary, a rational person would expect a defense or justification for a failure to comply with them. The reason for expecting such a justification is that failure to comply with these standards tends to *destroy the social and economic relationships* that cause a society to function. We suggest the following as components of the moral minimum, fully recognizing that these components sometimes will overlap and that they could be organized and labeled in a variety of ways.

Honesty

A rational person does not have to justify telling the truth. The notion that one should correctly represent the facts is so firmly ingrained in human relations that we expect a justification for not doing so. Without reasonable expectations of honesty, we cannot maintain the personal and business relationships that create order and economic well-being. As we have seen, there are also principles in the *legal* domain that are intended to encourage **honesty,** as with legal prohibitions against fraud. The moral obligation, however, is more encompassing.

Loyalty

In any culture there are certain voluntary relationships in which one party places a higher degree of trust and confidence in the other than one would place in a stranger. These relationships are not forced upon us; we consent to them either explicitly or implicitly. Examples include an agent or employee's relationship with her principal, the corporate manager's relationship with the company's shareholders, a trustee's relationship with the beneficiary, and each partner's relationship with the others. A moral duty of **loyalty** is based on two facts: First, by virtue of the relationship, we have created in the other person a legitimate expectation that we will further his or her interests. Second, the relationship has placed us in a position where we have the ability to cause serious harm if we do not act in that person's interests. For example, these relationships often give one party some degree of control over information or assets that are valuable to the other person.

When we enter such relationships we take on an affirmative obligation to (1) fully disclose to the other person all material information that is relevant to our dealings; (2) keep confidential any information that the other party reasonably expects us to protect; (3) avoid undisclosed conflicts of interest, (i.e., unless we obtain the other party's consent, stay out of situations that are likely to put pressure on us to act against the other party's best interests); and (4) generally act in the best interests of the other party, even if such action is not entirely in our own best interests. Relationships based on trust and confidence cannot exist without the observance of such behavioral standards, and these kinds of relationships contribute greatly to economic efficiency and social order. The moral duty of loyalty is one of those ethical obligations that has a very close analog in the legal domain. The law identifies certain *fiduciary* relationships, such as agent-principal, in which there are legally enforceable obligations of loyalty. Again, the legal obligation is usually less demanding than the moral one.

Keeping Commitments

Social and commercial relationships among people are quite difficult to maintain without accepting the notion that we should keep the promises we make to each other. For this reason, the rational person is not likely to feel it necessary to defend his actions in **keeping commitments.** Failing to keep them, however, normally requires justification.

Sometimes there can be difficult questions about whether a commitment has been made, and if so, about its scope, but once these questions are resolved the rational mind will find little need to justify keeping a promise.

Once again, we can find a narrower legal counterpart to this obligation—when a promise is part of a legally enforceable contract there are sanctions for breaking it.

Doing No Harm

The rational person does not have to defend himself when he refrains from *intentional, reckless,* or *careless conduct that can cause reasonably foreseeable harm to others.* To the contrary, justification is usually expected for such conduct. Our actions have both expected and unexpected effects on others, and these effects can be positive or negative. Negative effects are those that damage some legitimate interest of another person. It is generally recognized that people have legitimate interests in their physical, economic, and emotional well-being, as well as in their property, privacy, and reputation. There obviously is overlap among these interests but, taken together, they include most of the things that are important to people.

Sometimes our actions have negative consequences for others that we never could have foreseen. When, however, cautious concern for the welfare of others should lead us to anticipate that certain action or inaction may harm the legitimate interests of others, we should do what we can to avoid harm. Narrower legal counterparts for the obligation of **doing no harm** are found throughout the law of torts.

In the following case, the legal issue is whether the defendant committed the tort of fraud. After reading the court's legal analysis and conclusions, carefully consider the following questions: (1) Aside from the legal principles involved, are there any basic moral obligations that are possibly relevant? If so, what are they? (2) Is this a situation in which the extent of any relevant moral obligation is basically the same as the legal obligation? If not the same, is the moral obligation broader or narrower than the legal one? (3) If the moral and legal obligations are somewhat different in scope, can you think of any reasons why this is so?

GRENDELL V. KIEHL
Supreme Court of Arkansas, 723 S.W.2d 830 (1987)

Don Grendell had served as an insurance agent for Loretta and Ferdinand Kiehl since 1971. The Kiehls also relied on Grendell for financial advice. One investment that Grendell promoted to the Kiehls was an oil and gas drilling venture. Grendell told the Kiehls that the investment was "a good thing" and would "make money" for them. On another occasion he "guaranteed that they would make lots of money," and "were going to get 50 barrels a day." No oil was discovered, and the Kiehls lost their investment. They sued Grendell, claiming that he had committed fraud, and they received a judgment against him for $11,329.60. Grendell appealed.

Hays, Justice:

The essential elements of an action for [fraud] are well established: (a) a false, material representation of fact made by the defendant; (b) scienter—knowledge by the defendant that the representation is false, or an assertion of fact which he does not know to be true; (c) an intention that the plaintiff should act on such representation; (d) justifiable reliance by the plaintiff on the representation; and (e) damage to the plaintiff resulting from such reliance.

… The [statement] that the oil investment was a good thing and would make money, even the inference of "50 barrels a day," fails to rise to the level of misrepresentation of fact. Even at its strongest, the proof constitutes expressions of opinion in the nature of "puffing." Admittedly, Mr. and Mrs. Kiehl were relatively inexperienced in business affairs but we cannot conclude they were incapable of recognizing the difference between an opinion that a proposed investment in an oil lease looked promising and was a "good thing," as opposed to a factual assertion that an oil well would become a producer. Nothing in the testimony suggests the Kiehls were not mindful that while some oil ventures succeed, a good many others, just as inviting at the outset, do not. Indeed, Mrs. Kiehl candidly acknowledged recognizing the risk factor in oil leases and was aware that a "dry hole" was a possibility.

Finding the dividing line between misrepresentation of fact and expression of opinion is often troubling. Prosser and Keeton on Torts states that [a claim for fraud] cannot be based on "misstatements of opinion, as distinguished from those of fact. The usual explanation is that an opinion is merely an assertion of one man's belief as to a fact, of which another should not be heard to complain, since opinions are matters about which many men will be of many minds, and which are often governed by whim and caprice. [Expressions of] judgment and opinion in such a case implies no knowledge."

An opinion may take the form of a statement of quality, of more or less indefinite content. One common application of the opinion rule is in the case of loose, general statements made by sellers in commending their wares. No action lies against a dealer who describes the automobile he is selling as a "dandy," a "bear cat," a "good little car," and "a sweet job," or as "the pride of our line" and the "best in the American market," or merely makes use of broad, and vague, commendatory language comparing his goods favorably with others, or praising them as "good," "proper," "sufficient" and the like.

A statement that … a real estate investment will insure a handsome profit, that an article is the greatest bargain ever offered, and similar claims are intended and understood to be merely emphatic methods of urging a sale. These things, then, a buyer must disregard in forming a sober judgment as to his conduct in the transaction. If he succumbs to such persistent solicitation, he must take the risk of any loss attributable to a disparity between the exaggerated opinion of the seller and a reasonable or accurate judgment of the value of the article.

The Kiehls point out that their [longstanding] reliance on Don Grendell [in both insurance and financial matters] produced a special relationship of trust and confidence requiring the utmost in good faith and disclosure of all material facts. Even so, there was an absence of proof by the Kiehls that Grendell either knew the assurances made to them were false or made factual representations while lacking knowledge of their truthfulness.

[The court found that Grendell was not guilty of fraud. However, the evidence also showed that he had kept $3,500 of the Kiehl's money that had been deposited with him and not invested, so the court ordered him to pay back that money.]

Is There a Duty to "Do Good"?

The components of the moral minimum relate only to preventing harm that we may cause, or correcting harm that we have actually caused. What about situations in which harm is being caused through no moral fault on our part? Do we also have a fundamental moral obligation to affirmatively "do good" by trying to prevent or correct harm that we had no part in causing?

Many people, of course, help others without even thinking about the moral implications. They give to charities, volunteer their time, and perform other altruistic acts for many complex reasons. They may do so for religious reasons, because they want to help create a better world for their children, because of the attention it brings them, or just because it makes them feel good. The question we are raising here is whether there is a rationally based moral obligation to do such things and, if so, what are its limits. In other words, is there something resembling the moral minimum for doing good, and can it be defined in any useful way?

Many people do seem to feel a strong sense of obligation to help others. Again, the reasons why they feel this way are varied and complex. It is therefore difficult to isolate the phenomenon's purely rational element. If we study the question solely from the perspective of rational analysis, we will find less general agreement than we did in the case of the moral minimum. At least part of the reasoning process that supports the moral minimum, however, can also be used to argue in favor of a moral obligation to do good. Most rational people would not feel it necessary to defend their actions in doing good. Similarly, they usually would not expect others to defend such actions. On the other hand, does the rational mind expect a justification for not doing good? The answer, which is not very helpful, is that some rational minds would and some would not.

If one tries to build an argument that there is a rationally based moral obligation to do good, the argument probably should contain the following elements:

1. In many cases it can be practically impossible to assign a specific moral responsibility for the existence of needs. A family may be desperate because the breadwinner has lost a job from bad health or an economic recession, and they have no family or friends who can help. A Boy Scout troop may need volunteer adult leadership in order to fulfill its goals of teaching, guiding, and nurturing a group of youths.

The existence of such needs is really no one's "fault." Even if we can identify a responsible person or group, it may be totally unrealistic to expect them to take remedial action. The needy family's breadwinner may have lost the job because the company was recklessly or dishonestly managed and went bankrupt. In this case, we can trace moral fault but it is highly unlikely that the blameworthy person or group will correct the harm it has caused. Thus, in an organized society, the rational person should expect there to be unmet needs, and should understand that his efforts to meet these needs will improve the functioning of the society of which he is a member.

Although we should use government as one vehicle for meeting people's needs, government cannot serve effectively as our *only* social problem solver. For example, even though government programs can do much good in providing food and shelter for the poor, such programs will usually be inadequate by themselves. Resources will always be too scarce. Government agencies sometimes can be too impersonal, and too remote from the problem, to provide assistance as effectively as individuals or private groups. Moreover, government bureaucracy sometimes can make it a less efficient provider of assistance than individuals and private groups.

Helping others is clearly in harmony with the view that we generally should treat others as we would wish to be treated in similar circumstances.

In circumstances in which (1) a problem or need is brought to our attention, (2) we are in a good position to help, (3) we have the ability to help, and (4) taking positive action would not require an unreasonable risk or cost, our failure to do something positive is very similar to actually *doing harm by intentional, reckless, or careless conduct.*

If one argues that there is a moral obligation to do good, one must define some limits to the obligation. In item 4, we identified some possible limits which require a bit of further explanation. *First,* we can have no obligation to meet a need that we do not know about. This statement assumes, of course, that we have not consciously tried to avoid knowledge of the situation. If there is such an obligation, it cannot be avoided by intentional ignorance. *Second,* in a given situation we may not be the appropriate persons to take action. There are some cases in which our help is unwanted, or may actually do more harm than good. In addition, there may be some other person, organization or agency that is much better equipped to do the job than we are. This is not an excuse that one should look for, but sometimes good judgment suggests that we are inadequate to be useful. Of course, the fact that we are unable to solve the entire problem does not necessarily mean that we should do nothing at all. One person cannot solve the problem of world hunger, or even hunger in one city, but one person can do *something. Third,* any rational argument that there is a moral duty to do good must incorporate the concept of costs and benefits (or "risks and utility"). A rational person would not expect someone to take positive action that would entail far greater cost or risk to the provider than benefit to the recipient. One cannot be expected to impoverish oneself or one's family in order to give to a worthy cause. (Here, of course, a moral obligation to one's family would be violated at the same time.)

Although we have so far focused on personal situations, the preceding discussion serves as a necessary foundation for our later examination of corporate social responsiveness.

Excusing Conditions

There occasionally will be circumstances that may excuse one's violation of a basic moral obligation. The particular conditions surrounding a person's action or inaction may reduce the degree of moral responsibility or even completely remove it. Breaking a promise, for example, is *prima facie* wrong on moral grounds, but it may not always be absolutely wrong. **Excusing conditions** may be present. One must be careful about introducing this concept of excusing conditions into ethical analysis, however, because it so easily can be used improperly as a "cop-out." People are usually quite ready to offer "excuses" for their bad behavior, and they may have to be reminded that "reasons" are not necessarily moral excuses. When we speak of excusing conditions, we assume that they are not the result of carelessness, laziness, or conscious disregard of relevant information.

The kinds of circumstances likely to be viewed by a rational person as excusing conduct that otherwise would be morally blameworthy are those affecting a person's *knowledge* or *freedom of action*. Our status as fully responsible moral beings (or "moral agents") assumes that we act with knowledge of relevant and material information, and that our freedom of action is not substantially impaired by some external force.

Suppose, for instance, that Joe promises to deliver 100 laser printers to Sam by December 1. We are not likely to view Joe as morally blameworthy if he fails to deliver on time because, through no fault of Joe's, one of his main suppliers suddenly cuts him off or his own factory has to shut down for several weeks because of a strike by a labor union. His freedom of action has been impaired. Morally he is still expected, of course, to do everything legally within his power to minimize the harm caused to Sam or to come as close as he can to fulfilling the commitment. His moral responsibility is diminished, however, to the extent that his freedom of action is diminished. In a similar fashion, Joe's moral culpability is reduced to the extent that, when he made the promise, he neither knew nor had reason to know of existing facts that would make it impossible to deliver on time.

As is true of many ethical concepts, the idea of excusing conditions has a roughly similar counterpart in the law. In some situations, evidence showing that a person did not have the knowledge or freedom to have acted differently can prevent liability for breach of contract, negligence, or some other *legal* wrong. Moral excuses and legal excuses are not necessarily equivalent, but the general concepts exist in both domains. Thus, the actions or failures of one of Joe's suppliers might excuse Joe from the *moral* obligation to carry out a promise to deliver printers, but in some circumstances the law may hold that Joe had assumed the risk of such an occurrence and is *legally* responsible. In other situations, extenuating circumstances may provide a legal excuse but not a moral one. In still other cases, both kinds of excuses may exist.

Moral Dilemmas

On some occasions fundamental moral obligations may conflict. You know the familiar phrase for such a dilemma: "Caught between a rock and a hard place." Although **moral dilemmas** can arise in a wide variety of situations, *whistleblowing* presents a classic and often agonizing version of such an ethical conflict. The term whistleblowing normally refers to a situation in which an employee objects to or reports to the authorities the illegal or unethical activities of his employer. Because this kind of situation is frequently so rich in ethical questions, we will use the following hypothetical case for two purposes: as an illustration of how moral dilemmas arise and as a basis for our subsequent discussion of moral reasoning.

Suppose that Alexis works in the tax division of a large public accounting firm. One of the firm's major clients is Leviathan Corp. While working on one part of Leviathan's tax return, Alexis discovers that some expense items appear to have been overstated. No single item has been grossly inflated, and the total amount of expense overstatement is significant but not huge. Thus the risk of detection by the Internal Revenue Service probably is relatively small. Also Alexis cannot tell for sure whether the overstatements are intentional or simply resulted from honest mistakes or incompetence. She speaks with her immediate supervisor about the matter, but the supervisor dismisses the evidence as a "nonproblem." When Alexis presses the issue a little harder, the supervisor says, "Just do your job and don't stick your nose in too far." Should Alexis take up the matter with a higher level manager, perhaps even with the firm's top management? Suppose that she does so and receives the same kind of response at that level. What then?

Alexis owes a general moral duty of loyalty to her employer, an obligation that requires her to act in the firm's best interests. Moreover, in this case, she owes a duty of loyalty to the client. She also has made commitments, either explicitly or implicitly, to obey her superiors in the firm. Fulfilling these obligations, however, requires actions that are possibly dishonest and that may violate several conflicting moral obligations.

If Alexis refuses to overlook the problem, or if she reports it to the IRS, she stands an excellent chance of losing her job. How likely is it that she will be able to find a comparable job, especially if she cannot get a good reference from her current firm, a possibility that cannot be ignored? Does she have dependents who count on her for support? If so, she probably owes them a moral obligation that could be characterized as one of loyalty, or perhaps doing no harm. Is this duty strong enough to support a decision to keep quiet about something that is possibly dishonest?

Alexis owes a conflicting moral duty of honesty to the government, and to taxpayers who will have to pay more to make up for the underpayments by her firm's clients. It is true that the harm to any other single taxpayer will be extremely small, but the obligation exists nonetheless.

As an accountant, she also has made commitments to other members of her profession to uphold professional standards of honesty and competence. The failures of one member of a professional or trade group taint the reputation of the entire group and thus cause harm to every other member. To overlook the expense overstatements may violate this commitment and, if detected, harm the profession and its members.

Alexis faces a moral dilemma. Is there any way out of it? Of course, there are always ways out, but there may not be a painless way out. In the next section we will examine moral reasoning to see how ethical questions can be analyzed in a rational way. Part of this discussion will focus on moral dilemmas as a part of the overall process of moral reasoning. Clear, rational thinking about moral dilemmas does not necessarily eliminate the conflict or turn a difficult situation into an easy one. On the other hand, fuzzy or irrational thinking can certainly make matters worse. In the next section, we will explore the benefits that structured, rational thinking can bring to ethical problems, including moral dilemmas.

Moral Reasoning and Decision Making

Ethical issues frequently are emotionally charged. Although it can be quite difficult to think rationally about emotional issues, it is in such situations that clear, organized thinking is most needed. One of the most important lessons one can learn from a study of ethics is that moral questions are capable of being analyzed rationally. The process of analyzing moral questions is essentially the same as rational problem solving or decision making in other situations.

Identifying Issues

The necessary first step in problem solving is to figure out exactly what the problems are. In other words, one must identify the issues. If one is confronted with legal, financial, or marketing issues, for example, they first should be recognized and spelled out as clearly as possible. The same is true of ethical issues. In the hypothetical case involving Alexis, the issue she must cope with immediately is not (1) whether it is wrong in general to cheat on one's taxes; (2) whether her superiors are bad people; (3) whether her accounting firm or Leviathan Corp. has developed an organizational structure that is insufficient to establish lines of individual accountability for wrongdoing; or (4) whether she can sue her employer for the tort of wrongful discharge if she is fired for objecting to the expense overstatements or reporting them to the IRS.

Problems have to be defined narrowly enough so that we have the ability both to analyze them adequately *and* exercise some degree of influence over the outcome. The issue that Alexis must confront at the present time is whether her most morally defensible course of action is to keep quiet and go along with her firm's possibly inappropriate behavior or to resist it by "blowing the whistle." Other issues may arise later, but for now this is all she needs to deal with from an ethical perspective.

Identifying the Governing Principles

For every kind of issue there are governing principles or rules that guide or limit our decision. The source of these principles will vary, depending on the nature of the issue. There are legal rules, generally accepted accounting principles, marketing principles, generally accepted courses of medical treatment for particular illnesses, formulas for computing stress in the construction of bridges, and so on. In ethics we have the components of the moral minimum—the foundational moral obligations identified earlier in our discussion.

In some cases the principles will be relatively *specific* but in others they may be quite *general*. Whether they are specific or general, different principles may be characterized by varying degrees of *certainty or acceptance*. In the case of some legal principles, for example, it can be difficult to determine precisely what the rule is. This uncertainty can result from conflicting court decisions, ambiguous statutory language, or other reasons. In addition, some principles are more generally accepted than others, whether the relevant field is law, medicine, accounting, engineering, ethics, or another discipline. These qualifying remarks do not diminish the importance of guiding principles. They represent the collective knowledge gained from experience and rational thought, and should serve as the foundation for rational problem solving.

In ethics, the principles are fairly general. As indicated earlier, however, we think that the *prima facie* duties that constitute the moral minimum are widely accepted across time, culture, and circumstance. Their relative degree of acceptance as societal norms has varied, no doubt, at different times and in different cultures, but in general they have remained intact.

When analyzing ethical issues, it is important to identify the pertinent moral obligations as precisely as possible. What is the *nature* of the obligation? Honesty? Loyalty? Keeping commitments? Doing no harm? After identifying the nature of each moral obligation, we must make sure we understand exactly *who* owes which obligation to whom. In Alexis's case we have already done a pretty good job of identifying the obligations that she owes to various parties. If we are doing a complete ethical analysis of the entire situation, we also would find it necessary to identify the moral obligations owed to Alexis by her superiors. One can argue persuasively that they are violating their duty of doing no harm by intentionally, recklessly, or negligently engaging in conduct that may cause reasonably foreseeable harm to Alexis. Acting in behalf of the firm, essentially what they have done is ask her to participate in conduct that may be dishonest and possibly even illegal. Even if she does not get into any legal trouble, emotional trauma also can be viewed as "harm" when it is a reasonably foreseeable result of their actions.

Collecting, Verifying, and Drawing Inferences from Information

Issues of any kind always arise in a factual context— they do not exist in a vacuum. In our hypothetical case, the relevant information (i.e., "evidence" or "data) that initially caused Alexis to perceive a problem was the apparent inconsistency between entries in Leviathan's general ledgers used to prepare its tax return and the figures in supporting documentation. When information raises potential ethical, legal, or other issues, we should first do what we can to verify the accuracy, reliability, and completeness of that information. If the issues are sensitive, we obviously must exercise great care in doing this. Caution and good judgment are essential.

We may find that the true facts are very different than we initially suspected, and that there is no problem at all. Of course, we may find that things are much worse than we thought. Frequently we may conclude after an initial inquiry that our information is incomplete and that we need further evidence to understand the situation. Again, in the subsequent search for additional evidence, caution is the watchword. It is usually impossible to acquire information that is so complete and so clearly accurate and reliable as to resolve all doubt. Decisions always have to be made on the basis of information that is less than perfect. When analyzing important issues and preparing to make important decisions, however, it is essential that our information be as complete and accurate as circumstances will allow.

As with any fact-finding process that serves as a foundation for problem solving, in ethical analysis we infer relevant facts from the evidence. In other words, we infer that certain things have happened. In addition to inferring facts, we use the evidence as a basis for making predictions about likely future events. Thus, from the evidence she has at her disposal, Alexis might infer that her firm condones or possibly even assists in tax cheating by clients, although more information is needed to support this inference. Alexis also may have enough information to predict that any further objection to superiors within the firm is likely to be fruitless, and that she may even be penalized in some way for making a fuss.

Applying the Facts to the Principles

The remainder of the ethical problem-solving, or moral reasoning, process involves further application of the guiding principles to the facts that we have inferred from the evidence. In other words, we must determine how the identified moral obligations should apply to these particular facts. This determination should be relatively straightforward, of course, if there are no excusing conditions or moral dilemmas. Such complicating factors are present in many cases, however, and must be incorporated into the analysis.

In our hypothetical scenario, we already have identified the moral dilemmas created by several conflicting duties. The next step is to weigh and balance these obligations against one another. In doing so, we must keep in mind that this is not algebra. Despite being a rational analytical process, it is highly qualitative and involves a degree of subjectivity. The process of balancing conflicting obligations should incorporate at least the following factors.

Excusing Conditions

Are there any excusing conditions that might lessen the strength of one obligation relative to another? Remember that our moral accountability can be diminished or eliminated by genuine lack of knowledge or freedom. In Alexis's case, one can argue that her status as an employee who is acting under orders from her superiors causes her freedom of action to be considerably less than if she were in charge. No doubt this is true; the degree of her moral responsibility surely is not as great as it would be if she had more power over the firm's decisions. Is her freedom of action curtailed so much, however, that she has no moral duty at all? Certainly not—otherwise a person in a subordinate position could be morally answerable for his conduct only if he initiated and controlled the situation. In such a case, of course, either he would be acting outside his authority or else he really would not be acting as a subordinate at all. Completely relieving all subordinates of moral responsibility for their actions within the organization's chain of command has the potential to lower substantially the level of moral behavior within organizations and throughout society. Thus, Alexis should continue to have a moral duty of honesty with respect to her complicity in the firm's possible wrongdoing, although the strength of her obligation may be somewhat less than in other situations where she is not playing a subordinate role.

Conflict Reduction

Are there ways to minimize conflicts? As in this case, a *prima facie* moral duty usually is not eliminated by an excusing condition. Most of the time there either is no such condition or else the condition merely curtails the strength of a duty rather than doing away with it entirely. Thus, any moral dilemma that we previously identified still exists. Before getting to the point of having to make an all-or-nothing choice between conflicting duties, however, we should search for creative solutions that may diminish or remove the conflict.

Alexis might consider requesting reassignment within the firm, perhaps to another geographic location, so as to remove her from any direct role in the questionable activity. Reassignment may not be feasible, and even if it is feasible it may damage her future opportunities in the firm. Moreover, if the attitude of her current superiors is found throughout the organization, she may encounter similar problems in her new position. Assuming that she finds a higher level of ethical standards at her new location, Alexis still *knows* about the possible dishonesty at her previous one. If she remains silent about it, is she guilty of complicity in the questionable behavior even though she is no longer a participant? Many people would say yes. If we take the view that the duty of loyalty to her employer continues to exist, Alexis still owes the same basic duty because she has remained in the same organization. One can see that removing ourselves from direct involvement does not always eliminate a moral dilemma, although this course of action may reduce the acuteness of the conflict. There remain other options for Alexis, which we will not pursue here.

In other situations, creative ideas for minimizing the degree of conflict between obligations will take other forms. For example, in some cases a person caught in a moral dilemma might be able to work out agreements with one or more of the parties to whom duties are owed so that the duties no longer conflict and all can be fulfilled. If we cannot make agreements that enable us to fulfill all moral duties, it may be possible to work out compromises that permit us to comply fully with one and partially with another. Such opportunities will not always exist, but it is important to give careful consideration to the possibilities.

Prioritizing

When we cannot eliminate a moral dilemma, we must choose between the obligations that we will attempt to satisfy. The choice should be made only after carefully weighing the strength and importance of the conflicting duties. In other words, we must prioritize the obligations. We already may have gone a long way toward weighing and prioritizing our duties as we considered whether excusing conditions were present and sought creative ways to minimize the conflict. We may have found that excusing conditions reduce the significance of one moral duty with respect to another. Similarly, we may have worked out agreements or discovered alternative courses of action that strengthen or weaken different obligations and, consequently, make our choice easier.

If the relative importance of particular obligations, and thus their proper place on our list of priorities, still remains unclear, we should next attempt to evaluate the *harm* that may result from violating the various moral duties. A careful evaluation of harm will take into account both *degree* and *probability*. Other factors being equal, the relative importance of a moral obligation increases proportionately with increases in (1) the degree of harm that is likely to be caused by violating the obligation and (2) the probability (or likelihood) that the harm actually will occur.

In the case of Alexis, for instance, the harm done to taxpayers by this instance of expense overstatement, or even by all similar actions by her employer's clients, is probably pretty small in relative terms. On the other hand, we should also consider cumulative effects. When one tax cheater is reported and gets caught, other cheaters may change their behavior. Thus the harm to taxpayers caused by her firm's conduct, and the harm that may be prevented by her reporting it, could be a lot greater than one might think. With regard to probability, the harm caused by even a single instance of cheating is certain to occur even if it is very small.

The potential harm that Alexis's silence may cause to her profession apparently has a very low probability of occurrence. This harm will occur only if real tax cheating actually happened, she gets into trouble for going along with it, and the profession receives bad publicity as a result. This harm not only has a low probability of occurring, but if limited to this one event, it will also be relatively minor. Again, however, we should consider whether there may be cumulative harmful effects.

If Alexis reports the expense overstatements to the IRS, there is no doubt that short-term harm will be caused to both her employer and Leviathan, especially if the overstatements are found to have been intentional. They will incur penalties, and perhaps substantial legal fees and court costs. These harms appear to be high in both degree and probability. In addition, the accounting firm and Leviathan may suffer long-term harm in the form of damaged company reputations and the various costs associated with an increased level of future oversight by the IRS. This kind of harm probably is somewhat less certain to occur, but if it does occur it could be even more substantial than the short-term damage. At the same time, we must not overlook the possibility that, if Alexis's firm and Leviathan are reported and get into legal trouble now, this event could lead them to clean up their general level of ethical behavior. Arguably, more ethical behavior in the future will reduce their chances of encountering costly legal problems. This leads us to the question of whether ethical behavior produces economic benefit to the ethical company or person. "Does ethics pay?" is an exceedingly difficult and complicated question. We will discuss it later, although we will not even pretend to answer it.

Finally, we need much more information before evaluating the degree or probability of harm that might be caused to others if Alexis loses her job after "blowing the whistle." How likely is it that she will actually lose her job? If she gets fired, how likely is it that she will be able to recover damages from her former employer in a lawsuit claiming the tort of wrongful discharge? Will she have a difficult time finding comparable employment? Do others depend on her for support?

Making a Moral Decision

Ultimately Alexis must make a decision that reflects a choice. Even inaction is a choice. There may be no choice that is totally satisfactory, and there almost certainly will not be one that is completely free of doubt or negative consequences. Whatever course she takes, her choice should be the conscious result of a rational process similar to the one we have described.

It is true that quick decisions sometimes have to be made. If so, we may not have the luxury to gather as much information or reflect on our choices as much as we would like. There is almost always some time, however, for reflection and rational thinking. When emotionally charged ethical questions arise, we are far more likely to work them out through a rational analytical process if we have already anticipated and carefully thought about general problems of this nature. This is especially true when decisions have to be made under pressure and in relatively short periods of time. If we have not already practiced rational thinking about ethical issues in our actual experiences, we should at least have taken the time to examine our own values and to think about how we would deal with particular moral questions should they arise. Without some preparation, we run a much greater risk of making rash responses under pressure.

It is true that decisions, moral or otherwise, may turn out all right even if not preceded by sound analytical reasoning. Such a result probably represents simple good fortune more than anything else. Conversely, rational thinking does not guarantee optimal results. Although carrying no guarantees, such a process can have the following benefits:

1. It increases our chances of having better and more complete information on which to base a decision.
2. It lowers the risk of completely overlooking an important issue.
3. It improves our chances of making a decision that best balances the various conflicting interests that may be present.
4. If we are later called upon to defend our decision, we will be better prepared to do so. Difficult decisions that affect others are often challenged, and a decision resulting from the type of process described here is more defensible. We have our facts straighter, and our reasons for making particular choices can be presented more clearly and forcefully because they have been thought through carefully. In addition, we are able to demonstrate a good faith effort to do the right thing. Evidence of good faith is no small matter, and often can make the difference when close judgment calls are at issue.

Are Corporations Moral Agents?

There is nearly unanimous agreement that individuals are morally responsible for their actions within business organizations. Managers and employees in corporations, like other individuals in other settings, have moral obligations. These obligations can never be erased by joining anything, be it a club, fraternity, political party, or business organization. We do not, or at least should not, leave our values at the door when we enter the workplace.

There is less consensus, however, about whether a corporation itself can owe moral obligations independent of the individuals within the organization. A corporation is recognized as a **legal entity** that is capable of owning property, making contracts, being a party to legal proceedings, and so on. It can act, however, only through human beings. Thus, is a corporation a **moral agent** in addition to being a legal entity?

Does It Make Any Difference?

Before examining this question, it is legitimate to ask, "So what?" Does it make any difference? It is no doubt true that in many cases, we can resolve relevant moral questions in business by focusing only on the moral duties of particular individuals within the company. There are situations, however, in which it is impossible to trace decisions or actions to any given individual. So the question about corporate moral status is not a purely abstract one. Even if we recognize the question as being a real one, does the answer to it have any impact? Suppose that we conclude that corporations themselves do have moral responsibilities. If a particular corporation's actions do not violate the law, however, are there any meaningful consequences of a conclusion that it has "acted unethically"?

ETHICS AT WORK

Secret taping, an activity brimming with ethical and legal questions, has become increasingly common in the work place. Suppose an employee believes that his or her supervisor is "out to get" the employee for reasons that are unjust and possibly illegal. More and more frequently, the response of an employee in such a situation is secretly to tape conversations with the superior. Managers and company lawyers generally view such secret taping as dishonest and disloyal. Even many plaintiffs' lawyers say that the idea of secret taping makes them very uncomfortable. On the other hand, if the supervisor is actually treating the employee in a way that is at least unethical and perhaps illegal, the employee may have no other way to prove it. It is undoubtedly unethical for an employee to engage in secret taping when the employee has no good reason to believe that the supervisor is acting wrongly. However, if the employee does have good reason to believe that the supervisor is in the process of trying to get rid of the employee for wrongful reasons, such as age, race, or sex discrimination, does the employee have an adequate moral excuse for secret taping.? The ethical problem obviously is a difficult one; if there is an "answer" to the question, it depends very much on the particular facts of the case and demands thorough analysis.

From a legal perspective, federal law permits the secret taping of conversations so long as one party knows about the taping. Almost one-third of the states have similar legislation. Thus, an employee's secret taping does not violate federal law or the law of these states. Another group of states, again almost one-third, has laws prohibiting taping unless both parties to the conversation know about it. More than one-third of the states have no relevant legislation. If a fired employee files a lawsuit and has a secret tape that reveals evidence of illegal conduct by the supervisor, the tape certainly will be admissible evidence in the courts of states where such taping is expressly legal. It also is probably admissible in the courts of those states where there is no legislation on the subject of secret taping, and probably in federal courts if the employee is claiming a violation of a federal law such as the 1964 Civil Rights Act prohibition against race or sex discrimination. It is still unclear, however, whether such a tape will be admissible evidence in the courts of a state where the taping is expressly illegal.

We think there can be meaningful consequences. The consequences are not nearly as obvious or immediate as they may be when the law is violated, but they are there. The behavior of corporations is a frequent subject of discussion in the media, legislatures, regulatory agencies, classrooms, living rooms, and elsewhere. If there is a general perception in society that corporations are morally accountable for their actions, this perception will have an impact on the public debate over corporate behavior. It can alter the basic structure and direction of the debate, as well as the effect this debate has on people's attitudes about corporations. Feelings that a particular corporation, as an independent moral agent, has acted unethically can affect consumers' buying decisions. Similar feelings about an entire industry, or about corporations in general, can affect the decisions of legislatures and regulatory agencies as to the need for regulation. On the other hand, a company, industry, or the business community in general is much more likely to receive the benefit of the doubt in many different ways when there are no generally negative perceptions about its ethical standards.

The View That Corporations are Not Moral Agents

The most widely advanced view that corporations cannot have moral obligations is that of philosopher John Ladd, who regards corporations as purely formal organizations analogous to programmable robots or machines. Machines have neither a will nor any freedom of action. Similarly, according to Ladd, a corporation is merely an aggregation of legally binding documents such as a state charter and the corporate bylaws, organizational charts, operating procedures, and customs. The human cogs in this machine are role-players. Moreover, they are replaceable and often virtually interchangeable. Rule-governed activities and impersonal operating procedures prevent the application, or even the hint, of moral responsibility. Support for Ladd's view may be found, among other places, in Chief Justice John Marshall's description of a corporation in *Dartmouth College*, 17 U.S. 518(1819):

> A corporation is an artificial being, invisible, intangible, and existing only in contemplation of law. Being the mere creature of law, it possesses only those properties which the charter of creation confers upon it, either expressly, or as incidental to its very existence. These are such as are supposed best calculated to effect the object for which it was created.

The fact that corporations are mere "artificial being(s)," or "creature(s) of law," does seem to support the argument that corporations cannot be moral agents with separate moral obligations. The lifeless pieces of paper that bring the corporation into existence and provide governing rules for its operation do not provide it with autonomy or reason. Therefore, we must look elsewhere for support if we are to argue that corporations are moral agents.

The View That Corporations Do Have Moral Responsibilities

We mentioned that violations of moral obligations frequently cannot be traced to a particular individual within a corporation. As a rule, most actions and inactions of relatively large corporations cannot be tallied as the sum of individual actions—the whole is truly greater than the sum of its parts. As a result, individuals tend to escape moral accountability. This fact, in itself, provides considerable support for the argument that corporations should be viewed as separate moral agents.

Organization theory explains this phenomenon in terms of **group dynamics.** Groups often behave very differently than any member would have behaved, because the dynamics of the group transcend individual reason and autonomy. People sometimes just get "caught up in the spirit of things." Examples range all the way from the lynch mob to a corporate board that makes an ethically questionable decision despite the fact that each of its individual members has high personal moral standards. We find the phenomenon not only in groups of co-equal members, but also in chains of command. For example, managers at the top may set policies and give orders but deny any responsibility for conduct by their subordinates that they did not intend. Similarly, we often find those at the bottom denying responsibility because they did not make the policy and they themselves intended no harm; they were "just carrying out orders." Several complex factors seem to be responsible for the peculiarities of group dynamics in corporations:

Because the action is motivated by corporate purposes rather than personal reasons, participating individuals may not view their conduct as really their own. If they do not associate the action with themselves as human beings, they are not as likely to apply their own personal moral standards to it.

A member of a group may feel that there is "safety in numbers." As the number of individual participants in group action increases, each member's feeling of anonymity may also increase. Even if a person does recognize and feel somewhat responsible for the moral consequences of his group's proposed action, he nevertheless may go along with a plan because he doubts that he personally will ever be called upon to defend it.

Formal lines of authority and accountability within the organization may be fuzzy, thus increasing the chances that no single person really feels responsible. When people do not feel responsible, they are less likely to act responsibly.

Communication among individuals within the decision-making group may be less than perfect, and thus different individuals or subgroups may be acting on the basis of somewhat different facts and assumptions. One individual or subgroup within the organization may not be completely aware of the total picture, leading to the classic situation of the "right hand not knowing what the left hand is doing."

Peer pressure can cause a member of a group to be fearful of speaking up when he sees something wrong with the group's proposed action. Many of us do not want to be perceived as "different" or as a "prude." Peer pressure can produce some really strange results. One example is found in the actions preceding the so-called "Watergate cover-up" that ultimately led to President Nixon's resignation in 1974. Later interviews with the participants revealed that, when a group of Nixon's associates was planning to burglarize and plant microphones in Democratic Party headquarters in Washington, D.C.'s Watergate Hotel in the early 1970s, all of the major participants thought it was a dangerous, stupid thing to do. No one voiced this opinion at the time, however; each person thought that the others viewed the break-in as a good idea and no one wanted to risk being tagged as "not a team player." Similar things can happen in business when advertising campaigns, joint ventures, capital restructurings, mergers, new products, research and development programs, personnel policies, and countless other actions are being planned.

On balance, we believe that the arguments in favor of treating corporations as separate moral agents are stronger than those to the contrary. This conclusion is based upon three facts: (1) corporations can act only through the individuals they employ; (2) group dynamics is a reality, and often produces behavior very different than would have occurred had any individual in the group acted alone; and (3) it is frequently impossible to trace ethical failings to an individual in the organization and, consequently, there is no place to attach moral blame if we cannot attach it to the corporation.

Corporate Social Responsiveness

If a person accepts the notion that corporations are moral agents and thus owe separate moral obligations, another question arises. Is it appropriate for a corporation to go beyond the moral minimum and correct problems it did not cause? Should a corporation expend corporate resources "doing good" by meeting societal needs? Such actions are sometimes described by the phrase "corporate social responsibility," but "responsiveness" describes the idea better than "responsibility." Going further, if it is *appropriate* for a corporation to do these kinds of things, is there actually an *obligation* to do them?

We first must recognize that questions about corporate social responsiveness do not necessarily arise every time a corporation's management considers spending corporate funds for a socially worthwhile cause such as helping a local elementary school offer enrichment programs for gifted students. Voluntarily responding to community needs often can be justified solely on economic grounds. Such actions can provide excellent promotional opportunities for the company and enhance its reputation and goodwill in a variety of ways. Also improving the local community may improve the company's workforce and even its property values. Essentially, social responsiveness can provide some of the same economic benefits to a corporation that we mentioned earlier in our discussion of whether complying with the moral minimum can produce such benefits. Any attempt to justify socially responsive behavior on economic grounds must focus on long-term rather than short-term benefits, because the kind of benefit derived from such behavior is necessarily indirect and imprecise. Also we should not put any less value on a corporation's voluntary contribution to society just because management was motivated by the company's self-interest. Indeed, the motives of the managers may have been very complex and indeterminate.

Our main question here, however, is how to deal with the question on moral grounds. Is socially responsive conduct appropriate regardless of whether it pays, and are there any circumstances in which it is morally required?

The Agents of Capital View

One of the most well-known proponents of the view that corporations do not owe a moral duty to be socially responsive is Milton Friedman, a Nobel laureate in economics and an influential spokesman on the role of corporations in society. To begin with, Friedman does not view corporations as moral agents; only managers and employees as individuals have moral status. In addition, he contends that there is no obligation to spend corporate resources correcting problems the company did not cause and, going even further, he asserts that it is not even appropriate for the company's managers to do so. They are **agents of capital,** that is, agents of the shareholders who own the corporation and provide its capital. As such, their only duty is to earn as much money as possible for the shareholders, within the limits of the law and customary ethical practices.

Unless specially approved by shareholder resolution, decisions concerning the use of corporate resources to do good necessarily are made by individual managers. According to Friedman, it is completely inappropriate for them to do so. Corporate managers are free to devote their own time and money to whatever pursuits they deem morally or socially appropriate, but when they divert corporate resources to such projects they breach their duty of loyalty to shareholders. Friedman finds the social responsiveness movement to be a "fundamentally subversive doctrine" that resembles theft—managers are using "someone else's money." The proper function of government is to attend to matters of the common good and social welfare. Corporate managers are not, by training or otherwise, equipped to do that, and even if they were, it would be intolerable in a democracy for unelected, unaccountable "civil servants" to be charged with the responsibility. While government might be slow and unresponsive in addressing current social problems, the insistence that this gap be filled by corporate action is just an acknowledgment of defeat by proponents of corporate social responsiveness who "have failed to persuade a majority of their fellow citizens to be of like mind and [who] are seeking to attain by undemocratic procedures what they cannot attain by democratic procedures."

Another argument along the same lines is that when a social or religious organization or a government agency attempts to meet the needs of society, it usually does so with resources that were placed under the organization's control because of the merits of its social objectives. For example, grants from the American Cancer Society to researchers seeking a cure for cancer are made from funds that were donated to the Society because of the knowledge that the money would be used to fight the disease. Because of scarce resources, there is a "competition among good causes." Although it is unfortunate that all such needs cannot be fully met, this competition provides a method for roughly measuring the relative importance and value to the public of particular social needs. This prioritizing of needs by the marketplace is a very imperfect process that will always leave worthy needs unsatisfied. It does, however, introduce some necessary utilitarianism into the allocation of resources by reducing the chances that too much will go to causes that benefit too few. On the other hand, resources come into a corporation solely because of its business success, unless shareholders invest with the explicit understanding that certain corporate moneys will be spent on identified good causes. Thus, when managers use corporate funds to do good, the needs they meet have not withstood the test of this "market for donated funds."

The Agents of Society View

There are those who argue that it is both appropriate and morally obligatory for corporations to contribute to the correction of problems they did not cause. They place this duty on the corporation as a moral agent, as well as on managers whose individual and group decisions energize the company. In a speech to the Harvard Business School in 1969, Henry Ford II stated: "The terms of the contract between industry and society are changing.... Now we are being asked to serve a wider range of human values and to accept an obligation to members of the public with whom we have no commercial transactions." His words were foreshadowed by those of his grandfather some two generations earlier. "For a long time people believed that the only purpose of industry is to make a profit. They were wrong. Its purpose is to serve the general welfare."

This notion of a "social contract" forms the foundation for many of the arguments that corporate social responsiveness is morally required. Under this view, a corporation is the result of a contract between those forming the corporation and the society that permits its creation. Thus, the corporation has a contract-like obligation to contribute positively to society, and the corporation's managers are not just agents of the shareholders but are also agents of society. One noted proponent of this view, philosopher Thomas Donaldson, hypothesized the existence of a society in which individuals always work and produce alone, and never in corporate form. A society such as this, composed of rational persons, would permit the legal creation of corporations only if the benefits to the public are great enough to justify the privileges granted to corporations and to outweigh the potential drawbacks. The privileges include limited liability—only the corporate entity and its assets are liable for corporate debts, not the individual shareholders or managers. This limited liability can come at a cost to other members of society. One potential drawback is that permitting corporations to exist generally leads to much larger aggregations of resources being under the effective control of a smaller number of people. Large resource accumulations in corporations can bring both economic and political power that few, if any, individuals could ever match. Such power can create risks for society.

Supporters of the agents of society view also would use the same basic line of reasoning that one would use to argue that individuals have a moral obligation to do good. These arguments were discussed earlier in the chapter. Similarly, for those wishing to build a rational argument in favor of morally required corporate social responsiveness, the same limits that were applied to the individual's obligation to do good would apply to the corporation's duty to be socially responsive.

CSR Abroad

Corporate Social Responsibility (CSR) and related concepts such as sustainable development [the notion that economic development should not compromise the ability of future generations to enjoy the same standard of living as our own], and corporate citizenship [the idea that corporations are citizens of our society and owe duties to constituencies other than shareholders] are currently taken more seriously in Europe than in the U.S. Many major European companies routinely engage in "triple-bottom-line reporting," disclosing their performance on economic, environmental, and social matters.

In a recent survey, 70% of global CEOs believed that CSR is important to their companies' long-term success. In another, a near consensus of 1,000 people in 25 countries around the world was the corporation should go beyond financial philanthropy by using their particular skills and abilities to ameliorate world problems such as hunger and disease. PricewaterhouseCoopers recently reported that American companies are not doing a good job of considering socially acceptable behavior, environmentally sensitive policies, and related issues, though these are likely to become important measures of corporate performance in the near future. Companies that cannot take into account the risk that their businesses face in such areas may well pay a high price.

For example, the GAP stores have faced fierce criticism and consumer boycotts regarding the source of their products. Recently GAP deployed more than 80 employees whose sole responsibility was to ensure that factories around the world that produce clothing for GAP complied with ethical sourcing criteria when buying supplies. NIKE, facing similar criticism and boycotts arising from labor conditions in its third-world factors, recently quadrupled the number of employees dealing with labor practices.

Does Ethics Pay?

Earlier we alluded to the question of whether ethical behavior by a corporation and the people within it actually produces economic benefit for the company. Ethical behavior ought to be our ideal regardless of the economic consequences. A corporation is, however, created for the primary purpose of operating a business profitably and providing a sufficient return on the shareholders' investment to justify their continuation of that investment. So the question about economic consequences of ethical behavior is a legitimate one.

"Does ethics pay?" is a complex question that is exceptionally difficult to answer. Although there can be no doubt that ethics does pay in some ways some of the time, there is no clear-cut answer that covers all situations. In trying to work toward a general answer, we find a few relevant facts that are based on fairly concrete evidence, but we must rely on intuition and even speculation for many others.

Several possible economic benefits of ethical behavior seem likely to occur, although they are of a long-term nature and are incapable of being measured with any precision. The following are some of these possible economic benefits.

It seems almost certain that the maintenance of high ethical standards in a company creates an environment in which very costly violations of the law are less likely to occur.

As mentioned earlier, such standards also may reduce the likelihood of new government regulations that are costly to comply with. Although this potential benefit is rather speculative, we do have evidence that *bad* ethical behavior can produce more regulation. The Foreign Corrupt Practices Act, for example, was passed by Congress primarily in response to revelations about widespread bribery by American companies in overseas transactions. Sarbanes-Oxley was passed in response to stark evidence of fraudulent financial reporting by many large companies.

It also seems reasonable to assume that a high moral tone within a company will have a positive impact on employee morale and productivity. Intuitively, it would seem that, at least for most people, working in a company that observes and requires high ethical standards will be a much more pleasant experience than working in one with low standards. Employees and managers should experience less "cognitive dissonance," a disquieting and disruptive mental state caused by conflicting beliefs. Such a state can be created, for instance, when a manager or employee believes strongly that he should be loyal to the company, obey superiors, and work hard in pursuit of the company's interests, but where prevailing moral attitudes in the company are contrary to his personal moral standards. Since happier employees usually are more productive, the company should be more productive.

High ethical standards are likely to generate good will with suppliers and customers. The good reputation that results from ethical behavior does not substitute for quality products, good service, and competitive prices, but it can produce many intangible benefits over time. It makes it possible, for example, to develop long-lasting business relationships based on trust. These kinds of relationships are more economically efficient than those that are based solely on lengthy legal documents, legal threats, and keeping a close watch on the other party.

Balanced against these possible economic benefits is the fact that ethical behavior can sometimes be costly, and when these costs occur they are likely to be direct, immediate, and measurable. For example, it may be quite expensive to install better pollution control equipment than the law requires because of a strong moral commitment to those who drink the water and breathe the air. Competitors may not do the same thing, and their lower costs may enable them to undersell their more ethical brethren. Or a company may lose business in the short term because it refuses to pay a bribe or kickback.

And, unfortunately, an honest company can lose a business deal to a competitor who misrepresents the facts.

It takes a long-term view to properly assess the economic impact of ethical behavior. Whenever possible, of course, business firms should approach problems with a long-term perspective regardless of whether ethical questions are involved. It is probably impossible to prove that ethics pays in any conclusive fashion, of course, but several recent studies have pointed in that direction. One recent study analyzing thirty years of corporate data found that companies' social responsibility positively affected their financial performance more than 80% of the time. Of 80 or so studies of the issue, 42 have demonstrated a positive link between CSR and profits, 19 found no link, 15 produced mixed results, but only four showed a negative impact.

How does ethics pay? Obviously, many customers and investors prefer companies with reputations for good corporate citizenship. A smaller subset will actively avoid companies with bad reputations. Companies that commit fraud can damage their reputations in ways that are sometimes irreparable, as both Enron and Arthur Andersen discovered. Unethical activity can destroy the trust of customers, employees, suppliers, investors, and other constituents. A recent study of 132 cases of corporate fraud found that the average firm was punished by a $60 million drop in its market capitalization. Only a small percentage of that amount could be accounted for by potential civil and criminal penalties; the rest was reputational damage.

It has been reported that in a visit to the HarvardBusiness School, former Enron CEO Jeff Skilling was asked what he would do if his company was producing a product that caused death to its users. He responded: "I'd keep making and selling the product. My job as a businessman is to be a profit center and to maximize returns to the shareholders. It's the government's job to step in if a product is dangerous." Pursuant to his job as a profit center, Skilling was, of course, also doing everything he could through lobbying and campaign contributions to influence government not to step in. Some believe that Enron ultimately reaped what it sowed.

PART **II**

PRINCIPLES OF CONTRACT LAW

CHAPTER **11**

NATURE AND CLASSIFICATION OF CONTRACTS

- A Perspective
- Nature of a Contract
- Classification of Contracts
- Contract Law and Sales Law—A Special Relationship

A Perspective

In the preceding chapters we took a sweeping look at the aspects of our legal system that are common to all branches of law: the sources of our legal rules, the primary law-making processes, and the manner in which the rules of law are generally implemented by the courts. It is now time to move from the *environmental* approach to more *traditional, i.e.,* rule-oriented, areas of the law. The various branches of law that directly control all the legal aspects of business transactions—such as contracts, sales, and corporate dealings—are composed primarily of substantive legal rules.

Contract Law—Special Characteristics

Contract law, which is the subject of Part II, possesses several characteristics that make it the natural starting point for an examination of the other commercial law subjects. First, there is its pervasiveness in the average person's everyday activities. When a person buys a newspaper, leaves a car at a parking lot, or buys a ticket to a football game, a contract of some sort has been entered into. When someone borrows money, or hires someone to paint a house, or insures a car, a contract has again been made. And businesses—whether corner stores or large multinational corporations—must buy or lease office equipment, make agreements with employees, secure heat and light, buy materials from suppliers, and sell their goods and services to customers. All these transactions involve contracts.

Second, the basic principles of contract law are the underpinning of the more specialized business-related subjects, including sales and commercial paper, partnership and corporation law, and other areas.

Third, since the subject of contracts is essentially common-law in nature, the controversies that are presented usually require the courts to examine earlier decisions handed down in cases involving similar fact-patterns. Thus, the doctrine of *stare decisis* is illuminated; and an allied question—whether today's conditions have so changed as to justify a repudiation of earlier decisions— affords an opportunity to analyze more fully the process of judicial reasoning.

Nature of a Contract

A contract is a special sort of agreement—one that the law will enforce in some manner in the event that one party does not perform its promise. As will be seen in the next chapter, some agreements are not enforceable because their terms are too indefinite, or they are entered into in jest, or they involve obligations that are essentially social in nature (such as a date to go to a concert). Even seriously intended, definite business agreements, however, are generally not enforceable unless three additional elements are present—what the courts refer to as consideration, capacity, and legality. These concepts will be explored in later chapters also. Indeed, a comprehensive definition of contract cannot be attempted until these four elements have been examined in some detail.

One well-known source defines a contract in the following way: A more technical definition is the following: "A contract is a promise or set of promises for the breach of which the law gives a remedy, or the performance of which the law in some way recognizes as a duty." *Restatement, Contracts 2d,* §1, American Law Institute, 1979. A much simpler definition is that "a contract is an agreement that a court will enforce."

Classification of Contracts

Contracts have many facets and, consequently, may be categorized in a variety of ways. Different aspects may be important in different contexts. In one case it may be important that the contract is "bilateral" rather than "unilateral." The outcome of another case may turn on whether the contract is "voidable" rather than "void." An important purpose of this chapter is to introduce the various categories of contracts.

Bilateral and Unilateral Contracts

Most contracts consist of the exchange of mutual promises, the actual performance of which is to occur at some later time. When a manufacturer enters into a contract in May with a supplier, calling for the supplier to deliver 10,000 steel wheels during September at a specified price, each party has promised the other to perform one or more acts at a subsequent time. Such contracts, consisting of "a promise for a promise," are bilateral contracts.

The same terminology applies to offers (proposals) that precede the making of a contract. If the terms of an offer indicate that all the offeror wants at the present time from the offeree is a return promise— rather than the immediate performance of an act— then the proposal can be called a **bilateral offer.** The *offeror* is the person making the proposal; the *offeree* is the one to whom it is made. Thus, if a professional football club sends a contract to one of its players in June, offering him $800,000 for the coming season, it is clear that all the club presently wants is the player's promise to render his services at a later time. Such an offer is bilateral; and if the player accepts it by signing and returning the contract, a bilateral contract has been formed. (Note that, as in the previous example, people often say they are "sending a contract" when what they are really doing is sending an offer for a contract.)

Some offers, called **unilateral offers,** are phrased in such a way that they can be accepted only by the performance of a particular act. An example of such an offer would be the promise by a TV station to pay $5,000 to the first person who brings to its executive offices any piece of a fallen satellite. This offer can only be accepted by the actual physical production of a portion of the designated satellite, at which time a unilateral contract is formed; a mere promise by an offeree that he or she will bring in the item later does not result in the formation of a contract.

Offers for unilateral contracts occur much less frequently than offers for bilateral contracts—most contracts are bilateral. And, in cases where there is doubt as to the type of offer made, the courts generally construe them to be bilateral in nature, which means that the offeree can accept merely by indicating a definite intent to accept One type of unilateral offer, however, is made frequently in the real world—the promise by a seller of property to pay a real estate agent a commission when the agent finds a buyer for it. The real estate agent peforms a brokerage function, bringing together willing buyers and sellers. Brokers in other contexts are also frequently parties to unilateral contracts—typically, one using broker's services makes a unilateral offer of a commission if the broker finds what the party needs, such as financing. The following case presents another example, in which an employment agency offers to provide an employee to a company that is looking for someone. An employment agency is simply a broker in a labor market. The case also shows another consequence of an offer being a unilateral one, namely, if the offeree performs the requested act, he has accepted the offer even if he has verbally expressed reservations.

PRECISION CONCEPTS CORP. v. GENERAL EMPLOYMENT & TRIAD PERSONNEL SERVICES
Court of Appeals of Ohio, 2000 Ohio App. LEXIS 3322 (2000)

General Employment, an employment agency, contacted Precision, a computer company, regarding a job opening at Precision. General Employment sent a potential employee, Tavery Tan, to Precision for an interview. Precision eventually hired Ms. Tan but refused to pay General Employment its fee for procuring the employee. On September 11, 1998, Precision filed a complaint in the Franklin County Court of Common Pleas against General Employment. The complaint sought a declaration, in part, that there was no contractual relationship between Precision and General Employment. General Employment filed an answer and a counterclaim for breach of contract. The trial court dismissed Precision's complaint and rendered judgment to General Employment on its counterclaim in the sum of $ 17,624.99. Precision appealed.

Tyack, Justice:

To prove the existence of a contract, the elements of mutual assent (generally, offer and acceptance) and consideration must be shown. It must also be shown that there was a meeting of the minds and that the contract was definite as to its essential terms. Manifestation of mutual assent requires each party make a promise or begin to render a performance. Such manifestation of assent may be made wholly or partly by written or spoken words, or by other acts or the failure to act. Acceptance of an offer may be expressed by word, sign, writing or act.

As indicated above, the dispute in the case at bar centers on the fee allegedly owed by appellant (Precision Concepts Corp.) to appellee (General Employment) for procuring Ms. Tan. Appellant asserts it never agreed to pay a fee equaling one-third of Ms. Tan's first-year salary. The facts, construed most strongly in favor of appellant, establish the following. Appellant placed an ad in the newspaper indicating its desire to hire a senior applications developer. Charles E. Anthony, Jr., employed at Precision at the pertinent time, was the professional services manager and was contacted by appellee. Appellee's representative told Mr. Anthony that it had an applicant for the position. Mr. Anthony and the representative discussed the applicant's qualifications, and appellee sent appellant the applicant's resume.

Mr. Anthony testified that appellee informed him that it charged a fee of around thirty-three percent. Mr. Anthony told appellee that appellant did not generally pay that percentage and asked if the fee was negotiable. Appellee's representative responded that the fee was not negotiable.

On July 3, 1998, appellee's representative, Jasbir Sahota, sent a fax to Mr. Anthony informing him that the applicant, Tavery Tan, would be at appellant's office on Monday, July 6, 1998. On that Monday, Ms. Tan interviewed with Mr. Anthony. On that same day, appellant was faxed a fee schedule from appellee setting forth the terms and conditions should appellant hire Ms. Tan. The fee schedule contained a fee of one-third of the successful applicant's first-year salary. Such fee schedule was never signed by a representative of appellant.

After Ms. Tan's interview with Mr. Anthony, he recommended that she be hired. Mr. Anthony told appellant's president and co-owner, Robert W. Molitors, that he would like Ms. Tan to be hired but that he could not recommend hiring her if appellant had to pay the one third fee. Mr. Anthony testified that he thought Mr. Molitors "was looking to negotiate the fee down and basically he told me to go ahead and proceed with it." Mr. Anthony explained that he then continued the interview process with Ms. Tan and was going to have her "talk" to more people. Ms. Tan was interviewed by another employee of appellant who also recommended she be hired.

Ms. Tan was hired by appellant with an annual salary of $50,000. Mr. Molitors testified that appellant extended an offer to Ms. Tan without negotiating a lower fee "knowing that, hopefully, we could get to an agreement." Mr. Molitors further stated, "we went ahead and made the offer thinking we could work out the negotiations." Upon being asked if appellant ever negotiated a reduced fee, Mr. Anthony responded, "I am not 100 percent sure. I wasn't that involved with it, but I got from the gist of the conversation that we were going to go ahead and proceed with the hire since there was no contract in place and afterward we would negotiate a better fee."

Both Mr. Anthony and Mr. Molitors acknowledged that they were aware appellee charged a one-third fee for its services. However, Mr. Molitors testified that appellant had not signed any agreement and had not agreed verbally to any terms or conditions (relating to the fee). In an affidavit, Mr. Molitors stated that appellant rejected appellee's contract terms.

As a factual matter, the above evidence establishes that Mr. Molitors did not believe appellant had an agreement with appellee regarding the fee amount. However, it does not follow that there was no binding contract. The undisputed facts lead this court to conclude that as a legal matter, a unilateral contract was formed between the parties.

A unilateral contract is one in which the promisor receives no promise as consideration for his or her promise. By the promisor's offer, no obligation is imposed upon the offeree— only a condition, the performance of which is entirely optional with the offeree. As set forth in the Restatement of the Law 2d, Contracts (1981), Section 45(1), where an offer invites an offeree to accept by rendering a performance and does not invite a promissory acceptance, an option contract is created when the offeree tenders the invited performance. Such an offer has often been referred to as an offer for a unilateral contract. In such a situation, the contract is not formed until accepted by performance by the offeree. Consideration is not necessary prior to acceptance by performance and after acceptance, the obligation to pay becomes enforceable.

In the case at bar, appellee offered its services to appellant—the procuring of an employee. If appellant hired appellee's applicant, appellee's fee was one-third of the employee's annual salary. Appellant was under no obligation to interview and/or hire Ms. Tan. Appellant was aware of appellee's fee should Ms. Tan be hired. Appellant hired Ms. Tan and in doing so, accepted appellee's offer of procuring an employee for a one-third fee.

The fact that appellant did not like the fee appellee indicated it would charge should appellant hire Ms. Tan does not preclude the finding of a binding contract. Appellant intended and/or desired to negotiate the fee down; however, appellant never did so. Secretly held, unexpressed intent is not relevant to whether a contract is formed. There is evidence that Mr. Anthony initially told appellee that its fee was too high; however, appellee informed Mr. Anthony that such fee was not negotiable. Again, appellant hired Ms. Tan with knowledge of the fee charged by appellee, and it did so without negotiating down such fee. Accordingly, a unilateral contract was formed when appellant hired Ms. Tan, and appellant became obligated to pay appellee a fee equal to one-third of Ms. Tan's first-year salary.

Affirmed.

Express, Implied, and Quasi-Contracts

As has been indicated, the essence of a contract is an agreement (an understanding) that has been arrived at in some fashion. If the intentions of the parties are stated fully and in explicit terms, either orally or in writing, they constitute an **express contract.** The typical real estate lease and construction contract are examples of contracts normally falling within this category.

Express contracts are frequently in writing and of considerable length, but this is not necessarily so. If B orally offers to sell his used car to W for $450 cash, and W answers, "I accept," an express contract has been formed. The communications between B and W, while extremely brief and purely oral, are themselves sufficient to indicate the obligations of each.

An **implied contract** is one in which the promises (intentions) of the parties have to be inferred primarily from their conduct and from the circumstances in which it occurred. It is reasonable to infer, for example, that a person who is getting a haircut in a barbershop actually desires the service and is willing to pay for it. If the patron does not pay voluntarily, a court will have no hesitation in saying that by his conduct the patron had made an implied promise to pay a reasonable price, and will hold him liable on this obligation.

The words and conduct test is a good starting point in distinguishing between the two kinds of agreement, but it is also an oversimplification. This is primarily so because some agreements are reached through the use of words and conduct both—especially in the case where one person requests a service from another without specifying a price that he or she is willing to pay for it. For example, if T asks J to keep his lawn mowed during the two months that T will be in Europe, and if J performs the requested service, T's request for the service carries with it in the eyes of the law an implied promise that he will pay J the "reasonable value" of his services. Thus the contract that has been formed upon J's completion of the work is an implied contract, even though T requested the service expressly.

A **quasi-contract**, in contrast to express and implied contracts, exists only in those exceptional circumstances where a court feels compelled to impose an obligation upon one person regardless of whether he or she had any intention of making a contract. The technical name for implied contracts is *contracts implied in fact,* and for quasi-contracts *contracts implied in law.* We use the less formal terems "implied" and "quasi" for of simplicity.

One situation in which a quasi-contract obligation will be imposed is where it is necessary to promote an important public policy such as the performance of emergency medical care: The classic illustration is that of a doctor who renders first aid to an unconscious man and later sends a bill for his services. It is perfectly obvious that the patient neither expressly nor impliedly promised to pay for the services when they were rendered; yet to permit him to escape liability entirely on the grounds that a contract was not formed would be to let him get something for nothing—a result the law generally abhors. To solve this dilemma, the courts pretend that a contract was formed and impose a quasi-contractual obligation on the person receiving the service.

The other main situation in which a quasi-contractual obligation will often be imposed is where one party conferred a benefit on the other because of an honestly mistaken belief that he or she was under a legal or moral obligation to do so. In the Deskovic v. Porzio case, below, we see a situation in which a quasi-contractual obligation was imposed because money was paid as the result of an honestly mistaken belief that there was a strong moral obligation to do so.

A quasi-contractual obligation is imposed only in circumstances where the failure to impose such an obligation would result in one party receiving an "unjust enrichment"—a benefit which, on the grounds of fairness alone, he or she ought to pay for. Suppose, for example, that A plants and cultivates crops on land belonging to B, without B's knowledge. In such a case, B, upon learning the facts, is entitled to bring a *quantum meruit* action to recover from A the reasonable value of the benefit (the profit which A made as a result of the use of the land), for otherwise A would be unjustly enriched. *Quantum meruit* means, literally, "as much as is deserved." Three limitations on the quasi-contractual principle should be noted.

1. It cannot be invoked by one who has conferred a benefit unnecessarily or as a result of negligence or other misconduct. Thus, suppose that the X Company contracts to blacktop Y's driveway at 540 Fox Lane for $1,900, and the company's employees instead mistakenly blacktop the driveway of Y's neighbor, Z, at 546 Fox Lane, in Z's absence. In such a situation Z has no liability to the X Company, since his retention of the blacktop, while a benefit to him, is not an unjust benefit or an unjust retention under the circumstances.

2. Quasi-contracts are contracts in fiction only, since they are not based upon an agreement between the parties. Thus they are not "true" contracts. However, quasi-contractual remedies are often granted in contractual contexts. For example, suppose that A and B make a contract, but that it turns out to be unenforceable because the terms of the agreement are too vague, the contract was required to be in wrting but was not, or one party was induced by fraud or mistake to make the contract. In such a case, one party, thinking that there was a contract and that he had an obligation to fulfill, confers a valuable benefit on the other by providing services, money, or goods, the recipient is under a quasi-contractual obligation to compensate the other for the reasonable value of the benefit. These situations provide examples of a court's imposition of a quasi-contractual obligation on a recipient of something of value because the other conferred a benefit on the recipient as the result of an honestly mistaken belief that there was a legal obligation to do what was done.

3. A plaintiff generally will not be allowed quasi-contractual recovery from one person if he originally looked to another for compensation. Assume that C sells a house to B, and B hires A to plant shrubs around the house. A does so, but before he is paid, B dies and C generously allows B's widow to rescind the sales contract. If A sues C on quasi-contractual grounds, claiming that C was unjustly enriched by the planting of the shrubs, recovery will probably be denied because A originally looked to B for compensation and may still proceed against B's estate.

In the first of the following two cases, a state supreme court sets forth the general rules as to the nature and legal effects of implied contracts. The second presents a situation where a recovery of money by the plaintiffs quasi-contract doctrine is justified.

CARROLL V. LEE
Supreme Court of Arizona, 712 P.2d 923 (1986).

Judy Carroll with Paul Lee for fourteen years. Ultimately they settled in Ajo, Arizona where Paul operated an automobile repair shop. Although Judy used the name Lee during this time, the couple did not marry or ever seriously consider marriage. In 1982 they "went their separate ways."

Prior to the relationship little personal property was owned by either party, and neither owned any real property (i.e., land). During the course of the relationship the couple jointly acquired three parcels of land, several antique or restored automobiles, a mobile home, and various other items of personal property. The real property was titled to the couple in one of three ways. Title was held either (1) as joint tenants with the right of survivorship, (2) as husband and wife, or (3) as husband and wife as joint tenants with the right of survivorship. (The mobile home and some of the automobiles were titled to Paul T. Lee and Judy Lee, with other automobiles titled to Paul T. Lee alone.)

During the time the couple lived together Paul supplied virtually all of the money used to pay their living expenses, while Judy "kept the house" by cleaning, cooking, doing laundry, and working in the yard. After the couple *split up Judy filed this partition action claiming a one-half interest in the jointly titled property listed above. (The fact that the properties were titled to both parties did not, in and of itself, convey a one-half interest to Judy. This was because Paul proved that the money used in purchasing them came from the operation of the repair shop, which he owned personally. In such a case, the rule in Arizona—and in most states—is that "where property is paid for by one party and title is taken in the name of that party and a second party who are not husband and wife, it is presumed that the property was taken for the benefit of the one paying for the property." Thus it was necessary for Judy to prove an agreement existed between them that they be co-owners, in order to rebut this presumption.)*

The trial court ruled in favor of Judy, finding that an implied contract existed under which it was agreed that Paul and she would be co-owners of the property. (This finding was based on a 1984 case, Cook v. Cook, 691 P.2d 664, in which the Supreme Court of Arizona upheld an implied contract between an unmarried couple in circumstances similar to those presented by this case.) Paul appealed, and the court of appeals reversed the judgment (for reasons appearing below). Judy petitioned the Supreme Court of Arizona for review.

Gordon, Vice Chief Justice:

. . . In Cook v. Cook, supra, [this court approved] an agreement between unmarried cohabitants to pool income, acquire assets, and share in the accumulations. We compiled basic concepts of contract law:

"The sine qua non [essential element] of any contract is the exchange of promises. From this exchange flows the obligation of one party to another. Although it is most apparent that two parties have exchanged promises when their words express a spoken or written statement of promissory intention, mutual promises need not be express in order to create an enforceable contract. Restatement (Second) of Contracts 54. Indeed, a promise 'may be inferred wholly or partly from conduct,' id, and there is no distinction in the effect of the promise whether it is expressed in writing, or orally, or in acts, or partly in one of these ways and partly in others.' Id. §19. Thus, two parties may by their course of conduct express their agreement, though no words are ever spoken. From their conduct alone the trier of fact can determine the existence of an agreement. Id. §4."

The court of appeals [ruled that our decision in *Cook* was not applicable to the instant case because] "no evidence, in words or conduct, suggests mutual promises to contribute funds to a pool. . ." [In other words, the court of appeals refused to apply the *Cook* rule because in that case both parties were earning income, while in the instant case Paul was the sole income producer. The supreme court disagreed with the court of appeals decision, and continued:]

In Arizona we recognize implied contracts, and there is no difference in legal effect between an express contract and an implied contract. An implied contract is one not created or evidenced by explicit agreement, but inferred by the law as a matter of reason and justice from the acts and conduct of the parties and circumstances surrounding their transaction. Furthermore, in this state monetary consideration is not always required as consideration. . . Clearly a promise for a promise constitutes adequate consideration. . .

We believe Judy proved the property requested to be partitioned was acquired through joint common effort and for a common purpose. It is not necessary for her to prove that she produced by her labor a part of the very money used to purchase the property. The parties had an implied partnership or joint enterprise agreement at the very least, based on the facts and circumstances presented. Recovery for Judy should be allowed in accordance with these implied expectations. [The court here reviewed testimony by Paul in which he stated that it was his "preference" that Judy stay at home, cook meals, do washing and yard work, and that she did, in fact, perform these services. This testimony ended with the following:]

Q. Did you ever intend that she be an owner with you at that time, at the time that you were acquiring these properties, that she be an owner of those properties at that time?

A. You mean a co-owner? Q. Yes.

A. I suppose at the time I had it planned that way...

[Judy's relevant testimony is as follows:]

Q. All right. What type of an arrangement, if any, did you and Paul discuss about what he expected from your relationship in terms of contribution?

A. We didn't really discuss it. It just was there. He went to work. I stayed home and kept the house and, mostly because that's what he wanted me to do.

There was evidence from which the trial court could find the existence of an agreement for property to be acquired and owned jointly, as such was the method in which Paul took title in both the real and personal property... Since Judy was a co-owner of the property under a contract theory, she had the right [under Arizona law] to seek partition and divide the jointly owned assets...

We therefore vacate the opinion of the court of appeals and remand the case to the trial court for a redistribution of property not inconsistent with this opinion.

Comment

CommentThis case has been edited to emphasize the implied contract question. An additional question of equal importance was also presented: whether a finding that an implied contract existed even though the plaintiff's services were entirely of a "home-making" nature was contrary to public policy, on the ground that enforcement of such a contract might discourage marriage. The court of appeals, by refusing to apply the *Cook* rule, felt that the enforcement of such a contract would have that effect. The higher court, in a part of its decision omitted here, set forth reasons why enforcement of an implied contract in the circumstances presented here was not contrary to the public policy of the state.

DESKOVICK ET AL. V. PORZIO
Superior Court of New Jersey, 187 A.2d 610 (1963)

Plaintiffs in this action are brothers, Michael and PeterDeskovick, Jr. Their father, Peter Deskovick, Sr., was hospitalized in 1958 until his death in 1959. During this period Michael paid the hospital and medical bills as they came in, under the impression that the father was financially unable to do so. (This impression was based on statements made by the senior Deskovick in which he indicated an apparently genuine fear that he would not be able to pay the expenses of the hospitalization.) After the father's death it was discovered that, in fact, his estate was adequate to cover all of the payments made by Michael.

The plaintiffs thereupon brought this action against the executor of their father's estate, Porzio, to recover the amounts paid out.

In the trial court, plaintiffs proceeded on the theory that an implied contract existed between them and their father in the foregoing fact-pattern. (No mention of quasi-contractual liability was made.) While the evidence was somewhat conflicting as to whether Michael intended to be repaid out of his father's estate at the time he made the payments, the trial judge ruled as a matter of law that no such intention was present, and, for that reason, no implied contract had been formed. Accordingly, the court directed a verdict for the defendant. On appeal, plaintiffs contended for the first time that the estate should be liable on the theory of quasi-contract. (As a general rule, the parties cannot raise new issues on appeal. It does not appear why this was permitted in this case.)

Conford, Justice:

. . . If the question whether plaintiffs intended to be repaid at the time they advanced the monies in question were the sole material issue, we would conclude the trial court erred in taking the case out of the jury's hands [because of the conflicting evidence on that point]. However, . . . their intent to be repaid was immaterial in the factual situation presented, for the following reasons.

It is elementary that the assertion of a contract implied in fact [an "implied contract"] calls for the establishment of a consensual understanding as to compensation or reimbursement inferable from the circumstances under which one furnishes services or property and another accepts such advances. Here an essential for such a mutual understanding was absent *in that the decedent, on behalf of whom these advances were being made, was totally ignorant of the fact.* [Emphasis added.]

[After thus concluding that the proper reason why no implied contract was formed was

that the father could not give his implied consent to his sons' actions when he was not aware of them, the appellate court turned to the question of whether recovery might be allowed under the quasi-contract theory, as follows:]

It is elementary that one who pays the debt of another as a volunteer, having no obligation or liability to pay nor any interest menaced by the continued existence of the debt, cannot recover therefor from the beneficiary. Nor can such a volunteer claim the benefit of the law of subrogation. If plaintiffs were mere volunteers, therefore, they would not, within these principles, be entitled to be subrogated to the creditor position of the hospitals and physicians whose bills they paid.

Notwithstanding the foregoing principles, however, we perceive in the evidence adduced at the trial, particularly in the version of the facts reflected in the deposition of Michael, adduced by defendant, a quasi-contractual basis of recovery which in our judgment ought to be submitted to a jury at a retrial of the case in the interests of substantial justice.

It is said that a "quasi-contractual obligation is one that is created by the law for reasons of justice, without any expression of assent. . . 1 *Corbin on Contracts* (1950), §19, p. 38; 1 *Williston, Contracts* (1957), §3A, p. 13. This concept rests "on the equitable principle that a person shall not be allowed to enrich himself unjustly at the expense of another, and on the principle that whatsoever it is certain that a man ought to do, that the law supposes him to have promised to do." The Restatement of Restitution(1937) undertakes to formulate a number of rules growing out of recognized principles of quasicontract. Id., at p. 5 et seq. Section 26(p. 116), entitled "Mistake in Making Gifts," reads: "(1) A person is entitled to restitution from another to whom gratuitously and induced thereto by a mistake of fact he has given money if the mistake (a) was caused by fraud or material misrepresentation. . ." An innocent misrepresentation by the donee is within the rule. Id., comment, at p. 117. A "mistaken belief in the existence of facts which would create a moral obligation upon the donor to make a gift would ordinarily be a basic error" justifying restitution. Id., at p. 118...

We think the foregoing authorities would apply in favor of sons, who, during their father's mortal illness, believing him without means of meeting medical and hospital bills as a result of what he had previously told them, and wishing to spare him the discomfort of concern over such expenses at such a time, themselves assumed and paid the obligations. The leaving by the father of an estate far more than sufficient to have met the expenditures would, in such circumstances, and absent others affecting the basic equitable situation presented, properly invoke the concept of a *quasi contractual obligation* of reimbursement of the sons by the estate. [Emphasis added.] Such circumstances would take the payors out of the category of voluntary intermeddlers as to whom the policy of the law is to deny restitution or reimbursement...

Judgment reversed and remanded.

Valid, Voidable, and Void Contracts

A valid contract is one in which all of the required elements are present. As a result, it is enforceable against both parties.

In some circumstances, one of the parties to a contract has the legal right to withdraw from it at a later time without liability. Such contracts are referred to as **voidable contracts.** Contracts in which fraud is present fall within this category, because the law permits the one who has been defrauded to set aside the contract. Minors' contracts are another common example of voidable contracts. (Because of their importance, voidable contracts are considered separately in Chapter 15.)

Courts occasionally designate a third type of contract as being void. Such contracts are those which, so far as the law is concerned, never existed at all. Contracts are usually void for either of two reasons: (1) one of the parties is wholly incompetent at the time of contracting (such as a person who has been legally declared insane) or (2) the purpose of the contract is totally illegal (such as an agreement calling for the commission of a crime). The designation **void contract** is admittedly self-contradictory—an improper combination of terms. Nevertheless, this label is used by the courts to distinguish such contracts from those which are merely voidable; and in that sense it is a useful term.

Another type of contract is referred to as being "unenforceable." An **unenforceable contract** was valid at the time it was made but was subsequently rendered unenforceable because of the application of some special rule of law. For example, if a debtor goes through bankruptcy proceedings, the debtor's nonexempt assets are distributed among creditors and the debtor ultimately receives a discharge in bankruptcy. Under bankruptcy law, this discharge prevents a creditor who was not paid in full from bringing legal action to recover the balance of the debt; thus the contract that created the indebtedness was rendered unenforceable by virtue of the discharge. Other examples of unenforceable contracts include those sued upon after the statute of limitations has expired, oral contracts that should have been in writing under the statute of frauds (see Chapter 16), and those calling for performance of personal services by a person who died after the agreement was made.

Negotiated Contracts and Contracts of Adhesion

The terms of many contracts are agreed upon only after a certain amount of bargaining, or "dickering," takes place between the parties. After one party makes an offer to the other, for example, the latter— the offeree—may indicate that he or she will accept only if a specified change is made in the terms of the offer. Or the offeree may respond with a counteroffer, a different proposal from that of the original offer. Contracts that result from these kinds of exchanges are "negotiated contracts."

Contracts of adhesion, by contrast, are formed where one party—usually having greatly superior bargaining power than the other—prepares the terms of a proposed contract and presents it to the other party on a *take-it-or leave-it* basis. Examples of such "standard form" contracts are apartment leases, hospital admission forms, and sales contracts of new car dealers. While the terms of contracts of adhesion usually favor the parties who have prepared them, such contracts are generally enforceable unless the terms are so shockingly one-sided as to be, in the opinion of the courts, "unconscionable" in nature. (Unconscionable contracts are considered further in Chapter 14.)

HARTLAND COMPUTER LEASING CORP. v. THE INSURANCE MAN, INC.
Missouri Court of Appeals, 770 S.W.2d 525 (1989)

Appellant Hartland, the lessor, leases computers. Respondent The Insurance Man, Inc. (lessee), selected computer equipment sold by vendor Multitask. Hartland bought the equipment and in turn leased it to Insurance Man for $229.16 per month for 36 months. Respondents Saulsberry, the sole shareholder of Insurance Man, and Reese guaranteed that they would make the monthly payments if Insurance Man did not. The printed lease stated that the lessor Hartland made no warranties (promises that the computer equipment would perform properly) and that the lessee should look to the vendor for any needed repairs. Lease payments were due regardless of the condition of the machine.

After problems arose with the equipment, respondents stopped making payments. When contacted by Hartland's agent, Hogan, they stated that they did not want the machine and that Hogan should sell it and they would settle the difference.

Hartland sued under the terms of the lease for the payments not made. The trial judge, concluding that the contract was an adhesion contract, disregarded the disclaimers of liability and ruled against Hartland, which appealed.

Gaertner, Judge:
Apparently the trial court concluded that, because he found it to be a contract of

adhesion, he was free to disregard appellant's clear and unambiguous express disclaimer of all warranties. This conclusion, under the circumstances of this case, is a misapplication of the law requires reversal.

In Missouri, an adhesion contract, as opposed to a negotiated contract, has been described as a form contract created and imposed by a stronger party upon a weaker party on a "take this or nothing basis," the terms of which unexpectedly or unconscionably limit the obligations of the drafting party. Robin v. Blue Cross Hospital Service, Inc., 637 S.W.2d 695, 697 (Mo. ban 1982). Some writers view any pre-printed standardized form with filled-in blank spaces to be a contract of adhesion insofar as the pre-printed provisions are concerned. Thus, in *Corbin On Contracts*, §559A at 660 (Supp. 1989), it is said "the bulk of contracts signed in this country, if not every major Western nation, are adhesion contracts..." Such form contracts are a natural concomitant of our mass production-mass consumer society. Id. Therefore, a rule automatically invalidating adhesion contracts would be completely unworkable. *Corbin, supra* §559A at 660. Accordingly, courts do not view adhesion contracts as inherently sinister and automatically unenforceable. Rather, as with all contracts, the courts seek to enforce the reasonable expectations of the parties garnered not only from the words of a standardized form imposed by its proponent, but from the totality of the circumstances surrounding the transaction. *Robin, supra,* 637 S.W.2d at 697. Only such provisions of the standardized form which fail to comport with such reasonable expectations and which are unexpected and unconscionably unfair are held to be unenforceable. Corbin, supra, §559A at 660. Because standardized contracts address the mass of users, the test for "reasonable expectations" is objective, addressed to the average member of the public who accepts such a contract, not the subjective expectations of an individual adherent.

We look then to all the evidence surrounding this transaction to determine the objectively reasonable expectations of the parties and to the question of unconscionable unfairness imposed upon respondents under the terms of the form contract. We note first that Saulsberry was engaged in the operation of an insurance agency, presumably accustomed to form contracts. The contract at issue is clearly a lease of computer equipment for a term of years. It contains no option to purchase and requires that the equipment be returned to the lessor at the expiration of the term. Indeed, despite Mr. Saulsberry's references at trial to Mr. Hogan as the salesman, Saulsberry's own testimony was that he contacted Multitask, Inc., the vendor, and was referred to "Hartland Computer Leasing about leasing a computer system for my business." The lease provides and the evidence shows that, in fact, the equipment Saulsberry selected was purchased by Hartland from Multitask, and delivered to Saulsberry. The lease contains an assignment by Hartland of all warranties by the manufacturer and seller to Saulsberry. At the time of the first malfunction of the equipment Saulsberry exercised his rights under this assignment and took the equipment to the vendor where it was repaired under the warranty. His refusal to follow the same procedure at the time of the second malfunction, explainable perhaps as exasperation, does not indicate an objectively reasonable expectation that the lessor was obligated under any implied warranty of merchantability or of fitness.

This assignment of warranties did not leave Saulsberry without a remedy, thus militating against any finding of oppressive unconscionability. The retention of full warranty rights against the seller prevents the disclaimer of warranty obligations by the financing lessor from being unconscionable.

Much as we may wish to sympathize with the unrepresented respondents, we cannot escape the fact that it was the equipment, not the terms of the contract, which failed to live up to respondents' expectations. They pos-sessed the right to seek full and complete relief under the express and implied warranties made by the vendor. The fact is they sought relief from the wrong party.

[Reversed.]

Formal and Informal Contracts

Some specialized types of contracts are referred to as **formal contracts.** The term usually is used to refer to sealed contracts—ones that the parties have formalized either by making a physical impression on the paper on which the agreement was written or, in some instances, simply by having the word seal or the letters L. S. appear at the end of the document. The letters stand for *Locus Sigilli,* meaning "the place for the seal."

The great majority of ordinary business contracts are not sealed and are therefore **informal contracts** (or "simple contracts"). Thus any unsealed contract can be referred to as "simple," even though it may be several pages long and contain complex provisions.

Executory and Executed Contracts

Once a contract is formed, it is an **executory contract** until both parties have fully performed their obligations. When performance has taken place, the contract is said to be an **executed contract.** If one party has fully performed his or her part of the bargain but the other party has not, the contract is executed as to the former and executory as to the latter.

Contract Law and Sales Law—A Special Relationship

Contracts for the sale of goods—tangible articles of personal property such as automobiles, machine tools, grain, and items of clothing—are governed by both the general rules of contract law and provisions in Article 2 of the Uniform Commercial Code (UCC). Article 2 of the UCC covers sale of goods contracts in all states except Louisiana.

So-called "sales law" is simply a branch of contract law. The general rules of contract law apply unless there is a provision in Article 2 of the UCC that applies a different rule. On many questions, such as what constitutes an offer, the UCC is silent, and general rules of contract law apply. Also, some provisions of the UCC simply restate the general rules. However, for sale of goods contracts, Article 2 of the UCC does sometimes prescribe a different rule that the general common law rules would. In these chapters on contract law, we focus mainly on the general common law rules that apply to all types of contracts, but we also discuss special rules applying to sale of goods contracts when they are meaningfully different than the general rules.

CHAPTER **12**

THE AGREEMENT

THE FIRST AND FOREMOST element of any contract is an agreement—a reasonably definite understanding between two or more persons. It is for this reason that the liability or obligation resulting from the making of a contract (as distinguished from that imposed by the law of torts or the criminal law) is sometimes described as being "consensual" in nature. The usual view taken by the law today is that if two or more persons, expressly or by implication, have reached a reasonably clear agreement as to what each party is to do, then that agreement shall be enforceable by the courts (assuming, of course, that the additional elements of consideration and legality are also present). This means that if either party refuses to perform his or her part of the agreement without a lawful excuse, the other party is entitled to recover damages in a breach of contract action. On the other hand, if it is found that a legally sufficient agreement has not been formed, neither party has contractual liability to the other.

Because the word agreement encompasses a broad spectrum of situations where some kind of understanding has been reached (ranging from the extremely concise to the hopelessly vague), the courts are faced with the problem of deciding just what kinds of agreements are sufficiently definite to warrant judicial relief if they are breached. The best approach to this problem is to break the agreement down into two parts—the offer and the acceptance. The inquiries then become whether either party made an offer to the other, and, if so, whether the offer was followed by an acceptance. Before considering the legal definitions of these terms, we will briefly mention the rules used by the courts to ascertain the intentions of the parties—with emphasis upon the applicability of these rules to the offer and acceptance.

Intention of the Parties

In cases where the parties disagree as to whether their communications constituted an offer and an acceptance, the court will frequently emphasize the principle that the intention of the parties is controlling. If the court finds that their intentions were the same (that there was a "meeting of minds," as it is sometimes phrased), then there is a contract.

One caution about this principle, however, should be noted. When the courts view the parties' communications for the purpose of determining whether their intentions were one and the same, it is the parties' manifested (or apparent) intentions that control, rather than their actual intentions. A person's manifested or apparent intent is frequently referred to by the courts as "objective" intent, while actual or secret intent is called "subjective" intent. Thus the test used by the courts that is described here is referred to as the "objective test." For example, if X writes a letter to Y containing a proposal which meets the legal requirements of an offer, and if Y promptly accepts the offer in a return letter, there is a contract—even if X later claims to have had some mental reservations about the proposal, or says that he really did not intend his letter to be an offer. Thus, when it is said that there must be a meeting of minds to have a contract, this usually means that there must only be a legal, or apparent, meeting of minds.

There are two compelling reasons for the frequent use of this objective view:

1. It is virtually impossible for a court to determine what a person's actual intent was at a specific moment.
2. It would be unfair to allow someone to indicate a particular intention to another person and then to come into court and claim that he or she did not mean what was apparently meant.

Requirements of the Offer

Inherent in the many definitions of the word offer is the idea that it is a proposal made by one person, called the offeror, to another, the offeree, indicating what the offeror will give in return for a specified promise or act on the part of the offeree. That is, the offeror must manifest a definite, present willingness to enter into a contractual relationship with the other party. Sometimes the manifestation is referred to as a "conditional statement" of what the offeror will do for the offeree. Used in this manner, the term statement is broad enough to include both words and conduct by which the offeror indicates a willingness to contract. Thus, if a person in a drugstore shows a magazine to the cashier and deposits $2.50 (the stated price) on the counter, it is perfectly clear that he or she has made an offer to purchase the item without speaking a word. Similarly, when a company delivers an unordered article of merchandise under circumstances which indicate to the recipient that a charge will be made for the article if it is accepted, the company's act constitutes an offer to sell the product at the stated price. Of course, the recipient of such unsolicited merchandise does not incur a duty to pay for it unless he or she actually uses it or otherwise indicates acceptance of the sender's offer. (If the unsolicited goods are sent by *mail*, ordinarily no duty to pay arises even if the recipient uses the goods. Sec. 3009 of Title 39 of the U.S. Code, the Postal Reorganization Act of 1970, provides in part that, except for "merchandise mailed by a charitable organization soliciting contributions," the mailing of any unsolicited merchandise "may be treated as a gift by the recipient, who shall have the right to retain, use, discard, or dispose of it in any manner he sees fit without any obligations whatsoever to the sender.")

The courts have never tried to specify the exact language or the particular kinds of conduct that must exist in order for one person to make an offer to another, for any attempt to do so would be quite unrealistic in the "real world." What the courts have done, instead, is to formulate several general requirements that must be met in order for a particular communication (or act) to achieve the legal status of an offer. These requirements are (1) a manifestation of an intent to contract; (2) a reasonably definite indication of what the offeror and the offeree are to do; and (3) a communication of the proposal to the intended offeree.

The Intent to Contract

Preliminary Negotiations

Some language is so tentative or exploratory in nature that it should be apparent that an immediate contract is not contemplated. Such communications do not constitute offers;

they are designated preliminary negotiations, or "dickering." For example, the statement "I'd like to get $4,000 for this car" would normally fall into this category, as would a letter indicating "I will not sell my home for less than $56,000." If the addressee in either of these instances were to reply, "I accept your offer," a contract would not result since no offer was made in either case. Along similar lines, it is usually held that requests for information—called inquiries—do not manifest a genuine intent to contract, and consequently such questions do not constitute offers in most circumstances. Thus, if A writes B, "Would you rent your summer home for the month of June for $900?" and B replies, "Yes, I accept your offer," there is no contract. (The most that can be said in this situation is that B has now made an offer to A, and it will ripen into a contract only if A subsequently accepts it.)

Difficult questions sometimes arise when there are multiple offerees. Suppose that A writes to B: "I hereby offer to sell my farm to you for $120,000." The letter informs B that A is simultaneously making the same offer to several other potential purchasers. B should know that although the language appears to be an offer, this letter is merely preliminary negotiation because A does not intend to be bound to sell the farm to several different persons. On the other hand, if the letter does not disclose that the offer is being made to others, B can make an effective acceptance. (If another offeree, not knowing of the offer to B, also effectively accepts, A faces certain liability in a breach of contract action.)

The decision in the well-known case below helps show how the courts try to draw the lines between preliminary negotiations and offers in several common situations.

RICHARDS v. FLOWERS ET AL.
District Court of Appeal, California, 14 Cal. Reptr. 228 (1961)

Mrs. Richards, plaintiff, wrote defendant Flowers on January 15, 1959, as follows: "We would be interested in buying your lot on Gravatt Drive in Oakland, California, if we can deal with you directly and not run through a realtor. If you are interested, please advise us by return mail the cash price you would expect to receive."

On January 19, 1959, Flowers replied: "Thank you for your inquiry regarding my lot on Gravatt Drive. As long as your offer would be in cash I see no reason why we could not deal directly on this matter Considering what I paid for the lot, and the taxes which I have paid I expect to receive $4,500 for this property. Please let me know what you decide."

On January 25, 1959, Mrs. Richards sent the following telegram to Flowers: "Have agreed to buy your lot on your terms will handle transactions through local title company who will contact you would greatly appreciate your sending us a copy of the contour map you referred to in your letter as we are desirous of building at once...."

On February 5, 1959, Flowers entered into an agreement to sell the property to a third party, Mr. and Mrs. Sutton. Mrs. Richards, after learning of the Sutton transaction, called *upon defendant to deliver his deed to her, claiming the above correspondence constituted a contract between him and her. Flowers refused to do so, denying that his letter of January 19 constituted an offer to sell, whereupon Mr. and Mrs. Richards brought suit, asking for specific performance of the alleged contract. (The Suttons intervened in this action to protect their interest by supporting Flowers' contention that a contract was not formed between him and plaintiffs.)*

The trial court ruled that defendant's letter of January 19 did constitute an offer to sell, but it further ruled that plaintiff's telegram of January 25 was not a valid acceptance under a particular section of the California Code known as the "statute of frauds" (the provisions of which are not necessary to our consideration of this case). Accordingly the court entered judgment for the defendant. The Richardses appealed.

Shoemaker, Justice:

. . . Under the factual situation in the instant case, the interpretation of the series of communications between the parties is a matter of law and an appellate court is not bound by the trial court's determination. Respondent Flowers argues that the letter of January 19th merely invited an offer from appellants for the purchase of the property and that under no reasonable interpretation can this letter be construed as an offer. We agree with the respondent. Careful consideration of the letter does not convince us that the language therein used can reasonably be interpreted as a definite offer to sell the property to appellants. As pointed out in *Restatement of the Law, Contracts*, Section 25, comment a: "It is often difficult to draw an exact line between offers and negotiations preliminary thereto. It is common for one who wishes to make a bargain to try to induce the other party to the intended transaction to make the definite offer, he himself suggesting with more or less definiteness the

nature of the contract he is willing to enter into. . . ." Under this approach our letter seems rather clearly to fall within the category of mere preliminary negotiations. Particularly is this true in view of the fact that the letter was written directly in response to appellants' letter inquiring if they could deal directly with respondent and requesting him to suggest a sum at which he might be willing to sell. From the record, we do not accept the argument that respondent Flowers made a binding offer to sell the property merely because he chose to answer certain inquiries by the appellants. Further, the letter appears to us inconsistent with any intent on his part to make an offer to sell. In response to appellants' question, respondent stated that he would be willing to deal directly with them rather than through a realtor as long as their "offer would be in cash." We take this language to indicate that respondent anticipated a future offer from appellants but was making no offer himself.

Appellants refer to the phrase that he would "expect to receive" $4,500 and contend this constitutes an offer to sell to them at this price. However, respondent was only expressing an indication of the lowest price which he was presently willing to consider. Particularly is this true inasmuch as respondent wrote only in response to an inquiry in which this wording was used. We conclude that respondent by his communication confined himself to answering the inquiries raised by appellants, but did not extend himself further and did not make an express offer to sell the property. We have before us a case involving a mere quotation of price and not an offer to sell at that price.

The cause, therefore, comes within the rule announced in such authorities as Nebraska Seed Co. v. Harsh, 1915, 152 N.W. 310, wherein the seller had written the buyer, enclosing a sample of millet seed and saying, "I want $2.25 per cwt. for this seed f.o.b. Lowell." The buyer telegraphed his acceptance. The court, in reversing a judgment for plaintiff buyer, stated: "In our opinion the letter of defendant cannot be fairly construed into an offer to sell to the plaintiff. After describing the seed, the writer says, 'I want $2.25 per cwt. for this seed f.o.b. Lowell.' He does not say, I offer to sell to you.' The language used is general,... and is not an offer by which he may be bound, if accepted, by any or all of the persons addressed, and Owen v. Tunison,1932, 158 A. 926, wherein the buyer had written the seller inquiring whether he would be willing to sell certain store property for 6,000. The seller replied: "Because of improvements which have been added and an expenditure of several thousand dollars it would not be possible for me to sell it unless was to receive $16,00.00 cash...." The court, in holding that the seller's reply did not constitute an offer, stated: "Defendants letter... may have been written with the intent to open negotiations that might lead to a sale. It was not a proposal to sell." It would thus seem clear that respondent's quotation of the price which he would "expect to receive" cannot be viewed as an offer capable of acceptance

Since there was never an offer, hence never a contract between respondent Flowers and appellants, the judgment must be affirmed, and it becomes unnecessary to determine whether an appellant's purported acceptance complied with the statute of frauds or whether appellants failed to qualify for specific performance in any other regard.

Judgment affirmed.

Other Evidence on the Question of Intent

Up to this point, we have seen that the courts lay great stress on the actual language of a particular communication in determining whether it evidences an intent to contract. In addition, courts will take into account relevant evidence from several other sources if it sheds light on what reasonable people in the circumstances probably would have intended, such as: (1) Evidence of a well-established custom in the industry in which the parties are members, assuming that the parties have not stated otherwise in this transaction; (2) Evidence of a custom that these parties may have established between themselves in a series of previous similar transactions, assuming that the parties have not stated otherwise in this transaction; (3) Evidence from the conduct of the parties both before and after the alleged agreement was made. Regarding evidence of the parties' conduct before the alleged agreement was made, courts almost always consider any relevant evidence about the factual background—the surrounding circumstances in which the communication was made. Examination of the background sometimes makes it quite clear that an intent to contract was not present, even though the language taken by itself meets the requirements of an offer, as where a statement is apparently made in jest, excitement, or anger. In Higgins v. Lessig, 49 Ill.App. 459 (1893) , for example, a man who learned that his $15 harness had been stolen became so angry that he launched into a tirade in which he stated that he would "give $100 to any man who will find out who the thief is." The court held that this was not an enforceable offer, but merely the "extravagant exclamation of an excited man."

Higgins is consistent with the "objective theory" of contracts mentioned above, because a reasonable person hearing the owner's statement would have realized that once he calmed down he would not seriously wish to pay $100 for the return of a $15 harness. However, under this view parties are not required to read each others' minds. In Lucy v. Zehmer, 84 S.E.2d 516 (Va. 1954), for example, a man who claimed that he was only jesting when he offered to sell his farm to his neighbors was held to the bargain because the buyers reasonably believed that he was serious. Although the parties were drinking, they twice reduced their agreement to writing and its terms were reasonable.

This does not mean, however, that parties' intentions are always gauged totally objectively. Suppose, for example, that A promises to pay B $1,000,000 for his ranch. A stranger overhearing the promise might well believe that it was a serious offer because it outwardly appeared to be such. However, if B knows that A is a practical joker and nearly flat broke then B also knows that the statement is not a serious offer. If B attempted to accept the offer, no contract would result because of B's subjective knowledge. A's apparently serious offer does not bind him if B knows or should know that A is jesting.

LEONARD V. PEPSICO, INC.
U.S. District Court, Southern District of New York (1999)

Plaintiff Leonard saw a television commercial advertising a promotion that defendant PepsiCo was sponsoring for its products. The ad stated that one could accumulate "points" by buying Pepsi products and exchange the points for merchandise with the Pepsi logo on it. At the end of the ad, a high school student was shown landing a Harrier Jet at a school with a subtitle indicating that the cost of the jet was 7 million points. Additional terms of the promotion indicated that points could be purchased for ten cents each. Plaintiff sought investors and accumulated $700,000, enough to purchase 7 million points. He sent a check to defendant and demanded his jet. Defendant refused. Plaintiff filed this suit for breach of contract. Defendant moved for summary judgment. The following ruling was later affirmed by the Court of Appeals.

Wood, District Judge:

Plaintiff's understanding of the commercial as an offer must be rejected because the court finds that no objective person could reasonably have concluded that the commercial actually offered consumers a Harrier Jet. In evaluating the commercial, the Court must not consider defendant's subjective intent in making the commercial, or plaintiff's subjective view of what the commercial offered, but what an objective, reasonable person would have understood the commercial to convey. If it is clear that an offer was not serious, then no offer has been made.

Plaintiff's insistence that the commercial appears to be a serious offer requires the Court to explain why the commercial is funny. Explaining why a joke is funny is a daunting task; as the essayist E.B. White has remarked, "Humor can be dissected, as a frog can, but the thing dies in the process." The commercial is the embodiment of what defendant appropriately characterizes as "zany humor."

First, the commercial suggests, as commercials often do, that use of the advertised product will transform what, for most youths, can be a fairly routine and ordinary experience.

The military tattoo and stirring martial music, as well as the use of subtitles in a Courier font that scroll terse messages across the screen, such as "MONDAY 7:58 AM," evoke military and espionage thrillers. The implication of the commercial is that Pepsi Stuff merchandise will inject drama and moment into hitherto unexceptional lives. The commercial in this case thus makes the exaggerated claims similar to those of many television advertisements: that by consuming the featured clothing, car, beer, or potato chips, one will become attractive, stylish, desirable, and admired by all. A reasonable viewer would understand such advertisements as mere puffery, not as statements of fact, and refrain from interpreting the promises of the commercial as literally true.

Second, the callow youth featured in the commercial is a highly improbable pilot, one who could barely be trusted with the key to his parents' car, much less the prize aircraft of the United States Marine Corp. Rather than checking the fuel gauges on his aircraft, the teenager spends precious preflight minutes preening.

Third, the notion of traveling to school is an exaggerated adolescent fantasy. In this commercial, the fantasy is underscored by how the teenager's schoolmates gape in admiration, ignoring their physics lesson. The force of the wind generated by the Harrier Jet blows off one teacher's clothes, literally defrocking an authority figure.

Fourth, in light of the Harrier Jet's well-documented function in attacking and destroying surface and air targets, armed reconnaissance and air interdiction, and offensive and defensive antiaircraft warfare, depiction of such a jet as a way to get to school in the morning is not serious even if, as plaintiff contends, the jet is capable of being acquired "in a form that eliminates its potential for military use."

Fifth, the cost of a Harrier Jet is roughly $23 million, a fact of which plaintiff was aware when he set out to gather the amount he believed necessary to accept the alleged offer. Even if an objective, reasonable person were not aware of this fact, he would conclude that purchasing a fighter jet plane for $700,000 is a deal too good to be true.

Plaintiff argues that a reasonable, objective person would have understood the commercial to make a serious offer of a Harrier Jet because there was "absolutely no distinction in the manner in which the items in the commercial [caps, t-shirts, jackets, Harrier Jet] were presented. Plaintiff also relies upon a press release highlighting the promotional campaign issued by defendant, in which "no mention is made by [defendant] of humor, or anything of the sort." These arguments suggest merely that the humor of the promotional campaign was tongue in cheek. Humor is not limited to what Justice Cardozo called "the rough and boisterous joke [that] evokes its own guffaws." Murphy v. SteeplechaseAmusement Co., 166 N.E. 173 (1929). In light of the obvious absurdity of the commercial, the Court rejects plaintiff's argument that the commercial was not clearly in jest.

Defendant's motion for summary judgment is granted.

Advertisements

Advertisements are usually considered to be preliminary negotiations, rather than offers to sell. The general rule is that a store advertisement that merely names the company, describes the article to be sold, and gives the price of the article "constitutes nothing more than an invitation to patronize the store." And this is usually true even if the terms "offer" or "special offer" appear in the advertisement.

The historic rationale for this rule is based (1) on the fact that most advertisements are silent on other material matters, such as the available quantity and credit terms, (2) on the traditional principle that sellers of goods have the right to choose the parties with whom they deal and do not intend to commit themselves to sell to the potentially unlimited numbers of persons who might read advertisements, and (3) on the fact that a merchandiser cannot exactly predict the volume of responses from customers. The rule also applies to catalogs, price quotations, and even articles displayed on a shelf with a price tag; these also are generally treated as not being offers to sell the merchandise.

Thus, when a customer goes to the advertiser's store and tenders the advertised price, a contract is normally not formed. Rather, the customer is making an offer to purchase, which the store can accept or reject.

Exceptions can arise in a few circumstances, however, in which advertisements can be offers. An advertisement may be an offer in several related types of situations in which the quantity is clearly limited, or the number of possible persons who can accept is clearly limited, and other language is used indicating that the seller is making a promise to sell to the first ones who respond in the way called for in the advertisement. For example, many courts probably would treat the following advertisement as being an offer to sell: "Three 2006 Mazda Miata convertibles with R305 trim package at $22,395.00 each, on sale Saturday only while they last!" Thus, the first three buyers who show up the following Saturday ready, willing, and able to pay the advertised price are accepting the offer and creating an enforceable contract. A similar example, from Lefkowitz v. Great Minneapolis Surplus Store, 86 N.W.2d 689 (Minnesota 1957), involved an advertisement stating: "1 Black Lapin Stole, Beautiful, Worth $139.50 …$1.00, Saturday 8 a.m., First-Come, First-Served." The court found that this was a definite offer, and when the first customer showed up after the store opened at 8 a.m. ready and able to buy the fur stole, there was an acceptance creating a contract. Yet another example would be: "Any person entering our store on Christmas Day wearing a bathing suit can buy an XYZ CD Player for only $220." Likewise, an ad (or instructions on a product package) that instructs customers to send in a "proof-of-purchase" from a product package, in return for which the seller will provide a rebate or something else to the customer, will be an offer. An advertisement or product package providing a coupon that a customer is instructed to send or bring, with some benefit being promised in return, will typically be an offer.

In a similar vein, advertisements of rewards are often treated by the courts as being offers. For example, an advertised reward for the return of a missing dog would be an enforceable offer if it is clear and definite, since realistically there can be only one person accepting (or, say, two people who act together and share the reward), and because it calls for specific action that will constitute acceptance—returning the dog. Likewise, advertisements promising rewards for information leading to the apprehension of criminals are usually held to constitute offers. Even though several people might be in a position to accept by providing the information, the normally be very small, and reward offers call for specific action by the responder. Obviously, the evidence must show that the person returning the dog, providing the information about the criminal, and so on, must have known of the offer before taking the action. If there was no such knowledge, the person returning the dog or providing the information was not an offeree of the offer. One can see that advertisements found by the courts to constitute offers are either offers for a unilateral contract or otherwise make it clear that something is being definitely promised in return for specific conduct on the part of the person or persons responding.

Consumer Protection

The general rule on advertising creates the potential for abuse by unscrupulous merchants who might place advertisements, never intending to live up to their terms. Virtually all states have enacted consumer protection statutes which generally impose civil and/or criminal liability upon businesspersons who unfairly refuse to sell goods or services in conformity with the terms of their advertisements. For example, statutes in many states list deceptive trade practices, among which is the "advertising of goods or services with the intent not to sell them as advertised." Other states have special "bait and switch" advertising statutes which typically impose liability upon advertisers who lure readers into the store by offering fabulous deals on products, but then either have an insufficient quantity for an expected reasonable demand or focus all their sales efforts at convincing the shoppers to buy more expensive items that were not advertised.

Auctions

If conducted openly and fairly, auctions are an efficient way of determining a reasonable price in transactions between willing sellers and buyers. The UCC auction provision, Sec. 2-328, is generally consistent with common-law auction rules. In the typical with reserve auction, the act of putting a particular item up for auction indicates only a willingness to consider offers to purchase. A bidder's ensuing bid is treated as an offer which may be accepted when the auctioneer (the seller's agent) announces "sold" either verbally or through the fall of the hammer or some other customary means. Because no contract is formed until the hammer falls, the bidders are free to withdraw their bids prior to that event and, more importantly, the seller is free to withdraw the item from sale if no bids are as high as the seller desires.

   Auctions are presumed to be with reserve unless they are explicitly represented as being without reserve. The act of putting an article up for sale in a without reserve auction is treated as a definite offer. The first bid creates a contract binding on the seller, unless a higher bid is made. The seller can no longer withdraw the item (though, surprisingly, bidders may withdraw their bids until the hammer falls). The highest bidder has a contract for sale that he can enforce.

Reasonable Definiteness

The requirement that the offer be reasonably definite is largely a practical one. The terms of an agreement have to be definite enough that a court can determine whether both parties lived up to their promises, in the event that a question of breach of contract arises. If the offer is too indefinite, the court is unable to do this.

As a general rule, then, a communication must cover all major matters affecting the proposed transaction in order to constitute an offer. If one or more of these is missing, the communication is merely a preliminary negotiation. Thus if S makes a written proposal to sell his farm Blackacre to B upon specified terms and conditions, "at a mutually agreeable price," and if B promptly sends an acceptance, there is no contract for the reason that S's proposal was not an offer. In a similar case, a company told an injured employee that it would "take care of him" and offer him "light work" when his doctor certified that he was capable of doing such a job. The company later refused to rehire him, and he sued to recover damages, alleging that this was a breach of contract. In ruling against the employee, the court said that since no specific position was mentioned, and there was no discussion of rates of pay or hours of employment, it had no way of determining the amount of the employee's loss. The statement of the company, in other words, was held to be too indefinite to constitute an offer. Laseter v. Pet Dairy Products Company, 246 F.2d 747 (1957) . Similarly, if X writes Y, "I will sell you my car for $1,000, credit terms to be arranged," and Y replies, "I accept," there is no contract. X's statement does not constitute an offer, since there is no way of knowing what credit terms would be acceptable to her or whether any credit terms will ever be agreed on.

Despite the foregoing, the requirement of "reasonable definiteness" is, as the term itself indicates, relative rather than absolute. Thus it is not necessary that every detail be set forth in a contract, so long as there is agreement on major points. Where there is such agreement, missing terms about routine or mechanical matters may be supplied by the courts to "save" the contract; they may say in regard to such matters that there was implied agreement. For example, if X agrees to do certain clean-up work around a construction site for Y for $1,000, neither party can successfully contend that the agreement was too vague simply because no time of performance was specified. In this situation, it is implied that X will have a reasonable time in which to perform.

It also is important to note that, when courts believe that the parties intended to commit themselves to a contract, but some terms are either missing or ambiguous, they will examine other relevant evidence of what reasonable people probably would have intended the particular terms to be. Because this is another question of intent, courts will consider relevant evidence of the same kinds mentioned earlier in connection with determining the initial question of whether there was any intent to make a contractual commitment in the first place. Courts will not engage in guess-work, however, but must have actual evidence from which reasonable evidence may be drawn.

The case below presents a typical "definiteness" problem in a modern-day setting.

HINC V. LIME-O-SOL C.
382 F.2d 716 (7th Cir. 2004)

Through his experience in the paint industry, Hinc became aware of the recurring problems of surfactant leaching and tannin bleeding, which cause brown surface stains on painted exteriors. Often, because of this discoloration, paint manufacturers and insurance companies were forced to repaint entire commercial complexes at their own expense. Hinc sought to find a cost-effective remedy by inventing a product that would remove the stains, eliminating the need to repaint. Hinc mixed different ingredients and tested them on stains, eventually finding one that worked. Hinc's product, which he named Less Work Painted Surface Stain Remover ("Stain Remover"), combined a certain proportion of a secret ingredient with a shower-cleaning product manufactured by LOS ("Shower Cleaner").

Hinc tested a handmixed batch of his Stain Remover and it worked extremely well. Lacking knowledge of the Shower Cleaner formula but understanding the commercial potential of Stain Remover, Hinc contacted LOS about his invention in early 1999. In August of 1999, Hinc and LOS signed a contract providing that while Hinc would retain ownership of the secret ingredient, he would divulge it to LOS. LOS would produce and distribute Stain Remover while keeping Hincs secret ingredient confidential. Hinc would receive $10 per galon sold. Without discussion between the parties as to its meaning, the contract contained a term obligating both parties to use their "best efforts" to market the product "in a manner that seems appropriate."

After he signed the contract, Hinc supplied LOS with the secret ingredient and secured orders for Stain Remover with Sherwin-Williams. LOS filled these orders with its Shower Cleaner, not the combined product containing Hinc's secret ingredient. LOS claims production difficulties prohibited filling the orders with Stain Remover, and, in order to deliver the orders on time, Hinc agreed to allow LOS to ship Shower Cleaner instead of Stain Remover. Hinc denies he ever agreed to this. Ultimately, LOS never produced, marketed, or sold Stain Remover during the duration of the contract.

When, by summer 2001 LOS had not sold any of Hinc's product or divulged its portion of the Stain Remover formula, Hinc sued for breach of contract. The district court dismissed the suit, determining that the "best efforts" provision contained in the contract was vague and unenforceable. Hinc appealed.

Kanne, Circuit Judge:

Where possible, Indiana courts will construe contracts as being valid, rather than void. In applying Indiana contract law, the primary purpose is to ascertain and give effect to the intentions of the parties. This requires courts to "read the agreement in a manner which harmonize its provisions as a whole and to give effect to the parties' expressed intent." Kelly v. Smith, 611 N.E.2d 118 (Ind. 1993) . "In most cases, the intent of the parties to a contract is to be determined by the 'four corners' of the contract[,]" Dick Corp. v. Geiger, 783 N.E.2d

368 (Ind. App. 2003), "giving the words contained therein their plain, usual, and ordinary meaning," Samar, Inc. v. Hofferth, 726 N.E.2d 1286 (Ind. App. 2000). "When a court finds a contract to be clear in its terms and the intentions of the parties apparent, the court will require the parties to perform consistently with the bargain they made." First Fed. Sav. Bank of Ind.v. Key Markets, Inc., 559 N.E.2d 600 (Ind. 1990). An ambiguous contract is construed against the drafting party. MPACT Constr. Group LLC v. Superior Concrete Constructors, Inc., 802 N.E.2d 901 (Ind. 2004).

Keeping in mind the general principles and rules of construction of Indiana contract law outlined above, we now turn to the contract in this case. The clause at issue here states: "This is a 'best efforts' agreement on the part of Lime-O-Sol and Thomas P. Hinc to market such product in a manner that seems appropriate." The phrase, "in a manner that seems appropriate," is obviously indefinite and could mean different things to different people, but we do not believe that the clause as a whole is so vague as to be unenforceable as a matter of law. LOS, which drafted this provision of the contract, agreed to put forth its "best efforts" to market Stain Remover and required the same of Hinc. "Best efforts," as commonly understood, means, at the very least, some effort. It certainly does not mean zero effort— the construction LOS urges here to escape any obligation under its contract. Cf. E. Allen-Farnsworth, *On Trying to Keep One's Promises: The Duty of Best Efforts in Contract Law,* 46 UNIV. PITT. L. REV. 1, 8 (1984) (noting that fifty years ago it was generally accepted that a duty defined only in terms of best efforts was too indefinite to be enforced, but that such a view is no longer widely held today). We believe that Indiana's highest court would take the approach that "best efforts" provisions can be contractually enforced. REVERSED.

Definiteness of the Agreement: Sales Law

Among the most significant modifications of the common law achieved by the UCC is a general relaxation of the degree of definiteness required in the agreement. Several provisions indicate that the drafters of the UCC wanted to make the formation of binding contracts somewhat easier than under common law. They recognized that businesspersons frequently intend to enter into enforceable agreements in situations where it is impracticable to make those agreements as definite as required by common law. A prime example of this approach is found in Sec. 2-204(3). This section broadly states that a sales contract is enforceable even if one or more terms are left open, so long as (1) the court feels that the parties intended to make a binding contract and (2) the agreement and the surrounding circumstances give the court a reasonably certain basis for granting an appropriate remedy (such as money damages). Of course, there is a line beyond which the courts will not go. For instance, the larger the number of undecided terms, the less likely it is that a court will find that the parties intended to be legally bound. For this reason, a seller and buyer who wish to make an agreement with one or more terms left for future determination would do well to state specifically whether they intend to be bound in the meantime.

In addition to Sec. 2-204, a number of other sections of the UCC deal with specific omissions or ambiguities often occurring in sales contracts. We will examine the most important of these "gap-fillers" here.

Open Price Provisions

In some circumstances a seller of goods may be primarily concerned with being assured of a market for the goods he or she is producing. Or perhaps a buyer wants a guaranteed supply of certain needed products. In either case price may be of only secondary importance. Thus buyer and seller might draw up a contract for the sale and purchase of goods at a later date, with the contract providing that the price shall be agreed upon later. Or the contract may say nothing about price at all. (open price terms may be especially desirable in a market where the going price is subject to daily or weekly fluctuation.)

At common law many courts refused to enforce either type of agreement because of its indefiniteness. Under Sec. 2-305 of the UCC, however, agreements of this nature are now enforceable if the court feels that the parties did intend to be bound by them. (Of course, if the evidence indicates that the agreement was merely tentative and the parties intended to be legally bound only if and when the price was ultimately set, there is no contract until that condition is met. The UCC cannot supply missing contractual intent.)

Whenever a court is called upon to enforce a contract in which the price (for one reason or another) was never actually set, and where it finds that the parties intended to be bound by the open price agreement, the court is faced with the task of providing a price term. Sec. 2-305 establishes a number of principles to guide the court in such a situation.

1. If the parties had expressly left the price for later agreement and then failed to agree, the price set by the court should be a "reasonable price at the time for delivery."

2. If the agreement had said nothing at all about price, and the price was never settled on, the method of determining it should depend on the circumstances. If the price had failed to be set through no fault of either party, the court should fix a "reasonable price at the time for delivery," as in item 1. But if the failure to set a price was caused by the fault of either party, the party not at fault can either treat the contract as cancelled or fix a "reasonable price" himself or herself. This price is binding and the court will uphold it, so long as it is found to be actually reasonable.

3. If the agreement had provided that the price was to be subsequently fixed according to a definite standard set or recorded by a third party, the rules for determining the unresolved price are exactly as they were in item 2. For example, the parties might have agreed that the contract price was to be the market price reported in a certain trade journal on a given date, but no such price was reported in the journal on that date. Or they might have agreed that an impartial third person was to set the price at a future date, but the third party later failed to do so. In either case, the price will be a "reasonable price at the time for delivery." This reasonable price will be set by the

court if neither party was at fault; if one party caused the agreed upon method to fail, the other party may set a reasonable price.

4. If the parties had agreed that one of them was to set the price at a later time, the deciding party is obligated to set the price in good faith. Although good faith is defined differently for merchants and nonmerchants, the most compelling evidence of good or bad faith generally is whether the price fixed was a reasonable market price at that time. Good faith is generally defined in Sec. 1- 201(19) of the UCC as "honesty in fact." In the case of a merchant, it is defined in Sec. 2-103(1)(b) as "honesty in fact and the observance of reasonable commercial standards of fair dealing in the trade." Generally, the merchant definition will apply, since open price terms are rare among nonmerchants.If the party responsible for setting the price fails to do so or if he or she fixes a price in bad faith, the other party can either treat the contract as cancelled or set a reasonable price.

Open Time Provisions

The absence of a time provision does not cause a sales contract to be unenforceable. Sec. 2-309 states that, where a contract calls for some type of action by the seller (such as shipment or delivery) but does not specify the time for such action, a court may infer a "reasonable time" for performance. Of course, a reasonable time in a given case depends on all the circumstances known to the parties. For instance, suppose that the parties did not set a specific time for delivery but that the seller knew the reason for the buyer's purchase and the use to which the buyer intended to put the goods. A reasonable time for delivery would certainly be soon enough for the buyer to put the goods to their intended use.

Open Delivery Provisions

A sale of goods contract may also be enforceable even if certain delivery terms are to be decided at a later time. Another delivery term that might be absent is a provision for the place of delivery. Where the parties have not included this provision in their contract, Sec. 2-308 sets forth the following rules to serve as "gap-fillers."

1. The goods should be delivered to the buyer at the seller's place of business.
2. If the seller has no place of business, they should be delivered to the buyer at the seller's residence.
3. Where the contract refers to specifically identified goods, and both parties knew when making the contract that the goods were located at some other place, that place is where delivery should be made.

The UCC also attempts to account for other omitted details relating to delivery. For example, if the agreement contemplates shipping the goods but does not mention shipping arrangements, the seller has the right under Sec. 2-311 to specify these arrangements. (His or her actions are subject only to the limitation that they be in good faith and within limits set by commercial reasonableness). Another example is the situation where the contract fails to indicate whether the goods are to be delivered all at once, or in several lots. In such a case Sec. 2-307 obligates the seller to deliver them all at one time. However, there is one exception to this duty. If both parties, when making the contract, know that the circumstances are such that delivery in a single lot is not practicable, then the seller can deliver in several lots. This would apply, for instance, to a situation where the quantity involved is so large that both parties realize that a single shipment is not feasible. In that case, the UCC provides that the seller should deliver in the smallest number of shipments that are reasonably feasible.

Open Payment Provisions

UCC Sec. 2-310 is a "gap-filler" for contracts that are silent as to the time of the buyer's performance—that is, the time of payment. The basic rule is that unless the parties have otherwise agreed, payment is due at the time and place at which the buyer is to receive the goods. The buyer generally has the right to inspect the goods (and reject them if they do not conform to the contractual requirements) before making the payment, unless the contract provides otherwise.

Communication of the Offer

Returning to the common-law principles applicable to the formation of all types of contracts, it is a primary rule that an offer has no effect until it has legally reached the offeree. This requirement of communication is based on the obvious proposition that an offeree cannot agree to a proposal before knowing about it. To illustrate: A city council, via a public advertisement, offers to pay $200 to the person or persons who apprehend an escaped criminal. If X captures the fugitive on his farm, only to learn of the offer later, his act does not constitute an acceptance of the offer and he is not entitled to the reward under the principles of contract law. The relatively few cases that involve this kind of fact pattern generally follow this view. (However, a *few* courts have allowed recovery on noncontract grounds, such as public policy.)

The principle takes on broader scope—and is more difficult to apply—in situations where there has been clear-cut communication of some terms of the agreement but questionable communication of others. The so-called fine print cases illustrate the problem. For example, statements printed on the back of parking lot tickets frequently provide that "the company shall not be liable for loss of, or injury to, the automobile, regardless of cause," or words of similar import. The usual view is that such provisions have not been legally communicated to the owner of the car and that the owner is not bound by them unless they were actually brought to his or her attention when the contract was made.

One should not conclude, however, that an actual communication of all terms is required in all cases. If a court feels that the offeror has made a reasonable effort, under the circumstances, to call the terms of the offer to the offeree's attention, then a legal communication has occurred. A subsequent acceptance of the offer would be binding on the offeree in such a case, even though he or she might not have been aware of all its terms.

The case of Green's Executors v. Smith, 131 S.E. 846 (1926) is particularly instructive. In that case Smith sent a folder to each of his garage patrons, which indicated on the cover, in large type, that "new storage rates" would be effective at a future date. Inside the folder various rates were set forth, followed by a "note" which provided, in effect, that commencing with the new rates, patrons would third parties caused by Smith's drivers while taking the ars to an from patrons' homes. Subsequent litigation raised the question whether patrons were bound by the note even if they had not read it. The court held that they were not. Quoting from an earlier decision, the court said: "When an ofer contains various terms, some of which do not appear on the face of the offer, the question whether the acceptor is by the terms depends on the circumstances. . . . The question arises when a person accepts a railroad or steamboat ticket, bill of lading, warehouse receipt, or other document containing conditions. He is bound by all the conditions whether he reads them or not if he knows that the document contains conditions. But he is not bound by conditions of which he is ignorant. . . unless he knows that the writing contains terms or unless he ought to know that it contains terms, by reason of previous dealings, or by reason of the form, size, or character of the document." The court continued: "There was nothing on the face of the folder, nor in its form or character, to indicate that it contained [a liability change]. The paper only purported to contain a schedule of rates for services at plaintiff's garage, and defendant had no reason, on account of her previous dealings with plaintiff or otherwise, to know that plaintiff proposed . . . a new contract of such unusual terms."

The case below presents a communication of the offer problem in a more modern setting.

Termination of the Offer

Because of the rule that an offer can be accepted at any time before it is legally terminated, it becomes necessary to see what events will cause the offer to die. The rules in this area of the law are rather mechanical in their operation, and we need touch upon them but briefly.

Termination by Act of the Parties

Most offers are terminated by the conduct of the parties themselves by (1) revocation, (2) rejection, or (3) lapse of time.

Revocation

A revocation is a withdrawal of the offer by the offeror. Like the offer itself, it is effective only when it has been communicated to the offeree. Thus, in almost all states, a revocation sent my mail, courier service, or other independent intermediary is effective to terminate the offer only when actually received. (However, in one state, California, a revocation is effective when sent by such means.)

NEWMAN V. SCHIFF
U.S. 8th Circuit Court of Appeals, 778 F.2d 460 (1985)

Irwin Schiff, defendant, is a self-styled "tax rebel" who has made a career (and substantial profits) out of his tax protest activities. On February 7, 1983, Schiff appeared on CBS News Nightwatch in New York, a program with a viewer participation format. During the program he repeated his long-standing position that "there is nothing in the Internal Revenue Code which I have here, which says anybody is legally required to pay the (federal income) tax." After a number of viewers called in questioning this position, Schiff stated on the air: "If anybody calls this show I have the Code and cites any section of this Code that says an individual is required to file a tax return, I will pay them $100,000. A two-minute segment of the program, in which the reward proposal was made, was rebroadcast early the next day on the CBS Morning News.

Newman, plaintiff, is a St. Louis lawyer who saw the rebroadcast (but not the original broadcast). On February 9, a day after viewing the rebroadcast, Newman called the CBS Morning News and cited six sections of the Internal Revenue Code as authority for his position that individuals are legally required to pay federal income taxes. The same day he wrote a letter to CBS Morning News citing the same sections, and stated that the letter represented "performance of the consideration requested by Mr. Schiff in exchange for his promise to pay $100,000."

Some additional correspondence ensued between CBS, Schiff, and Newman, which culminated in a letter from Schiff to Newman dated April 20, 1983. In that letter Schiff said, in part, "I did make an offer on the February 7, 1983, news."

However, he went on to say that Newman had not properly accepted the offer, and was thus not entitled to the money. Newman then brought this action in federal district court to recover damages for breach of contract.

The court entered judgment for Schiff, ruling (1) that Schiff's offer remained open only until the conclusion of the live broadcast; (2) that the rebroadcast did not renew the offer, and (3) that Newman's acceptance was "untimely" (i.e., too late to result in the formation of a contract). Upon reconsideration of the case at Newman's request, the court ruled, in essence, that the offer was renewed when Schiff learned of the rebroadcast "and failed to object to it." The court concluded, however, that Newman's response to the renewed offer still was untimely. (While the court did not give a reason for this conclusion, it was apparently on the theory that Newman's phone call of February 9 was not an acceptance because it was directed to CBS rather than to Schiff, the offeror.) Accordingly, the court affirmed its original judgment that no contract was formed; Newman appealed.

Bright, Senior Circuit Judge:

. . . Newman contends that the district court applied the wrong standard in judging the timeliness of his response to the rebroadcast. We do not [need to decide that issue], however, because we conclude that the district court erred by ruling that Schiff renewed his Nightwatch offer [by failing to disavow] the CBS Morning News rebroadcast. Consequently, we affirm the judgment of the district court on grounds that Newman did not accept Schiff's initial and only offer that had been made on the Nightwatch program.

The present case concerns a special type of offer: an offer of a reward [if a particular act is performed]. At least since the time of Lilli Carlill's unfortunate experience with the Carbolic Smoke Ball, courts have enforced public offers to pay rewards [if the offers have been legally communicated to the claimants]. . . . In that case, frequently excerpted and discussed in student law books, the Carbolic SmokeBall Company advertised that it would pay a "100 £ reward" to anyone who contracted "the increasing epidemic of influenza, colds, or any disease caused by taking cold, after having used the Carbolic Smoke Ball three times daily for two weeks according to the printed directions supplied with each ball." Ms. Carlill, relying upon this promise, purchased and used a Carbolic Smoke Ball. It did not, however, prevent her from catching the flu. The court held that the advertised reward constituted a valid offer which Ms. Carlill had accepted, thereby entitling her to recover. . . . Carlill v. Carbolic Smoke Ball Co. 1 Q.B. 256 (1892).

[The court here ruled that the legal principle relied upon by the trial court to find that the offer was renewed was not applicable to contract law, and thus should not have been invoked by that court. The court continued]: Schiff may have [impliedly] authorized CBS's act of rebroadcasting an excerpt of his Nightwatch interview, yet this did not give the rebroadcast legal effect as a renewed offer. The rebroadcast itself was not an offer, only a news report. Schiff's subsequent conduct and letter do not convert it into an offer.

[After thus distinguishing this case from *Carlill*, the court concluded by saying:]

Schiff's claim that there is nothing in the Internal Revenue Code that requires an individual to file a federal income return demands comment. The kindest thing that can be said about Schiff's promotion of this idea is that he is grossly mistaken, or a mere pretender to knowledge in income taxation. We have nothing but praise for Mr. Newman's efforts which have helped bring this to light. Section 6012 of the Internal Revenue Code . . . provides that individuals having a gross income in excess of a certain amount "shall" file tax returns for the taxable year. Thus section 6012 requires certain individuals to file tax returns. . . . The district court stated that Schiff's argument is "blatant nonsense," [a ruling that] Schiff did not challenge. . . in his cross-appeal.

We affirm the judgment of the district court for the reasons discussed above.

Although Newman has not "won his lawsuit in the traditional sense of recovering a reward that he sought, he has accomplished an important goal in the public interest of unmasking the "blatant nonsense" dispensed by Schiff. For that he deserves great commendation by the public. Perhaps now CBS and other communication media who have given Schiff's mistaken views widespread publicity will give John Newman equal time in the public interest.

Affirmed.

The ordinary offer can be revoked at any time—assuming, of course, that it is communicated to the offeree before an acceptance has occurred. This is generally true even if the offeror had promised to keep the offer open a certain length of time. Thus, if X makes an offer to Y, stating that the offer will remain open thirty days, X can revoke it the very next day if he wishes. While this may seem unfair to Y, the reason for this view lies in the fact that Y has not given "consideration" (something of value) in return for X's promise to keep the offer open.

There are two notable exceptions to the general rule that an offer may be revoked at any time prior to its acceptance.

Option. In an **option** (or option contract, as it is frequently called) the offeree—either at the request of the offeror or acting on his or her own initiative—does give the offeror some consideration (usually a sum of money, but it can take other forms) in return for the offeror's promise to keep the offer open. once the consideration is accepted by the offeror, the offer cannot be revoked during the specified period of time.

Thus, assume that X says to Y: "I offer to sell my farm to you for $100,000, this offer to remain open for 30 days." Y knows the general rule is that X may revoke this offer at any time before acceptance, yet Y truly wishes to buy the farm and needs time to line up his financing. Y may offer to pay X $50 in exchange for X's promise to keep the offer open for 30 days. If X accepts, an option contract is formed and X must keep the offer open. The amount paid for the option need not be a large sum, and a counteroffer will not terminate the offer.

Sales Law—The Firm Offer. The general rule and exception noted above apply with equal force to sales transactions. However, for sale of goods transactions, the UCC has added a second exception to the general rule by creating another type of irrevocable offer, referred to in Sec. 2-205 as a **firm offer.**

The following requirements must exist for an offer to be irrevocable under this section:

1. It must be an offer to buy or sell goods.
2. It must be made *by* a merchant—though it does not necessarily to a merchant. That is, only the offeror need be have to be made *to* a merchant.
3. It must be written and signed by the offeror.
4. It must give assurance that it will be held open.

If all these requirements are met, the offer is irrevocable even if the offeree gives no consideration for the assurance that it will remain open.

The period of time during which the offeror cannot revoke the offer is the time stated in the offer so long as it does not exceed three months. If the offer contains an assurance that it will be held open but mentions no time period, it will be irrevocable for a reasonable time, again not exceeding three months. (The three-month limitation applies only where the offeree is relying on Sec. 2-205 to make the offer irrevocable. If he or she gives consideration for the offeror's assurance that the offer will remain open, an option exists, and the three-month limitation does not apply. Likewise, the other conditions necessary for Sec. 2- 205 do not apply if an option has been created.)

Rejection

A rejection occurs when the offeree notifies the offeror that he or she does not intend to accept. Like the offer and the revocation, it takes effect only when it has been communicated (in this case, to the offeror). Thus, if an offeree mails a letter of rejection but changes his or her mind and telephones an acceptance before the letter arrives, there is a contract. One form of rejection is the counteroffer—a proposal made by the offeree to the offeror that differs in any material respect from the terms of the original offer. Thus, if the price stated in an offer is $500, and the offeree replies, "I'll pay $400," the original offer is ended forever. A recent case, Thurmond v. Weiser, 699 S.W.2d 680 (Tex. 1985), provides a further illustration. There the owner of a small Texas farm offered to sell it for $260,000. The buyer made a counteroffer of $250,000, which was rejected by the seller. Several negotiations ensued, which ended with the buyer sending a written "acceptance" of the $260,000 offer. The owner refused to convey the land, and in subsequent litigation it was held that there was no contract. The court ruled (1) that the original offer to sell for $260,000 was terminated by the buyer's counteroffer of $250,000, and (2) that because the seller did not renew her offer of $260,000 during the negotiations following the counteroffer, there was no outstanding offer capable of being accepted by the buyer.

A response in which the offeree deletes a term from, or adds a term to, the terms of the offer also constitutes a counteroffer. In the preceding case, for example, if the buyer had replied to the original offer, "Accept offer of $260,000; assume highway commission's proposed plan to relocate road on north side will be abandoned," the offer is again terminated.

Lapse of Time

If revocation and rejection were the only recognized means of terminating offers, many offers would remain open forever. To prevent such an unworkable result, a third method of termination is recognized—termination by the mere passage of a reasonable length of time. If not otherwise terminated, and if not accepted, an offer will terminate after the passage of a time stated in the offer as being its duration. If the offer does not state a time when it will expire, it will termination upon the passage of a reasonable period of time. What is reasonable depends on the circumstances of each case; thus it is virtually impossible to formulate general rules in this area of law.

What we will do instead is list the circumstances or factors that the courts consider in reaching an answer in a given case.

1. A circumstance of particular importance is the language used in the offer. Obviously, if an offeror states, "I must hear from you very soon," the time within which the offeree must accept is somewhat shorter than if such language were not used.
2. Another important circumstance is the means of communication used by the offeror. Sending the offer by overnight express (express mail or courier service) normally implies an urgency that the use of regular mail does not.
3. Yet another factor of special importance is based upon prevailing market conditions. If the price of a commodity is fluctuating rapidly, for example, a reasonable time might elapse within hours or even minutes from the time the offer is received.
4. A final factor to be taken into consideration is the method by which the parties have done business in the past.

An offer in some circumstances may thus lapse soon after it has been made, while in other circumstances it may remain open weeks or even months. While there are surprisingly few cases in this area of law, Ward v. Board of Education, 173 N.E. 634 (1930) is one of them. In that case Ward received an offer of employment for the following school year on June 18, and she mailed her acceptance on July 5. In subsequent litigation, the higher court stated the applicable rule as follows: "It is a primary rule that a party contracting by mail, as she did, when no time limit is made for the acceptance of the contract, shall have a reasonable time, acting with due diligence, within which to accept." Applying that rule, where Ms. Ward had no explanation for her delay other than the fact that she was hoping to hear from another school board, the court held that the offer had lapsed prior to July 5 and there was, therefore, no contract.

Termination by Operation of Law

The rule that a revocation must be communicated to the offeree in order for it to take effect is based on the grounds of both fairness and logic. In ordinary circumstances, it seems reasonable that the offeree ought to be legally able to accept any offer until he or she has been put on notice that the offer has been terminated.

Certain exceptional events, however, will terminate an offer automatically—without notice to the offeree. These events fall into three categories: (1) death or adjudication of insanity of either party, (2) destruction of the subject matter of the contract, and (3) intervening illegality. The termination of an offer by any of these events is said to occur by operation of law.

To illustrate: On September 10, B offers a specific TV set to W for $525. On September 13, B dies. If W mails a letter of acceptance on September 14, there is no contract even if W is unaware of B's death. In the same example the result would be identical if, instead of B's death on September 13, the TV set were destroyed that day through no fault of B's. As another example, X offers to loan $1,000 to Y for one year with interest at the rate of 20 percent. Before the offer is accepted, a state statute takes effect which limits the rate of interest on that particular type of loan to 14 percent. The offer is terminated automatically.

The various events that automatically terminate unaccepted offers generally do not terminate existing contracts (except those calling for the rendering of personal services, which we will discuss in Chapter 18). Thus, in the first example, if B's offer of September 10 had been accepted by W before B's death on September 13, B's estate would remain bound by the obligation to deliver the TV set.

By the same token, the various terminations by operation of law do not generally apply to options because they are actually contracts themselves. Thus, if B had promised on September 10 to keep his offer open for ten days, and if W had given B a sum of money in return for this promise, B's death on September 13 would not terminate the offer.

Figure 12.1 summarizes the various ways by which an offer may terminate.

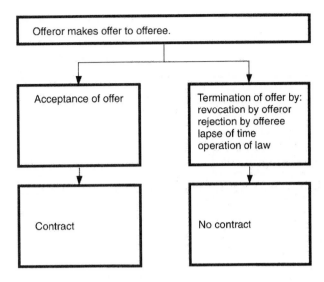

Figure 12.1 Methods of Terminating an Offer

The Acceptance

An offer ripens into a contract if, and only if, it is accepted by the offeree. Remember that a bilateral offer is accepted by the offeree's making the return promise that the offeror has requested, while a unilateral offer is accepted only by the actual performance of the requested act.

In the average situation, the offeree's response to the offer is so clearly an acceptance or so clearly is not an acceptance that there are no misunderstandings between the parties. Sometimes, however, legal difficulties do crop up—as, for example, where the offeree "accepts" the offer but then adds new terms to it or where the offeree's response is vague or indecisive. Another difficulty is the determination of the precise moment at which the acceptance becomes effective—specifically, whether the acceptance has to be actually communicated to the offeror before it becomes legally effective.

In the following discussion, emphasis is given to the acceptance of offers for bilateral contracts—those in which the offeror merely wants a return promise on the part of the offeree. Special problems raised by the acceptance of unilateral offers are considered later in the chapter.

Requirements of the Acceptance

An acceptance is an expression on the part of the (An acceptance is an expression on the part of the intent to out) offeree by which he or she indicates a definite intent to be bound by the terms of the offer. Under general contract law, the acceptance must be a "mirror image" of the offer. Thus if a purported (intended) acceptance varies from the terms of the offer in any way—sometimes called a conditional acceptance—it ordinarily

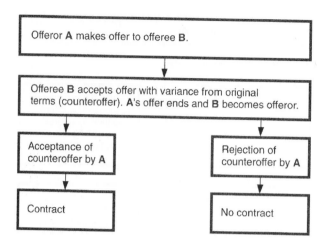

Figure 12.2 Legal Ramifications of the Counteroffer

constitutes a counteroffer rather than an acceptance, as illustrated in Figure 12.2. While an offeree usually states expressly that he or she is "accepting" the offer, it is not necessary that this particular term be used. Any language showing that the offeree is definitely assenting to the proposal is sufficient. Regardless of the particular words used by the offeree in his or her response to the offer, the response must meet certain requirements in order to constitute an acceptance. An acceptance (1) must demonstrate a definite, present intent to accept the offer, (2) must be unconditional and not add any terms that are additional to or different from those of the offer, and (3) must be legally communicated to the offeror or to the offeror's agent.

Requirement of a Definite Indication of Intent to Accept

An acceptance is an expression on the part of the offeree by which he or she indicates a definite intent to be bound by the terms of the offer. Here, the same rules apply and the same types of evidence are considered as when the question was whether the alleged offeror had actually made an offer. Both parties must manifest a definite intent to be legally bound to a contract on reasonably definite terms.

To illustrate: X, in response to an advertisement placed by Y, sends a bid to Y offering to perform the described landscaping work for $23,000. Y replies by telegram: "offer satisfies all requirements; will give it my prompt attention." Subsequently, Y hires another landscaper to do the job, and, when X sues Y to recover damages for breach of contract, Y contends that his response did not constitute an acceptance of the offer. Applying the general rule to this case, Y's reply is too indefinite and tentative to satisfy the requirement that there be a definite manifestation of intent to accept. Thus Y is correct in his contention that a contract was not formed. On the other hand, each case has to be decided on its own merits, including consideration of the circumstances surrounding the communications. Thus a different result might be reached in the foregoing example if the evidence indicated that X and Y had in the past considered such language to be binding.

Silence

As a general rule, there is no duty on the offeree to reply to an offer. Silence on the part of the offeree, therefore, does not usually constitute an acceptance. This is true even when the offer states, "If you do not reply within ten days, I shall conclude that you have accepted," or contains language of similar import. The reasons underlying this view are fairly obvious: (1) the view is consistent with the basic idea that any willingness to contract must be manifested in some fashion, and (2) it substantially prevents an offeree from being forced into a contract against his or her will.

In exceptional circumstances, however, the courts may find that the general rule is unfair to the offeror—that under the facts of the particular case, the offeree owed the offeror a duty to reject if he or she did not wish to be bound. In such cases, silence on the part of the offeree does constitute an acceptance. While it is difficult to generalize about these exceptional situations, two types of case present little controversy.

If an offeree initially indicates that silence on his or her part can be taken as acceptance, there is no reason why that person should not be bound by the statement. For example: "If you do not hear from me by March 1, you can conclude that we have a contract."

If a series of past dealings between the parties indicates that the parties consider silence to be an acceptance, it can be assumed by the offeror that this understanding continues until it is expressly changed. For example: a retail jewelry store has, over the years, received periodic shipments of both ordered and unordered jewelry from a large supplier; during this time, the retailer-buyer has always paid for any unordered goods not returned within two weeks. A failure by the retailer to reject a particular shipment, or to give notice of such rejection, within two weeks would very likely operate as an acceptance under the circumstances.

In both the preceding kinds of cases, the courts are likely to say that the offeror "had reason to understand" that silence on the part of the offeree was to be taken as a manifestation of assent, and that the offeree should have been well aware of this fact.

There is another, smaller group of cases in which it has been held that the offeror is justified in believing silence to be a manifestation of assent. These are situations in which a retail buyer gives a salesperson an order (offer) for certain goods, which the salesperson forwards to his or her company. If a reasonable period of time elapses without the company taking action, some courts hold that the buyer can justifiably view such silence as an acceptance of the offer and can hold the company liable for damages if it refuses to deliver the goods. Such courts reason that a company which sends salespeople out to solicit offers owes a duty to buyers to reject their offers within a reasonable time if it does not intend to accept them. (The same rule has sometimes been applied to mail order houses when they have failed to reject buyers' orders within a reasonable time.)

Requirement that an Acceptance be Unconditional and Not Add to or Change the Terms of the Offer

We have already seen that when an attempted acceptance changes the terms of the offer, it becomes a counteroffer and a rejection rather than an acceptance. The same is true when the attempted acceptance adds new terms or conditions to those of the offer.

Thus, if S writes to B: "I hereby offer to sell my farm to you for $50,000," no acceptance would result if B responded: "I accept, if I can pay $2,000 for each of the next 25 years" or "I accept if you promise to repaint the barn before sale." The general common law rule is that the acceptance must be a "mirror image" of the offer in order for a contract to result.

The following case presents an intriguing situation in which both parties originally assumed, quite understandably, that an agreement had clearly been reached—until the sharp-eyed bus driver began to compare the language of the school board's "acceptance" with the language of his offer. At that point, the fun began.

LUCIER V. TOWN OF NORFOLK
Supreme Court of Errors of Connecticut,
122 A. 711 (1923)

Lucier, plaintiff, operated a school bus for the defendant town for the school years of 1915, 1916, 1918, and 1919. In the summer of 1920 plaintiff and defendant began negotiating a contract for the coming year.

After several communications between the parties, plaintiff was asked by the Norfolk Town School Committee to submit a bid covering transportation of students for the 1920 - 1921 school year. On August 12, plaintiff submitted his bid, offering to provide transportation at '$175 per week each school week for that year.

On August 17 the board passed the following resolution: "Voted to award the contract for transporting children to and from Gilbert school and to and from various points in town to Mr. E.A. Lucier for the sum of $35 per day." The next day, a member of the committee, one Stevens, told plaintiff that the board

"had voted to award him the contract" and requested plaintiff to have his buses ready.

On the first day of school, September 7, plaintiff transported the students as agreed. On the evening of September 7 the board presented plaintiff with a formal contract for him to sign, the contract embodying the wording of the August 17 resolution. Plaintiff refused to sign the contract, on the ground that it was not in accordance with his bid for compensation at the rate of $175 per week, but at the rate of $35 per day instead. Thereupon defendant refused to employ plaintiff and awarded the transportation contract to a third party.

Plaintiff brought action to recover damages for breach of contract, alleging that a contract was formed on his terms and was breached by defendant. (Specifically, plaintiff's argument was that his bid was accepted on August 18 *when Stevens told him that the board "had voted to award him the contract.") Defendant contended that a contract was formed on its terms and that plaintiff was guilty of the breach. The trial court ruled that no contract was formed in this situation (but did award plaintiff $35 dollars, the reasonable value of his services performed on September 7). Plaintiff appealed.*

Keeler, Justice:

... Summarily stated, the contentions of the plaintiff are: that the negotiations between him and the school board [resulted] in a contract express or implied, and the minds of the negotiating parties met; that Stevens, by reason of his position, had authority to make a contract binding the town; and that [plaintiff's bid, followed by Stevens' actions] resulted in a contract being formed...

[Other] than as to the price to be fixed for the service, there is no dispute between the parties as to the terms submitted in the notice to bidders, and the plaintiff bid with reference to them, his offer conforming to these terms, the price for the service being the only open item in the transaction. The dispute turns upon the question of a rate per week as contrasted with a rate per day. The committee received from the plaintiff a bid of $175 per week; this undoubtedly meant to it the same as $35 per day, a result arrived at by a simple act of division of the larger number by five, the number of school days in the ordinary school week. It would seem that the committee were justified in reaching this conclusion, in that the plaintiff's pay in the contract for the year just past had been at a sum per day, and the notice for bids had called for a bid by the day.. ... When, therefore, the committee received a bid by the week they very naturally in their vote awarding the contract to the plaintiff substituted what they deemed an equivalent sum by the day, to accord with the requirement of the notice. This also was evidently the understanding of Stevens, when he afterward informed the plaintiff that the contract had been awarded to the latter. Subsequent events showed that this construction of his bid was not intended by the plaintiff, and that he intended to insist on the distinction between pay by the day and pay by the week, in that the latter afforded him compensation for work which would not in fact be required, when in any week a school day came upon a holiday.

In the pleadings, each side claimed the equivalence in fact and in effect of the expressions in the bid with those in the vote, each resolving the question of intent favorably to the contention by each, and each consequently claimed a contract which had been broken by the other party. Both are wrong. It clearly appears from the facts found that the trial judge correctly found that there was no meeting of minds, and hence no contract. The plaintiff had the burden of establishing his construction of the claimed contract and has failed.

But the plaintiff further insists that he was in effect informed by Stevens that his bid had been accepted by the committee, that the latter was bound by Stevens' statement, and that he [the plaintiff] acted in accordance with the information conveyed to him. Further, that Stevens was the agent of the committee, and had authority to bind it, and that the committee was so bound when Stevens told him that the contract had been awarded to him, which information was in his mind equivalent to a statement that his bid had been accepted in the form tendered.... So he says that whatever the committee really intended in the matter, it was bound by Stevens' statement that the contract had been awarded to him on the terms of his bid, even though the vote stated the price of the service at a sum differing therefrom. [The court rejected this contention of plaintiff, ruling that Stevens was simply informing plaintiff

of the board's action so that he could get his equipment in readiness, and that Stevens did not intend—nor did he have the authority—to
bind the board to anything other than the specific resolution as passed.]

Judgment affirmed.

A Note of Caution

In some situations the offeree's response does constitute an acceptance even though it contains one or more terms that were not set forth in the offer itself. This is true where a reasonable person, standing in the place of the offeree, would justifiably believe that the "new" terms were within the contemplation of, and were agreeable to, the offeror despite the failure to include them in the offer. Following are two illustrations.

For several years X has been performing maintenance work upon Y Company's assembly line equipment, and has always granted Y Company 90 days in which to pay for the work. If X writes to Y, offering to perform preventive maintenance on various equipment for $1,000, and Y responds, we accept on condition that we will have 90 days in which to pay," Y's response very likely constitutes an acceptance. Under the circumstances—the manner in which they had been doing business in the past—Y could assume that it was implied that X would grant the usual credit. (Custom in the industry could give rise to a similar implication, if clearly proved by Y.)

F offers to sell certain land to D for $55,000 cash. D replies by telegram, "I accept, assuming you will convey good title." This is an acceptance, even though F did not mention the quality of his title, because it is implied (under real property law) that a seller of land guarantees good or marketable title unless he or she indicates a contrary intention.

The purpose of the foregoing is simply to warn the student that it is possible for a term or condition to be literally new without necessarily being new in the legal sense. Thus, while the responses of the offerees in the preceding examples appear at first glance to constitute counteroffers, in the eyes of the law they add nothing new and therefore constitute valid acceptances.

Additional or Different Terms in Sale of Goods Contracts

Under the UCC's provisions for sale of goods contracts, an acceptance may be effective even though it contains terms that conflict with, or add to, the terms of the offer. A major reason for rejection of the mirror-image rule by the drafters of the Code lies in the manner in which many sales contracts are entered into. Generally, such contracts are not fully negotiated. For example, commercial buyers often use their own printed forms in ordering goods from manufacturers or wholesalers, and the latter companies frequently use their own forms in notifying buyers of their acceptance. Naturally, the terms and conditions of the two forms are rarely identical, because the order forms used by buyers contain buyer-oriented terms, while forms used by sellers to invite, acknowledge, or accept orders contain seller-oriented terms.

In the vast majority of situations, the parties do not pay much attention to the other's forms. The seller provides the goods, the buyer pays for them, and the forms are filed away and forgotten. However, in the occasional situation where problems result and one side or the other wishes to sue for breach of contract, strict adherence to the mirror-image rule would always allow the potential defendant to claim that there was no binding contract because of differences in the forms.

To illustrate: Suppose that on its purchase order form buyer B ordered a quantity of goods at a certain price from seller S, and that seller S sent a purchase acknowledgment form to B indicating that the goods would be shipped. S's form, however, contained a clause stating that interest would be charged on late payments. Later B notified S that he did not want the goods and would not go through with the deal, whereupon S sued B to recover damages for breach of contract. Both parties look at the forms for the first time. In such a case the common law presumes that by responding with the varying term on interest rates, S intended to make a counteroffer, which B has not accepted. Thus no contract was ever formed, with the result that B has no liability to S.

In the modern era where so much commercial activity occurs through "form swapping," the mirror image rule provides a haven for weshers such as B in the foregoing example. The drafters of the UC sought to eliminate such results in situations where the parties truly intended to contract. Section 2207, which is often caled the "Battle of the Forms" provision, addresses this problem. As our analysis will show, Sec. 2-207 reverses the common-law assumption, and presumes instead that an offeree who responds with varying terms intends to contract, unless he clearly indicates that he intends a counteroffer instead. Unfortunately, Sec. 2- 207 is one of the most complicated, controversial, and inconsistently applied provisions of the entire Code.

Text of Section 2-207

This section reads, in material part, as follows (emphasis added):
1. A definite and seasonable expression of acceptance or a written confirmation which is sent within a reasonable time *operates as an acceptance* even though it states terms *additional to or different from* those offered or agreed upon unless acceptance is expressly made conditional on assent to the additional or different terms.
2. The additional terms are to be construed as proposals for addition to the contract. *Between merchants, such terms become part of the contract unless:*
   a. the offer expressly limits acceptance to the terms of the offer;
   b. they materially alter it; or
   c. notification of objection to them . . . is given within a reasonable time after notice of them is received.
3. Conduct by both parties which recognizes the existence of a contract is sufficient to establish a contract for sale although the writings of the parties do not otherwise establish a contract. . . [T]he terms of the particular contract consist of those terms on which the writings of the parties agree [together with terms provided by UCC "gap-filler" rules].

Subsection 1—Is There a Contract?

The primary import of this provision is that, in a sale of goods transaction, an offeree's response that clearly indicates a definite intent to accept *constitutes an acceptance* even if it contain one or more terms additional to or different from those found in the offer. Thus Sec. 2- 207 clearly rejects the mirror-image rule.

Assume that Buyer B orders 2,000 A-20 widgets from seller S for $9,000, the price appearing in S's catalog. S sends his acknowledgment form as follows: "Accept your sales order #1379; 2,000 A-20 widgets/$9,000"; but on the back of the form is the new term "seller makes no warranties, express or implied, as to goods sold." *A contract now exists*, despite the new term in S's response. In other words, under subsection 1, S's acknowledgment constitutes an acceptance rather than a counteroffer, resulting in a binding contract. If S did not wish to be bound unless the buyer accepted the warranty exclusion, S should have made the matter a subject of negotiation by clearly condition-ing the acceptance upon B's approval of the exclusion. If S does not make this condition clear and if it appears that S's response is intended primarily as an acceptance, a contract results.

In situations where the offeree's form agrees with the offeror's as to key terms, such as price, quantity, and date of delivery, differing only as to nonbargained ancillary terms, courts are likely to hold that the offeree's primary purpose was to form a con-tract. On the other hand, if the offeror's form orders 100,000 pounds of plastic at $2.00 per pound and the offeree's form confirms the order of 100,000 pounds of plastic at $2.25 per pound, the second document is not an acceptance.

Subsection 2—Is the New Term Included in the Agreement?

If subsection 1 analysis leads to the conclusion that a contract has been formed, the remaining question is whether the warranty exclusion has become part of it.

If B notices the clause and agrees to it, then it is, of course, included. If B notices the clause and objects to it, then it does not become part of the contract. But what about the usual case where B does not notice the clause, or, if he does notice it, simply ignores it? In this situation, a distinction is made between terms that are "different from" those of the offer, and those which are "additional to" those of the offer.

Different Terms. If the term in the acceptance is different from (i.e., conflicts with) a term of the offer, the term does not become a part of the contract unless the offeror expressly agrees to it. Thus, in the above example, if B's order form had contained a clause setting forth certain warranties that were to be made by the seller (e.g., "seller warrants the widgets to be in conformity with U.S. Department of Defense specification #497 dated 6-15- 90"), S's warranty exclusion clause would clearly not be part of the contract.

Additional Terms. As to any term in the acceptance that is an additional term (i.e., regarding a matter not addressed in the offer), Sec. 2-207(2) provides that, if both parties are merchants, the term becomes a part of the contract without any further assent on the part of the offeror, unless (a) the offer stated that acceptance is limited to the terms of the offer itself; or (b) the term "materially alters" the contract; or (c) the offeror objects to the new term within a reasonable time after receiving the offeree's acceptance. Thus, in our example involving the widget purchase, if both B and S were merchants, and if B's order form made no reference to warranties. S's warranty-exclusion clause would automatically become part of the contract, unless barred by a, b, or c. (Therefore, in determining whether there is a contract (under subsection 1), it is not necessary that the parties be merchants. But their status as merchants is important in determining whether the additional term becomes part of the contract under subsection (2). The reason for this is that the drafters of the UCC felt that additional terms should be included in the contract without express agreement only where the transaction is between two professionals.

In this case, most courts would hold that a warranty exclusion clause does materially alter an offer and therefore *does not* become part of the contract. Thus, the goods would be covered by any warranties implied by the law—because the seller was a merchant, and the seller's attempted disclaimer was not part of the contract, the UCC would imply a warranty that the goods are fit for the ordinary purposes for which such goods are used (the "implied warranty of merchantability"). The courts decide whether or not there was a material alteration on a case-by-case basis. The basic thrust of subsection 2(b) is that the offeree is not allowed to slip anything really important past the offeror by simply including it in the acceptance form. Rather, the offeree should call the matter to the offeror's attention and make it a subject of negotiation.

Written Confirmation of Informal Agreement

A second situation in which UCC Section 2-207 is important occurs when (1) a seller and buyer have made an informal agreement of sale, such as a purely oral agreement (say, over the telephone) or an agreement formed by various "pieces" of informal notes, memos, messages, and so on (or a combination of oral statements and informal writings); (2) either (a) one of the parties subsequently prepares and sends a formal written confirmation of the agreement to the other party, or (b) the two parties subsequently exchange forms; and (3) the subsequent written confirmation or the subsequently exchanged forms add to or change the terms that were first agreed upon informally. If the evidence proves that the parties had truly made a contract informally, then there is a contract based on that informal understanding. Thus, the first part of 2-207 dealing with the question of whether there was a contract is irrelevant. The second part of 2-207 is then applied to determine whether the additional or different terms are part of the contract. In other words, the additional or different terms are treated as proposals for adding to or changing the informal.

Agreement Implied from Conduct

A third situation in which UCC Section 2-207 is important occurs when the parties do not have a prior informal agreement and, their exchanged forms did not create a contract for one reason or another—such as when the offeree does not definitely indicate an intent to accept, or when the offeree does indicate an intent to accept but its attempted acceptance specifically states that it should not be considered an acceptance unless the offeror expressly consents to the new or different terms. In such a case the documents do not produce a contract, yet sellers often ship goods and buyers often pay for them in such instances. Here, subsection 3 of 2-207 implies a contract from the conduct of the parties under the same circumstances that common-law rules of contract law find implied contracts to exist. The terms of the contract consist of those matters that the two forms do agree upon, supplemented by any evidence from their conduct showing what they intended particular terms to be, and also supplemented as necessary by the "gap-filler" provisions of the UCC.

For example, in one case a buyer and seller exchanged a series of purchase orders, acknowledgments and letters regarding a purchase of aluminum. At no time did the buyer's forms and the seller's forms agree as to a date of delivery. Buyer committed itself to purchase on September 1 and demanded delivery within seven weeks. Seller immediately acknowledged the order, but set a delivery date of nine weeks, later changed to eleven. Buyer stated that this was not acceptable. Seller told buyer either to accept it or obtain the aluminum elsewhere. Nonetheless, seller delivered the aluminum after eleven weeks and buyer accepted and partially paid for the aluminum. Certain defects were found and litigation resulted. The court held that the parties' correspondence did not create a contract. Seller's response materially altered the buyer's offer. In short, the communications indicated that the parties "dickered" over a key term, but never reached agreement. Nonetheless, the conduct of the parties (the seller's shipping the goods and the buyer's partially paying for them) did establish formation of a contract under subsection 3 of 2-207 (as under common-law rules pertaining to implied contracts). The court then used the UCC "gap-fillers" to establish a reasonable time of delivery in order to determine whether seller had breached. Alliance Wall Corp. v. Ampat Midwest Corp., 477 N.E.2d 1206 (Ohio App. 1984).

The following case illustrates the application of UCC section 2-207 to a typical sale of goods transaction.

REVIEW VIDEO LLC V. ENLIGHTEN TECHNOLOGY
2005 U.S. Dist. LEXIS 442 (N.D. Iowa 2005)

The plaintiff, Review Video, LLC, sued defendant Enlighten Technologies for breach of contract, claiming that between July and October of 2002, the defendant sent seven orders to plaintiff and thereby purchased and received goods that it never paid for. Plaintiff sent defendant an invoice in response to each of the orders and the parties agree that the goods that the defendant purchased from the plaintiff totaled $161,591.00. The plaintiff issued purchase orders for the goods and the defendant agreed to pay the purchase prices. The defendant admits liability for the purchase price, but resists plaintiff's summary judgment motion seeking to recover interest charges on the past-due amounts at a monthly *rate of 1.5 %. Defendant claims that it cannot be liable for interest because it never signed a document indicating that it would pay interest on past due accounts.*

Miner, Circuit Judge:

The defendant argues that the 1.5% monthly interest charge on past-due accounts, as contained in the plaintiff's invoices, was not a term of the contracts because the defendant never assented to such a term in writing. Iowa has adopted the Uniform Commercial Code, which governs transactions between merchants. It is clear that the defendant's ordering of goods, on each of the seven occasions, constituted a separate offer for contract purposes. "An order or other offer to buy goods for prompt or current shipment shall be construed as inviting acceptance either by prompt promise to ship or by the prompt or current shipment of conforming or nonconforming goods…" 2-206(l)(b). Likewise, the plaintiff's sending of the conforming goods to the plaintiff constituted an acceptance of the defendant's offer. The issue, therefore, is whether the additional term setting forth the 1.5 % monthly interest charge on past-due accounts, as contained in each of the plaintiff's seven invoices, is part of the contracts between the plaintiff and the defendant.

The court finds that the monthly interest charge term is properly construed as part of each of the contracts in this case. "A definite and seasonable expression of acceptance or a written confirmation which is sent within a reasonable time operates as an acceptance even though it states terms additional to or different from those offered or agreed upon, unless acceptance is expressly made conditional on assent to the additional or different terms." 2-207(1). Section 2-207 determines whether an additional term, as opposed to a different term, contained in a written confirmation but not expressly negotiated, is appropriately considered to be part of a contract.

According to that provision, an additional term, in this case the monthly interest charge, is to be construed as a proposal for addition to the contract. 2-207(2)

The mere acceptance of goods, even if done repeatedly, does not by itself constitute a valid acceptance of newly proposed contract terms. Between merchants, such as the plaintiff and the defendant, the additional term becomes part of the contract unless:

a.   the offer expressly limits acceptance to the terms of the offer;

b.   [the additional term] materially alter[s] [the contract]; or

c.   notification of objection to [the additional term] has already been given or is given within a reasonable time after notice of them is received. 2-207(2)(a-c).

The defendant does not contend that it limited acceptance of its offer to the terms of the offer. Further, the defendant does not contend that it notified the plaintiff of any objection to the additional monthly interest charge term within a reasonable time after receiving notice of the term. Accordingly, the court must determine whether the additional monthly interest charge term is a term that materially alters the contract, and therefore should not be considered part of the contract.

"Whether an additional term materially alters an agreement is a question of fact which must be resolved on a case by case basis." TRWL Financial Establishment v. Select Intern., Inc., 527 N.W.2d 573 (Minn. App. 1995). An agreement is materially altered if the inclusion of the additional term would "result in surprise or hardship if incorporated without express awareness by the other party." *Id.*

Courts in Iowa and elsewhere have held that a reasonable rate of interest on past due accounts, even if substantially greater than the default interest rate provided by law absent a finding of an agreement, does not constitute a material alteration of the contract. 2-207 (cmt. 5)

("Examples of typical clauses which involve no element of unreasonable surprise and which therefore are to be incorporated in the contract unless notice of objection is seasonably given are . . . a clause providing for interest on overdue invoices . . . "). *See also* Carson Grain & Implement, Inc. v. Dirks, 460 N.W.2d 483 (Iowa App. 1990) (no interest rate specifically mentioned in oral contract at issue, but court found that interest in amount of 18% was due when bills sent pursuant to the contract included a finance charge of 18% on late accounts). Accordingly, the court finds that the term setting forth a 1.5% monthly interest charge on past due amounts is part of the contract between the plaintiff and the defendant in this case. So ordered.

Special Problems with Shrink-Wrap Licenses and Similar Situations

Courts have had particular problems with situations involving the purchase of software. All or practically all courts have treated software transactions as involving a sale of goods that is governed by Article 2 of the UCC, which is sometimes a logical thing to do and sometimes is not, because the customer actually buys only a CD or other storage medium plus one copy of the software's intangible object code (the 1's and 0's), and is merely a licensee of the right to use the software subject to certain restrictions. Moreover, in the case of software "purchased" by downloading it from the Internet, nothing tangible at all is purchased. On the other hand, when someone buys a computer with software preloaded on the computer's hard drive, the predominant part of the transaction is the purchase of a tangible commodity, and it does make logical sense to treat the transaction as a sale of goods. Regardless of the sometimes questionable logic of treating software as a good, the courts do so and apply Article 2 of the UCC with respect to determining whether there is a contract, what the terms of the contract, and other matters such as warranties. It should also be recalled, however, that many of the traditional common-law rules of contract law continue to apply to sale of goods transactions, such as the rules for determining whether there is a definite expression of intent to make an offer or a definite expression of intent to make an acceptance. Thus, in software transactions, common-law rules apply unless altered by Article 2 of the UCC.

With respect to the determination of whether an agreement has been made, and with respect to what the terms of that agreement are, courts have had encountered difficulty with software transactions, especially in the case of software "purchases" by consumers.

Recall that courts have traditionally concluded that no offer is made when a seller makes goods or services available for a price, whether by advertising on the TV, radio, print media, or the Internet, or by placing goods on a shelf in a retail store. The customer makes an offer to buy when he or she indicates a definite desire to purchase. This approach continues to be used in all types of transactions, except that a majority of courts have switched the roles of the parties in software licensing transactions. Failure to follow the more sensible approach that is followed in all other types of merchant-consumer transactions is the source of most of the difficulty and confusion that has occurred in software transactions. As we will see shortly, failing to follow the traditional approach and instead treating the seller who merely makes software available for purchase as the offeror greatly increases the chances that a consumer will be legally obligated by the many detailed and often burdensome terms that one finds in the typical software license. These terms may include arbitration clauses, choice of law clauses, choice of forum clauses, warranty disclaimers, clauses prohibiting the reverse engineering of software to discover trade secrets, and many others that most consumers never know about when they "buy" the software. A few courts have taken the traditional approach, under which consumers are less likely to be bound by such terms, but the majority of courts have treated the seller of software as the offeror, and the trend is clearly in that direction.

There are two general scenarios in which the situation arises:

1. The first occurs when the customer does not have a reasonable opportunity to review the detailed license terms before buying and paying for the product. For example, suppose that a customer goes into a store and takes a box from a shelf. The box contains the software on a CD. The customer then pays for the software, takes it home, and installs it on a computer. Inside the box is a document containing various terms for the customer's license of the right to use the software. Or, if not on a document in the box, the detailed license terms might appear on a screen display when the customer first uses the software. In this scenario, the customer has not had an opportunity to review the detailed license terms before paying money for the software. Contrary to the approach taken in other kinds of transactions when goods or services are simply made available for sale, a majority of courts have treated the seller as the offeror in a software transaction such as this. Under this view, the majority of courts have held that, if the customer has a reasonable chance to review the terms after paying for the software, and does not return the software within a time stated in the license terms (or within a reasonable time if no time is stated), the customer is bound by the terms. Sometimes this situation is referred to as "money now, terms later." If a court were to take the traditional view of the roles of the seller and the customer, as a minority of courts have, the customer would be the offeror, and the license terms would be treated as additional or different terms under UCC section 2-207 and analyzed accordingly. All of what has just been said applies also to a situation in which the software comes preloaded on the hard drive of a computer, with the license terms on a document inside the box holding the computer or on the screen display when the customer sets up the new computer and first uses the preloaded software. A clear majority of courts have used the same approach when software is downloaded from the Internet and the customer has not had an adequate opportunity to review the detailed license terms before buying the software. (The most notable case to the contrary, using the minority approach, is Specht v. Netscape Communications, in which the U.S. Court of Appeals for the Second Circuit held in 2002 that the consumer was not bound by license terms because he did not have a reasonable chance to read them before paying for and downloading the software.)

An additional note is in order: In purchases of airline tickets, even though courts have used the traditional view of the customer as the offeror and the airline as the offeree, they have held the customer to be bound by detailed terms that are not available to the customer until after the ticket is purchased. The most common example is a term severely limiting the scope of the airline's liability for loss of or damage to luggage, a term that is allowed under an international treaty. Airline tickets are simply an exception.

2. The second situation occurs when the customer does, in fact, have a reasonable opportunity to review all the license terms before paying for the software. Such a scenario is likely to occur only in a case where the customer is downloading software from the Internet. Suppose that a customer is given an opportunity to read the license terms (say, in a window on the computer screen that the customer can scroll through) before arriving at the point at which a button is clicked indicating a desire to buy the software. In this situation, the customer is bound by the terms regardless of whether a court treats the seller as an offeree (traditional contract law approach) or as an offeror (newer, majority approach in software license cases). If a court follows the traditional contract law view, the customer is the offeror and the terms he had a chance to view before buying are part of the offer to the seller. If a court follows the different approach that a majority of courts have taken in software license cases, the seller is the offeror, the terms are part of that offer, and the customer accepts all of the terms when accepting the offer to buy the software.

When Does Acceptance Take Effect? Reasonable Medium or Mailbox Rule

Offers, revocations, and rejections are effective when received. Acceptances are also effective upon receipt, but they often are effective even sooner than that. That is, under the "mailbox rule" or "reasonable medium rule," an acceptance may be effective as soon as it is sent if the medium chosen is reasonable. The "mailbox rule" originally applied only when the offeree used the U.S. mail for sending the acceptance, and this term is often still used even though it has been generally expanded by the courts to apply to any medium that is reasonable under the circumstances. Although there is variation from state to state in this area of the law, courts typically deem a chosen medium to be reasonable if (1) it is the same one used by the offeror; (2) it is one customarily used in prior dealings between the parties; (3) it is customarily used within the trade or industry in which the parties are doing business; or (4) it is one which is impliedly authorized by the language of the offer (for example, an acceptance by mail is probably reasonable in response to an offer by telegram if the offer indicated that there was no urgency about reaching an agreement).

If the offeree uses a medium that is not reasonable, the acceptance will be effective only when received. However, if the medium chosen by the offeree is reasonable, the acceptance will be effective when dispatched (out of the possession of the offeree). Assume that A mails an offer to B. If B mails an acceptance, there is a contract the minute the acceptance is dispatched even if the post office delays the acceptance or even loses it altogether. (Of course, if the acceptance is lost, the offeree will bear the burden of proving by other evidence that it was, in fact, mailed.) If A calls B to revoke the offer after B has mailed the acceptance, it is too late for the revocation to be effective. The offer, already accepted, has ripened into a binding contract.

Exceptions. There are at least three situations where the reasonable medium rule is not applicable. First, and most important, the offeror may specifically state in the offer that an acceptance will be effective only when actually received by the offeror. This is simply part of the general rule that the offeror is the "master of the offer," and can put any terms or conditions he or she wants in the offer. The offeree can take them or leave them. It is an excellent idea for any offeror to do this, because it removes the possibility that the offeror will be legally bound by a contract for a period of time (while the message of acceptance is in transit) without knowing about it.

Second, also because of the rule that the offeror is the master of his or her offer, the offeror may require that an acceptance be made by a particular medium. If a particular medium (such as first-class mail) is clearly specified, then an acceptance sent by any other medium will not result in a contract being formed upon dispatch. Note that there can be a factual question of what the offeror actually intended when he or she merely stated that the offeree "may" use a particular medium for accepting. Unless there is other evidence showing that the offeror actually meant the suggestion to be a requirement, "may" or other merely suggestive language will not be treated as requiring that the offer use that method of accepting.

Third, if an offeree mails a rejection first, and only later changes his mind and sends an acceptance, the acceptance is not effective until received. Therefore, an offeror who receives the rejection first may assume that it is effective. In other words, in such a situation, the first message to be received by the offeror (rejection or acceptance) will be the effective one.

Also, courts have generally not applied the mailbox rule to e-mails. They have held instead that an acceptance is effective not when sent by when it arrives at the recipient's e-mail *server.*

Examples

The following examples will illustrate the sequence of events leading to the formation of a contract, given the use of a reasonable medium.

Case 1:   June 1— Y receives an offer in the mail from X.

June 2—X mails letter of revocation.

June 3—Y mails acceptance at 5 p.m.

June 4—Y receives the revocation.

June 5—X receives Y's acceptance.

Result: A contract was formed at 5 p.m. on June 3, since use of mail by Y was clearly reasonable. Since a revocation is usually not effective until it is received, the letter that X mailed on June 2 had no effect until June 4, when Y received it. And by that time a contract had already been formed. (This is the result in almost all states; as noted earlier, however, the rule in California is that a revocation is effective when sent.)

Case 2: June 1— Y receives an offer in the mail from X.

June 2— Y mails letter of rejection.

June 3— Y changes his mind and at 10 a.m. calls X on the telephone and accepts the offer, telling X to disregard his letter of rejection.

June 4— X receives letter of rejection.

Result: A contract was formed at 10 a.m. on June 3, when Y gave X actual notice of acceptance. (Since a rejection is usually not effective until it is received, Y's letter of rejection had no effect on June 2. The offer was thus open on June 3, when Y accepted it.)

CUSHING V. THOMSON
Supreme Court of New Hampshire, 386 A.2d 805 (1978)

An anti-nuclear protest group, the Clamshell Alliance, sent an application in March of 1973 to the New Hampshire Adjutant General's office, seeking permission to rent the national guard armory in Portsmouth the night of April 29.

The Alliance hoped to use the armory facilities for a dance it had scheduled on that date.

On March 31 the adjutant general mailed a "contract offer" to the Alliance, agreeing to rent the armory upon specified terms. The offer required that a signed acceptance be returned to the adjutant general's office.

Cushing, a member of the Alliance, received the offer at the alliance's office on Monday, April 3.

That same day he signed it on behalf of the organization, put the acceptance in an envelope, and placed the letter in the office's "outbox."

At 6:30 in the evening of the next day, Tuesday, April 4, Cushing received a phone call from the adjutant general stating that he was withdrawing the offer on orders of Governor Meldrim Thomson.

Cushing replied that he had already accepted the offer, but the adjutant general repeated the statement that the offer had been withdrawn. (The alliance's acceptance, postmarked April 5, reached the adjutant general's office on April 6.)

When the adjutant general continued in his refusal to give the Alliance permission to use the armory, Cushing and other members of the organization brought suit against Governor Thomson and the adjutant general, seeking specific performance of the contract that had allegedly been formed. Defendants contended that there was no contract, claiming that they had revoked the offer prior to plaintiff's "acceptance." Although there was no direct evidence indicating the precise moment at which the outgoing mail was placed in the hands of the U.S. Postal Service, the trial court found that this had presumably occurred prior to the time of the attempted revocation on Tuesday evening. It thus ruled that a contract had been formed, and granted plaintiffs decree of specific performance. Defendants appealed.

Per Curiam:

. . . The [primary] issue presented is whether the trial court erred in determining that a binding contract existed. Neither party challenges the applicable law. [The court quoted the rule from a prior New Hampshire decision as follows:] "To establish a contract of this character, there must be an offer and an acceptance thereof in accordance with its terms. Where the parties to such a contract are at a distance from one another and the offer is sent by mail, the reply accepting the offer may be sent through the same medium, and the contract will be complete when the acceptance is mailed . . . and beyond the acceptor's control." Withdrawal of the offer is ineffectual once the offer has been accepted by posting in the mail.

The defendants argue, however, that there is no evidence to sustain a finding that plaintiff Cushing had accepted the adjutant general's offer before it was withdrawn. Such a finding is necessarily implied in the court's ruling that there was a binding contract. The implied finding must stand if there is any evidence to support it.

Plaintiffs introduced the sworn affidavit of Mr. Cushing in which he stated that on April 3 he executed the contract and placed it in the outbox daily and put in the U.S. mail. No [other evidence bearing on this point] was submitted in this informal hearing, and . . . the court's order appears to be [based] in part . . . [on representations made by attorneys for both sides,] a procedure which was not objected to by the parties.

Thus the representation that it was customary office procedure for the letters to be sent out the same day that they are placed in the office outbox, supported the implied finding that the completed contract was mailed before the attempted revocation [was received]. Because there is evidence to support it, . . . the trial court's finding that there was a binding contract. . . must stand.

Decree affirmed.

The following case applies the reasonable medium approach in a common-law context, the question being when the acceptance was actually "sent."

When Acceptance Takes Effect: UCC Changes for Sale of Goods Transactions

The Uniform Commercial Code generally adopts the reasonable medium rule of the common law, UCC Sec. 2- 206(1)(a), providing that an offer may be accepted by "any medium reasonable in the circumstances." However, whereas the common law holds that if an unreasonable method of acceptance is utilized, it is not effective until received, UCC Sec. 1-201(38) provides that such an acceptance will be deemed effective as of the time it is sent if it is received within the time that a seasonably dispatched acceptance using a reasonable medium would normally arrive.

Acceptance of Unilateral Offers

Offers for unilateral contracts pose two unique problems insofar as offer and acceptance principles are concerned: (1) whether it is necessary for the offeree, having performed the requested act, to notify the offeror of that fact, and (2) whether the offeror has the right to revoke the offer after the offeree has commenced to perform but before the performance is completed.

Is Notice Required?

The general rule is that a unilateral offer is accepted the moment the offeree performs the requested act; giving notice that the act has taken place is usually not required. This rule does not apply, obviously, to offers that expressly request notification. In such offers, a contract is not formed until the requisite notice is given. Another type of case requiring notice involves those exceptional situations where the act is of such a nature that the offeror "has no adequate means of ascertaining with reasonable promptness and certainty" that the act has taken place. The typical cases in this category are contracts of guaranty—those in which one person guarantees a loan made to another. For example: A, in Columbus, asks B, in Miami, to lend $1,000 to C, a Miami resident, A promising to pay the debt if C fails to do so. In this situation, most courts take the view that while a contract is formed between A and B the moment that B makes the loan, A's resulting obligation is discharged (terminated) if B fails to notify him within a reasonable time that the loan has been made.

When Can Revocation Be Made?

Where the requested act will take a period of time for completion, the traditional rule has been that the offeror can revoke the offer at any time before full performance has taken place, even if the offeree has started to do the job. In such a case a contract is never formed. (However, under the quasi-contract theory, the offeree is ordinarily entitled to recover the reasonable value of his or her performance prior to the revocation. In the event that this partial performance is of no value to the offeror, the offeree will, of course, recover nothing.)

In recent years a growing number of courts have felt that the traditional view is unfair to the offeree in many circumstances, and they have abandoned it in favor of several other approaches. The most widely accepted of the newer views is that where the act is one that of necessity will take a period of time to complete, the right of revocation is suspended once the offeree starts to perform and remains suspended until the offeree has had a reasonable time to complete the act. This view is consistent with the traditional view to the extent that no contract is formed until the act has been completed, but it affords an interim protection to the offeree that the traditional view does not. Thus we have yet another illustration of the courts' freedom, within the framework of the common law, to modify those earlier principles whose application has brought about results of questionable merit.

Unilateral-Bilateral Contracts: UCC Changes for Sale of Goods Transactions

Most sale of goods contracts are clearly bilateral in nature. For example, a buyer on September 10 sends an order for goods at a specified price for November shipment, and the

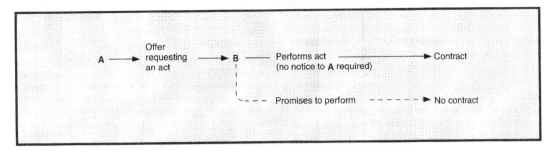

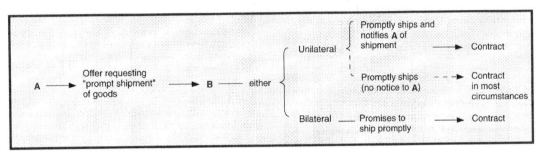

Figure 12.3 Acceptance of a Unilateral Offer under Common-Law and UCC Rules

seller accepts the offer—i.e., promises to ship the goods as ordered—by mailing his or her acknowledgment to the buyer on September 16. Because Sec. 2-206 provides that "an offer to make a contract shall be construed as inviting acceptance in any manner and by any medium reasonable in the circumstances," a bilateral contract is formed the moment the acceptance is deposited in the mail on the 16th (assuming the offeror had not stated otherwise and that mail was a reasonable medium).

"Prompt Shipment" Offers

Prior to adoption of the UCC, if a buyer ordered goods using such terms as "prompt shipment," "for current shipment," or "ship at once," the offer was usually construed as being an offer for a unilateral contract. Under this common-law view, actual shipment was the only way in which the offer could be accepted; a promise to ship would not cause a contract to come into existence (a result that sometimes came as a surprise to one or both of the parties). Sec. 2-206(1) of the UCC rejects that view by providing that an offer containing such language shall be construed as inviting acceptance either by prompt shipment or by a prompt promise to ship. Therefore, an offeree's sending of a return promise to ship forms a bilateral contract in such circumstances (although prompt shipment must follow or the contract will be contract wil be breached). The buyer can still require acceptance of the offer only by the act of shipment itself, but he or she now must explicitly state this in the offer.Sec. 2-206 thus blurs the common-law distinction between bilateral and unilateral offers by permitting the offeree, in this limited instance, a choice as to how his or her acceptance shall be made. The differences between common law and the UCC on this point are illustrated in Figure 12.3.

CHAPTER **13**

CONSIDERATION

AN ELUSIVE THING called **consideration** is the second element ordinarily required in a contract. Generally, if an agreement lacks consideration, neither party can enforce it, even if it is in writing. As a practical matter, consideration is present in most agreements; but since this is not always the case, we need a basic understanding of the doctrine of consideration in order to determine when an agreement is legally binding.

Historical Note

Courts have long struggled with the question of what agreements ought to be enforced. No system of law has ever enforced all promises, nor could this feasibly be done. Present—day concepts of consideration have resulted from a mixture of logic and historical accident. At one time, contracts had to be "sealed" in order to be enforced. A **sealed contract** had to have a bit of wax affixed to it, on which the initials or other distinctive marks of each of the parties were imprinted. Today, sealed contracts are virtually unknown, though a few jurisdictions will enforce such a contract even in the absence of consideration. Most jurisdictions, however, will enforce no contract, sealed or unsealed, in the absence of consideration.

The present—day requirements of consideration center in part on the notion that one party to an agreement should not be bound by it if the other party is not similarly bound. A's promise to give a present to B should not be binding on A because B is not bound to do anything. Promises to make gifts are generally unenforceable. Another important aspect of consideration is that it prevents one contracting party from exploiting another, as shall be illustrated later in this chapter in connection with a discussion of the "preexisting obligation" rule.

The Basic Concept of Consideration

Courts agree substantially about the kinds of promises or acts constituting consideration in most situations. Although several definitions of and tests for consideration have been formulated over the years, most lead to the same conclusion when applied to agreements where the existence of consideration is questioned. Our discussion focuses on a popular approach that emphasizes the "bargain" element of a transaction, which helps distinguish a promise of a mere gift (which may not be enforced) from an enforceable commercial promise to do something that the other party has bargained for.

Assume that Company A promised to deliver 5,000 tires to Company B on July 1 in exchange for Company B's promise to pay $200,000. Assume further that Company B breached the promise; Company A sued for breach of contract; and Company B raised the defense that no consideration existed to support its promise. How would B's contention be analyzed?

The *first* determination is whether the promisee (Company A, the party that received the promise that was not performed) suffered a **legal detriment**, defined as (a) doing (or promising to do) something that it was not obligated to do, or (b) refraining from doing (or promising to refrain from doing) something that it had a right to do. Unless Company A had a preexisting legal or contractual obligation to deliver the 5,000 tires, it is clear that Company A did suffer a legal detriment in this transaction. It promised to do something it did not otherwise have to do—to deliver 5,000 tires.

The *second* element of consideration is that the detriment (A's promise to deliver the 5,000 tires) must induce the promise that was not performed (B's promise to pay $200,000). Unless there is some other explanation for why Company B promised to pay $200,000 to Company A, it is clear that the detriment did induce the promise in this case.

The *third* element of consideration is that the promise (B's promise to pay $200,000) must induce the detriment (A's promise to deliver the 5,000 tires). Again, unless some other reason appears to explain why A promised to deliver the 5,000 tires, it seems clear that it was in order to earn the $200,000 promised by B. All three elements of consideration are present, so the contract is enforceable.

Sometimes, the second and third elements are combined and referred to as a requirement that there must have been a **bargained–for exchange**. This simply means that the parties must have bargained, or agreed, that each was giving something up in return for what the other party was giving up.

Viewed in this light, consideration at a general level is easy to understand and, obviously, is present in most cases. Companies and individuals promise to deliver goods and services because they want the money that other companies and individuals are willing to pay for those goods and services.

Consider another example. Assume that X promises to install a home air–conditioning unit for Y, and Y promises to pay X $1,100 for the job. Consideration will become important if one of the parties, let us say X, breaches the promise, is sued by Y, and claims lack of consideration as a defense. A court will quickly find: (1) The promisee (Y) has suffered a legal detriment (promising to do something he did not have to do—pay $1,100). (2) The detriment (Y's promise to pay $1,100) induced the promise (X's promise to install the air–conditioning unit). Obviously X bargained for Y's promise of payment; that is how X makes his living. (3) The promise (X's promise to install the air–conditioning unit) induced the detriment (why else would Y have promised to pay $1,100?). Try to analyze the following cases using the three basic elements of consideration.

HAMER V. SIDWAY
Court of Appeals of New York, 27 N.E. 256 (1891)

William E. Story, Sr., promised to pay his nephew, William E. Story, II, $5,000 if he would refrain from drinking, using tobacco, swearing, and playing cards or billiards for money until he became twenty-one years of age. The nephew refrained from all the specified activities as he was requested to do, and on his twenty-first birthday he wrote his uncle a letter asking him for the money.

The uncle, in reply, assured the nephew, "You shall have the $5,000 as I promised you." The uncle went on, however, to explain that he had worked very hard to accumulate that sum of money and would pay it "when you are *capable of taking care of it, and the sooner that time comes the better it will suit me."*

Two years later the uncle died, without having made payment. The administrator of the uncle's estate Sidway, refused to pay the $5,000, and suit was brought to recover that sum. (The plaintiff is Hamer, rather than the nephew, for the reason that at some time before litigation was begun the nephew had assigned—that is, sold—his rights against the estate to Hamer. Thus Hamer's right to recover is entirely dependent upon whether the nephew had a valid contractual claim against his uncle.)

The trial court ruled that the uncle's promise to pay the $5,000 was not supported by consideration on the part of the nephew (the promisee) and entered judgment for the defendant. The plaintiff appealed.

Parker, Justice:

The defendant contends that the contract was without consideration to support it, and therefore invalid. He asserts that the promisee, by refraining from the use of liquor and tobacco, was not harmed, but benefited; that that which he did was best for him to do,... and insists that it follows that, unless the promisor was benefited, the contract was without consideration—a contention which, if well founded, would [inject into the law, in many cases, an element so difficult to measure that needless uncertainty would result]. Such a rule could not be tolerated, and is without foundation in the law....

Pollock, in his work on Contracts, page 166, says: "Consideration' means not so much that one party is profiting as that the other abandons some legal right... as an inducement for the promise of the first." Now, applying this rule to the facts before us, the promisee used tobacco, occasionally drank liquor, and he had a legal right to do so. That right he abandoned for a period of years upon the strength of the promise of the [uncle] that for such forbearance he would give him $5,000. We need not speculate on the effort which may have been required to give up the use of those stimulants. *It is sufficient that he restricted his lawful freedom of action within certain prescribed limits upon the faith of his uncle's agreement, and now, having fully performed the conditions imposed, it is of no moment whether such performance actually proved a benefit to the promisor, and the court will not inquire into it;* ... [Emphasis added.] Few cases have been found which may be said to be precisely in point, but such as have been, support the position we have taken....

Judgment reversed.

Comment

CommentTwo consideration principles are underscored here, as a result of the higher court's rejection of the defenses raised by the uncle's estate. First, if a *promisee* incurs a detriment by giving up a legal right, the promisee has given consideration even though he or she may have received an incidental benefit at the same time. Thus, the nephew gave consideration by giving up certain rights—such as the right to smoke—even though he may have also been physically benefited by this forbearance). Second, even though the promisor typically receives some benefit from what the promisee gave up in return for the promisor's promise, it is not a requirement that the promisor have received any such benefit, and the courts normally do not make any inquiry into whether the promisor received a benefit.

Although consideration is usually present in contracts, and indeed is typically proved by the same evidence that proved that there was an agreement, obviously it is not always present. Consider the following examples.

- Company A to Company B: "Because you are having such tough times, we will charge you 20 percent less for custodial services than our contract with you calls for" In most jurisdictions, a court would not hold A to this promise. It is basically a gift, since B *suffered no legal detriment.*
- Company A to Company B: "We have an old metal press that we are no longer using If you would like to come over some time and pick it up, you may have it." If A reneges on this promise, it will not be deemed enforceable. Even if we assumed that B suffered a detriment in the transaction (making the effort to pick up the press), *that detriment did not induce A's promise.* A was not "bargaining for" that act. Rather, this is basically a promise to make a gift and is unenforceable.
- Wife attacks her husband (D) with an ax, knocking him down As she is about to decapitate him, P intervenes, catching the ax on its downward flight. P's hand is badly mutilated. D jumps up and promises to pay P $1,000 for saving his life. P has clearly suffered a detriment, and it is exactly what D bargained for. However, the *promise did not induce the detriment.* That is, because D made his promise after P acted, we cannot say that his promise caused her to do what she did. Thus, most courts would not enforce this promise. See Harrington v. Taylor, 36 S.E.2d 227(N.C. 1945).

Performance of Preexisting Obligations

As a general rule, a promisee does not incur a detriment by performing, or promising to perform, an act that he or she was under a preexisting duty to perform. One can be under a **preexisting obligation** because of the general law of a state or the federal government, or because a prior contract has not yet been carried out.

Obligations Imposed by Law

The following is a simple illustration of an obligation imposed by law. X's store has been burglarized, and X promises a local policeman $75 if he uncovers, and turns over to the authorities, evidence establishing the identity of the culprit. If the policeman furnishes the requested information, he is not entitled to the reward. Under city ordinances and department regulations he already has a duty to do this; therefore it does not constitute a detriment to him.

Contractual Obligations

Greater difficulty is presented in situations where the preexisting obligation exists (or may exist) as the result of a prior contract between the parties. While such situations involve varying fact–patterns, the starting point can be illustrated as follows. D contracts to drill a seventy–foot well for G for $200. After he commences work, D complains that he is going to lose money on the job and may not finish it unless he gets more money. G then says, "All right. Finish up and I'll pay you $100 extra," and D completes the job. G now refuses to pay the additional $100, and D brings suit to hold G to his promise. In this situation most courts would rule that D's act of completing the well was simply the performance of his original obligation—that he incurred no detriment thereby, and cannot enforce G's promise to pay the additional money. Thus, as a general rule, a **modification contract**—a contract that alters the terms of an existing contract—requires some new consideration in order to be enforceable. (Consideration would have been present in the above case, for example, had the modification contract required something extra of D—such as drilling the well to a depth of eighty feet.)

The primary rationale for the rule that performance of one's preexisting obligations does not constitute consideration is the prevention of coerced modification contracts. In other words, referring to the original example, the purpose is to prevent D—by threatening to stop work, or by actually stopping it—from enforcing the new promise made by G to pay more, in these circumstances.

Application of the preexisting obligation rule in most instances makes sense and brings about reasonable results. The following case is typical of those in which the rule prevents the enforceability of the modification contract. Following this case, a number of exceptions to the rule (and the reasoning underlying them) will be noted.

QUARTURE V. ALLEGHENY COUNTY ET AL.
Superior Court of Pennsylvania, 14 A.2d 575 (1940)

Quarture, plaintiff, owned land in Pennsylvania. A portion of it was taken when the defendant county relocated and widened a state highway. Plaintiff needed legal help to recover damages from the county, and he employed a lawyer, Sniderman, to represent him in this effort.

A written contract was entered into, under the terms of which Sniderman was to "institute, conduct, superintend or prosecute to final determination, if necessary, a suit or suits, action or claim against the County of Allegheny on account of taking, injuring, and affecting (my, our) property in the relocation, widening, and opening of the State Highway known as Route No. 545." The contract further provided that Sniderman was to receive, as a fee for his services, "10 percent of all that might be recovered."

Sniderman represented plaintiff before the Board of Viewers of Allegheny County, and the board awarded plaintiff $1,650 damages.

Plaintiff was dissatisfied with this amount and wished to appeal that award.

Subsequently, a new agreement was entered into between plaintiff and Sniderman. This agreement provided that Sniderman would appeal the case to the court of common pleas and that Quarture would pay him a fee of 33 percent of whatever recovery might be obtained on appeal.

Plaintiff, represented by Sniderman, then brought this action in the court of common pleas, appealing the award of the Board of Viewers, and the court awarded him a judgment of $2,961. At this point Sniderman filed a petition with the court, asking it to distribute to him 33 percent of the judgment—$987.

Quarture objected, contending that his promise to pay the larger percentage was not supported by consideration and that Sniderman was thus bound by his original contract (a fee of 10 percent). The court rejected this *contention and awarded Sniderman $987. Plaintiff appealed.*

Stadtfeld, Justice:

. . . Our first duty is to construe the original [contract]. What is meant by the terms "final determination?" . . . In the case of *Ex parte Russell*, 20 L.Ed. 632, it was said: "The final determination of a suit is the end of litigation therein. This cannot be said to have arrived as long as an appeal is pending."

The proceedings before the Board of Viewers cannot be considered as a "final determination," as their award is subject to appeal by either the owner of the property or by the municipality. If it were intended to provide for additional compensation in case of appeal from the award of viewers, it would have been a simple matter to have so provided in the contract. We cannot rewrite the contract; we must construe it as the parties have written it. . . .

The general principle is stated in 13 C.J. 351, as follows: "A promise to do what the promisor is already bound to do cannot be a consideration, for if a person gets nothing in return for his promise but that to which he is already legally entitled, the consideration is unreal." Likewise, at p. 353. "The promise of a person to carry out a subsisting contract with the promisee or the performance of such contractual duty is clearly no consideration, as he is doing no more than he was already obliged to do, and hence has sustained no detriment, nor has the other party to the contract obtained any benefit. Thus a promise to pay additional compensation for the performance by the promisee of a contract which the promisee is already under obligation to the promisor to perform is without consideration."

There are many cases in which this rule of law is laid down or adhered to, but one that clearly sets out the reason for the rule is Lingenfelder v. Wainwright Brewing Co., 15 S.W. 844. In that case, plaintiff, an architect engaged in erecting a brewery for defendant, refused to proceed with his contract upon discovering that a business rival had secured one of the subcontracts. The company, being in great haste for the building, agreed to pay plaintiff additional compensation as an inducement to resume work. It was held that the new promise was void for want of consideration, the court saying:

It is urged upon us by plaintiff that this was a new contract. New in what? Plaintiff was bound by his contract to design and supervise this building. Under the new promise he was not to do any more or anything different. What benefit was to accrue to defendant? He was to receive the same service from plaintiff under the new [contract] that plaintiff was bound to render under the original contract. What loss, trouble, or inconvenience could result to plaintiff that he had not already assumed? No amount of metaphysical reasoning can change the plain fact that plaintiff took advantage of defendant's necessities, and extorted the promise of 5 percent on the refrigerator plant as the condition of his complying with his contract already entered into. . . What we hold is that, when a party merely does what he has already obligated himself to do, he cannot demand an additional compensation therefor, and although by taking advantage of the necessities of his adversary he obtains a promise for more, the law will regard it as *nudum pactum*, and will not lend its process to aid in the wrong. . . .

While we do not question the value of the services rendered by Mr. Sniderman, we are nevertheless constrained by reason of our interpretation of the [first] agreement, *to limit the right of recovery to the amount stipulated therein [in view of the fact that the carrying on of the appeal was nothing more than what the first agreement required of him].* [Emphasis added.] It is unfortunate that [that] agreement did not stipulate additional compensation in case of an appeal.

Judgment reversed.

Exceptions to the Preexisting Obligation Rule

Generally, the preexisting obligation rule applies to both coerced promises and uncoerced promises. Thus if a party to a contract later makes a modification contract under which he or she agrees to pay a higher price for property or services to be received under the first contract, such party is not liable on the promise even if it was an entirely voluntary one on his or her part. Because the freeing of the promisor from liability on the second promise when made voluntarily, is sometimes felt to be unfair to the promisee, the courts (or legislatures) of the various states have fashioned a number of exceptions that cause the voluntary modification contract to be enforceable. The exceptions noted below are often recognized (although the circumstances to which they apply are rather limited ones).

The Unforeseen Difficulties Exception

The unforeseen difficulties rule is most easily illustrated by reference to a leading case in which a builder, Schuck, contracted to dig a cellar under a portion of an existing house, to a depth of seven feet, for $1,500. (The contract was made after the parties examined an excavation across the street, where the soil appeared to be normal.) After commencing work, Schuck discovered that the ground below the three—foot level was "swamp-like, black muddy stuff," and that this condition would require the use of piling, which the parties did not contemplate under the contract. Thereupon the home owner, Linz, told Schuck to do whatever was necessary to dig a seven foot cellar, adding that he would "pay him whatever additional cost" was involved. Schuck completed the job. In ensuing litigation, Linz denied that there was consideration on Schuck's part to support his promise to pay more than the $1,500. The court rejected this contention and permitted Schuck to recover his additional costs. Linz v. Schuck, 67 Atl. 286 (1907). The facts of this case must be distinguished from those presented by the earlier well-drilling example. In that example, the well driller threatened to quit simply because he was losing money, not because of some unknown condition of the soil that required unanticipated efforts.

In reaching this conclusion, the court stated that, in its opinion, *the preexisting obligation rule should not be applied to a situation of this sort.* To support its reasoning the court relied upon these statements from a prior decision:

> It is entirely competent [legally possible] for the parties to a contract to modify or waive their rights under it and ingraft new terms upon it, and in such a case the promise of one party is the consideration for that of the other; but, where the promise to the one is simply a repetition of a subsisting legal promise, there can be no consideration for the promise of the other party, and there is no warrant for inferring that the parties have voluntarily rescinded or modified their contract. But where the party refusing to complete his contract does so by reason of some *unforeseen and substantial difficulties in the performance of the contract, which were not known or anticipated by the parties when the*

contract was entered into, and which cast upon him an additional burden not contemplated by the parties, and the opposite party promises him extra pay or benefits if he will complete his contract, and he so promises, the promise to pay is supported by a valid consideration. [Emphasis added.] (Bryant v.Lord, 19 Minn. 396, 1872.)

Situations where the rule is applied are admittedly exceptional; the courts of a few jurisdictions do not recognize it at all. And, among courts that do, they have historically taken the view that such circumstances as increased costs, unexpected labor difficulties, or loss of expected sources of materials do not fall within the unforeseen difficulties (or "unanticipated circumstances") rule. However, among such courts today there is a clear trend to recognize such circumstances as being within the rule if (1) the circumstance was truly unanticipated when the contract was made, and (2) the increased compensation is "fair and equitable under the circumstances"—i.e., the extra money promised is no more than a reasonable compensation to the promisee for the additional effort or costs he or she expended in finishing the job. To illustrate: C contracts to build a home for B for $95,000. After work is under way C is unable to get the Pella windows called for in the contract from his local supplier, because of a strike in the Pella plant. C learns, however, he can get the identical Pella windows from a distant supplier at a cost of $500 higher than he originally expected to pay for them. When C tells B this, B tells C to go ahead with the window installation and he will pay C the additional cost. If C completes the job, he is entitled to the extra $500.

The Mutual Rescission Exception

If the parties to the original contract expressly or impliedly rescind (cancel) it before it is fully performed, and enter into a new contract involving the same subject matter, the new contract is enforceable. To illustrate: C contracts to do certain work for B for $1,000. After C starts the job he complains on several occasions that he is going to lose money on the deal. B says that he will consider paying more, and suggests a new contract be made. C, with B's consent, then tears up the contract, and the parties make a new contract under which B agrees to pay C $1,200 for the job. When C finishes the work, he is entitled to the $1,200. The rationale is that the mutual cancellation of the first contract freed C of his preexisting duty to do the job, and when C later assumed the same obligation under the new agreement he thus incurred a new detriment sufficient to support B's promise to pay the larger sum. (While this view has been criticized by several authorities, it continues to be followed by most courts today.)

Modification Contracts: Sales Law

The drafters of the UCC made several modifications of the common law aimed at preventing technical rules from impeding enforcement of the parties' factual bargain. As an example, the drafters believed that if the parties to a sales contract subsequently modified it voluntarily, that modification should be enforceable whether or not supported by consideration. Accordingly, UCC Sec. 2−209(1) rejects the general common−law rule by providing that "an agreement modifying a contract [for the sale of goods] needs no consideration to be binding." To illustrate: S and B have agreed that S will sell a certain quantity of goods (such as 10,000 gallons of fuel oil) to B at a certain price. S later finds that he is not going to be able to deliver by the agreed—upon date. He contacts B, who agrees to an extension of the time for delivery. B subsequently has a change of heart and demands the goods on the original date. Under the UCC, B is bound by the agreed—upon modification even though S gave no additional consideration for the extension of time. (The reasoning behind Sec. 2–209 has prompted several states, including California, New York, and Michigan, to adopt a similar rule for common—law contracts.)

Although the modification agreement need not be supported by new consideration, it must still meet two requirements that the UCC imposes on all contracts falling within its scope. First, the modification must be made in good faith—that is, it must not be a coerced modification. And, second, the contract must not be "unconscionable"— i.e., shockingly one—sided. (The concepts of coercion [duress] and unconscionability are discussed in later chapters.)

To avoid difficulties caused by claims of subsequent modifications, many parties place in their written contracts clauses stating that subsequent modifications not evidenced by a writing shall have no effect. Such NOM ("no oral modification") clauses are expressly made enforceable by Sec. 2–209(2).

Adequacy of Consideration

Whenever the enforceability of a promise is at issue, a finding that the promisee incurred a legally recognized detriment results in the promisor being bound by the contract. This is usually true even if the actual values of the promise and the detriment are unequal— as is reflected in the oft—repeated statement that "the law is not concerned with the adequacy of consideration."

To illustrate: X contracts to sell an acreage in Montana to Y for $60,000. Y later discovers that the actual value of the land is under $30,000. Y is liable on his promise to pay $60,000, even though what he received was worth much less. Under the usual test, X incurred a detriment when he promised to convey the land—the surrender of his right to retain the property. The presence of this detriment constituted a consideration sufficient to support Y's promise to pay; and Y's claim of inadequacy is therefore of no relevance. The legal sufficiency of an act or promise, rather than its adequacy, is controlling.

Mutuality of Obligation

The requirement of mutuality of obligation dictates that there must be consideration on the part of both parties to the contract. As we have indicated, in the typical bilateral contract each party's promise is supported by the promise of the other, and the requirement is met. If, however, in a particular case there is no mutuality because consideration is lacking on the part of one of the parties, neither party is bound by the agreement. Such an agreement is called an **illusory contract.** For example, A and B enter into a written agreement under the terms of which A promises to employ B as his foreman for one year at a salary of $22,000 and B promises to work in that capacity for the specified time. The last paragraph of the agreement provides that "A reserves the right to cancel this contract at any time." Because A has thus not absolutely bound himself to employ B for the year, A has incurred no detriment (no unconditional obligation) by such a promise, with the result that B's promise to work for the year is not binding upon him. Thus, he can quit work at any time without liability to A. In such a case the requirement of mutuality of obligation has not been met, since A is said to have a "free way out" of the contract, and his promise is therefore "illusory."

In the next case the right of cancellation was a restricted one. See if you agree with the distinction which the higher court makes between this kind of a clause, on the one hand, and one where the right to cancel is absolute, on the other.

LACLEDE GAS COMPANY V. AMOCO OIL COMPANY
U.S. Eighth Circuit Court of Appeals, 522 F.2d 33 (1975)

In 1970 a number of mobile home parks were being built by developers in Jefferson County, Missouri. At this time there were no natural gas mains serving these areas, so that persons living in them needed propane gas until the mains would be built.

In order to meet this demand, the Laclede Gas Company (Laclede) entered into a written contract with the American Oil Company (Amoco), under the terms of which Amoco would supply Laclede with propane for its customers living in the parks for a minimum period of one year. The contract contained a clause giving Laclede the right to cancel the agreement after one year upon 30 days written notice to Amoco, but it did not give Amoco any corresponding right to cancel the contract.

For several months Amoco made the required deliveries of propane to Laclede, but thereafter Amoco sent a letter to Laclede saying that it was "terminating" the contract. When Laclede brought this action to recover

damages for breach of contract, Amoco contended that it was not bound by the contract because it lacked mutuality (that is, Amoco claimed that its promise to supply the propane was not supported by consideration on the part of Laclede because of the cancellation clause.) The trail court agreed with this contention, and Laclede appealed.

Ross, Judge:

. . . The [trial] court felt that Laclede's right to "arbitrarily cancel the agreement". . . rendered the contract void "for lack of mutuality." We disagree with this conclusion. . . .

A bilateral contract is not rendered invalid and unenforceable merely because one party has the right to cancellation while the other does not. There is no necessity that for each stipulation in a contract binding the one party there must be a corresponding stipulation binding the other.

The important question in the instant case is whether Laclede's right of cancellation rendered all its other promises in the agreement illusory, so that there was a complete [absence] of consideration. This would be the result had Laclede retained the right of immediate cancellation at any time for any reason.

However, in 1 *Williston, Law of Contracts* §104, Professor Williston notes:

Since the courts do not favor arbitrary cancellation clauses, the tendency is to interpret even a slight restriction on the exercise of the right of cancellation as constituting such detriment as will satisfy the requirement of sufficient consideration; for example, where the reservation of right to cancel is for cause,... or after a definite period of notice, or upon the occurrence of some extrinsic event....

Professor Corbin agrees, and states simply that when one party has the power to cancel by notice given for some stated period of time, "the contract should never be held to be rendered invalid thereby for lack of mutuality or for lack of Missouri appears to be in conformity with this general contract rule that a cancellation clause will invalidate a contract only if its exercise is unrestricted.

Here Laclede's right to terminate was neither arbitrary nor unrestricted. It was limited by the agreement in at least three ways. First, Laclede could not cancel until one year had passed after the first delivery of propane by Amoco. Second, any cancellation could be effective only on the anniversary date of the first delivery under the agreement. Third, Laclede had to give Amoco 30 days written notice of termination. These restrictions on Laclede's power to cancel clearly bring this case within the rule [and consideration on Laclede's part thus did exist]....

Judgment reversed.

Requirements Contracts

Buyers and sellers of goods will sometimes enter into contracts where the quantity of the goods being sold—such as gasoline or coal—is not specified; rather, the quantity is to be determined by subsequent events. In some instances, the language of the contract is such that the buyer clearly has a "free way out"; that is, under the terms of the contract the buyer does not absolutely promise to buy any specific amount of goods. For example, S and B enter into a contract under the terms of which B promises to buy from S all the coal that he "might with" over the next six months at a specified price per ton, with S promising to sell such quantity. Because of the language used, either intentionally or accidentally, B has not bound himself to buy any quantity of coal at all; thus the contract is illusory, since B has incurred no detriment. Because mutuality of obligation is lacking, the result is that if B later desires some coal, he is free to buy it from whomever he chooses. Conversely, if B orders coal from S, S has no duty to supply it.

Application of the mutuality of obligation requirement to cases such as the above soon began to cast doubt on the validity of all sales contracts in which buyers did not absolutely commit themselves to purchase some specified minimum quantity of goods. Many contracts, for example, were phrased in such a manner that the quantity of goods the buyer was committed to purchase depended on his or her subsequent needs (whatever they might prove to be) rather than on an obligation to take a fixed number of units at the outset. For example: An ice company contracts to sell to an ice cream manufacturer "all the ice you will need in your business for the next two years" at a specified price per ton.

The courts recognized the practicality of such **requirements contracts** and wanted to enforce them if they could; but the theoretical difficulty was that these contracts did not, by their terms, absolutely bind the buyer to take even a single unit of the product or commodity in question. The courts therefore sought a theory by which many of these contracts could be upheld without demolishing the concept of mutuality.

They accomplished this, in large measure, by adopting the following view. If the parties, by the language of the contract, indicate that the quantity of goods is to be dependent upon the requirements of the buyers business, then the contract is not void for want of mutuality and both parties are bound by it. The determination of the exact quantity of goods is simply postponed, of necessity, until expiration of the period in question. In other words, such contracts are to be distinguished from illusory contracts, in which the quantity is solely dependent upon the buyer's whim or will. Under this theory, while the buyer might not require any of the item or commodity in question, consideration on the part of the buyer exists as follows. In the event that the buyer subsequently requires the product, he or she is obligated to buy it solely from the seller. That is, the buyer gives up the right to buy it from others. Thus contracts such as the one in the ice case are generally binding on both parties.

This discussion simply sketches out the basic distinction between illusory and requirements contracts. There are many cases, however, where the courts have difficulty determining whether the contract falls into one category or the other. This is due largely to the fact that the language is frequently vague—terms much less rigid than require or need are commonly used. As one illustration, the courts by no means agree as to the effect of contracts in which the buyer promises to purchase all goods that he or she "wants" over a specified period. Many feel that this creates a requirements contract; others do not. Thus questions of interpretation arise. And in determining the effect of such terms, an examination of the surrounding circumstances—which differ from case to case—is always relevant. For these reasons, particularly, the results of some cases inevitably conflict with others.

Output Contracts

Output contracts are essentially similar to and governed by the same principles as requirements contracts. A seller contracts to sell his or her entire output of a particular article, or of a particular plant, for a specified period of time to the buyer at a designated unit price. The implied promise of the seller (in the event he or she does produce the articles) not to sell them to anyone other than the buyer constitutes a detriment to the seller. And the promise of the buyer to purchase the output, in the event there is any, constitutes a corresponding detriment to the buyer. As a result, such contracts are usually enforceable.

Sec. 2-306 of the UCC implicitly adopts the general principles stated above in regard to requirements and output contracts. It also tries to limit certain abuses that have occasionally cropped up. For example, a seller under an output contract might take advantage of the buyer by increasing his or her productive capacity far beyond anything the buyer could have anticipated on entering the contract. A similar hardship can exist in a requirements contract when the buyer's requirements skyrocket far above what was reasonably contemplated by the seller or when the buyer shuts down operations solely for the purpose of escaping liability on the contract. Sec. 2–306(1) tries to prevent such abuses by providing: "A term which measures the quantity by the output of the seller or the requirements of the buyer means such actual output or requirements as may occur in good faith, except that no quantity unreasonably disproportionate to any stated estimate or in the absence of a stated estimate to any normal or otherwise comparable prior output or requirements may be tendered or demanded."

Settlement of Debts

After a debt becomes due, sometimes the creditor and debtor enter into a *settlement agreement*. This occurs when the creditor, either on his or her own initiative or that of the debtor, promises to release the debtor of all further liability if the debtor pays a specified sum of money. If, after the specified sum is paid, the creditor seeks to recover the balance of the debt on the ground that the agreement lacked consideration on the part of the debtor, the success of the suit usually depends on whether the original debt was "unliquidated" or "liquidated."

Unliquidated Debts

An **unliquidated debt** is one where a genuine dispute exists between the debtor and creditor as to the existence or amount of the indebtedness. Compromise agreements as to such debts are usually binding. The amount of a claim in a tort case is always subject to doubt, and thus the debt of the one who committed the tort is always an unliquidated debt. Three can also be unliquidated debts in many other situations. For example, suppose that B buys a boat from S, and promises to pay $40,000 for it. B makes a down payment of $20,000, and they agree that the balance is due in 60 days. After taking possession of the boat, B determines that there is a defect in the boat's motor. B then refuses to pay the full balance of $20,000. This is an unliquidated debt because there is a genuine dispute about whether the seller has breached the contract by selling a defective boat or whether the buyer has breached the contract by not paying the full balance. Therefore, a settlement agreement between the parties for, say, $17,000, will be legally enforceable. In the case of an unliquidated debt, the debtor gives up the right to claim in good faith that he owes less, and the creditor gives up the right to claim in good faith that he is entitled to more. Each side has given consideration. Such a settlement agreement is sometimes called an "accord and satisfaction."

Payment by Check The above rule—preventing a further recovery by the creditor—is also applicable to payments by check if the debtor indicates that the tendered payment is meant to be in full satisfaction of the indebtedness (rather than a partial payment). For example: suppose that in the prior situation, before the parties had reached any agreement on the $17,000 settlement amount, B simply mailed S a check for $17,000, bearing the inscription "payment in full," "in full satisfaction," or similar words indicating an offer to settle the debt for that amount. If S endorses the check in the usual manner by signing her name on the back of it, she is—because of B's statement that the check is offered as full payment— impliedly promising to free B of any remaining balance. This promise is binding on S because B, the promisee–debtor, by making the payment again gave up his right to contend in court that he owed less than $7,000 (or, indeed, that he had the right to return the boat and get his down payment back).

Suppose that a creditor such as S in the previous example attempts to protect herself by crossing out B's words "payment in full" or "in full satisfaction" and adding her own inscription, such as "under protest" or "without prejudice," indicating an intent to collect the remainder of the asserted debt. The general common–law rule has been that this action has no effect—the act of cashing or depositing the check implies an acceptance that overrides the words written on the check. For a number of years, there was doubt about whether a particular provision of the UCC changed the common law rule in the case of such checks, with various courts coming to different conclusions. However, a provison in the UCC dealing with checks (UCC 3–311) was revised so as to make it clear that the common–law rules continue to apply to part–payment checks in this type of situation.

Another problem arose with part–payment checks marked "payment in full" (or similar words). What if the recipient never even noticed the words "payment in full" or "in full satisfaction" on the check? This is particularly a problem with large organizations having very large numbers of customers who regular pay their bills by check, like credit card companies, electrical utilities, and so on. It is virtually impossible for them carefully examine thousands of checks a day. As a result, a number of courts have held that accepting and processing a check in such circumstances does not support an inference that the creditor agreed to the compromise. Revised Article 3–311 helps resolve this problem by allowing large corporate payees to notify customers that instruments that are "in full satisfaction" must be sent to a designated office. If the customer does not comply by sending the instrument to the designated office, the claim is not discharged.

Liquidated Debts

In the case of **liquidated debts**, those in which there is no genuine basis for a good faith dispute as to the existence or the amount of the indebtedness, compromise agreements are less frequently binding. For example: A agrees to lend $10,000 to B, and B agrees to repay the debt on a specific date along with 6% interest on the total amount. On or after the date for repayment, B says that he is unable to repay the full amount, and they agree that A will accept $9,000 in full settlement of the debt. B pays that amount, but A later seeks to recover the additional amount (another $1,000 plus the interest).

The common–law rule here is that A's promise to release B from the remainder of the debt is not binding, and he can therefore recover the unpaid balance. The reasoning is that, because there was no basis for a genuine, good faith dispute about the existence or amount of the debt, the payment of $9,000 by B did not constitute a detriment to him, since it was less than what he was already obligated to pay under the loan contract. He was simply performing a "pre–existing duty." This rule is followed by the courts of most states even where the promise to release is in writing. It should be noted, however, that a growing number of states (but still a minority) have rejected the latter view by enacting statutes providing that all settlement agreements, if in writing, are binding upon the creditor even though consideration is absent. Typical of such statutes is Sec. 1541 of the California Civil Code, which reads as follows: "An obligation is extinguished by a release therefrom given to the debtor by the creditor upon a new consideration, or in writing, with or without new consideration."

Payment by Check The common–law view discussed above, permitting further recovery by the creditor in the liquidated debt situation, is also applied by the courts of most states where the partial payment is made by a check that is marked "payment in full" (or words of the same import). Again, however, several states having the "written release" statutes referred to above, the blank endorsement of the check by the creditor is often held to constitute a release "in writing." In such states a recovery by the creditor is thus barred.

Composition Agreements

A different situation is presented when a debtor makes an agreement with two or more creditors, under the terms of which he or she agrees to pay each creditor who joins in the agreement a stated percentage of that person's claim, with the creditors agreeing in return to accept that percentage as full satisfaction of their claims. Such agreements, called **composition agreements** (or creditors' composition agreements), are ordinarily held to be binding on the participating creditors even though each of them receives a sum less than what was originally owed.

To illustrate: X owes Y $1,000 and Z $600. The three parties agree that X will pay each creditor 60 percent of the amount owed and that Y and Z will accept the 60 percent as payment in full. X then pays Y the $600 and Z the $360. If either Y or Z brings suit to recover an additional sum on the theory that his promise to release was not supported by X's payment of the lesser sum, the usual view is that the composition is binding; therefore, the creditor's suit will be dismissed. To reach this result, the courts of many states find consideration to be present in that the promise of each creditor to accept the smaller sum supports the promise of the other creditors to do likewise. Other courts reach the same result by simply ruling that such agreements are binding on the ground of public policy, without trying to find consideration.

Special Situations

Up to this point, we have emphasized the usual situations where the courts require consideration to be present in order for promises to be enforced. (Occasional references to minority views were made only for purposes of completeness.) In the remainder of this chapter, we will focus on three exceptional situations where promises can be enforced by the same courts when consideration clearly is not present. The three are promissory estoppel, promises to charitable institutions, and promises made after the statute of limitations has run.

Promissory Estoppel

While it is well established that a promise to make a gift is generally unenforceable by the promisee even where he or she has performed some act in reliance upon the promise, unusual circumstances exist where the application of this view brings about results that are grossly unfair to the promisee. In such circumstances, the courts occasionally will invoke the doctrine of **promissory estoppel** (or "justifiable reliance" theory, as it is often called) to enforce the promise.

The basic idea underlying this doctrine is that if the promisor makes a promise under circumstances in which he or she should realize that the promisee is almost certainly going to rely on the promise in a particular way, and if the promisee does so rely, thereby causing a substantial change in his or her position, the promisor is bound by the promise even though consideration is lacking on the part of the promisee. To illustrate: Tenant T leases a building from Landlord L from January 1, 1985, to December 31, 1986. In early December 1986, T indicates that he is thinking of remodeling the premises and wants a renewal of the lease for another two years. L replies, 'We'll get to work on a new lease soon. I don't know about two years, but you can count on one year for sure." T then spends $500 over the next few weeks in having the first—floor rooms painted, but the parties never execute a new lease. If L seeks to evict T in March 1987 on the ground that his promise to renew was not supported by consideration, he will probably be unsuccessful—that is, he will be held to his promise regarding the year 1987. In this case, where L should have realized the likelihood of T's conduct in consequence of his promise, L is said to be "estopped by his promise"; that is, he is barred by his promise from contending that the lack of consideration on T's part caused his promise to be unenforceable.

To illustrate further: "A has been employed by B for forty years. B promises to pay A a pension of $200 per month when A retires. A retires and forbears to work elsewhere for several years while B pays the pension. B's promise is binding." *Restatement, Contracts 2d*, The American Law Institute, Section 90, 1973.

Applications of Promissory Estoppel

Promissory estoppel is a doctrine of increasing importance and broadening application. We discuss promissory estoppel in this chapter because it is most commonly thought of as a method of enforcing a variety of promises that lack consideration. However, many courts invoke promissory estoppel in a variety of situations where they believe that contractual formalities are unnecessarily blocking attainment of the reasonable intentions and expectations of the parties. Consideration is one such formality; the requirement that some contracts be in writing in order to be enforceable is another. When the writing requirement is discussed in Chapter 16, we will see how promissory estoppel often

LEGAL FOCUS

Ethics

The law's traditional approach to consideration emphasizes the bargain element. As a general rule, the moral obligation that results from making a promise is not sufficient to cause it to be enforceable. Neither are the motives or feelings of the promisor. Thus, an uncle's promise to pay $500 to his niece "in consideration of the love and affection that I have for you" is not binding. Nor is a promise made "in consideration of your many acts of kindness over the years." These acts (commonly referred to as acts of past consideration), which were performed earlier and, presumably, without expectation of payment, have not been bargained for. Thus, under the traditional approach they do not make a promise enforceable. Should this be the state of the law? Should courts refuse to enforce promises based solely on a moral obligation?

The question becomes more problematic when we address situations such as that arising in Harrington v. Taylor, discussed in the text, where a reward promise by a rescue victim to the rescuer made after the rescue was held to be unenforceable. This traditional rule is slowly being modified by a trend to allow recovery to the extent of the moral obligation involved, that is, by enforcing a promise that was no more than what the promisor ought to have done. Thus, if a millionaire without close relatives promised a woman who had already rendered household services to him without compensation for 20 years that upon his death he would leave $25,000 to her, this promise would, in the eyes of some courts, be enforceable against his estate even if the value of her services was much less. Restatement (Second) of Contracts, Sec. 86. Also, in Webb v. McGowin, 168 So. 196 (Ala. 1935), D's grateful promise to pay P $15 every two weeks for the rest of P's life, made after P permanently injured himself saving D's life, was held enforceable. Does the better rule come from Harrington v. Taylor or Webb v. McGowin? How far can the law feasibly go in enforcing promises that our moral sense tells us should be performed, but that fall short of meeting legal requirements applicable to all other promises?

---

provides an alternative means of enforcing oral promises that the parties intended to be enforceable, but did not put in writing.

Promissory estoppel doctrine is not completely consistent from jurisdiction to jurisdiction, but typical examples of the wide variety of uses of promissory estoppel include:

- X worries about floods and asks his insurance company whether his current policy protects his house from flood damage, indicating that he will procure a different policy if it does not The company assures X that his current policy does cover flood

Garwood Packaging, Inc. v. Allen & Co.
378 F.3d 698 (7th Cir. 2004)

Plaintiff Garwood Packaging, Inc. (GPI) had flopped in its food–packaging system and by 1993 had run up debts of $3 million and was broke. It engaged Martin to help find investors. Martin told GPI that Allen & Co., an investment company for whom he worked, would consider investing $2 million of its own money if another investor could be found to make a comparable investment. Allen also decided to reduce its risk exposure by finding other investors to put in half of the promised $2 million.

Martin located Hobart Corporation that was prepared to manufacture $2 million worth of GPI packaging machines in return for equity in the company. As a precondition, Hobart demanded releases from other GPI creditors, as did the other investors that Allen was bringing into the deal.

Martin told Garwood and McNamara, GPI's principals, that he would see that the deal went through "come hell or high water." Based on several statements of that nature, Garwood and McNamara moved from Indiana to Ohio to be near Hobart's plant where they expected their equipment to be made. They also forgave their personal loans to GPI and incurred other costs. And GPI did not explore other funding opportunities.

Eventually, however, the investors Allen was bringing in to pay half of its promised $2 million got cold feet, so Allen decided not to invest. The deal collapsed and GPI took bankruptcy. When Allen withdrew, no contract had been signed and no agreement had been reached as to how much stock either Allen or Hobart would receive in exchange for their promised contributions to GPI. Nor had releases been obtained from the creditors.

GPI sued Allen on a promissory estoppel theory. The trial judge granted summary judgment to Allen, and GPI appealed.

Posner, Circuit Judge:

GPI claims that Martin's unequivocal promise to see the deal through to completion bound Allen by the doctrine of promissory estoppel, which makes a promise that induces reasonable reliance legally enforceable. Restatement (Second) of Contracts Sec. 90(1). If noncontractual promises were never enforced, reliance on their being enforceable would never be reasonable, so let us consider why the law might want to allow people to rely on promises that do not create actual contracts and whether the answer can help GPI.

The simplest answer to the "why" question is that the doctrine merely allows reliance to be substituted for consideration as the basis for making a promise enforceable. On this view promissory estoppel is really just a doctrine of contract law. The most persuasive reason for the requirement of consideration in the law of contracts is that in a system in which oral contracts are enforceable—and by juries, to boot—the requirement provides some evidence that there really was a promise that was intended to be relied on as a real commitment. Actual reliance, in the sense of a costly change of position that cannot be recouped if the reliance turns out to have been misplaced, is substitute evidence that there may well have been such a promise. The inference is especially plausible in a commercial setting, because most businesspeople would be reluctant to incur costs in reliance on a promise that they believed the promisor didn't consider himself legally bound to perform.

In other words, reasonable reliance is seen as nearly as good a reason for thinking there really was a promise as bargained—for reliance is. In many such cases, it is true, no promise was intended, or intended to be legally enforceable; in those cases the application of the doctrine penalizes the defendant for inducing the plaintiff to incur costs of reliance. The penalty is withheld if the reliance was unreasonable; for then the plaintiff's wound was self—inflicted—he should have known better than to rely.

A relevant though puzzling difference between breach of contract and promissory estoppel as grounds for legal relief is that while the promise relied on to trigger an estoppel must be definite in the sense of being clearly a promise and not just a statement of intentions, its terms need not be as clear as a contractual promise would have to be in order to be enforceable. The reason for this difference between breach of contract and promissory estoppel is unclear.

But even though the court is not precluded from finding a promise by its vagueness, the vaguer the alleged promise the less likely it is to be found to be a promise. And if it is really vague, the promisee would be imprudent to rely on it —— he wouldn't know whether reliance was worthwhile. The broader principle, which the requirement that the promise be definite and at least minimally clear instantiates, is that the promisee's reliance must be reasonable; if it is not, then not only is he the gratuitous author of his own disappointment, but probably there wasn't really a promise, or at least a promise intended or likely to induce reliance. The "promise" would have been in the nature of a hope or possibly a prediction rather than a commitment to do something within the "promisor's" power to do ("I promise it will rain tomorrow"); and the "promisee" would, if sensible, understand this. He would rely or not as he chose but he would know that he would have to bear the cost of any disappointment.

We note, returning to the facts of this case, that there was costly reliance by GPI, and by Garwood and McNamara. The reliance was on statements by Martin, of which "come hell or high water" was the high water mark but is by no means an isolated example. Martin repeatedly confirmed to GPI that the deal would go through, that Allen's commitment to invest $2 million was unconditional, that the funding would be forthcoming, and so on; and these statements induced the plaintiffs to incur costs they would otherwise not have done.

But were these real promises, and likely to be understood as such? Those are two different questions. A person may say something that he intends as merely a prediction, or as a signal of his hopes or intentions, but that is reasonably understood as a promise, and if so, as we know (this is the penal or deterrent function of promissory estoppel), he is bound. But what is a reasonable, and indeed actual, understanding will often depend on the knowledge that the promisee brings to the table. McNamara, with whom Martin primarily dealt, is a former investment banker, not a rube. He knew that in putting together a deal to salvage a failing company there is many a slip 'twixt cup and lips. Unless blinded by optimism or desperation he had to know that Martin could not mean literally that the deal would go through "come hell or high water," since if Satan or a tsunami obliterated Ohio that would kill the deal. Even if Allen had dug into its pockets for the full $2 million after the investors who it had hoped would put up half the amount defected, the deal might well not have gone through because of Hobart's demands and because of the creditors. GPI acknowledges that the Internal Revenue Service, one of its largest creditors, wouldn't give a release until paid in full. Some of GPI's other creditors also intended to fight rather than to accept a pittance in exchange for a release. Nothing is more common than for a deal to rescue a failing company to fall apart because all the creditors' consent to the deal cannot be obtained——that is one of the reasons for bankruptcy law. Again these were things of which McNamara was perfectly aware.

The problem, thus, is not that Martin's promises were indefinite, but that they could not have been reasonably understood by the persons to whom they were addressed (mainly McNamara, the financial partner in GPI) to be promises rather than expressions of optimism and determination. To move to Ohio, to forgive personal loans, to forgo other searches for possible investors, and so forth were in the nature of gambles on the part of GPI and its principals. They may have been reasonable gambles, in the sense that the prospects for a successful salvage operation were good enough that taking immediate, even if irrevocable, steps to facilitate and take advantage of the expected happy outcome was prudent. But we often reasonably rely on things that are not promises. A farmer plants his crops in the spring in reasonable reliance that spring will be followed by summer rather than by winter. There can be reasonable reliance on statements as well as on the regularities of nature, but if the statements are not reasonably understood as legally enforceable promises there can be no action for promissory estoppel.

Suppose McNamara thought that there was a 50 percent chance that the deal would go through and believed that reliance on that prospect would cost him $100,000, but also believed that by relying he could expect either to increase the likelihood that the deal would go through or to make more money if it did by being able to start production sooner and that in either event the expected benefit of reliance would exceed $100,000. Then his reliance would be reasonable even if not induced by enforceable promises. The numbers are arbitrary but the example apt. GPI and its principals relied, and may have relied reasonably, but they didn't rely on Martin's "promises" because those were not promises reasonably understood as such by so financially sophisticated a businessman as McNamara. So we see now that the essence of the doctrine of promissory estoppel is not that the plaintiff has reasonably relied on the defendant's promise, but that he has reasonably relied on its being a promise in the sense of a legal commitment, and not a mere prediction or aspiration or bit of puffery.

Affirmed.

damage. After X's house is damaged by a flood, examination of the policy clearly indicates that flood damage is excluded. The insurance company refuses to pay. Many courts would allow X to enforce the company's promise on grounds of promissory estoppel. See Travelers Indemnity Co. v. Holman, 330 F.2d 142 (5th Cir. 1964).

- P interviews for a job with D Co, telling D that he has a good job with X Co. but would quit there if D offered him a job. D offers P a job, realizing that he will now resign his job with X. When P reports for work, D tells him that it no longer needs him and points out that his employment was "at—will" anyway (so that D is within its rights to terminate P at any time). Many courts would allow P to recover from D on promissory estoppel grounds. See Roberts v. Geosource Drilling Co., 757 S.W.2d 48 (Tex. App. 1988).

- Just before L, a general contractor, submits a bid on a construction project, M, a paving subcontractor, calls L and submits an $8,000 bid for the paving work This is the lowest paving bid, so L reduces his overall bid, submits the bid, and is awarded the contract. Before L can inform M of the bid's success, M calls L to revoke its $8,000 offer, refusing to do the work for less than $15,000. M argues that it revoked its offer before L accepted it and that as of the time of revocation there was nothing to indicate to M that it had a contract it could enforce against L. Many courts would bind M to its promise through the doctrine of promissory estoppel. See Drennan v. Star Paving Co., 333 P.2d 757 (Cal. 1958).

Formal Promises to Charitable Institutions

The law generally looks favorably upon charitable institutions, such as churches, hospitals, and colleges. One result of this policy is that many courts enforce formal promises (e.g., charitable subscriptions) to make gifts to such institutions, even though technically there is no conventional consideration. Among the approaches that courts use to enforce promises to make such gifts are (1) invention of consideration, by finding that each donor's promise is made in consideration of the promises of the other donors (i.e., a donor's promise is supported by the detriment incurred by other donors who made similar promises); (2) promissory estoppel, by finding that donors should foresee that the donee institution will rely on the promised gift, for example, by drawing up plans and beginning construction; and (3) where all else fails, many courts will simply enforce the promise on grounds of public policy.

Promises Made Subsequent to the Running of a Statute of Limitations

All states have **statutes of limitations** limiting the time a creditor has in which to bring suit against the debtor after the debt becomes due. These periods of time vary widely among the states, and there is no typical statute. If the specified period of time elapses without the initiation of legal proceedings by the creditor, the statute is said to have "run." While the running of a statute does not extinguish the debt, it does cause the contract to be unenforceable—that is, it prevents the creditor from successfully maintaining an action in court to collect the debt.

New Promise to Pay. To what extent is the situation altered if the debtor, after the statute of limitations has run, makes a new promise to pay the debt? One might conclude that such a promise is unenforceable, since there is clearly no consideration given by the creditor in return. This, however, is not the case.

In all states, either by statute or by judicial decision, such a promise, if in writing, is enforceable despite the absence of consideration. In such a case, the debt is said to have been "revived," and the creditor now has a new statutory period in which to bring suit. (If the new promise was to pay only a portion of the original indebtedness, such as $200 of a $450 debt, the promise is binding only to the extent of that portion—in this case, $200.)

Part Payment or Acknowledgment. The debt is also revived if a part payment is made by the debtor after the statute has run. If, for example, a five-year statute had run on a $1,000 debt, and the debtor thereafter mailed a check for $50 to the creditor, the creditor now has an additional five years in which to commence legal action for the balance. A mere acknowledgment by the debtor that the debt exists will also revive the obligation to pay.

Imposition of liability in the above instances is based on the theory that the debtor has, by making the part payment or acknowledgment, impliedly promised to pay the remaining indebtedness. The debtor can escape the operation of this rule by advising the creditor, when making the payment or acknowledgment, that he or she is not making any promise as to payment of the balance.

It bears mentioning that these rules regarding the reviving of a debt by part payment or acknowledgement after the statute of limitations has expired *do not apply* to debts that have been discharged in *bankruptcy*. A debt that has been discharged in bankruptcy is not revived by part payment or acknowledgement

CHAPTER **14**

ILLEGALITY

- Contracts Contrary To Statute
- Contracts Contrary To Public Policy
- Effect Of Illegal Contracts

IN the case of Everet v. Williams, 9 Law. Quart. Rev. 197 [England], a lawsuit was filed by one partner against another, alleging that they had gone into business together and that the defendant had kept more than his share of partnership profits. The complaint was rather vague regarding the nature of the business alleging that the parties "proceeded jointly in [dealing for commodities] with good success on Hounslow Heath, where they dealt with a gentleman for a gold watch"; that in Finchley they "dealt with several gentlemen for divers watches, rings, swords, canes, hats, cloaks, horses, bridles, saddles, and other things"; and that a gentleman of Blackheath had items the defendant thought "might be had for little or no money in case they could prevail on the said gentleman to part with the said things." It is told that when it dawned on the court that the partners were highwaymen (the English equivalent of American stagecoach robbers), the solicitors (attorneys) for both parties were jailed and the plaintiff and defendant were both hanged. This possibly apocryphal case vividly makes the point that courts do not generally enforce illegal contracts. Indeed, the third element of an enforceable contract is legality of purpose—the attainment of an objective that is not prohibited by state or federal law.

In this chapter we will examine some of the most common kinds of contracts that are ordinarily illegal under state law. Within a given state, a contract is illegal because it is either (1) contrary to that state's statutes (including the regulations of its administrative agencies) or (2) contrary to the public policy of that state, as defined by its courts.

All states have criminal statutes (many of which, as we saw in Chapter 7, are directed towards various kinds of misconduct in the business world). Such statutes not only prohibit certain acts but, additionally, provide for the imposition of fines or imprisonment on persons who violate them. Any contract calling for the commission of a crime is clearly illegal. Many other statutes simply prohibit the performance of specified acts without imposing criminal penalties for violations. Contracts that call for the performance of these acts are also illegal. (An example of the latter is lending money under an agreement that obligates the borrower to pay interest at a rate in excess of that permitted by statute.)

Still other contracts are illegal simply because they call for the performance of an act that the courts feel has an adverse effect on the general public. (Examples of contracts contrary to public policy are those under which a person promises never to get married or never to engage in a certain profession.)

As a general rule, contracts that are illegal on either statutory or public policy grounds are void. This means that (1) in cases where the contract is entirely executory, neither party is bound by the agreement, and (2) in cases where one of the parties has performed his or her part of the bargain, such party cannot recover the consideration, or the value of the consideration, that has passed to the other party. (Exceptions to this general rule will be discussed later in the chapter.) Furthermore, courts will not allow even quasi–contractual recovery where illegal action is involved. By denying recovery to the parties to an illegal transaction, courts reason that they will deter illegal activity.

Contracts Contrary to Statute

Wagering Agreements

All states have statutes relating to **wagering agreements,** or gambling contracts. Under the general language of most of these statutes, making bets and operating games of chance are prohibited. Any obligations arising from these activities are void (nonexistent) in the eyes of the law, and thus completely unenforceable by the "winner."

Bets and Lotteries

In most instances wagering agreements are easily recognized. Simple bets on the outcome of athletic events and lotteries such as bingo (when played for money) are the most common of them. On the other hand, merchants holding promotional schemes such as supermarket drawings sometimes have difficulty determining if they are holding an illegal lottery, especially because definitions vary widely from state to state. Courts tend to rule that a scheme that does not require a purchase of goods by the participant is not a **lottery** because consideration (which most courts view as an essential part of a lottery) is lacking. That is why so many contests state "no purchase necessary." The following case illustrates a common approach to the lottery issue.

PEPSI–COLA BOTTLING CO. OF LUVERNE V. COCA–COLA BOTTLING CO., ANDALUSIA
Supreme Court of Alabama, 534 So.2d 295 (1988)

Coca–Cola Bottling of Andalusia and Alabama Citizens Action Program sued, claiming that Pepsi–Cola Bottling Company of Luverne had violated a 1982 court order which permanently enjoined Coke and Pepsi "from operation of promotional campaigns whereby consumers of soft drink beverages are participants in 'under the crown or 'on the tab games of chance for which a purchase is necessary all instances except for the right to obtain free crowns, tabs, or chances at some place other than the point of purchase of the beverage." The injunction order found that a 1981 "Pepsi Spirit" campaign in which participants could win cash and "NFL Prizes" (football jerseys and gift certificates) was an illegal lottery that violated the Alabama

Constitution. The court found that other than by buying the soft drink, the only way to participate was to request free bottle tops by mail or to visit the Pepsi bottling plant. Only 60 people had done so, and the trial court declared the free participation option to be a sham.

At issue in this case is Pepsi's 1987 "Instant Cash" promotion, in which certain caps were marked $0.25, $1.00, or $100.00, and others were marked with the letters needed to spell "Pepsi Instant Cash" (which could be worth $10,000 to a person with caps containing all the letters).

For this campaign, Pepsi distributed 25,000 cards with a similar opportunity at participating stores, and advertised by means of store displays and radio that no purchase was required. Cards could also be obtained by telephone request and by writing the bottling plant.

The trial court found that Pepsi's "Instant Cash" promotion was a lottery that placed Pepsi in contempt of the 1982 injunction. Pepsi appealed.

Per Curiam:

The three elements of a lottery are (1) a prize, (2) awarded by chance, and (3) for a consideration. Admittedly, the first two elements are present in Pepsi's promotion; however, the element of consideration is absent.

The very question on appeal was recently answered in our response to the Alabama House of Representatives' inquiry as to whether a bill proposing to allow "[a]ny contest for prizes or money as rewards, which is for promotional or advertising purposes, sponsored or conducted by any . . . soft drink bottler in this state . . . not requir[ing] . . .; consideration therefor" was constitutional *Opinion of the Justices* No. 277, 397 So.2d 546 (Ala. 1981). In finding that the proposal did not offend § 65 of the Constitution, this Court relied upon Clark v.State, 80 So.2d 308 (1954), stating that "the fact that the business enterprise may be 'expected to gain some benefit by way of increased sales' [does not] constitute [the necessary] consideration." *Opinion of the Justices* No. 277, 397 So.2d at 547.

For the same reason, the "Pepsi Instant Cash" game is not a lottery, because participants were not required to purchase cards in order to play. Any incidental profit or benefit to Pepsi in the sale of the soft drinks containing the "under the crown" chance neither provides the consideration to make the game a lottery nor negates the free participation aspect of the game.

We also find that the promotion did not violate the 1982 injunction. That order prohibited promotional campaigns in which purchases were necessary in all instances; it did not preclude "the right to obtain free crown[s], tabs, or chances at some place other than the point of purchase of the beverage." Less than one month after the promotion began, of the 25,000 free cards distributed, 252 winning free cards had been redeemed. There was also evidence that Pepsi's salesmen were instructed to keep records of the free cards dispersed and to check for the availability of such cards at each store.

The aspect of Pepsi's prior promotions that led to the injunction was the unavailability of free chances. A careful reading of the language of the injunction leads to but one conclusion: that Pepsi complied in good faith with the mandates of the injunction and that Pepsi was within its rights in conducting the "Instant Cash" campaign.

Reversed.

In recent years a growing number of state statutes have been liberalized to permit wagering and lottery activities within narrow limits. For example, so–called "friendly bets"—those defined as not producing substantial sources of income—are frequently exempted from the basic wagering statutes, as are some lotteries operated by religious or charitable organizations. Additionally, several states have sanctioned state–operated lotteries by special statutes.

Insurance Contracts

Many contracts whose performance is dependent upon an element of chance are clearly not wagers. This is particularly true of **risk–shifting contracts** (as distinguished from **risk−creating contracts**). If a person insures his or her home against loss by fire, for example, the contract is perfectly legal even though it is not known at the time the policy is issued whether the insurer will have liability under it. The contract is legal despite this uncertainty because the owner had an "insurable interest" in the home prior to taking out the policy—that is, a financial loss would have resulted if a fire had occurred. Thus an insurance policy is simply a contract by which an existing risk is shifted to an insurance company for a consideration paid by the owner. By contrast, an insurance policy on a building which the insured does not own and in which he or she has no other financial interest is clearly a wager and is unenforceable.

Licensing Statutes

All states have **licensing statutes,** requiring that persons who engage in certain professions, trades, or businesses be licensed. Lawyers, physicians, real estate brokers, contractors, electricians, and vendors of milk and liquor are but a few examples of persons commonly subject to a wide variety of such statutes. In many instances, particularly those involving the professions, passing a comprehensive examination (along with proof of good moral character) is a condition of obtaining a license. In others, only proof of good moral character may be required.

To find out whether an unlicensed person can recover for services rendered under a contract, one must check the particular statute involved. Some licensing statutes expressly provide that recovery by unlicensed persons shall not be allowed (no matter how competent their work). Others, however, are silent on the matter, in which case their underlying purposes must be determined. Most courts take the view in such instances that if the statute is *regulatory*—its purpose being the protection of the general public against unqualified persons—then the contract is illegal and recovery is denied. On the other hand, if the statute is felt to be merely *revenue raising*, recovery is allowed.

The reasoning behind this distinction, of course, is that allowing recovery of a fee or commission by an unlicensed person in the first category would adversely affect public health and safety, while the enforcement of contracts in the second category does not have this result. Thus an unlicensed milk vendor who has sold and delivered a quantity of milk will ordinarily not be permitted to recover the purchase price from the buyer. Similarly, an unlicensed physician, real estate agent, or attorney will be denied his or her fee. On the other hand, a corporation that has merely failed to obtain a license to do business in a particular city is still permitted to enforce its contracts, because city licensing ordinances applicable to corporations are normally enacted for revenue raising purposes.

The possibility that a regulatory statute might be passed for the protection of some persons, but not others, is presented in the following case.

BREMMEYER V. PETER KIEWIT SONS COMPANY
Supreme Court of Washington, 585 P.2d 1174 (1978)

The State of Washington awarded Peter Kiewit a prime contract to construct several miles of Interstate 90. The highway right–of–way was overgrown, and needed to have the trees and debris cleared before construction could begin. For this purpose, Peter Kiewit subcontracted the necessary clearing operation to Bremmeyer. Under the subcontract, Bremmeyer agreed to pay Peter Kiewit $35,000 for the right to fall, yard, buck, load and haul to a mill all the merchantable timber within the right–of–way. (Bremmeyer was to keep the proceeds of the sale of the timber as his compensation.)

Bremmeyer paid the $35,000 and began clearing the right–of–way, but before he had finished the job the state terminated Peter Kiewit's prime contract. Peter Kiewit, in turn, cancelled Bremmeyer's subcontract. Peter Kiewit received $1,729,050 from the state for "cancellation costs," but offered to pay Bremmeyer only $38 for cancellation of the contract. Bremmeyer refused the $38 and brought this action to recover the value of the merchantable timber that was still uncut at the time of termination.

In defense, Peter Kiewit's primary argument was that a state statute, RCW 18.27, required contractors to be registered with the state, and that Bremmeyer's failure to register barred his recovery. The trial court, citing a 1973 Washington State case, agreed with this contention and summarily dismissed the action. Bremmeyer appealed.

Stafford, Justice:

... We first considered whether the legislature intended RCW 18.27 to bar actions by unregistered subcontractors against prime contractors in Jeanneret v. Rees, 511 P.2d 60 (1973). A majority of the court agreed the legislature intended to preclude such actions.

[The court then went on to say, however, that it now felt that its decision in that case was based on too literal a reading of the statute and thus was not necessarily controlling. The court continued:]

Continued reliance upon the literal expression of RCW 18.27 is particularly inappropriate in light of the legislature's amendment to the statute after our divided opinion in *Jeanneret*... A new section now provides:

It is the purpose of this chapter to afford protection *to the public* from unreliable, fraudulent, financially irresponsible, or incompetent contractors. [Emphasis supplied by the court.]

In view of this newly declared statutory purpose and the minimal protections afforded the public by the statute, we are convinced the legislature did not intend to protect prime contractors from actions initiated by unregistered subcontractors. The statutory purpose clearly provides protection to the public, i.e., the customers of building contractors. In light of the amendment, and considering the judicial history of RCW 18.27, we do not believe the legislature also intended to protect contractors from each other...

Our conclusion that the legislature did not intend to bar actions by unregistered subcontractors against prime contractors is also supported by the practicalities of the contracting trade. Members of the trade are in a more nearly equal bargaining position with respect to each other. Not only is information concerning financial responsibility and competence readily attainable within the trade, but each contractor is knowledgeable concerning the financial protections needed for any particular job involved...

Judgment reversed, and case remanded for trial.

Usury

Partly as a result of religious views going back to early biblical statements, and partly because of the practical hardships resulting from high interest rates charged desperate borrowers, all states have statutes establishing the maximum rate of interest that can be charged on ordinary loans. Charging interest in excess of the permitted rate constitutes **usury.**

The interest ceilings that are imposed by the usury statutes vary from state to state. Traditionally the basic statutes have varied from 6 percent to 12 percent per annum. However, as a result of inflationary pressures over the years, the basic statutes now generally range from 10 percent to 16 percent per annum.

More important, many kinds of loans are not governed by the basic state statutes. For example, most states put no limit on the rate of interest that can be charged on loans made to corporations. And, under federal regulations, national banks are permitted to charge interest rates that are usually in excess of those permitted by the state usury laws.

Additionally, all states in recent years—again, partly because of inflationary pressures—have adopted special statutes permitting higher rates of interest on other specified kinds of loans. For example, most state laws today provide that interest rates charged by issuers of bank credit cards (such as Visa and MasterCard), and by department stores on their revolving credit accounts, can be at an annual percentage rate of 18 percent. Similarly, home purchase and construction loans, car loans, and loans by credit unions may generally carry annual interest rates ranging from 18 to 25 percent. It should also be noted that most states have adopted special statues that expressly permit mall loan companies, such as "personal loan companies," to charge rates of interest that are considerably higher than those of the general interest statutes. For example, a loan company that qualifies under such statutes may be allowed to charge interest at the rate of 3 percent *per month* on the first $150 of a loan, 2 percent per month on the amount from $151 to $300, and 1 percent on the balance. These statutes usually provide that if interest is charged in excess of the specified rates, the loan is void. In such a case, neither principal nor interest can be recovered.

The basic statutes also vary widely insofar as the effect of usury is concerned. Many states permit the usurious lender to recover the principal and interest at the lawful rate, but not the excess interest. In such states the lender suffers no penalty. In others, the lender is permitted to recover the principal only, forfeiting all interest. And in three or four states, the lender forfeits both interest and principal.

It is thus clear that no determination can be made as to the legality or effect of a given loan without inspecting the statutes of the state in which the transaction took place.

Ethics

In deciding which promises they will enforce or not enforce, courts and legislatures make public policy—engage in "social engineering—just as they do when deciding which types of acts (such as invasion of privacy) will be actionable in tort.

For example, courts have held that contracts in which men pay women to have an abortion are illegal and unenforceable as against public policy. The moral underpinnings of such a ruling are obvious, although to some extent the entire range of arguments underlying our intense national debate over abortion is implicated.

Courts and legislatures have also tended to hold that contracts to pay women to have babies—to be "surrogate mothers"—are unenforceable. So, contracts to terminate fetuses are both contrary to public policy. Is the law consistent? What moral or practical considerations support such policies?

Along related lines, the federal Transplant Act of 1984 makes it a felony to contract to buy or sell organs such as kidneys or hearts for medical transplants. Many experts believe that the provision is part of the reason for this current shortage of organ donors. For example, in 1991, there were 28,000 prospective kidney recipients, but only 6000 or so available donors, and more than 5000 prospective heart recipients, but only 2000 available donors. What moral or public policy considerations justify the refusal to enforce such contracts? Are those considerations likely to be persuasive to a prospective recipient whose life is on the line?

Contracts Contrary to Public Policy
Contracts in Restraint of Trade

Many contracts that unreasonably restrain trade or competition in interstate commerce are in violation of one or more federal antitrust statutes, such as the Sherman and Clayton acts. Long before the enactment of these statutes, however, many other contracts in restraint of trade were illegal under the common law of the various states, and this continues to be the case today. Thus a contract that is not subject to the Sherman or Clayton acts may still result in such restraint of trade that courts will set it aside under common law principles. These principles are briefly summarized here.

Contracts that contain **restrictive covenants**—promises by one party not to engage in a particular occupation or to operate a certain kind of business—compose one group of contracts that are in restraint of trade. However, such promises (sometimes called *covenants not to compete*) are not necessarily illegal. Generally, covenants not to compete are lawful if two conditions are met. First, the covenant must be of an "ancillary" nature, and second, the restriction (the covenant) must be reasonable under the circumstances.

The Ancillary Requirement

An **ancillary covenant** is one that is a subsidiary or auxiliary part of a larger agreement. A common example of an ancillary covenant is that found in a contract calling for the *sale of a business,* where the contract contains a promise by the seller of the business not to engage in the same type of business within a prescribed geographical area for a certain length of time after the sale. Equally common are covenants in *employment contracts,* under which the employee promises not to compete with the business of his or her employer for a specified period of time after the employment is terminated. (Nonancillary promises, on the other hand, stand alone; they do not protect any existing, legally recognized interest such as that in the prior examples. These covenants— such as a promise by a father to pay $10,000 for the son's promise not to engage in medical practice—are generally considered to be an unreasonable restraint of trade in all circumstances, and are thus illegal and unenforceable on public policy grounds.)

Reasonableness—Sale of Business Contracts

When a business is being sold, the interest to be protected relates to the goodwill of the business. A restrictive covenant on the part of the seller, in a particular case, is thus enforceable if its space and time limitations are no broader than are reasonably necessary to afford such protection. For example, a promise by the seller of a retail grocery in Kalispell, Montana, that he will not engage in the retail grocery business "within the City of Kalispell for the period of one year after the sale" is probably reasonable and thus lawful. Similarly, in Gann v. Morris, 596 P.2d 43 (1979), a promise by the seller of a silk-screening business in Tucson, Arizona, that he would not operate a competing business within a hundred–mile radius of Tucson for a specified period of time was held to be reasonable in view of the fact that at least one of the business's customers was located that distance away. Thus, in the above instances, if the seller should violate his or her promise, the purchaser of the business is entitled to an injunction against him or her. (On the other hand, if the restraint is found to be excessive—as would be the case if the seller of the grocery in Kalispell was prohibited from engaging in the grocery business "anywhere within the state of Montana" for one year—the restraint is illegal, and thus unenforceable by the buyer.)

Reasonableness—Employment Contracts

Restrictive covenants in employment contracts are reasonable (1) if the restriction is reasonably necessary to protect the employer, and (2) if the restriction is "not unreasonably excessive" as to the employee. Because of this second requirement, geographical restraints in employment contracts are more likely to be set aside by the courts than those in contracts where businesses are being sold. Courts will also be stricter with time restraints in employment contracts than in sale of business contracts. In one recent case, a one–year covenant was held to be unreasonably long, the court commenting that one year could be several generations in the fast–moving high–tech industry in which defendant employee worked. Earthweb, Inc. v. Schlack, (S.D.N.Y.1999),aff'd 2000 U.S. App. LEXIS 1146 (2d Cir. 2000). In other words, because such restraints may operate with particular harshness upon the employee insofar as his or her ability to make a living is concerned, they are scrutinized with particular care. In contrast to geographical restraints are those covenants under which the employee promises not "to contact or deal with persons who are customers of the employer at the time the employment relationship is terminated" for a stated period of time. Where the time period is found to be reasonable, these kinds of covenants are more likely to be enforced.

PROFESSIONAL BUSINESS SERVICES CO. v. ROSNO
589 N.W.2d 826, Supreme Court of Nebraska, 1999

Plaintiff Professional Business Services Co.(PBS) provides accounting servicesLincoln Nebraska. On October 1, 1992, defendant Rosno signed a contract in which he promised to work for PBS from that date until September 30, 1993, unless the term of employment was extended by PBS from year–to–year. Rosno was a CPA and tax specialist who would manage PBS's accounting and payroll taxes and service its clients. The contract contained a covenant–not–to–compete in which Rosno promised not to solicit, contact or perform services for any of PBS's clients for a period of two years following his leaving PBS for whatever reason within a twenty–five mile radius of Lincoln. In the event of violation, Rosno agreed to pay a liquidated damages amount of the total amount of his billings during that two–year period.

In November 1995, Rosno informed PBS that he was resigning effective 90 days later and that he did not consider the provisions of the non–compete clause to be valid. After leaving PBS, Rosno went into competition with PBS in Lincoln. PBS sued to enforce the covenant–not–to–compete. The trial judge held the covenant invalid and PBS appealed.

Miller–Lerman, Justice:

To determine whether a covenant not to compete is valid, a court must determine whether a restriction is reasonable in the sense that it is not injurious to the public, that it is not greater than is reasonably necessary to protect the employer in some legitimate interest, and that it is not unduly harsh and oppressive on the employee. There is no indication or claim that enforcement of the noncompete clause in Rosno's contract will be injurious to the public or that the restriction is "unduly harsh" as that expression is used in the cases. Accordingly, we focus our analysis on whether or not the restriction of the covenant is no greater than reasonably necessary to protect PBS' legitimate interest.

An employer has a legitimate business interest in protection against a former employee's competition by improper and unfair means, but is not entitled to protection against ordinary competition from a former employee. In Moore v. Eggers Consulting Co., 562 N.W.2d 434(1997), we stated:

To distinguish between "ordinary competition" and "unfair competition," courts and commentators have frequently focused on an employee's opportunity to appropriate the employer's goodwill by initiating personal contacts with the employer's customers. Where an employee has substantial personal contact with the employer's customers, develops goodwill with such customers, and siphons away the goodwill under circumstances where the goodwill properly belongs to the employer, the employee's resultant competition is unfair, and the employer has a legitimate need for protection against the employee's competition.

PBS alleges that Rosno had substantial personal contact with virtually all of PBS has a legitimate interest in protecting customer goodwill. A determination that an employer had a legitimate business interest in customer goodwill does not automatically validate a covenant not to compete. The issue before us, therefore, is whether it can be conclusively determined from the pleadings that the restriction of the noncompete covenant in Rosno's contract is greater than reasonably necessary to protect legitimate interests of PBS.

The relevant postterm noncompete clause in Rosno's contract, section 7b, with the handwritten addendum included, provides as follows:

> Rosno further covenants and agrees that in the event of the termination of his employment, for whatever reason, he shall not directly or indirectly solicit, contact or perform services for any of Employer's clients for his own benefit or as an officer, director, shareholder, partner, advisor, consultant or employee of any third party. Said Post—Term Covenant shall continue for a period of two (2) years following such termination or separation for any reason whatsoever and shall include the area located within twenty—five (25) miles of Lincoln, Nebraska. The post—term covenant shall not apply to clients listed on Exhibit I.

With respect to the propriety of the scope of the noncompete covenant, Rosno cites *Moore* and argues that PBS failed to state a cause of

action because its covenant not to compete generally prohibits Rosno from soliciting PBS' clients, regardless of whether or not Rosno had personal contact with these clients while at PBS, and that the petition shows on its face that the noncompete covenant is unenforceable. PBS responds that the rule set out in *Moore* is a general rule and that it should have been allowed to produce evidence to support the facts alleged and to show that the noncompete provision in Rosno's contract was not more restrictive than necessary to protect PBS' legitimate interests under the facts.

PBS alleged that the noncompete provision was placed in Rosno's contract at Rosno's request, that Rosno insisted that approximately 95 of PBS' clients be omitted from the noncompete provision as reflected in exhibit I to the contract, that Rosno had substantial contact with PBS' clients before he came to work for PBS, that PBS expected that Rosno would continue to have substantial personal contact with PBS' clients upon joining PBS, and that Rosno did in fact have substantial personal contact with virtually all of PBS' clients while at PBS. We conclude that PBS' petition stated a cause of action and that Rosno's demurrer to this petition should have been overruled, thereby allowing PBS to proceed to produce evidence as to the propriety of the inclusion of this non—compete covenant in Rosno's contract.

In *Moore*, this court repeated the general rule that a covenant not to compete may be valid only if it restricts the former employee from working for or soliciting the former employer's clients or accounts with whom the former employee actually did business and had personal contact. In *Moore*, the covenant involved precluded the employee from entering into business with anyone of whom he had knowledge due to his employment with the corporation, rather than those clients of the corporation with whom the employee merely did business and had personal contact. In addition, the covenant in question precluded the employee from working in employment recruitment anywhere in the continental United States. In *Moore*, the summary judgment evidence showed that while with the employer, Moore worked primarily with clients of the employer in the Midwest, indicating that Moore had little personal contact with the employer's clients outside the Midwest. The employer failed to rebut the evidence of over–breadth or otherwise propose a rationale for such a broad restriction. The restriction was, thus, untenable.

PBS' petition taken as a whole states a cause of action. In this regard, we note that PBS has alleged, inter alia, that Rosno has had substantial contact with virtually all of PBS' clients. The inferences of law and fact from the petition are that Rosno is being restricted from working for or soliciting PBS' clients or accounts with whom Rosno actually did business and had personal contact and that in his employment contract the covenant not to compete with respect to all of PBS' clients could be enforceable. PBS should be permitted to present evidence to support the facts alleged. REVERSED.

Will the Courts Rewrite the Contract?

Some courts find that an unreasonably broad time, geography, or activity restriction renders a restrictive covenant completely unenforceable. The modern trend, however, is use of the "blue pencil" rule. Under this approach, courts finding that a contract's restrictions on competition serve an employer's legitimate interests but are unreasonably broad (either in terms of geography or time), will simply rewrite the covenant so that the restrictions are reasonable in scope and then will enforce them to that extent. Thus, a promise not to compete in the entire state of New York for three years might be rewritten to cover only a few counties in New York (where the promisor had worked) for one year.

Exculpatory Clauses

The law of torts imposes certain duties on all persons, one of which is to carry out one's activities in a reasonably careful manner. If a person violates this duty by performing an act carelessly, he or she is guilty of the tort of negligence and is answerable in damages to anyone who was injured thereby.

Businesspersons, and others, often try to avoid this potential liability through the use of **exculpatory clauses** that purport to excuse them from liability resulting from their own negligence. Such clauses are generally—though not always—held to be contrary to public policy, and thus unenforceable against the injured party.

Some exculpatory clauses do *not* attempt to free a party from his or her negligence, but only from liability for injury caused by circumstances outside his or her control; this kind of clause, not contravening public policy, is ordinarily lawful and binding. One example: a school district's form requiring parental permission for a student's attendance at a field day might provide "The district shall have no liability for injuries arising out of transportation of student to and from said location, other than those directly resulting from negligence of district–employed drivers."

The Public Interest Inquiry

The legality of the exculpatory clause depends almost entirely upon the relative strength of the bargaining powers of the contracting parties. Where the party utilizing the clause has *vastly superior bargaining power* over the other, the clause is clearly void. Such disparity is normally found only in those contracts that "substantially affect the public interest"—in other words, in contracts of parties who furnish goods or services that are routinely used by companies and individuals in the carrying on of their everyday business or personal activities.

An early landmark case is instructive on the public policy aspects of exculpatory clauses. Little Rock &Fort Smith Ry Co. v. Eubanks, 3 S.W. 808 (1886). A brakeman was hired by a railroad only after he promised not to sue the company for any injuries that resulted from the company's negligence. When the company raised the clause as a defense in a negligence suit filed by the brakeman's family after his death in an accident caused by a defective switch, the court stated that parties' contracts are normally enforceable as written. However, parties to contracts are not allowed to make agreements that violate express provisions of the law or injuriously affect public policy. If such clauses as that signed in this case were enforced, the court stated:

> [t]he consequence would be that every railroad company, and every owner of a factory, mill, or mine, would make it a condition precedent to the employment of labor, that the laborer should release all right for injuries sustained in the course of the service, whether by the employer's negligence or otherwise. The natural tendency of this would be to relax the employer's carefulness in those matters of which he has the ordering and control, such as the supplying of machinery and materials, and thus increase the perils of occupations which are hazardous even when well managed. And the final outcome would be to fill the country with disabled men and paupers whose support would become a charge upon the counties or upon public charity.

Most of courts will give effect to exculpatory clauses where they involve only recreational activities, such as where people go rafting, skydiving, or horseback riding, or other activities that are completely optional on the part of the participant and thus do not affect the public interest. On the other hand, such clauses typically are not effective to bar a negligence claim in situations where the party in whose favor the clause operates has much greater bargaining power than the other and where the activity involves a matter that affects the public interest—that is, an activity that is not purely optional, such acquiring lodging (as in a residential apartment lease), medical services, utility services, legal services, and so on.

In a situation in which an exculpatory clause is potentially effective because it does not involve a matter affecting the public interest, it will be effective to bar a negligence suit only if the clause is (1) either very conspicuous or specifically called to the attention of the potential plaintiff, and (2) written in a way that clearly informs the potential plaintiff that the drafter of the clause seeks to be relieved from liability for its negligence or the negligence of its employees. An exculpatory clause buried in the fine print of a lengthy form—contract will not be given effect.

Finally, keep in mind that exculpatory clauses can only relieve defendants of liability for simple negligence. Clauses that attempt to avoid liability for acts of intentional wrongdoing or even gross negligence are not effective.

Seigneur v. National Fitness Institute, Inc. 752 A.2d 631, Maryland Court of Special Appeals, 2000

Defendant NFI operates an exercise and fitness facility which plaintiff Seigneur chose to help her on a weight loss and fitness program because (a) her chiropractor recommended NFI, (b) NFI advertised that it employed "degreed, certified fitness, clinical exercise and health specialists," and (c) NFI promised to "provide advice based upon scientific evidence." To apply for membership, plaintiff had to sign a contract containing a clause that provided in emphasized print: "Important Information: I, the undersigned applicant, agree and understand that I must report any and all injuries immediately to NFI, Inc. staff. It is further agreed that all exercises shall be undertaken by me at my sole risk and that NFI, Inc. shall not be liable to me for any claims, demands, injuries, damages, actions, or courses of action whatsoever, to my person or property arising out of or connecting with the use of the services and facilities of NFI, Inc., by me, or to the premises of NFI, Inc. Further, I do expressly hereby forever release and discharge NFI, Inc. from all claims, demands, injuries, damages, actions, or causes of action, and from all acts of active or passive negligence on the part of NFI, Inc., its servants, agents or employees."

Josties, defendant's employee, performed an initial evaluation of plaintiff. She asked plaintiff to use an upper torso machine and placed a 90–pound weight on it, despite her knowledge that plaintiff had a history of lower back problems, a herniated disk, and was in poor physical condition. While attempting to lift the load as instructed, plaintiff felt a tearing sensation in her right shoulder. She informed Josties, who ignored the complaint and completed the evaluation. Since the incident, plaintiff has had pain and difficulty using her shoulder. A doctor attributes plaintiff's difficulties to the injury on the upper torso machine. Plaintiff filed a negligence lawsuit against NFI which moved for summary judgment on grounds of the exculpatory clause quoted above. The trial court granted the motion and plaintiff appealed.

Salmon, J.:

To decide this case, we must first determine whether the exculpatory clause quoted at the beginning of this opinion unambiguously excused NFI's negligence. In construing the Participation Agreement, we are required to give legal effect to all of its unambiguous provisions. Our primary concern when interpreting a contract is to effectuate the parties' intentions. Not all attempts to limit liability by way of exculpatory clauses are successful. For instance, in Calarco v. YMCA of Greater

Metropolitan Chicago, 501 N.E.2d 268 (Ill.App. 1986), the court considered a contract purporting to exculpate the YMCA from liability to a plaintiff who was injured when a weight machine fell on her hand while she was exercising. In *Calarco,* the clause in question read:

"In consideration of my participation in the activities of the Young Men's Christian Association of Metropolitan Chicago, I do hereby agree to hold free from any and all liability the YMCA of Metropolitan Chicago and its respective officers, employees and members and do hereby for myself, my heirs, executors and administrators, waive, release and forever discharge any and all rights and claims for damages which I may have or which may hereafter accrue to me arising out of or connected with my participation in any of the activities of the YMCA of Metropolitan Chicago. I hereby do declare myself to be physically sound, having medical approval to participate in the activities of the YMCA."

The *Calarco* court concluded that the above–quoted clause did not contain a clear and adequate description of covered activities, such as "use of the said gymnasium or the facilities and equipment thereof," to clearly indicate that injuries resulting from negligence in maintaining the facilities or equipment would be covered by the release. "Participation in any of the activities of the YMCA" could be read to mean that the exculpatory clause from liability only pertains to participating in the activities at the YMCA, but not to liability from use of the equipment at the YMCA. Pertinent to this case, plaintiff at the time of the occurrence was not even using the equipment herself, but was assisting someone else who was using a universal machine which was apparently stuck. It is unclear whether this was "participation" in an "activity" under the meaning of the clause. Thus, the court held that "the language of the clause here is not sufficiently clear, explicit and unequivocal to show an intention to protect the YMCA from liability arising from the use of its equipment" at the YMCA.

Powell v. American Health Fitness Center of Ft. Wayne, 694 N.E.2d 757 (Ind. App. 1998) is another case in which the Court found that the exculpatory clause in question was too ambiguous to be enforced. In *Powell,* a health club member was injured while using a fitness club's whirlpool. Referring to the exculpatory clause contained in the club's agreement with the injured member, the court stated:

"Nowhere does the clause specifically or explicitly refer to the negligence of American Health. As a matter of law, the exculpatory clause did not release American Health from liability resulting from injuries she sustained while on its premises that were caused by its alleged negligence. Therefore, the exculpatory clause is void to the extent it purported to release American Health from liability caused by its own negligence."

In the foregoing cases where the clause was held to be ambiguous, the common thread was that the clause did not clearly indicate that the injured party was releasing the health clubs from liability for the clubs' own negligence. Without this clear expression of intent, the courts in those cases felt compelled to invalidate the exculpatory clauses in question. Nevertheless, given the judiciary's reluctance to interfere with the right of parties to contract, courts are almost universal in holding that health clubs, in their membership agreements, may limit their liability for future negligence if they do so unambiguously.

In Maryland, for an exculpatory clause to be valid, it "need not contain or use the word 'negligence' or any other 'magic words.'" Adloo v. H.T. Brown Real Estate, Inc., 686 A.2d 298 (1996). An exculpatory clause "is sufficient to insulate the party from his or her own negligence 'as long as [its] language . . . clearly and specifically indicates the intent to release the defendant from liability for personal injury caused by the defendant's negligence . . . .'" In the instant case, there is no suggestion that the agreement between NFI and Ms. Seigneur was the product of fraud, mistake, undue influence, overreaching, or the like. The exculpatory clause unambiguously provides that Ms. Seigneur "expressly hereby forever releases and discharges NFI, Inc. from all claims, demands, injuries, damages, actions, or courses of action, and from all acts of active or passive negligence on the part of NFI, Inc., its servants, agents or employees." Under these circumstances, we hold that this contract provision expresses a clear intention by the parties to release NFI from liability for all acts of negligence.

More than one hundred years ago, it was noted that "the right of parties to contract as they please is restricted only by a few well defined and well settled rules, and it must be a very plain case to justify a court in holding a contract to be against public policy. This legal principle continues to hold true today.

Three exceptions have been identified where the public interest will render an exculpatory clause unenforceable. They are: (1) when the party protected by the clause intentionally causes harm or engages in acts of reckless, wanton, or gross negligence; (2) when the bargaining power of one party to the contract is so grossly unequal so as to put that party at the mercy of the other's negligence; and (3) when the transaction involves the public interest.

Ms. Seigneur has not alleged that NFI's agents intentionally caused her harm, or engaged in reckless, wanton, or gross acts of negligence. She does assert, however, that the second and third exceptions are applicable.

Appellants argue that NFI "possesses a decisive advantage in bargaining strength against members of the public who seek to use its services." She also claims that she was presented with a contract of adhesion and that this is additional evidence of NFI's grossly disproportionate "bargaining power."

It is true that the contract presented to Ms. Seigneur was a contract of adhesion. But that fact alone does not demonstrate that NFI had grossly disparate bargaining power. There were numerous other competitors providing the same non–essential services as NFI. The exculpatory clause was prominently displayed in the Participation Agreement and Ms. Seigneur makes no claim that she was unaware of this provision prior to her injury.

To possess a decisive bargaining advantage over a customer, the service offered must usually be deemed essential in nature. ("As [teaching the art of parachute jumping] is not of an essential nature, [Parachutes Are Fun, Inc.] had no decisive advantage of bargaining strength against any member of the public seeking to participate.") Winterstein v. Wilcom, 293 A.2d 821 (1972). In Shields v. Sta-Fit, Inc., 903 P.2d 525 (Wash. App. 1995), the Court pointed out that: "Health clubs are a good idea and no doubt contribute to the health of the individual participants and the community at large. But ultimately, they are not essential to the state or its citizens. And any analogy to schools, hospitals, housing (public or private) and public utilities therefore fails. Health clubs do not provide essential services."

The following is as true today as when it was first uttered:

"I, for one, protest . . . against arguing too strongly upon public policy; it is a very unruly horse and when once you get astride it you never know where it will carry you. It may lead you from the sound law. It is never argued at all but when other points fail."

Anne Arundel County v. Hartford Ace. And Indem. Co., 621 A.2d 427 (1993) (quoting Richardson v. Mellish, 2 Bing. 229, 130 Eng. Rep. 303 (1824)). As it relates to exculpatory clauses, unless the clause is patently offensive, Maryland has this unruly horse securely in the stable. Here, the clause passes the not patently offensive test.

AFFIRMED.

Bailment Contracts

Bailment contracts are similar to leases and employment contracts in that they, too, are so widely used as to substantially affect the public interest. Accordingly, the status of exculpatory clauses in such contracts is essentially the same as those in leases and employment contracts—that is, highly suspect in the eyes of the law. A *bailment* occurs when the owner of an article of personal property temporarily relinquishes the possession and control of it to another. The person who has parted with the possession is the *bailor,* and the one receiving it is the *bailee.* Typical bailments result from checking a coat at a nightclub, leaving a car at a garage for repairs, and storing goods at a warehouse.

The existence of a bailment creates a duty on the part of the bailee to use reasonable care in taking care of the property in his possession and, thus, the bailee is liable to the bailor for loss of or damage to the property resulting from the bailee's negligence. In most states, when there is loss of or damage to the property while in the bailee's possession, negligence is presumed and the burden is on the bailee to explain how this happened without negligence.

Commercial bailees such as auto repair shops frequently attempt to escape this liability by the use of an exculpatory clause in the bailment contract. These are typically not effective to bar the owner of the property, such as a car, from suing for negligence if the property is stolen or damaged.

When a person leaves a car at a parking lot, it may or may not be a bailment transaction. Most courts hold that there is not a bailment in the first place unless the parking lot operator has control of the car by having an attendant on duty and keeping the car keys. If there is no bailment, there typically is not duty to exercise reasonable care in taking care of the care, and the exculpatory clause is irrelevant. When the parking lot owner does have such control and there is thus a bailment, an exculpatory clause seeking to relieve the lot owner from liability for negligence in the event the car is stolen or damaged, the clause typically will not be effective.

However, courts are much more likely to give effect to clauses in bailment contracts that seek to limit the extent of the bailee's liability rather than excuse the bailee of liability entirely. Thus, in the case of a parking lot having control of the car so that there is a bailment, many courts will enforce a clause that places a dollar limit on the parking lot owner's liability, assuming that the clause is conspicuous and very clear. Such a liability limitation printed on the back of an identification ticket or receipt, for example, is not sufficiently conspicuous.

Additionally, some bailees are expressly permitted by statue to limit their liability by contract. Under federal law, for example, common carriers in interstate commerce such as railroads and airlines are permitted to do so within certain limits: thus the limitations on the amount of liability commonly found in bills of lading and other transportation contracts are generally enforceable.

Unconscionable Contracts

As a general rule, the courts are not concerned with the fairness or unfairness of a particular contract. In other words, where competent parties have struck an agreement it will normally be enforced even if it proves much more advantageous to one party than to the other. However, occasionally the freedom to contract is abused so that the terms of a particular contract are so extremely unfair to one of the parties in light of common mores and business practices that they "shock one's conscience." Courts will not enforce such an **unconscionable contract** against the abused party.

A case vividly illustrating the common law approach to unconscionability is Williams v. Walker-Thomas Furnitur e Co., 350 F.2d 445 (D.D.C. 1965). There, a Mrs. Williams purchased some furniture in Washington, D.C., in 1957 on credit under a contract which contained the standard provision that the company would retain title to the goods until all monthly payments were made, and that the company could repossess in event of default. The contract also contained a clause that if Mrs. Williams purchased additional goods on credit, the company had the right to "credit pro—rata" her monthly payments against all such goods. She did, in fact, buy a number of additional items between 1957 and 1962, and the company, as permitted by the pro—rata clause, during that time had applied her payments so that a small balance remained due on all items, even those purchased in 1957 and 1958. In 1962, by which time Mrs. Williams had made payments of over $1,400, she was unable to make additional payments. When the company then sought to repossess all of the goods in her hands, the court refused repossession as to the first items that she had purchased. In part, the court said: When a party of little bargaining power, and hence little real choice, signs a commercially unreasonable contract with little or no knowledge of its terms, it is hardly likely that his consent, or even an objective manifestation of consent, was ever given to all the terms. In such a case the usual rule that the terms of the agreement are not to be questioned should be abandoned, and the court should consider whether the terms of the contract are so unfair that enforcement should be withheld."

The common law of unconscionability has been introduced to the sale of goods through UCC Sec. 2—302, which allows a court finding a sales contract or any clause of the contract to be unconscionable to: (1) refuse to enforce the contract, or (2) enforce the remainder of the contract without the unconscionable clause, or (3) limit the application of any unconscionable clause so as to avoid any unreasonable result.

Regardless of the type of contract involved—a sale of goods or some other type of contract—a court will refuse to enforce the contract because of unconscionability only if the party seeking to avoid the contract proves *both* procedural and substantive unconscionability. **Procedural unconscionability** exists when there is a lack of meaningful choice on the part of one of the parties. Courts must analyze the contract formation process, including such matters as the inability of one of the parties to bargain because of immaturity or old age, lack of sophistication, mental disability, inability to speak English, lack of education or business acumen, and the like; relative bargaining power; whether the party in the strongest economic position simply offered a printed form or boilerplate contract on a take—it—or—leave—it basis to the weaker party (adhesion contracts); whether the terms were explained to the weaker party; whether there were alternative sources for the goods or services; whether high—pressure or deceptive sales tactics were used; and whether important clauses were hidden in the fine print.

Contracts entered into in a commercial context are generally presumed not to be unconscionable; businesspersons should be able to protect themselves. Courts are much more likely to find unconscionability in order to aid a consumer than to aid a business, but commercial transactions are not immune from such a finding.

In order to ascertain **substantive unconscionability**, the courts examine the terms of the contract itself to determine whether they are oppressive, perhaps because they involve unfair disclaimers of warranty, inflated prices, denial of basic rights and remedies to consumers, penalty clauses, and the like. The courts will decide whether or not a particular contract is unconscionable on a case–by–case basis in light of the overall commercial context in which it was made and as of the time it was made. Just because a bargain has turned out poorly for one party does not mean that the contract was unconscionable when made. Courts will not use the concept to reallocate the risks taken by the parties when they entered into the contract, as the following case demonstrates.

DOUGHTY V. IDAHO FROZEN FOODS CORP.
Idaho Court of Appeals, 736 P.2d 460 (1987)

In 1983 Doughty contracted to sell a portion of his anticipated potato crop to Idaho Frozen Foods (IFF), a processor of potato products. The parties used a form contract developed through negotiations between IFF and the Potato Growers of Idaho (PGI), an independent bargaining organization which represented 1200 potato growers. Under the contract, Doughty was to receive a base price if the potato crop contained a certain percentage of potatoes weighing ten ounces or more. If the crop contained a higher percentage, the price would be increased; if it contained a lower percentage, the price would be decreased. Size was critical to IFF's processing needs. The contract provided that IFF could refuse any deliveries containing less than 10 percent ten–ounce or larger potatoes.

Unexpected weather conditions resulted in only 8 percent of Doughty's potatoes being ten ounces or more, so he was entitled to only $2.57 per hundredweight under the IFF contract. After four days of delivery to IFF, Doughty breached the contract, delivering the remainder of his potatoes to the "fresh pack" market where he could receive $4.69 per hundredweight. Pursuant to an agreement with IFF, the proceeds of this sale were placed in a court–controlled bank account.

Doughty then filed this declaratory judgment action, asking the court to declare the contract unconscionable and therefore not binding on him. The trial Judge ruled for IFF and Doughty appealed.

Walters, Chief Judge:

Doughty argues that the contract is unconscionable because the terms were disproportionately skewed in favor of IFF. Specifically, Doughty invites a comparison of the built–in step decreases in the contract price based on the percentage of smaller potatoes and the step increases in price for higher percentages of larger potatoes. Doughty contends the contract is unconscionable because the price decreases are steeper than the price increases. Doughty also contends that it was unconscionable for IFF to have the option not to accept the potatoes if they consisted of less than ten percent ten–ounce or larger size potatoes.

In, 111 Idaho 196, 725 P.2d 196 (Ct. App. 1986), this court recognized that a claim of unconscionability may have procedural and substantive aspects. We stated that procedural unconscionability may arise in the bargaining process leading to an agreement. Procedural unconscionability "is characterized by great disparity in the bargaining positions of the parties, by extreme need of one party to reach some agreement (however unfavorable), or by threats short of duress. These circumstances taint the bargaining process, producing a result that does not reflect free market forces." Regarding substantive unconscionability, we stated that "[o]nly in special circumstances may a court of equity set aside contracts fairly and freely negotiated." We further noted that such "special circumstances" turn on "whether at the time of making of the contract, and in light of the general commercial background and commercial needs of a particular case, [the contract is] so onesided as to oppress or unfairly surprise one of the parties."

Doughty's allegations encompass aspects of both procedural and substantive unconscionability. Under either aspect, we do not find the contract to be unconscionable. Although Doughty was not a member of PGI, the group which negotiated the contract with IFF, PGI represented a significant number of growers. Doughty has not shown that he was in any way different from those potato growers who were members of PGI. Moreover, the record clearly establishes that PGI did have substantial bargaining power and negotiating expertise.

Doughty entered into the contract freely and sought the benefits which the collective bargaining power of PGI had obtained. Apparently, Doughty was not dissatisfied with the contract until his crop produced small potatoes. There is no indication that Doughty tried or wanted to negotiate different terms under the contract. In fact, the contract would appear to be to the advantage of a farmer such as Doughty one who through innovation, skill, and aggressiveness sought to produce a crop that would fulfill not only the FF contract, but also his other processing contract, plus produce potatoes for the "fresh pack" market. Had Doughty's efforts produced the tenounce potatoes he sought, Doughty would have had a very beneficial contract. There was no indication that Doughty was forced by "extreme need" into the contract. Finally, there is no indication from the record of any threats to Doughty that caused him to enter into the IFF contract.

The contract also does not reflect any substantively unconscionable aspects. The prices were based on the size and quality of potatoes that IFF desired and that Doughty hoped he could produce. The pricing variations, as well as the option to refuse potatoes not meeting the contract requirements, do not appear to be unreasonable considering the product the contract was intended to produce— ten–ounce or larger potatoes. The contract was a preharvest contract. Therefore Doughty could attempt to manipulate and manage the crop to produce exactly the size potatoes that would be most financially rewarding. Doughty was thwarted by unexpected weather conditions. Doughty's assertions reflect an attempt to reap the benefits that the contract would have produced if he had grown the kind of potatoes he intended to, yet escape the negative aspects resulting from his inability to produce that type of potato. The contract simply does not appear to be "so one–sided as to oppress or unfairly surprise one of the parties.

Each party accepted certain risks by signing the preharvest contract. IFF took a chance that market prices might decline, while Doughty took a chance on growing a certain size potato. IFF did have an option to reject potatoes that did not meet IFF's size criteria. However, contracts do not necessarily give identical rights to all parties. That is part of the bargaining process. It does not necessarily make a contract unconscionable. We conclude that the contract was not unconscionable in this case.

[Affirmed.]

Other Illegal Contracts

Many other contracts are generally held to be contrary to public policy. Of these, one broad class deserves comment—contracts that "injure the public service." Promises to pay legislators money in return for their votes and similar promises to judges in return for favorable rulings are clearly injurious to the public and therefore illegal. On the other hand, **lobbying contracts**, under which a person is employed by a third party to influence a legislator's vote or an administrator's decision in the awarding of a contract, are not necessarily illegal. The legality of such contracts largely depends on the propriety of the means used by the lobbyist. If, for example, an engineer simply agrees, for a fee, to present to a lawmaker or administrator factual information tending to show the superiority of one product or material over another, the means are proper and the agreement is not contrary to public policy. A contract, however, that contemplates influencing a government official essentially by reliance on the lobbyist's long personal friendship with that person would be illegal.

In regard to **contingent fee contracts**, under which payment of the fee is conditional upon passage of a particular bill or awarding of a contract, many courts flatly deny the lobbyist recovery of his or her fee under any circumstances—on the ground that the tendency of such contracts to induce improper activities is, by itself, sufficient to cause them to be contrary to public policy. Other courts, in such cases, permit the lobbyist to recover if he or she can prove proper conduct—that is, conduct free of deception, undue pressure, and the like.

Effect Of Illegal Contracts

As noted early in the chapter, illegal contracts are generally void and unenforceable. This means that neither party to such a contract will be assisted by the courts in any way, regardless of the consequences to the parties involved. Thus, if S brings suit to recover the purchase price of a quantity of liquor that he has sold and delivered to B in violation of law, his action will be dismissed. Conversely, if B had paid the purchase price when the contract was made and S subsequently failed to deliver the liquor, any action brought by B to recover the price will also be unavailing.

Courts feel that such a hands–off policy is, in most cases, the best way to discourage the making of illegal contracts. There are exceptional situations, however, in which the courts feel that the results obtained under such a policy are so questionable as to warrant some measure of judicial relief. We will examine three of these situations.

Rights of Protected Parties

Some statutes have as their clear purpose the protection of a certain class of persons. Any contract made in violation of such a statute is enforceable by persons within that class, despite its illegality. For example: a Nebraska insurance company, not licensed to sell insurance in Colorado, issues a fire insurance policy on K's home in Denver. The home is destroyed by fire, and the company refuses to pay on the ground that the contract was illegal. The company is liable on its policy. It would be a ludicrous result if K, a person for whose benefit the licensing statutes were enacted, were to be denied recovery on the ground of illegality.

Parties Not Equally at Fault

In most illegal contracts the parties are equally at fault (or substantially equally at fault). In such instances when an action is brought to enforce the contract, the defendant may successfully assert the defense of *in pari delicto* (literally, "at equal fault").

In some situations, however, the plaintiff may convince the court that he or she was not equally at fault with the defendant—i.e., that his or her guilt was substantially less than the defendant's. In such a case the plaintiff's action may be maintained. The exception applies particularly—but not exclusively— where the plaintiff was ignorant of essential facts when the contract was made, through no fault of his or her own. For example: X forges a warehouse receipt, which makes it appear that he is the owner of certain goods stored at a warehouse. X takes the receipt to a trucking company and employs it to pick up the goods at the warehouse and to deliver them to his place of business. The trucking company does so, not knowing that X is not the owner of the goods. The company is entitled to receive its transportation charge from X, even though it was a participant in an illegal transaction.

Severable Contracts

Sometimes a single contract turns out on analysis to be two separate agreements. This can be illustrated by a contract under which a retiring restaurant owner agrees to sell to a former competitor his "ten pinball machines for $50 and one electric broiler for $75." In such a contract, called a severable contract, the fact that one of the agreements may be illegal does not prevent the other from being enforced. Thus, if the sale of the pinball machines is prohibited by law, the seller is still under an obligation, enforceable in court, to deliver the broiler. However, most contracts that contain several promises on the part of both parties are not severable. The promises of the two parties usually are so interdependent that the court must rule that they resulted in the creation of a single, indivisible contract. In such cases, if any part of the contract is illegal, the entire agreement is unenforceable.

CHAPTER **15**

VOIDABLE CONTRACTS

- Capacity
- Minors
- Mentally Impaired And Intoxicated Persons
- Reality Of Consent
- Fraud
- Innocent Misrepresentation
- Mistake
- Duress
- Undue Influence

AVOIDABLE CONTRACT IS a contract which may be avoided—that is, may be legally set aside—by one of the parties, even though the contract consists of a definite agreement, is supported by consideration, and has a lawful purpose. In this chapter we will examine the most common grounds for the avoidance (disaffirmance) of a contract: *lack of capacity,* and *lack of reality of consent.*

Capacity

The term **capacity** means the legal ability—the ability or "competence" in the eyes of the law—to perform a particular act. Within the context of this chapter, the particular act under consideration is the making of a binding contract.

A person's capacity to contract may be limited (or entirely lacking, in some instances) for any of three primary reasons: *minority, mental infirmity,* and *intoxication.* We will consider these subjects in order.

Minors

Centuries ago, the English courts became aware of the fact that many of the contracts entered into by young persons displayed a shocking lack of judgment; such persons assumed obligations and made purchases that they probably would not have had they possessed greater maturity and experience. The courts, desirous of protecting the young from the consequences of their own folly," began to wrestle with the question of how this protection could best be brought about.

They initially approached the problem by devising what came to be known as the *harm–benefit test.* Under this view, the courts permitted persons who had entered into contracts while under the age of twenty–one to disaffirm them if they were shown to be harmful to these individuals. This approach was followed for a time in the United States. Its application, however, produced such conflict and uncertainty in the law that a new solution became necessary.

The Common–Law Rule

The U.S. courts finally adopted the sweeping rule that, virtually without exception, *all minors' contracts are voidable at their option.* The right thus given to minors to escape their contractual obligations is no longer dependent upon a showing that the contract is harmful or unwise, or that they have been taken advantage of in some way. To effect a disaffirmance of any contract, all the minor has to do is indicate to the other party his or her intention not to be bound by it. The disaffirmance can be express or implied and the right to disaffirm continues until the minor reaches the age of majority, plus a "reasonable time thereafter."

Note that a minor's contract is enforceable against the minor *until* an effective disaffirmance occurs. Furthermore, only the minor has the right to disaffirm; the other party to the contract has no corresponding right to disaffirm. If the minor chooses, he or she may enforce the contract against the adult on the other side (assuming that adult's mental competence).

Definition of Minority

In the past twenty years or so virtually every state has lowered the age of majority from the common law's 21 years to 18 years of age for most purposes, including the making of valid contracts. These statues almost uniformly confer upon 18–year–olds the rights to sue and be sued in their own names, to make wills, to marry without parental consent, and to choose their own domiciles; but generally they do not sanction the right to buy alcoholic beverages until the age of 21 is reached. Thus, a **minor** is a person who has not yet attained the age of 18. The agreements of minors of "tender years—children so young that their minds have not matured sufficiently to understand the meaning of contractual obligations—are void rather than voidable. Because legal actions against this type of minor are virtually nonexistent, the rules considered below are those applicable to the contracts of "older minors—typically, teenagers.

There are at least two unusual situations where minors may be treated as adults. First, a few states provide that married persons should be treated as adults for purposes of entering into contracts even if they are not yet 18. Second, several states have procedures where, under court supervision, minors may be created as adults for purposes of making contracts. Such a procedure allows a child actor, for example, to contract with a movie studio. The studio is protected because the child is unable to disaffirm the contract. The child is protected because the funds he or she is paid under the contract typically go into a trust fund that is administered for the child's benefit.

We will now examine the results of the general rule permitting minors to disaffirm contracts at their option in three basic situations: (1) ordinary contracts—that is, contracts under which the goods or services being purchased are not necessities of life; (2) contracts for the purchase of "necessaries," and (3) contracts in which the minor has misrepresented his or her age.

Minors' Liability on Ordinary Contracts
Executory Contracts

Few problems arise where the minor's repudiation occurs before either party has started to perform the obligations under the contract (that is, where the contract is still *executory*). Since the other party is caused little hardship in such a case, all states take the view that the disaffirmance entirely frees the minor of liability. For example, suppose that M, a minor, contracts on July 1 to buy a home stereo system from X for $1,200, the contract providing that the system will be delivered and the purchase price paid on July 15. If M notifies X on July 10 that he will not go through with the deal, the contract is at an end and X has no recourse against M. Similarly, if M contracts to paint Y's house for

$400 and later refuses to do the job, the refusal absolves M of liability. If either X or Y were to bring suit against M to recover damages for breach of contract, the suit would be dismissed.

Executed Contracts

Surprising as it may seem, the same rule is also generally applied to executed contracts—those that have been fully performed before the repudiation takes place. Thus, in virtually all states, a minor can purchase a car for cash, drive it until he or she becomes an adult, and still disaffirm the contract (assuming, as is usually the case, that the car is not a necessity of life). Standard forms of many car dealers contain a statement that the buyer "hereby certifies that he or she is eighteen years of age, or over." The minor's right to disaffirm this kind of contract is discussed later under the "misrepresentation of age" section.

While virtually all courts agree as to the minor's *right to disaffirm* a contract in a situation such as the above, they do not agree about the extent of the relief that should be given to the minor in some circumstances. This can be illustrated by amplifying the facts about the car purchase. Suppose that the purchase price of the car was $2,800 and that the minor brings suit to recover that amount. At the trial, the seller offers evidence establishing that the value of the car at the time the minor offered to return it was $1,500. In such a case the seller can make at least two contentions: (1) that the minor should be charged with the benefit received—that is, the reasonable value of the use of the car prior to disaffirmance or (2) if this contention is rejected, that the minor should at least be charged with the depreciation of the car while it was in the minor's hands.

The Majority View. The courts of most states reject both contentions, permitting the minor to recover the full price of $2,800. Assuming that the automobile does not constitute a necessity, the majority rule is that the minor's only obligation is *to return the consideration if able to do so.* Under this view, the return of the car—even though it has greatly depreciated in value by reason of use or accident—entitles the minor to recover his or her *entire payment.* Furthermore, if the minor is unable to return the consideration, as would be the case if the car were stolen, the minor is still permitted to recover the $2,800 from the unfortunate seller. And regardless of whether the consideration has depreciated in value or cannot be returned, the minor is not charged with the benefit received from the possession and use of the consideration.

Freedom from liability would also exist if the minor had purchased the car on credit rather than for cash. In that case, if the minor disaffirmed the contract before paying off the balance, and if the seller then brought action to recover that balance, the minor would again be freed of all liability (subject, again, only to the obligation to return the car if he or she is able to do so). A procedural note: as the above examples illustrate, minority cases ordinarily arise in one of two ways. In the first (and most common) situation the minor has paid cash for the goods or services, and, upon disaffirmance, the minor is the plaintiff seeking return of his or her payment. In the second case, where the minor purchases goods or services on credit and then disaffirms, the unpaid seller is the plaintiff, seeking to recover the contract price. Regardless of how the cases arise, the applicable minority rules apply with equal force. (That is, if under the applicable rules the minor in the first case is permitted to recover the full purchase price, he or she in the second case will be entirely freed of the obligation to pay for the goods.)

Some Other Views. The courts of a growing number of states, feeling that the majority view imposes unreasonable hardship on the other party to the contract, *do* impose liability on the minor under one of two theories. Some states hold the minor liable for the reasonable value of the benefit received prior to the disaffirmance, while others reach a similar result by holding the minor liable for the depreciation that has occurred to the goods while in his or her possession. Going back to the original illustration, where the minor had paid cash for the car, the courts of these states would permit the minor to recover the purchase price minus the value of the benefit (or depreciation), whatever the jury finds this to be.

Most of these minority jurisdictions would not require a disaffirming minor who had purchased on credit to produce the funds necessary to "make the adult whole" in order to disaffirm. Thus, these minority jurisdictions give less protection to adults who sell to minors on credit than to those who protect themselves by demanding the minors' money "up front."

The case below illustrates the broad protection the majority view affords the minor in a typical fact pattern. (The rationale underlying this view follows the case.)

HALBMAN V. LEMKE
Supreme Court of Wisconsin, 298 N.W.2d 562 (1980)

James Halbman, a minor, worked at a gas station in Greenfield, Wisconsin. During his employment he contracted to buy a 1968 Oldsmobile from Michael Lemke, the station manager, for $1,250. At the time the contract was made Halbman paid Lemke $1,000 cash and took possession of the car. (Title to the vehicle was retained by Lemke.) Under the contract Halbman agreed to pay $25 per week until the balance was paid off.

A little more than a month later, at which time Halbman had paid $1,100 of the price, a connecting rod in the engine broke. He took the car to a garage, where it was repaired at a cost of $637. Halbman did not pay the repair bill. Shortly thereafter Lemke endorsed the car's title over to Halbman, even though the full purchase price had not been paid, in an

effort to avoid any liability for the operation and maintenance of the vehicle (including the repair bill). Halbman returned the title to Lemke, with a letter saying he was disaffirming the contract and demanding the return of the $1,100 he had paid. Lemke did not return the money and did not pay the bill. (The car remained in possession of the repair shop.) Five months later, with the repair bill still unpaid, the garage removed the car's engine and transmission in satisfaction of the debt. The garage then towed the vehicle to the home of Halbman's father. While there it was subjected to vandalism which made the car "unsalvageable."

Halbman then brought this action to recover the $1,100 he had paid, and Lemke counterclaimed for $150, the amount still *owing on the contract. The trial court granted judgment for Halbman, ruling that when a minor disaffirms a contract for the purchase of an item, his or her only obligation is to return the property remaining in his hands. The court of appeals affirmed, and Lemke petitioned the Supreme Court of Wisconsin for review.*

Callow, Justice:

. . . The sole issue before us is whether a minor, having disaffirmed a contract for the purchase of an item which is not a necessity and having tendered the property back to the vendor, must make restitution to the vendor for damage to the property prior to the disaffirmance. Lemke argues that he should be entitled to recover for the damage to the vehicle up to the time of disaffirmance, which he claims equals the amount of the repair bill.

Neither party challenges the absolute right of a minor to disaffirm a contract for the purchase of items which are not necessities. That right, variously known as the doctrine of incapacity or the "infancy doctrine," is one of the oldest and most venerable of our common—-law traditions. Although the origins of the doctrine are somewhat obscure, it is generally recognized that its purpose is the protection of minors from foolishly squandering their wealth through improvident contracts with crafty adults who would take advantage of them in the marketplace. . . .

As a general rule, a minor who disaffirms a contract is entitled to recover all consideration he has conferred incident to the transaction. In return the minor is expected to restore as much of the consideration as, at the time of disaffirmance, remains in the minor's possession. The minor's right to disaffirm is not contingent upon the return of the property, however, as disaffirmance is permitted even where such return cannot be made. . . .

The law regarding the rights and responsibilities of the parties relative to the consideration exchanged on a disaffirmed contract is characterized by confusion, inconsistency, and a general lack of uniformity as jurisdictions attempt to reach a fair application of the infancy doctrine in today's marketplace. [The court then analyzed a number of cases which, Lemke contended, barred recovery by Halbman in this action. The court rejected the rules of those cases, saying: Because these cases would at some point force the minor to bear the cost of the very improvidence from which the infancy doctrine is supposed to protect him, we cannot follow them. As we noted in [a prior Wisconsin case], modifications of the rules governing the capacity of infants to contract are best left to the legislature. Until such changes are forthcoming, however, we hold that, absent misrepresentation or tortious damage to the property, a minor who disaffirms a contract for the purchase of an item which is not a necessity may recover his purchase price without liability for use, depreciation, damage, or other diminution in value. . . .

The decision of the court of appeals is affirmed.

Rationale

There is no question but that the majority rule, as applied to specific situations, frequently results in a severe financial loss to the party who has dealt with the minor. It is also possible that some young people, aware of the rule, enter into contracts with the intention of getting something for nothing. Nevertheless, most courts justify the occasional hardships that result under the majority rule by noting that "the primary purpose of the common–law rule is to afford protection to minors by discouraging others from contracting with them," and this rule no doubt tends to bring about such a result. Thus we have once again a situation where the rights of some individuals, under certain circumstances, must give way to the rights of others because of public policy considerations.

A competent person can, of course, ordinarily escape such hardships by refusing to deal with minors. All persons are presumed to know the law, so that (in theory at least) one who deals with a minor is on notice that it is at his or her peril. A second solution for someone who wishes to make a sale is to refuse to deal with the minor and to contract instead with one of the minor's parents. In such a case the possibility of a disaffirmance is eliminated, since both parties to the contract are competent. A third solution, in situations where the competent party does not know whether the person with whom he or she is dealing is a minor, is to have that person make a statement, preferably in writing, that he or she is over the age of eighteen. (The protection afforded to the competent party by such a representation is considered later in the chapter.)

Some persons, such as common carriers, have a legal duty to deal with everyone who requests (and is able to pay for) their services. Disaffirmance against such persons is generally not permitted once the contract has been executed. Thus, a 17–year–old who purchases and uses an airline ticket is not permitted to recover his or her fare.

Ratification

Once a minor reaches the age of majority, he or she has the ability to ratify any contracts made earlier. A **ratification** occurs when the minor indicates to the other party, expressly or impliedly, the intent to be bound by the agreement. Thus, if a minor, after reaching the age of 18, promises that he or she will go through with the contract, an express ratification has taken place and the right of disaffirmance is lost forever. Similarly, if a minor has received an article, such as a typewriter, under a contract and continues to use it for more than a "reasonable time" after reaching the age of 18, an implied ratification has occurred. Another situation in which a ratification can take place involves purchases made under installment contracts. Suppose, for example, that a minor has purchased a motorcycle, agreeing to pay the seller $25 a month until the purchase price has been paid in full. If he continues to make payments for any length of time after reaching the age of 18, it is probable that such payments will be held to constitute a ratification of the contract. It is obvious, then, that any young person should review all of his or her contracts upon becoming an adult, and refrain from any conduct that would indicate to the other party an intent to be bound by them if he or she wishes to set any of them aside.

Minors' Liability on Contracts to Purchase "Necessaries"

When a minor purchases **necessaries** (goods that the law considers necessary to life or health), he or she incurs a greater liability than that imposed (by the majority rule) under contracts calling for the purchase of goods that are not necessities. The rule applicable to contracts calling for the purchase of "necessaries" is that the minor is liable to the other party for the *reasonable value of the goods actually used*. This is the quasi-contractual measure of recovery, because the minor is being held liable not on the contract but, instead, to avoid unjust enrichment. To illustrate: M, 17, buys a topcoat from C, contracting to pay the price of $150 one year later. At the end of that time, when the coat is completely worn out, C brings suit to recover the purchase price. If the court rules that the coat is a necessary, then it must determine what its reasonable value was at the time of the purchase, and M is liable to C in that amount. (In contrast, if the coat is held not to constitute a necessary, M is usually freed of all liability—as has been seen earlier.) This imposition of liability occurs only where the goods or services have been used by the minor; contracts calling for the purchase of necessaries can still be set aside as long as they are executory. Thus, if M contracts to purchase a coat from C, which is to be delivered one week later, he can set aside the contract without liability if he notifies C of his disaffirmance before the week is out— and indeed, even later as long as he does not use the coat.

What Constitutes a Necessary?

In answering the question of what constitutes a necessary, it is possible to draw a clear line in most cases. Minimum amounts of food, clothing, and medical services are clearly necessary. So, too, is the rental of a house or apartment by a minor who is married. Many items, on the other hand, are clearly luxuries—such as TV sets, sporting goods, and dancing lessons, under most circumstances. Other items held to be necessaries include legal services, taxes on real property owned by minors, and medical care for a minor's child. In determining whether a doubtful item is a necessary, the courts take into account the "station in life" occupied by the particular minor. Thus a fourth sport coat might be ruled a necessary for a minor who is a member of high society, while it would not be so ruled in regard to others.

A few states reason that items essential for a minor to earn a living (and therefore to have money to buy necessaries) should also be treated as necessaries. Thus, a minority of states would treat as necessaries such things as a car that a minor uses in his or her work or the services of an employment agency that the minor used to obtain a job. See Gastonia Personnel Corp. v. Rogers, 172 S.E.2d 19 (N.C. 1970).

It should be noted that an item is a necessity only if it is actually needed at the time of purchase. Thus if a minor purchases an item that appears to be a necessity, such as an article of clothing, the minor still has no liability to the seller if he or she can prove that a parent or guardian was "willing and able" to furnish clothing of the type purchased under that particular contract.

Rationale

Why is it that under the majority rule, a minor who buys something frivolous may disaffirm the contract and recover the entire purchase price, whereas a minor who buys something truly needed can disaffirm only where the seller can retain the fair value of what the minor used? These rules seem paradoxical, but the clear rationale is, on the one hand, to discourage merchants from dealing with minors for the frivolous items (by allowing the minors to disaffirm even when it is unfair to the merchant), but on the other hand to induce merchants to sell minors the things they need for survival (by ensuring that the minors will pay at least fair value).

Minors' Liability on Contracts Involving Misrepresentation of Age

We have assumed so far that the minor has not led the other party to believe that he or she is an adult. If such misrepresentation does occur, the minor is guilty of a kind of fraud, and the courts of most jurisdictions will deny the protection that otherwise would be given that person.

Some states have provided by statute that a minor who has misrepresented his or her age is liable on the contract exactly as if he or she were an adult. Most states, however, have left the matter up to the courts, and a spate of rules has resulted. Without attempting to consider all of them, we can make one or two generalizations.

First, where the minor repudiates the contract while it is entirely executory, most courts permit the disaffirmance just as if there had been no misrepresentation. Although this does not penalize the minor for wrongdoing, it also does not cause particular hardship to the other party in most instances.

Second, where a contract calling for the purchase of a nonnecessary item has been fully or partially executed before the attempted disaffirmance, many courts allow the disaffirmance *only if it will not cause a loss to the other party.* Under this approach, each case is analyzed separately to determine the effect of the disaffirmance. Two illustrations follow.

1. M, a minor, purchases a car from C, a competent party, for $2,500 cash, after telling C that she is 18. A year later, just before becoming 18, M wishes to disaffirm; at this time the market value of the car is $1,400. Despite the misrepresentation, disaffirmance will be permitted. C, however, will be allowed to withhold from the $2,500 the amount of the depreciation, $1,100, which—added to the $1,400 car—will restore him to his original position. M's recovery is thus only $1,400.

2. M purchases a car from C under a contract providing, "Buyer certifies that he or she is 18 years of age or older." The purchase price is $2,500, with $100 paid at the time of purchase and the balance of $2,400 payable in 24 monthly installments. Six months later, when the car is stolen, M notifies C that she wants to be relieved of the balance of the contract. Disaffirmance will probably not be allowed since this would cause a loss to C; thus a suit by C to recover the unpaid balance will be successful. This example is based on Haydocy Pontiac, Inc. v. Lee, 19 Ohio App.2d 217 (1969). The minor in this case was held to be "estopped" from disaffirming, in view of her misrepresentation; and she continued to be liable for the "fair value of the property."

The contract liability of minors regarding both executory and executed contracts is illustrated in Figure 15.1.

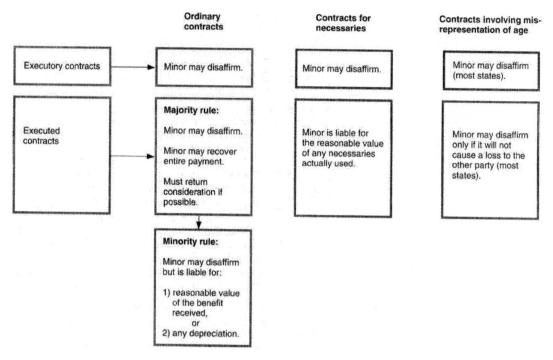

Ordinary contracts	Contracts for necessaries	Contracts involving misrepresentation of age

Executory contracts → Minor may disaffirm.

Minor may disaffirm.

Minor may disaffirm (most states).

Executed contracts

Majority rule:

Minor may disaffirm.

Minor may recover entire payment.

Must return consideration if possible.

Minor is liable for the reasonable value of any necessaries actually used.

Minor may disaffirm only if it will not cause a loss to the other party (most states).

Minority rule:

Minor may disaffirm but is liable for:

1) reasonable value of the benefit received,
   or
2) any depreciation.

Figure 15.1 Contract Liability of Minor

Contracts that Cannot be Disaffirmed

Not all contracts can be disaffirmed on the ground of minority. For example, disaffirmance of marriage contracts and contracts of enlistment in the armed forces is not permitted on the ground of public policy. For certain other contracts, such as those approved by a court or those made with banks or insurance companies, the same result is generally brought about by statute. For example, a North Carolina statute authorizes banks "in respect to deposit accounts and the rental of safe deposit boxes" to deal with minors as if they were adults. And another North Carolina

statute authorizes minors of 15 and insurance contracts to the same extent as adults. Still other states have held that releases signed litigation are enforceable; otherwise, minors could be effectively settled out of court.

Torts and Crimes

The rules permitting minors to disaffirm most contracts do not apply to acts that are tortious or criminal in nature. Generally, minors are fully liable for any torts or crimes they commit (except, of course, minors of "tender years," such as two- or three-year olds). Thus, if a minor drives a car negligently, anyone injured thereby can recover damages from him or her. Such liability cannot be disaffirmed. Similarly, if a minor operates a motor vehicle while intoxicated, the usual criminal penalties can be imposed (although in the criminal area, the penalties may be tempered under juvenile court procedures).

Mentally Impaired and Intoxicated Persons
Mentally Impaired Persons

Persons with impaired mental capacity are, like minors, given substantial protection by the law insofar as their contractual obligations are concerned. We will briefly examine the general rules within this broad category which include mentally retarded, brain damaged, and senile persons, and persons suffering from mental illness.

Adjudicated Insane

Some mentally impaired persons are formally declared to be incompetent by a court after hearings and examination by psychologists or psychiatrists. After a person has been **adjudicated insane,** a guardian is appointed. Thereafter, any "contract" made by the insane person rather than by the guardian is absolutely void—that is, creates no liability whatever, even if it is never disaffirmed by the incompetent person or the guardian. (However, if any goods or services furnished under the contracts were necessities not being furnished by the guardian, the impaired person would be liable for their fair market value under a quasi-contract theory.)

Insane in Fact

Many mentally impaired persons have never been the subject of incompetency proceedings, but are nonetheless **insane in fact.** If at the time the contract was made, the person was so impaired that he or she was *incapable of understanding the nature and effect of the particular agreement,* then the contract is voidable. A court may order rescission of the contract at the request of the impaired party after he or she regains full mental capacity. (Again, if rescission is allowed, liability for the fair market value of any *necessities* furnished under the contract would exist under the quasi-contract principle.)

Hanks v. McNeill Coal Corporation, 168 P.2d 256 (1946), is typical of those controversies in which the evidence on the "understanding" issue was in sharp conflict. In that case Hanks, a farmer who had never been adjudicated insane, sold coal lands in Colorado to the coal company. At his death his executor sought to rescind the contract on the ground that Hanks was insane in fact— actually insane—at the time of the transaction. In support of this contention, the executor introduced evidence that in the months prior to the sale Hanks was increasingly interested in the "emotional type" of religion, was increasingly abusive to his family members; and manufactured a medicine for horses made of brick dust, burnt shoe leather, and pieces of ground glass. Despite this evidence, the court ruled Hanks to be sane with respect to the sale, on the basis of testimony by lawyers and a banker who had other dealings with him about the time of the sale, who testified that, as to business matters, he appeared to be "in grasp of his affairs" and "rational." In explaining its ruling, the court said: "One may have insane delusions regarding some matters and be insane on some subjects, yet [be] capable of transacting business concerning matters wherein such matters are not concerned, and such insanity does not make one incompetent to contract unless the subject matter of the contract is so connected with an insane delusion as to render the afflicted party incapable of understanding the nature and effect of the agreement, or of acting rationally in the transaction."

Intoxicated Persons

People occasionally seek to escape liability under a contract on the ground that they were intoxicated when it was made. Success in doing so depends primarily on the degree of intoxication found to exist at that time. Disaffirmance is allowed only if a person can establish that he or she was so intoxicated as not to understand the nature of the purported agreement. Thus a question of fact is presented, for a lesser degree of intoxication is not grounds for disaffirmance.

If the required degree of intoxication is found to have existed, the intoxicated person's right to disaffirm, upon regaining sobriety, also substantially parallels that of a minor—again, however, with one basic exception. While we have seen that minors may, as a general rule, disaffirm contracts even though unable to return the consideration that they received, intoxicated persons are required by most courts to return the full consideration as a condition of disaffirmance in all cases (unless they are able to show fraud on the part of the other contracting party). For apparent reasons, contracting parties who are intoxicated receive less protection from the law than do minors or the mentally impaired.

Reality of Consent

A contract that has been entered into between two persons having full capacity to contract, and which appears to be valid in all other respects, may still be voidable if it turns out that the apparent consent of one or both of the parties was, in fact, not genuine. Contracts that are tainted with *fraud, innocent misrepresentation, mistake, duress,* or *undue influence* can ordinarily be voided (set aside) by the innocent parties. In such instances the courts will allow rescission on the ground that there was "no reality of consent." That is, although it *appears* from the form of the contract alone that the consent of both parties was genuine (or "real"), in fact it was not.

Many areas of law are essentially made up of rules that discourage conduct that is deceitful or otherwise injurious to individuals or to society in general. Some types of conduct are felt to be so detrimental to a stable society that they are flatly prohibited, and punishment for violators is prescribed. From hence have our bodies of criminal law been built up.

In other areas of law rules have come about that attempt to insure at least some degree of care and fairness when private citizens have dealings with one another, and which grant civil remedies against persons who violate them. We have seen, for example, that tortious conduct causes the wrongdoer to answer in damages to the injured party. This continuing filament of thought, to the effect that a person should not be allowed to profit by conduct that is patently offensive, is woven into the law of contracts. It is most apparent in that part of law having to do with fraud and duress and, to a lesser extent, mistake and undue influence.

Fraud

Leaving aside, for the moment, any attempt to define the term, the essence of **fraud** is deception—the intentional misleading of one person by another. Perhaps the most common type of fraud occurs when one person simply lies to another about a material fact, as a result of which a contract is made. Thus, if S, the owner of a current model car, tells B that he purchased it new six months ago, S knowing that it was in fact "second–hand" when he acquired it, S is guilty of fraud if B, believing this statement to be true, subsequently purchases the car. In this case, B—after learning the true facts—ordinarily can either rescind the contract and recover the purchase price or keep the car and recover damages from S.

Elements of Fraud

One person can mislead another in so many ways that the courts have been reluctant to fashion a hard and fast definition of fraud; any precise definition almost certainly could be circumvented by person's intent on getting around it. Instead, the courts generally recognize that the various forms of deception they wish to forestall usually contain common elements. When a court is called upon to decide in a given case whether the conduct of one of the parties was fraudulent, its usual approach is to see if the required elements are present. If so, fraud has been established and the victim will be afforded relief.

To be successful in a fraud action, the plaintiff is required to show all of the following:
1. That defendant made a misrepresentation of a material fact.
2. That the statement was made with the *intent to deceive(i.e.,* defendant knew or should have known the statement was false).
3. That plaintiff *reasonably relied* on the misrepresentation.
4. That plaintiff suffered an *injury* as a result.

Misrepresentation of a Material Fact

Misrepresentation of a material fact (or misstatement) is broadly interpreted to include any word or conduct that causes the innocent person to reach an erroneous conclusion of fact. Thus a seller of apples who selects the best ones in a basket and puts them on top of others of inferior quality has, in the eyes of the law, made a "statement" to a prospective buyer that all the apples are of the same quality as those which are visible.

In order for a misstatement to be fraudulent, it must be a **statement of fact**—an actual event, circumstance, or occurrence. Statements about the age of a horse, the number of acres in a tract of land, and the net profit made by a business during a given year are all statements of fact—that is, statements about a fact. And, the misstatement must be material (important). A statement that a 640–acre tract of land holds 642 acres would be false, but probably not materially so, a statement that it contained 670 acres probably would be materially false. If the innocent person can prove that a particular statement made to him or her was false in a material way, the first element of fraud has been established.

Predictions

Statements as to what will happen in the future are clearly not statements of fact and therefore are not fraudulent even if they turn out to be in error. Thus, if a seller of stock tells a buyer that the stock is "bound to double in value within six months," the buyer is not entitled to relief in the event the increase in value does not come about. The same is true when the seller of a motel states that "it will certainly net $14,000 in the coming year." The reason for the view that such statements do not constitute fraud, of course, is that no one can predict what will happen in the future, and a reasonable person would not put faith in such statements.

One important type of statement about a present or future event or condition does impose a legal obligation on the one making it if it proves to be false: statements that are "warranties"—guarantees as to existing fact or assurances about future performance of a product by the seller. For example: A manufacturer of house paint states on the cans that "this paint, when applied according to the manufacturer's instructions above, will not crack, fade, or peel within two years of its application." If the statement proves to be false, a buyer who has purchased the paint in reliance on the statement can recover damages. The recovery in such a case would be on breach of warranty rather than on fraud, except in the rare situation where the buyer can prove that the seller knew the representation to be false when he or she made it. However, statements that are clearly matters of opinion do not create warranties. Most warranties on goods are governed by provisions in Article 2 of the UCC, including sections 2–312, 313, 314, 315, and 316. It is important to note that damages for breach of warranty will almost always be much lower than damages for fraud; moreover, punitive damages are available in fraud cases and not in warranty cases.

Opinion

Statements of opinion, like predictions, are also distinguished from statements of fact. Contracts cannot be set aside on the ground of fraud simply because one of the parties, prior to making the contract, expressed an opinion that later turned out to be incorrect.

Most statements of opinion, in which the declarant is merely expressing personal feelings or judgments on a matter about which reasonable persons might have contrary views, are usually easy to recognize. For example, statements that "this is an excellent neighborhood in which to raise children" or that "this painting will harmonize beautifully with the colors of your living room" involve conclusions with which others might disagree; thus they cannot be the basis of an action of fraud brought by one who relied upon them.

Other statements, however, are not so easily placed in the "opinion" or "fact" categories. A statement by the seller of a boat that it is "perfectly safe" or a statement by a home owner that "the foundation is sound" are closer to being statements of fact than the previous representations about the neighborhood and the painting. But there are varying degrees of safety and soundness, so these statements too can be held in given situations to constitute only expressions of opinion—particularly if the declarant and the innocent party were on a relatively equal basis insofar as their experience and general knowledge of the subject matter were concerned. (On the other hand, if the declarant is considerably more knowledgeable than the other party, such statements are likely to be viewed as statements of *fact*, and thus fraudulent if false. For example, in the case of Groening v. Opsata, 34 N.W.2d 560 1948,, it was held that a false statement by the seller of a summer home located on an eroding cliff on the shore of Lake Michigan that "it isn't too close [to the lake]" and that "there is nothing to fear, everything is all right" constituted fraud, in view of the fact that the seller was a builder of homes in the area.)

Value

Statements about an article's *value* have also caused difficulties. Nevertheless, the courts today adhere to the traditional view (in most circumstances) that the value of an article or piece of property is a matter of opinion rather than fact. Two practical reasons are the basis for this view: (1) an awareness that many types of property are prized by some people but are considered of little value by others, and (2) a recognition of the fact that sellers generally overvalue the things they are attempting to sell, and prospective buyers must accordingly place little or no reliance upon such statements. Consequently, if a seller states that "this apartment building is easily worth $80,000," the buyer normally can not rescind the contract on the ground of fraud, even though he or she relied on the statement and can prove later that the actual market value of the building at the time of sale was nowhere near the stated figure and that the seller knew this at the time.

Again, the general rule is not followed when the declarant's experience and knowledge of the particular subject matter are *markedly superior* to those of the other party—especially if they are so great that the declarant is considered an "expert" in the eyes of the law. (In order to prevent such a person from taking grossly unfair advantage of those who are clearly less knowledgeable, his or her intentional misrepresentations *are* held to be fraudulent.)

The next case presents an allegation of fraud in a modern setting.

SARVIS V. VERMONT STATE COLLEGES
Supreme Court of Vermont, 772 A.2d 494 (2001)

On March 13, 1995, plaintiff Sarvis was convicted of five counts of bank fraud, sentenced to serve fortysix months in prison, and ordered to pay over $ 12 million in restitution to five banks, including the Proctor Bank. He was incarcerated from April 4, 1995 to

August 17, 1998 in the Allenwood federal penitentiary, where he worked in the electrical department. In August of 1998, two weeks after he was released from prison, plaintiff applied for an adjunct professor position at Community College of Vermont (CCV), a division of defendant. Plaintiff provided defendant with a resume, in which he indicated that from 1984–1998 he was "President and Chairman of the Board" of "CMI International Inc., Boston, Massachusetts." In describing his duties, plaintiff indicated he was "responsible for all operations and financial matters. He ended his summary with the following: "from 1995– 1998 this company was sold off by various divisions and I have retired."

Later, he added a line, "1998– present" "Semi–retired. Adjunct Instructor of Business at Colby–Sawyer College and Franklin Pierce College." In a memorandum to a CCV administrator, plaintiff also advised that "I have not 'worked' for almost four years," and discouraged defendant from contacting management at Franklin Pierce for additional references.

Plaintiff provided defendant with additional application materials, attempting to secure a teaching position. Plaintiff listed for defendant the classes he believed defendant would find him "well equipped to teach." He highlighted business law and business ethics as courses in which he had "the highest level of capability and interest." He alerted defendant that he had "a great interest and knowledge of business law" and that he believed he would do "an excellent job" teaching a business ethics class because this subject was "of particular concern" him.

In response to the information plaintiff provided, defendant entered into three employment contracts with plaintiff, covering plaintiff's duties as academic coordinator, teacher, and independent studies instructor. After plaintiff commenced performance on the coordinator and independent study contracts, his probation officer alerted defendant to plaintiff's criminal history. Defendant terminated plaintiff before the expiration of his contracts of employment, citing the nature of the federal offenses (involving dishonesty), the gravity of the offenses (multiple counts of bank fraud, over $ 12 million dollars in restitution) the presence of local victims (Proctor Bank and any other Vermont victims) and the potential harm to CCV's reputation, [as] substantial factors contributing to the termination decision.

Plaintiff filed a complaint alleging that defendant was liable for breach of all three contracts and wrongful termination. He later added other claims. Defendant claimed plaintiff's resume fraud rendered his contracts voidable and provided grounds for termination. Both sides moved for summary judgment. The trial court ruled for defendant and plaintiff appealed.

Skoglund, Justice:

It is well established that a party induced into a contract by fraud or misrepresentation can rescind the contract and avoid liability for any breach thereon. A misrepresentation is fraudulent when made with knowledge of its falsity. Where the procurer of a statement knew it was false, materiality is not required. Materiality is required where the mistake or false statement was not intentionally made and may be proved where the statement is "likely to induce a reasonable person to manifest his assent, or if the maker knows that it would be likely to induce" such assent. Restatement (Second) of Contracts § 162(2)(1981). Unlike a fraud action seeking damages in tort, a party seeking to rescind a fraudulently induced contract is not required to prove its case by clear and convincing evidence.

Principles of fraudulent inducement support a rule allowing an employer to avoid liability for breach of contract arising from an employment relationship induced by an employee's fraud. Thus, misrepresentation during the hiring process can be a basis for rescission of an employment contract. Further, we hold as a matter of law, such misrepresentation can constitute misconduct sufficient to support a just cause dismissal.

Plaintiff fraudulently induced defendant into entering into the employment contracts. Plaintiff misrepresented material facts related to his candidacy upon which defendant relied in making its employment decision. In both resumes, plaintiff omitted the fact that he was in prison from 1995 through 1998. Instead, he misrepresented his work history with the intent of creating the false impression of how he spent those years. During that time, he claimed he was, as president and chairman of the board of CMI, "responsible for all operations and financial matters" of CMI. In reality, he was in prison and working in the prison's electric department. Also during the hiring process, in a written response to defendant's coordinator of academic services, plaintiff declared that he had not worked for almost four years and that he had not worked for someone else since 1984. Plaintiff knew this statement was false and deceptive because four months earlier, seeking district court approval for employment in Maine under a post–prison relocation plan, he admitted that "at Allenwood FPC I currently work in the Electrical Department." Defendant's assertions and omissions were not in accord with the facts, and were offered for the sole purpose of affecting the employment decision.

Plaintiff seeks to avoid rescission and enforce the contracts by faulting defendant for failing to discover his criminal background. Plaintiff, however, cannot enforce the contract where his own actions hampered defendant's inquiry. Plaintiff discouraged defendant from contacting his current employers at Franklin Pierce for references. In a letter to defendant's academic services coordinator, plaintiff demurred that he did "not believe Franklin Pierce management could give an evaluation of me at this short date and I feel it would be unfair of me to ask that." What plaintiff failed to reveal to defendant was that he had disclosed his criminal history to Franklin Pierce. Plaintiffs effort to discourage defendant from contacting Franklin Pierce management for a reference succeeded in dissuading defendant from making full inquiry into his background.

Plaintiff also argues that his nondisclosure of his criminal history does not constitute fraud or misrepresentation because he had no duty to disclose his criminal past. Contrary to plaintiffs claim, plaintiff's misrepresentation involved more than nondisclosure. We have found fraud from partial disclosure.

Where one has full information and represents that he has, if he discloses a part of his information only, and by words or conduct leads the one with whom he contracts to believe that he has made a full disclosure and does this with intent to deceive and overreach and to prevent investigation, he is guilty of fraud against which equity will relieve, if his words and conduct in consequence of reliance upon them bring about the result which he desires.

The misrepresentation in this case occurred through plaintiffs partial disclosure of his past work history and references and his effort to limit defendant's inquiry into his past. Plaintiff was not silent; he carefully drafted his resumes and supplemental materials to lead defendant to believe he had made a full disclosure about his past and his qualifications. He listed classes in business ethics and law in which he claimed he had the highest level of capability and knowledge but failed to mention his felony bank fraud conviction. Plaintiff assured defendant that making additional inquiries into his background would have revealed "more of the same" type of information as that offered by the references plaintiff supplied. This was not true.

Contact with plaintiffs probation officer or supervisor at the Allenwood prison would have notified defendant of plaintiffs fraud convictions, period of incarceration, and work history at the prison. We agree with the trial court's conclusion that plaintiff misrepresented material facts related to his candidacy upon which defendant relied in making its employment decision.

[The trial court correctly held that plaintiff misrepresented his past and that this was reason to disaffirm the contract. It was also justifiable grounds for termination of employment. Affirmed.]

Law

Under the early common–law rule of this country, *statementsof law* made by lay persons were clearly held not to constitute statements of fact and thus could not be the basis for actions of fraud. If the seller of a vacant lot that carries a C–1 zoning classification assures the buyer that "this classification permits the erection of duplex rental units," a statement that the seller knows is not true, the buyer who purchases the property in reliance on the statement ordinarily cannot maintain an action for damages. The rule was based on two grounds: (1) the generally reasonable feeling that a statement made by a nonlawyer about a point of law should not be relied upon by the one to whom it is made, and (2) the somewhat more questionable maxim that "everyone is presumed to know the law."

While this is still the rule applied to most cases, it is subject to an increasing number of exceptions. One major exception comprises statements of law made by persons who—because of their professional or occupational status— can reasonably be expected to know the law relating to their specialty, even though they are not attorneys. Thus intentional misrepresentations of law by persons such as real estate brokers and bank cashiers as to legal matters within their particular specialties are frequently held to be fraudulent.

Silence

The traditional common-law rule was *caveat emptor* ("let the buyer beware"). Under this rule, buyers had the responsibility to look out for themselves in making a purchase. Thus, assume that a seller knew that a car had been involved in an accident that bent the car's frame. If the seller told the buyer: "This car has never been in an accident," a clear misstatement of material fact would have occurred. When the buyer learned the truth, he could rescind due to fraud. But what if the seller did not make such a statement, but simply kept silent about the accident? The traditional rule stated that mere silence (failure to disclose a material fact) does not constitute fraud. The reasoning was that in most instances the parties are dealing at arm's length, possessing roughly the same amount of experience and knowledge relating to the subject matter of the contract. Parties are said to deal at "arm's length" when their relationship is such that neither part owes a duty to divulge information to the other party, as distinguished from such "fiduciary" relationships such as attorney client, guardian–ward, employer–employee, principalagent, and business partner relationships. And, in many instances, the facts not disclosed could have been ascertained by the buyer with reasonable inspection or inquiry.

Today, however, *caveat emptor* has been so riddled with exceptions that in many jurisdictions it is difficult to speak of it as being the general rule. Court rulings and state consumer protection statutes have created so many situations where sellers must volunteer adverse information or be charged with fraud that many claim the new general rule is *caveat venditor* ("let the seller beware").

Silence and the Duty to Speak

The courts have found several types of situations where the withholding of information is so manifestly unfair that silence should be held to constitute fraud.

To prevent unfairness of this degree, the courts say that, in such situations, a "duty to speak" exists. It is difficult to summarize the duty–to–speak categories with precision, because the silence cases involve such a wide variety of fact–patterns, and because the rules of the various states applicable to duty to speak situations are often couched in general terms (to give the courts substantial discretion in their application). Additionally, the law is continuing to evolve in this area, as the courts seek to raise moral standards in the marketplace by applying the rules to situations that were earlier outside their scope.

Despite these factors, several fairly well–defined situations do exist in which the courts generally agree that a duty to speak exists. (In such instances the courts often speak of "intentionally withheld information," of "concealment," and of silence as part of a "plan" to deceive.)

The first of these instances is the sale of property that contains a **latent defect** (or *hidden defect*)—one that a simple or casual inspection by a prospective purchaser ordinarily would not disclose. Common examples are a cracked motor block in an automobile and a termite infestation in a house. A property owner who has knowledge of such conditions is guilty of fraud if he or she does not apprise the prospective purchaser of them— assuming, of course, that the innocent purchaser subsequently enters into a contract to buy the property.

While the latent defect rule, abstractly stated, is highly commendable, the practical protection it affords is less than one might hope for. Frequently it is difficult for the buyer to prove that the defect actually existed at the time of purchase—particularly if a long period of time has elapsed before its discovery. And even if this hurdle is cleared, the buyer has to establish that the seller knew, or should have known, of the defect when the sale occurred. The seller's contention that he or she was honestly unaware of the defective condition is frequently accepted by a jury.

Normally the rule on hidden defects does not work in reverse. Thus, if the buyer possesses information about the property that causes its value to be higher than the seller believes it to be, the buyer does not have a duty to divulge this information to the seller (unless the buyer is an expert in the field by reason of training or experience).

A second duty to speak situation occurs where a **fiduciary relationship** exists— that is, where one of the parties occupies a position of "trust and confidence" relative to the other. (This differs from the ordinary situation, where the parties are dealing "at arm's length.") For example, when a partnership is considering a land purchase, a partner who is part owner of the land under consideration has a duty to divulge his or her interest to the co–partner before the purchase is made. Similarly, a corporate officer who is purchasing stock from a shareholder has a duty to disclose any special facts of which he or she has knowledge, by virtue of that position, which would affect the value of the stock.

The third category comprises situations in which one party has **superior knowledge** about the subject matter of the contract as a result of his or her experience, training, or special relationship with the subject matter. In this type of circumstance the rule has obvious application where the silent party— the one possessing the superior knowledge—is an "expert" in the area, but it often applies to other parties as well. The rule commonly applied is that if one party has superior knowledge, or knowledge which is not within the reasonable reach of the other party (and which such party could not discover by the exercise of means open to both parties), there is a duty on the party possessing the knowledge to disclose it. Under this rule, for example, a buyer of Oklahoma land who, by virtue of his employment with an oil company, learns of an oil "strike" on an adjacent ranch would be guilty of fraud if he did not disclose this information to the seller, a rancher. On the other hand, if the buyer was simply another ranch owner in the area, his or her nondisclosure of this information would probably not be fraudulent.

Outside of these situations, most courts take the view that neither party has a duty to volunteer information to the other, even though it might bear materially on the other's decision of whether to contract. Thus the seller of a trash collection business probably has no duty to tell a prospective purchaser of indications that the city is going to institute a collection service of its own—especially if this information is as available to the buyer as it is to the seller.

The following case illustrates, in a rather unusual setting, the courts' struggle to establish fairer rules than a blanket application of *caveat emptor*.

STAMBOVKSY V. ACKLEY
New York Supreme Court, Appellate Division, 572 N.Y.S.2d 672 (1991)

After making a $32,000 down payment on a $650,000 house in Nyack, New York, plaintiff learned that (1) both Readers' Digest in 1977 and local newspapers in 1982, defendant seller had claimed that she and members of her family had several times over the previous nine years seen poltergeists in the house, and (2) in 1989 the house was included in a five-home walking tour of Nyack and was described in a November 27 newspaper article as "a riverfront Victorian (with ghost)." Plaintiff refused to close on the house and sued both the seller and the seller's real estate agent, seeking both monetary damages and rescission of the contract. The trial court dismissed the suit. Plaintiff appealed.

Rubin, Justice:

While I agree with [the trial court] that the real estate broker, as agent for the seller, is under no duty to disclose to a potential buyer the phantasmal reputation of the premises and that, in his pursuit of a legal remedy for fraudulent misrepresentation against the seller, plaintiff hasn't a ghost of a chance, I am nevertheless moved by the spirit of equity to allow the buyer to seek rescission of the contract of sale and recovery of his down payment. New York law fails to recognize any remedy for damages incurred as a result of the seller's mere silence, applying instead the strict rule of caveat emptor. Therefore, the theoretical basis for relief, even under the extraordinary facts of this case, is elusive if not ephemeral.

"Pity me not but lend thy serious hearing to what I shall unfold" (William Shakespeare, Hamlet, Act I, Scene V [Ghost]).

From the perspective of a person in the position of plaintiff herein, a very practical problem arises with respect to the discovery of a paranormal phenomenon: "Who you gonna' call?" as the title song to the movie "Ghostbusters" asks. Applying the strict rule of caveat emptor to a contract involving a house possessed by poltergeists conjures up visions of a psychic or medium routinely accompanying the structural engineer and Terminex man on an inspection of every home subject to a contract of sale.... In the interest of avoiding such untenable consequences, the notion that a haunting is a condition which can and should be ascertained upon reasonable inspection of the premises is a hobgoblin which should be exorcised from the body of legal precedent and laid quietly to rest.

It has been suggested by a leading authority that the ancient rule which holds that mere non–disclosure does not constitute actionable misrepresentation "finds proper application in cases where the fact undisclosed is patent, or the plaintiff has equal opportunities for obtaining information which he may be expected to utilize, or the defendant has no reason to think that he is acting under any misapprehension" (Prosser, Law of Torts, at 696 [4th ed. 1971]). However, with respect to transactions in real estate, New York adheres to the doctrine of caveat emptor and imposes no duty upon the vendor to disclose any information concerning the premises unless there is a confidential or fiduciary relationship between the parties or some conduct on the part of the seller which constitutes "active concealment" [such as constructing a dummy ventilation system or covering foundation cracks]. Normally, some affirmative misrepresentation is required to impose upon the seller a duty to communicate undisclosed conditions affecting the premises.

Caveat emptor is not so all encompassing a doctrine of common law as to render every act of nondisclosure immune from redress, whether legal or equitable. "In regard to the necessity of giving information which has not been asked, the rule differs somewhat at law and in equity, and while the law courts would permit no recovery of damages against a vendor, because of mere concealment of facts under certain circumstances, yet if the vendee refused to complete the contract because of the concealment of a material fact on the part of the other, equity would refuse to compel him so to do, because equity only compels the specific performance of a contract which is fair and open, and in regard to which all material matters known to each have been communicated to the other."(Rothmiller v. Stein, 143 N.Y. 581). Even as a principle of law, long before exceptions were embodied in statute law [for example, the implied warranty provisions of the UCC], the doctrine was held inapplicable to contagion among animals, adulteration of food, and insolvency of a maker of a promissory note and of a tenant substituted for another under a lease. Common law is not moribund. Where fairness and common sense dictate that an exception should be created, the evolution of the law should not be stifled by rigid application of a legal maxim.

Where a condition which has been created by the seller materially impairs the value of the contract and is peculiarly within the knowledge of the seller or unlikely to be discovered by a prudent purchaser exercising due care with respect to the subject matter, nondisclosure constitutes a basis for rescission as a matter of equity. Any other outcome places upon the buyer not merely the obligation to exercise care in his purchase but rather to be omniscient with respect to any fact which may affect the bargain. No practical purpose is served by imposing such a burden upon a purchaser. To the contrary, it encourages predatory business practice and offends the principle that equity will suffer no wrong to be without a remedy.

In the case at bar, defendant seller deliberately fostered the public belief that her home was possessed. Having undertaken to inform the public at large, to whom she has no legal relationship, about the supernatural occurrences on her property, she may be said to owe no less a duty to her contract vendee. It has been remarked that the occasional modern cases which permit a seller to take unfair advantage of a buyer's ignorance so long as he is not actively misled are "singularly unappetizing" (Prosser, Law of Torts, at 696 [4th ed. 1971]). Where, as here the seller not only takes unfair advantage of the buyer's ignorance but has created and perpetuated a condition about which he is unlikely even to inquire, enforcement of the contract (in whole or in part) is offensive to the court's sense of equity. Application of the remedy of rescission, within the bounds of the narrow exception to the doctrine of caveat emptor set forth herein, is entirely appropriate to relieve the unwitting purchaser from the consequences of a most unnatural bargain.

[Reversed. The first cause of action seeking rescission of the contract is reinstated.]

Intent to Deceive

The second element of fraud is *knowledge of falsity* (or, as it is sometimes called, "scienter"). Thus the innocent party must ordinarily prove that the person making the statement knew, or should have known, that it was false at the time it was made. However, the knowledge of falsity requirement is also met if a person makes a statement "with a reckless disregard for the truth," even if the declarant did not actually know it was false. Thus, if the seller of a used car has no idea as to its mileage but nevertheless states that "it has not been driven more than 30,000 miles," the statement constitutes fraud if it is later proven that the true mileage materially exceeded that figure.

Reliance

The victim of a misrepresentation must show that he or she reasonably relied on the misstatement at the time of contracting. Sometimes this is not difficult to establish. The innocent party does not have to prove that the fact in regard to which the misrepresentation was made was the primary factor in inducing him or her to make the contract. It is sufficient that the misrepresentation involved a matter tending to influence the decision.

Reliance does not exist, of course, if the one accused of fraud can prove that the other party actually knew the true facts before making the contract. Also, a charge of fraud will fail if the victim's reliance was not reasonable under the circumstances. While the old rule of *caveat emptor* is much less significant than formerly, a buyer still cannot blindly accept everything he or she is told. For example, a buyer given an opportunity to view the property is presumed to observe any patent (obvious) defects that might exist. To illustrate—the seller of a used television set tells the buyer it "produces an excellent picture on all channels." If the buyer viewed the set in operation prior to the sale and complained of reception on one channel, that person could hardly contend after the sale that he had reasonably relied on the seller's representation.

Injury

The last element of a successful fraud action is a showing by the innocent party that he or she suffered an injury, usually an economic loss, as a result of the misrepresentation. In most cases proof of injury (or "damage") is the easiest of the fraud elements to prove. For example, in a typical case involving the sale of property, the buyer is able to show that the value of the property he or she received is substantially less than it would have been if the seller's representations had been true.

Remedies for Fraud

Once fraud is established, the defrauded party always has the right to rescind the contract. When such a person chooses the remedy of *rescission*, he or she must ordinarily return the consideration, if any, that was received from the other party. Rescission, then, is designed to restore the parties to their original positions.

In some instances the defrauded party may wish to keep the consideration, for example, a parcel of land, even though it had been misrepresented by the seller. In such a case the buyer may keep the consideration (i.e., "affirm the contract") and bring suit for *damages*—which in the usual situation is, at the minimum, the difference between the actual value of the property the buyer received, and the value it would have had if the representations had been true. (Additionally, because fraud is a tort, the innocent party may be awarded punitive damages as well.)

As a general rule, the defrauded party must elect either to rescind the contract or to recover damages. However, where the fraud involves the making of a sales contract, such an election need not be made. Sec. 2–721 of the UCC provides, in part, that where fraud is established, "Neither rescission nor a claim for rescission of the contract ... shall bar or be ... inconsistent with a claim for damages or other remedy. Thus in circumstances where a buyer or seller seeking rescission can show that he or she will suffer a loss notwithstanding the rescission, damages may also be recovered.

Innocent Misrepresentation

If all the elements of fraud are present in a particular case, except that the person making the misstatement honestly (and reasonably) believed the statement to be true, that person is guilty of innocent misrepresentation rather than fraud. Under the rule of most states, the victim can rescind the contract on that ground, but is usually not given the alternative remedy of damages. Innocent misrepresentation and fraud are contrasted in Figure 15.2.

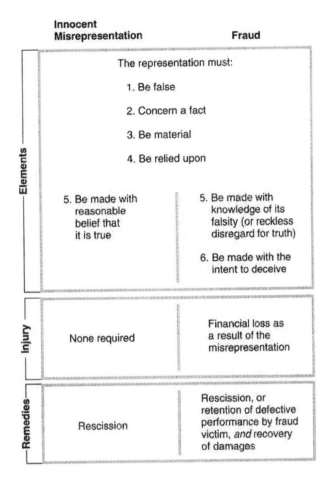

Figure 15.2 Fraud and Innocent Misrepresentation

Mistake

Cases are continually arising where one of the parties to a contract attempts to have it set aside by the court on the ground that he or she was mistaken in some respect at the time the contract was made. Often the mistake involves opinion or judgment rather than fact, in which case no relief will be granted. For example, a person contracts to buy land for $30,000 thinking this is its true value. If its actual value proves to be much less, he or she has shown bad judgment and will not be permitted to rescind the contract. Similarly, if a person purchases stock in the belief, that it will greatly increase in value in a short time, he or she obviously cannot have the contract set aside in the event that it does not perform as hoped. If rescission were permitted on grounds such as these, the basic value of all contracts would be destroyed.

However, in certain limited situations a plea of mistake will afford grounds for rescission of a contract, if the mistake was one of fact. The general rule is that if both parties were mistaken as to a material fact at the time of contracting, either party can rescind the agreement. On the other hand, if only one of the parties was mistaken, rescission will not be granted unless that person can show that the other party knew, or should have known, of the mistake at the time the contract was made. When both parties are mistaken, the mistake is a **bilateral mistake;** when only one is mistaken, it is a **unilateral mistake.**

Bilateral Mistake

The following examples illustrate the general principle that a contract can be set aside if there is a mutual mistake as to the *existence*, the *identity*, or the *character* of the subject matter of the contract.

1. B purchases S's summer home on April 10. Subsequently, B learns that, unknown to either party, the home was destroyed by fire on April 1. Since both parties entered into the contract under the mistaken assumption that the subject matter of the contract actually existed at that time, B can have the contract set aside.
2. P owns two properties outside Woodsfield, Ohio. G, after viewing both acreages, makes P a written offer to purchase one for $18,000. P accepts the offer. It later develops that G had one property in mind while P, after reading the description contained in G's offer, honestly and reasonably believed that G was referring to the other property. Either party can rescind the agreement, because there was a mutual mistake about the identity of the contract's subject matter.
3. C purchases a gemstone from D for $25. At the time of contracting, both parties believe the stone is a topaz. In fact, it turns out to be an uncut diamond worth $700. Since both parties were mistaken about the true character of the contract's subject matter, D can have the contract rescinded, thereby recovering the stone.

    The principle is not applicable to situations where both parties realize that they are *in doubt* as to a particular matter, but enter into a contract nonetheless. Thus, in example 3 above, if neither C nor D had any idea what the stone was when they made the contract, D could not rescind the contract when the E stone proved to be an uncut diamond (nor could C have rescinded had the stone turned out to be a worthless one). In such an instance both parties had, by contract, "assumed the risk" as to the stone's value. With these general rules of law in mind let us examine the problem presented by the following case.

BEACHCOMBER COINS, INC. V. BOSKETT
Superior Court of New Jersey, Appellate Division,
400 A.2d 78 (1979)

Boskett was a part-time dealer coins in New Jersey. He owned a 1916 dime which bore the letter indicating that it had been minted *Denver. Because of the rarity of such coins, their market value was greatly excess of their monetary worth.*

Beachcomber Coins, plaintiff, was interested in buying the coin, and one of its owners examined the coin to determine its genuineness. After an examination of forty-five minutes he was satisfied that the coin was, in fact, minted in Denver, and he purchased it on behalf of plaintiff for $500. Later plaintiff was advised by the American Numismatic Society that the "D" was a counterfeit. When Boskett, the seller, refused to take back the coin and refund the purchase price, plaintiff brought this action asking rescission of the contract.

The trial judge, sitting without a jury, found that there was a mutual mistake of fact (a mistake as to the coin's genuineness) that would ordinarily justify rescission of the contract. However, he further found that under customary coin dealing procedures a buyer of a coin who was permitted to examine it before purchase "assumed the risk" that it might be counterfeit. He therefore dismissed the action and plaintiff appealed.

Conford, Judge:

. . . The evidence and trial judge's findings establish this as a classic case [in which rescission should be allowed on the basis of] mutual mistake of fact. As a general rule, "where parties on entering into a transaction that affects their contractual relations are both under a mistake regarding a fact assumed by them as the basis on which they entered into the transaction, it is voidable by either party if enforcement of it would be materially more onerous to him than it would have been had the fact been as the parties believed it to be." Restatement, Contracts, 5502(1932). . . .

Moreover, [the Restatement provides that] "negligent failure of a party to know or discover the facts as to which both parties are under a mistake does not preclude rescission or reformation on account thereof." The law of New Jersey is in accord. . . .

Defendant's contention that plaintiff assumed the risk that the coin might be of greater or lesser value is not supported by the evidence. It is [true that] a party to a contract can assume the risk of being mistaken as to the value of the thing sold. The Restatement states the rule this way:

Where the parties know that there is doubt in regard to a certain matter and contract on that assumption, the contract is not rendered voidable because one is disappointed in the hope that the facts accord with his wishes. The risk of the existence of the doubtful fact is then assumed as one of the elements of the bargain.

However, for this rule to apply, the parties must be conscious that the pertinent fact may not be true and make their agreement at the risk of that possibility. [That rule is not applicable] in this case, because both parties were certain that the coin was genuine. . . .

[The court then turned to the trial judge's finding that it was customary in the coin dealing business for buyers of coins to assume the risk of genuineness. After examining the testimony on this point at the trial, the court concluded that it was too weak to support the finding of "custom and usage" under New Jersey law. The court thus reversed the judgment, and ordered rescission of the contract.]

Unilateral Mistake

Where only one party to a contract is mistaken about a material fact, rescission is ordinarily not allowed unless the mistake was (or should have been) apparent to the other party. Two examples follow.

1. B purchases a painting from S for $300; B believes it was painted by a well-known artist. B does not, however, disclose this belief to S. In fact, the painting is the work of an amateur and consequently worth no more than $50. Since only B was mistaken as to the identity of the artist, the mistake is unilateral and the contract cannot be rescinded. On the other hand, B would have been permitted to rescind if S had been aware of B's mistake and had not corrected it.

2. X furnishes three contractors with specifications for a building project and asks them to submit construction bids. C submits a bid for $48,000 and D submits one for $46,500. E's bid, because of an error in addition, is $27,000 rather than the intended $47,000. If X accepts E's bid, E can have the contract set aside if the jury finds (as is likely to be the case) either that X actually knew of the mistake when he accepted the bid or that he should have been aware of the mistake because of the wide discrepancy in the bids.

Cautions

The "bilateral–unilateral mistake" rule of thumb, while widely followed, by no means settles all cases that arise in the general area of mistake. In the first place, there is some disagreement as to what constitutes a bilateral mistake. Many courts, for example, take the view that such a mistake exists only where the parties have arrived at their erroneous conclusions independently of one another, rather than one party simply relying on information supplied by the other.

Second, a few states have statutes relating to contracts entered into under mistake of fact that sometimes permit rescission where common–law principles would not.

Third, the court will sometimes settle cases purely on "equitable principles"—the basis of overall fairness in particular situations—thereby giving little or no weight to the bilateral–unilateral factor. Many unilateral mistake cases arise in construction contracts when erroneous bids are made. A common approach allows rescission if three factors are present: (1) The mistake was one of mere negligence—for example, the misreading of plans or the erroneous adding of a column of figures due to exhaustion or haste. (2) Rescission would cause no injury to the nonmistaken party other than loss of the erroneous bargain—for example, if the mistake is discovered and called to the attention of the nonmistaken party before the contract is awarded or soon thereafter (i.e., before construction commences while the lowest nonmistaken bid could still be accepted). (3) Holding the mistaken party to his or her bid would be "unconscionable." Thus, a mistaken bidder in a school construction contract was allowed to rescind on the basis of unilateral mistake where the day after the contract was awarded he called the school district's attention to a simple error in addition that had led to a bid of $534,175 rather than the intended $634,175. Taylor v. Arlington ISD, 335 S.W.2d 371(Tex. 1960).

Additional types of Mistake

Occasionally a mistake involves the provisions of the contract itself rather than the contract's subject matter. For example, an offeree might accept an offer that he or she has misread, only to learn later that the offer was in fact substantially different than it seemed. This is a unilateral mistake, and the offeree is bound by the resulting contract (unless the acceptance itself discloses the mistake to the offeror).

Mutual mistakes as to the value of an article being sold generally are held to constitute mistakes of opinion rather than fact, and rescission is not permitted in such cases. Thus, if B buys a painting from S for $10,000, both parties correctly believing that the artist was Andrew Wyeth, B obviously cannot have the contract set aside simply because he later learns that the painting's true value is only $5,000.

There is somewhat greater uncertainty insofar as mistakes of law are concerned. The courts at one time refused to permit rescission of contracts where a *mistake of law* existed, either bilateral or unilateral, on the theory that such a mistake was not a mistake of fact. (This idea was consistent with the view that a *misstatement of law* does not constitute a misstatement of fact, under the law of fraud.) Today, however, most courts treat *mistakes of law* and *fact* the same— that is, they will set aside contracts which both parties entered into under a mistake of law as well as those in which the mistake of one party was apparent to the other.

Duress

Occasionally a person will seek to escape liability under a contract on the ground that he or she was forced to enter into it. Often the courts find that the "force" is insignificant in the eyes of the law, and the complaining party is held to the contract. For example, if a person enters into a contract simply because he or she knows that failure to do so will incur the wrath of some third person, such as his or her employer or spouse, relief will not be granted. If, on the other hand, the degree of compulsion is so great as to totally rob the person of free will, duress exists, and the contract can be rescinded.

One early definition of **duress** that still remains authoritative is the following:

> (1) any wrongful act of one person that compels a manifestation of apparent assent by another to a transaction without his volition, or (2) any wrongful threat of one person by words or other conduct that induces another to enter into a transaction under the influence of such fear as precludes him from exercising free will and judgment, if the threat was intended or should reasonably have been expected to operate as an inducement. *Restatement, Contracts.* §492. The American Law Institute, 1932.

A necessary element of duress is fear—a genuine and reasonable fear on the part of the victim that he or she will be subjected to an injurious, unlawful act by not acceding to the other party's demands. Thus, if a person signs a contract at gunpoint or after being physically beaten, duress exists, and the victim can escape liability on that ground. Duress also exists when a person makes a contract as a consequence of another person's threat of harm (for instance, kidnapping a child) if the contract is refused.

Generally, the innocent party must show that the act actually committed or threatened was a wrongful one. For instance, a contract entered into between a striking union and an employer cannot be set aside by the latter on the ground of duress if the strike was a lawful one—as, for example, if the strike occurred after an existing "no–strike" contract between union and employer had expired.

The threat of a criminal suit is generally held to constitute duress. For example: X proposes a contract to Y and tells him that if he refuses to sign the agreement, X will turn over evidence to the prosecuting attorney's office tending to prove that Y had embezzled money from his employer six weeks earlier. To prevent this, Y signs the contract. Y can have the contract rescinded on the ground of duress, because a threat to use the criminal machinery of the state for such a purpose is clearly wrongful—regardless of whether or not Y had actually committed the crime in question. Threat of a civil suit, on the other hand, usually does not constitute duress.

While a contract cannot be set aside simply because there is a disparity of bargaining power between the parties, the courts are beginning to accept the idea that *economic duress* (or business compulsion) can be grounds for the rescission of a contract in exceptional situations. The decision in the next case sets forth three requirements that ordinarily must be met in order for a plaintiff to be successful in a suit asking rescission on this ground.

TOTEM MARINE TUG & BARGE V. ALYESKA PIPELINE
Supreme Court of Alaska, 584 P.2d 15 (1978)

Totem Marine Tug and Barge, Inc., entered into a contract with Alyeska Pipeline Services under which Totem was to transport large quantities of pipeline construction materials from Houston, Texas, to Alaska. After Totem began its performance, many problems arose. One major difficulty was the fact that the tonnages to be shipped were six times greater than Alyeska had indicated. Additionally, long delays occurred in getting Totem's vessels through the Panama Canal, which resulted from Alyeska's failure to furnish promised documents to Totem by specified dates. After these and other problems, Alyeska cancelled the contract without cause.

At the time of the wrongful termination, Alyeska owed Totem about $300,000. Officers of Alyeska at first promised that it would

pay Totem invoices promptly, but later they told Totem that it would have its money "in six to eight months." (Totem alleged that the delay in payment occurred after Alyeska learned through negotiations with Totem lawyers that Totem's creditors were pressing it for their payments, and that without immediate cash it would go into bankruptcy— allegations that Alyeska did not deny.)

After further negotiations, a settlement agreement was made in 1975 under which Alyeska paid Totem $97,000 in return for surrender of all claims against it. In early 1976 Totem brought this action to rescind the settlement agreement on the ground of economic duress, and to recover the balance allegedly due under the original contract. The trial court ruled as a matter of law that the *circumstances under which the settlement occurred did not constitute duress, and dismissed the complaint. Totem appealed.*

Burke, Justice:

. . . This court has not yet decided a case involving a claim of economic duress, or what is also called business compulsion. . . . [In recent cases] this concept has been broadened to include myriad forms of economic coercion which force a person to involuntarily enter into a particular transaction. . . .

There are various statements of what constitutes economic duress, but as noted by one commentator, "The history of generalization in the field offers no great encouragement for those who seek to summarize results in any single formula." Dawson, *Economic Duress*, 43 Mich. L. Rev. (1947). . . . [However, many states adopt the view that] duress exists where: (1) one party involuntarily accepted the terms of another, (2) circumstances permitted no other alternative, and (3) such circumstances were the result of coercive acts of the other party. . . .

One essential element of economic duress is that the plaintiff show that the other party, by wrongful acts or threats, intentionally caused him to enter into a particular transaction. . . . This requirement may be satisfied where the alleged wrongdoer's conduct is criminal or tortious, but an act or threat may also be wrongful if it is wrongful in the moral sense. . . .

Economic duress does not exist, however, merely because a person has been the victim of a wrongful act; in addition, the victim must have no choice but to agree to the other person's terms or face serious financial hardship. Thus, in order to avoid a contract, a party must also show that he had no reasonable alternative to agreeing to the other party's terms, or as it is often stated, that he had no adequate remedy if the threat were carried out. . . .

Turning to the instant case, we believe that Totem's allegations, if proved, would support a finding that it executed a release of its contract claims against Alyeska under economic duress. Totem has alleged that Alyeska deliberately withheld payment of an acknowledged debt, knowing that Totem had no choice but to accept an inadequate sum in settlement of that debt; that Totem was faced with impending bankruptcy; that Totem was unable to meet its pressing debts other than by accepting the immediate cash payment offered by Alyeska; and that through necessity, Totem thus involuntarily accepted an inadequate settlement offer from Alyeska and executed a release of all claims under the contract. If the release was in fact executed under these circumstances, we think that . . . this would constitute the type of wrongful conduct and lack of alternatives that would render the release voidable by Totem on the ground of economic duress. . . .

Reversed, and case remanded.

Undue Influence

There are some circumstances in which a person can escape contractual liability by proving that his or her consent was brought about by the **undue influence** of the other party to the contract. While many kinds of influence are perfectly lawful, influence is undue (excessive) where one party so dominates the will of the other that the latter's volition actually is destroyed. A common example occurs where one person, as the result of advanced age and physical deterioration, begins to rely more and more upon a younger, more energetic acquaintance or relative for advice until the point is reached where the older person's willpower and judgment are almost totally controlled by the dominant party. If the older, weaker person can show (1) that he or she was induced to enter into a particular contract by virtue of the dominant party's power and influence, rather than as the result of exercising his or her own volition, and (2) that the dominant party used this power to take advantage of him or her, undue influence is established and he or she is freed of liability on this ground.

The same general rules for undue influence in the making of contracts also apply to the making of wills. Therefore, it may be helpful to read the Casper v. McDowell case in Chapter 27, which discusses wills and estate law

Home Solicitation Statutes

Several states have passed **home solicitation statutes** which protect persons who are subjected to high–pressure sales tactics by salespersons who come to their homes. These statutes supplement the common–law concepts discussed above. The general rule is that a buyer has an automatic three–day period in which to cancel a contract where: (1) the contract is for land, goods or services worth over $25; (2) the sale was initiated by the seller; and (3) the contract was completed at a place other than the seller's place of business (usually the buyer's home). The buyer need not show fraud, undue influence, or mistake. The three–day right to rescind is automatic. The federal government has passed a similar statute which applies to all sales affecting interstate commerce.

CHAPTER 16

CONTRACTS IN WRITING

Many People Have the idea that contracts are never enforceable unless they are in writing; thus we hear movie magnate Sam Goldwyn's famous aphorism, "Oral contracts aren't worth the paper they're written on." Insofar as the law is concerned, however, most oral contracts are just as enforceable as written contracts *if their terms can be established in court*. In this chapter we will examine the relatively few kinds of contracts that are required by law to be in writing; then we will consider general problems relating to written contracts. In a situation where the law requires a contract to be in writing, any contract that does not meet that requirement— i.e., one that is entirely oral in nature, or that is written but ambiguous—is an "unenforceable" contract, rather than a "void" or "voidable" one. Thus, as the term indicates, neither party is bound by such a contract—with limited exceptions noted later. Note, however, that although many types of contracts are enforceable even if there is little or no written documentation, many lawsuits based on oral contracts that are otherwise valid are dismissed by the courts because their terms cannot be sufficiently established. Thus, if a contract is important, it is always wise to document it in writing even if the law does not require this. Also, even if a contract is required to be in writing, if both parties have fully performed the contract, a court will not "undo" the contract because it was supposed to be in writing but was not.

The Statute of Frauds

In England, prior to the latter part of the seventeenth century, all oral contracts were enforceable as long as their existence and terms could be established. Under this approach, it became apparent that many unscrupulous plaintiffs were obtaining judgments against innocent defendants by the use of *perjured testimony*—false testimony given under oath. To illustrate: P claimed that D had breached a particular oral contract, a contract that D denied making. If P could induce his witnesses (usually by the payment of money) to falsely testify that they heard D agree to the alleged contract, and if D could neither refute such testimony by witnesses of his own nor otherwise prove that P's witnesses were lying, a judgment would ordinarily be granted in favor of P. D's situation was particularly difficult because, at the time we are speaking of, the parties to a civil suit were not permitted to testify in their own behalf; thus the testimony of their witnesses was all—important. To reduce the possibility that this could happen, Parliament in 1677 passed "An Act for the Prevention of Frauds and Perjuries"—or, as it is commonly called, the **statute of frauds.**

The statute of frauds required certain types of contracts to be in writing in order to be enforceable.

Virtually every American state has its own statute of frauds patterned after the original English version, which required the following types of contracts or promises to be in writing (or evidenced by a written memorandum):
1. A contract calling for the sale of an interest in land.
2. A contract that cannot be performed within one year of its making.

3. A promise by one person to pay the debt of another.
4. A promise made in consideration of marriage.
5. A promise by the administrator or executor of an estate to pay a debt of the estate out of his or her own funds.

Modern Rationale

Obviously, a continuing rationale for the statute of frauds is the hope that written agreements will diminish the chances that a plaintiff will simply fabricate the existence of a contract an sue. It also represents a policy judgment that written evidence is more reliable than fading memories. Additionally, the requirement of a writing serves the cautionary function of reminding the parties of the significance of their acts. On the other hand, the statute of frauds also allows some parties to evade obligations that they have willingly undertaken. Indeed, it appears that it is used more often for this purpose than to defeat a fabricated lawsuit. This concern has led England, where the statute of frauds originated, to virtually discard it. Indeed, most nations do not have a requirement that contracts be in writing, and the Convention on Contracts for the International Sale of Goods (CISG) provides that "a contract for sale need not be concluded in or evidence by writing and is not subject to any other requirements as to form."

Introduction to Exceptions

Criticisms of the statute of frauds have also led courts in America to devise various rules which in certain circumstances will either take oral contracts out of the statute of frauds or grant relief to a party who has performed his or her half of an oral agreement. Thus, even before we address the types of contracts that generally must be in writing to be enforceable, we should mention that each rule has judicially created exceptions.

Most courts will find an exception to the Statute of Frands and enforce an oral contract where the elements of promissory estoppel are present (if the promisee foreseeably relied on *the oral promise in circumstances where injustice would result if it were not enforced), or part performance (if the promisee has completely or in some instances partially performed his part of the bargain), or even quasi—contract (to avoid unjust enrichment of the promisor).*

These exceptions vary substantially from jurisdiction to jurisdiction and even from category to category among the types of contracts that are supposed to be in writing. It is almost impossible to delineate exactly the scope of these exceptions. However, this chapter will give many examples and notes the strong trend among the courts to use promissory estoppel or related doctrines to enforce oral promises, notwithstanding the statute of frauds, where needed to avoid unfair results. The framers of the Uniform Commercial Code agreed with this trend. As we shall see when we address UCC Sec. 2—201, there are even more exceptions to the sales contract's writing requirement than to the traditional statute of frauds.

Contracts that Must Be in Writing
Contracts Calling for the Sale of Land

As a practical matter, the most important contracts required by the statute to be in writing are those calling for the sale of land—real estate. With an exception to be noted later, unwritten agreements of this kind are absolutely unenforceable. Thus, if X orally agrees to sell a farm to Y for a specified price, neither X nor Y can recover damages from the other if one of even in the unlikely event that both parties admit in court that they made the contract.

In most cases it is easy to determine whether a contract does or does not involve the sale of land. Land, or *real property,* essentially consists of the earth's surface, vegetation, buildings, and other structures permanently attached to the soil. Growing crops, being physically attached to the ground, are also generally considered to be real property when sold in conjunction with the land. Thus, if S, by a written agreement, contracts to sell his farm to B for $50,000, B is entitled to receive any crops then growing on it, as well as the land itself— unless the contract provides otherwise. On the other hand, if S contracts merely to sell the crop to B, the crop is considered *personal property* and the contract does not have to be in writing under the statute of frauds. (If, however, the price of the crop were $500 or more, the contract would then be required to be in writing under a special section of the Uniform Commercial Code, which will be discussed later in the chapter.)

Interests in land include real estate mortgages and easements. A real estate **mortgage** is a conveyance of an interest in land by a debtor to a creditor as security for the debt. An **easement** is the right of one person to do something on someone else's land. Easements can be created in two general ways—expressly or by implication. If created in an express manner, the granting of the right must be evidenced by a writing—either specific language in a deed or a written contract. An easement created by implication, on the other hand, need not be evidenced by a writing. (One example of such an easement is an "implied easement of necessity." This is created when a landowner sells part of his or her property to another, the land being situated in such a way that the buyer has no access to it except by going across the seller's remaining land.) While real estate leases also convey interests in land and thus normally fall within the Statute of Frauds, most states have enacted special statutes providing that oral leases of a year's duration or less are valid—if for a term of more than one year, leases must be written.

Effect of Part Performance—Estoppel

As noted earlier, in some circumstances the courts have generally felt that oral contracts ought to be enforceable even though they are not in writing. Accordingly, they have recognized limited exceptions to the rules embodied in the statute of frauds.

One of these exceptions involves oral contracts calling for the sale of land. Such contracts are generally held to be enforceable if the buyer, in reliance upon the oral contract, has (1) paid all or part of the consideration for the land, (2) taken possession of the land, and (3) added substantial improvements to it. (In regard to oral leases of land of over one year, requirement 1 is, of course, dispensed with.) writing.

In these circumstances the courts will permit the buyer to enforce the contract for either of two reasons. First, the actions of the buyer, in and of themselves, may be felt to be "referable" to the oral contract that the buyer alleges has been formed—that is, the buyer's actions are fairly good evidence that an oral contract has, in fact, been entered into. These are actions that a person would normally take only if he or she expected to become the owner of the land. The second reason often cited for permitting the buyer to enforce the oral contract is the doctrine of **promissory estoppel** (discussed in Chapter 13). The reasoning here is that where the seller of the land has permitted the buyer to take such actions, it would be manifestly unfair to permit the seller to evict the buyer on the ground that the contract was not in writing. In such a case, the courts are increasingly taking the view that the seller is estopped (i.e., prevented) from using the statute of frauds as a basis for having the oral contract set aside.

CASTILLO V. RIOS
Texas Court of Appeals, 2001 Tex. App.
LEXIS 2552 (2001)

In 1992, Castillo and his wife moved into a house at 8905 Quinn in Dallas. They signed a two–year lease/purchase agreement to pay a rental payment each month and an additional amount to be credited to the down payment once the lease expired and the Castillos bought the property. As the end of the lease term neared, Castillo was about to be arrested and his marriage was ending; thus, he could not afford to purchase the home. In April 1994, Castillo asked Rios, his employer, if he wanted to buy the house from him. According to Rios, he and Castillo reached an oral agreement by which Rios gave Castillo a Ford Taurus, $ 1,000 for the down payment, and an additional $ 500 in exchange for the house. Thereafter, Castillo closed on the house.

In reliance on the oral agreement, Rios testified he completely remodeled the house, installing sheetrock, new cabinets, flooring, and carpeting. According to Rios, Castillo and other members of his work crew were paid to perform the labor on these

improvements. Rios valued the improvements at $ 35,000, but no receipts were offered into evidence. After making the improvements, he moved into the home and made the mortgage payments each month. However, Castillo refused to transfer title to the property and provide Rios with a deed.

Four years later, Castillo sued to evict Rios. Rios then brought this action to establish his right to title. At the time of trial, Rios had been in possession of the house for five-and–one–half years. The trial court overruled Castillo's statute of frauds defense and ordered him to convey the property to Rios by general warranty deed. Castillo appealed.

Roach, Justice:

In Hooks v. Bridgewater, 229 S.W. 1114 (Tex. 1921), the Texas supreme court established a three-prong test that must be met to exempt an oral contract for the sale of real estate from the statute of frauds. Pursuant to Hooks, an oral contract for the purchase of real property is enforceable if the purchaser: (1) pays the consideration, whether it be in money or services; (2) takes possession of the property; and (3) makes permanent and valuable improvements on the property with the consent of the seller or, without such improvements, other facts are shown that would make the transaction a fraud upon the purchaser if the oral contract was not enforced. These steps are seen as sufficient evidence of the agreement because they provide affirmative corroboration of the agreement by both parties to the agreement.

In this case, the evidence on the second prong (possession) was undisputed: Rios took possession of the property in 1994 and continued to reside there at the time of trial. Further, at all times, he made the required mortgage payment.

With respect to the first prong, i.e., payment of consideration, [the trial court believed Rios' testimony that] he gave Castillo a car, $ 1000 for the down payment, and an additional $ 500 in exchange for the house.

With respect to the third prong, i.e., the making of valuable and permanent improvements with Castillo's consent, Rios testified that he replaced the sheetrock and installed new cabinets and flooring in the house. Rios, who was a building contractor, valued these improvements at $ 35,000. [The trial judge believed Rios' testimony that] Castillo knew about the improvements because Castillo helped with the labor on them. In addition, Rios also put in a concrete driveway.

We conclude there was more than a scintilla of evidence from which the trial judge could reasonably conclude that Rios paid the consideration, took possession of the house, and made valuable and permanent improvements to the property with Castillo's consent. [Affirmed.]

Contracts Not Performable Within One Year

The section of the statute requiring that *agreements not to be performed within one year of the making thereof* be in writing is based on the fact that disputes over the terms of long—term oral contracts are particularly likely to occur; witnesses die, the parties' memories become hazy, and so on. Despite the logic underlying this provision, it has posed numerous problems in practice.

In deciding whether a particular agreement falls within this section, the usual (but not the only) approach taken by the courts is to determine whether it was *reasonably possible,* under its own terms, for the contract in question to have been performed within one year from the time it was made. If so, the contract is outside the statute and need not be in writing.

The fact that performance *actually* may have taken more than one year is immaterial. Consider these examples.

1. A, on June 1, 2000, orally agrees to work for B as a personal secretary at a salary of $3,000 per month "as long as this arrangement is satisfactory to both parties." This is known as an "at—will" employment contract. It gives either party the right to terminate it at any time. It does not have to be in writing to be enforceable, because it can be fully performed *by its own terms* in less than a year. Assume that A worked for B for two years, and in the third year, B refused to pay wages for work A had performed. If A sued, most courts would hold that B could not successfully raise a statute

of frauds defense. Even though performance actually took longer, the contract could have been fully performed in less than one year. A minority of courts, rejecting the "reasonably possible" test, would hold that if performance longer than one year was *within the contemplation of the parties*, the contract would have to be in writing.)

2. On June 1, 2000, A promises to work for B "as long as you [B] shall live." Most courts, but not all, would hold that this contract also need not be in writing to be enforceable. B might die in less than a year. If he did, the contract would have been fully performed in less than a year. Again, it is irrelevant if B actually did live longer than a year.

3. A promises on June 1, 2000, to work for B "for the next two years." This contract must be in writing to be enforceable, because it is not possible to work for two years in less than one year. True, it is again possible that B might die in less than a year, but the contract will not have been fully performed as written. (Instead, B's death would have *excused* performance under the doctrine of impossibility discussed later in Chapter 18.)

4. A promises on June 1, 2000, to sing a two-hour concert at XYZ University on August 12, 2001. This contract must be in writing to be enforceable. Even though the performance itself will take only two hours, by the contract's terms that performance must occur more than one year after the contract was made.

Exceptions

As with other categories of contracts that usually must be in writing, many courts have enforced oral contracts that would take more than one year from the making to perform where they believed that this was necessary to bring about just results. For instance, in example 1 above, even courts that choose the "contemplation of the parties" approach and conclude that the contract should be in writing would allow A to recover for *work performed* on a part performance basis. The case below is typical of those in which the exceptional result is largely based on the principle of promissory estoppel. This jurisdiction, however, appears to be one of the minority jurisdictions that also requires an ancillary promise (in this case, a promise to put the contract in writing) in order to invoke the exception.

HARMON V. TANNER MOTOR TOURS OF NEVADA, LTD.
Supreme Court of Nevada, 377 P.2d 622 (1963)

This litigation came about as a result of a dispute over which one of two competing common carriers had the exclusive limousine *ground transportation franchise for servicing the Las Vegas, Nevada, airport for a period of ten years. The carriers were Tanner Motor*

Lines, Ltd., plaintiff and Las Vegas—Tonopah—Reno Stage Lines, Inc. (LTR), one of the defendants.

Five legal issues were involved, one which had to do with the enforceability of an oral contract entered into between Tanner and the Board of Clark County Commissioners (Board), which was the governing authority of the Las Vegas airport. (Only that part of the fact—pattern and decision of the case relating to this issue is considered below.)

In late 1959 Tanner submitted a written bid for the limousine service, and that bid was orally accepted by the board members. Despite this acceptance, the board entered into a written contract in 1960 with the second carrier, LTR, giving it the exclusive transportation rights.

Tanner then brought this action against Harmon, a representative of the board, and LTR, defendants, asking for specific performance of its 1959 contract. The defendants contended, among other things, that that oral contract was unenforceable under the statute of frauds, because its performance was to take more than one year. The trial court ruled against the defendants on all points, and entered a decree of specific performance. (That is, the court ruled that Tanner's contract was valid and that he thus did possess the exclusive transportation rights, and it accordingly ordered the board to recognize these rights.) Defendants appealed.

Thompson, Justice:

. . . [The Nevada statute of frauds] provides that every agreement which, by its terms, is not to be performed within one year from the making thereof, shall be void, unless such agreement, or some note or memorandum thereof, expressing the consideration, be in writing and subscribed by the party charged therewith. The Tanner proposal which the board accepted was to provide limousine airport transportation service over a ten year period. It could not be performed within one year and is, therefore, squarely within the mentioned statute. [The court, however, continued:]

Following the acceptance of the Tanner bid, the board [orally] assured Tanner that a formal written agreement would be prepared for signature. *In reliance, Tanner continued to provide limousine service to the airport, paid $3,600 as the minimum guarantee for the ensuing year, and purchased two new limousines at the cost of about $9,000.* [Emphasis added].

We acknowledge the general rule that, in the absence of fraud, a promise to reduce an agreement to writing is not, standing alone, a basis for invoking an estoppel against raising the statute of frauds in defense [that is, such a promise alone does not make the moral agreement enforceable]. It is likewise true, as a general rule, that part performance of an agreement within the "one year provision" of the statute of frauds [does not alone make the oral agreement enforceable]. However, where both occur, i.e., a promise to reduce an agreement to writing *and* part performance, an *estoppel* is properly invoked [by the one seeking specific performance], and the main agreement [is enforceable]. We conclude, therefore, that the board cannot rely upon [the statute of frauds] as a defense to this action. . . . The lower court [did not err] in directing the board to execute a formal contract with Tanner and thereafter specifically perform the same. . . .

Affirmed.

Promises to Pay Debts of Another

If A has received a benefit from B, then B's claim that A has made a promise to B is more plausible than if A has received no such benefit. To avoid perjury, the statute of frauds requires that if A has not received such a benefit, A's "promise to answer for the debt, default or miscarriage of another" must be in writing to be enforceable. The classic example is a "guaranty contract" in which A promises B that he will pay C's debt to B *if* C does not. Because A received no benefit in this transaction, the law is suspicious and demands that B provide written evidence of A's promise.

There are three standard elements of a guaranty contract. First, the guarantor promises to pay the debtor's obligation *if* the debtor does not. In other words, guaranty contracts occur in situations of "secondary liability." The creditor is to look primarily to the debtor for repayment, and only if the debtor does not pay is the creditor to look to the guarantor. If, on the other hand, A tells B: "Send C's bills to me," A is the primary debtor to whom B is to look first for payment. A is making the debt his own, not promising to pay the debt of another. Such a promise is not a guaranty and therefore need not be in writing to be enforceable.

Second, a guaranty promise is made for the benefit of the debtor. If the guarantor's "main purpose" in making the promise is to benefit himself, it is not a guaranty contract and need not be in writing to be enforceable. An aunt who, out of pity, promises a landlord that she will pay her niece's rent if the niece does not pay is making a guaranty promise that must be in writing to be enforceable. On the other hand, assume that Guarantor Company has a government contract to build a wind tunnel to test airplanes. Guarantor hires Joe Debtor to do the concrete work. Because Joe does not pay his bills, Creditor Concrete Supply stops delivering concrete, halting construction and endangering Guarantor's contract with the government. If an official of Guarantor called Creditor on the phone and said: "Please keep delivering concrete to Joe Debtor, and we'll pay the bills if he doesn't," the promise would be enforceable though never put in writing because Guarantor's main purpose in making the promise is obviously to benefit itself. Therefore, this is not a guaranty promise and need not be in writing to be enforceable.

Third, a guaranty promise is made to the creditor, not to the debtor. If in the previous example, Guarantor Company had told Joe Debtor: "Keep ordering concrete, and we'll pay the bill if you don't," such a promise is not a guaranty and need not be in writing in order to be enforceable.

Copyright Transfer

Under Sec. 204(a) of the federal Copyright Act, transfers of copyright ownership (including via exclusive license) are not valid unless the copyright owner signs a written "note or memorandum of the transfer."

Other Promises

Two other relatively insignificant categories of contracts—*promises made in consideration of marriage and executors' contracts*—fall within the statute. Thus, if A promises to pay B $5,000 when and if B marries C, A is liable only if his promise is in writing. The same is true in regard to prenuptial agreements, in which parties about to be married to each other expressly spell out their interests in the other's properties. (Indeed, some states have passed statutes requiring that "palimony" contracts—agreements for support or division of property between live—in lovers who are not married—be in writing to be enforceable.) Finally, if the administrator or executor of an estate promises personally to pay a debt of the deceased, the creditor can hold the promisor liable only if the promise is in writing.

In addition, recently many borrowers have sued banks claiming some form of breach of an oral promise to lend, to refinance an existing loan, or to refrain from enforcing remedies contained in a written loan agreement. In one case, for example, a jury awarded $28 million for breach of an alleged oral promise to extend an existing line of credit. In another, a jury awarded $69 million for breach of an alleged oral promise to make a loan. To protect banks and other lending institutions from such liability, many states have recently passed laws barring the enforcement of oral lending agreements without a signed contract.

Contracts Calling for Sale of Goods
The UCC Statute of Frauds

Section 2–201 of the code, known as the **UCC statute of frauds**, states that a contract for the sale of goods for a price of $500 or more must be in writing to be enforceable (with exceptions noted subsequently). As is true of other statute of frauds provisions applicable to nongoods transactions, the requirement of Sec. 2–201(1) can be satisfied either (1) by having the contract itself in writing, or (2) by having a subsequent written memorandum of the oral agreement. In either situation, *the writing must be signed by the party against whom enforcement is sought.*

The UCC Confirmation

The language of Sec. 2–201(1) in regard to enforceability parallels that of the basic statute of frauds. That is, if an oral sales contract is followed by a writing signed by only one of the parties, the signer is bound by the contract but the nonsigner is not. To eliminate this one sidedness in certain circumstances, subsection 2 of Sec. 2 201 provides another method (in addition to the two set forth above) for satisfying the writing requirement of subsection 1.

Suppose that two parties have orally agreed on a sale of goods. One of the parties then sends a signed letter or other written communication to the other party, saying: "This is to confirm that on June 20 we entered into an agreement for the sale of 175 men's suits on the following terms [the terms being stated in the letter]." If this is the only writing the parties make, the question is whether it can be used to satisfy the requirements of Sec. 2–201(1). If the sender breaches the contract, the letter can be used in a lawsuit by the recipient against the sender because the sender signed it. But if it is the recipient who breaches the contract, can the sender use the letter in his lawsuit to recover damages from the recipient, the nonsigner? In transactions not governed by the

UCC, as we have seen, the answer is no. But as to sales of goods, however (as in the above example 3), the answer sometimes is yes.

Under Sec. 2–201(2), the **UCC confirmation rule,** a confirmation such as the above can be used by the sender against a nonsigning recipient if the following requirements are met:

1. The writing must be "sufficient against the sender." In other words, the *sender* must have *signed* the confirmation, and its contents must meet the relatively lenient sufficiency requirements discussed later in the chapter.
2. Both parties must be *merchants.*
3. The recipient must have had reason to know of the contents of the confirmation *but had not objected to it in writing within ten days after receiving it.*

UCC Exceptions

Section 2–201(3) defines three situations in which an oral contract, if proved, will be enforceable despite the total absence of a writing, even when it involves a sale of goods for a price of $500 or more. The first exception can be used only by a seller; the other two can be used by either a seller or a buyer.

1. If the oral contract is for goods to be specifically manufactured for the particular buyer, it is enforceable against the buyer if two requirements are met:
   a. The goods must be of a type not suitable for sale to others in the ordinary course of the seller's business. For example: Suppose that C is an importer of small, foreign–made pickup trucks, and D is a manufacturer of campers that are mounted on pickups. C orally orders from D a number of campers made to fit the pickups imported by C (that is, they will fit no other pickups on the market). If C repudiates the bargain after the campers are made, D will be hard–pressed to sell them elsewhere. He might eventually be able to do so, but considerable effort would probably be required. Thus the goods cannot be sold in the ordinary course of his business.
   b. The seller must either have substantially started the manufacture of the goods, or have made commitments for procuring them, before he or she learned of the buyer's repudiation of the agreement.
2. If the defendant "admits in his pleading, testimony or otherwise in court that a contract for sale was made," it will be enforceable even though oral. (The common–law court decisions on this point are conflicting, most courts holding that such an admission does *not* remove the requirement of a writing. Thus the UCC exception represents a significant innovation in this regard.) Observe that not just any admission will suffice; the admission by the defendant must become part of official court records.
3. An oral agreement will be enforced to the extent that payment has been made and accepted or that the goods have been received and accepted. Suppose, for example, that X and Y have made an oral contract for Y to sell X twenty– five television sets at a price of $300 each. Before any of the sets are delivered, X makes a prepayment

of $1,800, which Y accepts. Y then refuses to honor the contract. Even if Y were not bound by the contract, X could of course get her money back under the unjust enrichment theory (seeChapter 11). But under the UCC her part payment will make the contract partially enforceable, and she will be able to maintain a suit for breach of a contract obligation to deliver six of the twenty–five television sets. Similarly, if X has made no payment but Y has made a partial shipment which X has accepted, the oral contract is again partially enforceable. That is, if Y delivers and X accepts six television sets, and X then repudiates the agreement, Y can maintain a suit for breach of a contract obligation to pay $1,800. Prior to enactment of the UCC, part performance of this type made the *entire contract* enforceable. Also, the statutory language in this exception does not address the situation in which the buyer has made a partial prepayment that cannot be allocated to a certain number of individual units of goods. For example, what if buyer makes and seller accepts a $5,000 down payment on a single $20,000 automobile? In the few cases involving this question since enactment of the UCC, most courts have applied the common–law rule and have held the entire contract to be enforceable despite the absence of a sufficient written document.

The rationale underlying these exceptions is entirely consistent with the purpose of the basic writing requirement of Sec. 2–201(1), which is to forestall the possibility of a party successfully maintaining a fabricated breach of contract suit by the use of perjured testimony. By providing these exceptions, the drafters of the UCC have recognized that, in cases falling within them, it is extremely unlikely that plaintiff's claim will be a complete fabrication. Therefore, because the original purpose for the writing requirement no longer exists in such instances, the oral agreements ought to be binding. Compliance with the statute of frauds under UCC 2–201 is summarized in Figure 16.1

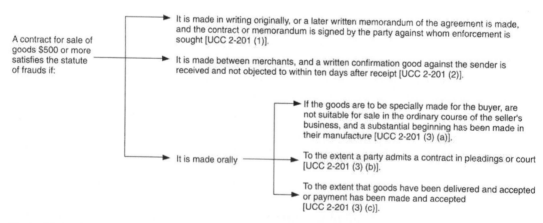

A contract for sale of goods $500 or more satisfies the statute of frauds if:

→ It is made in writing originally, or a later written memorandum of the agreement is made, and the contract or memorandum is signed by the party against whom enforcement is sought [UCC 2-201 (1)].

→ It is made between merchants, and a written confirmation good against the sender is received and not objected to within ten days after receipt [UCC 2-201 (2)].

→ It is made orally

→ If the goods are to be specially made for the buyer, are not suitable for sale in the ordinary course of the seller's business, and a substantial beginning has been made in their manufacture [UCC 2-201 (3) (a)].

→ To the extent a party admits a contract in pleadings or court [UCC 2-201 (3) (b)].

→ To the extent that goods have been delivered and accepted or payment has been made and accepted [UCC 2-201 (3) (c)].

Figure 16.1 Compliance with the Statute of Frauds in Contracts for the Sale of Goods, UCC 2–201

Modification Contracts

Under Section 2–209 of the UCC, agreements that modify existing sales contracts must be in writing in order to be enforceable in two situations:

1. The modification must be in writing if the original agreement had provided that it could be modified only by a writing. Section 2–209(2) has an additional provision applicable to those sales contracts entered into between a merchant and a non–merchant. In such a case, if the contract results from use of the *merchant's form* (with that form containing the requirement that any later modification had to be in writing), that requirement must itself be "separately signed" by the non–merchant in order to be binding upon him or her.

2. The modification must be in writing if the whole contract, *as modified,* is required to be in writing under the UCC statute of frauds (Sec. 2–201, discussed above).

Other Statutes Requiring a Writing

In addition to the basic statute of frauds and Sections 2–201 and 2–209 of the UCC, all states have additional statutes— usually narrow in scope—that require still other kinds of contracts to be in writing. For example, most states require real estate listing contracts and insurance contracts to be in writing. Additionally, Sec. 9–203 of the UCC imposes the same requirement upon most "security agreements" governed by Article 9 (i.e., agreements that create security interests in favor of lenders of money or unpaid sellers of goods).

When Is the Writing Sufficient?
Contract Law

The original statute of frauds began: "No action shall be brought [upon the following kinds of contracts] unless the agreement upon which such action shall be brought, *or some memorandum or note thereof,* shall be in writing and signed by the party sought to be charged therewith or some other person thereunto by him lawfully authorized." Thus, even if the full contract is not in writing, a "sufficient written memorandum" may satisfy the statute of fraud's requirements. In such situations, the courts *generally require that the writing include at least the following:* (1) names of both parties, (2) the subject matter of the contract, (3) the consideration to be paid, and (4) any other terms that the court feels are material under the circumstances. Under this fairly strict approach, if any basic term is missing, the contract continues to be unenforceable.

This does not mean, however, that the writing must be in any particular form, or be complete in every detail. And because of the provision that a memorandum or note of the contract may satisfy the statute, it is entirely possible that an oral contract can be validated by the production in court of a confirming telegram, sales slip, check, invoice, or some other writing—assuming, of course, that it contains all the material terms of the agreement.

Additionally, it frequently happens that the contract is evidenced by two or more separate writings, none of which alone is sufficiently complete to satisfy the statute. In such cases the writings may be construed together, thus satisfying the memorandum requirement, if the writings clearly refer to one another (expressly or impliedly), or if they are physically attached to one another.

The requirement that the contract or written memorandum be signed by the party against whom the agreement is to be enforced (or a duly authorized representative) is somewhat loosely applied. It may be satisfied by a signature, by initials, by the letterhead on a sheet of paper, or even by a company's trademark appearing on the paper.

Digital Signatures

In order to facilitate the rise of the Internet and e—commerce, governments on every level have enacted laws meant to ensure the validity of digital signatures. Numerous states enacted a patchwork of individual state laws that were well—intended but created confusion that inhibited e—commerce. To create some uniformity, the federal government passed the Electronic Signatures in Global and National Commerce Act of 2000 (E—Sign) giving presumptive validity to digital signatures (as well as digital contracts and records) and preempting statutes in states that had not yet acted to adopt the Uniform Electronic Transactions Act (UETA), promulgated by the National Conference of Commissioners on Uniform State Laws (NCCUSL). The fundamental premise of E—Sign was that the medium in which a record, signature or contract is created, presented or retained does not affect its legal significance. Form is irrelevant, so it does not matter whether information is set forth in an electronic rather than paper format. E—Sign was meant to bolster e—commerce until the states could widely adopt UETA, which has a similar philosophy. Most states have now done so, automatically preempting E—Sign.

Although E—Sign and UETA both bolster e—commerce, they do not mandate that all documents be digital. Indeed, under UETA most UCC documents, wills, codicils, testamentary trusts, and certain legal notices must all continue to be in paper form. Over time, that will likely change.

On an international level, many nations have passed digital signature laws and the United Nations Commission on International Trade Law (UNCITRAL) promulgated a Model Law on Electronic Commerce. Matters of authentication of signatures (and choice of technology for authentication) will continue to cause problems for some time.

SHATTUCK V. KLOTZBACH
Massachusetts Superior Court, 2001 Mass. Super. Lexis 642 (2001)

In April 2001, the plaintiff and the defendants began discussions concerning the sale of a *property at 5 Main Street, Marion, MA. On April 9, 2001, the plaintiff sent an e—mail to* the defendants which contained an offer for the property. Defendant responded and noted that e—mail was the "preferred" manner of communication during their negotiations.

The parties ultimately entered into a purchase and sale agreement, but prior to closing it was terminated because defendants could not procure a "wharf license" as the contract required. Nevertheless, commencing in July 2001, the parties again began communicating via e—mail concerning the sale of the same property. In an e—mail sent July 24, 2001, the plaintiff wrote to the defendant that he was increasing his offer to $ 1.825 million. Multiple e—mails were exchanged during the summer, and finally, on September 10, 2001, the plaintiff sent the defendant an e—mail which stated that the plaintiffs attorney had told him there were no complications and the attorney would draft a very standard purchase and sale agreement for $ 1,825,000 "with no usual contingencies." The defendant responded the same day by e—mail stating "once we sign the P&S we'd like to close ASAP. You may have your attorney send the P&S and deposit check for 10% of purchase price $ 182,500) to my attorney." The e—mail concluded by stating that "I'm looking forward to closing and seeing you as the owner of '5 Main Street,' the prettiest spot in Marion village." All e—mails detailed above contained a salutation at the end which consisted of the type written name of the respective sender.

Defendant later refused to perform and plaintiff sued for specific performance. Defendant raised statute of frauds defense. Plaintiff admitted that a real estate contract must be in writing to be enforceable, but argued that the statute was satisfied by the e—mails.

Murphy, Justice:
Where the defendant pleads the statute of frauds, the burden is on the plaintiff to prove the existence of a memorandum complying with the statute's requirements. "A memorandum is signed in accordance with the statute of frauds if it is signed by the person to be charged in his own name, or by his initials, or by his Christian name alone, or by a printed, stamped or typewritten signature, if signing in any of these methods he intended to authenticate the paper as his act." Irving v. Goodimate Co., 70 N.E.2d 414 (1946). Here, all e-mail correspondences between the parties contained a typewritten signature at the end. Taken as a whole, a reasonable trier of fact could conclude that the e—mails sent by the defendant were "signed" with the intent to authenticate the information contained therein as his act.

Moreover, courts have held that a telegram may be a signed writing sufficient to satisfy the statute of frauds. This court believes that the typed name at the end of an e—mail is more indicative of a party's intent to authenticate than that of a telegram as the sender of an e—mail types and sends the message on his own accord and types his own name as he so chooses. In the case at bar, the defendant sent e—mails regarding the sale of the property and intentionally and deliberately typed his name at the end of all such e—mails. A reasonable trier of fact could conclude that the e—mails sent by the defendant regarding the terms of the sale of the property were intended to be authenticated by the defendant's deliberate choice to type his name at the conclusion of all e—mails.

The defendant finally contends that the e—mails, even if sufficiently authenticated, do not contain the essential terms. A memorandum sufficient to satisfy the statute of frauds need not be a formal document intended to serve as a memorandum of the oral contract, but must contain the essential terms of the contract agreed upon: in the case of an interest in real estate, the parties, the locus, the nature of the transaction, and the purchase price. Multiple writings relating to the subject matter may be read together in order to satisfy the memorandum requirement so long as the writings, when considered as a single instrument, contain all the material terms of the contract and are authenticated by the signature of the party to be charged. The writings may, but need not, incorporate each other by reference. Tzitzon Realty Co. v. Mustonen, 227 N.E.2d 493 (1967).

In the case at bar, the e—mails contain terms for the sale of 5 Main Street, Marion Village, Marion, Massachusetts. The e—mails further refer to a purchase price of $ 1,825,000 and the defendant explicitly asked the plaintiff to send a "deposit check for 10% of [the] purchase price ($ 182,500) . . ." Finally, the multiple e—mails demonstrate the parties to the sale, to wit the plaintiff and the defendant. Thus, a reasonable trier of fact could conclude that the parties had formed an agreement as to the essential terms of a land sale contract; the parties, the locus, the nature of the transaction, and the purchase price.

Defendant's motion to dismiss is denied.

Sales Law

Contracts calling for the sale of goods are often made in the business world under circumstances where, because of the press of time or other factors, the parties put only the barest essentials of the agreement in writing. Recognizing this reality, Sec. 2—201 of the UCC (requiring a contract for the sale of goods for a price of $500 or more to be in writing) has *greatly relaxed the requirements of the sufficiency of the writing*. For sales of goods, that section provides that the writing (whether the contract itself, or memorandum, or subsequent confirmation) merely has to be "sufficient to indicate that a contract for sale has been made between the parties." The only term that *must be included in the writing is the quantity*. Other terms that are orally agreed upon can be proved in court by oral testimony. Terms that are not agreed upon at all can be supplied by Article 2 itself (as we saw in Chapter 12).

Cases have arisen presenting the question of whether a written "requirements contract" satisfies the quantity requirement of Sec. 2—201. For example, a seller might obligate himself or herself to sell and deliver "all of the 21 oz. plastic your plant can use" over a specified period of time at a specific unit price. In a case in which such language was utilized, Fortune Furniture Co. v. Mid—South Plastic Co., 310 So.2d 725 (1975) , the Supreme Court of Mississippi—following the majority rule—held that this type of provision satisfied the requirement that the writing state a quantity.

The Parol Evidence Rule

Whenever a contract (or a memorandum thereof) is reduced to writing, the writing ought to contain *all* the material terms of the agreement. This is true not only for contracts that fall within the statute of frauds, but for all other contracts where a writing is utilized as well. One reason for this, as to statute of frauds contracts, is to make sure that the writing meets the sufficiency requirement under the statute. An equally powerful reason lies in the **parol evidence rule**. This rule provides, in general, that when any contract has been reduced to writing and shows that the parties intended the written document to be the "final word" as to the terms the parties agreed on, neither party can introduce "parol" (outside) evidence in court for the purpose of adding to or changing the terms of that contract. More specifically, the rule prohibits a party to a written contract from unilaterally introducing either oral or written statements or agreements made at (or prior to) the time the written contract was made which either conflict with, or add to, the clear, unambiguous terms of the written contract.

Among the policy reasons for the existence of the parol evidence rule are (1) because a written contract is more reliable than oral testimony, it helps prevent perjury or fraud; (2) it encourages the parties to put their important agreements in writing, thus increasing the reliability of commercial transactions; and (3) it emphasizes a longstanding rule of contract interpretation to the effect that final expressions of intent should prevail over earlier tentative expressions of intent.

As to sales contracts, the UCC's parol evidence rule in Sec. 2–202 is essentially the same as the common–law parol rule, discussed above. However, its wording may increase the chances that extrinsic evidence will be allowed by narrowing the traditional view of what constitutes a *final* expression of the parties' agreement. Obviously, expressions of intent that are only preliminary are not protected by the rule from contradiction by parol sources.

Exceptions

The courts feel that the parol evidence rule brings about clearly undesirable results in some circumstances; accordingly, they have recognized a number of exceptions to it. (In general, these exceptions apply both to cases governed by common–law principles and those governed by sales law.) Following are the most important situations in which a party to a written contract is permitted to introduce parol evidence in subsequent legal proceedings:

1. The written contract itself appears to be incomplete. The parol evidence rule applies only to final *and complete* expressions of intent.
2. The written contract is ambiguous, and the parol evidence tends to clear up the ambiguity. Such evidence does not contradict or add to the writing.
3. The written contract contains an obvious mistake, such as a typographical or clerical error, and the parol evidence tends to correct the error.
4. The parol evidence shows that the contract was not a valid one, as, for example, that it was induced by fraud or duress on the part of the other party, or was formed under mutual mistake of fact. Alleged fraud is the major exception under which parol evidence is admitted.
5. The evidence shows that the contract was subject to a condition precedent, i.e., that the parties had agreed that a specified event had to occur before the contract would be effective, and that the event had not occurred.
6. The evidence tends to prove that the parties made either an oral or written agreement that modified the written contract after the written contract had been entered

into. Parties to written contracts often change their minds and later alter the agreements. Admission of such evidence does not contradict the basic reasoning behind the parol evidence rule which is that preliminary contract terms, which may vary substantially as the contract is negotiated, become merged into the final written contract.

A seventh exception, applicable only to sales contracts, allows evidence about the course of prior dealings of the parties or custom of the trade in which the parties are engaged to explain or supplement a writing, even when the evidence appears to contradict its unambiguous terms.

Cumulatively, these exceptions arm the courts with tools to avoid the operation of the parol evidence rule in instances where they believe its application would cause injustice. Thus, a substantial gap may exist between the theory underlying the formal rule on the one hand, and the rule's practical operation on the other.

CHAPTER **17**

RIGHTS OF THIRD PARTIES

- Third–Party Beneficiaries
- Assignments
- Delegation of Duties

As A General rule, the rights created by the formation of a contract can be enforced only by the original parties to the agreement. A contract is essentially a private agreement affecting only the contracting parties themselves; both legal and practical difficulties would arise if a stranger to the contract (a **third party**) were permitted to enforce it. Suppose, for example, that X employed B to paint her house and that B subsequently refused to do the job. If Y, one of X's neighbors, were to bring suit against B to recover damages for breach of contract, it would be ludicrous if he were permitted to get a judgment. Since Y was not a party to the contract, he clearly has "no standing to sue," and his suit would be dismissed.

However, in certain exceptional circumstances a third party is permitted to enforce a contract made by others, particularly (1) where it appears, expressly or by necessary implication, that at the time the contract was made the parties to the contract intended that that person receive the benefit of the contract, or (2) where one of the parties, after making the contract, assigned (transferred) his or her rights to a third party. In the former situation the third party is called a *third–party beneficiary,* and in the latter he or she is designated an *assignee* of the contract.

Third–Party Beneficiaries

The law recognizes three kinds of beneficiaries—creditor, donee, and incidenal. Generally, creditor and donee beneficiaries (also known as "intended" beneiciaries) can enforce contracts made by others, while incidental beneficiaries cannot.

Creditor Beneficiaries

When a contract is made between two parties for the express benefit of a third person, the latter is said to be a **creditor beneficiary** if he or she had earlier furnished consideration to one of the contracting parties. To illustrate: A owes X $500. A later sells a piano to B, on the understanding that B, in return, is to pay off A's indebtedness to X. Here X is a creditor beneficiary of the contract between A and B, inasmuch as she originally gave consideration to A, which created the debt in her (**X's**) favor. Once A has delivered the piano, X is entitled to recover the $500 from B—by suit, if necessary. If A refused to deliver the piano to B, should B be required to pay X? Obviously, the answer is "no." The promisor (B) can raise the same defenses against an intended beneficiary (X) as he or she can raise against the promisee (A). In this case, the defense is A's failure to perform. Defenses such as lack of consideration, incapacity, fraud, mistake, or statute of frauds would also be effective. If B raises an effective defense to avoid paying X, clearly X could sue A on the original $500 debt.

Assumption of Mortgage

One typical situation involving a creditor beneficiary arises when mortgaged real estate is sold, with the purchaser agreeing to pay off the existing mortgage. For example: S owns a home subject to a $15,000 mortgage held by the Y Bank. S finds a buyer for the home, Z, who is willing to assume the mortgage. Thereupon S and Z enter into a contract, under the terms of which S agrees to convey the property to Z, and Z promises to pay S's existing indebtedness to the bank. The Y Bank now has become a creditor beneficiary of the contract between S and Z, since it originally gave consideration to S by making the loan, and it can hold Z liable on his promise to pay the indebtedness. (The assumption of the mortgage by Z does not by itself free S of his liability. Thus the bank can look to either party for payment in case Z defaults—unless it has expressly released S from his obligation.) However, in most mortgages today, Z, even if willing, would not be allowed to assume the mortgages. "Due on sale clauses" (provisions in the mortgage which make the entire balance owed by S due immediately upon sale of the property) would render the loan "non–assumable."

Donee Beneficiaries

Where a contract is made for the benefit of a third person who has not given consideration to either contracting party, that person is designated a **donee beneficiary** of the contract. To illustrate: P, an attorney, agrees to perform certain legal services for Q, with the understanding that Q will pay the $200 legal fee to R, P's son–in–law. Here P has made a gift of $200 to R, and R—the donee beneficiary of the contract—can enforce it against Q if Q refuses to pay him voluntarily.

Life Insurance Contracts

The most common type of contract involving donee beneficiaries is that of the ordinary life insurance policy. If A insures his life with the B Insurance Company, and the policy expressly designates C as the beneficiary of the proceeds of that policy, C—the donee beneficiary—can enforce the contract against the company. The fact that C has not furnished consideration to the company is immaterial; it is sufficient that A, the insured, has done so by making his premium payments. If A did not pay the premiums that the contract required, obviously B Insurance Co. would not have to pay C the proceeds of the policy, again illustrating that claims of intended beneficiaries against the promisor are subject to the same defenses that could be raised against the promisee.

Incidental Beneficiaries

An **incidental beneficiary** is a person whom the contracting parties did not intend to benefit by making the contract, but who nevertheless will benefit in some way if the contract is performed. Such a beneficiary, unlike a donee beneficiary, has no rights under the contract and thus is not entitled to enforce it. For example, a retail merchant in a college town would benefit from a contract between a construction firm and the university calling for the construction of a four–level parking facility on campus property just across the street from his (or her) store. However, if the builder breaches the contract with the university by refusing to go ahead with the project, the merchant cannot recover damages from the builder.

In determining whether a beneficiary is a donee beneficiary or an incidental beneficiary, the usual test is whether the contract was made primarily for his or her benefit. If so, the beneficiary is a donee beneficiary; if not, he or she is merely an incidental beneficiary. Strong evidence that a beneficiary is intended arises where the contract expressly designates the third party as such or where the promisor's performance is to be rendered directly to the third party. Consider these illustrations:

1. A hires B Co. to construct a building. Soon after construction begins, A breaches the contract; as a result, B Co. lays off employee X. If X sued A for breach of contract, he would lose. His employment was an incidental benefit of the contract, but clearly A and B Co. did not make the contract for the purpose of benefiting X.

2. A promises to build an office building for B. The plans and specifications call for use of electrical wiring made by L Company. A uses wiring made by M Company instead. L could not sue A for breach of contract because the purpose of this requirement was not to provide business for L.

3. City hires ABC Water Co. to provide water for its citizens' needs at an agreed rate. If ABC charged more than the agreed rate, the citizens would probably be allowed to sue as intended beneficiaries for breach of contract. ABC's performance, after all, was to be directed to the citizens. However, assume that citizen X's warehouse burns down, in part because ABC did not provide adequate water pressure for the fire fighters. Although the same reasoning would appear to apply, most courts would deny recovery by X against ABC on *public policy* grounds. For fear that allowing recovery in the latter instance would impose crushing financial burdens on entities with government contracts, such as public utilities, most courts would characterize X as a mere incidental beneficiary. H. R. Moch Co. v. Rensselaer Water Co., (159 N.E. 896 N.Y. 1928.,)

The following is a recent creditor beneficiary case.

UNITED STATES V. STATE FARM MUTUAL AUTOMOBILE INSURANCE CO.
U.S. Court of Appeals, Fifth Circuit, 936 F.2d 206 (5th Cir. 1991)

Defendant State Farm issued to various armed services members standard boating and automobile accident insurance policies. Twenty-four of these army personnel were injured in accidents that entitled them to recover medical and hospital expenses under the policies. The United States treated these people free of any personal expense at government medical institutions as it is required to do by federal statute 10 U.S.C. Sections 1074, 1076. The government then brought this action seeking reimbursement as a *third–party beneficiary to the insurance policies for the value of the medical services provided. The trial court granted summary judgment to the government. State Farm appealed.*

Higginbotham, Circuit Judge:

Under Mississippi law, in order for a stranger to a contract to sue to enforce its term, "the contract between the original parties must have been entered into for his benefit, or at least such benefit must be the direct result of the performance within the contemplation of the parties." Burns v. Washington Savings, 171 So.2d 322 (Miss.1965). The third party need not be expressly identified in the contract; it is enough that the beneficiary is a member of a class intended to be benefited. At the same time, the right of the third party beneficiary to maintain an action on the contract must "spring" from the terms of the contract itself.

The State Farm policies at issue here contained the following emphasized provisions:

Persons for Whom Medical Expenses are Payable.

We will pay medical expenses for bodily injury sustained by:
1. a. The firm person named in the declarations;
   b. his or her spouse; and
   c. her relatives.
Payment of Medical Expenses.

We may pay the injured person or any person or organization performing the services.

We have read similar policy language to support third party claims by medical care providers . . . State Farm urges that it is obligated only for medical expenses actually incurred by the insured. No such limitation is imposed by the terms of the policies. State Farm is obligated to pay the costs of reasonable medical services, whether such costs were borne personally by the insured or, as here, directly by the medical care provider. We also cannot accept State Farm's contention that the policies' facility of payment clause— which provides, "We may pay the injured person or any person or organization performing the service"— makes the government an optional payee or incidental beneficiary.

[Affirmed.]

Assignments
Assignment of Rights

All contracts create certain rights and duties. With exceptions to be noted later, the *rights* a person has acquired under a contract can be transferred, or *assigned,* by that person to a third party. Suppose, for example, that A agrees to add a family room to B's home for $13,500 and that A performs the required work. A thereafter assigns his right to collect the $13,500 to C, in which case A is the assignor and C the **assignee.** C can now recover the $13,500 from B, just as A could have done had there been no assignment. The relationship among the parties toan assignment is set forth in Figure 17.1. While a person's duties under a contract can also be transferred to a third party in some circumstances, such a transfer is a delegation rather than an assignment. The delegation of duties is discussed later in the chapter.

Status of the Assignee

Whenever an assignment takes place, the assignee acquires no greater rights than those possessed by the assignor. Putting it another way, the obligor (the person with a duty to perform) can assert the same defenses (if any) against the assignee that he or she had against the assignor.

This can be easily illustrated by referring again to Figure 17.1. If B refuses to pay C and C brings suit against him on the contract, B can escape liability if he can prove that A breached his contract in some material way—by failing to complete the job, for example, or by using materials inferior to those required by the contract. In such a case C's only redress is the right to recover from A any consideration he had given to A in payment for the assignment.

What Rights Can Be Assigned?

Occasionally, when an assignee requests the obligor to perform his or her part of the bargain, the obligor refuses to do so on the ground that the assigned right was of such a nature that it could not be legally transferred without his or her consent. Usually, this contention is not accepted by the courts; most contractual rights can be assigned without the obligor's consent. This is especially true where the assigned right was that of *collecting a debt*. The reasoning is that it is ordinarily no more difficult for a debtor (obligor) to pay the assignee than to pay the assignor (the original creditor); hence the obligor has no cause to complain.

Some rights, however, cannot be assigned without the obligor's consent. Following are the most common of these situations:

1. The terms of the contract expressly prohibit assignment by one or both parties. (Such clauses are narrowly construed, however, often being interpreted to impose a duty on the assignor not to assign, but not to render invalid an assignment that does occur.)
2. The contract is "personal" in nature; specifically, the right in question involves a substantial personal relationship between the original parties to the contract. If X, for example, agrees to be Y's secretary for one year, any assignment by Y of the right to

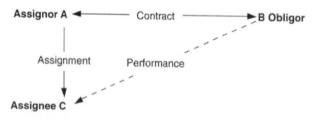

Figure 17.1 Assignment of Rights

LEGAL FOCUS

Ethics

As the text points out, assignees generally stand in the shoes of assignors and are subject to the same defenses that could be raised against assignors. Therefore, if a retail store (X) sells an item on credit to a customer (Y) and then assigns the customer's note to a financial institution (Z), Y can raise any defenses against Z that she could have raised against X. For example, if the item turns out not to be merchantable, Y may return the item and avoid paying Z just as she could have avoided paying X.

Not satisfied with their shaky position in this setting, many financial institutions added a new wrinkle. Under this plan, retailer X would have customer Y sign a *negotiable promissory* note to pay for the item. X would then negotiate the note to financial institution Z, under circumstances qualifying Z as a *holder in due course*. A holder in due course generally takes free of any defenses that could have been raised by the customer. Therefore, Z could still enforce the note against Y even if the item that Y bought turned out to be unmerchantable or was never even delivered by X.

This situation led to some easily envisioned abuses. Many state legislatures, and the federal government through Federal Trade Commission rule 433, virtually eliminated this process by holding that financial institutions in this situation could not be holders in due course and would remain subject to any defenses that could be raised by the customer against the retailer.

Is this a sensible result? Laws that interfere with the freedom to contract must be justified. This law clearly prevents the customers and retailers from making a type of contract that had been commonly used for years. Is the interference justified in this situation?

X's services would be invalid unless X consented to it. In fact, many (perhaps most) employment contracts fall within this category.

3. The assignment would materially alter the duties of the obligor. For example: S, of Columbus, Ohio, agrees to sell certain goods to B, also of Columbus, with the contract providing that "S will deliver the goods to the buyer's place of business." If B assigned this contract to the X Company of Cheyenne, Wyoming, S's obligation would be drastically increased and he would not be bound by the assignment unless he consented to it.

Additionally, the assignment of some rights is prohibited by statute. For example, a federal law (31 U.S.C.A. §3727) generally prohibits the claims against the federal government, and some state statutes prohibit the assignment of future wages by wage earners. When the assignment of rights is prohibited by statute, such rights cannot be assigned even with the obligor's consent.

The following case poses a question of assignability in a modern business setting.

PROFESSIONAL BUSINESS SERVICES CO. v. ROSNO
589 N.W.2d 826, Supreme Court of Nebraska, 1999

McDonald's, defendant, is the corporation that grants all McDonald's fast food restaurant franchises. In 1959 defendant granted a franchise to a Mr. Copeland, giving him the right to own and operate McDonald's first store in the Omaha Council Bluffs area. A few days later, in conformity with the negotiations leading up to the granting of the franchise, McDonald's sent a letter to Copeland giving him a "Right of First Refusal"—the right to be given first chance at owning any new stores that might subsequently be established in the area. In the next few years Copeland exercised this right and opened five additional stores in Omaha. In 1964 Copeland sold and assigned all of his franchises to Schupach, plaintiff, with McDonald's consent.

When McDonald's granted a franchise in the Omaha–Council Bluffs area in 1974 to a third party without first offering it to Schupach, he brought this action for damages resulting from establishment of the new franchise, claiming that the assignment of the franchises to him also included the right of first refusal.

A number of issues were raised in this litigation. Defendant contended, among other things, that the right it gave to Copeland was personal in nature, and thus was not transferable without its consent. Plaintiff alleged, on the other hand, that the right was not personal in nature, or, in the alternative, that its transfer was, in fact, agreed to by defendant.

On these issues the trial court ruled that the right was personal in nature. It also ruled, however, after analyzing voluminous correspondence between the parties, that defendant had consented to the transfer. It entered judgment for plaintiff, and defendant appealed. (Only that part of the higher court's opinion relating to these two issues appears below.)

White, Justice:

... McDonald's was founded in 1954 by Mr. Ray Kroc. Kroc licensed and later purchased the name of McDonald's [and all other rights relating thereto] from two brothers named McDonald, who were operating a hamburger restaurant in San Bernardino, California. In 1955 Kroc embarked on a plan to create a nationwide standardized system of fast–food restaurants. . . .

At the trial, Kroc testified about the image he sought to create with McDonald's. . . He wanted to create "an image people would have confidence in. An image of cleanliness. An image where the parents would be glad to have the children come and/or have them work there."

Kroc testified that careful selection of franchisees was to be the key to success for McDonald's and the establishment of this image. . . People were selected "who had a great deal of pride, and had an aptitude for serving the public, and had dedication."

Fred Turner, the current president of McDonald's, testified [in a similar vein]... He stated that by 1957 it became apparent that McDonald's could only achieve its goal by careful selection of persons who would adhere to the company's high standards. He stated that an individual's managerial skills and abilities were a matter of prime importance in the selection process...

Summarizing, the evidence is overwhelming, [and establishes the conclusion that] the Right of First Refusal was intended to be personal in nature, and was separately a grant independent of the terms of the franchise contract itself. [It also establishes the fact that] the grant depended upon the personal confidence that McDonald's placed in the grantee, and that to permit the assignability by the grantee without permission of McDonald s would serve to destroy the basic policy of control of the quality and confidence in performance in the event any new franchises were to be granted in the locality...

[The court then reviewed the same correspondence which was examined by the trial court, and ruled that McDonald's had not given its permission to the transfer of the right. The judgment for plaintiff was therefore reversed.]

Form of the Assignment

As a general rule, no particular formalities need be observed in order for an assignment to be legally effective. Any words or conduct that indicate an intention on the part of the assignor to transfer his or her contractual rights are normally sufficient. Some assignments, however, are required by statute to be in writing. Thus the assignment of a contract that falls within the statute of frauds must be evidenced by a writing; similarly, under the statutes of most states, the assignment of one's rights to collect wages from an employer must also be in writing.

Absence of Consideration

Once a valid assignment has occurred, the assignee is entitled to enforce the contract against the obligor even if the assignee did not give consideration for the assignment to the assignor. Because the assignment without consideration is essentially a gift, it may be terminated by death of the assignor, subsequent assignment of the same right to another person, or revocation. The assignor can no longer revoke if (a) the obligor has already performed, (b) the assignor has delivered to the assignee the "symbolic writing" that contains the right, such as a bond, savings account book, life insurance policy, or stock certificate, (c) the assignor has delivered to the assignee a written assignment of right, or (d) the elements of promissory estoppel are present so that the assignor can reasonably foresee that the assignee will change positions to his or her detriment in reliance on the promised assignment.

Notice of Assignment

A valid assignment takes effect the moment it is made, regardless of whether the obligor is aware that the assignment has occurred. However, the assignee should give *immediate notice* to the obligor whenever an assignment is made, in order to protect the rights received under it.

A primary reason for giving notice is that an obligor who does not have notice of an assignment is free to go ahead and render performance to the assignor, thereby discharging his or her contractual duties. Suppose, for example, that X is owed $500 by Y and that X assigns the right to collect the debt to Z. If Y, not knowing of the assignment, pays the debt to X (assignor), Z has lost her right to collect the indebtedness from Y. Any other result would be patently unfair to Y. Z's only redress in such a case is to recover payment from X, who clearly has no right to retain the money. On the other hand, if Y did pay the $500 to X *after* being informed of the assignment, Z could still collect from Y.

Notice of assignment can also be important in a case where successive assignments occur. To illustrate: R owes money to S. S assigns his right to collect the debt to A on June 10, then assigns the same right to B on June 15, B not knowing of the prior assignment. Suppose that the first assignee, A, does not give notice of assignment to until June 25, while the second assignee, B, gives notice on June 20. In such a situation, a number of courts—though not a majority— would rule that B is entitled to payment of the debt, rather than A; in other words, the assignee who first gives notice prevails. (In states adopting this minority view, A's only redress is to recover the consideration, if any, that he gave to S in exchange for the assignment.) The majority view is that A, the first assignee, collects, even if he did not give notice first.

Sales Contracts

The Uniform Commercial Code's provisions on assignments, primarily Sec. 2−210, are generally similar to the common−law rules discussed above, rendering ineffective only assignments that would (1) materially change the obligor's duties; (2) increase materially the burden or risk imposed on the obligor by contract, or (3) impair materially the obligor's chance of obtaining return performance. The Code is perhaps even more "pro−assignment" than the common law. For example, it contains numerous restrictions on anti−assignment clauses that are not present in the common law.

Most important, perhaps, several types of assignments come within the scope of Article 9's provisions relating to secured transactions. These rules are discussed in some detail in Chapter 29 and will not be repeated here. However, we emphasize that Article 9 does alter several of the common law's rules on assignments where secured transactions occur. For example, it may give priority to a second assignee over a first assignee if the second assignee was the first to file a proper financing statement covering the assignment (UCC 9−312(5)).

Delegation of Duties

Our discussion so far has been directed to those cases in which contractual rights alone have been transferred, or assigned—in other words, to those common situations in which it is reasonably clear that the parties understood that the assignor alone would be the party who would perform the contract, as he or she originally contracted to do. In many circumstances, however, a **delegation of duties**— the transfer of one party's contractual duties to another— is intended as part of the assignment of rights, and in other circumstances a delegation of duties may occur without an assignment of rights. We will briefly examine these situations.

Delegation in Conjunction with an Assignment

If an assignment occurs in which the assigning party also delegates his or her contractual duties to the assignee, that party is the **delegator** (or assignor delegator), and the party to whom the duties are transferred is the **delegatee** (or assignee–delegatee). The remaining party—the party to the original contract to whom the performance is owed—is the **obligee.** When a delegation occurs in conjunction with an assignment, the delegatee usually (but not necessarily) expressly or impliedly promises that he or she will perform the delegator's duties under the contract. Assuming such a promise, the relationships are diagrammed in Figure 17.2. This discussion is based upon the assumption of a valid delegation— i.e., one in which the obligee has consented to the delegation, or in which the duty is of such nature that it can be delegated without the obligee's consent. (Nondelegable duties—those that cannot be assigned without the obligee's consent—will be examined later.)

Obligations of the Parties

Where a delegation occurs, and where the delegatee expressly or impliedly promises to perform the delegator's duties, the delegatee assumes the primary responsibility for performance of those duties. The delegator, however, remains secondarily liable for performance of those duties. To illustrate: X contracts to put in a driveway for Y, and X then delegates the duty to Z. If Z fails to do the job, X must either perform the job or be

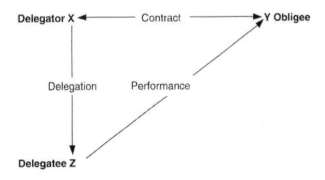

Figure 17.2   Delegation of Duties

liable to Y, the obligee, for damages for breach of contract. Thus, where the contract is never performed, the obligee has causes of action against both the delegatee and delegator. In other words, a delegation of duties— even when consented to by the obligee— does not in and of itself free the delegator of liability. (Thus, although a delegation is generally defined as a "transfer" of duties, this term is not entirely accurate in view of the retention of secondary liability by the delegator.)

The above discussion has assumed that the delegatee has promised, expressly or by clear implication, to perform the delegator's duties. In some situations, however, it is unclear whether the delegatee has made an implied promise to perform. Going back to the driveway illustration, for example, the assignment document might state that X hereby assigns to Z "all of my rights and obligations under my contract with Y," or it may simply say that X hereby assigns to Z the "entire contract" that he (X) has with Y. In either case, if Z accepts the assignment of rights but neither expressly promises to perform the contract nor commences performance, is he or she liable to Y if the driveway is never built? While there is disagreement on this point, the trend among the courts of most states is to find an implied assumption of duties by Z in both cases—with Z thus incurring liability in case he or she fails to perform.

Novation

As noted in the previous section, in the typical delegation, the delegator is secondarily liable on the contract if the delegatee assumes the duty but does not perform. An exception arises where the obligee agrees to substitute the delegatee for the delegator and to look no further to the delegator for performance in exchange for the delegatee's assumption of the duty. Such a consensual substitution of parties is called a **novation**. Mere approval by the obligee of a delegation does not constitute a novation, absent approval of the complete substitution of the delegatee for the delegator. The novation is discussed further in the next chapter.

Delegation in Absence of Assignment—Subcontracts

A delegation of duties may be made without an assignment of the delegator's rights under his or her contract with the obligee. In such cases, where the delegatee by contract promises to perform the delegator's duties, the general rule is that the delegatee's only obligation is to the delegator. In the "real world" a delegation of duties in the absence of an assignment most often involves a partial delegation of duties. To illustrate: X, a builder, contracts to build a home for Y for $92,000. X then subcontracts the electrical work to the Z Company, an electrical firm. If the Z Company fails to do the work, or does it in an unacceptable manner, it is liable to X but not to Y. (Similarly, it should be noted in passing that if the Z Company does perform, it may look only to X, the delegator, for payment. In other words, in the usual situation, the subcontractor is neither an intended beneficiary nor an assignee of the contract between the prime contractor— delegator and the obligee.)

What Duties Are Delegable?

In exceptional circumstances the obligee, upon learning of the delegation, will notify the parties that he or she will not accept performance by the delegatee. The general rule applicable to such a controversy is that any contractual duty may be delegated without the obligee's consent except (1) duties arising out of contracts which expressly prohibit delegation, and (2) contracts in which the obligee has a "substantial interest" in having the obligor–delegator perform personally.

Under the latter rule, contracts calling for the performance of *personal services*— such as those of a teacher, physician, or lawyer—are clearly non–delegable without the obligee's consent (even if the delegatee is as professionally competent as the delegator). Most other contracts call for the performance of duties that are described as essentially routine in nature, such as the repair of a building, the sale of goods, or the overhaul of machinery, and these duties are generally held to be delegable. (This result is not as unfair to the objecting obligee as it might appear, because, as we noted earlier, he or she may hold the delegator liable if the delegatee's performance is defective.) The UCC's rules on delegation are virtually identical to those of the common law.

CHAPTER **18**

DISCHARGE OF CONTRACTS

- Discharge By Operation of Conditions
- Discharge By Performance
- Discharge By Breach
- Discharge By Legal Impossibility
- Discharge By Commercial Impracticability
- Discharge By Frustration of Purpose
- Discharge By Parties' Agreement
- Discharge By Operation of Law

Sooner Or Later all contractual obligations come to an end. When this occurs in a particular case, the contract is said to be *discharged*. What is meant by this is that the *duties* of the contracting parties have been discharged.

There are many ways in which a discharge, or termination, can come about. Most of these result from the conduct of the parties themselves, while others involve events completely outside the control of either party. One leading treatise on contract law recognizes at least twenty separate and distinct ways in which a person's contractual obligations can be discharged. *Restatement, Contracts 2d.* The American law Institute, 1979. The most important of these are discharge by (1) operation of conditions; (2) performance; (3) breach by the other party; (4) circumstances excusing performance (impossibility, impracticability, and frustration); (5) agreement of the parties; and (6) operation, of law.

Discharge By Operation of Conditions
Conditions, Generally

In many contracts the parties simply exchange mutual promises to perform specified duties, with neither promise being conditioned or qualified in any way. Once such a contract is formed, each party is said to have incurred a "duty of immediate performance"—even though the performance of one or both parties may not be due until some specified time in the future.

In some situations, however, the performance of the contemplated contract is beneficial to one or both of the parties only if a certain event occurs in the future. And in other situations a contract may be mutually beneficial to the parties when entered into, but would be of little benefit if some event should occur before the stated time of performance arrives.

In these situations the parties can achieve substantial protection by the use of conditions in their contract. The term **condition,** in its broadest sense, can be defined as an express or implied provision in a contract which, upon the occurrence or nonoccurrence of a specified event, either creates, suspends, or terminates the rights and duties of the contracting parties. (While this definition refers to a provision or clause in a contract creating the condition, the terms may also be used to refer to the event itself that is designated in such provision.)

The law recognizes three kinds of conditions—*conditions precedent, conditions subsequent*, and *conditions concurrent*. Each type of condition can be further classified as *express or implied*. (Our discussion initially will focus on the nature of express conditions, with consideration of implied conditions precedent and implied conditions subsequent being delayed until we reach the subjects of performance and impossibility, respectively.)

Conditions Precedent

A **condition precedent** is a clause in a contract which indicates that the promises made therein are not to be operative until a specified event occurs. For example, X makes this offer to Y: "If the city rezones your property at 540 Fox Lane from C−3 to C−1 within thirty days, I will pay you $18,000 cash for it." Y accepts the offer. While a contract has now been formed, it is clear that the specified event must occur before either party incurs "a duty of immediate performance." The act of rezoning, therefore, is a condition precedent. And, because the condition resulted from the language of the contract, rather than by implication, the rezoning constitutes an express condition precedent. Conditions precedent can usually be identified by clauses containing the words if, in the event, or when. Thus the following language creates a condition precedent: "If X is able to obtain a building permit from the city within sixty days" (or "In the event X is able to obtain a building permit …"), "it is agreed that Y will construct a swimming pool for her, according to the attached specifications, for $9,000."

Discharge By Failure (or Nonoccurrence) of a Condition Precedent

Where a contract clearly creates a condition precedent, no "duty of immediate performance" arises until the specified event occurs. In the above case, then, should the rezoning not occur within the specified time, the condition is said to have "failed" and both parties are accordingly discharged of their obligations. In other words, the parties' duties under the contract are terminated.

Conditions Subsequent

Occasionally both parties to a contract are willing to incur a duty of immediate performance, but want to be freed of their obligations if a particular circumstance arises before the performance date. The parties can achieve this protection by use of an express **condition subsequent**—a clause in a contract providing that upon the happening of a specified event, the contract shall be inoperative (or void). Thus the essential difference in legal effect between the two basic kinds of conditions is that the occurrence of a condition precedent imposes a duty of immediate performance, while the occurrence of a condition subsequent removes such a duty. True conditions subsequent are rare, but consider this example: An insurance policy states "If written notice is given to the Company of Mr. A's death within 30 days of its occurrence, the Company will pay $100,000 to the beneficiaries. If the Company refuses to pay, and the beneficiaries do not file suit within one year of the death, any obligation of the Company under this contract shall be discharged."

Discharge By Occurrence of Condition Subsequent

In the above example, the death and the giving of written notice are conditions precedent which give rise to the Company's duty of immediate performance. However, that duty may be extinguished by the occurrence of a condition subsequent—the failure to file suit within one year. Conditions precedent are contrasted to conditions subsequent in Figure 18.1.

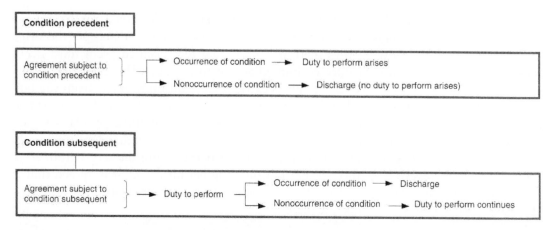

Figure 18.1 Conditions Precedent and Conditions Subsequent

Most conditions subsequent (as is true of conditions generally) are express rather than implied. They can ordinarily be recognized by language providing that the contract is to be void, inoperative, or canceled if a certain event occurs in the future. (The relatively few situations in which implied conditions subsequent exist will be discussed later in the chapter.)

Conditions Concurrent

Conditions concurrent exist when a contract expressly provides (or if one can reasonably infer from its terms) that the performances of the parties are to occur at the same time. A common example is a land sale contract which provides that the seller is to deliver the deed on payment of the purchase price. The duty of each party is thus conditioned on performance by the other. The seller has no duty to deliver the deed until the buyer pays (or tenders) the purchase price, and the buyer has no duty to pay until the seller delivers (or tenders) the deed. (A tender is an offer to perform one's obligation.)

The legal consequences that result from the use of express conditions precedent and subsequent are clear, once either condition is proven to exist. It is, however, often a more difficult question whether the parties conditioned their obligations at all, and, if so, whether the condition in the particular case fell in the precedent or subsequent category. The following case highlights the impact that such a determination might have on the outcome of a particular controversy.

Discharge By Performance

Most contracts are discharged by performance—by each party completely fulfilling his or her promises. In such cases, obviously, no legal problems exist. Nevertheless, the subject of performance merits special attention for several reasons.

RINCONES V. WINDBERG
Court of Appeals of Texas, Austin, 705 S.W.2d 846 (1986)

Rincones and Mena, plaintiffs, entered into a contract with Windberg, defendant, under which they were to "compile, research and edit material for academic and student services for a migrant program handbook." The contract was termed a "Consultant Agreement," and under it each plaintiff was to write specified chapters, for which Windberg would pay each $1,250 per chapter for their respective chapters.

The handbook was ultimately to be used by California authorities, and the parties were aware that the funds to pay plaintiffs would ultimately come from the State of California. The consultant agreement, however, made no mention of Windberg's obligation to pay being contingent upon his receipt of funding by California. Plaintiffs submitted the drts of their repective chapters to Windberg, but he refused to pay for them because "the publication was not accepted by alfia, and no funding from that state, therefore, was available for the project.

Plaintiffs then brought this action to recover the monies promised them. The primary question was whether Windberg s receipt of funding from aifornia was a condition precedent to his obligations under the contract, as Windberg contended. The trial court found () that the contract was partly written and partly oral; (2) that, under the oral agreement and the circumstances surrounding it, the parties had agreed that the contract was contingent upon California s funding of the project and (3) that alfornia refused to fund the project. The court concluded that a "condition precedent" existed that proof of the condition was not barred by the parol evidence rule; that the condition precedent had not been met that the contract was of no furtherforce and effect, and that Windberg thus had no liability under it.

The plaintiffs appealed.

Shannon, Chief Justice:

... The meaning of "condition precedent" in Texas jurisprudence is less than clear. For purposes of the parol evidence rule, however, we think that the definition from [a previous case] correctly states that a condition precedent is a condition "which postpones the effective date of the instrument until the happening of a contingency." ... By way of contrast, a condition subsequent "is a condition referring to a future event, upon the happening of which the obligation is no longer binding upon the other party, if he chooses to avail himself of the condition." *Id*. [The court here noted that parol evidence of a condition *precedent* is admissible to vary or contradict a complete written contract, while parol evidence of a condition *subsequent* is not admissible to vary or contradict such a written contract. The reason is that the parol evidence rule, discussed in Chapter 16, allows parol evidence to be introduced for the purpose of showing that there was never a valid contract in the first place.]

We now examine the record in an effort to determine whether the evidence supports the court's conclusion that funding from California was a condition precedent to the contract, or whether, to the contrary, the evidence shows an already effective and binding contract subject to a condition subsequent. The admissibility of the parol evidence turns on whether the contract was binding and effective from its inception, or whether it would become binding and effective only upon the occurrence of the contingency.

The evidence shows that all parties devoted substantial amounts of time and money attempting to perform their obligations under the Consultant Agreement. Appellants (plaintiffs) prepared and submitted a first draft of their manuscript, which Hardy [an associate of Windberg] took to California for revisions and recommendations. Thereafter, appellants worked on revisions and submitted a second draft for approval. Hardy, meanwhile, made several trips to California and spent $4,000 of her own money attempting to gain approval and receive funding from the state. All parties initially thought approval and funding for the project was certain, and performed under the contract accordingly. Only after several months had passed did they learn that political changes in California had placed their funding in jeopardy.

In our opinion the evidence shows that the parties understood that they had a binding and effective contract, and performed accordingly. The evidence is not [consistent] with a determination that the parties had agreed to postpone the effective date of the contract until the condition, funding from California, occurred.... [We conclude] that the parol payment condition [is a condition subsequent rather than a condition precedent].

As such, it written contract and is therefore in admissible under the parol evidence rule....

The judgment is reversed and the case is remanded to the trial court for new trial consistent with this opinion.

In the first place, many cases arise in which the actual performance of a promisor is, to some extent, defective. Sometimes the performance falls far short of what was promised; other times it deviates from the terms of the contract in only minor respects. As one might expect, the legal consequences of a major breach of contract are more severe and far—reaching than those resulting from a minor breach.

Second, in some cases the courts must determine whether the defective performance constituted a breach of a condition or a mere breach of a promise. A breach of a condition, no matter how slight, usually frees the nondefaulting party, while a breach of a promise generally does not unless it is a material one.

Promises: Degree of Performance Required

Many agreements consist simply of the exchange of mutual promises, with neither party's obligations expressly conditioned in any way. In most of these contracts, however, it is usually apparent from their nature that one of the parties is to perform his or her part of the bargain before the other is obligated to do so. For example: If X contracts to landscape Y's new home for $1,500, it can reasonably be inferred that the work is to be done by X before he can demand payment of Y. In this regard, it is sometimes said that the actual performance of one's promises constitutes an implied condition precedent that must be met by that person.

Thus, in general, when a promisor seeks to recover the contract price, that person must show that he or she has *fully* performed the promise in some cases or *substantially performed* it in others—depending on the nature of the obligation involved. If it is determined that this performance has met the applicable minimum standard, the promisor is entitled to recover the contract price minus damages (if any) suffered by the promisee. However, if the performance falls short of this minimum, the promisor's obligation has not been discharged, and he or she will recover little or nothing. (The rules determining the extent of recovery in each of these situations will be discussed immediately after the next case in the chapter.)

Total Performance

Some promises are of such a nature that they can be discharged only by complete performance. If a promisor's performance falls short of that called for under such a contract, even though the breach is minor, his or her obligation is not discharged. Suppose, for example, that B contracts in May to buy a car from S for $2,000—the contract providing that the price is to be paid in full by B on June 1, at which time S is to assign the car title to her. If, on June 1, B tenders S a check for $1,950, S has no obligation to transfer the title. A contract under which a seller of land is obligated to convey "merchantable title" falls into the same category; delivery of a deed conveying any interest or title less than that specified will not discharge the seller's obligation.

Substantial Performance

Many obligations are of such a nature that it is unlikely (indeed, not even to be expected, given the frailties of mankind) that a 100 percent performance will actually occur. The typical example involves a construction contract under which a builder agrees to build a home according to detailed plans and specifications. It is quite possible that the finished building will deviate from the specifications in one or more respects no matter how conscientious and able the builder is. In contracts of this sort, if the promisee–owner seeks to escape liability on the ground of nonperformance of the promisor–builder, it is ordinarily held that the promisor has sufficiently fulfilled the obligation if his or her performance, though imperfect, conformed to the terms of the contract in all major respects. This rule is known as the doctrine of **substantial performance.**

In order for the doctrine to be applicable, two requirements must ordinarily be met:

1. Performance must be "substantial"—that is, the omissions and deviations must be so slight in nature that they do not materially affect the for the purposes for which it was intended.
2. The omissions or deviations must not have been occasioned by bad faith on the part of the builder. (This is ordinarily interpreted to mean that the omissions or deviations must not have been made knowingly by the builder.)

Using the illustration involving the construction of a house, let us examine three cases where the builder is bringing suit against the owner to recover the last payment of

$5,000 called for under the contract and where the owner is refusing to pay on the ground of inadequate performance.

1. The owner proves that the following defects exist: (a) the plaster in all rooms is considerably softer than expected, because the builder used one bag of adamant for each hod of mortar instead of the two bags called for by the contract, and (b) water seepage in the basement is so great as to make the game room virtually unusable, as a result of the builder's failure to put a required sealant on the exterior of the basement walls. Here the defects are so material, and so affect the enjoyment and value of the home, that the builder has not substantially performed his obligations. Thus recovery will be denied, even if the breaches on the part of the builder are shown to be accidental rather than intentional.

2. The owner proves that the following defects exist: (a) the detached garage was given but one coat of paint rather than the two required; (b) the water pipes in the walls were made by the Cohoes Company rather than the Reading Company as was specified (though otherwise the two types of pipe are virtually identical); and (c) the wallboard installed in the attic is 1/8 inch sheeting instead of the 1/4 inch that was called for. Here the defects are so slight in nature, even when taken in total, that the builder has substantially performed the contract and can thus probably recover under the doctrine.

3. Same facts as case 2, but, in addition, the owner can show that one or more of the deviations were intentional; for example, he produces evidence tending to prove that the builder ordered the installation of the substitute pipe and wallboard knowing that they were not in conformity with the contract. Here the deviations are willful (rather than the result of simple negligence); therefore the builder is guilty of bad faith and the doctrine is not applicable.

Obviously, the requirement that performance be "substantial" is a somewhat elastic one, and necessitates a comparison of the promisor's actual performance with that which the terms of the contract really required of him. The following case is typical of those presenting substantial performance problems.

LANE WILSON COMPANY, INC. V. GREGORY
Court of Appeal of Louisiana, Second Circuit, 322 So.2d 369 (1975)

Lane Wilson Company, plaintiff, contracted to build a swimming pool for Gregory, defendant, at Gregory's KOA Campground outside Monroe, Louisiana, for $12,000. Under the written agreement, the pool was to be thirty by sixty feet, with a depth varying from three feet to six feet. Later the parties orally modified their contract by agreeing that plaintiff would add a diving board and increase the depth of the pool to *accommodate persons using the diving board. It was also orally agreed that a walkway around the pool would be enlarged and a longer fence built than was originally contemplated. The cost of these modifications raised the contract price to $13,643.*

During construction, defendant paid $8,400 on the contract. After the job was completed, however, he refused to pay the balance due because of various defects in the pool's construction (the most important of which are described in the appellate court's decision following). Plaintiff then brought this action to recover the balance allegedly due. The trial court held that plaintiff had substantially performed the contract, and that plaintiff was thus entitled to the balance of the contract price minus a credit of $300 to remedy one of the defects (the installation of a chlorinator). Defendant appealed.

Burgess, Judge:

. . . Defendant alleged [in his answer] that plaintiff had not constructed the pool according to the terms of the contract. . .. This appeal presents two issues. First, has plaintiff substantially performed the contract, thereby enabling him to recover the balance due on the contract price? Second, if plaintiff has substantially performed, are there any defects in the construction which entitle defendant to damages in an amount sufficient to remedy the faulty performance?

In Airco Refrigeration Service, Inc., v. Fink, 134 So.2d 880(1961), the supreme court considered . . . the meaning of "substantial performance." The court stated:

The principal question presented in this ease is whether or not there has been substantial performance so as to permit recovery on the contract. This is a question of fact. Among the factors to be considered are the extent of the defect or non-performance; the degree to which the purpose of the contract is defeated;

the ease of correction, and the use or benefit to the defendant of the work performed.

In light of the factors enumerated above, we cannot say the trial court was manifestly erroneous in finding that plaintiff substantially performed the contract. Defendant contracted for a 30 by 60 foot swimming pool deep enough to accommodate persons using a diving board. The defects alleged by defendant are not such that defeat the purpose of the contract or prevent defendant from using the pool. In addition, the defects for which plaintiff may be held accountable are easily remedied.

[The court here examined all of the defects in the job in order to determine whether or not plaintiff had substantially performed the contract. The most important of these defects were described as follows:]

Rather than measuring 30 by 60 feet as called for by the contract, the pool's measurements fluctuate from 59 feet six inches to 59 feet three and one half inches in length, and from 29 feet one—half inch to 29 feet three and one—half inches in width.

The walls of the pool are not vertical, but slope severely to form a bowl—shaped pool.

Plaintiff installed only six water inlets as opposed to twelve water inlets called for by the contract; this deficiency coupled with the poor placement of the inlets results in insufficient water circulation in the pool.

The pool is not ten feet deep as the parties allegedly agreed.

[The court here expressed its opinion as to the materiality of these defects as follows:]

(a) In the instant case we find the deviations in dimensions, which could be discovered only by measuring the pool, *in no way defeat the purpose of the contract.* [Emphasis added.] Plaintiff also testified the method of constructing the pool made it impossible to achieve perfect compliance with the exact measurements called for by the contract. Therefore, under the authority of [earlier cases in this state], we find the slight deviation in measurements did not constitute a breach of the contract.

Defendant made no complaint about the shape of the pool walls until after suit was filed. The defect, if it be one at all, was apparent and defendant is held to have accepted same since he made no objection to the walls until suit was filed.

The number of water inlets was changed at the suggestion of the supplier of the equipment because twelve water inlets would have lowered the water pressure and caused improper circulation in the pool. Defendant agreed to the change in plumbing and cannot now claim that change as a defect.

Defendant failed to prove that the parties agreed to a ten-foot depth for the pool. We find the pool, as constructed, is deep enough to accommodate a diving board and, therefore, there is no defect in regard to the depth of the pool.

[On the basis of this analysis, the court agreed with the trial court that plaintiff had substantially performed the contract. The court then turned to the question of defendant's damages. On this point the court ruled that, in addition to the $300 damages (credit) allowed by the trial court, additional damages should have been allowed to compensate defendant for his removal of incorrect depth markers and the installation of new markers; for his removal of waste cement and cement forms; and to compensate defendant for 200 feet of pipe owned by him that plaintiff used in building the pool. The court summarized these adjustments as follows:]

Totaling the amounts listed above, we find defendant is entitled to $331.02 as damages to correct defects in plaintiff's performance, in addition to the $300 allowed by the trial court for the cost of an additional chlorinator which plaintiff admitted the pool needed.

For the reasons assigned the judgment in favor of plaintiff is amended to reduce the award from $4,943.36 to the sum of $4,612.34, and as amended is affirmed.

Substantial Performance—Amount of Recovery

As noted earlier, if the rule of substantial performance *is* applicable to a particular case, the promisor-plaintiff is entitled to recover *the contract price* minus damages (that is, the promisor may recover the amount that the promisee agreed to pay under the contract, minus damages—if any—which the promisee sustained as a result of the deviations). Since the damages are typically inconsequential, the promisor usually recovers a high percentage of the contract price. By contrast, where the doctrine is not applicable, the recovery may be little or nothing. The general rules for such situations can be summarized as follows:

1. Where the performance falls short of being substantial and the breach is intentional, the promisor receives nothing. The rationale, of course, is that an intentional wrongdoer should not be rewarded— particularly where the promisee has not received the performance he or she was entitled to. (The rule of nonrecovery also has an affirmative aspect—it strongly "persuades" the promisor to actually finish the job, since he or she will receive nothing otherwise.)

2. In the somewhat rarer case where the performance is not substantial but the breach is unintentional, recovery is allowed on the basis of quasi-contract. For example, if

the promisor is permanently injured when only halfway through the job, he or she is entitled to receive the reasonable value of the benefit received by the promisee as a result of the partial performance.

3. If the performance is clearly substantial but the breach is willful, there are conflicting views. Some courts deny any recovery, regardless of other circumstances, embracing the principle that aid should never be given the intentional wrongdoer. Most courts, while endorsing this principle in the abstract, in practice allow the promisor to recover "the reasonable value of the benefit resulting from the performance, minus damages" (as distinguished from the "contract price, minus damages" recovery allowed in situations where the substantial performance requirements are met). Such a recovery is especially common where a failure to allow the promisor anything would result in the promisee being unjustly enriched—a result most likely to occur in cases where the performance is of such a nature that it cannot be returned by the promisee.

Special Problems Relating to Performance Personal Satisfaction Contracts

Under the ordinary contract, a person who has undertaken the performance of a job impliedly warrants only that he or she will perform in a "workmanlike manner," i.e., the performance will be free of material defect and of a quality ordinarily accepted in that line of work. If the performance meets this standard, he or she is entitled to recover the contract price even if the person for whom the work was done is not satisfied with it.

Some contracts, however, provide that "satisfaction is guaranteed," or contain other language of similar nature. In such cases, it is usually held that such satisfaction is a condition precedent that must be met in order for the promisor to recover under the contract; workmanlike performance alone will not suffice. In determining whether the condition has been met, the courts distinguish between two kinds of contracts: (1) those in which matters of personal taste, esthetics, or comfort are dominant considerations, and (2) those that entail work of mere "mechanical utility."

For contracts in the first category, the condition is fulfilled only if the *promisee is actually satisfied* with the performance that was rendered—no matter how peculiar or unreasonable that person's tastes may be. For example: X, an artist, contracts to paint a portrait of Y for $500 "that will meet with Y's complete satisfaction." When the portrait is completed, Y refuses to pay on the ground that he simply does not like it. If X brings suit to recover the $500, a question of fact is presented: Is Y's claim of dissatisfaction genuine; If the jury so finds, the condition has not been met and X is denied recovery. (Of course, if the jury finds that Y's claim of dissatisfaction is false—that is, he is actually satisfied and is simply using this claim as a ground to escape an otherwise valid contract—then the condition has been met and recovery is allowed.)

For contracts in the second category, where the performance involves work of mere mechanical fitness (or mechanical utility), an objective test is used. For example: M agrees to overhaul the diesel engine in T's tractor–trailer for $200, guaranteeing that T will be "fully satisfied" with the job. In this case, the condition precedent is met if the jury finds that *a reasonable person would have been satisfied* with M's job, even though T himself is dissatisfied.

Performance By an Agreed Time

If a contract does not provide a time by which performance is to be completed, the general rule is that each party has a reasonable time within which to perform his or her obligations. Whether the performance of a promisor in a given case took place within such a time is ordinarily a question for the jury. In practice this rule poses few problems and seems to produce acceptable results.

A more troublesome situation is presented by contracts that do contain a stated time of performance. For example: A printer agrees to print up 15,000 letterheads for a customer, with the contract specifying "delivery by April 10." If delivery is not made until April 14, and the customer refuses to accept the goods because of the late performance, the question for the jury is whether the stated time of performance legally constituted a condition precedent. If it did, the condition has obviously not been met and the customer has no obligation to accept the shipment.

The general rule is that such a provision, of and by itself, *does not create a condition precedent*. Under this view, it is sufficient if the performance occurs within a reasonable time after the date specified. Thus, in the preceding illustration, the customer is very likely obligated to accept the letterheads where delivery was only four days late. The customer may recover any damages caused by the delay in accordance with rules of recovery discussed in the next chapter.

Time–of–the–Essence Clauses. In some situations, however, the parties clearly intend that performance must actually take place by the specified time in order for the promisor to recover from the other party. In such situations, *performance by the agreed upon time does constitute a condition precedent*. The intention can be manifested in two ways: (1) by the express wording of the agreement itself and (2) by implication (reasonable inference from the nature and subject matter of the contract alone). Two examples may be helpful.

1. P agrees to print up and deliver 15,000 letterheads to Q by April 10, the contract further providing that *time is of the essence*. By this clause, the parties have made the stated time of performance an express condition precedent. Thus, if P fails to deliver the letterheads until April 11, Q can refuse to accept the belated performance. P's failure to meet the condition frees Q of her obligations under the contract. Additionally, Q can recover damages from P in a breach of contract suit. (An alternative open to Q is to accept the late performance and "reserve her rights" against P—in which case she is entitled to an allowance against the purchase price to the extent that she has suffered damages as a result of the late performance.)

2. A chamber of commerce purchases fireworks, for a Fourth of July celebration it is sponsoring, with the contract providing that "delivery is to be made prior to July 4th." The fireworks arrive too late on July 4th to be used. From the nature of the *subject matter alone it* can be inferred that the stated time is a condition precedent,

and the late delivery obviously did not meet that condition. In such a case it is said that time was made a condition "by operation of law" (that is, without regard to other factors). The courts are reluctant to rule—from the subject matter of the contract or from the nature of the contract alone—that time is of the essence. Limited instances in which such a ruling *may* be made, however (in addition to the rare case typified in example 2), are option contracts—where, for example, a seller of land contracts to keep an offer open ninety days and contracts in which the value of the subject matter, is fluctuating rapidly.

At one time, many courts ruled that time was presumed to be of the essence in sales contracts. Today, however, this is not the general rule. Thus, in most states, a late delivery does not free the buyer unless he or she can clearly prove that delivery by the date contained in the contract was material, and that the seller knew or should have been aware of the materiality.

Morevoer, a number of states have adopted legislation in modern times specifying that a time—is—of—the—essence condition cannot be implied, and that time is never of the essence unless the contract expressly indicates that it is. Thus, one must check the law of a particular state to be certain.)

Discharge By Breach

Actual Breach

It would be contrary to common sense if a person who had materially breached a contract were nevertheless able to hold the other party liable on it, and the law does not tolerate such a result. As the preceding section on performance indicates, an a **ctual breach**—failure of the promisor to render performance that meets the minimum required by law (full performance in some cases and substantial performance in others)—ordinarily results in the other party's obligations being discharged. In such cases the promisor's breach operates as "an excuse for nonperformance" insofar as the other's obligation is concerned.

This principle has found its way into the law of sales. Thus, if Seller S on May 1 contracts to deliver a thousand gallons of crude oil to Buyer B on August 15, and on that date S delivers only two hundred gallons with no indication that the balance will be delivered shortly thereafter, B can cancel the entire contract, returning the oil already delivered (see Secs. 2—610 and 2—711 of the UCC).

Anticipatory Breach

If one contracting party indicates to the other, before the time of performance arrives, that he or she is not going to perform his or her part of the bargain, an **anticipatory breach** has occurred; in most cases this has the same effect as an actual breach. For example: In March, X contracts to put in a sewer line for a city, with the contract providing that the work will be commenced by June 1. On April 10, X tells the city that he will not do the job. The city can immediately hire a new contractor to do the work and can institute a suit for damages against X as soon as the damages can be ascertained, without waiting until June to do so. (Such action is not mandatory; the city may ignore the repudiation in the hope that X will have a change of heart and actually commence the work on schedule.)

The doctrine of anticipatory breach does not apply to promises to pay money debts, such as those found in promissory notes and bonds. To illustrate: S borrows $500 from T on February 1, giving T a promissory note in that amount due September 1. If S tells T on August 6 that he will not pay the debt, T must nevertheless wait until September 2 before bringing suit to recover the $500. The UCC has detailed provisions addressing anticipatory breach that are discussed in detail in Chapter 23.

Discharge By Legal Impossibility

Between the time of contracting and the time of performance, some event may occur that will make the performance of the contract—for one party, at least—considerably more difficult or costly than originally expected. When this happens, a promisor may contend that the occurrence legally discharged his or her obligations under the contract—that is, it created a **legal impossibility.** (A related subject, the doctrine of *commercial impracticability,* will be discussed subsequently.) For example: A, an accountant for a large corporation who "moonlights" in his spare time, contracts in May to perform certain auditing services for B during the first three weeks of August, A's regularly scheduled vacation. In June A is transferred to a city five hundred miles away; as a result, he does not perform the promised services. If B were to seek damages for breach of contract, the issue presented would be whether A's transfer discharged his obligations under the contract.

In such a case, the courts resort to a two–step process. The first question to be decided is whether one of the parties had assumed the risk in some manner. For example, in the case above, a court might conclude—from a reading of the entire contract, or from testimony regarding the negotiations leading up to the contract—that B had, in fact, agreed that A need not perform if he were relocated. If so, B had assumed the risk, and A need not perform.

If no assumption of risk is apparent (as is often the case), the court must proceed to the second question: whether it can rule, on the basis of the circumstances under which the contract was made, that the contract necessarily contained an implied condition subsequent. In other words, in the case above, A would be excused from performing the contract only if he could convince the court that he and B agreed by implication that the contract would be voided if he were transferred before the date of performance.

In most cases of this sort, the promisor's contention that an implied condition subsequent existed is rejected by the courts. The usual view is that such possibilities should have been guarded against by an express condition in the contract. Thus, when a corporation promises to manufacture engines by a certain date under a contract containing no express conditions, the fact that it is unable to do so because of a strike at one of its plants is no legal excuse for its nonperformance of the contract. And when a contractor agrees to construct a building by a certain date, with a monetary penalty imposed for late completion, the law normally does not excuse late performance simply because unexpectedly bad weather delayed the work. Nor will a court normally free a builder from his obligations, in the absence of an express condition, merely because unexpectedly high labor or materials costs will cause him to suffer a loss if he is held to the contract.

Notwithstanding these generalizations, there are limited situations in which the defense of legal impossibility is accepted by the courts. We will discuss them briefly.

True Impossibility

Essentially, a contract is rendered impossible of performance only where the supervening event—the event occurring between the making of the contract and the time of performance—was unforeseeable at the time of contracting, and creates an objective impossibility. An objective impossibility results in a situation where, as a result of the unanticipated occurrence, no one can perform the contract—that is, performance is physically impossible. By contrast, an occurrence that makes performance by the promisor, only, impossible (but does not make performance by others impossible) does not discharge the promisor's obligations. For example, the inability of a buyer of a condominium to make a cash payment of $10,000 at the time of closing, as required by the contract, is not excused because his or her business suffered a catastrophic loss just prior to that time (The difference between the two types of impossibility is often summarized thus: where a promisor is claiming objective impossibility, he is saying "*No one* can perform," while in the subjective impossibility situation he is simply saying I cannot perform.")

Up until recent years, implied conditions subsequent— i.e., conditions resulting in legal (objective) impossibility— have been recognized by the courts in only three situations: (1) in contracts calling for personal services, (2) where the subject matter of the contract is destroyed without the fault of either party, and (3) where the performance of the contract becomes illegal after the contract is formed.

The view is commonly held among lay persons, and sometimes finds its way into court decisions, that promisors are freed of their obligations by any "act of God," or "force majeure"—i.e., a force of nature of such degree that it could not be guarded against or prevented by any degree of care or diligence (such as an earthquake or unprecedented flood). This generalization is true when the subject matter of a contract is destroyed by such an occurrence, but it is not necessarily true in other cases. For example, the destruction of a partially completed building by a tornado may be accepted by a court as grounds for permitting the contractor additional time in which to complete the job, but as a general rule, it does *not discharge* the contractor from the obligation to rebuild. Because of this rule, and because of uncertainty as to application of the act-of-God defense to other contracts, construction contracts (and many others) typically contain *express* conditions subsequent excusing delays in performance, or completely excusing performance, in the event of adverse weather conditions, strikes, and so forth. The following clause, in a maritime shipping contract, is typical: 'FORCE MAJEURE: In the event of any strike, fire or other event falling within the term 'Force Majeure' preventing or delaying shipment or delaying reception of the goods by the buyer, then the contract period of shipment or delivery shall be extended by 30 days on telex request made within seven days of its occurrence. Should shipment or delivery of the goods continue to be prevented beyond 30 days, the unaffected party may cancel the fulfilled balance of the contract. Should the contract thus be cancelled and/or performance be prevented during any extension to the shipment or delivery period *neither party shall have any claim against the other.*" [Emphasis added.]

Personal Services

In contracts calling for the rendering of *personal services,* such as the ordinary employment contract, the death or incapacity of the promisor (employee) terminates the agreement. The same is true of contracts that contemplate a *personal relationship* between the promisor and the other party. In such cases the courts will accept the argument that the performer's promise was *subject to the implied condition* that his or her death prior to the time of performance (or illness at the time of performance) rendered the contract null and void.

Note, however, that many obligations are not personal in nature. For example: If B contracts to sell his land to W for $30,000, and B thereafter dies, the agreement is not terminated. The reason is that B's estate, acting through the executor, is just as capable of delivering a deed to W as was B, had he lived. Nor would the contract be terminated if W rather that B had died. W's estate is just as capable of paying the $30,000 as W would have been, had he lived.

Destruction of the Subject Matter

The principle is well established that destruction of the subject matter of a contract without the fault of either party, before the time for performance, terminates the contract. Where such a situation occurs, the courts will accept the argument that the destruction *constituted an implied condition subsequent* and will rule, as in the personal service contracts, that a legal impossibility has occurred. For example: If C contracted in January to move D's house in March, the contract would be discharged if the house were destroyed by flood in February. In this regard, it can be said that the destruction of the subject matter of a contract by an act of God creates a legal impossibility. It should be noted, however, that it is the fact of destruction that discharges, rather than the cause (as long as the destruction is not attributable to neglect or misconduct of the parties). To illustrate: X contracts with an investors' syndicate to drive its race car at the next Indianapolis 500, and the night before the race the car is destroyed by a fire set by an arsonist. Both parties are discharged from their obligations, although the arsonist's act is not an act of God.

Beyond cases such as the above, it is often difficult to determine what is meant by the "subject matter" of a contract; the term is often used by the courts to include not only the precise subject matter involved, but any other "thing" or property that performance of the contract necessarily depends on. For example, the X Company in January agrees to manufacture and deliver five hundred widgets to the Y Company in March. In February the X Company's only plant is destroyed by fire, with the result that the widgets cannot be manufactured. In this case the courts will ordinarily rule that the existence of the plant is so necessary to the fulfillment of the contract that its destruction excuses the X Company from its obligations. (Such a ruling would not be made, however, if the X Company operated several plants and if there was no indication in the contract, expressly or impliedly, that the parties intended for the widgets to come from the particular plant that was destroyed.) Special problems arise in the "destruction" cases involving sales of goods. Specific "risk of loss" rules in article 2 of the UCC govern situation of this sort, and are considered in Chapter 21.

Subsequent Illegality

If, after a contract is made, its performance becomes illegal because of a change in the law (including a promulgation of an administrative agency's regulation), a legal impossibility is created. Thus if B in September contracts to sell fifty pinball machines to G in December, the parties' obligations would be discharged if a state statute prohibiting such a transaction took effect in November.

The case below raises a "destruction of the subject matter" issue in regard to the performance of a construction contract that contained no express conditions subsequent. (However, as noted earlier, the general subject of impossibility should also be considered with a related view, the **doctrine of "commercial impracticability,"** which is discussed immediately after this case.)

LA GASSE POOL CONSTRUCTION CO. v. CITY OF FORT LAUDERDALE
Florida District Court of Appeal, Fourth District, 288 So.2d 273 (1974)

The La Gasse Company, plaintiff, made a contract with the City of Fort Lauderdale under which it was to repair and renovate one of the city's swimming pools for a specified price. One night, when the job was almost completed, vandals damaged the pool so badly that most of the work had to be redone.

When the city refused to pay more than the contract price, plaintiff brought this action to recover compensation for the additional work. The primary contention of plaintiff was that the damage to its work constituted a destruction of the subject matter of the contract, and that it was consequently discharged from any obligation to redo the work. Accordingly, plaintiff argued, when it did do the work over again it was entitled to additional compensation for its services.

The trial court rejected this contention, holding that plaintiff had the responsibility under the original contract to redo the work, and it entered judgment for defendant. Plaintiff appealed.

Downey, Judge:

. . . The question presented for decision is: Where the work done by a contractor, pursuant to a contract for the repair of an existing structure, is damaged during the course of the repair work, but the existing structure is not destroyed, upon whom does the loss fall where neither contractor nor the owner is at fault?

The general rule is that under an indivisible contract to build an entire structure, loss or damage thereto during construction falls upon the contractor, the theory being that the contractor obligated himself to build an entire structure, and absent a delivery thereof he has not performed his contract. If his work is damaged or destroyed during construction he is still able to perform by rebuilding the damaged or destroyed part; in other words, doing the work over again.

In the case of contracts to repair, renovate, or perform work on existing structures, the general rule is that total destruction of the structure . . . without fault of either the contractor or owner, excuses performance by the contractor and entitles him to recover the value of the work done. The rationale of this rule is that the contract has an implied condition that the structure will remain in existence so the contractor can render performance. Destruction of the structure makes performance impossible, and thereby excuses the contractor's nonperformance.

But where the building or structure to be repaired is not destroyed, [and] the contractor's work is damaged so that it must be redone, performance is still possible, and it is the contractor's responsibility to redo the work so as to complete the undertaking. [Emphasis added.] In other words, absent . . . some other reason for lawful nonperformance, the contractor must perform his contract. Any loss or damage to his work during the process of repairs which can be rectified is his responsibility. The reason for allowing recovery without full performance in the case of total destruction (i.e., impossibility of performance) is absent where the structure remains and simply requires duplicating the work. . . . Accordingly, the judgment for [defendant] is affirmed.

Discharge By Commercial Impracticability

Under the traditional views just discussed, most contracts did not present situations in which legal impossibility was recognized. Thus most contracting parties were not freed from their obligations even in cases where their performance was clearly made more difficult by events that occurred after the contracts were entered into. Today, however, courts are more likely to free contracting parties than was the case earlier, because of increasing recognition of the **doctrine of commercial impracticability.**

The drafters of the UCC felt that sellers of goods should be excused from their obligations not only where the strict conditions of impossibility existed, but also where performance was literally possible but would necessarily be so radically different from that originally contemplated by the parties that it was impracticable.

LEGAL FOCUS

Ethics

Parker was a 37–year–old bachelor who lived alone in an attic apartment. He went to Arthur Murray Dance Studios to redeem a certificate for three free dance lessons. The instructor told Parker that he had potential to be a great dancer and talked him into signing up for more lessons. And more lessons. And more lessons. Before long, the blandishments of the Arthur Murray instructors had induced Parker to sign up for 2734 hours of lessons at an advance payment of $24,812.80. Long before Parker could begin to take all these lessons, he was seriously injured in a car accident.

His injuries effectively prevented him from ever taking advantage of the dance lessons.

Parker asked to have his money refunded, but Arthur Murray refused. Parker then sued, seeking rescission of the contract based on impossibility of performance. Arthur Murray agreed that the doctrine would normally apply, but pointed out that every contract Parker had signed specifically stated that it was "Non-Cancelable" or that "No Refund Will Be Made Under The Terms Of This Contract."

Once again, we are faced with a question raising both practical and ethical dimensions. Should the contract be enforced as written? Parker was a college graduate. A gullible college graduate, perhaps, but a college graduate nonetheless. Should the law protect him from his own agreement? Under what ethical theory?

Ultimately, the court in this case did protect Parker. It did so by construing the contract very narrowly. As we shall see in the next chapter, ambiguities are generally construed against the party who drafted the contract–Arthur Murray in this case. The court held that "plaintiff never contemplated that by signing a contract with such terms as 'NON–CANCELABLE' and 'NO REFUNDS' he was waiving a remedy expressly recognized by Illinois courts." Do you think the court ruled correctly? Parker v. Arthur Murray, Inc., 295 N.E.2d 487(Ill.App. 1973)

Commercial Impracticability Under the UCC

Section 2–615 of the UCC reads, in part, as follows: "Delay in delivery or nondelivery in whole or in part by a seller ... is not a breach of his duty under a contract for sale if performance as agreed has been made impracticable by the occurrence of a contingency the non–occurrence of which was a basic assumption upon which the contract was made."

While a full discussion of the scope and ramifications of the commercial impracticability doctrine cannot be undertaken here, several of its basic characteristics can be noted. These characteristics are best explained in Comment 4 following Sec. 2–615, which reads as follows:

Increased cost alone does not excuse performance unless the rise is due to some unforeseen contingency which alters the essential nature of the performance. Neither is a rise or a collapse in the market in itself a justification, for that is exactly the type of business risk which business contracts made at fixed prices are intended to cover. But a severe shortage of raw materials or of supplies due to a contingency such as war, embargo, local crop failure, unforeseen shutdown of major sources of supply or the like, which either causes a *marked increase in cost or altogether prevents the seller* from securing supplies necessary to his performance, is within the contemplation of this section. [Emphasis added.]

Thus this section clearly recognizes certain kinds of contingencies *in addition* to those constituting true impossibilities that may free the seller of his or her obligations under the contract. (In that regard, however, under both Comment 1 to Sec. 2–615 and the case law that has developed with respect to this section, the seller must show that the contingency was not within the contemplation of the parties at the time of contracting.)

A second change brought about by the impracticability doctrine is its recognition that a "marked increase" in cost will free the seller, if caused by an unforeseen contingency. (By contrast, increased cost of performance alone is almost never recognized under the impossibility doctrine as a ground for excusing performance.) However, determination of what constitutes a marked increase in cost is left to the courts to decide on a case–by–case basis, and the courts have interpreted this term quite narrowly. That is, under the decisions, the courts have generally taken the view that the seller must prove that the cost of performance (as a result of the contingency) would at least be double or triple the original cost of performance. Thus the increased cost provision does not afford sellers relief in as many cases as would at first appear.

After adoption of the UCC, the courts generally recognized commercial impracticability as an excuse for nonperformance in sales contracts only, continuing to require a showing of strict impossibility where other types of contracts were involved. Today, however, *there is a growing tendency among the courts to apply the commercial impracticability yardstick to all kinds of contracts.*

Discharge By Frustration of Purpose

Occasionally, after a contract is entered into, some event or condition will occur that clearly does not fall within the impossibility or commercial impracticability doctrines, yet one of the parties will argue that it so frustrated the purposes of the contract that its occurrence ought to free him nonetheless. (In other words, such a party is contending that the happening of the event caused the contract to become worthless to him.) To illustrate: D, a car dealer embarking on an ambitious expansion program, makes a contract with C, a contractor, under the terms of which he is to pay C $250,000 for the construction of new showroom facilities. Shortly thereafter, because of an unanticipated national defense emergency, the federal government orders a 90 percent reduction in the production of new automobiles. D contends that this action constitutes grounds for cancelling its construction contract, since he will obviously have few new cars to sell.

Here the courts are on the horns of a dilemma. On the one hand, they understand that the virtual stoppage of new car production substantially eliminates the purpose for which the contract was made—and may even drive D into bankruptcy if he is held to its terms. On the other hand, the adoption of a general rule to the effect that contracts are discharged whenever the *purposes* of one of the parties cannot be attained as a result of unanticipated future occurrences would cast great uncertainty on the enforceability of almost all contracts.

While it is dangerous to generalize about the kinds of cases in which the doctrine of frustration may be accepted as grounds for avoiding contractual liability, it can safely be said that the courts—while giving the doctrine due consideration in their decisions—actually find it to be *inapplicable* in the great majority of cases. Thus, in the example above, D's contention that he was freed on the ground of frustration of purpose will probably (though not certainly) be rejected. The following case discusses the entire bundle of doctrines—impossibility, commercial impracticability, and frustration of purpose—tracing their origins and rationale.

Northern Indiana Public Service Co. v. Carbon County Coal Co.
U.S. Seventh Circuit Court of Appeals, 799 F.2d 265 (1986)

In 1978 Northern Indiana Public Service Company (NIPSCO), an electric utility in Indiana, contracted to buy 1.5 million tons of coal every year for 20 years, at a price of $24 a ton (subject to various provisions for escalation which by 1985 had driven the price up to $44 a ton) from Carbon County Coal Co., which operated a coal mine in Wyoming. NIPSCO's rates are regulated by the Indiana Public Service Commission which, because of complaints from consumers about higher rates, ordered NIPSCO ("the economy purchase orders") to make a good faith effort to find and purchase electricity from other utilities that could produce it at prices lower than NIPSCO's internal generation. NIPSCO was able to buy substantial amounts of electricity from other utilities at costs below the costs of generating its own electricity using Carbon County's coal. Therefore, NIPSCO stopped accepting coal deliveries from Carbon and brought suit seeking a declaration that it was excused from its obligations under the contract. The trial court ruled against NIPSCO and it appealed.

Posner, Judge:

In the early common law, a contractual undertaking unconditional in terms was not excused merely because something had happened (such as an invasion, the passage of a law, or a natural disaster) that prevented the undertaking.

See Paradine v. Jane, Aleyn, 26, 82 Eng.Rep. 897(K.B. 1647). Excuses had to be written into the contract; this is the origin of *force majeure* clauses. Later it came to be recognized that negotiating parties cannot anticipate all the contingencies that may arise in the performance of the contract; a legitimate judicial function in contract cases is to interpolate terms to govern remote contingencies—terms the parties would have agreed on explicitly if they had had the time and foresight to make advance provision for every possible contingency in performance. Later still, it was recognized that physical impossibility was irrelevant, or at least inconclusive; a promisor might want his promise to be unconditional, not because he thought he had superhuman powers but because he could insure against the risk of nonperformance better than the promisee, or obtain a substitute performance more easily than the promisee. Thus the proper question in an "impossibility" case is not whether the promisor could not have performed his undertaking but whether his nonperformance should be excused because the parties, if they had thought about the matter, would have wanted to assign the risk of the contingency that made performance impossible or uneconomical to the promisor or to the promisee; if to the latter, the promisor is excused.

Section 2–615 of the Uniform Commercial Code takes this approach. It provides that "delay in delivery . . . by a seller . . . is not a breach of his duty under a contract for sale if performance as agreed has been made impracticable by the occurrence of a contingency the non–occurrence of which was a basic assumption on which the contract was made. . . ." Performance on schedule need not be impossible, only infeasible—provided that the event which made it infeasible was not a risk that the promisor had assumed. Notice, however, that the only type of promisor referred to is a seller;

there is no suggestion that a buyer's performance might be excused by reason of impracticability. The reason is largely semantic. Ordinarily all the buyer has to do in order to perform his side of the bargain is pay, and while one can think of all sorts of reasons why, when the time came to pay, the buyer might not have the money, rarely would the seller have intended to assume the risk that the buyer might, whether through improvidence or bad luck, be unable to pay for the seller's goods or services. To deal with the rare case where the buyer or (more broadly) the paying party might have a good excuse based on some unforeseen change in circumstances, a new rubric was thought necessary, different from "impossibility" (the common law term) or "impracticability" (the Code term), and it received the name "frustration". . .

The leading case on frustration remains Krell v. Henry, [1903] 2 K.B. 740(C.A.). Krell rented Henry a suite of rooms for watching the coronation of Edward VII, but Edward came down with appendicitis and the coronation had to be postponed. Henry refused to pay the balance of the rent and the court held that he was excused from doing so because his purpose in renting had been frustrated by the postponement, a contingency outside the knowledge, or power to influence, of either party. The question was, to which party did the contract (implicitly) allocate the risk? Surely Henry had not intended to insure Krell against the possibility of the coronation's being postponed, since Krell could always relet the room, at the premium rental, for the coronation's new date. So Henry was excused. . . .

Since impossibility and related doctrines are devices for shifting risk in accordance with the parties' presumed intentions, which are to minimize the costs of contract performance, one of which is the disutility created by risk, they have no place when the contract explicitly assigns a particular risk to one party or the other. . . . [A] fixed—price contract is an explicit assignment of the risk of market price increases to the seller and the risk of market price decreases to the buyer, and the assignment of the latter risk to the buyer is even clearer where, as in this case, the contract places a floor under price but allows for escalation. If, as is also the case here, the buyer forecasts the market incorrectly and therefore finds himself locked into a disadvantageous contract, he has only himself to blame and so cannot shift the risk back to the seller by invoking impossibility or related doctrines. . . . It does not matter that it is an act of government that may have made the contract less advantageous to one party. Government these days is a pervasive factor in the economy and among the risks that a fixed price contract allocates between the parties is that of a price change induced by one of government's manifold interventions in the economy. Since "the very purpose of a fixed—price agreement is to place the risk of increased costs on the promisor (and the risk of decreased costs on the promisee)," the fact that costs decrease steeply (which is in effect what happened here—the cost of generating electricity turned out to be lower than NIPSCO thought when it signed the fixed—price contract with Carbon County) cannot allow the buyer to walk away from the contract. *In re Westinghouse Electric Corp. Uranium Contracts Litigation*, 517 F.Supp. 440, 452 (E.D.Va. 1981).

[Affirmed.]

Discharge By Parties' Agreement

Once a contract has been formed, it is always possible for the parties to make a new agreement that will discharge or modify the obligations of one or both parties under the original contract. The new agreement can take any of several forms, the most common of which are rescission, novation, and accord and satisfaction.

Rescission

A contract can always be canceled by mutual agreement. When this agreement occurs, the contract is *rescinded*, and the obligations of both parties are thereby discharged. An oral rescission agreement is generally valid and binding, even where the original contract was in writing—with one major exception. A rescission agreement must be in writing if it involves a retransfer of real property. (Additionally, under Sec. 2—209(2) of the UCC, modification or rescission of a written *sales contract* must be evidenced by a writing if the original contract so provides.)

Novation

A novation occurs when the party entitled to receive performance under a contract agrees to release the party who "owes" the performance and to permit a third party to take that person's place. It is simply a three—sided agreement that results in the substitution of one party for another. For example: X and Y have a contract. Later, they and Z agree that Z will perform X's obligations, with Y expressly releasing X from the original contract. X's obligations are now discharged.

Accord and Satisfaction

After a contract has been formed, the parties may agree that one of them will accept, and the other will render, a performance different from what was originally called for. Such an agreement is an accord. Thus, if B owes W $1,800, and they subsequently agree that B will air-condition W's home in satisfaction of the debt, an accord exists. The reaching of an accord does not, of and by itself, terminate the existing obligation. To effect a discharge, a *satisfaction* must take place—the actual performance of the substituted obligation. Thus B's indebtedness is discharged by **accord and satisfaction** only when he completes the air–conditioning job.

Discharge By Operation of Law

In addition to the types of discharge already discussed, other events or conditions can bring about a *discharge by operation of law*. The most common of these are bankruptcy proceedings, the running of a statute of limitations, and the fraudulent alteration of a contract.

Bankruptcy Proceedings

If an individual has been adjudged bankrupt after proper bankruptcy proceedings have taken place, he or she receives a *discharge in bankruptcy* from a court which covers most—but not all—of his or her debts. While the discharge technically does not extinguish the debts that are subject to it, it does so as a practical matter by prohibiting creditors from thereafter bringing court action against the debtor to recover any unpaid balance.

Running of Statutes of Limitations

All states have statutes providing that after a certain amount of time has elapsed, a contract claim is barred. The time limits vary widely from one jurisdiction to another. In some states, for example, claimants are given three years in which to bring suit on oral contracts and five years on written ones; in others, the times vary from two to eight years on oral contracts and from three to fifteen years on written ones.

In any event, if a contract claimant lets the applicable time elapse without initiating legal proceedings, the statute of limitations has run and subsequent court action by that person is barred. The period of time begins the day after the cause of action accrues. Thus, if X promises to pay Y $500 on June 10, 1987, in a state having a three-year statute, the statute begins to run on June 11, with the result that Y has until June 10, 1990, to institute suit. (As in the case of a discharge in bankruptcy, the running of the statute does not extinguish the debt or claim itself; it simply prevents the claimant from subsequently bringing a legal action to recover the indebtedness.)

Alteration

The law generally strives to discourage dishonest conduct. Consistent with this policy is the rule that the fraudulent, material **alteration** of a written contract by one of the parties discharges the other party as a matter of law. Suppose, for example, that A makes a written contract with B under the terms of which he is to sell 1,000 gallons of paint to B at a specified price per gallon. If B subsequently changes the quantity to 1,200 gallons without A's knowledge, A is excused from delivering any paint at all, if that is his desire. (A also has the right to enforce the contract according to its original terms or as altered—that is, he can tender either 1,000 or 1,200 gallons to B and hold him liable for the quantity chosen.)

CHAPTER **19**

CONTRACT INTERPRETATION AND REMEDIES FOR BREACH

- Contract Interpretation
- Remedies for Breach of Contract

This Chapter Addresses two of the most practically important areas in all of contract law. Often a contract exists, in that all the basic elements of a binding contract (agreement, consideration, capacity, legality) are present, but its meaning is not clear. It expresses the general rights and obligations of the parties, but what it means *exactly* in relation to the events that have occurred since the contract was formed cannot be agreed upon by the parties to the contract. Indeed, questions regarding the meaning of contracts generate more litigation than any other type of contract question. The first portion of this chapter discusses the basic rules which courts apply when resolving disputes as to the meaning of a contract's terms.

If a plaintiff convinces the court that a contract exists, and that the defendant has breached that contract as interpreted by the court, he has gained nothing unless the law provides him a full and appropriate remedy. The second half of this chapter explores the various avenues of remedy available to a party injured by a breach of contract.

Contract Interpretation

It is told that the defenders of the bastion of Sebasta surrendered to Temures, their besieger, after he promised that "no blood would be shed" should they do so. Temures was good to the letter of his word. But, upon being buried alive, the defenders probably wished they had asked their lawyer to check the fine print. Most modern breach–of–contract lawsuits also involve, often among several issues, a dispute as to the meaning of the contract generally or some of its specific terms. It is a rare situation indeed when both parties to a contract agree as to the meaning of all of its provisions. Such difficulties are perhaps inevitable, a combination of the imprecision of human language, inattention to detail by the drafters of the agreement, and the inability of the parties to foresee events as they will eventually transpire. In Chapter 4, we discussed statutory law and learned that legislators face similar limitations in drafting statutes, giving rise to that "necessary evil"—judicial interpretation.

Similarly courts are often called upon to determine the meaning of contracts and their provisions.

Courts do this through the processes of interpretation and construction. According to some sources, the process of **interpretation** focuses on determining the meaning of words as used in the contract while **construction** deals with the legal effect to be given those words. Generally, however, courts use the terms interchangeably because there is much disagreement as to their technical meaning and as to where one process ends and the other begins. No matter which term is used, the process is complicated.

Intent of the Parties

The primary role of a court asked to interpret a contract is to determine the intent of the parties at the time the contract was made and to give effect to that intent. The court's job is not to improve the contract or to rewrite it to address matters that the parties should have considered but did not. As with the process of statutory interpretation, the parties' intent is the centerpiece of the process. The court's own evaluation as to how the contract should have been written is irrelevant.

There is disagreement as to the optimum approach to determining contract intent. Most courts speak of an "objective" test that gauges the meaning of a contract's words by how a hypothetical "reasonably intelligent person" would understand them. However, it is not at all rare to see courts strive to determine the common intent of the contracting parties at the time they made the contract.

Contractual interpretation generally raises questions of law to be resolved by the court. However, if a contract's wording is ambiguous, extrinsic evidence may be admitted to determine the parties' intent. Juries often play a role in resolving this question of fact.

While determination of the parties' intent is the overarching goal of contract interpretation, the courts, once they have determined that intent, are constrained by considerations of public policy. In other words, they cannot give effect to a contract where the intent is to produce illegal, unethical, or unconscionable activity.

Plain Meaning Rule

We learned in Chapter 4 that the primary source of legislative intent is the wording of the statute itself. It should not be surprising, then, that in determining the intent of the parties to a contract, courts look first to the language of that contract. The parties' own words are the main evidence of their intentions at the time they made the contract.

Indeed, the words of the contract may be the only evidence of the parties' intentions that a court will consider. As in statutory interpretation, there is a well-recognized **plain meaning rule**. If the language of the contract appears clear and unambiguous, the plain meaning rule requires that the courts determine the intent of the parties solely from the face of the instrument. Absent ambiguity, the courts should not resort to extrinsic evidence (such as the actions of the parties, the testimony of the parties, or even the past practices of the parties) in their search for intent. Any attempt to alter the obvious meaning of the words with outside evidence would likely stray from the parties' intent at the time they made the agreement.

A few courts have rejected the plain meaning rule, concluding that it "asserts a semantic perfection which cannot hope to be achieved." PG&E v. G. W. Thomas Drayage Rigging Co., 442 P.2d 641 (Cal. 1968). Even in plain meaning rule jurisdictions, courts often conclude that the language of the parties, though it appears clear, is not in fact "plain and unambiguous." When that happens, courts resort to extrinsic evidence such as all relevant writings and oral statements, other conduct of the parties manifesting their intent, negotiations, prior course of dealing, and other relevant factors.

The following case examines these divergent approaches to the introduction of extrinsic evidence.

If courts decide to resort to evidence outside the language of the contract, the best evidence of the parties' intent may be their subsequent conduct in carrying it out. For example, in one case both Jewell and Thomas signed a promissory note. Jewell claimed that he had signed only to assist Thomas in getting the loan and that, therefore, Thomas should repay Jewell for the payments he made to the bank. Thomas claimed that Jewell was the primary obligor on the note. The evidence showed that as soon as the note was signed, Jewell treated the note as his own obligation, taking over complete responsibility for servicing the debt. Thomas never dealt with the bank. Thus, the court concluded, the intent of the parties appeared to be as asserted by Thomas Marvin E. Jewell & Co. v. Thomas, 434 N.W.2d 532 (Neb. 1989).

ISBRANDTSEN V. NORTH BRANCH CORPORATION
Supreme Court of Vermont, 556 A.2d 81(1988)

Plaintiff (grantee) bought from defendant (grantor) a townhouse at a ski resort. Defendant operated recreational facilities, ski trails, parking areas, and assorted outbuildings. There were four townhouses and all adjoined a common area known as the "club" which contained a kitchen, restaurant, and sitting room. Defendant operated and maintained all these areas. Defendant's business depended in part upon rental income derived from lessees of owners of the townhouses who did not use them on a year round basis. The development was designed so that the temporarily unoccupied townhouses could be rented out to paying guests. This benefited the owners, who derived a percentage of income from the rentals, and it assured the defendant the income required to continue providing the maintenance services necessary to all occupants.

The deed through which defendant sold the townhouse to plaintiff contained this clause: "The premises hereby conveyed shall be used only for private, single family residence purposes, except that, under express agreement between Grantor and Grantee, the premises may be rented or used for paying guests in connection with Grantor's operations."

Plaintiff asked the lower court to declare that she could rent her townhouse to paying guests without defendant's knowledge or consent. Defendant claimed that this clause prohibited plaintiff from any such rental except by and with defendant's express consent. The trial judge ruled for the defendant and the plaintiff appealed.

Gibson, Justice:

The question of whether a contract term is ambiguous is a matter of law for the court to decide. A provision in a contract is ambiguous only to the extent that reasonable people could differ as to its interpretation. Here, plaintiff argues that the deed contains internal inconsistencies which render its terms ambiguous and therefore subject to rules of construction that would warrant judgment in her favor. In particular, plaintiff contends that before the restriction on commercial rental can be given effect, there must first be an agreement between the parties, and that since there is no such agreement, plaintiff is free to do as she wishes.

Before extrinsic evidence may be used to aid in the construction of a written instrument, ambiguity must first be found. In determining whether an ambiguity exists, many courts have adopted the traditional "four corners" test or "plain meaning rule," which states that if a writing appears to be plain and unambiguous on its face, its meaning must be determined from the four corners of the instrument without resort to extrinsic evidence of any nature: "If the term in question does not have a plain meaning it follows that the term is ambiguous."J. Calamari & J. Perillo, The Law of Contracts §3-10, at 166-67(3d ed. 1987).

A number of courts, recognizing that "plain meaning" cannot exist in a vacuum, have allowed the admission of evidence as to the circumstances surrounding the making of the agreement as well as the object, nature and subject matter of the writing. See, e.g., Pacific Gas &Elec. Co. v. G. W. Thomas Drayage & Rigging Co.,442 P.2d 641(1968).

We believe it appropriate, when inquiring into the existence of ambiguity, for a court to consider the circumstances surrounding the making of the agreement. Ambiguity will be found where a writing in and of itself supports a different interpretation from that which appears when it is read in light of the surrounding circumstances, and both interpretations are reasonable.

If ambiguity is found on that basis, the court may then rely on subordinate rules of construction in order to interpret the meaning of the disputed terms. If, however, no ambiguity is found, then the language must be given effect in accordance with its plain, ordinary and popular sense.

In making its determination as to ambiguity in the instant case, the trial court properly considered evidence as to the circumstances under which the conveyance was made.

In the late 1960s, plaintiff and her family stayed at North Branch (presumably under a rental agreement as described above) on at least three separate occasions before her husband decided to purchase a townhouse for her. This purchase, which was a gift from Mr. Isbrandtsen to his wife, consisted of one of two new townhouses built in 1969, both of which were joined to the original four buildings. The new townhouses, which had no common "club" areas (having been built after the main buildings), each contained six bedroom units.

At the time defendant conveyed the property to plaintiff, she was asked, like every other owner, to sign a "Business Use Agreement" allowing defendant to rent out the property when she was not in actual occupancy. She declined to do so, advising defendant that she and her family intended to occupy the entire townhouse for their own use. It was uncontested at trial that of the other townhouse owners, all five had executed a "Business Use Agreement."

Plaintiff acknowledges that the restriction to use the property only "for private, single-family residence purposes" limits its use to residential purposes as opposed to business or commercial uses. The clause immediately following that phrase provides one exception to the restriction: the premises may be rented or used for paying guests under express agreement between defendant and the owner. The words "under express agreement" were inserted for a purpose and may not be ignored. The law is clear that an agreement must be viewed in its entirety, with an eye toward giving effect to all material parts in order to form a harmonious whole.

While the language of the restrictive clause is somewhat awkward, that in itself does not render it ambiguous. "If a contract, though inartfully worded or clumsily arranged, fairly admits of but one interpretation, it may not be said to be ambiguous or fatally unclear." Allstate Ins. Co. v. Goldwater, 163 Mich.App. 646, 648, 415 N.W.2d 2, 4(1987). Likewise, the fact that a dispute has arisen as to proper interpretation does not automatically render the language ambiguous. Such an approach would merely invite court interference any time a litigant alleged a dispute as to a contractual term.

Viewing the language of the deed in light of the surrounding circumstances, we hold that only one reasonable interpretation exists: that absent an express agreement between plaintiff and defendant, plaintiff is prohibited by the deed from renting her property to paying guests. Likewise, absent such an express agreement, defendant may not rent out plaintiff's property in part or in whole. The restriction serves to protect defendant's interest in maintaining and operating its innkeeping business while serving also to protect plaintiff, who may not want her property rented out indiscriminately to transient individuals.

[Affirmed.]

Rules of Interpretation

As in statutory interpretation, various rules of contract interpretation have developed over the years to assist the courts in determining the parties' intent from the words that they used. Courts should not apply the rules so conservatively as to obstruct the parties' true intentions, nor so liberally as to allow one of the parties to escape his obligations. As noted earlier, the courts are not at liberty to rewrite the contract while purporting to interpret it.

The first task in contract interpretation is to determine to the extent possible the parties' *principal* objective in forming the contract. This principal objective is accorded great weight, and all the contract's terms are construed in order to carry out that objective.

The parties' intentions are generally (though not exclusively) judged in an objective fashion from their expressed intent. Secret intentions are deemed irrelevant. Intentions expressed through either words or actions are given effect unless they conflict with law, morals, or public policy.

Contracts often contain conflicting and inconsistent terms. These will be interpreted, insofar as possible, to achieve the intentions of both parties. If possible, a contract will be construed so as to give effect to all of its provisions. The courts disfavor a construction which requires that a portion of the contract be ignored.

The courts also presume that the parties intended their agreement to be legal, reasonable, and effective. If alternative constructions are both plausible, the one that is preferred is the one least likely to render it illegal, unreasonable, or ineffective. Assume that a contract grants a patent licensee "exclusive use in the U.S.A." of the patented product. If the licensee argues that the right is to be perpetual and the licensor argues that it is to last only the life of the patent, the latter interpretation would be favored because the former would be inconsistent with antitrust laws.

Other aids to interpretation include the following:

1. Words and phrases are given their ordinary meaning, unless the parties indicate otherwise. Although the courts are not slaves to dictionaries, they do frequently consult them. Similarly, technical words are presumed to be used in their commonly accepted technical sense.
2. Specific language controls general language. For example, if a contract provided in one clause that a sole shareholder guaranteed payment for electrical service provided to his company, and another clause provided that the sole shareholder guaranteed electrical service provided to his company at a specific address, the court would likely conclude that the sole shareholder was not liable for electrical service provided to the company at other addresses.

3. When a contract is embodied in a printed form, any conflicting provisions added by the parties will prevail. Handwriting will prevail over typewriting. Thus, if a pre-printed form contained a provision limiting liability to $1,000, but the figure $2,500 was handwritten into the relevant blank on the form, the latter would set the limit of liability.

4. Ambiguous language is construed against the party who prepares the agreement. This is especially true where the contract is a preprinted adhesion contract where there is little opportunity for negotiation. In Comprehensive Health Ins. Ass'n v. Dye, 531 N.E.2d 505 (Ind.App. 1988), for example, an insurance contract prepared by the insurance company contained two different definitions of "preexisting conditions" that would not be covered by the policy. One excluded any sickness that had been diagnosed or treated before the policy was issued; the other excluded any sickness for which a reasonable person would have sought diagnosis or treatment. The court chose to apply the first definition because it was narrower and therefore more favorable to the insured.

5. Where numbers are expressed, words prevail over figures where they are in conflict. For instance, if a typed contract indicated in one place that the purchase price was "four hundred dollars" but in another place indicated that it was "$405," the former would prevail.

6. In every contract, courts will imply a duty of good faith, fair dealing, and cooperation on the part of both parties. The law of the jurisdiction at the place and time the contract is made is also generally read into the contract. Courts will not imply any other terms, unless a contract is silent on a particular point. In such an instance, courts may occasionally imply terms. For example, a contract that is silent as to duration will generally be construed to last for a reasonable time. An obligation to pay money is construed to require that the money be paid in legal tender.

These rules of interpretation, when applied to a specific contract, will not always point in the same direction, as the following case illustrates.

HANIL BANK V. PT. BANK NEGARA INDONESIA
U.S. District Court 2000 U.S. Dist. LEXIS 2444
(S.D.N.Y.)

Texas Court of Civil Appeals, 538 S.W.2d 237 (1976)

Appellee Webb wished to buy a house owned by Huller. Appellant Innes, a real estate broker, prepared an earnest money contract between Webb and Huller. Webb gave Innes a check for $2,000 as earnest money; Innes gave the money to Huller. Huller left town and never completed the contract. Webb seeks return of his $2,000, pointing to a provision in the standard preprinted form that was used for the earnest money contract which provided that if the seller did not comply with the contract for any reason, "Purchaser may demand back the earnest money...." In essence, Webb alleged that Innes held the *funds as stakeholder subject to Webb's demand for return of the funds should Huller breach.*

Innes emphasized a provision that was typed onto the form which stated: "$2,000 escrow to be turned over to Seller for initial deposit on materials and administrative costs."

The trial court held for Webb in the sum of $2,000 and broker Innes appealed.

Young, Justice:

... All of which brings us to the construction of a contract that was prepared by a broker and that contains two apparently inconsistent clauses: one, a printed clause, requiring the return by the broker to the purchaser of the earnest money on purchaser's demand if the seller fails to comply with the contract; and the other, a typewritten clause, requiring the broker to turn over the "$2,000.00 escrow" to the seller "for initial deposit for materials and administrative costs." Appellant urges that we should be guided here by the rule of construction which provides that the written or typewritten part of a contract controls in the event of any conflict thereof with the printed portion of the contract. The rationale for this rule is that the written or typed words are the immediate language of the parties themselves whereas the language of the printed form is intended for general use only, without reference to the particular aims and objectives of the parties. Leslie Lowry & Co. v. KTRM, Inc., 239 S.W.2d 898, 900 (Tex.Civ.App.—Beaumont 1951, no writ).

On the other hand, appellee contends that our case should be controlled by the rule which requires that an agreement be construed most strictly against the party who drafted it and thus was responsible for the language used.

When we attempt to apply these rules to our case, we find that we apparently have two conflicting rules urged by the parties. The question then arises which rule should prevail here. Our answer to that question is that the rule should be applied which says typed matter controls the printed instead of the rule which says that a contract will be construed against the author. Universal C.I.T. Credit Corp. v. Daniel, 150 Tex. 513, 243 S.W.2d 154 (1951); Leslie Lowry & Co. v. KTRM, Inc., supr a; 17A C.J.S. Contracts § 324, p.217.

The rule of strict construction against the author has been dealt with in those authorities as follows: In *Daniel,* our Supreme Court held that the rule applies only after ordinary rules of interpretation (such as the typed controls the printed) have been applied. In *KTRM, Inc.,* that Court simply applied the typed controls the printed rule over the authorship rule. In 17A C.J.S., the statement is made that the authorship rule is the last one the courts will apply.

For all of those reasons, we hold that the typewritten clause in the contract determines the responsibility of the appellant for his disposition of the "$2,000.00 escrow"; that he delivered that money to the seller under the clause; that, therefore, he did not breach the contract in so delivering the money.

[Reversed.]

Uniform Commercial Code

The UCC in Sec. 2-202 alters common–law practice by permitting more liberal use of extrinsic evidence in determining the parties' intent in sale–of–goods contracts. That is, the UCC backs away from the plain meaning rule, which focuses attention primarily on the language of the parties, by assuming that the parties considered matters such as (1) course of performance, (2) course of dealing, and (3) usage of trade. Thus, in construing a sales contract courts may resort to this extrinsic evidence without finding that the words of the contract are ambiguous.

A **course of performance,** according to UCC 2–208, arises out of "repeated occasions for performance by either party with knowledge of the nature of the performance and opportunity for objection to it by the other." Such performance which is accepted and acquiesced in without objection by the other party is a strong indication of what the parties intended.

A **course of dealing,** according to UCC 1–205, is "a sequence of previous conduct between the parties to a particular transaction which is fairly to be regarded as establishing a common basis of understanding for interpreting their expressions and other conduct." Thus, whereas course of performance arises out of the same contract the court is trying to interpret, course of dealing arises out of earlier transactions between the parties.

Finally, a **usage of trade,** according to UCC 1–205, is "any practice or method of dealing having such regularity of observance in a place, vocation, or trade as to justify an expectation that it will be observed with respect to the transaction in question."

It certainly makes sense to assume that the parties' conduct in performing the contract evidences their intentions and to assume that their intent at the time of making the contract took into account their prior dealings and the customs of their industry. UCC 1– 205(4) establishes a priority for interpretation. Express terms of the agreement are the primary source for interpretation. Next in line is course of performance which, where conflicting, controls course of dealing. Course of dealing, in turn, prevails over a conflicting usage of trade. Use of this type of extrinsic evidence is, of course, consistent with the UCC's various "gap–filler" provisions that we studied in Chapter 12.

Remedies for Breach of Contract

Assuming that a valid contract exists and that one of the parties to that contract has breached its obligations (as those obligations were interpreted by the court), the matter of remedies arises. We have already touched on the concept of remedies in several chapters. For example, in Chapter 15 we learned that rescission is available as a remedy where contracts were induced by fraud. In Chapter 18, we discussed remedies that are available where parties have only partially, but not completely, performed their contracted obligations.) The party who received the promises that were not performed will often look to the judicial system for a remedy (though, as we learned in Chapter 3, remedies may also be provided by alternative means of dispute resolution, such as arbitration). The form, availability, and extent of remedies will play a big part in a party's decision whether to litigate. If the law does not provide a remedy, or provides an inappropriate or inadequate remedy, the wronged party may never sue.

In our legal system, the freedom to contract entails the freedom to breach one's obligations. Our system of remedies aims not at coercing parties into performing their obligations, but at providing adequate remedies for the other party when breaches do occur. The distinction is subtle, but our free enterprise system's main goal is to encourage people to do business with those who make promises by assuring them that adequate remedies will be available to compensate them should the promisors not perform.

Our discussion is divided into two major sections because of the historical distinction (explored in the introductory chapters) between actions at law and actions in equity. Because the law/equity distinction has largely disappeared, virtually every court can grant remedies that traditionally were available in courts of law (i.e., money damages) and those traditionally available in courts of equity (e.g., orders of specific performance and injunction).

As with earlier contract-law chapters, we will note areas where the Uniform Commercial Code alters common–law rules because of the special needs of sale–of–goods transactions.

Money Damages

The primary remedy available for breach of contract is money damages. Because this remedy originated in courts at law, a jury trial is available to plaintiffs seeking such damages. The main goal of an award of damages is to compensate the plaintiff for losses caused by the defendant's failure to perform as promised. We will emphasize **compensatory damages** in this discussion, but also explore other types of damages, including nominal damages and liquidated damages.

Compensatory Damages

The amount of money a jury might award depends upon which interest the law is attempting to compensate. There are three such interests that we must address.

1. *Expectation Interest.* The law usually seeks to compensate the plaintiff's expectation interest. That is, the law seeks to put the plaintiff in the position in which he expected to be after the defendant performed his promise. In other words, the law attempts to give the plaintiff the "benefit of his bargain."

2. *Reliance Interest.* In situations where it is not feasible or fair to award the plaintiff expectation damages, the law may seek to return the plaintiff to where he was before the contract was entered into. Because this frequently entails reimbursing the plaintiff for funds he spent (or other detriment incurred) in reliance on the defendant's promise, this is called the *reliance* interest.

3. *Restitution Interest.* Finally, a defendant who fails to perform a promise should not be allowed to keep a benefit conferred by a plaintiff who did perform his promise. Therefore, in a breach–of–contract action, the defendant is often ordered to compensate the plaintiff for such a benefit. This is called making restitution, and the law is compensating the plaintiff's *restitution* interest.

Illustration: Assume that D Company hired Ralph to build a storage shed for D for the sum of $10,000. Soon after the contract was made, D repudiated it. If Ralph sued for breach of contract, proving that he could have built the shed for $7,500, he will likely recover $2,500, the profit that he expected to receive from the transaction. This award gives Ralph the benefit of his bargain by placing him in the position he expected to occupy (a $2,500 profit in his pocket) if D performed its promise.

Assume, on the other hand, that sometime after Ralph began building the shed, D breached the contract, telling Ralph not to finish because D would pay nothing. If Ralph could not prove the profit he would have made had the shed been completed, but could show that he had spent $3,400 on labor and materials before the breach, the law would award Ralph that $3,400 to compensate his reliance interest. Ralph spent that amount in reliance on D's promise. (If Ralph could also establish the $2,500 expected profit, he would recover $5,900, because this is the sum required to place him in as good a position as he expected to be in when D performed.)

Assume, on the other hand, that on the day the contract was made, D paid Ralph $2,000 as an advance. Ralph told D the next day that he would not go through with the job, but was keeping the $2,000. If D sued Ralph, it would recover at least $2,000 to compensate its restitution interest.

Expectation Measure. The matter of expectation damages must be explored more thoroughly. Placing a plaintiff in the position he or she expected to be in had the defendant performed as promised is a complicated matter. The general term "expectation damages" can be broken down into at least three subcategories. "Direct" or "general" damages are those losses clearly and directly caused by the defendant's breach. "Consequential" or "special" damages include lost profits and injury to persons or property resulting from the defendant's defective performance. "Incidental" damages include such matters as costs incurred by the plaintiff in arranging for substitute performance.

Assume that D Corporation promised to repair a plastic–molding machine for P Corporation for $15,000 by June 1. D understood that time was of the essence, because P had a big contract to produce plastic cups that called for a June 1 start–up date. On May 20, D informed P that it would not perform its promise. P quickly but thoroughly investigated and found that X Company was willing to make the repairs for $17,000. Working quickly, X completed the repairs on June 15, but P lost $5,000 in profits because the machine was idled for two weeks. Because it cost P $2,000 more to have the machine repaired than it would have had D performed as promised, P can recover $2,000 in *direct damages*. P will also recover $5,000 in *consequential damages* to compensate for the lost profits. Finally, any costs incurred by P in finding X could be recovered as *incidental damages*.

Although this illustration gives a general idea as to calculation of compensatory damages to redress the expectation interest, remember that there are some very important limitations on the plaintiffs recovery:

1. *Causation.* Plaintiff must prove that the defendants breach was a "substantial factor" in bringing about his or her injury. Assume that Pam proves that she runs a retail clothing store, that Dan promised to deliver winter coats to Pam by September 1, that the coats were not delivered until October 1, and that Pam's revenues for the month of September were down 40 percent from the previous year. Pam appears to have a strong case, but if evidence adduced at trial discloses that the street leading to Pam's store was under construction during the entire month of September so that it

was very difficult for customers even to reach Pam's store, and that other stores in the area also sustained lost revenue, a jury might conclude that Dan's delay was not a "substantial factor" in bringing about the plaintiff's loss.

2. *Reasonable Certainty.* Judges and juries should not have to speculate as to the amount of damages the plaintiff sustained that was due to the defendant's breach. Therefore, the plaintiff must establish losses with "reasonable certainty," a higher standard of proof than is demanded for other issues. This is often a problem in consequential damages, such as lost profits at a sports event.

Assume, for example, that Pete, a candidate for governor in a primary election, contracted to have D Newspaper Co. run one of his ads on the Sunday before election day. The newspaper failed to run the ad, and Pete lost the election. If Pete sued for the salary he would have received as governor, it would be pure speculation to conclude that the missing ad caused Pete to lose the primary election or that Pete would have won the general election had he succeeded in the primary. Therefore, a court probably would deny Pete's claim for these consequential damages.

While the law does not wish to compensate the plaintiff for losses that did not occur, at the same time persons who have breached their promises should not escape liability simply because the plaintiff cannot prove the amount of damages to the penny. For that reason, the law requires reasonable, not absolute, certainty. The UCC reflects the trend in the common law by requiring the plaintiff to prove damages not with mathematical certainty, but with "whatever definiteness and accuracy the facts permit, but no more" (Sec. 1–106, comment 1).

Courts often are less demanding of a plaintiff's proof where the defendant's breach was willful and in situations where precision of proof is inherently impossible (such as in calculation of loss to "goodwill"). Similarly, where a defendant's wrong has caused the difficulty in proof of damages, many courts hold that the defendant "shall not be heard to complain." In short, where the courts are certain that a breach has occurred and that the plaintiff has suffered a loss, they hesitate to deny recovery on grounds that the plaintiff has failed to establish the amount of damages to a reasonable certainty. On the other hand, where the evidence is not clear that a loss even occurred, the reasonable certainty requirement is more likely to bar recovery. An interesting illustration of these general rules follows.

SOLDANO V. O'DANIELS
California Court of Appeal, 190 Cal. Rptr. 310 (1983)

California Court of Appeals, 140 Cal.Rptr. 921 (1977)
Plaintiff John Ericson, in an attempt to boost his career as an actor, agreed that defendant

Playgirl, Inc., could publish without compensation as the centerfold of its January 1974 issue of Playgirl photographs of Ericson posing naked. No immediate career boost to Eric-

son resulted. In April 1974, defendant wished to use the pictures again for its annual edition entitled Best of Playgirl, a publication with half the circulation of Playgirl and without the advertising. Ericson agreed to a rerun of his pictures in Best of Playgirl on two conditions: that certain of them be cropped to more modest exposure, and that Ericson's photograph occupy a quarter of the front cover, which would contain photographs of five other persons on its remaining three—quarters. Defendant honored the first of these conditions but, due to an editorial mix—up, Ericson's photograph did not appear on the cover of Best of Playgirl. Ericson sued for breach of contract, seeking to recover for the loss of publicity he would have received had his picture appeared on the cover as agreed.

The trial court entered a $12,500 judgment on behalf of Ericson, based in large part on the testimony of an advertising manager for TV Guide who placed the value to an entertainer of an appearance on the cover of a national magazine at $50,000. (1/4 cover x $50,000 = $12,500.) Playgirl appealed.

Fleming, Acting Presiding Justice:

Damages must be clearly ascertainable and reasonably certain, both in their nature and origin. (Civ. Code, § 3301.)

Plaintiff's claim of damages for breach of contract was based entirely on the loss of general publicity he would have received by having his photograph appear, alongside those of five others, on the cover of *Best of Playgirl*. Plaintiff proved that advertising is expensive to buy, that publicity has value for an actor. But what he did not prove was that loss of publicity as the result of his non—appearance on the cover of *Best of Playgirl* did in fact damage him in any substantial way or in any specific amount. Plaintiffs claim sharply contrasts with those few breach of contract cases that have found damages for loss of publicity

reasonably certain and reasonably calculable, as in refusals to continue an advertising contract. In such cases the court has assessed damages at the market value of the advertising, less the agreed contract price. Plaintiffs claim for damages more closely resembles those which have been held speculative and conjectural, as in the analogous cases of Jones v. San Bernardino Real Estate Board (1959) 168 Cal.App.2d 661, 665, 336 P.2d 606 where the court declined to award purely conjectural damages for loss of commissions, contacts, business associations, and clientele allegedly occasioned by plaintiff s expulsion from a local realty board; and of Fisher v. Hampton(1975) 44 Cal.App.3d 741, 118 Cal.Rptr. 811, where the court rejected an award of damages for defendant's failure to drill a $35,000 oil well when geological reports opined that oil would not be found and no evidence whatever established that plaintiff had been damaged.

An examination of the cases allowing recovery of damages for loss of publicity as a result of breach of contract discloses that in each instance the lost publicity grew out of the loss of the artist's exercise of his profession, i.e., loss of the opportunity to act, to broadcast, to sing, to conduct an orchestra, to entertain; or resulted from the loss of credit to the artist for professional services connected with a particular work, i.e., a script, play, musical composition, design, production, and the like. Publicity in both these categories performs a similar function in that it permits patrons and producers to evaluate the artist's merits in connection with the performance of his art. Damages for the loss of such publicity do not present insuperable difficulties in calculation, for the artist's future earnings can be directly correlated to his box office appeal or to his known record of successes.

A yawning gulf exists between the cases that involve loss of professional publicity and the instant case in which plaintiff complains of loss of mere general publicity that bears no relation to the practice of his art. His situation is comparable to that of an actor who hopes to obtain wide publicity by cutting the ribbon for the opening of a new resort— hotel complex, by sponsoring a golf or tennis tournament, by presenting the winning trophy at the national horse show, or by acting as master of ceremonies at a televised political dinner. Each of these activities may generate wide publicity that conceivably could bring the artist to the attention of patrons and producers of his art and thus lead to professional employment. Yet none of it bears any relation to the practice of his art. Plaintiff's argument, in essence, is that for an actor all publicity is valuable, and the loss of any publicity as a result of breach of contract is compensable. Carried to this point, we think his claim for damages becomes wholly speculative. It is possible, as plaintiff suggests, that a television programmer might have seen his photograph on the cover of *Best of Playgirl*, might have scheduled plaintiff for a talk show, and that a motion picture producer viewing the talk show might recall plaintiffs past performances, and decide to offer him a role in his next production. But it is equally plausible to speculate that plaintiff might have been hurt professionally rather than helped by having his picture appear on the cover of *Best of Playgirl*, that a motion picture producer whose attention had been drawn by the cover of the magazine to its contents depicting plaintiff posing naked in Lion Country Safari might dismiss plaintiff from serious consideration for a role in his next production. The speculative and conjectural nature of such possibilities speaks for itself.

Assessment of the value of general publicity unrelated to professional performance takes us on a random walk whose destination is as unpredictable as the lottery and the roulette wheel. When, as at bench, damages to earning capacity and loss of professional publicity in the practice of one's art are not involved, we think recovery of compensable damages for loss of publicity is barred by the Civil Code requirement that damages for breach of contract be clearly foreseeable and clearly ascertainable.

Plaintiff, however, is entitled to recover nominal damages for breach of, contract. We evaluate plaintiff's right to nominal damages by analogy to Civil Code section 3344, which provides minimum statutory damages of $300 for knowing commercial use of a person's name or likeness without his consent.

The judgment is modified to reduce the amount of damages to $300, and, as so modified, the judgment is affirmed.

3. *Foreseeability.* Another important limitation on recovery of compensatory damages is that the loss sustained by the plaintiff should have been reasonably foreseeable to the defendant. Assume that Sam's Repair Shop promised to fix Al's car and deliver it to him on June 1. Sam was a day late, delivering the car on June 2. However, on June 1, Al had been bitten by a rabid dog and his injuries had been exacerbated because he had had no car with which to drive himself to the emergency room. The extra medical injuries (potential consequential damages) could not be compensated because the injury was not reasonably foreseeable to Sam.

The leading case in this area is Hadley v. Baxendale, 156 Eng.Rep. 145 (1854), where plaintiff's flour mill suffered a broken gear. Plaintiff hired defendant to transport the gear and its attached drive shaft to the manufacturer for repairs. Plaintiff told defendant that the gear was part of his milling machinery and that defendant should act promptly. Plaintiff did not, however, tell defendant that his entire mill would be shut down until the repairs were made. Defendant breached the contract by performing two days late. Plaintiff sued for the profits lost during this two-day period. The court held that it was not reasonably foreseeable to defendant that plaintiff's entire operation would be shut down for two days; therefore, the lost profits could not be recovered. In so ruling, the English court set forth two important rules. First, it held that a plaintiff can recover direct damages "as may fairly and reasonably be considered . . . arising naturally, i.e., according to the usual course of things" from the breach itself. Second, the court held that plaintiff may recover consequential damages "such as may reasonably be supposed to have been in the contemplation of both parties, at the time they made the contract, as the probable result of it." Thus, the court introduced reasonable foreseeability as an important aspect of recovery for consequential damages.

The following case applies these general rules of foreseeability.

KENFORD COMPANY, INC. V. COUNTY OF ERIE
Court of Appeals of New York, 540 N.Y.S.2d 1 (1989)

In May of 1968, the County of Erie adopted enabling legislation authorizing it to finance and construct a domed sports stadium in the vicinity of the City of Buffalo. Kenford Co., through its president and sole shareholder, Cottrell, had acquired options on various parcels of land. It offered to sell that land to the county for construction of the stadium; the county rejected the offer. Kenford then offered to donate to the county the land upon which the stadium was to be built, in exchange for which the county was to permit Cottrell and his associate Hofheinz (who together had formed the management company of Dome Stadium Inc. [DSI]) to lease or manage the proposed stadium.

In June 1969, the county adopted a resolution accepting this offer, after which the parties began contract negotiation. During this time, Kenford exercised the options to buy several parcels of land. The contract was signed requiring Kenford to donate 178 acres of land and the county to commence construction within 12 months. The county agreed to negotiate a 40-year lease with DSI under which the county was to receive revenues of not less than $63.75 million over the 40-year term, comprising (1) all tax revenues received by the county generated by operation of the stadium site; (2) rental payments from DSI; and (3) increased real property taxes resulting from increased assessments received from the "peripheral lands"—those lands near the stadium owned or to be acquired by Kenford.

When the county was unable to raise enough revenue to build the stadium, it adopted a resolution cancelling the contract with Kenford and DSI. DSI and Kenford sued for breach of contract and were awarded summary judgment on the issue of liability. A nine-month trial followed on the matter of damages. Appeals and a retrial followed. The matter then came before New York's highest court for review of a lower court judgment that Kenford was entitled to recover $6.5 million in lost appreciation in the value of its property located on the periphery of the stadium.

Mollen, Judge:

It is well established that in actions for breach of contract, the nonbreaching party may recover general damages which are the natural and probable consequence of the breach. "[I]n order to impose on the defaulting party a further liability than for damages [which] naturally and directly [flow from the breach], i.e., in the ordinary course of things, arising from a breach of contract, such unusual or extraordinary damages must have been brought within the contemplation of the parties as the probable result of a breach at the time of or prior to contracting." Chapman v. Fargo, 223 N.Y. 32, 36, 119 N.E. 76; see also, Booth v. Spayten Duyvil Rolling Mill Co., 60 N.Y. 487 Hadley v. Baxendale, 9 Exch 341, 156 Eng.Rep. 145; McCormick, Damages § 138, at 562). In determining the reasonable contemplation of the parties, the nature, purpose and particular circumstances of the contract known by the parties should be considered as well as "what liability the defendant fairly may be supposed to have assumed consciously, or to have warranted the plaintiff reasonably to suppose that it assumed, when the contract was made" (Globe Ref: Co. v Landa Cotton Oil Co., 190 U.S. 540)

In the case before us, it is beyond dispute that at the time the contract was executed, all parties thereto harbored an expectation and anticipation that the proposed domed stadium facility would bring about an economic boom in the County and would result in increased land values and increased property taxes.

We cannot conclude, however, that this hope or expectation of increased property values and taxes necessarily or logically leads to the conclusion that the parties contemplated that the County would assume liability for Kenford's loss of anticipated appreciation in the value of its peripheral lands if the stadium were not built.

Similarly, there is no provision in the contract between Kenford and the County, nor is there any evidence in the record to demonstrate that the parties, at any relevant time, reasonably contemplated or would have contemplated that the County was undertaking a contractual responsibility for the lack of

appreciation in the value of Kenford's peripheral lands in the event the stadium was not built. This conclusion is buttressed by the fact that Kenford was under no contractual obligation to the County to acquire or maintain ownership of any land surrounding the 178 acres it was required to donate to the County. Although the County was aware that Kenford had acquired and intended to further acquire peripheral lands, this knowledge, in and of itself, is insufficient, as a matter of law, to impose liability on the County for the loss of anticipated appreciation in the value of those lands since the County never contemplated at the time of the contract's execution that it assumed legal responsibility for these damages upon a breach of the contract. As this court noted in Booth v. Spayten Duyril Rolling Mill Co., 60 N.Y. 487, 494, supra) "bare notice of special consequences which might result from a breach of contract, unless under such circumstances as to imply that it formed the basis of the agreement, would not be sufficient [to impose liability for special damages]" (see also, Czarnikow Rionda Co. v. Federal Sugar Ref. Co.,255 N.Y. 33, 173 N.E. 913, supra [the defendant supplier of sugar was not made aware at the time of the contract that the plaintiff purchaser could not acquire sugar on the open market and, therefore, was not liable for the plaintiff s special damages arising out of the breach of contract]; Baldwin v. United States Tel. Co., 45 N.Y. 744, supra [the defendant telegraph company was not liable for special damages caused by delay in delivery of message since it was without notice or information indicating that extraordinary care or speed of delivery was necessary].

Thus, the constant refrain which flows throughout the legion of breach of contract cases dating back to the leading case of Hadley v. Baxendale provides that damages which may be recovered by a party for breach of contract are restricted to those damages which were reasonably foreseen or contemplated by the parties during their negotiations or at the time the contract was executed. The evident purpose of this well–accepted principle of contract law is to limit the liability for unassumed risks of one entering into a contract and, thus, diminish the risk of business enterprise. In the case before us, although Kenford obviously anticipated and expected that it would reap financial benefits from an anticipated dramatic increase in the value of its peripheral lands upon the completion of the proposed domed stadium facility, these expectations did not ripen or translate into cognizable breach of contract damages since there is no indication whatsoever that the County reasonably contemplated at any relevant time that it was to assume liability for Kenford's unfulfilled land appreciation expectations in the event that the stadium was not built.

[Reversed.]

If the plaintiff establishes causation, reasonable certainty, and foreseeability of loss, recovery often will be calculated according to the following formula:

Damages = Direct Loss + Consequential Loss + Incidental Loss – Cost Avoided – Loss Avoided.

Assume that P had a contract to sell a tract of land to D for $50,000. In order to induce D to make the deal, P also agreed to do $500 worth of grading on the tract and to sell to D a smaller lot for $5,000. The fair market value of the two tracts was $40,000 and $6,000, respectively. D breached his promise and cancelled the deal after P had done half of the grading. P hired a real estate agent who sold the larger tract to X for $40,000, taking an 8 percent commission. P's direct loss is $10,000 ($50,000 – $40,000), his consequential loss is $250 (the cost of grading), and his incidental loss is $3,200 (the real estate commission). At the same time, P had avoided a cost of $250 (the remainder of the grading) and avoided a loss of $1,000 (for sale of the smaller tract). Therefore, P's recovery would be $10,000 + $250 + $3,200 – $250 – $1,000 = $12,200.

Reliance Measure. If the law cannot compensate the plaintiff's expectation interest, perhaps because the plaintiff cannot establish with reasonable certainty the profit he would make on the transaction, the courts often protect the reliance interest instead.

Other situations where the reliance interest is compensated include cases where a contract is frustrated by impossibility of performance or where there has been partial performance of an oral contract that the statute of frauds required to be in writing.

Plaintiffs suing for the reliance interest are allowed to recover such items as expenses incurred in preparing to perform their part of the contract, expenses incurred in actually performing, and losses incurred due to forgone opportunities that they would have pursued absent the contract with the defendant.

Assume that defendant promises to deliver a model stove to plaintiff at a trade fair. Plaintiff plans to demonstrate the stove and take orders from customers. Defendant fails to deliver the stove in time for the fair. If plaintiff could prove with reasonable certainty the profits he would have made from demonstrating the stove, he can recover them under the expectation interest. However, this is likely to be too speculative to establish with reasonable certainty. Therefore, at the very least, the court can compensate plaintiff's reliance interest by making defendant pay the costs, such as rental of the space at the trade fair and of materials to construct a booth, that plaintiff incurred in reliance on defendant's promise.

Restitution Interest. Assume that in the trade fair case, the plaintiff had made an advance payment to the defendant of $400. Because the defendant did not perform, the plaintiff should recover that amount also. The defendant has received a benefit and the law requires the defendant to make restitution to the plaintiff. The key to restitution is "unjust enrichment"—the defendant should forfeit benefits he received from the plaintiff's performance in cases where the defendant did not do as he promised. The concept of restitution pervades the law of both legal and equitable remedies, and we shall return to it later in this chapter.

Mitigation of Damages

There is no reason for the law to compensate the plaintiff for losses arising from the defendant's breach that the plaintiff could reasonably have avoided. Therefore the mitigation of damages doctrine requires plaintiffs to take reasonable steps to minimize the accumulation of damages.

Once aware of the other party's breach, a potential plaintiff may not continue his activities so as to increase his damages. For example, assume that Deeco, Inc., hires Peeco, Inc., to build a parking garage. After Peeco has spent $10,000 in commencing performance, Deeco unequivocally tells Peeco that it no longer wants the parking garage built and will not pay for it. If Peeco continues to work on the garage, spending another $8,000, it clearly has failed to mitigate its damages. It may recover the first $10,000, but not the subsequent $8,000, which was clearly avoidable.

A party may even be obliged to take positive steps to minimize damages. For example, assume that Juanita has a five–year contract to work for Acme Corporation as a research chemist. After one year, Acme fires Juanita without cause. Juanita should not sit home for the next four years. If she does, passing up several opportunities to obtain comparable jobs at comparable pay, the law will not compensate her for her lost salary. Instead, the law places on Juanita the obligation to make reasonable efforts to find comparable work. She needs not take a job that does not utilize her education, nor need she move across the country in order to find a position. Reasonableness is the key. At the same time, any reasonable expenses Juanita incurs (e.g., hiring an employment agency) in attempting to mitigate her damages are compensable, even if ultimately unsuccessful.

The duty to mitigate is incorporated in Article 2 of the Uniform Commercial Code. When a buyer of goods breaches a contract, the seller is often obliged to make conscientious efforts to find another buyer for those goods. If the second buyer pays less, the seller may recover from the breaching party not only the difference in purchase price but also the incidental expenses incurred in finding a new buyer.

Although almost every party in every situation has a duty to mitigate, a majority of jurisdictions make an exception for landlords where a lease has been executed. They do not require the landlord to search for a new tenant when the current tenant breaches its lease by moving out and refusing to pay rent. Many jurisdictions, on the other hand, do not recognize this exception.

Consider one other wrinkle. Assume that Acme has contracted to rent a truck from We–Haul Leasing, Inc. Acme breaches, but points out to We–Haul that it can mitigate its damages by leasing the truck to the next customer that comes in needing a truck. However, if We–Haul has a different truck that it would have rented to that next customer, then it cannot effectively mitigate its damages. It could have had two rentals if Acme had lived up to its part of the lease. Therefore, We–Haul may recover from Acme.

The following case illustrates some important mitigation principles in the employment context.

Nominal Damages

Nominal damages are a form of compensatory damages given in a trivial amount (such as six cents or one dollar). It is appropriate to grant nominal damages, for example, where the plaintiff establishes a breach of contract but cannot prove his or her damages with reasonable certainty. Ericson v. Playgirl, Inc. is an example (although a special statute established a minimum recovery of $300).

KENFORD COMPANY, INC. v. COUNTY OF ERIE
Court of Appeals of New York, 540 N.Y.S.2d 1 (1989)

In 1974, plaintiff Stewart was a "permanent teacher" under the Teacher Tenure Act, having taught for 15 years in defendant school district. The Board of Education terminated plaintiff in June 1974. Plaintiff sued. After multiple trials and appeals, the termination was held to be wrongful and damages were assessed. However, the case was heard one more time by the trial court on the issue of mitigation of damages. Despite Stewart's statement that she had made no efforts to secure any type of teaching position during the five years that she was unemployed, the trial judge refused to reduce the damages it had assessed against the Board in the sum of $108,948.01. The Board appealed.

Simon, Judge:

. . . The Board contends that Stewart failed to use reasonable diligence to secure similar employment. In Wolf v. Missouri State Training School for Boys, 517 S.W.2d 138, 142-43 (Mo. banc 1974), our Supreme Court stated: "the employer . . . [may] reduce damages recoverable by a wrongfully discharged employee by whatever the employee has earned or by reasonable diligence could have earned during the period of wrongful discharge." *Wolf* involved a wrongfully discharged state corrections officer. Our court, following *Wolf* held that the doctrine of mitigation applies to wrongfully discharged teachers protected under the Teacher Tenure Act.

A great deal of confusion surrounds the doctrine of mitigation. While it is often stated that the employee has the "duty" to mitigate damages, this characterization is misleading. As Professor Corbin notes, "The law does not penalize . . . [plaintiffs] inaction; it merely does nothing to compensate . . . [plaintiff] for the loss that he helped to cause by not avoiding it." 5 Corbin on Contracts 5 1039 (1954). Thus, the doctrine of avoidable consequences is the basis for most rules of general damages. Missouri law is in clear agreement with that of the overwhelming majority of jurisdictions to the effect that the Board has the burden of proving that Stewart could have mitigated her damages.

Furthermore, McCormick states "It is not enough for the employer to prove that the plaintiff made no effort to get other employment, but he must go further and prove that such employment could have been secured." McCormick, Damages 628 (1975 reprint).

In Ryan v. Superintendent of Schools of Quincy, 374 Mass. 670, 373 N.E.2d 1178, 1181 (1978), the Massachusetts Supreme Court outlined the defendant's burden:

A former employer meets its burden of proof of 'mitigation of damages' if the employer proves that (a) one or more discoverable opportunities for comparable employment were available in a location as, or more convenient than, the place of former employment, (b) the improperly discharged employee unreasonably made no attempt to apply for any such job, and (c) it was reasonably likely that the former employee would obtain one of those comparable jobs.

In *Ryan*, defendant school committee wrongfully discharged plaintiff Ryan, a fifty-nine year old art teacher. After winning reinstatement, Ryan sought damages in the form of back pay. As in the case at bar, Ryan did not apply for any teaching positions during the five years of her unemployment. The court stated that "[t]his fact alone . . . is not sufficient to establish that the employee could have mitigated damages."

The court proceeded to examine the facts of the case to determine whether "it was reasonably likely that Ryan could have obtained a comparable job." *Id*. The court noted that the facts indicated that during the period in question the number of art teachers greatly exceeded demand. The court also noted that Ryan would not have been able to get favorable references from her former employer. Finally, the court concluded that Ryan's age would probably have been viewed unfavorably by any prospective employers. On these facts the court held that "the defendants did not sustain their burden of proving that it was 'reasonably likely that the former employee would obtain one of . . . [the] comparable jobs'."

Likewise, we do not believe that the Board met their burden of proof. The evidence introduced at trial reveals that there were teaching jobs available in the St. Louis area during Stewart's period of unemployment for which she was qualified. The Board presented three witnesses who were in charge of hiring teaching personnel in different metropolitan school districts. They testified that in every year from 1974 to 1979, each of their districts hired from zero to 27 teachers in Stewart's subject area. Generally, the number of applicants exceeded the number of vacancies. For example, Dr. BurchardNeel, Associate Superintendent for Personnel for the St. Louis Public Schools, testified that in 1976 when the St. Louis Public Schools hired 27 teachers there were several hundred applicants. The witnesses further testified that from 1974 to 1979 none of their districts had hired a teacher in Stewarts age bracket, with Stewart's qualifications, who had been discharged from another district. None of the evidence indicated that there was a reasonable likelihood that Stewart could have received a teaching position. In fact, the evidence indicated that Stewart's chances of finding a teaching job were slim at best.

Dr. Ellen Harshman, Director of Career Planning and Placement at St.Louis University, testified that a person in Stewart's position would have "very poor" possibilities. Viewing the record in its entirety, we conclude that the Board did not meet its burden of proof to constitute our approval of a discharged employee's reaping a "reward" as a consequence of her failure to make a reasonable effort to mitigate her damages. Our holding is simply a result of the Board's failure to carry its burden of proof, i.e., of showing there was a reasonable likelihood that Stewart could have obtained one of the available positions. Therefore, we affirm the trial court's decision that Stewart's recovery should not be reduced for her failure to mitigate.

Nominal damages are also appropriate to remedy a technical breach of contract in situations where the plaintiff did not suffer any injury. Assume that P contracts to sell a tract of land to D for $50,000. D breaches, refusing to pay anything, and P sues. Before the suit progresses very far, a new buyer appears and pays P $70,000 for the land. P has not suffered any injury from D's breach. Still, D has breached a promise and the court will, as a matter of principle, allow P to recover nominal damages. In addition to the principle at stake, P is now the prevailing party in the lawsuit, making D responsible for paying court costs (but usually not attorney's fees) in many jurisdictions. (Other jurisdictions do not allow the plaintiff to recover court costs unless a specified minimum amount has been recovered. Such statutes are aimed at discouraging litigation over valid but trivial claims.)

Liquidated Damages

A **liquidated damages** provision is a clause in a contract that stipulates the amount of damages that will be paid in the event of a breach. Such a clause has several purposes. It may avoid a protracted dispute and trial on the issue of damages. This will lower the parties' costs of proof and society's cost of providing a judge and jury. Such a clause may diminish the losses of the defaulting party or, conversely, establish a minimum level of recovery from the nondefaulting party in a case where losses may well be speculative. It allows both parties to better calculate their level of risk in a given transaction.

Courts generally wish to enforce contracts as made by the parties, but they do tend to be leery of liquidated damages clauses, mostly out of a fear that such clauses may be used as a "penalty" to unfairly punish or coerce one of the parties. Typically, courts set forth three criteria for an enforceable liquidated damages clause. First, the injury arising from the breach must be difficult or impossible to estimate accurately. If the amount of damages arising from a breach is easy to determine, a liquidated damages clause does not save trial time and expense and therefore loses much of its justification. Second, the parties must intend for the clause to provide a remedy for the injured party, not a penalty for the defaulting party. This relates back to the notion that part of the freedom of contract is the freedom to breach a contract.

In virtually every case involving the enforceability of a liquidated damages clause, the focus of the court becomes the third criterion—whether the amount established as liquidated damages is a *reasonable* estimate of the actual loss caused by the subsequent breach. The courts will not enforce a clause that sets an amount so far above the true damages sustained that it constitutes a "penalty" imposed on the defendant rather than legitimate compensation for the plaintiffs loss. The reasonableness of the estimate is judged as of the time the contract is entered into, although UCC 2- 718(1) allows amounts that are reasonable considering anticipated *or* actual harm. (Indeed, even under the common law if the estimate turns out to be wildly inaccurate as a gauge of the actual damages, even if it seemed reasonable when the contract was made, the courts are unlikely to enforce it.)

THE LAW AT WORK

Box 19.1 The Law at Work

The general rule in contract law is that punitive damages are not recoverable in breach-of-contract actions, even if the defendant intentionally refused to perform his or her promise. However, several jurisdictions do allow recovery of punitive damages when they find that the breach constitutes an independent intentional tort or an independent breach of fiduciary duty. These exceptions have been invoked increasingly in recent years to benefit consumers who have been mistreated by businesses. For example, many jurisdictions recognize that an insurance company's intentional refusal to pay an insured's valid claim may constitute not only a breach of contract, but also an intentional tort often called the bad faith tort. Such jurisdictions allow plaintiffs to recover punitive damages in amounts that often dwarf the sum due under the policy.

Although the rationale underlying the bad faith tort seemingly applies to a wide range of situations, most courts have been reluctant to extend their holdings beyond the insurance context. Indeed, courts and academics have struggled with the theory underlying this combination of contract law and tort law, sometimes denominated a contort.

Consider two California cases. In the 1984 case Seaman's Direct Buying Service v. Standard Oil Co., 206 Cal.Rptr. 354(1984), the California Supreme Court expanded the bad faith tort in a lawsuit in which a would-be oil dealer sued an oil company that breached a contract to supply oil. The court stated that the bad faith tort should be available where defendant "in addition to breaching the contract, . . .seeks to shield itself from liability by denying, in bad faith and without probable cause, that the contract exists." However, just four years later in Foley v. Interactive Data Co., 254 Cal.Rptr. 211(1988), the court refused to apply the bad faith tort to an employee's suit against an employer for wrongful discharge, criticizing the "uncritical incorporation" by some lower California courts "of the insurance model into the employment context, without careful consideration of the fundamental policies underlying the development of tort and contract law in general or of significant differences between the insurer/insured and employer/employee relationship."

If an employer wrongfully fires an employee and then claims in bad faith and without probable cause that no contract exists, should the bad faith tort apply? Most courts would say "no," relegating the plaintiff to simple breach of contract damages. Do you agree with this approach? Do you see principled distinctions between this situation and the insurance scenario?

Whether a liquidated damages clause is an unenforceable penalty provision is a matter of law for the judge to decide. The labels used by the parties in the contract do not control. In U.S. v. Bethlehem Steel Co., 205 U.S. 105 (1907), because of a promise for early delivery, the government agreed to buy guns from defendant even though its bid was higher than those of competitors. The contract provided that for each day defendant's delivery was late, a "penalty" of $35 would be imposed. Because this sum represented the average difference in price between defendant's bid and those of the cheaper, but slower, suppliers, it was enforced as a genuine attempt to gauge the government's actual damages.

One form of liquidated damages clause that is almost always enforced is that calling for the breaching party to pay the attorney's fees of the nondefaulting party who is forced to bring a lawsuit.

UNITED AIR LINES, INC. V. AUSTIN TRAVEL CORP.
U.S. Second Circuit Court of Appeals, 867 F.2d 737 (1989)

Plaintiff United Air Lines owns and markets to travel agents the Apollo CRS, a computerized reservation system that provides subscribers access to a vast data bank through which they may make airline reservations, issue tickets, and reserve car rentals and hotel rooms. United is paid a monthly subscription fee and charges airlines a booking fee each time a travel agent uses Apollo to book a flight on another airline. United also markets its ABS, a back-office accounting and management system for travel agents.

Defendant Austin is a travel agency that formerly used a different CRS. However, in 1985 it acquired two small travel agencies (Karson and Fantasy) that subscribed to Apollo. Austin assumed their contracts with United and then executed a five-year Apollo contract to cover its Oceanside and Mitchell Field locations. The contract for Oceanside and Mitchell Field provided for liquidated damages consisting of (1) 80 percent of the remaining monthly fees due under the contract, (2) 80 percent of the
variable charges accrued by generation of tickets and itineraries for the month preceding termination, multiplied by the number of months remaining on the contract, and (3) 50 percent of the average monthly booking fee revenues, using the first six months of the contract as a basis for calculation, multiplied by the number of months remaining on the contract. The Fantasy contract contained only the first two elements of liquidated damages.

Austin breached the agreement when one of United's rivals offered to indemnify Austin for any damages incurred for breach if it would terminate the Apollo contracts and buy the rival's system. United brought this breach of contract action. The trial judge held for United, ruling, most importantly, that the liquidated damages clauses were valid and enforceable. Austin appealed.

Miner, Circuit Judge:
It is commonplace for contracting parties to determine in advance the amount of

compensation due in case of a breach of contract. 5 Corbin on Contracts § 1054, at 319 (1964). A liquidated damages clause generally will be upheld by a court, unless the liquidated amount is a penalty because it is plainly or grossly disproportionate to the probable loss anticipated when the contract was executed. Liquidated damages are not penalties if they bear a "reasonable proportion to the probable loss and the amount of actual loss is incapable or difficult of precise estimation." Leasing Service Corp v. Justice, 673 F.2d 70, 73 (2d Cir.1982).

The liquidated damages fixed in the Apollo contracts were, as the district court found, reasonable at the time the contracts were executed. Most of United's costs when providing Apollo service are either fixed or determined in the early stages of the contractual relationship. The few costs that United would avoid by an early termination of an Apollo contract are estimated to be "less than 20 percent of the amount of revenue from the monthly fixed usage fees and variable charges." The Apollo contracts' liquidated damages clauses provide for recovery by United of only 80% of the fixed and variable charges. Austin is thus provided with better than adequate credit for the costs United is able to avoid by the early removal of the Apollo CRSs from Austin premises.

Austin complains that the 20% discount incorporated by the liquidated damages provisions underestimates the savings realized by United in the event of early contract termination. Austin points to testimony by a representative of a competing CRS vendor that United's avoidable costs likely equal forty to fifty percent of United's total costs. The testimony of a competitor about United's costs and savings is inherently suspect, and United presented sufficient evidence to justify the 20% figure. The appropriate analysis is not whether a better quantification of damages could have been drafted by the contracting parties, but whether the amount of liquidated damages actually inserted in the contract is reasonable. We note as well, as the district court did, that CRS contracts of United's competitors often call for 100% of rent due on the unexpired term of the contract; United obligated Austin for only 80%. There is no indication that the estimate of probable loss, identified in the contracts as liquidated damages, is either unfair or unreasonable. Indeed, the liquidated damages provisions edge closer toward over–generousness to Austin than they do toward unreasonableness.

Austin further depicts the liquidated damages clauses as imposing penalties because they provide the same amount of damages for each possible breach of the contract, no matter how insignificant. Austin argues that establishing a single liquidated damages amount for any breach indicates that a fair estimation of probable loss for each breach was not conceived when the contract was drafted and executed.

Austin, however, ignores basic tenets of contract law. "A party may terminate a contract only because of substantial nonperformance by the other party so fundamental 'as to defeat the objects of the parties in making the agreement'." Maywood Sportservice, Inc. v. Maywood Park Trotting Ass'n, Inc., 14 Ill.App.3d 141, 302 N.E.2d 79, 84 (1973). Neither United nor Austin can terminate the contracts because of a non–material breach. Thus, liquidated damages can only be owed to United in the event of a material breach by Austin.

Furthermore, the presumed intent of the parties is that a liquidated damages provision will apply only to material breaches. Additionally, for a non–material breach to allow an aggrieved party to abrogate the contract it must be explicitly stated in the agreement of the parties. We are not persuaded that the liquidated damages outlined in the Apollo contracts were meant to apply to trivial breaches. Article 12 of the Lease Agreement states in unexceptional language that liquidated damages are to be awarded for a failure of "any of the covenants, agreements, terms or conditions." We take this language to refer to material breach. Absent a more explicit dem-onstration of intent to apply the termination provisions to trivial breaches, the liquidated damages clauses must be enforced.

[Affirmed.]

Equitable Remedies

Courts of equity developed in England because the early courts at law could give only one form of remedy—money damages. In other words, they could award a landowner damages caused by a neighbor's trespassing, but could not order the neighbor not to trespass again in the future. Courts of equity developed in large part to provide more flexible forms of remedy in situations where fairness seemed to demand them. Several forms of equitable remedy are available to the party injured by breach of contract. Whereas damages are generally assessed by juries, equitable remedies are within the province of the court and are enforced through the court's authority to hold in contempt persons who violate its orders.

Specific Performance

When a plaintiff asks the court for an order of **specific performance,** he or she is asking the judge to order the defendant to perform the promise that was made. Obviously there may be many instances where specific performance is a remedy that a plaintiff would prefer. If the judge orders specific performance, the plaintiff receives exactly what was bargained for and need not worry about collecting a money judgment or searching for someone to provide substitute performance.

Nonetheless, the courts presume that an award of money damages is the primary remedy in breach–of– contract cases. Specific performance is reserved for the "extraor-dinary" cases where money damages are inadequate to fully compensate the plaintiff. Specific performance is most frequently ordered when "unique" property is at stake, so that an award of money damages would not fully compensate the plaintiff who could not take the money anywhere to buy the item originally contracted for. Assume, for example, that plaintiff contracted to buy a secret recipe from defendant. If defendant breached its promise to deliver the recipe, an award of damages to plaintiff would not enable plaintiff to obtain the recipe elsewhere, because it remains defendant's trade secret.

Other items often held to be "unique" include rare books and coins, family heir-looms, priceless works of art, items in extremely short supply, patents, copyrights, and shares of closely held corporations which cannot be bought through any market or stockbroker. For historical reasons, courts view every tract of land as unique (even though it may be the same size and have the same characteristics as a tract adjacent to it). Therefore, contracts to sell real property are always enforceable through orders of specific performance. The same may be said of contracts to sell businesses, for these are also presumed to be unique.

Courts will often specifically enforce contracts against *insolvent* defendants, because an award of money damages against a defendant who cannot pay is certainly not adequate compensation. (Conflicts with the priorities given creditors under the bankruptcy laws must be avoided, however.) Specific performance is often granted in cases where the plaintiffs monetary damages are difficult to measure with reasonable certainty; absent specific performance, the plaintiff might be relegated to mere nominal damages.

Limitations. There are several factors that limit the availability of the specific performance remedy. First and foremost, specific performance is available only within the *discretion* of a court of equity. In attempting to achieve fairness and equity, courts must consider such factors as hardship to the defendant and impact on societal interests.

Additionally, courts consider traditional equitable rules such as the "clean hands" doctrine (no equitable remedy will be granted to a plaintiff who has breached his or her obligations in any material way), the doctrine of unconscionability (the courts will not be a party to enforcing an extremely one–sided bargain), and the doctrine of laches (no remedy for a party who has "slept on his rights" by unduly delaying the bringing of suit). Obviously courts will not order specific performance in contracts that involve illegality, mistake, or fraud.

Specific performance will not be granted in *personal service contracts*. Assume that Sally hires Waldo to paint her portrait because he is the best-known portrait artist in the state and Sally's personal favorite. If Waldo refuses to live up to his obligations the court might allow Sally to recover damages, but would not order specific performance. One reason often given is that it would violate the Thirteenth Amendment's proscription against involuntary servitude to force Waldo to paint against his will. A more plausible policy ground is the *difficulty of supervision* involved. How could a court effectively enforce Waldo's obligation? How could it supervise him to ensure that he did a "good job"? A court can transfer title to land, but it cannot paint for Waldo or sing for a reluctant rock star. For the same reason, courts often refuse to order specific performance in long–term contracts that might require them to undertake years of supervision.

Specific performance and damages are normally thought of as alternative forms of remedies. However, a plaintiff might be able to obtain both in the same case, especially if a court could feasibly order only partial performance by the defendant.

UCC. If there has been any trend in the common law of specific performance in recent years, it has been to soften the "adequacy" of remedy test, thereby increasing the availability of specific performance. That trend is reflected in UCC 2-716, which authorizes specific performance in sale–of– goods contracts "where the goods are unique or in *other proper circumstances*." [Emphasis added.] Still, even under the UCC, specific performance remains an "extraordinary" remedy.

Injunction

Assume that Chuck, a football coach, has a five–year contract with the Armadillos, an NFL franchise. In the second year of the contract, Chuck is offered a much more lucrative deal by Big State University and announces that he is accepting it. Obviously the Armadillos will wish to force Chuck to live up to his contract. Just as obviously, no court would order Chuck to specifically perform that contract. In addition to the "involuntary servitude" consideration, there is the difficulty of supervision. How could a court ensure that Chuck hired the right assistants, kept the best players, or called the appropriate plays? However, while a court could not feasibly order Chuck to do what he had promised to do (coach the Armadillos), it could order him not to do what he had promised not to do (coach Big State U). By signing a full–time contract with the Armadillos, Chuck had implicitly promised not to take any conflicting obligations. Such an order is called an **injunction.**

As with orders of specific performance, injunctive orders are within the court's equitable discretion. Courts will consider factors of fairness, unconscionability, and the plaintiff's "clean hands" in deciding whether to issue such orders. Injunctions are often used in cases involving sports and entertainment, and in normal employment relationships when a party seeks to enforce a covenant not to compete signed by a former employee. We studied the enforceability of these covenants in Chapter 14.

Reformation

Assume that Sharon and Nick reach an oral agreement that Nick's attorney reduces to writing. After the contract is signed, Sharon realizes that because of the attorney's error, the writing does not accurately reflect the oral agreement. Sharon may ask a court for an order of **reformation.** In effect, Sharon is asking the court to rewrite the contract, but only for the limited purpose of enforcing its true terms. The court is not making a new contract, but simply enforcing the parties' agreement as made. Sharon should have read the contract before she signed it, but if she can prove that an error has caused a discrepancy between the oral agreement and the written contract, her negligence would not bar reformation in most courts.

The parol evidence rule (see Chapter 16), which prevents introduction of oral testimony to vary the terms of a written contract, would not block Sharon's efforts in this case. It applies only when the writing was intended to be the final and complete statement of the parties' agreement. Most courts conclude that such is not the case where an error in reducing the oral agreement to writing has occurred.

However, the statute of frauds (see Chapter 16, again) does pose serious problems. What if the agreement is the type that the statute of frauds requires to be in writing? Is Sharon asking the court to enforce an oral agreement in contravention of the statute of frauds? Some courts think that this is exactly what she is asking, and will refuse reformation. Other courts reason that they are simply correcting the mistaken written agreement, and will grant reformation.

In relatively rare instances, some courts will reform contracts not to enforce the parties' original agreement, but to modify that original agreement to conform to the law. For example, we learned in Chapter 14 that if a covenant not to compete is drawn too broadly, many courts will rewrite it to cover a smaller geographic area or a shorter time span and will then enforce the modified version.

Rescission

An order of **rescission** is a court order terminating the contractual duties of each party. Usually (but not always) such an order will also allow each party to obtain restitution for any performance rendered to the other party.

Rescission is granted as a remedy in a wide variety of contracts, including those involving voidable agreements (e.g., fraud, mistake, undue influence, innocent misrepresentation, or parties lacking capacity) and those involving illegal activity.

Restitution

An order of **restitution** seeks to place a party in the position he or she was in before the contract was entered into. As noted earlier in this chapter, sometimes such an order will take the form of a damages award telling the defendant to pay the plaintiff the monetary value of the benefit the plaintiff conferred on the defendant. But the notion of restitution is very broad. It can also include an equitable order for the defendant to return specific property that the plaintiff transferred to the defendant pursuant to the agreement that the defendant has breached or the court is rescinding (on grounds of mistake, indefiniteness, lack of capacity, statute of frauds violation, etc.).

Assume, for example, that plaintiff transferred a cow to defendant, both parties believing that the cow was barren but having since discovered that the cow was pregnant at the time of the contract (see mistake cases, Chapter 15). Plaintiff will ask the judge for rescission and for an order of specific restitution, requiring defendant to return the cow. Courts are generally willing to grant restitution in mistake cases (unless defendant has already transferred the cow to an innocent third party). However, had this been a breach case where no mistake was made but the defendant simply failed to pay the purchase price, most courts would refuse to issue an order of rescission, reasoning that money damages would adequately compensate the plaintiff.

Restitution, generally speaking, is used not to enforce promises, but to prevent unjust enrichment by returning the parties to their precontract positions following rescission or breach.

Part III Begins By briefly surveying the subjects of sales law and products liability. Chapter 20 contains a brief introduction to sales law, which governs the sale of goods. This law is provided in most states by Article 2 of the Uniform Commercial Code. The chapter also mentions some related commercial law topics, such as Article 2A's provisions for leases of goods.Chapter 21 covers the important topic ofproducts liability. Much, but not all of the law governing products liability is contained in Article 2 of the UCC.-Chapter 22 concludes Part III by surveying the various methods for dealing with unpaid debts and then focusing on bankruptcy proceedings under federal law.

PART **III**

SALES, COMMERCIAL TRANSACTIONS, AND BANKRUPTCY

CHAPTER **20**

INTRODUCTION TO THE LAW OF SALES

- Scope of Article 2 of the Ucc
- Review of Basic Principles of Sales Contracts
- Documents of Title

A COLLEGE STUDENT PURCHASES a television. A home owner buys several cans of house paint. A manufacturer of tires purchases raw rubber, sulphur, and other materials and ultimately sells tires to automobile owners. A mining company sells coal to an electric utility company. All of the above have at least two things in common. First, they are quite ordinary transactions, occurring countless numbers of times. Second, they involve sales of goods. Thus we can hardly question the relevance of studying the law of sales.

The principles governing sales of goods do not exist in a vacuum. Indeed, Article 2 of the UCC, which provides the legal rules for contracts selling goods, is closely related to the common law which governs other types of contracts. Thus, in Part II's discussion of general contract law (Chapters 11-19), we have already noted pertinent instances where the UCC altered the common law in order to facilitate commercial transactions in goods. (These concepts are briefly recapitulated later in this chapter.) In Chapters 20-21, we will explore in more detail the law governing the sale of goods. In so doing, we will also treat a few closely related matters, such as for example, the law regarding leases of goods and another subject known as *documents of title*.

Scope of Article 2 of the Ucc

Article 2 of the UCC deals with the sale of goods. It forms the basis for most of the following discussion of the law of sales.

Sales

A **sale** is defined in Sec. 2–106 of the UCC as "the passing of title from the seller to the buyer for a price." Thus Article 2 does not apply to leases—such as the lease of an automobile—or to other types of bailments—such as the storage of furniture in a warehouse—because only temporary possession of the goods (rather than title) is transferred in these transactions. Neither does Article 2 apply to gifts, because no price is paid. (The section on documents of title later in this chapter briefly discusses bailments,) A barter transaction (i.e, the trading of goods for other goods or services without the exchange of money) would be within the scope of Article 2.

Goods

In the majority of cases there is no problem ascertaining whether the subject matter should be classified as **goods**. Occasionally, however, the term may present problems. Essentially, two requirements must be met before a particular item of property is classified as a good:

1. It must be *tangible*. In other words, it must have a physical existence. Thus intangible property such as a patent, copyright, trademark, investment security, or contract right would not come within the scope of Article 2.
2. It must be *movable*. This requirement obviously excludes real estate, which is tangible but not movable. (Of course, almost anything, even real estate, is capable of

being moved, shovel by shovel, if enough effort is expended. But the word is intended reasonably rather than literally.)

Using these two requirements we can easily envision the wide variety of products that are classified as goods, from airplanes to toothpaste.

Should things that are attached to real estate be considered goods? Because of the movability requirement this question would involve considerable conceptual difficulty were it not for Sec. 2–107 of the UCC, which sets forth the following basic rules:

1. A contract for the sale of *minerals or a structure* (such as a building or its materials) is a contract for the sale of goods if they are to be severed from the land by the *seller.* If, however, they are to be severed from the land by the *buyer,* the transaction is a sale of real estate and is governed by the principles of real estate law rather than by the UCC. Two examples may be of some help. First, suppose that S and B agree that S will sell to B a quantity of gravel to be taken from beneath the surface of land owned by S. If their agreement states that S will dig and remove the gravel, the transaction is a sale of goods. If, on the other hand, B is to dig and remove the gravel, the transaction is a sale of real estate. Second, suppose that S and B agree that S will sell to B a storage building (or perhaps the lumber from the building) located on land owned by S. If their agreement indicates that B will remove the building from the land, the transaction is a sale of real estate. If removal is to be by S, it is a sale of goods.

2. A contract for the sale of *growing crops or timber* is a contract for the sale of goods, regardless of who is to sever them from the land.

3. A contract for the sale of *anything else attached to real estate* is a sale of goods if it can be severed *without material harm* to the real estate. This rule is, perhaps, not as important as the two rules just discussed, simply because most of the problems regarding things attached to real estate have involved minerals, structures, timber, or growing crops. Situations might exist, however, where this third rule would be pertinent. For example: X and Y agree that X will sell to Y a window air conditioner that is now attached to X's home. (We are assuming it is attached, for otherwise the question would never arise—it would obviously be a sale of goods.) The air conditioner is bolted to a metal shelf supported by braces that are secured to the side of the house by bolts. It is fairly evident that the air conditioner can be removed without material harm to the real estate. Suppose, however, that the subject of the sale is a floor furnace. In this case a gaping hole in the floor would result. This might be a material harm, causing the sale to be treated as a sale of real estate rather than goods.

The rules regarding sales of goods attached to real estate apply to those contracts under which the items are being sold apart from the land. However, if two parties agree that one will sell a tract of land to the other, including a building or some timber located on the land, the sale is treated as a sale of real estate.

The UCC also gives special attention to three other potential problems of classification. It provides that (1) unborn animals are goods; (2) money treated as a commodity, such as a rare coin, is a good (though money used as a medium of exchange is not); and (3) things that are specially manufactured for the buyer are goods. Although item 3 seems clear—cut, the framers of Article 2 felt that such a sale might be seen as predominantly a sale of services rather than goods and therefore stated it definitely.

Sales of services (such as employment contracts) are obviously not within the scope of Article 2. However, as we saw in item 3, goods and services sometimes are so entwined that classification is no easy task. For example, when a hospital supplies blood to a patient, is the hospital selling a good or supplying a service? When a beautician applies hair dye to a customer's hair in a beauty parlor, is it a contract for goods or services? In such contracts involving both goods and services, most courts attempt to determine whether the *predominant factor, thrust, and purpose* of the transaction as a whole is that of selling a good or supplying a service. This determination often turns on the intent of the buyer, as gauged by several factors, including the relative dollar value involved.

For example, in De Filippo v. Ford Motor Co., 516 F.2d 1313 (3d Cir. 1975), the court held that the sale of a car dealership, which included sales of items that were clearly goods (e.g., cars, parts, and accessories) as well as items that clearly were intangible and therefore not goods (e.g., goodwill, notes receivable, and used car warranties), was predominantly a sale of goods because the contract's terms assigned little dollar value to the intangible items. The court refused to split the contract into two parts, applying the UCC to one portion but not to the other.

And in Grossman v. Aerial Farm Service, Inc., 384 N.W.2d 488 (Minn.App. 1986), the court held that a contract for the aerial spraying of a herbicide on a farm was predominantly a contract for services because the farmers could have applied the herbicide through several methods of ground spraying, but chose a method of application that could only be performed by a contractor equipped to handle their specific request. Thus, the farmers' selection of this type of service gave the contract its predominant character.

The UCC does provide in Section 2–314(1) that food sold in restaurants is a sale of goods (at least as far as creation of the implied warranty of merchantability is concerned), although an argument could be made that the predominant reason a person dines out is the service. The following case illustrates how tricky these issues can be.

MICRO-MANAGERS, INC. v. GREGORY
Court of Appeals of Wisconsin, 434 N.W.2d 97 (1988)

Stanley Gregory was hired to develop a new programmable controller for a manufacturing firm. Gregory contacted Micro–Managers, Inc. (MMI), which indicated an interest in designing and developing the software required for the controller. After some negotiation, MMI drafted a letter incorporating what it believed to be its working arrangement with Gregory. The letter provided that "all MMI time will be billed by MMI at a rate of $40/hour for software, $50/hour for engineering, and $75/hour for *supervision. Direct expenses will be billed as charged MMI."*

After MMI delivered the software, Gregory complained that it was unsatisfactory. During litigation that resulted, the question arose as to whether MMI had breached an implied warranty which depended, in turn, upon whether this was a contract for "goods" governed by the UCC. The trial court held for MMI, ruling that Article 2 did not govern the contract and therefore there was no implied warranty to be breached. Gregory appealed.

Dykman, Judge:

It is undisputed that this was a mixed contract, i.e., a contract for both goods and services. The issue is whether the mixed contract was predominantly for goods or for services.

"The test for inclusion or exclusion [within the U.C.C.] is not whether [contracts] are mixed, but, granting that they are mixed, whether their predominant factor, their thrust, their purpose, reasonably stated, is the rendition of service, with goods incidentally involved (e.g., contract with artist for painting) or is a transaction of sale, with labor incidentally involved (e.g., installation of a water heater in a bathroom)."

Bonebrake v. Cox, 499 F.2d 951, 960 (8th Cir. 1975).

[W]e conclude that Data Processing v. L.H. Smith Oil Corp., 492 N.E.2d 314 (Ind. App. 1986) is on point and more compelling [than cases cited by Gregory]. In that case, as here, the parties contracted for custom computer programming. The trial court had reasoned that the contract was for the development and delivery of a "program," which it concluded was a specially manufactured good covered by U.C.C. warranty provisions. The appellate court phrased the issue as "whether a contract to provide computer programming is a contract for the sale and purchase of goods and thus subject to the provisions of Article 2 of the UCC, or one for the performance of services, and thus subject to common law principles." The court noted that "DPS was to act with specific regard to Smith's need. Smith bargained for DPS's skill in developing a system to meet its specific needs." The court concluded that the "mere means by which DPS's skills and knowledge were to be transmitted to Smith's computers was incidental."

In the present case, the contract provided that all MMI charges to Gregory would be on the basis of time, at stated rates, and materials. Under *Bonebrake*, we must determine whether the contract's predominant factor, thrust and purpose is the rendition of a service or the transaction of a sale. We may look to evidence of billing to determine this issue. On January 18, 1983, TerryColeman, an agent for Gregory, wrote the following in a letter to SallyPeterson, president of MMI: "3. The projected total, excluding bonus, is therefore approximately $59,828, of which $55,968 is labor." In addition, we may look to the language of the contract to determine whether it is more in accord with services instead of sales. The contract speaks in terms of "man–days," "development," "time," "design," etc. These words connote the rendition of services and not a sales transaction.

Based on this evidence, we conclude that this was primarily a service contract. The method by which MMI transmitted that service was merely incidental. Therefore the transaction is not subject to the provisions of the U.C.C.

[Affirmed.]

Merchants

For the most part, Article 2 applies to all sales contracts, even those in which neither the seller nor the buyer is a merchant. However, a few provisions of Article 2 do require one or both of the parties to be merchants in order for such provisions to be applicable. For this reason, we will now examine the UCC definition of a **merchant.**

Most people who see the word *merchant* probably think of someone engaged in the retail grocery business, the retail clothing business, or similar endeavors. While such people (or corporations) are indeed merchants, the UCC definition includes many others as well.

Sec. 2–104 of the UCC details three different ways in which a person or organization can be considered a merchant.

1. One who "deals in goods of the kind" that are involved under the particular contract in question is a merchant; thus, not only retailers but also wholesalers and even manufacturers are merchants. A party is considered a merchant, however, only for the types of goods dealt with regularly in his or her business. That is, a merchant in one type of goods is not a merchant for all purposes. Thus a retail shoe seller is a merchant with respect to transactions involving the purchase or sale of shoes. But if that person buys a new car or sells a secondhand lawn mower, he or she is not a merchant in those transactions.

2. Even if a person does not regularly "deal" in a particular type of goods, he is nevertheless a merchant if he "by his occupation holds himself out as having knowledge or skill peculiar to the practices or goods involved in the transaction." While most persons who fall within this provision are also merchants under the first provision by dealing in the particular goods, there are a few who do not really deal in goods but who are merchants within this second category. For example, if we assume that the word deal means "to buy and sell goods," a building contractor does not actually deal in goods. He buys building materials but does not resell them; instead he uses them in the performance of a service—constructing a building. However, he does, by his occupation, hold himself out as having "knowledge or skill peculiar to the practices or goods" involved in certain transactions and thereby is a merchant by definition. Of course, his status is irrelevant in any agreement to construct a building, because that agreement is essentially for services and not within the scope of Article 2. But his status as a merchant can be important with respect to a dispute arising from the sale contract between him and his materials supplier.

3. If a party is not a merchant under either of the first two categories, he or she may nevertheless be treated as one by *employing a merchant* to act in his or her behalf in a particular transaction. The UCC states that one is a merchant if one employs "an agent or broker or other intermediary who by his occupation holds himself out" as having knowledge or skill peculiar to the goods or practices involved in the transaction. Suppose, for example, that Smith, who does not regularly deal in grain, hires a professional grain broker to procure a large quantity of feed for Smith's cattle. In this situation Smith is considered a merchant.

The common thread running through all the above categories of merchants is the possession of or access to a degree of commercial expertise not found in a member of the general public. The UCC occasionally treats merchants differently than nonmerchants. For example, it imposes a higher duty of "good faith" on them. Also, some provisions of the UCC apply only to merchants who are deemed such because they deal in goods, while others apply only to merchants who are deemed such because they hold themselves out as having skill peculiar to practice. In most provisions, both types of merchants are treated in the same manner.

Courts in different states have taken various views as to whether a farmer or rancher is a "merchant" for UCC purposes. The following case represents one point of view.

DAVIS V. FLAGSTAR COMPANIES
Seventh Circuit U.S. Court of Appeals, 1997 U.S. App. LEXIS 17531 (1997)

In 1991 Larry Davis began a business to find and organize opportunities for economically disadvantaged minority farmers. Davis negotiated with defendants, exploring the possibility of Davis' company coordinating the supply of vegetables to the defendants. Davis asserts that they subsequently entered into an oral agreement in January 1995 under which Davis would sell 500,000 cases of white potatoes to the defendants. A purchasing agent from Flagstar who had met with Davis in January sent a letter to Davis in early February enclosing a copy of Flagstar's produce product specifications and a supplier profile questionnaire, and stating that he looked forward to receiving the "growing schedule" which they had discussed at the meeting. Davis responded in early March with a growing schedule and delivery dates "per [their] agreement" as well as the projected annual volume for white potatoes which would be required by the defendants. Davis never received a reply to this letter and he claims that further attempts to set up another meeting regarding the alleged oral agreement were rebuffed by the defendants.

Davis sued for breach of contract. Defendants filed a motion for summary judgment asserting that the statute of frauds precluded enforcement of any oral agreement. Davis responded asserting that because both parties were merchants and because he had sent a confirmation letter which was not disputed by the defendants, then the statute of frauds did not apply. The district court granted the defendants' motion for summary judgment stating that while it might find Davis to be a merchant in a transaction for supplying marketing research data, he was not a merchant regarding the sale of potatoes. Davis appealed.

Per Curiam:
The Illinois Commercial Code provides that any oral contract for the sale of goods over $ 500 is not enforceable. However, "[b]etween merchants if within a reasonable time a writing in confirmation of the contract and sufficient against the sender is received and the party receiving it has reason to know its contents, it satisfies [the statute of frauds] against

such party unless written notice of objection to its contents is given within 10 days after it is received."

The defendants assert that Davis is not a merchant and thus that the "merchant exception" is not applicable in the present case. The UCC defines "merchant" as "a person who deals in goods of the kind or otherwise by his occupation holds himself out as having knowledge or skill peculiar to the practices or goods involved in the transaction." 2–104(1). Illinois case law sheds little light on how an Illinois court would decide the issue. The cases cited by defendants and the district court deal with the definition of merchant as one "who deals in goods of the kind: or otherwise by his occupation holds himself out as having knowledge or skill peculiar to the practices of goods involved in the transaction. Oloffson v. Coomer, 296 N.E.2d 871(Ill.App. 1973) (grain dealer who was in the business of merchandising grain was grain dealer while farmer who was merely in the business of growing was not merchant).

We agree that Davis did not deal in the sale of potatoes. However, a party asserting the merchant exception need not regularly sell the kind of goods that are the subject of the transaction. A party may also be a merchant because he "by his occupation holds himself out as having knowledge or skill peculiar to the practices or goods involved in the transaction." UCC 2–104(1).

The Comment portion of the Illinois Code provides some guidance when it indicates that the special provisions applicable to merchants become relevant in three different situations, including the statute of frauds. Specifically, the Comment states that: "Section[] 2–201(2), . . . dealing with the statute of frauds,. . . rest[s] on normal business practices which are or ought to be typical of and familiar to any person in business. For purposes of [this] section[] almost every person in business would, . . . , be deemed to be a 'merchant' under the language 'who . . . by his occupation holds himself out as having knowledge or skill peculiar to the practices. . . involved in the transaction' since the practices involved in the transaction are non–specialized business practices such as answering mail." Cmt. 2. *See also* County of Milwaukee v. Northrop Data Systems, 607 F.2d 767(7th Cir. 1979) (stating that county's argument that it was not a merchant under Wisconsin law because it was not engaged in the manufacture of laboratory computer systems and sought only to purchase a system "ignores the broad U.C.C. definition of a merchant"); Heinrich–Titus–Will v. Sales, 868 P.2d 169(Wash. 1994) (stating that "it is not necessary to possess an inventory to fit within the broad statutory definition of merchant" and holding that automobile broker/dealer "was a merchant who dealt in automobiles; he held himself out as a dealer in automobiles and appeared to be a dealer in automobiles [and] both parties treated him as one."). *But see* Chisolm v. Cleveland, 741 S.W.2d 619 (Tex.App. 1987)(dairy farmer who had never bought or sold "green chop" and had only bought other types of feed occasionally held not to be a merchant because the evidence established that "the plaintiff is a casual or inexperienced buyer, not that he was a professional buyer or seller of green chop, or any other kind of cattle feed.").

Under the broader definition, Davis properly could be characterized as a merchant. In *County of Milwaukee,* this court addressed whether the county of Milwaukee was a merchant for purposes of the U.C.C. when it purchased a computerized laboratory information system. The County asserted that it was not a merchant because "it [was] not engaged in the manufacture, sale or marketing of a laboratory system or other products, but is engaged in the procurement of supplies, materials, and equipment for the operation of the hospital." This court stated that this position "ignored the broad U.C.C. definition of a merchant." It stated that the facts indicated that the County "arguably . . . '[held] (itself) out as having knowledge or skill peculiar to the practices (or goods) involved in the transaction' because the bid itself indicated knowledge peculiar to the goods being solicited by the County." This court concluded that this reasoning was incorporated into the third definition of merchant, that the County's use of an agent who held himself out as having knowledge and skills peculiar to the goods or practices involved in the transaction "allowed the attribution of his knowledge to the County." This court noted that the hospital's agents, including one who was a certified public accountant whose responsibilities included management of the hospital's finances and business operations, solicited the bids and "extensively negotiated" the contract.

Here, Davis had been researching and working to organize business opportunities for minority farmers for approximately five years prior to the alleged contract in dispute and thus has some knowledge of supplying agricultural products to buyers. Davis held himself out as being knowledgeable in this field as is indicated by the letter sent by Flagstar's employee Gene Harris to Davis less than two weeks after their January 1995 meeting. The letter was addressed to "Mr. Larry Davis" of "The Davis Group," referred to Davis' "company" and included detailed specifications regarding the defendants' requirements for agricultural products. We can only assume that such specifications were sent to Davis with the understanding that he would know how to interpret and use them in responding to the defendant's needs.

We conclude only that the district court erred in finding Davis was not a merchant for purposes of the merchant exception to the statute of frauds. REVERSED AND REMANDED.

Leases

Thousands of times a day, Americans rent cars, garden equipment, machines to clean rugs, and numerous other goods. Leasing is also quite common in industry. For example, assume that Company A needs to buy 100 new delivery trucks from Company C, but cannot afford them. Company B ("lessor") agrees to buy the 100 trucks and then to lease them to Company A ("lessee"). Every day, innumerable such transactions occur in our economy.

Leases of goods present many of the same legal issues that arise in sales of goods. Indeed, some courts held that Article 2 applied to leases because UCC 2–102 states that it applies to "transactions in goods." Although most courts disagreed, many extended provisions of Article 2 to leases by analogy, reasoning that the rules governing sales could be helpful in resolving lease disputes. This proved unsatisfactory, however, because Article 2 was not designed to address leasing problems.

Therefore, almost all states have adopted Article 2A, which is designed to cover leases of goods in the same manner that Article 2 covers sales. It is intended to apply to virtually every type of lease of tangible personal property.

Article 2A's provisions resemble the common law of bailment for hire. This is the most–litigated pre–Article 2A issue related to the difference between a true lease (governed by bailment law) and a lease intended as security for a loan (subject to UCC Article 9). Return, for example, to the hypothetical involving the lease of 100 trucks. If Company A falls behind in its payments, the rights of Company B vis−a−vis Company A's other creditors will depend on whether the agreement is structured as a true lease or as a security interest.

Although Article 2 receives most of our attention in this chapter and the next, we should highlight a few of Article 2A's provisions.

Lessee's Remedies

Remedies are usually set forth in the lease contract. The parties to the lease generally have the right to set their own terms and to vary any provision of Article 2A. However, when the lease does not establish remedies, Article 2A provides that in event of default by the lessor, the lessee has the right, among others, to cancel the lease, to recover paid−in rents and security deposits to the extent "just under the circumstances," to obtain substitute goods, and to recover damages.

Lessor's Remedies

If the lessee breaches the lease by wrongfully refusing delivery or failing to make payments when due, the remedies available to the lessor include cancellation of the lease, repossession and disposition, and damages. "Reasonable" liquidated damages clauses will be enforced. Mitigation of damages by re−leasing is not required, but if an item is re−leased, the lessor is not entitled to recover double profits.

Warranties

Finance lessors (those who do not select, manufacture, or supply goods out of inventory, but simply serve as a financial conduit so that the lessee may obtain use of goods—such as Company B in the aforementioned truck example) are automatically exempted from implied warranties. For other lessors, Article 2A's warranty provisions generally track those of Article 2, which will be discussed in detail in Chapter 22. Warranties not affecting third parties may be disclaimed by written and conspicuous provisions.

Consumer Leases

A consumer lease is one that a lessor regularly engaged in the business of leasing or selling makes to an individual lessee who takes primarily for a personal, family, or household purpose, providing total payments do not exceed $25,000. Article 2A contains several provisions to protect consumers in such leases, including one allowing a consumer to recover attorney's fees when a court finds a provision in the lessor's form lease to be "unconscionable."

Review of Basic Principles of Sales Contracts

In explaining basic contract law, Chapters 11- 19of Part II focused on the common law of contracts but highlighted changes that Article 2 makes for sales contracts. The first part of this chapter examined the scope of Article 2's coverage. The next chapter will go into great detail regarding some very important features of Article 2. Before leaving this chapter, however, we will present a quick overview of some basic Article 2 rules on contract formation, enforcement, and interpretation.

Contract Formation

The basic elements needed to form a contract at common law (agreement, consideration, capacity of the parties, legality of purpose) are also essential to formation of a sales contract under Article 2. However, the drafters of the Code meant it to be nontechnical and to operate fairly. For example, the common law says that even if an offeror promises to keep an offer open for a specified period of time, he may revoke the offer at any time before acceptance (unless he has been given consideration to keep it open). As explained in Chapter 12, Sec. 2–205's "firm offer rule" provides a fairer rule, holding merchants to their signed promises to keep offers open for a specified time less than three months' duration even in the absence of consideration.

Even more importantly, the Code's rules on formation of an agreement do not turn on whether there existed a detailed offer and a detailed acceptance, each containing all important elements of the contract. Rather, the drafters of the Code realized that parties often, perhaps pursuant to a quick telephone conversation, intend to form a contract but fail to agree as to a specific term such as price or date of delivery. Therefore, Sec. 2–204 provides that a contract is made if the parties clearly intend one to exist and there is a reasonably certain basis for giving an appropriate remedy. Resort may be had to the "gap–fillers" to provide terms the parties omit. For example, 2–305 will provide the price if that term has been omitted, 2–308 fills in the gap if the parties did not determine the place for delivery, 2–309 fills in the time of delivery, and 2–310 fills in the time of payment.

The common law also generally requires that an acceptance be the "mirror image" of the offer on all important terms before a contract exists. The framers of the UCC realized that this requirement was unduly technical, given the modern commercial world's reliance on form contracts that cannot feasibly be fully negotiated for each transaction. Therefore UCC 2–207, the "battle of the forms" provision, states that a contract is formed if the offeree's primary intent is to accept an offer even if the offeree's form does not match the offeror's form in all particulars. That section then gives rules to decide the content of that contract. The essence of 2–207 is that no party is allowed to unfairly surprise the other with contract provisions hidden in fine print.

The area of consideration also illustrates the Code's nontechnical approach. As noted in Chapter 13, Sec. 2-209 states that, unlike at the common law, an agreement modifying a sales contract *needs no consideration to be binding*. Parties are bound to their promises to modify an existing contract, and another technical defense is eliminated. (Somewhat surprisingly, perhaps, the doctrine of promissory estoppel plays almost no role in Article 2.)

Contract Enforcement

No body of commercial law can be free of technical rules, of course. Like the common law, Article 2 carries a statute of frauds requirement that certain contracts for the sale of goods—those of $500 or more—must be in writing in order to be enforceable (Sec. 2–201). However, consistent with its overall approach, the Code makes several exceptions to this technical defense, providing that oral contracts of over $500 are enforceable where (1) the seller has already substantially begun producing specially made goods; (2) payment has been made and accepted or goods have been received and accepted; (3) between merchants there has been a confirmatory memorandum sent and the receiving party did not object to its terms in writing within 10 days; or (4) the party against whom the contract is to be enforced admitted in court proceedings that an oral agreement existed. The Code also has its own parol evidence rule, Sec. 2–202, which again is more generous than the common law, allowing unambiguous final written agreements to be explained or supplemented by course of dealing, usage of trade, or course of performance (see Chapter 16).

The Code also grants the parties the right to shape the contract's terms as they please. For example, they can establish their own remedies with very few limitations. However, in the interests of fairness, the Code does impose some limitations. As explained in Chapter 14, a contractual provision that is unconscionable will not be enforced. A party with superior bargaining power or sophistication will not be allowed to impose unfair terms on an inferior party (UCC 2-302). For example, we will see in Chapter 22 that if a seller with superior bargaining power contractually limits the remedies of the buyer of a defective product so severely that the remedy fails of its essential purpose depriving the buyer of the substantial value of the bargain, the limitation is unenforceable (UCC 2–719(2)).

Contract Interpretation

The Code follows general rules of contract interpretation, but, as noted in Chapter 19, allows more liberal use of extrinsic evidence to determine the parties' intent in sale–of–goods contracts. The Code assumes that the parties considered three important concepts when they formed their agreement. First is *course of performance,* which arises out of "repeated occasions for performance by either party with knowledge of the nature of the performance and opportunity for objection to it by the other." Second is *course of dealing,* "a sequence of previous conduct between the parties to a particular transaction which is fairly regarded as establishing a common basis of understanding for interpreting their expressions and other conduct." Third is *usage of trade,* defined as "any practice or method of dealing having such regularity of observance in a place, vocation or trade as to justify an expectation that it will be observed with respect to the transaction in question." In essence, this means that in determining the meaning of the contract, the courts may consider, in order of importance, the previous course of performance of this particular contract, the past course of dealing between the parties in

LEGAL FOCUS

International

As will be discussed in Chapter 31, the United Nations Convention on Contracts for the International Sale of Goods (CISG) is a multilateral treaty drafted in 1980. The United States adopted the treaty in 1988, and approximately 70 nations, including most of the world's important trading nations, have adopted the CISG. In a sale of goods transaction in which the seller and buyer are from different nations, and both nations have adopted the treaty, the CISG is the governing law unless the seller and buyer expressly agree that some other body of law should apply. (The treaty can also apply in some other situations that are too complex to discuss here.) Even if the seller and buyer do not expressly agree to be bound by some other body of law, they can modify any of the CISG's provisions by agreement.

The ability of the parties to modify the rules of contract law by their agreement is nothing new, of course; the same is true with regard to almost all of the common law of contracts and the rules of our UCC.

Although much of the CISG resembles Article 2 of our UCC, there are some significant differences. For example, under the UCC a sale of goods contract for $500 or more has to be in writing, but the CISG expressly provides that written documentation is not required so long as other evidence proves the existence and terms of the contract. This difference is more theoretical than real, however, because almost all international sales contracts are actually evidenced by documents that would satisfy the requirements of our UCC.

Another difference between the UCC and CISG relates to an acceptance containing terms that are additional to or different from the terms of the offer. As you have read, the UCC modifies the common–law "mirror–image" rule and consequently makes it easier to form an enforceable sale of goods contract than under common–law rules. The CISG, however, includes a provision that is virtually identical to the common–law mirror image rule: under the CISG, an acceptance containing a term that materially adds to or changes the offer is a counteroffer rather than an acceptance. One other difference relates to the creation of irrevocable offers., The "firm offer" provision of UCC Sec. 2–205 makes it somewhat easier to create an irrevocable offer than do traditional common law contract rules; the CISG makes it even easier than the UCC. Under the CISG, an offer for the sale or purchase of goods is irrevocable if it includes language indicating that it is irrevocable or even if it merely states a time for acceptance. Unlike the UCC, the CISG does not require the offer to be written, and does not include a time limit on an offer's irrevocable status.

other contracts they have had, and, finally, the usage of the trade in general as established by contracts and performance of other persons in the industry.

Duty of Good Faith

Finally, interpretation and enforcement of contracts for the sale of goods are favored not only by Article 2's specific policies against surprise, unfairness, and unconscionability, but also by its "good faith" requirements. UCC 1–203 specifically states that "[e]very contract or duty within this Act imposes an obligation of good faith in its performance or enforcement." Section 2–103(1)(b) goes further, defining the "good faith" duty of a merchant to mean acting with "honesty in fact and the observance of reasonable commercial standards of fair dealing in the trade." This again highlights that Article 2 is not a collection of dry rules, but an attempt to establish a framework promoting efficient, but also fair, commercial transactions in goods.

Documents of Title

Before concluding this introductory chapter, we need to present some terms that will aid understanding of the subsequent sales chapters. When goods are shipped by a carrier or stored in a warehouse before sale, a *bailment* often occurs. The owner of the goods is the *bailor,* the warehouseman or carrier is the *bailee*. An owner of goods who sends them through a carrier receives a receipt called a **bill of lading,** which contains instructions to the carrier regarding destination and the like, as well as the terms of the shipping agreement. If goods are stored with a bailee/warehouseman before sale, the owner will receive a warehouse receipt, which will also contain the terms of the storage agreement. Both instructions are sometimes referred to as documents of title, because they provide evidence of title to goods.

Documents of title—such as bills of lading, warehouse receipts, dock warrants, dock receipts, and other orders for delivery of goods which are treated in the regular course of business as adequate evidence that the holder is entitled to receive, hold, and dispose of the goods covered, are governed by Article 7 of the UCC. A **negotiable document of title** is one which by its terms specifies that the goods are to be delivered to "bearer" or to the "order" of a named person. Documents not meeting this requirement are **nonnegotiable documents of title.** A negotiable document of title (e.g., "Deliver to bearer" or "Deliver to order of Dan Owens") entitles whoever is in legal possession of it (as bearer or as Dan Owens's endorsee) to possession of the underlying goods. A nonnegotiable document of title (e.g., "Delivery to Dan Owens"), on the other hand, is not equivalent to ownership of the goods. Regardless of who presents the document, the bailee is under a duty to deliver the goods only to the party who is supposed to receive them under the bailor's instructions. (The difference between a negotiable and a nonnegotiable document is somewhat akin to the difference between a five–dollar bill and a copy of a contract.)

CHAPTER **21**

SALES: WARRANTIES AND PRODUCT LIABILITY

- Warranty
- Negligence
- Strict Liability
- Federal Consumer Legislation
- Legislative Limitations on the Products Liability Revolution

IN RECENT YEARS, courts have found themselves plagued with the problem of manufacturer liability, specifically the extent to which a manufacturer should be liable to a consumer who is injured by its product. To address this problem, various rules and legal theories for determining liability have been developed, and these make up the expanding area of law known as products liability. Since the 1960s, products liability has become one of the most rapidly changing areas in the history of common law, its bias having undergone a dramatic shift away from the seller to favor, instead, the consumer. The pendulum has taken such a sudden swing that sellers' liability has emerged as one of the most controversial subjects in the business world today.

Under products liability law and sales law, three legal theories may be available to an injured consumer seeking redress: (1) warranty, (2) negligence, and (3) strict liability. The first is a contract theory and is governed by the UCC; the other two are tort theories. The elements of negligence have been discussed in Chapter 8 and are applied here in the context of products liability. The principles of strict liability are taken from section 402A of the American Law Institute's Restatement (Second) of Torts. Unlike the UCC, the Restatement is not a statute, but a model code of law whose recommendations have been adopted by courts or legislatures in many states. Like the UCC, the strict liability theory applies primarily to transactions involving goods and not to those involving real estate or services.

Warranty

A **warranty** is an assurance or guarantee that goods will conform to certain standards. If the standards are not met, the buyer can recover damages from the seller, under a breach of warranty theory.

Such has not always been the case, for although suits involving warranties date as far back as fourteenth century England, a recovery theory was slow in developing. *Caveat emptor* ("let the buyer beware") governed the state of law until recent times—here in America, until the beginning of the twentieth century. The concept of *caveat emptor* allowed the seller to escape liability altogether, in the absence of fraud.

With the growth of business and industry came a clear need to move away from laissez–faire values and to place legal strictures on sales transactions. Chains of distribution were widening the distance between manufacturers and ultimate consumers, and an increasing sophistication in product design made inspection for defects more difficult. As a result, courts came to recognize the existence of three types of warranties, discussed in the following pages: express warranties, implied warranties, and warranties of title.

Express Warranties

Express warranties are those that originate from the words or actions of the seller. To create an express warranty, the seller does not have to use the word *warranty or guarantee,* and the buyer does not have to show that the seller intended to make a warranty.

Under Sec. 2–313 of the UCC, a seller can create an express warranty in three different ways: (1) by an affirmation of fact or a promise relating to the goods, (2) by a description of the goods, or (3) by providing a sample or model of the goods. Such representations by the seller create contractual obligations to the extent that they become "part of the basis of the bargain."

Affirmation of Fact or Promise

By making an affirmation of fact or a promise relating to the goods, the seller tacitly guarantees that the goods will conform to the specifics he or she sets forth. For example, the seller might claim, "This boat is equipped with a two–year–old, 100–horsepower engine that was overhauled last month." The statement contains several affirmations of fact: (1) the boat is equipped with an engine, (2) the engine is two years old, (3) it generates 100 horsepower, and (4) it was overhauled last month. The seller might further state, "I assure you that this boat will not stall when run in choppy water." The affirmations concern past and present conditions; the promise, by contrast, relates to future events. Both affirmations and promises may create express warranties.

A seller's *commendation or expression of opinion* does not constitute an express warranty; neither does a statement that relates only to the value of the goods. Thus, the seller could claim that his boat was a "first–class vessel, worth $25,000 at retail" without creating a warranty. The law is not so rigid as to disallow "puffing" of products; it assumes that a consumer can distinguish between sales talk and fact.

But at times the distinction between fact and opinion is not easy to make. Consider, for example, the following statement: "The steering mechanism on this boat has been thoroughly engineered." The claim is rather vague, and as a descriptive phrase, "thoroughly engineered" may not be appreciably different from "first class." Yet the reference to engineering may create an impression of technological excellence in the mind of an unsophisticated buyer and thus create a wrong impression.

In such cases, the courts tend to consider a number of factors, principally the buyer's frame of reference. If the buyer has limited knowledge of the goods involved, the statement from the seller is apt to be an affirmation of fact. If, however, the buyer is more knowledgeable than the seller, vague statements will be treated as mere expressions of opinion.

These additional generalizations can be made about the creation of express warranties: Statements that are specific and absolute are more readily construed as warranties than indefinite ones. Terms put in writing are more likely to create warranties than those given orally. A warranty is more likely to be found if the statement is objectively *verifiable* (for example, "This machine is one year old."). The nature and seriousness of the defect may also have a bearing on the determination.

Description of Goods

A descriptive word or phrase used in a sale of goods may create an express warranty that the goods will conform to the description. The word *pitted* or *seedless* on a box of prunes or raisins warrants that the fruit will have no seeds. Recognized trade terms may also constitute descriptions. For example, the term Scotchguard, used in connection with furniture upholstery, describes fabric that has been treated to make it water- and stain-resistant. Goods described by trade terms are warranted to possess those characteristics generally associated with the terms in the trade or business involved.

Sample or Model

If the seller provides to the buyer a sample or model of the goods to be sold, a warranty arises that the goods will conform to the sample or model. A sample is a single item taken from the mass to be sold, whereas a model is used to represent the goods. In a sale of wheat, a sample of one bushel might be drawn from the thousand bushels to be sold. But when the item being sold has not yet been manufactured or is too difficult to transport, a model might be used instead.

Although the UCC makes no distinction between express warranties arising out of sales by sample or by model, a sample is more likely to create such a warranty than a model. Because a sample is actually taken from the inventory to be sold, it is usually easier for the buyer to prove that a sample was intended to establish a standard of quality for the sale.

Basis of the Bargain

Under Sec. 2–313, an express warranty is created only if the affirmation or promise, description, model, or sample is "part of the basis of the bargain." Courts have applied this phrase to two types of circumstances. First is the case in which the seller makes a statement about the goods, and circumstances indicate that both parties intended the statement to be a part of the agreement. This would certainly be true if the statement appeared in the sales contract itself and would apply also when it is reasonably clear that the statement played a material part in the buyer's decision to purchase the goods. The second type of case involves statements of fact contained in a brochure, provided to the buyer by the seller. Under pre–Code law, the burden of proof was generally on the buyer to show that he or she had read the statement and relied on it. If reliance could not be shown, the buyer could not recover on the breach of warranty theory. By contrast, under the "basis of the bargain" language, courts *assume* that the statement became a part of the contract unless the seller can show "good reason" for the contrary (Sec. 2–313, comment 8).

A different question arises when, after the sale has been made, the buyer requests a promise from the seller that the goods meet certain standards. If given, does this promise become "part of the basis of the bargain"? Before the enactment of the UCC, the answer probably would have been *no;* today it is probably *yes.* Under Sec. 2–209(1), the seller's postsale promise is a modification of the contract and becomes an integral part of the agreement, even without additional consideration from the buyer.

A similar problem occurs sometimes in a sales negotiation, during which the seller makes statements that fail to appear in the written contract. Buyers who attempt to base a claim for breach of warranty on a recollection of oral statements are often thwarted by the parol evidence rule of UCC Sec. 2–202. Under this rule, if the court finds that the written form was intended as the final expression of the parties' agreement, any oral statement in contradiction of the written terms will not be admissible as evidence.

The following case illustrates how a company's advertising may expand the scope of an express warranty.

COMMUNITY TELEVISION SERVICES, INC. v. DRESSER INDUSTRIES, INC.
U.S. Court of Appeals, 8th Circuit, 586 F.2d 637 (1978)

In 1965, two television stations in South Dakota created a separate corporation, Community Television Services, Inc. (Community) for the purpose of constructing and operating a 2000–foot tower that would broadcast signals for both stations. Community contracted with Dresser Industries, Inc. (Dresser), who designed, manufactured, and erected the tower for a price of $385,000. The tower was completed in 1969, and Community used it until 1975. During this time, Community regularly inspected and properly maintained the tower. On January 10 and 11, 1975, a severe winter blizzard occurred in the area where the tower was located. During the early morning hours of January 11, as the storm reached its height with wind speeds of up to 80 miles per hour near the top of the tower, the structure collapsed. Dresser denied responsibility, and Community sued in federal district court for breach of an express warranty. The verdict and judgment in the trial court were in favor of Community, the plaintiff, for damages of $1,274,631.60. Dresser, the defendant, appealed.

Lay, Circuit Judge:

. . . Expert witnesses called by both sides differed in their opinions as to the cause of the collapse. Community's experts testified that they had eliminated metallurgical or mechanical failure or abnormal wind loading as the cause of collapse. They theorized that the cause was high winds setting up a phenomenon known as mechanical resonance. They concluded that because of the resonance, the tower members "were inadequate to support the load that they sustained." On the other hand, Dresser's experts testified that a combination of ice, snow and wind subjected the tower to a total force greater than the ultimate capacity of its structural elements. They theorized that a substantial accumulation of ice on the upper fourth of the tower enlarged the tower members to a greater load than their designed wind loading capacity. Community attempted to refute Dresser's ice theory by calling several witnesses who testified that they did not see any such ice on or near the area where the tower collapsed. In turn, Dresser countered Community's theory through expert testimony that relatively constant winds were necessary for resonance to begin, and the winds were gusty and varied in speed and direction at the time of collapse. Furthermore, Dresser argued that the warranty did not guarantee against mechanical resonance and experts testified that its prevention was beyond the current state of the art.

The specifications incorporated in the sale contract included a specified "Design Wind Load," which set forth the tower's capacity to withstand wind velocity as measured in pounds of pressure per square foot against the flat surface of its members. The specification reads: "The tower shall be designed to resist a uniform wind load per drawing T–5172, sheet S–1, 60 psf on flats." The trial court instructed the jury that this specification constituted an express warranty that the structure would withstand wind exerting pressure of 60 pounds per square foot on the flat surfaces of the tower. Dresser's advertising materials and the testimony of experts at trial revealed that the wind velocity necessary to create 60 pounds of pressure on the flat surfaces of the tower would be approximately 120 miles per hour. The evidence showed that the wind loading specifications referred, at least in engineering parlance, to "a force caused by the wind that is introduced parallel to the ground . . . [which] would be tending to blow the structure over."

Dresser argues that the trial court erred in failing to direct a verdict on the express warranty claim or grant it judgment notwithstanding the verdict, because expert testimony that the tower met the design specification was uncontradicted. Community's own experts stated unequivocally that in their opinion the tower conformed in a mathematical or analytical sense to the 60 pounds per square foot wind loading specification. If the warranty may be restricted to the technical specification set forth in the written contract, we would find Dresser's argument convincing. However, we agree with Community that the warranty was amplified, in advertising materials Dresser gave to Community prior to purchase of the tower, to promise more than mere compliance with technical measurements. In an advertising catalog, Dresser made the following supplementary affirmation:

"Wind force creates the most critical loads to which a tower is normally subjected. When ice forms on tower members thereby increasing the surface area resisting the passage of wind, the load is increased.

"Properly designed towers will safely withstand the maximum wind velocities and ice loads to which they are likely to be subjected. Dresser–Ideco can make wind and ice load recommendations to you for your area based on U.S. Weather Bureau data.

"In the winter, loaded with ice and hammered repeatedly with gale force winds, these towers absorb some of the roughest punishment that towers take anywhere in the country . . . yet continue to give dependable, uninterrupted service."

Although we agree with Dresser that a seller cannot be held to be the insurer of its product, Dresser nevertheless provided the catalog to Community to induce purchase of its product, and in the absence of clear affirmative proof to the contrary, the above affirmation must be considered part of the "basis of the bargain." Standing alone, the statements provide a warranty that Dresser's tower would be properly designed so as to safely withstand the maximum wind velocities and ice loads to which it would likely be subjected. Dresser did not indicate that this broad affirmation was superseded or cancelled by the technical specification in the contract. When the affirmation is read in tandem with the contract, as part of the "fabric" of the agreement of the parties, it enlarges the warranty created by the technical wind loading specification, giving evidence of its full intent and scope.

We find that the statements in the advertising catalog, which supplement the wind loading specification, could reasonably have been found by the jury to be an affirmation of fact or a promise concerning the actual durability or performance of the tower during the wind and ice storms to which it was likely to be subjected.

Although Dresser's defense was that the tower collapsed by reason of excessive loading due to ice on the tower members, no disclaimer or limitation of the warranty that a properly designed tower would safely withstand the maximum wind and ice loads to which it was likely to be subjected appeared in the advertising materials or the contract.

Under the integrated warranty given, a purchaser could reasonably assume that the tower, if properly designed for its location, would withstand maximum wind speeds to which it was likely to be subjected, even if ice accumulated on the tower members. While the blizzard was a severe one, the evidence does not support the conclusion that the wind alone, or the combination of wind and ice which Dresser claimed caused the collapse, was not within the range of storm conditions to be reasonably contemplated for the tower's location. Breach of a warranty created by standards describing the specific capacity of goods is proved when the product is shown by direct or circumstantial evidence to have failed to perform reasonably and safely the function for which it was intended by the manufacturer. In view of the affirmation made in the catalog, there was sufficient evidence for the jury to reasonably find that the tower was not as durable as it was warranted to be.

[Affirmed.]

Implied Warranties

An implied warranty is created through the mere act of selling and is imposed on the seller by law. Its purpose is to protect buyers who suffer economic and commercial losses when products fail to serve their needs. Unlike with express warranties, specific representations about a product have not actually been made. The consumer has been guided, instead, by the belief that his or her purchase is suitable for its intended use. In Secs. 2–314 and 2–315, the UCC names two types of implied warranties: the implied warranty of merchantability and the implied warranty of fitness for a particular purpose.

Merchantability

The law injects into the sales contract a warranty that the goods are "merchantable," if the seller is a *merchant with respect to the type of goods being sold.* (When a student sells his or her 2000 Mini Cooper to a neighbor, no implied warranty of merchantability exists because the student is not a merchant in automobiles.)

Merchantable means essentially that the goods are *fit for the ordinary purpose for which such goods are used.* The warranty of merchantability requires, for example, that shoes have their heels attached well enough that they will not break off under normal use. The warranty does not require, however, that ordinary walking shoes be suitable for mountain climbing. To be merchantable, goods must also serve their ordinary purpose safely. A refrigerator that keeps food cold but that gives an electric shock when the handle is touched is not merchantable. This is not to say that the seller becomes an insurer against accident or malfunction; the purchaser is expected to maintain his or her goods against the attrition of use.

The **implied warranty of merchantability** also does not guarantee that goods will be of the highest quality available. They are required to be only of *average or medium* *grade,* in addition to being adequately packaged and labeled. Some jurisdictions apply the implied warranty of merchantability to sales of used goods; most limit the warranty to sale of new goods.

When applied to food, the implied warranty of merchantability can be related to wholesomeness. A tainted pork chop, for instance, is not merchantable. A number of cases decided before enactment of the UCC held that food purchased at a restaurant, hotel, or other such establishment carried no warranty because the sale involved a service rather than a product. The UCC, however, explicitly states that the implied warranty of merchantability extends to food sold at service establishments such as restaurants and hotels, whether the food is consumed on or off the premises.

Many cases alleging a breach of the implied warranty of merchantability have involved objects in food that caused harm to the consumer. Exceptional examples range from a mouse in a bottled soft drink to a screw in a slice of bread. In such cases the courts traditionally have distinguished between "foreign" and "natural" objects. They usually find that if the object is foreign to the mass (such as the mouse or screw mentioned above), the warranty of merchantability has been breached. If, however, the object is natural (such as a bone in a piece of fish), no breach of warranty has occurred.

A growing number of courts have rejected this approach and have based their decisions instead on the "reasonable expectation" of the consumer. The controlling factor in this approach is whether a consumer can reasonably expect the object in question to be in the food. A piece of chicken may be expected to contain a bone but not when in a chicken sandwich; an olive may be expected to contain a pit but not when a hole at the end indicates that it has been pitted. Bones and olive pits will not render food unmerchantable under the "foreign–natural object" test *but may do so under the reasonable expectation test.* Thus, the results of a legal suit may vary considerably, depending on which approach is used. A famous case in this area follows.

EBSTER V. BLUE SHIP TEA ROOM, INC.
Supreme Judicial Court of Massachusetts, 198 N.E.2d 309 (1964)

Plaintiff, Webster, who was born and brought up in New England, ordered a cup of fish chowder while dining at the defendant's "quaint" Boston restaurant. She choked on a fish bone contained in the soup, necessitating two esophagoscopies at the Massachusetts General Hospital. The plaintiff sued for breach of the implied warranty of merchantability. A jury returned a verdict for the plaintiff. The defendant appealed the trial judge's refusal to direct a verdict for the defendant.

Reardon, Justice:
We must decide whether a fish bone lurking in a fish chowder, about the ingredients of which there is no other complaint, constitutes a breach of implied warranty under applicable

provisions of the Uniform Commercial Code. As the [trial] judge put it, "Was the fish chowder fit to be eaten and wholesome? Nobody is claiming that the fish itself wasn't wholesome. But the bone of contention here—I don't mean that for a pun—but was this fish bone a foreign substance that made the fish chowder unwholesome or not fit to be eaten?"

The plaintiff has vigorously reminded us of the high standards imposed by this court where the sale of goods is involved.

The defendant asserts that here was a native New Englander eating fish chowder in a "quaint" Boston dining place where she had been before; that "[f]ish chowder, as it is served and enjoyed by New Englanders, is a hearty dish, originally designed to satisfy the appetites of our seamen and fishermen"; that "[t]his court knows well that we are not talking of some insipid broth as is customarily served to convalescents." We are asked to rule in such fashion that no chef is forced "to reduce the pieces of fish in the chowder to miniscule size in an effort to ascertain if they contained any pieces of bone." In so ruling, we are told (in the defendant's brief), "the court will not only uphold its reputation for legal knowledge and acumen, but will, as loyal sons of Massachusetts, save our world—renowned fish chowder from degenerating into an insipid broth containing the mere essence of its former stature as a culinary masterpiece."

Chowder is an ancient fish dish preexisting even "the appetites of our seamen and fishermen. ' It was perhaps the common ancestor of the "more refined cream soups, purees, and bisques." Berolzheimer, The American Woman's Cook Book (Publisher's Guild Inc., New York, 1941) p. 176. The all embracing Fannie Farmer states in a portion of her recipe, fish chowder is made with a "fish skinned, but head and tail left on. Cut off head and tail and remove fish from backbone. Cut fish in 2—inches pieces and set aside. Put head, tail, and backbone broken in pieces, in stewpan; add 2 cups cold water and bring slowly to boiling point."

Thus, we consider a dish which for many years, if well made, has been made generally as outlined above. It is not too much to say that a person sitting down in New England to consume a good New England fish chowder embarks on a gustatory adventure which may entail the removal of some fish bones from his bowl as he proceeds. We are not inclined to tamper with age old recipes by any amendment reflecting the plaintiff's view of the effect of the Uniform Commercial Code on them. We are aware of the heavy body of case law involving foreign substances in food, but we sense a strong distinction between them and those relative to unwholesomeness of the food itself, e.g., tainted mackerel, and a fishbone in fish chowder. We consider that the joys of life in New England include the ready availability of fresh fish chowder. We should be prepared to cope with the hazards of fish bones, the occasional presence of which in chowders is, it seems to us, to be anticipated, and which, in the light of a hallowed tradition, do not impair their fitness or merchantability.

Judgment for the defendant.

Fitness for a Particular Purpose

In Sec. 2–315, the UCC provides 'Where the seller at the time of contracting has reason to know any particular purpose for which the goods are required and that the buyer is relying on the seller's skill or judgment to furnish suitable goods, there is … an implied warranty that the goods shall be fit for such purpose" (hence the name **implied warranty of fitness for a particular purpose,** sometimes referred to as warranty of fitness). Note that the seller is not required to be a merchant, although merchants are defendants in most cases.

Often the liability incurred by the seller under the implied warranty of fitness is greater than one incurred under the implied warranty of merchantability—a difference that can be best illustrated by a simple example Suppose a buyer purchases an electric clock and discovers that its hands do not glow in the dark. The packaging carries no reference to visibility of the dial; neither does the instruction card. No breach of the implied warranty of merchantability exists here, for visibility of the dial under all conditions is not within the realm of a clock's "ordinary purpose." Yet, the seller may be liable to the buyer for breach of the implied warranty of fitness for a particular purpose if he or she knew that the buyerhad a particular reason to need a clock with a lighted dial.

Some confusion exists because courts are split as to whether the "particular purpose" must be something other than the ordinary purpose for which the goods are used for the implied warranty of fitness to arise. Assume that Sally tells the salesman at the ABC Shoe Store that she wants some running shoes for jogging. He selects shoes clearly labeled as running shoes, which turn out to be unsuitable. Some courts would find that there was a breach of the implied warranty of fitness. Others would hold that because running was the ordinary purpose for which the shoes were intended, only an implied warranty of merchantability arose.

A close examination of facts is required to ascertain whether a warranty of fitness exists, because such a warranty arises only if the following conditions exist:

1. The seller had "reason to know" of the particular purpose for which the goods were purchased. This requirement is obviously met if the seller was actually informed of the intended purpose, but such knowledge does not have to be proven. The requirement is also met if the circumstances dictate that the seller, as a reasonable person, should have known that the buyer was purchasing the goods for a particular purpose.
2. The seller also had reason to know that the buyer was relying on the seller's skill or judgment to furnish suitable goods. That is, the buyer must have relied on the seller's recommendation and the seller must have known or should have known of this dependence. If the buyer shows initiative by presenting brand names or introducing other specifications, recovery will be less likely.
3. Items 1 and 2 above must have existed at the time of contracting. If the seller learns the relevant facts only after the sale contract is made, a warranty does not exist.

These elements are applied in the following unique case.

Warranties in Leases

Article 2A of the UCC contains warranty provisions for leases of goods. Except for "finance leases," Article 2A's rules regarding imposition and disclaimer of ex- press and implied warranty liability are generally the same as those of Article 2 that we have just discussed.

DEMPSEY V. ROSENTHAL
Civil Court, City of New York, 448 N.Y.S.2d 441
(1983)

Plaintiff bought a poodle, Mr. Dunphy, from defendant for $541.25. Five days later, an inspection by a veterinarian disclosed that Mr. Dunphy had one undescended testicle. The plaintiff returned the dog and demanded a refund. The defendant refused. The plaintiff brought this suit in small claims court, claiming breach of the implied warranties of merchantability and fitness.

Saxe, Judge:

[The judge first found that Mr. Dunphy's condition breached the implied warranty of merchantability because a dog with an undescended testicle would not pass without complaint in the trade. Although fertile, the dog could pass the condition on to future generations. The judge then turned to the matter of implied warranty of fitness.]

The next issue to be resolved here is whether warranty of fitness for a particular purpose has been breached. [The UCC] makes it clear that the warranty of fitness for a particular purpose is narrow, more specific, and more precise than the warranty of merchantability which involves fitness for the ordinary purposes for which such goods are used. The following are the conditions that are not required by the implied warranty of merchantability but that must be present if a plaintiff is to recover on the basis of the implied warranty of fitness for a particular purpose:

The seller must have reason to know the buyer's particular purpose.

The seller must have reason to know that the buyer is relying on the seller's skill or judgment to furnish appropriate goods.

The buyer must, in fact, rely upon the seller's skill or judgment.

Nevertheless, I find that the warranty of fitness for a particular purpose has also been breached. Ms. Dempsey testified that she specified to [defendant's] salesperson that she wanted a dog that was suitable for breeding purposes. Although this is disputed by the defendant, the credible testimony supports Ms. Dempsey's version of the event. Further, it is reasonable for a seller of a pedigree dog to assume that the buyer intends to breed it. But, it is undisputed by the experts here (for both sides) that Mr. Dunphy, with only one descended testicle, was as capable of siring a litter as a male dog with two viable and descended testicles. This, the defendant contends, compels a finding in its favor. I disagree. While it is true that Mr. Dunphy's fertility level may be unaffected, his stud value, because of this hereditary condition (which is likely to be passed on to future generations) is severely diminished.

The fact that Mr. Dunphy's testicle later descended and assumed the proper position is not relevant. "The parties were entitled to get what they bargained for at the time that they bargained for it. The right of the buyer to rescind must be determined as of the time the election to rescind was exercised. The parties' rights are not to be determined by subsequent events." White Devon Farm v. Stahl, 389 N.Y.S.2d 724 (Sup.Ct.N.Y.Co. 1976). *White De von Farm* involved the "tale of a stud who was a dud." The court there held that the warranty of fitness for a particular purpose was breached despite the fact that the horse's fertility later rose and the stallion sired 27 live foals.

A judgment for the claimant in the amount of $541.25 shall be entered by the clerk.

Warranties of Title

In most sales of goods, a warranty as to the validity of the seller's title automatically exists. Sec. 2–312 of the UCC imposes two basic types of **warranty of title.** The first is a warranty that the *title conveyed shall be good and its transfer rightful.* This warranty is obviously breached if the seller has stolen the goods from some third party and therefore has no title at all. Other breaches, however, are not so obvious. Suppose that A buys goods from B and then is approached by C who claims to be the rightful owner. Inquiries reveal that there is some basis for C's claim and that the matter can be resolved only through a lawsuit. Will A have to become involved in a lawsuit initiated by C to determine if she bought a good title from B? Or has B breached his warranty of title by conveying a "questionable" title? The answer is that A has the option of returning the goods to B and getting her money back or defending against C's claim. If A takes the latter route and wins the lawsuit, she can recover her legal expenses from B. If A loses the lawsuit, she can recover from B not only her legal expenses, but also the value of the goods lost to C. A breach of the warranty of title exists if C's claim places a "substantial shadow" on the title, even if it ultimately might be proved invalid.

The second type of title warranty is that the goods shall be delivered free from any security interest or other lien or encumbrance of which the buyer at the time of contracting has no knowledge. This warranty will be breached, for instance, if B sells mortgaged goods to A without telling A of the mortgage.

Warranties of title accompany a sale of goods unless the seller indicates by specific language that no such assurances are being made or unless the circumstances indicate as much (for example, in a public sale of goods seized by the sheriff to satisfy a debt, rightful transfers of title are generally not guaranteed).

An additional obligation—not, strictly speaking, a warranty of title—is imposed on some sellers by Sec. 2–312: Unless otherwise agreed, a seller who is a merchant in the type of goods involved is deemed to warrant *that the goods sold do not infringe on the patents, copyrights, or trademarks of a third party.* If a claim of infringement is made by a third party against the buyer, the seller is responsible—unless, of course, the goods were manufactured according to the buyer's specifications.

Conflicting and Overlapping Warranties

Two or more warranties sometimes exist in a single sales transaction. For example, a machine might be warranted to perform certain functions and to last for a specified time. In addition to these express warranties, an implied warranty of merchantability or of fitness for a particular purpose, or both, might exist.

When more than one warranty is created in a given transaction, the buyer does not have to choose among them. The warranties are *cumulative*, such that the buyer can take advantage of any or all of them. According to Sec. 2–317, courts should interpret the warranties as being "consistent" whenever such an interpretation is reasonable. In the unusual event that two warranties are in conflict and cannot both be given effect, the court must attempt to determine the intent of the parties as to which warranty should prevail. Several rules offer guidance in determining intention:

1. Exact or technical specifications take precedence over inconsistent samples or models or general language of description.

2. A sample drawn from the goods to be sold takes precedence over inconsistent general language or description.

3. An express warranty, regardless of how it was created, takes precedence over the implied warranty of merchantability if the two are inconsistent. (An express warranty does not take precedence over the implied warranty of fitness for a particular purpose, although it is difficult to imagine a situation in which the two would be inconsistent.)

These rules are not absolute and can be disregarded by the court if they produce an unreasonable result. The following case illustrates a situation in which a seller's express promise conflicted with a claimed implied warranty.

MOHASCO INDUSTRIES, INC. v. ANDERSON HALVERSON CORP.
Supreme Court of Nevada, 520 P.2d 234 (1974)

Anderson Halverson Corp., owner of the Stardust Hotel in Las Vegas, Nevada, ordered carpeting to be manufactured by Mohasco and installed in the hotel lobby and casino showroom of the Stardust. After installation the buyer refused to pay, claiming that the carpet "shaded" excessively, giving it a mottled effect and the appearance of being water stained. Mohasco, the plaintiff, sued Anderson Halverson, the defendant, to recover the price of $18,242.50. The trial court held in favor of the defendant, and the plaintiff appealed.

Thompson, Justice:

. . . One Fritz Eden, an interior decorator selected and hired by Stardust, designed a pattern for the carpet to be used in the hotel lobby and casino showroom. A sample run of the chosen pattern was taken to the hotel by Eden, and was approved. Eden then specified the material and grade of carpet which the Stardust also approved. The Stardust then issued a detailed purchase order designating the type and length of yarn, weight per square yard, type of weave, color and pattern. No affirmation of fact or promise was made by any representative of . . . the seller to . . . the buyer. The carpet which was manufactured, delivered and installed was consistent with the sample and precisely conformed to the detailed purchase order. There were no manufacturing defects in the carpet.

Upon installation, however, the carpet did shade and, apparently, to a much greater extent than the Stardust or its representative had anticipated. It is clear from the testimony that "shading" is an inherent characteristic of all pile carpeting. When the tufts of the carpet are bent in different angles, the light reflection causes portions of the carpet to appear in different shades of the same color. The only explanation in the record for the "excessive shading" was that Fritz Eden, the decorator for Stardust, decided not to specify the more expensive "twist yarn." That type yarn causes the tufts to stick straight up (or at least tends to do so) thus aiding in the elimination of excessive shading.

The trial court found that the sale of the carpet was a sale by sample which was made a part of the basis of the bargain and created an express warranty that the carpet delivered for installation would conform to the sample. Moreover, [the trial court found] that the express warranty was breached by the seller, thus precluding its claim for relief. [Emphasis added.]

That finding is clearly erroneous. The installed carpet conformed precisely to the description of the goods contained in the purchase order. Moreover, it conformed precisely to the sample which the buyer approved. Whether the sale be deemed a sale by description or by sample, in either event the express warranty of conformity was met. The seller delivered the very carpet which the buyer selected and ordered.

Although there is substantial evidence to support the trial court's finding that the installed carpet shaded excessively, that consequence may not be equated with a breach of an express warranty since the seller delivered and installed the very item which the buyer selected and ordered. Had the buyer, through its interior decorator, selected the more expensive carpet with "twist yarn," perhaps this controversy would not have arisen. The buyer, not the seller, must bear the consequence of that mistake.

[The court then turned to the implied warranty of merchantability question, as follows:] As already noted the judgment below rests upon an erroneous finding that the seller breached an express warranty that the whole of the carpet would conform to the sample which the buyer had approved. The buyer suggests, however, that the judgment should be sustained in any event since it is otherwise clear that the seller breached the implied warrant[y] of merchantability. . .. We turn to consider this contention.

Unless excluded, or modified, a warranty of merchantability is implied in a contract if the seller is a merchant with respect to the goods in question. We have not, heretofore, had occasion to consider the impact, if any, of the implied warranty of merchantability upon a case where the goods are sold by sample or description and the buyer's specifications are so complete that it is reasonable to conclude that he had relied upon himself and not the seller with regard to the merchantability of the goods. . ..

It is apparent that in a case where the sample or description of the goods may, for some reason, result in an undesirable product, the seller is placed in a dilemma. In Hawkland, A Transactional Guide to the Uniform Commercial Code, at 65, the following example is given. Suppose a buyer provides his seller with minute specifications of the material, design and method of construction to be utilized in preparation of an order of shoes, and the seller delivers to the buyer shoes which exactly conform to the specifications. If the blueprints are in fact designs of defective shoes, the buyer should not be able to complain that the shoes are defective. For such an order might put the seller in the dilemma of being forced to breach either the express warranty of description or the implied warranty of merchantability.

The matter at hand is similar to the example just given. Although the carpet was not defective, it did shade excessively and was, in the view of the buyer, an undesirable product. Yet, it was the product which the buyer specified and ordered. The manufacturer seller was not at liberty to add "twist yarn" and charge a higher price. The buyer relied upon its decorator, Fritz Eden, and the seller performed as directed. . .. [W]e hold that the implied, warranty of merchantability is limited by an express warranty of conformity to a precise description supplied by the buyer, and if the latter warranty is not breached, neither is the former.

Disclaimers Excluding and Limiting Warranties

As we have seen, a sales transaction can give rise to three types of warranties: express warranties, implied warranties, and warranties of title. But the creation of these warranties is by no means automatic. The UCC allows a seller to disavow the existence of warranties or to limit the circumstances in which liability will apply by including a **disclaimer** in the sales contract. Theoretically, disclaimers can be justified on the grounds that their use advances freedom of contract, permitting parties to bargain over contract terms and to allocate the risk of loss. Yet in reality, the arrangement tends to be one–sided: consumers usually are in no bargaining position and often do not read disclaimers when making a purchase. For this reason, courts may find a particular disclaimer *unconscionable* under UCC Sec. 2−302.

Disclaimers of Express Warranties

A seller who wishes to avoid liability on an express warranty obviously should not do anything to create a warranty in the first place (a highly impractical measure to take in making sales!). An alternative would be to include a disclaimer in the contract. However, if a warranty has actually become part of the contract, an attempt to disclaim liability will usually not be effective. Sec. 2−316(1) states that a disclaimer will be disregarded if it is inconsistent with the words or conduct that created the express warranty. Suppose that an express warranty has been created by a statement of the seller, by the use of a sample, or by a written description of the goods. Liability could not then be disclaimed by specifying: "These goods are sold without warranties." Such a statement would almost always be inconsistent with the words or conduct that created the warranty. In short, it is extremely difficult for a seller to disclaim an express warranty which has become part of the contract.

Disclaimers of Implied Warranties

Because the existence of an implied warranty depends on circumstances rather than on the precise words used by the seller, such a warranty is relatively easy to disclaim. The UCC permits disclaimers of implied warranties through (1) the use of language specified in Sec. 2−316 of the Code, (2) the buyer's examination of the goods, or (3) custom and usage.

    Disclaimer by Language. In the case of the *warranty of merchantability*, the language used by the seller to disclaim liability does not have to be in writing. If written, however, the disclaimer must be "conspicuous" enough to be noticed by any reasonable person involved in the purchase. (A disclaimer printed in larger type or in a different color than the remainder of the document will probably be considered conspicuous.) In addition, the word *merchantability* must be used—unless the seller uses a phrase such as a "with all faults" or "as is," language that serves to disclaim *both* or *either* of the implied warranties.

In the case of the *warranty of fitness for a particular purpose,* the disclaimer must be in writing and must be conspicuous. Yet the statement itself can be a general one, such as, "There are no warranties extending beyond the description on the face hereof."

Disclaimer by Examination. If before making a contract, the buyer fully examines the goods (or a sample or model of them) or deliberately refuses to examine them at all, no implied warranty exists for *reasonably apparent* defects. Yet if the buyer has no opportunity to examine the goods before contracting, the seller becomes liable for such defects.

When defects are hidden, the seller is always liable, unless it can be proved that the buyer had knowledge of the defects before contracting. When deciding whether a defect is "reasonably apparent" or "hidden," a court will take into account the buyer's knowledge or skill. Such a factor obviously has a bearing on what an examination should have revealed to the buyer. For example, in Dempsey v. Rosenthal, Mr. Dunphy's defective condition—the undescended testicle—was not readily observable. A manual manipulation of the scrotal area would have been the only means to verify the condition. The court found that. Ms. Dempsey, the buyer, did not know this and should not be charged with knowledge of the fact. The type of examination that would be undertaken by the average buyer of a male puppy would not disclose the defective condition, so recovery was not barred by the inspection provisions of UCC Sec. 2–316.

Disclaimer by Custom or Usage. Implied warranties are sometimes excluded or modified by *trade usage* (industry–wide custom) or by a custom that has been established between the contracting parties. An industrywide custom will have no effect, however, on a buyer who is not a member of the particular industry and is unaware of the custom.

Limitation on Damages. In contract cases, punitive damages traditionally have not been available to plaintiffs. For this reason, express and implied warranty suits usually involve two types of damages: basis–of–the–bargain damages (the value of the goods warranted less the value received) and consequential damages (personal and property damages proximately caused by the warranty breach, along with any indirect economic loss foreseeable by the defendant). The buyer injured by a breached warranty also has the option to rescind the contract.

The Code allows limitations to be placed by the seller on damages that may be recovered by a breach of warranty. For example, recovery may be limited to *liquidated damages*—that is, a specified amount to be paid in the event of a breach. A limitation may also be placed on the type of remedy available, guaranteeing, for example, only the replacement of the product without charge.

However, such limitations will not be given effect if they are *unconscionable.* For example, UCC Sec. 2–719(3) provides that "[l]imitation of consequential damages for injury to the person in the case of consumer goods is prima facie unconscionable. ... Furthermore, comment 1 to Sec. 2– 719 provides that "it is of the very essence of a sales contract that at least minimum adequate remedies be available...." Even a clause that appears not to be unconscionable may be ignored if "because of circumstances [it] fails in its purpose or operates to deprive either party of the substantial value of the bargain."

GREAT DANE TRAILER V. MALVERN PULPWOOD
Supreme Court of Arkansas, 785 S.W.2d 13 (1990)

The plaintiff, Malvern Pulpwood, Inc., bought two drop–deck, 65,000– pound weight-- rated pulpwood trailers from the defendant, Great Dane Trailer Sales, Inc. Great Dane issued warranties on the trailers that were limited to the repair or replacement of defective parts, and remedies were limited by the exclusion of consequential and incidental damages. The drop–deck trailers exhibited serious defects as did their replacements, two straight–decked trailers. Malvern Pulpwood sued for breach of the implied warranties of merchantability and fitness. Great Dane defended on the basis of the "repair or replacement" warranty and disclaimer. Great Dane appealed after a jury verdict in Malvern's favor for $40,000.

Glaze, Justice:

Under [UCC] 2–719, parties to an agreement may limit the buyer's remedies to the repair and replacement of nonconforming goods or parts and to make the remedy agreed upon the sole remedy, unless circumstances cause the exclusive or limited remedy to fail of its essential purpose. When there is substantial evidence tending to show that a particular piece of machinery obviously cannot be repaired or its parts replaced so that it is made free of defects, a jury verdict, which implicitly concludes that a limitation of the remedy to the repair and replacement of nonconforming parts deprived the purchaser of the substantial value of the bargain, should be sustained. Such a limited remedy fails whenever the warrantor,

given the opportunity to do so, fails to correct the defect within a reasonable period.

In connection with the sale of two drop–deck trailers sold to MalvernPulpwood, Great Dane offered the following warranty:

Great Dane Trailers, Inc.'s sole obligation under this warranty shall be limited to the repair or replacement, at its option, of any defective part of said trailer which is the result of defective materials and/or defective workmanship of parts furnished and installed by Great Dane Trailers, Inc. This warranty will expire sixty (60) months from date of delivery to the purchaser, and repairs under this warranty shall be at repair facilities designated by Great Dane Trailers, Inc. Transportation expenses to the repair facility are to be borne by the purchasers. THE EXPRESS WARRANTY HEREIN IS IN LIEU OF ANY AND ALL OTHER WARRANTIES, EXPRESSED OR IMPLIED. NO IMPLIED WARRANTY OF MERCHANTABILITY IS MADE AND THERE ARE NO WARRANTIES WHICH EXTEND BEYOND THE DESCRIPTION ON THE FACE HEREOF.

Although the foregoing five-year warranty was given to repair or replace the 65,000 pound GVWC rated dropdeck trailers, we believe the evidence sufficiently shows the limitation failed of its essential purpose. The drop–deck trailers were described as ten–year trailers with a five–year warranty. Both drop–deck trailers "broke" in the same spot within one year from the time Malvern Pulpwood acquired them. Malvern Pulpwood offered testimony that Great Dane's repair job was sloppy and rendered the trailers unsafe. One witness, a welder, stated he did not believe the repairs would fix the trailers; he said that any time steel is welded, the steel would not be as strong as it was before. Great Dane finally replaced the drop–deck trailers with straight–deck trailers. Nevertheless, the replacements, too, broke in the same spot as the drop–deck trailers. [W]e have no doubts that substantial evidence existed to support Malvern Pulpwood's claims that Great Dane failed to correct the trailers' defect within a reasonable period and that the limitation failed of its essential purpose.

[Affirmed.]

Defenses

Privity Defense

Privity is a legal term for the direct relationship between buyer and seller. **Privity of contract** means relationship of contract: If Manufacturer A sells a yacht to Retailer B who in turn sells it to Consumer C, there is privity of contract between A and B and between B and C, but not between A and C. Because a warranty arises from the formation of a contract, privity of contract between the plaintiff and the defendant used to be required for the plaintiff suing for breach of warranty. Warranties did not "run with the goods" to subsequent purchasers and users. Thus, C could sue B but not A.

The privity requirement was not a major hindrance in the early days of our country, when consumers bought most of their goods directly from artisans or local manufacturers. Today, however, when goods travel through chains of distribution, a privity requirement imposes an intolerable burden on consumers. Therefore, it has been greatly relaxed today *and is in the process of being eliminated*. All parties in the chain of distribution (manufacturers, wholesalers, and retailers) are now usually responsible to the last buyer for failure of the goods to live up to the standards of any warranties, especially for personal injuries.

Innocent Bystanders. A final problem with the privity requirement is that defects in goods often injure persons other than the purchaser; yet the privity requirement prevented nonpurchasers (for example, innocent bystanders or persons who borrowed the product from the buyer) from suing anyone in the chain of distribution for breached warranties.

Sec. 2-318 of the UCC has somewhat alleviated this problem by extending warranty protection to (1) members of the buyer's family, (2) members of the buyer's household, and (3) guests in the buyer's home, "if it is reasonable to expect that such person may use, consume or be affected by the goods, and [such person] is injured [physically] by the breach of the warranty." As the language indicates, the extended protection applies only when defective goods have caused a *physical injury to the individual*.

In recent years the drafters of the UCC have proposed alternative versions of Sec. 2-318 to relax the privity requirement further—primarily by granting protection to *any* injured person who could reasonably have been expected to use, consume, or be affected by the goods. Although only 15 or so states have enacted these versions of Sec. 2−318 to date, the trend in most jurisdictions is toward a loosening of the privity requirement in breach of warranty actions.

Plaintiff Misconduct Defenses

When a plaintiff's carelessness contributes to a products−related accident, the defendant can use that carelessness as a defense to warranty claims in most jurisdictions. Because the plaintiff's carelessness defenses to warranty claims are generally the same as such defenses to a strict liability claim, which we are about to discuss, we defer discussion of the matter to the strict liability section.

Statute of Limitations and Notice Requirements

Under UCC Sec. 2−725, an action for breach of contract for sale of goods must be commenced within four years after the cause of action accrues. A traditional tort statute of limitations begins to run only when the right to sue is or should be discovered (and typically lasts two years). The UCC has a similar rule where a warranty *explicitly* extends to future performance of the goods and discovery of the breach must await the time of such performance. In such cases, the statute of limitations does not begin to run until the breach is or should be discovered. However, for all other suits under Article 2, the UCC statute of limitations begins to run when the goods are tendered for delivery. Thus, if the defect is not discovered for four years, the suit may well be timebarred before the defect is discovered. Many potential plaintiffs lose the right to sue by allowing the seller to attempt to effect repairs until after the four year limit has expired. Furthermore, the Code provides that by agreement the parties may reduce the period of limitation to not less than one year but may not extend it. Thus, the statute of limitations often bars warranty suits.

Some warranty actions are barred by a plaintiff's failure to comply with UCC Sec. 2−607(3), which imposes on the buyer a duty to notify the seller of a breach within a reasonable time after he or she discovers or should discover any breach, or be barred from remedy. The purpose of such a requirement is to minimize litigation by giving the seller a chance to effect repairs or otherwise satisfy the buyer. Courtshave generally been reluctant to allow this provision to bar recovery by consumers who suffered personal injuries caused by a breach of warranty. Courts are inclined to construe a "reasonable time" as being a longer period in a personal injury case than in a suit brought for economic loss by a commercial purchaser. The courts are split as to whether a person who bought an item from a retailer must give notice not only to that retailer but also to the manufacturer to be allowed to sue the manufacturer.

Negligence

Because the elements of negligence have been discussed at length in Chapter 8, our purpose here is simply to apply them to the area of products liability. Remember that in an action based on negligence, the defendant must have owed a duty to the plaintiff, and this duty must have been breached. Where a sales transaction is involved, the seller's duty to use reasonable care arises from the mere act of placing goods on the market. The economic benefit derived from a sale generates a responsibility to consumers, for the act of selling directly affects the interests of those who have no choice but to rely on the integrity of sellers. Privity of contract is no longer required in the usual negligence suit.

The manufacturer's liability for negligence is often predicated on negligent design or manufacture; in addition, *both* manufacturer and seller may be liable for failure to inspect or failure to adequately warn.

If the seller is a retailer, distributor, or wholesaler, he or she usually has no duty to inspect new goods, barring knowledge of defects. A duty to inspect does exist, however, when the seller is involved in the installation of goods (new or used) or in their preparation for eventual sale. Liability is imposed to the extent that defects are *reasonably apparent*. By the same token, a manufacturer is charged with taking reasonable measures to discover flaws created during the production process.

A *duty to warn* arises when a product's design (or its intended use) subjects the user to hazard or risk of injury. The danger in question need only be reasonably foreseeable—discoverable only within the limits of existing technology. Warnings given must be adequate in their specifics and must extend to all individuals whose harm is reasonably foreseeable. There is no duty to warn of obvious dangers—no duty, for example, to warn about fire on a box of matches.

Negligent manufacture is often cited in cases in which defects are the result of oversight, human or mechanical error, or lack of judgment. For example, production line employees might not be properly trained, or materials selected for construction might not have sufficient strength to resist the stresses of normal use.

In contrast, actions based on charges of *negligent design* hold the manufacturer responsible for more than the exercise of care in production. In addition to warning about risks and hazards inherent in a design, the manufacturer is expected to design a product with optimal safety as the ideal, compromised only when the costs of improving the design exceed the benefits derived therefrom. Under the rule adopted by most states, there is a duty to design products so that accidents are unlikely to occur and so that injuries suffered will be minimal if an accident does occur. To illustrate, say X is driving a car that explodes when struck in the rear by Y, who has negligently maneuvered his truck. X may recover from Y for initial injuries and may possibly recover from the car's manufacturer for additional injuries resulting from the impact if, for example, the gas tank was located vulnerably close to the rear bumper.

Of course, it would be unreasonable to expect cars to be accident-proof in all situations. (If this were the law, some courts have observed, manufacturers would produce nothing but tanks.) In evaluating the adequacy of design standards, courts have considered such factors as the state of existing technology, the expectation of the ordinary consumer, the danger of a product in relation to its social use, and compliance with government safety standards.

To conclude, the negligence theory became viable as an avenue of recovery to injured plaintiffs when the privity requirement was finally abandoned. This theory offers some advantages over the warranty theory; for example, the buyer does not have to prove that a warranty existed, the buyer does not have to notify the seller within a reasonable time after discovering the defect, and disclaimers in the sales contract usually do not allow the seller to escape liability resulting from his or her negligence.

Yet certain disadvantages exist as well. A plaintiff must prove negligent conduct on the part of the manufacturer or seller, and proof of negligence is at times almost impossible to establish. Only in relatively rare cases have courts inferred negligence pursuant to the doctrine of *res ipsa loquitur* ("the thing speaks for itself"). The doctrine of *res ipsa loquitur* may presume negligence from the fact that the accident did indeed occur. A plaintif who can show that (1) the defendant controlled the product and (2) the defect would not normally occur absent negligence can benefit from *res ipsa loquitur's* presumption of negligence. The presumption would be applicable, for example, if a product exploded immediately on being removed from a container that was sealed at the defendants' factory.

Another impediment to recovery under the negligence theory is that any type of plaintiff misconduct, even simple plaintiff carelessness, will reduce or bar recovery.

In addition, most jurisdictions hold that the UCC provides the only avenue for product liability recovery for mere *economic* loss (generally defined as all losses other than personal injury and tangible damage to property other than the product itself). For example, the majority rule is that if a piece of equipment contains an electrical defect that causes it to be destroyed in a fire resulting in no other loss, warranty provides the buyer's only avenue for recovery. Suit on a negligence theory (and, as we are about to see, a strict liability theory) is precluded in most states.

Strict Liability

Most courts and legislatures have concluded that the warranty and negligence theories do not afford consumers as much protection as they ought, in fairness, to have. Many warranty claims are barred, for example, by disclaimers or because of the statute of limitations or failure to give notice of breach within a reasonable time. Many negligence suits fail because the plaintiff is not able to prove specific acts of negligence on the part of the manufacturer.

Recognizing these deficiencies, most jurisdictions have adopted the theory of **strict liability** by which manufacturers and sellers are held liable irrespective of fault. (See Figure 22.1 for a comparison of strict liability with negligence.) Today, strict liability is the most common basis for imposition of product liability for personal injuries.

Justification for the strict liability theory lies in the notion that merchants and manufacturers are better able to bear losses than injured consumers and that, in many cases, losses will be transferred to the buying public in the form of higher prices on products. Thus, society at large assumes the cost of damages suffered by a few— an

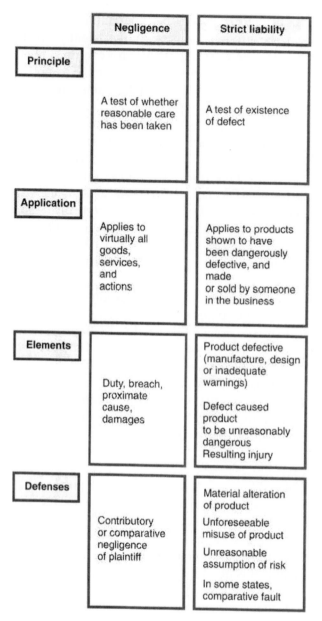

	Negligence	Strict liability
Principle	A test of whether reasonable care has been taken	A test of existence of defect
Application	Applies to virtually all goods, services, and actions	Applies to products shown to have been dangerously defective, and made or sold by someone in the business
Elements	Duty, breach, proximate cause, damages	Product defective (manufacture, design or inadequate warnings) Defect caused product to be unreasonably dangerous Resulting injury
Defenses	Contributory or comparative negligence of plaintiff	Material alteration of product Unforeseeable misuse of product Unreasonable assumption of risk In some states, comparative fault

Figure 21.1 Differences between Negligence and Strict Liability

arrangement that is perhaps more equitable in that it offers relief for those injured by defective products.

Proponents of strict liability argue, in addition, that eliminating the need to prove negligence in a tort action will make manufacturers and sellers more mindful of accident prevention.

Finally, there is an economic basis for adopting this liability theory. Because negligence is often difficult to prove, litigation becomes excessively costly. From an overall economic standpoint, then, it can make sense to abandon proof of negligence in a products liability action.

Elements of Strict Liability

The elements of strict liability are recorded in section 402 of the American Law Institute's *Restatement (Second) of Torts,* a summary and clarification of American common-law principles. Section 402A reads:

1. "One who sells any product in a defective condition unreasonably dangerous to the user or consumer or to his property is subject to liability for physical harm thereby caused to the ultimate user or consumer, or to his property, if
   a. "the seller is engaged in the business of selling such a product, and
   b. "it is expected to and does reach the user or consumer without substantial change in the condition in which it is sold.
2. " The rule stated in Subsection (1) applies although
   a. "the seller has exercised all possible care in the preparation and sale of his product, and
   b. "the user or consumer has not bought the product from or entered into any contractual relation with the seller."

Two points regarding section 402A merit special emphasis. First, subsection (1)(a) limits application of the strict liability theory to those engaged in the business of selling the products in question. Second, subsection (2) makes it clear that negligence and privity are not issues under the strict liability theory.

Thus in certain respects, strict liability may be viewed as an extension of the implied warranty of merchantability, where the warranty theory was applied to foreign objects in food and drink. (Recall our discussion of the "reasonable expectation" and "foreign–natural object" tests.) Taken further, strict liability is applied in cases involving virtually all kinds of goods. Although there is, in fact, some overlapping here with the warranty theory, actions based on strict liability are nevertheless considered to be actions in tort rather than under warranty.

The crux of a section 402A action is the sale of a *defective product that is unreasonably dangerous* to the *user* or *consumer* or to his or her property. Section 402A covers only sales of products, not services. A product is defective if it is unreasonably dangerous because of a flaw in the product or a weakness in its design or because adequate warning of risks and hazards related to the design has not been given.

A strict liability action differs from a negligence action in that the plaintiff need not prove the defect resulted from the defendant's failure to use reasonable care. Although in failure–to–warn cases the manufacturer will almost always be found negligent, the same cannot be said of resellers. New products packaged with inadequate warnings may be resold without subjecting intermediaries and retailers to liability under the negligence theory; yet these very resellers could be held liable under section 402A because no fault is required under the strict liability theory.

Defective conditions may result not only from flaws or harmful ingredients within the product but also from foreign objects in its composition and defects in its container. In this regard, a product is not defective "when it is safe for normal handling or consumption." For example, beer consumed only occasionally and in moderate amounts is probably not harmful. If an adult drinks too much beer at a party and then becomes ill, the seller is not liable.

To be safe, a product should be properly packaged and otherwise treated so that it will not deteriorate or be rendered dangerous within a reasonable period of time under normal conditions.

The question of what constitutes an "unreasonably" dangerous product is taken up in section 402A, comments i and k. Presumably, certain products are reasonably dangerous or "unavoidably unsafe"—that is to say, existing technology and scientific knowledge are insufficient to produce a completely safe result. An example often cited is that of the rabies vaccine, which has dangerous side effects but which is the only existing treatment against a deadly disease. Drugs sold under prescription and experimental treatments also fall within this category. Unavoidably unsafe products must be accompanied by instructions and warnings, so that the user can decide whether to undergo the risks involved. If the harmful consequences of using a product generally exceed the benefits and if safer alternatives are available, a product will be considered unreasonably unsafe. In defining what is meant by "unreasonably unsafe," section 402A also considers the expectations of the ordinary consumer, stating: "The articles sold must be dangerous to an extent beyond that which would be contemplated by the ordinary consumer who purchases it, with the ordinary knowledge common to the community as to its characteristics. . . . Good butter is not unreasonably dangerous merely because, if such be the case, it deposits cholesterol in the arteries and leads to heart attacks; but bad butter, contaminated with poisonous fish oil, is unreasonably dangerous."

Another stipulation in section 402A is that products must be in a defective condition when they leave the seller. The burden of proof lies with the plaintiff to show that the product was defective at the time of sale. Subsequent alteration or further processing may operate to relieve the seller of liability.

In addition, the plaintiffs injury must occur as a result of a defect in the product itself, rather than from conditions surrounding its use or consumption. For example, if an Africanized "killer" bee stings a longshoreman unloading crates of tropical fruit, the fruit company is not liable under section 402A because even if there is proof that the bee was a stowaway in the fruit, there is no defect inherent in the fruit itself.

Among the most problematic strict liability cases are those based on a product's allegedly defective warning. The following case is illustrative.

KNIGHT v. JUST BORN, INC.
United States District Court for the District of Oregon, 2000 U.S. Dist. LEXIS 9716 (2000)

Mr. Knight regularly ate Hot Tamales candy, manufactured by Just Born, Inc. One day Knight picked up a small handful of the Hot-Tamales, walked into his living room where he turned on the television and "popped a couple of candies in [his] mouth." He described his injury as follows: "And it was the next two I popped in my mouth. I chewed the first one, and I kind of had the second one over in the side of my mouth. And that was the one that when I bit in to [sic] it, instantly I had a sensation of like a fireball inside of my mouth. I knew there was something wrong, because instead of the usual gumdrop, jelly-type consistencies that those candies always had had, this one had inside the shell like a syrupy liquid that I bit in to. And instantaneously, this fire spread through my mouth, is the only way I can describe it."

After the incident, the skin sloughed off the inside of Mr. Knight's mouth. He could not eat anything for several days. He suffered headaches, an inability to swallow or speak, and a tongue "so swollen that it didn't feel like it fit inside [his] mouth." He didn't feel normal again for ten days to two weeks.

Knight sued both Just Born, Inc., the manufacturer, and Costco, the retailer in strict liability. Both plaintiff and defendants moved for summary judgment.

Stewart, Magistrate Judge:

In Oregon, a product liability civil action is: "a civil action brought against a manufacturer, distributor, seller or lessor of a product for damages for personal injury, death or property damage arising out of: (1) Any design, inspection, testing, manufacturing or other defect in a product; (2) Any failure to warn regarding a product; or (3) Any failure to properly instruct in the use of a product." (ORS 30.900.) [The court then quoted the language of 402A.]

"The justification for strict liability has been said to be that the seller, by marketing his product for use and consumption, has undertaken and assumed a special responsibility toward any member of the consuming public who may be injured by it; that the public has the right to and does expect . . . that reputable sellers will stand behind their goods; that public policy demands that the burden of accidental injuries caused by products intended for consumption be placed upon those who market them, and be treated as a cost of production against which liability insurance can be obtained; and that the consumer of such products is entitled to the maximum of protection at the hands of someone, and the proper persons to afford it are those who market the products." RESTATEMENT (SECOND) OF TORTS, §402A.

Liability for unreasonably dangerous defective products normally arises either from manufacturing defects or design defects (including a failure to warn). Mr. Knight does not contend that Hot Tamales are defectively designed. Rather, as described above, his claim is focused on a manufacturing defect and a failure to warn.

All product liability actions are premised on a product that is "in a defective condition unreasonably dangerous to the user." ORS 30.920(1). The standard by which "unreasonably dangerous" is measured is the "consumer contemplation test" set forth in Comment i from RESTATEMENT

(SECOND) OF TORTS, §402A. According to Comment i from the RESTATEMENT (SECOND) OF TORTS, §402A, "unreasonably dangerous" means that "the article sold must be dangerous to an extent beyond that which would be contemplated by the ordinary consumer who purchases it, with the ordinary knowledge common to the community as to its characteristics."

A plaintiff proceeding under the consumer expectation test need not produce specific evidence of defect. Instead, this test applies when the plaintiff cannot point to a specific manufacturing flaw. "In some cases the plaintiff can produce direct evidence of a mistake in fabrication," but: "[i]n the type of case in which there is no evidence, direct or circumstantial, available to prove exactly what sort of manufacturing flaw existed . . . the plaintiff may nonetheless be able to establish his right to recover, by proving that the product did not perform in keeping with the reasonable expectations of the user."

If a product fails in an unusual, unexpected fashion, "the inference is that there was some sort of defect, a precise definition of which is unnecessary." Thus, Mr. Knight need not produce direct evidence as to whether and how the Hot Tamale contained a "hot spot" of extra cinnamic aldehyde in order to create a question for the jury. Rather, if he has presented enough evidence to satisfy the consumer expectations test, then a jury will be allowed to infer a defect in the Hot Tamale. This court's function is to determine whether the evidence in this case would allow a jury to make an informed decision as to whether the allegedly defective Hot Tamale "performed as an ordinary consumer would have expected."

In order to satisfy the consumer expectations test, a plaintiff must prove: "(1) what an ordinary consumer would expect from the allegedly defective product, and (2) that the product failed to meet those expectations." By placing a food item into the marketplace, a seller represents to consumers that the product is safe for consumption. That is the one and only purpose for which a food product is intended. Viewing the evidence in the light most favorable to Mr. Knight, the Hot Tamale which he consumed did not live up to either the explicit representation of great taste or the implicit representation of safe to eat. Therefore, given the mix of explicit and implicit representations that Hot Tamales are safe to consume, a jury could reasonably believe that the Hot Tamale at issue did not satisfy a reasonable consumer's expectations.

In sum, Mr. Knight's claim is not foreclosed by the lack of definite and specific direct evidence regarding the alleged defect in the Hot Tamale. Although Mr. Knight is not entitled to summary judgment on this claim, he is nonetheless entitled to present his case to a jury. Therefore, both motions for summary judgment are denied.

Restatement (Third) of Torts: Products Liability

As strict liability law developed, most alleged product defects sorted into three categories: manufacturing defects (as alleged in *Just Born*), design defects (perhaps alleging that a machine should have featured a safety device that its design omitted), and warning defects. Most courts initially used the "consumer expectation" test to determine whether a particular defect rendered a product "unreasonably dangerous." This test worked pretty well for manufacturing defects and warning defects, but the complicated factors often involved in design defect cases led many courts to con- clude that the average consumer had no basis upon which to form a reasonable expectation regarding the safety of product designs. Therefore, most courts adopted a "risk/utility" test in cases of claimed design defects. Under this test, plaintiffs are required to demonstrate that the foreseeable risks presented by the product's current design outweigh the design's utility. A lawnmower without a blade would be much safer for consumers to use, but it would not cut much grass. Note that the risk/utility test reintroduces negligence factors into its calculation, arguably inconsistent with overall strict liability theory.

Judicial disagreement on this and other strict liability issues led the American Law Institute to issue in 1997 the Restatement (Third) of Torts focusing specifically on strict liability. The Restatement (Third) explicitly recognizes the three types of strict liability claims. Section 2(a) essentially replicates that traditional 402A approach for manufacturing defects, imposing liability whenever a product "departs from its intended design even though all possible care was exercised."

Section 2(b), on the other hand, replaces strict liability in design cases with an explicit negligence standard, providing that "[a] product... is defective in design when the foreseeable risks of harm posed by the product could have been reduced or avoided by the adoption of a reasonable alternative design by the seller..., and the omission of the alternative design renders the product not reasonably safe." Section 2(b) requires plaintiffs in most cases to demonstrate the availability of a reasonable alternative design and to show that defendant acted unreasonably in not adopting that alternative design. It explicitly rejects the consumer expectation test for design defects.

Restatement (Third) Section 2(c) similarly imposes a negligence standard in warning defect cases, providing that a product "is defective because of inadequate instructions or warnings when the foreseeable risks of harm posed by the product could have been reduced or avoided by the provision of reasonable instructions or warnings by the seller..., and the omission of the instructions renders the product not reasonably safe."

It is too early to tell whether the courts will embrace the Restatement (Third's) approach to these related issues, but it seems to reflect to at least some extent prodefendant developments in the products liability case law in recent years.

Limitations and Defenses

The strict liability theory is not an answer to every plaintiff's prayer. Various limitations and defenses operate against him or her, a number of which are effective in some states but not in others.

Limitations

Although strict liability makes recovery easier in certain respects, the requirement that a defective product be "unreasonably dangerous" precludes recovery in many instances. Damages resulting from the failure of a product to perform its ordinary purpose, for example, would not be covered under section 402A. As a result, some states have eliminated the "unreasonably dangerous" requirement.

In addition, section 402A limits recovery to users and consumers (including family members, guests, and employees of the purchaser; and individuals who prepare a product for consumption, who repair a product, and who passively enjoy the benefit of a product, as in the case of passengers on an airplane). Recovery is not always allowed to injured bystanders or others who are brought into contact with the defective product; courts differ on this point, depending on the state. Most states have extended application of the theory to anyone suffering reasonably foreseeable injury because of the defect (such as the driver of a car struck from behind by another vehicle whose brakes were defectively manufactured).

Another limitation to the strict liability theory is that the plaintiff may find it difficult to prove that a product left the hands of the seller in a defective condition. A related requirement is that the product undergo no material change in condition after leaving defendant's hands.

Where the technology involved in production is complex, witnesses who can testify to defective manufacture may not be available. For this reason, failure–to–warn cases are more common than those alleging errors in the production process.

Finally, damage limitations exist. Plaintiffs can usually recover only for property damages and personal injuries but, as in negligence cases, not for basis–of–the–bargain damages. Recovery for mere economic losses is usually disallowed as inconsistent with the UCC's scheme for warranty recovery. Punitive damages are available in *some* jurisdictions if the defendant evinces utter disregard for the safety of consumers and users of the product. Finally, as we shall discuss in more detail later in the chapter, many states have recently imposed statutory limitations on recoveries in products liability cases in an attempt to stem the "products liability revolution."

Privity Defense

Most states, but not all, follow the section 402A(2)(b) position abolishing the privity requirement. In some states an intermediary is protected from section 402A liability by requirements that the manufacturer be included in the plaintiff's suit whenever possible or that the manufacturer be sued instead of the intermediary.

Sophisticated Purchaser Defense

Some courts recognize a **sophisticated purchaser defense** in strict liability cases based on a defective warning. For example, in Smith v. Walter C. Best, Inc., 927 F.2d 736 (3d Cir. 1990) , the defendant sold sand to a foundry firm. The plaintiff, an employee of the buyer, allegedly contracted cancer from long–term inhalation of silica dust contained in the sand. Because the buyer was knowledgeable as to the risks of silica sand, the court granted summary judgment to the defendant seller, allowing it to rely on the knowledgeable intermediate purchaser to supply appropriate warnings. The defense succeeded because most courts treat a duty to warn claim, even under strict liability, according to negligence standards.

Plaintiff Misconduct Defenses

In negligence cases, of course, a plaintiff's carelessness is simply compared with the defendant's in most jurisdictions. The plaintiff's own carelessness can reduce or even bar recovery. In strict liability claims (and, in most jurisdictions, express and implied warranty claims), "plaintiff carelessness" is not treated as a single concept. Rather, several types of plaintiff misconduct are recognized, with differing effects on liability.

One category is simple plaintiff carelessness, often described as the **failure to discover or guard against** a defect in a product. Although some jurisdictions compare such plaintiff carelessness with the defendant's fault under a comparative negligence statute, others conclude that consumers are entitled to assume that products are defect-free. Unwilling to impose an obligation on consumers to assume that products they use might be defective, these latter jurisdictions hold that simple plaintiff carelessness is no defense at all to strict liability (or warranty) claims.

Another category of plaintiff misconduct is **product misuse,** which occurs when a plaintiff uses a product for a purpose for which it was not designed. For example, a consumer might use a pop bottle as a hammer or a lawn mower as a hedge trimmer. In some jurisdictions, unforeseeable product misuse indicates that the product is not defective and constitutes a complete defense to strict liability (and warranty) claims; in other jurisdictions, it is merely evidence of plaintiff misconduct to be compared with the defendant's fault. However, when the plaintiffs misuse is foreseeable to the defendant (for example, that the purchaser of a sports car might exceed the speed limit), many jurisdictions impose on the defendant a duty to warn against the misuse, or perhaps even to install safety devices to guard against the misuse. Therefore, foreseeable misuse typically is no defense.

A final category of plaintiff misconduct is **assumption of risk,** which occurs when a plaintiff, having discovered a defect in the product and fully appreciating its danger, voluntarily uses the product anyway. In Sargia v. Skil Corp., 1985 U.S. Dist. LEXIS 12752(S.D.N.Y), the plaintiff (a professional carpenter) was using the defendant's portable saw when he noticed that the "bumper" for the saw's protective blade guard had fallen off, causing the lower guard to obstruct the front of the blade, preventing it from beginning to cut. Although he had two similar saws on the job site, the plaintiff continued to use the defective one, manually retracting the blade guard before each cut. Six hours later, the plaintiff started the saw and then reached over with his left hand to retract the guard with its lift lever. Unfortunately, he missed the lever and hit the blade, amputating 3/8 inch of his finger. This was held to be an assumption of the risk by the plaintiff. In some jurisdictions, assumption of the risk is a complete bar to recovery; in others, it is evidence of the plaintiff's fault to be compared with that of the defendant under a comparative fault statute.

There is great variation among the states regarding application of these plaintiff misconduct defenses. The following case illustrates one court's thinking regarding a common issue.

Smith v. Goodyear Tire & Rubber Co.
U.S. District Court, District of Vermont, 600 F.Supp. 1561 (1985)

The plaintiff, Smith, was injured in an automobile accident. He brought this action alleging negligence on the part of the driver, Young, in whose car Smith was riding at the time of the accident, and alleging a strict liability claim against the defendant tire manufacturer, the Goodyear Tire & Rubber Company.

The defendants raised a "seat belt defense," asserting that their liability should be reduced or completely erased because Smith was not wearing a seat belt although one was available to him and that wearing it would have reduced, if not eliminated, his injuries. The plaintiff moved to strike this defense. The following is the trial judge's ruling on the plaintiff's motion.

Coffrin, Chief Judge:

Courts are divided on the issue of whether evidence regarding the nonuse of automobile seatbelts should be admissible in comparative negligence cases. Plaintiff relies heavily in his brief on the fact that regulations adopted pursuant to Vermont statutes, although they do require that pleasure cars be equipped with seat belts in their front seats, do not require that the seat belts be used. Plaintiff also points out that Vermont courts have never imposed such a duty.

Plaintiff asserts that courts' reluctance to "find a duty to buckle up" stems from a concern that requiring seat belt use would lead to a flood of litigation in which defendants would argue that, as a matter of law, any plaintiff who fails not only to use his seat belt but also to install an air bag in his car, to adjust his head rest, or, indeed, "to drive a Mack Truck" would be more vulnerable to injury and, thus, guilty of contributing to his own injury.

We are unpersuaded by such reasoning. First, admitting such evidence would not create a duty but would merely allow the jury to consider the information on the question of negligence. Second, the test of negligence would continue to be whether the person acted reasonably under the circumstances presented. We do not presume to decide whether or not Plaintiff's failure to fasten his seat belt in the instant case was reasonable. We do believe, however, that the arguments on both sides of the issue are such that a reasonable jury could decide either way. As stated by a New York court,

"[T]he seat belt affords the automobile occupant an unusual and ordinarily unavailable means by which he or she may minimize his or her damages prior to the accident. [T]he burden of buckling an available seat belt may, under the facts of the particular case, be found by the jury to be less than the likelihood of injury when multiplied by its accompanying severity." Spier v Barker, 323 N.E.2d 164 (Ct.App. 1974), .

We hold that the jury should be given the task of making this assessment.

. . . Comment (c) to §402A explains that the justification for this special doctrine of liability is "that the seller, by marketing his product for use and consumption, has undertaken and assumed a special responsibility. . .." Comment (n) goes on to say that contributory negligence "is not a defense to strict liability when such negligence consists merely in a failure to discover the defect in the product, or to guard against the possibility of its existence."

Instead, the Comment states, Plaintiff will be barred from recovery only if he "discovers the defect and is aware of the danger, and nevertheless proceeds unreasonably to make use of the product."

Even if Goodyear cannot prove the latter, however, we decline to follow the rigid requirements of Comment (n), and hold that Goodyear should be able to introduce evidence of Plaintiff's failure to use his seat belt as a defense to strict liability. Because Vermont follows the doctrine of comparative negligence, it need not be swayed by the "all or nothing" considerations present in the Comment to the Restatement or in contributory negligence jurisdictions. The purpose behind the strict liability doctrine is to hold certain sellers to a higher standard of care due to their assumption of a special responsibility. Our holding does not thwart that purpose, since Plaintiff still would not have to prove negligence on the part of Goodyear. Although we would be reluctant to completely excuse defendants simply because some of a plaintiff's injuries might have resulted from his own actions, it also does not seem fair to allow a negligent plaintiff, who may have contributed to as much as fifty percent of his injuries, to pay for none of them and to recover as much as a plaintiff who had taken all precautions reasonable under the circumstances.

There is a split of authority among other states on this issue. For the reasons stated above, we choose to follow the reasoning of many other comparative fault jurisdictions, and hold that juries may consider evidence of plaintiffs' negligence in assessing damages as to strict liability claims as well as to negligence claims.

Plaintiff's motion is Denied.

In conclusion, the strict liability doctrine favors plaintiffs in that it possesses several advantages (1) few defenses against liability can be raised by the defendant; (2) disclaimers are ineffectual; (3) privity is not required; and (4) buyers must prove only that goods were *dangerously defective* when they left the seller's hands and that this defect caused the buyer's injury.

However, disadvantages to the plaintiff include (1) applicability of section 402A only against sellers who are merchants, and (2) availability of damages only for physical injuries to person and property and not for economic injuries.

Federal Consumer Legislation

Over the years Congress has enacted a number of federal regulatory laws dealing with the safety and quality of goods. For the most part these laws have focused solely on protecting ultimate consumers from physical harm, and until recently, they were enacted piecemeal and were rather narrow in scope. Examples include the Food, Drug and Cosmetic Act (1938), the Flammable Fabrics Act (1953), the Refrigerator Safety Act (1956), the Hazardous Substances Act (1960), and the Poison Prevention Packaging Act (1970).

Consumer Product Safety Act

In 1972 Congress enacted the **Consumer Product Safety Act**—the first law to deal with the safety of consumer products in general—and created a federal agency, the

Consumer Product Safety Commission (CPSC), to administer it. Some consumer products are not covered by the Consumer Product Safety Act because they come under the aegis of other federal laws. The most important of these are food, drugs, and cosmetics, which are regulated by the Food and Drug Administration under the Food, Drug, and Cosmetic Act. Automobiles are also excluded because of coverage by the other legislation.

The CPSC possesses broad powers and performs many functions, ranging from safety research and testing to preparing safety rules and standards for more than 10,000 products. It has the power to ban or recall products and to require special labeling in certain circumstances. It can levy civil penalties on those who violate the Act and criminal penalties on those who willfully violate it. Yet despite the extensive range of its power, the CPSC has been criticized for not issuing sufficient standards to ensure the integrity of consumer products. Additionally, the CPSC has been woefully underfunded and understaffed in recent years, making it very difficult for the agency to effectively perform its tasks.

Because the maximum fine the CPSC can impose upon companies for failing to disclose problems with their products is $1.65 million, a relatively small amount compared to the losses defective products can cause, some believe that the CPSC lacks the enforcement threat to be effective. When Wal-Mart was caught failing to report safety hazards with fitness machines, the $750,000 fine it was assessed cost the company the equivalent of sales rung up in only 1 minute and 33 seconds. The Commission often attempts to punish companies through bad publicity.

Magnuson-Moss Warranty Act

In 1975 Congress passed the **Magnuson-Moss Warranty Act.** Like the federal legislation just discussed, this statute is consumer-oriented. It applies only to purchases by ultimate consumers for personal, family, or household purposes and not to transactions in commercial or industrial settings. The Warranty Act, which is usually enforced by the Federal Trade Commission (FTC), does not regulate the safety or quality of consumer goods. Instead it prevents deceptive warranty practices, makes consumer warranties easier to understand, and provides an effective means of enforcing warranty obligations. The federal Warranty Act is limited to consumer transactions, and it modifies the UCC warranty rules in some respects; in nonconsumer transactions, the UCC rules continue in effect.

The type of warranty to which the Warranty Act applies is much more narrowly defined than is an express warranty under the UCC. Specifically, it is (1) any written affirmation of fact made by a supplier to a purchaser relating to the quality or performance of a product and affirming that the product is defect free or that it will meet a specified level of performance over a period of time; or (2) a written undertaking to "refund, repair, replace, or take other action" if a product fails to meet written specifications. Obviously express warranties that are not in writing, such as those created by verbal description or by sample, will continue to be governed solely by the UCC, even though a consumer transaction is involved.

The Warranty Act does not require anyone to give a warranty on consumer goods. It applies only if the seller *voluntarily chooses* to make an express written warranty (perhaps in an effort to render a product more competitive). When a written warranty is provided for a product costing $10 or more, it must be labeled as either "full" or "limited." When the cost of goods exceeds $15, the warranty must be contained in a single document, must be written in clear including (1) a description of items covered and those excluded, along with specific service guarantees; (2) instructions on how to proceed in the event of product failure; (3) the identity of those to whom the warranty is extended; and (4) limitations on the warranty period.

Under a full warranty, the warrantor (and no one else in che chain of distribution) must assume certain minimum duties and obligations. For instance, he or she must agree to *repair or replace* any malfunctioning or defective product within a "reasonable" time and without charge. If the warrantor makes a reasonable number of attempts to remedy the defect and is unable to do so, the consumer can choose to receive a *cash refund or replacement* of the product without charge. No *time limitation* can be placed on a full warranty; and consequential damages (such as for personal injury or property damage) can be disclaimed only if the limitation is *conspicuous*.

A written warranty that does not meet the minimum requirements must be designated conspicuously as a *limited warranty*. It may cover, for example, parts but not labor, or it may levy shipping and handling fees. If a time limit (such as 24 months) is all that prevents the warranty from being a full one, it can be designated as a "full 24-month warranty."

Because its purpose is to regulate *written* warranties, the Warranty Act generally does not cover implied warranties of merchantability and fitness for a particular purpose. These are governed by the UCC, and as we have seen, the UCC allows implied warranties to be disclaimed. However, drafters of the Warranty Act saw fit to limit the use of disclaimers where written warranties are involved, because of certain abusive practices prevalent at the time: Sellers were providing limited express warranties in bold print and then disclaiming implied warranties, thus leaving the consumer with few rights while appearing to offer substantial protection.

For this reason, the Magnuson–Moss Act *prohibits a disclaimer of implied warranties* (1) when an express written warranty is given, whether full or limited, or (2) when a service contract is made with the consumer within 90 days after the sale. (Under a service contract the seller agrees to service and repair a product for a set period of time in return for a fixed fee.) If the written warranty specifies a *time* limitation, however, implied warranties may be suspended by a disclaimer effective *after* the written warranty expires.

The Warranty Act is usually enforced by the FTC, but the Attorney General or an injured consumer can also initiate an action if informal procedures for settling disputes prove ineffective. Sellers are authorized to dictate the informal procedures by which a particular dispute is to be settled. If these procedures follow FTC guidelines, the consumer cannot resort to court action until all established means have been exhausted.

Legislative Limitations on the Products Liability Revolution

From 1960 until the mid-1980s, the general trend in products liability law was strongly pro-plaintiff. New theories allowed new classes of injured persons to sue defendants that had never before been vulnerable to suit. Injured consumers have been well served, and it is certainly arguable that products liability litigation has been the most influential factor in bringing about improved product designs and safety practices that have saved thousands of lives.

Recent years, however, have seen a countervailing pressure to reform products liability law in order to roll back the "products liability revolution." Damage awards have increased insurance premiums, raised the prices of some products, induced some companies to cease manufacturing certain products, and arguably, caused American business to suffer a competitive disadvantage abroad. The expense of designing eminently safe products, coupled with insurance rates much higher than those in Europe, has added significantly to the costs of production. The apparent "explosion" of products liability has raised a storm of protest among manufacturers and sellers, and at present, almost every state has enacted or is considering tort reform.

Among reforms passed in many states are: (a) ceilings on damage awards in product liability suits, (b) caps on punitive damage awards, (c) elimination or modification of joint & several liability, (d) requiring plaintiffs to show the economic and technological feasibility of alternative designs in design defect cases, (e) statutes of repose providing a time period (often from 5 to 15 years) after which the manufacturer is not liable for injuries caused by a product, the statute of limitations notwithstanding, and (f) creation of "state of the art" defenses that prevent defendants' engineering and other decisions from being judged by 20–20 hindsight.

Some of these reforms (especially severe caps on damage awards) have been declared unconstitutional by state courts that believed plaintiffs were being denied their fair day in court. Because of these reforms, the number of products liability lawsuits has been declining in recent years, although the median award in such suits has risen in recent years as plaintiffs' attorneys have been more selective and serious cases such as the asbestos and tobacco litigation have buoyed recoveries.

The issue of punitive damages may be overblown, as they are granted in only three percent or so of all jury verdicts. Still, some awards are shockingly high. The Supreme Court put vague limits on punitive damages in a products liability case, Gore v. BMW of North America, 517 U.S. 559 (1996), when it struck down a $2 million punitive damages award (reduced from $4 million by the Alabama Supreme Court) on grounds that it was so grossly excessive as to violate the 14th Amendment's Due Process Clause. Although the Court failed to draw clear lines regarding what constitutes "grossly excessive" for purposes of creating a constitutional violation, it set out guidelines for review—consideration should be given to the degree of reprehensibility of defendant's conduct, the ratio of punitive damages to compensatory damages or other actual harm to plaintiff, and the difference between the award and comparable penalties under the law—and sent a message that should stiffen the spines of judges reviewing large jury assessments of punitive damages.

Federal product liability reform has been suggested repeatedly over the years for the twin purposes of reining in the products liability revolution and creating uniformity of standards so that manufacturers and other products liability defendants will not be subjected to varied and conflicting standards as they operate in many states and plaintiffs will not be able to forum shop in filing products liability suits. President Clinton vetoed a version of federal product liability reform; President Bush would likely sign such a bill. Even under the Clinton administration, Congress passed numerous federal acts limiting product liability, including: (a) the General Aviation Revitalization Act which set an 18-year statute of repose for small aircraft and aircraft parts, (b) the Aviation Disaster Family Assistance Act of 1996 which prohibits lawyers from contacting the survivors or families of people killed in airline crashes for 30 days after the crash, (c) the Good Samaritan Food Donation Act of 1996 which protects people or companies from most civil suits that might otherwise arise from food donations, and (d) the Year 2000 Information and Readiness Act which established numerous procedural and substantive requirements for plaintiffs filing suits for Y2K–related problems.

All lawsuits shape our society in at least minor ways, but massive products liability class action suits can have huge impacts and are often designed to change public policy in ways that the legislative and executive branches have resisted. Tobacco litigation has threatened the very existence of the giant tobacco industry. Proponents of the litigation argue that the lawsuits successfully brought to justice tobacco companies that because of their size and wealth were seemingly beyond regulation.

Industry's widespread use of asbestos in manufacturing long after its cancer-causing tendencies were discovered has led to litigation that has bankrupted numerous companies. Indeed, the civil justice system is so overwhelmed with 600,000 asbestos claims that even the American Bar Association urged Congress to restrict legislatively the class of potential asbestos plaintiffs.

Proponents of gun control who have not been able to defeat the National Rifle Association in the halls of Congress have taken their case to the courts in an attempt to impose liability on gun manufacturers comparable to that imposed upon cigarette makers. Although their success has been minimal, that did not stop other activists from filing a lawsuit against McDonalds in an attempt to force the fast food industry to change its menus and more clearly warn consumers of the health hazards of its food.

PELMAN V. MCDONALD'S CORP.
U.S. District Court, Southern District of New York, 237 F.Supp.2d 512 (2003)

Plaintiff consumers filed this class action against McDonald's, alleging that it sells fast food that is high in unhealthy substances and thereby contributes to a burgeoning obesity problem among Americans. The complaint alleged deceptive advertising claims and negligence claims. The trial judge held that plaintiffs had failed to produce any advertisements that could be viewed as deceptive and turned to the product liability claims based in negligence.

Sweet, District Judge:

Plaintiffs allege that McDonalds' products are inherently dangerous because of the inclusion of high levels of cholesterol, fat, salt and sugar. McDonald's argues that because the public is well aware that hamburgers, fries and other fast–food fare have such attributes, McDonald's cannot be held liable. McDonald's cites to the Restatement (Second) of Torts and claims that because plaintiffs' claims hinge on injuries resulting from excessive consumption of food, they face a high bar indeed:

Many products cannot possibly be made entirely safe for all consumption, and any food or drug necessarily involves some risk of harm, if only from over–consumption. Ordinary sugar is a deadly poison to some diabetics, and castor oil found use under Mussolini as an instrument of torture. That is not what is meant by "unreasonably dangerous".... The article sold must be dangerous to an extent beyond that which would be contemplated by the ordinary consumer who purchases it, with the ordinary knowledge common to the community as to its characteristics. Good whiskey is not unreasonably dangerous merely because it will make some people drunk, and is especially dangerous to alcoholics; but bad whiskey, containing a dangerous amount of fuel oil, is unreasonably dangerous. Good tobacco is not unreasonably dangerous merely because the effects of smoking may be harmful; but tobacco containing something like marijuana may be unreasonably dangerous. Good butter is not unreasonably dangerous merely because, if such be the case, it deposits cholesterol in the arteries and leads to heart attacks; but bad butter, contaminated with poisonous fish oil, is unreasonably dangerous.

When asked at oral argument to distinguish this case from those cases involving injuries purportedly caused by asbestos exposure, counsel for the defendants stated that in this case, the dangers complained of have been well-known for some time, while the dangers of asbestos did not became apparent until years after exposure. The Restatement provision cited above confirms this analysis, recognizing that the dangers of over–consumption of items such as alcoholic beverages, or typically high-in–fat foods such as butter, are well–known. Thus any liability based on over–consumption is doomed if the consequences of such over-consumption are common knowledge.

It is worth noting, however, that the Restatement provision cited above included tobacco as an example of products such as whiskey and butter, the unhealthy over–consumption of which could not lead to liability. As the successful tobacco class action litigation and settlements have shown, however, the fact that excessive smoking was known to lead to health problems did not vitiate liability when, for instance, tobacco companies had intentionally altered the nicotine levels of cigarettes to induce addiction.

Thus, in order to state a claim, the Complaint must allege either that the attributes of McDonald's products are so extraordinarily unhealthy that they are outside the reasonable contemplation of the consuming public or that the products are so extraordinarily unhealthy as to be dangerous in their intended use. The Complaint –– which merely alleges that the foods contain high levels of cholesterol, fat, salt and sugar, and that the foods are therefore unhealthy –– fails to reach this bar. It is well-known that fast food in general, and McDonald's products in particular, contain high levels of cholesterol, fat, salt, and sugar, and that such attributes are bad for one.

If a person knows or should know that eating copious orders of supersized McDonald's products is unhealthy and may result in weight gain (and its concomitant problems) because of the high levels of cholesterol, fat, salt and sugar, it is not the place of the law to protect them from their own excesses. Nobody is forced to eat at McDonald's. (Except, perhaps, parents of small children who desire McDonalds' food, toy promotions or playgrounds and demand their parents' accompaniment.) Even more pertinent, nobody is forced to supersize their meal or choose less healthy options on the menu.

As long as a consumer exercises free choice with appropriate knowledge, liability for negligence will not attach to a manufacturer. It is only when that free choice becomes but a chimera —— for instance, by the masking of information necessary to make the choice, such as the knowledge that eating McDonald's with a certain frequency would irrefragably cause harm —— that manufacturers should be held accountable. Plaintiffs have failed to allege in the Complaint that their decisions to eat at McDonald's several times a week were anything but a choice freely made and which now may not be pinned on McDonald's.

In an attempt to save their common law causes of action, plaintiffs raise [additional arguments] to show that McDonald's has a duty toward plaintiffs [including that McDonald's products have been processed to the point where they have become completely different and more dangerous than the run-of-the-mill products they resemble and than a reasonable consumer would expect.]

Plaintiff's attempt to show that over—consumption of McDonald's is different in kind from, for instance, overconsumption of alcoholic beverages or butter because the processing of McDonald's food has created an entirely different —— and more dangerous —— food than one would expect from a hamburger, chicken fnger or french fry cooked at home or at any restaurant other than McDonald's. They thus argue that McDonald's food is "dangerous to an extent beyond that which would be contemplated by the ordinary consumer who purchases it, with the ordinary

knowledge common to the community as to its characteristics." Restatement (Second) Torts § 402A, cmt. i. If true, consumers who eat at McDonald's have not been given a free choice, and thus liability may attach.

Plaintiffs argue that McDonald's products have been so altered that their unhealthy attributes are now outside the ken of the average reasonable consumer. They point to McDonalds' ingredient lists to show that McDonald's customers worldwide are getting much more than what is commonly considered to be a chicken finger, a hamburger, or a french fry.

For instance, Chicken McNuggets, rather than being merely chicken fried in a pan, are a McFrankenstein creation of various elements not utilized by the home cook. A Chicken McNugget is comprised of, in addition to chicken: water, salt, modified corn starch, sodium phosphates, chicken broth powder (chicken broth, salt and natural favoring (chicken source)), seasoning (vegetable oil, extracts of rosemary, mono, di—and triglycerides, lecithin). Battered and breaded with water, enriched bleached wheat four (niacin, iron, thiamine, mononitrate, riboflavin, folic acid), yellow corn four, bleached wheat four, modified corn starch, salt, leavening (baking soda, sodium acid pyrophosphate, sodium aluminum phosphate, monocalcium phosphate, calcium lactate), spices, wheat starch, dried whey, corn starch. Batter set in vegetable shortening. Cooked in partially hydrogenated vegetable oils, (may contain partially hydrogenated soybean oil and/or partially hydrogenated corn oil and/or partially hydrogenated canola oil and/or cottonseed oil and/or corn oil). TBHQ and citric acid added to help preserve freshness. Dimethylpolysiloxane added as an anti—foaming agent.

In addition, Chicken McNuggets, while seemingly a healthier option hamburgers because they have "chicken" in their names, actually contain twice the fat per ounce as a hamburger. It is at least a question of fact as to whether a reasonable consumer would know--without recourse to the McDonald's Web site--that a Chicken McNugget contained so many ingredients other than chicken and provided twice the fat of a hamburger. Similarly, it is hardly common knowledge that McDonald's french fries are comprised, in addition to potatoes, of: partially hydrogenated soybean oil, natural favor (beef source), dextrose, sodium acidpyrophosphate (to preserve natural color). Cooked in partially hydrogenated vegetable oils, (may contain partially hydrogenated soybean oiland/or partially hydrogenated corn oil and/or partially hydrogenated canola oil and/or cottonseedoil and/or corn oil). TBHQ and citric acid added to preserve freshness. Dimethylpolysiloxaneadded as an anti--foaming agent.

This argument comes closest to overcoming the hurdle presented to plaintiffs. If plaintiffs were able to flesh out this argument in an amended complaint, it may establish that the dangers of McDonald's products were not commonly well known and thus that McDonald's had a duty toward its customers. The argument also addresses McDonald's list of horribles, i.e., that a successful lawsuit would mean that "pizza parlors, neighborhood diners, bakeries, grocery stores, and literally anyone else in the food business (including mothers cooking at home)," could potentially face liability. Most of the above entities do not serve food that is processed to the extent that McDonald's products are processed, nor food that is uniform to the extent that McDonald's products are throughout the world. Rather, they serve plain—jane hamburgers, fries and shakes —— meals that are high in cholesterol, fat, salt and sugar, but about which there are no additional processes that could be alleged to make the products even more dangerous. In addition, there is the problem of causation; hardly any of the entities listed above other than a parent cooking at home serves as many people regularly as McDonald's and its ilk. [The court also held that the complaint did not adequately specify proximate cause and should be dismissed for that reason as well. Plaintiffs' complaint did not clearly draw the link between their obesity and McDonald's fast food alone. How many times a week plaintiffs ate at McDonald's and the nature of the rest of their diet were not adequately indicated. The judge dismissed the complaint, granting plaintiff permission to replead.]

Plaintiffs' subsequent attempts to adequately plead a cause of action failed. The suit was dismissed, and that dismissal was affrmed on appeal. Pelman v. McDonald's Corp., 396 F.3d 508 (2d Cir. 2005) . That is not to say that the suit, and others like it, had no impact. Many fast-food companies are today trying to serve healthier food, and it is unlikely that those efforts are totally unconnected to the prospect of more *Pelman*--like litigation. Interestingly, in February 2005, McDonald's paid $8.5 million to settle a consumer group's suit alleging that after McDonald's promised in 2002 to lower transfat in its cooking oils and to implement the change within five months, it delayed the conversion without adequately informing consumers.

Advocacy groups announced in early 2006 that they were suing the Nickleodeon TV network and Kellogg Co., the cereal maker, in an attempt to reduce junk food marketing to kids. At the same time, Congress was considering the Personal Responsibility in Food Consumption Act (the "Cheeseburger Bill"), which would prevent lawsuits such as *Pelman* from succeeding. Many state legislatures are considering similar legislation. In other words, there is a public policy battle going on in this area that shows signs of escalating.

CHAPTER 22

BANKRUPTCY

- Overview of Debtor Creditor Relations
- Bankruptcy Proceedings
- Liquidation Proceedings
- Business Reorganization
- Adjustment of Debts

As this edition of the text went to press in the spring of 2006, a major bankruptcy reform law that became effective on October 1,2005 was just starting to have a major impact. Passage culminated more than a decade of attempts to enact such reforms, many of them controversial. Supporters hoped to stem a large increase in personal bankruptcy filings occurring in recent years. In 2004, 1.6 million individual Americans filed for bankruptcy, a small decline after several years of increases. Opponents claimed that the banks and credit card companies supporting the reforms had targeted broad groups of people whom they knew with actuarial certainty would get into financial difficulty if given easy credit, yet were still earning record profits. Opponents called the new law an attack on the middle class, while supporters termed it a needed return to personal fiscal responsibility. Many of the changes enacted by the Bankruptcy Abuse Prevention and Consumer Protection Act of 2005 (BAPCPA) will be noted in this chapter's discussion.

Overview of Debtor Creditor Relations

The treatment of debtors has varied greatly over the years. During certain early periods, debtors were forced to become servants of their creditors, were thrown into prison, or even had body parts removed for failure to pay a debt. History finally demonstrated to both creditors and society that very little was accomplished by such methods. In seeking more humane solutions, the general problem has been how to balance the creditor's rights with the debtor's desire for relief from debts.

Numerous devices have been developed through the years for resolving debtor-creditor disputes. In this chapter we will deal primarily with one such procedure—**bankruptcy** under federal law. However, many of the other methods available under state common-law principles, state statutes, and private agreements may actually be preferable to bankruptcy when it is possible to use them. Bankruptcy has traditionally been viewed as an avenue of last resort. Before we turn to a detailed examination of the federal bankruptcy law, we first will survey some of the alternatives.

Alternatives to Bankruptcy

Although time and space do not permit a detailed analysis of each method of debt resolution, the following methods are frequently used when a debtor cannot pay his or her obligation: (1) foreclosure on a real estate mortgage, (2) enforcement of a secured transaction (Article 9 of the UCC), (3) enforcement of an artisan's lien, (4) enforcement of a mechanic's lien, (5) writ of execution on a judgment, (6) garnishment, (7) attachment, (8) receivership, (9) cancelling a fraudulent conveyance, (10) composition of creditors, and (11) assignment for the benefit of creditors.

Foreclosure on a Real Estate Mortgage

Under the terms of a mortgage agreement, the mortgagee (creditor) has the right to declare the entire mortgage debt due and enforce his or her rights through a remedy called **foreclosure.** In most states the mortgagee is required to sell the mortgaged real estate (even if it is the person's homestead) under the direction of the court, using the proceeds to pay the foreclosure costs and the balance of the debt. If any proceeds are left over, the surplus goes to the mortgagor. If the proceeds are insufficient to cover the costs of foreclosure and the remaining indebtedness, the mortgagor is liable to the mortgagee for the unpaid balance of the debt. However, before the actual foreclosure sale and for a certain period of time thereafter (set by state statute), the mortgagor can redeem the property by full payment of costs, indebtedness, and interest.

Enforcement of a Secured Transaction

Under Article 9 of the UCC, when a debtor defaults on the security agreement made with a secured party (the creditor), the **collateral** (personal property) that is the subject of the security agreement can be used to satisfy the debt. The secured party can retain possession of the collateral or take it from the debtor, either by court order or without court action if it can be accomplished peaceably. He or she can then either (1) keep the collateral in satisfaction of the debt by giving proper notice to the debtor of such intention (assuming the debtor does not object), or (2) sell the collateral through a "commercially reasonable" process. The secured party must always sell the collateral if proper objection is made by the debtor to the party keeping it or if the collateral is classified as "consumer goods" and the debtor has paid 60 percent or more of the debt.

If the collateral is kept by the secured party, the debt is discharged. If the collateral is sold and the proceeds are insufficient to pay the debt and the costs of enforcing the security interest, the secured party is usually entitled to seek a deficiency judgment for the balance. The debtor can redeem the collateral at any time until its sale or disposal.

Enforcement of an Artisan's Lien

The **artisan's lien,** a possessory lien given to creditors who perform services on personal property or take care of goods entrusted to them, was developed at common law. If the debtor does not pay for the services, the creditor is permitted to obtain a judgment and/or to foreclose and sell the property in satisfaction of the debt. Any proceeds remaining from the sale of the property after paying the debt and costs of sale must be returned to the debtor. In order to exercise this lien, the creditor must have retained possession of the property and must not have agreed to provide the services on credit. Many states have passed statutes governing the procedures to be followed in enforcing such a lien. If the creditor operates a warehouse and the claim arises from unpaid storage charges, the procedures which must be followed are set forth in Article 7 of the Uniform Commercial Code.

Enforcement of a Mechanic's Lien

Certain other liens have been made available to creditors by state statutes. One of the most common is the **mechanic's lien**—a lien against real estate for labor, services, or materials used in improving the realty. When the labor or materials are furnished, a debt is incurred. To make the real property itself security for the debt, the creditor must file a notice of lien in a manner provided by statute. To be effective, it usually must be filed within a specified period (usually 60 to 120 days) after the last materials or labor were furnished. If the notice is properly filed and the debt is not paid, the creditor can foreclose and sell the realty in satisfaction of the debt. (This is similar to a foreclosure of a real estate mortgage.)

Writ of Execution on a Judgment

Once a debt becomes overdue, a creditor can file suit for payment in a court of law and, if successful, be awarded a "judgment." If the judgment is not satisfied by the debtor, the creditor has the right to go back to court and obtain a **writ of execution.** The writ, issued by the clerk of the court, directs the sheriff or other officer to levy upon (seize) and sell any of the debtor's nonexempt property within the court's jurisdiction. The judgment is paid from the proceeds of the sale, and any balance is returned to the debtor. One limitation on the writ is that it can be levied only on nonexempt property. That is, exempt property, such as the debtor's homestead, cannot be taken to satisfy the judgment.

Garnishment

Another limitation of the writ of execution is that it usually cannot reach debts owed to the judgment debtor by third parties or the debtor's interests in personal property legally possessed by third parties.

However, the law does permit the creditor (using the proper court procedure) to require these persons to turn over to the court or sheriff money owed or property belonging to the debtor. This method of satisfying a judgment is called **garnishment;** the third party, called the garnishee, is legally bound by the court order. The most common types of "property" garnished are wages and bank accounts. The federal Consumer Credit Protection Act limits garnishment of a debtor's current wages to 25 percent of take home pay, and prohibits the debtor's employer from discharging him or her because of garnishment for "any one indebtedness." Some state laws place greater restrictions on garnishment of wages.

Attachment

The seizing of a debtor's property under a court order, known as **attachment,** is a statutory remedy and can be exercised only in strict accordance with the provisions of the particular state statutes. It is available to a creditor even before a judgment has been rendered, under some statutes. Statutory grounds for attachment prior to judgment are limited, usually including situations where the debtor is unavailable to be served with a summons or where there is a reasonable belief that the debtor may conceal or remove property from the jurisdiction of the court before the creditor can obtain a judgment.

To employ attachment as a remedy, the creditor must file with the court an affidavit attesting to the debtor's default and the legal reasons why attachment is sought. Additionally, the creditor must post a bond sufficient to cover at least the value of the debtor's property, the value of the loss of use of the goods suffered by the debtor (if any), and court costs in case the creditor loses the suit. Most states require the opportunity for some form of hearing before a judge. The court then issues a **writ of attachment,** directing the sheriff or other officer to seize nonexempt property sufficient to satisfy the creditor's claim. If the creditor's suit against the debtor is successful, the property seized can then be sold to satisfy the judgment.

Receivership

Attachment may prove inadequate to protect creditors while they pursue their claims if the debtor's property requires care (such as crops, livestock, etc.). In such cases, on essentially the same grounds as for attachment, the court may appoint a receiver to care for and preserve the property pending the outcome of the lawsuit in which one or more creditors are seeking to collect unpaid debts. It is then said that the debtor's property is placed in **receivership.** The object of receivership is to prevent a debtor from "wasting" assets while being pursued by creditors. Receivership may also be the appropriate protective device where the debtor has a going business and where creditors can convince the court that it is being grossly mismanaged.

Cancelling a Fraudulent Conveyance

A debtor may transfer property to a third party by gift or contract under circumstances in which his or her creditors are defrauded. If such fraud can be established, any creditor can have the conveyance (transfer) set aside and the property made subject to his or her claim—even if the property is in the hands of a third party.

The fraud necessary to have a conveyance set aside can be either fraud in fact or fraud implied in law. **Fraud in fact** occurs when a debtor transfers property with the specific intent of defrauding his or her creditors. A creditor will usually encounter difficulty in having a conveyance voided on this ground, simply because of the inherent problems in proving fraudulent intent. The creditor's chances of proving this intent will, however, be somewhat greater the transfer was to the debtor's spouse or other relative. In addition, it is often the case that the debtor actually had no such fraudulent intent, but the creditor is harmed nevertheless.

To assist the creditor, most states have enacted laws (such as the Uniform Fraudulent Conveyance Act) which create a presumption of fraud under certain circumstances. This means that, in some situations, the burden of proof shifts to the debtor. If the debtor fails to prove the absence of fraud, there is **fraud implied in law** and the transfer is voided. Generally speaking, these statutes create a presumption of fraud whenever a debtor transfers property without receiving "fair consideration" in return and the debtor has insufficient assets remaining to satisfy creditors.

Composition of Creditors

Sometimes a debtor or his or her creditors recognize early (before bankruptcy) that the debtor is in financial difficulty. Instead of pursuing remedies under bankruptcy, the debtor and creditors make a contract to resolve the debts. The contract—referred to as a **composition of creditors**—calls for the debtor's immediate payment of a sum less than that owed and for the creditor's immediate discharge of the debt. This payment can be made from any of the debtor's assets, including exempt property. Such contracts are held to be binding by the courts. The advantage of an immediate payment and minimum costs makes the composition attractive to creditors. Whether the composition agreement is binding on nonparticipating creditors depends on state law. At common law the agreement was not binding on these creditors.

Assignment for the Benefit of Creditors

Under common-law principles and, in some states, under statute, an **assignment for the benefit of creditors** is available as an alternative to bankruptcy In such an arrangement, the debtor voluntarily transfers title to some or all assets to a "trustee" or "assignee" for the creditors' benefit. By such a transfer, the debtor irrevocably gives up any claim to or control over the property. The trustee or assignee liquidates (sells) the property and makes payment to the creditors on a pro rata basis according to the debt amounts.

Creditors can either accept or reject the partial payment. One accepting such a payment may in effect be releasing the balance of his or her claim. In most states, creditors who do not participate in the assignment cannot reach the assets that have been so assigned. They do, however, have rights to any surplus remaining after participating creditors have been paid, any nonexempt property not assigned, and any nonexempt property acquired after the assignment.

Nonparticipating creditors may also be able to force the debtor into bankruptcy.

Bankruptcy Proceedings
History of Bankruptcy Statutes

Bankruptcy as a legal device was initially applied only to commercial business failures. The first Bankruptcy Act in England was adopted in 1542 and applied only to traders or merchants who were unable to pay their debts. It was not until 1861 that bankruptcy was extended to other types of debtors.

The founders of the United States were well acquainted with the problems of debtors. In drafting the U.S. Constitution they stated in Article I, Section 8, clause 4: "The Congress shall have the power ... to establish ... uniform laws on the subject of bankruptcies throughout the United States."

Bankruptcy Proceedings Today

Today's bankruptcy law comes primarily from the 1978 Bankruptcy Reform Act, also known as the Bankruptcy Code, as amended several times (most importantly by the Bankruptcy Abuse Prevention and Consumer Protection Act of 2005). Before 1978, federal district courts handled bankruptcy cases, often delegating the responsibility for hearing them to "bankruptcy referees" who were not federal judges but who performed many of the same functions. The 1978 Code established a set of bankruptcy courts, with one such court in each federal district. Bankruptcy judges are complemented by U.S. Trustees who, as we shall see, usually select the trustees who administer the debtors' estates.

Bankruptcy courts hear and decide all of the issues directly involving the bankruptcy proceeding itself, but related nonbankruptcy matters, such as a tort claim by or against the debtor, are decided by the federal district court. An appeal from a bankruptcy court decision is heard by a federal district court or, under certain conditions, by a bankruptcy appellate panel or even a Court of Appeals.

As we noted earlier, bankruptcy has traditionally been a solution of last resort. Despite this fact, staggering numbers of cases are filed each year under the federal bankruptcy law. The large number of cases is not, however, the only reason for the importance of modern bankruptcy law. Many people have their only direct exposure to our legal system in bankruptcy proceedings. In bankruptcy court debtors and creditors alike find final, if not totally satisfactory, conclusions to disputes that may have seemed endless. In bankruptcy court businesses of all sizes are liquidated or rehabilitated, often affecting the livelihoods of many employees, the security of suppliers and customers, and even the economies of local communities.

The Code provides for three different kinds of proceedings: (1) liquidation; (2) reorganization; and (3) adjustment of the debts of an individual with regular income. These provisions are contained in Chapters 7, 11, and 13 of the Bankruptcy Code. Additionally, Chapter 12 provides a provision primarily available to family farmers. Our discussion will focus primarily on Chapter 7s liquidation proceeding, often referred to as "straight bankruptcy," because it is the most common type. We will, however, devote some attention to the other three types of proceedings at the end of this chapter. It should also be noted that current bankruptcy law contains a special section dealing with the rehabilitation of bankrupt municipalities, which is beyond the scope of our discussion.

Liquidation Proceedings

Stated very generally, the object of a **liquidation proceeding** under Chapter 7 of the Bankruptcy Act is to sell the debtor's assets, pay off creditors insofar as it is possible to do so, and legally discharge the debtor from further responsibility.

Commencement of the Proceedings

A liquidation proceeding will be either a **voluntary case,** commenced by the debtor, or an **involuntary case,** commenced by creditors.

Voluntary Case

The filing of a **voluntary case** automatically subjects the debtor and its property to the jurisdiction and supervision of the Bankruptcy Court. Any debtor, whether an individual, a partnership, or a corporation, may file a petition for voluntary bankruptcy, with the following exceptions: (1) banks, (2) savings and loan associations, (3) credit unions, (4) insurance companies, (5) railroads, and (6) governmental bodies. These exempted organizations are covered by special statutes and their liquidation is supervised by particular regulatory agencies.

A debtor does not have to be insolvent in order to file a petition for voluntary bankruptcy, but as a practical matter it is usually insolvency that prompts such a petition. In addition, a husband and wife may file a joint case if both consent.

BAPCPA contains two primary provisions aimed at reducing the number of Chapter 7 voluntary filings by individuals. First, is a requirement that people undergo credit counseling before filing for bankruptcy. Second, is a requirement that they undergo a "means test" to determine if they can really pay their debts and if they can, the courts should shift them from the liquidation bankruptcy of Chapter 7 to Chapter 13s provisions for adjustment of debts of individuals with regular income where the debtors will be required to make payments to creditors rather than receive a full discharge. The means test is a rough calculation which deems it an abuse of Chapter 7 for a debtor who can make payments to seek discharge of all obligations. These requirements will be discussed in more detail in the section relating to Chapter 13

Involuntary Case

The types of organizations that are not permitted to file a voluntary liquidation case also cannot be subjected to an involuntary case. In addition to these exemptions, creditors also cannot file an involuntary case against **farmers, family farmers** or **nonprofit corporations.**

If the debtor has twelve or more creditors, at least three must join in filing the case. If there are fewer than twelve creditors, the involuntary case may be filed by one or more of them. Regardless of the number of creditors, those filing the petition must have noncontingent unsecured claims against the debtor totaling in the aggregate at least $12,300 [Note: Most of the dollar values in these statutes are periodically adjusted for infation.]

The debtor and its property automatically become subject to the jurisdiction and supervision of the bankruptcy court if the involuntary petition is not challenged. However, if the debtor contests the creditors' petition, they must prove either (1) that the debtor has not been paying debts as they became due or (2) that the debtor's property has been placed in a receivership or an assignment for the benefit of creditors within

120 days before the involuntary petition was filed. If the filing creditors prove either of the above, the debtor and its property are then under the supervision of the court. If no such proof is made, the petition is dismissed.

Automatic Stay

As soon as the petition is filed in either a voluntary or involuntary case, an automatic stay is in operation. The automatic stay puts creditors' claims "on hold" until they are dealt with in the bankruptcy proceeding, and prevents creditors from taking any judicial administrative, or other action against the debtor. A secured creditor, however, may petition the bankruptcy court and receive protection against the loss of its security. The court- ordered protection for **secured creditors** may take the form of cash payments from the debtor, substitute collateral, or an express grant of relief from the automatic stay permitting foreclosure of the security interest. BAPCPA created several exceptions to the automatic stay provision, which no longer stops or postpones (a) evictions by landlords (in cases where a judgment of possession was obtained prior to the bankruptcy filing or the eviction is based on endangerment of the rental property or illegal use of controlled substances), (b) actions to withhold, suspend, or restrict a driver's license, (c) actions to withhold, suspend or restrict a professional or occupational license, (d) lawsuits to establish paternity, child custody, or child support, (e) divorce proceedings, or (f) lawsuits involving domestic violence.

The Trustee

After the debtor becomes subject to the bankruptcy proceeding, the U.S. Trustee must appoint an interim trustee to take over the debtor's property or business. A U.S. Trustee is appointed to monitor certain aspects of bankruptcy cases and to appoint and supervise the standing and panel trustees. Within a relatively short time thereafter, a permanent trustee will take over. This trustee may be elected by the creditors, but if they do not do so, the interim trustee receives permanent status.

The trustee is an individual or corporation who, under the court's supervision, administers and represents the debtor's estate. (Which property is included within the debtor's estate is discussed later.) The basic duties of the trustee are to: (1) investigate the financial affairs of the debtor; (2) collect assets and claims owned by the debtor; (3) temporarily operate the debtor's business if necessary; (4) reduce the debtor's assets to cash; (5) receive and examine the claims of creditors, and challenge in bankruptcy court any claim which the trustee feels to be questionable; (6) oppose the debtor's discharge from its obligations when the trustee feels that there are legal reasons why the debtor should not be discharged; (7) render a detailed accounting to the court of all assets received and the disposition made of them; and (8) make a final report to the court when administration of the debtor's estate is completed. To fulfill these duties as representative of the debtor's estate, the trustee has the power to sue and be sued in that capacity, to use or sell property of the estate, and to employ account-ants, attorneys, appraisers, auctioneers, and other professionals with court approval.

If they wish, unsecured creditors may elect a creditors' committee of three to eleven members for the purpose of consulting with the trustee. This committee may make recommendations to the trustee or U.S. Trustee regarding the latter's duties and may submit questions to the court or U.S. Trustee concerning administration of the debtor's estate.

Creditors' Meetings

Within a reasonable time after commencement of the case, the U.S. Trustee must call and preside at a meeting of unsecured creditors. The debtor will have already supplied the court with a list of creditors, so that they may be notified of the meeting. The judge of the bankruptcy court is not permitted to attend a creditors' meeting.

At the first meeting, creditors may elect the trustee. In order for such election to be possible, at least 20 percent of the total amount of unsecured claims which have been filed and allowed must be represented at the meeting. A trustee is elected by receiving the votes of creditors holding a majority, in amount, of unsecured claims represented at the meeting.

The other major item of business at the first creditors' meeting is an **examination of the debtor.** The debtor, under oath, will be questioned by the creditors and the trustee concerning (1) the debtor's assets, and (2) matters relevant to whether the debtor will be entitled to a discharge.

Duties of the Debtor

The bankruptcy law imposes the following duties on the debtor: (1) within a reasonable time after commencement of the proceedings, file with the court a list of creditors, and liabilities, a schedule of income and expenditures, and a statement of financial affairs; (2) file with the court a statement of intention with respect to the retention or surrender of any property of the estate which secures consumer debt, specifying that such property shall be claimed as exempt, redeemed, or the debt reaffirmed thereon, and perform these intentions within 45 days after filing the notice; (3) cooperate and respond truthfully during the examination conducted at the first creditors' meeting; (4) surrender to the trustee all property to be included in the debtor's estate, as well as all documents, books, and records pertaining to this property; (5) cooperate with the trustee in whatever way necessary to enable the trustee to perform his or her duties; and (6) appear at the hearing conducted by the court concerning whether the debtor should be discharged.

A debtor who fails to fulfill any of these duties may be denied a discharge from liabilities.

The Debtor's Estate

Types of Property

The property owned by the debtor which becomes subject to the bankruptcy proceeding, ultimately to be sold by the trustee, is the **debtor's estate.** This includes all tangible and intangible property interests of any kind, unless specifically exempted. For example, the estate could consist of consumer goods, inventory, equipment, any of the various types of interests in real estate, patent rights, trademarks, copyrights, accounts receivable, and various contract rights.

After-Acquired Property

In addition to property owned at the time the bankruptcy petition (either voluntary or involuntary) was filed, the debtor's estate also includes after-acquired property under some circumstances. Specifically, the estate includes any type of property that the debtor acquires, or becomes entitled to acquire, within 180 days after the petition filing date (1) by inheritance, (2) as a beneficiary of a life insurance policy, or (3) as a result of a divorce decree or a property settlement agreement with the debtor's spouse. And, of course, if a particular item of property is part of the estate, any proceeds, income, production, or offspring from it will also be part of the estate. However, the debtor's earnings from his or her own labor or personal service after the filing date are not included in the estate.

Exemptions

A debtor who is an individual (rather than a partnership or corporation) may claim certain **exemptions.** This means that certain types of property are **exempt** and are not included in the debtor's estate. The debtor may keep such property and still receive a discharge from liabilities at the close of the proceedings. Every state has exemption statutes setting forth the types of property which are exempt from seizure under a writ of execution. Before passage of the 1978 Bankruptcy Code, the debtor's exempt property in a federal bankruptcy case was determined solely by the exemption statutes of the state where he or she lived. The 1978 Code, however, included for the first time a list of federal exemptions that are available to the debtor in bankruptcy regardless of the state of domicile.

Under the federal exemption a debtor may claim, among others, the following exemptions (and each spouse may claim them in a joint case): (1) the debtor's interest in a homestead used as a residence, up to a value of $18,450; (2) the debtor's interest in a motor vehicle, up to a value of $2,950; (3) the debtor's interest, up to $475 per item, in household furnishings, household goods, appliances, wearing apparel, animals, crops or musical instruments used primarily for personal, family, or household (nonbusiness) uses, subject to a total of $9,850 for all such items; (4) the debtor's interest in jewelry, up to a total of $1,225 in value, held primarily for personal purposes; (5) the debtor's interest in any kind of property, not to exceed in value $975, and any unused portion of the $18,450 homestead exemption, subject to a limit of $9,250; (6) the debtor's interest in implements, tools, or professional books used in his or her trade, not to exceed $1,850 in value; (7) any unmatured life insurance policies owned by the debtor (except for credit life policies); (8) professionally prescribed health aids; (9) the debtor's right to receive various government benefits, such as unemployment compensation, social security, and veteran's benefits; (10) the debtor's right to receive various private benefits, such as alimony, child support, and pension payments, to the extent reasonably necessary to support the debtor and dependents; and (11) the right to receive (a) awards under crime victim's reparation laws, (b) payments on account of wrongful death of a dependent, (c) payments on life insurance contracts due to the death of one upon whom the debtor depended, (d) payments on account of bodily injury not to exceed $18,450, and (e) payment in compensation for loss of future earnings of the debtor or one on whom the debtor was dependent. The amounts in # 11 are generally limited to a sum reasonably necessary for the support of the debtor and dependents. (Remember that the dollars amounts in the bankruptcy laws are periodically adjusted, primarily to account for inflation.)

The 1978 Code did not bring national uniformity to bankruptcy exemptions for two reasons. First, it permitted debtors to choose either the federal exemption or those of the state where the debtor lived. Because many states' exemptions are more liberal than federal exemptions, debtors in those states naturally choose the state exemptions. Second, the Code allows state legislatures to prohibit debtors in their states from using the federal exemptions, and a majority of states did so.

Because Florida and Texas have particularly liberal homestead exemptions, O.J. Simpson, disgraced WorldCom CFO Scott Sullivan, and many others moved to those states to shield assets from creditors. BAPCPA contains several provisions aimed at preventing debtors from simply picking the most liberal state exemption around.

First, debtors seeking to invoke a state exemption must choose the law of the place where their domicile was located in the two years before filing. They can no longer simply move to Florida or Texas in the weeks or months before filing for bankruptcy and build a mansion to claim as their homestead.

Second, whenever in the 10 years preceding bankruptcy filing a debtor converts nonexempt property into homestead value with the intent to hinder, delay or defraud creditors, the homestead exemption is reduced by that amount. In other words, if within 10 years of filing for bankruptcy, a debtor sells his nonexempt vacation home in Colorado and takes $300,000 of the proceeds and uses it to pay for an addition to his homestead in Florida, that amount is not protected if the debtor acted with the intent of hindering or defrauding creditors.

Third, regardless of intent, any value in excess of $125,000 that is added to a homestead during the 1215 days before filing may not be included in a state homestead exemption unless it was transferred from another homestead in the same state (or the homestead is the principal residence of a family farmer). This federal cap on state exemptions prevents debtors within 3-1/4 years of filing for bankruptcy from taking the proceeds from sale of that hypothetical vacation home in Colorado and adding more than $125,000 in value to their Florida homestead, even if there is no bad intent.

Fourth, the new law imposes an absolute federal cap of $125,000 for the state homestead exemption under certain circumstances. Those circumstances are that either (a) the court determines that the debtor has been convicted of a felony demonstrating that the filing of the bankruptcy petition was an abuse of the provisions of the Bankruptcy Code, or (b) the debtor owes a debt arising from a violation of federal or state securities laws (Congress may well have had Scott Sullivan of WorldCom and Andy Fastow of Enron in mind), fiduciary fraud, racketeering, or crimes or intentional torts that caused serious bodily injury or death in the preceding five years. There is a loophole if more valuable homestead property is "reasonably necessary for the support of the debtor.

Voidable Transfers

In a number of circumstances, the trustee has the power to sue and restore to the debtor's estate property or funds which the debtor (or someone acting in the debtor's behalf) had transferred to some third party. These situations, called **voidable transfers,** are as follows:

1. The trustee generally may cancel any transfer of property of the debtor's estate which was made **after** the debtor became subject to the bankruptcy proceeding. The trustee must exercise this power within two years after the transfer was made, or before the bankruptcy case is concluded, whichever occurs first.
2. The trustee may cancel **any fraudulent transfer** made by the debtor within two years prior to the filing of the bankruptcy petition. This power of the trustee applies to both **fraud in fact** and **fraud implied in law,** as discussed earlier in the chapter. It will be remembered that insolvency is an element of fraud implied in law. In determining the fair value of assets for this purpose under the bankruptcy law, exempt property and the property transferred in the particular transaction being challenged are not included.
3. The trustee has the power to cancel a property transfer on any ground that the debtor could have used, such as fraud, mistake, duress, undue influence, incapacity, or failure of consideration.
4. A new BAPCPA provision allows a trustee to avoid any transfer by a debtor to a self-settled trust (or similar device) within 10 years of filing of the petition, if the debtor had "actual intent to hinder, delay, or defraud any entity to which the debtor was or became, on or after the date that such transfer was made, indebted."

Voidable Preferences

One of the fundamental objectives of the bankruptcy law is to insure equal treatment of most types of unsecured creditors. The primary reason why we are so concerned with equal treatment of creditors, of course, is that a bankrupt debtor's assets are usually sufficient to pay only a fraction of creditors' total claims. As a result of this concern, the trustee has the power to cancel any transfer by the debtor to a creditor which amounted to a **preference.** A preference is essentially a transfer of property or money, in payment of an existing debt, which causes that creditor to receive more of the debtor's estate than he or she would be entitled to receive in the bankruptcy proceeding had the transfer not occurred.

General Rules for Cancelling Preferences

In the ordinary situation, a preferential transfer to a creditor can be cancelled by the trustee, and the property or funds returned to the debtor's estate, if (1) it occurred within **90 days** prior to the filing of the bankruptcy petition, and (2) the debtor was **insolvent** at the time of the transfer. In this situation, however, insolvency is **presumed.** In other words, if a creditor has received a preferential transfer within the 90-day period prior to the filing of the bankruptcy petition, that creditor must prove that the debtor was not insolvent at the time.

Insiders

If the creditor receiving the preference was an **insider,** the trustee's power of cancellation extends to any such transfer made within one year before the bankruptcy petition was filed. In general, an insider is an individual or business firm which had a close relationship with the debtor at the time of the transfer. Examples would include a relative or partner of the debtor, a corporation of which the debtor was a director or officer, or a director or officer of a corporate debtor. In such a case, however, the presumption of insolvency only applies to the 90 days prior to the petition filing. Therefore, if the preference being challenged by the trustee had taken place more than 90 days but less than a year before the petition filing, the trustee must prove that the debtor was insolvent. Figure 22.1 illustrates the rules for cancelling preferences to insiders and other creditors.

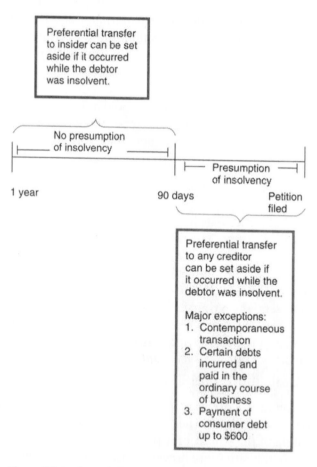

Figure 22.1　Trustee's Recovery of Voidable Preference

Exceptions

In certain circumstances, a payment or transfer to a creditor cannot be cancelled even though it meets the basic requirements of a voidable preference. Three of the most important exceptions are:

1. A transaction which involved a "contemporaneous"(that is, within a very short period of time) exchange between debtor and creditor cannot be cancelled by the trustee. For example, the debtor may have bought goods from the creditor and either paid for them immediately or within a few days. This type of transaction is treated differently than one in which the debtor was paying off a debt which had existed for some time. Such a contemporaneous exchange will be left standing even though it occurred during the 90-day period prior to the filing date.

2. Even though there is no contemporaneous exchange, a payment or transfer to a creditor within the 90-day period will not be cancelled if (1) the particular debt had been incurred by the debtor in the ordinary course of business, (2) the payment was made in the ordinary course of the debtor's business, and (3) the payment was made according to ordinary business terms. An example would be the debtor's payment, during the 90-day period, of the previous month's utility bill.

3. A debtor's repayment of up to $600 in **consumer debt** is not treated as a voidable preference.

    Voidable preferences can occur in an almost infinite variety of circumstances. The following case illustrates one such situation, and also shows one of the many reasons why it is so important for a creditor to obtain and perfect a security interest whenever possible.

In Re Fisher
U.S. Bankruptcy Court, S.D. Ohio,
100 Bankr. Rptr. 351 (1989)

Defendant Almiro Case Fur Fashion Design ("Almiro") was a furrier who supplied furs to Kinston LeeFurriers when it was formerly owned and operated by debtor Julius Fisher under an arrangement giving Fisher the right to return unsold furs. A "sale or return" is a sale transaction in which the buyer has a right to return the items to the seller within an agreed time period. A true sale or return actually transfers title to the buyer until a particular article is returned. In contrast, a "sale on approval" is a transaction in which

the buyer has an agreed period of time to decide whether to keep the goods, with no title passing until the expiration of that time or until the buyer affirmatively indicates a desire to keep them. In other words, a sale on approval is a "consignment," the supplier being the "consignor" and the one holding them being the "consignee." A consignee is merely an agent for the purpose of selling the principal's goods, and owns no interest in them. When a right of return exists and the parties have not specified whether it is a sale or return or a sale on approval, the UCC provides that it usually is a "sale or return" if the goods are taken by the buyer for the purpose of resale, and a sale on approval if they are taken by the buyer for the purpose of use.

Under this arrangement with Almiro, Fisher received and held several mink coats ("Minks") having an approximate total wholesale value of $11,155. Almiro did not take a security interest in the Minks. Fisher returned the Minks to Almiro. Less than three months later, Fisher filed a voluntary petition under Chapter 7 of the Bankruptcy Code. The bankruptcy trustee (plaintiff) claimed that Fisher's return of the Minks to Almiro was a voidable preference and filed a complaint against Fisher (defendant) seeking to have the value of the Minks restored to the bankrupt debtor's estate.

Cole, Bankruptcy Judge:

Section 547(b) of the Bankruptcy Code provides as follows:

(b) Except as provided in subsection

(c) Of this section, the trustee may avoid any transfer of an interest of the debtor in property—

(1) to or for the benefit of a creditor;

(2) for or on account of an antecedent debt owed by the debtor before such transfer was made;

(3) made while the debtor was insolvent;

(4) made—

(a) on or within 90 days before the date of the filing of the petition; . . .

(5) that enables such creditor to receive more than such creditor would receive if—

(a) the case were a case under Chapter 7 of this title;

(b) the transfer had not been made; and

(c) such creditor received payment of such debt to the extent provided by the provisions of this title.

According to the Trustee, the transfers of the Minks satisfy each and every element of Sec. 547(b) and, therefore, such transfers may be avoided. In response, Almiro submits that it was not a creditor of the Debtor. And, no transfer of property of the Debtor was made, Almiro argues, inasmuch as Debtor had no property interest in the Minks to transfer. This argument is premised upon Almiro's contention that the shipments of the Minks "were not for the purpose of transferring property, but for the sole purpose of consigning the goods to the Debtor for inspection only."

To establish that a transfer constitutes an avoidable preference, the threshold requirement of a transfer of an interest of the debtor in property must be met. "Transfer" is defined in [the Bankruptcy Code] as "every mode direct or indirect, absolute or conditional, voluntary or involuntary, of disposing of or parting with property or with an interest in property. . . .." In returning the Minks to Almiro, Debtor obviously physically parted with the property in question. The dispute here centers upon whether Debtor possessed a transferable property interest in the Minks. According to Almiro, because the Minks were transferred on a consignment basis, for inspection only, Debtor never obtained a transferable property interest in the Minks. This argument ignores Ohio law. Debtor's affidavit, as well as Almiro's interrogatory answers, establish that the Minks were shipped to Debtor to be sold on consignment. Because the Minks were delivered to Debtor primarily for resale, and the Debtor could return the Minks to Almiro for credit even if the Minks conformed to the contract, pursuant to Ohio law, this transaction would be classified as a "sale or return." Under [UCC 2-326(b)], goods held on a "sale or return" basis are subject to the claims of the buyer's creditors while in the buyer's possession unless compliance with one of the provisions of [UCC 2-326(c)] is demonstrated.

Absent such a showing, then, the Minks were subject to the claims of Debtor's creditors while in his possession and must be deemed to be "property" of the Debtor within the meaning of Sec. 547(b).

Under [UCC 2-326(c)], goods held on "sale or return" are subject to the claims of the buyer's creditors while they are in the buyer's possession, unless the seller of such goods does one of the following:

1. complies with an applicable state law providing for a consignor's interest to be evidenced by a sign;
2. establishes that the person conducting the business is generally known by his creditors to be substantially engaged in selling the goods of others; or
3. complies with the filing requirements of [UCC Article 9].

Almiro's failure to comply with any of the requirements of [2-326(c)] is clear as a matter of fact and law. Ohio has no applicable law providing for a consignor's interest to be evidenced by a sign. And, Almiro does not assert that Debtor was generally known by his creditors to be substantially engaged in the sale of goods of others. Finally, Almiro's failure to file [Article 9] financing statements with respect to the Minks is likewise undisputed. Hence, the relationship between Almiro and the Debtor is not that of consignor- consignee under Ohio law. Rather, the transaction was a "sale or return" and, . . . the Minks were subject to the claims of Debtor's creditors while in Debtor's possession. It follows, therefore, that under Ohio law Debtor possessed a transferable property interest in the Minks for purpose of Sec. 547(b). Thus, the initial element of an avoidable transfer—transfer of an interest of the Debtor in property—has been established.

According to Almiro, it was not a creditor of the Debtor during the preference period. Hence, Almiro asserts, the Trustee cannot meet the requirement of Sec. 547(b)(1). This contention is without merit. Under [the Bankruptcy Code], a "creditor" is an "entity that has a claim against a debtor that arose at the time of or before the order for relief concerning the debtor." A "claim" is a "right to payment or a right to an equitable remedy." Here, Debtor had the obligation to either return the Minks or to pay for the merchandise. Put differently, Almiro had a right to payment for the Minks or to an equitable remedy for their return. Accordingly, Almiro was a creditor as defined in [the Code] and the transfers in question were to or for Almiro's benefit.

The transfers of the Minks from Debtor to Almiro were "for or on account of an antecedent debt owed by the Debtor before such transfer[s] . . .[were] made." As noted above, Almiro is a creditor of the Debtor because Debtor had the obligation to either pay for the Minks or return them to Almiro. By the same reckoning, the transfers in question clearly were made on account of claims owned by Debtor to Almiro before such transfers were made.

The third element of a preferential transfer is set forth in Sec. 547(b)(3): the transfer must be made while the Debtor was insolvent. Sec. 547(f) creates the presumption that a debtor is insolvent for the 90 days preceding the petition date. This places the burden of going forward with evidence of the debtor's solvency on the recipient of the alleged preferential transfer. Here, Almiro has offered no evidence, by affidavit or otherwise, to overcome the statutory presumption of insolvency. . .. Hence, the Court finds that Debtor was insolvent at the time of the transfer of the Minks [which admittedly occurred within 90 days preceding the petition date].

The final element which must be shown to establish a preferential transfer is Almiro's receipt of more than it would have received had no transfer taken place and its claim was provided for pursuant to the distributive scheme of the Bankruptcy Code. The affidavit of the

Trustee establishes that there will be insufficient assets in the estate for payment of a 100% dividend to general unsecured claimholders. Because the transfer of the Minks, Almiro received more by virtue of the transfers than it would have under a Chapter 7 liquidation.

[Therefore] each element of Sec. 547(b) has been established; hence, the transfers of the Minks are subject to avoidance. Judgment is hereby entered in favor of the Trustee and against Defendant in the amount of [$11,155.00].

Claims

As a general rule, any legal obligation of the debtor existing pre-petition gives rise to a claim against the debtor's estate in the bankruptcy proceeding. There are, however, several special situations we should mention.

1. If the claim is **contingent** on the happening or nonhappening of some future event or, if its **amount is in dispute**, the bankruptcy court has the power to make an estimate of the claim's value.

2. If the claim against the debtor is for breach of contract, it will include any damages which accrued prior to the filing of the bankruptcy petition, and also those damages attributable to the debtor's failure to perform any future obligations under the contract. Of course, this is no different from an ordinary breach of contract claim when bankruptcy is not involved. However, under the bankruptcy law, if the claim arises out of an **employment contract** or a **real estate** lease, limits are placed on a claim for damages relating to future nonperformance. In the case of an employment contract, such damages are limited to a term of one year from the filing date or the date the contract was repudiated, whichever is earlier. In the case of a real estate lease, damages are limited to either **oneyear** or **15 percent** of the remaining term of the lease, whichever is greater, up to a maximum of three years. The starting point for measuring this time is the same as for employment contracts. One reason for these limits is that contracts of these two types are frequently long-term ones, and the farther in the future we try to compute damages, the more speculative they get.

3. A creditor who has received a voidable transfer or preference may not assert a claim of any kind until the wrongfully received property or funds are returned to the debtor's estate.

Subject to the above limitations, any claim filed with the bankruptcy court is allowed unless it is contested by an interested party, such as the trustee, debtor, or another creditor. If challenged, the court will rule on the claim's validity after pertinent evidence is presented at a hearing held for that purpose. In this regard, claims against the debtor's estate will be subject to any defenses that the debtor could have asserted had there been no bankruptcy. The fact that a claim is allowed, of course, does not mean that the particular creditor will be paid in full; it just means that the creditor has the hope of receiving **something**.

Distribution of Debtor's Estate

A secured creditor—one having a security interest or lien in a specific item of property can proceed directly against that property for satisfaction of his or her claim. This is true even though the debtor is or is about to become subject to a bankruptcy proceeding. In a sense, then, **secured creditors** have priority over all classes of unsecured creditors (usually referred to as **general creditors**). However, if a portion of a secured creditor's claim is not secured, that portion is treated like any other unsecured claim.

When the trustee has gathered all the assets of the debtor's estate and reduced them to cash, these proceeds will be distributed to unsecured creditors. There are certain unsecured claims which are given priority in this distribution. These claims are paid in full in **the order of their priority,** assuming there are sufficient proceeds available. The following classes of debts are listed in order of priority. Each class must be fully paid before the next is entitled to anything. If the available funds are insufficient to satisfy all creditors within a class, payment to creditors in that class is made in proportion to the amounts of their claims.

1. Domestic support obligations. BAPCPA elevated such claims to top priority.
2. Costs and expenses of administration (trustees', auctioneers' and attorneys' fees, for example).
3. If the proceeding is an involuntary one, any expense incurred in the ordinary course of the debtor's business or financial affairs after commencement of the case but before appointment of the trustee.
4. Any claim for wages, salaries, or commissions, including vacation, severance, and sick leave pay earned by an individual within 180 days before the filing of the petition or the cessation of the debtor's business, whichever occurs first, limited to $10,000 per individual.
5. Any claim for contributions to an employee benefit plan arising from services performed within 180 days before filing or business cessation, limited to $10,000 per individual. However, a particular individual cannot receive more than $10,000 under the fourth and fifth priorities combined.
6. Claims of grain producers or U.S. fishermen against a debtor who owns or operates a grain or fish storage facility for the produce or its proceeds, limited to $4,925 for each such individual.
7. Claims of individuals, up to $2,225 per person, for deposits made on consumer goods or services that were not received.
8. Claims of governmental units for various kinds of taxes, subject to time limits that differ depending on the type of tax.

If all priority claims are paid and funds still remain, general creditors are paid in proportion to the amounts of their claims. Any portion of a priority claim that was beyond the limits of the priority is treated as a general claim. An example would be the amount by which an individual's wage claim exceeded $10,000. Figure22.2 outlines the process of distributing the debtor's estate.

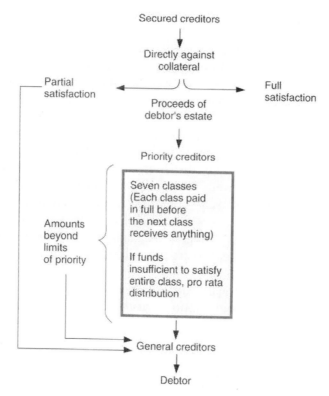

Figure 22.2 Distribution of Debtor's Estate

Discharge

After the debtor's estate has been liquidated and distributed to creditors, the bankruptcy court may conduct a hearing to determine whether the debtor should be discharged from liability for remaining obligations.

Grounds for Refusal of Discharge

Under certain circumstances the court will refuse to grant the debtor a discharge. Among these are the following:

1. Only an **individual** can receive a discharge in a liquidation proceeding. For a corporation to receive a discharge it must go through a reorganization proceeding (discussed later in the chapter), or be dissolved in accordance with state corporation statutes.

2. A debtor will be denied a discharge if he or she had previously received such a discharge within **eight years** before the present bankruptcy petition was filed. For many years this period had been only six years, but BAPCPA extended the period by two years in 2005 in order to make this provision more creditor-friendly.

3. The debtor will be denied a discharge if he or she has committed any of the following acts (a) intentionally concealed or transferred assets for the purpose of evading creditors, within one year before the filing of the petition or during the bankruptcy proceedings; (b) concealed, destroyed, falsified, or failed to keep business or financial records unless there was reasonable justification for such action or failure; (c) failed to adequately explain any loss of assets; (d) refused to obey a lawful court order or to answer a material court-approved question in connection with the bankruptcy case; or (e) made any fraudulent statement or claim in connection with the bankruptcy case.

4. If a discharge has been granted, the court may revoke it within one year if it is discovered that the debtor had not acted honestly in connection with the bankruptcy proceeding. BAPCPA instructs the Attorney General to conduct audits of a certain percentage of bankruptcy cases to detect inaccuracies in debtor filings and prevent fraud. It also provides that discharge may be revoked if a debtor fails to cooperate with an auditor or to explain satisfactorily a material misstatement in an audit.

In the following case, creditors of the bankrupt debtor claimed that the debtor should not be discharged from his obligations because he had demonstrated an actual intent to defraud his creditors. The case demonstrates the importance of looking at a debtor's overall pattern of conduct when determining whether he or she has acted fraudulently.

Norwest Bank Nebraska, N.A. v. Tveten
U.S. Eighth Circuit Court of Appeals, 848 F.2d 871 (1988)

Tveten was a 59- year-old physician and sole shareholder of Omar A. Tveten, P.A., a professional corporation. He began investing in real estate, initially quite successfully. Joined by other doctors,

Tveten organized ventures that were highly leveraged. Debts were personally guaranteed by Tveten and the other doctors. In mid-1985, Tveten's investments began to sour. Appellees Norwest Bank and Business Development Corporation, and Harold Panuska became creditors of Tveten as a result of his various investment ventures.

Tveten filed a bankruptcy petition on January 7, 1986. Meanwhile, several creditors already had commenced lawsuits against him.

Panuska had obtained a $139,657 judgment against him on October 9, 1985. Norwest Bank and Business Development had commenced an action against him but had not obtained a judgment when Tveten filed for bankruptcy. On the date the petition was filed, Tveten owed his creditors close to $19,000,000.

Before filing for bankruptcy, Tveten consulted a lawyer. As part of his pre-bankruptcy planning, he liquidated almost all of his nonexempt property, converting it into exempt property worth approximately $700,000. This was accomplished through some 17 separate transfers. The non-exempt property he liquidated included land sold to his parents *and his brother, respectively, for $70,000 and $75,732 in cash; life insurance policies and annuities with a for-profit company with cash values totaling $96,307.58; his net salary and bonuses of $27,820.91; his KEOGH pension plan and individual retirement fund of $20,487.35; his corporation's profit-sharing plan worth $325,774.51; and a home sold for $50,000. All of the liquidated property was converted into life insurance or annuity contracts with the Lutheran Brotherhood, a fraternal benefit association, which, under Minnesota law, cannot be attached by creditors. Tveten concedes that the purpose of these transfers was to shield his assets from creditors. Minnesota law provides that creditors cannot attach any money or other benefits payable by a fraternal benefit association. Unlike most exemption provisions in other states, the Minnesota exemption has no monetary limit. Indeed, under this exemption, Tveten attempted to place $700,000 worth of his property out of his creditors' reach.*

The bankruptcy court held that, even if the exemptions were permissible, Tveten had abused the protections permitted a debtor under the Bankruptcy Code. His awareness of Panuska's judgment against him and of several pending lawsuits, his rapidly deteriorating business investments, and his exposure to extensive liability well beyond his ability to pay, all led the court to find that Tveten intended to hinder and delay his creditors. Accordingly, the bankruptcy court denied Tveten a discharge. The federal district court affirmed and Tveten appealed.

Timbers, Circuit Judge:

At the outset, it is necessary to distinguish between (1) a debtor's right to exempt certain property from the claims of his creditors and (2) his right to a discharge of his debts. The Code permits a debtor to exempt property either pursuant to the provisions of the Code if not forbidden by state law, or pursuant to the provisions of state law and federal law other than the minimum allowances in the Code. When the debtor claims a state-created exemption, state law determines the scope of the claim. It is well established that under the Code the conversion of nonexempt to exempt property for the purpose of placing the property out of the reach of creditors, without more, will not deprive the debtor of the exemption to which he otherwise would be entitled.

The rationale behind this policy is that "[t]he result which would obtain if debtors were not allowed to convert property into allowable exempt property would be extremely harsh, especially in those jurisdictions where the exemption allowance is minimal." This blanket approval of conversion is qualified, however, by denial of discharge if there was extrinsic evidence of the debtor's intent to defraud creditors.

A debtor's right to a discharge, unlike his right to an exemption, is determined by federal, not state, law. The Code provides that a debtor may be denied a discharge under Chapter 7 if, among other things, he has transferred property "with intent to hinder, delay, or defraud a creditor" within one year before the date of the filing of the petition.

[T]he standard applied consistently by the courts is the same as that used to determine whether an exemption is permissible, i.e., absent extrinsic evidence of fraud, mere conversion of non-exempt property to exempt property is not fraudulent as to creditors even if the motivation behind the conversion is to place those assets beyond the reach of creditors.

As the bankruptcy court correctly found here, therefore, the issue in the instant case revolves around whether there was extrinsic evidence to demonstrate that Tveten transferred his property on the eve of bankruptcy with intent to defraud his creditors. The bankruptcy court's finding that there was such intent to defraud may be reversed by us only if clearly erroneous.

In the instant case, the state exemption relied on by Tveten was unlimited, with the potential for unlimited abuse. Indeed, this case presents a situation in which the debtor liquidated almost his entire net worth of $700,000 and converted it to exempt property in seventeen transfers on the eve of bankruptcy while his creditors, to whom he owed close to $19,000,000 would be left to divide the little that remained in his estate. Borrowing the phrase used by another court, Tveten "did not want a fresh start, he wanted a head start." His attempt to shield property worth approximately $700,000 goes well beyond the purpose for which exemptions are permitted.

The bankruptcy court, as affirmed by the district court, examined Tveten's entire pattern of conduct and found that he had demonstrated fraudulent intent. We agree. While state law governs the legitimacy of Tveten's exemptions, it is federal law that governs his discharge. Permitting Tveten, who earns over $60,000 annually, to convert all of his major non-exempt assets into sheltered property on the eve of bankruptcy with actual intent to defraud his creditors "would constitute a perversion of the purposes of the Bankruptcy Code." Tveten still is entitled to retain, free from creditors' claims, property rightfully exempt under relevant state law.
Affirmed.

Nondischargeable Debts

Even if the debtor is granted a general discharge from obligations, there nevertheless are a few types of claims for which he or she will continue to be liable. These **nondischargeable debts** include the following:

1. Obligations for payment of taxes are not discharged if (a) the particular tax was entitled to a priority in the distribution of the debtor's estate, but was not paid; or (b) a tax return had been required but was not properly filed; or (c) the debtor had willfully attempted to evade the particular tax.
2. Claims arising out of the debtor's fraud, embezzlement, or larceny are not discharged.
3. The debtor is not excused from liability for a willful and malicious tort.
4. Claims for alimony and child support are not discharged.
5. The debtor is not discharged from a claim that he or she failed to list in the bankruptcy case if this failure caused the creditor not to assert the claim in time for it to be allowed.
6. A fine, penalty, or forfeiture payable to a governmental unit, which is neither compensation for actual pecuniary loss nor a tax penalty, is not discharged.
7. Obligations to repay student loans, scholarships, stipends or other educational benefits are not dischargeable unless to refuse discharge would impose an undue hardship on the debtor or the debtor's dependents. BAPCPA expanded this provision beyond student aid provided by governmental units.
8. Any judgments or awards of damages resulting from the debtor's operation of a motor vehicle while legally intoxicated are not dischargeable.
9. Primarily because of credit card abuse by debtors shortly before filing for bankruptcy, two types of **consumer debts** have been made nondischargeable: (a) debts of more than $500 to a particular creditor for **luxury goods or services,** if incurred

within 90 days of the order for relief (i.e., the petition); and (b) cash advances total-ing more than $750 obtained by using a credit card or other open-ended consumer credit arrangement, if incurred within 70 days of the order for relief.

Redemption, Ride-Through, and Reaffrmation

Assume that a Chapter 7 debtor has a car (or other personal property). Debtor bor-rowed money from a creditor to buy the car and is currently making payments. Creditor has a lien on the car. If the debtor would like to keep the car, he or she has had three pri-mary routes through which to do so.

Redemption. First, the debtor may redeem the car by paying off the lien. Before BAPCPA, the debtor was required to make a lump sum payment of the value of the collat-eral or the unpaid balance of the debt, whichever was less, within 45 days after the first meeting of creditors. Now, it is clear that the debtor must pay the full amount of the claim and may not redeem by paying the value of the collateral if it is a lesser sum. BAPCPA also reverses the majority court interpretation by providing that the value of collateral for pur-poses of redemption should be measured by the replacement cost to the debtor not the typ-ically lower amount that the creditor would receive for the property upon repossession.

Ride-Through. The courts developed a system by which debtors who were not behind in their payments could continue to retain their car (or other collateral) by con-tinuing to make payments. The lien was not released until the debtor had paid the full price, if the debtor later quit making payments, the creditor was limited to retaking col-lateral; no deficiency judgment was allowed. BAPCPA eliminates this alternative.

Reaffirmation. Because ride-through is no longer available, the other option for debtors (which is likely to be much more popular than redemption), is reaffirmation. Debtors may renew obligations on debts that have been discharged in bankruptcy. Reaf-firmations are obviously good for creditors, who may be paid sums that the debtor is otherwise no longer legally obligated to pay. Reaffirmations can also be good for debt-ors who can use them to settle disputes as to the nondischargeability of claims or to rees-tablish credit, as well as to retain collateral.

Before the 1978 Bankruptcy Code, debtors could renew their obligations on a dis-charged debt simply by expressing a willingness to be bound. No consideration was required, although some states mandated that the reaffirmation be in writing. Because many creditors induced debtors to reaffirm obligations by use of coercion or deception, the 1978 Code established strict procedures governing reaffirmations. Those changes reduced abuse, but in 1999 the giant retailer Sears paid a $60 million fine for violating the procedures by leading bankruptcy debtors to believe that they had no choice but to reaffirm their obligations.

Therefore the BAPCPA of 2005 imposed lengthy disclosure requirements and new procedures in an attempt to ensure that debtors know the law and understand fully the consequences of reaffirming a debt. The law even requires the Attorney General of the United States to designate individuals to have primary responsibility to enforce prohibi-tions on abusive reaffirmations.

Business Reorganization

If it is felt that reorganization and continuance of a business is feasible and is preferable to liquidation, a petition for reorganization may be filed under Chapter 11 of the 1978 Bankruptcy Code. The reorganization procedure is intended for use by businesses, but it does not matter whether the owner of the business is an individual, partnership, or corporation. A **reorganization case** can be either voluntary or involuntary, and the requirements for filing an involuntary case are the same as for a liquidation proceeding. In general, the types of debtors exempted from reorganization proceedings are the same as those exempted from liquidation proceedings. The major difference in coverage is that a railroad can be a debtor in a reorganization proceeding. The most important aspects of a reorganization case are summarized below.

As soon as the petition is filed, an **automatic** stay is in operation just as in a liquidation proceeding. The automatic stay is even more important in a reorganization proceeding, because without such a stay the debtor often would find it impossible to continue operating its business.

There may or may not be a trustee in a reorganization case. If a trustee is appointed, he or she will take over and will have basically the same duties and powers as in a liquidation case. Essentially, the court will appoint a trustee if requested by an interested party (such as a creditor) and if it appears that such an appointment would be in the best interests of all parties involved. Obviously a trustee will be appointed if the court feels there is a possibility of the debtor's business being mismanaged or assets being wasted or concealed. If a trustee is not appointed, the debtor remains in possession and control of the business. In this situation, the debtor is called the **debtor in-possession**, and has all the powers of a trustee.

After commencement of the case, the U.S. Trustee must appoint a committee of unsecured creditors. If necessary, the court or the U.S. Trustee may appoint other creditors' committees to represent the special interests of particular types of creditors. A committee of shareholders may also be appointed to oversee the interests of that group, if the debtor is a corporation.

The creditors' and shareholders' committees, and the trustee, if one was appointed, will investigate the business and financial affairs of the debtor. A **reorganization plan** will then be prepared and filed with the bankruptcy court. This plan must divide creditors' claims and shareholders' interests into classes according to their type. For instance, claims of employees, secured creditors, bondholders, real estate mortgage holders, and government units might be segregated into different classes. The plan must indicate how claims within each class are going to be handled and to what extent each class will receive less than full payment, as well as provide adequate means for the plan's execution. Treatment of claims within each class must be equal.

The court will "confirm" (approve) the reorganization plan if (a) each class has approved the plan and (b) the court rules that the plan is "fair and equitable" to all classes. A plan is deemed to be accepted by a class of creditors if it received favorable votes from those representing at least two-thirds of the amount of claims and more than half of the number of creditors within that class. Acceptance by a class of shareholders requires an affirmative vote by those representing at least two-thirds of the shares in that class. If the parties are unable to produce an acceptable plan or if the plan subsequently does not work as expected, the court may either dismiss the case or convert it into a liquidation proceeding.

After the plan has been confirmed, the debtor is discharged from those claims not provided for in the plan. However, the types of claims that are not discharged in a liquidation case are also not discharged in a reorganization case.

Certain procedural changes were made in 1991 in order to facilitate use of **prepackaged bankruptcies**—reorganization plans negotiated with the debtor's creditors prior to filing as a way to abbreviate the period the debtor company will have to stay in bankruptcy. And in 1994, Congress established a "fast-track" Chapter 11 provision for small businesses. Under this provision, they can save time and expense over the normal Chapter 11 rules. For example, orders in small business cases do not require creditor committee consent.

Policy Issues in Reorganizations

The attempt by bankruptcy laws to achieve equity among debtors and creditors has always raised questions of ethics and public policy. Indeed, the provisions of the Bankruptcy Code dealing with voidable preferences, refusal of discharge, and nondischargeable debts have ethical and policy questions at their core. The fact that the 1978 Code no longer requires that a debtor be insolvent to file a voluntary case has made these ethical questions even more important: If it is in the best interest of society to provide relief to an insolvent debtor, how far should public policy go in letting a debtor start afresh when that debtor is financially beleaguered but not insolvent?

Since the enactment of the 1978 Code, which increased the flexibility and acceptability of business reorganization cases, ethical and policy questions have arisen with increasing frequency under Chapter 11 of the Code. Again, there is no insolvency requirement, and the ultimate objective of a reorganization is to permit the debtor to continue as a viable entity. Although the reorganization provisions of Chapter 11 pursue worthwhile goals, the process of reorganization does present opportunities for abuse. As we mentioned previously, if a trustee is not appointed in a reorganization proceeding, the debtor becomes a so-called **debtor-in-possession,** with all the powers of a trustee. Although the exercise of such power obviously is under the supervision of the bankruptcy court, creditors, employee unions, and other groups often are understandably concerned about the actions of the debtor-in-possession. Bankruptcy reorganization is today being successfully utilized by major corporations to defer pre-petition debts in order to improve cash flow for post-petition operating costs, to alter obligations under burdensome labor contracts and underfunded pension plans, and to block products liability litigation.

One of the most important powers of the debtor in- possession, like a trustee, is the power to cancel **executory contracts.** For a time, there was a question whether a debtor-in-possession could cancel a collective bargaining agreement covering its unionized employees. Unions claimed that a debtor-in-possession should not have the power to cancel collective bargaining agreements because an employer could then use a Chapter 11 reorganization as a "union busting" device. The Supreme Court ruled, however, in NLRB v. Bildisco & Bildisco, 465 U.S. 513 (1984), that collective bargaining agreements, like other contracts, can be cancelled by the debtor-in-possession when cancellation is in the best interests of a successful reorganization. Shortly thereafter, Congress amended the law so as to place restrictions on this power. Specifically, Congress provided that the debtor-in possession (i.e., the employer) must first propose reasonable modifications to the existing union contract. If the union rejects these proposed modifications, the Bankruptcy Court then conducts a hearing to determine whether the union has "good cause" for the rejection. A union has good cause for rejecting the proposed modifications if the employer has failed to prove that the contract changes are "fair and equitable" to all parties and necessary for the company's survival. If it is found that the union does have good cause, the burden is then upon the employer to make further proposals. If the court finds that the union did not have good cause for rejecting a particular proposal for modifying the collective bargaining agreement, the employer then has the power to cancel the agreement and set new employment terms unilaterally.

Bankruptcy has become unpopular with workers, as companies seem to increasingly be using Chapter 11 to force union concessions. For example, in 2005, Delphi filed for Chapter 11, threatening union workers with default on the company's defined-benefit pension plan. As one observer noted, "managers in Chapter 11 cases have their eyes on the prize of cash and equity bonuses if they can work the company into shape speedily without it having to be broken up. Delphi plans to award up to $87m in bonuses and 10 per cent of equity in a new company to its 600 most senior managers. They can get richer by persuading the hourly-paid workers to become poorer." (John Gapper, "The Danger of Rewriting Chapter 11," Financial Times, Oct. 13, 2005, at 13.)

One of the most important effects of the filing of a Chapter 11 bankruptcy is the imposition of the automatic stay. This prohibition of collection efforts with regard to pre-petition debts or against the reorganizing debtor raises various ethical and policy questions. Suppose, for example, that a large, profitable company is faced with a great many claims for injuries allegedly arising from products made by the company. A large number of claims have already been filed, and many others are anticipated in the future, making it necessary for the company to set aside extremely large reserves to cover contingent liabilities. Can the company use a Chapter 11 reorganization proceeding to obtain settlements of these claims in an organized, hopefully uniform fashion? This is the question faced by the court in the following case.

IN RE JOHNS-MANVILLE CORPORATION
U.S. Bankruptcy Court, S.D. New York, 36 Bankr. Rptr. 727 (1984)

Johns-Manville Corp. (Manville) was a large, highly successful manufacturing enterprise. It and several other companies were major producers of several products, such as insulation, that contained asbestos. After many people who had been exposed to asbestos for lengthy periods of time developed very serious diseases such as asbestosis and lung cancer, large numbers of lawsuits began to be filed against asbestos producers.

Manville filed a petition for reorganization under Chapter 11 of the Bankruptcy Code, claiming that such filing was made necessary by the "uncontrolled proliferation" of asbestos related lawsuits. At the time of the court's initial decision in the reorganization case, over 16,000 such suits had been filed against Manville. The company stated that its problems were compounded by the "crushing economic burden to be suffered by it over the next 20-30 years by the filing of an even more staggering number of suits by those who had been exposed but who will not manifest the asbestos-related diseases until some time during this future period." In addition, Manville showed that the insurance industry had generally disavowed coverage for asbestos-related claims under products liability insurance policies carried by the company. The question of insurance coverage had been tied up in state court litigation in California for several years.

Several different groups of creditors and asbestos-lawsuit plaintiffs challenged Manville's reorganization petition as inappropriate, and asked that it be dismissed. These groups contended that Manville was a healthy company and was misusing the Bankruptcy Code by attempting to use a reorganization proceeding to resolve products liability claims. The opinion of the Bankruptcy Court follows.

Lifland, Bankruptcy Judge:

Clearly, Manville meets the requirements... for debtors under all chapters of the Code in that it is domiciled and has its place of business in the United States... In addition, Manville meets the eligibility requirements applicable to Chapter 11 debtors ... Moreover, it should also be noted that neither Section 109 [containing eligibility requirements] nor any other provision relating to voluntary petitions by companies contains any insolvency requirement... This is in striking contrast to the requirement of insolvency ... with regard to the commencement of involuntary cases...

The filing of a Chapter 11 case creates an estate for the benefit of all creditors and equity holders of the debtor wherein all constituencies may voice their interests and bargain for their best possible treatment...

A principal goal of the Bankruptcy Code is to provide open access to the bankruptcy process... [According to congressional reports,] the rationale behind this "open access" policy is to provide access to bankruptcy relief which is as "open" as "access to the credit economy." Thus, Congress intended that "there should be no legal barriers to voluntary petitions." Another major goal of the Code, that of "rehabilitation of debtors," requires that relief for debtors must be "timely." Congress declared that it is essential to both the open access and rehabilitation goals that [i]nitiating relief should not be a death knell. The process should encourage resort to it, by debtors and creditors, that cuts short the dissipation of assets and the accumulation of debts. Belated commencement of a case may kill an opportunity for reorganization or arrangement.

Accordingly, the drafters of the Code envisioned that a financially beleaguered debtor with real debt and real creditors should not be required to wait until the economic situation is beyond repair in order to file a reorganization petition. The congressional purpose in enacting the Code was to encourage resort to the bankruptcy process. This philosophy not only comports with the elimination of an insolvency requirement, but also is a corollary of the key aim of Chapter 11 of the Code, that of avoidance of liquidation. The drafters of the Code announced this goal, declaring that reorganization is more efficient than liquidation because "assets that are used for production in the industry for which they were designed are more valuable than those same assets sold for scrap." Moreover, reorganization also fosters the goals of preservation of jobs in the threatened entity.

In the instant case, not only would liquidation be wasteful and inefficient in destroying the utility of valuable assets of the companies as well as jobs, but, more importantly, liquidation would preclude just compensation of some present asbestos victims and all future asbestos claimants. This unassailable reality represents all the more reason for this Court to adhere to this. . . liquidation avoidance aim of Chapter 11 and deny the motions to dismiss. Manville must not be required to wait until its economic picture has deteriorated beyond salvation to file for reorganization. . . All of the motions to dismiss the Manville petition are denied in their entirety.

The Johns-Manville Corporation bankruptcy was described as "one of the most significant Chapter 11 bankruptcy proceedings" by the circuit court that affirmed confirmation of the reorganization plan on appeal. That plan, which resulted from more than four years of negotiations, is described in the opinion that follows.

KANE V. JOHNS-MANVILLE CORP.
U.S. Second Circuit Court of Appeals, 843 F.2d 636 (1988)

The Bankruptcy Court confirmed Johns-Manville's reorganization plan and the district court affirmed. Kane, representing 765 "Class-4 creditors"—persons with asbestos related disease who had filed personal injury suits against Manville prior to Manville's Chapter 11 status—appealed. Kane's primary argument is that the plan does not adequately protect the interests of asbestos victims.

Newman, Circuit Judge:
The cornerstone of the Plan is the Asbestos Health Trust (the "Trust"), a mechanism designed to satisfy the claims of all asbestos health victims, both present and future. The Trust is funded with the proceeds from Manville's settlements with its insurers; certain cash, receivables, and stock of the reorganized Manville Corporation; long term notes; and the right to receive up to 20% of Manville's yearly profits for as long as it takes to satisfy all health claims. According to the terms of the Trust, individuals with asbestos-related disease must first try to settle their claims by a mandatory exchange of settlement offers with Trust representatives. If a settlement cannot be

reached, the claimant may elect mediation, binding arbitration, or traditional tort litigation. The claimant may collect from the Trust the full amount of whatever compensatory damages he is awarded. The only restriction on recovery is that the claimant may not obtain punitive damages.

The purpose of the Trust is to provide a means of satisfying Manville's ongoing personal injury liability while allowing Manville to maximize its value by continuing as an ongoing concern. To fulfill this purpose, the Plan seeks to ensure that health claims can be asserted only against the Trust and that Manville's operating entities will be protected from an onslaught of crippling lawsuits that could jeopardize the entire reorganization effort. To this end, the parties agreed that as a condition precedent to confirmation of the Plan, the Bankruptcy Court would issue an Injunction channeling all asbestos-related personal injury claims to the Trust. The Injunction provides that asbestos claimants may proceed only against the Trust to satisfy their claims and may not sue Manville, its other operating entities, and certain other specified parties, including Manville's insurers. Significantly, the Injunction applies to all health claimants, both present and future, regardless of whether they technically have dischargeable "claims" under the Code.

Manville presented extensive evidence on feasibility at the confirmation hearing, while Kane presented no evidence. The Bankruptcy Judge found that "the Debtor's reasonable and credible projections of future earnings have established that the reorganized corporation is unlikely to face future proceedings under this title." With specific reference to the Trust, the Court found that "[t]he evidence submitted by the Debtor ...provides a reasonable estimation, based upon known present claimants and reasonable extrapolations from past experience and epidemiological data, of the number and amount of asbestos-related claims that the AH Trust will be required to satisfy. The Debtor has also established that the Trust will, in fact, meet this burden.

[Affirmed.]

Adjustment of Debts
Of an Individual with Regular Income

Debtors who have a regular income can and generally should pay more to creditors than those without regular income. For debtors without regular income,Chapter 7 may be the only real choice. For others, 13Chapter provides for "Adjustment of Debts of an Individual with Regular Income." Individuals with regular income who owe fixed unsecured debts less than $307,675 or fixed secured debts less than $922,975 may choose this method, which has parallels to Chapter 11s reorganization plan for businesses, but is less complex and expensive). Sole proprietors, salaried employees, individuals living on fixed incomes, and others are eligible to use Chapter 13.

As noted earlier, a major goal of the 2005 BAPCPA was to force individuals into Chapter13 rather than allowing them to just write the slate clean in Chapter 7 liquidation. While the Bankruptcy Code has always allowed a bankruptcy court to dismiss a Chapter 7 proceeding, or to convert it to a Chapter 11 or Chapter 13 proceeding if it constituted an "abuse" of the bankruptcy process, BAPCPA added a requirement that a court must presume that abuse exists if debtors have an income above their state's median income and can pay at least \$6,000 (\$100 per month) over five years. These individuals are generally to be shifted to Chapter 13 and ordered to make payments on credit card and other bills. It was predicted that as high as 20% of individual debtors may be shifted out of Chapter 7 and into Chapter 13 by these provisions that became effective in the fall of 2005. However, an early post-BAPCPA study found that 97% of the individual debtors examined had no realistic way to pay their debts. Therefore, the claim by creditors that many people who could pay their debts were simply choosing not to do so may have been greatly exaggerated.

To further discourage filing of bankruptcy petitions by consumers, BAPCPA requires that debtors must undergo credit counseling before being allowed to file. That requirement is discussed in the following case. The judge does not appear to be too pleased by BAPCPA.

IN RE SOSA
U.S. Bankruptcy Court, Western District of Texas, 336 B.R. 113 (2005)

Mr. and Mrs. Sosa filed for bankruptcy under Chapter 13. Their filing did not include a Certificate of Credit Counseling. They appeared without an attorney, but had copies of a pleading by an attorney, Chapman, who helped them respond to the Court's Order to Show Cause why their petition should not be dismissed.

Monroe, Bankruptcy Judge:

The Congress of the United States of America passed and the President of the United States of America signed into law the Bankruptcy Abuse Prevention and Consumer Protection Act of 2005 (the "Act"). It became fully effective on October 17, 2005. Those responsible for the passing of the Act did all in their power to avoid the proffered input from sitting U. S. Bankruptcy Judges, various professors of bankruptcy law at distinguished universities, and many professional associations filled with the best of the bankruptcy lawyers in the country as to the perceived flaws in the Act. This is because the parties pushing the passage of the Act had their own

agenda. It was apparently an agenda to make more money off the backs of the consumers in this country. It is not surprising, therefore, that the Act has been highly criticized across the country. In this writer's opinion, to call the Act a "consumer protection" Act is the grossest of misnomers.

One of the more absurd provisions of the new Act makes an individual ineligible for relief under the Bankruptcy Code unless such individual, "has, during the 180-day period preceding the date of filing of the petition by such individual, received from an approved nonprofit budget and credit counseling agency described in Sec. 111(a) an individual or group briefing (including a briefing conducted by telephone or on the Internet) that outlined the opportunities for available credit counseling and assisted such individual in performing a related budget analysis." No doubt this is a truly exhaustive budget analysis.

An individual who does not receive such counseling can only receive an exemption from such requirement if such debtor "submits to the court a certification that - (i) describes exigent circumstances that merit a waiver of the requirements of paragraph (1); (ii) states that the debtor requested credit counseling services from an approved nonprofit budget and credit counseling agency, but was unable to obtain the services referred to in paragraph (1) during the 5-day period beginning on the date on which the debtor made that request; and (iii) is satisfactory to the court." In the event such waiver is granted, the debtor must complete such counseling within 30 days after the petition date.

Simply stated, if a debtor does not request the required credit counseling services from an approved nonprofit budget and credit counseling service before the petition is filed, that person is ineligible to be a debtor no matter how dire the circumstances the person finds themselves in at that moment.

This Court views this requirement as inane. However, it is a clear and unambiguous provision obviously designed by Congress to protect consumers.

In this case the Debtors admit they did not seek or request the required credit counseling services from an approved nonprofit budget and credit counseling agency before filing their case even though they talked to Mr. Chapman by telephone prior to filing and he rightfully advised them to do so. Instead they filed this Chapter 13 case on December 6, 2005, "as an emergency measure to stop foreclosure on their homestead." The Debtors responded to the Court's question as to why they waited so long to file their case by stating that they had been working with the mortgage company to determine the exact amount that was owed but that the lien holder had refused to accept payment at the last moment and that was what

necessitated the emergency filing of bankruptcy.

Mr. Sosa has now undergone his credit counseling and filed a Certificate. No certificate has been filed by Mrs. Sosa.

One Debtor has now substantially complied with the intent of the Act by undergoing the required credit counseling. One has not but still could within the time limit if a waiver could be granted. However, because the Debtors did not request such counseling before they filed their case, Congress says they are ineligible for relief under the Act. Can any rational human being make a cogent argument that this makes any sense at all?

But let's not stop there. If the Debtors' case is dismissed and they re-file a new case within the next year, it may be that some creditor will take the position that the new case should be presumed to be filed not in good faith. *See* Sec. 362, which further states that if it applies, then stay in that second case will be good for thirty days unless the debtor (i) files a motion, (ii) obtains a hearing and ruling by the Court within such thirty-day period and (iii) proves by clear and convincing evidence that the second case was filed in good faith. It should be obvious to the reader at this point how truly concerned Congress is for the individual consumers of this country. Apparently, it is not the individual consumers of this country that make the donations to the members of Congress that allow them to be elected and re-elected and re-elected and re-elected.

The Court's hands are tied. The statute is clear and unambiguous. The Debtors violated the provision of the statute outlined above and are ineligible to be Debtors in this case. It must, therefore, be dismissed. Congress must surely be pleased.

The Petition

When an individual voluntarily files a Chapter 13 petition or a court converts a Chapter 7 proceeding to Chapter13, a trustee will be appointed to make payments under the plan.

Filing of the plan activates an automatic stay that applies to consumer debt, but not the debtor's business debt.

The Repayment Plan

The debtor will be file a repayment plan. It may provide for payment of all obligations, or a lesser percentage. Before BAPCPA, payment plans could not exceed three years without court approval. Today, plans will typically run for five years.

The plan must provide for turning over to the trustee the debtor's future earnings or income as needed to execute the plan. Priority claims must be respected, and all claims within a particular class must be treated equally.

The bankruptcy court will hold a confirmation hearing at which interested parties may lodge objections to the plan. Regarding claims of secured creditors, courts will confirm the plan if (a) the secured creditors have accepted it, (b) it provides that they retain their liens and receive property not less than the secured portion of their claims, or (c) the debtor surrenders the secured property to the creditors.

Unsecured creditors are not entitled to vote regarding the plan, but may object to it. The court can approve the plan over their objection if (a) the value of the property to be distributed is at least equal to the amount of the claims, or (b) when all the debtor's projected "disposable income" (all income minus amounts needed to support debtor and dependents and/or needed to meet ordinary expenses to continue operation of a business) will be paid to creditors.

A plan will not be confirmed if the debtor is not current in payments on any post-petition domestic support obligation.

The provisions on redemption and reaffirmations under Section 7, discussed earlier, generally apply under Chapter 13 as well.

Discharge

In order to induce individual debtors to choose Chapter 13 rather than Chapter 7 so that creditors will likely gain a greater recovery, somewhat more liberal discharge has been accorded debtors under Chapter 13. However, the so-called "superdischarge" provision of Chapter 13 was pared down somewhat by BAPCPA. Chapter 13 had allowed discharge of virtually all debts except those arising from (a) alimony or child support obligations, (b) student loans, (c) judgments caused by driving while intoxicated, and (d) restitution orders or fines resulting from conviction of a crime.

BAPCPA restricts the Chapter 13 discharge to more closely resemble that of Chapter 7 by adding that obligations also cannot be discharged if they arise from: (a) unfiled, late-filed, and fraudulent tax returns, (b) fraud, including credit card misuse, (c) failure to notify creditors of the bankruptcy filing in order for them to file a timely claim, (d) embezzlement and breach of fiduciary duty, (e) willful or malicious injury to another or another's property.

No discharge will be granted if the debtor does not certify that he or she is current on all domestic support obligations. As you may have noticed, several

Legal Focus

International

In the age of large, multinational corporations owning assets and owing obligations in several countries, bankruptcy law has become an exceedingly complex matter. Most nations have traditionally operated under the "grab" rule. That is, creditors in Country X will be allowed by its courts to grab the debtor's assets in County X. Outside creditors will be relegated to whatever crumbs, if any, are left when Country X's creditors are satisfied. Country Y's creditors will grab the debtor's assets located in Country Y, and so on. When Robert Maxwell' worldwide business empire collapsed in 1991 and the Bank of Credit and Commerce International (BCCI) went under a year later, it became exceedingly clear that some order needed to be brought to the field of international bankruptcy.

The United Nations Commission on International Trade Law (UNCITRAL) developed a model law by 1997. Its primary purpose is to reduce uncertainty and costs by establishing at the outset which country will have the responsibility to handle the bankruptcy proceedings involving a multinational enterprise. The United States adopted this new provision in October of 2005 as Chapter 15 of the U.S. Bankruptcy Code. On April 1, 2006, the UK adopted the provision as well. So, if a company with headquarters in the U.S. goes bankrupt, the U.S. liquidator will be able to go to the UK where the bankrupt firm has assets, and induce UK courts to freeze assets, sell assets, or otherwise assist in winding up the business. Before the new provision, the courts might have cooperated, but they might not have. Now they will.

A leading bankruptcy expert from the University of Texas has described the essence of the new approach:

> "In general, universalism would treat a multinational bankruptcy ideally as a unified global proceeding administered by a single court assisted by courts in other countries, while territorialism is the traditional approach by which each court in a country in which assets are found seizes them (the "grab rule") and uses them to pay local creditors. Both approaches have become considerably more sophisticated in recent years. Universalism is now characterized as modified universalism, meaning a pragmatic approach that seeks to move steadily toward the ideal of universal proceedings while accepting the reality of step-by-step progress through cooperation. Territorialism has changed also, moving toward cooperative territorialism, which seeks to ameliorate some of the most wasteful features of the grab rule by a measure of judicial cooperation." (Jay Westbrook, "Chapter 15 at Last," 79 AMERICAN BANKRUPTCY LAW JOURNAL 713(2005)).

Canada, Mexico, and Japan have also signed on. The biggest current question is whether other Western European nations such as France and Germany will agree as well. The EC has similar rules, in that they also focus on the company's home country and place courts in that nation in charge of handling the international bankruptcy proceedings. However, there are enough differences between UNCITRAL's model law and the EC's Regulation on Insolvency to create some complications.

provisions of BAPCPA are aimed at ensuring that domestic support obligations are enforced.

The following case illustrates that creditors must be vigilant in protecting their rights in Chapter 13 proceedings.

IN RE DOREEN ANDERSEN
Tenth Circuit Court of Appeals, 179 F.3d 1253 (1999)

Andersen filed for bankruptcy under Chapter 13 while owing various student loan obligations, including four promissory notes she had signed held by Higher Education Assistance Foundation (HEAF). HEAF filed proofs of claim for the balance due on the notes.

Andersen then filed a plan providing for payment of only 10% of these notes with the rest being discharged on grounds that to do otherwise would impose an undue hardship on her and her dependents. HEAF filed an untimely objection to the plan which was denied for that reason. The plan was later confirmed and HEAF did not appeal the order of confirmation. Educational Credit Management Corporation (ECMC) acquired HEAF's loan portfolio. Andersen completed all payments under the confirmed plan and was granted a discharge.

ECMC reviewed Andersen's account during the course of processing the discharge and determined that two of the promissory notes had not reached default status before Andersen filed for bankruptcy. ECMC initiated repurchase proceedings and then collection

proceedings. Andersen reopened her bankruptcy case for the purpose of filing a complaint to determine the discharge-ability of the debt which ECMC was attempting to collect.

The bankruptcy judge held that the language of the discharge did not constitute a binding conclusion that Andersen would suffer a hardship if the debts were not discharged. Andersen appealed to the Bankruptcy Appeals Panel (BAP), which reversed, holding that confirmation of the plan did constitute a finding of undue hardship, rendering the student loans dischargeable. ECMC appealed.

Cook, District Judge (sitting by designation)

The Bankruptcy Code generally provides that a discharge does not discharge a debtor from a debt arising from an educational loan unless excepting such debt from discharge will impose an undue hardship on the debtor and the debtor's dependents. . . .We note at the outset that ECMC is correct in stating that the "debtor bears the burden of demonstrating undue hardship" with respect to the dischargeability of educational loans. And, we may assume that the Bankruptcy Court correctly held that a debtor must normally prove undue hardship by bringing an adversary proceeding directed to that issue. However, these statements do not resolve the present issue before us. The real issue here is not whether Andersen properly met her burden of proving an undue hardship, which she clearly did not, but whether confirmation of the plan constitutes a binding adjudication of hardship.

In the present case, Andersen placed language in her proposed plan that, if confirmed, would clearly have a negative impact on [HEAF's claims]. The plan provided that these claims shall be paid ten percent, and the balance of each claim shall be discharged. Recognizing the requirement that such claims may only be discharged upon a finding of undue hardship, Andersen further provided in her plan that excepting such loans from discharge will impose an undue hardship, that confirmation of the plan shall constitute a finding to that effect, and that the debt is dischargeable

Despite the inclusion of this adverse provision in the proposed plan, HEAF failed to file a proper objection. The objection that was ultimately filed by HEAF was denied as untimely. Indeed, these claims were only pursued by the successor guaranty agency ECMC after the plan was confirmed, all payments under the plan had been made, and an order of discharge had been entered.

Clearly, then, HEAF failed to take an active role in protecting its claims. While a debtor unquestionably has the burden or proving undue hardship in order to obtain a discharge of her student loan, a student loan creditor, like every other creditor, has a duty to ensure that its interests are adequately protected. A creditor cannot simply sit on its rights and expect that the bankruptcy court or trustee will assume the duty of protecting its interests. We do not believe that ECMC can now excuse

HEAF's failure to protect its interests by arguing that Andersen failed to prove undue hardship in an adversary proceeding. This argument should have been raised in a timely filed objection to the plan prior to confirmation, or argued subsequently in a timely filed appeal attacking the confirmed plan. Neither was done here.

Aside from HEAF's failure to protect itself during the bankruptcy proceedings, the strong policy of finality also justifies the result reached by the BAP. We may assume that student loan debts are presumptively nondischargeable and that the debtor is under an obligation to prove undue hardship by bringing an adversary proceeding. While Andersen did not properly prove undue hardship pursuant to the requirements of the Code, we agree with the Third Circuit that, "after the plan is confirmed the policy favoring the finality of confirmation is stronger than the bankruptcy court's and the trustee's obligations to verify a plan's compliance with the Code." *In re Szostek*, 886 F.2d 1405 (8th Cir. 1989).

There must be finality to a confirmation order so that all parties may rely upon it without concern that actions which they may thereafter take could be upset because of a later change or revocation of the order." 5 Collier on Bankruptcy ¶1327.01[1] (15th ed. 1996).

By the time ECMC began its collection efforts on the student loan obligation after Andersen emerged from bankruptcy, she certainly possessed a reasonable expectation that her student loans had been discharged as provided for in the plan; HEAF had previously failed to properly challenge the plan at any time, either by objection or appeal, Andersen had completed her payments under the plan, and she ultimately received an order of discharge. To permit ECMC to prevail at this late stage, subsequent to the order of discharge and several years after the plan was confirmed, would not only diminish the reliability and finality of the confirmed plan, but would surely disrupt Andersen's reasonable and settled expectations regarding her future financial planning.

We understand that Congress has sought to progressively limit the instances in which student loan debts may be discharged in bankruptcy, and this intent is most recently seen in the 1998 amendments which eliminated the "seven- year rule" of dischargeability of educational loans. Higher Education Amendments of 1998, Pub. L. No. 105-244, § 971, 112 Stat. 1581, 1837(1998). Recognizing Congress' clear desire to restrict dischargeability in this area, we emphasize that our holding does not in any manner lessen a debtor's burden of proof on the issue of undue hardship when seeking to discharge an educational loan, nor do we suggest that this is an easy burden to overcome. Rather, under the particular facts of this case, we merely conclude that the strong policy favoring finality, coupled with the creditor's complete failure to properly protect its interests during the course of the bankruptcy proceedings, permit us to affirm the BAP's decision. AFFIRMED.

Of a Family Farmer with Regular Income

In 1986 in response to the farm economy crisis, Congress enacted Chapter 12, entitled "Adjustment of Debts of a Family Farmer with Regular Annual Income" to provide relief to family farmers who wished to retain and reorganize their farming operations. Most farmers are not eligible for such relief under Chapter 13 because their debts exceed statutory limits. Others are ineligible because they operate as a corporation or partnership.

Chapter 11 reorganizations were considered by Congress to be excessively expensive, time-consuming, complicated, and unlikely to result in a confirmed plan for the family farmer. Chapter 12 expired briefly in 2004, but was permanently reenacted by BAPCPA in 2005.

Chapter 12 was generally modeled after Chapter 13 so that the procedures are basically the same as the Chapter 1313 procedures outlined above. The most striking distinctions found in Chapter 12 are set forth below.

1. The eligibility requirements of Chapter 12 are specifically aimed at the family farmer and exclude large agricultural operators. The debtor must be a family farmer defined as an individual engaged in farming whose aggregate debts do not exceed $3,237,000 and not less than 50 percent of whose debts (excluding debt on the principal residence) arise out of farming operations owned and operated by them and who received more than 50 percent of their gross income during the preceding taxable year from such farming operation. Only those partnerships and corporations are included in which more than 50 percent of the outstanding stock or equity is held by one family and its relatives who conduct the farming operation and more than 50 percent of the value of whose assets relate to the farming operation. In addition, the family farmer must have "regular income" defined as income sufficiently regular to enable the debtor to make payments under the Chapter 12 plan.
2. The family farmer's plan need not be filed for 90 days. Moreover, while a Chapter 13 debtor must commence payments to the trustee within 30 days of filing his or her

plan, Chapter 12 has no provision requiring immediate payments so that a plan may be confirmed even though no payments are provided until the next harvest.

3. Congress has expressly provided that the adequate protection provision which applies in all other bankruptcy cases does not apply in Chapter 12 and has redefined the term more favorably for farmers. In Chapter 12 the customary, reasonable rental value of farmland constitutes adequate protection. Such rental payments should be significantly lower than adequate protection payments in a Chapter 11 case, where costs for lost opportunity to repossess may be included.

4. A Chapter 12 plan may provide for modification of the mortgage on a debtor's principal residence, which is prohibited in Chapter 13. It may also provide for the sale of farmland by parcels or farm equipment by items free and clear of blanket liens as long as the creditor's lien attaches to the proceeds. These modifications of creditors' liens, which would be objectionable in a Chapter 11 or 13 plan, are intended by Congress to permit the family farmer to scale down his operations by selling unnecessary property.

5. In 2005, Congress amended the Bankruptcy Code to allow family fishermen, as well as family farmers, to take advantage of Chapter 12s provisions. The rules governing family fishermen are quite similar to, but not identical to, those governing family farmers.

PART **IV**

AGENCY AND PARTNERSHIPS

CHAPTER **23**

AGENCY NATURE, CREATION, DUTIES, AND TERMINATION

- Nature of the Agency Relationship
- Creation of the Agency Relationship
- Duties of Principal and Agent
- Termination of the Agency Relationship

Nature of the Agency Relationship

In a legal context the term agency ordinarily describes a relationship in which two parties—the principal and the agent—agree that one will act as a representative of the other. The **principal** is the person who wishes to accomplish something, and the **agent** is the one employed to act in the principal's behalf to achieve it.

At one time or another, almost everyone has come into contact with the agency relationship. Anyone who has purchased merchandise at a retail store almost certainly has dealt with an agent—the salesclerk. Similarly, anyone who has ever held a job probably has served in some type of representative capacity for the employer.

The usefulness of the agency relationship in the business world is obvious. With few exceptions, no single individual is capable of performing every act required to run a business enterprise. Furthermore, many businesses are organized as corporations, which by definition can act only by employing agents. As a result, most business transactions throughout the world are handled by agents.

The term *agency* is often used loosely to describe many different types of relationships in which one party acts in a representative capacity for another. *Principal* and *agent* are also sometimes used loosely to denote the parties to various types of arrangements. However, throughout our discussion these terms are used narrowly to describe a particular type of relationship. The **principal-agent relationship,** as we use it, means a relationship in which the parties have agreed that the agent is to represent the principal in negotiating and transacting business; that is, the agent is employed to make contracts or enter similar business transactions on behalf of the principal. The term will ordinarily be used in discussions of contractual liability.

Two similar relationships are the **employer-employee relationship** (which is still sometimes referred to by the older term *master-servant relationship),* and the **employer independent contractor relationship.** The distinction between an employee and an independent contractor is important to many different kinds of legal questions. For example, state workers' compensation laws, federal antidiscrimination statutes, and many other laws regulating employment are applicable only to employees and not to independent contractors. Similarly, federal tax laws requiring the employer to withhold income and social security taxes and to contribute to the worker's social security account are applicable only to employees and not to independent contractors. In the law of agency, the distinction is important when a third party tries to hold the employer legally responsible for a tort committed by the employee. As we will see toward the end of the next chapter, an employer often can be held liable for the job-related torts of its employees, but usually cannot be held liable for such torts committed by those working for it as independent contractors.

It also is important to note that the same worker can be both an agent and an employee or both an agent and an independent contractor. Which relationship is relevant depends on the nature of the legal issues in the dispute. When the legal question involves either (1) the rights and duties between the superior and subordinate or (2) the superior's liability to third parties for contracts or other transactions executed by the subordinate, the relevant question usually is whether the subordinate was an agent who acted with authority. On the other hand, if the legal question involves the superior's liability for a tort committed by the subordinate, the relevant question usually is whether the subordinate was an employee who acted within the scope of his or her employment.

Sometimes, however, it is appropriate to use the term agent and to discuss the agent's authority when the legal issue is the superior's tort liability. This happens mainly in two situations. First, it is appropriate to use agent and authority concepts when the superior has directly authorized the agent to engage in the wrongful conduct. In such a case, the superior is liable to the third party for the subordinate's tort regardless of whether the latter is an employee or an independent contractor. Second, courts sometimes use agent and authority concepts when the subordinate's tort was *nonphysical* in nature, such as fraud, defamation, and so on.

Most of our discussion in these two chapters involves the principal-agent relationship; the employer-employee and employer-independent contractor relationships are dealt with in the latter part of the next chapter.

Creation of the Agency Relationship
Necessary Elements

The agency relationship is consensual—that is, based on the agreement of the parties. Many times it is created by a legally enforceable employment contract between the principal and the agent. A legally binding contract is not essential, however. An agency relationship that gives the agent authority to represent the principal and bind him or her by the agent's actions can generally be established by any words or actions that indicate the parties' consent to the arrangement. Consideration is not required.

In fact, no formalities are required for the creation of an agency relationship in most circumstances. For example, it is not usually necessary to spell out the agent's authority in writing; oral authority is ordinarily sufficient. Exceptions do exist, however. The most common one occurs when an agent is granted authority to sell real estate. In a majority of states an agent can make a contract for the sale of real estate that will bind the principal only if the agent's authority is stated in writing.

Even though formalities are usually not required for the creation of an agency, it is certainly wise to express the extent of an agent's authority and any other relevant matters in writing. This precaution often prevents misunderstandings between the principal and agent or between the agent and third parties with whom he or she is dealing. The formal written authorization given by a principal to an agent is frequently referred to as a **power of attorney.** When a formal power of attorney is used, the agent is sometimes referred to as an **attorney-in-fact.** This is simply another term for an agent, and should not be confused with attorney-at-law (a lawyer). Courts generally scrutinize powers of attorney very carefully and interpret their language strictly.

In the following case, an agent learned the hard way about the rule that powers of attorney are interpreted very strictly, and found that good intentions are no substitute for authority.

KING V. BANKERD
Court of Appeals of Maryland, 492 A.2d 608 (1985)

Howard R. Bankerd (Bankerd) and his wife Virginia owned, as "tenants by the entirety, " a home in Montgomery County, Maryland. "tenancy by the entirety" is one type of joint ownership created by the marriage relationship in some states. They lived there until 1966 when Mrs. Bankerd moved out as a result of marital problems. Bankerd continued to live at the property until July, 1968, when he "left for the west. " Mrs. Bankerd then resumed living on the property. For the next twelve years, Bankerd lived at various locations in Nevada, Colorado, and Washington, and made no payments on the mortgage, for taxes, or for the maintenance of the home.

Before Bankerd's departure, he executed a power of attorney to King, an attorney with whom he was acquainted. From 1971 to 1974, Bankerd did not communicate with King in any way. In 1975, however, King sent Bankerd a letter enclosing an updated power of attorney because the Suburban Sanitary Commission was about to put a sewer adjacent to the property, and King believed the new power would be needed. This power of attorney, dated October 30, 1975, was executed by Bankerd and returned to King. It stated:

KNOW ALL MEN BY THESE PRESENTS, that I, Howard R. Bankerd, hereby make, constitute and appoint ARTHUR V. KING,, my attorney for me, and in my name to convey, grant, bargain and/or sell the property designated in the Montgomery County land record as Lot 9 of an unrecorded subdivision as recorded in Liber 3027 at folio 293, situated at 14026 Travilah Road, Rockville, Maryland on such terms as to him may seem best, and in my name, to make, execute, acknowledge and deliver, good and suffcient deeds and conveyances for the same with or

without covenants and warranties and generally to do and perform all things necessary pertaining to the future transfer of said property, and generally to do everything whatsoever necessary pertaining to the said property.

After granting this power of attorney, Bankerd had no further communication with King until 1978.

Mrs. Bankerd, who had been living at and maintaining the property since 1968, requested King in September 1977 to exercise the power of attorney and to transfer Bankerd's interest in the property to her. King was aware that Mrs. Bankerd was nearing retirement and that she was "saddled" with a property she could neither sell nor mortgage because of her husband's legal interest in it. Consequently, King made several attempts to find and communicate with Bankerd, but was unsuccessful.

Mrs. Bankerd informed King that her husband had once attempted to give the property away to a neighbor on the condition that the neighbor assume the mortgage payments. As a result, King asserted that he believed Bankerd "didn't give a damn" about the property, and that given Bankerd's age (approximately sixty-nine years), King believed that Bankerd might even be deceased. King therefore conveyed Bankerd's interest in the property to Mrs. Bankerd by deed in 1978. Mrs. Bankerd paid no consideration for the transfer and King received no compensation for executing the deed. Mrs. Bankerd then sold the property to a third party for $62,500.

In 1981 Bankerd filed suit against King alleging that King had acted negligently and had exceeded his authority as Bankerd's agent. The trial court granted summary judgment to Bankerd against King and awarded

$13,555.05 in damages. The intermediate appellate court affirmed, and King appealed to Maryland's highest court.

Cole, Judge:

The single issue presented in this case is whether a power of attorney authorizing the agent to "convey, grant, bargain and/or sell" the principal's property authorizes the agent to make a gratuitous transfer [i.e., a gift] of that property. . . .

Broadly defined, a power of attorney is a written document by which one party, as principal, appoints another as agent (attorney-in-fact) and confers upon the latter the authority to perform certain specified acts or kinds of acts on behalf of the principal. . . . Various rules govern the interpretation of powers of attorney. . . . One well-settled rule is that powers of attorney are strictly construed . . . and are held to grant only those powers which are clearly delineated. . . .

Another accepted rule of construction is to discount or disregard all embracing expressions found in powers of attorney. Because powers of attorney are ordinarily very carefully drafted and scrutinized, courts give the terms used a technical rather than a popular meaning. In addition, ambiguities in an instrument are resolved against the party who made it or caused it to be made, because that party had the better opportunity to understand and explain his meaning. Finally, general words used in an instrument are restricted by the context in which they are used, and are construed accordingly. . . .

For the reasons below, we conclude that an agent holding a broad power of attorney lacks the power to make a gift of the principal's property, unless that power (1) is expressly conferred, (2) arises as a necessary implication from the conferred powers, or (3) is clearly intended by the parties, as evidenced by the surrounding facts and circumstances.

First, the power to make a gift of the principal's property is a power that is potentially hazardous to the principal's interests. Consequently, this power will not be lightly inferred from broad, all-encompassing grants of power to the agent. Accordingly, "the agent must be circumspect with regard to the powers created—or the lack of them."

Second, the main duty of an agent is loyalty to the interest of his principal. Thus, in exercising granted powers under a power of attorney, the attorney in fact is bound to act for the benefit of his principal and must avoid where possible that which is detrimental unless expressly authorized. It is difficult to imagine how a gift of the principal's real property would be to the benefit of the principal when the power of attorney does not authorize such a gift or the principal does not intend to authorize such a gift. In short, the agent is under a duty to serve his principal with only his principal's purposes in mind. Third, it would be most unusual for an owner of property to grant a power of attorney authorizing the attorney in fact to give his property away. If a person has decided to make a gift of property, he or she usually decides as to who is going to be the donee. . . .

The facts and surrounding circumstances presented in this case do not give rise to any fact or inference that King was authorized to make a gift of Bankerd's real property. In arguing that his conduct was reasonable under the circumstances, King points to his "beliefs" that Bankerd had abandoned the property, that Bankerd did not care about the property, and that Bankerd might be deceased. These arguments completely miss the mark. King's conduct could only be "reasonable" if Bankerd intended for King to give the property away. Although the facts and surrounding circumstances to which King points suggest reasons why he made the gift, they do not support an inference that Bankerd intended to authorize the gift.

Furthermore, the only evidence before the trial court that was relevant to this issue indicated that Bankerd did not intend to authorize

King to give the subject property to Bankerd's wife or anyone else. In a letter Bankerd sent to King along with the executed power of attorney, Bankerd wrote that "[y]ou know if I outlive Va., (and I'm ornery enough) you would certainly have a job on that Travilah Road bit if you would accept it, that is." Nothing could more clearly belie an assertion that Bankerd authorized any gift of the property. Bankerd, by virtue of this correspondence, notified King that he clearly anticipated maintaining his interest in the property. Furthermore, King wrote Bankerd assuring him that if the latter executed the new power of attorney he would do nothing detrimental to Bankerd's interests. Certainly, had King believed that he was acquiring the authority to give away Bankerd's property, King would not have made this representation. In sum, there is no genuine dispute as to any material fact. The trial court did not err in granting Bankerd's motion for summary judgment.

Judgment affirmed. [Note: Instead of suing his agent for damages, Bankerd could have sued to set aside the transfer of his interest to his wife, which, in turn, would have invalidated the transfer by her to the third party.]

Capacity

If an agent, acting on behalf of a principal, makes a properly authorized contract with a third party, the contract is viewed legally as being one between the principal and the third party; that is, it is the principals contract, not the agent's. For this reason the principal's capacity to make contracts may be important in determining the validity of the contract in question. The minority, insanity, or other incapacity of the principal has the same effect on contracts made through an agent as it does on contracts made personally.

On the other hand, the agent's capacity is usually immaterial. The reason is the same—the contract made by the agent for the principal is the principal's contract. A minor, for example, can serve as an agent; his or her lack of contractual capacity ordinarily has no effect on a contract made in behalf of the principal. (Of course, the agent's lack of contractual capacity has an effect on his or her own contract of employment with the principal, and can also be important if for any reason the third party attempts to hold the agent personally responsible on a contract made with that party.)

Duties of Principal and Agent

The principal-agent relationship is a **fiduciaryrelationship**—one of trust. Each party owes the other a duty to act with the utmost good faith. Each should be entirely open with the other, not keeping any information from the other that has any bearing on their arrangement. Other duties, some of which are merely specific applications of the general fiduciary obligation, are discussed below and outlined in Fig. 23.1.

The primary duty owed by the principal to the agent is simply that of complying with the terms of their employment contract, if one exists. Failure of the principal to do so will render him or her liable to the agent for damages; if the breach is material, it will justify the agent in refusing to act for the principal any further. For example: P and A

LEGAL FOCUS

International

As we have seen, the general rule under state law in the United States is that powers of attorney are interpreted very strictly. The United States is not the only place where this attitude is taken toward powers of attorney. In the French case, Societe Generale v. Erulin [1991] ECC 132, , Madeline Wrulin opened a bank account in her name with Societe Generale. Shortly thereafter, she executed a general power of attorney to her sister-in-law, Francoise Erulin, giving the latter the authority to operate the account as if she were the owner. About three weeks later, Francoise applied to the bank for a "credit card" on the account, signing the application as the owner. Francoise executed a guarantee to the bank for up to 100,000 French Francs (FF). The card operated as a debit card for withdrawing money so long as the account had a positive balance. If the balance became negative, the card served as a credit card that permitted overdrafts.

When the card was issued to Francoise, the account had a significant positive balance. During the next three months, however, Francoise used the card for purchases and withdrawals in huge amounts, resulting in a negative balance of 107,000 FF. During these three months, bank statements were sent to Madeline; she did not examine these statements but forwarded them directly to Francoise. When the negative balance passed 100,000 FF, the bank notified Francoise, not Madeline. The overdraft of 107,000 FF plus interest was not paid, and the bank sued both Madeline and Francoise. Both of the defendants filed counterclaims against the bank.

Ultimately, the Court of Appeals held that the bank acted wrongfully by issuing the credit card to Francoise without notifying Madeline. Although the court spoke in terms of the bank's negligence, its holding clearly was also based on a restrictive view of powers of attorney. The general power of attorney did not specifically give Francoise authority to obtain "extra facilities" such as the credit card; as a consequence, she had no such authority. Although the court admitted that Madeline was somewhat negligent by simply forwarding the bank statements to Francoise without examining them, the court placed the burden of the loss on the bank and Francoise. The bank was held responsible for two-thirds of the loss, and Francoise the other one-third.

have agreed that A is to be paid a specified percentage of the sales she makes for P. If P refuses or fails to pay A, A can rightfully terminate their arrangement and hold P responsible for damages.

In addition, the principal is under a duty to reimburse the agent for any expenditures reasonably incurred by the agent in furthering the interests of the principal. For example, if P directs A to travel from Chicago to Los Angeles to transact business for P, but does not provide her with any funds for travel expenses, P will be under a duty when A returns to reimburse her for amounts she reasonably expended in making the trip, such as her round-trip air fare.

Similarly, the principal has an obligation to indemnify the agent for liabilities or losses the latter suffers while acting lawfully and within the scope of his or her authority.

Duties Owed By Agent to Principal

Obedience

It is the duty of the agent to obey the clear instructions of the principal, so long as such instructions are legal. If the instructions are ambiguous, the agent cannot disregard them altogether, but he or she can fulfill the duty by acting in good faith and interpreting them in a manner that is reasonable under the circumstances.

Where the instructions are both legal and clear, the agent is justified in departing from them on only rare occasions. One such occasion is when an *emergency* occurs and following the principal's original instructions is not in that person's best interests. The agent should, of course, consult with the principal and obtain new instructions if

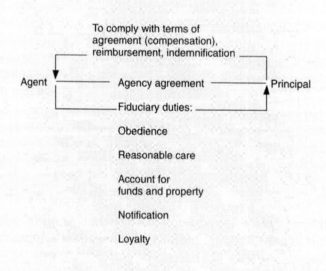

Figure 23.1   Duties of Agents and Principals to Each Other

possible. But if there is no opportunity to consult, the agent is justified in taking reasonable steps to protect the principal, even if it means deviating from prior instructions. Indeed, the agent may even be under a duty to depart from instructions if following them in the emergency can be considered so unreasonable as to be negligent. (The agent's authority to act in emergencies is discussed more fully in the next chapter.)

Reasonable Care

Unless special provisions in the agreement say otherwise, an agent is normally expected to exercise the degree of care and skill that is reasonable under the circumstances. In other words, the agent has a duty not to be negligent. For example, suppose that B has funds which he wishes to lend to borrowers at current interest rates. He employs C to act in his behalf in locating the borrowers. C lends B's money to T without investigating T's credit rating and without obtaining from T any security for the loan. T turns out to be a notoriously bad credit risk and is actually insolvent at the time of the loan. If B is later unable to collect from T, C will probably be liable to B, because he failed to exercise reasonable care in making the loan.

Under some circumstances, an agent may be under a special duty to exercise more than an ordinary degree of care and skill. For example, if a person undertakes to serve in a capacity that necessarily involves the possession and exercise of a special skill such as that of a lawyer or stockbroker, he or she is required to exercise the skill ordinarily possessed by competent persons pursuing that particular calling.

In any agency relationship, the principal and agent can by agreement change the agent's duty of care and skill, making it either stricter or more lenient.

Duty to Account

Unless principal and agent agree otherwise, it is the agent's duty to keep and make available to the principal an account of all the money or property received or paid out in behalf of the principal. In this regard, an agent should never mix his or her own money or property with that of the principal. The agent should, for example, set up a separate bank account for the principal's money. If the agent commingles (mixes) his or her own money or property with the principal's in such a way that it cannot be separated or identified, the principal can legally claim all of it.

Duty to Notify

Another important duty of the agent is to notify the principal of all relevant facts—just about any information having a bearing on the interests of the principal—as soon as reasonably possible after learning of them. For example, if A (the agent) discovers that one of P's (the principal's) creditors is about to foreclose a lien on P's property, A should promptly notify P. Or, if A learns that one of P's important customers, who owes P a substantial amount of money, has just filed for bankruptcy, A should contact P as soon as possible.

Loyalty

Perhaps the most important duty owed by the agent to the principal is that of loyalty. Violation of this duty can occur in numerous ways. A few of the more significant actions constituting a breach of the duty are discussed below.

Quite obviously, the agent should not *compete* with the principal in the type of business he or she is conducting for the principal, unless the principal expressly gives consent. To illustrate: X, who owns a textile manufacturing business, employs Y to act as his sales agent. Y will be violating his duty of loyalty if, without X's consent, he acquires a personal interest in a textile manufacturing business that competes with X's.

The law presumes that a principal hires an agent to serve the principal's interests and not the personal interests of the agent. Thus the agent should avoid any existing or potential conflict of interest. For example, if B is hired to sell goods for R, he should not sell to himself. Or if he is hired to buy goods for R, he should not buy them from himself. It is difficult, if not impossible, for the agent to completely serve the principal's interests when his or her own personal interests become involved. Of course, such things can be done if the principal is fully informed and gives consent.

In a similar fashion, the agent should not further the interests of any third party in his or her dealings for the principal. The agent also should not work for two parties on opposite sides in a transaction unless both parties agree to it.

If the agent, in working for the principal, acquires knowledge of any *confidential information,* he or she should not disclose this information to outsiders without the principal's consent. To illustrate: G hires H, a lawyer, to represent G in defending a lawsuit filed against G by T. T alleges that his factory was damaged in a fire caused by certain chemicals, purchased by T from G, that were highly flammable and not labeled with an adequate warning. In order to properly defend G, H must learn the secret formulas and processes for producing the chemicals. After learning them, he should not disclose them to anyone without G's consent, either at that time or at any time in the future.

The following case illustrates the strictness of the duty of loyalty owed by an agent to the principal.

GLADES PHARMACEUTICALS, LLC v. MURPHY
U.S. District Court, Northern District of Georgia, 2005 U.S. Dist. LEXIS 36198 (2005)

Plaintiff, Glades Pharmaceuticals, LLC develops, markets, and distributes generic versions of dermatological products. Glades is a wholly-owned subsidiary of Stiefel Laboratories, Inc., a privately held corporation. Stiefel maintains direct control over all aspects of Glades's business operations. Defendant Murphy, a Georgia resident, served as the President of Glades from 1991 until 2002. He served as Glades's Vice President of Business Development and Outsourcing from January 2003 until approximately May 2, 2003. Murphy also served as Stiefel's Vice President of Sales from June 2001 until approximately October 23, 2002.

As a senior executive officer and employee, Murphy was responsible for exploring, developing, and pursuing business opportunities for Glades, including securing the right to market and distribute non-branded dermatological products. In early 2003, while still employed as Vice President for Glades, Murphy allegedly entered into discussions with Janssen Pharmaceuticals, Inc. regarding the distribution of a generic version of a Nizoral shampoo currently being sold by Janssen. Murphy allegedly pursued the opportunity himself while actively concealing the opportunity and his activities from Glades. Glades further alleges that Murphy, while still employed by Glades, discussed joining forces with Bi-Coastal Pharmaceutical Corporation ("Bi-Coastal") and Pharm Force to market and distribute the generic Nizoral shampoo. In 2003, Murphy founded River's Edge Pharmaceuticals, LLC ("River's Edge") to develop and market generic dermatological products. In addition to the Nizoral shampoo, the Plaintiff alleges that Murphy also diverted opportunities to market and distribute other products.

Glades maintains that, in order to pursue the generic Nizoral shampoo and other opportunities, Murphy misappropriated a PowerPoint presentation and converted other confidential product information belonging to Glades. Glades sued Murphy and Rivers Edge, asserting, among other claims, that Murphy breached his fiduciary duty to Glades. Defendants moved for summary judgment.

Thrash, District Judge:

Glades has alleged that Murphy, as an officer and employee, abused his position of trust and authority by usurping business opportunities from his employer and misappropriating its property for his own personal financial gain. Murphy argues that he did not owe a duty of loyalty as an employee of the Plaintiff. However, Georgia law has continually implied "a duty of loyalty, faithful service and regard for an employer's interest." Wilson v. Wilson, 596 S.E.2d 392 (Ga. 2004). In Lane Co. v. Taylor, 330 S.E.2d 112 (Ga. 1985), an apartment management company sued a former employee who had left the plaintiff and taken three of the plaintiffs clients with her to a new company. Among its claims, the plaintiff alleged that the defendant had breached her duty of good faith and loyalty to the company. The defendant moved for summary judgment on the duty of loyalty claim, which the trial court granted. In reviewing the lower court's decision, the Georgia Court of Appeals examined the following facts: (1) the plaintiffs former customers had terminated their contracts and moved to the defendant's new company, where they were assigned to her; (2) the defendant and the officers of her new company conducted meetings prior to this happening; and (3) the defendant used the plaintiffs forms, documents and management techniques for her new employer. After examining both the master-servant and principal-agent relationships, the Court of Appeals held that "even if defendant be classified as a servant, there still remains the duty of loyalty, faithful service and regard for the employer's interests." Thus, even though "uncontroverted evidence" showed the defendant had not contacted the plaintiffs former customers in an attempt to "pirate them away from the plaintiff," the court still reversed the lower court's grant of summary judgment for the defendant.

Similarly here, the Court finds that a triable issue exists as to whether Murphy violated his duty of loyalty. The Plaintiff has presented evidence that Murphy pursued opportunities in the generic drug market for his own benefit while employed by the Plaintiff and to the detriment of the Plaintiff. The Plaintiff has also offered evidence that Murphy appropriated the presentation and market and sales information contained within it. Thus, triable issues of fact remain, leaving the matter within proper purview of a jury.

An employee breaches no fiduciary duty to the employer simply by making plans to enter a competing business while he is still employed. Even before the termination of his agency, he is entitled to make arrangements to compete and upon termination of employment immediately compete. He is not, however, entitled to solicit customers for a rival business before the end of his employment nor can he properly do other similar acts in direct competition with the employer's business.

The motion for summary judgment is denied.

Termination of the Agency Relationship

Like most private consensual arrangements, the agency relationship usually comes to an end at some point. Termination can occur because of something done by the parties themselves or by operation of law (something beyond their control). Our discussion focuses on the termination of the relationship between the principal and the agent, ignoring for the moment the effects of termination on third parties who might deal with the agent. (The circumstances under which third parties should be notified of the termination and the type of notice required are dealt with in the next chapter.)

Termination by Act of the Parties

Fulfillment of Purpose

Many times an agent is employed to accomplish a particular object, such as the sale of a tract of land belonging to the principal. When this object is accomplished and nothing else remains to be done, the agency relationship terminates.

Lapse of Time

If principal and agent have agreed originally that the arrangement will end at a certain time, the arrival of that time terminates their relationship. If nothing has been said as to the duration of the agency, and if nothing occurs to terminate it, the relationship is deemed to last for a period of time that is reasonable under the circumstances. This generally is a question of whether, after passage of a particular period of time, it is reasonable for the agent to believe that the principal still intends for him or her to act as earlier directed. Of course, if the principal knows that the agent is continuing to make efforts to perform, and if the principal does nothing about the situation, the agency relationship may remain alive for a period of time longer than would otherwise be held reasonable.

Occurrence of Specified Event

In a similar fashion, if the principal and agent have originally agreed that the agency, or some particular aspect of it, will continue until a specified event occurs, the occurrence of the event results in termination. For example: P authorizes A to attempt to sell P's farm, Blackacre, for him "only until P returns from New York." When P returns, A's authority to sell Blackacre as P's agent comes to an end. An analogous situation occurs when principal and agent have agreed that the agency, or some aspect of it, will remain in existence only during the continuance of a stated condition. If the condition ceases to exist, the agent's authority terminates. For instance: X directs Y, X's credit manager, to extend $10,000 in credit to T, so long as T's inventory of goods on hand and his accounts receivable amount to $50,000 and his accounts payable do not exceed $25,000. If T's combined inventory and accounts receivable drop below $50,000, the agency terminates insofar as it relates to Y's authority to grant credit to T.

Mutual Agreement

Regardless of what the principal and agent have agreed to originally, they can agree at any time to end their relationship. It makes no difference whether the relationship has been based on a binding employment contract or whether no enforceable employment contract exists; their mutual agreement terminates the agency in either case. It is a basic rule of contract law that the parties can rescind (cancel) the contract by mutual agreement.

Act of One Party

Since the agency relationship is consensual, it can usually be terminated by either the principal or the agent if that person no longer wants to be a party to the arrangement. In most circumstances termination occurs simply by one party indicating to the other that he or she no longer desires to continue the relationship. This is true even if the parties had originally agreed that the agency was to be irrevocable.

If no binding employment contract exists between the two of them, the party terminating the agency normally does not incur any liability to the other by this action. If an enforceable employment contract does exist, one party may be justified in terminating it if the other has violated any of the duties owed under it. Of course, if there are no facts justifying termination, the party taking such action may be responsible to the other for any damages caused by the breach of contract. But the agency relationship is ended nevertheless.

One major exception exists to the ability of either party to terminate the relationship. If the agency is not just a simple one but instead is an agency coupled with an interest (that is, the agent has an interest in the subject matter of the agency), the principal cannot terminate the agent's authority without the agent's consent. (Note, however, that an agent is not considered to have an interest in the subject matter simply because he or she expects to make a commission or profit from the activities as agent.) To illustrate: P borrows $5,000 from A. To secure the loan, P grants A a *security interest* (a property interest for the sole purpose of securing a debt) in P's inventory. As part of the agreement, P makes A his agent for the sale of the inventory in case P defaults on the loan. Since A has an interest in the subject matter of the agency (the inventory), the arrangement is an agency coupled with an interest, and P cannot terminate A's authority to sell without A's consent (unless, of course, P repays the loan, in which case A no longer has an interest in the subject matter).

The reason for the exception is that the agent is not really acting for the principal in this situation. By exercising this authority, the agent is acting in his or her own behalf to assert a personal interest.

Termination By Operation of Law
Death or Insanity

The death or insanity of the *agent* immediately terminates an agency relationship. The death or insanity of the *principal* also terminates an agency relationship. In most cases the termination of an agency by the principal's death or insanity occurs immediately, regardless of whether the agent knows what has happened.

Bankruptcy

The insolvency or bankruptcy of the *agent* does not always terminate the agency, but will do so in those circumstances where it impairs the agent's ability to act for the principal. To illustrate: B is authorized by I, an investment house, to act as its agent in advising I's local clients about investments. If B becomes bankrupt, he will no longer be authorized to act for I. The reason is simple; the agent in this situation should realize that the principal probably would not want him to act in its behalf any longer if it knew the facts.

Suppose, however, that the *principal* becomes insolvent or bankrupt, and the agent knows about it. In this case the agent might no longer have authority to act for the principal—but only under circumstances where the agent ought to realize that the principal would no longer want such transactions to be conducted in his or her behalf. For example: P has authorized A to buy an expensive fur coat on credit for P. If P becomes bankrupt, this will probably terminate the agency when A learns of it. A should reasonably infer that under the circumstances P will no longer want him to make such a purchase. However, if A is P's housekeeper and has been authorized to buy groceries for P's household, P's bankruptcy probably will not extinguish that authority. The inference that A should reasonably draw when learning the facts is that P will want her to continue buying necessities such as food until informed otherwise. It is simply a matter of reasonableness.

Change of Law

If a change in the law makes the agency or the performance of the authorized act *illegal*, the agent's authority is ordinarily extinguished when he or she learns of the change. To illustrate: S is a salesperson for T, a toy manufacturer. If a federal agency determines that certain of T's toys are dangerous and bans them, S's authority to sell them to retailers probably will be terminated when she learns of the government ban. That is, upon learning the facts, S should reasonably assume that T will no longer want her to sell the banned items.

Even if the change in the law does not make the agency or the authorized act illegal, termination can still occur if the agent learns of the change and should reasonably expect that the principal will no longer want him or her to act in the manner previously authorized. For instance: A is authorized to purchase fabricated aluminum from a foreign supplier. The federal government imposes a new tariff on imported aluminum that results in substantially higher prices. It is likely that A's authority to buy foreign aluminum will be terminated when he learns of the change.

Loss or Destruction of Subject Matter

The loss or destruction of the subject matter of an agency relationship will terminate the agent's authority. If, for example, X employs Y to sell grain belonging to X that is being stored in a particular storage elevator, the destruction by fire of the elevator and the grain will ordinarily extinguish Y's authority.

Whether the agent's authority terminates automatically or only when he or she learns of the facts depends on the nature and terms of the original agreement between principal and agent. In the instant case, if, instead of a fire, X himself sells the grain to a buyer (which actually amounts to X revoking Y's authority), Y's authority may or may not be automatically terminated. If X has given Y *exclusive authority* to sell, that authority ends only if X notifies Y that he has sold the grain himself. On the other hand, if the authority is not exclusive and Y should realize that X may try to sell the grain himself, Y's authority will terminate when X sells the grain even if Y does not know of the sale.

If the subject matter of the agency (such as the grain) is not lost or destroyed but is merely damaged, Y's authority is terminated if the circumstances are such that Y ought to realize that X would not want the transaction to be carried out.

Miscellaneous Changes of Conditions

The various occurrences we have discussed that terminate an agency by operation of law are by no means an exclusive list. For instance, in some circumstances the outbreak of war, a sudden change in the market value of the subject matter of the agency, or an unexpected loss of some required qualification by the principal or the agent (such as a license) may terminate the agency. Again, if all the circumstances known to the agent are such that he or she, as a reasonable person, ought to realize that the principal would no longer wish him or her to continue in the endeavor, the authority is ended. The agent simply must act in a reasonable fashion until there is an opportunity to consult with the principal.

CHAPTER **24**

AGENCY LIABILITY OF THE PARTIES

- Liability of the Principal
- Liability of the Agent
- Liability of the Third Party
- Nonexistent, Partially Disclosed, and Undisclosed Principals
- Tort Liability
- Criminal Liability

WE HAVE ALREADY discussed the formation and termination of the agency relationship and the duties existing between the parties. Now we will focus our attention on the legal consequences of this relationship, primarily the *contractual liability* of those involved: principal, agent, and third parties. Near the end of the chapter we will deal with a superior's liability for the torts and crimes of his or her subordinates.

Liability of the Principal

The principal is, of course, liable to the agent if he or she breaches a valid employment contract with the agent or violates any other duty owing to the agent. However, the most important questions in this area relate to the principal's liability to the third parties with whom the agent has dealt. If A, acting on behalf of P, makes a contract with T, what is P's legal responsibility to T? If P does not perform as required in the contract, is P required by law to compensate T for T's losses resulting from P's breach?

The answers to these questions usually depend on the court's decision on another question: Was the agent acting within the scope of his or her *authority* in making this particular contract? We will now examine the approach taken by the courts in arriving at an answer.

The Agent's Authority to Act for the Principal

The fact that you have hired someone to act as your agent does not mean that the person can represent you in any way he or she sees fit. An agent ordinarily can act for the principal in such a way as to make the principal legally responsible only when he or she has **authority** to act that way. The agent's authority can be divided into two basic types: actual and apparent. **Actual authority** is the authority that the agent does, in fact, have. For convenience it can be further divided into *express authority* and *implied authority*. On the other hand, *apparent authority* is something of a contradiction in terms. It describes a concept which, because of unusual circumstances giving rise to an appearance of authority, occasionally holds the principal responsible for certain of the agent's actions that were not really authorized at all.

Express Authority

Express authority is the most obvious and the most common type of authority—that which is directly granted by the principal to the agent. To illustrate: P authorizes A to sell P's farm for at least $25,000. If A sells the farm to T for $30,000, P is bound by the transaction and must honor it. The obvious reason is that A's actions are within the scope of his express authority. Conversely, under most circumstances, P will not be required to honor the transaction if A sells the farm for $20,000.

Implied Authority

As is the case with most business transactions, the principal and agent rarely, if ever, contemplate and provide for every possible event that might occur during the existence of their relationship. The law seeks to allow for this fact through the concept of implied authority. **Implied authority** is primarily a matter of what is *customary*. In other words, where the principal has said nothing about a particular aspect of the agent's authority, whether the agent has such authority normally depends on what type of authority a person in a similar position customarily has. Of course, the principal has the final word as to what authority the agent possesses and can grant more or less authority than such an agent usually has. The concept of implied authority serves only to fill in gaps where the principal has not spoken specifically on the subject but where it is reasonable to assume that the principal would have granted such authority if he or she had thought about it.

Many examples of implied authority can be found. For instance, unless the principal has given indications to the contrary, a traveling salesperson ordinarily has authority to take orders but not to make a binding contract to sell the principal's goods. He or she often will be in possession of samples but there usually is no implied authority to sell them. If, however, the salesperson is one who possesses goods for *immediate sale* (such as a salesclerk in a retail store or a door-to-door sales agent who actually carries the principal's merchandise), he or she ordinarily has authority to sell them and collect payment. But this type of agent still does not have implied authority to grant credit or accept payment from the customer for prior credit purchases.

Such authority usually exists only if expressly given by the principal, because it is simply not customary for a salesperson to do these things.

Another common application of the concept of implied authority enables an agent to perform those acts which are merely incidental to the main purpose of the agency. (Some legal writers, in fact, use the term *incidental authority.*) Again, the key is what is customary. The rule regarding such authority is: *Unless the principal has indicated otherwise, his or her agent has implied authority to do those things which are reasonably and customarily necessary to enable that person to accomplish the overall purpose of the agency.*

To illustrate: O, the owner of a retail clothing store, hires M to act as manager of the store and gives M express authority to act in certain ways. For instance, M probably will be expressly authorized to purchase inventory and make sales. In addition, M will have implied authority to handle matters that are incidental to the main purpose of the agency. Thus, if the plumbing in the store begins to leak, M can hire a plumber, and O is bound to pay for the services. Similarly, unless instructed otherwise, M can hire an electrician to repair a short in the wiring or a janitorial service to clean the floors. He can also hire a salesclerk or other necessary assistants.

Of course, if the transaction is out of the ordinary or involves a substantial expenditure, the agent should first consult with the principal, because the agent's implied authority may not extend to such matters. Thus, if the electrician hired by M to repair a shorted wire informs him that the wiring in the building is badly worn and does not comply with city building code requirements, M should not act on his own to contract for the rewiring at a substantial cost. Instead he should consult with O before taking further action.

Interesting questions regarding an agent's authority are sometimes raised by the occurrence of an *emergency*. Although it is often said that the scope of an agent's implied authority is "expanded" in emergency situations, this is only sometimes true. If an emergency occurs and there is no opportunity to consult with the principal, the agent has implied authority to take steps that are reasonable and prudent under the circumstances— including actions that may be contrary to prior instructions by the principal.

To illustrate: A has been ordered by P to purchase badly needed raw materials from country X and to ship them through country Y, which has the nearest port facility where the goods can be loaded on vessels. A makes the purchase but then learns from a usually reliable source that a revolution is imminent in country Y and will probably break out while the goods are en route. Fearing that transportation may be impaired or that the goods may be seized by the revolutionaries, A attempts to contact P but is unable to do so. Since he knows that P needs the goods quickly, A arranges for shipment to another port through country Z. Shipment over the other route will be slightly more expensive and time-consuming but also presumably safer, and P will still receive the goods in time to meet his needs.

In this case, A was impliedly authorized to act as he did—even if no revolution actually occurred. What is important is that two elements were present: (1) A, the agent, *was unable to consult with his principal*; and (2) he acted reasonably, in light of all the knowledge available to him, to protect the interests of his principal.

Apparent Authority

Thus far we have dealt with situations where the agent has actual authority, either express or implied. Now we will examine the peculiar concept of **apparent authority** (sometimes called **ostensible authority**). As we mentioned earlier, speaking of apparent authority as a specific type of authority is something of a contradiction, because the phrase describes a situation where the agent actually has no actual authority. If the agent acts outside the scope of his or her actual (express or implied) authority, the principal is normally not responsible on the unauthorized transaction. However, if the principal, by *his or her own conduct*, has led reasonable third parties to believe that the agent actually has such authority, the principal may be responsible. In discussing implied authority, we were concerned with what appeared reasonable to the agent. But for apparent authority, our concern is with the viewpoint of reasonable *third parties*. Obviously, some situations can fall within the scope of either implied or apparent authority. In such cases we usually speak in terms of implied authority; apparent authority is used as a basis for holding the principal responsible only where no express or implied authority is present.

The importance of apparent authority can be illustrated by two examples:

1. S, a salesman for R, has in his possession R's goods (not just samples). It is customary for an agent in S's position who is handling this type of goods to have authority to actually sell and collect payment for them. While making his rounds, S calls the home office. R tells him that he is afraid some of the items S has are defective and instructs him not to sell the goods in his possession but merely to take orders for a period of time. Contrary to instructions, S sells the goods. R is bound by the transactions and will be responsible to T, the buyer, if the goods actually are defective. It appears that R

has acted in a reasonable fashion under the circumstances. However, by allowing S to have possession of the goods, he has led T to believe that S is authorized to sell—because it is customary. T has no way of knowing that S's actual authority has been expressly limited to something less than what is customary. The basis of R's liability is not S's implied authority, because S knew that he had no authority and was acting contrary to express instructions. Instead, the basis for R's liability is apparent authority—arising out of the fact that T has been misled by the *appearance of authority.*

2. When the agency is terminated, the agent's *actual authority* is also terminated. (Note that a few courts have held that where the agency is terminated by the principal's *death,* his or her estate can continue to be liable for the agent's actions, under the doctrine of apparent authority, until the third party of learns of the death.) But this does not automatically dispose of the problem of *apparent authority.* It is sometimes necessary to notify third parties of the termination in order to keep the principal from being liable under the concept of apparent authority. As a general rule, where termination has occurred *as a matter of law* (see Chapter 23 for details), all authority ceases automatically and the principal is not responsible for the agent's further actions regardless of whether the third party has been notified. Most problems involving termination and apparent authority arise when the agency has been ended *by act of the parties* (such as the principal firing the agent). Where termination is by act of the parties, the principal may still be bound by the agent's actions (because of apparent authority) unless and until the third party is notified of the termination. The principal must notify third parties with whom the agent has dealt in the past by letter, e-mail, telephone, or some other method of *direct communication* if their identities are reasonably easy to ascertain. Regarding all other third parties, the principal can protect himself simply by giving *public notice.* An advertisement in a local newspaper is the most common form of such notice, but other methods may be sufficient if they are reasonable under the circumstances.

Ratification of Unauthorized Transactions

If an agent's action is not within the scope of his or her actual (express or implied) authority, and if the facts are such that no apparent authority is present, the principal generally is not liable to the third party for that action. Even in the absence of actual or apparent authority, however, the principal may become responsible if he or she *ratifies* (or *affirms)* the agent's unauthorized actions. An unauthorized act ratified by the principal is treated by the courts in the same manner as if it had been actually authorized from the beginning. The two forms of **ratification**— express and implied—are discussed below.

Express Ratification

If, upon learning of the agent's unauthorized dealings, the principal decides to honor the transaction, he or she can simply inform the agent, the third party, or someone else of that intention. In this situation an **express ratification** has obviously occurred.

Implied Ratification

Even if the principal has not expressly communicated the intent to ratify, the person can nevertheless be deemed to have done so if his or her words or conduct reasonably indicate that intent. *Inaction* and *silence* may even amount to ratification if, under the circumstances, a reasonable person would have voiced an objection to what the agent had done. The following five examples will help clarify the concept of **implied ratification**. For each example, no actual authority exists, and there are no facts present to indicate apparent authority.

Example 1. A, who is a driver of a truck owned by P, enters into an unauthorized agreement with T, under which A is to haul T's goods on P's truck. Sometime later, while A is en route, T becomes concerned about the delay and calls P. Upon learning of the transaction, P does not repudiate it but instead assures T that "A is a good driver and the goods will be properly cared for." P has ratified the agreement.

Example 2. Same facts as Example 1. This time, however, T does not call P. The goods arrive safely at their destination, and T sends a check for the shipping charges to P. This is when P first learns of the transaction. If P cashes or deposits the check and uses the money, he will be deemed to have ratified the agreement. Even if he simply retains the check for an appreciable period of time and says nothing, he will probably be held to have ratified.

Example 3. A makes an unauthorized contract to sell P's goods to T. Upon learning of the contract, P says nothing to A or T but assigns the right to receive payment for the goods to X. P has ratified the agreement.

Example 4. Same facts as Example 3. This time, however, P does not assign the right to receive payment. Instead he ships the goods to T. P has ratified the agreement.

Example 5. Same facts as Example 4, but the goods are shipped to T without P's knowledge. P then learns of the transaction, and when T does not make payment by the due date, P files suit against T to collect the purchase price. P has ratified the transaction (P would not have ratified if he had filed suit to rescind the sale and get his goods back.)

Requirements for Ratification

Certain requirements must be present for ratification to occur. Following are the most important of them:

1. The courts generally hold that a principal can ratify only if the agent, in dealing with the third party, has indicated that he or she is acting *for a principal* and not in his or her own behalf.

2. At the time of ratification, the principal must have *known* or *had reason to know* of the essential facts about the transaction. What this means is that the principal must have had either actual knowledge of the relevant facts or sufficient knowledge so that it would have been easy to find out what the essential facts were. The requirement of knowledge is usually important when the third party tries to hold the principal liable by claiming that some words or actions of the principal had amounted to ratification.

3. Ratification must occur within a *reasonable time* after the principal learned of the transaction. What constitutes a reasonable time will, of course, depend on the facts of the particular case. However, a court will automatically rule that a reasonable time period has already expired, and thus that there can be no ratification, if there has been a fundamental change in the facts that had formed the basis of the transaction. An example would be damage to or destruction of the subject matter of the transaction. Similarly, the principal will not be permitted to ratify if the third party has already indicated a desire to withdraw from the transaction. The third party has the right to withdraw prior to ratification and, when he or she does so, any later attempt by the principal to ratify will be treated as being too late.

4. If the principal ratifies, he or she must ratify the *entire transaction* rather than ratifying that part which is to his or her advantage and repudiating that which is to his or her disadvantage. For example, a principal ratifying a contract for the sale of goods to a third party is obligated on any warranties that accompany the goods.

5. The transaction obviously must be *legal*, and the principal must have the *capacity* required to be a party to the transaction.

6. If any *formalities* (such as a writing) would have been required for an original authorization, the same formalities must be met in ratifying the transaction. Of course, if formalities are required, the ratification will have to be express—it cannot be implied. Since most authorizations do not require any special formalities, this usually poses no problem.

The following two cases both deal with the question of apparent authority. The second case also involves the issue of ratification.

INDUSTRIAL MOLDED PLASTIC PRODUCTS, INC. V. J. GROSS & SONS, INC.
Superior Court of Pennsylvania, 398 A.2d 695 (1979)

Industrial Molded Plastic Products (Industrial) is in the business of manufacturing custom injection molded plastics by specification for various manufacturers. Industrial also manufactures various 'fill-in' items during slack periods, such as electronic parts, industrial components, mirror clips, and plastic clothing clips. J. Gross & Sons (Gross) is a wholesaler to the retail clothing industry, selling mostly sewing thread, but also other items such as zippers, snaps, and clips.

Sometime in the fall of 1970, Stanley Waxman (Gross's president and sole stockholder) and his son Peter (a twenty-two-year-old salesman for Gross) appeared at the offices of Industrial's president, Judson T. Ulansey. They suggested to him that they might be able to market Industrial's plastic clothing clips in the retail clothing industry, in which they had an established sales force. At this initial meeting, there was no discussion of Peter Waxman's authority or lack thereof in the company. After this meeting,

Stanley authorized Peter to purchase a 'trial' amount of clips (not further specified) to test the market, but neither this authorization nor its limitation was communicated to Ulansey. All subsequent negotiations were between Ulansey and Peter Waxman only. Deceiving both his father and Ulansey, Peter himself out as vice-president of Gross, and on December 10, 1970, signed an agreement obligating Gross to purchase from Industrial five million plastic clothing clips during the calendar year of 1971, at a price of $7.50 per thousand units, delivery at Industrial's plant in Blooming the execution of this agreement, Ulansey telephoned Stanley Waxman, who told Ulansey that Peter could act on behalf of Gross. There was no discussion of the specific terms of the agreement, such as the quantity purchased.

Industrial immediately began production of the five million clips during 'fill-in' time. As they were manufactured, they were warehoused in Industrial's plant as specified in the contract. In February 1971, PeterWaxman picked up and paid for 772,000 clips. Stanley Waxman, who had to sign Gross's check for payment, thought that this was the "trial amount" he had authorized Peter to buy. These were the only clips which Gross ever took into its possession. On numerous occasions during the year Ulansey urged Peter to pick up more of the clips, which were taking up more and more storage space at Industrial's plant as they were being manufactured. Peter told Ulansey that he was having difficulty selling the clips and that Gross had no warehousing capacity for the inventory that was being accumulated. At no time, however, did Peter repudiate the contract or request Industrial to halt production. By the end of 1971, production was completed and Industrial was warehousing 4,228,000 clips at its plant.

On January 19,1972, Industrial sent Gross an invoice for the remaining clips of $31,506.45. However, Gross did not honor the invoice or pick up any more of the clips. Ulansey wrote to Stanley Waxman on February 7, 1972, requesting him to pick up the clips. Receiving no response, Ulansey wrote to Stanley Waxman again on February 23, 1972, threatening legal action if shipping instructions were not received by March 1, 1972. Finally, on March 30, 1972, Peter Waxman responded with a letter to Ulansey, which stated that Gross's failure to move the clips was due to a substantial decline in the clothing industry in 1971 and competition with new lower-cost methods of hanging and shipping clothes. The letter asked for Industrial's patience and predicted that it would take at least the rest of the year to market the clips successfully. At this point, Industrial sued. Stanley Waxman learned of the five million clip contract for the first time when informed by his lawyer of the impending lawsuit. At this time, Peter began an extended (four years) leave of absence from Gross.

The trial court ruled in favor of Industrial, the plaintiff, but awarded damages of only $2,400. Both parties appealed, plaintiff claiming that it should be entitled to the entire contract price of over $31,000, and defendant claiming that it should not be liable at all.

Hoffman, Judge:

. . . Gross contends that it was not bound by the agreement to purchase the clips because Peter Waxman had no authority to sign the contract for Gross. However, Peter was an agent of Gross and did have express authority to purchase for Gross, as its president instructed him to purchase a "trial amount" of clips. A principal's limitation of his agent's authority in amount only, not communicated to the third party with whom the agent deals, does not so limit the principal's liability.

Although the agent violates his instructions or exceeds the limits set to his authority, he will yet bind his principal to such third persons, if his acts are within the scope of the authority which the principal has caused or permitted him to possess. Such limitations will be binding [only] upon third persons who know of them.

An admitted agent is presumed to be acting within the scope of his authority where the act is legal and the third party has no notice of the agent's limitation. The third person must use reasonable diligence to ascertain the authority of the agent, but he is also entitled to rely upon the apparent authority of the agent when this is a reasonable interpretation of the manifestations of the principal.

Here, the limitation on Peter's authority was not communicated to Industrial. As Stanley Waxman brought Peter into the initial meeting soliciting business from Industrial, Ulansey could reasonably presume his authority to act for Gross in consummating the deal. Gross complains that Ulansey was not diligent in ascertaining Peter s authority, but in fact Ulansey telephoned Stanley Waxman precisely for the purpose of verifying Peter's authority. As Stanley said that Peter was authorized to act on behalf of Gross, the principal thus completed clothing the agent in apparent authority to bind the corporate entity on the agreement. If anybody was lacking in diligence, it was Stanley Waxman in not inquiring as to the amount of the contract Peter proposed to sign. Thus, we affirm the conclusion of the court below that Gross was bound by the agreement to purchase the clips.

[The court then held that the trial court had incorrectly computed damages, and that Industrial was entitled to the total contract price of $31,506.45.]

CITY ELECTRIC V. DEAN EVANS CHRYSLER-PLYMOUTH
Supreme Court of Utah, 672 P.2d 89 (1983)

Dave Sturgill was a salesman for Dean Evans Chrysler-Plymouth, a retail automobile dealership. Dean Evans was president of the firm, and his son Mike Evans was assistant secretary. Mike Evans was also a partner with Johnny Rider in another business, Johnny Rider's Backstage Restaurant. On one occasion, Mike Evans and Johnny Rider were discussing the remodeling of their restaurant. Sturgill happened to be present during the discussion, and volunteered to contact City Electric, an electric materials supplier that Sturgill had previously worked for. Sturgill said that he might be able to get a good price on the electrical materials they would need for the remodeling project. Sturgill called Don Hatch, a salesman for City Electric, and told Hatch that Sturgill was trying to do a favor for his boss (Mike Evans). Sturgill asked if City Electric would give Mike Evans a fair price, and if the restaurant could establish an account. Shortly after this conversation, and before City Electric had time to set up an account for the restaurant, Mike Evans told Sturgill that the materials should be purchased on the auto dealership's account with City Electric.

The next day, Sturgill again called Hatch and placed an order for materials, stating that the materials were to be charged to the account of Dean Evans Chrysler-Plymouth. Sturgill said that he was acting pursuant to

Mike Evans's directions, but there was never any representation that the auto dealership owned or was affiliated with the restaurant. Hatch checked his firm's computer printouts of open accounts and found that the auto dealership did have such an account with City Electric. Hatch put this and several later orders on the account, and the materials were delivered to the restaurant. Several invoices were sent to the auto dealership, and two of them dated October 8 and 9, 1978, were paid in December, 1978. There was no evidence indicating who paid these two invoices in behalf of the auto dealership. Thereafter, the dealership refused to make any further payments, leaving an unpaid balance of $2,332.70. City Electric, plaintiff, filed suit against Dean Evans Chrysler-Plymouth, defendant, for this unpaid balance. The trial court held that both Mike Evans and Dave Sturgill had apparent authority to charge the orders to the dealership's account, and ruled in favor of plaintiff. Defendant appealed.

Howe, Justice:

It is well settled law that the apparent or ostensible authority of an agent can be inferred only from the acts and conduct of the principal. Where corporate liability is sought for acts of its agent under apparent authority, liability is premised upon the corporation's knowledge of and acquiescence in the conduct of its agent which has led third parties to rely upon the agent's actions. Nor is the authority of the agent "apparent" merely because it looks so to the person with whom he deals. It is the principal who must cause third parties to believe that the agent is clothed with apparent authority. (See Forsyth v.Pendleton, 617 P.2d 358 (Utah 1980), where the referral by seller to her attorney of a letter written to her by buyers constituted an act sufficient to clothe the attorney with apparent authority to act for seller.) It

follows that one who deals exclusively with an agent has the responsibility to ascertain that agent's authority despite the agent's representations. Moreover, it has been held that apparent authority vanishes when the third party has actual knowledge of the real scope of the agent's authority.

Under the applicable standard of review this Court will accord the findings of the trial court a presumption of validity and correctness so long as there is support for them in the evidence. That support is singularly absent in this case... Sturgill's apparent authority was never established. His request for electrical materials for the remodeling of the restaurant fell wide of the mark of his scope of employment... His own statement could not establish any authority in him.

Plaintiff's credit manager testified that all purchases made between October and December of 1978 were made out to Johnny Rider of the Backstage Restaurant and that none of the receipts was signed by anyone on behalf of the defendant. None of the materials was delivered to the defendant and most of them were picked up by workers involved with the remodeling. Hatch testified that Sturgill told him he was trying to do his boss (Mike Evans) a favor by getting him good prices. Hatch never talked to Mike, who he knew was a son of Dean Evans and who he assumed had a management position with defendant. His only contact was with Sturgill, who he assumed had no management position with the defendant. Sturgill made no representation to Hatch that defendant owned the Backstage Restaurant and the only authority Hatch relied upon was Sturgill's telling him that Mike told Sturgill to call and arrange for the materials. When questioned whether he took credit information from Sturgill from which he could determine whether to extend credit, Hatch answered "No. I looked on our computer printout for addresses and open accounts, and Dean Evans Chrysler-Plymouth had an account with us." Hatch did not claim that plaintiff had an agreement with the defendant relating to the materials. Hatch's dealings were exclusively with Sturgill and on a matter unrelated to the business of the defendant. Whatever apparent authority Sturgill might have otherwise had vanished for that reason alone. Unless otherwise agreed, general expressions used in authorizing an agent are limited in application to acts done in connection with the act or business to which the authority primarily relates.

Plaintiff's argument that the contract was ratified by payments made of the October 8 and October 9 invoices fares no better.

Plaintiff's exhibit offers no clue as to who paid them. A penciled notation "Paid in Dec 1978" does not rise to the level of ratification by defendant as required by law. Ratification is premised upon the knowledge of all material facts and upon an express or implied intention on the part of the principal to ratify. There is not a shred of evidence in the record that defendant paid the two mentioned invoices, nor is the court's statement that "everybody knew that Mike was connected" sufficient to impute knowledge of Sturgill's actions to the defendant, let alone an intent to subsequently ratify those actions.

The plaintiff failed to establish its case and it was error for the trial court to find in its favor. The judgment is reversed.

Importance of the Agent's Knowledge

In deciding the question of a principal's liability to a third party, sometimes a key issue is whether the principal has received notice of a particular fact. For example, P is obligated under a contract to make payment to T. T assigns her right to receive this payment to X, an assignee. Assuming that T's right is assignable, P is bound to honor the assignment and pay X instead of T only if he has received notice of the assignment. But what if P's agent, A, receives this notice rather than P himself? If A promptly relays the information to P, there is usually no problem. What happens, though, if A fails to do so and P, not knowing of the assignment, pays T instead of X? Is P liable to X because P's agent had received notice?

Ordinarily, in any case where notice to the principal is important, notice to the agent is treated as notice to the principal if the agent's receipt of the notice is within the scope of his or her actual or apparent authority. In other words, in such cases the law will treat the principal as if he or she had received notice even if the agent did not transmit it. Obviously, however, this does not apply where the third party who notifies the agent knows that the agent is acting adversely to the interests of the principal (as where the third party and the agent are conspiring to defraud the principal).

Liability of the Agent

When the agent is acting for the principal, the agent ordinarily incurs no personal responsibility if he or she acts in a proper fashion. However, circumstances do exist where the agent can become liable.

Breach of Duty

If the agent violates any of the duties owed to the principal, he or she naturally is liable for the damages caused by the breach. Where the duty which has been violated is that of loyalty, the penalties may be even more severe. A disloyal agent is not only responsible to the principal for any resulting loss sustained by the latter but also usually forfeits his or her right to be compensated for services rendered. Furthermore, the agent must turn over to the principal any profits made from his or her disloyal activity.

Exceeding Authority

The agent who exceeds his or her actual authority is personally responsible unless the principal ratifies the unauthorized actions. Whether this responsibility is to the principal or to the third party depends on the circumstances. If the agent exceeds his or her actual authority, but the principal is liable to a third party on the ground of apparent authority, the agent's liability is to the *principal*. On the other hand, if the agent exceeds his or her actual authority and the facts are such that the principal is not liable to a third party under apparent authority, then the agent's liability is to the *third party*.

Assuming Liability

If the agent personally assumes liability for a particular transaction, then he or she obviously is responsible. For instance: A is attempting to purchase goods for P on credit. T, the seller, is wary of P's credit rating and refuses to grant credit unless A also becomes obligated. A signs the agreement as P's agent and in his own individual capacity. A is in effect a *co-principal* and therefore personally liable to T if P defaults.

Nondisclosure of Principal

If the agent, in dealing with a third party, fails to disclose that he or she is *acting for a principal* or fails to disclose the *principal's identity*, the agent is personally responsible to the third party. Additionally, the agent will sometimes beliable if he or she acts for a nonexistent principal or for one not having legal capacity. (These subjects are dealt with specifically later in the chapter.)

Commission of a Tort

If the agent commits a *tort*, he or she is personally responsible to the injured party for the resulting harm. This is true regardless of whether the agent was working for the principal at the time. (Sometimes the principal also is responsible. This problem is discussed later in the chapter.)

Liability of the Third Party

Relatively little need be said about the liability of the third party. Since that party is acting on his or her own behalf, he or she is personally responsible to the other party to the transaction. This ordinarily means that:

1. If the third party fails to live up to his or her part of the bargain, that person will be liable to the principal.
2. The third party owes no responsibility to the agent unless the agent has personally become a party to the transaction.
3. The third party is liable for his or her torts to any party injured as a result.

Nonexistent, Partially Disclosed, and Undisclosed Principals

In discussing the principal-agent relationship we have thus far assumed that the principal exists when the agent executes the transaction in question and that both the existence and the identity of the principal are disclosed to the third party. This is usually, but not always, the case. The special problems that arise in connection with *nonexistent, partially disclosed,* and *undisclosed principals* are discussed below.

Nonexistent Principals

If an agent purports to act for a principal who does not exist at the time, the agent is usually liable to the third party. Of course, since there is no principal, the agent is not really an agent at all; he or she merely *claims* to be one.

While this situation does not occur frequently, it is by no means rare. A common instance of the **nonexistent principal** is that of a person attempting to act for an organization that is not legally recognized as a separate entity. (A *legal entity* is an organization—such as a corporation—that is recognized by the law as having the rights and duties of a person, although it is not flesh and blood. It can, for example, make contracts, sue, and be sued in its own name.) Thus a member of an unincorporated association, such as a church, club, fraternity, or the like, may attempt to contract in behalf of the association. Since the "principal" is not legally recognized as one, the members who make the agreement are personally responsible. It is for this reason that many churches and other such organizations form corporations.

The contracts of *corporate promoters* (those who play a part in the initial organization of a corporation) have posed similar problems. Quite often, these people make various types of agreements before the proposed corporation is formed. They may, for example, enter contracts for the purpose of raising capital, purchasing a building site, or procuring the services of an attorney, an accountant, or other professionals.

A similar situation occurs when a principal has existed but is now dead or lacks contractual capacity when the agent contracts with the third party. Such an occurrence often terminates the agency, and the principal (or that person's estate) is not bound. If the agency is not terminated, the principal's status affects his or her own liability in the same way as if the principal had personally dealt with the third party.

Whether the *agent* is personally liable depends on the circumstances. If the principal is *dead* or has been *declared insane by a court* at the time of the transaction, the agent invariably is held personally liable to the third party. On the other hand, if, at the time the transaction is made, the principal is either a *minor* or *insane* (but not officially declared insane by a court), the agent is personally responsible to the third party in only two situations:

1. The agent is liable if he or she has made representations to the effect that the principal has contractual capacity. This is true even if the agent is honestly mistaken.
2. The agent who has made no such representations is still liable to the third party if he or she *knew or had reason to know* of the principal's lack of capacity *and* the third party's ignorance of the facts.

Partially Disclosed Principals

As we indicated earlier, an agent usually is responsible to the third party if the agent discloses the fact that he or she is acting for a principal but does not *identify* that person. If the agent acts with authority, the principal is also responsible and may be held liable when the third party learns his or her identity. (There is conflict among the courts on whether the third party must make a choice (or *election*) between the agent and the principal in such a case or whether he or she can hold both of them responsible.) Since the third party knows that the agent is acting for someone else, the third party is, in turn, liable to the principal. In sum, the liability of the principal and the third party is the same as in the case of a completely disclosed principal. The only difference is that in the case of a **partially disclosed principal,** *the agent is also liable,* unless the agent and the third party agree otherwise.

Undisclosed Principals

Individuals and business organizations sometimes prefer not to have their connection with a transaction be known. If an agent acts in behalf of a principal but does not disclose to the third party the fact that he or she is representing another, it is said that the agent acts for an **undisclosed principal.** In other words, the third party, not knowing that a principal-agent relationship exists, thinks that the agent is dealing solely for himself.

In a case such as this, the agent is personally liable to the third party. If and when the principal makes himself known, that person is also liable to the third party if the agent acted within the scope of his authority. In such an event, the third party must *elect* whether to hold the agent or the principal responsible.

Thus far we have focused on the liability of the undisclosed principal and the agent. But what about the liability of the *third party?* Since the agent is a party to the contract, he or she can enforce the agreement against the third party. Once revealed, the principal ordinarily can also enforce the agreement. In three situations, however, the third party can refuse to perform for the undisclosed principal and can continue to treat the agent as the sole party to whom he or she is obligated.

1. If the third party has already performed for the agent before the principal is revealed, the third party is not required to render a second performance.
2. If, prior to the transaction, the third party has indicated that he or she will not deal with the one who is the undisclosed principal, the third party is not required to perform for that principal. Similarly, the third party is not responsible to the undisclosed principal if the former has indicated beforehand or in the agreement that he or she will not deal with *anyone* other than the agent.
3. In all other situations the undisclosed principal is treated in much the same way as an *assignee* from the agent. He or she can demand performance from the third party only if the contract is of a type that can be assigned. Thus, if the contract calls for personal service by the agent or if the agent's personal credit standing, judgment, or skill played an important part in the third party's decision to deal with that individual, the third party cannot be forced to accept the undisclosed principal as a substitute.

Tort Liability

Until now, our discussions of legal responsibility have focused almost exclusively on the parties' contractual liability. Now we will turn to their *tort liability*.

Circumstances in Which the Superior Is Liable for the Suborinate's Torts

Obviously, if either the superior, the subordinate, or the third party personally commits a tort, that person is liable to the one injured by the wrongful act. If the *subordinate* commits a tort, the additional question often arises whether his or her *superior* is also liable to the injured third party. This is often important because ordinarily the superior is insured or otherwise more financially capable of paying damages.

If the superior is personally at fault, that person obviously is liable because he or she has committed a tort. This can be seen in the following situations:
1. If the superior *directs* the subordinate to commit the tort (or even if the superior intends that the tort be committed), he or she is responsible.
2. If the superior carelessly allows the subordinate to operate potentially dangerous equipment (such as an automobile or truck), even though he or she knows or should know that the subordinate is unqualified or incapable of handling it safely, the superior is responsible for any resulting harm. The phrase *negligent entrustment* is often used to describe this situation.
3. Similarly, the superior is held liable if he or she is negligent in *failing to properly supervise a subordinate*.

Most often, however, the superior has not directed or intended the commission of a tort and has no reason to suppose that he or she is creating a dangerous situation. Therefore, the third party usually seeks to impose **vicarious liability** (liability imposed not because of one's own wrong but solely because of the wrong of one's subordinate) on the superior. The imposition of liability on the superior for a tort committed by a subordinate is based on the doctrine of **respondeat superior** ("let the master answer").

The theoretical justification for holding the superior responsible is that he or she can treat the loss—or the premiums for liability insurance—as a cost of doing business. The cost is thus reflected in the price of his or her product, and the loss is ultimately spread over that segment of the population benefiting from that product.

When the superior is required to pay damages to a third party because of the tort of a subordinate, the superior usually has a legal right to recoup the loss from that subordinate. As a practical matter, this is an illusory right in many cases, because the subordinate frequently is unable to pay.

Of course, the superior is not always responsible for the torts of subordinates. In this regard, two issues must ordinarily be dealt with:

1. Was the relationship that of employer-employee (i.e., master-servant) or employer-independent contractor?
2. If an employer-employee relationship existed, was the employee acting within the scope of his or her employment at the time of committing the alleged tort?

Employer-Employee or Employer-Independent Contractor

Legal Significance of the Distinction

The imposition of vicarious liability often depends on the nature of the relationship involved. If it is found to be that of employer-employee, the employer is liable for a tort committed by the employee if it was committed in the scope of the employee's employment for the employer.

On the other hand, if the relationship is found to be that of employer and independent contractor, the employer generally is not liable for a tort committed by the independent contractor. Those few instances in which the employer is liable for a tort are as follows.

1. If the task for which the independent contractor was hired is *inherently dangerous,* the employer will be responsible for harm to third parties caused by the dangerous character of the work. The employer's responsibility in such a case is based on the tort concept of *strict liability.* That is, the responsibility exists solely because of the nature of the activity, regardless of whether any negligence or other fault brought about the damage. Activities deemed to be inherently dangerous include blasting, using deadly chemicals, or working on buildings in populated areas where people must pass below the activity.

2. If the employer owes a *nondelegable duty,* he or she cannot escape ultimate responsibility for performing that duty by obtaining an independent contractor to perform it. Thus, if the independent contractor is negligent or commits some other tort in the performance of such a task, the employer is liable to the injured third party. Nondelegable duties are those duties owed to the public which legislatures or courts feel to be of such importance that responsibility cannot be delegated. Activities recognized as involving nondelegable duties vary widely from state to state, but examples

include (a) the statutory duty of a railroad to keep highway crossings in a safe condition; (b) the duty of a city to keep its streets in a safe condition; (c) the duty of a landlord who has assumed responsibility for making repairs to the premises to see that those repairs are done safely; and (d) the duty of a business proprietor whose premises are open to the public to keep the premises in a reasonably safe condition.

3. As is usually the case regardless of the exact nature of the relationship between the superior and subordinate, an employer is liable for the independent contractor's tort if the employer specifically directed, authorized, or intended the wrongful conduct.

Making the Distinction

The determination of whether a particular subordinate is an employee or an independent contractor depends essentially on the issue of *control*. If the employer has hired the subordinate merely to achieve a result and has left decisions regarding the method and manner of achieving that result up to the subordinate, the latter is an independent contractor. On the other hand, if the superior actually controls or has the right to control the method and manner of achieving the result, then the subordinate is an employee. Thus a construction contractor hired to erect a building is usually an independent contractor, while a secretary hired to type and take dictation is usually an employee.

However, the delineation is not always easy, and sometimes it produces problems of extreme conceptual difficulty. The most important question, of course, is whether the employer *controls or has the right to control the method and manner of doing the work*. Where the matter of control is not so obvious as to make the determination readily apparent, other factors can be taken into account. Some facts which would increase the likelihood of a subordinate being viewed as an independent contractor are: (1) the subordinate has his own independent business or profession; (2) the subordinate uses his own tools, equipment, or workplace to perform the task; (3) the subordinate is paid by the job, not by the hour, week, or month; (4) the subordinate has irregular hours; and (5) the subordinate is performing a task that is not part of the employer's regular business. None of these facts automatically makes a subordinate an independent contractor; each is simply a factor to be weighed along with all the other evidence.

The following case illustrates the importance of the employer's right of control when there is a question about the subordinate's status as an employee or an independent contractor.

Branco Wood Products, Inc. v. C.C. Huxford Trust
Court of Civil Appeals of Alabama, 521 So. 2d 73 (1988)

The defendant, Branco Wood Products, is a corporation engaged in the business of supplying wood to large purchasers, such as Container Corporation of America (CCA), the purchaser in this case. Branco has a number of individuals who act as its wood producers, i.e., individuals who cut and deliver the timber which Branco then supplies to its purchasers.

CCA buys wood from Branco by means of a "ticket system." The way this system works is that the wood producer cuts and delivers to CCA the amount of wood indicated on the ticket. CCA then pays Branco for the wood delivered, and Branco pays the wood producer. On the occasion that led to this dispute, CCA gave tickets to Branco which entitled the bearer to deliver a certain amount of wood to CCA. Branco gave the CCA tickets to Edward Bell, one of its producers, who began cutting timber on property located adjacent to land owned by the C.C. Huxford Trust, the plaintiff in this case. Mistakenly, Bell crossed the boundary line between the two tracts and cut timber on the Trust's property. When the Trust learned that Bell was cutting timber on its property, it immediately informed Branco's president who told Bell to stop cutting the timber.

The Trust sued Branco, claiming that it was liable for the damages caused by Bell's trespass because Bell was Branco's employee and was acting in the scope of his employment. Branco claimed that it was not responsible because Bell was an independent contractor. The trial court ruled in favor of the Trust, and Branco appealed.

Holmes, Judge:

Under the doctrine of respondeat superior, [an employer] may be liable for the acts of his [employee] that are done in the interest of and in the prosecution of the [employer's] business if the [employee] is acting within the scope of his employment.

The test for determining if one is an agent or employee, as opposed to an independent contractor, is whether the alleged employer has reserved the right of control over the means and agencies by which the work is done, not the actual exercise of such control. Moreover, the control reserved by the employer must be over the manner in which—or the means by which—the employee's work is done, as well as the result accomplished. In other words, the employer must have the right to control, "not only what shall be done, but how it shall be done."

Because working relationships take a wide variety of forms, each case must depend upon its own facts, and all features of the relationship must be considered together. Thus, whether an [employer–employee] relationship exists is determined by the facts of the case, not by how the parties characterize their relationship.

Applying these rules to the case now before us, we can only conclude that the evidence does not support the trial court's conclusion that Bell was acting as the defendant's agent or employee when he cut timber on the plaintiffs land. In other words, the evidence does not show that the defendant had a reserved right of control over the means, or the manner, by which Bell performed his job of producing the quantity of timber called for by the CCA tickets that could make the defendant liable under the theory of respondeat superior.

The testimony of George I. Edwards, the defendant's president, was that the defendant did not direct or supervise Bell or its other wood producers in their work. Edwards testified that he did not tell Bell how to cut down trees, load his truck, or haul the wood; that he did not offer Bell any advice on cutting and removal techniques; that the defendant did not supply Bell with any equipment, trucks, or gas to use in his wood producing; that Bell was not on the "payroll per se" of the defendant; and that he did not tell Bell when he was supposed to go to work or when he was to quit work or how long he was to work each day.

Moreover, in this particular instance, the defendant did not direct Bell as to where he was to cut timber to fill the amount called for by the CCA tickets. Rather, the testimony indicated that Bell made arrangements independently with the property owner to cut timber on her land.

We do note that the testimony was to the effect that Edwards does go out periodically to the sites where the defendant's wood producers are cutting to check on their work. In addition, Bell testified that "whenever [Edwards] told me something I was cutting for him or something like that and he told me, that is what I did."

We do not think that any of the testimony, even that last recited, shows that the defendant retained the right to control the manner in which Bell performed his job of producing wood to fill the amount called for by the CCA tickets given to him by the defendant.

The control necessary for the existence of an employer-employee relationship is not established merely because the employer retains the right to supervise or inspect the work of an independent contractor to determine if he is performing in conformity with the contract...

We must reverse [because the trial] court's conclusion that the defendant is liable for the trespass of Bell is not supported by the evidence when the applicable law is applied. This case is reversed and remanded to the trial court for entry of a judgment [consistent with this opinion].

Scope of Employment

If the subordinate is deemed to be an employee, the employer is liable to third parties for those torts committed by the employee in the *scope of his or her employment*. There exists no simple definition of the **scope of employment** (sometimes called course of employment) concept. Obviously, an employee is acting within the scope of employment while performing work that he or she has been expressly *directed to do by the employer*. To illustrate: X has directed Y to drive X's truck from Dallas to Houston via a certain route. While on that route, Y drives negligently and injures T. X is liable to T.

In the absence of a specific directive given by the employer, an act usually is in the scope of employment if it is *reasonably incidental to an activity that has been expressly directed*. Thus, in the above example, if Y had stopped to buy gasoline and had negligently struck a parked car belonging to T, X would have been liable to T.

Deviations

The employer sometimes can be held liable even though the employee has deviated from the authorized activity. The employer's liability in such cases depends on the *degree* and *foreseeability* of the deviation. If the deviation is great, the employer usually is not responsible. Suppose that Y, in driving X's truck from Dallas to Houston, decides to go a hundred miles off his authorized route to visit an old friend. On the way there, Y negligently collides with T. In this situation, X is not liable.

But what if Y has been to see his friend and was returning to his authorized route when the collision occurred? Three different viewpoints have been taken by various courts. Where there has been more than a slight deviation from the scope of employment, as in this case, some courts have held that the reentry into the scope of employment occurs only when the employee has *actually returned to the authorized route or activity*. Others have held that there is reentry the moment that the employee, with an intent to serve the employer's business, *begins to turn back toward the point of deviation*. However, a majority of courts have held that reentry occurs when the employee, with an intent to serve the employer's business, *has turned back toward and come reasonably close to the point of deviation*.

If the deviation from the authorized route or activity is only slight, many courts have held that the employee is still within the scope of employment if the type of deviation was *reasonably foreseeable* by the master. For example: While driving from Dallas to Houston, Y stops at a roadside establishment to get something to eat or buy a pack of cigarettes. While pulling off the road, he negligently strikes a parked car. In this situation X is liable. Although buying something to eat or smoke may not be necessary to drive a truck from Dallas to Houston (as is the purchase of gasoline) and although Y was not really serving his employer, the deviation was only slight and was of the type that any employer should reasonably expect.

Many examples of the scope of employment issue—such as the next two cases—involve auto accidents (though certainly the issue is not limited to them). These two cases illustrate some typical problems in this area.

LAZAR V. THERMAL EQUIPMENT CORP.
Court of Appeals of California, 195 Cal. Rptr. 890 (1983)

Richard Lanno was employed as a project engineer for Thermal EquipmentCo., which was a manufacturer of heating equipment and pressure vessels for the aerospace industry. In connection with his job, Lanno was sometimes required to proceed from his home directly to a job site in the mornings. In addition, he was constantly on call as a trouble-shooter, and, consequently, Thermal's customers occasionally called him at his home after hours and on weekends. In order to answer these calls, Lanno needed the company truck, in which he sometimes carried tools; if the truck was not at his home, he would stop at Thermal to pick up needed tools on the way to answer the call. To facilitate these duties, Thermal allowed Lanno to take the company truck home with him on a daily basis. Thermal provided Lanno with gasoline for the truck, and allowed him to use it for personal purposes.

On one occasion, Lanno finished work and left Thermal's business premises. Driving the company truck, he headed in a direction away from both the workplace and his home; Lanno testified that he planned to stop at a store, purchase something, and then go home. Before reaching the store, Lanno was involved *in an accident with Lazar who suffered bodily injury and damage to his car. Lazar filed suit against Thermal, claiming that Lanno had driven the truck negligently and that Lanno was within the scope of his employment at the time of the accident. The jury found that Lanno was not acting within the scope of his employment at the time of the accident, but the trial court granted Lazar's motion for judgment notwithstanding the verdict, holding that Lanno was within the scope of employment as a matter of law. The jury had found Lazar's damages to be $81,000, and the trial court rendered judgment for Lazar against Thermal in this amount. Thermal appealed.*

Schauer, Presiding Judge:

Under the doctrine of respondeat superior, an employer is responsible for the torts of his employee if these torts are committed within the scope of employment. The "going and coming" rule acts to limit an employer's liability under respondeat superior. This rule deems an employee's actions to be outside the scope of employment when these actions occur while the employee is going to or returning from work. The "going and coming" rule, in turn, has been limited in recent years. Under the modern rule, if the employee's trip to or from work "involves an incidental benefit to the employer, not common to commute trips made by ordinary members of the work force," the "going and coming" rule will not apply. Thus in Hinmanv. Westinghouse Electric Co., 2 Cal.3d 956 (1970), it was held that the "going and coming" rule did not apply where the employer had made the commute part of the workday by compensating the employee for his travel time. Similarly, in Huntsinger v. Glass Containers Corp., 22 Cal. App.3d 803 (1972), an employee was required to drive to and from work in order to have his vehicle available for company business. The court

held that these circumstances, if confirmed by a jury, would support a finding that the employee's commute conferred an incidental benefit on the employer; a jury could therefore find that the commute fell within the scope of employment.

In the [present] case, the trial court was presented with uncontroverted evidence that Thermal derived a special benefit from Lanno's commute. This commute was made in the company vehicle, and an object of the commute was to transport the vehicle to Lanno's home where it would be ready for business use in case Lanno received emergency after-hours calls for repair from the employer's customers. In traveling to and from work, Lanno was thus acting in the scope of his employment, conferring a tangible benefit on his employer; the "going and coming" rule is thus inapplicable.

A further issue, however, is presented in this case. . . Lanno decided that, before going home, he would stop at a shop and buy a certain, now forgotten, item. To further complicate the question, this shop and item were located in the opposite direction from Lanno's home. . .

Categorization of an employee's action as within or outside the scope of employment. . . begins with a question of foreseeability. . . Foreseeability as a test for respondeat superior merely means that in the context of the particular enterprise an employee's conduct is not so unusual or startling that it would seem unfair to include the loss resulting from it among other costs of the employer's business.

One traditional means of defining this foreseeability is seen in the distinction between minor "deviations" and substantial "departures" from the employer's business. The former are deemed foreseeable and remain within the scope of employment; the latter are unforeseeable and take the employee outside the scope of his employment.

Witkin [an authority on the law of agency] describes the traditional distinction as follows:

"The question is often one of fact, and the rule now established is that only a substantial deviation or departure takes the employee outside the scope of his employment. If the main purpose of his activity is still the employer's business, it does not cease to be within the scope of the employment by reason of incidental personal acts, slight delays, or deflections from the most direct route..."

In the [present] case, we are asked to decide whether Lanno's personal errand was a foreseeable deviation from the scope of his employment, or whether evidence or inferences therefrom have been presented which would lead a jury to believe that this errand was an unforeseeable, substantial departure from his duties...

The evidence presented to the trial court was not controverted. Lanno testified that on the day of the accident he left work and headed away from his home, planning to buy an item and then return directly home. The evidence thus clearly showed that Lanno planned a minor errand to be carried out, broadly speaking, on the way home. Lanno further testified that this type of errand occurred with his employer's permission. No evidence was presented, nor could any inference be drawn from the evidence, showing that Lanno had any other object in mind that day than a brief stop at a store before going home.

The evidence, then, leads ineluctably to the conclusion that Lanno's errand was a minor deviation from his employer's business. While the specific act was one "strictly personal" to Lanno, it was "necessary to his convenience" under the standard [set forth in] Alma W. v. Oakland Unified School Dist., 123 Cal. App.3d 133. While this standard was suggested for deviations "at work," we think it is applicable to deviations made on the way home, in the employer's vehicle, when the trip home benefits the employer. Here, it would have been unreasonable and inconvenient for Lanno to drive his truck home, stop there, then return to purchase the needed item, passing work on the way. The decision to stop to buy the item on the way home was one reasonably necessary to Lanno's comfort and convenience. For this reason the detour must be considered a minor deviation.

The detour was foreseeable for much the same reason. While a decision to stop at a party, or a bar, or to begin a vacation, might not have been foreseeable, we can think of no conduct more predictable than an employee's stopping at a store to purchase a few items on the way home. Where, as here, the trip home is made for the benefit of the employer, in the employer's vehicle, accidents occurring during such minor and foreseeable deviations become part of the "inevitable toll of a lawful enterprise."

Finally, we note that Thermal makes much of the fact that Lanno was headed in the direction opposite his home at the time of the accident... An employer's liability, however, should not turn simply on a point of the compass; the fact that the store Lanno decided to visit was to the north of his workplace, rather than to the south, is not the controlling factor in this case. Instead, the modern rationale for respondeat superior requires that liability be hinged on the foreseeability and substantiality of the employee's departure from his employer's business. Where, as here, the deviation is insubstantial and foreseeable, the doctrine of respondeat superior will apply.

The judgment is affirmed.

Comment

CommentIf the deviation had been substantial and unforeseeable, such as a two-hour stop at a bar, Lanno would have been outside the scope of his employment during the deviation. However, because the "coming and going" rule did not apply to this case, Lanno would have reentered the scope of employment upon getting back into the truck and resuming the trip toward home.

Dinkins v. Farley
New York Supreme Court, Monroe County, 434 N.Y.S.2d 325 (1980)

As part of its personnel policy, Xerox Corporation maintained a National Tuition Aid Program that provided financial assistance to employees taking advanced college courses. An employee's application to participate in the program had to be approved by the employee's immediate supervisor. The company provided tuition assistance only for those courses directly related to a present job or to a future job to which an employee might reasonably aspire at Xerox. Upon approval of the employee's application, Xerox advanced 100 percent of the tuition and lab fees and then deducted 35 percent of that amount from the employee's paychecks in installments. Thereafter, the employee was required to verify enrollment by submitting itemized receipts from the college, and later to verify successful completion of a course by submitting a grade report to Xerox within 30 days after the end of the semester. If a grade report for a course was not submitted to Xerox within 50 days after semester's end, the company initiated steps to collect the other 65 percent of course expenses from the employee. However, if the employee ultimately received an advanced degree as a result of his participation in the tuition aid program, Xerox would refund the 35 percent that had been paid by the employee. A course taken under the program was expected to be scheduled outside of working hours if possible. Iif this was not possible, the employee could have limited time off during the workday to attend classes, subject to approval by the employee's supervisor. Such time off had to be made up at another time decided by the supervisor. Xerox spent about $1,000,000 annually on the program, and at the time of this case over 6,000 of Xerox's employees had participated.

Victor Farley, an employee of Xerox, had a bachelor's degree in engineering and wished to take a linear systems course that would better prepare him for pursuing a master's degree in that field. His application for the tuition aid program was approved by Xerox and he enrolled in the course at the Rochester Institute of Technology. He usually got out of work at 4:20 or 4:30 p.m., and frequently was a few minutes late for the class, which began at 4:20. One afternoon as Victor was driving to class, he was involved in an automobile accident at an intersection on campus. The other driver, Diane Dinkins, sued both Victor and Xerox, claiming that Victor was guilty of negligence and that Xerox was also liable because Victor was acting within the scope of his employment at the time of the accident. Before trial, Xerox filed a motion for summary judgment on the ground that, as a matter of law, Victor was not acting within the scope of his employment when the accident occurred. Below is the opinion of the trial court on this issue.

Boehm, Justice:

Although Xerox subsidizes the outside education of an employee who successfully completes course work for a degree, this alone should not be controlling in creating a "scope of employment" status, at least while the course is still in progress, because failure to complete the course would make the employee responsible to pay the entire tuition. Thus, if tuition payments alone were the criterion by which scope of employment was determined, one would not know whether or not an employee was within the scope of his employment during the course year until his work had been graded at the end of the school year. Until that time an employee's status would be a contingent one, ripening only after the grades were issued. If, in the meantime, the employee had an accident driving to or from class, Xerox would not know whether it could be held responsible as his employer until the employee had passed or flunked.

Further, the purpose of Victor Farley in working toward a master's degree was predominantly personal. Although it may also serve a purpose of Xerox to have its employees better trained or more satisfied on the job by being promoted from within the organization, this purpose is subservient to the personal motive of Victor to better his own employment and economic status by obtaining a master's degree, a degree which would remain his and continue to benefit him even if he should no longer work for Xerox.

No doubt there is a good business and policy reason for Xerox to subsidize the education of its employees within certain areas of value to Xerox, but it cannot be said that such a purpose is necessary or vital to its operation except insofar as ambitious, well-trained or satisfied employees are vital to any organization in the same way as healthy employees are.

Further, it is undisputed that Xerox does not direct the number of times an employee must attend class nor whether he must attend at all. Hypothetically, if an employee were able to successfully complete a course by home study and never attend class, Xerox would still be obligated for 100 percent of the tuition. It is not going to and from class which determines whether an employee is reimbursed; it is whether he successfully completes his educational course.

If Xerox could be held liable in this case under respondeat superior, other circumstances come to mind which would also appear to impose liability upon it. For example, if Victor Farley carelessly handled volatile materials in a chemistry class and another student were injured or property were destroyed, Xerox could be held responsible. If Xerox is responsible for what an employee does on his way to class, why would it not be equally responsible for what an employee does in class? Or, if educational sabbaticals funded by scholarship grants under the same aid program were encouraged by Xerox, it could be responsible for injuries caused by one of its employees during such a sabbatical driving to or from class at a university hundreds of miles away from the plant. Or, if Xerox encouraged its employees to take paid leaves of absence to participate in worthwhile community organizations or projects, it could be responsible for injuries caused by an employee while so participating.

Other areas of liability come to mind. If Xerox encouraged noontime physical activity by its employees, such as jogging, would it be responsible for an injury caused to a pedestrian by one of its jogging employees in the area around Xerox Square? . . .

In none of these examples would an employee be acting in the scope of his employment as that term has been historically understood. Scope of employment "refers to those acts which are so closely connected with what the servant is employed to do, and so fairly and reasonably incidental to it, that they may be regarded as methods, even though quite improper ones, of carrying out the objectives of the employment." (Prosser, Law of Torts [4th ed], pp. 460-461.)

The Restatement of Agency sets forth the requirements as follows: (1) Conduct of a servant is within the scope of employment if, but only if (a) it is of the kind he is employed to perform; (b) it occurs substantially within the authorized time and space limits, (c) it is actuated . . . by a purpose to serve the master. . .(2) Conduct of a servant is not within the scope of employment if it is different in kind from that authorized, far beyond the authorized time or space limits, or too little actuated by a purpose to serve the master.

Victor's activity at the time of the accident in driving to a course whose successful completion was of primary and direct benefit to him cannot be said to be in the scope of his employment. Taking the course was not "closely connected" with what he had been employed to do nor was it "fairly and reasonably incidental" to the carrying out of the objectives of his employment. It was "too little actuated by a purpose to serve the master;" his own purpose was clearly the prevailing one. Nor was Xerox exercising control over him, directly or indirectly, at the time. He was driving a car not owned by Xerox; he selected his own mode of transportation; he chose the course which he was attending, but he could have gone or not gone as he saw fit and if he failed to attend class after enrolling the jeopardy he suffered was not his job but only the tuition Xerox had advanced on his behalf. It is difficult to see how Xerox was in control or could have been in control of Victor when the accident happened.

The case of Makoske v. Lombardy, 47 A.D.2d 284, is not to the contrary for there the employees were required to attend the training session at Saratoga. They were obliged to go. They did not have the same option which Victor had...

The motion of defendant Xerox Corporation is granted. [Thus, Xerox would not be liable even if Victor was found to have been guilty of negligence. The question of Victor's liability for negligence would be decided at trial, because genuine fact issues existed with regard to this question.]

Intentional Torts

Thus far we have assumed the tort to be that of *negligence* (simple carelessness). Most cases in fact are concerned with the employee's negligence. However, an employee's *intentional tort,* such as assault and battery, libel, slander, fraud, trespass, or the like, can also subject the employer to liability. The test is the same. The employer is liable if the employee was acting within the scope of his or her employment at the time. It should be emphasized, though, that an employer is *less likely* to be responsible if the employee's tort was *intentional* rather than merely negligent. The reason is that when an employee intentionally commits a wrongful act, he or she is more likely to be motivated by personal reasons rather than by a desire to serve the employer. Those cases where the employer *has* been held liable for his or her employee's intentional torts usually fall within one of four broad categories.

1. *Where the tort occurs in a job in which force is a natural incident.* An example is a bouncer in a saloon, who is naturally expected to use force occasionally. But if excessive force is used, the employer may well be liable.

2. *Where the employee is actually attempting to promote the employer's business but does it in a wrongful manner.* For example, two competing tow truck drivers are attempting to beat each other to the scene of an accident to get the business for their respective employers. One intentionally runs the other off the road. The employer of the one committing the tort is liable.

3. *Where the tort results from friction naturally brought about by the employer's business.* For instance, the employee, who works for a building contractor, argues with

an employee of a subcontractor about the method for laying a floor. They become angry, and the building contractor's employee strikes the other party. The building contractor, as employer, is probably liable.

4. *Where the tort was directly authorized or clearly intended by the employer.* This situation usually, but not always, involves a nonphysical tort such as fraud or defamation. As mentioned at the beginning of this discussion of the employer's tort liability, an employer who authorizes or intends the subordinate's wrongful act is usually held liable regardless of the kind of tort or the type of relationship between superior and subordinate.

There are different points of view regarding the appropriate test for determining when a principal should be liable for an agent's intentional tort. The following case applies the majority view.

PATTERSON V. BLAIR
Kentucky Supreme Court, 172 S.W.3d 361 (2005)

Plaintiff Patterson agreed with defendant Courtesy Autoplex to trade his Camaro for a new GMC Jimmy. He incorrectly informed Courtesy that he owned only $9,500 on the Camaro, when he really owed $3,000 more. Because the bank was closed and Courtesy could not verify Patterson's statement, it allowed him to take possession of the Jimmy, but did not transfer title. When Courtesy learned the truth and Patterson refused to make an extra payment or to return the Jimmy, Courtesy twice attempted unsuccessfully to repossess the Jimmy.

On October 4, 1995, after investigating where he could find Patterson, defendant Blair, Jr. and another Courtesy employee encountered Patterson, who was driving the Jimmy, on a public road. At a stoplight, Blair, Jr. exited his car and knocked on the Jimmy's driver-side window, demanding that Patterson get out of the vehicle. When Patterson refused, Blair, Jr. drew a pistol he was carrying and fired two shots in the front tire and two shots in the rear tire of the Jimmy. Ultimately, the disabled truck was impounded and returned to Courtesy by the police.

Blair, Jr. was criminally prosecuted and was convicted of wanton endangerment in the first degree, a felony. Patterson sued Blair, Jr. and Courtesy under several tort theories, including assault. A jury found that Courtesy was responsible for Blair, Jr.'s actions. Courtesy appealed, and the appellate court held that Blair, Jr. was not acting within the scope of employment and therefore Courtesy should not be liable. Patterson appealed.

Roach, Justice:

Stated generally, the doctrine of respondeat superior, also called vicarious liability, provides the legal rationale for holding a master responsible for a tort committed by his servant. An employer's liability is limited only to those employee actions committed in the scope of employment. The central difficulty in applying the rule of respondeat superior focuses on this concept, especially when the tort in question was intentional (as opposed to merely the result of negligence). Thus, the question inevitably arises: What does "scope of employment" mean?

In Ira S. Bushey & Sons,Inc. v. U.S., 398 F.2d 167(2d Cir. 1968), one of the most cited respondeat superior cases involving an intentional tort, Judge Friendly rejected many of the traditional justifications for the doctrine, focusing instead on the activities of the business enterprise. In *Bushey*, a drunken sailor returned to his ship and opened valves that flooded a drydock, damaging both the ship and drydock. Judge Friendly rejected many of the traditional policy arguments that have been offered in support of respondeat superior liability. He noted that even though the drunken sailor was not motivated by a purpose to serve his employer, respondeat superior liability was proper. This liability rested on the fact that the "business enterprise cannot justly disclaim responsibility for accidents which may be fairly said to be characteristic of its activities" and that the sailor's conduct "was not so unforeseeable as to make it unfair to charge the government with responsibility."

Judge Friendly applied the standard of forseeability as the benchmark for scope of employment. He discussed forseeability in the following manner: "Here it was foreseeable that crewmembers crossing the drydock might do damage, negligently or even intentionally, such as pushing a Bushey employee or kicking property into the water. Moreover, the proclivity of seamen to find solace for solitude by copious resort to the bottle while ashore has been noted in opinions too numerous to warrant citation. Once all this is granted, it is immaterial that Lane's precise action was not to be foreseen."

The most prominent alternative to the foreseeability standard is the principle that an action is only within the scope of employment when the employee intends to further the employer's business or advance the employer's goal. Prosser and Keeton state that "in general, the master is held liable for any intentional tort committed by the servant where its purpose, however misguided, is wholly or in part to further the master's business." Prosser and Keeton, TORTS, at 505. In explaining this principle, they offer the following example of the rule in action: "Thus a railway ticket agent who assaults, arrests or slanders a passenger, in the belief that he has been given a counterfeit bill for a ticket, is within the scope of employment, although the employer has not authorized such conduct, or has even expressly prohibited it. But if he acts from purely personal motives, because of a quarrel over his wife which is in no way connected with the employer's interests, he is considered in the ordinary case to have departed from his employment, and the master is not liable."

This rule differs significantly than the one proffered by Judge Friendly in that it depends on the employee's motivation in acting, not on whether his or her action is foreseeable. We must ultimately turn to our precedent to define the standard to be applied in Kentucky. In Frederick v. Collins,, 378 S.W.2d 617(Ky. 1964), an employee of a neighborhood grocery shot and killed a frequent patron of the store who disguised his voice and said "Stick'em up; this is a hold up." The employee turned around, hit the patron in the face with a gun, and shot him without realizing who it was. The employee was the storeowner's son. The owner testified that he did not know his son had a gun and that he had frequently instructed all of his employees, including his son, never to resist a holdup. The question before the Court was whether the owner could be held vicariously liable for the shooting, an intentional tort. The Court noted that Prosser had recognized "that even intentional torts may be so reasonably connected with the employment as to fall within the scope of it. The present tendency is to extend the employer's responsibility for such conduct." The Court then favorably cited Section 245 of the Restatement (Second) of Agency, which states that the master is liable "for the intended tortious harm by a servant to the person or things of another by an act done in connection with the servant's employment, although the act was unauthorized, if the act was not unexpectable in view of the duties of the servant."

In finding that the employee was acting within the scope of employment, the Court placed great weight on his motive for the shooting. The Court stated: "Without doubt RobertFrederick was under obligation generally to manage and protect the appellant's store and its contents. There is no evidence that Robert sought to serve any personal purpose in his activity toward Collins. So it is obvious that this case is not governed by any of the authorities which deny liability because the employee has acted in furtherance of a personal motive as distinguished from a motive connected with the employer's business."

The court went on to note: "In order to hold an employer responsible to a third person for the tortious act of an employee of the former, such act must have been committed while the employee was engaged in furthering his employers business or interests, without any deviation by the employee to a pursuit of his own business or interest, and there must have been a general similarity between the tortious act committed and the usual, ordinary, everyday acts commonly pursued by the employee in prosecuting the regular routine of his employment."

In the area of intentional torts, we have, with few exceptions, focused on the motive of the employee in determining whether he or she was acting within the scope of employment. Although in certain cases we have paid lip service to the principle of the forseeability of the misconduct that was advanced by Judge Friendly in *Bushey*, our substantive focus has remained on the servant's purpose or motive. It is quite possible that had *Bushey* been decided under Kentucky law, the employer would not have been held liable for the drunken sailor's conduct because the

drunken sailor was "not actuated by a purpose to serve the employer." It is clear, however, that Kentucky law has rejected Judge Friendly's approach, which focuses exclusively on foreseeability and refuses to consider motive.

Instead, Kentucky's approach is precisely the standard advanced by Prosser and Keeton when they explained that "in general, the master is held liable for any intentional tort committed by the servant where its purpose, however misguided, is wholly or in part to further the master's business." Prosser and Keeton at 505. Thus, if the servant "acts from purely personal motives ... which [are] in no way connected with the employer's interests, he is considered in the ordinary case to have departed from his employment, and the master is not liable." This sound approach also conforms to the economic theory of vicarious liability, because when the employee acts for solely personal reasons, the employer's ability to prevent the tort is limited.

Clearly, in confronting Patterson and shooting out the truck's tires, Blair, Jr. was acting to further the business interests of Courtesy. At the very least, his conduct was at least incidental to the conduct that was authorized by Courtesy. Here, just as in *Frederick*, Blair, Jr. was acting to protect his employer's property. In fact, Blair, Jr.'s testimony explicitly confirmed this motive. And perhaps most importantly, there is no evidence that he sought to serve any personal purpose by his actions. Quite simply, he engaged in the act to further his employer's business interests. Although the act was criminal, it was not so outrageous to indicate that the motive was a personal one. Therefore, the jury's finding that Blair, Jr. acted within the scope of employment, thereby imposing vicarious liability on Courtesy, is supported by the evidence and the law of this Commonwealth. The decision of the Court of Appeals on the issue of vicarious liability is reversed.

Concluding Note on Tort Liability

Two additional problems regarding an employer's tort liability need to be discussed:

1. A minor is not necessarily the employee of his or her parents. Thus, in the absence of a special statute, the parent is not liable for the torts of a minor child unless the child was acting as an employee in the scope of employment for the parent. The parent can, of course, be held liable for his or her own wrongful act in negligently supervising the child. Also, several states have passed statutes making parents liable within set limits for intentional property damage caused by a minor child.

2. Although the subject of bailments is beyond the scope of this discussion, it should be mentioned that a bailee is not necessarily the employee of the bailor. A bailment occurs when the owner of an item of property (the bailor) turns over temporary custody (not ownership) of the item to the bailee for any reason. The bailor ordinarily is *not* liable to third parties for torts committed by the bailee while using the bailor's property. The bailor is liable, however, if he or she was negligent in entrusting the item to one whom he or she knew not to be qualified or capable of handling it safely. Otherwise, the bailor generally is liable only if the bailee was acting as the bailor's employee in the scope of employment at the time of the tort. Two exceptions exist with regard to *bailments of automobiles:*

    a. A few states follow the *family purpose doctrine.* Under that judge-made doctrine, a member of the family is treated as the employee of the head of the household when driving the family car, regardless of whether such a relationship actually existed.

    b. A few states have passed *owner-consent* statutes, which hold the owner of an automobile liable to a third party injured by the negligence of anyone who is driving it with the consent of the owner. This liability exists regardless of any employer-employee relationship and regardless of whether the owner was personally negligent.

Criminal Liability

As a general rule, a superior cannot be criminally prosecuted for a subordinate's wrongful act unless the superior expressly authorized it. Thus, if Y, a subordinate, while acting within the scope of her employment, injures T, and T dies, Y's superior can be held liable in a civil suit for damages but cannot be subjected to criminal liability. Any criminal responsibility rests on the shoulders of the subordinate. The rule exists because crimes ordinarily require intent, and the superior in this situation had no criminal intent.

Exceptions to the rule usually fall within one of two categories:

1. The statute making the particular act a crime may specifically provide for placing criminal responsibility on the superior. For example, the federal antitrust laws provide for criminal penalties to be levied against corporations, which can commit crimes only through their human agents.

Legal Focus

International

The legal concept that an employer can be held liable for the wrongful acts of an employee committed within the scope of employment is not just an American rule. It has been applied for centuries in various legal systems, including those derived from the English common law, the Roman civil law, and others. Today, it operates to impose both tort liability and criminal responsibilities on employers throughout the world. In fact, it is used to impose criminal liability on employers in many nations to a greater extent than in the United States.

An example is found in Anklagemyndigheden [Public Prosecutor] v. Hansen & Son, decided in 1990 by the European Court of Justice (the judicial organ of the European Union (EU). In that case, an EU regulation required truck drivers to drive no more than eight hours consecutively and to have a rest period of at least eleven hours between eight-hour driving stints. Hansen & Son was a trucking company based in Denmark. One of its drivers was found to have violated the EU rest-period regulation while hauling cargo in the Netherlands. The regulation provided for criminal penalties; both the driver and his employer were prosecuted, convicted, and ordered to pay fines in Denmark. The European Court of Justice ultimately upheld both convictions. The employer's conviction was upheld because the driver was acting within the scope of his employment at the time of the violation. The court held that it was irrelevant that the employer, Hansen & Son, had taken all reasonable steps to ensure that its drivers complied with the regulation and was not blameworthy in any other way. The company's liability was based purely on the concept of respondeat superior.

2. A superior can sometimes be criminally prosecuted under statutes that do not require intent for a violation. A specific example is the offense of selling adulterated food under the federal Food, Drug, and Cosmetic Act. Other examples can be found in some state laws regulating liquor sales and the accuracy of weights of goods sold on that basis.

CHAPTER **25**

PARTNERSHIPS NATURE, FORMATION, AND PROPERTY

- The Nature of Partnerships
- Formation of a Partnership
- Partnership Property

The Nature of Partnerships
Governing Law

Court-developed common law provided the governing rules for partnerships until 1914, when the Uniform Partnership Act (UPA) was promulgated by the American Law Institute and the National Conference of Commissioners on Uniform State Laws. The UPA codified most of the common law rules and significantly altered some of them. It was updated by the Revised Uniform Partnership Act (RUPA) of 1994 (amended in 1997). UPA is still in effect in many states. The rest have adopted some version of RUPA. The discussion in this chapter will focus on rules that the two uniform acts have in common, although some important differences will be noted.

Defining a Partnership

Both UPA and RUPA define a *partnership* as "an association of two or more persons to carry on as co—owners a business for profit." This definition can be broken into elements as follows.

Association

The term *association* indicates that a partnership is a voluntary arrangement formed by agreement.

Person

The term *person* includes not only individuals but also corporations, other partnerships, and other types of associations. With regard to minors and insane persons, the same basic rules apply to partnership agreements as to other types of contracts. Thus a minor may treat the partnership agreement with the other partners as voidable. The minor usually can also repudiate personal liabilities to creditors beyond the amount of his or her investment in the business. But this investment is subject to the claims of partnership creditors, although it is the maximum liability that the minor ordinarily can incur.

Co—owners

The partners are co—owners of the business, which distinguishes them from those who are merely agents, servants, or other subordinates. Courts often say that true partners share in three communities of interest: capital, management, and profits. Typically, partners will contribute money, property, or services to the enterprise's capital, have a voice in management, and enjoy a right to share in the profits.

To Carry on a Business

The term *business* includes "every trade, occupation, or profession."

For Profit

An association cannot be a partnership unless the purpose of forming it is to make profits directly through its business activities. Associations for other purposes (including religious, patriotic, or public improvement purposes, or furtherance of the *separate* economic interests of members) are not partnerships, even if they engage in business transactions. Thus the local chapter of a fraternal lodge cannot be a partnership, and the rights and duties of partners cannot attach to its members. For example, individual members are not personally liable for debts incurred for the lodge by its officers unless an agency relationship has been expressly created.

The Entity Theory Versus the Aggregate Theory

Drafters of the UPA could not agree as to whether a partnership should be treated (1) like a corporation, as an *entity*, separate and apart from its owners, or (2) as it traditionally had been at common law as a mere *aggregation* of its partners. They eventually reached a compromise so that a partnership today is treated as an entity for some purposes and as a mere aggregation for others. In a sense, the UPA has retained the **aggregate theory** by defining a partnership as "an association of two or more persons. . ." The pass–through taxation feature of partnerships is also consistent with an aggregation theory.

On the other hand, the UPA uses the **entity theory** for selected purposes. For example, the UPA recognizes the concept of partnership property and allows a partnership to own and convey property in the partnership name. In addition, it places liability for acts of the partners in conducting partnership business primarily on the partnership itself and the partnership property, and only secondarily on individual partners and their individual property. Also, under various UPA provisions every partner is an agent *of the partnership,* capital contributions are made *to the partnership,* books are kept *for the partnership*, and every partner is accountable as a fiduciary *to the partnership*. The UPA even defines the term *person* to include partnerships.

RUPA specifically provides that a partnership is an entity. Although it retains pass-through taxation, of course, RUPA provides that a partnership is distinct from its partners, that property can be owned and transferred in the partnership name, and that the partnership entity can survive the death of one of its partners.

Formation of a Partnership
The Partnership Agreement

Unlike corporations, which are created by statute and require filings with the state, partnerships are formed by the parties' agreements express or implied. Although no formal filing is requisite to the formation of a general partnership, under RUPA a "Statement of Partnership Authority" may be voluntarily filed with the Secretary of State's office. The primary purpose is to facilitate the sale of real property, because the statement must specify the partners required to sign a transfer of real property held in the partnership name. The statement may contain other information, including the authority (or limitations upon the authority) of various partners.

Because parties need not have any written (or even oral) agreement before becoming partners, UPA and RUPA serve as "form contracts" that provide the rules for partnerships in the absence of express agreement. By agreement, the partners may vary the form terms to suit their purposes, with some limitations. Under RUPA, for example, partners may not prejudice rights of third parties, waive the duties of loyalty or good faith and fair dealing that partners owe one another, unreasonably restrict partners' access to books and records, or unreasonably reduce the duty of care partners owe each other.

Despite the fact that a written partnership agreement is usually not required, it is highly desirable. Formation of a business is a substantial undertaking and should not be left to the oral declarations of the parties—for several reasons:

1. There are many inherent problems in proving the exact terms of an oral agreement.
2. Numerous problems (such as those relating to taxation) can be satisfactorily resolved only by a carefully drafted written instrument.
3. If the parties go through the process of drafting a formal document with the aid of an attorney, they are much more likely to foresee many problems they otherwise would not have thought about. For example, matters such as procedures for expulsion of a partner or for settlement of disputes between partners are easily overlooked because they seem so remote when the partnership is first formed.

Desirable Elements of a Partnership Agreement

The formal partnership agreement, often referred to as the articles of partnership, should clearly reflect the intent of the partners as to the rights and obligations they wish to assume in the business. What is contained in these articles will depend on the nature of the business and the desires of the partners, but ordinarily the written instrument should include such items as the following:

1. Name of the firm. The partnership is not required to have a firm name, but it is usually a good idea to have one. The name can be that of one or more of the partners, or it can be fictitious. (But it cannot be deceptively similar to that of another business for the purpose of attracting its customers.) If the name is fictitious, it usually must be registered. Most states have **assumed name statutes** (sometimes called **fictitious name statutes**) that require any firm, including a partnership, to register with a state official the fictitious name under which the firm is doing business. The purpose of such statutes is to enable creditors of the firm to learn the identities of those responsible.
2. Nature and location of the business.
3. Date of commencement and duration of the partnership.
4. Amount of contributions in money or property each partner is to make (in other words, the amount of their investments in the business).
5. Time within which the contribution of each partner is to be made.

6. Salaries and drawing accounts of each partner, if such are desired.
7. Division of work and duties of each partner, including rights in management.
8. Admission requirements for new partners.
9. Each partner's proportionate share of net profits while the business is continuing to operate and upon dissolution.
10. Any proposed restrictions on the power of individual members to bind the firm.
11. Clear delineation of partnership assets as distinguished from individual partners' assets.
12. Bookkeeping and accounting methods to be used and location of and access to books.
13. Procedures for withdrawal or exclusion of a partner.
14. Indication of whether withdrawal or exclusion causes dissolution, and if not, rules for continuing the business after such an event.
15. Method for determining the value of a withdrawing or excluded partner's interest.
16. Requirements and procedures for notice to partners and partnership creditors in case of dissolution.
17. Which partner or partners will be in charge of winding up the business upon dissolution.
18. Procedures for settling disputes between partners, such as submitting them to arbitration.

Determining the Existence of a Partnership

When the parties have clearly expressed their intentions in a written instrument, there is ordinarily no difficulty in determining whether a partnership exists. But when the parties have not been explicit in declaring their intentions, problems frequently arise. The most fundamental, of course, is whether a partnership has even been *created*. This issue arises with surprising frequency, because of its importance in regard to the rights and obligations of the "partners" and third parties as well. For example, a creditor may seek to hold several persons liable for the transactions of one of them on the ground that they are partners. Or one party might claim that he and another are partners and that the other party has violated a resulting fiduciary duty by having a conflicting business interest.

When the existence of a partnership is disputed by an interested party, such existence becomes a question of fact to be decided on the basis of all the circumstances. Typically, no single factor is controlling, and the court's ultimate decision commonly is based on several considerations. *Intent* of the parties is important, but not the labels that they use. If persons associated in business call themselves *partners*, that label is indicative, but not necessarily controlling. Similarly, the fact that persons believe and perhaps even explicitly state that they are *not* partners is irrelevant if the actual substance of the relationship they intend to create is what the law calls a *partnership*.

Substance controls over form. The most important substantive factors in determining the parties' intent are (1) sharing of profits and losses, (2) joint control of the business, and (3) joint ownership and control of capital or property.

Sharing of Profits and Losses

If there has been no sharing of profits or agreement to share them, a court is very likely to find that no partnership exists. On the other hand, the sharing of *net profits* (as opposed to mere *gross revenues*) usually gives rise to a rebuttable presumption that a partnership exists. That the presumption is rebuttable means that it may be overcome by the weight of contrary evidence, but it remains a potent aid to the party seeking to establish the existence of a partnership who has the burden of proof in such matters.

There are certain situations, however, where the sharing of profits does *not* give rise to a rebuttable presumption of partnership existence. These are situations where logical alternative explanations for the sharing of profits are present. Following are several situations that fall in this category.

First, no presumption of partnership exists where the profits are received by a creditor in payment of a debt. For example, O, the owner of a business in financial difficulty, owes a debt to X. In settlement of this debt, X agrees to accept a certain percentage of O's profits for a period of time. No inference of partnership is created by the sharing of profits, and no partnership exists between O and X (unless, perhaps, X takes title to a portion of the business property and takes an active role in managing the business).

Second, no presumption of partnership arises where profits are received as wages by an employee. Employers often key salary bonuses to profits in order to encourage employees to work harder. This is an obvious and common explanation for the sharing of profits that indicates nothing more than an employment relationship, so long as X withholds federal taxes from employees' salaries, exercises control over the employees, and does not allow them any management powers or co-ownership of business property.

Third, where the profits are received as consideration for the sale of property no presumption of partnership exists. When an item of property having uncertain value is sold to someone who expects to use it in carrying on a business, it is sometimes agreed that the price payable to the seller will include a share of the profits made from use of the property.

Two common examples are *goodwill* and *trademarks*. The seller often retains no ownership of the property or control over its use; nor is he or she usually expected to share any losses incurred by the buyer. In many instances this is simply the best way of computing the value of a particular property right. No partnership presumption is created by such an arrangement.

Other situations where sharing of profits does not give rise to a presumption of partnership are where the profits are received as rent by a landlord, as an annuity by a spouse or representative of a deceased partner, or as interest on a loan by a creditor.

Absence of an agreement to share losses does not necessarily weigh heavily against the existence of a partnership. Often partners will agree to share profits, but they may not even consider that they might suffer a loss, or they may believe it will bring bad luck to even think about the possibility. Hence, they will have no agreement as to losses even though they clearly intended to be partners. On the other hand, if there is an agreement to share losses, an extremely strong presumption of partnership arises. As noted previously, there are many non−partnership explanations for why persons would agree to share profits, but there are few nonpartnership reasons that would explain an agreement to share losses.

Joint Control and Management

Although sharing of profits is a cardinal element of the partnership, another factor often felt to be important by the courts is whether the parties have *joint control* over the operation of the business. For instance, where sharing of profits by itself is not sufficient to indicate existence of a partnership, the addition of the factor of joint control might well cause a court to hold that a partnership has been created. *Exercise of management powers* is obviously very strong evidence of control. But the fact that management powers have been expressly delegated to one or more of the partners or to one more nonpartner managers does not mean that those who do not manage are not true partners if the other facts indicate that they are. In a sense, agreeing to relinquish control is itself an exercise of the right of control.

Joint Ownership of Property

Another factor that frequently finds its way into court opinions is *joint ownership of assets*. Of the three basic tests for existence of a partnership, this is the least important, although it certainly is taken into account by the court, along with all the other evidence. The UPA takes the position that co−ownership of property does not, of itself, establish a partnership. An inference of partnership is also not necessarily created by the fact that the co−owners share any profits made by the use of the property. This seems at first to be inconsistent with our earlier discussion of the presumption of partnership that is usually engendered by profit sharing. But there is no real inconsistency. In the case of co−owners of property, the sharing of profits made from the property is a basic part of co−ownership. In most cases the owner of property wishes to receive whatever income it generates; thus it is reasonable to assume that co−owners will want to share the income from their jointly owned property. A partnership should not be presumed simply because the owners act in a way totally consistent with simple co−ownership.

On the other hand, if the property and its use are only part of a larger enterprise, and the parties share profits from the whole enterprise, an inference of partnership is justified. For instance, co−ownership of a commercial building and sharing of its rental income by A and B does not necessarily make them partners. If, however, they use part of the building as premises for the operation of a going business of some type, sharing not only the rental income from the remainder of the building but also the profits and management of the business, they are quite likely to be considered partners.

The following case illustrates the type of evidence considered by courts in determining whether a partnership exists.

H2O'C LTD V. BRAZOS
Missouri Court of Appeals, 114 S.W.3d 397 (2003)

O'Connor was an engineering professor and around 1980 Brazos began to work in O'Connor's lab. Later, O'Connor employed Brazos to work on externally funded research projects on an as–needed basis. In 1993, O'Connor and Brazos began conducting drinking water analysis for profit. Initially, they were paid directly and individually. In October of 1993, O'Connor incorporated H2O'C Ltd. with himself and his wife as the only shareholders. The corporation was formed by O'Connor to handle the money received from the consulting projects and for tax purposes. Brazos did most of the lab and field work, while O'Connor handled budgeting and other paperwork. Until their business relationship ended in March 1997, O'Connor and Brazos provided consulting services on several projects, including a five–year project with Premium Standard Farms that Brazos brought in as a client.

The men did not sign a partnership agreement nor file partnership tax returns. During their association, both Brazos and O'Connor were consulting and receiving compensation on projects that were not a part of H2O'C. From 1993 through 1996, Brazos filed his individual income tax returns listing his occupation as a sole proprietor consultant.

According to Brazos, he and O'Connor agreed to split the revenues equally. He also said "He told me I was a partner; he allowed me to act like a partner; he encouraged me to act like a partner. I'm a partner." Further, he presented at trial the testimony of two individuals who stated that the relationship was characterized as a partnership. In addition, Brazos offered a letter written by O'Connor in which O'Connor said he was worried about Brazos purchasing a $40,000 microscope. In the letter, O'Connor stated "I've been fretting about your microscope dilemma all night. So, I thought I would write as both friend and business partner to share my thoughts."

In 1997, the men's relationship began deteriorating. Brazos complained that his amount of compensation, specifically from the Premium Standard Farms project, was being reduced from that which they had agreed. Brazos testified that in July before the end of their association he confronted O'Connor and asked, "Are we in a partnership or not" Brazos then began trying "to separate along financial lines." When the separation was complete, Brazos filed for unemployment. The Division of Employment Security determined that he was not qualified for benefits because he left work voluntarily without good cause attributable to the work or the employer.

Following the end of their business relationship in March 1997, the O'Connors sued requesting the return of certain items in Brazos' possession. Brazos filed a counterclaim, requesting a determination of a partnership and distribution of assets.

The trial court found that a partnership existed, and this appeal followed.

Lowenstein, Judge:

In Meyer v. Lofgren, 949 S.W.2d 80 (Mo.App. 1997), this court addressed the statutory and judicial definitions of partnership:

"A partnership is statutorily defined as 'an association of two or more persons to carry on as co–owners a business for profit.' A partnership has been judicially defined as a contract of two or more competent persons to place their money, effects, labor and skill, or some or all of them, in lawful commerce or business and to divide the profits and bear the loss in certain proportions. The partnership agreement need not be written but may be expressed orally or implied from the acts and conduct of the parties . . ., with the intent of the parties serving as the primary criterion for determining whether such a relationship exists."

Brazos, as the party seeking to establish the existence of a partnership, has the burden to prove its existence by clear, cogent and convincing evidence. The intent necessary to find a partnership is not the intent to form a partnership, but the intent to enter a relationship that legally constitutes a partnership. "Indicia of a partnership relationship include a right to a voice in management of the partnership business, a share of the profits of the partnership business, and a corresponding *risk of loss* and liability to partnership creditors." Morrison v. Labor & Indus. Rel. Com'n, 23 S.W.2d 902 (Mo.App. 2000).

Since there is no written partnership agreement in this case, the agreement or existence of a partnership, or lack thereof, may be implied by the conduct of the parties. The conduct of the parties does not support a finding that a partnership existed. Brazos alleges that he and O'Connor formed a partnership and that the establishment of H2O'C "in no way affected the partnership relationship." In fact, he testified that he considered himself one partner and H2O'C or the O'Connor family the other partner. However, H2O'C was incorporated after Brazos alleges that the partnership began. H2O'C was the primary entity that handled all aspects of the consulting services. For example, all of the contracts for the projects named H2O'C, and not Brazos and O'Connor individually or as partners, as a party; the payments resulting from the contracts were paid to H2O'C; Brazos received compensation through H2O'C; he had no interest in H2O'C; and all advertisements and papers were completed in the name of H2O'C. No evidence suggests that a partnership existed separate from H2O'C.

Brazos argues that he and O'Connor split the gross profits equally, and each bore his own expenses. While the decision to divide profits may be prima facie evidence of a partnership, assuming there was a division of the profits, "the sharing of profits 'is far from conclusive, and this is particularly true where the parties, although agreeing to divide profits, do not agree to share any possible losses." Nesler v. Reed, 703 S.W.2d 520 (Mo.App. 1985). Although a specific agreement to share losses may, in some instances, be implied, the implication may be overcome by evidence to the contrary. Here, the presumption of an agreement to share in the losses is rebutted by Brazos' testimony——there is utterly no evidence that O'Connor and Brazos agreed or intended to share in any loss. Brazos testified that he did not intend to match any losses and that O'Connor "never agreed to match any losses" that he incurred.

Further, the testimony at trial was that this was a sharing of gross revenues, not net income. Brazos testified that the agreement was to pay their own expenses, and it appears that most of the overhead was paid by O'Connor. The fact that expenses were not borne by the partnership further refutes the existence of a partnership since this fact suggest that there was no true sharing of profits in this case. Brinkley v. Palmer, 10 S.W.3d 166 (Mo.App. 1999) held that "gross revenues are not profits and an agreement to pay a percentage of gross revenues is not the sharing of profits."

Moreover, no inference of a partnership is drawn where a share of the profits was received by an employee in payment of wages. Here, O'Connor prepared budgets for each of the projects based upon the amount of work he expected to expend. Brazos' compensation was based upon these amounts. He even testified that the "division of the profits" in the initial contract was a "division of what we considered to be compensation for our work and our expenses." Thus, it is clear that he was being paid for services rendered on each project. Brazos' received compensation from H2O'C in which taxes, social security and unemployment was withheld. He also received W-2 forms from the corporation. While testimony from Brazos' brother, a CPA, indicates that it is not unusual for a partner to consider himself an employee and receive W-2 forms, there is no evidence that any other "sharing of profits" occurred apart from this compensation for services. Further, Brazos' individual income taxes during this time list his occupation as a sole proprietor and consultant. Finally, and likely the most significant indication that a partnership did not exist, when his association with O'Connor ended, he filed an unemployment claim with the Division of Employment Security. This was after consultation with his brother who was an accountant. He did not petition the court at that time to dissolve the partnership and enter an accounting to distribute the assets of the partnership, but chose instead to seek unemployment benefits.

Apart from his assertion that there was a sharing of profits, Brazos has failed to point to an intention or agreement to become partners or to enter into a relationship that legally constitutes a partnership. Brazos has provided no indication that a discussion occurred between him and O'Connor concerning an intent or agreement to create a partnership to perform the consulting work. Brazos testified that he questioned O'Connor about their relationship several times before the March 1997 break-up. If there was an agreement to enter into a partnership, then Brazos would have

had no question about the relationship. Brazos may have wanted to be a partner, but the evidence does not support a co-ownership of a business. The overwhelming evidence is that H2O'C was the business entity involved in the consulting services and O'Connor exercised control over the business enterprise. Brazos has provided no evidence of a "definite and specific agreement" to enter into a partnership or to conduct business as partners. Shea v. Helling, 826 S.W.2d 419 (Mo.App. 1992).

Likewise, as indicated above, there is no evidence that Brazos had a voice in the management of the business. Because each of the contracts were executed in the name of H2O'C, Brazos, who stated that he did not have any interest in H20'C, did not have the authority to enter into contracts on its behalf. It does not appear from the testimony that he had any control over the financial aspects of the relationship. While he may have had authority to order items needed for the project, he had no ability to disperse funds to pay for those items since they were paid through H20'C, nor was there any other separate partnership account from which Brazos could disperse funds to pay partnership expenses.

The conduct of the parties in this case does not evidence the existence of a partnership. There was no true sharing of the profits. More importantly, under the facts here there was absolutely no evidence of any agreement or even thought given to sharing in the losses of the partnership or in assuming the burden of the partnership expenses. Nor was there evidence of a specific intention to enter into a partnership relationship. Brazos did not participate in the management of the partnership. He had no authority to issue checks or enter into contracts on behalf of the partnership. Thus, there are no indicia of a partnership relationship.

Reversed.

Partnership By Estoppel

Under both RUPA and UPA, people may be deemed partners for liability purposes, even if they are not truly partners. Under RUPA they are called "purported partners," and under UPA they are called "partners by estoppel." Under both approaches, the essential notion is that someone who holds himself out as a partner, or who allows himself to be held out as a partner, may be liable as a partner to a third party who relied upon the appearance to her detriment. Thus, if the ABC Bank loans money to the XYZ partnership because wealthy Ms. Q holds herself out as an XYZ partner (or allows X, Y, and Z to do so), it is equitable to hold Ms. Q liable for the debt even if she did not meet the legal criteria of a partner and did not intend to be a partner.

These doctrines apply much more often to contract cases than tort cases because tort plaintiffs are seldom able to meet the reliance requirement. Obviously, Mrs. Q could not be held liable as a purported partner on the basis of XYZ's representations that were unknown to her.

Partnership Property

A partnership commonly requires various types of property for the operation of its business, including, for example, real estate, equipment, inventory, or intangibles such as cash or securities. Under the UPA, a partnership is recognized as an entity insofar as property ownership is concerned and can own either real estate or other types of property. The UPA uses the phrase **tenants in partnership** to describe the status of individual partners with respect to the partnership property. (The rights that individual partners have regarding partnership property will be discussed in the next chapter.)

Although today a partnership can (and quite often does) own such property itself, it is not essential that it own any property at all. The partners themselves may wish to individually own the property needed for the operation of the business.

One of RUPA's most important changes is elimination of the tenancy−in−partnership concept. RUPA eliminates any mention of a partner's rights in specific partnership property, making it clear that partners are not co−owners of partnership property and have no interest in it that can be transferred. The partnership entity owns partnership property under RUPA.

For a number of reasons it is sometimes important to determine whether an item of property belongs to the partnership or to an individual partner. Among them:

1. In most states, creditors of the partnership must resort to partnership property for satisfaction of their claims before they can take property of individual partners.
2. The right of a partner to use partnership property is usually limited to purposes of furthering the partnership business.
3. The question of ownership can also be important with regard to taxation, distribution of assets upon dissolution of the partnership, and other matters.

Factors in Determining Ownership

Agreement

The ownership of property is determined by *agreement* of the partners. Sound business practices dictate that the partners should explicitly agree on the matter and keep accurate records of their dealings with property. Unfortunately, partners often fail to indicate clearly their intentions as to whether ownership of particular items of property rests with the partnership or with one or more individual partners. In such cases, the courts consider all pertinent facts in an attempt to discover the partners' *intent*. Where it appears that the matter of property ownership never occurred to the partners, so that they actually had no definite intention, the court determines which of the possible alternatives— partnership or individual ownership—more closely accords with their general intentions and objectives for the business as a whole and which is fairer both to partners and to third parties.

Legal Title

In the absence of a clear agreement as to ownership, the strongest evidence of property ownership is the name in which the property is held, often referred to as the **legal title.** If an item of property is held in the name of the partnership, courts will hold it to be partnership property in almost every case. This principle most often plays a part where *real estate* is involved, because a deed has been executed in the name of some party and usually has been "recorded" (made part of official county records). Such formal evidence of ownership is frequently not available for property other than real estate, but if it is available, it will play the same important role. For example, this principle applies to motor vehicles, for which there is usually a state–issued certificate of title.

Problems regarding ownership seldom arise if title to the property in question is held in the partnership name. Those that do arise usually occur in either of two situations: (1) where the property is of a type for which there is no deed, certificate, or other formal evidence of ownership; or (2) where title is held in the name of one or more individual partners, but there is a claim that it is actually partnership property. In the first instance, evidence must be presented to establish just where ownership actually rests. In the second, evidence must be introduced to overcome the presumption of individual ownership and prove that the property actually belongs to the partnership. No single factor is controlling; the court's determination ordinarily is based on the cumulative weight of several factors.

Specific Factors

Property *purchased with partnership funds* is presumed to be partnership property. This presumption is rebuttable, but typically it is very difficult to overcome.

Evidence indicating that the property has been used in the business of the partnership also weighs in favor of the conclusion that it is partnership property. This factor, however, is not conclusive because courts realize that it is not uncommon for an individual partner to allow his or her property to be used in the partnership business without intending to surrender ownership of it.

If property is carried in the partnership books as an asset of the firm, this strongly indicates that it is partnership property. The inference is even stronger if an unpaid balance on the property's purchase price is carried in the records as a partnership liability.

Among other factors that a court may consider in determining whether specific property belongs to the partnership or an individual partner are the following:

1. If property had been purchased with funds of an individual partner, the fact that partnership funds were later used to improve, repair, or maintain the property *tends* to show that it now belongs to the partnership. (But additional evidence usually is required, because most courts have been unwilling to infer that the property is owned by the partnership *solely* on the basis that partnership funds were later used to maintain it.)

2. The fact that *taxes* on the property have been paid by the partnership can be important.

3. The receipt by the partnership of *income* generated by the property is evidence that the partnership is the owner.

4. Any other conduct of those involved is considered if it tends to indicate their intent regarding property ownership.

This discussion and the *Eckert* case are based on the UPA, but RUPA provisions are comparable.

The following case illustrates the strong presumption that property acquired with partnership funds or labor is partnership property, as well as some of the problems that may sometimes result from having partnership property in the name of one of the partners instead of the partnership.

ECKERT V. ECKERT
Supreme Court of North Dakota, 425 N.W. 2d 914 (1988)

Ben Eckert was Donovan Eckert's uncle. In 1959 the two formed a farming and ranching partnership called the "E-7 Ranch." No formal partnership agreement was ever executed. Donovan died in 1982, and Gaila Eckert, the representative of Donovan's estate, filed suit seeking dissolution and liquidation of the partnership.

Ben and Gaila agreed on the division of all partnership property except for cooperative patronage credits with the Minot Farmers Union Elevator, Minot Farmers Union Oil, and Harvest States Cooperative. Gaila asserted that these patronage credits are partnership property which should be equally split. Ben asserted that these credits were titled in his name individually and are not partnership property.

A portion of the cooperatives' profits each year are allocated to each member–patron and the cooperative is required to pay out at least 20 percent of this amount in cash to the member–patron. The remaining 80 percent is retained by the cooperative but shows on its books as a patronage credit to the member patron. Although this portion is not distributed to the member–patron at the time it is earned, the member patron must report it as income. These unpaid distributions typically are retained by the cooperative until the member–patron reaches a certain age or the cooperative's board of directors votes to "retire" the credits for a specified past year.

In this case, patronage credits were earned on business generated by the partnership. The 20 percent annual cash distributions were paid to Ben Eckert, who placed them in the partnership account and included them as income to the partnership on the partnership tax return. The partnership return then allocated one–half of this income to Ben and one–half to Donovan. The 80 percent patronage credits were also included as partnership income each year, and again one–half of this income was allocated to each partner.

Upon reaching age 65 in 1978, Ben began receiving distributions of the retained patronage credits from Farmers Union Oil. Between 1978 and 1983, Ben received $28,612.28 of those credits. Ben kept all of these funds. None of the retained patronage credits earned on partnership business with Farmers Union Elevator and Harvest States had been distributed at the time of trial.

The trial court placed the burden on Gaila to prove that the patronage credits earned through partnership business were partnership property. In large part because the credits were held in Ben's name, the trial court concluded that Gaila had failed to meet her burden of proof and dismissed her claim. Gaila appealed.

Gierke, Justice:

The trial court relied heavily upon the fact that the patronage credits were held in Ben's name, but that fact is not conclusive of the issue of ownership. Property which is titled in the name of an individual partner may nevertheless be partnership property. The determination whether property held in the name of an individual partner belongs to the partnership is a question of fact. The relevant inquiry is whether the partners intended that the property in question be partnership property or individual property.

Section 45–05–07, N.D.C.C. [U.P.A. § 8], provides:

1. " All property originally brought into the partnership stock or subsequently acquired by purchase or otherwise, on account of the partnership, is partnership property.
2. " Unless the contrary intention appears, property acquired with partnership funds is partnership property."

The above–quoted provisions of the Uniform Act have consistently been construed to create a presumption that property acquired with partnership funds is partnership property. The presumption extends beyond purchases with partnership funds to any acquisition of property derived from partnership labor, materials, or other assets.

In this state, a presumption shifts the burden of proof to the party against whom it is directed. A review of the record in this case establishes that the presumption should have been applied and the burden of proof shifted to Ben. Ben does not dispute that the vast majority of the patronage credits were derived from partnership business with the cooperatives. Inasmuch as these credits were property acquired or derived through partnership funds, assets, labor, or materials, they are presumed to be partnership property... The burden then shifts to Ben to establish that there was an intention between the partners that the patronage credits earned through partnership business were to be Ben's individual property.

The judgment of the district court is reversed and the matter is remanded for a new trial in accordance with this opinion.

LEGAL FOCUS

In recent years accounting firms, and to a lesser degree law firms, have taken a beating from liability judgments. Traditionally, all major accounting firms were generally partnerships, but that created the real possibility that the individual partners might have to dip into their personal assets to pay massive judgments that have been assessed against accounting firms, especially for their audit activities, in recent years.

In light of this situation, most accounting firms (and law frims) have abandoned the traditional partnership form and sought alternative ways of organizing themselves to avoid this open–ended liability exposure. For example, some regional accounting firms are reorganizing from partnerships into separate professional corporations–one corporation for each state in which the firm does business. Under state professional corporation or professional association statutes, partners remain individually liable for their own malpractice, but their liability for the negligent acts of their former partners (now co–share–holders) is limited to the amount of money they have invested in the partnership.

More popular are limited liability partnerships (LLPs). All state have authorized LLPs in the past fifteen years or so. In Texas, for example, if a lawyer, doctor, accountant or similar professional files a proper statement with the secretary of state indicating that the firm is reorganizing into a limited liability partnership and that it maintains a certain level of liability insurance to cover typical malpractice cases, that professional will be individually liable only for his or her own malpractice (and the malpractice of those they directly supervise). Malpractice committed by other partners must be compensated out of the liability policy and firm assets only.

Such reforms are controversial because protection for the professionals may come at the expense of compensation for clients and others injured by malpractice. The struggle continues to be an effort to protect the economic viability of professional firms on the one hand, while adequately compensating malpractice victims and encouraging careful performance of professional obligations on the other. LLPs, along with the related new development— Limited Liability Companies (LLCs), are creating a revolution in the form of business organizations used by small firms (and some large firms) in this country.

PART V

SECURITIES REGULATION AND WILLS, TRUSTS, AND ESTATE PLANNING

CHAPTER **26**

SECURITIES REGULATION

- Introduction to Securities Regulation
- 1933 Act: Regulating the Issuance of Securities
- 1934 Act: Regulating the Trading of Securities
- State Regulation
- International Implications

THE GREAT STOCK market crash of 1929 was one of the most dramatic turning points in American economic history. That event not only ushered in the Great Depression but also heralded the creation of modern securities regulation. The much more recent Enron scandal again brought securities regulation to the headlines and caused Congress to pass the most significant amendments to the securities laws since they were originally enacted in the 1930s. Securities regulation is one of the most complicated areas of the law; and attorneys who practice in the securities field are among the most specialized and well paid of all lawyers. Although this vast, ever–changing subject may be intimidating to the novice, few persons in business can afford to remain ignorant of its effects on the way business is done in this country.

Many aspects of securities regulation are highly visible. Most Americans are familiar with the hustle and bustle of the New York Stock Exchange. Because of the popularity of mutual funds, tens of millions of Americans own stock, at least indirectly, in major corporations such as Microsoft and General Motors. Through securities regulation, the federal government, and to a lesser degree the states, regulate trading on the stock exchanges, protect the interests of shareholders, and attempt to ensure that the collapse of 1929 and the corporate fraud scandals of the early 21st Century are never repeated.

In this chapter, some of the more important aspects of the law of securities regulation are surveyed.

Introduction to Securities Regulation

A security such as a stock or a bond has no intrinsic value—its value lies in the ownership interest that it represents. The value of that ownership interest may be difficult to discover and easy to misrepresent. Securities may be produced in nearly limitless supply at virtually no cost by anyone with access to a printing press. For all these reasons, fraud, manipulation, and deceit have been frequent companions of the security. Government regulation of securities dates back to at least 1285, when King Edward I of England attempted to gain some control over the capital markets by licensing brokers located in London.

Securities regulation in the United States was almost nonexistent until 1911, when Kansas enacted securities laws. Other states soon followed suit, but without federal laws, companies could evade regulation by operating across state lines.

The 1920s were an especially active time for the issuance and trading of securities. The securities business was then characterized by price manipulation, deceitful practices, buying on excessive credit, and the abuse of secret information by corporate insiders. Of the $50 billion of new securities offered for sale in the United States in the 1920s, about one–half were worthless. The public and the national economy were devastated when stock market prices fell 89 percent between 1929 and 1933, a situation that finally produced federal action.

Federal Legislation

The first federal securities law was the *Securities Act of 1933* (the 1933 Act), which regulated the initial issuance of securities by companies. Fraudulent and deceptive practices were outlawed, and registration was required before a new security could be offered or sold, unless that security was entitled to an exemption from registration.

A year later, Congress passed the *Securities Exchange Act of 1934* (the 1934 Act), which extended federal regulation to trading in securities already issued and outstanding, required registration of securities brokers and dealers, and created the Securities and Exchange Commission (SEC), the federal agency that enforces the federal securities laws through its extensive powers.

During the next decade, Congress passed several other laws, including (a) the Trust Indenture Act of 1939, which helped protect persons investing in bonds, debentures, notes, and other debt securities by imposing qualification requirements on trustees of such instruments; (b) the Investment Company Act of 1940, which regulates mutual funds; and (c) the Investment Advisers Act of 1940, which required persons or firms who engaged in the business of advising others about investments for compensation to register with the SEC, as brokers and dealers are required to register under the 1934 Act. The Securities Investor Protection Act of 1970 amended the 1934 Act in response to a rash of failures in the late 1960s in the broker–dealer business. The act creates the Securities Investor Protection Corporation (SIPC), which manages a fund to protect investors from the failure of broker–dealers in the same manner as the Federal Deposit Insurance Corporation protects the customers of banks.

Courts have interpreted the 1934 Securities Exchange Act to allow injured investors to sue companies for securities fraud under Section 10(b) and Rule 10b–5. Each year many large class action lawsuits are filed, claiming huge amounts of damages. Lobbying by Silicon Valley high–tech firms and large accounting firms convinced Congress that many of these lawsuits were without merit and motivated primarily by the interests of plaintiffs' attorneys. Therefore, in 1995 Congress passed the Private Securities Litigation Reform Act (PSLRA) in 1995. The main thrust of the PSLRA was to make it harder for plaintiffs to win these class action fraud suits and more difficult for plaintiffs' attorneys to profit from them.

Perhaps coincidentally, just a few years after the PSLRA provided protection for potential defendants in securities fraud suits, the Enron scandal prompted Congress to pass the Sarbanes–Oxley Act (SOX) of 2002. SOX made many important changes in the other direction, including (a) stiffening penalties for securities fraud, (b) creating a new board to regulate audit firms, the Public Company Accounting Oversight Board (PCAOB), (c) requiring CEOs and CFOs to swear to the accuracy of their companies' major financial disclosure, upon penalty of prosecution, (d) restricting the types of non-audit services that accounting firms may provide to public company audit clients, (e) requiring that public companies have audit committees that are composed entirely of independent directors, (f) reducing investment banker influence over financial analysts in order to reduce conflicts of interest, and (g) requiring more and prompter disclosure of important corporate developments and of insider trading activity.

What Is a Security?

Securities are commonly thought of as the stock issued by corporations. The shares of common and preferred stock issued by corporations constitute a major type of security. These are *equity securities* which evidence an ownership interest in the corporation. Holders of equity securities are normally entitled to vote on important corporate matters and to receive dividends as their share of the corporate profits. The other major type of security is the debt security, such as the bond, note, or debenture. Holders of *debt securities* are creditors rather than owners. They have no voice in corporate affairs but are entitled to receive regular interest payments according to the terms of the bond or note.

Because the inventive human mind has devised an inordinate variety of investment interests, securities regulation goes beyond items that are clearly labeled *stocks or bonds*. Sec. 2(1) of the 1933 Act broadly defines *security* to include

> any note, stock, treasury stock, bond, debenture, evidence of indebtedness, certificate of interest or participation in any profit–sharing agreement, . . . investment contract, voting–trust certificate, fractional undivided interest in oil, gas or other mineral rights, or, in general, any interest or instrument commonly known as a 'security.''

This broad definition has, of necessity, been liberally construed by the courts. Interests in limited partnerships, condominiums, farm animals with accompanying agreements for their care, franchises, whiskey warehouse receipts, and many other varied items have been deemed to be securities.

The inclusion of the term *investment contract* in the 1933 Act's definition of security has produced much litigation. Some very interesting investment opportunities have been held to constitute investment contracts, as the following case illustrates.

SMITH V. GROSS
U.S. Ninth Circuit Court of Appeals, 604 F.2d 292 (1979)

Gross used a promotional newsletter to solicit buyer–investors to raise earthworms to help him reach his quota of selling earthworms to fishermen. Buyers were promised that the seller's instructions would enable them to have a profitable worm farm, that the time required was similar to that of a garden, that the worms doubled in quantity every 60 days, and that Gross would buy back all bait–size worms produced by buyers at $2.25 per pound.

The Smiths invested but later sued claiming that contrary to Gross's representations, the worms multiplied at a maximum of eight rather than 64 times per year and that the promised profits could be achieved only if the multiplication rate were as fast as represented and if Gross repurchased the Smiths' production at $2.25 per pound, which was much higher than the true market value. Gross could pay that amount only by selling the worms to new worm farmers at inflated prices.

The Smiths claimed that Gross made false representations, which violated the federal securities laws.

The federal district court dismissed the action for want of subject matter jurisdiction after concluding that no "security" was involved in the case. The Smiths appealed.

Per Curiam:

... The Smiths contend that the transactions between the parties involved an ... investment contract type of security. In SEC v. W. J. Howey Co., 328 U.S. 293, 301 (1946), the Supreme Court set out the conditions for an investment contract. "[t]he test is whether the scheme involves [1] an investment of money [2] in a common enterprise [3] with profits to come solely from the efforts of others." This court in SEC v. Glenn W. Turner Enterprises, Inc., 474 F.2d 476, 482 (9th Cir.), held that, despite the Supreme Court's use of the word "solely," the third element of the *Howey* test is "whether the efforts made by those other than the investor are the undeniably significant ones, those essential managerial efforts, which affect the failure or success of the enterprise." The *Turner* court defined a common enterprise as "one in which the fortunes of the investor are interwoven with and dependent upon the efforts and success of those seeking the investment or of third parties."

We find this case virtually identical with Miller v. Central Chinchilla Group, Inc., 494 F.2d 414 (8th Cir. 1974). In *Miller,* the defendants entered into contracts under which they sold chinchillas to the plaintiffs with the promise to repurchase the offspring. The plaintiffs were told that it was simple to breed chinchillas according to the defendants' instructions and that the venture would be highly profitable. The plaintiffs alleged that the chinchillas were difficult to raise and had a high mortality rate, and that the defendants could return the promised profits only if they repurchased the offspring and sold them to other prospective chinchilla raisers at an inflated price.

The *Miller* court focused on two features in holding there was an investment contract: (1) the defendants persuaded the plaintiffs to invest by representing that the efforts required of them would be very minimal; and (2) that if the plaintiffs diligently exerted themselves, they still would not gain the promised profits because those profits could be achieved only if the defendants secured additional investors at the inflated prices. Both of these features are present in the instant case. We find *Miller* to be persuasive and consistent with *Turner.*

There was a common enterprise as required by *Turner.* The Smiths alleged that, although they were free under the terms of the contract to sell their production anywhere they wished, they could have received the promised profits only if the defendants repurchased above the market price, and that the defendants could have repurchased above the market price only if the defendants secured additional investors at inflated prices. Thus, the fortune of the Smiths was interwoven with and dependent upon the efforts and success of the defendants.

We also find that here, as in *Miller* the third element of an investment contract set forth in *Turner*—that the efforts of those other than the investor are the undeniably significant ones— was present here. The *Miller* court noted that the plaintiffs there had been assured by the sellers that the effort needed to raise chinchillas was minimal. The significant effort necessary for success in the endeavor was that of the seller in procuring new investors who would purchase the chinchillas at inflated prices. Here, the Smiths alleged that they were promised that the effort necessary to raise worms was minimal and they alleged that they could not receive the promised income unless the defendants purchased their harvest.

We find the analysis in *Miller* persuasive and hold that the Smiths alleged facts that, if true, were sufficient to establish an investment contract. . . .

The judgment of the district court is reversed.

1933 Act: Regulating the Issuance of Securities

A major portion of federal securities regulation concerns the issuance of securities by companies. Congressional investigations after the 1929 stock market crash disclosed that enthusiasm for investment opportunities in the 1920s was often so great that large offerings of stock would be gobbled up by an investing public that knew virtually nothing about the selling company.

The goal of the 1933 Act is to protect the investing public. The 1933 Act is a disclosure statute frequently called the "Truth in Securities" law. The Act requires full disclosure by companies wishing to issue and sell stock to the public. By requiring such companies to file a registration statement with the SEC and to use an offering called a **prospectus** when attempting to sell securities, the law attempts to enable the investor to make an informed decision. The SEC, which is charged with enforcement of the law, does not attempt to pass on the value of the securities offered nor to advise investors to purchase or not purchase the securities of particular companies.

The 1933 Act also protects investors by prohibiting fraud and deceit in the distribution of shares that are registered. (Section 10(b) and Rule 10b–5 of the 1934 Act also punish such fraud, as well as fraud in the distribution of shares that the law does not require to be registered.)

Registration Process

Elements of the Process

Securities are distributed much like any product. The corporation selling securities to raise capital, the issuer, is analogous to the manufacturer of goods. *Underwriters* act as wholesalers, *dealers* act as retailers, and the investor is a consumer. By regulating the activities of the issuer, underwriter, and dealer, the 1933 Act seeks to ensure that the investor has access to adequate information before purchasing a particular security.

The keystones to the disclosure process are the registration statement and the prospectus, the contents of which are discussed presently. From 1933 until 2006, it was fair to say that: (i) Sec. 5(a) of the 1933 Act made it unlawful to sell or deliver any security without first filing with the SEC a registration statement that had become effective; (ii) Sec. 5(b)(2) made it unlawful to sell a security by means of a prospectus that did not meet statutory standards; (iii) Sec. 5(b)(2) made it unlawful to sell securities that were not accompanied or preceded by a prospectus; and (iv) Sec. 5(c) it illegal even to *offer* to sell or buy securities before a registration statement is filed. In December 2005, major changes became effective that will be discussed presently.

SEC Approval

The registration statement filed with the SEC is not automatically effective (with the exception of those filed by WKSIs that we are about to discuss). Rather, the staff of the SEC may review the statement for omissions and inaccuracies. Some reviews may be more thorough than others. Because of budgetary cutbacks and staff reductions, the SEC in recent years has had to give cursory reviews to many registration statements, reserving the full review process primarily for statements filed by new issuers selling to the public for the first time. Indeed, today most registration statements are not reviewed at all.

Sec. 8(a) of the 1933 Act provides that if the SEC is silent, the registration statement automatically becomes effective on the twentieth day after its filing. The registration process may be analyzed in terms of its three major time periods. The first stage of the process is the period before the registration statement is filed (the *prefiling period*). The second stage lasts from the filing of the statement until it becomes effective (the *waiting period*). The final stage is, of course, after the statement becomes effective (the *post–effective period*).

Prefiling Period. To prevent circumvention of the provisions of Sec. 5, issuers have traditionally been strictly limited during the prefiling period. The issuer could not sell or even offer to sell a security before the registration statement was filed. The term offer was broadly construed and encompassed not only formal sales campaigns, but any type of activity meant to "precondition" the market. A simple speech by a corporate executive or a press release about how well the company was doing could be improper if it "just happened" to be soon followed by the filing of a registration statement.

The only activities permitted during the prefiling period, other than normal advertising and communications with shareholders by an issuer, were preliminary negotiations between the issuer and underwriters. This was necessary because a large distribution of securities might require that an entire syndicate of underwriters be assembled.

Waiting Period. The purpose of the waiting period is to slow the distribution process so that the dealers and the public have time to familiarize themselves with the information disclosed in the registration process. Although traditionally no sales could be consummated during this period, certain types of offers were allowed, and underwriters could make arrangements with dealers for their assistance in distribution.

In addition to oral offers, certain types of written offers were permissible during the waiting period. For example, an issuer could place in *The Wall Street Journal* a short announcement known as a *tombstone ad* because it is usually surrounded by a black border. It could contain only minimal information about the offering.

The other primary goal of the waiting period, besides to slow the process down, was to ensure that the type of information that Congress thought investors needed would be widely distributed. Therefore, offers could also be made by use of a preliminary prospectus, which contains information from the registration statement then under review. These are called *red herring prospectuses*, because SEC rule 430 requires that a special legend be printed in red ink on each one labeling it a preliminary prospectus, stating that a registration statement has been filed but is not yet effective, that no final sale can be made during the waiting period, and that it does not constitute an offer to sell.

Post–Effective Period. Traditionally, once the registration statement became effective, sales of securities could be completed. However, the law still imposed requirements aimed at encouraging dissemination of information. With some exceptions, the issuer, underwriter, and dealer had to provide a copy of the final prospectus with every written offer, supplemental sales literature (call "free writing"), written confirmation of sale, or delivery of securities.

Thus, from 1933 to 2006, it is fair to say that the basic rule, simplistically put, was that (a) before the registration statement was filed, neither sales nor offers could occur; (b) during the waiting period, no sales could occur but oral offers and certain written offers...primarily those via red herring prospectus could be made; and (c) after the effective date, both offers and sales were permitted. This is still the case for most issuers, but the rules for the largest corporations have changed, as we are about to see.

Shelf Registration

Originally, an insurer was required to file a new registration statement every time it sought to initiate a new distribution of stock. However, in 1980 the SEC promulgated Rule 415 which established a system known as **shelf registration.** Under this system, the largest 2,000 or so companies in the nation were allowed to file one registration statement announcing their plans for sales of securities during the following two years. Then, whenever the company believed market conditions and its own financial needs required the sale of securities, it could issue the additional securities without going through the registration process described above to achieve SEC approval because it already had a registration statement and a prospectus "on the shelf." The shelf registration statement was periodically updated as the company filed its annual, quarterly, and interim reports with the SEC and they were incorporated by reference. Rule 415 enhanced the ability of large corporations to raise capital on short notice with a minimum of fuss.

The 2005 Amendments and WKSIs

Shelf registration worked so well and its theory seemed so sound that eventually the SEC got around to promulgating what might be called limited "company registration." The basic theory is that certain companies reveal so much about themselves through their periodic filings with the SEC (that we are about to discuss) and are so closely followed in the market that it makes little sense to require them to file registration statements every time they want to have a public offering of securities. Indeed, the restrictive rules regarding the types of offers that can be made in the pre–filing and waiting periods seem rather silly when applied to these companies.

So, in December 2005, new rules became effective that tailored the requirements we have just described for different types of issuers. For example, the most freedom was granted to Well–Known Seasoned Issuers (WKSIs)(pronounced "wick–sees"). These are the largest 30% of companies that are publicly traded in the U.S. They own approximately 90% of the assets controlled by public companies.

Under the new rules, WKSIs should file a registration statement every three years indicating roughly what securities they intend to issue during the following three–year period. After that, they need not worry about quiet periods, waiting periods, or the like. Whenever they wish to sell securities, they may file a registration statement supplement with the SEC that is immediately effective.

Furthermore, WKSIs are entitled to use "free writing prospectuses (FWPs) at all times. FWPs are written communications used to sell the companies' stock (other than the preliminary and final prospectuses). They may be used before or after the WKSI starts selling. The old rule of "no offer and no sale" before the registration statement is filed no longer applies to WKSIs. WKSIs need not worry about traditional waiting period restrictions. However, FWPs usually must be filed with the SEC and any misleading statements in them are actionable.

The new rules create a second cateory of issuer known as seasoned issuers. These firms meet the general requirements for being WKSIs in that they file regular reports with the SEC and have not suffered any major reporting problems or financial complications recently, but they are smaller than the WKSIs. Under the new rules, seasoned issuers can use FWPs after they file a registration statement, but not before. The new rules increase seasoned issuers' freedom to distribute information under such provisions as Rule 134, mentioned earlier.

Other new categories of issuers include unseasoned issuers, non–reporting issuers, and ineligible issuers. They also have more freedom from traditional restraints than existed before 2005, but they do not have all the flexibility of WKSIs and seasoned issuers. Firms doing IPOs, for example, must generally follow the pre–2005 rules. They are allowed to use FWPs after filing their registration statements (not before), but must precede or accompany the FWP with the red herring or final prospectus.

Disclosure Requirements

The information disclosure requirements of the 1933 Act and the 1934 Act were for a long time separate, often overlapping and sometimes conflicting. In 1980, with the shelf registration rules and then in 2005 with the new WKSI rules, the SEC has obviously attempted to harmonize and coordinate disclosure under the two acts.

Registration and Reporting

Section 12 of the 1934 Act requires all companies whose shares are traded on national exchanges such as the New York Stock Exchange, the American Stock Exchange, and any other companies with more than $10 million in assets and more than 500 shareholders in any one class to register their securities with the SEC. These companies are referred to as registered or reporting companies. The required registration statement must contain extensive information about such areas as the organization, financial structure, and nature of the business; the structure of present classes of stock; the directors and officers and their remuneration; important contracts; balance sheets; and profit–and–loss statements for the three preceding fiscal years.

Sec. 13 requires that the registration statement be continually updated with annual reports (called 10–Ks) and quarterly reports (10–Qs). In addition, if important facts change between quarterly reports, the company should amend the registration statement by use of an 8–K report. It is the contents of these reports that keep the investing public up to date regarding reporting companies' affairs and convinced the SEC to allow WKSIs to dispense with filing traditional registration statements.

Materiality

Exactly which details must be included in the registration statement and prospectus is a matter governed not only by statutes and rules but also by the concept of **materiality**. The most important element in the disclosure provisions of both the 1933 and 1934 Acts is that all matters that are important or material to an investor's decision should be disclosed. Materiality is an elusive concept, but the Supreme Court has described information as material "if there is a substantial likelihood that a reasonable shareholder would consider it important" in making an investment decision. This is usually limited to matters having a significant bearing on the economic and financial performance of the company.

Examples of material facts include an erratic pattern of earnings, an intention to enter into a new line of business, adverse competitive conditions, litigation with the government that might lead to imposition of a financially damaging fine, and a substantial disparity between the price at which the shares are being offered to the public and the cost of the shares owned by officers, directors, and promoters. The following case illustrates one application of the concept of materiality in the context of the 1933 Act disclosure requirements.

IN RE DOMAN HELICOPTERS, INC.
Securities and Exchange Commission, 41 S.E.C. 431(1963)

Doman Helicopters, Inc., was formed in 1945 but never was able to do business on a profitable basis. Except for one experimental model sold in 1950, two prototypes delivered to the Army in 1956 and 1957 (both subsequently repurchased by Doman), and one helicopter on loan to its Italian licensee, by 1962 Doman had never manufactured or sold any *helicopters. Instead, it had continually flirted with bankruptcy. By September 30, 1961, its accumulated losses totalled more than $5.7 million. On January 31, 1962, Doman's current liabilities were $292,446, whereas its assets were only $13,178.*

On April 19, 1962, Doman filed a Form S–1 registration statement proposing to offer publicly 681,971 shares, some to current shareholders, some to creditors, and some to the public. The contemplated price was $1.50 per share. Doman's future plans were predicated on development of a proposed helicopter, the D–10B.

The SEC commenced a proceeding under Sec. 8(d) of the 1933 Act to determine whether a stop order should issue suspending the effectiveness of Doman's registration statement. The focus of the investigation was on deficiencies in the prospectus.

The Commission:

. . .

1. Status and Prospectus of the Model D–10B. The prospectus describes the D–10B as though it were an existing and operational helicopter possessing superiority in specified respects [economy of operation, range, payload per dollar invested] over other helicopters offered on the market. . . . There is no adequate factual foundation for the[se] statements, and they were false and misleading.

The D–10B has never been flown or tested or even assembled in prototype form, crucial facts which are nowhere disclosed in the registration statement.

2. The Doman Hingeless Rotor System. The prospectus makes the following claims for the so–called "Doman Hingeless Rotor System": "In comparison with other devices, this system provides greater inherent stability in forward flight, less vibration in any flight attitude or maneuver, long life for the rotor and blade assembly, relatively low initial and maintenance costs and exceptional permissible range of the center of gravity of the fuselage and its cargo.". . .

These representations present in their totality a misleading picture of uniqueness and substantiated superiority of the Doman rotor system. That system has been used only on a few converted or prototype models. No production model using the Doman rotor system has ever been subjected to normal day to day usage by a user or customer. In such circumstances the unqualified claims as to superior durability and lower maintenance costs were not warranted, and it was deceptive to describe the system as 'fully developed and proven.'". . .

3. Efforts to Secure Defense Contracts. The prospectus makes only a passing reference to the fact that registrant unsuccessfully attempted to secure a military market for its helicopters. It does not disclose the nature of those attempts or of the action of the Department of Defense with respect to them. Registrant had from 1951 to 1962 made strenuous and persistent efforts to interest that Department in its proposals and devices. The Department made a number of tests with the two prototype helicopters that it purchased from the registrant and made an extensive study of the Doman rotor system. It found "no significant advantages in the Doman rotor system over other types, and those findings were reaffirmed upon successive reviews following objections raised by registrant. . . . Irrespective of the correctness of the Department's conclusions, they constitute a determination by the technical staff and responsible authorities of the largest single purchaser of helicopters that for their purposes registrant's rotor system had no special merit. Such determination was a significant adverse factor, and the failure to disclose it rendered the prospectus misleading.

4. Application of Proceeds. The prospectus stated that the proceeds of the offering would be used to develop the D–10B, but failed to state the order of priority in which the proceeds would be applied as required by Instruction 2 to Item 3 of Form S–1. The prospectus did not adequately disclose that except to the extent that the creditors to whom part of the offering is to be made elected to take stock in exchange for their debt claims, $292,466 of the proceeds from the public offering would first have to be applied to the liquidation of registrant's outstanding indebtedness, thereby reducing and perhaps exhausting the funds that the prospectus stated would be allocated to the D–10B. It also failed to disclose that approximately $13,000 of the estimated proceeds would have to be used to pay the accrued salaries of certain officers and directors, and that a large portion of the proceeds would have to be used to meet current expenses, which were being incurred at the rate of $11,000 per month, and would be used for that purpose even if the proceeds of the offering were insufficient to permit registrant to go forward with its D–10B program.

5. Dilution Aspects of Offering. The prospectus fails to disclose the dilution aspects of the offering. As of January 31, 1962, registrant's shares had a book value of minus 30 cents per share. If all the shares that the registrant proposes to offer to its existing stockholders and to its creditors were in fact sold at the proposed offering prices, that book value would increase to 55 cents per share. Purchasers paying $1.50 per share would therefore suffer an immediate dilution of 95 cents per share, the benefit of which will inure entirely to the present stockholders. It was pertinent to an informed appraisal by the persons to whom the securities being offered may be sold that this dilution be described in the prospectus. . . .

A stop order will issue.

Exemptions

In certain situations where there is less need for regulation, Secs. 3 and 4 of the 1933 Act provide exemptions from Sec. 5's registration requirements (although not from the antifraud provisions of the 1933 and 1934 Acts). Firms other than WKSIs must be vitally interested in these exemptions.

Perhaps the most important exemption is that for "transactions by any person other than an issuer, underwriter, or dealer" provided by Sec. 4(1). This simply means that once the issue is sold to the investing public, the public may trade, and the dealers may handle most transactions, without any worry about registration or prospectus delivery requirements. Thus, the 1933 Act does not generally apply to so–called secondary trading, which is regulated by the 1934 Act.

Sec. 3(a) exempts from registration the securities of governments (state and federal), charitable organizations, banks, savings and loans, and common carriers, which are regulated under other federal laws. These are exempt securities. There are also three major categories of exemption for transactions in nonexempt securities: private placement exemptions, small offering exemptions, and the intrastate offering exemption.

Private Placements

Sec. 4(2) of the 1933 Act exempts from registration "transactions by an issuer not involving any public offering," an exemption used primarily in connection with so–called "private placements"— privately negotiated sales of securities to large institutional investors and the promotion of business ventures by a few closely related persons. Because sophisticated investors with access to the same information that is normally available in a registration statement can protect themselves without SEC assistance, private placements are exempt from registration. Section 4(2)'s requirements are fleshed out in a "safe harbor" provision, Rule 506 of Regulation D.

Rule 506 allows a company, including reporting companies, to sell an unlimited amount of securities so long as the investors are either sophisticated or represented by "purchaser representatives" who can help them make wise decisions. No more than 35 of these investors may be "unaccredited." But the issuer may sell to an unlimited number of "accredited investors," persons who are presumed to be sophisticated. Rule 501 defines them as as pension funds, banks, corporate insiders, and millionaires—who because of their very nature are unlikely to need government protection in making investment decisions.

Small Offerings

Sec. 3(b) authorizes the SEC to exempt securities if it finds that registration "is not necessary in the public interest and for the protection of investors by reason of the small amount involved [a $5 million ceiling] or the limited character of the public offering." Rules 504 and 505 of Regulation D provide the requirements that issuers must meet in order to utilize these exemptions. Rule 504 exempts from registration any offering in a 12–month period totaling less than $1 million (reduced by amounts sold in reliance on other exemptions). This exemption is aimed at smaller businesses and is not available to 1934 Act reporting companies. Rule 505 allows even reporting companies to raise up to $5 million in a 12–month period so long as certain requirements are met, including that the issuer sell to no more than 35 nonaccredited investors.

Additionally, small companies may also solicit indications of interest from investors before proceeding to raise up to $5 million annually (with minimal SEC filings) under Regulation A, another small offering exemption.

Local Offerings

A final important exemption is Sec. 3(a)(11)'s exemption for intrastate offerings, which applies where a selling company doing business in a state offers and sells securities only to residents of the same state and intends to use the proceeds there. An issuer, according to rule 147, is doing business within a state if (1) it derives 80 percent or more of its revenue from operations within the state, (2) at least 80 percent of its assets are located within the state, (3) at least 80 percent of the net proceeds of the issuance will be used within the state, and (4) the issuer's principal office is located there. Offer of the shares for sale to a single nonresident will void the exemption. Federal regulation is deemed unnecessary because of the availability of state regulation and the close proximity of purchaser to seller.

Institutional Investors

Buyers of private placement securities under rule 506 have traditionally been hindered in attempts to resell them. To encourage trading in the private placement markets by large institutional investors, in 1990 the SEC adopted rule 144A, which exempts a sale of securities so long as (1) they are not of the same class as those listed on an exchange or quoted on the National Association of Securities Dealers Automated Quotation (NASDAQ) system, (2) the buyer is a qualified institutional buyer (QIB), and (3) the seller and prospective purchaser may request basic financial information from an issuer. A QIB must in the aggregate own and invest at least $100 million, ensuring that QIBs are large institutions that can take care of themselves. Rule 144A functionally allows large investors to trade among themselves without worrying about registration and disclosure requirements. Creation of the WKSI rules will likely reduce the popularity of Rule 144A because its provisions will no longer be necessary. It will be so easy for WKSIs to comply with the registration process that exemptions from registration will simply not be as important.

Enforcement and Civil Liabilities

Government Action

The SEC has numerous powers to enforce compliance with the provisions of the 1933 Act. For example, if the SEC believes that a registration statement is incomplete or inaccurate, Sec. 8(b) authorizes issuance of a "refusal order," which prevents the statement from becoming effective until SEC objections are satisfied. If inaccuracies are discovered after the effective date, the SEC may issue a *stop order* pursuant to Sec. 8(d), as was done in the *Doman Helicopters* case, to suspend the effectiveness of the statement. Sec. 8(e) authorizes the SEC to conduct an "examination" to investigate fully whether a stop order should issue.

More generally, Sec. 19(b) gives the SEC power of subpoena to aid investigations of any potential violation of the 1933 Act. Sec. 20(b) allows the SEC to go into federal district court to seek an injunction whenever it appears that any person is violating the 1933 Act.

The 1933 Act even contains criminal provisions. Sec. 24 provides that any person who willfully violates any provision of the act or any SEC rule or any person who willfully makes an untrue statement or omits a material fact in a registration statement is subject to fine and imprisonment. The Department of Justice enforces these criminal provisions.

Private Suit

The 1933 Act provides remedies for violation of its provisions in the form of lawsuits that may be brought by injured investors.

Sec. 11. An investor who is injured after buying securities with reliance on a rosy picture falsely painted in a prospectus will probably not be satisfied with the SEC's injunction remedy or even criminal prosecution. The investor will desire to recoup losses through a civil action for damages, and the 1933 Act has express provision for such lawsuits. Sec. 11 states that if "any part of the registration statement, when such part became effective, contained an untrue statement of a material fact or omitted to state a material fact required to be stated therein or necessary to make the statements therein not misleading, any person acquiring such security" may file a civil action. Potential defendants in such an action include every person who signed the registration statement (which includes the issuer, its principal executive officers, chief financial officer, principal accounting officers, and most of the board of directors), every person who was a director or identified as about to become a director, every accountant, every appraiser or other expert who is named as having helped prepare it, and every under-writer.

The Sec. 11 cause of action is loosely patterned after a common–law fraud action but is modified to greatly ease a plaintiff's burdens in seeking recovery in many ways. For example, the common–law fraud elements of privity of contract and reliance are not necessary in a Sec. 11 claim.

If the plaintiff proves the registration statement contained misstatements or omissions of material facts, the law presumes that these caused the plaintiff's damages, and the burden of proof shifts to the defendants to prove that other factors were the true cause of the plaintiff's losses.

Furthermore, Sec. 11 does not require proof of fraudulent intent. Proof of misstatement or omission shifts the burden of proof to the defendants to establish that they were guilty of neither fraudulent intent nor negligence in preparing the registration statement. Individual defendants must establish that they used "due diligence" in preparing the registration statement. The amount of diligence that is due from a defendant depends on his or her position as an insider (with full access to key information) or an outsider, and a defendant is generally allowed to rely on "expertised" portions of the statement—those portions prepared by experts such as independent auditors. The due diligence defense is not available to the issuing company, which is strictly liable for inaccuracies in the registration statement.

One aspect of the Sec. 11 cause of action that is very pro–defendant, however, is the requirement that plaintiffs be able to "trace" their shares to a defective registration statement and to establish conclusively that the shares they purchased were not shares that has been previously issued. In practice, this makes it exceedingly difficult for most investors to recover under Sec. 11 except in the case of an initial public offering (IPO).

Sec. 12. Complementing Sec. 11 are Sec. 12(a)(1), which allows an investor to recover when offers or sales are made in violation of Sec. 5 (that is, without the filing of a required registration statement, by use of a defective prospectus, or where securities are delivered without an accompanying prospectus), and Sec. 12(a)(2), which allows recovery by investors injured by misrepresentations made outside a prospectus (such as in an oral sales pitch or in literature accompanying a registered offering). The Supreme Court held that Sec. 12(a)(2) does not apply to shares purchased in the secondary market or in a private placement. The elements of recovery and defenses in Sec. 12 suits are roughly the same as under Sec. 11, although the range of potential defendants is limited to "sellers" of securities—those who actually pass title or those who "solicit" transactions, such as brokers and dealers.

1934 Act: Regulating the Trading of Securities

Although the 1933 Act regulates primarily the initial issuance of securities, the 1934 Act regulates the trading of those securities. An array of complex problems comes within the purview of the 1934 Act. The general registration and reporting requirements of the 1934 Act have already been discussed. Attention is now turned to several other major concerns of the act.

Insider Trading

Knowledge of the inner workings of a corporation can be very valuable in making investment decisions. For example, if a corporate vice–president learned that his company's scientists had just been granted an important patent that will open up a new sales field, he would have a distinct and arguably unfair trading advantage over the general investing public. Insider trading was a widespread phenomenon in the 1920s, yet the common law provided little protection from such abusive practices.

Sec. 16(b)

One response to the insider trading problem is Sec. 16 of the 1934 Act, which applies to three categories of persons: officers, directors, and owners of more than 10 percent of the shares of any one class of stock of a 1934 reporting company. Thus, the provision applies only to persons reasonably assumed to have influence in and — therefore access to inside information of large, publicly traded companies. Subsection (a) of Sec. 16 requires that these three categories of insider file three types of reports with the SEC. The two most important are an initial report revealing the holdings when a director or officer takes office or when a stockholder first obtains a 10 percent holding, and an additional report each month there after in which a change in holdings occurs. Because many insiders had been lax in filing such reports, in 1991 the SEC added a requirement that in their proxy statements sent to shareholders, issuers list any insiders who did not comply with Sec. 16(a). In 2002, Sarbanes–Oxley required that the insiders begin reporting their covered trades to the SEC within two days. Previously, they could often wait for a month and sometimes longer.

Subsection (b) of Sec. 16 provides that any profits realized (or losses avoided) by such an insider in connection with a purchase and sale (or sale and purchase) within a six–month period is an illegal "short–swing" profit. Any such profit may be recovered on the issuer's behalf. The striking thing about Sec. 16(b) is the near absolute nature of the liability it imposes. Thus, assume that Sherry, a director of ABC Company, buys ABC shares on January 1. If she sells any ABC shares (not necessarily the same ones she bought on January 1) within six months thereafter at a higher price than she purchased, she is liable to forfeit her profit even if she did not use any inside information. A classic Sec. 16(b) case follows.

SMOLOWE V. DELENDO CORPORATION
U.S. Court of Appeals, Second Circuit, 136 F.2d 231 (1943)

Litigation over a tax claim disrupted Delendo Corporation's negotiations for sale of its assets to Schenley Distillers. Four years later, negotiations were reopened and the sale was completed on April 30, 1940. In the six months before the sale, defendants Seskis and Kaplan— both officers, directors, and major shareholders of Delendo—bought Delendo shares, which they then sold at substantial profits in the Schenley deal.

Plaintiff shareholders of Delendo sued to recover those profits for the benefit of the corporation, apparently claiming that Seskis and Kaplan had inside information that the tax problem with the government was being negotiated away, thus clearing the way for the profitable sale of assets.

The defendants claimed they did not use inside information in making their purchases, thus raising the issue of whether such use is a necessary element of recovery in a Sec. 16(b) claim. The trial court ruled for the plaintiffs; the defendants appealed.

Clark, Circuit Judge:

The primary purpose of the Securities Exchange Act . . . was to insure a fair and honest market, that is, one which would reflect an evaluation of securities in the light of all available and pertinent data. Furthermore, the Congressional hearings indicate that Sec. 16(b), specifically, was designed to protect the "outsider" stockholders against at least short–swing speculation by insiders with advance information. It is apparent too, from the language of Sec. 16(b) itself, as well as from the Congressional hearings, that the only remedy which its framers deemed effective for this reform was the imposition of a liability based upon an objective measure of proof. This is graphically stated in the testimony of Mr. Corcoran, chief spokesman for the drafters and proponents of the Act, in Hearings before the Committee on Banking and Currency: "You hold the director, irrespective of any intention or expectation to sell the security within six months after, because it will be absolutely impossible to prove the existence of such intention or expectation, and you have to have this crude rule of thumb, because you cannot undertake the burden of having to prove that the director intended, at the time he bought, to get out on a short swing."

A subjective standard of proof, requiring a showing of an actual unfair use of inside information, would render senseless the provisions of the legislation limiting the liability period to six months, making an intention to profit during the period immaterial, and exempting transactions wherein there is a bona fide acquisition of stock in connection with a previously contracted debt. . . . And its total effect would be to render the statute little more of an incentive to insiders to refrain from profiteering at the expense of the outside stockholders than are the common law rules of liability; it would impose a more stringent statute of limitations upon the party aggrieved at the same time that it allowed the wrongdoer to share in the spoils of recovery. Had Congress intended that only profits from an actual misuse of inside information should be recoverable, it would have been simple enough to say so.

The present case would seem to be of the type which the statute was designed to include. Here it is conceded that the defendants did not make unfair use of information they possessed as officers at the time of the transactions. When these began they had no offer from Schenley. But they knew they were pressing the tax suit; and they, of course, knew of the corporate offer to settle it which reestablished the offer to purchase and led to the favorable sale. It is naive to suppose that their knowledge of their own plans as officers did not give them most valuable inside knowledge as to what would probably happen to the stock in which they were dealing. It is difficult to find this use "unfair" in the sense of illegal; it is certainly an advantage and a temptation within the general scope of the legislature's intended prohibition. . .

Affirmed.

Sec. 10(b)

Another provision of the 1934 Act that regulates insider trading, as well as many other facets of securities trading, is Sec. 10(b). This provision makes it unlawful to "use or employ, in connection with the purchase or sale of any security, . . . any manipulative or deceptive device or contrivance in contravention of such rules and regulations as the Commission may prescribe. . . ."

Pursuant to Sec. 10(b), the SEC has issued the most famous of all its rules, rule 10b–5, quoted in full:

It shall be unlawful for any person, directly or indirectly, by the use of any means or instrumentality of interstate commerce, or of the mails, or of any facility of any national securities exchange,

1. to employ any device, scheme or artifice to defraud,
2. to make any untrue statement of a material fact or to omit to state a material fact necessary in order to make the statements made, in the light of the circumstances under which they were made, not misleading, or
3. to engage in any act, practice, or course of business which operates or would operate as a fraud or deceit upon any person, in connection with the purchase or sale of any security

General Provisions. One important category of rule 10b–5 cases involves insider trading. Although a Sec. 10(b) case is more difficult to prove, its coverage is broader than Sec. 16(b)'s. The broad purpose of Sec. 10(b) and rule 10b–5 is to protect the investing public by preventing fraud and equalizing access to material information. Sec. 10(b) applies to any purchase or saleby any person of any security—there are no exceptions. Thus, small, close corporations (the shares of which are not offered to the public for sale but are typically held by just a few, perhaps members of a single family) are covered as well as the largest public corporations. Transactions covered include those occurring on the stock exchanges, in over–the–counter sales through stockbrokers, or even in privately negotiated sales. Any person connected with the transaction is regulated, not only insiders as in Sec. 16(b).

Unlike Sec. 16(b), Sec. 10(b) requires proof of actual use of inside information to establish a violation. There is no automatic presumption. Furthermore, the information must be material, and it must be nonpublic.

Enforcement. A willful violation of any provision of the Antifraud provisions of 1934 Act, including those banning insider trading, subjects the violator to the criminal provisions of Sec. 32, which carry penalties of imprisonment up to 25 years, and/or a fine of up to $10 million for individuals. Corporations can be fined up to $25 million.

The SEC refers criminal cases to the Department of Justice for prosecution. But the SEC itself can take steps against inside traders. It can hold disciplinary proceedings if a regulated broker, dealer, or underwriter is involved. It can go to federal district court to obtain an injunction to halt illegal practices and perhaps an order rescinding the fraudulent sale. In 1988, the SEC was authorized to seek civil fines against securities firms that "knowingly and recklessly" fail properly to supervise their employees who engage in insider trading. Additionally, the SEC is authorized in civil insider trading cases to seek relief in the form of disgorgement of illicit profits and assessment of a civil penalty of up to three times the profit gained or loss avoided.

The SEC also has broad civil powers to impose fines, seek injunctions, bar bad actors from serving as officers and directors of public companies, seek disgorgement of ill–gotten gains, and the like

In addition to government civil and criminal actions, a private civil lawsuit for damages may be brought by victims of fraud, such as insider trading, against the perpetrators. Although the 1934 Act does not explicitly provide for such a right of action, the courts have implied one since 1946. Private lawsuits brought under Sec. 10(b) and rule 10b–5 in the 1960s and 1970s dramatically altered the law of securities regulation in the United States.

Potential Defendants. The key to insider trading liability is the disclose or abstain rule, which requires that certain persons either disclose material nonpublic information that they possess or abstain from trading in the relevant company's stock until that information becomes public. The disclose or abstain rule promotes fairness in securities trading by equalizing access to important information affecting the value of securities. Equal information is not the goal, only equal access. Although the goal cannot be perfectly achieved, small investors will likely be more willing to enter the market if they know the SEC is actively promoting equal access.

Four major categories of persons owe a duty to disclose or abstain. The first category consists of *corporate insiders,* a term defined more broadly than in the Sec. 16 provisions to include any corporate employee with access to material inside information, not just officers and directors.

A second major category of potential insider trading defendants are *temporary insiders.* These are persons who receive confidential corporate information for a corporate purpose and with the expectation that it will be kept confidential but then use it in insider trading. Classic examples are attorneys, accountants, and investment bankers hired temporarily by a corporation. For example, if an attorney is hired to help Corporation A merge with Corporation B and the attorney realizes that this will be a very favorable arrangement for Corporation A, she may be tempted to trade in its stock. That would be illegal so long as the information is nonpublic.

A third category of potential insider trading defendant consists of *misappropriators*—noninsiders who misappropriate confidential inside information for their own purposes. The "disclose or abstain" obligation must rest on a fiduciary duty to someone. Insiders, their tippees, and temporary insiders all owe a fiduciary duty to the corporation in whose shares they trade. It can be a little more elusive to determine the duty owed by a misappropriator.

The fourth category includes any *tippee* of any of the first three categories. Unless tippees are covered, a corporate president could tip his or her spouse and then enjoy the fruits of the spouse's trading. The Supreme Court has held that a tippee cannot be liable for insider trading unless he or she knows that the tipper breached a duty in passing along the information. Such a breach occurs if the information is passed for personal benefit (whether monetary or otherwise) rather than for a corporate purpose.

The "misappropriation" category of insider trading is the most controversial and is illustrated in the following case.

United States v. O'Hagan
U.S. Supreme Court, 541 U.S. 642 (1997)

James O'Hagan was a partner in the law firm of Dorsey & Whitney. After Grand Metropolitan PLC (Grand Met) retained the law firm of Dorsey & Whitney to represent it regarding a potential tender offer for the Pillsbury Company's common stock, respondent O'Hagan, who did no work on the representation, began purchasing call options for Pillsbury stock, as well as shares of the stock. Dorsey & Whitney withdrew from representing Grand Met. Grand Met publicly announced its tender offer, the price of Pillsbury stock rose dramatically, and O'Hagan sold his call options and stock at a profit of more than $4.3 million.

A Securities and Exchange Commission (SEC) investigation culminated in a 57–count criminal indictment alleging that O'Hagan

defrauded his law firm and its client, Grand Met, by misappropriating for his own trading purposes material, nonpublic information regarding the tender offer. O'Hagan was charged and convicted of several counts of violating section 10(b) of the Securities Act of 1934 and SEC Rule 10b–5.

The Eighth Circuit reversed all of the convictions, holding that section 10(b) and Rule 10b–5 liability may not be grounded on the "misappropriation theory" of securities fraud. The government appealed.

Ginsburg, Justice:

Is a person who trades [in securities for personal profit, using confidential information misappropriated in breach of a fiduciary duty to the

source of the information, guilty of violating §
10(b) and Rule 10b–5? Our answer is yes.

The "misappropriation theory" holds that a person commits fraud "in connection with" a securities transaction, and thereby violates § 10(b) and Rule 10b–5, when he misappropriates confidential information for securities trading purposes, in breach of a duty owed to the source of the information. Under this theory, a fiduciary's undisclosed, self–serving use of a principal's information to purchase or sell securities, in breach of a duty of loyalty and confidentiality, defrauds the principal of the exclusive use of that information. In lieu of premising liability on a fiduciary relationship between company insider and purchaser or seller of the company's stock, the misappropriation theory premises liability on a fiduciary–turned–trader's deception of those who entrusted him with access to confidential information.

The misappropriation theory outlaws trading on the basis of nonpublic information by a corporate "outsider" in breach of a duty owed not to a trading party, but to the source of the information. The misappropriation theory is thus designed to "protect the integrity of the securities markets against abuses by 'outsiders' to a corporation who have access to confidential information that will affect the corporation's security price when revealed, but who owe no fiduciary or other duty to that corporation's shareholders."

In this case, the indictment alleged that O'Hagan in breach of a duty of trust and confidence he owed to his law firm, Dorsey & Whitney, and to its client, Grand Met, traded on the basis of nonpublic information regarding Grand Met's planned tender offer for Pillsbury common stock. This conduct, the Government charged, constituted a fraudulent device in connection with the purchase and sale of securities.

We agree with the Government that misappropriation, as just defined, satisfies § 10(b)'s requirement that chargeable conduct involve a "deceptive device or contrivance" used "in connection with" the purchase or sale of securities. We observe, first, that misappropriators, as the Government describes them, deal in deception. A fiduciary who "[pretends] loyalty to the principal while secretly converting the principal's information for personal gain," Brief for United States 17, "dupes" or defrauds the principal.

Deception through nondisclosure is central to the theory of liability for which the Government seeks recognition. Under the misappropriation theory urged in this case, the disclosure obligation runs to the source of the information, here, Dorsey & Whitney and Grand Met.

Full disclosure forecloses liability under the misappropriation theory: Because the deception essential to the misappropriation theory involves feigning fidelity to the source of information, if the fiduciary discloses to the source that he plans to trade on the nonpublic information, there is no "deceptive device" and thus no § 10(b) violation—although the fiduciary–turnedtrader may remain liable under state law for breach of a duty of loyalty.

Reversed.

False or Inadequate Corporate Disclosures

A second major category of Sec. 10(b) cases relates to disclosures of information about corporations. Already noted are the registration and reporting requirements of the 1934 Act. The registration forms— the 10–Ks, 10–Qs, and 8–Ks– are all designed to promote full disclosure of information important to the investing public. When a corporation or some person fraudulently misstates or fails to disclose material information, a Sec. 10(b) violation may occur.

An investor who is injured because he or she bought or sold shares on the basis of inaccurate or incomplete corporate information may bring a private cause of action under the antifraud provisions of Sec. 10(b). The requirements of a valid claim in such a lawsuit are patterned after those of common law fraud: (1) a misrepresentation of material fact, (2) made by defendant with knowledge of the falsity, (3) an intent to induce the plaintiff to rely, (4) actual reliance by the plaintiff, (5) privity of contract between the plaintiff and the defendant, and (6) damage sustained. Modification of some of these common–law elements has been a source of controversy in this type of Sec. 10(b) case.

Privity

Privity of contract has been largely eliminated as a requirement of a Sec. 10(b) cause of action in the corporate disclosure setting. An injured shareholder is normally allowed to sue those persons responsible for false statements whether or not the stockholder purchased shares from or sold shares to the defendants.

Intent

Actual intent to defraud arising from knowledge of the falsity of a statement is a traditional element of common–law fraud. It is also an element of Section 10(b), as the Supreme Court has held that 10(b) defendants are not liable "in the absence of any allegation of scienter— intent to deceive, manipulate, or defraud."

The PSLRA of 1995 raised the pleading requirement regarding scienter. Plaintiffs must now plead very specific facts about what false statement was made, when it was made, by whom it was made, why it is false, and why the source of the statement knew it was false. This pleading requirement has caused plaintiffs' attorneys to be much more careful about the lawsuits they file and has led to a big increase in the number of such suits that are dismissed at an early stage.

Reliance

In a common-law fraud case, the plaintiff must normally prove that he or she relied upon the defendant's fraudulent statement in making the sale or purchase. To advance the broadly remedial purposes of the 1934 Act, some adjustments have been made to the traditional reliance requirement.

A misleading corporate disclosure can occur either when a material fact is concealed or when it is misrepresented. Because it is impractical to require an investor to prove reliance on a fact that was concealed from him or her, the Supreme Court has eliminated the reliance requirement in concealment cases. In Affiliated Ute Citizens v. United States, 406 U.S. 128 (1972), the plaintiffs, mixed–blood Ute Indians, sold shares in the Ute Development Corporation through the defendants, bank officials. The defendants failed to disclose to the plaintiffs their own interest in the transactions or the fact that shares were trading at higher prices among whites. The Court held:

> Under the circumstances of this case, involving primarily a failure to disclose, positive proof of reliance is not a prerequisite to recovery. All that is necessary is that the facts withheld be material in the sense that a reasonable investor might have considered them important in the making of this decision. This obligation to disclose and this withholding of a material fact establish the requisite element of causation in fact.

In cases of active misrepresentation, proof of reliance is practicable; nonetheless, there have been some important modifications of the reliance requirements even in misrepresentation cases, partly because of the impersonal nature of transactions that occur through the stock exchanges. The leading case for what is called the "fraud on the market" theory of reliance follows.

Although the outer limit of permissible rule 10b–5 actions is not completely settled, the Supreme Court has attempted to confine the actions to situations involving deceit and manipulation. Simple corporate mismanagement or breaches of fiduciary duty by corporate officials, not involving deceit, are not actionable under rule 10b–5.

BASIC, INC. V. LEVINSON
U.S. Supreme Court, 485 U.S. 224 (1988)

In 1965, Combustion Engineering, Inc. expressed an interest in acquiring Basic, Inc. That interest was reawakened by regulatory developments in late 1976. Beginning in September 1976, Combustion representatives had meetings and phone calls with Basic officers and directors about a possible merger. During 1977 and 1978, Basic made three public statements denying that it was engaged in merger negotiations. On December 18, 1978, Basic was asked by the New York Stock Exchange to suspend trading in its shares. It issued a press release stating that it had been "approached" about a merger. On December 19, Basic's board accepted Combustion's offer, and this was publicly announced on December 20.

Former Basic shareholders (respondents), who sold their stock after Basic's first denial that it was engaged in merger talks (October 21, 1977) and before the suspension of trading, sued Basic and its directors (petitioners). The respondents claim that petitioners' misleading statements caused them to miss the opportunity to sell at the higher merger price, in violation of Sec. 10(b) of the 1934 Securities Act.

The district court (1) granted class action status to the respondents adopting a presumption that they had relied on petitioners' public statements, thereby satisfying the "common question of fact or law" requirement of the Federal Rules of Civil Procedure; and (2) granted summary judgment to petitioners on the merits, holding that petitioners had no obligation to disclose the ongoing merger negotiations.

The circuit court affirmed on the class action issue, adopting the district court's fraud on the market" theory, but reversed on the merits, finding that a duty to disclose the merger talks might have existed. Petitioners appealed.

Blackmun, Justice:

[The Supreme Court first rejected the circuit court's resolution of the merits of the case. Unlike the circuit court, which held that almost any misleading statement about merger negotiations could be material, the Supreme Court held that materiality must depend on a balancing of (1) the indicated probability that the merger will occur, and (2) the anticipated magnitude of the merger in light of the totality of the company's activities. It then catalogued various factors, such as board resolutions and instructions to investment bankers (which might show probability that the merger would occur) and the size of the corporations involved and of the premium over market price being discussed (which might show magnitude of the event), for lower courts to consider in applying its subjective, fact specific approach.]

We turn to the question of reliance and the fraud–on–the–market theory. Succinctly put:

The fraud–on–the–market theory is based on the hypothesis that, in an open and developed securities market, the price of a company's stock is determined by the available material information regarding the company and its business. . . . Misleading statements will therefore defraud purchasers of stock even if the purchasers do not directly rely on the misstatements. . . . The causal connection between the defendants' fraud and the plaintiffs' purchase of stock in such a case is no less significant than in a case of direct reliance on misrepresentations. Peil v. Speiser, 806 F.2d 1154 (CA3 1986).

We agree that reliance is an element of a rule 10b–5 cause of action. See Ernst & Ernst v. Hochfelder, 425 U.S. 185 (1976). Reliance provides the requisite causal connection between a defendant's misrepresentation and a plaintiff's injury. . . . There is, however, more than one way to demonstrate the causal connection. . . .

The modern securities markets, literally involving millions of shares changing hands daily, differ from the face–to–face transactions contemplated by early fraud cases [that required a showing of privity], and our understanding of Rule 10b–5's reliance requirement must encompass these differences.

In face–to–face transactions, the inquiry into an investor's reliance upon information is into the subjective pricing of that information by that investor. With the presence of a market, the market is interposed between the seller and buyer and, ideally, transmits information to the investor in the processed form of a market price. Thus the market is performing a substantial part of the valuation process performed by the investor in a face–to–face transaction. The market is acting as the unpaid agent of the investor, informing him that given all the information available to it, the value of the stock is worth the market price.

Requiring a plaintiff to show a speculative state of facts, i.e., how he would have acted if omitted material information had been disclosed, . . . or if the misrepresentation had not been made . . . would place an unnecessarily unrealistic evidentiary burden on the Rule 10b–5 plaintiff who has traded on an impersonal market.

The presumption of reliance employed in this case is consistent with, and, by facilitating Rule 10b–5 litigation, supports the congressional policy embodied in the 1934 Act. In drafting that Act, Congress expressly relied on the premise that securities markets are affected by information, and enacted legislation to facilitate an investor's reliance on the integrity of those markets....

The presumption is also supported by common sense and probability. Recent empirical studies have tended to confirm Congress' premise that the market price of shares traded on well developed markets reflect all publicly available information, and, hence, any material misrepresentation. It has been noted that "it is hard to imagine that there ever is a buyer or seller who does not rely on market integrity. Who would knowingly roll the dice in a crooked crap game? Schlanger v. Four Phase Systems, Inc., 555 F.Supp. 535, 538 (SDNY 1982)....

Any showing that severs the link between the alleged misrepresentation andeither the price received (or paid) by the plaintiff, or his decision to trade at a fair market price, will be sufficient to rebut the presumption of reliance.

[Court of Appeals' judgment is vacated and remanded.]

Proxy Regulation

Although most corporate decisions are made by the officers and directors, shareholders do occasionally vote on matters of importance. At the annual shareholders' meeting required by state incorporation laws, the shareholders elect directors to the board of directors. Their approval may also be required for certain extraordinary matters, such as amendments to corporate bylaws or articles of incorporation, mergers, or sales of major assets.

Valid shareholder approval requires at least a majority vote (and sometimes two–thirds or three–fourths approval) of a quorum of shares eligible to vote. However, in a large corporation with thousands of shareholders, it is very unusual for more than a small percentage of shareholders to appear at the annual meeting. To obtain a quorum, corporate management is usually required to solicit *proxies* from the shareholders. A **proxy** is an authorization to vote shares owned by someone else. At a typical corporation's annual meeting, incumbent management will solicit and receive proxies from a sufficient number of shareholders to vote itself into control for another year.

Sec. 14(a) of the 1934 Act prohibits solicitation of proxies for any shares registered under the Act in contravention of rules promulgated by the SEC. The rules that the SEC has issued have three broad goals: full disclosure, fraud prevention, and increased shareholder participation.

Full Disclosure

State laws have not always required corporate management to be responsive to the informational needs and desires of shareholders. The SEC, knowing that most major corporations solicit proxies at least annually, requires in rule 14a–3 that no soliciting occur unless each person solicited is furnished with a written proxy statement containing the information specified in Schedule 14A.

Schedule 14A contains more than 20 items, some of which are applicable only if specified matters, such as merger approval, are involved. In the typical solicitation by management relating to election of directors, the proxy statement must be accompanied by an annual report to contain, inter alia, comparative financial statements for the last two fiscal years, a summary of operations, a brief description of the business done by the issuer and its subsidiaries, and identification of the issuer's directors and executive officers and their principal occupations. This information must be clearly presented. Indeed, unfavorable publicity given to the extremely high pay of many American executives, whose companies were performing less well than foreign competitors whose executives were paid much less, led to a 1992 SEC reform that requires proxy materials to spell out for shareholders the specifics of executive compensation via charts rather than often unreadable legalistic text. Indeed, in many areas of securities disclosure there is now a "plain English" requirement that important disclosures be easily understandable rather than couched in confusing legalese.

Proxy Contests

Normally, incumbent management will face no organized opposition in the election of directors at the annual meeting. But if the corporation is floundering financially, perhaps a group of "insurgent" shareholders will attempt to elect its own slate of candidates to the board of directors. Or perhaps the insurgents have lined up a merger with or tendered their shares to another corporation, which intends to fire incumbent management, and incumbent management has negotiated a proposed defensive merger with yet another company, which would be willing to retain the incumbents in their present positions. In these and other situations, proxy contests arise over the control of the corporation. Incumbent managements and insurgent shareholders vie for sufficient proxies to prevail in the shareholders' vote. Federal regulations specify the procedure for such contests and punish any fraud that may occur.

Changes promulgated in 1992 made it easier for dissident shareholders to communicate with each other. Previously, any time 10 or more shareholders communicated, they were required to file a Schedule 14B with the SEC disclosing such matters as employment history, stock holdings, and past criminal violations. The 1992 changes make it much easier for dissident shareholders to cooperate in formulating plans to reform a poorly performing company.

Antifraud. Proxy contests sometimes become quite heated. To prevent fraud, rule 14a–9 prohibits the use of false or misleading statements to solicit proxies. The term solicitation is broadly defined to cover both statements seeking proxies and communications urging shareholders to refuse to give proxies. Thus, if incumbent management falsely states or omits to state a material fact in urging shareholders not to grant proxies to an insurgent group, a violation of rule 14a–9 and Sec. 14(a) occurs. A private cause of action is available to remedy such a violation.

Tender Offers

A final important area of federal securities law regulates a method of taking control of a corporation, called a **tender offer.** In a typical tender offer, one corporation (the *offeror*) will publicly offer to purchase a controlling interest (more than 50 percent of the shares) in another corporation (the target). The target's shareholders are invited to tender their shares to the offeror in return for cash or the offeror's equity or debt securities (or a combination) in an amount usually well above the prior market price of the target's stock.

Because of the easy availability of credit and lack of government regulation, the tender offer gained widespread usage in the 1960s. One variety, termed the *Saturday Night Special*, featured a"take–it–or–leave–it" offer to the target's shareholders with a very short time for them to make up their minds. Afraid of losing an opportunity to sell shares at above the market price, shareholders frequently would tender their shares with little time to learn much about the offeror or to evaluate the possibility of a higher offer from a different source.

Federal Legislation

Comprehensive federal regulation of tender offers began with the passage of the Williams Act of 1968. That Act amended Secs. 13 and 14 of the 1934 Act with the basic purpose of increasing both the amount of information flowing to target shareholders and the time available to use that information.

Filing Requirements. Sec. 13(d) of the 1934 Act requires that any person or group acquiring more than 5 percent of the shares of any corporation must file a Schedule 13D within 10 days with the SEC. That schedule requires disclosure of the background of the person or group, their source of funds, their purpose, the number of shares owned, relevant contracts or other arrangements with the target, and any plans for change of the target's affairs.

Procedural Rules. Sec. 14(d) and rule 14d–2 provide that a tender offer is commended on the date of public announcement of the offer. On that date, rule 14d–3 requires the offeror to file with the SEC a Schedule TO (for Tender Offer), which requires informational disclosures similar to those of Schedule 13D.

The target's management may support a tender offer; perhaps the management even negotiated it. But tender offers frequently are "hostile," and the offeror intends to replace the target's management with its own people. Even if the target's management opposes the offer, Sec. 14(d) and rule 14d–5 require the target's management to mail the tender offer to the target's shareholders or promptly to provide the offeror with a shareholder list so it can do the mailing itself.

Target management must also file with the SEC a Schedule 14D–9. This document (1) discloses whether the officers and directors intend to hold their shares or to tender, (2) describes any contractual arrangement management may have with the offeror (for instance, the offeror sometimes can obtain management's support through monetary incentives), and (3) disclose any concrete negotiations with a "white knight"—a company willing to make a competing tender offer that is more advantageous to incumbent management.

Substantive Rules. Substantively, Sec. 14(d) and rule 14e–1 provide that a tender offer must be held open for a minimum of 20 business days, so the target's shareholders will have an opportunity to evaluate the offer fully. No more Saturday Night Specials will occur. If more shares are tendered than the offeror wishes to purchase, the offeror must purchase from each shareholder on a pro rata basis. This requirement promotes equal treatment of shareholders.

What if an offeror initiates the tender offer at $40 per share, seeking to purchase 51 percent of the target's shares, but only 25 percent is tendered? The offeror may choose to extend the offering period and amend the offer to $50 per share. This higher price must be given to all tendering shareholders, including those who were willing to sell at the lower price.

The final important provision of the Williams Act is Sec. 14(e), the prohibition of fraud or manipulation in either supporting or opposing a tender offer.

Remedies. Violations of Secs. 13(d), 14(d), and 14(e) may be remedied by civil actions for injunctive relief. Injured shareholders who, relying on fraudulent statements, either tendered when they would not have done so had they known the truth, or failed to tender when they would have had they not been defrauded, also can sue for damages under Sec. 14(e).

Defensive Tactics

A recent controversy has focused on the latitude that should be accorded target management in opposing hostile tender offers. Normally, courts hesitate to review the business judgments of any corporation's management, but the recent use by target managers of such tactics as "poison pills," sale of "crown jewels," recruiting of "white knights," and other devices has brought two major types of legal challenges. First is a state law challenge based on a claim that target managers using these devices are breaching their fiduciary duty to target shareholders.

The second basis for attacking defensive tactics is the argument that they are "manipulative" in violation of Sec. 14(e) of the Williams Act. The Supreme Court rejected this argument in the following case— thus relegating any significant court review to state jurisdiction.

SCHREIBER V. BURLINGTON
U.S. Supreme Court, 472 U.S. 1 (1985)

On December 21, 1982, Burlington Northern, Inc. made a hostile tender offer for 25 million shares of El Paso Gas Co. at $24 per share. Although El Paso's manage– ment initially opposed the offer, its shareholders fully subscribed it. Burlington did not accept the tendered shares, however. Instead, after negotiations with El Paso's manage– ment, Burlington rescinded the December tender offer, purchased 4 million shares from El Paso, substituted a new tender offer for only 21 million shares at $24 each, and recognized certain contractual arrangements between El Paso and its management that guaranteed the managers substantial compensation upon a change of control ("golden parachutes"). More than 40 million shares were tendered in response to the second tender offer.

Rescission of the first offer diminished payment to those shareholders who had tendered during the first offer. Not only were fewer shares purchased, but the shareholders who retendered were subjected to substantial proration. Petitioner Schreiber sued on behalf of similarly situated shareholders, alleging that Burlington, El Paso, and members of El Paso's board had violated § 14(e). She claimed that withdrawal of the first tender offer coupled with substitution of the second was a "manipulative" distortion of the market for El Paso stock.

The trial court dismissed the suit for failure to state a claim. The U.S. Court of Appeals for the Third Circuit affirmed. Schreiber petitioned to the Supreme Court.

Burger, Chief Justice:

We are asked in this case to interpret § 14(e) of the Securities Exchange Act. The starting point is the language of the statute. Section 14(e) provides:

It shall be unlawful for any person to make any untrue statement of a material fact or omit to state any material fact necessary in order to make the statements made, in the light of the circumstances under which they are made, not misleading, or to engage in any fraudulent, deceptive or manipulative acts or practices, in connection with any tender offer or request or invitation for tenders, or any solicitation of security holders in opposition to or in favor of any such offer, request, or invitation. The Commission shall, for the purposes of this subsection, by rules and regulations define, and prescribe means reasonably designed to prevent, such acts and practices as are fraudulent, deceptive, or manipulative.

Petitioner reads the phrase "fraudulent, deceptive or manipulative acts or practices" to include acts which, although fully disclosed, "artificially" affect the price of the takeover target's stock. Petitioner's interpretation relies on the belief that § 14(e) is directed at purposes broader than providing full and true information to investors.

Petitioner's reading of the term "manipulative" conflicts with the normal meaning of the term. We have held in the context of an alleged violation of § 10(b) of the Securities Exchange Act:

Use of the word "manipulative" is especially significant. It is and was virtually a term of art when used in connection with the securities markets. It connotes intentional or willful conduct designed to deceive or defraud investors by controlling or artificially affecting the price of securities. Ernst &Ernst v. Hochfelder, 425 U.S. 185, 199(1976)

The meaning the Court has given the term "manipulative" is consistent with the use of the term at common law, andwith its traditional dictionary definition.

Our conclusion that "manipulative" acts under § 14(e) require misrepresentation or nondisclosure is buttressed by the purpose and legislative history of the provision. "The purpose of the Williams Act is to insure that public shareholders who are confronted by a cash tender offer for their stock will not be required to respond without adequate information." Rondeau v. Mosinee Paper Corp., 422 U.S. 49, 58(1975).

The expressed legislative intent was to preserve a neutral setting in which the contenders could fully present their arguments. The Senate sponsor [said]:

We have taken extreme care to avoid tipping the scales either in favor of management or in favor of the person making the takeover bids. S. 510 is designed solely to require full and fair disclosure for the benefit of investors. The bill will at the same time provide the offeror and management equal opportunity to present their case.

Congress' consistent emphasis on disclosure persuades us that it intended takeover contests to be addressed to shareholders. In pursuit of this goal, Congress, consistent with the core mechanism of the Securities Exchange Act, created sweeping disclosure requirements and narrow substantive safeguards. The same Congress that placed such emphasis on shareholder choice would not at the same time have required judges to oversee tender offers for substantive fairness. It is even less likely that a Congress implementing that intention would-dexpress it only through the use of a single word placed in the middle of a provision otherwise devoted to disclosure.

We hold that the term "manipulative" as used in § 14(e) requires misrepresentation or nondisclosure. Without misrepresentation or nondisclosure, § 14(e) has not been violated.

Applying the definition to this case, we hold that the actions of respondents were not manipulative. The amended complaint fails to allege that the cancellation of the first tender offer was accompanied by any misrepresentation, nondisclosure or deception. The District

Court correctly found, "All activity of the defendants that could have conceivably affected the price of El Paso shares was done openly."

Petitioner also alleges that El Paso management and Burlington entered into certain undisclosed and deceptive agreements during the making of the second tender offer. The substance of the allegations is that, in return for certain undisclosed benefits, El Paso managers agreed to support the second tender offer. But both courts noted that petitioner's complaint seeks redress only for injuries related to the cancellation of the first tender offer. Since the deceptive and misleading acts alleged by the petitioner all occurred with reference to the making of the second tender offer— when the injuries suffered by petitioner had already been sustained— these acts bear no possible causal relationship to petitioner's alleged injuries.

Affirmed.

State Regulation

Because every state has its own system of securities regulation, corporations must always be cognizant of these rules also. The Commissioners on Uniform State Laws have produced the Uniform Securities Act, which has been used as a pattern for many states' laws. Still, because many large states have not followed this act and many have amended it to varying degrees, there is a lack of uniformity that complicates the marketing of securities.

Registration

Most states have laws that, like the 1933 Securities Act, regulate the original distribution of securities. A corporation that intends to market its shares nationwide must comply with not only the 1933 Act but also approximately 40 separate state registration laws.

There are three basic systems of state registration. Some states use *registration by notification* which requires the filing of certain material and then a waiting period before the securities may be sold, similar to the procedure under the 1933 Act.

Registration by qualification is used by some states. This process goes beyond the simple disclosure philosophy of the 1933 Act and actually involves merit review of the securities by state officials. Typically, states using merit review refuse to allow sales of

LEGAL FOCUS

Ethics

If ethical standards were sufficiently high and widely practiced, there would be little need for much of the securities regulation currently performed by the federal and state governments. Indeed, there is a school of thought that most areas of securities law should be deregulated and investors should be left to look out for themselves in terms of gathering information about companies in which they might wish to invest. There is substantial evidence, however, that vigorous securities regulation is needed now and will continue to be a necessary fixture.

At one level, scam artists continually victimize unsophisticated (and sometimes sophisticated) investors with whatever is the latest "get rich quick" scheme. For example, the SEC has investigated such scams as (1) a company claiming to have developed a fuel–processing device that could turn low–grade coal, rubber, and household garbage into crude oil (the company demonstrated the machine without disclosing that hidden inside its works was a 23–gallon tank that promoters filled with oil before each demonstration); (2) a company that falsely claimed to have developed a "self–chilling" soda can; and (3) a company that raised $300 million be claiming to have a secret process for turning sand from Costa Rica's black sand beaches into gold.

These scam artists are a recurring problem for the SEC, but their tricks seem somewhat modest in light of the huge frauds pulled by Enron, Global Crossing, World-Com, Tyco, and so many other high–flying companies at the turn of the century. Those companies overstated profits and net worth by *billions* of dollars. Often times, earning were exaggerated so that securities analyst forecasts could be realized. This kept the companies' stock prices from dropping and often enabled corporate executives to pocket huge bonuses or to convert stock options into large profits. The companies would have to pay real taxes on these illusory profits.

In many of these frauds the top officers—CEOs and CEOs––were the driving forces behind the frauds. But the frauds could succeed only with the passive acquiescence of a broad circle of subordinates. Furthermore, so–called guardians of the marketplace such as outside directors, independent auditors, stock analysts, and others seem to have often just looked the other way, frequently because they were hopelessly conflicted. Auditors, for example, seemed more interested in selling consulting services to audit clients than in doing competent audits.

What does this say about the state of ethics in American business?

By enacting Sarbanes–Oxley in 2002, Congress attempted to raise the standards of ethics in corporate America. As noted elsewhere in this text, Sarbanes–Oxley created the PCAOB to regulate public audit firms, increased the penalties for a wide variety of securites–related transactions, created protections for whistleblowers such as Enron's Sherron Watkins, required CEOs who pocketed bonuses based on misleading financial statements to disgorge them, required firms to adopt codes of ethics for their CFOs or explain why they had failed to do so, and made many other changes aimed at reminding corporate actors of their ethical responsibilities.

securities that do not meet a "fair, just, and equitable" standard. The standard may not be met, for example, if the organizers and promoters of the corporation intend to sell to the public at per share prices much greater than they themselves paid.

The third type is *registration by coordination*, which results in automatic state approval whenever a security's registration has become effective under the 1933 Act at the federal level.

Some states allow registration by more than one method.

Exemptions

State registration laws contain exemptions, as does the 1933 Act. There is an ongoing effort to coordinate state and federal exemption to produce uniformity. A uniform system of exemptions would greatly simplify matters for a corporation planning a widespread distribution of securities, but the chances of achieving complete uniformity appear slim. Nonetheless, substantial progress has been achieved.

Other Provisions

Many state securities laws also contain antifraud provisions similar to those in the 1933 and 1934 federal laws. In states without such laws, the courts have extended the common law of fraud to prohibit deceitful securities practices.

Many states also regulate tender offers in a manner that burdens offerors and therefore discourages such transactions. The Supreme Court held one such state act to be constitutional in CTS Corp. v. Dynamics Corp., 481 U.S. 69 (1987).

Many states also regulate stockbrokers and investment advisers, although Congress has taken steps to minimize the overlap between federal and state regulation so that these professionals to not face conflicting or overlapping rules.

International Implications

Each year, Americans buy tens of billions of dollars worth of foreign securities, and foreign investors purchase tens of billions of dollars of U.S. securities. Many American investors watch the London and Tokyo stock markets almost as closely as they monitor the New York Stock Exchange. Because our economy increasingly intersects with those of other nations, international concerns affect virtually every sphere of U.S. securities law.

Registration Exemptions

Earlier we listed the important domestic exemptions to the registration requirements of the 1933 Act. To encourage foreign issuers to raise equity in American markets, in 1990 the SEC added a foreign exemption—Regulation S. Generally speaking, Regulation S provides that Sec. 5's registration requirement does not apply to sales or resales of securities if two requirements are met. First, the sale must be an off–shore transaction, defined as one in which no offer is made to a person in the United States, and either

(1) at the time the buy order is originated the buyer is outside the United States or (2) the transaction is executed through the facilities of a designated offshore securities market. Second, there can be no "directed selling efforts" in the United States. Issuers must take additional precautions to assure that the shares, once purchased outside the United States, are not quickly resold in the United States as a means of circumventing the registration requirements.

Regulation S provides an exemption only from registration, not from antifraud rules. Therefore, Sec. 10(b) and rule 10b–5 continue to apply whenever (1) fraudulent conduct occurs in the United States (even if the impact is on American or foreign investors in other countries), or (2) fraudulent conduct occurs abroad, having significant effects in the United States. To illustrate the *conduct test:* Foreign investors who bought the issuer's shares abroad were allowed to sue an American accounting firm for a fraud involving allegedly fraudulent certified financial statements that occurred primarily in Ireland, because, in large part, the audit was directed primarily by the firm's American office where engagement partner responsibility lay (even though the field work was performed mostly in Ireland). To illustrate the *effects test* American investors were allowed to sue in the United States the directors of a Canadian corporation who allegedly authorized the sale of the company's stock in Canada at an unfairly low price, thus affecting the value of the company's shares that were traded on the American Stock Exchange.

Insider Trading

Many of the insider trading schemes occurring in the United States in the 1980s were aided by the bank secrecy laws of Switzerland and other countries. In recent years, with pressure from the United States, many of these nations have become more cooperative in divulging information, thereby allowing the SEC to prosecute more successfully foreign citizens who are inside traders as well as U.S. citizens who attempt to cover their tracks with use of foreign bank accounts. Over the past 20 years, often because of American urging, most developed nations have outlawed insider trading.

Tender Offers

As foreign investors from Japan, Europe, and elsewhere have bought American companies through tender offers, some Americans have become uneasy with the implications of these purchases. Therefore, Congress passed the Exon–Florio Amendment to a 1988 trade bill. Exon–Florio authorizes the President or the President's delegates to prevent or even reverse such a takeover if it threatens national security.

Conclusion

Securities laws impose substantial burdens on public companies. Section 404 of the Sarbanes–Oxley Act, for example, requires public companies to install and audit internal controls to increase the likelihood that their publicly–reported financial statements will actually reflect the true value of the firm. Implementation of this law has proved substantially more expensive than the SEC envisioned. The SEC should always be looking for ways to minimize the burdens and expense of the securities rules for issuing companies. The 2005 creation of the WKSI rules is an example of the SEC doing just that.

At the same time, capital markets are essential for economic development and they seem to flourish only where the law protects investors' interests and encourages them to "play the game." There is substantial empirical evidence that only by enacting mandatory disclosure, antifraud rules, and prohibitions against insider trading can countries create vigorous capital markets. Nations all over the world have learned this lesson and in the last 20 years or so virtually all developed countries have adopted securities law regimes largely patterned after the American system.

CHAPTER **27**

WILLS, TRUSTS, AND ESTATE PLANNING

- Wills
- Intestacy—Statutes of Descent and Distribution
- Administration of the Estate
- Trusts
- Estate Planning

ALTHOUGH FEW PEOPLE amass large fortunes in their lifetimes, most will not die penniless. Many people are surprised at the actual value of what they may have considered to be modest holdings. Real estate acquired early in life may appreciate dramatically; life insurance, both individual and group, may be owned in substantial amounts, and investment in the stock market through mutual funds is commonplace. One's personal property, slowly acquired over a period of years, may constitute a sizable asset. Some knowledge of wills, trusts, and other estate planning devices is essential to make informed decisions about one's personal situation.

The case of Pablo Picasso is a good example of what can happen when a person with a substantial estate fails to provide for its orderly disposition. When the famous artist died in 1973 he left a tremendous fortune—millions of dollars in assets. To whom did he leave it¿ As a matter of fact, Picasso died **intestate;** that is, at the time of his death he had not prepared a document—a will—to provide specific and detailed instructions about what to do with his property. A properly planned, drafted, and executed will might have eliminated most of the bitter controversy that arose among those close to him over the disposition of his wealth.

Picasso apparently felt that making a will was an act in contemplation of death and therefore an unpleasant subject to be avoided. He resisted all efforts by those who anticipated protracted legal proceedings to persuade him to make a will to provide for an orderly disposition of his property. When any person of considerable means refuses to provide for his or her estate's distribution on death, controversy is almost as certain as death itself.

Wills

A will transforms a person's wishes about the disposition of his or her property into a valid, legal instrument. This section covers formal, written wills in detail and mentions other types briefly. Following are some commonly used terms with which the student may be unfamiliar. A man who makes a will is a **testator,** a woman is a **testatrix.** A person who dies is a **decedent.** A decedent leaving a valid will is said to die testate. It is customary for a testator to designate a personal representative to carry out the provisions of the will. This person is an **executor** if male and an **executrix** if female. If there is no will or the will does not designate a personal representative, the court will appoint an **administrator** (or administratrix) to handle the decedent's estate. With regard to the testator's property, disposition of real estate is properly called a **devise,** money passing under a will is a **legacy,** and other property is disposed of by **bequest.** The Uniform Probate Code, which has been largely adopted in about 15 states and partially in some others, uses the term **devise** to refer to any sort of testamentary gift, whether of land, money, or personal property. In any event, today, lawyers tend to use these terms interchangeably.

Testamentary Capacity

A will is valid only if the testator had **testamentary capacity** at the time of its making. In most states the testator must have attained a specific minimum age, usually 18. In all states the testator must possess the mental capacity to dispose of the property intelligently. Testamentary capacity is not identical to capacity to contract. In general, testators have the capacity to make wills if they have attained the statutory age, if they know what property they own, and if they reasonably understand how and to whom they want to leave their property. The following case illustrates this principle.

HOLLADAY V. HOLLADAY
Court of Appeals of Kentucky, 172 S.W.2d 36 (1943)

This action was a will contest involving the will of Lewis Holladay. A college graduate, Holladay lived on his mother's farm with her and a sister until his mother's death in 1929. He remained on the farm until he died in 1940 at age 66. He was survived by a brother, Joe, and three sisters. Joe was the sole beneficiary under Lewis's will. When he submitted the will for probate, the sisters opposed the proceeding, alleging that Lewis did not possess sufficient mental capacity to execute a will.

The sisters (contestants) bring this appeal from a trial court judgment upholding the will.

Sims, Justice:

. . . Lewis Holladay had a college education and made his home on his mother's farm with her and a maiden sister, Miss Denia, until his mother's death in 1929. His mother was quite old and her death greatly upset him. The testimony for contestants is that Lewis was far from normal mentally years before his mother died, but was much more unstable afterwards. It was testified he shot and killed his pet dog without reason in 1917 or 1918. During electrical storms he would take his seat under a tree, saying it was safer there than in the house. He was afflicted with stomach ulcers and could not sleep at nights and would roam over the premises and farm, and on occasion would stand like a statue in the county road even at midnight, requiring travelers to drive

around him. At times he would go to the barn during the night and throw down hay for his stock when it was not in the barn but was out on pasture. He would bathe at night in a pond which was little more than a hog wallow, saying it gave him relief. It was testified that if the least thing went wrong, such as some meat falling down or the spilling of some lard from a bucket, he became so upset that it was necessary to put him to bed to quiet him. Pages could be consumed in reciting the testimony relative to his queer, weird and unnatural actions. There were many suicides and much insanity on both sides of his family, and it appears in the evidence that he threatened to destroy himself.

The judgment is affirmed.

Opposing such testimony, twenty—six of his neighbors, friends, business acquaintances and associates testified he was perfectly sane and normal; that he was a good farmer and a successful business man. These twenty—six witnesses made up a cross section of the community and included people from all walks of life: doctors, bankers, veterinarians, livestock buyers, farmers and shop keepers, practically all of whom had business or social contacts with him. Upon the written request of his sisters, he and his brother, Joe, were named administrators of his mother's $23,000 estate, which testator wound up practically without assistance from Joe. In 1930, the year he wrote his will, Lewis contracted with his sisters that he would bid $137.50 per acre for his mother's farm of 146 acres if it were sold at public auction; and he carried out his contract and purchased the_farm. He raised and sold registered sheep; was the moving spirit in some important and successful litigation in 1929 involving damages to farm lands in the community when a water dam broke. From 1929 to 1933 he served twice on the petit jury and twice on the grand jury; and in the interim between 1927 and 1940 he wrote more than 2,000 checks aggregating $29,000.

... The court did not err in refusing to give contestants' proffered instruction on the alleged insane delusions Lewis had against his sisters. His feelings toward them were unkind and even bitter, but they were based upon facts and not delusions. His sisters had objected to the fee allowed him as administrator of his mother's estate, although it was slightly less than the statutory limit of 5 percent. They had insinuated that when he and Joe, the morning after the death of their brother Felix, went through the deceased's personal effects they were looking for his will with the sinister motive of destroying it if they found one in favor of the sisters. Miss Denia had intimated that Lewis had sensual plans in bringing in a housekeeper after his mother's death. Then after Lewis had agreed to bid $137.50 per acre on his mother's farm, his three sisters attempted to raise the price. This combination of incidents had turned Lewis against his sisters, but it cannot be said his feelings were insane delusions, which are ideas or beliefs springing spontaneously from a diseased or perverted mind without reason or foundation in fact. A belief which is based upon reason and evidence, be it ever so slight, cannot be an insane delusion....

Undue Influence

Even if a testator or testatrix has the legal capacity to make a will, that will should not be admitted to probate if it is the product of fraud, duress, or, more typically, undue influence. Many courts use a four–factor test to determine the existence of undue influence. That test is applied in the following case.

CASPER V. MCDOWELL
Wisconsin Supreme Court, 205 N.W.2d 753 (1973)

On April 2, 1970, 78–year–old Joseph Casper died. His will, drafted ten months before his death by a local attorney, provided for payment of debts and funeral expenses, bequeathed $1,500 to each of Casper's two sons (Alger and Richard), and left the residue and remainder of the estate to Wilma Jean McDowell, who had lived with Casper as housekeeper and friend from October 1964 to his death. Nothing was left to Joseph's brother, John. The will specified Wilma Jean's father or her brother as executor.

After the will was submitted for admission to probate, objections were filed by Alger and Richard. Later they also challenged, on undue influence grounds, transactions in which Joseph had named Wilma Jean a joint tenant on a bank account and two deposit certificates. A jury found no undue influence in the transactions, and the trial court admitted the will to probate. Alger and Richard appealed.

Wilkie, Justice:

This court has often reiterated the elements necessary to establish undue influence. In Will of Freitag [101 N.W.2d 108 (Wis. 1960)]they were capsulized as follows:

... Susceptibility, opportunity to influence, disposition to influence, and coveted result; stated more completely: 1. A person who is susceptible of being unduly influenced by the person charged with exercising undue influence; 2. the opportunity of the person charged to exercise such influence on the susceptible person to procure the improper favor; 3. a disposition on the part of the party charged, to influence unduly such susceptible person for the purpose of procuring an improper favor either for himself or another; 4. a result caused by, or the effect of such undue influence.

Joseph Casper's first marriage ended in divorce in the early 1930s. After the divorce the sons [Alger and Richard] lived with their mother but continued to see their father. Both sons eventually moved to California in the 1950s. Joseph Casper remarried but ... his second wife died in 1950. In October 1964, the testator placed an advertisement in the Kenosha newspaper for a housekeeper. Wilma JeanMcDowell, then twenty–two years old, answered the ad ... and continuously resided in the testator's home until his death in 1970. Although Jean McDowell testified that she had not had sexual relations with the testator, several witnesses testified the two were intimate. There was very little contact [between testator and his sons] after 1965. The testator' s brother, John, testified that after 1965 he did not see his brother very often.

A. *Susceptibility.* As evidence of Joseph Casper's susceptibility to undue influence, appellants cite his deteriorating physical condition, his dissociation from family members, former friends and associates, and his inordinate attraction to this young girl. Testimony from various witnesses regarding Casper's odd conduct included his failure to recognize a grandchild and an old friend; his cutting off the top of several of his trees and one of his neighbor's trees; the severe cutting of his_hand by placing it in his lawnmower. Appellants also cite as conclusive proof of susceptibility a boast made by Jean McDowell to a neighbor that she could get anything she wanted from Casper.

The prevailing evidence, however, is that Joseph Casper was a strong willed and independent person. A neighbor, Frank Novelen, stated: "Well, he had a mind of his own.... Yeah, I'd say if he wanted to do something, he'd do it." Casper's stockbroker, Harry Myers, testified he had talked with Casper a couple of days before his death. According to Myers the two men had a conversation for fifteen minutes concerning the stock market. Myers stated the only difference he perceived in Casper was that his hair was a "shade grayer than the time I'd seen him before."

His personal physician testified that, in his opinion, Casper was "orientated" during the fourteen years they were acquainted. We conclude from this evidence that Casper, during the last half dozen years of his life, did not lose his characteristic independence. He was not susceptible to undue influence as claimed by appellants. While his health declined with age, his mental condition did not deteriorate severely.

B. *Disposition.* The disposition to influence is shown by "a willingness to do something wrong or unfair, and grasping or overreaching characteristics." Estate of Brehmer, 164 N.W.2d 318 (Wis. 1969). Not every act of kindness may be considered as indicating a disposition to influence a testator. In *Estate of McGonigal*, 174 N.W.2d 205 (Wis. 1970), we noted: "There is nothing wrong with aiding and comforting a failing testator; indeed, such activity should be encouraged."

While Jean McDowell's aid and comfort to Joseph Casper may have exceeded that which is normally expected of a nurse or housekeeper, this fact, standing alone, does not require the inference of a disposition to unduly influence.

While Casper's diminished contacts with his friends and family may give rise to the suspicion that Jean McDowell was "poisoning" the testator's mind, such inference or suspicion is not necessarily true. Casper's friend, John Schanock, stated that he felt Casper's interests simply turned to love. Quite natural is Casper's diminished need to depend upon friends and family after Jean McDowell's arrival. The two, despite several spats, were quite close.

[Also] on June 2, 1964, [testator] designated Linda Corn as beneficiary of [a savings] account. This indicates that Casper, although maintaining contact with friends and family, did not regard them as potential recipients of his bounty even before he and Jean McDowell met.

C. *Coveted result*. At first blush, the will and [property] transfers in the instant case appear unnatural. Indeed, as stated in Estate of Culver [126 N.W.2d 536 (Wis. 1964)], they raise a "red flag of warning." It does not automatically follow, however, that Joseph Casper's giving the majority of his wealth to non–kin is unnatural. The naturalness of a will depends upon the circumstances of each case.

D. Here, the testator's closest kin, his two sons, lived in California and had for many years. It appears that Casper's closest friend was JeanMcDowell.

E. Although there is a claim that Casper deviated from socially acceptable behavior for a man of his age in hiring Jean McDowell, fifty years his junior, as a resident housekeeper and in considering her as his closest friend through his last years, this does not necessarily lead to but one inference that his giving the majority of his estate to her was an unnatural testamentary result obtained by undue influence.

F. *Opportunity*. The only element of the four essential to a finding of undue influence that is present here is the "opportunity" to influence the testator.

G. [Affirmed.]

The Formal Will

The term *formal* indicates that the will has been prepared and executed in compliance with the state's law of wills ("probate code"). Although the right to make a will generally exists independent of statute, the procedures for drafting, executing, and witnessing the formal written document are governed by statute. Such statutory requirements, although basically similar, vary from state to state. Therefore the drafter must be thoroughly acquainted with the law of the state in which the testator's will is to be effective and must be sure to comply with its provisions. Noncompliance usually means that the will is declared invalid. If this happens, the decedent's property passes in accordance with the state's law of descent and distribution. (Such statutes and their application are discussed later in another section.)

General Requirements

A will must be written; it must be signed by the testator or testatrix or at his or her direction. In most states, the signing must be witnessed by two competent persons who themselves must sign as witnesses in the presence of each other and of the testator or testatrix. A few states require three witnesses. Most states require an **attestation clause,** a paragraph beneath the testator's signature to the effect that the will was *published*—that is, declared by the testator to be the last will and testament, and signed in the presence of the witnesses, who themselves signed as attesting witnesses. These are the formalities required by statute, and they must be strictly observed. The witnesses do not need to read or know the contents of the will. The testator or testatrix simply announces to them that the document is the will and that he or she is going to sign it. The function of the attestation clause is to serve as a self—proving affidavit to relieve the witnesses of the burden of testifying when the will is submitted for admission to probate after the death of the testator or testatrix.

Specific Provisions

The main function of a will is to provide for the disposal of property. However, it can appoint an executor and cancel all previous wills if it so states. It can also provide for an alternative disposition of property in the event the primary beneficiary predeceases the testator. If the testator or testatrix is married, the surviving spouse is usually appointed as the executor or executrix; if unmarried, a close relative or friend may be designated.

A will can also cover the disposition of property in the event that husband and wife die nearly simultaneously. It is essential for the will to state that it revokes any and all prior wills. The existence of two or more wills can create insurmountable problems. Sometimes none are admitted to probate (the court proceedings whereby a will is proved and the estate of the decedent is disposed of), in which event the state's statutory provisions for the division of an estate are followed.

The will can also name a guardian for minor children. If both husband and wife die, the guardian they have appointed in their wills can be confirmed by the court if he or she is qualified and willing to serve in that capacity. This will obviate the necessity for a court—appointed guardian and a possible controversy between the two competing, though well—meaning, sides of the family.

Modification

While it is possible in some states to change one's will by erasure, by striking out portions, or by interlineation, such procedures are risky undertakings at best. The proper method is to modify by means of a **codicil.** This is an addition to the will and must be executed with the same formalities as the original document. Consequently, if extensive modification is necessary, the testator would be well—advised to consider making a new will.

Revocation

A will becomes effective only at the death of the testator. The testator can revoke or amend the will at any time until death. Revocation can be accomplished in several ways, but usually must be done in strict compliance with statute by means evincing a clear intent to revoke. Executing a new will with a clause expressly revoking all prior wills and codicils is a customary method of revoking a will. The necessity for strict statutory compliance is illustrated in the following case.

IN RE ESTATE OF HAUGK
Wisconsin Supreme Court, 280 N.W.2d 684 (1979)

On January 6,_1965, MarieHaugk executed a will naming the Lutheran Children's Friend Society and the Easter Seal Society of Milwaukee County (appellants) as residual beneficiaries. On September 2, 1976, Marie's husband, Horst Haugk, burned the 1965 will in the family basement, while Marie, who was suffering from a heart condition and was thus unable to descend the stairs into the basement, stayed upstairs in the kitchen. Soon there— after, Marie spoke to her attorney about execution of a new will which would have eliminated appellants as beneficiaries, purportedly because she had wearied of their repeated requests for funds. However, Marie died before the new win could be executed.

Haugk filed a petition with the probate court claiming his wife died intestate, leaving him as sole beneficiary of her $130,000 estate. Appellants then petitioned the court for admission of the 1965 will. The trial court found that the 1965 will was properly revoked and ruled for Haugk. Appellants challenge this ruling on appeal.

Coffey, Justice:

The common law requirements for revocation of a will by physical act have been codified in sec. 853.11(1)(b), Stats., which recites:

"853. Revocation. (1) subsequent writing or physical act. A will is revoked in whole or in part by: . . .(b) Burning, tearing, canceling or obliterating the will or part, with the intent to revoke, by the testator or by some person in the testator's presence and by his direction."

Thus the revocation statute clearly delineates that, in order for the revocation of Marie's will to be effective, Haugk had to burn the will: (1) in Marie's presence, and (2) at her direction.

The record discloses that Marie was in the kitchen of her apartment while Haugk was in the basement burning the will in the incinerator. He explained that Marie's heart condition prevented her from going to the basement because of the strain of climbing the stairs. Contrary to the strict wording of sec. 853.11(1)(b), Stats., the trial court found that Marie, being in near proximity in the same house, 13 steps away, was in Haugk's "constructive presence at the time the will was destroyed.

In state of Murphy, E 259 N.W. 430(1935), this court discussed the necessity of the testator's presence during the destruction of a will.

In as much as revocation involves intention, the inference arises that the physical act must be performed by the testator himself or under his sanction and direction. . . . Both presence and direction of the testator being usually essential where the act is performed by another, a will is not legally revoked though destroyed by the testator's own order, if burned or torn where he did not or could not see or take cognizance of the deed done, as statutes commonly require the revocation by physical act to be by testator himself or in his presence and in such states cancellation by a third party out of the presence of testator is of no effect.

In the present case, a valid revocation could have been achieved if Haugk had torn up and destroyed the will in Marie's presence; thus she would not have had to endanger her health by climbing the basement stairs. It makes even more sense and eliminates all suggestion of fraud if the testator personally revoked the will, defacing each page of the document and placing her initials thereon.

The requirement that a will must be destroyed in the "testator's presence" must be strictly construed. This strict construction is necessary so as to prevent the inadvertent or more importantly the fraudulent destruction of a will contrary to the testator's intentions. Each element must be established by adequate evidence as this court will not adopt a position that will promote either intestacy or the fraudulent destruction of an individual's last will and testament.

Reversed.

Revocation can also be caused by operation of law. Marriage, divorce, or the birth of a child subsequent to making a will may affect its validity by revoking it completely or partially. State laws on wills are not uniform—the birth of a child may revoke a will completely in one state but only partially in another. Marriage and divorce also affect wills differently from state to state.

Limitations

There are a few limitations on a person's right to dispose of property through a will. For example, if a married person's will leaves no provision for inheritance by the spouse, many states allow the spouse to claim a share of the estate, typically one—third, under what is called a "forced share," "widow's share," or "elective share." If the spouse is left less than the statutory "forced share," the spouse has the right to renounce the actual devise and take the larger "forced share." In addition, many states provide the spouse a "homestead right" to a specific amount of land (for example, 1 acre in town or 160 acres in the country).

In community property states, each spouse owns one—half of the community property. In most of these states, the surviving spouse receives title to half the community property and the deceased spouse's share passes by will, if one exists, or by intestacy if no will_exists. In no event can either spouse dispose of more than one—half the community property by will.

Holographic Wills

Many states allow testators to execute their own wills without formal attestation. These **holographic wills** must be entirely in the testator's own handwriting, including the signature. These wills differ from formal wills in that no attestation clause or witnesses are required. However, most states allowing holographic wills require that the testator's handwriting and signature be proved by two witnesses familiar with them during probate of the will. Competent witnesses would include persons who had received correspondence from the testator. A holographic will is purely statutory—that is, it must be made in accordance with the appropriate state's law and is subject to prescribed conditions and limitations. The principal requirement is that it be entirely in the testator's own handwriting. In *Estate of Thorn*, 192 P. 19 (Cal. 1920), a testator in a holographic will used a rubber stamp to insert "Cragthorn" in the phrase "my country place Cragthorn." The will was held to be invalid since it was not entirely in the testator's handwriting. In some jurisdictions the holographic will must be dated in the testator's handwriting. The requirements of testamentary capacity and intent are the same as those for formal wills, but a holographic will is otherwise informal and may even take the form of a letter if it conveys testamentary intent (the mental determination or intention of the testator that the document constitute the person's will).

Nuncupative Wills

Some states permit **nuncupative wills,** or *oral wills.* These are also known as "soldiers' and sailors' wills." In general, statutes impose strict limitations on the disposal of property through a nuncupative will. Most states require that it be made during the testator's "last sickness"; that it be written down within a short period; that it be proved by two witnesses who were present at its making; and that the value of the estate bequeathed not exceed a certain amount, usually quite small. Some states also require that the decedent have been a soldier in the field or a sailor at sea in actual contemplation or fear of death. Nuncupative wills, where recognized, usually effect distribution of personal property only, not real property.

Nuncupative wills are difficult to establish, and the restrictions placed on them are intended to discourage their use. There is always the possibility of mistake or fraud and, except on rare occasions, a testator can easily plan sufficiently ahead to use the more traditional and acceptable type of will.

Intestacy—Statutes of Descent and Distribution

State laws govern the disposition of a decedent's estate when the decedent has died without a will—intestate. Such laws are called statutes of descent and distribution. They provide for disposition of the decedent's property, both real and personal, in accordance with a prescribed statutory scheme. Real property descends; personal property is distributed. Consequently, the law of the state where the decedent's real estate is located will determine the heirs, by class, to whom it will descend. The decedent's personal property will be distributed in accordance with the law of the state in which he or she is domiciled. In addition to prescribing the persons who will inherit a decedent's property, statutes of descent and distribution also prescribe the order and proportions in which they will take. The effect of this

The Surviving Spouse

Without exception, statutes of descent and distribution specify the portion of a decedent's estate that will be taken by his or her lawful, surviving spouse. Variation in this area is significant from state to state. Formerly, under common law, the surviving spouse was entitled only to a life estate (ownership for life) or *dower* (to the widow) or *curtesy* (to the widower) in the real property owned by the decedent. Personal property was divided among the surviving spouse and any children of the marriage. Today, the law of dower and curtesy has been either abolished or altered significantly by statute in all jurisdictions. *Typically, if a husband or wife dies intestate, the statutes provide that the surviving spouse takes one–half or one–third of the estate if there are children or grandchildren. If there are no children or grandchildren, in most jurisdictions the surviving spouse takes the entire estate. However, the states vary considerably in their treatment of this matter. In one jurisdiction, for example, children of the decedent take the real estate, to the exclusion of a surviving spouse, with the spouse taking one–third of the personal property. If there are no children or descendants of children the spouse takes the entire estate. In another, if there are children or representatives of deceased children, the surviving wife takes a child's share but not less than one–fifth of the estate.*

In general, if there are children the surviving spouse must share the estate with them. The number of children or grandchildren will determine the share which is to pass to the surviving spouse. If there are no children or grandchildren, or none have survived the decedent, the surviving spouse takes everything.

As noted earlier, in a community property state, the surviving spouse owns one–half of the community property. The remaining half is subject to intestacy rules if no will exists.

Descendants of the Decedent

There is little disparity in the statutes that govern the shares of an intestate's children or other lineal descendants (those in a direct line from the decedent— children and grandchildren). It is generally the case that, subject to the statutory share of a surviving spouse, children of the decedent share and share alike, with the children of a deceased child taking that child's share. This latter provision is known as a **per stirpes** distribution. For example, assume that a decedent dies after his spouse, leaving two children, a son and a daughter, who have two and three children of their own, respectively. If both son and daughter survive the decedent, each will take half the estate. However, if the son predeceases the decedent, his two children will take his share, each of them taking one–fourth of the estate with the daughter taking the other half. (If the decedent's spouse were still alive, the fractions described here would still apply, but only to that portion of the estate remaining after the spouse took her share.)

If the descendants are all of one class, that is, children or grandchildren, they will take **per capita**, each getting an equal share. Thus, if the intestate had a son and daughter who predeceased him, but those children left behind five living grandchildren, each grandchild would take one–fifth of what is left after the surviving spouse's share has been provided for. Figure 27.1 illustrates these differences.

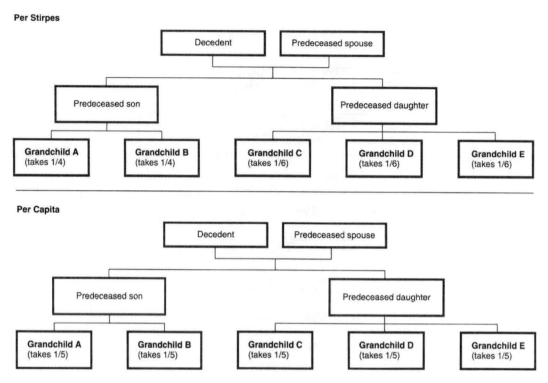

Figure 27.1   Per Stirpes and Per Capita

Adopted children are generally treated the same as natural children; illegitimate children generally inherit only from their mother unless their father's paternity has been either acknowledged or established through legal proceedings.

The Surviving Ascendants

There is general agreement that children of the decedent and subsequent generations of lineal descendants will take to the exclusion of other blood relatives such as parents or brothers and sisters. With regard to the ascendants of the intestate (parents and grandparents), there is much less uniformity in state law. In most states, where decedents leave no descendants, their parents will take the estate, with brothers and sisters (known as collaterals) taking if the parents are not living. In other jurisdictions, brothers and sisters share with the parents. Nephews and nieces may take the share of a predeceased parent if other brothers and sisters of the decedent are still living. If not, the nephews and nieces, as sole survivors, share and share alike in a per capita distribution. In any event, a distribution to ascendants and collaterals is made only if there are no surviving descendants or spouse.

Other than the surviving spouse, relatives by marriage have no claim on the decedent's estate. If the intestate has died leaving no heirs or next–of–kin whatsoever—no spouse, children, grandchildren, ascendants, or collaterals —the estate will pass to the state by a process known as escheat. This rarely happens, but it is provided for by law.

Administration of the Estate

Administration of decedents' estates is accomplished by a proceeding in **probate** if they die leaving a will. The word derives from the Latin *probatio,* proof. In the law of wills it means the proof or establishment of a document as the valid last will and testament of the deceased. In most states, the court having jurisdiction is called the probate court, and the principal question to be decided by judicial determination is the validity or invalidity of the will. Once the will has been admitted to probate—that is, determined to be valid—the probate court insures efficient distribution of the estate. Funeral expenses, debts to creditors and taxes are paid first. Then homestead rights and forced shares must be taken into account. Finally, the remaining assets are distributed impartially to heirs, devisees, legatees, and others, in accordance with the testator's wishes.

The *personal representative* of the decedent (called the executor if appointed by will and the administrator if appointed by the court) administers the estate under the supervision of the court—to collect decedent's assets, to pay or settle any lawful claims against the estate, and to distribute the remainder to those who will take under the will. If there is no will, the state's law of descent and distribution will determine how the estate is to be distributed.

Probate and the administration of decedents' estates are strictly regulated by statute and can be complex procedures when the estate is substantial and the interest in property of the deceased is not clear. Many parties may be affected by the administration process, so attention to detail and compliance with the state's probate law or code are essential. A personal representative who has effectively handled the estate and wound up its affairs may petition the court and be discharged from any further responsibilities.

Avoiding Administration

Quite frequently, the formal administration of decedents' estates can be wholly or partially avoided. In fact, it is safe to say that fewer than half the deaths in this country result in administration proceedings. Obviously, if the decedent died with no assets or a very small estate, there is no need for an involved administration. Most jurisdictions permit the handling of decedents' affairs without official administration in such cases.

There are, however, still other situations in which probate or formal administration can be avoided, at least for a portion of the decedent's assets. For example, if some or all of the property was co–owned with others as a "joint tenancy" with a right of survivorship, it passes to the surviving owners and not to the estate. Joint tenancy bank accounts or securities or a residence owned as a joint tenancy or as a tenancy by the entirety all pass to the surviving owner. This method of owning property is sometimes referred to as the "poor man's will." It should be noted, however, that even though the decedent's interest in such property bypasses the estate, it can still be subject to an estate or inheritance tax.

If the decedent owned one or more life insurance policies, they will not be subject to administration if a beneficiary has been named. If one has not been named or if the one named has predeceased the decedent, the proceeds pass to the estate.

Trusts

The trust is a versatile legal concept that is typically used to conserve family wealth from generation to generation, to provide for the support and education of children, and to minimize the tax burden on substantial estates. Trust law recognizes two types of property ownership, legal and equitable. One person can hold legal title to property while another can have the equitable title.

To establish a trust, the party intending to create a trust, called a **settlor** or *trustor,* transfers legal ownership of property to a *trustee* for the benefit of a third party, the **beneficiary.** The trustee is the legal owner of the property, called the **res** or *corpus,* but it is owned in trust to be used and managed solely for the benefit of others, who own the equitable title. A trust established and effective during the life of the settlor is known as an *inter vivos* or "living" **trust.** If it is created by the settlor's will, to be effective on that person's death, it is a **testamentary trust.** Trusts are also classified as *express, implied, private,* or *charitable,* depending on the purpose they serve and how they are created.

The Express Private Trust

An express private trust is created when a settlor, with clear intent to do so, and observing certain formalities, sets up a fiduciary relationship involving a trustee, the beneficiaries, and management of the it trust res for a lawful purpose. There is little uniformity in the statutes that govern trusts and their creation. It is a general requirement, however, that trusts be established by a_writing or, if oral, subsequently proved by a writing. The writing need not be formal so long as it clearly identifies the trust property and the beneficiary and states the purpose for which the trust is created. The intent of the settlor to create a trust must be clear from the circumstances and the action taken. No particular language is required, but the settlor's instructions should be direct and unambiguous. If the purpose of the trust is to put children through college, this should be stated clearly. Language that "requests," or "hopes," or "desires" that the trustee do certain things is considered to be precatory in nature (a mere request and not an order or command) and may not be binding on the trustee. Further, words or phrases that fall short of appointing a trustee or imposing positive responsibilities should be avoided. For example, in Comford v. Cantrell, 151 S.W. 1076 (Tenn. 1941), a husband left his estate to his wife, stating in the will that it was his "request" that upon her death his wife "shall give my interest to each of my brothers." The court viewed the language as purely **precatory.** The brothers had no legal right to object when the wife gave the land to her nephew instead.

Legal Focus

Several years ago, Jamaican reggae singer and songwriter Bob Marley became a star with such songs to his credit as "I Shot the Sherif," "War," "Jammin," and others. Many of his songs were made even more popular when recorded by others such as Eric Clapton. When he died in 1981 at age 36 from brain cancer, Marley had an international network of music publishing and recording companies and was personally worth over $30 million. After his death, his estate continued to earn millions of dollars annually from royalties on his music. Marley died without leaving a will, despite the advice he had received many times that he should have one. Marley was of the Rastafarian religion; many people believed that his religious beliefs caused him to spurn the making of a will. His mother stated that "[h]is" mind wasn't on those material t'ings because he know no man never bring nuttin' into this world. Naked they come and naked shall they go." Other claim that Marley simply got too busy and forgot to have a will prepared.

Under Jamaican law, which applied to the disposition of his estate because this was his domicile, the lack of a will meant that his wife Rita was entitled to only 10 percent of his assets. The other 90 percent was to be divided among his eleven children, of whom Rita was the mother of four. Rita thought, perhaps correctly, that Marley would have left her far more than 10 percent if he had make his wishes known by executing a will. Several years after his death, the court-appointed administrator of Marley's estate charged Rita and her accountant and lawyer with fraud and other legal violations. The basis for the administrator's claims was the assertion that Rita and her advisors had forged Marley's signature to a number of documents that were backdated to a time before his death.; these documents purported to transfer controlling ownership of several companies to Rita, thus removing them from the assets of his estate. Several years of litigation have now taken place, with no end in sight. A will does not guarantee that there will be no disputes after a person's death, but it certainly improves the odds either that there will not be any significant disputes or that any such issues will be resolved more quickly. In this case, knowing Marley's true wishes probably would have had a substantial impact on the actions of various interested parties, especially in light of the fact that he very likely would have provided more for Rita if he had made a will.

The Trust Property

The subject matter of a trust may be any property of value. Money, interests in real estate, securities, and insurance are commonly used. However, settlors must own the property at the time they create the trust. They cannot transfer in trust property they expect to acquire and own at a later date. When the property is transferred to the trustee it becomes his or hers to manage for the benefit of the beneficiaries and in accordance with the terms of the trust. If the essential elements of a valid trust are missing or if the trust fails, the property will revert to the settlor, if living, or to that person's estate, if deceased.

The Trustee

A **trustee** is, of course, essential; a trust without one cannot be effective. However, the courts will not let an otherwise valid trust fail for want of a trustee. If the named trustee dies or declines to serve or is removed for cause, the court will appoint a replacement. The court will also appoint a trustee when the settlor fails to name one in the trust. No special qualifications are necessary. Since trustees take title to property and manage it, they must be capable of owning property. Minors and incompetents can own property, but they are under a disability in regard to contractual capacity. Consequently, since their contracts are voidable, they cannot function as trustees. Settlors can appoint themselves trustees and, in fact, designate themselves as beneficiaries. The settlor cannot, however, be the sole trustee and the sole beneficiary of a single trust. This relationship would merge both legal and equitable titles to the trust property in the trustee, and he or she would hold it free of any trust.

If a corporation (an artificial person) is not prohibited by its charter from doing so, it can act as a trustee. Trust companies and banks, for example, frequently serve as trustees for both large and small trusts. They typically charge fees amounting to 1 percent of the value of the *res* per year.

Beneficiaries

The express private trust is ordinarily created for the benefit of identified, or identifiable, beneficiaries. A father can establish a trust for the care and education of his minor children—and can name them in the trust instrument. However, a settlor can also simply specify as the beneficiaries a class of persons, such as "my minor children" or "my brothers and sisters." In either case, the persons who are to benefit are readily identifiable. Trusts have also been held to be valid when established for domestic animals, household pets, and even inanimate objects. Such trusts present problems though, *since nonhuman and inanimate beneficiaries are incapable of holding title to property. Additionally, there will be no beneficiary with the capacity to enforce the provisions of the trust against the trustee. This is not to say that a charitable trust for animals in general or a trust for humane purposes will fail. (The charitable trust is discussed in a following section.)*

The beneficiary does not have to agree to accept the benefits of the trust. It is presumed that beneficiaries accept the trust unless they make a specific rejection. Their interest in the trust can, in general, be reached by creditors, and they can sell or otherwise dispose of their interests. However, beneficiaries can transfer only the interests they hold—the equitable title. If a beneficiary holds more than a life estate, and the trust does not make other provisions, this interest can be disposed of in a will or can pass to the beneficiary's estate after death.

Managing the Trust

The administration of a trust is highly regulated by statute. Trustees must know the law of their jurisdictions. In general, they must make every effort to carry out the purpose of the trust. They must act with care and prudence and use their best judgment, and at all times they must exercise an extraordinary degree of loyalty to the beneficiary— the degree of loyalty required of those in a fiduciary position.

In carrying out the purposes of a trust, the trustees ordinarily have broad powers that are usually described in the trust instrument. In addition, they may have implied powers that are necessary to carry out their express duties. For example, trustees can have express authority to invest the trust property and pay the beneficiary the income from such investments. They can also have the implied power to incur reasonable expenses in administering the trust.

Insofar as it is possible trustees should exercise the care and skill of a "prudent person" in managing the trust. A reasonable goal for a trustee is to exercise the diligence necessary to preserve the corpus and realize a reasonable return on income from "prudent" investments at the same time. State laws often specify the types of investments a trustee can make. In Georgia, for example, trust law authorizes investment in bonds or securities issued by the state and by the U.S. government and certain of its agencies and in certain banks or trust companies insured by the Federal Deposit Insurance Corporation. With certain exceptions, any other investment of trust funds must be under an order of the superior court or at the risk of the trustee. If the trust instrument gives the trustee wide discretion to invest in "other" securities, many jurisdictions allow this. Statutes often indicate that prudent persons should diversify their investments. However, the trustee can still be held accountable for a failure to exercise proper care. In other words, the law discourages bad investments.

The relationship between the trustee and the beneficiary is fiduciary in nature. Consequently, in managing trusts, trustees must act solely for the benefit of the beneficiaries. For example, trustees cannot borrow any portion of the trust funds or sell their own property to the trust. Neither can they purchase trust property for themselves. Even though the trustee's personal dealings with the trust may prove to be advantageous to the beneficiary, the duty of loyalty is breached and the trustee can be charged with such breach. If there are multiple trustees, an innocent trustee may well be held liable for not preventing a co–trustee's breach of fiduciary duty.

The duties of a trustee are highlighted in the following case.

WITMER V. BLAIR
Missouri Court of Appeals, 588 S.W.2d 222 (1979)

At his death in 1960, Henry Nussbaum's will created a trust for the education of his grandchildren. Defendant Jane Ann Blair, Nussbaum's niece, was named trustee. Nussbaum's daughter, Dorothy Janice Witmer (defendant's cousin) was given a reversionary interest in the residue of the trust should none of the grandchildren survive to inherit the estate. Marguerite Janice Witmer (Dorothy's daughter) became the only beneficiary of the trust.

Defendant Blair received the trust estate in 1961. It consisted of $1,905 in checking and *savings accounts $5,700 in certificates of deposit, and a house valued at $6,000. The house was sold in 1962, netting $4,467 to the trust estate, which amount was deposited in a trust checking account. For the next several years, the trustee kept funds in checking and savings accounts and in certificates of deposit. As of December 31, 1975, the trust assets consisted of $2,741 checking account, $5,474 savings, and $8,200 certificates of deposit.*

Marguerite was 23 years old at the time of trial. She had not attended college, but various sums of money had been expended from the trust for her benefit, including a typewriter, clothes, glasses, modeling school tuition and expenses, and a tonsillectomy, all totaling some $1,250. The trust also spent $350 for dentures for Dorothy.

Marguerite and Dorothy brought this suit against Blair for breach of trust for failure to properly invest the funds of the trust. The trial judge removed the trustee and surcharged her account for $309 in unexplained expenditures, but refused to assess actual or punitive damages for breach of trust. Plaintiffs appealed.

Welborn, Special Judge:

The trust was handled by appellant rather informally. She kept no books for the trust. The expenditures were in most cases advanced by her from her personal account and she reimbursed herself from the trust income. In 1965, the bank erroneously credited the trust account with $560 which should have gone to the trustee's personal account. The mistake was not corrected and that amount remained in the trust account. The trustee received no compensation for her services. Asked at the trial whether she had ever been a trustee before, she responded negatively, adding "And never again." She explained the large checking account balances in the trust account by the fact that college for Janice "was talked about

all the way through high school.... [I]n my opinion, it was the sensible way to keep the money where I could get it to her without any problems at all in case she needed it quickly."

An accountant testified that had $500 been kept in the checking and savings accounts (the $800 was based upon the maximum disbursement in any year) and the balance of the trust placed in one—year certificates of deposit, $9,138 more interest would have been earned as of September 30, 1976.

A concise summary of the law applicable to the situation appears in 76 Am. Jur.2d Trusts §379(1975):

It is a general power and duty of a trustee, implied if not expressed, at least in the case of an ordinary trust, to keep trust funds properly invested. Having uninvested funds in his hands, it is his duty to make investments of them, where at least they are not soon to be applied to the purposes and objects or turned over to the beneficiaries of the trust. Generally, he cannot permit trust funds to lie dormant or on deposit for a prolonged period, but he may keep on hand a fund sufficient to meet expenses, including contingent expenses, and he need not_invest a sum too small to be prudently invested. A trustee ordinarily may not say in excuse of a failure to invest that he kept the funds on hand to pay the beneficiaries on demand.

The trustee is under a duty to the beneficiary to use reasonable care and skill to make the trust property productive. Restatement (Second) of Trusts §181(1959).

A breach of trust is a violation by the trustee of any duty which as trustee he owes to the beneficiary. Restatement (Second) of Trusts §201(1959).

Comment b to this section states:

Mistake of law as to existence of duties and powers. A trustee commits a breach of trust not only where he violates a duty in bad faith, or intentionally although in good faith, or negligently, but also where he violates a duty because of a mistake as to the extent of his duties and powers. This is true not only where his mistake is in regard to a rule of law, whether a statutory or common–law rule, but also where he interprets the trust instrument as authorizing him to do acts which the court determines he is not authorized by the instrument to do. In such a case, he is not protected from liability merely because he acts in good faith, nor is he protected merely because he relies upon the advice of counsel."

Under the above rules, there has been a breach of trust by the trustee in this case

and her good faith is not a defense to appellants' claim. In 1962, appellant Marguerite was some nine years of age. Obviously there was no prospect of the beneficiary's attending college for a number of years. However, when Marguerite became of college age [around 1971] and was considering a college education, the respondent should not be faulted for keeping readily available a sum of money which would permit the use of the trust fund for such purpose.

Reversed, and remanded with directions to enter judgment for plaintiffs for $2,840.

The Uniform Prudent Investor Act, adopted in most states, requires trustees to consider modern portfolio theory in making investments on behalf of beneficiaries, providing that "[a] trustee's investment and management decisions respecting individual assets must be evaluated not in isolation but in the context of the trust portfolio as a whole and as part of an overall investment strategy having risk and return objectives reasonably suited to the trust." Among the factors that trustees are directed to consider are (a) general economic conditions, (b) possible effects of inflation or deflation, (c) expected tax consequences of investment decisions, (d) the role that each investment plays within the overall trust portfolio, (e) expected total return from income and appreciation of capital, (f) the beneficiaries' other resources, (g) needs for liquidity, regularity of income, and preservation of capital; and (h) an asset's special relationship or special value, if any, to the purposes of the trust or to the beneficiary.

The Spendthrift Trust

Settlors may be concerned that beneficiaries may be incapable of managing their own affairs either because of inexperience and immaturity or simply because they are "spendthrifts." Settlors can therefore determine that beneficiaries will not sell, mortgage, or otherwise transfer their rights to receive principal and income and that the beneficiaries' creditors will not reach the income or principal while it is in the hands of the trustee. Such a provision no longer applies after the income or principal has been paid over to the beneficiary. Further, some modern statutes limit the **spendthrift trust.** They either limit the income that is protected from creditors or they permit creditors to reach amounts in excess of what the beneficiary is considered to need.

Because most states have traditionally had little statutory law relating to trusts, courts made created most of the trust law, often relying upon the persuasive authority of various versions of the Restatement of Trusts. However, in 2000 the **Uniform Trust Code(UTC)** was promulgated. It has now been adopted largely by 15 states and in part by a few others. It is largely patterned after the Restatement and should not do much to alter the preexisting law of trusts in the states in which it is adopted.

The following case applies the UTC in a case that raises a common question—how can beneficiaries of spendthrift trusts get their hands on the trust's assets?

Trust Termination

In most states, settlors can revoke a trust at any time if they have reserved that power. However, most trusts are terminated when the stated period has elapsed or when the trust purpose has been served. In a trust for the care of minor children, it logically ends when the beneficiaries have reached their majority. In a trust for the college education of the beneficiary, it will terminate when that goal has been attained. In any event, upon termination of a trust, any balance of funds remaining reverts to the settlor or is disposed of in accordance with the instructions contained in the trust.

ESTATE OF SOMERS
Kansas Supreme Court, 89 P.3d 898 (2004)

Eula Somers died in 1956, leaving a testamentary trust of $120,000 for her two grandchildren. By January 2001, the value of the Trust had increased to approximately $ 3,500,000. The trust provided for $100 monthly payments to the grandchildren, with the remainder of the trust after their deaths to be paid to the Shriners Hospital for Crippled Children. Firstar Bank is currently the trustee of the trust.

The Shriners Hospitals for Children (Shriners) and the Grandchildren reached an agreement to terminate the Trust. They agreed that the Grandchildren would each receive a distribution of $ 150,000 from the Trust and that the remainder of the Trust assets would immediately be distributed to Shriners. Shriners agreed to continue the $ 100 monthly payments to the Grandchildren. Firstar

opposed the termination of the Trust. Shriners and the Grandchildren then filed a joint petition in district court asking that the Trust be terminated immediately. Each side filed a motion for summary judgment. The district court denied the petition to terminate the Trust and the Grandchildren's request for individual distributions of $ 150,000. However, the district court concluded that it had equity jurisdiction and ordered an immediate, partial distribution of the corpus of the Trust to Shriners, but required that $ 500,000 remain in the Trust to fund the annuity payments to the Grandchildren. The court further ordered that the attorney fees and expenses of the Grandchildren's attorneys be paid from the Shriners' distribution. All the parties appealed.

Gernon, Justice:

This appeal requires us to determine whether the trial court ruled properly when it partially distributed funds from a spendthrift trust at the request of each of the beneficiaries. The beneficiaries acted in concert, and none were or are under any incapacity.

A spendthrift trust is defined in Estate of Sowers, 574 P.2d 224 (Kan. 1977), as "a trust created to provide a fund for the maintenance of a beneficiary and at the same time to secure the fund against his improvidence or incapacity. Provisions against alienation of the trust fund by the voluntary act of the beneficiary or by his creditors are its usual incidents."

The parties do not dispute that this Trust is a spendthrift trust. Thus, the question is whether a court can terminate a spendthrift trust at the request of the beneficiaries, who are all in agreement and competent to consent, if the settlor is not available to consent to the termination. This is an issue of first impression in Kansas, requiring the application and interpretation of the Kansas Uniform Trust Code (KUTC). Section 410(a) of the KUTC provides: "A trust terminates to the extent the trust is revoked or expires pursuant to its terms, no purpose of the trust remains to be achieved, or the purposes of the trust have become unlawful, contrary to public policy, or impossible to achieve."

And Section 411 provides:

"(a) A noncharitable irrevocable trust may be modified or terminated upon consent of the settlor and all qualified beneficiaries, even if the modification or termination is inconsistent with a material purpose of the trust. A settlor's power to consent to a trust's termination may be exercised by an agent under a power of attorney only to the extent expressly authorized by the power of attorney or the terms of the trust; by the settlor's conservator with the approval of the court supervising the conservatorship if an agent is not so authorized; or by the settlor's guardian with the approval of the court supervising the guardianship if an agent is not so authorized and a conservator has not been appointed.

"(b) A noncharitable irrevocable trust may be terminated upon consent of all of the qualified beneficiaries if the court concludes that continuance of the trust is not necessary to achieve any material purpose of the trust. . . .

"(c) A spendthrift provision in the terms of the trust is presumed to constitute a material purpose of the trust."

The Grandchildren claim that the district court had the power to terminate the Trust with all of the beneficiaries' consent because the spendthrift provision is not a material purpose of the trust. They appear to raise two arguments in this regard. First, the Grandchildren argue that the spendthrift provision is not a material purpose because it is a small fraction of the entire trust. The Grandchildren cite no authority for their proposition that a spendthrift provision must apply to a substantial portion of the trust to be considered a material purpose. The material purposes of a trust are subject to the settlor's discretion, which is limited "only to the extent its purposes are lawful, not contrary to public policy, and possible to achieve." (KUTC Sec. 404) Accordingly, we find no merit in this argument.

Second, the Grandchildren claim that an annuity could continue their lifetime payments, thereby continuing the material purpose of the trust after its termination. This argument overlooks the purpose of a spendthrift provision, which "restrains either voluntary or involuntary transfer of a beneficiary's interest." An annuity purchased by Shriners outside the confines of the trust is not protected from alienation or attachment by the annuitant's creditors. The only way to ensure the protection of the spendthrift provision is for sufficient funds to remain in the Trust. Thus, Eula Somers' purpose to protect the trust assets from her grandchildren's creditors cannot be accomplished by terminating the Trust and purchasing an annuity that would merely maintain the beneficiaries' lifetime payments.

It should be noted that KUTC Sec. 411, by its express terms, applies to the modification or termination of a noncharitable trust. Clearly, this is a charitable trust. Thus, we must consider whether, under these facts, a charitable trust with a spendthrift provision for certain beneficiaries for their lives may be modified, terminated, or partially terminated. When there is no law directly on point, Kansas courts turn to the Restatement of Trusts, which does not distinguish between charitable and noncharitable trusts, and provides in Sec. 337:

> "(1) Except as stated in Subsection (2), if all of the beneficiaries of the trust consent and none of them is under an incapacity, they can compel the termination of the trust.

> "(2) If the continuance of the trust is necessary to carry out a material purpose of the trust, the beneficiaries cannot compel its termination."

The Restatement's comment 1 to Sec. 337 specifically proscribes the termination of spendthrift trusts, stating: "If by the terms of the trust or by statute the interest of one or more of the beneficiaries is made inalienable by him, the trust will not be terminated while such inalienable interest still exists, although all of the beneficiaries desire to terminate it or one beneficiary acquires the whole beneficial interest and desires to terminate it."

[Existing authorities] support a conclusion that the tenet from KUTC Sec. 411 may be applied equally to charitable and noncharitable trusts. Thus, the beneficiaries are precluded from terminating the Trust while continuation of the Trust is necessary to achieve a material purpose of the Trust does not make a spendthrift provision a material purpose under all circumstances. Rather, it raises a rebuttable presumption that the spendthrift provision is a material purpose. The Grandchildren, however, offer no evidence to rebut the presumption that the spendthrift provision is a material purpose of the trust. As a result, we find the spendthrift provision of the Trust to be a material purpose of the Trust. The Grandchildren's proposal that Shriners would purchase an annuity to continue their monthly payments does not satisfy the protections required by the spendthrift provision. Thus, termination of the trust would frustrate a material purpose of the Trust. The trial court did not err when it reached the same conclusion and refused to terminate the Trust.

[The court then held that the trial court acted properly in ordering the $3,000,000 distribution to Shriners before the death of both grandchildren, especially in light of the fact that the reserved $500,000 would easily fund the continuing $100 monthly payments to the grandchildren. The payment to Shriners advanced an important purpose of the Trust and was proper because the accumulation of so much money in the Trust was unforeseen to the testator. The lower court also properly refused to order the Shriners to make the $300,000 distribution to the grandchildren, because EulaSomers' will and the Trust did not provide for any cash distributions to the grandchildren beyond the specified monthly payments.]

Affirmed.

Charitable Trusts

The purpose of a charitable trust is the general benefit of humanity. Its beneficiaries can be education, science, religion, hospitals, homes for the aged or handicapped, and a host of other charitable or public entities. Charitable trusts are much like private trusts.

Furthermore, the courts of most jurisdictions will find another suitable purpose for a charitable trust when the settlor's stated purpose is impossible or difficult to achieve. The courts do so under the doctrine of *cy pres,* meaning so near or as near. The doctrine is used to prevent a charitable trust from failing for want of a beneficiary. To illustrate: a testator establishes a testamentary trust for the support and maintenance of orphans in a specified orphanage. If the specified orphanage ceased to exist before the testator's death, the court could use the *cy pres* doctrine, find that the trustor's intent was to benefit orphans generally, and apply the trust to some other orphanage in the area. The *cy pres* doctrine applies only where there is definite charitable intent, never to private trusts.

Implied Trusts

An implied trust, constructive or resulting, is created by law. While the distinction is not always clear, a **constructive trust** is usually imposed upon property by the courts to correct or rectify fraud or to prevent one party from being unjustly enriched at the expense of another. In reality, it is a fiction or remedy to which a court of equity will resort to prevent injustice. Suppose that A and B have agreed to purchase a tract of land jointly with the deed to list both of them as grantees. If, despite the agreement, A secretly buys the land alone, and the deed fails to list B as grantee, the court will impose a constructive trust on the property to the extent of the half interest B should have. This procedure assumes that B is ready and willing to pay half the purchase price. In another case, directors of corporations who take advantage of their positions to make secret profits from corporate opportunities will be constructive trustees for the corporations to the extent of the profits they make. Constructive trusts commonly arise out of the breach of a fiduciary relationship where no trust intent is present or required.

The **resulting trust** arises out of, or is created by, the conduct of the parties. It is imposed in order to carry out the apparent intentions of the parties at the time they entered into the transaction that gave rise to the trust. The most frequent use of the resulting trust occurs when one party purchases property but records the title in the name of another. For example, A wants to purchase a tract of real estate but does not want it subjected to the hazards of his business ventures. He therefore buys the land but has the deed made out in the name of a friend, B. There is no problem if B conveys the real estate to A on demand in accordance with their understanding of the nature of the transaction. However, if B refuses to convey the land, the courts can impose a resulting trust on B for A's benefit. Some difficulty can arise if, in the situation above, A has title taken in the name of his wife or a close relative, because it could be valid to presume that A intended the land as a gift. And if A had purchased in the name of another to defraud his creditors, it is likely that the courts would refuse to impose the resulting trust, being reluctant to afford relief to a wrongdoer.

Estate Planning

"*Estate Planning* is applying the law of property, trusts, wills, future interests, insurance, and taxation to the ordering of one's affairs, keeping in mind the possibility of retirement and the certainty of death." (R. J. Lynn, *An Introduction to Estate Planning*, (1975) at 1.) Wills and trusts are the most commonly used estate planning devices. This final section briefly explores other aspects of the estate planning process, touching first on the philosophy that has previously guided or misguided many in the disposition of their property—a disposition that usually occurs after death, with dire results for the surviving heirs. The general public equates estate planning with death; lifetime planning is more important than death planning. The aim is not merely to dispose of one's estate at death but to organize resources during life in order to provide for the present and future well-being of one's family.

Perhaps the major consideration in preserving estate integrity is the impact taxes may have, if little thought is given to methods for reducing estate shrinkage. The decedent's survivors may find on settling the estate that the principal heir is the government. It is, of course, unlawful to evade taxes, but there is nothing illegal about doing everything possible to avoid paying unnecessary taxes. Various planning devices can keep unwanted heirs, in the form of estate and inheritance taxes, and the expense of probate and administration to a minimum.

Recent legislation in Congress to substantially reduce the estate tax (the "death tax" in the parlance of its opponents) has dramatically altered estate planning strategies. As presently structured, the law slowly reduces federal estate tax rates over the next several years as it increases exclusions. Then, in 2010 there will be no estate tax, but in 2011 the law will revert back to the pre-2001 exclusion of $1 million. Many Republicans are committed to eliminating the federal estate tax permanently.

Gifts

One of the keys to cutting estate taxes is to give away some assets before death. The gifts shift income to children or perhaps retired parents who may be in lower tax brackets. Giving, as an estate planning device, may be hard to accept for the donor who has spent a lifetime slowly accumulating an estate. Nevertheless, it is something to consider, keeping in mind one's personal situation. Amateur philanthropy, however, can be dangerous. Property given outright to a poor manager can be wasted away; a gift with too many strings attached can be something less than useful to the donee. Gift taxes must also be considered. Under current tax law, each parent may transfer $12,000 each year to any recipient, including children, without any gift tax liability.

Life Insurance

Life insurance, in its various forms, can serve many purposes in estate planning. Ownership can be so arranged that the proceeds will not become part of the insured's estate to be taxed. It is a good means of providing liquid funds so that forced sales of other property to pay estate charges or debts can be avoided. In general, life insurance is not subject to probate and administration expenses and is a good way to make *inter vivos* (during lifetime) gifts to children, to grandchildren, or, if the donor is so inclined, to charity. Many kinds of policies are available—term, whole life, and endowment, for example—and there may be a place for one or more types in an estate plan. For the average wage earner life insurance is the major, perhaps the only, means of providing security for the family. Indeed, it may be all that is necessary, other than a valid will. With regard to business ventures, the members of a partnership often enter into buy and sell agreements with a view to continuing the partnership after the death of a partner. The partnership agreement sometimes provides that the estates of deceased partners will sell their interests to surviving partners and that the partners will buy such interests. Insurance is frequently used by the partnership to fund the agreement.

The Marital Deduction

For federal estate tax purposes the **marital deduction** is a useful device in estate planning involving substantial assets. It reflects the social concept that property accumulated during marriage should be treated as community property, disregarding the fact that the husband and wife could have contributed differing amounts. The marital deduction was designed to more nearly equate tax treatment between residents of states that have community property laws and those of states which do not. No matter what amount a decedent spouse passes to a surviving spouse, that amount will not be taxed in the decedent spouse's estate. This allows the surviving spouse to continue to have the use of up to all of the "community" assets for the rest of his or her life. The amount passing to the surviving spouse is included in his or her estate and will be taxed at the surviving spouse's death. The amount passing to the surviving spouse under the marital deduction must be determined through careful planning to maximize tax savings and meet the objectives of a particular family. Competent legal counsel and financial advice should be sought early in the estate planning process.

PART VI

GOVERNMENT REGULATION OF BUSINESS

CHAPTER **28**

ANTITRUST LAW

Introduction

Although antitrust enforcement has been in decline for more than two decades in the United States, the landmark Microsoft antitrust litigation launched by the U.S. Department of Justice and supported by various state attorneys general demonstrates that this remains an important area of law that is capable of shaping the future of entire industries. The Microsoft case, popularly chronicled in such books as John Heilemann's *Pride Before the Fall,* demonstrates that companies are wise to avoid antitrust entanglements in the first place. In addition to massively expensive litigation here in the United States, some of which Microsoft lost and some of which it won, it was ordered by European Union antitrust authorities to make specific changes in how it markets its software as well as pay a $648 million fine. Over the last decade or so, antitrust problems have cost Microsoft billions of dollars. Microsoft's experience, plus the recent $1.05 billion judgment in an antitrust case involving U.S. Smokeless Tobacco and the $650 million in fines that Samsung and its competitors in the American market for dynamic random access memory chips paid in a price–fixing case in 2005, indicates that the strategic manager should most definitely have a solid grounding in the essentials of antitrust law.

This is especially true because there have also been several criminal antitrust cases brought lately, which can result in wrongdoers going to jail. The Department of Justice's Antitrust Division has been seeking higher fines and longer jail terms in its prosecutions. For example, when vitamin manufacturers from Switzerland, Germany, France, and Japan were caught agreeing to fix prices at a top secret meeting in the Black Forest in Germany, high ranking officers at two of the companies went to prison. In addition, the five companies paid $862 million in U.S. fines, 855 million euros in EU fines, $1.05 billion to settle private class action lawsuits by direct purchasers of vitamins and $335 million to settle lawsuits brought by indirect purchasers.

The Objectives of Antitrust Law

An economy such as that of the United States, which depends primarily on the operation of market forces, cannot function properly without competition. Although the word "competition" is subject to various shades of meaning, it most often refers to a condition of economic rivalry among firms. That is, firms should be engaged in a contest for customers, the outcome of that contest depending on each firm's ability to satisfy customer needs and wants. The primary purpose of antitrust law is to promote competition. In the various types of markets, competition can take somewhat different forms. In the case of many kinds of products, for example, price is a very important factor in customers' buying decisions (that is, "price elasticity" is high), and much of the competitive rivalry among sellers may focus on price. On the other hand, in some markets price may not be quite as important to most customers as good service, availability of many product options, convenience, or other factors. In such markets, competition among sellers is likely to emphasize these non–price attributes to a greater extent. Not only does the form of competition vary somewhat among markets, but the intensity of competition also is less in some markets than in others. The job of antitrust law is to encourage competition in its various forms and to preserve it to the extent feasible in a given market. Most economists feel that a competitive, market–based economy produces a number of beneficial results such as efficient allocation of scarce resources, lower prices, higher quality, greater innovation, and economic freedom. In the view of some authorities, there is another reason for having a strong antitrust policy in the United States—more competition in an economic sense may diminish the amount of power that large firms have over the political process and over the lives of large numbers of people. Has antitrust law achieved its goals? This question cannot be answered with certainty because it is practically impossible to measure the effects of antitrust law on the American economy. There are many markets (so–called **oligopolies**) in which most of the sales are made by a few large companies. Many of these firms are very efficient; some are not. Many do not abuse their power; some do. In some of these markets, competition appears to be quite vigorous, but in others it is rather stagnant. Moreover, in many of these markets concentration of power in a few firms is an inevitable result of extremely large capital requirements and economies of scale. On the other hand, the *degree* of economic concentration is clearly not always inevitable. Thus, it is not surprising to find substantial disagreement among authorities concerning the wisdom and effect of antitrust law. Some say the law has not been enforced aggressively enough, while others say that it has been applied too aggressively to the wrong things. Many points of criticism and support have been raised over the years. Only two conclusions are relatively certain: (1) although the interpretation of some of the antitrust rules will vary over time, the fundamental principles are probably going to remain with us; and (2) antitrust law will always be controversial. With that, we will examine the law itself.

The Federal Antitrust Statutes

The first, and still the most important, of the federal antitrust laws is the Sherman Act, passed by Congress in 1890. Section 1 of this Act prohibits "contracts, combinations, and conspiracies in restraint of trade." The focus of Section 1 is collusion among firms that are supposed to be acting independently when making basic business decisions. Section 2 prohibits "monopolization, attempts to monopolize, and conspiracies to monopolize." The prohibition of monopolization, which is the most important part of Section 2, focuses on single–firm domination of a market.

In 1914, Congress enacted the Clayton Act with two main purposes in mind: (1) to make the prohibitions against certain anticompetitive practices more specific, and (2) to make it easier to challenge certain practices, such as mergers, when the evidence shows only probable future anticompetitive effects and not actual present effects. Section 2 of the Act prohibits price discrimination; Section 3 prohibits some tying and exclusive dealing agreements; and Section 7 forbids anticompetitive mergers. In any of these cases, the law is violated only if the evidence demonstrates an actual or highly probable anticompetitive effect of a substantial nature. Section 8 of the Clayton Act prohibits interlocking directorates between certain large corporations that are in direct competition with each other. An interlocking directorate occurs when the same individual serves on the boards of directors of two corporations.

Also in 1914, Congress passed the Federal Trade Commission Act (FTC Act). In addition to creating the Federal Trade Commission (FTC) as an enforcement agency, the Act also prohibited "unfair methods of competition" in Section 5. Any conduct that violates one of the other antitrust laws, plus a few other types of conduct, constitutes an unfair method of competition. In 1938, Congress added another phrase to Section 5 prohibiting "unfair or deceptive acts or practices." Thus the first part of the statute deals with antitrust matters, and the second part deals with various forms of consumer deception such as false advertising.

In 1936 Congress passed the Robinson–Patman Act, which amended Section 2 of the Clayton Act in an effort to make the law against price discrimination more effective.

Even though antitrust law is based on statutory enactments, most of the language in those statutes is so broad that court interpretations account for most of the lawmaking process. Also, our attention in this chapter is focused only on *federal* antitrust law. Most states have their own antitrust laws, which usually apply to the same basic practices that are forbidden by federal law.

Coverage and Exemptions

Coverage

Like many other federal statutes that are based on the Commerce Clause of the U.S. Constitution, the federal antitrust laws apply to business activities that either directly involve or substantially affect interstate commerce. Business activities occurring in foreign commerce, such as imports and exports, are also covered by U.S. antitrust law if there is a substantial effect on an American market.

Exemptions

The actions of the federal government are exempt from the antitrust laws, as are most actions of state governments so long as they are acting pursuant to legitimate and clearly expressed state regulatory interests. In this regard, actions of cities and other local governments are treated as state action if the local government is essentially just carrying out some aspect of state regulatory policy. Actions by foreign governments also are not within the scope of the antitrust laws.

If particular activities of a firm are subject to special regulation by a federal agency, such as the Securities Exchange Commission or the Commodity Futures Trading Commission, any possible anticompetitive consequences of those activities will usually not be scrutinized under the antitrust laws if the responsible agency has approved the activities after carefully considering the impact on competition.

In addition, the formation and ordinary activities (collective bargaining and strikes, for instance) of labor unions are exempt. Similarly, the actions of firms are exempt to the extent that they form a legitimate part of the union–company collective bargaining agreement and do not affect parties outside the union–company relationship. Finally, the joint activities of two kinds of selling cooperatives are exempt from the antitrust laws: (1) those formed by agricultural or livestock producers and (2) export groups so long as the limitation on export competition among members of the group does not adversely affect a domestic U.S. market.

Enforcement

Enforcement of the federal antitrust laws can take one or more of several different forms. The Antitrust Division of the U.S. Department of Justice, which operates under the Attorney General as part of the executive branch, can institute civil lawsuits and criminal prosecutions in federal district court. In a civil suit, if the Justice Department proves a violation of the Sherman, Clayton, or Robinson–Patman Acts, the remedy it normally obtains from the court is an injunction. The injunction will order the cessation of particular illegal actions, and may even require substantial modification of a firm's everyday business practices so as to lessen the likelihood of future violations. Many times the terms of an injunction are the result of an agreed settlement between the Justice Department and the defendant. In such cases, the injunction issue by the court after approving the terms of the settlement is called a *consent decree*. A firm or individual violating the terms of an injunction will be held in contempt of court.

If the case falls under the Sherman Act and involves a flagrant violation, such as blatant price fixing among competitors, the Justice Department may file a criminal prosecution in federal court. Upon conviction (which is a felony), the maximum penalty in a criminal case is a $10 million fine for corporations, and a $350,000 fine and three years' imprisonment for individuals. If larger fines are needed to ensure that violators do not profit from their wrongdoing, the Criminal Fines Enforcement Act of 1984 permits fines of twice a wrongdoer's pecuniary gain.

The FTC also has authority to enforce the Clayton, Robinson–Patman, and FTC Acts. Even though it technically has no power to enforce the Sherman Act, any conduct that would violate the Sherman Act will also constitute an "unfair method of competition" under Section 5 of the FTC Act. FTC enforcement, which is civil in nature, consists of a hearing before an administrative law judge of the agency, with subsequent review by the five– member FTC. If a violation is found, the FTC will issue a "cease and desist order," which is essentially the same as an injunction. Violation of an FTC order is punishable by a penalty of up to $10,000 for each day of noncompliance.

A private party can file a civil lawsuit in federal court claiming a violation of the Sherman, Clayton, or Robinson–Patman Acts. The plaintiff sometimes can obtain an injunction in such a suit, but the remedy normally sought is *treble damages*. This means that if the plaintiff proves it was damaged by the defendant's violation, the law automatically multiplies the plaintiff's money damages by three.

In the following pages, we look first at that portion of the law concerned primarily with industry structure, namely the law of monopolization and mergers. We then turn to the antitrust laws that focus on particular kinds of conduct in our discussion of *horizontal restraints of trade, vertical restraints of trade,* and *price discrimination.*

Monopolization

In trying to formulate a working definition of **monopoly** under Section 2 of the Sherman Act, as a practical matter the courts could not simply adopt the classical economic model of monopoly: one seller, very high entry barriers to the market, and no close substitutes for the product. Instead, they defined a monopoly in more pragmatic terms as "a firm having such an overwhelming degree of market power that it is able to control prices or exclude competition."

The center of this definition is market power. Essentially, market power is the ability of a firm to behave differently than it could behave in a perfectly competitive market. Stated differently, market power is a firm's ability to exercise *some* degree of control over the price of its product, that is, to raise its price without losing most of its customers. In virtually every market, there will be firms with some control over the price they charge, although the degree of control varies greatly from case to case.

The concept of market power is critical to any examination of competition under the antitrust laws, because competition usually cannot be harmed unless one firm, or a group of firms acting together, possesses some degree of market power. With respect to other issues in antitrust law, degrees of market power that are less than monopolistic can be very important. However, in deciding whether there is a monopoly under Section 2 of the Sherman Act, courts look for an *overwhelming degree* of market power. This exists when one firm dominates a market to such an extent that it does not have to worry much about the response of competitors.

Measuring Market Power

Traditionally, the enforcement agencies and courts have looked primarily at the structure of a market when trying to draw inferences about degrees of market power. The most important structural factor is usually the firm's **market share.** In other words, what percentage share of the relevant market does the firm have? The courts have not developed hard and fast rules as to what market share definitely does or does not demonstrate overwhelming market power. However, the cases indicate that a market share of less than 50 percent will never be enough, and a share of 75 percent will frequently (but not always) be enough. Although other indicators of market power are always important, they become critical when the share is below or above this range.

Other structural factors include the following:

1. The *relative size of other firms* in the market can be important. If M has, say, 60 percent of the market, M generally will have less market power if there are at least one or two other very large firms with perhaps 20 or 30 percent shares than if the remainder of the market is occupied by a large number of very small firms. The reason is that if the other firms are themselves quite large, even though smaller than M, they are more likely to have economies of scale and costs similar to M. Thus, although oligopoly may not be the most desirable market structure, it is usually much better than monopoly.

2. The *size and power of customers* is also relevant, because the existence of large, powerful buyers can put a damper on the market power of a potentially monopolistic seller.
3. The market's **entry barriers** are quite important. Entry barriers are conditions that make entry into the market by a new competitor significantly more costly and risky. If a market has low entry barriers, and a powerful firm in the market earns very high returns by using its power to charge high prices, the high returns will attract new competition to the market that will diminish the dominant firm's power. High entry barriers, on the other hand, provide substantial insulation for the powerful firm so that it can fully exploit its market power. Examples of entry barriers include excess production capacity in the market, higher costs of capital for potential competitors than for the dominant firm, strong customer preferences for brands produced by the dominant firm, important technology or know–how that is protected by patents or by trade secret law, complex distribution channels, and so forth. Entry barriers are not necessarily good or bad; they are just conditions that may be relevant. It also should be noted that some entry barriers are inevitable, whereas some can be intentionally erected by a dominant firm. Although the importance of entry barriers has long been recognized, in recent years some authorities have come to view them as even more important to the question of market power than the internal composition of the market.
4. In addition to market share and other structural factors, the *dynamics* of the market can also be relevant to the question of how much power a firm has. For instance, if the market is characterized by rapidly developing technology, or if total market demand is expanding rapidly, it will be much harder for a firm to hold on to its dominant position for very long.

Defining the Relevant Market

Before seeking to determine whether a firm has overwhelming power, it is necessary to define the relevant market. Essentially, the process of market definition involves an attempt to identify a category of business transactions that accurately reflects the operation of competitive forces. A market can be thought of as the context within which competitive forces can be measured with reasonable accuracy. Any market must be defined in terms of two elements: (1) a particular product or service, or some grouping of products or services, and (2) a geographic area.

Product Market

Suppose that M Company is charged with monopolizing the market for the sale of zippers in the United States. Most of M's zippers are sold to clothing manufacturers, but some are sold to fabric stores and other retail outlets for resale to consumers. M produces 90 percent of the zippers sold in the United States. If "zippers" is the proper market definition, M's market share almost certainly demonstrates overwhelming market power. M argues, however, that zippers actually face stiff competition from buttons, snaps, hooks, and Velcro, and that the 90 percent figure does not accurately portray M's power. If buttons, snaps, hooks, and Velcro are included in the market definition, let us suppose that M's share of this larger "clothing fastener" market will be only 23 percent, a figure that certainly does not indicate overwhelming power.

The approach that most courts have taken to such a problem is to look first at the **cross elasticity of demand** among the products in question. The term describes the concept of interchangeability. If there is a substantial degree of cross elasticity of demand between two or more products, they usually will be treated as occupying the same product market. In other words, if the evidence indicates that a substantial portion of customers view two products as being reasonable substitutes for one another, a court is likely to treat the products as being part of a single market.

The evidence in such a case, like so many others, will usually not be very "neat." It probably will show that zippers are preferred by most customers for particular uses, and that these customers are willing to pay significantly more for zippers than other fasteners for these uses. Buttons are probably preferred for certain other uses, snaps for others, and Velcro for still others. For some uses, two or more types of fasteners may be viewed as basically equivalent, and customers may choose solely on the basis of price. Courts necessarily must employ some fairly rough approximations in such cases. Thus, if the evidence convinces a court that a substantial body of customers views two or more products as reasonably interchangeable for a substantial number of important uses, they probably will be included in a single product market. It is also possible, of course, that the evidence will justify a conclusion that fasteners for one particular use constitute a separate market, and that one or more other markets exist for other uses. This conclusion is likely only if the use is quite distinctive from other uses and the volume of business for this use is very substantial.

Another factor that sometimes is relevant to the process of product market definition is **cross elasticity of supply.** This refers to the relative ease or difficulty with which producers of related products may respond to increases in demand. Suppose, for example, that many customers view buttons and zippers as basically interchangeable for certain important uses. Thus, there may be a high degree of cross elasticity of demand. However, all button manufacturers are operating at close to their production capacity, and the building of additional button−making facilities is very costly and time−consuming. Therefore, if M raises the price of zippers substantially and many customers would consider switching to buttons, button manufacturers cannot absorb the additional demand. These zipper customers will have to keep buying zippers at a higher cost. Button makers will not build additional capacity unless they think that zipper prices will remain high for the foreseeable future, so they could count on the additional demand for buttons for a long enough time to justify the investment in new button−making capacity. Thus, even though *demand* cross elasticity may be relatively high, there is low *supply* cross elasticity, and courts will probably treat zippers and buttons as two separate markets. It is also true that high cross elasticity. Suppose, for example, that most customers view zippers an Velcro as not being interchangeable for a particular use. However, if a price increase for zippers causes many customers to look for a substitute, and if Velcro manufacturers could modify their product easily and inexpensively so that it would be a reasonable zipper substitute for this particular use, zippers and Velcro may be treated as one market.

Geographic Market

Depending on the situation, the relevant geographic market can be local, regional, national, or international. It represents the area within which buyers can reasonably be expected to seek alternative sources of supply. Retail geographic markets tend to be smaller than wholesale markets, which tend to be smaller than manufacturing markets, although there are many exceptions to this generalization. The factor that usually determines the size of a geographic market is the relative cost of searching for and shipping products from more distant geographic locations. When we speak of relative cost, we mean relative to the cost of the product itself. Buyers obviously will spend more time and money searching for better deals and shipping from more distant places when the desired purchase is 100 million computer chips than when it is a loaf of bread.

Intent to Monopolize

If a firm has overwhelming market power and thus is a monopolist, is there automatically a violation of Section 2 of the Sherman Act? Or must something else be proved? The answer is that the evidence must also demonstrate that the dominant firm had an intent to monopolize, that is, that it willfully acquired or maintained its monopoly power. This obviously means that there can be legal monopolies. For example, a monopoly is legal if it exists solely because of lawful patents or trade secrets, or because economies of scale are so large that the market will support only one profitable firm.

As in other areas of law, intent is inferred from conduct. In the case of monopolization, courts usually will infer an intent to monopolize only if the dominant firm has engaged in *predatory* conduct, that is, conduct which is aimed at inflicting economic harm on one or more other firms for reasons that are not related to greater efficiency or better performance. There are two very general categories of predatory behavior: predatory pricing and non–price predation.

Predatory pricing is usually found where the dominant firm has persistently sold at prices below its average variable cost. Such pricing is viewed as predatory because it cannot be justified by a legitimate profit motive; while these prices are being charged, it is a money–losing proposition for the dominant firm. Instead, predatory pricing can only pay off for the dominant firm if it permits that firm to maintain its monopoly position so that it can later recover its losses by charging very high prices and earning monopoly profits. Predatory pricing can be used to drive another firm out of the market, although this is so costly for the dominant firm and has such uncertain long–term payoffs for that firm that it may not happen very often. Strategic predatory pricing can also be used on a periodic basic to discourage other firms from entering the market, or to send a clear signal to smaller firms in the market that they had better not engage in aggressive price competition. Predatory pricing for these purposes is probably more common than for the purpose of actually driving a competitor out.

Nonprice predation is probably more common than any kind of predatory pricing because it does not cost the dominant firm as much. Most forms of non–price predation are aimed at increasing competitors' costs or increasing entry barriers for potential competitors. A few examples are (1) tying up customers with long–term contracts that are not justified by cost savings, so that it is much more difficult for existing and potential competitors to engage in a fair contest for those customers; (2) taking away key employees from a smaller competitor; (3) falsely disparaging the products of smaller competitors; (4) forcing smaller firms into completely unjustified lawsuits and administrative proceedings because the costs of such proceedings hurt the smaller firms more than the dominant firm; and (5) various forms of sabotage. Some kinds of nonprice predation may violate other laws as well, but many kinds do not.

LePage's Inc. v. 3M
U.S. Third Circuit Court of Appeals, 324 F.3d 141 (2003)

3M enjoys a monopoly in the Scotch tape home and office use market, with around 90% of market share. LePage's makes "second brand" and private label transparent tape. This tape sells at a lower price than branded tape. With the rise of office super-stores and large retailers, the demand for private label tapes rose. 3M therefore entered that business, selling its own second brand under the name "Highland."

LePage's claims that 3M engaged in a series of related, anticompetitive acts aimed at restricting the availability of lower–priced transparent tape to consumers, and that 3M devised programs that prevented LePage's and the other domestic company in the business, Tesa Tuck, Inc., from gaining or maintaining large volume sales and that 3M maintained its monopoly by stifling growth of private label tape and by coordinating efforts aimed at large distributors to keep retail prices for Scotch tape high.

LePage's brought this antitrust action asserting that 3M used its monopoly over its Scotch tape brand to gain a competitive advantage in the private label tape portion of the transparent tape market in the United States through the use of 3M's multi– tiered "bundled rebate" structure, which offered higher rebates when customers purchased products in a number of 3M's different product lines. LePage's also alleges that 3M offered to some of LePage's customers large lump–sum cash payments, promotional allowances and other cash incentives to encourage them to enter into exclusive dealing arrangements with 3M.

LePage's asserted several antitrust claims, including monopolization and attempted monopolization under Sec. 2 of the Sherman Act. A jury rendered a substantial verdict for LePage's on all counts ($68,486,697 when trebled), and 3M appealed, claiming that bundled rebates were legal as long as prices were not below cost. LePage argued that the below–cost standard was irrelevant in a case that did not involve predatory pricing. An appellate court panel first reversed the *judgment, but then decided to rehear the case en banc.*

Sloviter, Circuit Judge:

In this case, the parties agreed that the relevant product market is transparent tape and the relevant geographic market is the United States. Moreover, 3M concedes it possesses monopoly power, with a 90% market share. Therefore we need not dwell on the oft–contested issue of market power.

The sole remaining issue is whether 3M took steps to maintain that power in a manner that violated Sec. 2 of the Sherman Act. A monopolist willfully acquires or maintains monopoly power when it competes on some basis other than the merits. LePage's argues that 3M willfully maintained its monopoly in the transparent tape market through exclusionary conduct, primarily by bundling its rebates and entering into contracts that expressly or effectively required dealing virtually exclusively with 3M, which LePage's characterizes as de facto exclusive. 3M does not argue that it did not engage in this conduct. Instead, 3M argues that its conduct was legal as a matter of law because it never priced its transparent tape below its cost.

In its brief, 3M states "above–cost pricing cannot give rise to an antitrust offense as a matter of law, since it is the very conduct that the antitrust laws wish to promote in the interest of making consumers better off." For this proposition it relies on Brooke Group Ltd. v. Brown & Willliamson Tobacco Corp., 509 U.S. 209(1993).

Before turning to consider LePage's allegation that 3M engaged in exclusionary or anticompetitive conduct and the evidence it produced, we consider the type of conduct Sec. 2 encompasses. As one court of appeals has stated: " 'Anticompetitive conduct' can come in too many different forms, and is too dependent upon context, for any court or commentator ever to have enumerated all the varieties." Caribbean Broad. Sys. Ltd. v. Cable & Wireless PLC, 148 F.3d 1080(D.C. Cir. 1998). Numerous cases hold that the enforcement of the legal monopoly provided by a patent procured through fraud may violate Sec. 2. A monopolist's denial to competitors of access to its "essential" goods, services or resources has been held to violate Sec. 2. Even unfair tortious conduct [such as disparaging advertising about a competitor] unrelated to a monopolist's pricing policies has been held to violate Sec. 2.

A recent decision of the United States Court of Appeals for the Sixth Circuit, Conwood LP v. U.S. Tobacco Co., 290 F.3d 768(6th Cir. 2002), presents a good illustration of the type of exclusionary conduct that will support a Sec. 2 violation. That court upheld the jury's award to plaintiff Conwood of $350 million, which trebled was $ 1.05 billion, against United States Tobacco Company ("USTC") because of USTC's monopolization. USTC was the sole manufacturer of moist snuff until the 1970's when Conwood, Swisher, and Swedish Match, other moist snuff manufacturers, entered the moist snuff market. Not unexpectedly, USTC's 100% market share declined and it took the action that formed the basis of Conwood's complaint against USTC alleging unlawful monopolization in violation of Sec. 2.

The evidence that the court of appeals held proved that USTC systematically tried to exclude competition from the moist snuff market included the following: USTC (1) removed and destroyed or discarded racks that displayed moist snuff products in the stores while placing Conwood products in USTC racks in an attempt to bury Conwood's products; (2) trained its "operatives to take advantage of inattentive store clerks with various 'ruses' such as obtaining nominal permission to reorganize or neaten the moist snuff section" in an effort to destroy Conwood racks; (3) misused its position as category manager (manages product groups and business units and customizes them on a store by store basis) by providing misleading information to retailers in an effort to dupe them into carrying USTC products and to discontinue carrying Conwood products; and (4) entered into exclusive agreements with retailers in an effort to exclude rivals' products.

On appeal, USTC contended that Conwood had failed to establish that USTC's power was acquired or maintained by exclusionary practices rather than by its legitimate business practices and superior product. The court of appeals rejected USTC's argument, finding that there was sufficient evidence for a jury to find willful maintenance by USTC of monopoly power by engaging in exclusionary practices.

[Here, LePage's argues that 3M attempted to monopolize the market by use of two exclusionary practices, bundled rebates and exclusive dealing contracts.]

Bundled Rebates. 3M offered many of LePage's major customers substantial rebates to induce them to eliminate or reduce their purchases of tape from LePage's. Rather than competing by offering volume discounts which are concededly legal and often reflect cost savings, 3M's rebate programs offered discounts to certain customers conditioned on purchases spanning six of 3M's diverse product lines. The rebates were considerable, not "modest" as 3M states. Just as significant as the amounts received is the powerful incentive they provided to customers to purchase 3M tape rather than LePage's in order not to forgo the maximum rebate 3M offered. The penalty would have been $264,000 for Sam's Club, $450,000 for Kmart, and $200,000 to $310,000 for American Stores.

One of the leading treatises discussing the inherent anticompetitive effect of bundled rebates, even if they are priced above cost, notes that "the great majority of bundled rebate programs yield aggregate prices above cost. Rather than analogizing them to predatory pricing, they are best compared with tying, whose foreclosure effects are similar. Indeed, the 'package discount' is often a close analogy." Phillip E. Areeda & Herbert Hovenkamp, *Antitrust Law* P 794, at 83 (Supp. 2002).

The principal anticompetitive effect of bundled rebates as offered by 3M is that when offered by a monopolist they may foreclose portions of the market to a potential competitor who does not manufacture an equally diverse group of products and who therefore cannot make a comparable offer. The jury could reasonably find that 3M used its monopoly in transparent tape, backed by its considerable catalog of products, to squeeze out LePage's.

Exclusive Dealing. The second prong of LePage's claim of exclusionary conduct by 3M was its actions in entering into exclusive dealing contracts with large customers. 3M acknowledges only the expressly exclusive dealing contracts with Venture and Pamida which conditioned discounts on exclusivity. It minimizes these because they represent only a small portion of the market. However, LePage's claims that 3M made payments to many of the larger customers that were designed to achieve sole—source supplier status.

Even though exclusivity arrangements are often analyzed under Sec. 1, such exclusionary conduct may also be an element in a Sec. 2 claim. [And agreements which effectively foreclose the business of competitors can be illegal even if not expressly exclusive.] LePage's introduced powerful evidence that could have led the jury to believe that rebates and discounts to Kmart, Staples, Sam's Club, [and others] were designed to induce them to award business to 3M to the exclusion of LePage's. Many of LePage's former customers refused even to meet with LePage's sales representatives. A buyer for Kmart, LePage's largest customer which accounted for 10% of its business, told LePage's: "I can't talk to you about tape products for the next three years" and "don't bring me anything 3M makes." Kmart switched to 3M following 3M's offer of a $1 million "growth" reward which the jury could have understood to require that 3M be its sole supplier. The purpose and effect of 3M's payments to the retailers were issues for the jury which, by its verdict, rejected 3M's.

The Court of Appeals for the District of Columbia relied on the evidence of foreclosure of markets in reaching its decision on liability in U.S. v. Microsoft Corp., 253 F.3d 34 (D.C. Cir. 2001). In that case, the court of appeals concluded that Microsoft, a monopolist in the operating system market, foreclosed rivals in the browser market from a "substantial percentage of the available opportunities for browser distribution" through the use of exclusive contracts with key distributors. Microsoft kept usage of its competitor's browser below "the critical level necessary for [its rival] to pose a real threat to Microsoft's monopoly." The Microsoft opinion does not specify what percentage of the browser market

Microsoft locked up—merely that, in one of the two primary distribution channels for browsers, Microsoft had exclusive arrangements with most of the top distributors. Significantly, the Microsoft court observed that Microsoft's exclusionary conduct violated Sec. 2 "even though the contracts foreclose less than the roughly 40% or 50% share usually required in order to establish a Sec. 1 violation."

Section 2, the provision of the antitrust laws designed to curb the excesses of monopolists and near—monopolists, is the equivalent in our economic sphere of the guarantees of free and unhampered elections in the political sphere. Just as democracy can thrive only in a free political system unhindered by outside forces, so also can market capitalism survive only if those with market power are kept in check. That is the goal of the antitrust laws.

The jury heard the evidence and the contentions of the parties, accepting some and rejecting others. There was ample evidence that 3M used its market power over transparent tape, backed by its considerable catalog of products, to entrench its monopoly to the detriment of LePage's, its only serious competitor, in violation of Sec. 2. [Affirmed.]

Mergers
Basic Principles

A **merger** between two companies clearly is a "combination" that could be scrutinized under Section 1 of the Sherman Act, which prohibits "contracts, combinations, and conspiracies in restraint of trade." In the early years after Congress passed the Sherman Act, however, the Supreme Court interpreted Section 1 in such a narrow way, at least as applied to mergers, that a merger could be illegal only if it occurred between two direct competitors with very large market shares. Because Congress intended antitrust law to reach some other mergers as well, in 1914 it enacted Section 7 of the Clayton Act. The statute was amended substantially by the Cellar—Kefauver Act of 1950, further demonstrating congressional intent to prevent mergers when the evidence indicates either actual harm to competition or a substantial probability of such harm in the future. Another amendment in 1976 requires the participants in most mergers of any significant size to give both the Justice Department and the FTC advance notice of a merger so that these agencies can assess its possible effects before it occurs.

Section 7 prohibits one company from acquiring the stock or assets of another company if the acquisition is likely to diminish competition in a substantial way. Total or partial acquisitions are covered. Obviously, however, a stock acquisition cannot raise any concerns about harming competition unless the acquiring company obtains a large enough stake in the acquired company either to control it or at least to have substantial influence over its board of directors. Similarly, an acquisition of assets cannot harm competition unless the assets are very important to competition in the particular market, such as major manufacturing facilities, airline routes, critical patented technology, and so on.

So long as there is an acquisition of assets or shares of stock, the exact form of the transaction does not matter. It may be a "friendly" merger or consolidation negotiated between the boards of the two firms and then approved by shareholders, a "hostile" stock acquisition by means of a public tender offer, a series of stock purchases either on the open market or through negotiations with individual shareholders, or any other form.

In attempting to assess a merger's actual or probable effects on competition, a court will first define the relevant market or markets. This is done in exactly the same way as in a monopoly case. As we will see in our discussion of the different types of mergers, the question of market power is also very important in merger cases. It is important to note, however, that a merger does not have to result in market power that is even close to being monopolistic in order to be ruled illegal. Although substantial market power is necessary for substantial anticompetitive effects, that power does not have to be overwhelming for such effects to occur.

Another important point about the law in this area is that periodic political changes in Washington affect the enforcement and interpretation of Section 7 to a greater extent than the other antitrust laws. Although such changes affect antitrust law in general, private lawsuits are much less important as an enforcement tool in the case of mergers than in other areas of antitrust. Most challenges to mergers are made by either the Justice Department or the FTC, rather than by private plaintiffs. Thus, when the current political climate is relatively conservative and pro–business, the enforcement attitude toward mergers is likely to be quite lenient. On the other hand, when an administration is in power that distrusts large concentrations of economic power and does not really believe that most mergers contribute to economic efficiency, more mergers are usually challenged under Section 7. In recent times, the attitude toward mergers has generally been more strict during Democratic administrations and more lenient during Republican administrations.

Types of Mergers

Mergers traditionally have been classified as horizontal, vertical, or conglomerate. A *horizontal merger* occurs if the two firms are competitors, and a *vertical merger* occurs if one of the firms sells something that the other firm buys. Any other is a conglomerate merger. Although these classifications are useful to describe very broadly some relevant differences in the various factual settings in which mergers occur, the same basic test applies to all mergers: does the merger substantially diminish competition, or is it quite likely to do so in the future? Moreover, a merger may sometimes fit more than one category. For instance, in Brown Shoe Co. v. United States, 370 U.S. 294 (1962), the challenged merger had both horizontal and vertical aspects because each of the merging firms, Brown Shoe Co. and Kinney ShoeCo., was both a manufacturer and a retailer of shoes.

Horizontal Mergers

A merger between competitors poses the greatest danger to competition because the market has one less competitor. In assessing the impact of a **horizontal merger,** the courts usually emphasize the same general kinds of evidence that are important in measuring market power in a monopoly case.

Market Share. The *combined market* share of the merging firms is often the first thing the courts look at. During earlier periods when the attitude toward mergers was very strict, a number of them were challenged and ruled illegal when the combined market share was above 10 percent and other evidence indicated a definite trend toward concentration of economic power in the relevant market. Today, however, a horizontal merger is not likely to get much attention under Section 7 unless the combined market share exceeds 30 percent.

Market Concentration. The *overall concentration of the market* is also important. In general, the more concentrated the market is at the time of the merger, the more likely it is that a questionable merger will be held illegal. Suppose, for example, that a merger occurs between two firms having market shares of 20 percent and 15 percent, and the remainder of the market consists of three other firms with shares of 25 percent, 20 percent, and 20 percent. This merger would be somewhat more likely to violate Section 7 than it would if the remainder of the market consisted of, say, six other firms with shares of approximately 11 percent each.

Acquisition by Leading Firm. In addition, if a single firm already dominates a market rather completely and there are no other firms that can come close to its resources and scale economies, any acquisition of a competitor by the dominant firm runs a great risk of being held illegal.

Entry Barriers. If the market is characterized by high entry barriers, a borderline merger is much more likely to be ruled illegal, and vice versa. Indeed, as we mentioned in the discussion of monopoly, an increasing number of authorities have begun to view a market's entry barriers as being at least as important to the market power question as the market's internal composition. One practical difficulty with this view, however, is that entry barriers usually are much more difficult to measure with any kind of precision than the market's internal structure.

Increased Risk of Collusion. Another relevant factor could be the existence of evidence indicating that collusion among competitors had been a problem in this market in the past, and that by further reducing the number of competitors this merger could make collusion even easier in the future. In general, the lower the number of competitors, the easier it is for them to put together and maintain a price–fixing conspiracy or other collusive anticompetitive arrangement.

Other Factors. Other factors can also be important to the evaluation of horizontal mergers. For example, a firm with 15 or 20 percent of a market ordinarily could acquire a firm with a 2 or 3 percent share without much fear of legal challenge. Suppose, however, that the smaller firm had recently developed patented technology of major significance to future competition in the market, or that it had traditionally been a very efficient "maverick" and frequently had led the way in vigorous price competition. In such a case, the acquisition would run a significantly higher risk of being challenged successfully under Section 7.

Vertical Mergers

Although a **vertical merger** is much less likely to harm competition than a horizontal one, it is possible for such a merger to diminish competition. Essentially, a vertical merger creates **vertical integration,** which occurs when one firm operates at more than one level of the distribution chain for a product. (Obviously, a firm can also become vertically integrated, without a merger, by creating new facilities to operate at another level.) Suppose that S Company is an important producer of a key component or ingredient used by B Company in manufacturing an end product, and that S acquires B. S would be using the merger to vertically integrate "downstream." If B had acquired S, B would be vertically integrating "upstream."

The Debate. There has been a long–standing debate about the merits of vertical integration. Some experts have viewed vertical integration as being primarily a vehicle for greater efficiency. Others have viewed it as being primarily a tool for locking up markets and supply sources, raising entry barriers, and making collusion easier. Still others have viewed vertical integration as something of a "mixed bag" of economic effects that is exceptionally difficult to sort out. Currently, the prevailing attitude among a majority of economists and enforcement officials toward vertical integration is basically a favorable one. Not everyone shares that view, however, and the pendulum of expert opinion could swing in the other direction at some point in the future.

Efficiency Argument. Undoubtedly, vertical integration can create efficiencies, primarily by saving transaction costs. If the vertically integrated firm ("S–B") is managed properly, it usually should be able to transfer goods and services from one level to another more cheaply than if it were two separate firms operating at the two levels. Being part of one company ideally should permit better coordination and planning. Having an assured source of supply for B and an assured market for S should permit better inventory control. This, in turn, should produce lower carrying costs by avoiding excess inventory and lower delay–related costs by reducing instances of shortage. Vertical integration also can reduce the various kinds of selling costs between S and B, such as those associated with promotion, sales personnel, and contract drafting and monitoring. Opponents of vertical integration reply that, even if these efficiencies are created, the cost savings are not going to be passed along to consumers unless competition in the downstream market is vigorous. They also argue that many of the same efficiencies can be achieved through relatively long–term contracts without creating the same degree of risk for competition.

Entry Barriers. Some observers argue that vertical integration can increase entry barriers and thus insulate firms in the market from new competition. The reason, they say, is that a firm thinking about entering a market in which the major competitors are vertically integrated will have to come into the market at two levels simultaneously, which is more costly and difficult. Those favoring vertical integration, however, reply that new entry into such a market is more difficult simply because the vertically integrated firms in the market are more efficient, and that it is more difficult to compete against efficient firms with low costs.

Making Collusion Easier. Some critics of vertical integration also claim that it can make collusion easier for the vertically integrated firms, especially those at the "upstream" level (in our example, S's level). This can happen, they claim, because removing the layer of independent buyers from the downstream level does away with an important set of "watchdogs" on the upstream firms. Those with a favorable view of vertical integration often admit that this is a possibility, but point out that it is likely to happen only if there are very few firms at both levels and if most of these large firms are already vertically integrated. Besides, they say, antitrust enforcers can just watch out for the collusion and take action if they find it.

Current Law. Because of today's generally favorable attitude toward vertical integration, a vertical merger will usually be legal. A successful challenge to such a merger is likely only if most of the firms in the market are already vertically integrated, this vertically combined market is a highly concentrated oligopoly, and both S and B have large market shares. It is mainly the fear of collusion being made easier in this kind of situation that creates the risk of a successful legal challenge.

Conglomerate Mergers

Mergers without horizontal or vertical characteristics are usually called **conglomerate mergers**. Although several grounds for striking down conglomerate mergers have been employed in the past, such a merger creates very little legal risk today. About the only situation where such a risk exists now is in the following circumstances: (1) X enters the widget market in the western U.S. by acquiring Y, a major producer of widgets in that area. (2) That market was already a highly concentrated oligopoly. (3) For a substantial period of time before the merger, X had a special incentive to enter the market and the resources to do it. Other potential new entrants did not have similar incentives. This special incentive may have existed because the widget market was an unusually attractive extension of X's product line, or perhaps because X already sold widgets elsewhere and this was an ideal geographic expansion. In either case, X could get into the market and compete more easily and cheaply than other new firms because of the product or geographic relationship. (4) The western widget market had high entry barriers that discouraged other firms from entering, but that were not so high as to discourage X because of its large resources and special incentive. (5) Prior to the merger, the major firms in the western widget market knew that X was a probable future entrant.

In this situation, the presence of X "on the edge" of the western widget market prior to the merger was probably having a beneficial effect by causing widget makers in the market to keep their prices lower than they would have otherwise, in the hope of discouraging X from actually entering. When X enters, this beneficial "edge effect" is removed. If X had entered by building new facilities, or by acquiring a very small firm in the market and expanding it into a major competitor, X's entry would have positive effects that would offset the removal of its former "edge effect." But when X enters by acquiring a firm that is already a major player, there is nothing positive to counteract the negative, and the merger may be illegal.

Failing Company Defense

Even if a merger is one that normally would violate Section 7 of the Clayton Act, proof of the failing company defense prevents a violation. This defense exists if (1) one of the merging firms probably will not be able to meet its financial obligations in the near future; (2) it appears unlikely that the failing firm will be able to reorganize successfully under Chapter 11 of the Bankruptcy Code and emerge as a viable company; and (3) the failing firm has made a good faith, but unsuccessful, effort to obtain a merger offer from another firm that would pose less danger to competition than does the merger being challenged.

Merger Guidelines

The Justice Department's Antitrust Division first issued Merger Guidelines in 1968. The guidelines, which are also followed by the FTC, were completely rewritten in 1982, and again revised slightly in 1984. These guidelines are not binding law but do provide business with a valuable planning tool by specifying the circumstances in which the two agencies can ordinarily be expected to challenge a merger.

One of the key innovations of the current guidelines is the use of the Herfndahl–Hirschman Index (HHI) for measuring the relative level of economic concentration in a market. This index involves squaring the market share of each firm in the market and then adding the squares. Thus, a market with 10 firms of equal size would have an HHI of 1,000. The guidelines consider a market with an HHI under 1,000 to be unconcentrated, between 1,000 and 1,800 to be moderately concentrated, and over 1,800 to be concentrated. The greater the level of concentration in the relevant market, the more likely it is that a merger will be challenged and that it will be ruled illegal. The following decision is from a case involving a horizontal merger between two relatively large competitors. It is an important decision because, among other things, it illustrates how evidence of surrounding economic circumstances may convince a court that such a merger is legal.

Horizontal Restraints of Trade

In examining the law pertaining to monopolies and mergers, we were concerned primarily with market structure and only secondarily with specific instances of conduct. We now turn our attention to particular types of business behavior. Market structure continues to be relevant here, but its role is a secondary one.

UNITES STATES V. ORACLE CORP.
U.S. District Court, Northern District of California, 331 F.Supp. 2d 1098 (2004)

Oracle sought to acquire Peoplesoft, a rival maker of software. The Department of Justice's antitrust division, in conjunction with various state attorneys general (plaintffs), sought to invoke Section 7 of the Clayton Act to prevent the acquisition, arguing that the relevant product market was providers of large–scale applications software for HRM (human resources management) and FMS (financial management systems), and that the relevant geographic market was the United States. Plaintiffs argued that if Oracle and Peoplesoft merged, the only remaining competitor would be Germany's SAP, creating a highly concentrated duopoly.

Oracle argued, to the contrary, that HRM and FMS products are just part of a broad range of ERP (enterprise resource planning) applications software, that many firms compete to provide such products, that price competition comes additionally from firms that providing outsourcing of data processing, that the geographic area of competition was worldwide or at least the U.S. and Europe, that many purchasers of ERP software are large, knowledgeable and sophisticated and would therefore impede any exercise of market power by a merged Oracle/Peoplesoft, and that potential competitors were poised to enter the market to counter any anticompetitive effects of the merger. After a lengthy trial, the judge ruled for defendant.

Walker, District Judge:

Section 7 of the Clayton Act prohibits a person "engaged in commerce or in any activity affecting commerce" from acquiring "the whole or any part" of a business' stock or assets if the effect of the acquisition "may be substantially to lessen competition, or to tend to create a monopoly." To establish a section 7 violation, plaintiffs must show that a pending acquisition is reasonably likely to cause anticompetitive effects. "Section 7 does not require proof that a merger or other acquisition [will] cause higher prices in the affected market. All that is necessary is that the merger create an appreciable danger of such consequences in the future." Hospital Corp. of Am. v. FTC, 807 F.2d 1381(7th Cir. 1986). Substantial competitive harm is likely to result if a merger creates or enhances "market power," a term that has specific meaning in antitrust law.

Market Definition. In determining whether a transaction will create or enhance market power, courts historically have first defined the relevant product and geographic markets within which the competitive effects of the transaction are to be assessed. This is a "necessary predicate" to finding anticompetitive effects. Market definition under the case law proceeds by determining the market shares of the firms involved in the proposed transaction, *Philadelphia Nat'l Bank*, 374 U.S. 321(1963), the overall concentration level in the industry and the trends in the level of concentration. A significant trend toward concentration creates a presumption that the transaction violates section 7. In other words, plaintiffs establish a prima facie case of a section 7 violation by showing that the merger would produce "a firm controlling an undue percentage share of the relevant market, and [would] result [] in a significant increase in the concentration of firms in that market." *Id.* Under *Philadelphia Nat'l Bank,* a post—merger market share of 30 percent or higher unquestionably gives rise to the presumption of illegality.

To rebut this presumption, defendant may show that the market—share statistics give an inaccurate account of the merger's probable effects on competition in the relevant market. Arguments related to efficiencies resulting from the merger may also be relevant in opposing plaintiffs' case. If the defendant successfully rebuts the presumption [of illegality], the burden of producing additional evidence of anticompetitive effects shifts to [plaintiffs], and merges with the ultimate burden of persuasion, which remains with the government at all times.

An application of the burden—shifting approach requires the court to determine (1) the "line of commerce" or product market in which to assess the transaction; (2) the "section of the country" or geographic market in which to assess the transaction; and (3) the transaction's probable effect on competition in the product and geographic markets. Both the Supreme Court and appellate courts acknowledge the need to adopt a flexible approach in determining whether anticompetitive effects are likely to result from a merger. Reflecting their "generality and adaptability," application of the antitrust laws to mergers during the past half—century has been anything but static. Accordingly, determining the existence or threat of anticompetitive effects has not stopped at calculation of market shares. In

Hospital Corp. of Am. the court upheld the FTC's challenge to the acquisition of two hospital chains, but noted that "the economic concept of competition, rather than any desire to preserve rivals as such, is the lodestar that shall guide the contemporary application of the antitrust laws, not excluding the Clayton Act." Hence, the court held that it was appropriate for the FTC to eschew reliance solely on market percentages and the "very strict merger decisions of the 1960s." In addition to market concentration, probability of consumer harm in that case was established by factors such as legal barriers to new entry, low elasticity of consumer demand, inability of consumers to move to distant hospitals in emergencies, a history of collusion and cost pressures creating an incentive to collude.

The trend in [recent] cases away from the "very strict merger decisions of the 1960s," is also reflected in the FTC Horizontal Merger Guidelines. The Guidelines view statistical and non—statistical factors as an integrated whole, avoiding the burden shifting presumptions of the case law. The Guidelines define market power as "the ability profitably to maintain prices above competitive levels for a significant period of time." Five factors are relevant to the finding of market power: (1) whether the merger would significantly increase concentration and would result in a concentrated market, properly defined; (2) whether the merger raises concerns about potential adverse competitive effects; (3) whether timely and likely entry would deter or counteract anticompetitive effects; (4) whether the merger would realize efficiency gains that cannot otherwise be achieved; and (5) whether either party would likely fail in the absence of the merger.

Once the market has been properly defined, the Guidelines set about to identify the firms competing in the market and those likely to enter the market within one year. Following these steps, the Guidelines calculate the market share of each participant, followed by the Herfindahl–Hirschman Index (HHI) concentration measurement for the market as a whole. The HHI is calculated by squaring the market share of each participant, and summing the resulting figures. The Guidelines specify safe harbors for mergers in already concentrated markets that do not increase concentration very much. Notwithstanding these statistical data, the Guidelines next focus on the likely competitive effects of the merger.

[Applying these standards after listening to expert testimony from both parties and additional evidence from a myriad of witnesses, the court ruled against plaintiffs because they had not established, among other points:]

- that the product market they allege, high function HRM and FMS, exists as a separate and distinct line of commerce;
- that the geographic market for the products of the merging parties is, as they allege, confined to the United States alone;
- that a post–merger Oracle would have sufficient market shares in the product and geographic markets, properly defined, to apply the burden shifting presumptions of *Philadelphia Nat'l Bank;*

- that the post–merger level of concentration (HHI) in the product and geographic markets, properly defined, falls outside the safe harbor of the Horizontal Merger Guidelines (Guidelines);
- that the ERP products of numerous other vendors, including Lawson, AMS and Microsoft, do not compete with the ERP products of Oracle, PeopleSoft and SAP and that these other vendors would not constrain a small but significant non–transitory increase in price by a post–merger Oracle;
- that outsourcing firms, such as Fidelity and ADP, would not constrain a small but significant non–transitory increase in price by a post–merger Oracle; and
- that the ability of systems integrators to adapt, configure and customize competing ERP vendors' products to the needs of the group of customers that plaintiffs contend constitute a separate and distinct product market would not constrain a small but significant non–transitory increase in price by a post–merger Oracle.

Judgment is entered in favor of defendant Oracle Corporation.

Our first inquiry into the behavioral side of antitrust is horizontal restraints of trade— arrangements between two or more competitors that suppress or limit competition. The applicable statute is Section 1 of the Sherman Act which, as stated earlier, prohibits "contracts, combinations, or conspiracies in restraint of trade."

The Requirement of Collusion

Section 1 of the Sherman Act can be applied only if there was collusion between two or more independent entities. Many different terms are used to describe the concept: joint action, concerted action, agreement, combination, conspiracy, and others. As is true of all things that must be proved in the law, the collusion requirement is sometimes obvious and sometimes not. An example of a case in which the requirement obviously was present is National Society of Professional Engineers v. United States, 435 U.S. 679 (1978), in which the Court held illegal an ethical rule of the society that prohibited competitive bidding by its 69,000 members. The collusion requirement was so obviously satisfied that it was not even an issue. In such a case, even if the association has been incorporated and thus is a single independent entity, its rules and other actions are in reality the collective actions of its members who explicitly or implicitly granted their approval.

If collusion is not obvious, courts normally have to rely on circumstantial evidence to decide the question. Evidence of any *communications* among the parties can be very important, but such evidence may or may not be strong enough to permit the fact finder to conclude that collusion has taken place. If there is no such evidence, or if it is not sufficient to prove collusion, there must at least be evidence demonstrating that the parties had an *opportunity to conspire*. To establish a circumstantial case of collusion, it usually is also necessary to prove *uniformity of action* among the defendants. Thus, a court is quite unlikely to find that collusion occurred unless the defendants acted in a very similar fashion in pricing, refusing to deal with another party such as a customer or supplier, or other important matter.

It is not enough, however, merely to prove that the firms did about the same thing, because there can be many legitimate reasons for such an occurrence. This is especially true in a market with a relatively small number of firms. In an oligopoly, for example, it sometimes is inevitable that several companies will make similar pricing moves within a relatively short time span, primarily because they all know what the others are doing and the actions of each one are quite important. In other situations, there also may be reasonable explanations for uniformity; for instance, the same external factor such as a supply shortage may have affected all firms simultaneously. If there is substantial uniformity, however, without any legitimate explanation, the situation is suspicious and the firms' parallel conduct is fairly strong evidence of collusion. Also, the greater the degree of uniformity, the more strongly this evidence points toward collusion.

The Rule of Reason

Assuming that collusion has been proved, the defendants' action violates Section 1 only if it "restrains trade." What this means is that their conduct must have suppressed or limited competition. Relatively early in the history of the Sherman Act, in Standard Oil Co. v. United States, 221 U.S. 1 (1911), the Supreme Court held that Section 1 does not forbid all arrangements that limit competition. If the statute had been interpreted in a literal, all–inclusive fashion, it could have produced strange and inefficient results such as prohibiting the formation of partnerships, corporations, and other business organizations because they involve the combination of individuals who might otherwise be competitors. Instead, the Court adopted the so–called **rule of reason,** under which arrangements are illegal only if they "unreasonably" restrict competition.

The next question, of course, is how do the courts decide whether a particular arrangement is reasonable or unreasonable? In essence, the rule of reason involves an examination of the *purpose* and the *effect* of the conduct being challenged.

Purpose

The firms will always claim that their purpose was legitimate—i.e., not anticompetitive. They may insist, for example, that their motive was to promote ethical conduct in their industry, prevent fraudulent practices by their suppliers or customers, encourage product standardization or safety, or any one of many other lawful purposes. The court will examine all pertinent evidence before deciding whether the defendants are to be believed, or whether their predominant motive was to restrict competition. If the court concludes that their primary motive was to limit competition, the arrangement is illegal if there is a likelihood of even a small restriction on competition. If, on the other hand, the court decides that their primary motive was a legitimate one, the court will find a violation of Section 1 only if the evidence indicates that competition will be diminished in a substantial way. There is actually something of a rough sliding scale. The greater the apparent bad effect on competition, the less weight the court will give to any legitimate motive.

Effect on Competition

Perhaps the most important factor in the analysis of an arrangement's effect on competition is the collective *market power* of the group. Market power is evaluated in the same way here as in the more structurally oriented situations of monopoly and merger. A group's aggregate market power does not have to be huge for an arrangement to violate the rule of reason, but if the group's purpose was apparently all right, its power must be substantial enough to convince a court that serious anticompetitive effects are likely to result.

Another factor that often plays a part in the court's analysis is the existence of a *less restrictive alternative*. Thus, if the evidence establishes that the firms could have achieved their claimed objectives by using some other arrangement that would have posed less danger to competition, a court is somewhat more likely to find a violation of Section 1. The existence of a less restrictive alternative does not automatically cause their arrangement to be illegal, but it does tip the scales a bit in that direction, for two reasons. First, it demonstrates that the firms caused a greater negative effect on competition than they really had to. Second, such evidence may even cause a court to view their alleged motive with more suspicion.

If evidence of market power and other relevant factors indicates that a substantial negative effect on competition is possible, the legality of the arrangement sometimes can be saved by clear evidence that it also will have offsetting procompetitive effects.

These are just positives to offset the negatives, and usually involve some aspect of the arrangement that will improve the efficiency of the market. The court will engage in a rough balancing of these effects against the anticompetitive ones and decide which seem to predominate. Examples of procompetitive effects include creating a new kind of market that otherwise would not exist, stimulating competition by bringing more transactions into the market, improving the quality or quantity of information available to buyers and sellers, and so on.

The following landmark Supreme Court case illustrates most of these aspects of rule–of–reason analysis. You will be able to see the Court examining (1) motives; (2) market power (although it does not use this term); (3) the fact that the scope of the arrangement seemed to be limited so that it was not any more restrictive than it had to be; and (4) what the judges viewed as offsetting procompetitive effects brought about by taking quite a few transactions from a few large dealers and bringing them into the organized market where information was more accurate and up–to–date and trading more open and competitive.

CHICAGO BOARD OF TRADE V. UNITED STATES
U.S. Supreme Court, 246 U.S. 231 (1918)

In the late 1800s and early 1900s Chicago was the leading grain market in the world, and the Board of Trade was the commercial center through which most of the trading in grain was done. Its 1,600 members included brokers, commission merchants, dealers, millers, manufacturers of corn products, and grain elevator owners. Grain transactions usually took one of three forms: (1) spot sales—sales of grain already in Chicago in railroad cars or elevators ready for immediate delivery; (2) future sales— agreements for delivery of grain at a later time; (3) sales "to arrive"—agreements for delivery of grain which was already in transit to Chicago or which was to be shipped almost immediately from other parts of the Midwest.

On each business day, sessions of the Board of Trade were held at which all bids and sales were publicly made. Spot sales and future sales were made during the regular session between 9:30 a.m. and 1:15 p.m. Special sessions, referred to as the "Call," were held immediately after the close of the regular session. During the Call, which usually lasted about 30 minutes, members of the Board of Trade engaged only in "to arrive" transactions. These transactions usually involved purchases from farmers or small dealers in one of the Midwestern states. Participation in the Call session was limited to members, but they could trade on behalf of nonmembers if they wished. Members also could make any of the three types of transaction privately with each other at any place, either during or after board sessions. Members could engage privately in any type of transaction at any time with nonmembers, but not on the board's premises.

With respect to 'to arrive' transactions, a particular market price would be established by the public trading during the short Call session. Until 1906, however, members were not bound by that price during the remainder of the day. In that year the Board of Trade adopted what was known as the "Call rule." The rule, which applied only to "to arrive" transactions, required members to use the market price established at the public Call session when they bought grain in private transactions between the end of that session and 9:30 the next morning.

The government filed suit in federal district court, claiming that the Call rule violated Section 1 of the Sherman Act. The board contended that the purpose and effect of the rule was to bring more of the "to arrive" transactions into the public market at the Call session. By bringing more of these transactions into the public market, the board felt that four or five large grain warehouse owners in Chicago would no longer have such a controlling grip over "to arrive" transactions. The district court, however, ruled that evidence relating to the history and purpose of the rule was irrelevant and issued an injunction against the operation of the rule. The Board of Trade then appealed to the U.S. Supreme Court.

Brandeis, Justice:

... Every agreement concerning trade, every regulation of trade, restrains. To bind, to restrain, is of their very essence. The true test of legality is whether the restraint imposed is such as merely regulates and perhaps thereby promotes competition or whether it is such as may suppress or even destroy competition. To determine that question the court must ordinarily consider the facts peculiar to the business to which the restraint is applied; its condition before and after the restraint was imposed; the nature of the restraint and its effect, actual or probable. The history of the restraint, the evil believed to exist, the reason for adopting the particular remedy, the purpose or end sought to be attained, are all relevant facts. This is not because a good intention will save an otherwise objectionable regulation or the reverse; but because knowledge of intent may help the court to interpret facts and to predict consequences. The District Court erred, therefore, in striking from the [Board's] answer allegations concerning evidence on that subject. But the evidence admitted makes it clear that the rule was a reasonable regulation of business consistent with the provisions of the Antitrust Law.

First: The nature of the rule: The restriction was upon the period of price–making. It required members to desist from further price–making after the close of the Call until 9:30 a.m. the next business day: but there was no restriction upon the sending out of bids after close of the Call. Thus it required members who desired to buy grain "to arrive" to make up their minds before the close of the Call how much they were willing to pay during the interval before the next session of the Board. The rule made it to their interest to attend the Call; and if they did not fill their wants by purchases there, to make the final bid high enough to enable them to purchase from country dealers.

Second: The scope of the rule It is restricted in operation to grain "to arrive." It applies only to a small part of the grain shipped from day to day to Chicago, and to an even smaller part of the day's sales members were left free to purchase grain already in Chicago from anyone at any price throughout the day. It applies only during a small part of the business day; members were left free to purchase during the sessions of the Board grain "to arrive," at any price, from members anywhere and from nonmembers anywhere except on the premises of the Board. It applied only to grain shipped to Chicago: members were left free to purchase at any price throughout the day from either members or nonmembers, grain "to arrive" at any other market. Country dealers and farmers had available in practically every part of the territory called tributary to Chicago some other market for grain "to arrive."

Thus Missouri, Kansas, Nebraska, and parts of Illinois are also tributary to St. Louis; Nebraska and Iowa, to Omaha; Minnesota, Iowa, South and North Dakota, to Minneapolis or Duluth; Wisconsin and parts of Iowa and of Illinois, to Milwaukee; Ohio, Indiana and parts of Illinois, to Cincinnati; Indiana and parts of Illinois, to Louisville.

Third: The effects of the rule: As it applies to only a small part of the grain shipped to Chicago and to that only during a part of the business day and does not apply at all to grain shipped to other markets, the rule had no appreciable effect on general market prices; nor did it materially affect the total volume of grain coming to Chicago. But within the narrow limits of its operation the rule helped to improve market conditions thus:

a. It created a public market for grain "to arrive." Before its adoption, bids were made privately. Men had to buy and sell without adequate knowledge of actual market conditions. This was advantageous to all concerned, but particularly so to country dealers and farmers.

b. It brought into the regular market hours of the Board sessions more of the trading in grain "to arrive."

c. It brought buyers and sellers into more direct relations; because on the Call they gathered together for a free and open interchange of bids and offers. (d) It distributed the business in grain "to arrive" among a far larger number of Chicago receivers and commission merchants than had been the case there before.

d. It increased the number of country dealers engaging in this branch of the business; supplied them more regularly with bids from Chicago; and also increased the number of bids received by them from competing markets.

e. It eliminated risks necessarily incident to a private market, and thus enabled country dealers to do business on a smaller margin. In that way the rule made it possible for them to pay more to farmers without raising the price to consumers.

f. It enabled country dealers to sell some grain "to arrive" which they would otherwise have been obliged either to ship to Chicago commission merchants or to sell for "future delivery."

g. It enabled those grain merchants of Chicago who sell to millers and exporters to trade on a smaller margin and, by paying more for grain or selling it for less, to make the Chicago market more attractive for both shippers and buyers of grain...

The decree of the District Court is reversed with directions to dismiss the [government's complaint].

The Per Se Rule

Also relatively early in the history of the Sherman Act, the Supreme Court recognized that certain types of practices are obviously anticompetitive and do not really have any redeeming social virtues. In such a case, the **per se rule** applies. This means that, once the particular type of activity is identified as one that falls within a per se category, it is automatically illegal and the inquiry ends. Of the various horizontal restraints of trade, price fixing, market division, and boycotts are per se illegal. It is very important to understand, however, that the per se rule has its greatest impact in situations where the challenged activity can be easily labeled as price fixing, market division, or a boycott. If there is a close question whether the arrangement should be characterized in this way, the court must analyze its purpose and effect in order to decide how to label it. This analysis is basically the same as in a rule–of–reason case.

Price Fixing

Price fixing among competitors is per se illegal. This activity occurs when two or more competitors agree explicitly to charge a specific price, or to set a price floor, but many other arrangements can also constitute price fixing because they substantially interfere with the price–setting function of the market. Some examples include agreements or understandings among competitors to (1) not submit competitive bids; (2) rotate the privilege of being low bidder on contracts; (3) artificially manipulate supply or demand in a way that affects price substantially; (4) not advertise prices; (5) not grant certain discounts; (6) maintain uniformity on a particular term that constitutes a component of price, such as shipping or credit charges; (7) keep prices within a particular range; and even (8) maintain a *ceiling* on prices.

Many other joint arrangements may have an arguable effect on the market's pricing mechanism. If the court is convinced that the parties' main purpose is to suppress price competition, it will probably call the arrangement price fixing and find it illegal. As mentioned earlier, however, if there is significant doubt about the question, a court will probably engage in a rule–of–reason type analysis, regardless of whether it uses that phrase.

Market Division

Market division among competitors is also per se illegal, assuming that such division is found to be the primary objective of a particular arrangement. The same rule can be applied to market division agreements involving potential competitors making decisions about entering new markets. Market division arrangements can take at least three forms: (1) in a *territorial* market division, the firms agree to refrain from competing with each other in designated geographic areas; (2) in a *customer allocation* arrangement, the firms assign particular customers or classes of customers to each seller and agree not to solicit customers of another seller; (3) in a *product line* division, the firms agree to limit their activities to particular types of products or services so as to avoid competing with each other.

Boycotts

A firm ordinarily has freedom to choose those with whom it will transact business. However, when two or more parties agree not to deal with some other party, antitrust problems arise. When the agreeing parties are competitors and their primary purpose apparently is to curtail competition, the resulting **boycott** is per se illegal. Two or more firms will violate Section 1, for example, if they agree to quit selling to a customer because the latter is trying to integrate upstream and become their competitor. Likewise, a group of firms would be engaged in an illegal boycott if they agreed to stop selling to certain customers unless those customers quit buying from a competitor of those in the agreeing group. A similar violation would occur if the group agreed not to buy from a supplier unless that supplier refrained from selling to a competitor or potential competitor of the group. Boycotts are sometimes used to drive a firm out of a market, keep it from entering in the first place, or discipline a firm by "showing it who's boss" and thus convincing it to stop competing so aggressively.

Although labeling problems occur with respect to all of the per se categories, they seem to be especially troublesome in the case of boycotts. The reason is that there are many group activities that have legitimate reasons for existing, but that also may have the tendency to *exclude* other firms. Suppose for example, that many of the automotive repair businesses in Missouri, Kansas, and Oklahoma form an organization called the Midwest Auto Repair Association (MARA). The stated purposes of the group are to promote the auto repair business in various ways and encourage high ethical standards in the industry. Like any organization, MARA establishes rules for membership that might require such things as full–time participation in the auto repair business, a fee to cover the organization's costs, fewer than a specified number of verified customer complaints during a given period of time, and so on. Jones does not meet one of the requirements and is either denied membership initially or is forced out later. He claims that he has been the victim of a boycott.

There are many other examples. Similar problems can arise if a group of firms in the same industry tries to establish uniform product standards for the purpose of either safety or reducing customer confusion and dissatisfaction. One firm's product does not meet the standard and thus does not receive the approval of the group. The firm claims a boycott.

Yet another example arises where a group of firms pool their resources to develop a facility such as a research lab. This can be legitimate where the great cost, risk, and uncertainty of constructing a major facility or engaging in a particular undertaking is too much for a single firm. (This last example describes a "joint venture," which will be discussed shortly.) A competitor is not permitted to join the venture and claims a boycott.

When confronted with such claims, courts first look at the group's apparent *purpose*. If the primary purpose was to exclude others and achieve some restriction on competition, it will be per se illegal as a boycott. If the main purpose appears to have been a legitimate one, the court engages in a rule–of– reason type of analysis. The court will try to determine just how important it is for a firm to participate. (This is just another kind of inquiry into a group's collective market power.) If exclusion really does not harm a firm's ability to compete in the relevant market, the arrangement is legal. On the other hand, if participation is very important to a firm's ability to compete, the rules or restrictions that have the result of excluding others must be *reasonable*. To be reasonable, they must (1) have a logical relationship to the group's legitimate objectives, and (2) not exclude others any more than is necessary to accomplish those objectives.

Trade Associations

A trade association is a loosely knit organization of firms with mutual interests. Its membership usually includes firms within the same industry, but sometimes also includes suppliers or customers of these firms, and perhaps others with an interest in the field, such as consultants. The mere existence of a trade association presents no antitrust problems—most industries have some type of trade association. Moreover, the activities of these associations usually are legitimate and socially useful. Associations in some industries have been instrumental, for example, in setting product safety standards, maintaining ethical norms, providing arbitration or other procedures for resolving disputes between members, forming group self–insurance pools, and so on.

The problem with trade associations is that they can present very tempting opportunities for illegal group activities such as price fixing, market divisions, boycotts, or other arrangements that stifle competition. Members must be vigilant to ensure that the association's activities do not harm competition, and have all proposals reviewed by attorneys with antitrust expertise. If a firm believes that action about to be taken by the group is legally questionable, the firm should voice its dissent and not participate.

Joint Ventures

Although the term **joint venture** has no precise meaning, it has been likened to a partnership for a limited purpose. The joint research lab used earlier as an illustration is a type of joint venture. When two or more firms collaborate for some reason, their joint undertaking may or may not be a joint venture. The basic characteristics of a legitimate joint venture are (1) a partial pooling of resources by two or more firms, (2) a limited degree of integration of some aspect of the firms' operations, and (3) an intent to accomplish a defined business objective that could not be accomplished as efficiently (or at all) by a single firm. Situations in which joint ventures are commonly accepted as legitimate include those in which extremely large economies of scale, very high risks, or unusually extended long–term payoffs are involved, or where the nature of the product is such that it cannot be produced or marketed efficiently without collaboration between two or more firms.

Joint ventures usually do not violate the antitrust laws, but they can do so on occasion. Section 1 of the Sherman Act is the primarily applicable statute, and joint ventures are normally judged under the rule of reason. If formation of the joint venture involves an asset or stock acquisition, Section 7 of the Clayton Act also can be applied, although the legal standards for joint ventures are basically the same under both statutes.

The risk of illegality obviously is greater when actual or potential competitors are involved. In addition, certain kinds of activities are more likely to limit competition than those involving other kinds of activities. A joint venture might involve matters ranging along a continuum from basic research to applied research, product development, production, promotion and other marketing activities, selling, and finally, distribution. The risk of harm to competition, and thus the degree of scrutiny under the antitrust laws, increases as the activity moves along the continuum away from research. Joint ventures involving activities farther along the continuum, such as production, can be valid, but their justification must be stronger.

Assuming that the basic objectives of the joint venture are legitimate, three basic types of antitrust questions can still be raised. First, the formation of a joint venture occasionally may create dangers to competition that probably will not be outweighed by increased efficiency or other positive effects. This may happen if the venture is just *too big*–that is, if it is larger than really necessary to accomplish its legitimate objectives. Second, even if the venture is not too large, it may include some *ancillary restriction* that limits competition among the participants more than necessary.

For example, participants might agree to exchange certain kinds of information which, if misused, could make it fairly easy to engage in horizontal price fixing. This restriction would require a very strong justification. Third, the joint venture may harm outsiders who are excluded from participation. This situation is analyzed as described earlier in the discussion of various group activities that tend to exclude others.

Vertical Restraints of Trade

When firms operating at different levels of the distribution chain enter some arrangement that may harm competition, we call it a **vertical restraint of trade.**

Resale Price Maintenance

Nature and Effects

Resale price maintenance (RPM), which is also called vertical price fixing, occurs when a seller and buyer agree on the price at which the buyer will resell to its own customers.

RPM usually is a method by which a manufacturer or other supplier limits price competition among its dealers or distributors in the market for resale of the product. Competition among such dealers for sales of the manufacturer's product is called **intrabrand competition,** in contrast with the **interbrand competition** that occurs between different manufacturers' brands.

RPM has always been controversial. Many economists and legal scholars believe that RPM and other forms of restriction on intrabrand competition are usually employed to increase efficiency. They claim that these limits on intrabrand competition can be used by a manufacturer to make sure that its dealers invest in the facilities, trained personnel, and promotional activities necessary to stimulate sales and properly serve customers. If one dealer makes such an investment and thereby stimulates demand for the manufacturer's product, but another dealer does not, the latter has lower costs and can underprice the former. The first dealer will then be discouraged and will stop making such investments. Because of some dealers' **free riding,** the argument goes, many (or most) of the manufacturer's dealers will not do those things necessary to compete vigorously with other brands. If the manufacturer uses RPM to put a floor below its dealers' resale prices, however, some argue that this will solve the problem by reducing dealers' incentives to take a free ride on the investment of other dealers. The incentive is gone because they cannot use their lower costs to underprice and take customers from another dealer. Those arguing that the law should treat RPM very leniently also claim that, because any potential harm to competition is only intrabrand, customers are protected so long as competition among different brands remains active.

Other experts have serious doubts about the "free rider" justification for RPM. They argue that free rider problems are really not that common, and that many cases of resale price maintenance have involved products like toothpaste or blue jeans, for which there is not much need for the kinds of costly facilities or services that are susceptible to free riding. They also claim that, even if free rider problems are common, other means are available for solving them that do not cause similar harm to price competition. Such means include contractual commitments from dealers to provide the necessary facilities, personnel, promotion, and services. Opponents of RPM claim that the true reason for the practice often may be the manufacturer's desire to keep dealers' prices up and relieve them from intrabrand competition so that they do not pressure the manufacturer to lower its prices to them. They also sometimes argue that RPM can be used as a device to carry out a horizontal price–fixing conspiracy among dealers.

Legal Standards

The statute applicable to RPM is Section 1 of the Sherman Act. From the early days of the Sherman Act, RPM was viewed as per se illegal. That recently changed as to vertical maximum pricing.

STATE OIL CO. V. KHAN
U.S. Supreme Court, 522 U.S. 3 (1997)

Respondents Khan and his corporation, entered into an agreement with petitioner, StateOil Company, to lease and operate a gas station and convenience store owned by State Oil. The agreement provided that respondents would obtain the station's gasoline supply from State Oil at a price equal to a suggested retail price set by State Oil, less a margin of 3.25 cents per gallon. Under the agreement, respondents could charge any amount for gasoline sold to the station customers, but if the price charged was higher than State Oil's suggested retail price, the excess was to be rebated to State Oil. Respondents could sell gasoline for less than State Oil's suggested retail price, but any such decrease would reduce their 3.25 cents–per–gallon margin.

About a year after respondents began operating the gas station, they fell behind in lease payments. State Oil then gave notice of its intent to terminate the agreement and commenced a state court proceeding to evict respondents. A state court appointed a receiver to operate the gas station. The receiver operated the station for several months without being subject to the price restraints in respondents' agreement with State Oil, obtaining an overall profit margin in excess of 3.25 cents per gallon by lowering the price of regular–grade gasoline and raising the price of premium grades.

Respondents sued State Oil, alleging in part that State Oil had engaged in price fixing in violation of §1 of the Sherman Act by preventing respondents from raising or lowering retail gas prices. They claimed that but for the agreement with State Oil, respondents could have charged different prices based on the grades of gasoline, in the same way that the receiver had, thereby achieving increased

sales and profits. The District Court found for State Oil; the Seventh Circuit reversed on appeal. State Oil appealed to the Supreme Court.

O'Connor Justice:

Under §1 of the Sherman Act, "every contract, combination . . ., or conspiracy, in restraint of trade" is illegal. In Albrecht v. Herald Co.,390 U.S. 145 (1968), this Court held that vertical maximum price fixing is a per se violation of that statute. In this case, we are asked to reconsider that decision in light of subsequent decisions of this Court. We conclude that *Albrecht* should be overruled.

Although the Sherman Act, by its terms, prohibits every agreement "in restraint of trade," this Court has long recognized that Congress intended to outlaw only unreasonable restraints. As a consequence, most antitrust claims are analyzed under a "rule of reason," according to which the finder of fact must decide whether the questioned practice imposes an unreasonable restraint on competition, taking into account a variety of factors, including specific information about the relevant business, its condition before and after the restraint was imposed, and the restraint's history, nature, and effect.

Some types of restraints, however, have such predictable and pernicious anticompetitive effect, and such limited potential for procompetitive benefit, that they are deemed unlawful per se. Per se treatment is appropriate "once experience with a particular kind of restraint enables the Court to predict with confidence that the rule of reason will condemn it." Arizona v. Maricopa County Medical Soc., 457 U.S. 332(1982). Thus, we have expressed reluctance to adopt per se rules with regard to "restraints imposed in the context of business relationships where the economic impact of certain practices is not immediately obvious." *FTC v. Indiana Federation of Dentists*, 476 U.S. 447 (1986).

Albrecht involved a newspaper publisher who had granted exclusive territories to independent carriers subject to their adherence to a maximum price on resale of the newspapers to the public. The Court concluded that it was per se unlawful for the publisher to fix the maximum resale price of its newspapers. The Court acknowledged that "maximum and minimum price fixing may have different consequences in many situations," but nonetheless condemned maximum price fixing for "substituting the perhaps erroneous judgment of a seller for the forces of the competitive market."

Albrecht was animated in part by the fear that vertical maximum price fixing could allow suppliers to discriminate against certain dealers, restrict the services that dealers could afford to offer customers, or disguise minimum price fixing schemes. The Court rejected the notion (both on the record of that case and in the abstract) that, because the newspaper publisher "granted exclusive territories, a price ceiling was necessary to protect the public from price gouging by dealers who had monopoly power in their own territories."

In a vigorous dissent, Justice Harlan asserted that the majority had erred in equating the effects of maximum and minimum price fixing. Justice Harlan pointed out that, because the majority was establishing a per se rule, the proper inquiry was "not whether dictation of maximum prices is ever illegal, but whether it is always illegal." He also faulted the majority for conclusively listing "certain unfortunate consequences that maximum price dictation might have in other cases," even as it rejected evidence that the publisher's practice of fixing maximum prices

counteracted potentially anticompetitive actions by its distributors. Justice Stewart also dissented, asserting that the publisher's maximum price fixing scheme should be properly viewed as promoting competition, because it protected consumers from dealers such as Albrecht, who, as "the only person who could sell for home delivery the city's only daily morning newspaper," was "a monopolist within his own territory."

Nine years later, in *Continental T.V., Inc. v. GTE Sylvania, Inc.*, 433 U.S. 36 (1977), the Court [rejected] application of a per se rule in the context of vertical nonprice restrictions. The Court concluded that, because "departure from the rule—of—reason standard must be based upon demonstrable economic effect rather than upon formalistic line drawing," the appropriate course would be "to return to the rule of reason that [had previously] governed vertical restrictions."

Our analysis is guided by our general view that the primary purpose of the antitrust laws is to protect interbrand competition. "Low prices," we have explained, "benefit consumers regardless of how those prices are set, and so long as they are above predatory levels, they do not threaten competition." Our interpretation of the Sherman Act also incorporates the notion that condemnation of practices resulting in lower prices to consumers is "especially costly" because "cutting prices in order to increase business often is the very essence of competition."

So informed, we find it difficult to maintain that vertically—imposed maximum prices could harm consumers or competition to the extent necessary to justify their per se invalidation. . . .We recognize that the *Albrecht* decision presented a number of theoretical justifications for a per se rule against vertical maximum price fixing. But criticism of those premises abounds. The *Albrecht* decision was grounded in the fear that maximum price fixing by suppliers could interfere with dealer freedom. In response, as one commentator has pointed out, "the ban on maximum resale price limitations declared in *Albrecht* in the name of 'dealer freedom' has actually prompted many suppliers to integrate forward into distribution, thus eliminating the very in-dependent trader for whom *Albrecht* professed solicitude." 7 P. Areeda, Antitrust Law, P1635, p. 395 (1989).

The *Albrecht* Court also expressed the con-cern that maximum prices may be set too low for dealers to offer consumers essential or desired services. But such conduct, by driving away customers, would seem likely to harm manufacturers as well as dealers and consum-ers, making it unlikely that a supplier would set such a price as a matter of business judg-ment. In addition, *Albrecht* noted that vertical maximum price fixing could effectively chan-nel distribution through large or specially—advantaged dealers. It is unclear, however, that a supplier would profit from limiting its mar-ket by excluding potential dealers. Further, although vertical maximum price fixing might limit the viability of inefficient dealers, that consequence is not necessarily harmful to com-petition and consumers.

Finally, *Albrecht* reflected the Court's fear that maximum price fixing could be used to disguise arrangements to fix minimum prices, which remain illegal per se. Although we have acknowledged the possibility that maximum

pricing might mask minimum pricing, we believe that such conduct——as with the other concerns articulated in *Albrecht*——can be appropriately recognized and punished under the rule of reason.

Not only are the potential injuries cited in *Albrecht* less serious than the Court imagined, the per se rule established therein could in fact exacerbate problems related to the unre-strained exercise of market power by monopo-list—dealers. Indeed, both courts and antitrust scholars have noted that *Albrecht's* rule may actually harm consumers and manufacturers. Other commentators have also explained that *Albrecht's* per se rule has even more potential for deleterious effect on competition after our decision [holding that vertical nonprice restric-tions] are not unlawful per se, the likelihood of dealer monopoly power is increased.

In overruling *Albrecht*, we of course do not hold that all vertical maximum price fixing is per se lawful. Instead, vertical maximum price fixing, like the majority of commercial arrangements subject to the antitrust laws, should be evaluated under the rule of reason. In our view, rule—of—reason analysis will effectively identify those situations in which vertical maximum price fixing amounts to anticompetitive conduct.

We therefore vacate the judgment of the Court of Appeals and remand the case for fur-ther proceedings consistent with this opinion. It is so ordered.

Proving a Vertical Agreement

Most of the difficult issues in RPM cases have involved the question of whether there actually has been an "agreement" to set resale prices. "Suggested" resale prices at the retail level are quite common. They do not constitute RPM unless there is evidence that there really has been an agreement (either voluntary or coerced) that gives the manufac-turer or other supplier effective control over the dealer's resale prices. This point also illustrates the fact that there can be an illegal RPM "agreement" even if one party has coerced the other into participating; Section 1 of the Sherman Act does not require that the agreement be completely voluntary.

One of the most difficult issues in this area involves the extent to which a seller lawfully may use a *refusal to deal* in an attempt to control buyers' resale prices. In United States v. Colgate &Co ., 250 U.S. 300 (1919), the Supreme Court stated that a "unilateral refusal to deal" cannot violate Section 1 of the Sherman Act even if controlling resale prices is the seller's ultimate goal. In other words, so long as a seller acts entirely on its own ("unilaterally") it can refuse to sell to anyone it chooses, regardless of the motive. The problem, of course, is distinguishing between unilateral action by the seller and action that is part of an RPM arrangement between the seller and others. Suppose that M, a manufacturer, either initially refuses to sell to R, a retailer, or later terminates an existing supplier–customer relationship with R. (When RPM is claimed, the second situation is the most common.) To create a genuine fact issue for the jury, R must present evidence indicating that (1) there was an agreement to fix resale prices at R's level, and (2) M refused to deal with R because R would not go along with the arrangement. The agreement to limit price competition at R's level could be between M and wholesalers who act as intermediaries between M and R, between M and other retailers who compete with R, or even between M and R if the evidence shows that R previously had been part of an RPM arrangement with M and then tried to get out of it.

Vertical Nonprice Restrictions

Nature and Effects

Vertical restrictions may relate to matters other than price. The vertical nonprice restrictions (VNRs) that can cause some concern under Section 1 of the Sherman Act generally are those involving some type of market division. VNRs take many forms, depending on several factors. These factors include the relative bargaining power of the manufacturer and its dealers or distributors, and the nature of the product and the markets in which it sells.

One type of VNR is the *territorial exclusive*, in which M, the manufacturer, guarantees its dealers that they will have the exclusive right to market M's product in their respective geographic areas. In order to honor this arrangement with each dealer, M obviously must keep all dealers from reselling outside their own areas. Because this restriction places a contractual limitation on M's freedom, M will not use exclusive territories in its distribution system unless it has relatively less bargaining power than its dealers. More often, M will use *territorial and customer restrictions*, without any promise of exclusive territories. Such an arrangement requires dealers or distributors to resell only within their respective territories or only to particular customers, but does not guarantee them exclusive rights to sell in those areas or to those customers. A similar provision that restricts dealers somewhat less is the *area of primary responsibility*, which does not absolutely prohibit a dealer from reselling outside its designated territory but requires only that the territory be thoroughly served before sales can be made outside the area. Another fairly common provision is the *location requirement*, which requires a dealer to sell only from a specified location. In most cases, a location requirement has the same effect as a territorial restriction.

Like RPM, all forms of VNRs have the common characteristic of limiting intrabrand competition. Also like RPM, there is a longstanding debate about the competitive benefits and dangers of VNRs. Today, and commonly during the past, the prevailing attitude toward these restrictions has been more favorable than the attitude toward RPM. Generally, the feeling has been that VNRs are more likely than RPM (1) to be based on legitimate motives and (2) to help intrabrand competition more than they hurt intrabrand competition. A significant number of authorities think, however, that the law should not treat VNRs and RPM any differently because they are usually employed for the same purposes, have basically the same effects, and can be difficult to distinguish in practice.

Legal Standards

The legal status of VNRs has varied over the years. Until 1967, they were analyzed under the rule of reason. In that year, a decision of the U.S. Supreme Court caused some kinds of nonprice restriction on dealers to be per se illegal. This decision was overruled by the Court in 1977, and since then the rule of reason has been applied to all forms of VNRs.

In the case of VNRs, the question of motive is usually not as important as it can be when the rule of reason is applied to horizontal restrictions. Courts generally accept as legitimate M's objective of using a VNR to limit intrabrand competition, so long as there apparently is some business justification for the limitation. Under the rule of reason, M's market share will be the most important factor. If it is below approximately 10 percent, the restriction usually will be legal without further inquiry. If the share is at or above this level, courts normally will look at other factors. Other factors that could increase the chances of illegality in a close case include (1) evidence that *interbrand competition* in this particular market is not very strong, and that intrabrand competition is especially important; (2) evidence that most other manufacturers in this market also use such restrictions to limit *intrabrand competition among* their dealers; and (3) evidence that M selected a form of VNR that limits intrabrand competition much more than is really necessary under the circumstances.

The following case is the one in which the U.S. Supreme Court switched from the per se rule back to the rule of reason for judging VNRs. The Court's discussion outlines and adopts some of the arguments made by those who feel that VNRs usually produce more economic benefits than harms.

CONTINENTAL T.V., INC. V. G.T.E. SYLVANIA, INC.
U.S. Supreme Court, 433 U.S. 36 (1977)

Sylvania manufactured and sold television sets through its Home Entertainment Products Division. Prior to 1962, like most other *television manufacturers, Sylvania sold televisions to independent or company—owned wholesale distributors who then resold them* to a large and diverse group of retailers. *Prompted by a decline in its market share to a relatively insignificant 1 to 2 percent of national television sales, Sylvania conducted an intensive reassessment of its marketing strategy and in 1962 adopted the franchise plan challenged here. Sylvania phased out its wholesale distributors and began to sell its televisions directly to a smaller and more select group of franchised retailers. The main purpose of the change was to decrease the number of competing Sylvania retailers in the hope of attracting the more aggressive and competent retailers, which Sylvania felt was necessary to improve its market position.*

Thus, Sylvania limited the number of franchises granted for any given area and required each retail dealer to sell Sylvania products only from the location or locations specified in the franchise agreement. These retailers were not prohibited from selling the products of competing manufacturers. A franchise did not constitute an exclusive territory, and Sylvania retained sole discretion to increase the number of retailers in an area in light of the success or failure of existing retailers in developing their market. The revised marketing strategy apparently was successful, and by 1965 Sylvania's share of national television sales increased to 5 percent, making it the eighth largest manufacturer of televisions.

In 1965 Sylvania proposed to franchise an additional retailer in San Francisco. This proposal upset Continental T. V., an existing Sylvania dealer in the city. Continental then proposed to open a new store in Sacramento. Sylvania denied Continental's request because it felt that Sacramento presently was being adequately served. Continental then began selling Sylvania televisions in Sacramento in defiance of Sylvania, and the manufacturer stopped selling to Continental.

Continental filed a treble damage suit against Sylvania, claiming that the restrictions on dealer location violated Section 1 of the Sherman Act. In federal district court Continental received a jury verdict against Sylvania for approximately $600,000 and a judgment for $1.13 million. In ruling for Continental, the district court applied the Supreme Court's 1967 decision in United States v. Arnold, Schwinn & Co., which had held vertical nonprice restrictions to be per se illegal. When Sylvania appealed to the court of appeals, that court reversed and ordered a retrial because it thought that the Schwinn case was inapplicable to the present situation. Continental then appealed to the U.S. Supreme Court. The Supreme Court felt that the Schwinn case was indeed applicable to the facts of the present case, but wished to decide whether Schwinn should still be the law. Thus, the issue for the Supreme Court was whether to follow its earlier decision in the Schwinn case and apply the per se rule, or to overrule that case and apply the rule of reason to vertical nonprice restrictions.

Powell, Justice:

. . . Since its announcement, Schwinn has been the subject of continuing controversy and confusion both in the scholarly journals and in the federal courts. The great weight of scholarly opinion has been critical of the decision, and a number of the federal courts confronted with analogous vertical restrictions have sought to limit its reach. In our view, the experience of the past 10 years should be brought to bear on this subject of considerable commercial importance. . .

Per se rules of illegality are appropriate only when they relate to conduct that is manifestly anti–competitive. As the Court explained in Northern P ac. R. Co. v. United States, 356 U.S. 1, 5, 78 S.Ct. 514, 518, 2 L.Ed.2d 545 (1958), "there are certain agreements or *(con*—practices which because of their pernicious effect on competition and lack of any redeeming virtue are conclusively presumed to be unreasonable and therefore illegal without elaborate inquiry as to the precise harm they have caused or the business excuse for their use."

In essence, the issue before us is whether *Schwinn's* per se rule can be justified under the demanding standards of *Northern P ac. R. Co...*

5The market impact of vertical restrictions is complex because of their potential for a simultaneous reduction of intrabrand competition and stimulation of interbrand competition...

Vertical restrictions reduce intrabrand competition by limiting the number of sellers of a particular product competing for the business of a given group of buyers. Location restrictions have this effect because of practical constraints on the effective marketing area of retail outlets. Although intrabrand competition may be reduced, the ability of retailers to exploit the resulting market may be limited both by the ability of consumers to travel to other franchised locations and, perhaps more importantly, to purchase the competing products of other manufacturers...

Vertical restrictions promote inter−brand competition by allowing the manufacturer to achieve certain efficiencies in the distribution of his products. These "redeeming virtues" are implicit in every decision sustaining vertical restrictions under the rule of reason. Economists have identified a number of ways in which manufacturers can use such restrictions to compete more effectively against other manufacturers. For example, new manufacturers and manufacturers entering new markets can use the restrictions in order to induce competent and aggressive retailers to make the kind of investment of capital and labor that is often required in the distribution of products unknown to the consumer. Established manufacturers can use them to induce retailers to engage in promotional activities or to provide service and repair facilities necessary to the efficient marketing of their products. Service and repair are vital for many products, such as automobiles and major household appliances. The availability and quality of such services affect a manufacturer's good will and the competitiveness of his product. Because of market imperfections such as the so called "free rider" effect, these services might not be provided by retailers in a purely competitive situation, despite the fact that each retailer's benefit would be greater if all provided the services than if none did...

Certainly, there has been no showing in this case, either generally or with respect to Sylvania's agreements, that vertical restrictions have or are likely to have a "pernicious effect on competition" or that they "lack ... any redeeming virtue." Accordingly, we conclude that the *per se* rule stated in *Schwinn* must be overruled. In so holding we do not foreclose the possibility that particular applications of vertical restrictions might justify *per se* prohibition under Northern P ac. R.Co. But we do make clear that departure from the rule of reason standard must be based upon demonstrable economic effect...

In sum, we conclude that the appropriate decision is to return to the rule of reason that governed vertical restrictions prior to *Schwinn*. When anti−competitive effects are shown to result from particular vertical restrictions they can be adequately policed under the rule of reason, the standard traditionally applied for the majority of anticompetitive practices challenged under secl of the Act. Accordingly, the decision of the Court of Appeals is affirmed.

Comment

CommentOn retrial, the district court found that Sylvania's vertical restrictions were valid under the rule of reason. This holding was based primarily on (1) Sylvania's legitimate business justification, (2) Sylvania's small market share, and (3) the court's feeling that Sylvania had chosen the "least restrictive alternative"—in other words, that the location clause was less restrictive of competition than other methods Sylvania might have used to accomplish its objectives.

Tying Agreements
Nature and Effects

When one party agrees to supply (sell, lease, etc.) a product or service only on the condition that the customer also take another product or service, a **tying agreement** has been made. The desired item is the *tying* product, and the item the customer is required to take is the *tied* product. Tying agreements are scrutinized under both Section 1 of the Sherman Act and Section 3 of the Clayton Act. Section 3 of the Clayton Act applies only to the tying of two tangible commodities. Section 1 of the Sherman Act applies to all tying arrangements, including those in which either or both products is not a tangible commodity (such as a service, an intangible property right, or land). Today tying agreements are analyzed the same way under the two statutes, so Section 3 of the Clayton Act is largely redundant.

An early landmark case provides a clear example of tying. In IBM v. United States, 298 U.S. 131 (1936), IBM was found guilty of illegal tying by requiring all customers leasing its tabulating machines to also purchase their tabulating cards from IBM.

In 2003, Visa and MasterCard settled a lawsuit brought by Wal–Mart (and claiming $3 billion in damages) that alleged defendants had illegally tied use of debit cards to credit card purchases. And in 2004, the EU fines Microsoft $600 million for, among other things, incorporating a media player into its Windows computer operating system and thereby "tying" the two products together.

The main concern about tying is that a supplier may use power in one market (the market for the *tying* product) to distort competition in another market (the market for the *tied* product). Such distortion can occur, it is argued, because the supplier's sales of the tied product are not based on the independent competitive merits of that product.

Several different motivations may lead a supplier to use tying arrangements. In some cases, the supplier may be trying to use the power it has in the tying market to expand its power in the tied market. Such a practice is sometimes referred to as leveraging. There is quite a bit of debate among experts as to the extent to which power actually can be leveraged from one market to another.

A supplier also might use tying in an attempt to *protect its goodwill*. This could be the motive, for example, where the supplier sells or leases product X, and where product Y must be used in conjunction with X. The supplier may be concerned that some customers might use inferior versions of Y that will cause X to perform poorly, and thus hurt the reputation of X. In such a case, the supplier might require buyers to buy the supplier's own version of Y along with X. The general feeling under the antitrust laws, however, has been that the supplier should accomplish its objective by requiring the customer to use any version of Y that meets specifications set by the supplier, unless the use of specifications is very difficult.

Another possible motive for tying is to *discriminate among customers* according to the intensity with which they use the supplier's product. Suppose that M manufactures a machine used by food processing companies to inject salt into foods during processing. If M feels that customers who use the machine more may be willing to pay more for it, M may try to charge them based on intensity of use so as to maximize its total revenues. Direct metering may be very difficult. Sometimes, however, intensity of use is directly proportional to the amount of a second product the customer uses in connection with M's product. In the case of the salt–dispensing machine, intensity of use can be measured by the amount of salt used by the customer. Thus, M may try to measure intensity by requiring customers of its machines also to buy its salt. Through the salt sales, M's total revenue will be greater in transactions with high–intensity users.

Legal Standards

Tying can occur only if two separate products are involved. Often this is obvious, but sometimes it is not, as for example in the case of various options on new automobiles. Generally, a transaction will be viewed as including two separate products if the evidence demonstrates that there really are two separate markets in which the different items are commonly demanded. However, even if there are two separate markets, courts usually will treat a transaction as involving only one product if packaging two items is significantly more efficient than selling them separately.

If there are two separate products, tying is illegal only if the supplier has *substantial power in the market for the tying product*. The reason for this requirement is the generally accepted proposition that tying cannot cause any substantial harm in the *tied* market unless the supplier has quite a bit of power in the tying market. Market power is measured in the same way here as in other cases. Today, a supplier probably has to have at least a 30 percent share of the tying market to be viewed as having substantial power in that market. Other factors, such as entry barriers, are also very important. According to the courts, there is a second requirement for tying to be illegal, namely, that the supplier's tying arrangements must generate a substantial amount of business in the tied market. This requirement is so easy to establish, however, that it is practically always present.

In recent years, courts have moved slowly from applying a per se illegality approach to tying when the defendant had market power for the high demand product, to a rule of reason approach. Although the U.S. Supreme Court in Jefferson Parish Hospital Dist. v. Hyde, 466 U.S. 2 (1984), seemingly applied a per se approach, clearly many justices on the court were more comfortable with a rule of reason approach. Because tying is so ubiquitous in commerce and often has economic benefits (consider the hotel that provides soaps and shampoos to customers and wraps those costs up into the overall room charge), several courts have reconsidered the legal tests in the area. For example, in U.S. v. Microsoft Corp., 253 F.3d 34 (D.C.Cir. 2001), the government charged that Microsoft was illegally tying its not–so–popular Web browser to its highly popular operating system by bundling the software all together. The court held, consistent with a rule of reason approach, that the government bore the burden of proving that the harm to competition from this integration of features outweighed efficiency benefits.

Exclusive Dealing

Nature and Effects

The most common form of **exclusive dealing** agreement is one in which the customer makes a commitment that it will purchase a particular product or service only from the supplier (and, implicitly or explicitly, *not* from the supplier's competitors). Many times these arrangements are called "requirements contracts" because the parties often speak in terms of the buyer's commitment to purchase its "requirements" of a product from the seller. The primary concern caused by this type of arrangement is that there may be fewer and less frequent opportunities for the seller's competitors to compete for those customers who are parties to the exclusive dealing. Widespread use of such agreements in a market may also increase entry barriers for potential competitors.

Another kind of exclusive dealing that occurs less often is one in which the seller agrees to sell only to a particular buyer (and, thus, not sell to the buyer's competitors). This is sometimes called an "output" contract, because the seller obligates itself to sell all of its output of a product to the buyer. Output contracts usually raise no competitive concerns, but occasionally might unreasonably prevent the buyer's competitors from acquiring products needed to compete.

Legal Standards

Today, exclusive dealing is likely to be illegal under Sections 1 or 2 of the Sherman Act or Section 3 of the Clayton Act only if a dominant share—probably more than 30 percent—of the relevant market is locked away from competitors. Thus, the practice creates a real legal risk only when a leading or dominant firm in a market makes widespread use of it.

In U.S. v. Dentsply, 399 F.3d 181 (3d Cir. 2005), the court held that the nation's largest false teeth manufacturer had illegally monopolized sales of false teeth to dental laboratories and dealers by prohibiting its distributors from carrying competing lines of false teeth. Although exclusive dealing arrangements can in proper circumstances create market efficiencies, this arrangement was held illegal under Section 2 of the Sherman Act because defendant's dominant market position meant that the exclusive dealing foreclosed others from competing by wrapping up vital outlets to the marketplace. Similarly, in U.S. v. Visa U.S.A., Inc.,344 F.3d 229 (2d Cir. 2003), exclusionary rules imposed by MasterCard and Visa that preventing their issuing banks from also issuing Discover or American Express cards were invalidated under Section 1 of the Sherman Act.

Price Discrimination

Although the original version of Section 2 of the Clayton Act contained a prohibition of **price discrimination,** it proved ineffective because of certain major loopholes. In 1936 Congress enacted the Robinson–Patman Act in an effort to make the law against price discrimination more effective. Congress's main purpose in passing this law was to protect small businesses from having to pay higher prices than larger companies. The specific complaint in 1936 was that large chain stores like the Great Atlantic and Pacific Tea Co. (A&P) were forcing suppliers to sell to them at lower prices than they sold to smaller "mom and pop" stores.

Basic Elements

The interstate commerce requirement in the Robinson–Patman Act is more difficult to prove than in any other of the antitrust laws. It is not enough that the seller or buyer is an interstate company or that the transaction affects interstate commerce—at least one of the relevant sales must actually cross state lines. Only a few states have laws prohibiting intrastate price discrimination within their borders. It should also be noted that many nations, including the United States, have *antidumping laws* that prohibit a foreign producer from selling goods in the country at a lower price than in that producer's home country.

Assuming that the interstate commerce requirement is met, the following must be proved to establish a violation of the Robinson–Patman Act. (1) The seller must have charged *different* prices to two or more different customers. (2) The transaction must have involved *tangible commodities,* not services, land, or intangibles. (3) The transactions must have been *sales,* rather than consignments, leases, or some other form of transaction. (4) The goods sold in the transactions being compared must have been *of like grade and quality,* which means that the products sold to different customers at different prices must have been essentially the same. Trivial differences are ignored. For example, when physically identical liquor was put into different bottles and sold as "premium" and as a cheaper brand, plaintiff's attorney noted that "Four Roses by any other name would still swill the same." (5) The evidence must demonstrate a likelihood of *substantial harm to competition.*

Injury to competition includes both injury to competitors of the seller (primary–line injury) and injury to competitors of the buyer (secondary–line injury). It is difficult to win primary–line cases (where defendant cuts prices just to plaintiff's customers in order to injure plaintiff, its competitor), because the Supreme Court requires such plaintiffs to demonstrate that defendants priced below cost (*predatory* pricing) and reasonably expected to recoup losses in the future primary line. These types of claims are similar to predatory pricing claims under the Sherman Act and normally are not winners unless there is a "dangerous probability of success" in defendant's attempt to monopolize.

Most courts are more receptive to secondary line claims (where plaintiffs are customers of defendant seller who favored some of its other customers at plaintiffs' expense). These plaintiffs must prove that they competed with the favored purchasers and they must show competitive injury. One way to show competitive injury is by direct evidence of lost sales or lost profits. If they cannot produce direct evidence, plaintiffs may still win by proving competitive injury by "inference" under the test of FTC v. Morton Salt, 334 U.S. 37 (1948). Under *Morton Salt*, courts will infer the existence of competitive injury if plaintiffs show a substantial price difference over a substantial time period.

Defenses

When the basic elements of a Robinson–Patman Act violation are proved, the seller is guilty unless it can prove one of three available defenses. The first is *cost justification*. There is no violation if the seller's different prices are simply a reflection of differences in the costs of "manufacture, sale, or delivery." Thus the seller wins if it proves that the higher prices to one buyer or group of buyers are directly attributable to the higher costs of providing the goods to that buyer or group. The second defense is *meeting competition*. A seller does not violate the Act if a lower price to one buyer "was made in good faith to meet an equally low price of a competitor." Suppose S generally charges $10 for a product, but learns that its competitor is offering the product to a certain customer for $9. S can legally meet the $9 price to that customer even while keeping its price to other buyers at $10. Another version of the meeting competition defense permits a seller to charge different prices in different geographic markets in order to meet different prevailing market prices in those different areas. The third defense is *changing conditions*. The seller is permitted to change prices in response to changing conditions that affect the marketability of the goods, such as imminent deterioration of perishable commodities or obsolescence of seasonal goods.

CHAPTER **29**

EMPLOYMENT LAW

- Labor Relations Law
- Employment Discrimination Law
- Protection of Safety and Welfare
- Employer's Right to Discharge Employees
- Protection of Employee Privacy

The law of employment relations has undergone a fundamental transformation within recent years and change continues even today. For much of our nation's history, the legal relationship between employer and employee was governed by general traditional principles of common law, which in practice typically tilted in the direction of the employer's authority. For example, employers lawfully could discharge their workers for any (or no) reason, including the individual employee's race, union membership, or job—related injury.

The growth of unions was the working person's first response to this legal regime, which seemingly favored employers to an inordinate degree. Unionization was frustrated at first by a series of judicial decisions, but once Congress provided statutory protection in the 1930s, the new labor organizations were able to thrive and provided considerable benefits to member workers.

Notwithstanding the advantages provided the majority of employees, unions had some serious shortcomings, especially when it came to protecting small groups of employees and dealing with noneconomic issues. In the 1960s Congress once again intervened to expand the protection of workers in areas where unions had contributed little. A number of antidiscrimination laws were enacted, the most significant being the Civil Rights Act of 1964. The Occupational Safety and Health Act of 1968 established a new agency and granted it considerable power to guard against workplace hazards. Legislation expanded worker rights in other areas as well. Perhaps prodded by this congressional activity, the courts also began to reexamine old precedents and initiate new common—law protections for employees. This chapter explores these developments in the law of employment relations and the complications the changes create for employers.

Labor Relations Law

In the early nineteenth century, attempts to unionize were stymied by the doctrine that they represented unlawful criminal conspiracies at common law. This theory gradually fell into disfavor and by the end of the century unions began to achieve some success, especially with the advent of industrialization and a rise in perceived employer abuse of power. Even in the early twentieth century, however, the courts continued to frustrate union development by enjoining critical functions of such organizations, such as striking and picketing. This was an era of much labor strife and periodic outbreaks of violence associated with labor/management disputes.

Recognizing the existence of a serious national problem, Congress passed several laws in an attempt to resolve labor/management difficulties, including the Railway Labor Act and the Norris—La Guardia Act, which prohibited, among other provisions, the use of injunctions against many union activities. Although these statutes eased the situation somewhat, it soon became clear that more extensive legislation was necessary. In 1935 Congress created a comprehensive framework for labor relations law by passing the National Labor Relations Act (NLRA). While this act has been amended, the basic rules established by the original NLRA survive today as the foundation of current law.

The NLRA unambiguously recognized an employee's right to organize by forming unions and authorized these labor organizations to bargain collectively with employers. Certain practices were declared to be unfair labor practices, and these were prohibited. Unfair labor practices were defined to include employer domination of unions, interference with employee organizing, discrimination against union members, and refusal to bargain collectively.

In order to enforce these requirements, the NLRA established a new agency, the National Labor Relations Board (NLRB). The NLRB consists of the General Counsel and the Board itself. The General Counsel investigates charges of unfair labor practices and, if they are found meritorious, initiates an action against the responsible party. These actions are heard by an administrative law judge and may be appealed to the entire Board. If the Board finds a violation, it can seek enforcement of a number of sanctions, including cease—and—desist orders and back pay awards. Board decisions may be appealed to the U.S. Courts of Appeals.

Coverage

The NLRA applies generally to all employers involved in or affecting interstate commerce. As discussed in Chapter 5 (Constitutional Law), this language is quite broad in scope. The act is limited to protection of employees, however, and does not cover independent contractors, a distinction explained in Chapter 32. In addition, some categories of employees are specifically excluded from the act's coverage. Government employees, as well as workers for railways and airlines (protected under a different statute) are outside the NLRA's coverage. Significantly, managerial and supervisory employees are not covered by the act, as they are considered to be part of "management" rather than "labor."

Right to Organize

Central to the NLRA is its guarantee of a right to form unions. Once a group of employees determines that it desires to form an organization for collective bargaining, the group seeks out other workers for support. Once 30 percent of the eligible employees in an appropriate job category sign authorization cards, the employee group may petition for an election to certify a union as the employees' bargaining representative. Conduct of such elections is carefully scrutinized by the NLRB to ensure "laboratory conditions" of fairness. Employers opposing unionization must take special care in their actions and statements lest they be found to have committed an unfair labor practice, in which case the union may be automatically certified by the Board, regardless of the election's outcome. The following case illustrates the care that an employer must take to avoid disturbing the laboratory conditions required for a unionization election.

NLRB v. Exchange Parts Co.
U.S. Supreme Court, 375 U.S. 405 (1964)

Exchange Parts Co. is in the automobile parts rebuilding business. On November 9, 1959, the International Brotherhood of Boilermakers, Iron Shipbuilders, Blacksmiths, Forgers and Helpers informed the company that majority of workers favored unionization and on February 19 the Board granted an election petition.

On February 25, the company held a dinner for employees, at which a vice–president announced that a previously granted extra vacation day could be either a floating holiday or could be taken on the individual employee's birthday. The workers chose the latter. The vice–president also mentioned the upcoming election as an opportunity for employees to "determine whether they wished to hand over their right to speak and act for themselves."

On March 4, the company sent its employees a letter that spoke of the "Empty Promises of the Union" and "the fact that it is the Company that puts things in your envelope..." After mentioning a number of benefits, the letter stated: 'The Union can't put any of those things in your envelope—only the Company can do that." The letter also went on to state that "it didn't take a Union to get any of those things and ...it won't take a Union to get additional improvements in the future." Past company benefits were summarized and new benefits were announced, including the new birthday holiday, a new system for computing overtime that had the effect of increasing wages, and a new vacation schedule that enabled employees to take more time off per year.

The election was held on March 18, and the union lost. The union promptly filed a charge with the Board, which held that the company actions had the intent to induce employees to vote against the union, thereby disrupting laboratory conditions and amounting to an unfair labor practice. The Board sought enforcement of its ruling in the Court of Appeals, which held against the Board. The Board then appealed this decision to the Supreme Court.

Harlan, Justice:

[The NLRA] makes it an unfair labor practice for an employer "to interfere with, restrain, or coerce employees in the exercise of [their rights to form labor unions]." ...We think the Court of Appeals was mistaken in concluding that the conferral of employee benefits while a representation election is pending, for the purpose of inducing employees to vote against the union does not "interfere with" the protected right to organize...

In Medo Photo Supply Corp. v. N.L.R.B., 321 U.S. 678, 686, this Court said: "The action of employees with respect to the choice of their bargaining agents may be induced by favors bestowed by the employer as well as by his threats or domination."

...The danger inherent in well–timed increases in employee benefits is the suggestion of a fist inside the velvet glove. Employees are not likely to miss the inference that the source of benefits now conferred is also the source from which future benefits must flow and which may dry up if it is not obliged...

We cannot agree with the Court of Appeals that enforcement of the Board's order will have the "ironic" result of "discouraging benefits for labor." The beneficence of an employer is a threat of unionization which is subsequently removed. Insulating the right of collective organization from calculated good will of this sort deprives employees of little that has lasting value.

Reversed. [The Board's order shall be enforced.]

In addition to benefits, employers must be careful not to say anything that may be interpreted as a "threat." An employer's statement that a plant shutdown was possible because the union would make company survival impossible was held to be unlawful.

Collective Bargaining

Collective bargaining is the term for negotiations between an employer and the union representative. Once a union has been certified as an official bargaining representative of a category of employees, the NLRA imposes a duty to bargain in good faith on both employer and union. Mandatory subjects of bargaining include wages and most working conditions. The good faith provision requires the parties to make a sincere effort to reach agreement. Approaches such as "take it or leave it" proposals may support an inference of bad faith and hence an unfair labor practice finding. An employer also must be willing to furnish certain information to the union and cannot delay unduly in doing so.

Strikes

The most powerful device possessed by unions under the NLRA is the right to strike. This right is available when collective bargaining has reached an impasse. For a strike to be legal it must be supported by a majority of members and cannot be a "wildcat" strike by a disgruntled minority. The NLRA also restricts strikes to those against the primary employer and prohibits strikes against third parties in an attempt to coerce that third party to pressure the primary employer. Even primary strikes are unlawful if they are violent or designed to compel "featherbedding" (the hiring of unnecessary employees) or other illegal contract terms.

The NLRA imposes other conditions on the conduct of strikes. For example, if workers are on strike against one employer at a multi–employer location (such as a construction site), the employees may not picket the entire site, as this applies unlawful secondary pressure against the other employers. Workers may picket a portion of the site that is used largely by their primary employer. If a strike is legal, the employer may be restricted in dealing with his striking employees. If the workers are engaged in an authorized strike protesting the employer's unfair labor practices, the strikers are automatically entitled to reinstatement after the strike is resolved. In the more traditional economic wage strike, the employer need not necessarily rehire strikers but never can discriminate against strikers, who have a right to seek reemployment on terms equal to those offered other prospective employees.

Nonunion Employees

Although the NLRA was designed primarily to protect unionization, it extends certain rights to nonunion workers as well. Where nonunion employees engage in concerted activity, such as a walkout in response to perceived unsafe working conditions, they are protected much like strikers on behalf of a union. In general, however, employers have a relatively free hand in dealing with nonunion workers. This situation gives rise to one potentially serious pitfall, however. If an employer sets up "employee committees" or other groups to address grievances in the absence of a union, the committee's independence from management must be carefully ensured. Otherwise, the employer may be found to have created a company–dominated labor organization, which is an unfair labor practice under the NLRA.

The above discussion represents an exceedingly brief review of labor relations law. There is a huge body of precedent under the NLRA elaborating on the above principles. Many of the legal rules in this field have become quite picayune. Consequently, employers must take special care in any controversy involving an organization of employees.

Employment Discrimination Law

For much of America's history, employers had the legal right to discriminate among employees on any basis other than union membership. Recently, however, antidiscrimination laws have been enacted that affect all phases of the employment process and that prohibit discrimination based on race, color, religion, sex, age, national origin, or perceived handicap. Worker use of these laws has grown to the point where they may exceed the NLRA as a source of litigation and potential employer liability.

Title VII of the 1964 Civil Rights Act Coverage

The Civil Rights Act of 1964 is a comprehensive federal enactment prohibiting discrimination in various settings, including housing, public accommodations, and education. Title VII of the Act deals specifically with discrimination in employment. Title VII prohibits discrimination against individuals because of their race, color, religion, sex, or national origin. Although Title VII was one of the earliest laws prohibiting employment discrimination, it remains the most significant.

The provisions of Title VII apply to employers, employment agencies, and labor unions. An employer is subject to Title VII if it (1) has 15 or more employees and (2) is engaged in business that affects interstate or foreign commerce. State and local governments are also within the definition of employer, and their employment practices are covered by Title VII. In most instances, the federal government's employment practices are also covered.

Scope of Protection

Title VII's prohibition against discrimination on the basis of race or color is very broad. It obviously protects blacks, but it also protects many other classes from unequal treatment, including Hispanics, American Indians, and Asian–Americans. Even whites are protected against racial discrimination.

The prohibition against national origin discrimination is violated if an employer discriminates on the basis of a person's country of origin. It is not illegal, however, for an employer to require employees to be U.S. citizens. (However, a government employer must have a very good reason for requiring its employees to be U.S. citizens, or the requirement will violate the equal protection clause of the U.S. Constitution.) Title VII also protects individuals against discrimination based on the race, color, or national origin of their family members or friends.

Title VII's prohibition against sex discrimination, which forbids unequal treatment based on gender is aimed primarily at discrimination against females, but it also protects males against gender–based discrimination. The law makes it illegal to use sex as a factor in employment decisions, and also to engage in sexual harassment. Title VII protects women from discrimination because of pregnancy or childbirth, as well. It does not apply to discrimination based on sexual practices, preferences, or lifestyles, so long as the employer treats employees of both sexes equally.

Although religious organizations can lawfully hire employees based on their religious beliefs, other employers cannot make distinctions for religious reasons. The term religion not only includes well–recognized religious faiths, but also unorthodox ones. For Title VII purposes, the courts use the same broad definition of religion that they use in freedom of religion cases under the first amendment to the Constitution: "a sincere and meaningful belief occupying in the life of its possessor a place parallel to that filled by the God of those admittedly qualified."

In addition to forbidding discrimination based on religion, the law also requires an employer to make "reasonable accommodation" for employees' religious beliefs and practices. Employers do not have to go to great lengths or incur significant expense in order to make reasonable accommodation, however. For example, in TWA v. Hardison, 432 U.S. 63 (1977), Hardison worked in a department of TWA that had to operate 7 days a week, 24 hours a day. He became an adherent of a religious denomination that observed a Saturday sabbath, and tried to get Saturdays off. The collective bargaining agreement between TWA and the labor union included a seniority system that controlled many aspects of employment, including priorities in getting particular days off. Hardison did not have enough seniority to get Saturdays off most of the time. TWA tried unsuccessfully to find other employees who would voluntarily switch days with him so that he would not have to work Saturdays. Hardison requested that TWA use supervisors to fill in for him, hire additional personnel, or require other employees to switch with him regardless of seniority. TWA declined, Hardison refused to work on Saturday, and the employer fired him. When Hardison claimed a Title VII violation, the Supreme Court ruled that TWA had acted properly. The company fulfilled its obligation to make reasonable accommodation by reducing weekend shifts to minimum crews and trying to find volunteers to trade shifts.

Procedures and Remedies

Title VII establishes special procedures for enforcing its dictates. An individual who believes himself or herself to be the victim of unlawful discrimination cannot simply take an employer to court. Rather, the Civil Rights Act created the Equal Employment

Opportunity Commission (EEOC) to receive complaints of violations. The EEOC investigates these complaints and, when they are adequately supported by facts, the Commission attempts conciliation measures between the employer and employees. If conciliation efforts fail, the EEOC may file suit in federal district court. Individuals may sue to enforce Title VII only after EEOC and the particular state equal employment opportunity agency has had the opportunity to take action.

Once a court finds that Title VII has been violated, the court is empowered to grant an injunction prohibiting future violations and correcting past actions.

Retroactive back pay or seniority may be ordered for employees who have suffered from unlawful discrimination. In addition, a court may compel an offending company to implement an "affirmative action" program to recruit and retain minority employees.

What Constitutes Discrimination Under Title VII?

Illegal discrimination can be proved in either of two ways. First, the plaintiff may show that the defendant had engaged in intentional discrimination—sometimes referred to as "disparate treatment." Second, the plaintiff may show that some employment practice or policy of the defendant has had a discriminatory effect, or impact—sometimes referred to as "disparate impact." The following discussion explains the use of these terms.

Intentional Discrimination—"Disparate Treatment"

In general, any employment decision or practice which treats individuals unequally because of race, color, religion, sex, or national origin violates Title VII. Illegal discrimination might occur, for example, in connection with firing, refusing to hire, refusing to train or promote, granting unequal compensation or fringe benefits, or practicing any type of segregation or classification of employees or applicants that tends to deprive them of employment opportunities.

A violation of Title VII may be proved by showing that an employer intended to discriminate for a prohibited reason. Intentional discrimination is often referred to as "disparate treatment." When there is a claim that the employer violated Title VII by committing disparate treatment, the employer's unlawful motivation can be proved in several ways.

Explicit exclusionary policy. If a company has a policy of excluding those of a particular gender, race, national origin, or religion, there is no question about whether there was intentional discrimination. This is clearly illegal unless it is one of the really unusual cases in which the employer can prove the so–called BFOQ defense (i.e., that being of a particular gender or national origin is a bona fide occupational qualification—a genuine necessity for doing the job). As discussed later, however, race cannot be a BFOQ. Also, a special provision in Title VII allows religious organizations to restrict hiring to those having particular religious beliefs.

Direct evidence of intentional discrimination. Even if there is not an explicit exclusionary policy, sometimes the evidence makes it obvious that an adverse employment action was intentionally based on a person's gender, race, national origin, or religion, so that there is no need for a court to carefully sift though many bits of circumstantial evidence. Suppose that Guy is hired to drive a delivery truck by Julie's Fashion Furniture, Inc. On one occasion, Julie is driving to lunch and observes one of her company's delivery trucks rolling through a stop sign without stopping. She saw the license number on the truck but not the identity of the driver. When she returns to work after lunch, she asks an assistant to ascertain who was driving the truck with that license number. Upon hearing that it was Guy, Julie says, "Oh, that doesn't surprise me. Stupid men drivers. They're too aggressive, and they let their testosterone drive for them. Or, when they're not being aggressive, they don't pay attention. He was probably reading his Penthouse while driving. Get the paperwork ready so that I can fire that Neanderthal!" Although these words would not have been illegal by themselves, when she follows up on them by firing Guy, evidence of her words clearly shows that she was motivated in large measure by Guy's gender. Many courts would call this direct evidence of a gender–based motivation. The fact that he was male does not have to be Julie's only reason for firing him, but just a substantial contributing factor to the employment decision.

Circumstantial evidence. In most cases in which there is an allegation of disparate treatment, the evidence is not clear–cut. In such cases, the plaintiff asks the court to draw an inference that there was an underlying discriminatory motivation from an aggregation of circumstantial evidence. The ultimate questions are the same as in other types of cases: First, has the plaintiff presented enough evidence to create a genuine fact issue regarding the employer's discriminatory motivation? An affirmative answer prevents the plaintiff from losing at the summary judgment or directed verdict stage. If so, the next question is whether the plaintiff has proved disparate treatment by a preponderance of the evidence—in other words, does this evidence show that it is more likely than not that the employer's adverse employment decision was based on the plaintiffs race, gender, national origin, or religion. Unlike cases in other areas of law, however, courts in these kinds of Title VII cases have used a three–stage process for analyzing circumstantial evidence. It accomplishes the same results that are accomplished in non–Title VII cases involving circumstantial evidence, but simply goes about it in a somewhat different way.

Prima Facie Case. A court in a Title VII disparate treatment case first seeks to determine whether the plaintiff has established a so–called prima facie case. If not, the plaintiff has not even created a genuine issue of fact on the question. If the plaintiff does so, however, he or she does not lose at a preliminary stage and the case goes forward. In general, a prima facie case is established when the EEOC or an individual plaintiff proves facts that permit (but do not compel) an inference that intentional discrimination on the basis of race, national origin, gender, or religion was the employer's motivation. More specifically, however, the courts have identified particular facts that must be proved in situations to establish a prima facie case.

Suppose, for example, that an individual job applicant is rejected and has reason to believe that the employer's refusal to hire was motivated by unlawful discrimination. In a hiring situation such as this, a prima facie violation of Title VII can be established by showing that (1) the applicant is within a protected class (racial or ethnic minority or female); (2) the applicant applied for a job for which the employer was seeking applicants; (3) the applicant was qualified to perform the job; (4) the applicant was not hired for the job; and (5) the employer either filled the position with a nonminority person or continued trying to fill it. If the claim of discrimination is based on a discharge rather than a refusal to hire, a prima facie case can be established by showing that (1) the plaintiff is within a protected class; (2) the plaintiff was performing the job satisfactorily; (3) the plaintiff was discharged; and (4) the plaintiff's work was then assigned to someone who was not within a protected class. In other employment decisions, the requirements of a prima facie case would similarly have to be modified to fit the circumstances. (It should be noted that when courts speak of "protected class," they are referring to the usual situation in which a female or nonwhite person is the plaintiff; it is possible, however, for a male or white to be the plaintiff.)

Employer's Rebuttal. When the plaintiff in such a case introduces evidence sufficient to create a prima facie case, the burden then shifts to the employer to bring forth evidence of a legitimate, nondiscriminatory reason for plaintiff's rejection. To overcome plaintiff's prima facie case, the employer can introduce evidence relating to matters such as the applicant's past experience and work record, letters of recommendation, or the superior qualifications of the person actually hired. An example is found in Peters v. Jefferson Chemical Co., 516 F.2d 447 (5th Cir. 1975), in which the employer successfully rebuted the female plaintiff's prima facie case by showing that she had not been hired as a laboratory chemist because she had not done laboratory work for several years. The court did not require the employer to prove that her skills were actually inadequate, but accepted the employer's assumption that laboratory skills diminish from nonuse over a substantial period of time. In another case, Boyd v. Madison County Mutual Insurance Co., 653 F.2d 1173 (7th Cir. 1981), a male employee established a prima facie case of sex discrimination against the employer by showing that the employer had a policy of awarding attendance bonuses only to clerical employees, all of whom were women. The employer was able to rebut the prima facie case successfully by demonstrating that there had been a serious absenteeism problem with clerical staff and that the bonus policy was aimed at correcting that problem.

In a case based on an allegedly discriminatory discharge, the employer might overcome the plaintiff's prima facie case by showing evidence of the plaintiff's poor performance, absenteeism, insubordination, and so on.

The types of reasons that are sufficient to rebut a plaintiff's prima facie case may vary from one kind of job to another. For instance, some jobs require skills that are quite subjective and extremely difficult to measure. Many executive and professional jobs are of such a nature, requiring traits such as creativity, initiative, ability to delegate and supervise, communicative skills, and a facility for persuasion. With regard to jobs that are inherently subjective, an employer usually will be permitted to use subjective justifications for the action taken. Thus, an attorney could be rejected because of "poor reputation," so long as the employer actually had some evidence of this fact. On the other hand, a court ordinarily will not accept an employer's purely subjective evaluation of an individual when the job in question requires little skill or responsibility or when it requires skills that can be objectively measured.

Pretext. If the plaintiff establishes a prima facie Title VII violation and the employer fails to come forth with acceptable evidence of a legitimate, nondiscriminatory reason, the plaintiff wins. If the employer does produce such evidence, the plaintiff will lose unless he or she can then convince the court that the employer's asserted reason was really just a "pretext"—that is, a cover-up for intentional discrimination. Plaintiff might be able to show, for example, that the employer's "legitimate reason" was applied discriminatorily. In Corley v. Jackson Police Dept., 566 F.2d 994 (5th Cir. 1978), the employer proved that the plaintiffs, black police officers, had been fired for accepting bribes. Although this clearly was a legitimate reason for firing them, the plaintiffs proved that white officers who also had been accused of the same conduct by an informant were not investigated as thoroughly and were not fired. The court held that the employer's reason was a pretext for racial discrimination and that Title VII had been violated.

Harassment as a Special Case of Disparate Treatment

Harassment of an employee because of his or her race, sex, religion, or national origin is a particular form of disparate treatment discrimination under Title VII. The following case explains how courts analyze these harassment claims. This case involves racial harassment, and later in the chapter we will separately discuss sexual harassment. The same basic principles apply to sexual harassment, but there can be some differences from other types of harassment when sexual demands or requests are made. Because of the special nature of harassment cases, the courts often do not follow the prima facie-rebuttal-pretext decision model.

DANIELS V. ESSEX GROUP, INC.
U. S. Court of Appeals, Seventh Circuit, 937 F.2d 1264 (1991)

In 1978, Robert Daniels, a black man, began working at the Essex Group. In April 1988, he resigned. He subsequently brought suit against his former employer under Title VI of the Civil Rights Act of 1964. Daniels' complaint enumerated multiple instances of racial *harassment at Essex that created a hostile work environment. The district judge ruled in favor of Daniels, and Essex appealed.*

Even before the first of the three most serious incidents occurred, Daniels' work environment was not discrimination-free. In his ten years at Essex, Daniels' colleagues told "ni***er jokes," nicknamed the plaintiff "Buckwheat" and teased him because he conversed with white women at work. Daniels complained to his coworkers, to his supervisor, and to the Personnel Director at Essex, none of whom did anything to nip the discriminatory treatment in the bud. Daniels endured the frequent harassment, earning high marks for his on—the—job performance.

The harassment escalated and intensified beginning in the fall of 1987 when events began to occur that were of a more menacing character than the ribbing Daniels endured. One morning Daniels clocked in at his usual arrival time of 7:00 a.m. and made the following discovery en route from the time clock to his work station. Hanging from a doorway was a human—sized dummy with a black head. The dummy wore white overalls and had what appeared to be simulated blood dripping on it. Daniels reported the existence of the dummy to his immediate supervisor, Mike Rohrer. Rohrer claimed to know nothing of the dummy and reassured Daniels: "Well, Bob, don't get excited. I will take care of it. Don't worry about it." Twelve hours later the dummy had not been removed.

The second of the three most grave incidents involved graffiti written on the bathroom walls of Daniels' department. Daniels found the initials "KKK" and the slogan "All ni**ers must die" scrawled onto the bathroom walls. From Daniels' testimony and from the supervisor's admission that he could not recall all of the slogans written on the bathroom walls over the years, the court concluded that someone wrote racial slurs onto the bathroom walls on several occasions. Describing the effect that the graffiti had upon him, Daniels said, "it put a little fear into me." As with the dummy, Daniels reported these slogans to his supervisor, who again said to the plaintiff: "Oh, Bob, don't get excited. I will take care of it." The slogans were painted over, but

according to the plaintiff, they reappeared three or four times. The district court found that no reasonable effort was made "to discourage further incidents despite the repetitive nature of their occurrences."

While the graffiti on the bathroom wall did not specifically mention Daniels by name, the writing on the scale—house wall did. (The scale house is a small shed—type building located outdoors where tools and other such items are kept.) On occasion, Daniels went to the scale house as part of his job. It appeared sometime before the dummy. The exact words were "hi Bob KKK." As with the other racial incidents, Daniels reported the graffiti to Rohrer, who again told Daniels not to get excited.

Daniels reported two other events during the same time frame. First, a co—worker by the name of Art Reimer ("Art") approached Daniels and called him a "ni**er" and threatened to "whip" Daniels, "take [him] out on [route] 30" and "beat" him. Art also threatened to injure the plaintiffs four—year—old son. This incident was reported to Essex supervisors, who brought Art and Daniels together in an attempt to resolve their differences. Daniels testified in court that Art continued to call him racist names such as "dumb ni**er" after the meeting occurred.

Second, at about 2:30 one morning, Daniels heard a loud noise on the porch of his home. When he investigated the noise later in the day, he found that someone had shot a bullet into the wall near his bedroom window. Although Daniels had no proof that an Essex employee had fired the shot into his house, he claimed that the incident precipitated his resignation a few weeks later. On appeal, counsel for defendant argued that because Daniels had failed to prove that an Essex employee had actually fired the shot, the district court improperly considered the evidence as probative of racial harassment. However, the district court discussed the incident, not as part *of its legal analysis of racial harassment at work, but in its summary of Daniels' testimony. As we will show below, the incident has bearing in its effect on plaintiffs own fear and feeling of persecution.*

All of the incidents took their toll on Daniels. He testified that the events described above made him nervous and that "I just couldn't work there and look around my shoulder all the time and what not. I didn't want to be out there no more. It was a threat to me. It was a threat to my family. I didn't want to go through that stress and strain." Daniels met with Vickie Churchward, who worked in the Personnel Department at Essex, two to three weeks before he quit. She suggested only a transfer to another department. When he submitted his formal resignation, Daniels wrote that he couldn't take it anymore: "I just got tired of the harassment and the writings on the walls and threats to me and it just kept me nervous all the time." At no time before his departure did a meeting of the Essex workforce take place to condemn the racial harassment. Nor did the management of Essex ever issue a warning announcing the employer's abhorrence of racial harassment. All the company did was issue a generic message about racial discrimination a few weeks before Daniel resigned.

Cummings, Circuit Judge:

Title VII covers claims of discrimination due to the existence of a hostile environment. [To prove that harassing language or conduct based on race, sex, national origin, or religion violates Title VII, the plaintiff must prove that it was sufficiently "severe and pervasive" to create a hostile working environment. A court will find that the harassment is severe and pervasive if the plaintiff actually perceived it as being severe and pervasive (a subjective standard) and if a reasonable person in the plaintiff's position would have viewed it as severe and pervasive (an objective standard). When

trying to decide whether a reasonable person of Daniels' race would have so viewed the harassment, the court considers several factors: seriousness of the incident or incidents, frequency of the incidents, duration of the incidents, and other factors such as the overall ambience in the workplace. Thus, the harassment may be severe and pervasive even though no single incident is terrible if relatively minor incidents occur with regularity over a significant period of time. Likewise, it is possible for one or two events to be sufficient if they are bad enough. In addition, evidence of an overall environment of hostility toward those of the plaintiff's race (or gender, religion, or national origin if those are the motivating reasons for the harassment) may tip the scales toward a finding of hostile environment in a close case. If the court concludes that the harassment was severe and pervasive, the employer is liable if a manager or supervisor was the one committing the harassment. If, as in this case, the harassment is committed by one or more co—workers who are not managers or supervisors, the employer is liable if the evidence shows that someone in management knew or reasonably should have known about it and failed to take prompt steps to stop it and prevent it from recurring.]

The effects of the changed work environment upon Daniels are undeniable. As the only black employee in his department, he took each individual act of racial harassment personally. [The dummy, the two incidents of graffiti, the racial slurs and threats by Art Reimer, and the gunshot fired into his home can all be reasonably construed as racially—motivated acts of harassment aimed at Daniels.] By the time that Daniels quit, the racial harassment profoundly affected him both physically and psychologically. He changed from being the diligent, good worker that he had been into an argumentative employee with whom it was hard to get along. Moreover, his absenteeism increased in the months after the dummy incident. He also lost 30 to 40 pounds.

Having determined that Daniels [subjectively perceived the racial harassment to be severe and pervasive], we turn to an inspection of the evidence in light of the objective standard. The work environment and the injuries suffered by Daniels are to be measured against a reasonableness standard. The number of instances of harassment is but one factor to be considered in the examination of the totality of the circumstances. A Title VII plaintiff does not prove racial harassment or the existence of a hostile working environment by alleging some "magic" threshold number of incidents. Conversely, an employer may not rebut a claim simply by saying that the number of incidents alleged is too few. Because a court must make a particularized inquiry into an employment environment that gives rise to racial harassment, it will consider a range of factors to determine whether the objective standard has been met, [including the seriousness of particular incidents and their duration].

We agree with the district court that the racial incidents described by Daniels were immediately threatening to him and that "they would have adversely affected the work performance and well–being of a reasonable person." Unlike other cases where a relatively small number of [minor] racial incidents have been found to be inadequate to give rise to Title VII liability, here each of the incidents was directed personally at Daniels over the course of a few months. The district court described in vivid terms the effect that the mention of the Ku Klux Klan would have on blacks: "The most violent threats to black society are well known to come from that organization. Furthermore, there is no more chilling image than that of a black man being hung by the KKK. Any reasonable person who is targeted by such a terrorist organization over a period of time without any protection from his employer would surely suffer similar adverse

effects as those experienced by Daniels." Plainly, any black person would find this graffiti threatening.

In addition to the instances of racial harassment directed at Daniels by his coworkers, a reasonable employee would have found the general workplace environment oppressive also. Daniels himself was the victim of racial taunts such as the nickname "Buckwheat" for the first ten years that he was employed at Essex. He asked his co–workers to back off, but, for the most part, he chose to turn the other cheek and endure the prejudice. These conditions place the hostile environment that emerged in the fall of 1987 into perspective. The appearance of the dummy did not represent an unexplainable aberration in a heretofore harmonious environment free of the taint of racial discrimination. Rather, the change in environment marked the outbreak of a more injurious strain of the virus of racism that had already infected the workplace. A black man who applied for a job at Essex was told by a supervisor that the workplace was "extremely prejudiced." Another employee suffered slurs because he "looked Mexican." Both of these examples help to fulfill the objective standard of a hostile work environment that provided fertile ground for an outgrowth of racial harassment. They serve to demonstrate that Daniels did not weave his allegations out of whole cloth, and bolster the confidence of the finder of fact in the plaintiffs veracity and in the objective reasonableness of his claims.

Having established that Daniels' injury was subjectively hurtful and objectively reasonable, we now consider the final predicate to liability for racial harassment in a hostile work environment. This Court has repeatedly recognized that an employer will be liable for discrimination by an employee "if the employer knew or should have known about an employee's acts of harassment and fails to take appropriate remedial action." The district court expressly found that two management level employees, Daniels' supervisor Mike Rohrer and Vickie Churchward of the Personnel Department, heard plaintiffs complaints as to the specific instances of racial harassment. Each time Daniels approached his supervisor, Rohrer shrugged off his employee, admonishing him not to worry about the dummy or the graffiti. As for Churchward, Daniels notified her of the graffiti and complained of the racial harassment generally when he first notified her of his intent to resign. Although management had knowledge of the harassment directed at Daniels, it was less than diligent in taking remedial action. The dummy remained hanging in the doorway for at least eighteen hours after Daniels first spotted it and complained to Rohrer; the restroom graffiti reappeared two to three times after plaintiff first noticed it; and the scale–house wall still contained the racial slur against him as of the time that he left. In addition to dragging its feet on responding to the discrete acts, the defendant made virtually no effort to investigate the incidents, nor did Essex independently warn employees verbally or in writing that racial harassment would not be tolerated in the workplace.

The law of racial harassment in a hostile work environment required us to conduct the foregoing three–pronged review: [After determining that the harassment was indeed racially motivated, then, (1) Did Daniels personally perceive the racially motivated harassment as being sufficiently severe and pervasive to create a racially hostile environment? (2) If so, would a reasonable person in Daniels' position have also viewed the harassment as being sufficiently severe and pervasive to create a racially hostile environment? (3) If so, did the employer take prompt remedial action? The answer to the first and second questions is yes, and the answer to the third question is no.]

The district court's judgment in favor of the plaintiff Daniels is affirmed in all respects.

Daniels is awarded back pay of $ 38,548.84, prejudgment interest of $ 3,782.76, and front pay and attorneys' fees in the amount of $35,455.20.

Comment

Three comments about the *Daniels* case are in order. First, the award of damages to Daniels probably would be substantially larger today. After the facts of this case arose, Congress amended Title VII in several ways with respect to disparate treatment (intentional discrimination) cases. Before this amendment, a successful plaintiff could receive back pay, interest on that amount, and attorney fees. If appropriate, a court could also order hiring, reinstatement, or promotion. An order of reinstatement certainly would not have worked in this case. When such an order was not feasible, the court could award "front pay"—an amount to account for lost wages between the time that the employee was terminated or had to quit because of the unlawful working conditions and the time at which the plaintiff probably should have found comparable employment if he acted with reasonable diligence. When Congress amended Title VII's remedy provisions for intentional discrimination cases in the 1990s, it provided that a successful plaintiff could still receive back pay, interest, and attorney fees, but on top of that could also receive actual and punitive damages computed in the way that such damages are calculated in intentional tort cases. The court has substantial discretion in determining the amount of such a damage award, but it can take into account a variety of harms such as mental anguish, physical harm, and various types of economic harm. Punitive damages added to that can be very substantial. In cases of intentional discrimination based on sex, national origin, or religion, the combined total of actual and punitive damages is capped at $300,000, but there is no upper limit placed on such damages in cases of intentional discrimination based on race. Thus, Essex probably would have had to pay a lot more if the case were decided today.

Second, the evidence showed that Daniels had actually suffered psychological harm, including severe depression requiring medication, and that this psychological harm even caused physical harm. Later, in another case, the U.S. Supreme court ruled that the victim of harassment can prove that it was sufficiently severe and pervasive to create hostile working environment without having to prove that there was actual psychological or physical harm. Evidence of such harm obviously bolsters the plaintiff's case very substantially, and will usually produce a larger damage award, but it is not required.

Third, also in another later case, the Supreme Court ruled that the determination of whether a reasonable person would perceive the harassing language and conduct as severe and pervasive should be viewed from the perspective of a reasonable person in the plaintiff's position. In other words, from the perspective of a reasonable person of Mr. Daniels' race. Or, in a sexual harassment case in which the plaintiff is a woman, from the perspective of a reasonable woman.

Sexual Harassment

Harassment or intimidation of an employee violates Title VII when it is based on that person's sex just as it does when based on race, color, religion, or national origin. Sexual harassment may take the same form that other illegal harassment normally takes, namely, slurs, taunts, epithets, or other abuses that create a hostile, intimidating, or offensive working environment. In some situations, however, sexual harassment may be quite different from harassment for racial or other reasons. Sexual harassment may take the form of unwelcome requests for sexual favors. Sexual harassment is a form of intentional sex discrimination because the harasser would not treat the victim this way if the victim were of the other gender.

The courts and the EEOC have recognized two general kinds of situations in which such unwelcome requests constitute illegal sexual harassment. These two varieties, which may sometimes overlap, are referred to as "quid pro quo" and "hostile environment" sexual harassment.

Quid Pro Quo Harassment. The term quid pro quo means "something for something," and refers to the situation in which continued employment, a favorable review, promotion, or some other tangible job benefit is explicitly or implicitly conditioned upon an employee's positive response to a requested sexual favor. Although there is no rule that only supervisors can commit quid pro quo harassment, as a practical matter it is only one with supervisory or managerial authority who has control over job benefits and who is thus capable of committing this form of sexual harassment. The evidence must convince a court that the sexual advances were unwelcome. When the unwelcome request or demand for sexual activities causes the target to believe that a negative response will lead to adverse job–related consequences, and when the evidence shows that a reasonable person would also believe this, there is quid pro quo harassment.

Hostile Environment Sexual Harassment. So called "hostile environment" sexual harassment occurs when a supervisor, manager, or co–worker engages in sexually oriented language or conduct that is unwelcome and that is sufficiently "severe and pervasive" to alter the terms and conditions of employment for an employee who has been targeted. Repeated sexual advances can constitute hostile environment sexual harassment, as can language and conduct that manifest gender–based hostility. Sometimes, hostile environment cases involve a mixture of unwelcome sexual advances and gender-based hostility.

The question whether the harassment is severe and pervasive is analyzed in the same way in sexual harassment cases as in the *Daniels* case involving racially motivated harassment. The same approach is also used in cases of harassment based on religion or national origin. Thus, the court first determines whether the unwelcome language and conduct is aimed at the victim because of her gender. Then, the court ascertains whether the language and conduct was sufficiently severe and pervasive to alter the work environment, both subjectively from the victim's perspective and objectively from the perspective of a reasonable person in the victim's position. In other words, when the victim is female, the objective determination is made from the perspective of a reasonable woman. The decision whether the harassment was severe and pervasive takes account of several factors, including the severity of particular instances, the frequency and duration of occurrences, and the overall workplace ambience.

Most victims of sexual harassment are females, but occasionally females victimize males. The Supreme Court also has ruled that same–sex sexual harassment is actionable under Title VII, as long as the evidence shows that the victim was harassed because of his or her gender. The courts have held, however, that if the evidence shows that the harassment based solely on the employee's homosexuality, it is not a Title VII violation because Title VII does not prohibit discrimination based on homosexuality. Obviously, it may sometimes be difficult to distinguish between sexual harassment by one person against another of the same gender from harassment based on hostility toward homosexuals.

Several cases have involved so–called "equal opportunity harassers," in which a manager has sexually harassed males in particular ways because they were males and females in somewhat different ways because they were females. The federal courts have been split in their decisions in such cases. A majority of them have held that there is not violation of Title VII in such situations because both males and females are being harassed. Some courts have found a Title VII violation, however, because the victims were targeted in different ways because of their particular gender. Although the latter is a minority view among the courts, it seems to us to be the more logical one.

Employer Liability for Sexual Harassment

For most alleged violations of Title VII, the only question is whether the evidence shows that there was such a violation. If there is a violation, the employer is liable. In the case of harassment, however, the rules for employer liability are somewhat different. The main reason for the difference is that illegal harassment can be committed by co–workers and not just by managers. We saw an example of this in the *Daniels* case involving racial harassment, where the harassers were coworkers, and the employer was liable because managers knew about the harassment and failed to take prompt remedial action. The question of employer liability is especially important in Title VII cases because only the employer can be held monetarily liable; an individual cannot be liable for damages in his personal capacity as he can in tort law. A court can issue an injunction against both the employer and particular individuals in a Title VII case, however. In harassment cases involving particularly egregious conduct the victim frequently asserts tort law claims such as intentional infliction of emotional distress, assault and battery, or false imprisonment against the individual wrongdoers, who can indeed be personally subjected to tort liability.

Until recently, the rules for deciding when employers were liable for sexual harassment were rather different in quid–pro–quo cases and hostile environment cases. Because of several recent Supreme Court decisions, however, employer liability is now based on other factors. Thus, the distinction between the two forms of sexual harassment is still helpful in deciding whether illegal harassment has actually occurred, but the rules for determining when the employer is liable do not depend on which form the harassment took.

As with other types of harassment, the employer can be held liable if the harassment is committed by a manager or supervisor. If committed by a coworker the employer can be liable only if a manager knows or should know about the harassment and fails to take prompt action to stop the harassment and prevent it from recurring. In sexual harassment cases, however, the Supreme Court has created a special defense for employers even when the requisite degree of managerial involvement exists. As seen below, the defense strongly encourages employers to have anti–harassment policies in the workplace. For this defense to be applicable, the following must be proved:

1. The employee did not suffer a tangible job detriment, such as discharge, demotion, undesirable reassignment, and so forth. If there was such a detriment to the employee, the defense does not exist.

2. The employer had a stated company policy condemning sexual harassment that provided a clear procedure for employees to make complaints. The policy must have been well publicized in the workplace, such as being prominently displayed in signs or being prominently included in a handbook for employees. The complaint procedure must provide a means for the employee to go over the head of a supervisor when the supervisor is the alleged harasser.

3. If the employee did not suffer a tangible job detriment, and the employer had a clear and well publicized policy against sexual harassment with adequate complaint procedures, the employer is not liable for the Title VII violation if the employee failed to use these complaint procedures. The courts have held, however, that an employee does not have to immediately report the harassment. In other words, the employee will be deemed to have used the available complaint procedures, thus removing the employer's defense, even when the employee waits a substantial period of time before complaining.

With regard to the first element of the employer defense, there is still some uncertainty among the lower federal courts about the question of what constitutes a tangible job detriment. There are, of course, many situations in which the fact of a tangible job detriment is obvious, such as those in which the employee's resistance to sexual harassment leads to being fired, demoted, or denied benefits. There also are situations in which the courts will have no difficulty in concluding that the employee did not suffer a tangible job detriment. For example, suppose that a supervisor commits quid pro quo harassment by making unwelcome sexual overtures to an employee and indicating that there will be negative consequences if the employee resists. But then nothing else happens—the supervisor does not carry out his threats and doesn't continue the behavior. In such a case, the employer is not liable if an adequate policy and complaint procedures were in place, and the employee failed to use them.

One question that several courts have had to face is whether an employee suffers a tangible job detriment when she submits to sexual demands because of a fear of losing her job. As long as it is clear that the sexual demands were unwelcome and the submission was coerced, courts have thus far treated the submission as a tangible job detriment, thus depriving the employer of any defense to the Title VII violation.

During the first few years after the Supreme Court created this new defense for employers, lower federal courts reached conflicting conclusions about whether a "constructive discharge" constituted a tangible job detriment. In employment law generally, a constructive discharge occurs when an employee voluntarily quits because working conditions are so bad that a reasonable person would find them to be intolerable. In other areas of employment law, the courts will treat the employee as having been actually fired when working conditions have become intolerable. Constructive discharge is not illegal by itself in U.S. law, but in any situation in which the cause for constructive harassment is illegal, the law treats the employee as having been actually fired for that illegal reason.

Lower federal courts were inconsistent in their application of traditional rules regarding constructive discharge in the sexual harassment context. Suppose, for instance, that an employee has been subjected to hostile environment sexual harassment. Because the courts will not find hostile environment harassment to have occurred unless the harassment has caused working conditions for the affected employee to be very bad, the same evidence that proves hostile environment harassment should usually be sufficient to prove that there was a constructive discharge when the employee quit her job because of the hostile environment. The most logical conclusion is that the employee has suffered a tangible job detriment when she suffered a constructive discharge. A few federal courts concluded, concluded, however, that there is no tangible job detriment when the employee quits because the sexually hostile environment has made working conditions intolerable to one of average sensibilities. In 2004, the U.S. Supreme Court sided with those lower courts concluding that constructive discharge, by itself, is not a tangible job detriment. The Court held that, if an employer has a well–designed anti–harassment policy with good complaint procedures and the harassed employee proves only that she quit because the sexually hostile environment created working conditions that would be intolerable to a reasonable victim. The employee must additionally prove that the employer did something concrete such as demoting her, decreasing her compensation or benefits, or giving her an undesirable reassignment. To the authors of this text, this decision seems to be quite illogical.

The following two cases illustrate some interesting concepts in the law of sexual harassment. The first one, Ross v. Double Diamond, discusses hostile environment harassment, as well as the rule that there is a separate violation of Title VII when an employee is fired because of having objected to illegal discriminatory practices such as sexual harassment. The second case, Ellison v. Brady, involves a situation in which a coworker committed hostile environment harassment by conduct and several bizarre letters over a substantial period of time, and managers learned of the harassment. Although both cases were decided before the Supreme Court created a defense for employers, such a defense would not have been available to the employer in either case. In Ross, there obviously was a tangible job detriment, and the employer did not have a policy against sexual harassment. In *Ellison*, a court today might not find that the plaintiff suffered a tangible job detriment, because she was not fired, demoted or penalized in any other way. She also did not submit to coercive sexual advances, and did not quit (so there could be no constructive discharge). The employer did have a strong policy against sexual harassment, with complaint procedures, but the employee used those complaint procedures and the employer did not promptly and appropriately remedy the situation, so it could not use the defense if the case were decided today.

Ross v. Double Diamond, Inc.
U.S. District Court, Northern District Of Texas, 672 F. Supp. 261 (1987)

Plaintiffs Beverly Ross and Sheila Stoudenmire were sisters. Ross was 20 years old and Stoudenmire was 23 when the events in this case occurred. Double Diamond was in the business of developing lakeside communities and selling property within such communities. Larry Womack was the manager of Double Diamond's facility at Canyon Creek in the Dallas–Fort Worth area of Texas. In response to an advertisement by Double Diamond, on August 5 Stoudenmire interviewed with and was hired by Womack to be a salesperson at Canyon Creek. She was told to report for her first day of training on Monday, August 8.

During the interview, Womack told Stoudenmire that he also was looking for a part–time receptionist/secretary. Stoudenmire recommended her sister, Ross, for the job. Womack interviewed and hired Ross on August 6, and Ross began work at 9:00 a.m. on August 7. During the first hour that she was on the job, Womack asked Ross if she "fooled around," to which she answered no. A short time later, Womack asked Ross to bring him a cup of coffee. After Ross entered his office with the coffee, Womack told her that he wanted to take her picture. Ross stated that she did not want to have her picture taken.

Womack ignored Ross's response and told Ross stand against the wall so that he could take her picture. Ross agreed to do this because she was scared about what Womack's reaction would be if she refused his request. After Ross was against the wall, Womack then told Ross to pull up her dress. Continuing to be scared of Womack's possible reaction if she did not comply, Ross lifted her dress up two inches to her knees. Womack then took the picture, and Ross left the office. A short time later, Ross went back into Womack's office and asked for the picture. Womack refused to give the picture to her. Later that same day, Womack called Ross on the telephone and asked her to pant heavily for him. Ross immediately hung up the phone.

During that evening, as was customary on most Sundays, Womack and several salesmen had a meeting in Womack's office. Ross entered Womack's office during the meeting to give a message to one of the salesmen. After she entered the office, a salesman, Larry West, placed a Polaroid camera on the floor directly under Ross and took a picture up Ross' dress. The salesmen laughed at the event. Ross, finding no humor in the photograph, attempted to take the camera. Womack prevented Ross from getting the camera and took the picture out of the camera. At this point, the telephone rang and Ross left the room to answer it. A short time later, Ross approached Womack and asked for the picture. Womack declined to give Ross the picture and, instead, chose to lie by stating that the picture did not turn out. Womack further stated that he had thrown the picture out, and that Ross could not look for the picture in the waste paper basket. Later on, Womack called Ross on the phone and again asked her to pant heavily on the phone. Ross immediately hung up.

Ross finally left work at 9:30 p.m. When she arrived home, Ross called her sister, Stoudenmire, and told her about the barrage of hostile treatment to which she was subjected on her first day at work. Her sister encouraged her to continue at the job and told her that things would improve in the future. After this conversation Ross decided to go to work the following day.

Ross reported to work at 8:30 a.m. on Monday, August 8. Shortly thereafter, Womack called Ross into his office to bring him some coffee. As she entered the office, Womack told her to come over to him by the desk. She did so, and Womack physically pulled her onto his lap. A salesman, Robert Chapman, entered the office and saw Ross on Womack's lap. Chapman testified that Womack had his arms around Ross' waist and that Ross was feverishly trying to pull away. Chapman later stated that he thought Womack had looked perverted. It was only after Chapman entered the office that Womack released his hold on Ross.

Monday, August 8, was Sheila Stoudenmire's first day of work at Double Diamond as a sales trainee. At approximately 3:00 p.m. Sheila heard some of the salesmen laughing while looking at a picture in Womack's office. She informed her sister, Ross, of this, and they both went to Womack's office to obtain the picture. When they entered the office, two of the salesmen were at the desk looking at something. One of the salesmen slipped a picture into Womack's desk drawer, and they left the office. Sheila took the picture out of the drawer. The picture was the one West took up Ross' dress on the previous evening. She showed the picture to Ross, whereupon Ross began to cry and went to the ladies' room. Later that day, Womack called Ross into his office. Womack told Ross to "bend over" and clean up some mustard on the office wall. Ross refused to do so and started to leave the office. Womack proceeded to close the door to prevent Ross from leaving the room and trapped Ross up against the door. Ross escaped from his grasp by crawling out from under his arms. At this point Ross said she would clean up the mustard. She did so and then left.

Also, in the afternoon of Monday, August 8, Womack entered the room in which Stoudenmire was studying to speak with her. In the course of the conversation, Womack said to Stoudenmire that he bet she liked to wear black boots and carry a whip in the bedroom.

On Tuesday, August 9, Stoudenmire went to work and studied sales presentations as she was supposed to under her training program. Ross did not work on this day because she was hired to work only on Fridays, Saturdays, Sundays and Mondays. After work on Tuesday, Stoudenmire, Ross, and Tina Karasek, a recently hired salesperson, went to the county Sheriffs office to complain about Womack's offensive actions. The Sheriff informed the women that there was nothing that he could do for them, but suggested that they complain to Womack's boss. The sheriff also told them that, if they weren't pleased with the response from Womack's boss, they might want to contact the district attorney or the EEOC.

During the morning of Wednesday, August 10, Stoudenmire and Karasek approached Womack's supervisor, Robert Gray, and asked to speak privately with him. Gray immediately suggested that they take a drive in his car. During the drive, Stoudenmire complained to Gray about Womack's deplorable conduct, the picture taking incident, and inadequate training procedures. Gray stated that he would immediately take care of the situations involving West and Womack. Upon return to the Double Diamond facility, Gray confronted Womack regarding the charges. Womack denied all of the allegations. Gray also confronted West. Gray told West to stop such activity and to apologize to Ross. West agreed to do both. After Gray spoke with Womack, Womack called Stoudenmire into his office and yelled at her

for discussing his conduct with his supervisor instead of first contacting him. Later, in a letter to the EEOC after Ross and Stoudenmire had filed a complaint with the agency, Gray claimed that during the car ride Stoudenmire had opened her blouse to reveal her breasts to him. Neither the EEOC nor the district judge believed him.

For the remainder of Wednesday, Womack required Stoudenmire to continue her studying as a sales trainee in a separate room, away from the male trainees. In addition, Stoudenmire could not take her training material home at the end of the day. She had been allowed to take the material home in the past.

On Thursday, August 11, Stoudenmire once again was required to study alone, away from the other trainees who were studying together. During the day on Thursday, West spoke with Stoudenmire. West stated that he was sorry about taking the picture of Ross. He also stated that Womack "put him up" to taking the picture. At the end of the day, Stoudenmire was not permitted to take her studying materials home.

On Friday, August 12, Stoudenmire arrived at work around 9:00 a.m. She noticed that a full—time secretary was sitting at the desk that Ross was to occupy on that day. Shortly after she arrived, Womack informed Stoudenmire that Ray Wylie, the vice president of sales for Double Diamond, wanted to speak with Stoudenmire on the telephone. Stoudenmire went into Womack's office to receive the call. Wylie informed Stoudenmire that she was "barking up the wrong tree" and that "we know how to handle girls like you." Wylie also stated that if Stoudenmire pursued this claim any further she would lose her home and her husband would lose his job. Wylie admitted that he spoke to Stoudenmire in a loud voice during this conversation. Stoudenmire left Womack's office in tears at the end of the conversation.

While Stoudenmire was in Womack's office, Ross entered the facility to report to work as she was supposed to do. Noticing that another secretary was at her desk, she requested to speak to Womack. At this point Stoudenmire exited Womack's office in tears. Stoudenmire and Ross called the Sheriff about the threats Wylie made to Stoudenmire and asked him to come over to the Double Diamond facility. The Sheriff arrived at the Double Diamond facility fifteen minutes later. He spoke with Womack about the incidents that had been occurring. Womack brushed them off, stating that everyone was just having fun. After speaking with Womack, the Sheriff went into a separate building and spoke with West, Ross, Stoudenmire, and Karasek.

After the meeting with West, Ross, Stoudenmire, and Karasek (??) went to Womack and requested to have the rest of the day off for personal reasons. Womack stated that if they left, their positions with the company would be terminated. The women chose to leave, and they were terminated. They went home and called the E.E.O.C. The following Monday, August 15, Ross, Stoudenmire, and Karasek went to the E.E.O.C. and filed charges. Ross and Stoudenmire were never paid for the work that they did at Canyon Creek. The evidence showed that other women who were later hired to work at the Canyon Creek facility were treated the same way. About six months later, Womack resigned as manager. His replacement, Oliver Mowatt, behaved similarly to Womack.

Mahon, District Judge:

This Court believes that there are four factors which a trial court should consider in determining whether [unwelcome sexually oriented language and conduct was sufficiently severe and pervasive to create a sexually hostile working environment.] First, a court should consider the nature of the unwelcome sexual acts or words. Generally, unwelcome physical touching is more offensive than unwelcome verbal abuse. However, this is only a generalization and in specific situations the type of language used may be more offensive than a type of physical touching. Second, a court should consider the frequency of the offensive encounters. It is less likely that a hostile work environment exists when, for instance, the offensive encounters occur once every year than if the encounters occur once every week. Third, the Court should consider the length of time during which all of the offensive meetings occur. Lastly, the court should consider the context in which the sexually harassing conduct occurred. The Court emphasizes that none of these factors should be given more weight than the others. In addition, the nonexistence of one of these factors does not, in and of itself, prevent a Title VII claim. The trier of fact must consider the "totality of the circumstances."

[The unwelcome sexually oriented language and conduct directed at Ross began in the first hour after she began working and continued unabated while she was there. The conduct actually worsened during the next several days, and escalated to physical confinement, physical touching, and taking pictures, including one picture from under her dress. There also were threats of dire consequences if the women complained. The nature of the harassing conduct was serious and highly offensive.]

Because of its importance in this case, the Court chooses to elaborate on the reasons why a short duration of sexual harassment does not obviate a Title VII claim. The courts are looking for a "pattern of sexual harassment inflicted upon an employee because of her sex" because this type of activity "is a pattern of behavior that inflicts disparate treatment upon a member of one sex with respect to terms, conditions, or privileges of employment." Sexual harassment need not exist over a long period of time for it to be considered a pattern. If the sexual harassment is frequent and/or intensely offensive, a pattern can be established over a short period of time. [In addition to the severity and frequency of the harassment, the evidence showed an overall ambience at Canyon Creek that treated women, all of whom were quite young, as sexual objects whose main purpose was to sexually gratify the male employees and managers.]

The Court finds that the acts and communications perpetrated against Ross at Double Diamond are sufficiently severe and pervasive to alter the conditions of Ross' employment and create an abusive work environment.

This court finds, however, that the type of language and conduct directed at Ross's sister, SheilaStoudenmire, was not sufficiently severe and pervasive to alter the conditions of employment or create an abusive work environment.

Womack suggested once that she wore black boots and carried a whip in the bedroom. She was segregated from the male employees who were also training to be sales persons on three separate days. She was not permitted to take her training books home with her at night after she complained about the treatment she and Ross received at Canyon Creek. Title VII is not a shield that protects people from all sexual conduct at the workplace. The type of conduct listed above does not rise to the level of harassment that is actionable under Title VII. [However, it is a separate violation of Title VII to fire or otherwise punish an employee for objecting to conduct that is illegal under Title VII. Even though this court concludes that Stoudenmire was not subjected to hostile environment sexual harassment herself, the main reason she was fired was that she had objected to the treatment of her sister. Prior to her termination, she made these objections to Womack, two managers higher than Womack, and to the county sheriff. With respect to Stoudenmire, Double Diamond is guilty of retaliatory discharge in violation of Title VII.]

[The court also concluded that the employer, Double Diamond, was liable because the harassment was committed by a supervisor, Womack. Strengthening this conclusion is the fact that two of Womack's superiors knew about his conduct. Also, Womack and his two superiors knew about the conduct of the non—supervisory employee, West. Double Diamond's management did not take effective action to stop the harassment and prevent its recurrence.

In addition to an award of damages and attorney fees to the plaintiffs, the court also issued an injunction that not only forbade sexually harassing conduct at Double Diamond, but also ordered Double Diamond to implement a comprehensive anti—discrimination program that included education of managers and employees, complaint procedures, and monitoring.]

ELLISON v. BRADY
U.S. Court of Appeals, Ninth Circuit 924 F. 2d 872 (1991)

Kerry Ellison worked as a revenue agent for the Internal Revenue Service in San Mateo, California. During her initial training in 1984 she met SterlingGray, another trainee, who was also assigned to the San Mateo office. The two co-workers never became friends, and they did not work closely together. Revenue agents in San Mateo office often went to lunch in groups. In June 1986 when no one else was in the office, Gray asked Ellison to lunch. She accepted. Ellison claimed that after the June lunch Gray started to pester her with unnecessary questions and hang around her desk. On October 9, 1986, Gray asked Ellison out for a drink after work. She declined, but she suggested that they have lunch the following week. She did not want to have lunch alone with him, and she tried to stay away from the office during lunch time. One day during the following week, Gray uncharacteristically dressed in a three-piece suit and asked Ellison out for lunch. Again, she did not accept.

On October 22, 1986, Gray handed Ellison a note he wrote her a on a telephone message slip, which read: "I cried over you last night and I'm totally drained today. I have never been in such constant term oil [sic]. Thank you for talking with me. I could not stand to feel your hatred for another day." When Ellison realized that Gray wrote the note, she became shocked and frightened and left the room. Gray followed her into the hallway and demanded that she talk to him, but she left the building. Ellison later showed the note to Bonnie Miller, who supervised both Ellison and Gray. Miller said that "this is sexual harassment." Ellison asked Miller not to do anything about it. She wanted to try to handle it herself. Ellison asked a male coworker to talk to Gray and to tell him that she was not interested in him and to leave her alone. The next day, Thursday, Gray called in sick.

Ellison did not work on Friday, and on the following Monday, she started four weeks of training in St. Louis. Gray mailed Ellison a card and a typed, single-spaced, three-page letter, which she described as a "twenty times, a hundred times weirder" than the prior note. Gray wrote, in part: "I know that you are worth knowing with or without sex ...Leaving aside the hassles and disasters of recent weeks. I have enjoyed you so much over these past few months. Watching you. Experiencing you from O so far away. Admiring your style and élan ... Don't you think it odd that two people who have never even talked together, alone, are striking off such intense sparks ...I will [write] another letter in the near future." Explaining her reaction, Ellison stated: "I just thought he was crazy. I thought he was nuts. I didn't know what he would do next. I was frightened."

She immediately telephoned Miller. Ellison told her supervisor that she was frightened. She requested that Miller transfer either her or Gray because she would not be comfortable working in the same office with him. Miller asked Ellison to send a copy of the card and letter to San Mateo. Miller then telephoned her supervisor, Joe Benton, and discussed the problem. That same day Miller had a counseling session with Gray. She informed him that he was entitled to union representation. During this meeting, she told Gray to leave Ellison alone. She reminded Gray many times over the next few weeks that he must not contact Ellison in any way. Gray subsequently transferred to the San Francisco office on November 24,1986. Ellison returned from St. Louis in late November and did not discuss the matter further with Miller. After three weeks in San Francisco, Gray filed union grievances requesting a return to the San Mateo office. The IRS and the union settled the grievances in Gray's favor, agreeing to allow him to transfer back to the San Mateo office provided that he spend four more months in San Francisco and promise not to bother Ellison.

On January 28, 1987, Ellison first learned of Gray's request in a letter from Miller explaining that Gray would return to the San Mateo office. The letter indicated that management decided to resolve Ellison's problem with a six-month separation, and that it would take additional action if the problem recurred.

After receiving the letter, Ellison was "frantic." She filed a formal complaint with the IRS. She also obtained permission to transfer to San Francisco temporarily when Gray returned. Gray wrote Ellison another letter, which still sought to maintain the idea that he and Ellison had some type of relationship. The IRS employee investigating the allegation agreed with Ellison's supervisor that Gray's conduct constituted sexual harassment. In its final decision, however, Treasury Department (of which the IRS is a unit) rejected Ellison's complaint because it believed that the complaint did not describe a pattern or practice of sexual harassment. The EEOC also ruled against Ellison because it concluded that the IRS took adequate action to prevent the repetition of Gray's conduct. Ellison filed a complaint in federal district court against Brady, Secretary of the Treasury, alleging a Title VII violation. The district court granted the defendant's motion for summary judgment on the ground that Elision had failed to state a case of sexual harassment caused by a hostile working environment; it characterized Gray's conduct as "isolated and genuinely trivial." Ellison appealed.

Beezer, Circuit Judge:

In Meritor Saving Bank v. Vinson, 477 U.S. 57 (1986), the Supreme Court held that sexual harassment constitutes sex discrimination in violation of Title VII. Courts have recognized different forms of sexual harassment. In "quid pro quo" cases, employers condition employment benefits on sexual favors. In "hostile environment" cases, employees work in offensive or abusive environments. This case, like Meritor, involves a hostile environment claim...

The Supreme Court in *Meritor* held that Michelle Vinson's working conditions constituted a hostile environment in violation of Title VII's prohibition of sex discrimination. Vinson's supervisor made repeated demands for sexual favors, usually at work, both during and after business hours. Vinson initially refused her employer's sexual advances, but eventually acceded because she feared losing her job. They had intercourse over forty times. She additionally testified that he fondled her in front of other employees, followed her into the women's restroom when she went there alone, exposed himself to her, and even forcibly raped her on several occasions." The court had no difficulty finding this environment hostile...

[A] hostile environment exists when an employee can show (1) that he or she was subjected to sexual advances, requests for sexual favors, or other verbal or physical conduct of a sexual nature, (2) that this conduct was unwelcome, and (3) that the conduct was sufficiently severe or pervasive to alter the conditions of the victim's employment and create an abusive working environment. Here, the [defendant] argues that Gray's conduct was not of a sexual nature. The three—page letter, however, makes several references to sex and constitutes verbal conduct of a sexual nature. We need not and do not decide whether a party can state a cause of action for a sexually discriminatory working environment under Title VII when the conduct in question is not sexual...

To state a claim under Title VII, sexual harassment "must be sufficiently severe and pervasive to alter the conditions of the victim's employment and create an abusive working environment."... [The court then reviewed the facts of two cases from other circuits, the Scott case and the Rabidue case, that found no sexually hostile environment despite much evidence of sexual language and conduct, offensive posters, and even some physical contact. The courts in those cases apparently would find a hostile environment only in circumstances in which the plaintiff has suffered serious psychological effects.] We do not agree with the standard set forth in Scott and Rabidue, and we choose not to follow those decisions... Surely, employees need not endure sexual harassment until their psychological well−being is seriously affected to the extent that they suffer anxiety and debilitation...Although an isolated epithet by itself fails to support a cause of action for a hostile environment, Title VII's protection of employees from sex discrimination comes into play long before the point where victims of sexual harassment require psychiatric assistance...

We ... believe that Gray's conduct was sufficiently severe and pervasive to alter the conditions of Ellison's employment and create an abusive working environment. We first note that,... although a single act can be enough... repeated incidents create a stronger claim of hostile environment, with the strength of the claim depending on the number of incidents and the intensity of each incident...

Next, we believe that in evaluating the severity and pervasiveness of sexual harassment, we should focus on the perspective of the victim. Courts "should consider the victim's perspective and not stereotyped notions of acceptable behavior."...Conduct that many men consider unobjectionable may offend many women. A male supervisor might believe, for example, that it is legitimate for him to tell a female subordinate that she has a 'great figure' or 'nice legs.' The female subordinate, however, may find such comments offensive; men and women are vulnerable in different ways and offended by different behavior. Men tend to view some forms of sexual harassment as "harmless social interactions to which only overly−sensitive women would object"; the characteristically male view depicts sexual harassment as comparatively harmless amusement.

We realize that there is a broad range of viewpoints among women as a group, but we believe that many women share common concerns which men do not necessarily share. For example, because women are disproportionately victims of rape and sexual assault,

women have a stronger incentive to be concerned with sexual behavior. Women who are victims of mild forms of sexual harassment may understandably worry whether a harasser's conduct is merely a prelude to violent sexual assault. Men, who are rarely victims of sexual assault, may view sexual conduct in a vacuum without a full appreciation of the social setting or the underlying threat of violence that a woman may perceive. One writer explains: "Their greater physical and social vulnerability to sexual coercion can make women wary of sexual encounters. Moreover, American women have been raised in a society where rape and sex− related violence have reached unprecedented levels, and a vast pornography industry creates continuous images of sexual coercion, objectification and violence...Because of the inequality and coercion with which it is so frequently associated in the minds of women, the appearance of sexuality in an unexpected context or a setting of ostensible equality can be an anguishing experience."

In order to shield employers from having to accommodate the idiosyncratic concerns of the rare hyper−sensitive employee, we hold that a female plaintiff states a prima facie case of hostile environment sexual harassment when she alleges conduct which a reasonable women would consider sufficiently severe or pervasive to alter the conditions of employment and create an abusive working environment...Of course, where male employees allege that coworkers engage in conduct which creates a hostile environment, the appropriate victim's perspective would be that of a reasonable man...

We note that the reasonable victim standard we adopt today classifies conduct as unlawful sexual harassment even when harassers do not realize that their conduct creates a hostile working environment... To avoid liability under Title VII, employers may have to educate and sensitize their workforce to eliminate conduct which a reasonable victim would consider unlawful sexual harassment . . . If sexual comments or sexual advances are in fact welcomed by the recipient, they, of course, do not constitute sexual harassment. Title VII's prohibition of sex discrimination in employment does not require a totally desexualized work place. . .

We cannot say a matter of law that Ellison's reaction was idiosyncratic or hyper−sensitive. We believe that a reasonable woman could have had a similar reaction. After receiving the first bizarre note from Gray, a person she barely knew, Ellison asked a co−worker to tell Gray to leave her alone. Despite her request, Gray sent her a long, passionate, disturbing letter. He told her he had been "watching" and "experiencing" her; he made repeated references to sex; he said he would write again. Ellison had no way of knowing what Gray would do next. A reasonable woman could consider Gray's conduct, as alleged by Ellison, sufficiently severe and pervasive to alter a condition of employment and create an abusive working environment. . .

We next must determine what remedial actions by employers shield them from liability under Title VII for sexual harassment by co−workers. [The question is, when management knows or has reason to know of the harassment, has it taken adequate steps to stop the harassment? Because the district court in this case granted a summary judgment against Ellison on the hostile environment issue, the court did not deal with the question of whether the employer took adequate steps upon learning of Gray's conduct. Before remanding the case to the district court for a trial on both the hostile environment question and the employer liability question, the Court of Appeals provided some general guidelines for the district court to follow in determining whether an employer has taken sufficient steps to avoid liability:] Employers have a duty to "express strong disapproval" of sexual

harassment, and to "develop appropriate sanctions" [that are]. . ."reasonably calculated to end the harassment ."... In Barrett v. Omaha National Bank, 726 F.2d 424 (8th Cir. 1984), the Eighth Circuit held that an employer properly remedied a hostile working environment by fully investigating, reprimanding a harasser for grossly inappropriate conduct, placing the offender on probation for ninety days, and warning the offender that any further misconduct would result in discharge. . .

An employer's remedy should persuade individual harassers to discontinue unlawful conduct. We do not think that all harassment warrants dismissal; rather, remedies should be "assessed proportionately to the seriousness of the offense." Employers should impose sufficient penalties to assure a workplace free from sexual harassment. . . [The Court of Appeals then noted some possible inadequacies in the employer's response to Gray's conduct: First, the employer had not indicated that he would be punished if he continued the behavior. Second, the employer had not disciplined Gray; neither the counseling nor the temporary transfer were disciplinary actions. Third, it was not appropriate for the employer to permit Gray to come back to the San Mateo office if his mere presence would continue to create a sexually hostile environment. Fourth, if Gray's mere presence would continue to create a hostile environment, it is not appropriate to transfer Ellison; the employer's response should not have negative consequences for the victim. The Court of Apeals concluded that there was a genuine fact issue as to the sufficiency of the employer's response.]

We reverse the district court's decision that Ellison did not allege a case of sexual harassment due to a hostile working environment, and we remand for [a trial on this question and on the question of whether the employer took sufficient remedial steps to avoid liability for a Title VII violation.]

Discriminatory Impact ("Disparate Impact")

Another way to prove that an employer has violated Title VII is to show that a particular employment rule or practice, although apparently neutral on its face, actually has an unequal impact on a protected group. Examples include height and weight requirements having the effect of excluding a disproportionate number of females, or a standardized test or educational requirement having the effect of excluding a disproportionate number of persons from a particular ethnic group. In such a case, the plaintiff is not required to show that the defendant had an intent to discriminate.

Prima Facie Case. The individual plaintiff, or the EEOC acting in the individual's behalf, must initially prove that the employment practice in question has an adverse impact on the protected group of which the individual is a member. This can be accomplished by the use of several different types of evidence. It could be shown, for example, that the employment practice has caused the employer to hire 40 percent of the whites who had applied, but only 20 percent of black applicants. Or, in another situation, discriminatory impact might be proved by showing that some action of the employer had the effect of eliminating 75 percent of all women from possible consideration, even though women comprise approximately one–half of the total population. Another method for proving discriminatory impact is to do a statistical comparison of the composition of the employer's work force with the composition of the relevant labor pool. For example, if the plaintiff alleges that a job criterion or selection method has a discriminatory impact on blacks, the plaintiff might attempt to show that the percentage of blacks working for the employer is much smaller than the percentage of qualified blacks in the available labor market. When a statistical disparity is used to prove discriminatory impact, the plaintiff must produce evidence linking the particular practice being challenged to the statistical imbalance in the employer's work force. If several employment practices are being challenged on the grounds that they have an aggregate discriminatory impact, the plaintiff will be permitted to lump them together if it is not feasible to single out a specific practice and show its impact alone.

It is important to realize, however, that the method used to prove discriminatory impact must be tailored to fit the particular employment practice being challenged and the particular group allegedly being affected. Thus, a court usually would not accept a comparison of the employer's minority hiring rate with general population statistics where the job in question required special qualifications. For example, if the job required a degree in mechanical engineering, the employer's experience in filling that job would need to be compared with the available population of mechanical engineers. The geographic area in which the statistical comparison should be made will also differ from one case to another. Suppose, for instance, that a plaintiff is trying to establish discriminatory impact in the case of an employer in San Francisco. If the job in question involves unskilled or semiskilled labor, general population statistics for the San Francisco–Oakland Bay area would probably be appropriate for comparison. However, if the job requires such special training and qualifications that the employer normally would have to recruit over a wider geographic area, the appropriate base for statistical comparison would be the population of qualified individuals in that larger area, such as the United States.

Employer's Rebuttal. As we have seen, an employer may rebut a prima facie case of discriminatory intent merely by producing some plausible evidence of a nondiscriminatory reason for the employer's action. When the plaintiff has established a prima facie case by proving discriminatory impact, however, the employer's task of rebuttal is somewhat more difficult. In an impact case, the employer has to prove (not just introduce some plausible evidence) "business necessity." To meet this burden, the employer must prove that (1) the challenged employment practice was necessary to achieve an important business objective, and (2) the practice actually achieves this objective.

Employee's Proof of Alternatives. If the employer has proved business necessity, the plaintiff loses unless he or she can then prove that the employer had some other feasible alternative for achieving its important business objective, that the alternative would have accomplished the objective without having a discriminatory effect, and that the employer failed to use this non-discriminatory alternative.

Disparate Impact in Recent Years. Proving a Title VII violation by showing disparate impact once was a fairly commonly used alternative to proving a violation by showing disparate impact. In recent years, however, the federal courts have made it far more difficult to prove disparate impact. In most cases, a plaintiff has to make a rather sophisticated statistical demonstration of disparate impact, and the courts have substantially raised the standards for doing this. Disparate impact can still be proved in some cases, such as height requirements that obviously have the effect of excluding a much larger portion of women than men. In most other situations, however, proving disparate impact has become much more difficult. This fact, coupled with the fact that Congress made *disparate treatment* cases much more attractive for plaintiffs several years ago by providing for jury trials and increasing the amount of damages that can be recovered, has led to the result that very few disparate impact cases are filed anymore.

Bona Fide Occupational Qualification Defense

Once discrimination has been proved, the employer has few defenses. One such defense in Title VII provides that it is not illegal to discriminate on the basis of religion, sex, or national origin in situations where religion, sex, or national origin is a bona fide occupational qualification (BFOQ). The law states that race or color cannot be a BFOQ, although a court probably would find some way to conclude that it is legal to cast an actor of a particular race to portray a historical figure of that race. Congress intended the BFOQ defense to be a very limited exception that would apply only to rare situations. The EEOC and the courts have followed this intent by recognizing the exception very infrequently.

Most of the situations in which the BFOQ defense has been an issue have involved sex discrimination, and most of those have involved employer policies that clearly excluded women from certain jobs. Stereotypes or traditional assumptions about which jobs are appropriate for males or females do not establish the BFOQ exception. A basic principle of Title VII is that the individual should decide whether the job is appropriate, assuming that person is qualified to perform it. Thus, males cannot automatically be barred from jobs such as airline flight attendant or secretary, and females cannot be barred from mining, construction, or other jobs requiring lifting, night work, and so forth. Even the fact that the employer's customers strongly prefer employees to be of one sex or the other does not create the BFOQ exception.

In a few circumstances, however, gender is an essential element of the job. For example, the BFOQ defense has been permitted where one sex or the other is necessary for authenticity, as in the case of models or actors. In addition, being a woman has been held to be a BFOQ for employment as a salesperson in the ladies' undergarments department of a department store, and as a nurse in the labor and delivery section of an obstetrical hospital. Being a man has been held to be a BFOQ for employment as a security guard, where the job involved searching male employees, and also as an attendant in a men's restroom.

The following case applies the BFOQ defense to a difficult problem faced by both employers and employees—exposure of women workers to substances that create risks of harm to fetuses.

United Automobile Aerospace & Agriculture Workers Union v. Johnson Controls, Inc.
US. Supreme Court, 111 S.Ct. 1196 (1991)

Johnson Controls, Inc., manufactures batteries. In the manufacturing process, the element lead is a primary ingredient. Occupational exposure to lead entails health risks, including the risk of harm to any fetus carried by a female employee. Lead exposure to men also carries some risk for their unborn children, but not to the same extent as in the case of exposure to women. Before the Civil Rights Act of 1964 became law, Johnson Controls did not employ any woman in a battery–manufacturing job. In 1977 adopted a policy of fully informing its female employees of the fetal risks associated with exposure to lead, permitting them to make a voluntary decision about whether they wished to work in a job that would expose them to lead. In 1982, the company changed its policy to one of exclusion. Under this policy, women *were absolutely excluded from jobs involving significant lead exposure unless they presented medical documentation of sterility.*

Several employees and the union filed a class action in federal district court, alleging that the company's fetal protection policy constituted sex discrimination in violation of Title VII. Among the individual plaintiffs were MaryCraig, who had chosen to be sterilized in order to avoid losing her job; Elsie Nason, a 50-year-old divorcee who had suffered a loss in compensation when she was transferred out of a job where she was exposed to lead; and DonaldPenney, a male employee who had been denied a request for a leave of absence for the purpose of lowering his lead level because he intended to become a father. The district court treated the fetal protection policy as a neutral employment practice having a discriminatory impact on women. The court concluded that the plaintiffs had established a prima facie case of discriminatory impact, but that the company had established business necessity, and the plaintiffs had failed to demonstrate reasonable alternatives that would not have such a discriminatory impact. It granted summary judgment for the company. The U.S. Court of Appeals affirmed. The plaintiffs appealed to the U.S. Supreme Court. In their appeal, they claimed that the fetal protection policy was not a gender–neutral practice, but was explicitly discriminatory on the basis of sex. Because it was explicit gender discrimination, they contended that the defendant could prevail only by proving the BFOQ defense, which is much more difficult than showing business necessity in an impact case.

Blackmun, Justice:

The bias in Johnson Controls' policy is obvious. Fertile men, but not fertile women, are given a choice as to they wish to risk their reproductive health for a particular job. The policy excludes women with childbearing capacity from lead–exposed jobs and so creates a facial [that is, explicit] classification based on gender...

[Johnson Controls] does not seek to protect the unconceived children of all its employees. Despite evidence in the record about the debilitating effect of lead exposure on the male reproduction system, Johnson Controls is concerned only with the harms that may befall the unborn offspring of its female employees... Johnson Controls' fetal–protection policy is [explicit] sex discrimination forbidden under Title VII unless respondent can establish that sex is a "bona fide occupational qualification."

Under section 703(e)(1) of Title VII, an employer may discriminate on the basis of "religion, sex, or national origin in those certain instances where religion, sex, or national origin is a bona fide occupational qualification reasonably necessary to the normal operation of that particular business or enterprise." ...The BFOQ defense is written narrowly, and this Court has read it narrowly. We have read the BFOQ language of section 4(f) of the Age Discrimination in Employment Act of 1967 (ADEA), which tracks the BFOQ provision in Title VII, just as narrowly... The wording of the BFOQ defense contains several terms of restriction that indicate that the exception reaches only special situations. The statute thus limits the situations in which discrimination is permissible to "certain instances" where sex discrimination is "reasonably necessary" to the "normal operation" of the "particular" business. Each one of these terms—certain, normal, particular—prevents the use of general subjective standards and favors an objective, verifiable requirement. But the most telling term is "occupational" this indicates that these objective, verifiable requirements must concern job–related skills and aptitudes...

Johnson Controls argues that its fetal–protection policy falls within the so–called safety exception to the BFOQ. Our cases have stressed that discrimination on the basis of sex because of safety concerns is allowed only in narrow circumstances. In Dothard v. Rawlinson, this Court indicated that danger to a woman herself does not justify discrimination. We there allowed the employer to hire only male guards in contact areas of maximum security male penitentiaries only because more was at stake than the 'individual woman's decision to weigh and accept the risks of employment." We found sex to be a BFOQ inasmuch as the employment of a female guard would create real risks of safety to others if violence broke out because the guard was a woman. Sex discrimination was tolerated because sex was related to the guard's ability to do the job— maintaining prison security. We also required in Dothard a high correlation between sex and ability to perform job functions and refused to allow employers to use sex as a proxy for strength although it might be a fairly accurate one. Similarly, some courts have approved airlines' layoffs of pregnant flight attendants at different points during the first five months of pregnancy on the ground that the employer's policy was necessary to ensure the safety of passengers. In two of these cases, the courts pointedly indicated that fetal, as opposed to passenger, safety was best left to the mother.

We considered safety to third parties in Western Airlines, Inc. v. Criswell, 472 U.S. 400(1985), in the context of the ADEA. We focused upon "the nature of the flight engineer's tasks," and the "actual capabilities of persons over age 60" in relation to those tasks. Our safety concerns were not independent of the individual's ability to perform the assigned tasks, but rather involved the possibility that, because of age connected debility, a flight engineer might not properly assist the pilot, and might thereby cause a safety emergency. Furthermore, although we considered the safety of third parties in Dothard and Criswell, those third parties were indispensable to the particular business at issue. In Dothard, the third parties were the inmates; in Criswell, the third parties were the passengers on the plane. We stressed that in order to qualify as a BFOQ, a job qualification must relate to the "essence," or to the "central mission of the employer's business."...

Third—party safety considerations properly entered into the BFOQ analysis in Dothard and Criswell because they went to the core of the employee's job performance. Moreover, that performance involved the central purpose of the enterprise. The essence of a correctional counselor's job is to maintain prison security; the central mission of the airline's business was the safe transportation of its passengers... The unconceived fetuses of Johnson Controls'

female employees, however, are neither customers nor third parties whose safety is essential to the business of battery manufacturing. No one can disregard the possibility of injury to future children; the BFOQ, however, is not so broad that it transforms this deep social concern into an essential aspect of battery making.

Our case law, therefore, makes clear that the safety exception is limited to instances in which sex or pregnancy actually interferes with the employee's ability to perform the job... Women as capable of doing their jobs as their male counterparts may not be forced to choose between having a child and having a job...

Pregnant women who are able to work must be permitted to work on the same conditions as other employees ... [E]mployers may not require a pregnant woman to stop working at any time during her pregnancy unless she is unable to do her work. Employment late in pregnancy often imposes risks on the unborn child, but Congress indicated that the employer may take into account only the woman's ability to get her job done... Congress made clear that the decision to become pregnant or to work while being either pregnant or capable of becoming pregnant was reserved for each individual woman to make for herself...

We have no difficulty concluding that Johnson Controls cannot establish a BFOQ. Fertile women, as far as appears in the record, participate in the manufacture of batteries as efficiently as anyone else. Johnson Controls' professed moral and ethical concerns about the welfare of the next generation do not suffice to establish a BFOQ of female sterility. Decisions about the welfare of future children must be left to the parents who conceive, bear, support, and raise them rather than to the employers who hire those parents...

A word about tort liability and the increased cost of fertile women in the workplace is perhaps necessary. One of the [concurring] judges in this case expressed concern about an employer's tort liability and concluded that liability for a potential injury to a fetus is a social cost that Title VII does not require a company to ignore... More than 40 States currently recognize a right to recover for a prenatal injury based either on negligence or on wrongful death. According to Johnson Controls, however, the company complies with the lead [exposure] standard developed by OSHA and warns its female employees about the damaging effects of lead... Without negligence, it would be difficult for a court to find liability on the part of the employer [in a case alleging injury to a fetus]. If...Title VII bans sex–specific fetal–protection policies, the employer fully informs the woman of the risk, and the employer has not acted negligently, the basis for holding an employer liable [under general tort principles] seems remote at best.

[Without ruling on the question because it was not presented, the Supreme Court then noted that Title VII's prohibition of gender-specific fetal protection policies might preclude a tort claim for injury to a fetus on the constitutional theory of federal presumption.] ...We, of course, are not presented with, nor do we decide, a case in which costs would be so prohibitive as to threaten the survival of the employer's business. We merely reiterate our prior holdings that [an] incremental cost of hiring women cannot justify discriminating against them...

It is no more appropriate for the courts than it is for individual employers to decide whether a woman's reproductive role is more important to herself and her family than her economic role. Congress has left this choice to the woman as hers to make. The judgment of the Court of Appeals is reversed and the case is remanded.

Seniority Systems

Seniority refers to the length of time an employee has worked for a company, or perhaps the time worked within a particular department or other division of the company. Many companies, especially those having collective bargaining agreements with unions, have seniority systems. These systems provide that many kinds of employment rights and privileges are to be determined on the basis of seniority. For example, the right to bid for another job or another shift within the company, or the right to be protected from lay–-off, may be determined by seniority. Although far from perfect, seniority systems are generally recognized as one of the few truly objective means for making many kinds of employment decisions. Such systems, however, can sometimes have a discriminatory impact on women and minorities, because these employees on the average are likely to have less seniority than white males. Because of their positive aspects, seniority systems are partially exempted from Title VII. A "bona fide" (good faith) seniority system does not violate Title VII just because it has a discriminatory impact; the system is illegal only if it is intentionally used to discriminate.

Affirmative Action in Employment

The primary strategy in the legal battle against employment discrimination has been simply to prohibit discriminatory practices and to strike them down when they are discovered. Another important weapon, however, has been affirmative action—actually giving preferences to minorities and women in the hiring process. In many cases, affirmative action programs include goals and timetables for increasing the percentage of minorities and women in the employer's work force. The purpose of affirmative action is to rectify the effects of previous discrimination.

Affirmative action has been used by some courts as a remedy in specific cases of discrimination. In other words, after concluding that an employer had practiced discrimination, some courts have both ordered the cessation of the practice and required the employer to implement an affirmative action program. In addition, some employers, either on their own or in connection with union collective bargaining agreements, have instituted voluntary affirmative action programs.

Since their inception, affirmative action programs have raised difficult legal questions. By granting preferences to minorities and women, these programs discriminate in some degree against white males. White males are protected against race and sex discrimination by Title VII; does so–called reverse discrimination, brought about by affirmative action programs, violate Title VII or other discrimination laws? In United Steelworkers of America v. Weber, 443 U.S. 193 (1979), the Supreme Court ruled that voluntary affirmative action programs are permissible under Title VII in certain circumstances. In several other cases, lower courts have upheld mandatory affirmative action programs in similar circumstances. As a limited exception to the basic prohibition against discrimination, reverse discrimination brought about by affirmative action programs is legal under the following conditions.

1. There must be a formal, systematic program— the employer cannot discriminate against nonminorities on an isolated, ad hoc basis.
2. Any such program must be temporary—it must operate only until its reasonable minority hiring goals are reached.
3. The program cannot completely bar the hiring or promotion of nonminority workers.
4. The program cannot result in the actual firing of nonminority workers.
5. The program cannot force the employer to hire or promote unqualified workers.
6. If the program is court–ordered, it must be based on evidence that there actually had been discrimination by the employer in the past. If the program is voluntary, it can be based either on evidence of past discrimination or merely on evidence that there has been a substantial underutilization of minorities or women by the employer.
7. In general, an affirmative action plan cannot override preexisting employee rights that have been established by a valid seniority system. The following case illustrates this additional limitation on the operation of an affirmative action program.

Comparable Worth

As we will see shortly, a separate federal statute, the Equal Pay Act of 1963, prohibits sex–based discrimination in rates of pay. This law applies only when a male and a female are doing jobs that are substantially the same. Therefore, the Equal Pay Act does not apply to a situation in which a male and a female receive different pay for jobs that are different, even if the evidence indicates that the two jobs are of equal economic value to the employer. Although the doctrine of comparable worth does not provide a basis for a claim under the Equal Pay Act, the fact that men and women receive different pay for jobs that are of comparable worth to the employer might be relevant in a Title VII case in some circumstances. Suppose, for example, that a female employee claims that her employer violated Title VII by intentionally placing males and females in different categories of job because of their sex, or by setting different rates of pay for different jobs because one category of job was held primarily by men and the other primarily by women. In such a situation, evidence that the two categories of job were of comparable economic value to the employer would be a relevant factor to be considered by a court when it decides whether an inference of discriminatory intent is warranted.

Although evidence of different pay for jobs of comparable worth may in some circumstances be relevant to a possible inference of discriminatory intent, the courts thus far have held that evidence of comparable worth, by itself, does not establish a violation of Title VII. In other words, the fact that an employer has different pay rates for two different jobs of comparable worth, one type of job being held primarily by males and the other primarily by females, does not establish a violation of Title VII. Other evidence of gender–based discrimination would have to be present.

It is quite common for employers to base pay rates for different jobs on prevailing market rates for such jobs in the area. If such dependence on the market creates a situation in which women and men are paid differently for jobs of comparable worth, has the employer violated Title VII? In the leading case on this question, American Federation of State, County, and Municipal Employees v. State of Washington, 770 F.2d 1401 (9th Cir. 1985), the court of appeals concluded that an employer does not violate Title VII merely by basing pay scales on prevailing market rates even if the result is a differential between men and women. After this case and some others, the doctrine of comparable worth probably is of limited value in challenging a compensation system under Title VII. It should be noted, however, that several state legislatures have adopted comparable worth systems for state government employees. Because government jobs usually are classified in a systematic fashion, with substantial uniformity within a classification, the concept of comparable worth may have its greatest utility in government employment.

Equal Pay Act

The first antidiscrimination in employment act, predating even Title VII, is the Equal Pay Act. This statute prohibits an employer from paying an employee of one sex less than an employee of the opposite sex, when the two are performing jobs that require "equal skill, effort, and responsibility" and "under similar working conditions." Proof that the pay differential is due to the workers' varying merit or pursuant to a legitimate seniority system are available defenses under the Act. The Equal Pay Act is limited to sex discrimination in the form of wages and overlaps considerably with Title VII. There are slight differences in employers covered by the two Acts, however, and the Equal Pay Act may be a worker's only recourse for wage discrimination in some companies with fewer than 15 employees.

Age Discrimination in Employment Act

Title VII expanded the scope of employment discrimination protection in 1967, when it passed the Age Discrimination in Employment Act (ADEA). The coverage of this Act is quite similar to Title VII, except that it applies only to situations where there is a minimum of 20 employees. The ADEA prohibits discrimination based on age against anyone age 40 and over. Almost all age discrimination cases involve alleged disparate treatment of individual workers. Although the U.S. Supreme Court held in 2005 that the disparate impact theory can be used in age discrimination cases, it is unlikely that we will see many such cases because, as in Title VII, disparate impact has come to be very difficult to prove in recent years.

Only the age of the victim of discrimination is relevant. Thus, an employer favoring a 45–year–old over a 60–year–old because of the age of the latter has violated the ADEA just as surely as if the employer had favored a 25–year–old. In such a situation, the "favored" employee just has to be sufficiently younger than the "disfavored" employee so that an inference of age discrimination is logical. The evidence must convince the court, however, that the plaintiff's age was the main reason for the disparate treatment.

The ADEA provides several statutory defenses for employers. An employee may always be discharged or otherwise penalized for good cause other than age. A bona fide occupational qualification defense also exists and closely resembles that under Title VII. Bona fide seniority systems or employee benefit plans are also exempted from ADEA violation. Courts have interpreted these defenses somewhat more expansively, in the employer's favor, than in most cases decided under Title VII.

OLSON V. NORTHERN FS, INC.
387 F.3d 632 (7th Cir. 2004)

Northern FS fired plaintiff Olson, who had won several sales awards in his more than 40 years with the company, and replaced him with Bloome, a 22–year–old with no sales experience. Olson filed an ADEA discrimination suit against Northern FS, but the district court granted Northern FS's summary judgment motion. Olson appealed.

Evans, Circuit Judge:
The fact that Bloome's supervisor described his performance as "substandard" in his 2 years as a crop salesman (Bloome no longer works for Northern FS) allows us to conclude that the company likely made a bad decision when it replaced Olson with Bloome. Whether the decision was also an illegal one, however, is a closer call. Having considered the case, we

think it should be resolved at a trial, rather than at the summary judgment stage where Olson's age discrimination claim came up a loser in the district court.

Olson began selling seeds, fertilizer, and feed in 1960. Beginning in 1991, Olson sold grain buildings and equipment for 3 years before returning to crop sales. Olson won the company's annual sales award in 1996 and 1997 before returning to building sales from 1997 until Northern FS stopped selling buildings in 2000.

Olson spent February to October 2000 answering phones and working in the warehouse of a Northern FS plant. In August of that year, SteveKeelen, who had supervised Olson's sales route in the mid–1990's before leaving the company, returned to Northern FS and met with Olson about Olson's future with Northern FS. Olson claims Keelen told him that, despite his experience, Olson was undesirable in the business world because of his age. Olson says he repeated Keelen's remark to Keelen's secretary on his way out of Keelen's office.

The following month, a crop sales position suddenly opened. Olson was tapped to fill the void. On the day Northern FS hired Bloome, Keelen took Olson off his sales route and moved him back into the warehouse. Eleven days after Bloome was hired, Northern FS fired Olson. At the time of his termination, Olson was 59 years old and had spent 41 years with Northern FS.

Summary judgment is appropriate if there is no genuine issue as to any material fact and the moving party is entitled to judgment as a matter of law. A plaintiff can prove discrimination under the ADEA by presenting direct or circumstantial evidence that an employer took an adverse job action against him because of his age (the direct method) or "by constructing a 'convincing mosaic' of circumstantial evidence that 'allows a jury to infer discrimination by the decision maker'" (the indirect

method). Cerutti v. BASF Corp., 349 F.3d 1055 (7th Cir. 2003). The district court rejected Olson's claims on both counts, finding that Keelen's statement that Olson's age made him undesirable in the business world was merely a "stray remark" and that Olson could not establish a prima facie case under the indirect method because he and Bloome were not similarly situated.

We have found a statement to be direct evidence of discriminatory intent where the statement was made around the time of and in reference to the adverse employment action. As the district court noted, Keelen's remark came 5 months before Olson's termination and was not made in direct reference to the firing. Therefore, it was not, as we have required, "an admission by the decision–maker that his actions were based upon the prohibited animus." Cerutti, 349 F.3d at 1061.

The district court's error, however, was ignoring Keelen's remark when evaluating Olson's claim under the indirect method set forth in McDonnell Douglas Corp. v. Green, 411 U.S. 792 (1973). Instead, the district court noted that, generally, to establish a prima facie case of employment discrimination under the indirect method, a plaintiff must show: (1) he was a member of a protected class; (2) he was meeting his employer's legitimate job expectations; (3) he suffered an adverse employment action; and (4) similarly situated employees not in the protected class were treated more favorably. Koski v. Standex Int'l Corp., 307 F.3d 672 (7th Cir. 2002). Since both sides agreed that Olson and Bloome were not simiarly situated because they had diferent acdemic credentials.

In its rigid adherence to Koski and McDonnell Douglas, however, the district court skirts the ultimate question––whether age was a motivating factor in the decision to fire Olson. See Hazen Paper Co. v. Biggins, 507 U.S. 604 (1993)("Liability depends on whether the protected trait (under the ADEA, age) actually motivated the employer's decision."). In an attempt to better reach the ultimate question of when, as here, an employee within the protected class has been discharged and replaced, we have required that the employee show only that "he was performing his job to the employer's legitimate expectations" and that the employer "hired someone else who was substantially younger or other such evidence that indicates that it is more likely than not that his age . . .was the reason for the discharge." Robin v. Espo Enginerring Corp., 200 F.3d 1081 (7th Cir. 2000).

Olson presented evidence showing that his job performance was satisfactory (Jeff Kimmel, the facility manager of the plant where Olson worked, said that Olson had done a good job as a crop salesman) and that Northern FS hired someone substantially younger to replace him, even though Bloome had no sales experience and, according to Kimmel, was not more qualified than Olson. Those facts, coupled with Keelen's remark, stray or otherwise, that Olson was undesirable because of his age, are sufficient to let a jury decide whether Olson's age actually played a role in Northern FS's decision to terminate his employment.

The district court found that, even if Olson presented a prima facie case, he did not present evidence that Northern FS's explanation—that Keelen did not know Olson was interested in a permanent position as a crop salesman—was pretextual, as required by McDonnell Douglas. But, again, a reasonable trier of fact could look at Keelen's remark and at Northern FS's unusual decision to hire someone with no sales experience to replace an experienced, highly successful salesman and determine that Keelen's explanation was pretextual. For these reasons, we REVERSE the district court's judgment and REMAND the case for further proceedings.

Discrimination Against Persons with Disabilities

In the Rehabilitation Act of 1973, Congress prohibited discrimination in employment against handicapped persons. That law, however, applied only to the employment practices of federal government agencies, businesses having contracts with the federal government, and organizations or programs receiving federal funding (such as universities receiving federal research funds). The Rehabilitation Act continues to apply to these three groups of employers.

In 1990, Congress passed the Americans with Disabilities Act (ADA), which provides comprehensive protection against discrimination to persons with disabilities. The ADA includes provisions dealing not only with discrimination in employment, but also with problems of discrimination and access in public transportation, public accommodations (such as restaurants and office buildings), and communications. Title I of the ADA, dealing with employment, is the only part relevant to our discussion in this chapter. The employment portions of the ADA cover the same employers as Title VII of the 1964 Civil Rights Act; in addition, the new law adopts most of the procedures and methods of proving discrimination from Title VII.

The ADA borrows most of its basic concepts and definitions, however, from the Rehabilitation Act. Instead of speaking of "handicapped persons," as did the Rehabilitation Act, the ADA speaks of "persons with disabilities." It uses the same basic definition for such persons as was used for handicapped persons under the Rehabilitation Act. Under the ADA, a person has a disability if he or she has a "physical or mental impairment that substantially affects one or more of the major life activities" of that person. Major life activities include functions such as caring for one's self, performing manual tasks, walking, seeing, hearing, speaking, breathing, learning, and participating in social relationships and activities. The law does not attempt to include an exhaustive list of disabilities. However, conditions that obviously would constitute disabilities include orthopedic, visual, speech, and hearing impairments; cerebral palsy; muscular dystrophy; multiple sclerosis; HIV infection; cancer; diseases of the heart or other major organs; diabetes; seizure disorders (epilepsy); mental retardation; emotional illness; serious learning disabilities; drug addiction; and alcoholism. Although alcoholism and drug addiction constitute disabilities, the ADA expressly provides that a current user of alcohol or illegal drugs is not protected by the law. Finally, the ADA also contains a list of conditions referred to as "behavioral" that are expressly excluded from the definition of disability, including homosexuality, bisexuality, gender identity disorders, exhibitionism, voyeurism, compulsive gambling, kleptomania, pyromania, and several others.

In addition to prohibiting discrimination in employment against a person actually having a "physical or mental impairment substantially affecting a major life activity," the ADA also prohibits discrimination against a person who either has a record of such an impairment or is regarded as having such an impairment. That part of the law dealing with having a record of an impairment is intended to protect those victimized by mistaken records (which are often difficult to correct) or by the stigma of a past affliction that no longer constitutes an impairment. Although that part of the law dealing with one who is "regarded" as having an impairment will sometimes overlap with the "record of" provision, its main purpose is to protect those who are victimized by stereotypes. In other words, there are some conditions that may cause no impairment at all, or at least no impairment for a certain kind of job, but because of stereotypes those with the condition are treated as if they are impaired.

Even if a person is protected by the ADA, an employer is under no obligation to hire unless the person is qualified to do the job. If the person can do the job without any special accommodation, the employer should not even bring up the subject of changing the job, changing the working environment, or similar subjects. However, if an individual is not qualified as the job now exists, but would be qualified if the employer makes a "reasonable accommodation" for the person's impairment, then the person is viewed by the law as being qualified. The question of reasonable accommodation should not be dealt with, however, unless the disabled person brings it up or unless the need to make some adjustment in the job becomes obvious after the individual has been performing it for a time. An adjustment of the work environment or schedules may be reasonable, or perhaps rearranging a job into different parts if such a change does not significantly affect efficiency. To meet the burden of making a reasonable accommodation for a person's disability, however, the employer is not required to incur an "undue hardship."

The ADA has generated lots of litigation, but statistics show that employers are winning 90% of the cases. One reason is that many courts have set a rather high hurdle for what constitutes a disability that limits a "major life activity." Another reason is that the Supreme Court has held that people are not disabled if their condition can be remedied by medicine or devices, as shown in the following case. One result of this and several other similar decisions by the Supreme Court in the late 1990s is that the "regarded as" category of disability is much less important than it was before then.

Sutton v. United Air Lines
U.S. Supreme Court, 527 U.S. 471 (1999)

Petitioners are myopic (nearsighted) twin sisters who unsuccessfully applied for jobs as airline pilots with defendant/respondent United Air Lines. Their myopia is correctable with appropriate lenses. They sued under the ADA claiming that United's failure to hire them as pilots because of their uncorrected visual acuity was based on their disability. The trial court ruled against petitioners, as did the appeals court.

O'Connor, Justice:

The ADA prohibits certain employers from discriminating against individuals on the basis of their disabilities. A disability is defined as "(A) a physical or mental impairment that substantially limits one or more of the major life activities of such individual; (B) a record of such an impairment; or (C) being regarded as having such an impairment. [Petitioners make a claim under provisions (A) and (C).]

Because petitioners allege that with corrective measures their vision "is 20/20 or better," they are not actually disabled within the meaning of the Act if the "disability" determination is made with reference to these measures. Consequently, with respect to subsection (A) of the disability definition, our decision turns on whether disability is to be determined with or without reference to corrective measures. [Justice O'Connor then examined the legislative history of the ADA in great detail and concluded that the subsection (A) definition

should, in fact, be made with reference to the corrective measures.]

The dissenting justices suggest that viewing individuals in their corrected state will exclude from the definition of "disabled" those who use prosthetic limbs, or take medicine for epilepsy or high blood pressure. This suggestion is incorrect. The use of a corrective device does not, by itself, relieve one's disability. Rather, one has a disability under subsection A if, notwithstanding the use of a corrective device, that individual is substantially limited in a major life activity. For example, individuals who use prosthetic limbs or wheelchairs may be mobile and capable of functioning in society but still be disabled because of a substantial limitation on their ability to walk or run. The same may be true of individuals who take medicine to lessen the symptoms of an impairment so that they can function but nevertheless remain substantially limited.

Because we decide that disability under the Act is to be determined with reference to corrective measures, we agree with the courts below that petitioners have not stated a claim that they are substantially limited in any major life activity.

Our conclusion that petitioners have failed to state a claim that they are actually disabled under subsection (A) of the disability definition does not end our inquiry. Under subsection (C), individuals who are "regarded as" having a disability are disabled within the meaning of the ADA. Subsection (C) provides that having a disability includes "being regarded as having . . . a physical or mental impairment that substantially limits one or more of the major life activities of such individual," There are two apparent ways in which individuals may fall within this statutory definition: (1) a covered entity mistakenly believes that a person has a physical impairment that substantially limits one or more major life activities, or (2) a covered entity mistakenly believes that an actual, nonlimiting impairment substantially limits one or more major life activities. In both cases, it is necessary that a covered entity entertain misperceptions about the individual — it must believe either that one has a substantially limiting impairment that one does not have or that one has a substantially limiting impairment when, in fact, the impairment is not so limiting. These misperceptions often "result from stereotypical assumptions not truly indicative of . . .individual ability."

There is no dispute that petitioners are physically impaired. Petitioners do not make the obvious argument that they are regarded due to their impairments as substantially limited in the major life activity of seeing. They contend only that respondent mistakenly believes their physical impairments substantially limit them in the major life activity of working. To support this claim, petitioners allege that respondent has a vision requirement, which is allegedly based on myth and stereotype. Further, this requirement substantially limits their ability to engage in the major life activity of working by precluding them from obtaining the job of global airline pilot, which they argue is a "class of employment." In reply, respondent argues that the position of global airline pilot is not a class of jobs and therefore petitioners have not stated a claim that they are regarded as substantially limited in the major life activity of working.

Standing alone, the allegation that respondent has a vision requirement in place does not establish a claim that respondent regards petitioners as substantially limited in the major life activity of working. By its terms, the ADA allows employers to prefer some physical attributes over others and to establish physical criteria. An employer runs afoul of the ADA when it makes an employment decision based on a physical or mental impairment, real or imagined, that is regarded as substantially limiting a major life activity. Accordingly, an employer is free to decide that physical characteristics or medical conditions that do not rise to the level of an impairment —such as one's height, build, or singing voice — are preferable to others, just as it is free to decide that some limiting, but not substantially limiting, impairments make individuals less than ideally suited for a job.

Considering the allegations of the amended complaint in tandem, petitioners have not stated a claim that respondent regards their impairment as substantially limiting their ability to work. The ADA does not define "substantially limits," but "substantially" suggests "considerable" or "specified to a large degree." See Webster's Third New International Dictionary 2280(1976).

When the major life activity under consideration is that of working, the statutory phrase "substantially limits" requires, at a minimum, that plaintiffs allege they are unable to work in a broad class of jobs. Reflecting this requirement, the EEOC uses a specialized definition of the term "substantially limits" when referring to the major life activity of working: "significantly restricted in the ability to perform either a class of jobs or a broad range of jobs in various classes as compared to the average person having comparable training, skills and abilities. The inability to perform a single, particular job does not constitute a substantial limitation in the major life activity of working."

The EEOC further identifies several factors that courts should consider when determining whether an individual is substantially limited in the major life activity of working, including the geographical area to which the individual has reasonable access, and "the number and types of jobs utilizing similar training, knowledge, skills or abilities, within the geographical area, from which the individual is also disqualified." To be substantially limited in the major life activity of working, then, one must be precluded from more than one type of job, a specialized job, or a particular job of choice. If jobs utilizing an individual's skills (but perhaps not his or her unique talents) are available, one is not precluded from a substantial class of jobs. Similarly, if a host of different types of jobs are available, one is not precluded from a broad range of jobs.

Because the parties accept that the term "major life activities" includes working, we do not determine the validity of the cited regulations. Assuming without deciding that working is a major life activity and that the EEOC regulations interpreting the term "substantially limits" are reasonable, petitioners have failed to allege adequately that their poor eyesight is regarded as an impairment that substantially limits them in the major life activity of working. They allege only that respondent regards their poor vision as precluding them from holding positions as a "global airline pilot." Because the position of global airline pilot is a single job, this allegation does not support the claim that respondent regards petitioners as having a substantially limiting impairment. See 29 CFR § 1630.2(j)(3)(i)("The inability to perform a single, particular job does not constitute a substantial limitation in the major life activity of working"). Indeed, there are a number of other positions utilizing petitioners' skills, such as regional pilot and pilot instructor to name a few, that are available to them. Even under the EEOC's Interpretative Guidance, to which petitioners ask us to defer, "an individual who cannot be a commercial airline pilot because of a minor vision impairment, but who can be a commercial airline copilot or a pilot for a courier service, would not be substantially limited in the major life activity of working."

AFFIRMED.

Protection of Employee Safety and Welfare

Although unions undoubtedly have improved the safety and welfare of individual employees, they have failed to provide full protection, at least in the judgment of Congress and the states. Numerous laws have been passed to protect workers from on—the—job injuries and the financial consequences of such injuries. Congress also has legislated to preserve the financial welfare of workers, especially in the context of pension and other employee benefit plans.

Workers' Compensation

In the 19th century, workers were frequently injured on the job and often without legal recourse to compensate them for their injuries. In response, state legislatures passed workers' compensation statutes. All fifty states have such laws and while they vary somewhat, the laws all share certain common features. Workers' compensation is paid without regard to employer negligence and workers receive a predetermined amount, based on the injury suffered. Benefits payable include medical costs, income replacement, death benefits, and rehabilitation costs. Levels of compensation are typically lower than a worker might receive in a lawsuit, but the statutory system avoids much of the attorney and other costs of litigation, while eliminating most employer defenses to payment of the lesser sum.

The main restriction on recovery under workers' compensation statutes is the requirement that the injury must have arisen "out of and in the course of employment." Although the majority of injuries are clearly job–related, a large number of cases lie on the disputed borderline of work. For example, an employee whose job requires travel will ordinarily be able to receive benefits for injuries incurred in the course of such travel. By contrast, a mere commuter will not be compensated if injured on the way to work.

Employees typically are also covered while engaging in activities reasonably incidental to job duties. Thus, an employee on a lunch break who slips and falls in the employer's cafeteria would be covered.

State laws also cover diseases arising out of employment, but proof of the source of disease is much more complicated to obtain than is proof of work injuries, and such cases are more often disputed.

Occupational Safety and Health Act

In 1970, Congress passed the Occupational Safety and Health Act to help prevent workplace disease and injuries. The Act created the Occupational Safety and Health Administration (OSHA), part of the U.S. Department of Labor, to administer its provisions. This statute applies to virtually every United States employer.

Central to OSHA's powers is its standard–setting authority. The agency promulgates regulations compelling employers to make their workplaces safer in a variety of ways. Most of the early standards were intended to prevent job injuries, and OSHA suffered considerable ridicule because of the highly detailed nature of its rules. For example, the agency devoted considerable effort to regulating the number of toilets to be available and the allowable design of such facilities. As the agency has gained experience, its standards have allowed more flexibility for employers, and the regulatory focus has shifted toward prevention of occupational diseases.

Unlike some agencies that have been largely co–opted by the industries they regulate, OSHA has maintained standards that are often quite strict. These rules have given rise to litigation that has helped define the extent of the agency's powers. In an attempt to prevent a cancer associated with the inhalation of benzene, a petroleum byproduct, OSHA promulgated a stringent standard without attempting to specify the magnitude of the harm created by existing levels. The agency believed that it was simply fulfilling its mandate to create the healthiest workplace feasible, but the Supreme Court overturned the regulation in Industrial Union Department v. American Petroleum Institute, 448 U.S. 607 (1980). The Court held that OSHA could regulate only "significant risks" and generally should quantitatively measure a risk before promulgating rules. Shortly after this decision, industry challenged an OSHA regulation limiting exposure to cotton dust, which causes several lung diseases. Industry contended that OSHA had to base regulation on a cost/benefit analysis, but the Supreme Court upheld the agency's regulation in American Textile Manufacturers Inst. v. Donovan, 452 U.S. 490 (1981). This decision held that OSHA possessed authority to require any health protection "feasible" for industry and was not required to weigh the costs of a rule against its benefits before acting.

While OSHA has broad standard–setting authority, the task of establishing rules against all workplace hazards is beyond the capabilities of any agency. In recognition of this limit, Congress created a "general duty clause" in the Safety Act. This provision requires all employers to provide a place of employment free from recognized hazards of death or serious harm. As an example of the application of this clause, one employer was found in violation for permitting untrained employees to attempt electrical repairs on a wet floor without any protective equipment. OSHA's General Duty Clause does not apply when there is a specific safety standard covering the situation.

Beyond standards development, OSHA is also responsible for enforcing the Act, and considerable controversy has circulated around these enforcement powers. The agency's compliance officers make unannounced inspections. While search warrants are required for the inspections, they are liberally granted. When violations are found, OSHA may issue citations to an employer that include penalties of up to $1000 per violation. An employer may contest these penalties before a separate, independent organization known as the Occupational Safety and Health Review Commission.

Fair Labor Standards Act

The Fair Labor Standards Act (FLSA) was among the federal government's first employment law statutes. Passed in response to the Great Depression, the FLSA regulates the hours that employees may be required to work and the wages they must be paid. As was the case in the statutes discussed above, the coverage of the FLSA is extremely broad. An employer involved in any way in interstate commerce falls under the Act's purview. An exception is made for managerial and supervisory employees, as well as those employed in the professions, such as lawyers and accountants.

Among the most controversial provisions of FLSA immediately after its passage was the Act's prohibition of certain forms of child labor. Employees under 18 years of age are excluded from occupations designated as hazardous, such as mining, logging, and excavation work. Hours are strictly regulated for employees who are less than 16 years old.

The FLSA is also the source of the federal minimum wage and overtime requirements. Any work in excess of 40 hours per week must be paid at a "time–and–a–half" rate—50 percent greater than the employee's normal wage. If employees are not paid on an hourly basis, the FLSA requires at least as much compensation as a per hour minimum wage rate would require for the hours they actually worked. Employers must maintain complete employment and payroll records for review by the Department of Labor. Substantial penalties are imposed for violations. With the exception of the above provisions, the Act imposes no other requirements on the employment relationship, such as mandatory vacations or rest periods.

Employer's Right to Discharge Employees

An employer must have considerable freedom to discipline or fire employees in order to manage its work force effectively and efficiently. If an employer is unable to discharge disgruntled or shirking workers, we all pay. On the other hand, many feel that employees deserve protection from unjustified dismissals. (Incidentally, when we speak of an employee being fired or discharged, we are referring not only to actual firing but also to "constructive discharges," where the employer creates such an intolerable situation for the employee that he or she is forced to quit.)

An employee who has a legally enforceable employment contract obviously has whatever job security the contract specifies. Most employees, however, do not have such a contract. An employee who is covered by a labor–management collective bargaining agreement usually enjoys considerable protection from improper discharge. Most such contracts provide that employees can be fired or otherwise disciplined only for "good cause." Approximately 16% of the total public and private workforce is covered by collective bargaining agreements, but only about 10% of the private sector American work force is covered by such agreements. Public employees, i.e., those who work for a federal, state, or local government agency, also enjoy significant job security under federal and state "civil service" laws even when they are not unionized. In general, after a designated probationary period, these employees can be fired only for good cause and only after specified procedures have been followed. Public employees account for about 19% of the American work force. With regard to public employees at the state and local government level, the extent to which they are protected by civil service systems varies greatly from state to state. In general, more state and local government employees have civil service protection in the northeastern and upper mid–western U.S. where laws traditionally have been more favorable to employees in many ways than in other parts of the country.

Employment at Will

All other employees (over 70% of the work force) are covered by the so–called employment–at–will doctrine. This traditional common–law rule provides that, in the absence of a contract, either the employer or employee can terminate the relationship at any time, for any reason or no reason. In recent years, however, many people have come to view this rule as overly harsh toward employees and, consequently, a number of exceptions have been created.

Statutory Exceptions

A few federal and state statutes provide protection for employees in specific situations. For example, federal employment laws like Title VII, FLSA, and OSHA include provisions making it illegal for an employer to punish an employee for filing a complaint or cooperating with an investigation or proceeding under the particular law. In some states, employees are protected from being penalized for filing a workers' compensation claim or taking time off to serve on a jury. Also, several states now have statutes giving an employee a right to sue an employer for damages if the employer fired the employee for "whistle—blowing." Whistle—blowing occurs when a worker objects to or reports the employer's suspected illegal activities. Even if the employee turned out to be wrong, and the employer was not actually doing anything illegal, these statutes apply so long as the employee was sincere and had a solid factual basis for believing that illegal practices were occurring.

The Public Policy Exception

Although a number of statutes such as these have been enacted during recent times, the most important developments in the area have been judicial ones. On their own, the courts in a majority of states have carved out several important exceptions to employment at will. The most notable of these exceptions can be grouped together under the idea of "public policy." In other words, these courts have ruled that an employee should be able to recover damages for the tort of "wrongful discharge" (or "retaliatory discharge") when the employer's conduct is contrary to a clearly established public policy. The public policy exception to the employment—at—will doctrine has been recognized to varying degrees by the courts in 45 states. Defining public policy is not always an easy task, however. Most courts are fully aware that a vague, expansive public policy concept will provide very little guidance to employers or employees. Without reasonable guidance, employers will find it very difficult to maintain an effective personnel management system because of the fear that every discharge might lead to an expensive lawsuit.

As a result, most courts have concluded that the public policy claimed to have been violated by the employer must be clearly stated in a federal or state statute, or widely recognized and accepted judicial decision. In those states permitting an employee to assert a claim for wrongful discharge based on public policy, a fired employee is likely to have a good claim in the following situations:

1. The employer may not discharge a worker for refusing to commit an act that is illegal under a federal or state statute. For example, courts have found employers liable for firing employees who refused to participate in an illegal price—fixing scheme, commit perjury, mislabel food products, falsify a pollution control test, perform a medical procedure for which the nurse—employee was not licensed, or pump a ship's bilges containing sewage and toxic waste into the water. Most of these states also recognize the public policy exception when a company has fired an employee for refusing to commit a tort, such as refusing to sign a false defamatory statement about a co—worker.

2. Generally, an employee has a good wrongful discharge claim if he or she has been fired for exercising a statutory right. For example, an employer has been held liable for damages to an employee who was fired for exercising the right to sign a union authorization card. Similarly, employers have been held liable for discharging

employees because they filed workers' compensation claims or served on juries, even if there was no specific antiretaliation statute in that state covering the situation.

3. An employer often will be held liable to an employee who was fired for whistle blowing— objecting to or disclosing the employer's violations of the law, even if there is not a state statute providing protection to whistleblowers. The employee normally has a valid claim if he or she (a) acted in good faith and (b) had reasonable cause to believe that the employer was violating the law, even if later investigation reveals that the employer actually did not act illegally. On the question of whether an employee must first give company management an opportunity to correct the problem before complaining to the authorities, the courts are split. A majority of them, however, recognize the wrongful discharge claim regardless of where the employee first lodged an objection. Although most of the 45 states recognizing the public policy exception do so in the case of whistle blowing, not all of them do.

Courts usually have stressed that an employee is not protected from discharge just because he or she acted out of strong, and even admirable, convictions if a purely private matter is involved that does not affect the public interest. For example, one court concluded that there was no wrongful discharge claim where the employee was fired for refusing to follow a particular research program. As a matter of personal conscience, the employee felt that the research was not proper, but there was nothing illegal, immoral, or hazardous about it. Two Illinois cases also provide an illustrative contrast. In one, the court found that no violation of public policy had occurred when a company's chief financial officer was fired for a continuing disagreement with the company's president about accounting methods. There was no plausible claim that the president's methods were deceptive or violated securities or tax laws or generally accepted accounting principles. In the other case, the court held that the employee did have a claim for wrongful discharge where he had been fired for complaining about the company's use of accounting methods that substantially overstated income and assets in a way that very likely would violate tax laws and the disclosure provisions of federal securities laws.

The following case illustrates an unfortunate situation that led one state supreme court to consider and adopt the public policy exception to employment at will.

WAGENSELLER V. SCOTTSDALE MEMORIAL HOSPITAL
Arizona Supreme Court, 710 P.2d 1025 (1985)

Catherine Wagenseller worked as an emergency room nurse for the Scottsdale Memorial Hospital. She had originally been recruited personally by the emergency department's manager, Kay Smith, and for four years maintained superior work record and enjoyed excellent professional and personal relationships with Smith and others in the department. She was an "at will" employee, with no contractual or other job guarantees.

Wagenseller, Smith, and a group of others from the emergency department, as well as a number of employees from other area hospitals, went on an eight-day camping and rafting trip down the Colorado River. While on the trip, Wagenseller became very uncomfortable because of the behavior of Smith and a few others. This behavior included heavy drinking group nude bathing and other public nudity, and a lot of unnecessary closeness while rafting. In addition, Smith and others staged a parody of the song "Moon River," which ended with members of the group "mooning" the audience. Wagenseller declined to participate in any of these activities. Smith and others also performed the "Moon River" skit twice at the hospital after the group's return from the river, but Wagenseller declined to participate there as well.

After the trip, relations between Wagenseller and Smith deteriorated. Smith began harassing Wagenseller, using abusive language and embarrassing her in the presence of other staff. These problems continued, and Wagenseller was fired about five months after the camping trip. Wagenseller appealed her dismissal to the hospital's administrative and personnel department, but the dismissal was upheld. She then filed suit for damages against Smith, the hospital, and several of its personnel administrators. In the suit, she alleged that her termination violated public policy and therefore constituted the tort of wrongful discharge. Although Wagenseller's claims had been substantiated by the pretrial statements of several others, the trial court refused to recognize any exception to the employment-at-will doctrine and granted the defendants' motions for summary judgment. The appeals court reversed part of the judgment, but still did not grant Wagenseller the relief she sought, so she appealed to the Arizona Supreme Court.

Feldman, Justice:

...Under the traditional employment-at-will doctrine, an employee without an employment contract for a definite term can be fired for cause, without cause, or for "bad" cause... In recent years there has been apparent dissatisfaction with the absolutist formulation of the common law at-will rule... The trend has been to modify the at-will rule by creating exceptions to its operation... The most widely accepted approach is the "public policy" exception, which permits recovery upon a finding that the employer's conduct undermined some important public policy... A majority of the states have now either recognized a cause of action based on the public policy exception or have indicated their willingness to consider it, given appropriate facts. The key to an employee's claim in all of these cases is the proper definition of a public policy that has been violated by the employer's actions.

Before deciding whether to adopt the public policy exception, we first consider what kind of discharge would violate the rule. The majority of courts required, as a threshold showing, a "clear mandate" of public policy. The leading case recognizing a public policy exception to the at will doctrine is Palmateer v. International Harvester Co., 421 N.E.2d 876, 878 (Ill. 1981), which holds that an employee stated a cause of action for wrongful discharge when he claimed he was fired for supplying information to police investigating alleged criminal violations by a co-employee. Addressing the issue of what constitutes "clearly mandated public policy, the court stated:

There is no precise definition of the term. In general, it can be said that public policy concerns what is right and just and what affects the citizens of the State collectively. It is to be found in the State's constitution and statutes and, when they are silent, in its judicial decisions. Although there is no precise line of demarcation dividing matters that are the subject of public policies from matters purely personal, a survey of cases in other States involving retaliatory discharges shows that a matter must strike at the heart of a citizen's social rights, duties, and responsibilities before the tort will be allowed. . . .

It is difficult to justify this court's further adherence to a rule which permits an employer to fire someone for a cause that is morally wrong. . . Certainly, a court would be hard––pressed to find a rationale to hold that an employer could with impunity fire an employee who refused to commit perjury. . .. We therefore adopt the public policy exception to the at–will termination rule. We hold that an employer may fire for good cause or for no cause. He may not fire for bad cause—that which violates public policy. . .

In the case before us, Wagenseller refused to participate in activities which arguably would have violated our indecent exposure statute. This statute provides that a person commits indecent exposure by exposing certain described parts of the body when someone else is present and when the defendant is "reckless about whether such other person, as a reasonable person, would be offended or alarmed by the act." . . .While this statute may not embody a policy which "strikes at the heart of a citizen's social rights, duties, and responsibilities" as clearly and forcefully as some other statutes, such as a statute prohibiting perjury, we believe that it was enacted to preserve and protect the commonly recognized right of public privacy and decency. The law does, therefore, recognize bodily privacy as a "citizen's social right." . . .We are compelled to conclude that termination of employment for refusal to participate in the public exposure of one's buttocks is a termination contrary to the policy of this state. . .

[The trial court's action granting summary judgment against Wagenseller was in error. The decision is reversed and remanded to the trial court for a trial where Wagenseller will have a full opportunity to prove her allegations.]

Protection of Employee Privacy
Lie Detector Testing

Employers have extremely important interests in learning certain kinds of background information about people who are applying for jobs. Incompetent, dishonest, or violent employees can cause untold harm to an employer. A company may need to know about a job applicant's past work record, criminal record, and general character when legitimately attempting to protect itself against lawsuits and against a damaged reputation, as well as to protect its customers and its other employees from physical harm. Employers also have a valid interest in obtaining information from existing employees when theft or other wrongdoing has occurred at the workplace.

During the past several decades, more and more employers used the lie detector (polygraph) examination in an effort to get accurate information from employees and job applicants. Because of mounting evidence that these examinations are not very reliable, and that thousands of employees and applicants were being harmed each year by erroneous results, Congress passed the Employee Polygraph Protection Act of 1988. This law prohibits most uses of the polygraph by private employers, subject only to a few limited exceptions. The most important exception permits a private employer to require an employee to take a lie detector test as part of an ongoing investigation of theft, sabotage, or other property loss, if this employee had custody of the property and if there is other independent evidence creating a reasonable suspicion that this employee was involved in the incident. The law also does not prohibit federal, state, or local government agencies from requiring their employees and job applicants to take lie detector tests, mainly because the Constitution applies to government employers. The constitutional right of privacy protects against many unreasonable uses of the polygraph by government employers, but clearly does not protect employees to the extent that the federal polygraph statute does.

Employee Drug Testing

Employees who are impaired by drugs or alcohol endanger the public and their fellow workers, and cost their employers millions of dollars annually as a result of accidents, absenteeism, higher health insurance claims, low productivity, and poor workmanship. Employers have legitimate interests in minimizing these costs; maintaining a safe, secure, and productive workplace; and protecting themselves against liability to those injured by the actions of impaired employees. Both co—workers and members of the public have a legitimate claim to protection against the unsafe conduct or defective products resulting from employees' drug or alcohol use.

Employees subjected to drug testing, on the other hand, have important interests in preventing harm to their reputations and economic security resulting from inaccurate test results and avoiding unwarranted intrusions into their personal lives. Drug tests are not always accurate, and the analysis of urine, blood, or hair specimens often reveals a lot of private information about the subject that has nothing to do with the use of illicit drugs. It is certainly true that alcohol use causes the same kinds of workplace problems as drug use, but alcohol—impaired employees often can be identified more easily without the risk of erroneous test results or the disclosure of irrelevant private information that may be revealed in drug testing. Most of the difficult legal issues, therefore, have involved employers testing for controlled substances other than alcohol.

Most employers take some kind of action against an employee who refuses a test or who tests positive for illicit drugs. This action can range from required enrollment in a rehabilitation program to immediate discharge. Similarly, job applicants who refuse testing or test positive are virtually assured of not getting the job. As a result, legal action by employees challenging drug—testing programs is becoming increasingly common. The legal system has not yet had sufficient time, however, to develop a coherent, uniform set of principles to balance the various interests that are involved. Although the law pertaining to employee drug testing is still in a formative stage, it is possible to make some generalizations.

If the employer is a federal, state, or local government agency, the Constitution provides a measure of protection for the legitimate privacy interests of employees. The Constitution also applies if the government requires a private employer to do drug testing.

The most obviously applicable constitutional provision is the Fourth Amendment prohibition of unreasonable searches and seizures. The taking of a urine, blood, or hair specimen is a "search and seizure." Generally, people and their belongings can be searched only if there is "probable cause" to believe that they possess evidence of a violation of the law. In National Treasury Employees Union v. Von Raub, 109 S.Ct. 1384 (1989)(involving testing by a government agency), and Skinner v. Railway Labor Executives Ass'n, 109 S.Ct. 1402 (1989) (involving government–required testing by private employers), the U.S. Supreme Court held that drug testing sometimes is constitutionally permissible even without any evidence that a particular employee is a drug user. The Court said that, in the case of employees whose work creates significant safety, health, or security risks, testing may be done on a random or mass basis so long as the testing program is conducted in a reasonable manner overall. To be reasonable, the program must include ample safeguards to ensure accuracy and privacy.

The Constitution does not apply to drug testing by private employers unless the testing is required by the government. Tort law does apply, however, if an employer conducts a test or uses the results in such a way that a tort is committed. If the employer intentionally reveals private information from the test to others who have no legitimate interest in receiving it, the employer may be liable to the employee for the tort of invasion of privacy. If the test produces a false positive result, and the employer reveals it to others without a legitimate interest in knowing it, the employer may be liable for defamation. In some cases, carelessness in the administration of the test or use of the results may cause the employer to be liable for the tort of negligence.

A few states have passed statutes specifically regulating the design and implementation of drug testing programs by private employers. The objective of these statutes is to increase the likelihood that results will be accurate and that employee privacy will be protected to the fullest extent possible.

In the case of unionized workers, the implementation of a drug testing program is a so called "mandatory subject of collective bargaining." This means that the employer cannot make such a decision on its own, but must submit the question to the process of collective bargaining with the union. If the company and the union cannot agree, either or both may use economic weapons such as lockouts or strikes to put pressure on the other side.

In April 2001, the EEOC successfully settled a case charging an employer with violating the Americans with Disabilities Act (ADA) by its practice of genetically testing its employees. In addition, more than 25 states have banned genetic testing in the workplace.

CHAPTER 30

ENVIRONMENT PROTECTION LAW

- Common Law and Pollution
- National Environmental Policy Act
- Water Pollution Control
- Air Pollution Control
- Solid Waste and Its Disposal
- Regulation of Toxic Substances
- Noise Pollution
- Indoor Pollution
- Endangered Species
- The Environment, Industry, and Society

CONCERN FOR THE environment is growing both domestically and internationally. As Americans have gradually become more aware of the adverse impact that human consumption of resources and human technology can have on the land, sea, and air, their support for more comprehensive governmental regulation of environmental matters has grown. Well—known incidents such as the accident at the Three Mile Island nuclear facility; the contamination by dioxins of Times Beach, Missouri; the indiscriminate dumping of hazardous wastes in Love Canal, New York; and the Alaskan oil spill caused by the Exxon *Valdez* have intensified public concern. Problems such as acid rain often create concerns that transcend national boundaries. And the phenomenon of global warming is quickly becoming a matter of major concern to people around the world.

In recent years these concerns have led to a strengthening of state and local regulation of pollution, to the creation of a mammoth array of federal pollution regulations, and to some initial efforts at international cooperation in pollution control. For businesses, these rules and regulations are decidedly a mixed blessing. On the one hand, the owners, officers, and employees of businesses are individuals who need a clean, safe environment for themselves and their employees as much as anyone else. On the other hand, many of these laws impose additional burdens on what many consider to be an already overregulated economy.

The Environmental Protection Agency (EPA) is the largest nonmilitary federal agency, and its thousands of rules and regulations have become a part of the legal environment of business with which companies must become familiar. Many small firms have gone out of business because they could not meet various antipollution requirements imposed by the EPA. Others, both large and small, have found that compliance has become an extremely costly budget item. As we shall see in this chapter, two obvious manifestations of the heightened level of environmental regulation lie in (1) the increasing use of *criminal* sanctions against environmental offenders and (2) regulations that require persons who did not actually pollute to pay for the cleanup of pollution caused by others (for example, landowners may be liable for millions of dollars to clean up pollution caused entirely by previous owners of the land).

Nothing could be more important than the saving of our planet's environment. However, the many governmental regulations outlined in this chapter place a tremendous burden on industry, much of which is passed on to the consuming public. During the coming years there will be continuing debate as to the proper balancing of environmental versus economic interests both domestically and internationally. However, there is no doubt that environmental regulation will continue to be a consideration of enormous importance in most domestic and multinational businesses. Modern managers must view the environment and its legal regulation as a challenge, as an opportunity, and as a factor that must be continuously considered as decisions are made. New rules and regulations will create costs that must be managed. They will terminate some lines of business but open up other opportunities.

In this chapter we examine several of the known causes of pollution and the major remedial measures designed to prevent further deterioration of the environment. We also briefly address the matter of *indoor* air pollution. And we will explore the fledgling international efforts to preserve the global environment by multinational cooperation. Initially, however, we will look at common–law remedies that have long been available at the state level to remedy certain types of pollution.

Common Law and Pollution

Common law remedies founded on the law of torts are totally inadequate to provide a comprehensive method of regulating air, land, and water pollution in the United States. However, as a remedial or loss–shifting device, common law torts may be useful to individual plaintiffs who may have suffered some environmental harm. A farmer's water supply may be contaminated by industrial discharge of pollutants into a stream. Homeowners near a sanitary landfill may be exposed to noxious fumes from the constant trash fires used by the landfill to dispose of burnable refuse. Or homeowners may suffer property damage when caustic fumes from a chemical plant blanket their property, killing vegetation and causing housepaint to peel and crack. In each case the individual plaintiff may seek injunctions to prohibit further damage from the pollutants and, in appropriate cases, recover money damages. The common–law tort remedies available include nuisance, negligence, trespass, and strict liability.

Nuisance

When property is used in such a manner that it inflicts harm on others, there may be a cause of action in tort for nuisance against the owner. If the harm is widespread, affecting the common rights of a substantial segment of a community, it is considered a public nuisance. Because fishing rights belong to the public, a discharge of pollutants into a navigable stream that killed fish would be a public nuisance. If an individual's right to quiet enjoyment of his or her land is disturbed by unreasonable and unwarranted use of property by another property owner, a private nuisance has occurred. Most public nuisances are abated through action by public officials charged with controlling the facility that is causing the harm. An action to abate a private nuisance is usually brought by the party affected against the party whose conduct gives rise to the nuisance.

In the case of either public or private nuisances, courts are often called on to balance the interests of plaintiffs and defendants. No court would eagerly close an offending industrial plant that employs an entire community. Similarly, residents near a large airport may be expected to endure some inconvenience caused by noise and vibration. A homeowner who buys near an existing airport or industrial facility may not find the courts sympathetic when a complaint is registered, but this is not invariably the case. To balance the interests of the community properly courts often cannot simply rule in favor of the party who arrived first.

For example, in Spur Industries, Inc. v. Del E. Webb Development Co., 494 P.2d 700 (Ariz. 1972), a major developer bought 20,000 acres of farm land near Phoenix to develop Sun City, a retirement village. Nearby were cattle feedlots, later purchased and expanded by Spur Industries. As the developer completed houses and Spur expanded, only 500 feet separated the two operations. Prevailing winds blew flies and odors from the cattle pens over the homesites, thus making it difficult to sell the sites most affected. The developer filed a nuisance suit against Spur, asking that Spur be enjoined from operating its cattle feedlots in the vicinity of the housing development. In an attempt to balance the parties' competing interests reasonably, the court permanently enjoined Spur from operating the feedlots but further held that Spur should be awarded damages, a reasonable amount of the cost of moving or shutting down, because the developer had brought people to the nuisance, thus causing Spur damage.

Negligence, Trespass, and Strict Liability

The tort of negligence involves the breach by the defendant of a duty owed to the plaintiff to use reasonable care to avoid injury to the plaintiff's person or property. If the operator of a plant negligently maintained its equipment so that harmful pollutants were discharged into a waterway, neighbors injured by the pollution would probably have a valid negligence claim against the careless plant operator.

An intentional entering onto another's land without permission is a trespass. So too, causing particles to be borne onto another's land may be a trespass if the owner of the source of the particles has reason to believe that the activity would cause damaging deposits. For example, a physical and obvious trespass occurs when cement dust from a plant is deposited, layer on layer, on the property of nearby residents. Of course, if the particles deposited are undetectable by human senses and not harmful to health, although undeniably real, a court, in balancing the interests of society, will likely dismiss any trespass action.

In certain cases in which the threat or damage is caused by abnormally or inherently dangerous activities, the theory of strict liability may be used to recover damages or to halt the activity. The spraying of crops with toxic chemicals and the storage of explosive or other hazardous materials are examples of activities that may result in a defendant being held strictly liable. In such cases, a defendant's reasonable care is no defense. The inherent danger of the activity and resulting damages are sufficient to justify the plaintiff's recovery.

Although much attention is focused on the federal regulations that we are about to discuss, the role of these state common law causes of action must not be overlooked. Even in situations addressed by federal laws, they provide a tremendously important supplement. For example, litigation over the costs of cleaning up hazardous waste sites is usually based on the federal "Superfund" statute to be discussed later. However, the New Jersey Supreme Court, for example, has ruled that a company that pollutes a property can be held strictly liable for cleanup and other costs, giving an important remedy to the purchasers of such sites. T&E Indus. v. Safety Light Corp., 587 A.2d 1249 (N.J. 1991).

These common law theories are of ancient origin but have been adapted to the environmental context in "toxic tort" litigation in recent years. In addressing the enhanced risk doctrine and the medical monitoring doctrine, the following case illustrates the modern evolution of the doctrine of negligence made necessary by the peculiar problems caused by exposure to environmental hazards.

IN RE PAOLI RAILROAD YARD PCB LITIGATION
U.S. Court of Appeals, Third Circuit,
916 F.2d 829 (1990)

The plaintiffs are 38 persons who have either worked in or lived adjacent to the Paoli railyard, an electric railcar maintenance facility in Philadelphia. Their primary claim is that they have contracted a variety of illnesses as the result of exposure to polychlorinated biphenyls (PCBs). PCBs are toxic substances that, as the result of decades of PCB use in the Paoli railcar transformers, can be found in extremely high concentration at the railyard and in the surrounding air and soil. Defendants include Monsanto (maker of PCBs), General Electric (maker of transformers), Amtrak (owner of the site since 1976), and Conrail (operator of the site).

The district court excluded much of the plaintiffs' proffered testimony and thereafter granted summary judgment to the defendants. The trial court also rejected as a matter of law the plaintiffs' claim based on the medical monitoring doctrine. The plaintiffs appealed.

Becker, Circuit Judge:

[The court held that the trial judge had improperly excluded plaintiffs' expert testimony and therefore concluded that summary judgment had been inappropriately granted. In the following excerpt, the court addressed the plaintiffs' medical monitoring theory.]

We turn ... to the viability of certain plaintiffs' "medical monitoring" claims by which plaintiffs sought to recover the costs of periodic medical examinations that they contend are medically necessary to protect against the exacerbation of latent diseases brought about by exposure to PCBs. [Pennsylvania state courts have not] decided whether a demonstrated need for medical monitoring creates a valid cause of action.

Therefore, sitting in diversity, we must predict whether the Pennsylvania Supreme Court would recognize a claim for medical monitoring under the substantive law of Pennsylvania and, if so, what its elements are.

Medical monitoring is one of a growing number of non–traditional torts that have developed in the common law to compensate plaintiffs who have been exposed to various toxic substances. Often, the diseases or injuries caused by this exposure are latent. This latency leads to problems when the claims are analyzed under traditional common law tort doctrine because, traditionally, injury needed to be manifest before it could be compensable.

Nonetheless, in an effort to accommodate a society with an increasing awareness of the danger and potential injury caused by the widespread use of toxic substances, courts have begun to recognize claims like medical monitoring, which can allow plaintiffs some relief even absent present manifestations of physical injury. More specifically, in the toxic tort context, courts have allowed plaintiffs to recover for emotional distress suffered because of the fear of contracting a toxic exposure disease, the increased risk of future harm, and the reasonable costs of medical monitoring or surveillance. ...

It is easy to confuse the distinctions between these various non–traditional torts. However, the torts just mentioned involve fundamentally different kinds of injury and compensation. Thus, an action for medical monitoring seeks to recover only the quantifiable costs of periodic medical examinations necessary to detect the onset of physical harm, whereas an enhanced risk claim seeks compensation for the anticipated harm itself, proportionately reduced to reflect the chance that it will not occur. We think that this distinction is particularly important because . . . in Martin v. Johns–Manville Corp., 494 A.2d 1088 (Pa. 1985), the [Pennsylvania Supreme Court] made clear that a plaintiff in an enhanced risk suit must prove that future consequences of an injury are reasonably probable, not just possible.

Martin does not lead us to believe that Pennsylvania would not recognize a claim for medical monitoring, however. First, the injury that the court was worried about finding with reasonable probability in Martin is different from the injury involved here. The injury in an enhanced risk claim is the anticipated harm itself. The injury in a medical monitoring claim is the cost of the medical care that will, one hopes, detect that injury. The former is inherently speculative because courts are forced to anticipate the probability of future injury. The latter is much less speculative because the issue for the jury is the less conjectural question of whether the plaintiff needs medical surveillance. Second, the Pennsylvania Supreme Court's concerns about the degree of certainty required can easily be accommodated by requiring that a jury be able reasonably to determine that medical monitoring is probably, not just possibly, necessary.

[We predict] that the Supreme Court of Pennsylvania would recognize a cause of action for medical monitoring established by proving that:

Plaintiff was significantly exposed to a proven hazardous substance through the negligent actions of the defendant.

As a proximate result of exposure, plaintiff suffers a significantly increased risk of contracting a serious latent disease.

That increased risk makes periodic diagnostic medical examinations reasonably necessary.

Monitoring and testing procedures exist which make the early detection and treatment of the disease possible and beneficial.

. . . The policy reasons for recognizing this tort are obvious. Medical monitoring claims acknowledge that, in a toxic age significant harm can be done to an individual by a tortfeasor, notwithstanding latent manifestation of that harm. Moreover, as we have explained, recognizing this tort does not require courts to speculate about the probability of future injury. It merely requires courts to ascertain the probability that the far less costly remedy of medical supervision is appropriate. Allowing plaintiffs to recover the cost of this care deters irresponsible discharge of toxic chemicals by defendants and encourages plaintiffs to detect and treat their injuries as soon as possible. These are conventional goals of the tort system as it has long existed in Pennsylvania. [Reversed.]

Note: This court guessed wrong. Pennsylvania's highest court later rejected medical monitoring. Nonetheless, the approach taken in *Paoli* is popular elsewhere.

Regulation By State Legislatures

In addition to the common–law role played by the courts, all state governments (and many subordinate governmental units) have passed laws dealing with the quality of the environment. These laws deal with all types of pollution—water, air, solid waste, noise, and others. Often state laws are patterned after federal laws. For example, several states have "mini–Superfunds" for hazardous waste site cleanup patterned after the federal Superfund law discussed later in this chapter. One popular type of state statute is the "bottle bill," designed to regulate the dumping of cans and bottles. Additionally, many federal laws presently provide a substantial state role in the establishing and enforcing of pollution standards.

National Environmental Policy Act

Although all states and many localities have significant environmental rules and regulations, federal regulations clearly dominate the regulatory landscape. Recognizing that a national environmental policy was needed, Congress enacted the National Environmental Policy Act (NEPA) in 1969 to "encourage productive and enjoyable harmony between man and his environment and biosphere and stimulate the health and welfare of man; to enrich the understanding of the ecological systems and natural resources important to the Nation; and to establish a Council on Environmental Quality." NEPA is a major step toward making each generation responsible to succeeding ones for the quality of the environment.

Environmental Impact Statements

NEPA requires that an environmental impact statement (EIS) be prepared by the appropriate agency whenever proposed major federal action will significantly affect the quality of the human environment. This requirement affects private enterprise as well because an EIS will be required if federal funds have been committed to a particular private venture. For example, a contractor building a federal highway or a naval base may have to help provide a detailed statement describing the environmental impact of the proposed action, unavoidable adverse effects, acceptable alternatives to the proposed project, and any irreversible and irretrievable commitments of resources involved.

Preparation of an EIS can be a costly and time–consuming task, even though regulations now limit the length to 150 pages (except in unusual circumstances.) NEPA requires that the statement be clear, to the point, and in simple English. It also requires that all key points and conclusions be set forth in a summary of no more than 15 pages. No matter how well prepared, an EIS is merely a prediction as to future environmental consequences of a proposed federal action. The proposed agency action, evaluated in light of the EIS, can be successfully challenged in court only if it can be shown to be "arbitrary and capricious."

Litigation over EISs often substantially delays and increases the costs of federal projects. Although very few federal projects have ever been halted by court actions based on NEPA, it is likely that many environmentally unsound projects have been abandoned or never begun because of EIS requirements. The EIS requirement remains controversial because it is impossible to quantify whether the environmental benefits of this process outweigh the additional time and expense incurred.

Environmental Protection Agency

In 1970 the EPA was created, consolidating into one agency the power to regulate various aspects of the environment that previously had been scattered across several federal agencies and departments. The EPA establishes and enforces environmental protection standards, conducts research on pollution, provides assistance to state and local antipollution programs through grants and technical advice, and generally assists the Council on Environmental Quality (CEQ). The CEQ was established to facilitate implementation of NEPA by issuing guidelines for the preparation of impact statements and generally to assist and advise the President on environmental matters. In its guidelines, CEQ has required that EISs be prepared as early in the decision-making process as possible and that other agencies and the public be given a chance to comment and criticize before any final decision is made to go ahead with major federal action.

Consolidation of diverse functions under the EPA has provided a center of control for the continuing war on pollution. How it works can be illustrated by studying the major areas of concern.

Water Pollution Control

As in other areas of environmental concern, federal regulation of water pollution is based on a series of measures passed over the years. For example, the Rivers and Harbors Act of 1890 prohibited the dumping of refuse into all navigable waters, and the 1899 Rivers and Harbors Appropriations Act made it unlawful for ships and manufacturing establishments to discharge refuse into any navigable waterway of the United States or into any tributary of a navigable waterway. Efforts to clean up the nation's waterways began in earnest with passage of the Federal Water Pollution Control Act in 1948, which has been repeatedly amended over the years.

Clean Water Act

The Clean Water Act (passed in 1971 and subsequently amended) is the major federal law governing water pollution. It provided a comprehensive plan to eliminate water pollution, setting standards and guidelines on an industry-by-industry basis for controlling water pollution from industrial sources. The types of discharges with which the law is concerned are as varied as the industries to be controlled. Thermal pollution from heat-generating plants and particulates and toxic wastes from manufacturing activities are subject to regulation and continual monitoring to assure that prescribed standards are being met. In general, industry is expected to control and eliminate its discharge of pollutants as soon as possible through the "best available technology (BAT) economically achievable."

The law placed primary responsibility on the states but provided for federal aid to local governments and small businesses to help them in their efforts to comply with the law's requirements. It also provided a licensing and permit system, at both state and federal levels, for discharging into waterways and a more workable enforcement program.

Citizen Suits

The Clean Water Act also allows citizens or organizations whose interests are affected by water pollution to sue violators of standards established under the law. Similar provisions are contained in several other environmental laws. The following case addresses a major issue raised by these "citizen suit" provisions. The factual summary sheds additional light on the working mechanism of the Clean Water Act.

FRIENDS OF THE EARTH, INC. v. LAIDLAW ENVIRONMENTAL SERVICES
U.S. Supreme Court, 528 U.S. 167 (2000)

In the Clean Water Act, Congress authorized citizen–suits initiated by "a person or persons having an interest which is or may be adversely affected." Judges may order injunctive relief or civil penalties payable to the U.S. Treasury. In 1986, defendant–respondent Laidlaw Environmental Services (TOC), Inc. bought a hazardous waste incinerator in South Carolina that included a wastewater treatment plant. Shortly thereafter, the South Carolina Department of Health and Environmental Control (DHEC) granted Laidlaw a National Pollutant Discharge Elimination System (NPDES) permit placing certain limitations on Laidlaw's discharges into the North Tyger River. Between 1989 and 1995, Laidlaw exceeded the limit on mercury discharges 489 times.

On April 10, 1992, plaintiff–petitioners, environmental groups collectively referred to as Friends of the Earth (FOE) sent a letter notifying Laidlaw of their intention to file a citizen suit against it within 60 days. Laidlaw then asked DHEC to file suit against it, hoping to bar FOE's suit. DHEC agreed. Laidlaw drafted DHEC's complaint and paid its filing

fee. On the last day before FOE's 60 day notice period expired, DHEC and Laidlaw reached a settlement requiring Laidlaw to pay $100,000 in civil penalties and to make "every effort" to comply with permit obligations.

On June 2, 1992, FOE filed this suit. Laidlaw moved to dismiss. On January 22, 1997, the trial court found that Laidlaw had violated its NPDES license 23 times after FOE had filed suit, but that the last reported mercury discharge violation occurred in 1995, after suit was filed but before well before judgment was issued. The court found that Laidlaw had gained an economic benefit of over a million dollars as a result of its extended period of noncompliance with the mercury discharge limit, but concluded that a $400,000 fine was sufficient. The court refused FOE's request for injunctive relief stating that an injunction was inappropriate because "Laidlaw has been in substantial compliance with all parameters in its NPDES permit since at least August 1992."

Both parties appealed. The Fourth Circuit held that the matter had become moot because the only remedy available to FOE (civil penalties payable to the government) would not redress any injury FOE had suffered. Therefore, the Court ordered dismissal of the suit and held that FOE's failure to gain a remedy on the merits precluded its recovery of attorney's fees. FOE appealed to the Supreme Court. Thereafter, Laidlaw permanently closed the offending plant.

Justice Ginsburg:

We reverse the judgment of the Court of Appeals. The appellate court erred in concluding that a citizen suitor's claim for civil penalties must be dismissed as moot when the defendant, albeit after commencement of the litigation, has come into compliance. A defendant's voluntary cessation of allegedly unlawful conduct ordinarily does not suffice to moot a cause. The Court of Appeals also misperceived the remedial potential of civil penalties. Such penalties may serve, as an alternative to an injunction, to deter future violations and thereby redress the injuries that prompted a citizen suitor to commence litigation.

[Regarding standing to sue, the Court first cited precedents indicating that citizen suitors lack standing to sue if the violator comes into compliance within the 60–day notice period required for the filing of such suits or where the EPA or a State agency has already commenced and is "diligently prosecuting" an enforcement action. The trial court found no diligent prosecution here.]

The relevant showing for purposes of Article III standing is not injury to the environment but injury to plaintiff. The District Court found that FOE had demonstrated sufficient injury to establish standing. For example, FOE member Kenneth LeeCurtis averred in affidavits that he lived a half–mile from Laidlaw's facility; that he occasionally drove over the North Tyger River, and that it looked and smelled polluted; and that he would like to fish, camp, swim, and picnic in and near the river between 3 and 15 miles downstream from the facility, as he did when he was a teenager, but would not do so because he was concerned that the water was polluted by Laidlaw's discharges. Other members presented evidence to similar effect.

Laidlaw argues next that even if FOE had standing to seek injunctive relief, it lacked standing to seek civil penalties. Civil penalties offer no redress to private plaintiffs, Laidlaw argues, because they are paid to the government, and therefore a citizen plaintiff can never have standing to seek them. Laidlaw is wrong to maintain that citizen plaintiffs facing ongoing violations never have standing to seek civil penalties.

Congress has found that civil penalties in Clean Water Act cases do more than promote immediate compliance by limiting the defendant's economic incentive to delay its attainment of permit limits; they also deter future violations. To the extent they encourage defendants to discontinue current violations and deter them from committing future ones, they afford redress to citizen plaintiffs who are injured or threatened with injury as a consequence of ongoing lawful conduct.

[Regarding the mootness issue, the] only conceivable basis for a finding of mootness in this case is Laidlaw's voluntary conduct—either its achievement by August 1992 of substantial compliance with its NPDES permit or its more recent shutdown of the facility. It is well settled that "a defendant's voluntary cessation of a challenged practice does not deprive a federal court of its power to determine the legality of the practice." City of Mesquite v. Aladdin's Castle, Inc., 455 U.S. 283. "If it did, the courts would be compelled to leave 'the defendant free to return to his old ways.'" City of Mesquite, citing U.S. v. W.T.Grant Co., 345 U.S. 629.

REVERSED.

Note: Groups as the National Resources Defense Fund, the Sierra Club Legal Defense Fund, and the Friends of the Earth often file notices of intent to sue under the Clean Water Act. Only a tiny percentage of such suits are preempted by governmental enforcement action, and most lead to negotiations and court–approved settlements and consent decrees. Such citizen suits have become quite controversial. Supporters believe that they are a beneficial supplement to actions brought by overworked agencies such as the EPA and its state counterparts. Critics believe that the suits have become so numerous (and arguably driven by provisions allowing for recovery of attorneys' fees) that they do not bring about cost–effective results and subvert consistency and fairness in national enforcement. The Supreme Court's decision to deny the right to sue to environmental groups in Lujan v. Defenders of Wildlife,, 504 U.S.555 (1992) , a citizens' suit brought under the Endangered Species Act, reflects a hostility to such suits that may foreshadow future imposition of restrictive procedural requirements.

Water Quality Act of 1987

In the Water Quality Act of 1987, Congress amended the Clean Water Act by emphasizing a state–federal program to control non–point source pollution. Whereas point sources such as municipal or industrial discharge pipes account for much water pollution, Congress determined that non–point source pollution such as oil and grease run-off from city streets, pesticide runoff from farmland, and runoff from mining areas must be addressed. The states were charged with developing programs to improve water quality by combating this pollution, which is so difficult to track.

The 1987 Act also clamped down on toxic water pollution and empowered the EPA to assess administrative penalties for water pollution. The penalties were placed on a sliding scale. For more serious offenses (considering the nature, circumstances, extent, and gravity of the violation, and the violator's ability to pay, history of violations, degree of culpability, and savings resulting from the violation), the EPA must provide relatively formal hearings but can assess larger penalties. Smaller penalties are assessed for minor violations after less formal procedures.

Responding to concerns about abuses of citizen suits, the 1987 Act also gave the EPA more supervision of settlement agreements in such cases, and a greater ability to preclude such suits administratively.

Oil Spills

All too frequently, vessels from small coastal barges to huge supertankers accidentally discharge their cargos into the sea near the coast. The ecologic effect on fish, shellfish, and waterfowl and on the public and private shorelines and beaches may be immense. Consequently, the Clean Water Act imposes severe sanctions on those responsible for such pollution. The owner or operator of a grounded oil–carrying vessel can be liable for up to $250,000 of the cost of cleaning up its spilled oil; if the oil spill is the result of willful negligence or misconduct, the owner or operator of the vessel can be held liable to the U.S. government for the full cost of cleaning up the shore. Operators of onshore and offshore facilities are also held liable for spillage and pollution, under ordinary conditions, to the extent of $50 million and, where willful negligence and misconduct are involved, to the full extent of the cost of cleanup and removal, including the restoration or replacement of natural resources damaged or destroyed by the discharge of oil or hazardous substances.

After the Exxon Valdez oil spill in Alaska, Exxon was charged with a variety of criminal offenses and sued by all manner of private and governmental officials. A wide variety of laws and regulations dealing with water pollution and wildlife were allegedly violated. Exxon settled state and federal litigation by agreeing to pay $900 million over 11 years (in civil penalties), plus $100 million for restoration of the injured area to be split between the United States and Alaska and $25 million in criminal fines. The settlement did not affect about $59 billion in private civil suits then pending against Exxon.

Additional Regulations

Of related concern are the Marine Protection, Research, and Sanctuaries Act, which regulates the discharge and introduction of pollutants into coastal waterways and marine areas, and the Safe Drinking Water Act of 1974, which gave the states primary responsibility for enforcing national standards for drinking water. Under the act, the EPA has set maximum drinking water contaminant levels of certain chemicals, pesticides, and microbiologic pollutants.

Air Pollution Control
Clean Air Act

The Clean Air Act of 1970 empowered the EPA to set standards to attain certain primary ambient (outside) air quality standards designed by Congress to protect public health. Because achieving the standards is costly, the EPA's role is to balance the economic, technological, and social factors that must be considered in attaining the clean air goals that have been set.

Several programs formed the essential elements of the Clean Air Act. Foremost was the setting of primary (health) and secondary (welfare) ambient air quality standards. Because the Clean Air Act's approach involved a federal–state partnership, another program required the states to draft State Implementation Plans (SIPs) for achieving ambient air quality standards. When approved by the EPA, such plans permitted the states to enforce air quality standards within their borders. Operators of air pollution sources could be required to monitor, sample, and keep appropriate records, all of which were subject to on–premises inspection by the EPA. When a proper SIP was not prepared, the burden fell to the EPA to adopt a Federal Implementation Plan (FIP).

To reduce emissions in accordance with prescribed schedules, the Act also set new source performance standards (NSPSs)—emission standards for various categories of large industrial facilities. Major polluters must use the best acceptable control devices, those with proven capabilities to reduce emissions. To ease the burden on industry, the EPA adopted the bubble concept, under which a large plant with multiple emission points (stacks) does not have to meet standards for each one. The plant instead is under a "bubble" with a single allowable emission level. Plant management can manage each point source within the bubble to meet the sum total of emission limits by the most economical means.

Finally, the Act addressed automobile pollution by developing emission standards and fuel additive regulations. Use of unleaded gasoline and catalytic converters has resulted in substantial progress. However, industry continues to complain that the standards are too burdensome, and environmentalists still claim that the rules are too lax and are ineffectually enforced.

1990 Amendments

Although measurable progress was made in many areas pursuant to the 1970 Clean Air Act, it is undeniable that serious air pollution problems remain. Therefore, in 1990, Congress enacted significant amendments to the Act. With predicted costs for implementation between $20 billion and $100 billion annually, the 1990 amendments emphasized four critical areas.

First, the amendments addressed ozone, carbon monoxide, and particulate matter—where there had been significant failures to attain established standards. For example, the amendments established five categories for ozone nonattainment, ranging from marginal to extreme, with attainment deadlines stretching from 1993 to 2010, and increasingly stringent control requirements tied to the degree of nonattainment.

A second key area is air toxics. A list of 139 hazardous substances or groups of substances was added to a previous list of eight air pollutants. The EPA is to target categories of major sources of such pollutants. For each source, the EPA is required to establish emission control standards based on maximum achievable control technology (MACT).

The third major area is acid rain. With a phased– in timetable, the amendments required a major reduction in emissions of sulfur dioxide by electric utility steam generating units. by 10 million tons from 1980 levels.

Fourth, in addressing automobile pollution, the law set emission standards that might add as much as $500 to the cost of a new car. Among other provisions, the 1990 amendments prohibited the sale of leaded gasoline for highway use after December 31, 1995, and prohibited the manufacture of an engine that requires leaded gasoline after 1992.

The amendments created increased expenses and record–keeping for giant corporations and many small businesses as well. As many as 50,000 points of pollution may be required to obtain permits under the amendments. Those who fail to comply face the stiffest penalties yet. For example, previously violations were generally misdemeanors, but now they are felonies with criminal penalties that may run up to $1 million per violation. Additionally, the EPA Administrator may assess civil administrative penalties up to $25,000 a day per violation, and the role of litigation by citizens and private organizations in the enforcement process has been expanded. For example in Gwaltney of Smithfield Ltd. v. Chesapeake Bay Foundation, 484 U.S. 49 (1987) , the Supreme Court held that citizens could sue only for ongoing violations of the Clean Water Act, a holding applied to the Clean Air Act as well. The 1990 amendments specifically permit citizens to file complaints over past violations that have been repeated.

Another form of citizen input comes in the permit process. All large pollution sources (except vehicles) must obtain permits from state pollution authorities specifying that their emissions do not violate Clean Air Act limits. Those permits are subject to EPA review, and if the EPA does not object to a permit, citizens may petition the agency to do so and may comment on permits and request public hearings during the approval process. Tens of thousands of facilities are covered by the permit program.

Proponents stress that the long–term benefits to the environment and public health may well outweigh the burdens that the act places on industry and on consumers who purchase products.

The 1990 Amendments are viewed as having been substantially successful, because American power plants have significantly reduced their output of sulfur dioxide under the EPA's Acid Rain Guidelines established by the Amendments.

In the area of air pollution, as well as most others, major environmental programs have been established in a sequential fashion. That is, instead of having a master comprehensive plan, major initiatives have been amended and then amended again to address new problems or old problems that have proved to be intractable. The following case involves a significant recent challenge by industry to the EPA's powers.

WHITMAN V. AMERICAN TRUCKING ASSOCIATIONS
U.S. Supreme Court, 531 U.S. 457 (2001)

Section 109(a) of the Clean Air Act (CAA) requires the EPA to promulgate national ambient air quality standards (NAAQS) for each air pollutant for which "air quality criteria" have been issued under Sec. 108. In 1997, the EPA's administrator (defendant and petitioner) pursuant to CAA Sec. 109(b)(1) revised the ozone and particular NAAQS. Plaintiff–respondents, including the American Trucking Association, challenged the revised NAAQS in the District of Columbia Court of Appeals on several grounds. The Court of

Appeals found, in part, (a) that compliance costs should not be considered in establishing the NAAQS, and (b) that the CAA included an unconstitutional delegation of legislative power to the EPA. The EPA appealed to the Supreme Court regarding the second holding and respondents appealed regarding the first..

Scalia, Justice:

Costs of implementation.

Section 109(a) of the CAA requires the Administrator of the EPA to promulgate NAAQS for each air pollutant for which "air quality criteria" have been issued under §108. Once a NAAQS has been promulgated, the Administrator must review the standard (and the criteria on which it is based) "at five-year intervals" and make "such revisions . . . as may be appropriate. These cases arose when, on July 18, 1997, the Administrator reviewed the NAAQS for particular matter (PM) and ozone.

In Lead Industries Assn., Inc. v. EPA, 647 F.2d 1027(D.C.Cir. 1980), the District of Columbia Circuit held that "economic considerations [may] play no part in the promulgation of ambient air quality standards under Section 109" of the CAA. [The lower court followed that rule in this case.] Respondents argue that this decision is incorrect. We disagree.

Section 109(b)(1) instructs the EPA to set primary ambient air quality standards "the attainment and maintenance of which . . . are requisite to protect the public health" with "an adequate margin of safety." Were it not for the hundreds of pages of briefing respondents have submitted on the issue, one would have thought it fairly clear that this text does not permit the EPA to consider costs in setting the standards. The language, as one scholar has noted, "is absolute." D. Currie, Air Pollution: Federal Law and Analysis 415(1981). The EPA, "based on" the information about health effects contained in the technical "criteria" documents complied under § 108(a)(2), is to identify the maximum airborne concentration of a pollutant that the public health can tolerate, decrease the concentration to provide an "adequate" margin of safety and set the standard at that level. Nowhere are costs of achieving such a standard made part of that initial calculation.

Against this most natural of readings, respondents make a lengthy, spirited, but ultimately unsuccessful attack. Respondents argue that many more factors than air pollution affect public health. In particular, the economic cost of implementing a very stringent standard might produce health losses sufficient to offset the health gains in cleaning the air—for example, by closing down whole industries and thereby impoverishing the workers and consumers dependent on those industries. That is unquestionably true, and Congress was unquestionably aware of it. [The 1970 Congress commissioned a study on this very issue and] armed with the results of this study, not only anticipated that compliance costs could injure the public health, but provided for that precise exigency. Section 110(f)(1) of the CAA permitted the Administrator to waive the compliance deadline for stationary sources if, inter alia, sufficient control measures were simply unavailable and "the continued operation of such sources is essential . . . to the public health or welfare." [Many provisions of the CAA expressly direct the Administrator to consider the cost of compliance.] We have therefore refused to find implicit in ambiguous sections of the CAA an authorization to consider costs that has elsewhere, and so often, been expressly granted.

Accordingly, to prevail in their present challenge, respondents must show a textual commitment of authority to the EPA to consider costs in setting NAAQS under § 109(b)(1). And because § 109(b)(1) and the NAAQS for which it provides are the engine that drives nearly all of Title I of the CAA, that textual commitment must be a clear one. Congress, we have held, does not alter the fundamental details of a regulatory scheme in vague terms or ancillary provisions—it does not, one might say, hide elephants in mouse holes.

Respondents first claim is that § 109(b)(1)'s terms "adequate margin" and "requisite" leave room to pad health effects with cost concerns. We find it implausible that Congress would give to the EPA through these modest words the power to determine whether implementation costs should moderate national air quality standards.

The same defect inheres in respondents' next two arguments: that while the Administrator's judgment about what is requisite to protect public health must be "based on [the] criteria" documents developed under § 108(a)(2), it need not be based solely on those criteria; and that those criteria themselves, while they must include "effects on public health or welfare which may be expected from the presence of such pollutant in the ambient air," are not necessarily limited to those effects. Even if we were to concede those premises, we would still not conclude that one of the unenumerated factors that the agency can consider in developing and applying the criteria is cost of implementation. That factor is both so indirectly related to public health and so full of potential for canceling the conclusions drawn from direct health effects that it would surely have been expressly mentioned in §§ 108 and 109 had Congress meant it to be considered.

Yet while those provisions describe in detail how the health effects of pollutants in the ambient air are to be calculated and given effect, they say not one word about costs.

[The unconstitutional delegation of legislative power.]

Section 109(b)(1) of the CAA instructs the EPA to set "ambient air quality standards the attainment and maintenance of which in the judgment of the Administrator, based on [the] criteria [documents of § 108] and allowing an adequate margin of safety, are requisite to protect the public health." The Court of Appeals held that this section as interpreted by the Administrator did not provide an "intelligible principle" to guide the EPA's exercise of authority in setting NAAQS.

In a delegation challenge, the constitutional question is whether the statute has delegated legislative power to the agency. Article I, § 1 of the Constitution vests "all legislative Powers herein granted . . . in a Congress of the United States. This text permits no delegation of those powers, and so we repeatedly have said that when Congress confers decision-making authority upon agencies, Congress must "lay down by legislative act an intelligible principle to which the person or body authorized to [act] is directed to conform." J.W. Hampton, Jr. & Co. v. United States, 276 U.S. 394 (1928).

The scope of discretion § 109(b)(1) allows is in fact well within the out limits of our nondelegation precedents. In the history of the Court we have found the requisite "intelligible principle" lacking in only two statutes, one of which provided literally no guidance for the exercise of discretion, and the other of which conferred authority to regulate the entire economy on the basis of not more precise a standard than stimulating the economy by assuring "fair competition." See Panama Refining Co. v. Ryan, 293 U.S. 388 (1935) ; A.L.A. Schechter Poultry Corp. v. United States, 295 U.S. 495 (1935) . We have, on the other hand, upheld the validity of the Public Utility Holding Company Act, which gave the Securities and Exchange Commission authority to modify the structure of holding company systems so as to ensure that they are not "unduly or unnecessarily complicated" and do not "unfairly or inequitably distribute voting power among security holders." American Power & Light Co. v. SEC, 329 U.S. 90 (1946) . We have approved the wartime conferral of agency power to fix the prices of commodities at a level that "will be generally fair and equitable and will effectuate the purposes of the Act." Yakus v. United States, 321 U.S. 414 (1944) .

And we have found an "intelligible principle" in various statutes authorizing regulation in the "public interest." In short, we have "almost never felt qualified to second-guess Congress regarding the permissible degree of policy judgment that can be left to those executing or applying the law." Mistretta v. United States, 488 U.S. 361(1989)(Scalia, J. dissenting).

Section 109(b)(l) of the CAA, which to repeat we interpret as requiring the EPA to set air quality standards at the level that is "requisite"—that is, not lower or higher than is necessary—to protect the public health with an adequate margin of safety, fits comfortably within the scope of discretion permitted by our precedent.

[The holding that the EPA need not consider compliance costs in revising air quality standards is affirmed. The holding that the CAA contains an unconstitutional delegation of legislative authority is reversed.]

International Cooperation

International cooperation can be important for combating many forms of pollution, but it is obviously especially important regarding air pollution. For example, the world recognizes with increasing alarm that global warming is a phenomenon that must be dealt with. Many multilateral approaches have been tried. The United States ratified the **United Nations Framework Convention on Climate Change,** committing itself to cooperate with other nations in seeking to develop multilateral solutions to global climate change. While the U.S. helped to negotiate the **Kyoto Protocol** to this Convention, it later withdrew from the Protocol on grounds that it called for disproportionate reductions in greenhouse gas emissions from developed nations but relatively little sacrifice by developing nations. This American action has been extremely controversial. It seems imperative that the nations of the world find an alternative means of getting global cooperation back on track.

Solid Waste and Its Disposal

The disposal of millions of tons of solid waste produced annually in this country presents a problem of staggering proportions. Periodic garbage pickups at residences or small businesses or weekly trips to the county or municipal sanitary landfill solve the problem for most people. However, less than 10 percent of solid waste is classified as residential, commercial, or institutional. The greater portion is classified as agricultural or mineral. Agriculture alone contributes more than 50 percent. Undisposed of, the waste creates enormous health and pollution problems; inadequate disposal methods often create greater hazards. If burned, solid waste pollutes the air. If dumped into waterways, lakes, or streams, the Clean Water Act is violated. Consequently, federal statutes have been enacted to combat the problem.

Solid Waste Disposal Act/Resource Conservation Recovery Act

The primary goal of the Solid Waste Disposal Act of 1965 and the 1976 amendment known as the Resource Conservation and Recovery Act (RCRA) is more efficient management of waste and its disposal through financial and technical assistance to state and local agencies in the development and implementation of new methods of waste disposal. RCRA defined hazardous waste as a solid waste, or combination of solid wastes, that because of its quantity, concentration, physical, chemical, or infectious characteristics may

A. cause, or significantly contribute to an increase in mortality or an increase in serious irreversible, or incapacitating reversible, illness, or

B. pose a substantial present or potential hazard to human health or the environment when improperly treated, stored, transported, or disposed of, or otherwise managed.

RCRA also established an Office of Solid Waste within the EPA to regulate the generation and transportation of solid waste (both toxic and nontoxic), as well as its disposal, thus providing "cradle–to–grave" regulation. Although RCRA focuses primarily on the regulation and granting of permits for ongoing hazardous waste activities, it does have a corrective action program for site cleanup. The EPA is authorized to sue to force the cleanup of existing waste disposal sites presenting imminent hazards to the public health.

These acts generally treat toxic wastes more harshly than nontoxic wastes. But where is the line drawn? The Hazardous and Solid Waste Amendments (to RCRA) of 1984 required the EPA to expand the list of constituents characterized as toxic. In 1990, the EPA issued its rules, adding 25 organic chemicals to a preexisting list of eight metals and six pesticides regulated for toxicity. Nearly 20,000 small (and large) businesses generating solid waste containing these substances must now comply with rules regarding hazardous waste, and a substantial number of landfills must now be treated as hazardous waste facilities, greatly expanding the costs of required disposal and cleanup. The 1984 amendments also created a comprehensive program for regulating underground storage tanks, such as gasoline tanks at service stations.

Comprehensive Environmental Response, Compensation, and Liability Act of 1980 (CERCLA/Superfund)

Although RCRA provides cradle–to–grave regulation of active hazardous waste sites, in the wake of the Love Canal incident referred to earlier, Congress passed the Comprehensive Environmental Response, Compensation, and Liability Act of 1980 (CERCLA), better known as the "Superfund" legislation, to clean up abandoned or inactive sites. CERCLA initially established a $1.6 billion Hazardous Substance Response Trust Fund to cover the cost of "timely government responses to releases of hazardous substances into the environment."

Addressing a much broader range of hazardous substances than RCRA, CERCLA holds the polluter, rather than society, responsible for the costs of cleaning up designated hazardous waste sites, instructing the EPA to list the nation's worst toxic waste sites, identify responsible parties, and sue them for cleanup costs, if necessary. The following potentially responsible parties (PRPs) were initially enumerated: (1) present owners and operators of facilities; (2) any person who, at the time of disposal, owned or operated such a facility; (3) generators of hazardous substances who arrange for disposal or treatment at another's facility; or (4) transporters of hazardous substances. These parties are strictly liable for cost of removal and remediation, response costs incurred by others, and damages to natural resources owned or controlled by any government. Due care and compliance with existing laws are no defense. Once determined to be responsible, a PRP may have to bear the entire cost of cleanup because liability is joint and several. In other words, if the government proves that owner A, prior owner B, and transporter C are all PRPs, and B and C are insolvent, A may have to pay for the entire cleanup. Furthermore, CERCLA is retroactive, covering both disposal acts committed and response costs incurred before the law was passed. Thus, potential CERCLA liability can be staggering.

The act also allows a category of exceptions, including owners of property incident to a security interest *(security interest exception)* and owners of land contaminated by the acts or omissions of third parties who are not contractually related to the owner *(third–party defense)*. CERCLA also allows a PRP to avoid liability when pollution is caused by an Act of God or war. The third–party defense is unavailable if the polluter is an employee or agent of the responsible party or one in a direct or indirect contractual relationship with that party.

Under the original version of CERCLA, completely innocent current owners of hazardous dumps faced liability for cleanup. In 1986, Congress passed the Superfund Amendments and Reauthorization Act (SARA), which provided an *innocent landowner defense* for those who could not only establish the third–party defense but also show (1) they had no reason to know of the contamination of the property when they purchased it and (2) they had made all appropriate inquiry into the previous ownership and uses of the property consistent with good commercial and customary practice. SARA also replaced the original CERCLA trust fund with the $8.5 billion Hazardous Substance Superfund (Superfund) financed by general revenue appropriations, certain environmental taxes, and monies recovered under CERCLA on behalf of the Superfund, and CERCLA–authorized penalties and punitive damages. SARA authorized civil penalties of up to $25,000 per day for willful failure to comply with EPA regulations.

Although in the earlier years, the costs of Super–fund fell primarily on large corporations, in recent years, those corporations have spread the pain by suing small businesses and even municipalities for contributions specifically authorized by CERCLA. For example, two large corporations, who had settled an EPA action by agreeing to pay for a $9 million cleanup of a landfill, sued a tiny pizzeria (among several other small businesses), surmising that it might have included cleanser, insecticide cans, or other items containing traces of toxins in its garbage sent to the landfill. Small companies often settle such cases out of court because the cost of defending would be so high.

The financial threat that CERCLA poses to industries that generate toxic wastes and companies that dispose of them is obvious. Additionally, CERCLA poses substantial hidden liabilities for a wide range of entities, including the pizzeria mentioned above; real estate buyers, lessees, and landlords; purchasers of corporations with unknown environmental liabilities; and indirect owners and operators such as lenders or parent corporations. For example, a lender might under certain circumstances be liable to clean up a borrower's waste site at an expense far in excess of the amount of the loan.

The follow case discusses both the broad scope of primary liability under CERCLA and the right of CERCLA defendants to seek contribution from other responsible parties.

ACUSHNET CO. V. MOHASCO CORP.
U.S. Court of Appeals for the First Circuit, 191 F.3d 69 (1999)

Sullivan's Ledge in New Bedford, Massachusetts was once a pristine area well suited for swimming, hiking, and picnicking. Over the years it became little more than an industrial dumping ground for scrap rubber, waste oils, telephone polls, and worse. The sludge became so toxic, the refuse so thick, and the stench so overwhelming that the area was closed down in the 1970s. The EPA eventually identified the business entities or their successors—in—interest that it believed were legally responsible for the decades of polluting. These thirteen entities (the Sullivan's Ledge Group) (plaintiffs) negotiated a consent decree with the United States. They commenced clean up efforts and brought this suit against various defendants for contribution.

Plaintiffs accused defendant New England Telephone & Telegraph (NETT) of dumping the butts of old telephone poles chock full of Polycyclic Aromatic Hydrocarbons (PAHs), alleged that defendant AFC discarded scrap cable containing lead, copper and zinc, claimed that defendant Mohasco's predecessor deposited waste sodium hydroxide and sulfuric acid, and asserted that defendant Ottaway's predecessor disposed of ink sludge containing sulfuric and nitric acids.

NETT moved for summary judgment, claiming that the poles it had discarded added so few PAHs to the mix compared with

the overall quantity of PAHs found at Sullivan's Ledge that NETT could not fairly be said to have contributed to the environmental harm or "caused" any of the remediation expenses. The trial judge granted the summary judgment motion, noting in part evidence that showed that the ground around NETT's poles had no more PAHs than popular foods and were miniscule compared to the 335,000 pounds of PAHs contributed by plaintiffs. After trial, the judge ruled for the other defendants as well, stating that their contribution to pollution at the site was so slight as to be insufficient to bring them within the group for which the calculus of appropriate proportional shares of liability for response costs could be made, and that plaintiffs had not shown a causal connection with respect to remediation costs. He noted, for example, that defendant AFC had discarded only two cubic yards of cable out of the million cubic yards of waste dumped at the site. Plaintiffs appealed.

Bownes, Senior Circuit Judge:

CERCLA, as we have said on other occasions, sketches the contours of a strict liability regime. Broad categories of persons are swept within its ambit, including the current owner and operator of a vessel or facility; the owner or operator of a facility at the time hazardous waste was disposed of; any person who arranged for the transportation of hazardous substances for disposal or treatment; and anyone who accepted hazardous waste for transportation. There are a few affirmative defenses available, but they are generally difficult to satisfy (they include showing that the release or threat of release was caused solely by an act of God or an act of war). By and large, a person who falls within one of the four categories defined in § 9607(a) is exposed to CERCLA liability.

While CERCLA casts the widest possible net over responsible parties, there are some limits to its reach. The courts of appeals have generally recognized that "although joint and several liability is commonly imposed in CERCLA cases, it is not mandatory in all such cases." In reBell Petroleum Servs., Inc., 3 F.3d, 889(5th Cir. 1993).

In O'Neil v. Picillo, 883 F.2d 176(1st Cir. 1989), we embraced the Restatement (Second) of Torts approach in construing the statute, stating that a defendant may avoid joint and several liability if the defendant demonstrates that the harm is divisible. In that event, damages should be apportioned according to the harm to the environment caused by that particular tortfeasor.

A responsible party, in turn, may bring an action for contribution under § 9613(f) to recover a portion of costs from "any other person who is liable or potentially liable under § 9607(a)." The standard for contribution liability is the same as that under § 9607(a), but in resolving contribution claims, a court may, in its discretion, "allocate response costs among liable parties using such equitable factors as the court determines are appropriate."

A plaintiff seeking contribution must prove that: (1) the defendant must fall within one of four categories of covered persons; (2) there must have been a "release or threatened release" of a hazardous substance from defendant's facility; (3) the release or threatened release must "cause[] the incurrence of response costs" by the plaintiff; and (4) the plaintiff's costs must be "necessary costs of response consistent with the national contingency plan."

Generators whose waste has been deposited in the facility from which there has been a release are presumptively responsible for the response costs, subject to the opportunity to prove (i) that the harm was solely caused by someone (or something) else or (ii) that the harm they caused is divisible, and subject further to the equitable allocation of relative shares of responsibility in an action for contribution.

The parties do not dispute that Sullivan's Ledge is a "facility" or that each of the defendants was a responsible person within the meaning of § 9607(a). Instead, they hotly contest the correct legal standard by which one could be said to have "caused" plaintiffs to incur remediation expenditures, and whether the record was adequate to allow any meaningful award of response costs.

The Sullivan's Ledge Group mounts a three—fold attack on the district court's reasoning in resolving the respective motions. Its arguments on appeal are broad—brushed in nature, focusing almost entirely on the legal meaning of "causation" and CERCLA's underlying policy goals. First, plaintiffs insist that reading any causal element into CERCLA is inconsistent with the principle of strict liability. Second, they contend that doing so would run counter to the remedial purpose of CERCLA because, among other things, it will let smaller polluters off the hook and discourage responsible parties from entering into consent agreements with the government. Third, to the extent the district court may have considered equitable factors in ruling in favor of Mohasco, Ottaway, and AFC, plaintiffs claim that the court did so without providing a "full and fair allocation trial" within the meaning of section 9613(f).

Defendants—appellees, for their part, contend that it makes sense to say that a de minimis polluter has not caused a responsible party to incur clean up costs; and that, in all events, plaintiffs' contribution claims against them founder for a more fundamental reason: the record did not permit a finding that each should bear a meaningful share of the costs associated with restoring Sullivan's Ledge. In their view, these fatal weaknesses in the plaintiffs' case justified judgment as a matter of law in their favor.

We have strong reservations about interpreting the statute's causation element to require that a defendant be responsible for a minimum quantity of hazardous waste before liability may be imposed. The text of the statute does not support such a construction — CERCLA itself does not expressly distinguish between releases (or threats of releases) by the quantity of hazardous waste attributable to a particular party. At least on its face, any reasonable danger of release, however insignificant, would seem to give rise to liability. On this point, the courts of appeals are in unison.

To read a quantitative threshold into the language "causes the incurrence of response costs" would cast the plaintiff in the impossible role of tracing chemical waste to particular sources in particular amounts, a task that is often technologically infeasible due to the fluctuating quantity and varied nature of the pollution at a site over the course of many years. Moreover, it would be extremely difficult, if not impossible, to articulate a workable numerical threshold in defining causation. How low would a polluter's contribution to the mix have to be before a judge could find, with equanimity, that the polluter was not a but—for "cause" of the clean up efforts? Less than 0.5% or 1%? We do not see how such a line, based on the quantity or concentration of the hazardous substance at issue, can be drawn on a principled basis in defining causation. To even begin down that path, we feel, is to invite endless confusion.

We have never discussed CERCLA causation in quantitative terms. To satisfy the causal element, it is usually enough to show that a defendant was a responsible party within the meaning of 9607(a); that clean up efforts were undertaken because of the presence of one or more hazardous substances identified in CERCLA; and that reasonable costs were expended during the operation. To the extent that the district court held that some minimal quantity of hazardous waste must be involved before a defendant may be held to have "caused" the expenditure of response costs, it was mistaken.

This does not mean, however, that the de minimis polluter must necessarily be held liable for all response costs. The approach taken by the Second Circuit is instructive. In Alcan I, 990 F.2d 711(2d Cir. 1993), the Second Circuit reaffirmed the Restatement (Second) of Torts approach to fleshing out the scope of CERCLA liability, holding that where environmental harms are divisible, a defendant may be held responsible only for his proportional share of the response costs. In extending the principle a half—step, the Second Circuit went on to say that:

[A defendant] may escape any liability for response costs if it either succeeds in proving that its [waste], when mixed with other hazardous wastes, did not contribute to the release and cleanup costs that followed, or contributed at most to only a divisible portion of the harm.

The court emphasized that this particular defense was limited to situations where a defendant's "pollutants did not contribute more than background contamination and also cannot concentrate."

It acknowledged that causation was, in some sense, "being brought back into the case through the backdoor, after being denied entry at the front door at the apportionment stage."

Id. Nevertheless, the court concluded that a defendant who successfully meets its burden can "avoid liability or contribution." The *Alcan I* panel took great pains to leave questions of liability, including the divisibility of environmental harm, and equitable apportionment of clean up expenses, to the sound discretion of the trial judge to be handled in the manner and order he or she deems best. We think the Second Circuit had it right.

We therefore hold that a defendant may avoid joint and several liability for response costs in a contribution action under § 9613(f) if it demonstrates that its share of hazardous waste deposited at the site constitutes no more than background amounts of such substances in the environment and cannot concentrate with other wastes to produce higher amounts. This rule is not based on CERCLA's causation requirement, but is logically derived from § 9613(f)'s express authorization that a court take equity into account when fixing each defendant's fair share of response costs. We caution, however, that not every de minimis polluter will elude liability in this way. As always, an equitable determination must be justified by the record. There are several reasons why, after all is said and done, an otherwise responsible party may be liable for only a fraction of the total response costs or escape liability altogether. In the first place, § 9613(f) expressly contemplates that courts will take equity into account in resolving contribution claims. We have in the past suggested that while a defendant in a direct EPA enforcement action invoking the divisibility of harm defense bears an "especially heavy burden," a defendant in a contribution proceeding seeking to limit his liability has a "less demanding burden of proof" by virtue of the equitable considerations that come immediately into play. A court, in evaluating contribution claims under § 9613(f), is "free to allocate responsibility according to any combination of equitable factors it deems appropriate." In an appropriate set of circumstances, a tortfeasor's fair share of the response costs may even be zero.

In the second place, there is nothing to suggest that Congress intended to impose far–reaching liability on every party who is responsible for only trace levels of waste. Several courts, albeit taking different paths to a similar result, have rejected the notion that CERCLA liability "attaches upon release of any quantity of a hazardous substance." Licciardi v. Murphy Oil USA, 111 F.3d 396 (5th Cir. 1997).

Third, allowing a CERCLA defendant to prevail on issues of fair apportionment, even at the summary judgment stage, is consistent with Congress's intent that joint and several liability not be imposed mechanically in all cases. Permitting a result that is tantamount to a no– liability finding is in keeping with the legislative goal that clean up efforts begin in a speedy fashion and that litigation over the details of actual responsibility follow. In fact, to require an inconsequential polluter to litigate until the bitter end, we believe, would run counter to Congress's mandate that CERCLA actions be resolved as fairly and efficiently as possible. On the whole, the costs and inherent unfairness in saddling a party who has contributed only trace amounts of hazardous waste with joint and several liability for all costs incurred outweigh the public interest in requiring full contribution from de minimis polluters.

Plaintiffs complain that any consideration of causation is at odds with CERCLA's objectives and would discourage responsible parties from entering into consent decrees. Because we ground the quantum inquiry solidly in § 9613(f), we are satisfied their prophesy will not come to pass. The ultimate failure of a contribution claim because someone did only a negligible amount of harm does not impede enforcement by the EPA or frustrate any of CERCLA's objectives.

[The court then reviewed the evidence in the case and concluded that the trial judge's decision to exonerate defendants from a contribution claim based on the extremely de minimis nature of their pollution and the tenuous causal connection their actions had to the damage at Sullivan's Ledge was justifiable, and it affirmed the judgment.]

The potentially crushing liability that CERCLA imposes created "brownfields" that no one wanted to touch. To encourage development of these areas, in 2000 Congress reduced CERCLA liability by passing the Small Business Liability Relief and Brownfields Revitalization Act, which:

1. Clarified the "innocent purchaser" defense which had not protected landowners because Congress had not defined the "all appropriate inquiry" that purchasers of land were supposed to take before buying land. The defense is now available to purchasers who (a) inquired as to the previous ownership and uses of the facility, and (b) took reasonable steps to prevent future releases of hazardous substances.

2. Created a "bona fide prospective purchaser" defense for those who knowingly buy contaminated properties, but can establish that all disposals of hazardous substances occurred before they brought the property and that they have exercised appropriate care to prevent releases of hazardous material, cooperated with clean–up authorities, and provided all necessary information.

3. Created a "contiguous property exemption" for innocent owners of downgradient property.

4. Created a "small business" exemption. The broad language of CERCLA meant that virtually all waste, including ordinary household waste or restaurant waste, contains hazardous substances. So, small business owners could find themselves liable as PRPs. The Brownfields amendments created exceptions for very small amounts of waste and for "municipal solid waste."

An important related issue that has been repeatedly litigated is the responsibility of corporate parents for the CERCLA liability of their subsidiaries. In United States v. Bestfoods, 524 U.S. 51(1998) , the Supreme Court held that state corporate law principles of corporate veil piercing should be applied and that CERCLA did nothing to broaden the liability of corporate parents in Superfund cases specifically. The Court did hold that under corporation law principles, parents are liable not only when the corporate form would otherwise be misused to accomplish wrongful purposes, but also where they directly participate in the operation of the offending facility that is owned by the subsidiary. The Court concluded that the parent in *Bestfoods* could potentially be liable because of evidence that its governmental and environmental affairs director actively participated in and exerted control over a variety of the subsidiary's environmental matters.

Regulation of Toxic Substances

In addition to the identifiable pollutants that are controlled at the source by the EPA, a more serious threat may be posed by the thousands of chemicals and compounds that are manufactured for commercial and generally beneficial use. These include herbicides, pesticides, and fertilizers, some of which may be highly toxic as single elements or may become toxic when combined with other elements. It is now apparent that toxic substances, initially applied to serve some useful purpose, are working their way into the environment, often with potentially dangerous results to humans exposed to those substances. An infamous example occurred at Times Beach, Missouri, where deadly dioxins deposited years before may have caused severe health problems for local residents.

Toxic Substances Control Act

In 1976 Congress enacted the Toxic Substances Control Act (TSCA) to create a review and control mechanism for the process of bringing chemical substances into the marketplace. The EPA is required to develop a comprehensive inventory of existing chemicals by calling on manufacturers to report the amount of each chemical substance they produce. TSCA imposes testing requirements on manufacturers and requires notice to the EPA when a new substance is being considered for development and production. The main purpose of the act is to prohibit the introduction of substances that would present an uncontrollable risk. Additionally, TSCA provides for testing, warnings, and instructions leading to the safe use of toxic chemicals with minimal effects on humans and the environment. Enforcement procedures permit the EPA to issue an order to prohibit the manufacture of high-risk substances. Pursuant to TSCA, the EPA has developed specific standards for PCBs, asbestos, chlorofluorocarbons, dioxins, and other substances.

Unlike some other environmental laws (the Clean Air Act, for example), TSCA orders the EPA to consider the economic and social impact of its decisions as well as the environmental effects. Therefore, more than some environmental regulations, TSCA seeks to avoid unnecessary burdens on the economy.

Pesticide Regulation

Obviously pests such as insects and mice cause significant crop damage and health problems. For that reason, chemicals that can kill or inhibit the reproduction of such pests are quite valuable for the health and economic welfare of Americans. Unfortunately, the widespread and long—term use of such substances can itself endanger the environment, injuring wildlife and human health. For that reason, Congress passed the Federal Environmental Pesticide Control Act in 1972, amending an earlier 1947 law, the Federal Insecticide, Fungicide, and Rodenticide Act (FIFRA). These acts together require that pesticides be registered with the EPA before they can be sold. Applicants for registration must provide comprehensive safety testing information to the EPA, which will approve the application only if the pesticide is properly labeled, lives up to its claims, and does not cause "unreasonable adverse effects on the environment." Such substances, when applied to crops that provide food for animals or people, may be used only within established limits. It is under this legislation that the EPA substantially banned the well-known insecticide DDT.

Food Quality Protection Act

FIFRA was altered with passage of the controversial Food Quality Protection Act (FQPA) of 1996 that mandated a cataloging of the nation's overall pesticide use to determine all the routes by which humans are exposed to pesticides and provided a single health−based safety standard for pesticide residues in all raw and processed food (replacing multiple standards for various residues). The law was supported by environmentalists and opposed by farmers who worried that it would put them out of business by unduly limiting their use of pesticides. Its goal was to protect America's children.

The FQPA required the EPA to determine that there is a "reasonable certainty of no harm" from exposure to the residue. The law required an additional safety factor of up to 10 times to account for uncertain data and ordered the EPA to consider children's special sensitivity and exposure to pesticides. The FQPA also limited consideration of economic benefits when setting pesticide tolerances, required the EPA to review all pesticide registrations every 15 years, and, required the distribution of brochures at food stores to provide consumers with more information about the health effects of pesticides. The Act has led to a phasing out of many pesticides previously used in producing foods, prompting agricultural producers to look for biopesticide replacements.

Noise Pollution

The Noise Control Act of 1972, the first major federal assault on excessive noise emanating from sources to which the public is exposed on a continual basis, empowers the EPA to establish noise emission standards for specific products in cooperation with agencies otherwise concerned with them and to limit noise emissions from those products that can be categorized as noise producers. The act specifically targets transportation vehicles and equipment, machinery, appliances, and other commercial products. The act subjects federal facilities to state and local noise standards and expressly reserves the right to control environmental noise in the state through licensing and regulation or restriction of excessively noisy products.

The thrust of the Noise Control Act is to reduce environmental noise in an effort to prevent what are recognized as long−range effects (hearing problems) on public health and welfare. Violations of the prohibitions of the act are punishable by fines, imprisonment, or both.

Many states and localities have their own noise pollution rules and regulations.

Indoor Pollution

Until recently, indoor pollution was given relatively little attention by environmentalists, businesses, and regulators. Recently, however, many experts have concluded that indoor air is many times more hazardous than outdoor air. Because Americans spend a very high percentage of their time indoors, a serious problem is presented by such indoor pollutants.

Among the most serious indoor pollutants are radon gas (a colorless, odorless gas that often percolates from the soil into homes and other buildings), asbestos (natural fibers often used as insulation and for other construction purposes), and formaldehyde (a chemical also often found in insulation and other construction materials). The tendency of these substances and others to cause cancer or other diseases is widely accepted.

Despite the dangers presented by these and other substances, as of this writing there is no comprehensive federal policy on indoor air quality. Nor have the states taken any uniform action. For example, the federal government's efforts at regulating radon have not yet moved past the research and study phase. Hit–and–miss attempts have led to substantial amounts being spent to clean up asbestos, especially in schools, and to the demise of the formaldehyde insulation industry. Nonetheless, the regulatory efforts have been incomplete. Therefore, the substantial dangers posed by indoor air pollution will undoubtedly lead to additional state and federal regulation in the near future.

Litigation in the area of indoor pollution is also in its infancy, but increased activity will likely be seen in coming years. In Pinkerton v. Georgia Pacific Corp., No. CV 186–4651CC (Mo. Cir. Ct. 1990), for example, $16.2 million was recovered to compensate for sensitivity reactions in the plaintiffs to indoor formaldehyde exposure caused by the defendant's negligence.

Endangered Species

The 1973 Endangered Species Act (ESA) has been called the world's most stringent environmental law because of its unstinting protection of plant and animal species endangered or threatened with extinction. Aside from the moral principles underlying preservation of endangered species, there is the simple utilitarian consideration that an extinct species can no longer provide food, medicine, and other benefits to mankind.

On the other hand, a tiny fish (the snail darter) interrupted the construction of a $100 million dam project, a bird (the northern spotted owl) arguably has endangered thousands of jobs in the lumber industry in the Northwest, and millions of acres of land have been subject to land use restrictions under the ESA.

More than two–thirds of the plants and animals on the ESA's protected list are stable or increasing in number, including the bald eagle. Nonetheless, the ESA remains deeply unpopular in many quarters and many are working to repeal or heavily amend it.

The Environment, Industry, and Society

At least two things should be clear from this chapter. First, businesses are faced with a myriad of environmental rules and regulations, some extremely costly and difficult to implement. To cover them fully would require a discussion hundreds of pages long. We have scarcely touched on the thousands of state and local antipollution ordinances and have not mentioned several matters of intense federal concern, such as the controversies over preserving national parks and drilling for oil and gas offshore. Nor have we mentioned some very important federal laws, including the Hazardous Materials Transportation Act (promoting safe movement of "hazardous materials" through our nation's transportation system), the Emergency Planning and Community Right–to–Know Act

LEGAL FOCUS

International

The various forms of pollution do not respect national borders. Therefore, pollution has a critical international dimension that cannot be overlooked. International law and international organization now play an increasingly important role in solving important environmental problems. Unfortunately, as in non-environmental areas, their weaknesses prevent truly effective action. Nonetheless, important strides have been made.

International Organizations

Naturally, a look at international organizations must begin with the United Nations. Unfortunately, the United Nations has no executive environmental agency. Its strongest arm is UNEP (United National Environment Programme), which has helped formulate international treaties on pollution but has a limited budget and therefore can neither fund major projects not comprehensively enforce international law.

The International Court of Justice plays at least a minor role in enforcing customary international law on transnational pollution. For example, in the *Corfu Channel Case*(Greece v. Italy, 1949 I.C.J. 18), that body ruled that countries have an obligation not to allow their territory to be used for acts (including polluting acts) contrary to the rights of other states. An International Joint Commission established a similar "good neighbor" principle in a pollution dispute between the United States and Canada in the *Trail Smelter Arbitration (*United States v. Canada3 R. Int'l. Arb. Awards 1907(1949),), which involved claims by citizens of the state of Washington against smelters located in the British Columbia province, ruling that "under the principles of international law, . . . no state has the right to use or permit the use of its territory in such a manner as to cause injury by fumes in or to the territory of another or the properties or persons therein, when the case is of serious consequence and the injury is established by clear and convincing evidence."

International Conventions

The international community has in recent years attacked various aspects of the pollution problem through conventions and conferences. For example, as a starting point, Principle 21 of the Stockholm Conference (1972) provides that

States have, in accordance with the Charter of the United Nations and the principles of international law, the sovereign right to exploit their own resources pursuant to their own environmental policies, and the responsibility to ensure that activities within their own jurisdiction or control so no cause damage to the environment of other States or of areas beyond the limits of national jurisdiction.

Pursuant to that principle, several important conventions have been formulated. To attack the problem of "garbage imperialism" (the exporting of waste by developed countries for disposal in underdeveloped countries), the Basel Convention (1989) sought to prohibit transboundary movement of hazardous wastes absent written consent by all countries involved. Another requirement is that the receiving country have an environmentally sound way to dispose of the waste.

Water pollution in the form of oil spills by tankers has been addressed several times, including through the Protocol of 1984 to Amend the International Convention of Civil Liability for Oil Pollution Damage and the Protocol of 1984 to Amend the International Fund for Compensation for Oil Pollution Damage. The goal of these conventions was to create international standards of liability and an internationally enforced insurance scheme.

The endangering of species has been addressed in the 1973 Convention on International Trade in Endangered Species and Wild Fauna and Flora and the 1979 Convention on Conservation of Migratory Species of Wild Animals. These conventions address such matters as the illicit international trade in ivory, exotic birds, and rhinoceros horns.

The matter of ozone depletion is of primary importance in the international legal community because of the potential for worldwide adverse effects. The Montreal Protocol called for industrialized nations to completely phase out the use of ozone–depleting chlorofluorocarbons (CFCs) by the year 2000. It also provided a $100 million "financial mechanism" trust fund to enable developing countries to reduce their reliance of CFCs and to fund the attempt to find nonpolluting substitutes.

The June 1992 U.N. Conference on the Environment and Development ("Earth Summit") in Brazil let to several potential advances in international cooperation, including two treaties— the U.N. Framework Convention on Climate Change and the Convention on Biological Diversity. These two treaties bind all countries that ratify them; 153 nations signed the Biological Diversity treaty (only the United States refused).

Limitations

Unfortunately, although most of these conventions look good on paper and all are important symbolic steps, most suffer in varying degrees from limitations that are common to all international legal measures. Most of the conventions were signed by substantially more nations than ultimately ratified them. Most do not apply to nations that did not ratify. Most lack methods of enforcement and suffer from vagueness in terminology. Many point to the United States' withdrawing support for the Kyoto Protocol relative to global warming as a classic example of the limitations of international approaches to environmental problems. Still, international cooperation seems essential to saving the planet, and every effective step in the right direction should be appreciated and supported.

(aimed at forcing communities to prepare for a Bhopal–type spill of hazardous chemicals in the United States), or the Occupational Safety and Health Administration's numerous rules to protect workers from chemical injury, including the Worker Right-to–Know Rule (under which chemical manufacturers and employers using hazardous chemicals must communicate their hazards to affected employees).

Second, it should be obvious that striking a balance among competing interests—protection of the environment, economic health of business, long–term health of citizens—is exceedingly difficult. For that reason, the national debate on our priorities in this area and the best way to meet them will continue long into the future.

CHAPTER **31**

THE LEGAL ENVIRONMENT OF INTERNATIONAL BUSINESS

Introduction

As early as 1816 in The Schooner Exchange v.McFadden, 11 U.S. 116(1812), Chief Justice Marshall wrote: "The world [is] composed of distinct sovereignties … whose mutual benefit is promoted by intercourse with each other, and by an exchange of those good offices which humanity dictates and its wants require." As long as nations have existed, there has been commercial activity among them. That activity is generally very beneficial to all the parties involved, and in our modern world the amount of international commercial activity is exploding.

For example, total worldwide trade in 2004 was estimated at $55 trillion. The United States alone exports around a trillion dollars of goods and services each year. (Unfortunately, for our trade balance, we import more than we export each year.) Many of the largest U.S. corporations derive more than half their profits from sales outside the country. On the flip side of the coin, most U.S. manufacturers face direct foreign competition for sales in the United States.

Cross-border direct investment, where the investor not only invests money but also takes an active role in the foreign enterprise, is also large and increasing quickly. In 1999, there was $865 billion in worldwide foreign direct investment. The U.S. was a primary source of that foreign direct investment, but also the largest recipient, receiving $275 billion of the total. Many millions of Americans are employed by companies directly owned by foreign investors. More than half of all products made in the U.S. have foreign components and more than half of all imports and exports are between companies and their foreign parents of affiliates. Increasingly, U.S. companies are forming joint ventures with foreign companies to do business overseas. Conversely, many foreign companies are entering U.S. markets through similar means.

This is only one aspect of the situation, because foreign entities also own well more than a trillion dollars of U.S. securities and total cross–border securities trading is estimated to have topped $5 trillion in 2000. Thousands of traders watching computer screens around the globe constitute an international financial market that sends a stream of capital 50 times the value of international trade flowing across international borders.

All in all, an already small world is growing smaller. Every day investors around the world watch the American stock markets, for what happens here will affect markets across the world. Similarly, happenings in the European and Asian stock markets will have a direct impact on U.S. markets. The fall of the Berlin Wall opened up new markets two decades ago, just as the events of Tiananmen Square in China in 1989 put a damper on the enthusiasm of foreign investors. Changes in U.S.–China relations influence international business trends almost daily.

Just as each company or investor hoping to do business abroad must be concerned with the events occurring in other countries, so must they be concerned with legal aspects of international transactions. The laws of the countries in which they intend to do business, as well as international law, must be considered in each and every transaction.

Legal problems are pervasive and inescapable. Can a U.S. company selling its goods in South Korea expect protection from trademark infringement by local companies Must a Japanese company operating its plant on American soil comply with U.S. laws when making its employment decisions Does a European company wishing to purchase an American company face any barriers that a potential U.S. purchaser would not face An endless variety of legal questions shape international commerce.

This chapter provides an introduction to the basic aspects of international legal rules as they bear most directly on persons and business organizations engaged in commercial transactions across national borders. It does not pursue in any detail many related and very important fields such as public international law, which regulates legal and political relationships among sovereign states.

Classifying international trade

Today we classify within the term international trade any movement of goods, services, or capital across national boundaries. In its normal use, the term includes three major components:
1. Export of goods, services, or commodities from one country to another.
2. Import of goods, services, or commodities into one country from another.
3. Of increasing importance since the end of the Second World War, foreign direct investment, such as the acquisition of interests in capital facilities in one country by investors from another.

Each of these components of international trade is distinct from the other; each raises particular legal and business issues; and each has been met with a distinct legal response intended to facilitate, harmonize, and regulate this aspect of global commercial and economic relations. With the growth in complexity of modern trade, the competition among nations as expressed in trade policy, and the shrinking presence of centrally planned economies in socialist bloc and Third World countries, the three main facets of international trade noted above have come to demonstrate, to varying degrees, three different sources of regulations:
1. Procedures developed by the *international trading community,* intended to ease trading relations and foster the resolution of disputes.
2. Regulations developed by *national governments* designed to protect national trading interests and to make them more competitive in international markets.
3. Laws and standards for international trade relations established by *international governmental organizations* such as the United Nations and the Organization for Economic Cooperation and Development, intended to harmonize trading community and national principles; to eliminate trade abuses; and to develop a greater participation in world trade, especially on the part of those nations that form the Third World.

This chapter looks at some of the major features of each of these components of the international trade framework.

International sales contracts

Although foreign direct investment and foreign portfolio investment have become increasingly important factors in world commerce in recent years, the transfer of goods across national frontiers remains extremely important. This type of transaction—an export from the buyer's point of view—is fundamentally a contract of sale, much like its domestic cousin in its essential features. However, special factors such as the great distances involved, accompanying insurance considerations, and differences in legal systems present special problems. An overriding factor in the formation of the international sales contract is that the parties do not, in the normal situation, know each other well; this ignorance can lead to uneasiness over the creditworthiness of the buyer and the dependability of the seller, and anxiety about the enforcement of the obligations of the parties if there should be a breach of contract.

In response to these and other concerns, international private sector traders have over time devised a series of specialized but fairly standard techniques and legal devices that take the form of a series of "side" contracts that supplement the basic sales contract.

Financing the transaction: the letter of credit

Because of the presumed lack of knowledge on the part of the seller as to the creditworthiness of the buyer, the export trade has developed a reliance on the **letter of credit** financing device. In the United States, Article 5 of the Uniform Commercial Code regulates letters of credit. However, in practice most letters of credit incorporate the provisions of the International Chamber of Commerce's Uniform Customs and Practice for Documentary Credits (UCP), creating some level of some level of international uniformity in practice.

Basically, the letter of credit is an irrevocable assurance by the bank of the importer/buyer that funds for the payment of goods sold by the exporter/seller are available beyond the control of the buyer and that these can be obtained by the seller on provision of documentary proof that the goods have been shipped and that other contractual obligations of the seller have been fulfilled and are thus beyond the arbitrary control of the seller.

The documents that the seller must produce to be paid can include (1) inland and ocean **bills of lading** to establish receipt of the goods by the shipper and to serve as "documents of title" for the merchandise; (2) commercial invoices and packing lists to attest to the contents of bulk and packaged materials; (3) an **export license** and shipper's export declaration to show compliance with any applicable export controls; and (4) any **import licenses,** consular invoices, or **certificates of origin** necessary to comply with the import laws of the receiving country.

Because the buyer's bank is typically a foreign bank, the seller may have no more confidence in it that in the buyer itself. It is not unusual, then, for the seller to involve its own bank in the transactions to transmit the funds or to confirm or guarantee the performance of the buyer's bank that is issuing the letter of credit. In these circumstances, the seller's bank may undertake only to accept the transfer of funds from the buyer's bank and to credit these to the account of the seller (an advising bank); it may go further, however, and contract to guarantee this payment to the seller (a standby or confirming bank).

In either event, an additional layer of contractual obligation will appear, this time between the seller and its bank and, further, between the seller's bank and the buyer's bank.

The letter of credit is essentially a means to make the seller comfortable that the goods will be paid for and to assure the buyer that the purchase money will not be released to the seller until proper, conforming goods are suitably shipped. Strict compliance with the letter of credit is generally required, as the following case illustrates.

The complexity of these multilayered arrangements is greatly reduced by the frequency with which they are used and their corresponding familiarity in the international trading community. It may help to chart the usual financing techniques of a typical international sales transaction in goods (see Figure 31.1).

In a high percentage of cases, there are discrepancies between the documents produced and the letter of credit. In almost all cases, the buyers waive these discrepancies; absent such waivers, the issuing bank may avoid its payment obligation. New York is arguably the world's center for commercial use of letters of credit. The following case shows how important compliance with technicalities can be.

Trade terms

Financing is, of course, only a means to an end, and a myriad of other factors—almost all of them bearing directly on the ultimate price paid for the goods—will be resolved in the terms of the international sales contract. The parties may wish to provide for a fixed rate of currency exchange or to specify the currency of payment for the contract; they may elect to identify the "official" language of the sales contract or to provide that two or more languages each represent the agreed terms of the transaction; they may choose the applicable law and identify the court that will have jurisdiction in the event of a subsequent disagreement; or they may decide to refer any contract disputes to binding or nonbinding arbitration. Clauses such as these, although very important, may or may not appear in the final contract, depending on a host of subtle factors, including the current economic and political climate, the degree of mutual trust and familiarity between the parties, and the extent to which they share common linguistic, cultural, business, or legal tradition. For instance, an

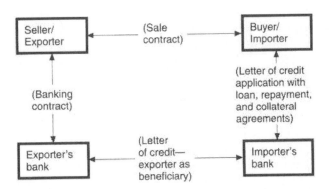

Figure 31.1   Financing Techniques of Typical International Sales Transaction

HANIL BANK V. PT. BANK NEGARA INDONESIA

U.S. District Court 2000 U.S. Dist. LEXIS 2444 (S.D.N.Y.)

Plaintiff Hanil Bank is a Korean banking corporation. Defendant PT. Bank Negara Indonesia (Pesero)("BNI") is an Indonesian banking corporation. On July 27, 1995, PT. Kodeco Electronics Indonesia ("Kodeco") applied to BNI to issue a letter of credit (the "L/C") for the benefit of "Sung Jun Electronics Co., Ltd." ("Sung Jun"). On July 28, 1995, BNI issued the L/C, No. IM1MHT0272.95, in the amount of $ 170,955.00 but misspelled the name of the beneficiary as "Sung Jin Electronics Co. Ltd." The beneficiary did not request amendment of the L/C to change the name of the beneficiary. On August 2, 1995 Sung Jun negotiated the L/C to Hanil. Hanil purchased the L/C and the documents submitted by Sung Jun thereunder from Sung Jun for $ 157,493.00, the face amount of the draft, less Hanil's commission. On August 2, 1995, Hanil submitted the documents, a draft, a commercial invoice, bill of lading, insurance policy, a packing list, and a fax advice, to BNI for payment. On August 16, 1995, BNI rejected the documents tendered by Hanil and refused to pay under the L/C. BNI alleges that it compared the documents with the L/C and identified four discrepancies, and based upon those discrepancies, refused the documents and demand for payment. The alleged discrepancies included the name of the beneficiary.

BNI contacted Kodeco to ask whether it would accept the discrepancies and approve the requested payment, but Kodeco declined to do so. BNI then returned the entire original package of documents back to Hanil on September 4, 1995. Hanil sued BNI for breach of contract, breach of the UCP, and breach of an implied covenant of good faith. Both parties moved for summary judgment.

Keenan, District Judge:

The principles of letter of credit law are embodied in the Uniform Customs and Practice for Documentary Credits (1993 Revision) International Chamber of Commerce Publication No. 500 (the "UCP"). The UCP is a compilation of internationally accepted commercial practices. Although it is not law, the UCP commonly governs letters of credit by virtue of its incorporation into most letters of credit. In this case, the L/C provides that it is governed by the UCP and both parties agree that the provisions of the UCP govern the L/C in this case. New York law provides that if a letter of credit is subject in whole or part to the UCP, as in this case, Article Five of the U.C.C. does not apply.

Typically, in a letter–of–credit transaction, the letter of credit substitutes the credit of the opening bank for that of the account party. International letters of credit permit quick and easy financing of international transactions by reducing the risks of non–payment. The Second Circuit has described the basic function of the letter of credit as follows:

> In its classic form, the letter of credit is only one of three distinct relationships between three different parties: (1) the underlying contract for the purchase and sale of goods between the buyer ("account party") and the seller ("beneficiary"), with payment to be made through a letter of credit to be issued by the buyer's bank in favor of the seller; (2) the application agreement between the bank and the buyer, describing the terms the issuer must incorporate into the credit and establishing how the bank is to be reimbursed when it pays the seller under the letter of credit; and (3) the actual letter of credit which is the bank's irrevocable promise to pay the seller–beneficiary when the latter presents certain documents . . . that conform with the terms of the credit.

Alaska Textile Co., Inc. v. Chase Manhattan Bank, N.A., 928 F.2d 813 (2d Cir. 1992).

A fundamental tenet of letter of credit law is that the obligation of the issuing bank to honor a draft on a credit is independent of the performance of the underlying contract. E & H Partners v. Broadway Nat'l Bank, 39 F.Supp.2d 275 (S.D.N.Y. 1998) ("The duty of the issuing bank to pay upon the submission of documents which appear on their face to conform to the terms and conditions of the letter of credit is absolute, absent proof of intentional fraud . . . ."). Because the credit engagement is concerned only with documents, "the essential requirements of a letter of credit must be strictly complied with by the party entitled to draw against the letter of credit, which means that the papers, documents and shipping description must be as stated in the letter." Marino Indus. v. Chase Manhattan Bank, N.A.,686 F.2d 112 (2d Cir. 1982). "There is no room for documents which are almost the same, or which will do just as well." *Alaska Textile*. Even under the strict compliance rule, however, "some variations . . . might be so insignificant as not to relieve the issuing or confirming bank of its obligation to pay," for example, if there were a case where "the name intended is unmistakably clear despite what is obviously a typographical error, as might be the case if, for example, 'Smith' were misspelled 'Smithh.'" Beyene v. Irving Trust Co., 762 F.2d 4 (2d Cir. 1985). The Court will now consider the alleged discrepancies in this case.

As set out above, the name of the beneficiary in this case was Sung Jun. Kodeco's application to BNI for the issuance of the L/C requested that the L/C be issued to Sung Jun. BNI, however, issued the L/C identifying the beneficiary as Sung Jin. BNI argues that under *Beyene* this discrepancy was a proper basis to reject the letter of credit presentation. Hanil argues, however, that the strict compliance rule does not permit an issuing bank to dishonor a letter of credit based on a discrepancy such as the misspelling in this case which could not have misled or prejudiced the issuing bank. The Court agrees with BNI.

In *Beyene,* Plaintiffs brought suit seeking damages for the alleged wrongful refusal of the defendant trust company, Irving Trust Co. ("Irving"), to honor a letter of credit. The district court granted Irving's motion for summary judgment because the bill of lading presented to Irving misspelled the name of the person to whom notice was to be given of the arrival of the goods, listing the name of the party as Mohammed Soran instead of Mohammed Sofan. As a result, the district court found that the bill of lading failed to comply with the terms of the letter of credit and that Irving was under no obligation to honor the letter of credit. The Second Circuit agreed, finding that "the misspelling in the bill of lading of Sofan's name as 'Soran' was a material discrepancy that entitled Irving to refuse to honor the letter of credit" and stating that "this is not a case where the name intended is unmistakably clear despite what is obviously a typographical error, as might be the case if, for example, 'Smith' were misspelled 'Smithh'". The Second Circuit also noted that it was not claimed that in the Middle East, where the letter of credit was issued, that "Soran" would be obviously recognized as a misspelling of the surname "Sofan." The Court finds the misspelling in the present case to be similar to the misspelling in Beyene and notes that Hanil likewise does not claim that Sung "Jin" would be obviously recognized as a misspelling of Sun "Jun."

Plaintiff argues that *Beyene* is distinguishable from the present case because in *Beyene* the beneficiary made the error, while in the present case, the issuing bank made the error. However, the Second Circuit has made it clear that under letter of credit law, "the beneficiary must inspect the letter of credit and is responsible for any negligent failure to discover that the credit does not achieve the desired commercial ends." Mutual Export Corp. v. Westpac Banking Corp., 983 F.2d 420 (2d Cir. 1993). Thus, in *Mutual Export,* even though the issuing bank had issued a letter of credit with an incorrect termination date, the Second Circuit reversed the district court's finding that the letter of credit should be reformed to reflect the appropriate date, and held that the beneficiary was responsible for failure to discover the error. The *Mutual Export* court explained that this rule is important because "the beneficiary is in the best position to determine whether a letter of credit meets the needs of the underlying commercial transaction and to request any necessary changes. . . . it more efficient to require the beneficiary to conduct that review of the credit before the fact of performance than after it, and the beneficiary that performs without seeing or examining the credit should bear the costs."

Pursuant to *Beyene* and *Mutual Export,* this Court concludes that BNI properly rejected payment on the ground that the documents improperly identified the beneficiary of the letter of credit. Although Hanil contends that BNI should have known that the intended beneficiary was Sung Jun, not Sung Jin, based on the application letter in BNI's own file, the Second Circuit has stated that in considering whether to pay, "the bank looks solely at the letter and the documentation the beneficiary presents to determine whether the documentation meets the requirements in the letter." *See Marino Indus.* (stating that compliance is to be determined from the face of the documents stipulated in the letter of credit).

Finally, as to Hanil's argument that BNI dishonored the L/C at the instruction of Kodeco and thereby violated its duty of good faith and fair dealing, the Court again disagrees. As noted above, the issuing bank's obligation under the letter of credit is independent of the underlying commercial transaction. Thus, BNI had an obligation to independently review Hanil's submissions to determine if there were any discrepancies. However, under the UCP, BNI is permitted to approach the payor of the letter of credit, in this case Kodeco, for a waiver of any discrepancies with or without the beneficiary's approval. *See Alaska Textile*, 982 F.2d at 824 (noting that allowing the issuer to seek waiver from the payor is efficient because the account party typically waives the discrepancies and authorizes payment). In this case there is no evidence that BNI communicated with Kodeco other than to ask whether Kodeco would accept the discrepancies and approve the requested payment. As a result, the Court finds that Hanil has not set forth facts showing there is a genuine issue as to whether BNI breached its duty of good faith and fair dealing by dishonoring the L/C. Summary judgment for BNI is therefore granted.

American exporter will have, in most cases, fewer questions about the conditions of commerce with a long–time Canadian business associate than, for instance, with a first–time trading partner in Sri Lanka or Liechtenstein.

Various commonly accepted **trade terms**, addressing matters of universal concern such as factors of distance, language barriers, and general unfamiliarity between the parties, have evolved over time within the international trading community. These terms are often used to allocate responsibility between the parties. For example, *CIF* stands for "cost insurance, and freight," meaning that the seller's quoted price is inclusive of the cost of goods, shipping charges, and marine insurance policy providing at least minimum coverage. This implies that the seller will bear the risk of loss during transit from the factory to the port of shipment; thereafter the risk shifts to the buyer who pays for the marine insurance policy that is usually arranged by the seller.

The term *AFS* (Free Alongside) implies that the risk of loss will pass from the seller/exporter when the goods are delivered alongside a vessel, usually designated by the buyer. Risk of damage in the onloading operation rests on the buyer. *FOB* (Free On Board) contemplates delivery of the goods by the seller, usually on a designated vessel where shipment has been arranged by the buyer; risk of loss passes at the ship's rail. *CAF* (Cost and Freight) is similar to *CIF* but the buyer arranges for insurance during carriage. *Ex* terms (exfactory) can be used to designate a place of delivery from seller to buyer that is other than the location of the carrier—for instance, at the factory, or perhaps at the ultimate destination of the goods.

Convention on contracts

In an attempt to add uniformity and certainty to the terms of international sales of goods contracts, several countries have ratified the 1980 United Nations Convention on Contracts for the International Sale of Goods (CISG). The CISG became part of American law on January 1, 1988, and has been ratified by nearly 70 nations, including most of America's major trading partners, except the UK and Japan.

Assume that Country A and Country B have both ratified the CISG. If a purchaser with a place of business in A makes a contract to buy goods from a company with a place of business in B, the CISG's provisions will automatically govern the contract unless the parties opt out of its coverage.

The CISG does not apply to consumer sales and has no provisions governing the validity of contracts, ownership claims of third parties, or liability claims for death or personal injury. However, it does have provisions governing most other issues that could arise in a contractual setting. The parties may provide their own variations, but the CISG augments contractual terms and provides the rules for situations the parties did not contemplate or address in their agreement.

The CISG could be loosely termed an international Uniform Commercial Code. It addresses most of the same subjects as Article 2 of the UCC, such as definiteness and revocability of offers, timeliness of acceptances, risk of loss, excuse from performance, and remedies. However, the CISG differs from the UCC in several respects. For example, Article 11 of the Convention largely abolishes the statute of frauds requirement of a written contract. Article 16 states that an offer cannot be revoked if it was reasonable for the offered has acted in reliance thereon. Article 35 alters the UCC's "perfect tender" rule. A seller must deliver goods fit for ordinary use of the buyer's particular purpose that is known to the seller. A buyer may reject goods only if there is a "fundamental breach." Article 50 addresses buyer's remedies, providing that a buyer may require a seller to perform in accordance with the promise or fix an additional time for the seller to perform. This latter option is not contained in the UCC but is derived from German law. A complete discussion of the CISG's provisions is beyond the scope of this chapter, but these differences and others (for example, the CISG contains no obligation to act in good faith, as does the UCC's Article 2), some American lawyers advise their clients to opt out of the CISG where possible. This is not always easy.

In Asante Technologies v. PMC-Sierra, Inc.,164 F.Supp.2d 1142 (N.D.Cal. 2001), a Canadian company bought electronic products from a California firm. The parties did not have a single contract with a clear choice–of–law provision, but four of five purchase orders specified that California law should apply. Nonetheless, the buyer argued that because both Canada and the U.S. are signatories of the CISG, it should govern. The court concluded that the purchase order provisions did not evidence a clear enough intent to opt out of the CISG. Furthermore, even if the law of California did apply, under the Supremacy Clause of the U.S. Constitution California law is subordinate to U.S. treaties. In the absence of clearer "opt out" language, the court held that the CISG applied even under California law. Had the choice of law provision stated "This contract is governed by the laws of the State of California, *not* including the 1980 United Nations Convention on Contracts for the International Sale of Goods," a successful opt out likely would have been recognized.

Other commercial confentions

The CISG's attempt to add uniformity to international sales law is representative of the work of the United Nations Commission on International Trade Law (UNCITRAL), which actively promotes conventions, including the Convention on the Limitations Period in the International Sale of Goods; on the Carriage of Goods by Sea; on International Bills of Exchange and Promissory Notes; and on Recognition and Enforcement of Foreign Arbitral Awards. UNCITRAL also promotes model laws, including the Model Law on International Awards; on International Credit Transfers; on Procurement of Goods, Construction and Services; and on Electronic Commerce.

Resolving international trade disputes

No contract—including one for an international busines transaction—can be so tightly drawn that it is totally impervious to later disagreement; similarly, unforeseen changes in circumstances may make performance of the contract impossible or, perhaps, more difficult or expensive than originally contemplated by the parties. An international trader should, therefore, have a clear understanding of the means available to resolve such disputes if they should arise.

Judicial litigation is rarely the best means to resolve any business dispute: The costs associated with it (attorneys' fees, court costs, and general expenses) will often offset any profit expected from the transaction. These factors are compounded in transnational litigation.

Difficulties often arise in identifying a court with proper jurisdiction over the subject matter of the action or the parties to the transaction. In many types of litigation the question will arise as to which state has the authority to assert its law over the transaction and the parties.

Domestic court jurisdiction

In business litigation, and in other types of litigation touching the international sphere, the rules of jurisdiction are evolving but are as yet unclear. The as yet unadopted American Law Institute *Restatement (Third) of the Foreign Relations Law of the United States* may be a good indicator of the direction in which the law is heading. Rather than use the traditional categories of subject matter jurisdiction and personal jurisdiction, the proposed revision to this Restatement establishes three categories: (1) *jurisdiction to prescribe*, that is, the authority of a state to make its law applicable to persons or activities; (2) *jurisdiction to adjudicate*, that is, the authority of a state to subject particular persons or things to its judicial process; and (3) *jurisdiction to enforce*, that is, the authority to use the resources of government to induce or compel compliance with its law.

Attempts by the United States to impose its legal regulations on activities occurring abroad have caused substantial resentment in foes and allies alike in recent years. The Restatement (Third)'s Sec. 402 would recognize a nation's *jurisdiction to prescribe* with respect to

1. (a) conduct, a substantial part of which takes place within its territory; (b) the status of persons, or interests in things, present within its territory; (c) conduct outside its territory which has or is intended to have substantial effect within its territory;
2. the activities, status, interests or relations of its nationals outside as well as within its territory; or
3. certain conduct outside its territory by persons not its nationals which is directed against the security of the state [example: terrorism] or a limited class of other state interests.

Thus, links of territoriality and nationality are ordinarily necessary to the power to prescribe law, although they are not sufficient in all cases. Furthermore, these criteria are expressly limited by Sec. 403, which states that even when they are present, jurisdiction to prescribe should not be exercised when it would be "unreasonable" as determined by an evaluation of all relevant factors, including (1) the extent to which the activity takes place in the regulating state and has a substantial, direct, and foreseeable effect there; (2) the connections, such as nationality, residence, or economic activity, between the regulating state and the persons responsible for the activity to be regulated or between the state and those whom the law is designed to protect; (3) the character of the activity to be regulated, the extent to which other states regulate it, and its general acceptability; (4) the existence of justified expectations that might be injured; (5) the importance of the regulation to the international political, legal, or economic system; the extent to which such regulation is consistent with the traditions of the international system; the extent to which another state may have an interest in regulating the activity; and (8) the likelihood of conflict with regulation by other states. A state should defer to another state whose interest in regulating the same conduct is clearly greater.

The *Timberlane* case, which soon follows, illustrates a court's independent formulation of a "reasonableness" approach.

Reasonableness also is the hallmark of the revised Restatement's approach to *jurisdiction to adjudicate*. According to Sec. 421, personal jurisdiction is to be exercised only if reasonable. Such exercise will generally be deemed reasonable if an individual defendant is present (other than transitorily) in the territory of the state; or is a domiciliary, resident, or national of the state; or regularly carries on business there; or has consented to the exercise of jurisdiction. Additionally, exercise of jurisdiction to adjudicate will be reasonable if the person has carried on activity in the state that created the liability in question or has carried on outside the state an activity having substantial, direct, or foreseeable effect within the state that created the liability in question.

Finally, under Sec. 431 of the Restatement, jurisdiction to enforce will be present only where a state had the power to prescribe, in accordance with Secs. 402 and 403, and the power to adjudicate as to the particular defendant. Enforcement measures must be proportional to the gravity of the violation and may be used against persons located outside the territory of the enforcing state only if such persons are given fair notice and an opportunity to be heard.

DEN NORSKE STATS OLJESELSKAP AS V. HEEREMAC V.O.F.

U.S. Seventh Circuit Court of Appeals, 241 F.3d 420 (2001)

Plaintiff, Den Norske Stats Oljeselskap As ("Statoil"), is a Norwegian oil company that owns and operates oil and gas drilling platforms exclusively in the North Sea. The defendants are providers of heavy–lift barge services in the Gulf of Mexico, the North Sea, and the Far East. Only six or seven heavy–lift barges exist in the world. These immense vessels have cranes capable of hoisting and transporting offshore oil platforms and decks weighing in excess of 4,000 tons. During the 1993–1997 time frame, the three defendants controlled these barges and two of hem sold services to Statoil in the North Sea.

Statoil alleges that the defendants conspired to fix bids and allocate customers, territories, and projects between 1993 and 1997. Defendants allegedly agreed that defendants HeereMac and McDermott would have exclusive access to heavy–lift projects in the Gulf of Mexico, while defendant Saipem would receive a higher allocation of North Sea projects in exchange for staying out of the Gulf. The defendants also allegedly agreed to submit embellished bids on heavy–lift projects, causing Statoil to pay inflated prices for heavy lift barge services. Statoil further argues that the conspiracy compelled it to charge higher prices for the crude oil it exported to the United States. Finally, Statoil asserts that purchasers of heavy–lift services in the Gulf of Mexico were forced to pay inflated prices for those services because of the conspiracy.

The trial court dismissed Statoil's complaint, finding no subject matter jurisdiction. Statoil appealed.

Jolly, Circuit Judge:

This appeal requires us to interpret the scope of the United States antitrust laws and their application to foreign conduct. Supreme Court precedent makes clear as a general proposition that United States antitrust laws "do not regulate the competitive conditions of other nations' economies," Matsushita Elec. Indus. Co. v. Zenith Radio Corp., 475 U.S. 574(1986). Sections 1 and 2 of the Sherman Act prohibit restraints of trade and monopolization. The Foreign Trade and Antitrust

Improvements Act (FTAIA), enacted by Congress in 1982 to clarify the application of United States antitrust laws to foreign conduct, limits the application of such laws when non–import foreign commerce is involved. The FTAIA states that the antitrust laws will not apply to non–import commerce with foreign nations unless the conduct at issue has a "direct, substantial, and reasonably foreseeable effect" on domestic commerce and "such effect gives rise to a claim under" the antitrust laws.

The issue presented to us is primarily one of statutory interpretation. Statoil argues that the FTAIA does not preclude the district court's jurisdiction over its antitrust claims. Specifically, Statoil argues that the FTAIA was enacted exclusively to ensure that the conduct providing the basis of the plaintiff's claim have the requisite domestic effects, and was not intended to preclude recovery to foreign plaintiffs based on the situs of the injury. Moreover, Statoil contends that Section 2 of the FTAIA was inserted only to ensure that the effect on United States commerce that provides jurisdiction is itself a violation of the antitrust laws; that is, the statute simply requires that there be some anticompetitive, harmful effect in this country.

Addressing specifically the FTAIA's requirement that the domestic effect "gives rise" to its antitrust claim, Statoil primarily argues that, because the defendants operating in the Gulf of Mexico were able to maintain their monopolistic pricing only because of their overall market allocation scheme (which included agreements regarding operations in the North Sea), Statoil's injury in the North Sea was a "necessary prerequisite to" and was "the quid pro quo for" the injury suffered in the United States domestic market. Statoil alleges that the market for heavy–lift services in the world is a single, unified, global market; therefore, because the United States is a part of this worldwide market, the effect of the conspiracy, whether in the United States or in the North Sea, "gives rise" to any claim that is based upon this conspiracy.

We begin with an analysis of the plain language contained therein. The Sherman Act itself applies only to conduct in "trade or commerce with foreign nations." The commerce that gives rise to the action here—the contracting for heavy lift barge services in the North Sea—was not United States commerce with foreign nations, but commerce between or among foreign nations—that is, between or among Statoil (a Norwegian corporation), Saipem (England), and HeereMac (The Netherlands). Therefore, we doubt that foreign commercial transactions between foreign entities in foreign waters is conduct cognizable by federal courts under the Sherman Act.

As we have noted, the FTAIA states that the antitrust laws will not apply to non–import foreign conduct unless (1) such conduct has a direct, substantial, and reasonably foreseeable effect on United States domestic commerce, and (2) such effect gives rise to the antitrust claim. The conduct of these defendants is foreign conduct that falls within the general parameters of the FTAIA and, thus, Statoil must show that the two specific requirements of the statute are met to establish subject matter jurisdiction over its claims. Statoil has sufficiently alleged that the defendant's conduct—that is, the agreement among heavy–lift service providers to divide territory, rig bids, and fix prices—had a direct, substantial, and reasonably foreseeable effect on the United States market. Statoil alleges that the conspiracy not only forced purchasers of heavy–lift services in the Gulf of Mexico to pay inflated prices, but also that the agreement compelled Americans to pay supra–competitive prices for oil. These allegations are sufficient to satisfy the first requirement of the FTAIA.

However, Statoil fails to show that this effect on United States commerce in any way "gives rise" to its antitrust claim. Based on the language of Section 2 of the FTAIA, the effect on United States commerce in this case, the higher prices paid by United States companies for heavylift services in the Gulf of Mexico must give rise to the claim that Statoil asserts against the defendants. That is, Statoil's injury must stem from the effect of higher prices for heavylift services in the Gulf. We find no evidence that this requirement is met here. The higher prices American companies allegedly paid for services provided by the McDermott defendants in the Gulf of Mexico does not give rise to Statoil's claim that it paid inflated prices for HeereMac and Saipem's services in the North Sea. This is not to say that any antitrust injury suffered by customers or competitors of McDermott that arose from the anticompetitive effect in the Gulf of Mexico cannot be addressed. This means only that, while we recognize that there may be a connection and an inter-relatedness between the high prices paid for services in the Gulf of Mexico and the high prices paid in the North Sea, the FTAIA requires more than a "close relation-ship" between the domestic injury and the plaintiffs claim; it demands that the domestic effect "gives rise" to the claim.

Statoil asks that we interpret the requirement of Section 2 that the domestic "effect" give rise to a claim under the antitrust laws as merely requiring that the defendants' domestic "conduct" (here, for example, agreements relating to the Gulf of Mexico) give rise to a claim. This interpretation is not true to the plain lan-guage of the FTAIA. Moreover, under such an expansive interpretation, any enti-ties, anywhere, that were injured by any conduct that also had sufficient effect on United States commerce could flock to United States federal court for redress, even if those plaintiffs had no commercial relationship with any United States market and their injuries were unrelated to the injuries suffered in the United States. Such an expansive reading of the extraterritorial application of the anti-trust laws was never intended nor contemplated by Congress.

In sum, we find that the plain language of the FTAIA precludes subject matter jurisdiction over claims by foreign plaintiffs against defendants where the situs of the injury is overseas and that injury arises from effects in a non–domestic market.

Although the plain language of the relevant statutes is clear and controlling, we nonetheless turn now to address briefly the legislative history of the FTAIA to illustrate how that history reinforces our interpretation of the extraterritorial reach of the antitrust laws.

[The court then determined that both the legislative history of the FTAIA and the interpretations of other courts supported its interpretation that the FTAIA was meant to exclude purely foreign transactions.]

Any reading of the FTAIA authorizing jurisdiction over Statoil's claims would open United States courts to global claims on a scale never intended by Congress. Without subject matter jurisdiction, United States federal courts are without power to entertain Statoil's claims. Affirmed.

Foreign sovereign immunities act

Even in circumstances in which the court should be willing to assert its jurisdiction over the defendant under the effects or reasonableness tests, it may be barred from doing so because of a personal immunity of the defendant. This bar is most often encountered when the defendant is a foreign state or state agency, a circumstance more frequently present today when many nations— especially those with centrally planned economies—are engaging directly in trading activities. The Foreign Sovereign Immunities Act (FSIA), passed by Congress in 1976, modifies the absolute sovereign immunity that the common law had recognized but continues to limit a plaintiff's ability to recover a judgment from a foreign state or state agency.

Under the FSIA, U.S. courts have jurisdiction over foreign sovereigns primarily in cases arising out of the latters' *commercial activities,* as illustrated in the following case.

GNSS, LIMITED V. AO TECHSNABEXPORT

U.S. Fourth Circuit Court of Appeals, 376 F.3d 282 (2004)

In 1993, the United States and the Russian Federation entered into an agreement "Concerning the Disposition of Highly Enriched Uranium (HEU) Extracted from Nuclear Weapons." The United States' Executive Agent under this agreement is the United States Enrichment Corporation (USEC), and Russia's is the Ministry of Atomic Energy (MINATOM), which has appointed defendant AO Techsnabexport (Tenex) to discharge its responsibilities. Under the agreement, Russia obligated itself to extract weapons-grade HEU from dismantled nuclear warheads, dilute the HEU by combining it with commercial reactor–grade Low–Enriched Uranium (LEU), and then deliver the resulting LEU to USEC. In exchange for this, USEC then pays Tenex partially in cash, and partially by transferring to Tenex title to uranium hexafluoride, which can be used to create LEU. Under the relevant U.S. and Russian legal framework, Tenex is then able not only to ship some of that uranium hexafluoride back to Russia for use in further dilution of weapons–grade HEU pursuant to the Agreement between the United States and Russia, but also to sell portions of that uranium hexafluoride for use in the United States.

Accordingly, in January 2000, Tenex entered into a contract with plaintiff Globe Nuclear Services and Supply (GNSS), by which Tenex obligated itself to supply GNSS with specified quantities of uranium hexafluoride from 2001 until 2013. In reliance on the Tenex Contract, and with full knowledge and cooperation of Tenex, GNSS then entered into long–term supply contracts with utility customers in the United States. In November 2003, Tenex informed GNSS that "further sales of [uranium hexafluoride] to GNSS are inimical to the interests of the Russian Federation," and that it was therefore unilaterally terminating the contract. GNSS brought this suit in federal district court, but that judge dismissed the suit for lack of subject matter jurisdiction under the Foreign Sovereign Immunity Act (FSIA), holding in particular that Tenex was an instrumentality of the Russian Federation that is generally immune from suit, and that Tenex's activity relevant to this lawsuit did not constitute a "commercial activity." GNSS appealed.

Luttig, Circuit Judge:

Because Tenex is wholly owned by the Russian Federation, it is an instrumentality of the Russian Federation and is thus itself considered to be a "foreign state" for purposes of the FSIA. Accordingly, it is presumptively immune from GNSS's suit unless one of the specifically enumerated exceptions in the FSIA applies to that suit. The only exception relevant here is the "comercial activity" exception, which provides: "(a) A foreign state shall not be immune from the jurisdiction of courts of the United States or of the States in any case ... (2) in which the action is based upon a commercial activity carried on in the United States by the foreign state; or upon an act performed in the United States in connection with a commercial activity of the foreign state elsewhere; or upon an act outside the territory of the United States in connection with a commercial activity of the foreign state elsewhere and that act causes a direct effect in the United States."

To determine whether the "commercial activity" exception of section 1605(a)(2) is applicable to GNSS's lawsuit against Tenex, we must engage in a two–step inquiry. First, we must precisely identify the conduct by Tenex upon which GNSS's lawsuit is "based." Second, we must determine under section 1605(a)(2) whether that conduct constitutes "a commercial activity carried on in the United States by the foreign state;" "an act performed in the United States in connection with a commercial activity of the foreign state elsewhere;" or "an act outside the territory of the United States in connection with a commercial activity of the foreign state elsewhere" and which "causes a direct effect in the United States."

Our first task is to identify precisely the conduct by Tenex upon which GNSS's lawsuit is "based." In Saudi Arabia v. Nelson, 507 U.S. 349 (1993), the Supreme Court provided the following guidance regarding the meaning of the words "based upon":: "In denoting conduct that forms the 'basis,' or 'foundation,' for a claim, the phrase is read most naturally to mean those elements of a claim that, if proven, would entitle a plaintiff to relief under his theory of the case."

The district court, without discussing *Nelson*, held that the conduct upon which GNSS's lawsuit is "based" is not limited to Tenex's entrance into a contract to supply GNSS with uranium hexafluoride and unilateral termination of this obligation, but includes the entire framework by which Russia has agreed to dismantle its nuclear weapons and convert weapons–grade HEU into commercial–grade LEU. The district court's capacious view of the conduct upon which GNSS's lawsuit is "based" cannot be reconciled with *Nelson*. Under that precedent, we must turn our attention not to "the reality of the situation in light of the agreements and the overall context of the contract," as the district court did, but to the specific claim GNSS has asserted against Tenex, and the elements of that claim that, "if proven, would entitle [GNSS] to relief under [its] theory of the case."

To establish likelihood of success on the merits, GNSS will need to prove that a valid contract exists between it and Tenex, that Tenex has unilaterally declared that it will no longer perform its obligations under the contract, and that this declaration by Tenex constitutes a breach of the contract. As this analysis shows, the entrance into the Tenex Contract and the unilateral declaration of non–performance by Tenex are the only conduct that constitute "elements" of GNSS's claim, and, if proven, would entitle GNSS to relief.

We do not deny that GNSS's complaint includes background information regarding the signing of the Agreement "concerning the disposition of highly enriched uranium extracted from the nuclear weapons" between the United States and the Russian Federation in 1993. But this is background information which, while factually relevant to explaining how the Tenex Contract came into existence, is not at all necessary for GNSS to prove in order to prevail in its suit for injunctive relief. Focus on the elements of GNSS's claim, as required by *Nelson*, yields the conclusion that the district court erred by taking an overly broad view of Tenex's conduct relevant to GNSS's lawsuit. For purposes of section 1605(a)(2), GNSS's action is "based upon" nothing more or less than Tenex's entrance into a contract to supply GNSS with uranium hexafluoride and subsequent repudiation thereof.)

Having precisely identified the conduct by Tenex upon which GNSS's lawsuit is "based," we now consider whether this particular conduct qualifies under section 1605(a)(2). In this case, our inquiry begins and ends with the first clause of that provision, because Tenex's conduct, we conclude, constitutes "a commercial activity carried on in the United States," and on this basis alone we must reverse the district court's holding that it lacked jurisdiction over the case. Our analysis of whether Tenex's conduct qualifies under 1605(a)(2)'s first clause proceeds in two stages. Initially, we consider the harder question of whether this conduct meets the definition of "commercial activity." We then proceed, albeit briefly, to consider the much easier question of whether this conduct is "carried on in the United States."

Republic of Argentina v. Weltover, 504 U.S. 607 (1992) makes clear that whether conduct is "commercial" within the meaning of the FSIA depends on whether that conduct is of the type "by which a private party engages in 'trade and traffic or commerce,'" regardless of the motive that leads the foreign state to engage in the conduct. In *Weltover,* Argentina had issued bonds, known as "Bonods," designed to refinance debts it had incurred while establishing a foreign exchange insurance contract program to overcome the instability of the Argentine currency. In holding that this bond issuance constituted "commercial activity" under the FSIA and that Argentina was not immune from suit for failure to make timely payments on the Bonods, the Supreme Court stressed that there was "nothing about the issuance of the[] Bonods (except perhaps its purpose) that is not analogous to a private commercial transaction."

Tenex's conduct upon which GNSS's lawsuit is based also constitutes "commercial activity." The entrance into a contract to supply a private party with uranium hexafluoride is the very type of action by which private parties engage in "trade and traffic or commerce." Urging the contrary conclusion, Tenex argues, "the Russian Federation is not merely dealing in uranium; it is *regulating* its inventory of [uranium hexafluoride] and LEU supply in a manner that no private player can." But this stylized usage of the term "regulation" proves far too much. Under Tenex's usage, it would also follow that a government which enters into a contract to purchase bullets for its army is "regulating" its bullet supply, or that the government of Argentina in *Weltover* was "regulating" its money supply. As these examples show, acceptance of Tenex's usage of "regulation" is not only inconsistent with the Supreme Court's decision in *Weltover,* but would also strip the "commercial activity" exception of much, if not all, of its meaning, for a foreign state would almost always be able to characterize its activities as sovereign "regulation" of some subject matter related to the conduct at issue.

We also hold that Tenex's "commercial activity" on which GNSS's lawsuit is based constitutes "commercial activity carried on in the United States" and thus satisfies the first clause of section 1605(a)(2). The FSIA provides that "a 'commercial activity carried on in the United States by a foreign state' means commercial activity carried on by such state and having substantial contact with the United States." It is readily apparent that Tenex's conduct has "substantial contact with the United States" and thus fits comfortably under this definition. First, GNSS is a United States corporation. Second, under the terms of the Tenex Contract, Tenex transfers to GNSS title to uranium hexafluoride that is located within the United States. Third, Tenex's notice of termination, the catalyst for GNSS's claim, was served upon GNSS at GNSS's principal place of business within the United States, in Bethesda, Maryland.

Reversed.

Act of state doctrine

Closely related in effect to the doctrine of sovereign immunity is the **act of state doctrine.** This doctrine is based on the concept that it is beyond the sensible exercise of judicial powers for a court in this country to sit in judgment on the actions of another sovereign nation taken in its own territory. Any redress of grievances caused by such actions should be obtained by the United States government dealing directly with the other sovereign. Thus, in Banco Nacional de Cuba v. Sabbatino, 376 U.S. 398 (1964), involving a challenge to Cuba's expropriation of a Cuban corporation that was largely owned by U.S. residents, the Supreme Court held:

> "[T]he Judicial Branch will not examine the validity of a taking of property within its own territory by a foreign sovereign government, extant and recognized by this country at the time of the suit, in the absence of treaty or other unambiguous agreement regarding controlling legal principles, even if the complaint alleges that the taking violates customary international law."

Also related to sovereign immunity is the doctrine of **sovereign compulsion,** under which American courts will refuse to hold a defendant liable for actions that it was compelled to take under the law of a recognized foreign sovereign.

The following case illustrates some of the difficult questions that can arise in application of the act of state doctrine.

International litigation: other concerns

In the domestic setting, it can be quite troublesome to obtain service of summons over a proper defendant; obtain evidence to support the claim through oral depositions, written interrogatories, and document production; and ultimately enforce the judgment against a recalcitrant defendant. In the international context, such tasks can be overwhelming. To reduce these barriers to the civil prosecution of a valid claim, several international agreements have been reached that are intended generally to increase international cooperation in these respects.

W.s. Kirkpatrick & co. v. Environmental Tectonics Corporation

U.S. Supreme Court, 493 U.S. 400 (1990)

Petitioner W. S. Kirkpatrick & Co. pleaded guilty to a violation of the Foreign Corrupt Practices Act for having paid a bribe to a Nigerian official to obtain a contract with the Republic of Nigeria. Respondent Environmental Tectonics Corporation, an unsuccessful bidder on the contract, then brought this suit claiming that petitioner had violated the Racketeer Influenced and Corrupt Organizations Act (RICO) among others. Despite having received a letter from the Department of State indicating its view that this case posed no "unique embarrassment" to execution of American foreign policy, the trial court granted summary judgment to the petitioner on grounds that the act of state doctrine barred the claim. The court of appeals reversed, concluding that no embarrassment of the executive in its conduct of foreign affairs was evident. Petitioner appealed.

Scalia, Justice:

This Court's description of the jurisprudential foundation for the act of state doctrine has undergone some evolution over the years. We once viewed the doctrine as an expression of international law, resting upon "the highest considerations of international comity and expediency," Oetjen v. Central Leather Co., 246 U.S. 297, 303-304 (1918). We have more recently described it, however, as a consequence of domestic separation of powers, reflecting "the strong sense of the Judicial Branch that its engagement in the task of passing on the validity of foreign acts of state may hinder" the conduct of foreign affairs. Banco Nacional de Cuba v. Sabbatino, 376 U.S. 398, 423 (1964). Some Justices have suggested possible exceptions to application of the doctrine where one or both of the foregoing policies would seemingly not be served: an exception, for example, for acts of state that consist of commercial transactions, since neither modern international comity nor the current position of our Executive Branch accorded sovereign immunity to such acts . . . or an exception for cases in which the Executive Branch has represented that it has no objection to denying validity to the foreign sovereign act, since then the courts would be impeding no foreign policy goals. The parties have argued about the applicability of these possible exceptions, and, more generally, about whether the purposes of the act of state doctrine would be furthered by its application in this case. We find it unnecessary, however, to pursue those inquiries, since the factual predicate for application of the act of state doctrine does not exist. Nothing in the present suit requires the court to declare invalid, and thus ineffective as "a rule of decision for the courts of this country," Ricaud v. American Metal Co., 246 U.S. 304, 310(1918), the official act of a foreign sovereign.

In every case in which we have held the act of state doctrine applicable, the relief sought or the defense interposed would have required a court in the United States to declare invalid the official act of a foreign sovereign performed within its own territory. . .. In the present case, by contrast, neither the claim nor any asserted defense requires a determination that Nigeria's contract with Kirkpatrick International was, or was not, effective.

The short of the matter is this: Courts in the United States have the power, and ordinarily the obligation, to decide cases and controversies properly presented to them. The act of state doctrine does not establish an exception for cases and controversies that may embarrass foreign governments, but merely requires that, in the process of deciding, the acts of foreign sovereigns taken within their own jurisdiction shall be deemed valid. That doctrine has no application to the present case because the validity of no foreign sovereign act at issue.

[Affirmed.]

The Hague Convention on Service Abroad of Judicial and Extrajudicial Documents in Civil or Commercial Matters provides that each signatory state will maintain a Central Authority to process judicial documents, such as complaints, and expedite their transmission. The Hague Convention on the Taking of Evidence Abroad in Civil or Commercial Matters of 1970 seeks to reduce the barriers raised by national laws to obtaining evidence for use in court and to streamline the discovery process in international litigation. The Convention creates Central Authorities in each signatory nation through which discovery requests ("Letters of Request") are channeled; it permits consuls to conduct some discovery procedures regarding their own nationals; and, finally, it allows the use of court-appointed commissioners for discovery purposes in limited circumstances. The United States is a signatory of both Conventions.

What happens if an American company, for example, receives a judgment against a foreign defendant in a foreign country's court and wishes to enforce that judgment against the defendant's property located in the United States Will U.S. courts recognize such foreign judgments Enforcement of foreign judgments is a matter of state law, which varies somewhat from jurisdiction to jurisdiction. Guidance is provided by the Restatement (Third) of the Foreign Relations Law of the United States, which provides that final money judgments of the courts of a foreign state will generally be enforced in the United States. However, a U. S. court is prohibited from enforcing a judgment that (1) was rendered by a judicial system that does not provide impartial tribunals or due process of law or (2) was rendered by a court lacking personal jurisdiction over the defendant under its own law or international law. Furthermore an American court has discretion to refrain from enforcing a foreign judgment on several grounds, including that the rendering court did not have subject matter jurisdiction, that the defendant did not receive notice of the proceedings in time to defend, that the judgment was obtained by fraud, or that the judgment is based on a cause of action repugnant to American public policy.

Arbitration

In view of the special difficulties encountered in international court litigation, it is not surprising that the international business community has actively sought alternative methods of commercial dispute resolution. Quite popular is **arbitration,** a process whereby parties to a transaction agree (either within the terms of their basic agreement or subsequently) to submit any future (or existing) disputes to an impartial third party (or panel) for nonjudicial resolution. The decision of the arbitrator—termed an award—may, depending on the agreement of the parties, be binding or nonbinding.

Binding arbitration within the international trading context has a long and colorful history and today is the preferred alternative to litigation in international commercial circles. The advantages of arbitration are many, including: (1) it is usually less expensive and faster than court procedures; (2) it is more private than litigation; and (3) the parties may choose knowledgeable experts (rather that generalist judges and untrained juries) to decide the matter based on commercial realities.

Arbitration is not, however, without its disadvantages. Arbitral panels generally do not have the power to compel the attendance of witnesses or the production of other information relevant to the case. The informality of the procedure can lead to an undesired degree of "looseness" in the process; and, because arbitrators are generally not bound by the strict letter of the law, final outcomes may be difficult to forecast.

Several organizations have sought to facilitate this means of dispute resolution by providing standard arbitral rules and procedures. Chief among these organizations are the International Chamber of Commerce (headquartered in Paris), the U.N. Commission on International Trade Law (UNCITRAL), the American Arbitration Association, the International Centre for Settlement of Investment Disputes (ICSID), the Inter-American Commercial Arbitration Commission, and the London Court of Arbitration.

So well accepted is the use of arbitration in international commercial disputes that most nations readily enforce such awards. In the United States, such enforcement is a matter of federal law. As with foreign court judgments, guidance is provided by the Restatement (Third) of Foreign Relations, which provides that awards pursuant to valid written arbitral agreements will generally be enforced, although a court may deny recognition on such grounds as: (1) the agreement to arbitrate was not valid under applicable law; (2) the losing party was not given an opportunity to present its case; (3) the award deals with matters outside the terms of the agreement to arbitrate; or (4) recognition of the award would be contrary to public policy. The Restatement's rules are based on the U.N. Convention on the Recognition and Enforcement of Foreign Arbitral Awards (known as the *New York Convention*). Almost 80 nations are parties to this Convention, reflecting the widespread acceptance of arbitration in the international sphere. The following case is illustrative.

Mitsubishi Motors Corp. v. Soler Chrysler-Plymouth, Inc.

U.S. Supreme Court, 473 U.S. 614 (1985)

Petitioner Mitsubishi, a Japanese corporation that manufactures automobiles, is the product of a joint venture between Chrysler International, S.A. (CISA), a Swiss corporation, and another Japanese corporation, aimed at distributing automobiles manufactured by the petitioner through Chrysler dealers outside the continental United States. Respondent Soler, a Puerto Rican corporation, entered into distribution and sales agreements with CISA. These agreements contained a clause providing for arbitration by the Japan Commercial Arbitration Association of all disputes arising out of certain articles of the agreement or for the breach thereof. Disagreements did arise, and petitioner filed suit in federal district court in Puerto Rico under the federal Arbitration Act and the Convention on the Recognition and Enforcement of Foreign Arbitral Awards, seeking an order to compel arbitration of the dispute in accordance with the arbitration clause. Respondent filed a counterclaim alleging antitrust violations by petitioner and CISA. The district court ordered arbitration of almost all issues. On appeal, the circuit court affirmed, except as to the antitrust issues, which it held to be inappropriate for arbitration.

Blackmun, Justice:

By agreeing to arbitrate a statutory claim, a party does not forgo the substantive rights afforded by the statute, it only submits to their resolution in an arbitral, rather than a judicial, forum. It trades the procedures and opportunity for review of the courtroom for the simplicity, informality, and expedition of arbitration. We must assume that if Congress intended the substantive protection against waiver of the right to a judicial forum, that intention will be deducible from text or legislative history. . . . Having made the bargain to arbitrate, the party should be held to it unless Congress itself has evinced an intention to preclude a waiver of judicial remedies for the statutory rights at issue. . . .

We now turn to consider whether Soler's antitrust claims are nonarbitrable even though it agreed to arbitrate them. in holding that they are not, the Court of Appeals followed the decision of the Second Circuit in American Safety Equipment Corp. v. J. P. McGuire&Co., 391 F.2d 821(1968) [finding] that "the pervasive public interest in enforcement of the antitrust laws, and the nature of the claims that arise in such cases, combine to make . . . antitrust claims . . . inappropriate for arbitration." We find it unnecessary to assess the legitimacy of the *American Safety* doctrine as applied to agreements to arbitrate arising from domestic transactions. As in Scherk v. Alberto-Culver Co., 417 U.S 506 (1974), we conclude that concerns of international comity, respect for the capacities of foreign and transnational tribunals, and sensitivity to the need of the international commercial system for predictability in the resolution of disputes require that we enforce the parties' agreement, even assuming that a contrary result would be forthcoming in a domestic context.

Even before *Scherk,* this Court had recognized the utility of forum selection clauses in international transactions. In The Bremen v. Zapata Of f-Shore Co., 407 U.S. 1(1972), an American oil company, seeking to evade a contractual choice of an English forum and, by implication, English law, filed a suit in admiralty in a United States District Court against the German corporation which had contracted to tow its rig to a location in the Adriatic Sea. Notwithstanding the possibility that the English court would enforce provisions in the towage contract exculpating the German party which an American court would refuse to enforce, this Court gave effect to the choice-of-forum clause. It observed:

The expansion of American business and industry will hardly be encouraged if, notwithstanding solemn contracts, we insist on a parochial concept that all disputes must be resolved under our laws and in our courts. . . . We cannot have trade and commerce in world markets and international waters exclusively on our terms, governed by our laws, and resolved in our courts.

. . . In *Scherk,* . . . this Court [enforced] the arbitration agreement even while assuming for purposes of the decision that the controversy would be nonarbitrable had it arisen out of a domestic transaction. Again, the Court emphasized:

A contractual provision specifying in advance the forum in which disputes shall be litigated and the law to be applied is . . . an almost indispensable precondition to achievement of the orderliness and predictability essential to any international business transaction.

A parochial refusal by the courts of one country to enforce an international arbitration agreement would not only frustrate these purposes, but would invite unseemly and mutually destructive jockeying by the parties to secure tactical litigation advantages. . . . [It would] damage the fabric of international commerce and trade, and imperil the willingness and ability of businessmen to enter into international commercial agreements.

. . . There is no reason to assume at the outset of the dispute that international arbitration will not provide an adequate mechanism. To be sure, the international arbitral tribunal owes no prior allegiance to the legal norms of particular states; hence, it has no direct obligation to vindicate their statutory dictates. The tribunal, however, is bound to effectuate the intentions of the parties. Where the parties have agreed that the arbitral body is to decide a defined set of claims which includes, as in these cases, those arising from the application of American antitrust law, the tribal therefore should be bound to decide that dispute in accord with the national law giving rise to the claim. And as long as the prospective litigant effectively may vindicate its statutory cause of action in the arbitral forum, the statute will continue to serve both its remedial and deterrent function. . . .

As international trade has expanded in recent decades, so too has the use of international arbitration to resolve disputes arising in the course of that trade. The controversies that international arbitral institutions are called upon to resolve have increased in diversity as well as in complexity. Yet the potential of these tribunals for efficient disposition of legal disagreements arising from commercial relations has not yet been tested. If they are to take a central place in the international legal order, national courts will need to "shake off the old judicial hostility to arbitration." Kulukundis Shipping Co. v. Amtorg Trading Corp., 126 F2d. 97S (CA2 1942), and also their customary and understandable unwillingness to cede jurisdiction of a claim arising under the domestic law to a foreign or transnational tribunal. To this extent, at least, it will be necessary for national courts to subordinate domestic notions of arbitrability to the international policy favoring commercial arbitration.

Accordingly, we "require this representative of the American business community to honor its bargain," . . . by holding this agreement to arbitrate "enforce[able] in accord with the explicit provisions of the Arbitration Act." *Scherk*, 417 U.S., at 520.

The judgment of the Court of Appeals is affirmed in part and reversed in part.

National regulation of the importerort process

The impact of export trade transcends, of course, the private interests of the parties to the international sales contract. Concerns at the national level touch on defense and security matters (especially in the export of high technology with military applications) and the depletion of national stocks of critical materials. Moreover, the volumes and direction of flow of export sales are inextricably bound up in the general economic posture of a nation and thus bear directly on its overall pattern of foreign relations. Not surprisingly, almost all nations have responded to these factors by adopting broad regulatory schemes to control exports. The implementation of these programs will directly affect the international trader and the methods used in that trade.

Export Controls

All nations wish to export their goods, but this desire must be weighed against national security concerns. If military weapons, nuclear materials, advanced technology, or the like are in the mix, concerns for national security may outweigh companies' desire to sell to foreign nations or companies.

In the United States, the power to regulate international trade is vested in the Congress under the provisions of the commerce clause of the federal Constitution. Congress has used this power repeatedly since the early days of the Republic and the trail of congressional legislation dealing with import and export matters continues into the present day. For many years, the Export Administration Act of 1979 was perhaps the most important piece of federal legislation affecting American export traders. It contained a comprehensive scheme scheme to regulate exports from the United States and, together with the regulations adopted pursuant to it, extended its controls in some instances to the reexport of certain American goods to third countries. The Act granted discretionary authority to the Office of Export Administration (OEA) of the Department of Commerce to impose export controls for three basic reasons: (1) national security (to prevent "dual use" products that might have military applications from reaching our enemies), (2) foreign policy (for example, to prevent goods from reaching countries that practice terrorism or apartheid), and (3) short supply of goods in the United States.

In 2001, the Export Administration Act was not renewed by Congress. Since that time, President Bush has maintained export controls pursuant to the International Emergency Economic Powers Act, as implemented by executive order. A recent court challenge claiming that the IEEPA delegated too much authority to the Executive Branch was denied. U.S. v. Esfahani, 2006 U.S. Dist. LEXIS 1839 (N.D.Ill.).

Since the tragic events of September 11, 2001, export controls have naturally evolved, in part to focus more on securities threats posed by non–nation entities.

Trade activity is also constrained by numerous other acts and conventions. For example, export control provisions are also found in the Nuclear Non–Proliferation Act (1978) and the Atomic Energy Act (1954), which govern nuclear materials. The Arms Export Control Act, the Trading with the Enemy Act, and the International Emergency Economic Power Act also contain important export restrictions. In B–BWest Imports, Inc. v. U.S., 75 F.3d 633 (Fed.Cir. 1996), the court held that the Arms Export Control Act's granting to the president the power to "control" arms imports included the authority to stop such importing altogether of munitions from China in light of human rights abuses occurring ithere.

In addition, after World War II the United States joined the Coordinating Committee for Multilateral Export Controls (COCOM) along with Japan and most NATO members. This international group cooperated in the control of exports of strategic goods to sensitive destinations. It was aimed largely at preventing military technology from being exported to Russia. COCOM expired in 1994 and two years later was replaced when thirty–three nations met to discuss the problem of export controls on conventional weapons and dual–use goods and technologies. The meeting ended in the Wassenaar Arrangement on Export Controls for Conventional Arms and Dual–Use Goods and Technologies. Wassenaar differs importantly from COCOM because it was arranged after the fall of the Berlin Wall, and Russia is a party to the arrangement rather than its target.

Given the post–9/11 terrorism concerns, the United States has urged the strengthening of the Wassenaar Arrangement; has advocated a "zero tolerance" policy for violations of nonproliferation treaties, has used the Cooperative Threat Reduction program to work bilaterally with other nations like Russia and China to help them develop and strengthen export controls; and has led 70 nations in the Proliferation Security Initiative to interdict shipments of materials that could be used in creating weapons of mass destruction.

Export incentives

U.S. export policy and legislation is not, however, totally negative. Important legislation has long been on the books to encourage increased export trade by manufacturers and suppliers in this country.

As early as 1918, Congress adopted the Webb–Pomerene Act to promote American export trade by granting limited exemptions to exporters from the application of U.S. antitrust laws, principally the Sherman and Clayton acts. Congress acted in the belief that American traders could better compete in foreign markets if they were permitted to form associations capturing the benefits of economies of scale and greater efficiency; such associations, however, involved a danger of criminal or civil liability under American antitrust laws. The Webb–Pomerene Act, therefore, relieved export associations of this risk but conditioned the exemption in important respects. Principally, such an association is prohibited by the act from entering into any agreement that "artificially or intentionally" depresses commodity prices within the United States or that "substantially lessens competition within the United States, or otherwise restrains trade therein." Further, the benefits of the act (obtained by registration of the association with the Federal Trade Commission) are limited to associations formed for the export of commodities; transactions for services or technology are not protected. As a result of these limitations and lingering anxiety about possible antitrust liability, comparatively few Webb–Pomerene associations are registered with the FTC.

Export trading company act

The failure of the 1918 legislation to promote greater American export trade, coupled with increasing U.S. trade deficits in the mid and late 1970s, created a sense of urgency in Congress to devise new and more effective means to encourage increased exports from this country, especially by small and medium–sized companies historically underrepresented in international trade transactions. The legislative response was the Export Trading Company Act of 1982.

At the heart of this Act is the provision that no criminal or civil action may be brought under the antitrust laws [of the United States] against a person to whom a certificate of review is issued [by the secretary of Commerce] which is based on conduct which is specified in, and complies with the terms of, a certificate ... which ... was in effect when the conduct occurred.

This exemption is available to individual persons residing in the United States, partnerships or corporations created under state or federal law, and significantly for antitrust purposes, "any association or combination, by contract or other arrangement" between or among any of these.

The Act's scope is comprehensive. It extends its antitrust protection to activities related to the export of goods and merchandise and (going beyond the reach of the Webb–Pomerene Act) to services. This latter category is defined to include services that are the subject of the transaction (as in trans–border management agreements) and includes accounting, architectural, data processing, business, communications, consulting, and legal services. Also eligible for exemption from possible antitrust liabilities are "export trade services," that is, international market research, product research and design, transportation, warehousing, insurance, and the like.

The European Commission is distrustful of these antitrust exemptions, viewing the activities of U.S. companies under Webb–Pomerene and the Export Company Trading Act as cartel–related. A collision between European interests and American interests over these activities seems inevitable.

Regulating imports

Compared with the elaborate nature of export controls and incentives, the regulation of imports into the United States is relatively straightforward. The application of these import control laws can, however, be quite complex.

Under the import export clause of the federal Constitution, the power to levy import customs and duties rests exclusively with the federal government. Using federal power in this regard, the government has established a comprehensive system of tariff schedules that apply to goods entering the United States—the Harmonized Tariff Schedules of the United States (HTSUS). Tariffs vary from nation to nation and product to product. The HTSUS will be applied by federal customs officials first to classify the entering goods and then to determine the applicable tariff rate to the goods so classified.

Because tariffs vary from nation to nation and product to product, fierce disputes can arise during the categorization processs.

BAUSCH & LOMB V. UNITED STATES

U.S. Circuit Court for the Federal Circuit, 148 F.3d 1363 (1998)

Bausch & Lomb imports several types of electric toothbrushes into the U.S. On February 6, 1991, U.S. Customs changed the classification of these items from "toothbrushes" to "electromechanical domestic appliances." Bausch & Lomb challenged this reclassification, but the Court of International Trade rejected the challenge. Bausch & Lomb appealed.

Plager, Circuit Judge:
When there is a dispute over which of two or more tariff classifications particular merchandise falls under, the court analyzes the problem in two steps: first, construe the relevant classification headings; and second, determine under which of the properly construed tariff terms the merchandise at issue falls. The first step of construing the tariff classification terms is denominated a question of law, while

the second step is, under the usual iteration of the rule, referred to as a factual inquiry.

We start first with the competing tariff headings. Customs classified the Interplak electric toothbrushes as "Other appliances" under Subheading 8509.80.00 of the HTSUS, which provides: "8509 Electromechanical domestic appliances, with self–contained electric motor; parts thereof: * * * 8509.80.00 Other appliances . . . [duty rate of 4.2% ad valorem]"

The plain language of Subheading 8509.80.00 covers electromechanical domestic appliances with self–contained electric motors—of which an electric toothbrush is undoubtedly one. This interpretation is supported by the Explanatory Notes under Heading 8509, which specifically classify "Electric tooth brushes" under that Heading, rather than under Heading 9603, as well as the Explanatory Notes under Heading 9603, which appear to limit that Heading to brushes "for" appliances, and not the appliances themselves. See Lonza, Inc. v. U.S., 46 F.3d 1098 (Fed. Cir. 1995). ("While the Explanatory Notes do not constitute controlling legislative history, they do offer guidance in interpreting HTS subheadings.").

Bausch & Lomb does not dispute that this provision literally covers the Interplak. Instead, it contends that electric toothbrushes are more specifically provided for under HTSUS Subheading 9603.21.00 in light of the legislative history and prior case law of this court and its predecessor. Under General Rule of Interpretation ("GRI") 3(a) of the Harmonized Tariff System, according to Bausch & Lomb, the more specific description "brush" in Heading 9603 is preferred to the more general description "electromechanical appliance with self–contained motor" contained in Heading 8509. Thus, even though the Interplak could literally fall within Heading 8509, the preferred classification is under Heading 9603, argues Bausch & Lomb. We must therefore construe Heading 9603.

The relevant provisions in Heading 9603 provide: "9603 Brooms, brushes (including brushes constituting parts of machines, appliances or vehicles) * * * Toothbrushes . . . for use on the person, including such brushes constituting parts of appliances: 9603.21.00 Toothbrushes . . . [duty rate of 0.2 cents each plus 3.4% ad valorem].

Bausch & Lomb advances the following dictionary definition for "brush"–"

brush: a hand–operated or power–driven tool or device composed of bristles set into a back or handle or attached to a roller and designed or adapted for such uses as sweeping, scrubbing, painting or smoothing." Without deciding whether this is the correct definition of brush, it is not inconsistent with definitions in prior opinions. It is enough at this juncture simply to agree that the word "brush," by itself, is broad enough to encompass motorized devices such as the Interplak.

The word brush, however, does not appear alone in Heading 9603; brush is limited by the parenthetical "including brushes constituting parts of machines, appliances or vehicles." We interpret this phrase to cover only brushes that are a part of a machine, appliance or vehicle that are imported separately. To interpret this phrase otherwise would require all "machines, appliances or vehicles" that include a brush such as a street sweeper to fall within this heading. Under our reading, only if the brush is separately imported would it fall under this provision. This interpretation is consistent with treating "appliances" separately under Heading 9603.

It is true, as Bausch & Lomb points out, that electric toothbrushes have long been classified under the toothbrush provision. The government does not argue to the contrary. In none of the earlier cases so holding, however, did the brush or toothbrush provision have the "including" parenthetical that now appears. As a result, Bausch & Lomb's reliance on those decisions, while not without merit, misses the mark because the Heading has been substantially changed.

Affirmed.

The federal government sets the actual rate, but does so subject to bilateral or multilateral restraints that it has assumed. For example, a treaty with another nation may stipulate the tariff level or, more generally, the applicable tariff may have been negotiated within the framework of a multinational commitment, for example, the General Agreement on Tariffs and Trade (GATT). In either event, the tariff generally must be paid before the goods are admitted into this country.

An important exception to this principle is the use of a foreign trade zone (FTZ). Established by federal law, these zones are fenced–off, policed warehouses and industrial parks usually located near American ports of entry. Goods entering the port from abroad may be taken into the FTZ and stored there without paying any applicable tariff and with a minimum of formality and procedure. As long as the goods are warehoused within the FTZ, no duty is payable and the goods may be further processed, assembled, or finished. Only when the merchandise leaves the confines of the FTZ will the duty be imposed, frequently at a reduced rate. The FTZ has shown itself to be an effective device for encouraging additional international trade in the United States.

Whereas import licenses are generally not required for imports into the United States, certain goods may be denied entry altogether. Bans on importation may be applied against undesirable imports such as narcotics, pornographic material, or printed materials advocating the violent overthrow of the United States. Import bans may be applied to prevent entry of automobiles that do not meet vehicle safety regulations or against other products not meeting standards established to protect public health and safety. Products violating the patent, trademark, and copyright laws of the United States may also be excluded. Moreover, certain goods may be subjected to tariff increases to offset foreign government subsidies that unfairly reduce their U.S. market price or to counteract a foreign producer's domestic production in the United States. These countervailing and *anti-dumping* measures are considered again in this chapter with regard to the GATT.

Trade and tariff act

One method of increasing the access of U.S. companies to foreign markets is retaliation against countries that treat U.S. companies unfairly. A series of acts over the years have authorized and encouraged the President to take such retaliatory action. In recent years Congress has been specifically concerned with the difficulty U.S. companies have had gaining access to markets in Asia, especially Japan. At various times Congress has authorized, and even mandated, the President to respond to unfair trade practices by use of higher tariffs, import quotas, or withdrawal from existing trade agreements with offending parties. Prying open new markets for U.S. companies without unduly antagonizing existing trading partners requires the striking of a delicate balance.

Protection from unfair competition

Various provisions of federal law protect U.S. companies from unfair practices by foreign competitors selling in this country. The primary protective provision is Sec. 337 of the Tariff Act of 1930, which protects "domestic industries" from "substantial injury" stemming from "unfair methods of competition and unfair acts in the importation of articles into the United States, or in their sale…." In the 10 years preceding 2005, 158 complaints in Section 337 investigations were filed. Ninety percent of such proceedings involve cases of alleged patent infringement, but it also protects U.S. businesses from copyright and trademark infringement, false advertising, trade secret misappropriation, palming off (misleading consumers into thinking they are buying another company's goods), and even "dumping."

Sec. 337 is activated by a domestic company's complaint to the U.S. International Trade Commission (ITC), an independent federal regulatory commission. The commission follows the Administrative Procedure Act in investigating the complaint and determining whether there has been a violation. The President has 60 days to review the commission's decision. Damages are not available under Sec. 337, but remedies can include cease and desist orders, temporary exclusion orders, and even permanent exclusion orders that will keep the infringing goods from entering the U.S. market.

Organizing for international trade

The massive devastation of the Second World War had among its many casualties the international trade infrastructure, which had been growing slowly but perceptibly since the middle of the nineteenth century. One of the major tasks of reconstruction following 1945 was the recreation of a framework for international trade. Negotiations focusing on trade, money, and finance led to establishment of the current international economic institutions, including the GATT, the International Monetary Fund, and the International Bank for Reconstruction and Development. More recently, regional trade agreements have become a prominent means of facilitating international trade.

The gatt

The United Nations Conference on Trade and Employment met in Havana in late 1947 and was attended by more than 50 countries. Although the conference was unsuccessful in creating a proposed International Trade Organization, it led almost two dozen countries to conclude the GATT (General Agreement on Tariffs and Trade), the essential purpose of which was to achieve a significant reduction of the general level of national tariffs and, further, to provide an institutional framework within which future tariff conflicts could be resolved. The GATT has, since its creation, shown itself to be of enduring significance in international economic and trade relations. According to its supporters, the GATT trading system has achieved unprecedented trade expansion and world prosperity. (Its detractors note that GATT provisions are often breached by participating countries.)

The GATT achieves its overall objective of liberalized international trade by addressing a series of key issues regarding important restrictions. It requires that each signatory state extend "most favored nation" tariff rates to goods from other signatory nations and, further, obligates participating nations to afford "national treatment" to the imported goods from other signatory countries. Article III of the agreement provides:

The products of the territory of any contracting party imported into the territory of any other contracting party shall be accorded treatment no less favorable than that accorded to like products of national origin in respect of all laws, regulations and requirements affecting their internal sale, offering for sale, purchase, transportation, distribution or use.

The GATT prohibits discrimination by participating states through quantitative trade restrictions by providing that import quotas, if adopted at all by a state, shall be applied equally to all nations that are parties to the agreement. An even more ambitious objective of the GATT is the elimination of all prohibitions or restrictions (other than duties, taxes, or other charges) on imports and exports among the member nations.

In large measure, the GATT implements its goals of free trade through a series of published tariff schedules that are developed through an intricate negotiation process within the framework of the organization and that, once published, are binding on each of the participating states. In recognition of inevitable trade anomalies and to secure the willing participation and cooperation of member states in its tariff reduction program, the GATT provides special circumstances when unilateral exceptions to the schedules of tariffs may be made. The most well known of these relate to antidumping duties and countervailing subsidies.

If the products of one country are "dumped" into another at prices below their fair market value in the exporting country in an effort to disrupt or destroy the domestic production of those goods in the receiving nation, the GATT contemplates that the government of the receiving country may impose an "antidumping duty" in an effort to equalize the domestic price in those goods with the prevailing fair market price in the exporting country. Similarly, when the production of certain goods in the exporting state is heavily subsidized by the government of that nation (leading to a reduced export price for that product), the GATT permits the receiving state to impose a "counter-vailing duty" to bring the market price up to a competitive level.

In its formative years, the GATT concentrated almost exclusively on measures to reduce tariff barriers to increase international trade. More recently, it has turned its attention to the reduction of nontariff barriers, such as unreasonably restrictive local standards and inaccessible national distribution systems, to further increase the volume of trade among nations.

During the rounds of negotiation, nations bargain to advance their positions. The United States, for example, seeks to induce Europe and Japan to lower subsidies for their farmers who compete with American agriculture and to induce Third World nations to refrain from pirating U.S. trademarks, copyrights, and patents. Many nations seek to induce Japan to open its economy to foreign sellers and urge the United States to reduce its protection for textiles. For their part, underdeveloped nations seek freer access to advanced technology and to markets for their agricultural products.

One of the most important GATT developments was the 1995 negotiation of the agreement on Trade–Related Aspects of Intellectual Property Rights (TRIPS) in which WTO members committed themselves to enacting and enforcing modern copyright, pat-ent, and trademark laws. Parties committed themselves to punishing intellectual prop-erty pirates. Compliance with TRIPS has been spotty in many nations and several disputes have arisen.

The world trade organization

The World Trade Organization (WTO) was created by GATT to resolve trade disputes, such as those arising under TRIPS. The WTO can resolve tariff and non-tariff barrier disputes among signatory nations. It may order compliance with GATT agreements and impose trade sanctions. Several nations were uncomfortable granting this much power to an international body. When Congress approved GATT, it created a panel of Ameri-can judges to review WTO decisions. The panel may recommend to Congress that the U.S. withdraw from GATT if it finds three unprincipled rulings against the United States within a five–year period.

WTO meetings have become very controversial as protestors who worry that GATT agreements exploit lesser–developed nations and endanger the environment often protest vigorously.

Although negotiations seem to become more and more contentious, the WTO has had some success in encouraging free trade through the gradual abolition of trade barriers like import duties, subsidies, and quotas. As the ninth round of negotiations since the 1940s, the Doha Round, proceeds, the average import duty has come down to less than 4%.

The imf and the ibrd

The International Monetary Fund (IMF), like the GATT, is intended to coordinate the activities of governments regarding international trade functions and does not primarily address the individual international trader. Growing out of discussions held at Bretton

Woods, New Hampshire, late in the Second World War, the IMF was designed to speed international financial and economic reconstruction by providing an institutional structure within which intergovernmental loans would be used to stabilize currency exchange rates and, through a system of credits (termed Special Drawing Rights or SDRs), to enable member countries to borrow from the fund or from each other as a means of stabilizing their national currencies with the international monetary system.

Affiliated with the International Monetary Fund is the International Bank for Reconstruction and Development (IBRD), which was founded to "assist in the reconstruction and development of territories of members by facilitating the investment of capital for productive purposes" and to "promote private foreign investment by means of guarantees or participations in loans and other investments made by private investors." The IBRD, located in Washington, D.C., is permitted under its charter to guarantee, participate in, or make loans to member states and to any business, industrial, or agricultural enterprise in the territories of a member state. The availability through IMF and IBRD of massive amounts of financial credit was particularly significant in Western Europe during the immediate postwar years and has had, in addition, a very significant role in the industrial development of Asia and Africa in the past several decades.

Regional trade agreements

The creation of cooperative organizations to break down trade in regions of the world is a new and important trend in international law. For example, the Association of South-East Asian Nations (ASEAN) seeks to reduce tariffs and duties among its members—Brunei, Indonesia, Lao, Malaysia, Myanmar, the Philippines, Singapore, Thailand, and Vietnam. And Mercosur hopes to do the same in trade among Argentina, Brazil, Paraguay, and Uruguay. Of greater importance to the U.S. are NAFTA and the EU.

North american free trade agreement

The North American Free Trade Agreement (NAFTA) signed by Mexico, Canada, and the United States in 1993, is designed to eliminate most tariff and non–tariff barriers in trade among the three nations. Any remaining trade barriers are to serve legitimate purposes such as protection of health, environment, and national security.

NAFTA has certainly increased the amount of trade among the three nations. The United States has essentially doubled its exports to Mexico and Canada. Two–way trade among the three nations has sky–rocketed.

Controversy persists, however. A decadelong economic boom followed passage of NAFTA, yet some studies indicate that 750,000 American jobs have been relocated to Mexico. The American trade balance with Mexico has gone from a pre–NAFTA surplus to a post–NAFTA substantial deficit. Some American interests believe that employee rights and environmental concerns have suffered under NAFTA. Old–time disputes still arise. For example, in 2001, U.S. timber interests lobbied President Bush to launch negotiations with Canada to limit its exports of soft timber to the U.S. The U.S. businesses claim that Canada is subsidizing the Canadian exports.

In May 2001, the presidents of the U.S. and Mexico stated their support for extending the NAFTA concept throughout the Americas. The U.S. has approved CAFTA–DR (Central American Free Trade Agreement—Dominican Republic), but at this writing controversy is delaying implementation that was supposed to have been completed by January 1, 2006. This controversy makes extension of NAFTA and CAFTA throughout South America seems a long way off.

The european union

The European Union (EU)(formerly known as the Common Market or EEC) is an attempt by European nations to break down barriers to trade among the many sovereign nations on that continent. Six founding members (Belgium, France, Luxembourg, Netherlands, West Germany, and Italy) were joined by nine others (Austria, Denmark, Finland, Greece, Ireland, Portugal, Spain, Sweden, and the United Kingdom) to create a powerful free–trade association. Among the purposes of the EU are elimination of trade barriers, creation of a common currency (the Euro), free movement of citizens, and establishment of common dispute resolution institutions. Recently membership in the EU has grown to 26 nations and at this writing four more have applied for membership.

Other ways of doing business

Thus far, we have spoken of international trade mainly in terms of direct sales from a seller in one country to a buyer in another. However, there are many other forms of international transactions. Take the case of an American corporation wishing to export its goods. Rather than send its own employees to the foreign markets to drum up business at the retail or wholesale level, it might hire an agent in that foreign country to act on its behalf. Such agents would typically have authority to contract on behalf of the American sellers. Complications would likely arise from the differences between agency law and customs in the United States and those of the foreign country.

Or the American company might choose to do business through a **licensee** in the foreign country. That licensee would pay a fee to the American company for the right to sell the company's goods. Such licensees, of course, will want exclusive rights to sell the American company's products, if possible. Legal problems here may result from antitrust laws of the United States and the foreign country. An increasingly popular form of such licensing arrangement is the franchising of trademarks, trade names, and copyrights. Many American service industries, such as fast food chains and convenience store chains, are expanding to foreign markets through use of this device.

Or an American seller may wish to have a foreign subsidiary corporation formed in the foreign nations in which it seeks to do business. This process is complicated by the many restrictions that most countries, especially in the underdeveloped world, place on such corporations. Such restrictions may take the form of **currency controls,** which make it difficult to take profits out of the country. Or the host country may require a certain percentage of host country ownership of the American company's subsidiary or require that the company enter into a joint venture with the host government or a local company.

India, for example has endeavored to "Indianize" foreign companies operating there. In the wake of the terrible 1984 Bhopal, India, gas leak that killed 2700 and injured perhaps 200,000, the Union Carbide Corporation has claimed that its subsidiary— Union Carbide India Ltd.—was so "Indianized" that Union Carbide could not have shut the plant down out of safety concerns had it wanted to. All 9000 employees of the company were Indian, and quasi–governmental Indian financial institutions owned 25 percent of its stock. Union Carbide itself retained only 50.9 percent of the subsidiary's stock. In many lesser developed countries, foreign corporations are limited to 49 percent ownership; local entities must retain control.

The following case illustrates legal issues that may arise with the use of one of these methods of doing business abroad—the franchise.

DAYAN V. MCDONALD'S CORPORATION
Appellate Court of Illinois, 466 N.E.2d 958 (1984)

In 1971, Dayan and McDonald's Corp. signed a master license agreement (MLA), granting Dayan a 30–year franchise right to use the McDonald's patents, trademarks, and trade names in Paris. The agreement bound Dayan to meet McDonald's Quality, Service, and Cleanliness (QSC) standards, because his departure from them would impede the successful operation of McDonald's restaurants in other parts of the world. If Dayan defaulted, McDonald's had the right to terminate the agreement. McDonald's issued operating licenses to Dayan for 14 restaurants. However, McDonald's was never satisfied with Dayan's compliance with QSC standards. In 1976, McDonald's told Dayan that his substandard operation could no longer be tolerated and that he would have six months to bring his restaurants into compliance with the QSC standards. When Dayan failed to do so, McDonald's sued in Paris to terminate the MLA. Dayan then brought this action in Illinois to enjoin the termination.

The trial judge, after 65 days of testimony, refused to issue the injunction, ruling that McDonald's properly terminated the MLA because of Dayan's breach of its QSC provisions. Dayan appealed.

Buckley, Presiding Justice:

[Several] cases reflect judicial concern over longstanding abuses in franchise relationships, particularly contract provisions giving the franchisor broad unilateral powers of termination at will. Taken collectively, they stand for the proposition that the implied covenant of good faith restricts franchisor discretion in terminating a franchise agreement to those cases where good cause exists.

After finding good cause for termination existed, the trial court found that McDonald's sole motive for termination was Dayan's failure to maintain QSC standards.

Our review of the evidence admits of no doubt; the trial court properly resolved this issue in favor of McDonald's. To characterize the condition of Dayan's restaurants as being in substantial noncompliance with McDonald's QSC standards is to engage in profound understatement. Throughout the trial the various witnesses struggled to find the appropriate words to describe the ineffably unsanitary conditions observed in these restaurants, as did the trial court in its memorandum opinion. Terms describing the uncleanliness—such as "indescribable," "extremely defective sanitary conditions," "filthy, grimy, cruddy," "deplorable," "significantly unsanitary," "contaminated," "insanitary," "very dirty," "very, very dirty," "disgusting," "abundance of filth," "pig pens"— tell only part of the story. The accuracy of these epithets is supported by voluminous, detailed testimonial evidence which consumed many weeks of trial and thousands of pages of transcript and is also corroborated by over 1,000 photographs admitted in evidence at trial. The conditions of filth were so widespread and reported by so many persons that any attempt to catalog them all would only unduly lengthen this opinion.

[Dayan's complaint that McDonald's did not provide a trained, French–speaking operations man] rings false. As the trial court correctly realized:

"It does not take a McDonald's trained French speaking operational man to know that grease dripping from the vents must be stopped and not merely collected in a cup hung from the ceiling, that dogs are not permitted to defecate where food is stored, that insecticide is not blended with chicken breading, that past–dated products should be discarded, that a potato peeler should be somewhat cleaner than a tirevulcanizer and that shortening should not look like crankcase oil."

[Affirmed.]

Regulating the multinational enterprise

The rise of huge and powerful **multinational enterprises (MNEs)** is one of the defining elements of the post-World War II global economic environment. MNEs such as IBM, Exxon, and Toyota can have tremendous impact on the economy, culture, and environment of developing host countries. In the early 1970s, a series of economic, political, and legal factors focused international attention on the role and impact of these MNEs in global economic relationships.

MNEs are naturally interested in gaining free entry to foreign economies and protecting the investments they make there. For their part, developing countries are concerned with avoiding repetition of the consequences of earlier colonialism. They wish to have their local laws and autonomy respected and to protect their resources, culture, environment, and workers. They wish to be fairly treated and assisted to develop and not merely exploited.

LEGAL FOCUS

International

The Foreign Corrupt Practices Act (FCPA) of 1977 bars American companies from paying bribes to get business from foreign governments. More specifically, the FCPA bans these companies (and their officers and agents) from offering money or "anything of value" to foreign officials, foreign political candidates, or foreign political parties if the purpose is to induce that entity to assist the American company in obtaining or retaining business. (In addition to antibribery provisions, the FCPA also has accounting provisions designed to prevent large corporations from maintaining "off–the book accounts" or "slush funds" from which such payments might be made without alerting auditors or senior corporate officials.)

Penalties for violation for the FCPA are severe. An American company maybe fined up to $2 million for criminal violations of

the FCPA. Individual agents of these companies may be fined up to $100,000, imprisoned for up to five years, or both. Lesser civil penalties may be imposed in actions brought by the Securities and Exchange Commission.

The antibribery provisions carry exceptions permitting (1) "grease" payments made to officials in order to obtain routine government actions, such as the issuing of permits or licenses, the processing of government papers such as visas, the providing of police protection or mail delivery, and the providing of telephone, electrical power, or water service; (2) any payments lawful under the written laws and regulations of the recipient's home country; and (3) bona fide expenses, such as for travel and lodging, directly related to promoting or demonstrating a product.

Congress assumed other nations would join the U.S. in banning bribery, but not until 1997 did the Organization for Economic Cooperation and Development (OECD) promulgate the Convention on Combating the Bribery of Foreign Public Officials in International Business Transactions. More than 33 nations have signed the Convention. Because of differences between the Convention and the FCPA, Congress had to amend the FCPA in several particulars via the International Anti–Bribery and Fair Competition Act of 1998. Most importantly, it (a) expanded the scope of prohibited activities to include paying bribes to secure "any improper advantage," (b) expanded the scope of prohibited payees to include officials of public international organizations such as the World Bank and the International Red Cross, and (c) eliminated the jurisdictional requirement that there be an act in the U.S. that utilized the mails or some other instrumentality of interstate commerce to further an improper payment.

For the past three decades efforts at balancing these competing interests have been ongoing in a number of spheres. Several bilateral treaties have been signed between developed and developing nations, wherein the former promised certain concessions to obtain the latters' protection of MNE investments. Some regional pacts have also have been signed.

Perhaps most importantly, the United Nations has played a major role. Fifteen years in the making, a draft U.N. Code of Conduct on Transnational Corporations was never adopted by the U.N. The code specified that treatment of MNEs by host countries should be fair and equitable. Specific standards on matters of nationalization and compensation, national regulation, transfer of payments, and settlements of disputes were all set forth.

Absent an overarching code of conduct, some guidance stems from such sources as an International Code of Marketing of Breast–Milk Substitutes (under the jurisdiction of the World Health Organization), Guidelines of Consumer Protection (adopted by the U.N. General Assembly), and Criteria for Sustainable Development (aimed at discouraging over–exploitation by MNEs).